March 17–20, 2019
Tempe, AZ, USA

Association for
Computing Machinery

*Advancing Computing as a Science & Profession*

# TEI'19

## Proceedings of the Thirteenth International Conference on Tangible, Embedded, and Embodied Interaction

*Sponsored by:*

***ACM SIGCHI***

*Supported by:*

***Arizona State University, Sands, Seeed, The Center for Philosophical Technologies & Synthesis @ ASU***

Association for
Computing Machinery

Advancing Computing as a Science & Profession

**The Association for Computing Machinery**
**2 Penn Plaza, Suite 701**
**New York, New York 10121-0701**



**ISBN:** 978-1-4503-6196-5 (Digital)

**ISBN:** 978-1-4503-7068-4 (Print)

Additional copies may be ordered prepaid from:

**ACM Order Department**
PO Box 30777
New York, NY 10087-0777, USA

Phone: 1-800-342-6626 (USA and Canada)
+1-212-626-0500 (Global)
Fax: +1-212-944-1318
E-mail: acmhelp@acm.org
Hours of Operation: 8:30 am – 4:30 pm ET

# Foreword

Welcome to ACM TEI 2019, the 13th International Conference on Tangible, Embedded and Embodied Interactions, hosted in Tempe, Arizona, United States, from the 17th to the 20th of March 2019. The TEI conference features top-tier work that addresses issues of human-computer interaction, novel tools and technologies, interactive art, and user experience. The work presented at TEI has a strong focus on how computing can bridge atoms and bits into cohesive interactive systems.

Over the past few years, TEI research has increasingly embraced hybridity, whether through material explorations of composites such as bioelectronic, on-body, or active materials, or theoretical inquiries into socio-technical systems as hybrid assemblies. Not confined to a single approach, we have seen advancements in new materials—such as conductive and thermochromic inks, OLEDs, biosensors, or bioelectronics—which have helped to embed computing in the physical world. Simultaneously, comparisons between tangible computing and crafting traditions—such as crocheting or weaving—have served to destabilize assumptions about 'low' and 'high' technologies, the cultures that surround them, and even which communities have been able to participate in the discussion. These hybrid, materially-oriented approaches are radically changing our understanding of what tangible interaction looks and feels like. The theme of Hybrid Materials will continue to catalyze this exciting trend of tangible interaction research at the intersection of social, technical, biological, and artistic systems.

The intimate size of this single-track conference provides a unique forum for exchanging ideas and presenting innovative work through talks, interactive exhibits, demos, hands-on studios, posters, art installations and performances. TEI 2019 hosts a four-day program, starting on Sunday, March 17th with the Graduate Student Consortium and a series of five Studios that engage participants in the concrete making of novel interfaces and interactions. The main program starts on Monday, March 18th with an opening keynote by Dr. Batya Friedman, which sets out to inspire reflection and action on the TEI community's engagement with human values and material matters. The keynote us followed by a series of talks on "Users with Abilities" and "Learning & Entertainment", followed by a hands-on session showcasing Work-in-Progress demonstrations as well as exemplar demos and posters of the full papers accepted to the proceedings.

Tuesday, March 19th starts with an exhibit of Student Design Challenge submissions that speculate on how humans will interact with future digital, physical, biological, social, and virtual materials, as well as the Graduate Student Consortium poster session. This is followed by a paper talks session titled "Matters Shape, Shape Matters". TEI is then hosting a Diversity and Inclusion Lunch, the first event of its kind at TEI. Organized by invited speaker Dr. Gopinaath Kannabiran, this event aims to 1) create and strengthen the diverse networks of our attendees and support mentorships across academia, research, and industry for those with traditionally marginalized backgrounds; and 2) reflect on current diversity/inclusion research and develop an agenda for future TEI work to explore previously under-studied diversity/inclusion themes. The afternoon features another hands-on session showcasing the remainder of the Work-in-Progress as well as demonstrations and posters of the full papers accepted to the proceedings.

The evening of March 19th finds the conference at the Tempe Center for the Arts (TCA), premier arts venue, which hosts *Hybrid Materials:* TEI Arts and Performance track. The evening begins with an exhibition of twelve art installations in the TCA Studio, followed by six live performances exploring hybridity on the TCA Theatre Stage. A total of 18 curated artworks are presented over the course of the evening, which is also open to the public.

On Wednesday, March 20th, paper talks are presented in sessions titled "Creating Together", "Move & Feel", and "How You Make It". The conference concludes with a closing keynote on "Design Experiments in Civics", presented by Dr. Carl DiSalvo to envision how design can support our lives in turbulent times.

This year we received 110 submissions to the Papers track. A total of 36 papers were selected after a double-blind peer review process of at least three reviewers and a meta-reviewer, resulting in an acceptance rate of 33%. These works are presented in three formats throughout the conference: fifteen of the works are presented as talks, eight are shown as a talk and a demo, while six are exhibited as posters, and seven are featured as demos. Our program also includes one talk and demo presentation of a full paper from the journal of Human-Computer Interaction.

For the Work-in-Progress track, we received 44 submissions, which were subjected to a double-blind peer review process of at least two reviewers each. This resulted in 29 accepted submissions, making for an acceptance rate of 66%. For the Arts track, we received 41 submissions, subject to a four-person curation committee who performed the selection based on the artistic merits of the work and their engagement with issues relevant to the field of tangible and embedded interactive art. 18 submissions (44%) were shown at the conference.

Of course, organizing this conference could not have been possible without the energy and commitment of many, many people. We would like to thank everyone who contributed to TEI 2019: the authors for submitting their quality work to the conference, all the organizing committee chairs for managing their part of the conference, the program committee and external reviewers for safeguarding the quality of the conference, the local organizing committee, the sponsors, supporters and partners, and the TEI steering committee.

**Stacey Kuznetsov**
*TEI 2019 General Chair*
*Arizona State University*
*USA*

**Daniel Saakes**
*TEI 2019 General Chair*
*KAIST*
*South Korea*

**Ron Wakkary**
*TEI 2019 General Chair*
*Simon Fraser University, Canada &*
*Eindhoven University of Technology, the Netherlands*

**Luc Geurts**
*TEI 2019 Program Chair*
*KU Leuven*
*Belgium*

**Lauren Hayes**
*TEI 2019 Program Chair*
*Arizona State University*
*USA*

**Manfred Lau**
*TEI 2019 Program Chair*
*Lancaster University, UK &*
*City University of Hong Kong, Hong Kong*

# Table of Contents

## Poster Session 1



## WIP Session 1

## Talk Session 3: Matters Shape, Shape Matters



## Demo Session 2

## WIP Session 2



## Hybrid Materials: TEI Arts and Performance Track

Session Chair: Shahabedin Sagheb, Kimberlee Swisher *(Arizona State University)*

## Talk Session 4: Creating Together

## Talk Session 5: Move & Feel



## Talk Session 6: How You Make It



## Studio

## GSC

# TEI 2019 Conference Organization

| | |
|---|---|
| **General Chairs:** | Stacey Kuznetsov *(Arizona State University, USA)*<br>Daniel Saakes *(KAIST, South Korea))*<br>Ron Wakkary *(Simon Fraser University, Canada & Eindhoven University of Technology, the Netherlands)* |
| **Program Chairs:** | Luc Geurts *(KU Leuven, Belgium)*<br>Lauren Hayes *(Arizona State University, USA)*<br>Manfred Lau *(Lancaster University, UK & City University of Hong Kong, Hong Kong)* |
| **Studio Chairs:** | Ambra Trotto *(RISE Interactive, Sweden)*<br>Daisuke Uriu *(University of Tokyo, Japan)* |
| **Work in Progress Chairs:** | Tom Jenkins *(Georgia Institute of Technology, USA)*<br>Alejandra Rodriguez Vega *(Arizona State University, USA)*<br>Bert Vandenberghe *(KU Leuven, Belgium)* |
| **Graduate Student Consortium Chairs:** | Alissa N. Antle *(Simon Fraser University, Canada)*<br>Ellen Do *(University of Colorado, Boulder, USA)*<br>Bart Hengeveld *(Eindhoven University of Technology, the Netherlands)* |
| **Arts and Performance Chairs:** | Shahabedin Sagheb *(Arizona State University, USA)*<br>Kimberlee Swisher *(Arizona State University, USA)*<br>Byron Lahey *(Arizona State University, USA)*<br>Hye Yeon Nam *(Louisiana State University, USA)*<br>Asta Roseway *(Microsoft Research, USA)*<br>Tim Shaw *(Newcastle University, UK)* |
| **Demo Arrangement Chairs:** | Piyum Fernando *(Arizona State University, USA)*<br>Cesar Torres *(University of California, Berkeley, USA)* |
| **Student Design Challenge Chairs:** | Sophia Brueckner *(University of Michigan)*<br>Joshua Tanenbaum *(University of California, Irvine)*<br>Anja Thieme *(Microsoft Research)* |
| **Local Chairs:** | Collin Smith *(Arizona State University, USA)*<br>Michelle Fehler *(Arizona State University, USA)*<br>Pamela Winfrey *(Arizona State University, USA)* |
| **Web Chairs:** | Heesun Kim *(Arizona State University, USA)*<br>Kyle Hoefer *(Arizona State University, USA)* |

**Social Media Chair:** Cyn Liu *(Indiana University Bloomington, USA)*

**Registration Chair:** Kayla Elizondo *(Arizona State University, USA)*

**Sponsorship Chair:** Loren Olson *(Arizona State University, USA)*

**Accessibility Chair:** Althea Pergakis *(Arizona State University, USA)*

**Diversity & Inclusion Lunch Chair:** Gopinaath Kannabiran *(Aarhus University, Denmark)*

**Publication Chairs:** Ren Bozgeyikli *(University of Arizona, USA)*
Suren Jayasuriya *(Arizona State University, USA)*

**Student Volunteer Chairs:** Jennifer Weiler *(Arizona State University, USA)*
Yanjun Lyu *(Arizona State University, USA)*

**Local Organizing Committee:** Luke Kautz *(Arizona State University, USA)*
Caroline Fernandez *(Arizona State University, USA)*
Daniel Jackson *(Arizona State University, USA)*
Peter Weisman *(Arizona State University, USA)*

**Visual Designer:** Nipuni Siyambalapitiya *(Arizona State University, USA)*

**Program Committee:** Leonardo Angelini *(HumanTech Institute, Switzerland)*
Jussi Ängeslevä *(Berlin University of the Arts, German))*
Saskia Bakker *(Eindhoven University of Technology, the Netherlands)*
Alvaro Cassinelli *(University of Tokyo, Japan & SinergiaTech, Uruguay)*
Liwei Chan *(National Chiao Tung University, Taiwan)*
Victor Cheung *(Carleton University, Canada)*
Jelle van Dijk *(University Twente, the Netherlands)*
Tanja Doering *(University of Bremen, Germany)*
Augusto Esteves *(Edinburgh Napier University, UK)*
Sarah Fox *(University of California, San Diego, USA)*
Domenique Van Gennip *(University of Technology Sydney, Australia)*
Tincutta Heinzel *(Berlin University of The Arts, Germany)*
Trevor Hogan *(Cork Institute of Technology, Ireland)*
Michaela Honauer *(Bauhaus-Universität, Germany)*
Eva Hornecker *(Bauhaus-Universität, Germany)*
Jörn Hurtienne *(University of Würzburg, Germany)*
Martin Kaltenbrunner *(Kunstuniversität Linz, Austria)*
Cindy Hsin-Liu Kao *(Cornell University, USA)*
Rohit Ashok Khot *(RMIT University, Australia)*
Andrew Kun *(University of New Hampshire, USA)*
Rong-Hao Liang *(Eindhoven University of Technology, the Netherlands)*
Lian Loke *(University of Sydney, Australia)*
Ali Mazalek *(Ryerson University, Canada)*
Robb Mitchell *(University of Southern Denmark. Denmark)*
Martin Murer *(University of Salzburg, Austria)*
Ian Oakley *(Ulsan National Institute of Science and Technology, South Korea)*
Steve Oney *(University of Michigan, USA)*
Nadya Peek *(University of Washington, USA)*
Raf Ramakers *(Hasselt University, Belgium)*
Claudia Rebola *(University of Cincinnati, USA)*
Michal Rinott *(Shenkar- Engineering. Design. Art, Israel)*
Enrico Rukzio *(University of Ulm, Germany)*
Jelle Saldien *(Ghent University, Belgium)*
Ehud Sharlin *(University of Calgary, Canada)*
Beat Signer *(Vrije Universiteit Brussel, Belgium)*
Andrew Smith *(CSIR Meraka Institute, South Africa)*
Paul Strohmeier *(University of Copenhagen, Denmark)*
Yuta Sugiura *(Keio University, Japan)*
Jakob Tholander *(Stockholm University, Sweden)*
Brygg Ullmer *(Clemson University, USA)*
Jean Vanderdonckt *(UC Louvain, Belgium)*
Vasilis Vlachokyriakos *(Newcastle University, UK)*
Raphael Wimmer *(Universität Regensburg, Germany)*
Katrin Wolf (*Hamburg University of Applied Sciences, Germany)*
Yingqing Xu *(Tsinghua University, China)*

# TEI 2019 Sponsors & Supporters

Sponsor:

SIGCHI

acm Association for Computing Machinery

Supporters:

ASU Center for Science and the Imagination
Arizona State University

ASU Knowledge Enterprise
Arizona State University

ASU School of Arts, Media and Engineering
Arizona State University

ASU School for the Future of Innovation in Society
Arizona State University

SANDS

seeed studio
The IoT Hardware Enabler

( C P T )
The Center for
Philosophical Technologies

Synthesis @ASU

# Material Matters: Human Values and the Longer View

**Batya Friedman**
University of Washington
Seattle, WA. USA
batya@uw.edu

## ABSTRACT

Whether you aspire to Weiser's [4] disappearing technology of ubiquitous computing or Negroponte's [3] atoms to bits or something in-between, there is something inescapably material about the digital. How much more so when the goal is hybridity: the bridging of atoms with bits. In this keynote, I examine the intersection of this hybridity with human values—in the present and in the longer term. I situate my remarks in the observation that our scientific and technological capacities have and will continue to far surpass our moral ones – that is our ability to use wisely and humanely the knowledge and tools that we develop. My reflections are grounded in the intellectual traditions of value sensitive design [1] and multi-lifespan design [2].

I take up such questions as: What human values and human impacts are implicated by hybridity and, in particular, hybrid materials? From this perspective of human values, are all hybrid materials the same? Is embedding computation in my glove the same as in my finger? Or are some materials deserving of special status? And, if so, in what ways? What cultural considerations come to the fore? What of non-humans? Turning to metaphor and mental models, what metaphors should be developed for hybrid materials? And in what ways will those highlight and hide embedded computation? What mental models should be associated with these materials? How will these models position people to think about their relationship with hybrid materials, including when to use them, how to adapt them, when to dispose of them, and when to eschew them? More generally, what constitutes responsible innovation around hybrid materials and how should we go about pursuing it?

To gain purchase on these questions, I use the frame of value scenarios and anticipatory futures. My comments highlight the importance of taking the material impacts of the digital seriously. At stake is nothing less than what sort of society we want to live in and how we experience our humanity.


*TEI'19, March 17--20, 2019, Tempe, AZ, USA.*

ACM ISBN 978-1-4503-6196-5/19/03.
DOI: https://doi.org/10.1145/3294109.3305256

## CCS Concepts

• **Human-centered computing~Human computer interaction (HCI)**
• Security and privacy~Human and societal aspects of security and privacy
• Social and professional topics~Computing / technology policy
• Applied computing~Law, social and behavioral sciences

## Author Keywords

Ethics; human values; hybridity; hybrid materials; materiality; multi-lifespan design; responsible innovation; time; value sensitive design

## BIOGRAPHY

Batya Friedman is a professor in the Information School and holds adjunct appointments in the Allen School of Computer Science & Engineering and Department of Human-Centered Design and Engineering at the University of Washington. She codirects the Value Sensitive Design Lab and the UW Tech Policy Lab.

Dr. Friedman pioneered value sensitive design (VSD), an approach to account for human values in the design of technology. First developed in human-computer interaction, VSD has since been used in architecture, civil engineering, computational linguistics, computer security, energy, human-robotic interaction, information management, legal theory, moral philosophy, and transportation.

Dr. Friedman has worked on technologies and values in a wide range of systems, from security for implantable medical devices to informed consent for cookies and web browsers, reputation in knowledge base systems, privacy in mobile technology, and equitable representation in large-scale computer simulation for land use and transportation planning.

To bring VSD into engineering, design and tech policy research and practice, she has developed practical methods and toolkits. Among these, *Envisioning Cards* help technologists consider stakeholders, values, time, and pervasive uptake in their technical work; *Security Cards*, with a focus on threat analysis, help to develop a security mindset; and *Diverse Voices* aims to create more inclusive tech policy. Her new book *Value Sensitive Design: Shaping Technology with Moral Imagination* will be published by MIT Press in spring 2019.

Dr. Friedman is currently working on multi-lifespan design—generating design knowledge for envisioning and building information systems to support sociotechnical solutions as they unfold over longer periods of time, on the order of 50 or 100 years. Voices from the Rwanda Tribunal, which explores the design of information systems to support transitional justice and healing from cyclical violence and genocide, is a first project in this multi-lifespan design research program.

Among her honors, Dr. Friedman was selected as the University of Washington's University Faculty Lecturer and received the ACM SIGCHI Social Impact Award in 2012. She is also a stone sculptor and mixed media artist. She received her BA and PhD from the University of California at Berkeley.

## REFERENCES


[1] Batya Friedman and David G. Hendry. 2019. *Value Sensitive Design: Shaping Technology with Moral Imagination.* MIT Press, Cambridge, MA.

[2] Batya Friedman and Lisa P. Nathan. 2010. Multi-lifespan information system design: A research initiative for the HCI community. In *Proceedings of Conference on Human Factors in Computing Systems* (CHI '10). ACM Press, New York, NY 2243-2246.

[3] Nicholas Negroponte. 1995. *Being Digital.* Knopf, New York, NY.

[4] Mark Weiser. 1991. The computer for the 21st century. *Scientific American,* 265 3 (September 1991) 94– 105.

# Design Experiments in Civics

**Carl DiSalvo**
Georgia Institute of Technology
Atlanta, Georgia, USA
cdisalvo@gatech.edu

## ABSTRACT

Often when we talk about or do critical and speculative design the work is future oriented, looking towards technologies or conditions that are yet to come. While such work is important and compelling, there is also an opportunity to turn the critical and speculative impulse towards our contemporary moment, to consider how design might participate in alternate forms of living now or in the near present. I call this kind of work "design experiments in civics" because it uses design processes and products as a mode of inquiry into how we might differently structure our collective lives.

What's more, given the pressing issues we are facing in 2019 there is an urgency to design that looks to address how we might live in the turbulent times. One move to make is to shift from thinking that design might solve the issues of climate-change or democracy or capitalism, and instead look to design as a way to contribute to different configurations of resources and action, through creativity and resourcefulness.

In this talk I will share examples from my own work as well as the work of other artists and designers doing these "design experiments in civics." From these projects, I will draw out a set of themes for critical practices aimed at exploring and -enabling alternate forms of living and speculating on more diverse forms of togetherness in the contemporary moment and near-present. In particular, for the TEI audience I will address the ways in which explorations of materialities and interactions can express and support alternative collective practices and consider what the unique contributions of this research community might be to broad field of "design experiments in civics."


*TEI'19, March 17--20, 2019, Tempe, AZ, USA.*

ACM ISBN 978-1-4503-6196-5/19/03.
DOI: https://doi.org/10.1145/3294109.3305257

## CCS Concepts

• Human Centered Computing → Interaction Design → Participatory Design.

## Author Keywords

Public Design, Participation, Politics

## BIOGRAPHY

Carl DiSalvo is an Associate Profe.sor at the Georgia Institute of Technology with joint appointments in the School of Interactive Computing and the School of Literature, Media, and Communication. At Georgia Tech he directs the Public Design Workshop: a design research studio that explores socially-engaged design and civic media. DiSalvo's scholarship draws together theories and methods from design, the social sciences, and the humanities to analyze the political qualities of design and prototype experimental systems and services. His first book, *Adversarial Design* (2012), is part of the Design Thinking, Design Theory series at MIT Press. He is also a co-editor of the MIT Press journal *Design Issues.* DiSalvo's experimental design work has been exhibited and supported by the ZKM, Grey Area Foundation for the Arts, Times Square Arts Alliance, Science Gallery Dublin, and the Walker Arts Center.

# SpinalLog: Visuo-Haptic Feedback in Musculoskeletal Manipulation Training

**D. Antony Chacon**
The University of Melbourne
Melbourne, Australia
antony@iis-lab.org

**Eduardo Velloso**
The University of Melbourne
Melbourne, Australia
evelloso@unimelb.edu.au

**Thuong Hoang**
Deakin University
Melbourne, Australia
thuong.hoang@deakin.edu.au

**Katrin Wolf**
Hamburg University of Applied Sciences
Hamburg, Germany
katrin.wolf@acm.org

## ABSTRACT
Current techniques for teaching spinal mobilisation follow the traditional classroom approach: an instructor demonstrates a technique and students attempt to emulate it by practising on each other while receiving feedback from the instructor. This paper introduces *SpinalLog*, a novel tangible user interface (TUI) for teaching and learning spinal mobilisation. The system was co-designed with physiotherapy experts to *look and feel* like a human spine, supporting the learning of mobilisation techniques through *real-time visual feedback* and deformation-based *passive haptic feedback*. We evaluated Physical Fidelity, Visual Feedback and Passive Haptic Feedback in an experiment to understand their effects on physiotherapy students' ability to replicate a mobilisation pattern recorded by an expert. We found that simultaneous feedback has the largest effect, followed by passive haptic feedback. The high fidelity of the interface has little effect, but it plays an important role in the perception of the system's benefit.

### Author Keywords
Spinal Mobilisation; Deformable Interface; Haptic Perception

### CCS Concepts
•**Human-centered computing** → **Haptic devices;**

## INTRODUCTION
Learning new motor skills is challenging, so practice and feedback are essential. An example domain where this challenge is evident is in physiotherapy education, in which among other skills, students must master *spinal mobilisation techniques*—complex manual fine motor skills to assess and treat physical conditions of the spine. The basic arrangement to perform them consists of the patient lying face down (prone) at the level of the practitioner's hip, who exerts a vertical force with the side of one hand on a specific vertebra of the patient's spine. The force is exerted following a repetitive sinusoidal pattern with a constant frequency at a certain amplitude.



*TEI '19,* March 17–20, 2019, Tempe, AZ, USA



ISBN 978-1-4503-6196-5/19/03...$15.00
DOI: https://doi.org/10.1145/3294109.3295626

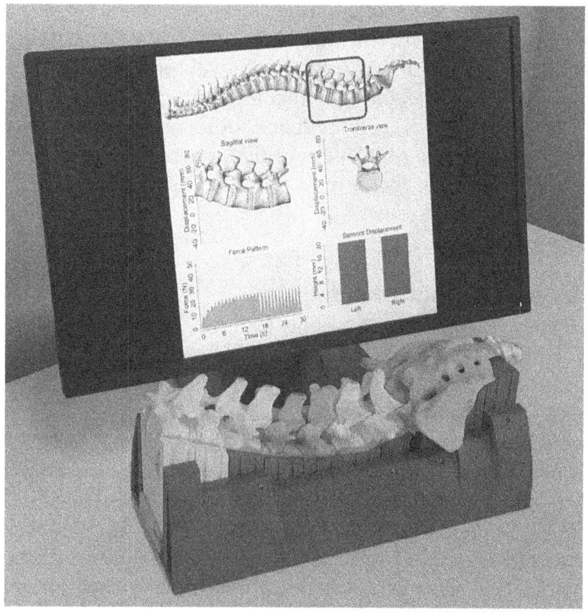

**Figure 1.** ***SpinalLog*. Our system senses force patterns on individual vertebrae and gives real-time feedback to physiotherapy students through the passive haptic sensation of deformation and through a GUI.**

Traditionally, to teach these skills, the instructor demonstrates the force pattern on a volunteer and asks students to practise on each other by replicating it. During such practice, a major challenge is that force-based movements are difficult to be visually observed, as the movements are subtle and barely perceptible. This is also an issue when students perform the movements themselves, as it is difficult for the instructor to assess and provide feedback solely based on visual observation.

Alternative approaches for addressing this problem include placing force-sensitive resistors (FSRs) either under the volunteer [23] or in standalone devices to measure force and to provide feedback [29]. However, these approaches usually suffer from either scalability or fidelity problems. On one hand, practising on a volunteer provides the authentic haptic sensation of a human spine, but it is difficult to scale to large classes. On the other hand, while practising on an FSR placed on a rigid surface can provide quantifiable force feedback at scale, it lacks haptic fidelity—a hard and rigid surface is substantially different to a real spine. To cope with the fidelity problem, devices can incorporate manikins [6] and spine models [12, 24]. However, they do not provide suitable visual aids about the force patterns or the bones' displacement, as deformation is only perceived haptically.

In this work, our goal is to understand how properties of tangible interfaces can support physiotherapy students as they practise spinal mobilisation techniques. We achieve this through a study with a prototype of the *SpinalLog* (Fig. 1). Our system consists of a tangible interface that *looks and feels* like a human spine, supporting the learning of mobilisation techniques through *real-time visual feedback* and foam-based *passive haptic feedback*. We investigate how these three properties—shape fidelity, visual feedback, and deformation—impact students' abilities to replicate the instructor's force demonstrations.

In summary, this paper contributes (1) an exploration of the use of resistive foam for the implementation of passive haptic feedback systems; (2) the design and development of *SpinalLog*, a novel tool for teaching spinal mobilisation; (3) an analysis of the effects of visual feedback, deformable passive haptic feedback, and tangible interface fidelity on participants' ability to replicate force patterns.

## RELATED WORK

### Motor Behaviour Learning

Motor control theory accounts for how the motor system controls the movement's trajectory length, velocity, acceleration, and force. It makes the distinction between *closed-loop* and *open-loop* control. Whereas a closed-loop system features feedback, error detection, and error correction, an open-loop system has no feedback or mechanisms for error regulation [1]. An expert would typically execute spinal mobilisation as an open-loop movement running a Motor Program, which is automated, fast, and precise as long as the context does not change [20]. However, when learning spinal mobilisation techniques, students have to build their own Motor Program by repeating movements through deliberate practice in a closed loop, which requires feedback to train a movement until it becomes automated. This led to the assumption that visual feedback could help students recognise the differences between their own force patterns and those recorded by the instructor.

Because learning happens in the brain, we can only measure whether it has occurred indirectly through behavioural measures, such as *persistent improvement, better consistency, stability of performance*, and *adaptability* [10]. The first three of these highlight that measuring the quality of a performance is a first step towards measuring learning. We draw from qualitative activity recognition the idea that we measure quality through comparisons with a benchmark, which we consider to be the instructor's performance [35].

### Motor Learning in HCI

A fundamental principle in human motor learning is the knowledge of results—the information provided to the learner about whether they met the task's goals [19]. In an HCI context, we aim at augmenting the proprioceptive sensory feedback with knowledge of results. Many devices provide visualisations as the single or main source for guidance or feedback due to visual dominance over other senses [17]. For example, *Andantino* [37] provides concurrent visual assistance for learning instruments, while in the context of sports, *Motion Echo Snowboard* provides visual feedback by embedding displays into the sports device [18]. Augmented and virtual reality are also widely used. For instance, in *LightGuide* [27], which projects images on users hands to guide them actively through specific motion activities. Another example with projected images is *SleeveAR* [28], which helps users perform arm rehabilitation exercises. Similarly, *MotionMA* [34], *Onebody* [9], and *YouMove* [2] interfaces employ camera-based motion tracking systems to guide users in improving gross motor skills through 2D and 3D overlays on their body. In this work, we explore how visual feedback impacts learners' ability to replicate a force pattern benchmark.

Haptic feedback is generally classified in two main categories: *tactile* or *cutaneous*, which include vibration and temperature sensation, and *kinaesthetic*, which involves the perception of forces and torques [4]. Gu et al. explored the use of vibrational haptics to learn correct arm postures in the context of archery, guiding the user through different levels of cutaneous vibrations in parts of the arm to reach the objective posture [7]. A similar approach has been used by Seim et al. to teach finger positioning during activities with a keypad [21]. Force feedback haptic devices have been used extensively both in research prototypes and commercial products in conjunction with visual feedback to enable immersive interaction in motor learning tasks with positive results [14]. These interfaces usually employ traditional robotic arms with a variety of tools as end-effectors mostly for the motor training in surgery related medical procedures [5]. These devices are typically employed in activities that involve the use of a tool, such as a scalpel. Tension-based interfaces allow more freedom in this aspect, but they have limited working space [11, 16]. Because scalability to large classes is a primary goal of our project, we do not explore audio feedback in our system, as it can be distracting if emitted by speakers or isolating if emitted by headphones.

### Force and Pressure Input

Early works in HCI force sensing and pressure input explored the implications of finger pressure for pointing in computers [22], while more recently the focus has shifted to touch-screen devices [32]. In recent times, FSRs are extensively used to sense force-based gestures [8, 13]. Because of the difficulty in gauging how much force we are applying at any point, studies have shown that there is a substantial loss of accuracy when there is no explicit visual feedback [30, 36].

While FSRs are often used on rigid surfaces, deformable user interfaces (DUIs), on the other hand, employ solid-state sensors embedded within soft mediums or rely on smart materials to sense forces. These devices have high flexibility and provide exciting opportunities for designing novel user experiences. An example of devices that work with inserted sensors is the *FuwaFuwa* sensor module [31]. This device can sense deformations of almost any soft object by measuring the emission and reception of electromagnetic waves within the medium. Thus, any soft object is a potential touch-input device that can detect both touch position and surface displacement.

Murakami and Nakajima used conductive soft materials to sense displacement by presenting a cuboid device made of conductive foam for 3D manipulation [15]. Smith et al., inspired by this idea, developed *Digital Foam*, a material that changes its electrical resistance when deformed, which was used to create a device that supports 3D sculpting [25, 26]. A more recent device that extends these works is the *HandLog* [3]. It consists of a cylindrical 3D-printed core covered with a matrix of conductive pieces within a non-conductive medium, similar to a soft handle, with the novel feature to measure individual finger flexion. This feature represents an opportunity for better measurement of forces in learning activities that demand high precision and accuracy. In this work, we explore the use of this type of foam to build sensor modules to measure the force being exerted at each vertebra on a spine model and to provide resistance to this force.

## SPINALLOG

### Design Process

This work contributes to the question of how emerging technologies can support physiotherapy teaching and learning. This is a domain in which embodiment and tangibility are core aspects of the user experience, creating rich opportunities for design. Hence, we applied a Human-Centred Design process to develop a system to support a key technique—spinal mobilisation. We began with a field study where we observed six two-hour practical classes, focusing on manual assessment skills, for students of the Doctor of Physiotherapy program at our university. We collected data from our observations and informal conversations with teachers and students. We found that tactile sensation and the ability to support "sense of feel" are crucial in learning manual skills. Students also indicated their struggle with identifying the correct anatomical structure on the body as they perform manual skills on one another.

Regarding spinal mobilisation, we learned that the instructor performs an oscillating force pattern on a volunteer, based on a graph drawn on a whiteboard, while the other students watch. The instructor also uses a plastic human spine model to indicate the specific vertebrae that students should focus on. After the demonstration, the students break into pairs to take turns practising the skills on each other. As they practise, the instructor approaches each group to provide feedback. To assess a student's technique, the instructor holds the student's hands as they apply pressure on the volunteer's back. As a consequence, the instructor can only give feedback to one student at a time, and students spend only half of the activity time practising while acting as a volunteer in the other half.

During the class, students struggle to discern the subtle movements demonstrated by the instructor. The force pattern graph on the whiteboard showed a pattern based on the tactile sensation of the spinal compliance, which is not reflected visually in the movement of the instructor's hands during demonstration.

We identified several opportunities for the design of a tangible interface for the practice of these skills. First, by practising on a system rather than on a volunteer, we can almost double the practice time in class, as students would not have to volunteer as patients. Second, because the instructor can only give feedback to one student at a time, by providing feedback during or immediately after each performance, an interactive system could substantially increase the amount of feedback students receive. Third, though practising on a fellow student lets students feel a real spine, these volunteers are usually healthy. A tangible system could simulate different spinal conditions. Fourth, an interactive system has the potential to make visible internal structures of the body, such as bones and muscles, which represents an important learning aid.

We validated these assumptions in three interviews with the instructor. These interviews directed us towards a design involving a 3D-printed model of the spine mounted on a deformable substrate aiming to match the haptic feeling of a human spine. In each interview, the expert tried multiple variations of our design that involved different foam configurations and levels of haptic perception of compliance, and provided feedback. The expert also guided the design of the graphical user interface of the system. We began with hand-drawn sketches, increasing the level of fidelity until we had a working prototype. We repeated this process until the expert was satisfied with the look and feel of both the hardware and software systems, which are described in the remainder of this section.

### Hardware

The hardware comprises the medium for haptic interaction of *SpinalLog*. It has a set of transducers to measure displacements and forces exerted on them while providing compliance as haptic feedback to the user. This system consists of four main components stacked one on top of the other in the following order: (1) a real-size lumbar spine model in prone position, (2) a set of pairs of L-shaped supports for each vertebra, (3) an array of foam-based sensor modules, and (4) a frame that holds the deformable sensor modules in its bottom and supports the motion of the other components (Fig. 2-Centre).

The spine model consists of seven 3D-printed vertebrae (L1 to L5, T11, and T12) and a sacrum, interconnected with polyurethane foam emulating intervertebral discs to allow soft relative movement between them. Each vertebra is supported individually by a pair of L-shape supports. Each of these supports moves independently according to the orientation of the vertebra that they support. We also used polyurethane foam in the upper contact with the vertebra for each L-shape support to allow small rotational movements (Fig. 2-Left). All L-shaped supports were inserted in a housing containing smooth-surface metal rods to facilitate their motion.

Below each pair of L-shape supports intended for individual vertebra, there is a sensor module made of a combination of conductive and non-conductive foam, inspired by Beven et al.'s *HandLog* [3] and Smith et al. [26]. The conductive foam changes its electrical resistance when deformed, increasing its value when elongated and decreasing when compressed. Therefore, by measuring its electrical resistance, we could estimate its displacement and the force being exerted upon it. This feature enabled its use as both a sensor and as a passive haptic actuator.

Given that when manipulating a vertebra the physiotherapist should feel two levels of compliance as they press it, we designed special sensor modules. They consist of three conductive foam cylinders surrounded by non-conductive foam for

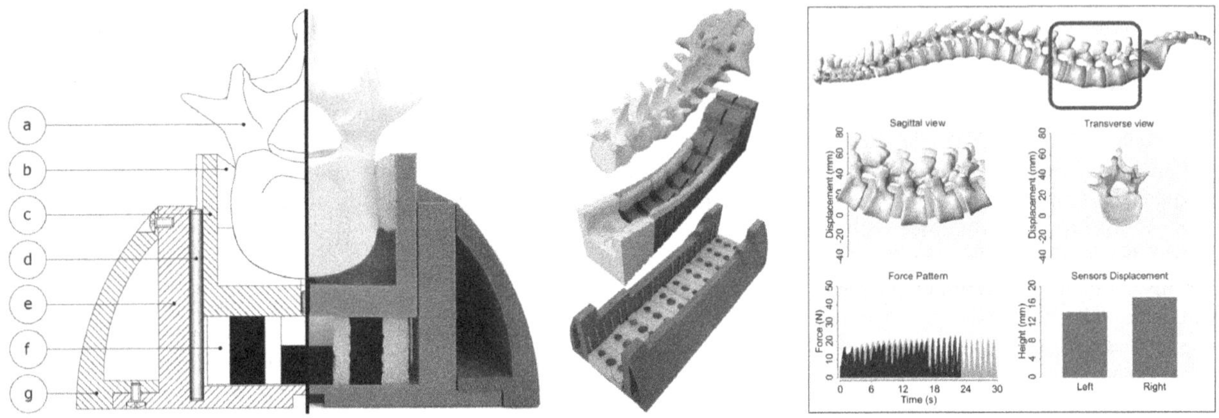


**Figure 2. SpinalLog hardware and software. Left: frontal section cut view showing (a) a vertebra, (b) lateral supportive foam, (c) L-shape support, (d) stainless steel rod for sliding, (e) the base, (f) sensor module and (g) the cover. Centre: exploded view of the spine model, supports and sensing foam components. Right: graphical user interface.**

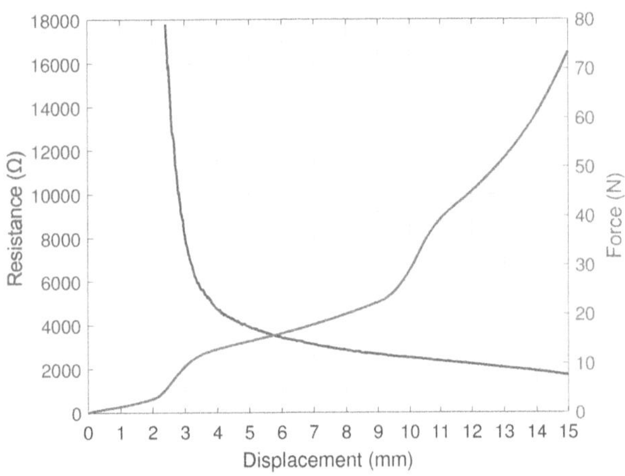


**Figure 3. Force-Displacement-Resistance graph.**

support in a rectangular shape (Fig. 2-Left and Middle). The cylinders in the sides allow estimating the vertebra's rotation in the transverse plane, whereas the cylinder in the middle provides an extra level of compliance when reaching its surface after pressing on the module. This arrangement allows students to identify the second level based on passive haptic feedback. Amongst multiple alternatives, our expert selected a configuration based on conductive low density polyethylene foam (Plastazote LD50CN) as the most similar to the compliance of the average human spine with some additional rigidity (as if they had a mild spinal condition). The modular design of our sensor modules allows them to be swapped or mixed to simulate different spinal injuries and levels of compliance.

To obtain precise estimates about the relationship between the module's sensors' deformation, resistance, and force upon them, we conducted a series of compression tests. We continuously varied the force applied on the unit with an Instron Universal Tester, measuring the corresponding change in the displacement, resistance, and force values on the foam. Figure 3 shows the Force-Displacement-Resistance graph from this experiment. We used these results and a voltage divider configuration to map the output of the sensor to the values displayed on our interface.

### Software

Given that visual feedback in closed-loop movements is important during motor learning [1], we designed a visual interface for *SpinalLog*. This captures the raw voltage values from each conductive foam sensor with a Data Acquisition System and processes them with LabVIEW, relaying them to the GUI at 50 Hz. We use these values to render the positions and forces of the elements in the displayed visual interface.

The GUI (Fig. 2-Right), developed with Processing 3.3/Java, includes a sagittal view of the entire human spine in a horizontal position with a window that highlights the area where most force is being applied during mobilisation. This highlighted area is zoomed in the middle left widget, showing the vertebrae being mobilised in real-time. Displacements of each vertebra in the area are rendered by overlaying their resting position in the background for reference. The widget in the middle right shows the transverse view of the vertebra being manipulated with its orientation and vertical displacement rendered over its resting position. The widget in the bottom left provides the reference force pattern that the user should try to replicate. The aggregate force exerted is displayed over the ideal pattern in real time, providing instant visual feedback. Lastly, the widget in the bottom right displays the heights of the two conductive foam cylinders below the main mobilised vertebra.

## EXPERIMENT

*SpinalLog* was designed under the assumption that receiving real-time **visual** and **passive haptic deformation** feedback about the force being exerted on a system that **looks and feels** like a human spine would have a positive effect on how well students can replicate the pressure patterns recorded by an expert. To test this assumption, we conducted a lab experiment with a $2 \times 2 \times 2$ design. In each trial, participants were shown a different reference force pattern recorded by the expert. All force patterns were recorded by the expert with all different devices, ensuring that all comparisons were made between data recorded from the same device and that the data from each device contained all patterns. Participants were then asked to replicate these patterns in different conditions created by the combinations of our independent variables:

- VISUAL FEEDBACK: We presented two types of visual feedback. In the **simultaneous** condition, the force values were plotted as the system recorded them, overlaying the reference pattern. In the **delayed** condition, a vertical bar moved from left to right over the reference indicating the force level that should be exerted at each point in time, and the generated forces were shown at the end of each trial.
- DEFORMATION: To isolate the effect of the passive haptic compliance feedback enabled by the foam deformation, we tested two types of devices. In the devices with **deformable** passive haptic feedback, we recorded force using the readings from the force-sensitive foam. In the **rigid** devices, we recorded the force with a flat FSR in a voltage divider configuration. Both types of sensors were calibrated to give the same output when the same force was exerted.
- FIDELITY: Given that an advantage of tangible user interfaces for simulation is that they are able to physically resemble their counterparts, we wanted to test whether the shape of the device resembling a spine had any effect on user performance. Our study had two types of devices. High fidelity devices (**Hi-Fi**) featured a 3D-printed model of a set of vertebrae mounted on the sensor, while low fidelity devices (**Lo-Fi**) featured a flat block mounted on the sensor.

This design was guided by the following hypotheses:

- **H1:** Simultaneous visual feedback hampers the timing of the movements. In other words, the time difference between the peaks in the reference curve and the corresponding peaks in the force exerted curve will be higher with simultaneous feedback. We hypothesised that the added cognitive load of visualising the force being exerted might lead to delays when matching the peaks in the reference curve.
- **H2:** Visual feedback helps users exert force levels more similar to the reference.
- **H3:** Deformable haptic feedback helps users exert force levels more similar to the reference.
- **H4:** Higher fidelity helps users exert force levels more similar to the reference.

### Participants and Experimental Setup

We recruited 16 participants (9M/7F), aged between 20 and 37 years (mean = 25.62, SD = 4.12). All were university students from physiotherapy or related courses and had completed or were currently enrolled in the Sports and Manual Therapy subject, where they learn spinal mobilisation techniques. We restricted our participant pool to these students to ensure that they performed the task using similar techniques and that they understood the instructions provided by the expert.

The study took place in a quiet laboratory setting, with participants standing in front of a 74.5 cm-high desk with four devices in front of two 23" displays, one for the video demonstration and one for the task instruction and feedback (Fig. 4). The four devices were (Fig. 5):

- **Deformable Hi-Fi:** *SpinalLog*, containing both deformable passive haptic feedback and high fidelity (Fig. 5-A).

**Figure 4. Experimental setup.**

- **Deformable Lo-Fi:** a flat 3D-printed block mounted on a piece of the resistive foam, thus containing deformable passive haptic feedback, but low physical fidelity (Fig. 5-B).
- **Rigid Hi-Fi:** a 3D-printed segment of a spine mounted on a platform containing an FSR, therefore providing high physical fidelity, but with no deformable passive haptic feedback (Fig. 5-C).
- **Rigid Lo-Fi:** a flat 3D-printed block mounted on a platform containing an FSR, hence providing low fidelity and no deformable passive haptic feedback (Fig. 5-D).

Sessions were video recorded, except for two in which the participants asked not to be recorded. All devices streamed their data to a laptop, which recorded it synchronously with the reference curve.

### Procedure

Upon arrival, participants signed a consent form and completed a demographics questionnaire. We explained the procedure both verbally and through a plain language written statement. Participants then completed a series of eight conditions, three times each, for a total of 24 tasks (2 VISUAL FEEDBACK $\times$ 2 DEFORMATION $\times$ 2 FIDELITY $\times$ 3 $Trials = 24$). We counter-balanced the condition order using a Latin Square, but all three trials within each condition were performed consecutively. At the beginning of each condition, we presented participants with a video recording of an expert demonstrating the reference pattern on the corresponding device. The same patterns were recorded with all devices, and the order of patterns was counter-balanced across participants. We also presented the reference curve of the pattern in a picture-in-picture frame while the expert performed it.

Then, participants performed each condition three times, but we only considered their final performance in our analysis in order to minimise learning effects. In the conditions with delayed feedback, we displayed the force plot to the user after each trial. Upon completion of all three trials, participants filled in a NASA-TLX questionnaire to measure the task workload and a custom questionnaire where we asked them to comment on the advantages and disadvantages of each device and to explain their preference towards delayed or simultaneous feedback. As quantitative subjective measures, we collected the ranking of devices and their preference towards the timing of visual feedback on a 5-point scale.

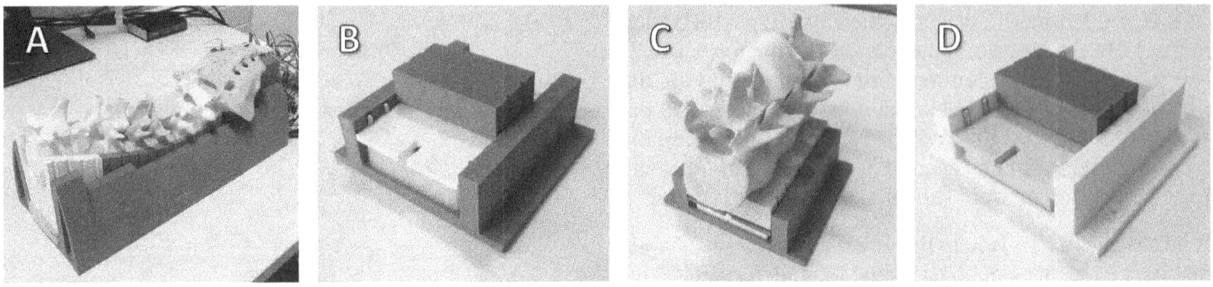


**Figure 5. The devices used in our experiment: (A) Deformable Hi-Fi; (B) Deformable Lo-Fi; (C) Flat Hi-Fi; and (D) Flat Lo-Fi.**

Finally, we collected qualitative feedback on the complete *SpinalLog* interface. We presented the system depicted in Figure 1 and walked participants through each visualisation widget. We let them manipulate the device and observe the changes in the interface. Participants then completed a questionnaire where we asked them about the visual feedback, passive haptic feedback, and physical fidelity of the device.

## RESULTS

### Task Performance

We quantified participants' performance on the task through the comparison between the force pattern exerted by them and the reference pattern recorded by the expert. The force patterns were characterised by pulses exerted at different baseline force levels. Thus, we evaluated three aspects of task performance:

- LAG: Were the user-exerted pulses executed in sync with the reference pulses?
- BASELINE DIFFERENCE: Were the user-exerted pulses executed around the same baseline as the reference?
- PULSE AMPLITUDE DIFFERENCE: Did the user-exerted pulses have the same amplitude as the ones in the reference?

To answer these questions, we first extracted the peaks and troughs of the reference curve and identified the corresponding peaks and troughs at the user-generated curve. To perform this matching, we iterated over these points in the reference curve and searched for local maxima or minima in the temporal vicinity of the point in the user-generated curve. We defined the vicinity to be half of the average pulse period in the pattern. This approach outperformed other time series matching approaches that do not take into account the cyclical nature of the signal or the previous knowledge that the two signals are approximately synchronised (e.g., dynamic time warping). This approach was also more appropriate than standard measures for curve fit, such as Root Mean Squared Error (RMSE). These are only meant to be used to compare different models for the *same* dataset, not *between* datasets as is our case, due to the variety of force patterns in each trial. To ensure that all patterns had the same range, we normalised all signals according to the corresponding reference curve, so that it had a mean of zero and a standard deviation of one.

To determine the LAG, we computed the absolute time difference between corresponding peaks and troughs. To determine the BASELINE DIFFERENCE, we ran a moving average over the force values at the peaks and troughs in the reference curve and the user-generated curve and computed the absolute difference between them. Finally, to determine the PULSE AMPLITUDE DIFFERENCE, we computed the absolute difference between consecutive peaks and troughs in each curve and calculated the absolute difference between corresponding pairs in the user-generated and reference curves.

We analysed the effect of our independent variables on our dependent variables using a multilevel linear regression model. We chose this test over a repeated measures ANOVA for its ability to model individual features of the participants and due to the different number of peaks and troughs being compared for each pattern. We built a model for each dependent variable with VISUAL FEEDBACK, DEFORMATION, and FIDELITY as fixed effects and PARTICIPANT as a random effect. We used Restricted Maximum Likelihood (REML) to fit the models and an $\alpha$ of .05 when testing for significant effects.

We tested for multicollinearity to ensure that the predictors in the model cannot be linearly predicted from any combination of the other predictors. A typical threshold for detecting multicollinearity is a variance inflation factor of 5 and above. In all of our models, the factors were in the range of [1, 1.004], substantially below this threshold.

Table 1 shows the model we built for the three dependent variables. In the LAG model, despite all of our independent variables showing a significant slope, the model overall only explained 7% of the variability in the data ($R^2 = .068$). Contrary to our beliefs, the simultaneous feedback actually helped participants exert the pulses more in sync with the reference than without. Even though the effect of all variables was significant, it is important to note that the magnitudes of these effects were quite small, in the order of a few milliseconds. These were within the range of 150 ms within which people would judge two visual stimuli to be simultaneous [33]. For example, despite the simultaneous feedback having a positive effect by reducing the lag, this reduction was in the order of 7 ms, which is practically imperceptible.

The BASELINE DIFFERENCE model is shown in normalised units (z-score of the reference curve normalised to mean of 0 and SD of 1). In its model, all independent variables had a significant slope, and the model explained 20% of the variability in the data ($R^2 = .204$). Simultaneous visual feedback, deformation, and high-fidelity, all contributed to a decrease in the baseline error, though the effect of the VISUAL FEEDBACK (-.22) and DEFORMATION (-.13) were substantially larger than the effect of the FIDELITY (-.04). Given that the intercept was

| | **Lag** | | | | **Baseline Difference** | | | | **Pulse Amplitude Difference** | | | |
|---|---|---|---|---|---|---|---|---|---|---|---|---|
| | Estimate | SE | t | $p$ | Estimate | SE | t | $p$ | Estimate | SE | t | $p$ |
| (Intercept) | 1.8e-1 | 5.8e-3 | 30.5 | 6e-15 | .56 | .040 | 14.2 | 4e-10 | .86 | .04 | 7.6 | 2e-6 |
| Visual Feedback | -7.4e-3 | 1.2e-3 | 6.3 | 3e-10 | -.22 | .005 | 41.0 | 2e-16 | -.26 | .01 | 27.0 | 2e-16 |
| Deformation | 5.8e-3 | 1.2e-3 | -4.9 | 9e-7 | -.13 | .005 | 2.5 | .013 | -.042 | .01 | 4.3 | 2e-5 |
| Fidelity | 2.1e-2 | 1.2e-3 | 17.7 | 2e-16 | .030 | .01 | 3.0 | .002 | .030 | .01 | 3.0 | .002 |

**Table 1. Linear regression models for the Lag, Baseline Difference, and Pulse Amplitude Difference**

.56, the effect of a high fidelity spine only decreased the error by approximately 7%.

The PULSE AMPLITUDE DIFFERENCE model is also shown in normalised units (z-score of the reference curve normalised to mean of 0 and SD of 1). All independent variables had a significant slope, and the model explained 23% of the variability in the data ($R^2 = .227$). While the simultaneous visual feedback and the sensor deformation contributed to pulses with more similar amplitudes to the reference, the high fidelity of the prototypes had a negative effect. However, the effect of the VISUAL FEEDBACK (-.26) was much more pronounced than those of both the DEFORMATION (-.042) and FIDELITY (.03). Given that the intercept was .86, the presence of a deformable sensor and a high fidelity spine led to changes of less than 5%.

### Task Load

We analysed the raw NASA Task Load Index score to determine if the perceived workload of the task was affected by our independent variables. Simultaneous visual feedback led to lower scores than the delayed feedback (47.29±16.68 SD and 54.97±16.7 SD). There was little difference in scores in the conditions with and without deformation (51.82±17.2 SD and 50.44±17.05 SD) and in the conditions with high and low fidelity (51.22±16.87 SD and 51.04±17.4 SD). We tested whether these effects were significant with a three-way repeated measures ANOVA, which revealed a significant effect on the score for VISUAL FEEDBACK ($F_{1,120} = 6.52, p = .012, \eta^2 = .052$), but neither for DEFORMATION ($F_{1,120} = .21, p = .647$) nor for FIDELITY ($F_{1,120} = .004, p = .952$). In other words, tasks were perceived to be significantly easier with simultaneous visual feedback than with feedback given at the end of each task. We found no significant effect of the DEFORMATION and FIDELITY on the task workload perception.

### Subjective Questionnaire

We asked participants to rank the four devices in order of preference. The most popular choice was the Deformable Hi-Fi device ($N = 8$). It was also the most popular among the top-2 devices ($N = 11$), followed by the Rigid Hi-Fi device ($N = 8$). No participant picked the Deformable Lo-Fi device as their first choice. We tested the ranking scores with a Friedman Rank Sum Test, but we did not find a significant effect of the device on the ranking at $\alpha = .05$ ($\chi^2 = 5.1, p = .15$).

We also asked participants to rate on a 5-point scale their preference for delayed or simultaneous visual feedback. Of the 16 participants, 9 strongly preferred simultaneous feedback, 5 slightly preferred simultaneous feedback, and 2 slightly preferred delayed feedback. The questionnaire also asked them to justify their answer. We clustered the comments using affinity mapping. Amongst the reasons for preferring the simultaneous feedback, participants cited the fact that it enabled them to correct mistakes immediately, demanded less mental effort, and made visual the force they were exerting on the device. Both participants that preferred the delayed feedback cited the fact that it facilitated their learning because they felt that with simultaneous feedback they were just copying the pattern and not actively thinking about the force they should exert.

We asked participants to compare the different devices and discuss advantages and disadvantages. Participants consistently cited the realism of the devices (or lack of) as advantages (or disadvantages), both in terms of the appearance of a spine (FIDELITY) and the amplitude of the movement (DEFORMATION). The Hi-Fi devices were praised for looking like a spine and making the bones visible, but participants felt it was "too bony" in comparison to a human patient and, as a result, uncomfortable to manipulate for a long period of time. The advantages for the Lo-Fi devices were that they distributed the pressure more evenly on the flat surface and were more comfortable, while lack of realism was the main disadvantage. The deformable devices were praised for the realism of the movement amplitude and the resistance of the foam, while the rigid devices were praised for being less physically demanding and being accurate in low amplitude movements.

After the controlled experiment trials, participants evaluated the full graphical user interface of *SpinalLog*, while we collected unstructured informal feedback in an interview and quantitative subjective feedback through a questionnaire. Participants rated the fidelity of the physical shape of *SpinalLog* in relation to a human spine at 6.1 out of 7. Suggestions for improvement included using an additional layer on top of the bones simulating muscles. Participants also rated the fidelity of the displacement in comparison to a real spine, on average 4.2 out of 7. Participants felt that *SpinalLog* was slightly more rigid than their previous experience with practising on their peers and that an additional muscle layer on top would also help to make the displacement more realistic. All participants thought *SpinalLog's* visual feedback helped them control the force exertion better, rating it at 6.3 out of 7. Two participants felt that the complete GUI showed too much information, but that it could be helpful in reviewing the movement after the fact. Participants were divided in the final question, about practice confidence with *SpinalLog* versus with a human, rating it at 4.8 out of 7, with 2 participants disagreeing and 5 participants feeling neutral about it. Among the advantages, participants cited the real-time feedback, its use as an additional practice tool, and its opportunity to safely make mistakes without harming anyone. However, participants also mentioned that ultimately, there is no replacement for a human volunteer to practise the force patterns, so *SpinalLog* could be used as a preliminary activity before practising on a human.

## DISCUSSION

We predicted that the simultaneous feedback would enable participants to better replicate the patterns on the screen, but we also assumed that the added cognitive workload of simultaneously exerting the force and observing the result would hamper how in sync the pulses would be. Our results showed that indeed it allowed users to better match both the baseline force and the amplitude of the pulses—in comparison to the delayed feedback condition, simultaneous feedback reduced the baseline difference by 40% and the pulse amplitude difference by 30%. However, contrary to the hypothesis, it did not introduce a significant lag in how in sync participants performed the pulses. In fact, we found a significant effect in the opposite direction, by reducing the lag by 7 ms (which is negligible for this particular application). We therefore reject **H1** and accept **H2**. However, as two participants noted, even though it is easier to replicate the pattern with simultaneous visual feedback, this does not necessarily lead to better learning. By forcing participants to try to replicate the pattern using only their muscle memory, delayed feedback might be better for learning. We hope to investigate this in future work.

We predicted that the passive haptic feedback enabled by the deformation of the foam would be beneficial to participants trying to replicate the force pattern. Though we found a significant reduction in the error due to the DEFORMATION on both the BASELINE DIFFERENCE and the PULSE AMPLITUDE DIFFERENCE, the effect on the latter was negligible. This means that while it does help users exert pulses with more similar amplitudes reducing the error by 5%, its effect is more pronounced in helping users find the correct baseline, where it helped reduce the error by 23%. This is likely due to the additional perceptual channel through which the baseline information is fed back to the user. As shown in Figure 3, the foam was quite responsive to changes in deformation, making it harder to deform the further the user presses on it. Because the force-feedback depends more on the baseline than on the amplitude of the pulse, it is natural that the effect will be more pronounced in the former. We, therefore, accept **H3**.

Participants' comments highlighted that the deformation felt too rigid. This was a design decision we made together with the subject expert. When presenting the different foam alternatives, the expert chose a foam that was realistic, though more rigid than a healthy spine, so as to give students practice with what a patient with a spinal injury might feel like. This highlights an advantage of *SpinalLog* as a practice tool. Its modular design allows us to replace the foam modules to simulate different spinal conditions, opening the opportunity for activities that involve a diagnosis component.

We hypothesised that more realistic looking devices would lead to better task performance. The effect of the FIDELITY on task performance was significantly beneficial for the BASELINE DIFFERENCE (7% error reduction) and detrimental for the PULSE AMPLITUDE DIFFERENCE (3% error increase). We reject **H4** due to mostly negligible effect. However, despite having little impact on the task performance, fidelity was highly praised in participants' qualitative comments. Participants who liked the Hi-Fi devices praised the realism of the bone structure, and the ones who did not like it felt that it needed an additional layer of muscles to make it even more realistic. Participants that preferred the flat design cited reasons that are not productive in the context of learning, such as how comfortable it is or that it allows them to distribute the force more evenly. Thus, although **H4** is rejected in terms of task performance, FIDELITY does seem to be an important component in how participants perceive the applicability of the device as a learning tool for the particular domain of physiotherapy. In future work, we hope to untangle this relationship.

Our results extend to other scenarios of motor learning where learning to exert correct force patterns is important. Examples include learning how to perform cardiopulmonary resuscitation (CPR) procedures with a dummy and stroke patients re-learning to perform gripping hand movements during rehabilitation with a grip strengthener.

Our study isolated the different properties of our spinal mobilisation simulator to unpack their effects in the participants' ability to replicate a force pattern. However, this does not necessarily mean that this translates to better learning. In order to test the effects of the variables on how they help students learn these patterns, we plan to conduct a future study where we measure transfer of learning: how do these variables impact students' performances when they move from practising on the simulator to practising on a human volunteer?

## CONCLUSION

In this paper, we presented *SpinalLog*, a spinal manipulation simulator that senses forces on each vertebra and gives visual feedback through a GUI and passive haptic feedback through foam deformation. We evaluated three aspects of its design—simultaneous vs delayed feedback, high vs low shape fidelity, and deformable vs rigid sensors—in a controlled user study. We measured their effects on how closely physiotherapy students could replicate a reference force pattern recorded by an expert. We found that simultaneous visual feedback has a strong beneficial effect on task performance without introducing a substantial lag. The sensor deformation helped participants exert forces at the correct baseline level, but it had little effect on the amplitude of the pulses. Though the physical shape of the device had little effect on task performance, it was the most important feature regarding participants' perceptions of the benefits of the device for learning spinal mobilisation.

Our results highlight the potential for the use of *SpinalLog* as a teaching aid and practice tool. A future deployment of *SpinalLog* in class could substantially increase the amount and quality of feedback students receive on their performance, increase practice time as it does not require a volunteer, and allow students to make mistakes without hurting volunteers.

## ACKNOWLEDGEMENTS

This work was partly funded by the University of Melbourne Learning and Teaching Initiative and the Melbourne Research Scholarship. Eduardo Velloso is the recipient of an Australian Research Council Discovery Early Career Award (Project Number: DE180100315) funded by the Australian Government. We thank Dr David Kelly from the Melbourne School of Health Sciences for his expertise in physiotherapy.

## REFERENCES

[1] Jack A Adams. 1971. A Closed-Loop Theory of Motor Learning. *Journal of Motor Behavior* 3, 2 (1971), 111–150. DOI: http://dx.doi.org/10.1080/00222895.1971.10734898

[2] Fraser Anderson, Tovi Grossman, Justin Matejka, and George Fitzmaurice. 2013. YouMove: Enhancing Movement Training with an Augmented Reality Mirror. In *Proceedings of the 26th Annual ACM Symposium on User Interface Software and Technology (UIST '13)*. ACM, New York, NY, USA, 311–320. DOI: http://dx.doi.org/10.1145/2501988.2502045

[3] Tristan Beven, Thuong Hoang, Marcus Carter, and Bernd Ploderer. 2016. HandLog: A Deformable Tangible Device for Continuous Input Through Finger Flexion. In *Proceedings of the 28th Australian Conference on Computer-Human Interaction (OzCHI '16)*. ACM, New York, NY, USA, 595–604. DOI: http://dx.doi.org/10.1145/3010915.3010933

[4] Timothy R Coles. 2011. *Investigating Augmented Reality Visio-Haptic Techniques for Medical Training*. Ph.D. Dissertation. School of Computer Science, Bangor University, Wales. http://diglib.eg.org/handle/10.2312/8257

[5] Timothy R Coles, Dwight Meglan, and Nigel W John. 2011. The Role of Haptics in Medical Training Simulators: A Survey of the State of the Art. *IEEE Transactions on Haptics* 4, 1 (January 2011), 51–66. DOI: http://dx.doi.org/10.1109/TOH.2010.19

[6] Martin Descarreaux, Claude Dugas, Jean Raymond, and Martin C Normand. 2005. Kinetic analysis of expertise in spinal manipulative therapy using an instrumented manikin. *Journal of Chiropractic Medicine* 4, 2 (2005), 53 – 60. DOI: http://dx.doi.org/10.1016/S0899-3467(07)60114-1

[7] Heng Gu, Kai Kunze, Masashi Takatani, and Kouta Minamizawa. 2015. Towards Performance Feedback Through Tactile Displays to Improve Learning Archery. In *Adjunct Proceedings of the 2015 ACM International Joint Conference on Pervasive and Ubiquitous Computing and Proceedings of the 2015 ACM International Symposium on Wearable Computers (UbiComp/ISWC'15 Adjunct)*. ACM, New York, NY, USA, 141–144. DOI: http://dx.doi.org/10.1145/2800835.2800893

[8] Seongkook Heo and Geehyuk Lee. 2011. Force Gestures: Augmenting Touch Screen Gestures with Normal and Tangential Forces. In *Proceedings of the 24th Annual ACM Symposium on User Interface Software and Technology (UIST '11)*. ACM, New York, NY, USA, 621–626. DOI: http://dx.doi.org/10.1145/2047196.2047278

[9] Thuong N Hoang, Martin Reinoso, Frank Vetere, and Egemen Tanin. 2016. Onebody: Remote Posture Guidance System Using First Person View in Virtual Environment. In *Proceedings of the 9th Nordic Conference on Human-Computer Interaction (NordiCHI '16)*. ACM, New York, NY, USA, Article 25, 10 pages. DOI: http://dx.doi.org/10.1145/2971485.2971521

[10] Jeffrey C Ives. 2013. *Motor Behavior: Connecting Mind and Body for Optimal Performance*. Lippincott Williams & Wilkins.

[11] Seahak Kim, Shoichi Hasegawa, Yasuharu Koike, and Makoto Sato. 2002. Tension Based 7-DOF Force Feedback Device: SPIDAR-G. In *Proceedings IEEE Virtual Reality 2002*. 283–284. DOI: http://dx.doi.org/10.1109/VR.2002.996540

[12] Shrawan Kumar. 1995. Teaching aid for spinal mobilization and manipulation therapy. (15 August 1995). US Patent 5,441,413.

[13] Bhoram Lee, Hyunjeong Lee, Soo-Chul Lim, Hyungkew Lee, Seungju Han, and Joonah Park. 2012. Evaluation of Human Tangential Force Input Performance. In *Proceedings of the SIGCHI Conference on Human Factors in Computing Systems (CHI '12)*. ACM, New York, NY, USA, 3121–3130. DOI: http://dx.doi.org/10.1145/2207676.2208727

[14] Dan Morris, Hong Tan, Federico Barbagli, Timothy Chang, and Kenneth Salisbury. 2007. Haptic Feedback Enhances Force Skill Learning. In *Proceedings of the Second Joint EuroHaptics Conference and Symposium on Haptic Interfaces for Virtual Environment and Teleoperator Systems (WHC '07)*. IEEE Computer Society, Washington, DC, USA, 21–26. DOI: http://dx.doi.org/10.1109/WHC.2007.65

[15] Tamotsu Murakami and Naomasa Nakajima. 1994. Direct and Intuitive Input Device for 3-D Shape Deformation. In *Proceedings of the SIGCHI Conference on Human Factors in Computing Systems (CHI '94)*. ACM, New York, NY, USA, 465–470. DOI: http://dx.doi.org/10.1145/191666.191823

[16] Jun Murayama, Laroussi Bougrila, YanLin Luo, Katsuhito Akahane, Shoichi Hasegawa, Béat Hirsbrunner, and Makoto Sato. 2004. SPIDAR G&G: A Two-Handed Haptic Interface for Bimanual VR Interaction. In *Proceedings of EuroHaptics*, Vol. 2004. 138–146. http://haselab.net/files/paperDB_uploads/pdf-eshhwpu9.pdf

[17] Keith Nesbitt. 2003. *Designing multi-sensory displays for abstract data*. Ph.D. Dissertation. School of Information Technologies, University of Sydney, Australia. http://hdl.handle.net/2123/4135

[18] Hyung Kun Park and Woohun Lee. 2016. Motion Echo Snowboard: Enhancing Body Movement Perception in Sport via Visually Augmented Feedback. In *Proceedings of the 2016 ACM Conference on Designing Interactive Systems (DIS '16)*. ACM, New York, NY, USA, 192–203. DOI: http://dx.doi.org/10.1145/2901790.2901797

[19] Alan W Salmoni, Richard A Schmidt, and Charles B Walter. 1984. Knowledge of Results and Motor Learning: A Review and Critical Reappraisal. *Psychological Bulletin* 95, 3 (1984), 355–386. DOI: http://dx.doi.org/10.1037/0033-2909.95.3.355

[20] Richard A Schmidt, Timothy D Lee, Carolee J Winstein, Gabriele Wulf, and Howard N Zelaznik. 2018. *Motor Control and Learning: A Behavioral Emphasis* (6th ed.). Human Kinetics.

[21] Caitlyn Seim, Nick Doering, Yang Zhang, Wolfgang Stuerzlinger, and Thad Starner. 2017. Passive Haptic Training to Improve Speed and Performance on a Keypad. *Proc. ACM Interact. Mob. Wearable Ubiquitous Technol.* 1, 3, Article 100 (September 2017), 13 pages. DOI: http://dx.doi.org/10.1145/3132026

[22] Ted Selker and Joseph D Rutledge. 1991. Finger Force Precision for Computer Pointing. *IBM RC* 17342 (1991), 2–7.

[23] Emma G Sheaves, Suzanne J Snodgrass, and Darren A Rivett. 2012. Learning Lumbar Spine Mobilization: The Effects of Frequency and Self-Control of Feedback. *Journal of Orthopaedic & Sports Physical Therapy* 42, 2 (February 2012), 114–124. DOI: http://dx.doi.org/10.2519/jospt.2012.3691

[24] Maureen J Simmonds, Shrawan Kumar, and Eugene Lechelt. 1995. Use of a Spinal Model to Quantify the Forces and Motion That Occur During Therapists' Tests of Spinal Motion. *Physical Therapy* 75, 3 (March 1995), 212–222. DOI: http://dx.doi.org/10.1093/ptj/75.3.212

[25] Ross T Smith, Bruce H Thomas, and Wayne Piekarski. 2008a. Digital Foam Interaction Techniques for 3D Modeling. In *Proceedings of the 2008 ACM Symposium on Virtual Reality Software and Technology (VRST '08)*. ACM, New York, NY, USA, 61–68. DOI: http://dx.doi.org/10.1145/1450579.1450592

[26] Ross T Smith, Bruce H Thomas, and Wayne Piekarski. 2008b. Tech Note: Digital Foam. In *2008 IEEE Symposium on 3D User Interfaces*. 35–38. DOI: http://dx.doi.org/10.1109/3DUI.2008.4476588

[27] Rajinder Sodhi, Hrvoje Benko, and Andrew Wilson. 2012. LightGuide: Projected Visualizations for Hand Movement Guidance. In *Proceedings of the SIGCHI Conference on Human Factors in Computing Systems (CHI '12)*. ACM, New York, NY, USA, 179–188. DOI: http://dx.doi.org/10.1145/2207676.2207702

[28] Maurício Sousa, João Vieira, Daniel Medeiros, Artur Arsenio, and Joaquim Jorge. 2016. SleeveAR: Augmented Reality for Rehabilitation Using Realtime Feedback. In *Proceedings of the 21st International Conference on Intelligent User Interfaces (IUI '16)*. ACM, New York, NY, USA, 175–185. DOI: http://dx.doi.org/10.1145/2856767.2856773

[29] Brynne E Stainsby, Michelle CS Clarke, and Jade R Egonia. 2016. Learning spinal manipulation: a best-evidence synthesis of teaching methods. *Journal of Chiropractic Education* 30, 2 (2016), 138–151. DOI: http://dx.doi.org/10.7899/JCE-15-8

[30] Craig Stewart, Michael Rohs, Sven Kratz, and Georg Essl. 2010. Characteristics of Pressure-based Input for Mobile Devices. In *Proceedings of the SIGCHI Conference on Human Factors in Computing Systems (CHI '10)*. ACM, New York, NY, USA, 801–810. DOI: http://dx.doi.org/10.1145/1753326.1753444

[31] Yuta Sugiura, Gota Kakehi, Anusha Withana, Calista Lee, Daisuke Sakamoto, Maki Sugimoto, Masahiko Inami, and Takeo Igarashi. 2011. Detecting Shape Deformation of Soft Objects Using Directional Photoreflectivity Measurement. In *Proceedings of the 24th Annual ACM Symposium on User Interface Software and Technology (UIST '11)*. ACM, New York, NY, USA, 509–516. DOI: http://dx.doi.org/10.1145/2047196.2047263

[32] Faisal Taher, Jason Alexander, John Hardy, and Eduardo Velloso. 2014. An Empirical Characterization of Touch-Gesture Input-Force on Mobile Devices. In *Proceedings of the Ninth ACM International Conference on Interactive Tabletops and Surfaces (ITS '14)*. ACM, New York, NY, USA, 195–204. DOI: http://dx.doi.org/10.1145/2669485.2669515

[33] Rob LJ van Eijk, Armin Kohlrausch, James F Juola, and Steven van de Par. 2009. Temporal Interval Discrimination Thresholds Depend on Perceived Synchrony for Audio-Visual Stimulus Pairs. *Journal of Experimental Psychology: Human Perception and Performance* 35, 4 (August 2009), 1254–1263. DOI: http://dx.doi.org/10.1037/a0014254

[34] Eduardo Velloso, Andreas Bulling, and Hans Gellersen. 2013a. MotionMA: Motion Modelling and Analysis by Demonstration. In *Proceedings of the SIGCHI Conference on Human Factors in Computing Systems (CHI '13)*. ACM, New York, NY, USA, 1309–1318. DOI: http://dx.doi.org/10.1145/2470654.2466171

[35] Eduardo Velloso, Andreas Bulling, Hans Gellersen, Wallace Ugulino, and Hugo Fuks. 2013b. Qualitative Activity Recognition of Weight Lifting Exercises. In *Proceedings of the 4th Augmented Human International Conference (AH '13)*. ACM, New York, NY, USA, 116–123. DOI: http://dx.doi.org/10.1145/2459236.2459256

[36] Graham Wilson, Craig Stewart, and Stephen A Brewster. 2010. Pressure-based Menu Selection for Mobile Devices. In *Proceedings of the 12th International Conference on Human Computer Interaction with Mobile Devices and Services (MobileHCI '10)*. ACM, New York, NY, USA, 181–190. DOI: http://dx.doi.org/10.1145/1851600.1851631

[37] Xiao Xiao, Pablo Puentes, Edith Ackermann, and Hiroshi Ishii. 2016. Andantino: Teaching Children Piano with Projected Animated Characters. In *Proceedings of the The 15th International Conference on Interaction Design and Children (IDC '16)*. ACM, New York, NY, USA, 37–45. DOI: http://dx.doi.org/10.1145/2930674.2930689

# Tangible Objects for Reminiscing in Dementia Care

**Stephan Huber**
Universität Würzburg
Würzburg, Germany
stephan.huber@uni-wuerzburg.de

**Renate Berner**
Demenz Support Stuttgart
Stuttgart, Germany
renny.b@gmx.de

**Martina Uhlig, Peter Klein**
User Interface Design GmbH
Ludwigsburg, Germany
Martina.uhlig@uid.com
peter.klein@uid.com

**Jörn Hurtienne**
Universität Würzburg
Würzburg, Germany
jörn.hurtienne@uni-wuerzburg.de

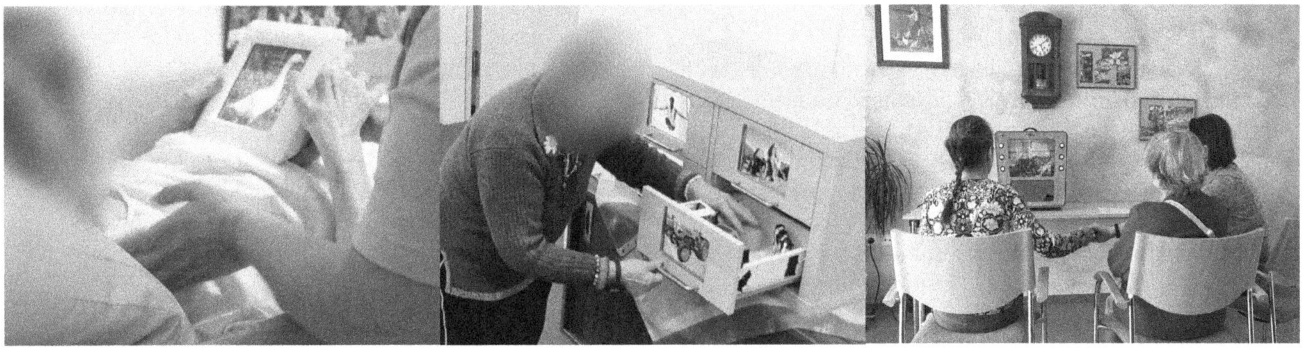

**Figure 1. The pictures show from left to right how people with dementia used prototypes of (a) the pyramid during an individual intervention, (b) the drawers in free exploration, and (c) the jukebox during a group session.**

## ABSTRACT
Reminiscence in dementia care often does not make use of interactive technology. In this work we present a study conducted in two dementia care facilities aimed at developing prototypes for reminiscence. We conducted contextual inquiries over a week to learn how 80 people with varying stages of dementia reminisce throughout the day. We present resulting needs and three tangible prototypes designed to facilitate reminiscence. These prototypes – the pyramid, the set of drawers and the jukebox – were tested in three exploratory field studies. We elaborate on the features of the prototypes that facilitated communication and reminiscence and share insights from failures that need to be considered when designing tangibles in the dementia context. To visualize both positive and negative aspects we introduce a model of successful interaction in the dementia context.

## Author Keywords
Dementia; Contextual Design; Reminiscence


*TEI '19, March 17–20, 2019, Tempe, AZ, USA*

ACM 978-1-4503-6196-5/19/03...$15.00
https://doi.org/10.1145/3294109.3295632

## INTRODUCTION
Dementia is a syndrome impairing cognitive function beyond what might be expected from normal ageing. Affected functionalities include memory, thinking, orientation, comprehension, learning capacity, language and judgement [31]. The proceeding depletion of memory and cognitive, emotional and social abilities negatively influences activities of daily living [32] and reduces the general quality of life [3]. Alleviating the decrease of quality of life is one of the great challenges in dementia care. Therefore many studies in clinical dementiology apply Quality of Life measures as the main evaluation criteria for interventions in dementia care facilities [1]. Quality of Life includes social and environmental conditions as well as the psychological state [30] and is typically measured by observing behaviours and general well-being in people with dementia, e.g. [20]. Lately the shift from technology for safety and security [21] towards designing for self-identity and quality of life [28] also arrived in HCI.

In this work we focus on tangible interactive systems in the context of *reminiscence activities*. Reminiscence activities are psychosocial interventions for people with dementia. They have been shown to have positive effects on cognition, mood and behaviour of people with dementia [38]. Their aim is to counteract the loss of self-identity [9] by presenting memory-triggers to evoke autobiographical memories. Memory-triggers can be provided by mentioning familiar locations, showing pictures, playing music, reading out tales or performing activities together that once were relevant for the person with dementia. This requires knowledge about the person's biography; care persons need to retrieve this knowledge in time and apply it in a validating manner to create a valuable experience for the person with dementia.

Today, reminiscence activities in care facilities primarily employ non-digital cues like pictures, music or household equipment from the past, mostly the formative years of self-identity [26]. Since the 1990s several attempts have been made to bring interactive technology into care facilities to support reminiscence activities. The CIRCA project [2] is a popular example where touchscreens were used to present different forms of media, like pictures, videos, or music. More recent research includes mobile applications [14] and even virtual reality experiences [6; 33], with some inspiration taken from other fields like art therapy [24; 25].

Designing and evaluating interfaces with people with dementia poses additional challenges. Standard methods for user-centered design or user-experience testing are hardly applicable since those methods rely on reflecting and self-reporting perceived emotions and meanings of actions – skills that are limited by the decline of cognitive and emotional abilities [18]. Direct questioning therefore often is replaced by ethnographically inspired observations of behavior [22]. However, it is difficult to measure whether a person is reminiscing. Only uttered memories or, in people with advanced aphasia, observed non-verbal emotional responses can indicate reminiscence and thus decide over the success or failure of interventions. Sometimes, attention alone (versus disinterest) is considered a good outcome [23].

We adapted and implemented a user-centered design process in the context of and in close collaboration with two dementia care facilities. As part of this process we designed three tangibles, the interactive pyramid, the interactive chest of drawers, and the jukebox. We deployed these in dementia care homes and explored how they can support reminiscing in people with dementia and how successful they are in terms of interaction, emotional outcomes and reminiscence events.

## PROTOTYPE DEVELOPMENT

From pilot observations, we learned how reminiscence activities were currently conducted in care homes. Some of the material used in group sessions does not work well. For example, when looking at pictures of popular politicians from the 50s, few people with dementia remember the person's name, others can barely recognise the picture over a distance. The caregiver often has no deeper knowledge of the time and culture than the information provided on the back of the picture. What works nicely in triggering memories and positive emotional responses are household activities that can be experienced on multiple sensory channels. Examples are the smell, sound and haptic feedback of using an old coffee mill or preparing and eating an apple pie. However, those sensory-rich activities require a high degree of preparation and therefore are not often employed. Specific memories may be evoked in planned activities but reminiscing also occurs outside of scheduled sessions. Therefore, in our user research we wanted to go beyond scheduled reminiscence activities and learn how people with dementia reminisce throughout the day.

| N° | Top User Needs and Requirements |
|---|---|
| N01 | People with dementia show a strong need to physically interact with objects. |
| N02 | Their "own territory" is important to residents. |
| N03 | Actions and activities of people with dementia appear to be meaningful even if the meaning is not immediately clear to outsiders. |
| N04 | People with dementia who are able to walk do so whenever they can - for example to look for interesting objects. |
| N05 | People with dementia must have the choice to opt out of activities. |
| N06 | Music, singing and games are important to approach people with dementia. |
| R01 | A system must be adaptable to different users so it can be used for several individuals. |
| R02 | A system must obtain a broad stock of media and topics to be adjustable to everyone's needs. |
| R03 | A system must be applicable for group activity but also for individuals. |
| R04 | A system shall promote interactions between residents. |
| R05 | Even though external stimuli may often be needed, self-initiative shall be promoted. |
| R06 | A system must not cause overstimulation. |
| R07 | A system must offer smooth interactions and transitions. |
| R08 | A system must offer experiences of success. |
| R09 | A system must be fitted for people with dementia's cognitive and sensorimotor skills. |
| R10 | A (physical) systems must be very robust. |

**Table 1. Top User Needs (N) and Requirements (R) for a reminiscence support system for the context of dementia care facilities, as extracted from user data.**

Ten researchers of the project *Interactive Memories* with backgrounds in HCI and dementia care spent two weeks observing and talking to people with dementia in several dementia groups in two care facilities. Our aim was to learn how people with dementia reminisced in everyday life and to gather affordances and needs of people with dementia in this context. From the two care facilities located in a rural (A) and an urban (B) environment, altogether 80 residents with dementia participated in our study. We followed a Contextual Design [15] approach adapted to the dementia context that involved more observing than interviewing and that stretched observation periods to multiple days [16; 17] – thus returning to the method's ethnographic origins.

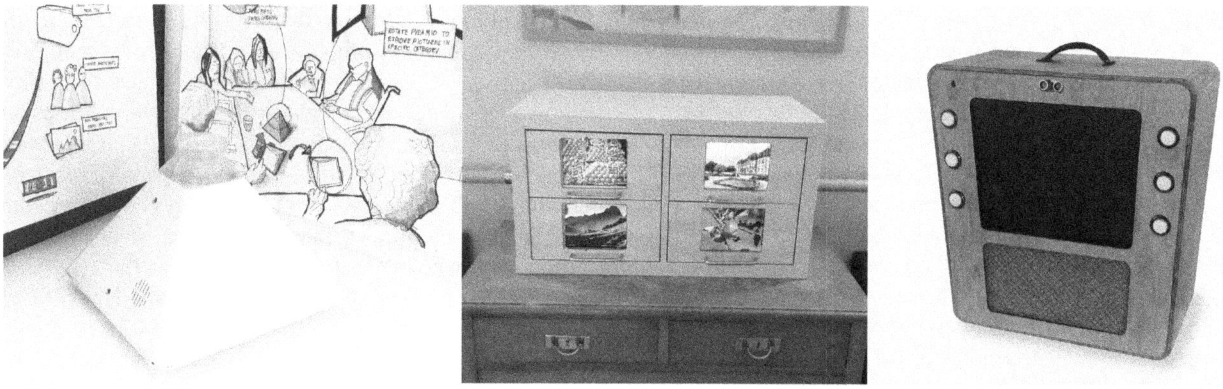

**Figure 2. The pictures show from left to right (a) the pyramid with the display facing down, (b) the interactive drawers displaying pictures relevant to the closest user, and (c) the jukebox able to play music from selected categories.**

Our design process incorporated the wall walk of an affinity diagram [15] to generate key findings and design ideas followed by a visioning workshop. Among our key findings were the observations that residents of all groups showed a strong need to physically interact with objects, and residents who were able to walk did so whenever they could – for example to look for interesting objects to manipulate. For a list of top user needs [15] and gathered requirements for people with dementia see Table 1. Caregivers, being the secondary user group, needed interfaces that allow for better care while being easy to administer and not causing any extra labor. Therefore, we attempted to minimize their role in our designs. Based on those findings and inspired by the design ideas, we created a set of visions [15], including tangible prototypes reported in this paper but also scenarios for an interactive wall [5] or table [4]. In the following we present three tangible prototypes that emerged in the visions and were further developed and iterated with the care facilities.

All tangible prototypes have in common that they supported some sort of simple tangible interaction (N01) to fit the sensorimotor skills of people with dementia (R01), foster their self-efficacy (R05) and provide them with experiences of success (R08). Additionally, we deployed generally popular topics and non-private pictures to promote interactions between residents (R02, R03).

### Pyramid

The 3D-printed prototype of the *pyramid* (see Figure 2a) contained speakers and a square 10" screen in its base as output channels. Input was possible through the pyramid's position sensors and its turnable top. The prototype was designed to stand on a side, so the user could watch the screen from a seated as well as a lying position. Pictures from the domains of gardening, animals, traveling, harbors, hiking or local monuments were shown on the screen, accompanied by matching sound (e.g. bird songs with the picture of a songbird). Each domain contained a sequence of 11...24 pictures. By turning the top of the pyramid, one could navigate between domains. Turning the entire pyramid by 90° in either direction changed the screen to show the next or previous picture within the sequence. Rotating the entire pyramid or its top were considered appropriate interactions for the typical sensorimotor skills of people with dementia. The pyramid was designed to be used in individual sessions as well as group activities.

### Drawers

The *interactive chest of drawers* consisted of a set of four smoothly sliding drawers (80 x 40 x 40 cm). These contained several tangible objects (like photographs or animal figurines) that were intended to trigger reminiscing. Integrated in the front of the drawers were four iPad minis. These served as picture frames to advertise the content of the drawers (see Figure 2b). Pictures displayed on the screens could be exchanged according to the current user's personal preferences or actions (for example in a Wizard of Oz setup in which the wizard knew about the preferences). Based on our insights from the contextual inquiry, we expected residents to be curious about the new furniture, approach it and open the drawers to see what's inside. Viewing the pictures and interacting with the content should trigger (autobiographic) memories and evoke positive emotions. As the drawers hold generic content they can be installed in a community area and allow for individual or group reminiscing activities. The prototype was designed to be explored by wandering people with dementia that could use these on their own to facilitate their self-efficacy.

### Jukebox

The *jukebox* was a rectangular box (about 45 x 45 x 23 cm size). The front of the jukebox was equipped with a speaker, a display and six large hardware buttons (Figure 2c). Each button started another predefined playlist: folk songs with vocals, folk songs without vocals, popular hits of the past, church songs, choral music, and lullabies. One or two pictures were shown with each song, that were thought to support the song's meaning (e.g. pictures of Paris when a chanson was playing). The jukebox was designed to be used by people with varying senso-motoric abilities and trigger memories through either sound, image or the combination of both. Its retro-design was thought to appear familiar to people with dementia and encourage them to approach the jukebox and initiate interaction.

## EVALUATION

The prototypes were evaluated in the same facilities where the contextual inquiry had been conducted. We recorded data through observation, video and follow-up interviews with caregivers and coded and interpreted the resulting protocols. Our focus lay on the prototypes' effects on reminiscence and meaningful moments during the intervention. Experienced evaluators identified and interpreted those meaningful moments through observation of non-verbal reactions and evocations as indicators of reminisced past events. Noting and interpreting meaningful interactions is common when designing in the dementia context [27]. More systematic methods were proposed but not yet evaluated [8; 18]. Observations took place in the setting of group sessions or individual interventions. Details on the evaluation of each prototype are provided in the respective section below.

### Pyramid

The pyramid was evaluated in four short single interventions and four group sessions that took 1...1.5 hours. Group sessions took place in a residential community area of the urban dementia care facility and 2...8 residents participated in each group session, including nonverbal people with dementia. All interactions with the pyramid were closely accompanied and guided by a caregiver. Data was gathered through direct observation, video (partly), transcript of interactions and reflection talks with 4 caregivers and 3 supervisors.

#### *Findings*

People with dementia were able to directly interact with the prototype and to switch between pictures. When a caregiver prompted residents to turn the pyramid, they at most stroke an edge of the prototype. After a demonstration of the interaction, however, residents who were physically fit enough, turned the pyramid on their own.

People with dementia often held the pyramid or reached out to it, as they watched a picture. They frequently touched the screen while talking about its content. One resident (P15) who was shown the picture of a dachshund said merrily that it was her dog from home and called him repeatedly by the name of her (remembered) pet. She also tried to pet the animal on the screen and was surprised by the heat radiation, exclaiming "Oh, nicely warm!" and petted the screen again.

The pyramid's size made it very mobile, so it could be handed around and turned in group sessions. Caregivers were also able to bring the prototype to the rooms of bedridden people who no longer could get up and participate in activities in the community area. On three occasions caregivers placed the pyramid on lying residents' lap, so they could reach it and watch the pictures (see Figure 1a). One of them (P63) was not responsive to either the pyramid or the caregiver. The other two bedridden residents and an additional resident who sat isolated from the group showed positive reactions like grasping the pyramid while attentively observing the pictures (P61) or smiling and even talking about the content (P62, P64).

Sounds and pictures triggered stories. As expected, pictures from residents' hometowns triggered memories. Additionally, we found travelling to be a very beneficial topic as it animated the residents to share their stories and experiences from vacations in the past. Even generic pictures of beaches and the sea for example triggered residents' memories of different countries and holidays. When a picture of the Big Ben with the Thames in London was shown, the group riddled whether that is "in Austria, no Italy [...] huh? France, yes?" (P15) or "Milan, there are many lakes" (P12). After the caregiver solved the puzzle, a former teacher remembered, that he had been to London with his class once (P13).

Sound emitted by the prototype potentially amplified the effect of the pictures, for example when light (holiday-) music accompanied the travel pictures. Sometimes the sounds stood on their own, for example when animal sounds, could also be heard by those participants of a group who could not currently see the picture. Residents' reaction varied from simply whistling in response to a bird song (P16) to wondering about the sound but still associating it with memories "where is the fair-music coming from?" (P21).

Animals triggered positive emotions and stories even when these were not recognized correctly. One group recited and enjoyed rhymes about singing birds, even though they were not sure whether the picture showed a blackbird or a raven. In another picture one resident took horses for kangaroos (P18) but then joined the group discussion about horse-riding and racetracks.

Generic content brings up important memories and facilitates group discussions. Group discussions were often based on one resident sharing an autobiographic experience that was triggered by a picture and other participants then built on the story. For example, when viewing pictures of birds, one resident said "in the garden" (P17). The caregiver confirmed "correct, there is an aviary in our garden". Another resident joined in, telling that she "had many budgies, most of the time even two in the cage" (P16). Generic pictures could also trigger personal memories, so a resident laughed and happily claimed "There, that's our car!" (P43) when viewing a historic image of the city of Freiburg.

Residents showed strong emotions when viewing the pictures. For example, a resident who was not able to speak anymore smiled and a tear ran down his cheek when the caregiver showed him a picture of the sea and reminded him of holidays he spent traveling with his family (P23).

People with mild to moderate dementia share their mental models of the interface. A resident who noticed the 'meow' sounds emitted by the pyramid, when it showed cat pictures, commented "oh they shout every time when one turns them? [laughs] 'no, no, we do not want to be turned!'" (P21). Another resident commented on the short lag when turning the pyramid "now [the picture] makes a headstand [...] now there is another one" (P16).

The display is of sufficient size for the user who is holding it. When pictures were viewed across the table residents were mostly able to identify the content, sometimes the displayed pictures were misinterpreted due to lack of size, brightness, or light reflections on the screen. Some bowed down towards the screen on the table to identify details. Overall, the caregivers enjoyed using the pyramid and asked frequently when the next prototype would be ready to test. They criticized that the sound level was only adjustable via an app and not directly on the pyramid. Also, the prototype was not very stable and lost its functionality to switch categories towards the end of both observation days, so it had to be repaired between days.

### Drawers

We evaluated the interactive drawers in two residential living groups of the rural dementia care facility. During the first three days we installed the prototype in a seating area alongside a corridor in group A that was highly frequented by residents as it connected their community area with the private rooms and an exit door. Additionally, we took the prototype for one day to a corridor leading towards the community area of group B. Pictures displayed on the screens of the drawers could be exchanged remotely by a Wizard-of-Oz according to the current user's known personal preferences or actions. We assigned a topic of interest (according to data from the initial observation, caregiver interviews and piloting) to each drawer and filled it with generic tangible memory-triggers that catered for the residents' observed need to explore their environment and interact with objects. Pilot test had shown that the most popular topics for the drawers' content among users were:

- nature (chestnuts, animal figurines and a box of postcards with nature-motives)
- sports (jump rope and balls of different sizes and materials)
- household (dustpan and brush, wooden spoon, rolling pin and a Bundt cake pan)
- farming (figurines of farm animals and models of a tractor, tools and fruits)

Care staff introduced us as visitors who brought something interesting and we acted mainly as overt observers but also assisted or engaged in conversation when the residents initiated contact. To facilitate unbiased, self-initiated interactions with the drawers we also observed covertly during some time slots. Based on our insights from the contextual inquiry, we expected residents to be curious about the new furniture, approach it and open drawers. Viewing the pictures and interacting with content should trigger (autobiographic) memories and evoke positive emotions.

In preceding pilot studies many residents were just walking around while looking down on the floor. Some chased caregivers or looked for a toilet, their shoes or a place to sleep; and they did not pay attention to the set of drawers as they walked by. Most walked past us several times, always facing down and appearing rather unsatisfied. So without forcing people to use the prototype we strived to draw more attention towards it and attached an LED strip that led from the floor towards the drawers. When the Wizard started the LED animation, a green light slowly moved towards the drawers. Data was gathered through direct observation and interaction transcripts from video data.

#### *Findings*

The drawers mediate communication with residents with mild to moderate dementia. Residents often approached us as observers and asked about the drawers' pictures or told us what they saw in them, e.g. "drawers – oh a tractor!" (D2). Together with a friend she (D2, D4) returned to the drawer after lunch and asked us, whether they "may have a look at that". When invited to open a drawer, D2 opened each drawer twice. She took out the dustpan and brush from the household drawer, laughed and found it to be "interesting and a diversion". D11 even initiated a conversation by pointing to a picture showing the church from her home town and informing the care giver that "that is at our place".

The drawers mediate interaction in group sessions. A caregiver who included the drawers in her scheduled group reminiscence session came with five residents to the prototype. One resident (D4) joked and laughed as she named the motives she saw in the pictures. After the caregiver encouraged residents to have a look inside the drawers, D2 opened all of them and exclaimed "oh how cute!" when she discovered the small tools. D4 kept her distance to the drawers and did not directly interact with it. However, she had fun commenting interactions performed by others.

The drawers facilitate the choice of subject by the residents. When caregivers tried to draw residents' attention to one of the pictures, residents often showed more interest in another picture. On our last day in the facility, we involved one of the caregivers as companion and gave him a one-minute instruction into the Wizard-App. He used the drawers as wall of pictures and involved a resident (D13) into an extended session on utility vehicles from the 50s. When D13 showed particular interest in one picture, the companion displayed associated pictures on other drawers and moderated the content well.

People with moderate to severe dementia did not benefit from the drawers. Two wandering ladies with moderate to severe dementia (D7, D10) were interested in the light animation and stopped to follow or observe it multiple times as they passed but did not pay attention to the drawers. Also, when D10 later initiates contact to an observer and is led to the drawers she only smiles at the observer and walks away.

The perception of repetitive content varies strongly between people with dementia. Few users were annoyed by looking at images they remembered. One lady said "oh – it's the same picture as yesterday" (D4), another answered when asked if she liked the drawers "no, [pictures] come and go" (D03).

Some users apparently were not disturbed by repetition and identified familiar content on two days as "look, that's the church from my home" (D11) or "yes it's beautiful - I was delighted yesterday already" (D2). A large third group only recognized content through repetition like D02 who sat close to the drawer for a longer time and commented on a "little girl" after she saw it for the second time. Observers tested the appropriateness of several roles. We conducted observations as covert observers (hiding in a room and observing through a small window), overt observers (sitting near the prototype while watching) and also steward observers (inviting residents to use the prototype while presenting ourselves as its owner or a steward). For research purposes steward observation was better than overt observation. Residents repeatedly expressed the concern of interrupting our work and left, as we sat there passively observing and taking notes. When we engaged them in conversations, however, they happily stayed, interacted with the drawer (see Figure 1b), and told stories. During all covert observations over four days, only two residents approached the drawers, inspected the pictures but then walked away without physically interacting. The presence of the overt observers appeared to be more interesting than the prototype.

### Jukebox

To evaluate the jukebox, seven group sessions took place over two days in the urban facility. One session was held with a larger group of 8-12 residents (four residents joined during the course of the session), the other sessions were smaller with 2-6 participating residents (see Figure 1c). Data was gathered through steward observation, supported by video recordings. The camera was positioned in the back of the room and recorded interactions but not facial expressions during interaction. The observer sat in the front for a good view on the users' behavior and emotional reactions.

#### *Findings*

People with dementia showed positive reactions to the music. Residents who were able to hear the music, sang (e.g. J15, J31, J32, J33, J42, J52, J61, J78) along with the lyrics, whistled the melody (J32), swayed (J42), bobbed their feet (J13, J14, J15), waved their hands to the rhythms (J41, J62) or even danced with a caregiver (J76). They enjoyed the music but hardly responded to the pictures. When asked about a picture by the caregiver, most residents did not respond at all or gave a short answer and whistled to the music again (J32). Across all sessions there were only two residents (J13, J51) who talked about the pictures rather than enjoying the music. Even though the pictures' content was selected to match the songs' lyrics and mediate reminiscence, this combination did not work for users. In contrast, the two types of media seemed to compete. Possibly listening to either the music or focusing on the pictures already consumed their cognitive resources and left no place for the other medium.

Finding an adequate sound volume of the music was a major issue. Residents sitting in the back of the room barely heard the music and had trouble understanding the lyrics or melody. Those residents became either restless or fell asleep. For residents sitting closer to the jukebox the music was perfect to sing along but too loud for having a conversation next to it. Reminiscence activities therefore took place between songs. For example, after a song was over, J32 talked about her "mum" and remembered, how she used to sing that song. After a song about blooming lilac, another participant (J78) explained how it reminds her of a wedding in April, where lilac served as decoration.

Interactions with the jukebox were never initiated by residents. Residents did not only need to be instructed but rather convinced by caregivers to push one of the buttons to

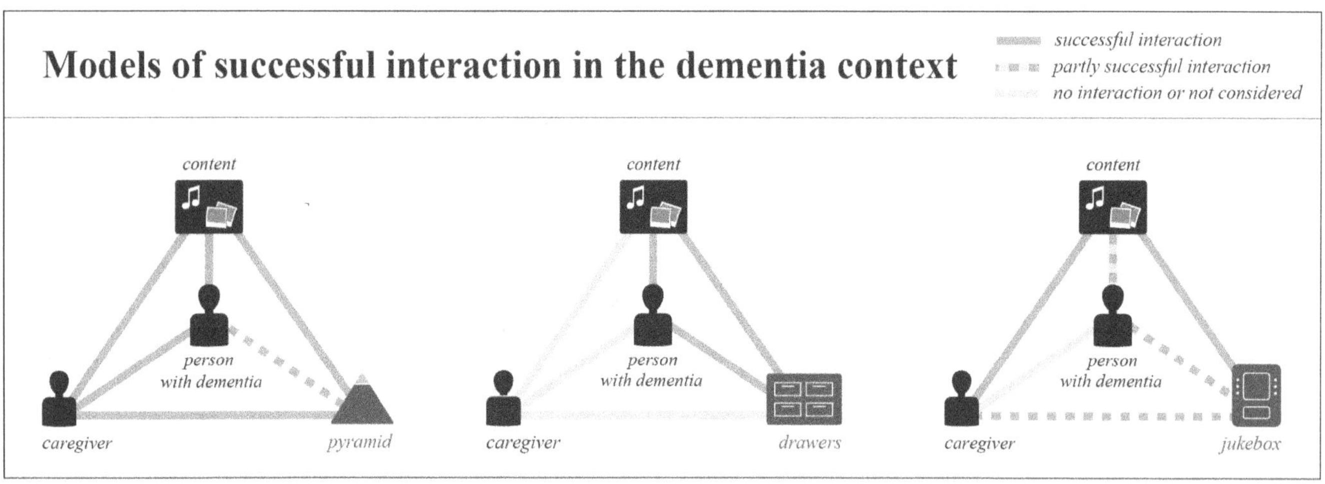


**Figure 3. The models of successful interaction in the dementia context for the pyramid (left), interactive drawers (middle) and jukebox (right). Green lines represent an interaction that was planned and worked well. Dotted lines represent interactions that only worked in part. Grey lines stand for interactions that were either not considered or did not work.**

start a playlist. So, on most occasions caregivers operated the jukebox. Additionally, residents were not able to read the labels next to the buttons.

Caregivers did not like the controls of the jukebox and that some of the settings, like volume or song selection could only be adjusted in the accompanying smartphone app. In sum they felt that there was no obvious advantage over a common CD player.

## DISCUSSION

In the following we discuss our findings and elaborate on why some aspects of our prototypes worked while others did not. For a better comparability of the three prototypes we have developed a model of successful interactions in the dementia context shown in Figure 3. The model acknowledges that a successful reminiscence activity depends on the interaction between the person with dementia, very often the caregiver, the system and its content. Therefore, in the center of the model is the person with dementia who, as an individual or in a group interacts with a system (here: pyramid, drawers or jukebox) that delivers content (here: images, sound, tangible objects) selected to trigger moments of reminiscence. We differentiate between systems and their content here for a more detailed analysis of interactions but explicitly do not recommend to separate those two aspects during the design process. The caregivers add three new relations to the model: they interact with the person with dementia, possibly select content and may also operate the system.

The pyramid was successful because it evoked the most emotional responses in people with all stages of dementia. The generic picture material with appropriate sound cues facilitated reminiscence for individuals as well as in group sessions. Residents often responded to different aspects of the prototypes and sometimes evaluators could not document the exact memory but only the resulting emotional response. Residents enjoyed the tangible experience of grasping the pyramid and even found pleasure in the unintended heat radiation. After a short instruction most residents who had the physical strength were also able to turn the pyramid to scroll through an image gallery. However, interesting pictures and sounds of the pyramid often caught the users' entire attention, so they forgot how to operate it. Possibly the content's reminiscing effect was stronger than the pyramid's affordance to be turned. Caregivers operated the pyramid with ease and assisted the residents in using the pyramid. They were familiar with the content, chose appropriate categories for each session and did a great job in moderating the interaction and validating residents' evocations. When moderated appropriately, the pyramid supported reminiscence sessions with people in all stages of dementia.

Our primary users, people with dementia, interacted most intuitively with the drawers. Each resident who attempted to look into a drawer knew how to open it. Apart from this, people with mild to moderate dementia only interacted with objects or named content in pictures when a caregiver or steward to talk to was nearby. Most positive reactions were evoked when a caregiver moderated the interaction and residents verbalized their associations triggered by the content or even shared their stories. Then the drawers successfully served as mediator of communication and choice of subject for people with dementia, when a companion was involved.

However, residents only dared to open drawers and happily interacted with the objects inside when invited to do so. Since our vision involved free exploration of the drawers by an individual wandering person with dementia, the drawer-experience was not optimized for multiple users or companions. So unfortunately, caregivers who knew the residents well were not instructed in the functionality of the drawers and were not familiar with the personalized content of pictures for each user, e.g. did not recognize a church from a resident's hometown. Steward observers were familiar with the tangible setup but did not know much about the residents apart from how some of the pictures linked to their biography. Because caregivers played no big role in the vision, an effective moderation of reminiscing processes was not catered for. It turned out that without this moderation the personalized pictures did not work better than the generic objects in the drawers, cf. [12]. The set of drawers failed its original purpose by providing an experience that left out the caregiver.

User data that led to the development of the drawers originated mainly from people with moderate to severe dementia. In our evaluation sessions, however, residents with moderate to severe dementia were most interested in the moving light animation towards the drawers. They barely payed attention to the pictures. Whether this was due to a lack of visual perception, cognitive processing, disinterest or a mixture of all three is unclear.

The jukebox activated people with dementia to move to the rhythm or even sing along with the music. However, the pictures provided hardly any additional value and for people sitting close to the jukebox, the music was too loud to have a conversation while for people sitting farther away, the sound was too quiet to properly understand the lyrics. Additionally, persons with dementia had to walk up to the jukebox to read the category names but then did not want to push the category buttons, even when prompted by caregivers. Caregivers' attempts to moderate reminiscence were hindered through the sound level of the music that was not programmable directly at the jukebox and neither was the title within a selected genre. Although the music triggered positive reactions in people with dementia, the jukebox was still deemed as unsuccessful by the caregivers as it had no additional value to a standard CD player, only at the cost of a more cumbersome interface.

For future work, we plan to examine the long-term effects of the pyramid when employed regularly in reminiscence sessions. For this purpose, the prototype needs to be made stable. The pyramid also has the potential to be employed in group interventions with people living with moderate to severe dementia, a setting barely covered in HCI so far. We will not investigate the drawers any further, as the aspect that worked best was a selectable set of pictures, a task that can be performed better on a large screen without the drawers. We will also not pursue the jukebox any longer. From successes and failures of all three prototypes we learned that:

- tangibles (e.g. drawers) have the potential of being familiar and thus intuitive to use for people with dementia.
- holding on objects (e.g. pyramid) while observing pictures adds value to interactions for people with dementia, especially when they emit warmth.
- reminiscence activities only make sense when a care person is involved to react with validation [11] to the persons' utterances and moderate the interaction.
- small is beautiful since it can be transported and therefore be used in several contexts, e.g. with bedridden people.
- repetition is ambiguous: some people with dementia enjoy the same content again while others are bored of repetition.
- addressing a new sensory channel only makes sense if it conveys the same meaning (e.g. the bird sounds supported the bird pictures in the pyramid, whereas the pictures in the jukebox distracted from the music).
- technical soundness is hard to be achieved with prototypes but needs to be maintained to increase acceptance among caregivers and create predictable experiences for residents.
- what represents a good concept in the Contextual Design vision does not necessarily work in the dementia care home - multiple concepts need to be tested with all potential stakeholders.
- generic content/triggers are fine (also supported by [10]) – personal connections to the content can be conveyed through supporting moderation by caregivers.
- technology in the reminiscence context should not be a mere diversion but must provide an additional value compared to analogue methods (e.g. experienced self-efficacy during interaction or higher contrast of displays opposed to laminated paper).
- people with dementia were most likely to interact with prototypes during steward observations (opposed to findings for healthy users by [37]).

## RELATED WORK

So far most research in tangible interfaces and reminiscence involves people without dementia as users. Tsai et al. [34] describe how tangible memory probes can be used to facilitate reminiscent dialogue in participants aged 22-78. In a case study with tangible photo cubes, a higher degree of interactivity of the cubes improved the reminiscing communication between parents and their teenage children [13]. With Nostalgia [29], a prototype that allowed selection of music or news from former decades, a tangible interface for reminiscing was brought into an old people's home. Old news led to discussions among the elderly and they sang along with the music.

There are also few participative approaches, involving highly individual artefacts or personal media. One example are Wallace et al. [36] who conducted a co-creative process with a woman living with dementia and her husband. From this "design-led inquiry into personhood in dementia" several design probes and tangible, interactive artefacts emerged, which supported the couple in reminiscing. In another study Wallace et al. [35] created a TV set with RFID tagged snow globes that triggered videos of different topics. Similar to our drawers this art piece was exhibited in the semi-public space of a hospital unit for people with dementia and facilitated communication between patients and staff or visiting family members. Opposed to our prototypes their design and particularly the themes were not based on user data but requests from caregivers.

Huldtgren et al. [19] designed a tangible multimedia book and tested it in individual sessions with people with dementia. With well instructed caregivers the book served as medium to support both reminiscence and communication. Bennett, Hinder and Cater [6] created a rocking chair that emitted sound when used and placed it in a care home for two weeks. The chair was popular among residents even though some did not notice the association between sound and the rocking motion. In the study, not enough data is provided to say whether the chair made users feel comfortable or actually triggered reminiscence. Nevertheless, the rocking chair apparently allowed unsupervised or uninstructed usage what our drawers could not achieve.

## CONCLUSION

In this work, we used an adapted contextual design approach to support reminiscing in people with dementia. We found that the tangibles emerging from our design process have the potential to be intuitive to use for people with dementia if their form is familiar. Where memories metaphorically "slip away" [7], a tangible object can still be held firmly while exploring its contents. Tangibles alone are not sufficient for reminiscing though – the process needs to be facilitated. Caregivers, who entertain trustful relationships to residents, are best qualified for this facilitation of interactions and validation of evoked memories. Well-designed technology can shift caregivers' valuable time from session preparation towards interaction with residents. Future work will show whether the combination of iterative optimized tangibles and well-trained caregivers can also benefit the understudied and difficult-to-approach user group of people with moderate to severe dementia.

## ACKNOWLEDGMENTS

We thank all project partners and participants with their families and gratefully acknowledge the grant from German Federal Ministry of Education and Research (project InterMem, 16SV7322). We also want to thank Clara Hüsch for graphically improving the model.

**REFERENCES**


[1] Katherine Algar, Robert T. Woods, and Gill Windle. 2014. Measuring the quality of life and well-being of people with dementia: A review of observational measures. Dementia(June 24, 2014). DOI= http://dx.doi.org/10.1177/1471301214540163.

[2] Norman Alm, Richard Dye, Arlene Astell, Maggie Ellis, Gary Gowans, and Jim Campbell. 2005. Making software accessible to people with severe memory deficits. In *Accessible design in the Digital World Conference*.

[3] Christian K. Andersen, Kim U. Wittrup-Jensen, Anette Lolk, Kjeld Andersen, and Per Kragh-Sørensen. 2004. Ability to perform activities of daily living is the main factor affecting quality of life in patients with dementia. *Health and Quality of Life Outcomes 2*, 1, 52. DOI= http://dx.doi.org/10.1186/1477-7525-2-52.

[4] Alexander Bejan, Patrizia Murko, Nadine Müller, Peter König, and Christophe Kunze. 2017. Using Surface Table Computers to Promote the Well-Being of People with Dementia. *Studies in health technology and informatics 242*, 23-26.

[5] Alexander Bejan, Markus Wieland, Patrizia Murko, and Christophe Kunze. 2018. A Virtual Environment Gesture Interaction System for People with Dementia. In *Proceedings of the Proceedings of the 2018 ACM Conference Companion Publication on Designing Interactive Systems* (Hong Kong, China2018), ACM, 3205440, 225-230. DOI= http://dx.doi.org/10.1145/3197391.3205440.

[6] Peter Bennett, Heidi Hinder, and Kirsten Cater. 2016. Rekindling Imagination in Dementia Care with the Resonant Interface Rocking Chair. In *Proceedings of the Proceedings of the 2016 CHI Conference Extended Abstracts on Human Factors in Computing Systems* (San Jose, California, USA2016), ACM, 2892505, 2020-2026. DOI= http://dx.doi.org/10.1145/2851581.2892505.

[7] Kathryn L Braun, Jeanette C Takamura, and Thanh Mougeot. 1996. Perceptions of dementia, caregiving, and help-seeking among recent Vietnamese immigrants. *Journal of Cross-Cultural Gerontology 11*, 3, 213-228.

[8] W. Chang, S. Šabanovic, and L. Huber. 2014. Observational study of naturalistic interactions with the socially assistive robot PARO in a nursing home. In *The 23rd IEEE International Symposium on Robot and Human Interactive Communication*, 294-299. DOI= http://dx.doi.org/10.1109/ROMAN.2014.6926268.

[9] Jiska Cohen-Mansfield, Aleksandra Parpura-Gill, and Hava Golander. 2006. Utilization of self-identity roles for designing interventions for persons with dementia. *The Journals of Gerontology Series B: Psychological Sciences and Social Sciences 61*, 4, P202-P212.

[10] Boyd H Davis and Dena Shenk. 2015. Beyond reminiscence: Using generic video to elicit conversational language. *American Journal of Alzheimer's Disease & Other Dementias® 30*, 1, 61-68.

[11] Anke Erdmann and Wilfried Schnepp. 2014. Conditions, components and outcomes of Integrative Validation Therapy in a long-term care facility for people with dementia. A qualitative evaluation study. *Dementia 15*, 5 (2016/09/01), 1184-1204. DOI= http://dx.doi.org/10.1177/1471301214556489.

[12] Gaupenraub. 2016. Memobil - ein Erinnerungs- und Kommunikationsmöbel für Menschen mit Demenz und deren Umfeld in Pflegeheimen [memobil - a reminiscence and communication furniture for people with dementia and their environment in carefacilities]. Retrieved July 09, 2018 from http://gaupenraub.net/memobil/

[13] Connie Golsteijn and Elise Den Hoven. 2013. Facilitating parent-teenager communication through interactive photo cubes. *Personal and Ubiquitous Computing 17*, 2, 273-286.

[14] Aimee V Hamel, Tai L Sims, Dan Klassen, Thomas Havey, and Joseph E Gaugler. 2016. Memory Matters: A Mixed-Methods Feasibility Study of a Mobile Aid to Stimulate Reminiscence in Individuals With Memory Loss. *Journal of Gerontological Nursing*.

[15] Karen Holtzblatt and Hugh Beyer. 2016. *Contextual Design: Design for Life*. Morgan Kaufmann.

[16] Stephan Huber, Jan Preßler, and Joern Hurtienne. 2018. Towards a public interface for self-determined reminiscing in residential groups. In *Proceedings of the Dementia Lab 2018* (Newcastle, UK2018), in press.

[17] Stephan Huber, Jan Preßler, and Jörn Hurtienne. 2016. Anpassung von Contextual Design für den Kontext Demenz [Adaption of Contextual Design for the Dementia Context]. *Mensch und Computer 2016-Tagungsband.*

[18] Stephan Huber, Jan Preßler, Nam Ly Tung, and Jörn Hurtienne. 2017. Evaluating Interaction-Triggered Emotions in People with Dementia. In *Proceedings of the 2017 CHI Conference Extended Abstracts on Human Factors in Computing Systems* ACM, Denver, CO, 2659-2667.

[19] Alina Huldtgren, Fabian Mertl, Anja Vormann, and Christian Geiger. 2016. Reminiscence of People with Dementia Mediated by a Tangible Multimedia Book. In *ICT4AgeingWell*, 191-201.

[20] A Innes and C Surr. 2001. Measuring the well-being of people with dementia living in formal care settings: The use of Dementia Care Mapping. *Aging & mental health 5*, 3, 258-268.

[21] M. Kinney Jennifer, S. Kart Cary, D. Murdoch Latona, and J. Conley Cheryl. 2004. Striving to Provide Safety Assistance for Families of Elders: The SAFE House Project. *Dementia 3*, 3 (2004/10/01),

351-370. DOI= http://dx.doi.org/10.1177/1471301204045165.

[22] T. Kitwood and K. Bredin. 1992. The Dementia Care Mapping Method Bradford, England: University of Bradford.

[23] M Powell Lawton, Kimberly Van Haitsma, and Jennifer Klapper. 1996. Observed affect in nursing home residents with Alzheimer's disease. *The Journals of Gerontology Series B: Psychological Sciences and Social Sciences 51*, 1, P3-P14.

[24] Amanda Lazar, Raymundo Cornejo, Caroline Edasis, and Anne Marie Piper. 2016. Designing for the Third Hand: Empowering Older Adults with Cognitive Impairment through Creating and Sharing. In *Proceedings of the Proceedings of the 2016 ACM Conference on Designing Interactive Systems* (Brisbane, QLD, Australia2016), ACM, 2901854, 1047-1058. DOI= http://dx.doi.org/10.1145/2901790.2901854.

[25] Amanda Lazar, Caroline Edasis, and Anne Marie Piper. 2017. Supporting People with Dementia in Digital Social Sharing. In *Proceedings of the Proceedings of the 2017 CHI Conference on Human Factors in Computing Systems* (Denver, Colorado, USA2017), ACM, 3025586, 2149-2162. DOI= http://dx.doi.org/10.1145/3025453.3025586.

[26] A. Conway Martin, Wang Qi, Hanyu Kazunori, and Haque Shamsul. 2005. A Cross-Cultural Investigation of Autobiographical Memory: On the Universality and Cultural Variation of the Reminiscence Bump. *Journal of Cross-Cultural Psychology 36*, 6 (2005/11/01), 739-749. DOI= http://dx.doi.org/10.1177/0022022105280512.

[27] Kellie Morrissey, John Mccarthy, and Nadia Pantidi. 2017. The Value of Experience-Centred Design Approaches in Dementia Research Contexts. In *Proceedings of the Proceedings of the 2017 CHI Conference on Human Factors in Computing Systems* (Denver, Colorado, USA2017), ACM, 3025527, 1326-1338. DOI= http://dx.doi.org/10.1145/3025453.3025527.

[28] Anja B Naumann, Jörn Hurtienne, Stefan Göllner, Patrick M Langdon, and P John Clarkson. 2011. Technology supporting the everyday life of people with dementia. *Helen Hamlyn Centre for Design, Include 2011 Proceedings, 18th-20th April, London: Royal College of Art.*

[29] Magnus Nilsson, Sara Johansson, and Maria Håkansson. 2003. Nostalgia: an evocative tangible interface for elderly users. In *CHI'03 Extended Abstracts on Human Factors in Computing Systems* ACM, 964-965.

[30] World Health Organization. Ageing and health technical report. Volume 5. A Glossary of terms for community health care and services for older persons. 2004 [consultafo 16 Nov 2015].

[31] World Health Organization. 1992. *The ICD-10 classification of mental and behavioural disorders: clinical descriptions and diagnostic guidelines.* Geneva: World Health Organization.

[32] Steven G Potkin. 2002. The ABC of Alzheimer's disease: ADL and improving day-to-day functioning of patients. *International Psychogeriatrics 14*, S1, 7-26.

[33] Panote Siriaraya and Chee Siang Ang. 2014. Recreating living experiences from past memories through virtual worlds for people with dementia. In *Proceedings of the SIGCHI Conference on Human Factors in Computing Systems* ACM, 3977-3986.

[34] Wenn-Chieh Tsai, Daniel Orth, and Elise Van Den Hoven. 2017. Designing Memory Probes to Inform Dialogue. In *Proceedings of the Proceedings of the 2017 Conference on Designing Interactive Systems* (Edinburgh, United Kingdom2017), ACM, 3064791, 889-901. DOI= http://dx.doi.org/10.1145/3064663.3064791.

[35] Jayne Wallace, Anja Thieme, Gavin Wood, Guy Schofield, and Patrick Olivier. 2012. Enabling self, intimacy and a sense of home in dementia: an enquiry into design in a hospital setting. In *Proceedings of the SIGCHI Conference on Human Factors in Computing Systems* ACM, 2629-2638.

[36] Jayne Wallace, Peter C Wright, John Mccarthy, David Philip Green, James Thomas, and Patrick Olivier. 2013. A design-led inquiry into personhood in dementia. In *Proceedings of the SIGCHI Conference on Human Factors in Computing Systems* ACM, 2617-2626.

[37] Julie R. Williamson and John Williamson. 2017. Understanding Public Evaluation: Quantifying Experimenter Intervention. In *Proceedings of the Proceedings of the 2017 CHI Conference on Human Factors in Computing Systems* (Denver, Colorado, USA2017), ACM, 3025598, 3414-3425. DOI= http://dx.doi.org/10.1145/3025453.3025598.

[38] Bob Woods, A. Spector, C. Jones, Martin Orrell, and S. Davies. 2005. Reminiscence therapy for dementia. *Cochrane Database Syst Rev 2.*

# SenseBox: A DIY Prototyping Platform to Create Audio Interfaces for Therapy

**Foad Hamidi, Sanjay Kumar, Mikhail Dorfman, Fayokemi Ojo, Megha Kottapalli, Amy Hurst**
University of Maryland, Baltimore County (UMBC)
Baltimore, MD, USA
{foadhamidi, skumar5, dorfman2, fkme, mkott2, amyhurst}@umbc.edu

## ABSTRACT
Customizable systems that let children and adults with disabilities control audio playback can support different forms of therapy, including music therapy and speech-language therapy. We present *SenseBox*, a low-cost, open-source, customizable hardware/software prototyping platform to turn everyday objects into audio triggers for people with disabilities. Users can add tags to physical objects that when in proximity to SenseBox trigger the playback of associated audio files. We designed SenseBox with input from three therapists and an assistive technology expert. We detail our human-centered design process that took place over 16 months and describe a detailed example use case where SenseBox was used to create an accessible music player for a child with cognitive disabilities. This project illustrates how to design physical computing prototyping platforms for therapists to create customized interfaces for their clients without requiring prior programming or design experience.

## Author Keywords
Accessibility; DIY Assistive Technology; Speech-Language Therapy; Music Therapy; Audio Interfaces

## INTRODUCTION
The emergence of a variety of low-cost electronic and computational prototyping platforms, such as Arduino, Raspberry Pi and compatible sensors and actuators, has made it possible for people with non-technical backgrounds to experiment with designing and implementing novel interactive interfaces [[11], [32]]. The relatively low technical barriers to using these devices, along with their affordability and customizability, are often cited as factors that make them accessible to a range of hobbyists, makers and amateur artists and designers with creative ideas but limited programming or digital prototyping experience [[6], [38]]. For people with disabilities and their therapists, special education teachers, parents and caregivers, the possibility of utilizing these platforms to create Do-It-Yourself (DIY) customizable interactive artifacts for expressive, educational and/or therapeutic activities is enticing [[15], [17]]. However, despite current efforts to create more accessible tools and processes to support participation in the creation of DIY interactive objects important technical barriers to participation still exist.


*TEI '19*, March 17–20, 2019, Tempe, AZ, USA

ACM 978-1-4503-6196-5/19/03…$15.00
https://doi.org/10.1145/3294109.3295633

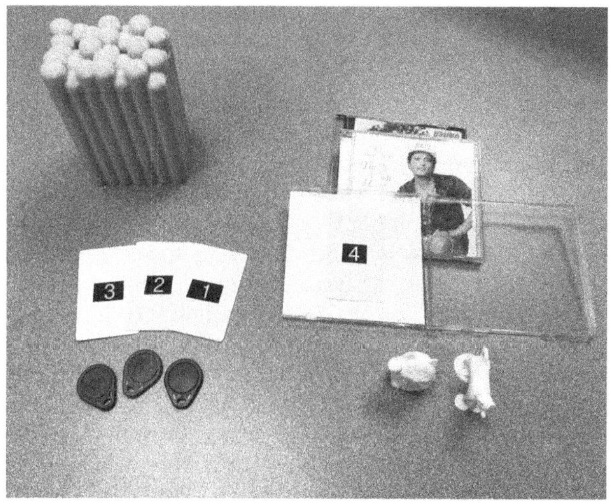


**Figure 1. SenseBox consists of an audio playback module, housed in a 3D printed case (Left, top) and a series of RFID tags (Left, bottom) that can be embedded into physical objects (Right).**

To better understand these barriers and to explore ways of overcoming them, we worked with two speech-language pathologists, a music therapist and an assistive technology specialist in a series of 10 sessions over 16 months to design a prototyping platform for users with little or no prior programming or physical computing experience to create customizable audio interfaces using physical objects. *SenseBox* (Figure 1) is a Raspberry Pi-based prototyping platform that consists of an audio playback module and a set of Radio-Frequency Identification (RFID) tags that can be embedded into existing or fabricated (i.e., 3D printed, or laser cut) physical objects to turn them into accessible audio triggers for use in therapeutic settings. Each tag is associated with a user-specified audio file that is played back when an object embedded with it is in close proximity to the playback module. Users can customize the system by (1) changing audio files, and (2) embedding tags in different objects. Neither of these mechanisms require any programming or electronics skills, making the system technically accessible to a wide group of users. We have incorporated these mechanisms to make it possible for

SenseBox to be used to create audio interfaces that are adapted for each user, a quality described in previous research as important in creating accessible electronic interfaces for use in speech-language therapy [[34]], music therapy [[25]], and the "Holy Grail" of designing music and audio interfaces for people with disabilities [[23]].

The simple functionality of SenseBox, along with its flexibility make it useful in the context of speech-language therapy and music therapy, in which it is desirable for a client to exercise agency in generating alternative speech or audio sounds [[9], [34], [41]]. *Speech-Language Therapy* is a clinical practice used to support clients who experience difficulties in exercising communication skills [[9]]. Exercises used by speech-language pathologists (SLPs) can support non-verbal clients or clients with very limited speech to find alternative ways to express themselves and can include the use of Alternative Augmentative Communication (AAC) devices, such as communication boards [[24], [34]]. While a range of commercial AAC devices exist, they are often expensive, complex and their hardware is difficult to customize and adapt to specific users. *Music Therapy* is another established form of therapy in which music is used within a therapeutic relationship to address physical, emotional, cognitive, and social needs of individuals [[9], [41]]. After assessing the strengths and needs of each client, the qualified music therapist provides customized treatments which can include creating and/or listening to music. Music therapists use a variety of tools, including conventional musical instruments and digital music playback devices (i.e., iPods and CD players). The use of conventional devices can pose accessibility barriers to participation in music making for clients with motor or cognitive disabilities [[33]].

We next describe previous research in this area, followed by a description of SenseBox and the process that informed its design. We also describe a use scenario in which SenseBox was used to create an audio interface for a child on the Autism Disorder Spectrum (ASD). Finally, we describe and summarize SenseBox's design features and limitations.

## RELATED WORK

The TEI and HCI communities have long been interested in developing systems that use physical objects to trigger and manipulate audio in different forms, including tabletop systems (e.g., [[20], [39]]), wearable instruments (e.g., [[35], [40]]), game controllers (e.g., [[22]]), and augmented physical objects (e.g., [[14], [18]]). These projects are complemented by the development of several physical computing platforms, such as Bela [[7]] or Satellite CCRMA [[12]] that have been specifically designed for high-quality music synthesis and playback.

While many of these systems are designed for use by artists, designers or researchers, several Do-It-Yourself (DIY) platforms and kits are specifically designed for use by non-technical users (e.g., [[14], [18], [28]]). An example is Makey Makey, a popular DIY "invention kit" designed to let users connect conductive objects, such as conductive tape or pieces of fruit, to a computer to trigger specific mouse or keyboard button presses when the objects are touched [[28]]. Using this mechanism, users can interact with a variety of computer applications, including games and audio applications, using connected physical objects as input devices. While Makey Makey was designed for the general public, Rogers et al. used it as a mechanism to engage groups of older adults [[32]]. They found that their participants enjoyed using the kit for musical expression and came up with new application ideas. The researchers found it particularly important that using the kit does not require programming skills and presents a low barrier of entry for participants. Despite its strengths, some of Makey Makey's design features, including the need to connect objects to a separate computer using wires, and for users to hold a ground wire for the system to work, make it difficult to use with children with disabilities. SenseBox is inspired by Makey Makey and other similar designs, such as the Lilypad Arduino platform [[11]], that allow the use of everyday physical objects in creating interactive interfaces. It aims to incorporate other features, such as using wireless contact between objects and the audio playback module, and avoiding the use of a separate computer, to make it easier to use by therapists to prototype accessible interfaces.

While some of the systems and platforms described above can be used to develop accessible interfaces for people with disabilities, they are not specifically designed for them. Several other research projects have developed audio and musical interfaces specifically for people with disabilities, including people with visual impairments (e.g., [[42]]), people with motor disabilities (e.g., [[5]]), and people with cognitive disabilities such as Autism Disorder Spectrum (e.g., [[31]]) and dementia (e.g. [[33]]). Larsen et al. conducted a review of the current state of development in music-supported therapy, as well as recent trends in designing accessible musical interfaces for people with physical disabilities [[23]]. They identified the development of accessible musical interfaces that can be adapted for each user as the "Holy Grail" of designing in this space. Similarly, in a study of switches designed for children with limited mobility, Schaefer and Andzik stressed the importance of choosing devices that match a child's abilities and customizing activity outcomes to keep the child motivated to continue the effort required for sustained use [[34]]. SenseBox is designed with these goals in mind: it is built as a platform to make it possible to create a wide range of audio interfaces, each adapted to the specific physical and cognitive needs of a user.

Several projects have explored the possibility of using tangible and embedded physical interfaces to create accessible customized therapeutic devices for occupational therapy (e.g., [[30]]), music therapy (e.g., [[21]]), speech-language therapy (e.g., [[13]]), and educational systems for children with autism (e.g., [[2]]), as well as, deaf children (e.g., [[16]]). These devices are often designed in collaboration with therapists and offer a degree of customizability to let them adapt interfaces for their clients. Moraiti et al. presented a DIY-toolkit for occupational therapists and caregivers to create customized computer user interfaces for their clients out of soft objects [[30]]. The Skweezee system allowed therapists to embed electronics into existing or newly fabricated soft objects, such as pillows or mats, that could then be used to detect a range of tactile interactions, including squeezing, pushing, grasping and pinching. The interactions could be mapped to computer input actions, such as mouse clicks or keyboard input, which would then turn the soft objects into input devices for interacting with a range of existing computer applications, including games. The system was evaluated with seven occupational therapists and one assistive technology expert who used it to create potential solutions for clients. The therapists found the development of the system and other similar DIY platforms valuable and emphasized the importance of not requiring the users of such platforms to have advanced programming or electronics prototyping experiences.

In a different study with three stroke patients, Kirk et al. found that using a digital drum set connected wirelessly to an iPad application to trigger percussion sounds in musical exercises led to significant levels of self-managements and an increase in functional measures [[21]]. The participants also reported high levels of motivation and enjoyment. The drum setup was fabricated in consultation with therapists who also helped choose a set of favorite songs to accompany for each of the participants. The researchers concluded that using digital musical instruments can offer health and therapeutic benefits to users and that it is important to have health professionals on board when deploying such systems to ensure their successful uptake.

Finally, several studies have explored design opportunities for new interactive interfaces in the context of speech-language therapy [[13], [19]]. In a study of five children with disabilities who use AACs in a special education school, Ibrahim et al. identified a series of design opportunities for future AAC solutions, including incorporating an embodied view of communication and designing to emphasize children's competence and agency [[19]]. The study found that the complexity of existing AACs creates a high entry barrier to their use by children. This often means the children have to undergo long trainings before being able to exercise agency in using the systems. The authors recommended the development of flexible communication technologies that place child users' agency in communication at the forefront of the interaction and develop and grow in complexity with their users over time.

In another study, Hamidi et al. presented TalkBox, a DIY low-cost open-source communication board for non-verbal users, that was designed as an affordable and customizable alternative to commercial AAC devices [[13]]. TalkBox was designed as a kit that could be assembled by therapists and adapted to meet the needs of each client. The researchers employed a participatory design process to develop the system in collaboration with special education teachers and therapists. While the physical form of the system could be adapted for each user, the users still needed to touch a conductive part of the system in order to activate audio sounds. While we take a similar approach to DIY interface design, our aim is to develop a more flexible approach to allow a range of physical objects as wireless audio triggers during interaction.

In summary, previous research has shown that there are design opportunities for developing DIY prototyping platforms for therapists to create customized audio and music interfaces for their clients. Further, these interfaces should be designed so that non-technical users can utilize them to create therapeutic experiences for their clients that support client agency and self-expression. As we will describe in the next section, we have designed SenseBox with these goals in mind.

## SENSEBOX: A PROTOTYPING PLATFORM FOR TURNING PHYSICAL OBJECTS INTO ACCESSIBLE AUDIO TRIGGERS

SenseBox (Figure 1) is a Do-It-Yourself (DIY) prototyping platform that allows users to create audio triggers out of existing or fabricated objects. It is primarily designed for use by therapists and special education teachers to create interactive audio experiences for children and adults with disabilities. In this section, we first describe SenseBox's design process which was informed by perspectives from its user community. This is followed by a description of SenseBox's design and functionality.

### Design Process

SenseBox was designed using a human-centered design approach in which representative users were included in the iterative design process early on. Participants provided several rounds of feedback on design ideas to ensure that the system reflects their desires and needs [[29]].

#### *Methods and Participants*

SenseBox's design process took place over a period of 16 months where we worked closely with two speech-language pathologists (SLPs), a licensed music therapist, and an assistive technology expert. The SLPs and assistive technology expert work with children and youth with cognitive and motor disabilities and the music therapist works with both children and adults, including older adults who experience cognitive disorders and difficulties due to aging. The participants were all female and had worked in their fields between 3-10 years.

In total, we conducted 10 interview sessions, each taking between 40 to 60 minutes, where we discussed different aspects of the system and how it could support therapy. Most of the sessions (7 out of 10) were conducted with two participants and the remainder with one participant. Employing an iterative design process, we fabricated and used a series of mockups and functional prototypes as objects for participants to reflect on and give us feedback about. These included a series of existing objects (e.g., empty CD cases) and newly fabricated ones (e.g., 3D printed rings and small animal shapes) to demonstrate the range of audio triggers that can be used with the system. Additionally, if they desired, participants could choose to keep the prototypes between meetings to think about them and provide us with their reflections afterwards. We incorporated participants' feedback into subsequent design iterations.

We encouraged the participants to ground their input on specific outcomes they desired in their practice and they often, anonymously, described how clients that they had worked with could benefit from aspects of the system. The design process resulted in a total of four working prototypes and six 3D printed mockups (Figure 2) and culminated in a functional prototype that we will describe in the next section.

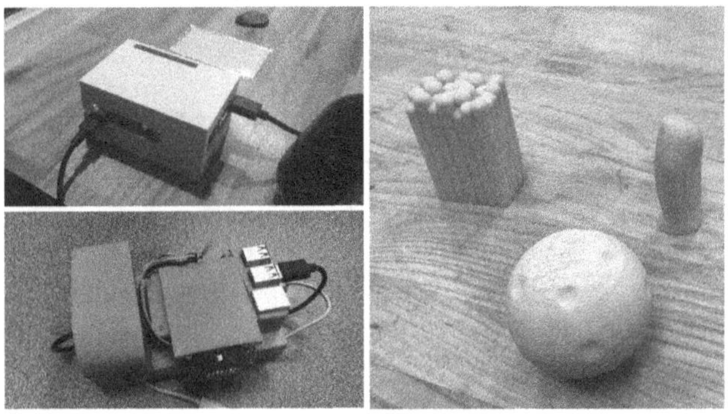

**Figure 2. Two functional SenseBox prototypes (Left), and three 3D printed mockups (Right) used during the design process.**

During the sessions, we took detailed notes that we annotated with our reflections after the meetings. We analyzed these notes using an inductive thematic analysis [[9]] where we coded the data and categorized them to identify emergent themes. The themes were then discussed with members of the research team and incorporated into the next design iteration of prototypes.

### *Design Considerations*

We identified three themes in our participants' input that we will use to structure our design considerations below:

*The Importance of Physical Objects in Therapy.* Both the SLPs and the music therapist described how they use physical objects with some of their clients during therapy sessions. The SLPs described how working with abstract symbols, such as images or words, can be challenging for some of their clients. One SLP described how some clients with cognitive disabilities have a hard time associating a 2D image (e.g., a picture of a ball) with a 3D object (e.g., a ball) or an activity (e.g., playing). For these clients, using physical objects, such as rubber balls, pieces of textile or wooden or plastic objects can be more effective. The SLPs described how using objects is often a stepping stone to learning more vocabularies and expanding the client's expressive abilities. One SLP uses a set of everyday objects, including a fork, a hand mirror, a pen and a cup, among other objects (Figure 3) to introduce her clients to new vocabulary and ask them about their preferences. She described how for some clients, she uses physical objects to refer to activities. These can include a small rubber ball to signify going to the gym and a small baby shoe to indicate going for a walk. The SLPs described how these objects are often chosen to be appealing or meaningful to their clients. Additionally, the SLPs described how they use a range of objects with different textures and materials (e.g., metal, fabric, …) for some of their clients who have low vision.

**Figure 3. A collection of physical objects used in speech-language therapy to introduce clients to new vocabulary: During therapy the therapist would ask a client to touch and hold an object (e.g., a fork or hand-held mirror) and would repeat its name with them.**

The music therapist utilizes physical objects differently in her practice: She described how she often encourages her clients to use existing musical instruments (e.g., drums or shakers) to express themselves musically or participate in group musical activities. She described these activities often involve her playing music on a piano or guitar with her clients listening, dancing, singing or playing along on an instrument. She stated that many of her clients find the use of existing instruments physically challenging and require guidance, practice and some level of customization of the instrument. For example, one of her clients, a lady in her late 80's, enjoyed accompanying music by playing a small hand drum. However, her motor control and strength had been declining and she had difficulty making audible sounds by hitting the drum with her hands. To accommodate for these changes, the music therapist had been experimenting with drums that the client could play with her feet or with a mallet attached the sleeve of her shirt rather than one that she needed to grasp in her hands. The music therapist described how she is often looking for instruments, such as percussion instruments or portable musical keyboards that do not require a high level of skill or hand dexterity to play for her clients. Additionally, she mentioned that multisensory experiences are important and when choosing instruments or objects for her clients she tries to select a variety of textures (e.g., objects with fluffy or smooth surfaces and handles) when possible.

*Supporting Client Agency and Self-Expression.* The therapists described how it is important in their practice to support clients in exercising agency, in the sense of making decisions that somehow impact them [[8]]. For the SLPs, making choices and acting on them are important therapy goals that can lead to increased independence and self-expression for their clients. The SLPs described how they deliberately choose words and phrases that are personally meaningful to their clients. They then respond consistently when clients express these words and phrases. For example, one of the SLPs described how she was teaching one of her clients to say "more" and "finished". When the client expressed these phrases clearly, the SLP would respond to them by pausing current activities or giving them more of something that they desired (e.g., a food item). She described that once the client mastered these phrases and the idea of them associating to consequences, she would move on to new ones. She described how the choices of words and phrases to practice also depends on a client's background and culture. For example, she described how for one of her clients whose parents speak Spanish at home, she sometimes used both English and Spanish phrases.

The music therapist described how supporting clients' self-expression and agency were important in her practice as well. She encouraged clients to express themselves musically and participate in group activities in order to find fulfilment and well-being. She described two elements that are important to her clients' successful self-expression and exercise of agency. The first element involves initiating and completing an action that has a desired outcome, for example hitting a drum with stick or pressing a button on an audio player. The second element involves perceiving that the completed action had a desired effect, for example by hearing the sound of a drum or music coming out of an audio player. She stated that this perception is important because otherwise clients might lose interest in the activity and become demotivated. She described how she considers both of these elements when choosing which instruments or objects to use with her clients. For example, she described how for one of her clients who had limited strength in her hands, she chose a drum that made a relatively loud sound when hit with a light stick. The drum's characteristics allowed the client to experience hitting the drum and perceiving the resulting sound in a manner that matched their abilities. In contrast to the drum, using a violin with an untrained client would pose a barrier as making a pleasant musical sound on this instrument requires a high level of skill and hand dexterity.

The music therapist also described another aspect of client agency that was important in her practice: agency over one's sound environment. She described how some of her clients are very sensitive to music that is nostalgic or holds strong emotional memories for them. Playing back such music without checking in with the clients can cause negative emotions in them, leading to sadness and hurt. She described how one of the hospitals she works at has guidelines on how staff should avoid playing music or tuning into radio stations without continuously checking in with clients. Further, the therapist stated that since emotions can shift over time and constant supervision is not practical in some cases, it is desirable to have accessible interfaces that older adults can use to stop or play music themselves.

*Customizing Client Experiences.* All of our participants underlined the importance of customizing therapy for each client based on their abilities, needs and interests. The SLPs described how they assessed a child's communication and cognitive abilities in initial consultations and used this information and any other available from previous assessments to customize therapeutic activities accordingly. The assistive technology expert also described that part of the initial assessment, often conducted in collaboration with an SLP, is a consideration of the types of assistive technologies that the client had successfully or unsuccessfully used before and deciding what existing solutions might be appropriate for them. She described a range of software and hardware solutions for speech-language therapy, including software apps, such as GoTalkNow [[4]], as well as, hardware solutions, such as Logan® ProxTalker® Modular [[26]].

For software systems, customization often took the form of changing parameters, such as the set of vocabulary or images used, for each client. A challenge for some clients was that using the visual interfaces of digital tablets, as well as, desktop and laptop computers, could be overwhelming or distracting. For these clients, the therapists opted for applications with simple interfaces with few onscreen elements. Other times, they would limit the use of digital systems altogether. For hardware systems, the form factor and physical features often needed to be customized and adapted for each client. One of the SLPs described how it is often difficult to change the physical form of existing commercial solutions beyond small changes since they are designed to be sturdy and not tampered with by users. Additionally, they are often expensive, making it risky to void their warranty by tampering with their form. For example, she described that in addition to communication disorders, some clients have visual impairments which makes it desirable to change the color, size and even texture of buttons or other areas of devices for them. However, the therapists often had difficulty implementing these changes and settled on more minor changes instead. Example modifications included adding a sturdy waterproof case to an iPad or a keyguard to a computer keyboard to make it easier to use by clients with limited motor abilities.

The music therapist also described how she customized musical activities based on specific clients' needs. Since she worked primarily with older adults her therapeutic goals were different from the ones described by the SLPs working with children and included motivating clients to make decisions, participate in group activities, exercise and make movements, and find ways to express themselves.

She identified how she often used her phone and speakers to find music that her clients liked and reacted positively to. She stated that, "*YouTube is a music therapist's best friend*", explaining how such streaming platforms provide access to large databases of music for engaging different clients. The music therapist also searched for ways to involve clients in music making or other activities participatory (e.g., dancing). To this end, she looked for instruments that were easy to use for clients in individual or group sessions. As described previously, these instruments had to be chosen to be both easy to use and also make sounds perceptible by clients to keep them motivated. She asserted that for many aging clients it is difficult to use conventional instruments because of weakening motor abilities, especially in the hands. Also, for clients who experience dementia and other condition due to old age, it is often difficult to use digital interfaces. She stated that often *"one of the first things to lose is computer access"*. Additionally, she described that for many older clients who do not have experience using digital technology, newer digital systems (e.g., iPads) can be overwhelming. Thus, having simple mechanisms to activate sounds would be useful in including these clients in musical activities.

*Summary*. Based on our participants' input, a prototyping platform that would let therapists easily create customized audio experiences for clients to express themselves and exercise their sense of agency would be useful in therapeutic contexts. Additionally, using augmented physical objects with different sizes, shapes and textures as part of the system can let therapists engage clients with a range of cognitive and physical abilities.

### SenseBox System Description

SenseBox consists of an audio playback module and a series of Radio-Frequency Identification (RFID) tags that can be embedded in existing or fabricated objects to turn them into audio triggers (Figure 1). A series of audio files, each corresponding to a tag are stored on the module (and can be customized by users, as described below). When a tagged object is detected in close proximity of the audio playback module, the corresponding audio sound is played back.

Figure 4 shows a schematic of the SenseBox audio module that consists of a Raspberry Pi microcomputer connected to a RC522 RFID Reader, a battery and a USB speaker. The electronics are housed in a 3D printed enclosure (approximately 2.3" X 4.2" X 3").

The 3D printed enclosure is designed to incorporate participants' recommendations to make the system engaging and durable. By incorporating geometric patterns and a fastening mechanism, it provides an appealing appearance and protects the electronics from direct touch. We also intended it to be small enough for young users to carry. After experimenting with several forms (Figure 2), we decided on a rectangular shape with rounded edges and a top surface that consists of a series of randomly generated geometric cone shapes. The 3D model was designed using the Rhino 3D modeling software with the Grasshopper algorithmic modeling plug-in. We are currently developing a library of 3D models for a range of enclosures that can house the electronics and that users can choose from in the future depending on the needs and desires of their clients.

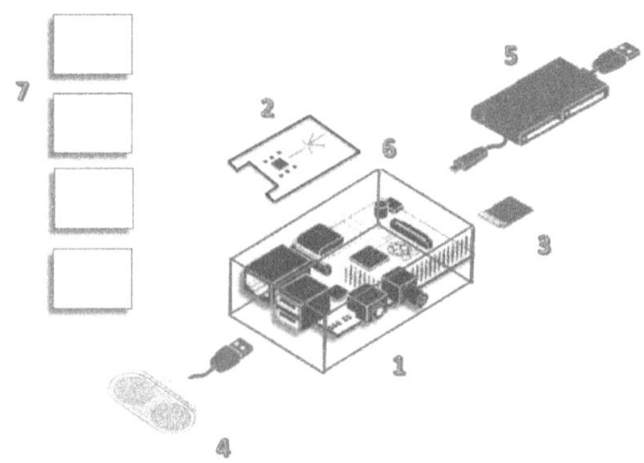


**Figure 4. SenseBox Schematic: The electronic components of the audio playback module consist of a Raspberry Pi (1) connected to an RFID reader (2), with software on a SD card (3), and connected to a speaker (4) and a battery (5). All of these components are housed in a 3D printed enclosure (6) whose shape, color and texture can be customized depending on user needs and desires. The audio module plays back sounds when in proximity to RFID tags (7).**

We have currently utilized three different sizes of RFID tags to embed in objects: credit card-sized tags (5" x 2.2"), keychain tags (1.1" X 0.8"), and small circular tags (0.8" X 0.8"). The RC522 RFID Reader operates at 13.56 MHz and can detect different commercially available tags. In our experience, the choice for which ones to use in an application depends on the size of the objects to be tagged: smaller tags are more suitable for smaller objects because they will not add to their size.

The software running the system is based on the open-source Linux operating system and is written in Python as firmware for the device that loads automatically upon power up. By default, the system stores a set of RFID tag ID keys in its memory, each associated with an audio file also stored as part of the software, as a Waveform Audio File Format (WAV) files. For tags to be detected, their ID key needs to be registered in a database stored as part of SenseBox's software. The system can work with a large number of tags.

Non-technical users can utilize SenseBox as a DIY prototyping platform to create customized audio interfaces using two mechanisms: 1) loading their own audio files onto the audio playback module, and/or 2) adding tags to existing or fabricated objects. For mechanism 1, users need to format their audio files as WAV files, naming each to correspond to the RFID tag that should trigger it (e.g., naming an audio file that should be triggered by RFID tag 1 as S1.WAV) and copying the files onto a USB stick. Inserting the USB stick into any of the audio module's USB ports would then automatically copy the sounds onto the module. The new sounds would subsequently play back when corresponding RFID tags are in proximity to the sensor. This mechanism is implemented such that users can switch SenseBox vocabularies without having to interact with any code or display.

Mechanism 2, adding tags to objects, can be accomplished using different methods, including using glue or Velcro strips to attach tags to existing objects (e.g., a table or a plate), or newly fabricated objects (e.g., a 3D printed, or laser cut object).

### SenseBox Usage Scenarios

SenseBox can be used in several ways. In one scenario, the audio playback module can be placed on a table or similar surface (e.g., a wheelchair tray). If more stability is needed, it can be fastened to the surface using Velcro or glue strips. When tagged objects are brought to the proximity of the sensor, a corresponding audio file is played back. Since in this scenario the audio playback module remains stationary and tagged objects are brought to its proximity, it is best suited to using small tagged objects and for users who would have difficulty with grasping and holding the audio module. The objects can then be used in different speech language therapy exercises, for example when therapists want to teach the name of objects to clients or encourage them to communicate using objects that symbolize activities or greetings. For music therapy exercises, musical sounds can be activated when a client brings an object close to the module.

In a second usage scenario, tags can be attached to potentially larger objects (e.g., tables, chairs, …) and a user can hold the audio playback module with their hands and move it close to the objects to trigger the playback of corresponding audio sounds. An example of this usage in the context of therapy is when a client with visual impairments is encouraged to explore a space or environment and scan tags in a room using SenseBox. Needless to say, the two scenarios described above can be combined in a single therapy session and a therapist may choose to keep the module stationary for only part of the time and for specific exercises.

Despite its strengths, the current design of the system presents limitations, including limited use beyond therapy contexts due to a practical limit of how many objects can be tagged and kept together with the playback module, and the need for audio files to be created elsewhere before being loaded onto the device. The system is unsuitable for socially contextualized communication (e.g., in a classroom setting) due to the limited number of tagged objects that are practical to use by a single individual. However, it can serve as an accessible bridging device to scaffold learning experiences needed before moving on to using more sophisticated AAC systems [[34]].

### Example Use Case

To illustrate how SenseBox can be used as a prototyping platform, we describe a real-world use case in which we used it to create a customized audio interface in the form of an accessible music player for a young client who is receiving therapy from two of the SLPs who participated in the project.

The music player is designed for a 16-years-old boy who is on the Autism Spectrum Disorder (ASD). He is non-verbal and has low-vision. He uses corrective lenses, which he occasionally refuses to wear and is generally more responsive to audio prompts than visual prompts. His SLPs have been using 3D objects, such as a rubber ball or a baby shoe to communicate activities, such as recreation or walking, on his schedule. He is interested in music and is especially fond of the popular artist Bruno Mars. Sometimes he finds Bruno Mars' YouTube videos on an iPad by looking for his pictures displayed as part of the website's interface. However, using YouTube poses difficulties because the many on-screen elements on the platform's interface can be confusing and also navigating through it can lead to undesired or inappropriate videos and needs to be done under adult supervision. The SLPs described that currently, one of their therapy goals for this individual is to teach him about cause and effect through the use of images and objects that correspond to specific outcomes and activities, a common activity in speech language therapy [[34]]. Acquiring these skills would improve his overall communication, leading to gains in independence and quality of life. To this end, the SLPs recommended using SenseBox to create a customized Bruno Mars music player for him that he could activate himself.

The customized music player was created by first identifying three Bruno Mars songs that the client liked and also finding images that correspond to them on YouTube (including album covers and pictures of the artist). The three songs were then copied to the SenseBox playback module using the process described above and each associated with an RFID tag. The RFID tags and images were each attached to one of three empty CD cases, that would serve as an audio trigger for the music player (Figure 1, Left). CD cases were chosen because they are large enough for the client to use and light enough for him to move close to the audio playback module to play a song. In the future, we plan to evaluate the music player and other similar designs, including both therapist and client perspectives.

## SENSEBOX'S DESIGN FEATURES

SenseBox's design incorporates several important features based on our participants' input. These features confirm and build on previous recommendations for designing accessible physical interfaces for people with disabilities. SenseBox's design illustrates how these features can be concretely incorporated in the design of DIY prototyping platforms for therapists, special education teachers and others who work with people with disabilities.

*Simplicity.* SenseBox does not require the use of a visual interface and only relies on audio and physical interactions. This feature is based on the participants' input that described how visual interfaces can be distracting or complicated for many users with disabilities, an observation made by previous research on systems designed for children with disabilities [[13], [19]]. Additionally, we have intentionally kept the functionality of the audio playback system simple and currently limited to the playing back of audio files, rather than other functionalities such as looping, adding effects to or recording new audio files. While these functionalities could be added to the system if users want them, we have prioritized simplicity and avoided adding extra features to the core functionality of the system.

*Customizability.* The importance of customizability was underlined both by input from our participants and by previous research (e.g., [[13], [19], [23], [25], [30]]). As described before, we incorporated two mechanisms for non-technical users to customize SenseBox's hardware (i.e., physical audio triggers) and software (i.e., embedded sounds). RFID tags can be attached to objects of different sizes and textures and users can load musical sounds, speech samples, or relaxing sounds among others onto the audio playback module. This DIY approach allows therapists to change the system's physical form to meet the needs and desires of specific users as well as, their preferences as to the appearance and attractiveness of the physical device. These are key differences of this approach from existing switches and other alternative input devices that have fixed form factors [[34]].

*Affordability.* We chose to use open-source, affordable and widely available computational components (i.e., the Raspberry Pi and RC522 RFID Reader) to implement SenseBox, to make it easier for users to fabricate and modify it themselves in the future. Currently, the cost of building a SenseBox from scratch is under $120. While more sophisticated physical computing platforms, such as Bela [[7]] or Satellite CCRMA [[12]], that are designed for high-quality music playback could possibly provide a better audio performance than the current implementation, we chose to build the system with materials that are more widely available. This approach is in accord with DIY and maker priorities that prioritize platforms that more people can assemble and fabricate themselves over highly specialized and technically complex ones [[15], [17]]. In the future, we plan to make SenseBox's design, including the software, 3D models and instruction on how to assemble the system, available online to let users assemble and fabricate variants of the system themselves.

*Accessibility.* The features described above all contribute to the overall accessibility of the system, in the sense of lowering barriers to use for its users. The simplicity and customizability of the system make it possible to use it to create audio interfaces adapted to a wide range of adults and children with different motor and cognitive abilities. The non-technical mechanisms to customize it lower technical barriers to its use for therapists and other professionals who might not have prior programming or design experience. Finally, its affordability lowers financial barriers of access and makes it possible for users situated in a range of socio-economic settings to use it. In these ways, we hope that SenseBox exemplifies a new generation of DIY prototyping platforms that make physical computing available for a wide range of applications and accessible to user populations beyond professional technologists and designers.

## LIMITATIONS AND FUTURE WORK

In this paper, we focused on the design process of SenseBox without a formal user evaluation of the system. In the future, we plan to evaluate the system with representative users including therapists, special education teachers and children with disabilities. We also currently focused on therapists' perspectives since they are the primary users of the system. However, we recognize the importance of including input from participants with disabilities, as pointed out in previous research [[37]], and plan to do that in the future. Additionally, we plan to refine SenseBox's design further using a participatory design approach in which we ask participants to identify new audio applications that we will then co-design with them.

In terms of technical features, we have so far focused on using a single audio playback module. We plan to explore implementing a network of multiple SenseBox units that can communicate and interact with each other using a Musical Instrument Digital Interface (MIDI) interface [[27]] or taking advantage of Raspberry Pi's Sonic Pi built-in open-source audio programming environment [[36]]. This approach might allow several users to interact with each other using a network of SenseBoxes.

## CONCLUSION

DIY prototyping platforms can enable users to create customized audio interfaces in support of music and speech-language therapy. We presented SenseBox, a DIY prototyping platform to enable therapists to design audio interfaces that fit the needs and desires of their clients. SenseBox is implemented using a Raspberry Pi microcomputer, sensors and corresponding electronic components. This project demonstrates that with appropriate design features open-source DIY components can be utilized by users without prior programming or design experience to create accessible interfaces for use in therapeutic contexts. We hope that SenseBox inspires future platforms that combine the computational power of low-cost embedded hardware with usability features that allow non-technical users to create their own therapeutic and expressive applications.

## ACKNOWLEDGMENTS

We would like to thank our participants for their time and input. We would also like to thank Melanie Baljko and Ray Feraday for their prior work on the TalkBox platform. This research is supported by NIDILRR grant #-90DP0061-01-00 and the National Science Foundation under Grant No. IIS-1451661. Any opinions, findings, and conclusions or recommendations expressed in this material are those of the authors and do not necessarily reflect the views of the National Science Foundation.

## REFERENCES

[1] Ankur Agrawal, Glen J. Anderson, Meng Shi, and Rebecca Chierichetti. 2018. Tangible Play Surface Using Passive RFID Sensor Array. In *Extended Abstracts of the 2018 CHI Conference on Human Factors in Computing Systems* (CHI EA '18), Paper D101, 4 pages.

[2] Andrea Alessandrini, Victor Loux, Gabriel Ferreira Serra, and Cormac Murray. 2016. Designing ReduCat: Audio-Augmented Paper Drawings Tangible Interface in Educational Intervention for High-Functioning Autistic Children. In *Proceedings of the 15th International Conference on Interaction Design and Children* (IDC '16), 463-472.

[3] Jesse Allison and Timothy Place. 2003. SensorBox: practical audio interface for gestural performance. In *Proceedings of the 2003 Conference on New Interfaces for Musical Expression* (NIME '03), 208-210.

[4] Attaiment Company. GoTalkNow. Retrieved August 3, 2018 from https://www.attainmentcompany.com/gotalk-now

[5] Amal Dar Aziz, Chris Warren, Hayden Bursk, and Sean Follmer. 2008. The flote: an instrument for people with limited mobility. In *Proceedings of the 10th international ACM SIGACCESS conference on Computers and accessibility* (ASSETS'08), 295-296.

[6] Chris Anderson. 2012. *Makers: The New Industrial Revolutions.* Crown Business, New York, NY.

[7] Bela. Retrieved August 1, 2018 from http://www.bela.io/

[8] Albert Bandura. 2006. Toward a psychology of human agency. *Perspectives on psychological science, 1*(2), 164-180.

[9] Virginia Braun and Victoria Clarke. 2006. Using thematic analysis in psychology. *Qualitative research in psychology, 3*(2), 77-101.

[10] Kenneth Bruscia. *Defining music therapy*. Barcelona Publishers, New Braunfels, TX, 1998.

[11] Leah Buechley, Mike Eisenberg, Jaime Catchen, and Ali Crockett. 2008. The LilyPad Arduino: using computational textiles to investigate engagement, aesthetics, and diversity in computer science education. In *Proceedings of the SIGCHI Conference on Human Factors in Computing Systems* (CHI '08), 423-432.

[12] CCRMA Satellite. Retrieved August 1, 2018 from https://ccrma.stanford.edu/~eberdahl/Satellite/

[13] Foad Hamidi, Melanie Baljko, Toni Kunic, and Ray Feraday. 2015. A DIY Communication Board Case Study. *Journal of Assistive Technologies,* 9(4), 187-198.

[14] Jiffer Harriman, Michael Theodore, and Mark Gross. 2015. The Kitsch-Instrument: Hackable Robotic Music. In *Proceedings of the Ninth International Conference on Tangible, Embedded, and Embodied Interaction* (TEI '15), 141-144.

[15] Jonathan Hook, Sanne Verbaan, Abigail Durrant, Patrick Olivier and Peter Wright. 2014. A study of the challenges related to DIY assistive technology in the context of children with disabilities. In *Proceedings of the 2014 conference on Designing interactive systems* (DIS'14), 597-606.

[16] Kevin Huang, Jesse Smith, Kimberly Spreen, and Mary Frances Jones. 2008. Breaking the sound barrier: designing an interactive tool for language acquisition in preschool deaf children. In *Proceedings of the 7th international conference on Interaction design and children* (IDC '08), 210-216.

[17] Amy Hurst, and Jasmine Tobias. 2011. Empowering individuals with do-it-yourself assistive technology. In *Proceedings of the International ACM SIGACCESS Conference on Computers and Accessibility* (ASSETS'11), 11-18.

[18] Hyunjoo Oh, Jiffer Harriman, Abhishek Narula, Mark D. Gross, Michael Eisenberg, and Sherry Hsi. 2016. Crafting Mechatronic Percussion with Everyday Materials. In *Proceedings of the TEI '16: Tenth International Conference on Tangible, Embedded, and Embodied Interaction* (TEI '16), 340-348.

[19] Seray B. Ibrahim, Asimina Vasalou, and Michael Clarke. 2018. Design Opportunities for AAC and Children with Severe Speech and Physical Impairments. In *Proceedings of the 2018 CHI Conference on Human Factors in Computing Systems* (CHI '18). Paper 227, 13 pages.

[20] Sergi Jordà, Günter Geiger, Marcos Alonso, and Martin Kaltenbrunner. 2007. The reacTable: exploring the synergy between live music performance and tabletop tangible interfaces. In *Proceedings of the 1st international conference on Tangible and embedded interaction* (TEI '07), 139-146.

[21] Pedro Kirk, Mick Grierson, Rebeka Bodak, Nick Ward, Fran Brander, Kate Kelly, Nicholas Newman, and Lauren Stewart. 2016. Motivating Stroke Rehabilitation Through Music: A Feasibility Study Using Digital Musical Instruments in the Home. In *Proceedings of the 2016 CHI Conference on Human Factors in Computing Systems* (CHI '16), 1781-1785.

[22] Miriam Konkel, Vivian Leung, Brygg Ullmer, and Catherine Hu. 2004. Tagaboo: a collaborative children's game based upon wearable RFID technology. *Personal Ubiquitous Comput*. 8, 5, 382-384.

[23] Jeppe V. Larsen, Daniel Overholt and Thomas B. Moeslund. 2016. The Prospects of Musical Instruments for People with Physical Disabilities. In *Proceedings of the International Conference on New Interfaces for Musical Expression*, 327-331.

[24] Janice Light and Kathryn Drager. 2007. AAC technologies for young children with complex communication needs: State of the science and future research directions. *Augmentative and Alternative Communication* 23, 3: 204–216.

[25] Wendy, L. Magee. 2006. Electronic technologies in clinical music therapy: A survey of practice and attitudes. *Technology and Disability*, 18, 3, 139-146.

[26] Logan® ProxTalker® Modular. Retrieved August 3, 2018 from https://logantech.com/collections/proxtalker-and-proxpad-modular-communication-systems/products/proxtalker

[27] Gareth B. Loy. Musicians Make A Standard: The MIDI Phenomenon. *Computer Music Journal,* 9, 4 (Fall 1985), 8-26.

[28] MaKey MaKey toolkit. Retrieved August 1, 2018 from http://www.makeymakey.com/

[29] Patrizia Marti and Liam J. Bannon. 2009. Exploring user-centered design in practice: Some caveats. *Knowledge, Technology & Policy,* 22 (1), 7-15.

[30] Argyro Moraiti, Vero Vanden Abeele, Erwin Vanroye, and Luc Geurts. 2015. Empowering Occupational Therapists with a DIY-toolkit for Smart Soft Objects. In *Proceedings of the Ninth International Conference on Tangible, Embedded, and Embodied Interaction* (TEI '15), 387-394.

[31] Ajit Nath and Samson Young. 2015. VESBALL: a ball-shaped instrument for music therapy. In *Proceedings of the International Conference on New Interfaces for Musical Expression* (NIME'15), 387-391.

[32] Yvonne Rogers, Jeni Paay, Margot Brereton, Kate L. Vaisutis, Gary Marsden, and Frank Vetere. 2014. Never too old: engaging retired people inventing the future with MaKey MaKey. In *Proceedings of the SIGCHI Conference on Human Factors in Computing Systems* (CHI '14), 3913-3922.

[33] P. Frazer Seymour, Justin Matejka, Geoff Foulds, Ihor Petelycky, and Fraser Anderson. 2017. AMI: An Adaptable Music Interface to Support the Varying Needs of People with Dementia. In *Proceedings of the 19th International ACM SIGACCESS Conference on Computers and Accessibility* (ASSETS'17)*,* 150-154.

[34] John M. Schaefer and Natalie Andzik. 2016. Switch on the Learning: Teaching Students with Significant Disabilities to use Switches. *Teaching Exceptional Children*, 48(4), 204–212.

[35] Sophie Skach, Anna Xambó, Luca Turchet, Ariane Stolfi, Rebecca Stewart, and Mathieu Barthet. 2018. Embodied Interactions with E-Textiles and the Internet of Sounds for Performing Arts. In *Proceedings of the Twelfth International Conference on Tangible, Embedded, and Embodied Interaction* (TEI '18), 80-87.

[36] Sonic-Pi: The Live Coding Music Synth for Everyone. Retrieved January 19, 2018 from http://www.sonic-pi.net/

[37] Katharina Spiel, Christopher Frauenberger, Eva Hornecker, and Geraldine Fitzpatrick. 2017. When Empathy Is Not Enough: Assessing the Experiences of Autistic Children with Technologies. In *Proceedings of the 2017 CHI Conference on Human Factors in Computing Systems* (CHI '17), 2853-2864.

[38] Joshua G. Tanenbaum, Amanda M. Williams, Audrey Desjardins, and Karen Tanenbaum. 2013. Democratizing technology: pleasure, utility and expressiveness in DIY and maker practice. In *Proceedings of the SIGCHI Conference on Human Factors in Computing Systems* (CHI '13), 2603-2612.

[39] Brygg Ullmer and Hiroshi Ishii. 1997. The metaDESK: models and prototypes for tangible user interfaces. In *Proceedings of the 10th annual ACM symposium on User interface software and technology* (UIST '97), 223-232.

[40] Katia Vega and Hugo Fuks. 2014. Beauty tech nails: interactive technology at your fingertips. In *Proceedings of the 8th International Conference on Tangible, Embedded and Embodied Interaction* (TEI '14), 61-64.

[41] Barbara L. Wheeler and Kathleen M. Murphy. 2016. *Music Therapy Research* (3rd. ed.). Barcelona Publishers, New Braunfels, TX.

[42] Ikuko Eguchi Yairi and Takuya Takeda. 2012. A music application for visually impaired people using daily goods and stationeries on the table. In *Proceedings of the 14th international ACM SIGACCESS conference on Computers and Accessibility* (ASSETS '12), 271-272.

# Beyond the Bare Stage: Exploring Props as Potential Improviser-Controlled Technology

**Claire Mikalauskas, April Viczko, Lora Oehlberg**
University of Calgary
Calgary, AB Canada
{crmikala, aaviczko, lora.oehlberg}@ucalgary.ca

## ABSTRACT
While improvised theatre (improv) is often performed on a bare stage, improvisers sometimes incorporate physical props to inspire new directions for a scene and to enrich their performance. A tech booth can improvise light and sound technical elements, but coordinating with improvisers' actions on-stage is challenging. Our goal is to inform the design of an augmented prop that lets improvisers tangibly control light and sound technical elements while performing. We interviewed five professional improvisers about their use of physical props in improv, and their expectations of a possible augmented prop that controls technical theatre elements. We propose a set of guidelines for the design of an augmented prop that fits with the existing world of unpredictable improvised performance.

### Author Keywords
Improvisational Theatre; Performer-Controlled Technology; Props

### CCS Concepts
•**Human-centered computing → User centered design;**

## INTRODUCTION
Improvised theatre (improv) is when actors create cohesive, interesting storylines and scenes without a script. Within improv, there is a wide variety of formats, from short-form games to long-form, complex storylines woven throughout multiple scenes or shows [6]. Actors often perform improv on a bare stage with only basic lighting to highlight their faces for the audience. Some improv troupes such as Loose Moose[1], Rapid Fire Theatre[2], and the Upright Citizens Brigade[3] incorporate improvised technical theatre elements (light, sound) controlled by a technician in a tech booth. The physical distance of the tech booth from the stage limits improvisation as there is a delayed reaction between an improviser's actions and a technical element being cued. Actors must slow down or over-exaggerate actions, like miming turning up a car radio, to convey their intended reaction from the tech booth.

[1]https://www.loosemoose.com/
[2]https://rapidfiretheatre.com/
[3]https://ucbtheatre.com/


*TEI '19,* March 17–20, 2019, Tempe, AZ, USA

ISBN 978-1-4503-6196-5/19/03...15.00
DOI: https://doi.org/10.1145/3294109.3295631

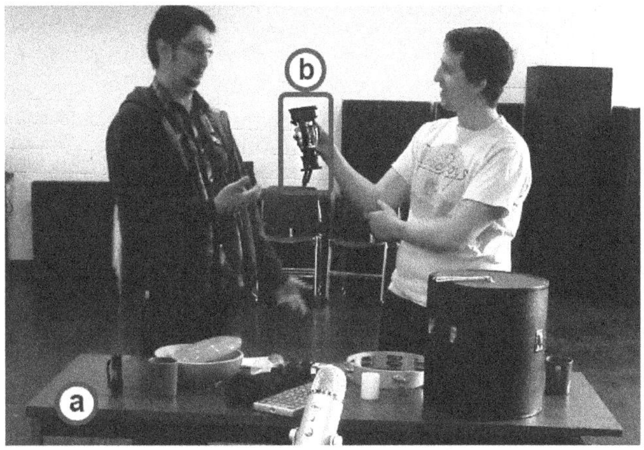


**Figure 1: Participants could select among (a) fourteen different objects as potential props. (b) Harvey and Henry hold a lantern upside-down while exploring its properties.**

Performers can control some technical elements. In improv formats such as improvised musicals [14], performers directly control their own diegetic (exists within the scene) and non-diegetic (exists for the audience but not the characters in the scene) sound by playing instruments. However, not all actors are able to improvise with a musical instrument, limiting the added layer of playfulness to those performers who are also musicians. Past performer-controlled technologies [4, 11, 17] have resulted in new formats of improv designed to serve the system's technical capabilities [1]. Our goal is to design technology that fits the existing world of improv, but where light and sound technical elements are controlled through actors' tangible interactions with on-stage props.

We conducted an exploratory qualitative study (see Figure 1) to understand existing improv practice and inform the design of an augmented prop. We interviewed five professional improvisers split into three groups, offering them a series of fourteen props to use throughout the interview. These props helped improvisers describe their existing use of props, reflect on characteristics of useful on-stage props, and speculate on the expected capabilities of an augmented prop in improv. Based on our findings, we propose a set of guidelines for the design of an augmented prop that controls technical elements in improvised theatre.

Our research offers the following contributions: (a) examples of existing uses of props and of technical elements in improvised theatre, (b) a discussion of suggested capabilities of performer-controlled technology, and (c) design guidelines for the creation of an augmented prop.

## RELATED WORK

In our related work, we primarily focus on tangibles as they relate to theatrical performance. While past work has looked at physical 'props' as controllers in the context of gaming [19, 20], we focus on the specific role of props in live theatre. First, we discuss past work on improvising with props, and improvising with technical theatre elements (light, sound). Then, we discuss past human-computer interaction research systems that offer performer-controlled technology.

### Improvising with Props

Props are *"a discrete, material, inanimate object that is visibly manipulated by an actor in the course of performance"* [16]. In a theatrical scene, props must be 'triggered' by an actor in order to become a prop [16]. Therefore, unless an object is touched by an actor, the object remains set dressing on-stage or a costume piece on the actor. For example, a handkerchief on a table is set dressing and a handkerchief in a suit jacket pocket is costume, but once the handkerchief is interacted with or held by a performer it is a prop.

*Props* is also an improv game[4] where players are tasked with repurposing a given prop in as many ways as possible. Improvisers are encouraged to think outside the box and explore different interpretations of the same object.

In a performance, props can constrain the possible space of actions, which can inspire innovative ideas [5]. When actors integrate a prop into a scene, it reflects both a creative constraint as well as inspiration or opportunity. While some amount of choice is necessary, having too much can be counterproductive. A narrowed focus in a creative space can push people to explore the problem in original ways [7]. Thus, the introduction of a prop can force the performer to think of new and creative ways to incorporate the object in a scene.

We go beyond the *Props* game and uncover how improvisers use props in a range of situations. Our goal is to identify object qualities that constrain or inspire, and show how those qualities affect how actors choose to use that prop within a scene. In our augmented prop concept, tangible interactions with props will ultimately be paired with technical elements.

### Improvised Technical Theatre Elements

Technical elements for rehearsed performances are often designed and created in advance by specialized professionals. However, several improv troupes also include technicians in a tech booth. The technicians, often trained improvisers themselves [15], must improvise light and sound technical elements based on the dialogue and actions of the performers on-stage. However, the physical distance of the tech booth from the improvisers can cause a time delay between the actions on-stage and the technician responding with a technical element.

Improvised musicals [14] are an established format of improvised theatre where the performers make up songs on the spot to create a musical. Music is used to heighten the emotions of a character, and provides a quick way for the audience to understand the mood of the scene. This format often includes improvising music with instruments on-stage as the performers create and sing new songs on the fly. However, both singing and playing an instrument require skill and training outside of acting. Improvising live music provides a low-cost alternative for incorporating sound and music into improv, but not all improvisers feel comfortable improvising a musical on-stage.

Our research goal is to better understand how improvisers use and respond to technical elements (light, sound) while creating a scene. We hope to clarify what controls for technical elements are appropriate via performer-controlled technology.

### Performer-Controlled Technology

Rehearsed performances incorporate technology as pre-made technical elements – the control and timing of technical elements are rehearsed alongside the on-stage performance. Performer-controlled technology allows performers – from music, dance, or theatre– to include some of these technical elements such that the technology is more responsive to their performance.

Previous HCI researchers have explored technology to enhance dance performance [9], including improvised dance. For example, MotionDraw [13] allows dancers to interact with a 3D trail of their movements. Using MotionDraw, dancers can use defined gestures with a Kinect to alter the color and width of the trail or change how the trail is captured. The researchers found that while dancers were excited to improvise with the technology to enhance their performance, they preferred having one person take the role of an external conductor rather than trying to simultaneously perform and control the technology. Clay et al. [3] discusses a similar need for external control with the "augmented reality engineer," a technician overseeing and sometimes controlling the augmentations on-stage. Although dance and theatre can both be improvised live, there are fundamental differences between the two disciplines. Therefore, technology made for dance does not necessarily translate to the needs of improvisers performing live.

For live theatre, The Dynamic Lighting System (DLS) [2] adjusts stage lighting based on a tracking system that monitors an actor's position using signals from their on-stage microphone. This provides perfectly timed lighting effects when an actor reaches specific scripted points on-stage – a cue that would otherwise be difficult to time consistently across performances from a tech booth. Thus, actors have limited direct control over effects during an otherwise tightly scripted performance.

Other systems are tailored for improvised theatre, and provide improvisers some creative control from the stage. Improv Remix [4] extends the idea of *callbacks* – improvised ideas that are re-referenced throughout a show – to create a system for long-form improv. Performers use defined gestures to

[4]http://improvencyclopedia.org/games/Props.html

| Object | Rationale for Inclusion |
|---|---|
| Lantern | Uses light, Uncommon |
| Flashlight | Uses light |
| LED Candle | Uses light |
| Tambourine | Instrument, Uses sound |
| Bike Horn | Uses sound |
| Rubber Gloves | Costume, Common |
| Umbrella | Common |
| Two Plastic Cups | Common |
| Jumbo Remote | Oversized, Controller |
| Wooden Bowl | Round, Could be repurposed |
| Frisbee | Round, Could be repurposed |
| Rubik's Cube | Square, Simple |
| Cardboard Box | Square, Container, Common |
| Old-Fashioned Hat Box | Container, Uncommon |

**Table 1: List of props used during the study, and research rationale for including the objects.**

record and interact with live playback of themselves and other performers on-stage. The gestures are distinctly different compared to existing techniques used to organize the format of an improvised show. For example, improvisers often run in front of fellow performers to "sweep" away a scene; Improv Remix allows a performer to stand over a playback performer and delete it with an arm gesture. This distinction of formats allows for the system to co-exist with current improv practice.

RIPT [11] allows audience members to create dialogue-gesture pairs for a robot arm who performs random dialogue-gesture pairs in scenes with an improviser. While the robot acts as a voice for the audience, an audience member or fellow improviser controls when the robot actually speaks. Performers can play with comedic timing as they choose the best time for the robot to interject random dialogue into the scene.

The above systems incorporate advanced technology into performances but also lead to performances made to serve the technical capabilities of the system [1]. Our goal is to provide performers direct, instantaneous control of light and sound technical elements. We hope to blend new performer-controlled technology with the existing world of improv such that it can handle the unpredictable nature of improv and fit with improvisers' existing tangible interactions with physical objects when building a scene on-stage.

## INTERVIEWING IMPROVISERS

We conducted a series of 90-minute semi-structured interviews with five professional improvisers. We scheduled our interviews based on the improvisers' availability, resulting in two sets of dyad interviews and one solo interview. This setup allowed for both a group dynamic and individual perspective [10]. The interview took place in a theatre studio space where the interviewer and improvisers stood the entire time to allow for any movement or demonstration that may occur when talking about the improvisers' experience.

| Selected Objects | Participant Selection Rationale | Groups |
|---|---|---|
| Lantern | Multiple features, Challenging | 1, 2, 3 |
| Rubber Gloves | Wearable, Soft | 1, 2 |
| Bike Horn | Simple | 1, 2 |
| Umbrella | Multiple features, Versatile | 1, 2, 3 |
| Jumbo Remote | Oversized, Controller | 1, 2, 3 |
| Wooden Bowl | Simple, Versatile | 2 |
| Frisbee | Simple, Versatile | 3 |
| Rubik's Cube | Distracting | 1, 2, 3 |

**Table 2: List of props that participant groups interacted with and talked about for longer than two minutes. Also, participant rationale for selecting the prop, and the specific groups that used each prop.**

The interview was structured into three sections. The first section focused on concrete examples of recent shows the participants had done and their experience improvising with props. During the second section, we introduced a box of fourteen potential props (see Table 1) displayed on a table for improvisers to use (see Figure 1). We obtained these objects from the prop room at a nearby theatre, and selected these props for their ubiquitous use in theatre, basic shapes, and the ability to produce light or sound. Participants were also told to consider the furniture in the studio space as objects for them to use (tables, chairs, black boxes). We asked the improvisers about their creative practice in relation to which objects they had seen in improv, which objects inspired them, and if anything was creatively limiting among the objects.

The last section tasked the participants to imagine an augmented prop and consider how performer-controlled technology could impact improv. We asked them to grab an object that inspires them for improv and, once selected, imagine how they would respond to being able to control light or sound directly with that prop. Improvisers could swap out what they were using for something they thought may work better throughout this portion of the interview.

### Data Collection

We collected demographic questionnaires, including improvisers' past experience with improv. We video and audio recorded interviews, and transcribed all audio and general movements of the participants. By asking open-ended questions in the interview, participants utilized their retrospective nature as improvisers to provide in-depth responses [10].

### Data Analysis

One researcher performed open coding [18] on transcribed video data over two iterations: the first iteration immediately after conducting and transcribing each interview, and the second iteration after completing and reviewing initial findings from all interviews.

### Participants

We recruited five professional improvisers from local improv troupes, four male and one female. Each participant had three to nine years of improv experience (average: 6 years) and had worked with at least two professional improv troupes;

our most veteran participant had worked with six professional improv troupes over the past nine years. When reporting our findings, we refer to our participants by pseudonyms. The researcher who conducted the interviews is a part of the improv community; all participants were recruited either directly or indirectly from this connection. Participants in the dyad interviews (Group 1: *Harvey-Henry*; Group 2: *Emily-Evan*) were acquaintances from performing together once or twice when their improv troupes had collaborated. This was a coincidence, but not surprising as the local improv community is small.

## FINDINGS

From our interviews, it is clear that *"props are not crucial, but they are a gift" (Todd).* Although improvisers can perform without props, they are happy to use anything they are given in a scene. In our findings we discuss current uses of props in improv, current uses of improvised technical elements, and the expectations for future performer-controlled technology for technical elements in improv.

### Current Use of Props

We looked at the properties of the eight objects commonly used among the study participants (see Table 2) to understand why the participants chose those objects during the study, and to help inform the design of an augmented prop. Through open coding [18], we identified five qualities that drew our improvisers to use particular props: *recognizability*, *functionality*, *stage-safe durable material*, *multiple possible interpretations*, and *avoiding distraction from the performance*. We also learned how the presence of a prop influences audience expectations of how it will be used in an improvised scene.

#### *Recognizability*

Distinct, recognizable objects help improvisers generate ideas for what to do with a prop and provide inspiration for creating a scene. However, if an object is too commonplace like *"a generic cup, ... it's not as inspiring" (Evan).* The lantern was a favored prop as participants found it inspiring because *"it's challenging" (Evan)* and *"not something normal" (Todd).* While at least one person in each group was inspired by the lantern at some point during the study, the participants were inspired in very similar ways (see Figure 2). These consistent interpretations were similar to *Lazzi*, stock comic routines spontaneously performed in traditional Commedia dell'Arte [8]. Participants fixated on the lantern because they had never used a lantern in improv, yet the lantern was recognizable and offered a clear story line. However, this initial inspiration could lose its appeal over time if the object only inspires one type of story line (e.g. navigating in the dark).

The objects were recognizable to participants, but some objects had unusual properties that provoked curiosity. The rubber gloves were intriguing because they were white, not a stereotypical yellow or blue dish glove color, and they were *"soft on the inside" (Henry).* The bike horn was an unusual prop for participants because *"[actors] use them to, like, end scenes [non-diegetically]" (Harvey)* rather than bringing the prop into a scene. The umbrella is a well-known, versatile object in theatre [16]. Our umbrella had additional appeal because *"it's a broken umbrella, and everyone owns a broken umbrella" (Todd).* Finally, the oversized remote, while recognizable, was presented at an unfamiliar scale: *"now I'm three years old again and everything's too big" (Emily).* Overall, these objects were decidedly "good" for improv among all the participants because they were recognizable but offered something slightly different than what the participants had used already.

*Harvey: You learn what inspires you. You learn what inspires your other improvisers, right? So I feel like, both [Henry] and I were very easily like "oh, that one, that one" (gestures at props table) ... I think as improvisers we need to know what specifically inspires us."*

#### *Functionality*

Functional items – *"the practical stuff" (Todd)* – were appealing as props *"because you can use them, like, [you] can open that umbrella on-stage" (Todd).* It is clear to the performers, and their audience, how or why a character would use a functional item during a scene. Our participants liked objects that could relate to a specific character or place because the object *"is actually something real, like, we're not make believing" (Emily).* It gives a starting point for creating a scene, *"and then from there [they're] creating the rest of the world" (Emily).*

Performers can mime practical props but scenes function better with the physical object because fellow performers may not understand how the mimed prop is functioning.

*Evan: Turning [the flashlight] on and off, like, that opens a lot of possibilities ... You don't have to be like, "okay, now the flashlight's on" or if you're in the dark and it's like, "okay, now the flashlight's off". So you're not ... trying to pretend not to see your fellow improvisers, it's like you actually can't.*

#### *"Stage Safe" Durable Material*

Performing improvised theatre is active and unpredictable. When given objects on-stage, the improviser must not be afraid of breaking the object or potentially hurting someone. With many objects in our study, the participants' first instinct was to grab them and wave them around to get a feel for the object. The rubber gloves are naturally soft so, *"I would slap someone across the arm, and/or face, depending on my comfort level with them" (Henry).* The lantern, although much more solid, also offered some carefree use as it was durable, lightweight plastic, but looked like it was made of glass.

*Harvey: Plastic! So, (waving lantern around) you know, if I do have to smack my fellow improvisers with it, I'm not going to hurt them as much (hits lantern on own hand) as if it were a real metal, glass, like (taps lantern).*

Although the ability to hit a fellow performer on-stage is not something we encourage as the goal of a prop, the improvisers should not be concerned that an object could cause harm. If a prop is safe, durable, and lightweight, the actors have more opportunity to be playful with it.

#### *Multiple Possible Interpretations*

Having multiple possible interpretations of an object offered the participants more ways to work with a prop. For example, the lantern had a handle, a compass, and a dial to turn it on/off. Since the object has multiple features, there is more to use as inspiration when exploring the possibilities of the object.

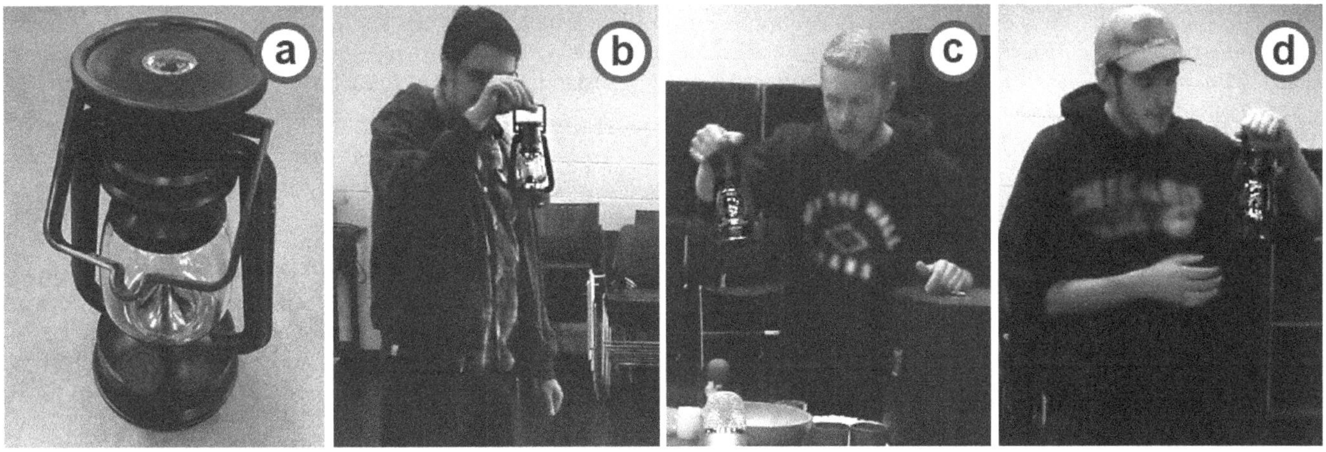


**Figure 2: Three participants from the three separate study groups being inspired in similar ways by (a) the lantern prop. (b) Harvey hunched over on a camping trip, (c) Evan hunched over navigating in the dark, and (d) Todd hunched over exploring a cave.**

*Henry: I think, like, maybe the more facets it has (playing with handle of old-fashioned hat box), the more, uh, well, intrigue it can inspire.*

Multiple interpretations of an object might offer more playfulness, especially if the improvisers want to re-purpose the prop into something new based on the scene. While objects like the bowl and Frisbee are simple and versatile, the desire to *"make it look real" (Todd)* is unnecessary with these objects because the task is simple and *"miming goes a long way" (Todd)*. For example, using a Frisbee as a plate while eating is simple to convey, either with the Frisbee or miming. Participants agreed simple objects are more outwardly versatile because they're *"not complex to the point where everyone's going to think it's one thing" (Evan)*. Although the participants spoke of the simple objects serving a purpose, none of the participants chose a simple object when initially told to choose an inspiring object for improv. Participants gravitated towards objects with more features as inspiration for improv: lantern (Harvey, Todd), rubber gloves (Henry, Evan), jumbo remote (Emily).

While some creative re-interpretation of objects is possible, there are limits to what an audience will accept. Some props can become a "gag" – an object or action that provokes an immediate audience reaction that is briefly funny: a cheap laugh.

*Henry: It's like the difference between a head laugh and a belly laugh. And a belly laugh is something that you're, like, you know it's hilarious because it comes up naturally. Where, like, a head laugh is, like, [when] someone says "dildo" or, like, "cock" or whatever.*

At one point, Henry suggested using the rubber gloves to become a chicken – a visually silly idea. While the immediate "gag" is that he is a chicken made from rubber gloves, the idea must then be integrated into the rest of the improvised scene.

*Harvey: We can use these props to, like, inform character. Or to, like, make yourself a chicken. But then after that, you're the chicken. You're committing [to the scene], don't keep worrying about the gag.*

This limits the types of re-interpretations that are reasonable to perform in a scene. While some re-interpretations are possible, improvisers are looking to push beyond the "gag" into something that works throughout the rest of the scene.

*Emily: I can't really pretend this [box] is a ball because [the audience isn't] going to believe me, they're not going to suspend their disbelief with me up until that point, ... they're just going to laugh at the fact that I'm using a box as a ball.*

Any "gag" element needs to have a purpose in the scene: *"A person [can] walk [on-stage] with a baseball bat and be like, 'oh, it's a pool noodle' or, ... 'nice dildo, right?' ... but [it's] not deeply, intelligently funny" (Henry)*. Being funny is not necessarily the goal of improv; objects that provoke an interesting story line will ultimately be more successful than a "gag." Thus, the actors do not need the audience to see, for example, an umbrella as more than an umbrella.

### *Avoiding Distraction from the Performance*

Our participants advocated for using props as a means to focus a performance, yet they felt that offering too many objects to select from on-stage could be distracting or problematic. They said they would feel pressured to use every object at some point in a show but *"with all [the] choices, it [is] almost too much because the improv [isn't] focused" (Evan)*.

Similarly, individual objects may distract from a performance and not necessarily benefit the audience. Each study group had one participant playing with the Rubik's cube while answering interview questions. However, the Rubik's cube was considered *"a very limiting object" (Henry)* for improv because *"it's not interesting unless you're playing with it" (Evan)*.

### *Presence and Audience Expectation*

Beyond the qualities of the prop itself, it is also important to consider how props are deployed within a performance. When an object is sitting on-stage, the audience expects the object to eventually be used in a particular way – "[obeying] Chekhov's famous dictum that a gun shown in the first act should always go off in the last" [16]. Even with minimal props, a single object sitting on-stage can dictate a format for using that prop for the duration of the scene or an entire show. Performers can *"never deny what the audience sees. ... If [they] have something sitting on-stage, [the audience] can see it" (Harvey).* If an object on-stage is never touched, the audience will spend the entire time wondering why the object is there at all.

*Todd: At the [school festival], um, we only had two chairs on-stage. There's a couple groups that, the chairs just sat on-stage and didn't move, ever. And I, as an audience member, ... if there's something on-stage, I want to see it used.*

Someone from each group had experience working with an improv troupe that has a supply of props backstage for use. However, there is no pressure to use everything because *"the audience doesn't know what they don't know, ... they don't know what the potentials are" (Harvey).* These backstage props can inform or dictate the start of a scene, particularly if an actor walks into a scene as a character based on the object. There is also little incentive to grab a backstage prop mid-scene because *"anything can be mimed if needed" (Todd).*

*Harvey: [If] we're starting a scene where we're in a dark campsite ... and I'm like, "there's a lantern backstage and I love it!" ... If I run [backstage], grab [the lantern] and guess what everyone? Now I have this cool lantern. ... I did a disservice by bringing [it] out and I should have just mimed it.*

If improvisers had every prop applicable to their scene location, they may feel overwhelmed when keeping track of all the props. Additionally, improv relies on the audience using their imagination. Not everything is physically needed in an improvised scene for the audience to suspend their disbelief.

*Todd: People don't rely on props, [they] just mime stuff. Like [an improvised] barber shop scene I [set the stage for], [the performers] just mimed shaving [someone's] head. They just mimed scissors, they mimed a comb, they mimed [a lot of small props]... In a scripted scene, having all those things is nice because you can work through them and work with ... the timing of everything. ... Whereas if you actually had [those small props in improv], you'd have to search for [them], you'd have to do all this stuff that you wouldn't necessarily want to waste time doing.*

Performers need to understand what is required of the format prior to the show to determine the correct amount of props and how they will be accessed on-stage. A participant in each group had experience with a professional improv troupe whose defined format includes stagehands that bring out objects when necessary. The stagehands are fellow improvisers, familiar with the backstage supply, taking turns determining what pieces need to come out, on the fly.

*Todd: Sometimes you'll have people come ... to you before their scene [starts] and say, "we need you to set up a doctors office with a knife." ... Other times [they're performing and] ... say, "we need a cave", and you're just like, "how do I make a cave?" and you just have to [improvise].*

Improvisers will also use *opportunistic props* – objects that are, by chance, on the improviser when performing and fit the scene. When doing a scene on an empty stage, *"[improvisers] still have [their] phone, wallet, [and] keys" (Todd).* Just like backstage props, the audience does not know what they are missing until the object is shown, but when the improviser can instantly access the right object it provokes a surprise.

*Henry: It's so rewarding. ... If someone's like, "twenty bucks for that" and you're like, "sure" and you take out a twenty dollar bill, people are like, "what? How did he know that was going to happen!"*

### Current Improvisation with Technical Elements

Of the fourteen objects provided during our study, three involved light and two involved sound (see Table 1). While some troupes, venues, or formats improvise technical elements, they are not an expected feature of improvised theatre. Our participants primarily discussed existing practices of improvising music and lighting.

#### *Improvised Sound & Music*

Performers already improvise sound and music. Improvised music is even a necessity in formats such as *"musical improv, where, like, there's an instrument and people are singing to it" (Emily).* Some participants felt *"it's such a joy to have [live music] on-stage" (Henry)* because they were confident performing improvised musicals themselves. Others were simply happy that other people could do it, but had no desire to improvise music as part of their own creative practice.

*Todd: (picks up tambourine) Musical improv is really cool. I'm really bad at it so I don't usually do it, but ... when people are good at musical improv, it's, like, one of the best things to watch.*

Although sound also adds a lot to a scene, a performer *"could always make the sound [themselves]" (Todd)* instead of relying on performer-controlled technology or an augmented prop.

#### *Improvised Lighting*

While actors can mime missing objects or use their voice to create sound effects, they cannot make light on their own while on-stage. For this, they rely on technicians in a tech booth who are able to control overall sound and lighting on-stage. Although technicians can change the lights whenever they see fit, they are always watching for cues from the actors that communicate an intended lighting change.

*Todd: A lot of the time you can mime lights. ... If you're [on-stage] having someone over for a date ... you can just do this (slowly mimes using a dimmer light switch) and the tech booth will see that and slowly lower the lights.*

In our study, two participants had experience doing improvised lighting. We currently see improvisers in the tech booth improvising lighting because, *"like an actor on-stage, you have to have that kind of mindset when you're in the tech booth" (Todd).* The resulting technical element responds to the performers on-stage and is, in its own right, a creative act.

*Emily: [The improvisers on-stage] asked to be in, like, a dream, so I was [in the tech booth] lowering dim, I was dimming and brightening the lights all throughout the scene while I was changing colors with it. ... We had, like, more blue when it was calmer, more red as [the scene content] got darker. There was some yellow and pink going on for, like, when [the scene content] was, like, light and fluffy and that was matched with brighter lights because it was nicer.*

These existing ways that performers improvise both sound and light influenced our participants' expectations for new performer-controlled technology.

### Expectations of Performer-Controlled Technology

The concept of performer-controlled technical elements conflicts with the traditional relationship between actors on-stage and the tech booth controlling technical elements on-stage. When discussing future uses of technology in theatre, participants initially had trouble looking beyond the connection with the tech booth that they are accustomed to on-stage: *"You could play fun games of, like, once the cup hits the ground, the lights come down" (Todd).* However, collaborating with the tech booth from the stage can sacrifice timing and creative decisions, since *"sometimes the tech booth nails it, and sometimes they just, like, put something really weird on" (Todd).*

Directly controlling stage lighting was clearly appealing to our improvisers. We also discuss two ways to integrate an augmented prop. In one approach, both the performer and the audience learn about the prop's interactivity live on-stage. In the second approach, the performer surprises the audience with the interactivity.

#### *Controlling Light*

By having an object on-stage that manipulates light, the improviser has the option to use that object purely as a light control. As discussed with improvised musicals [14] allowing performers to directly control their own diegetic and non-diegetic sound, an object that manipulates the light could now offer similar direct control.

*Evan: [The improviser is] not part of the scene but they're still operating music and lights, right? So, they have the power to alter mood and environment and all that stuff as well. ... If they were seen [on-stage], and they had like an object [that acts as the control] (picks up lantern and turns dial), I don't know. It would definitely be interesting.*

The idea of controlling lights on-stage offered more varied uses than controlling sound.

*Evan: (holding lantern) It's, like, a super emotional scene or something with, like, a grandma or whatever. ... Someone can come turn the light out (slowly turning off lantern), and that's a metaphor for, like, death.*

Among the groups, the bike horn and the umbrella stood out as "good" controls for lights on-stage. The simplicity of the bike horn offered a way of quickly changing the dynamics of the lighting. Coordinating lighting changes with the instantaneous sound from the horn would also be difficult to accomplish from a tech booth.

*Harvey: (squeaking bike horn) I think maybe the squeaking changes the color of the light.*

*Evan: (squeaks bike horn repeatedly) Like constantly changing lights and it's simple. ... It's hilarious, I think, like, if you just see a clown horn and then (squeaks horn) all of a sudden the lights shift.*

Participants from each group also felt a logical connection between the properties of stage lighting and the properties of the umbrella.

*Henry: (holding umbrella) It would be a level, like, it would get brighter as [the umbrella] opened.*

*Emily: (holding umbrella) Bigger is more expanded [light] and if you close it, it's more direct [light].*

*Todd: Whenever this umbrella is open, you're going to have the lights at full. And when it's closed, you're going to have the lights all the way off. And when it's, like, halfway, you could have, like, dimmer lights.*

#### *Learning Interactivity On-Stage*

While scripted performance mandates well-coordinated expertise with any technology interface before integrating it into a performance, an improviser can have a lot of fun learning about the possibilities and limitations of an object on-stage, in front of a live audience. Together, both the improviser and the audience learn what a prop can do (a "magical" creative experience [12]) and, from there, the improviser can creatively use it to their advantage (an "expressive" spectator experience [12]).

*Evan: If you had time before a show to use these props and figure it out, you'd almost be cheating yourself out of the discovery on-stage.*

*Todd: One time on-stage, [my fellow improviser's] character got super angry and she was on-stage with a couch and she grabbed the cushion off the couch and tried to pull it off and it didn't come off. Like, it was sewn on, but she pulled so hard that it tore. So then, as an actor they're like, "oh my God", and the audience is going, "wow, she didn't know it was going to tear. She actually just broke something on-stage." But now, ever since then, I don't think I've seen her get angry on-stage without tearing the couch apart, because now she knows that the couch, like, well now [the cushions] move.*

By controlling technical elements with a prop, the prop offers new uses within a scene. The improviser can choose to use it solely as the controller for a technical element, even within the scene, because the audience witnessed the discovery process.

*Todd: If [the audience] understands that [the umbrella] controls the lights, that I could just go like this (closes umbrella) and the lights would come down, then it doesn't need to be an umbrella anymore because it's just a light switch.*

However, an augmented prop still needs to be simple enough that an actor can learn what it does simply by playing with it briefly on-stage. Once the audience understands what the prop does, there is an expectation that the prop always works as demonstrated for the rest of the show.

*Todd: [If] I closed [the umbrella] and the lights came down, everyone would kind of get that the umbrella controls the lights. And then if [the umbrella] came back, it should probably [still] control the light, because the whole audience sees that umbrella and they're like, "it's going to happen again!"*

*Emily: If I figured ... out [how the controls worked], it would be fun. If I didn't, then I would probably just spend the entire show wondering who was screwing around with the lights.*

### *Surprising Audiences with Interactivity*

While one approach to an augmented prop is to slowly introduce the audience to its capabilities, an alternative approach is to surprise the audience with the augmented prop (a "secretive" spectator experience [12]). Once an improviser has discovered an objects capabilities on-stage, they will have that knowledge for future performances. The improvisers can use the object for its "normal" functionality, and the technology it controls becomes an external force in the scene. The audience may see an umbrella, but they may not necessarily see that it manipulates the lights.

*Todd: Someone walking in and then being like, "oh, thank God, we're inside now" and then (closing umbrella) "woosh" the lights come down and that's the scene.*

## DESIGN GUIDELINES

Given our findings on the use of props and technical elements in improv, as well as feedback on the augmented prop concept, we offer several design guidelines.

**Function as a real object.** Without purposely using any augmentation with technology, the object should still have it's "normal" function. For example, an augmented umbrella would still open, close, shield the performer from water, and communicate the idea of an umbrella to an audience just like a standard umbrella. These "normal" functions can serve as the controls for manipulating technical elements if desired.

**Avoid the "gag."** Any prop augmentation needs to avoid becoming a "gag." While an augmented prop that behaves like a whoopee cushion may get a cheap laugh from the audience, it may not ultimately fit the scene or help the improviser continue the story. The augmentation should instead blend with the original look of the object.

**Offer varied story lines.** Some objects may inspire similar story lines (e.g. the lantern used to navigate in the dark (see Figure 2)), which diminishes the long-term appeal of those props. Improvisers should continually want to find new inspiration from both the physical form and the technical elements of an augmented prop. By adding controls for technical elements, the object becomes a complex, versatile prop that offers varied story lines for different scenes.

**Actor- and Audience-discoverable interactions.** One suggestion for integrating the augmented prop into a performance was to allow the actor to familiarize themselves with the prop on-stage, during the show. In this format, both the actor and the audience learn about the augmented prop on-stage, and the actor can demonstrate how they can improvise scenes with the new, mystery object. This particular approach would require simple controls that can easily be discovered, and technical elements that are clearly visible and associated with the prop. While this design guideline is universally applicable to any system with good usability, it is particularly important in this setting as the interactivity must not only be discovered by the actor, but also by the audience.

**Technical element controls are always "ON."** If a feature on the augmented prop controls a technical element, it must consistently control that technical element for the duration of an improvised show. Any failure or inconsistency will indicate to the audience that the object is "broken."

## DISCUSSION & CONCLUSION

The design guidelines for an augmented prop are important, but fundamental to our approach is that an augmented prop be well-suited for improv:

- Recognizable to fellow actors and the audience
- Clear functional purpose
- Made of "stage safe" durable material
- Multiple ways to interpret the object
- Avoids distraction

While the above design guidelines offer some clear directions, there are still design trade-offs that remain open questions, even after our investigation: Should tangible controls for technical elements be obvious or hidden to the audience? Should the prop be visible on-stage or introduced from off-stage as needed? Should technical elements be triggered as part of the prop's "normal" function, or controlled independently of normal use? Should there be a clear semantic link between the object and the technical element (e.g., opening an umbrella cues light and sound for a rainstorm)?

Many of these design trade-offs depend on the improv format itself. A more subtle augmented prop may involve more subtle tangible interactions, subdued technical elements, or be hidden backstage only to be brought out when the prop makes sense in a scene. The augmentation may then require the semantic link between the object and the technical elements it controls.

If always on-stage, the augmented prop could, in itself, define a new format of improv, such as an improv game where players must make sense of a strange, multifaceted augmented prop. Such a prop may need big, obvious technical elements that may or may not have a clear connection to the prop itself.

By turning a prop into a tangible interface for controlling technical elements, we allow more room for play with instantaneous timing and provide a different layer of possibilities for the scene. Our work illustrates the critical role of both props and technical elements in improv, discusses how these elements fit within a broader improv performance, and proposes design guidelines for building augmented props for improv. Although our work is still in its preliminary stages, we hope our initial findings serve as a guide for integrating technical elements into the ever-changing world of improv. Our new-found understanding of props in improvisation could also inform technology support for improvising in the rehearsal process of scripted theatre, or tangible interfaces built into set and costume design.

## ACKNOWLEDGEMENTS

This research was supported by NSERC. We also thank Kevin Ta for their research assistance.

## REFERENCES


[1] Christopher Baugh. 2014. *Theatre, Performance and Technology: The Development and Transformation of Scenography*. Macmillan International Higher Education.

[2] Jeff Burke. 2002. Dynamic performance spaces for theatre production. *Theatre Design and Technology* 38, 1 (2002), 26–33.

[3] Alexis Clay, Nadine Couture, Laurence Nigay, Jean-Baptiste De La Riviere, Jean-Claude Martin, Matthieu Courgeon, Myriam Desainte-Catherine, Emmanuel Orvain, Vincent Girondel, and Gaël Domengero. 2012. Interactions and systems for augmenting a live dance performance. In *Mixed and Augmented Reality (ISMAR-AMH), 2012 IEEE International Symposium on*. IEEE, 29–38. DOI:http://dx.doi.org/10.1109/ISMAR-AMH.2012.6483986

[4] Dustin Freeman and Ravin Balakrishnan. 2016. Improv Remix: Mixed-Reality Video Manipulation Using Whole-Body Interaction to Extend Improvised Theatre. In *Proceedings of the ACM Conference on Designing Interactive Systems (DIS '16)*. ACM, 533–542. DOI: http://dx.doi.org/10.1145/2901790.2901894

[5] Steve Howard, Jennie Carroll, John Murphy, and Jane Peck. 2002. Using 'endowed props' in scenario-based design. In *Proceedings of the second Nordic conference on Human-computer interaction*. ACM, 1–10. DOI:http://dx.doi.org/10.1145/572020.572022

[6] Keith Johnstone. 2014. *Impro for Storytellers*. Routledge.

[7] Caneel Joyce. 2009. *The blank page: effects of constraint on creativity*. Ph.D. Dissertation. University of California, Berkeley.

[8] John Keefe and Simon Murray. 2007. *Physical theatres: A critical reader*. Routledge.

[9] Celine Latulipe, David Wilson, Sybil Huskey, Melissa Word, Arthur Carroll, Erin Carroll, Berto Gonzalez, Vikash Singh, Mike Wirth, and Danielle Lottridge. 2010. Exploring the design space in technology-augmented dance. In *CHI'10 Extended Abstracts on Human Factors in Computing Systems*. ACM, 2995–3000. DOI: http://dx.doi.org/10.1145/1753846.1753904

[10] Brian Magerko, Waleed Manzoul, Mark Riedl, Allan Baumer, Daniel Fuller, Kurt Luther, and Celia Pearce. 2009. An empirical study of cognition and theatrical improvisation. In *Proceedings of the ACM Conference on Creativity and Cognition*. ACM, 117–126. DOI:http://dx.doi.org/10.1145/1640233.1640253

[11] Claire Mikalauskas, Tiffany Wun, Kevin Ta, Joshua Horacsek, and Lora Oehlberg. 2018. Improvising with an Audience-Controlled Robot Performer. In *Proceedings of the 2018 Designing Interactive Systems Conference (DIS '18)*. ACM, New York, NY, USA, 657–666. DOI: http://dx.doi.org/10.1145/3196709.3196757

[12] Stuart Reeves, Steve Benford, Claire O'Malley, and Mike Fraser. 2005. Designing the spectator experience. In *Proceedings of the SIGCHI conference on Human factors in computing systems*. ACM, 741–750. DOI:http://dx.doi.org/10.1145/1054972.1055074

[13] Danilo Gasques Rodrigues, Emily Grenader, Fernando da Silva Nos, Marcel de Sena Dall'Agnol, Troels E Hansen, and Nadir Weibel. 2013. MotionDraw: a tool for enhancing art and performance using kinect. In *CHI'13 Extended Abstracts on Human Factors in Computing Systems*. ACM, 1197–1202. DOI:http://dx.doi.org/10.1145/2468356.2468570

[14] Tom Salinsky and Deborah Frances-White. 2013. *The Improv handbook: The Ultimate Guide to Improvising in Comedy, Theatre, and Beyond*. Bloomsbury Publishing.

[15] Sally Smallwood and Cameron Algie. 2011. Unsung Heroes Of Improv: The Tech. (2011). https://peopleandchairs.com/2014/10/06/unsung-heroes-of-improv-the-tech/

[16] Andrew Sofer. 2003. *The stage life of props*. University of Michigan Press.

[17] Flavia Sparacino, Glorianna Davenport, and Alex Pentland. 2000. Media in performance: Interactive spaces for dance, theater, circus, and museum exhibits. *IBM Systems Journal* 39, 3.4 (2000), 479–510.

[18] Anselm Strauss and Juliet M Corbin. 1990. *Basics of Qualitative Research: Grounded Theory Procedures and Techniques*. Sage Publications, Inc.

[19] Joshua Tanenbaum and Karen Tanenbaum. 2015. Envisioning the Future of Wearable Play: Conceptual Models for Props and Costumes as Game Controllers.. In *Foundations of Digital Games*.

[20] Joshua Tanenbaum, Karen Tanenbaum, Katherine Isbister, Kaho Abe, Anne Sullivan, and Luigi Anzivino. 2015. Costumes and Wearables as Game Controllers. In *Proceedings of the Ninth International Conference on Tangible, Embedded, and Embodied Interaction*. ACM, 477–480. DOI:http://dx.doi.org/10.1145/2677199.2683584

# IRelics: Designing a Tangible Interaction Platform for the Popularization of Field Archaeology

**Qi Lu**
Tsinghua University
Beijing, China
luq17@mails.tsinghua.edu.cn

**Shao-en Ma**
Colgate School
Hamilton, NY, USA
bma@colgate.edu

**Jiayin Li**
Tsinghua University
Beijing, China
lijiayin16@mails.tsinghua.edu.cn

**Haipeng Mi**
Tsinghua University
Beijing, China
mhp@mail.tsinghua.edu.cn

**Yingqing Xu**
Tsinghua University
Beijing, China
yqxu@mail.tsinghua.edu.cn

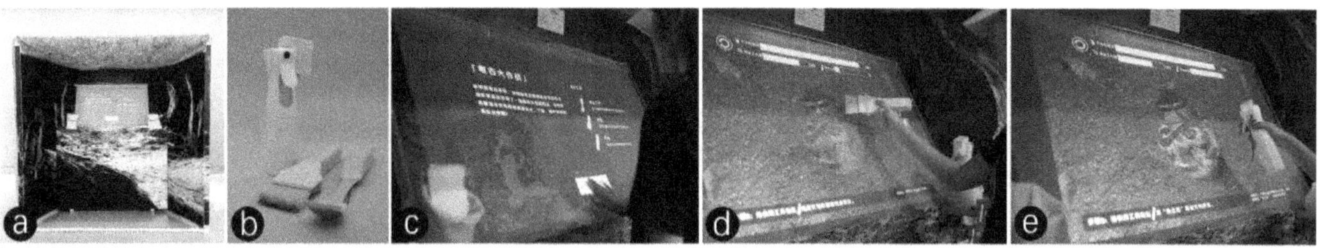

**Figure 1. An overview of IRelics. (a) Front view of the platform, (b) The tangible tools, (c) Bare hand touching interaction is supported, (d) & (e) Playing the field archaeological game by brushing and spraying liquid.**

## ABSTRACT

We present IRelics, a tangible interaction platform for the popularization of field archeology. IRelics allows users to experience archaeological field work activities as a serious game by using a set of tangible tools. We developed an innovative LWIR (Long Wavelength Infrared Rays) sensing system, which implements the design of tangible tools that provide real manipulation experiences. By interacting with IRelics, a player may experience different archaeological activities such as excavation and cleaning. We conducted two observations to evaluate the usability and effectiveness at archeology popularizing. Findings suggest that the IRelics platform can enhance the engagement of the participants by providing a positive and interactive environment while teaching them unfamiliar knowledge.

## CCS Concepts

**•Human-centered computing → User interface toolkits;**


*TEI '19, March 17–20, 2019, Tempe, AZ, USA.*

ACM ISBN 978-1-4503-6196-5 /19/03 ...$15.00.
http://dx.doi.org/10.1145/3294109.3295647

## Author Keywords

Tangible Interaction; Museum Education; Archaeological Popularization; Gamification; Thermal Imaging

## INTRODUCTION

Recent public interest in cultural heritage and archaeology has been growing as reflected by the increasing popularity of television shows [19] and documentary films [24] about this subject. The interest of the audience is not exclusively on the artifacts and relics themselves, but also on the process of how the relics were excavated by the archaeologists. However, many people have misconceptions about the field, considering it similar to treasure hunting. The popularity of novels and television series about tomb-raiding, especially in China, has led to misunderstandings about the nature of field archaeology [36, 37] (Storylines often feature protagonists obtaining relics through tomb-raiding, which is in fact illegal). These misconceptions may lead to threats of theft from archaeological sites, or improper handling of archaeological sites by non-archaeologists during accidental discoveries.

In reality, the field archaeological process is complex and includes various steps such as analysis, excavation, data recording and so on, in which the discovery methods may also vary based on the geographical and historical factors. Additionally, greater familiarity with archaeological knowledge would allow people to have a deeper understanding of the relics. Hence, there is a need to correct the misconceptions about field archaeology and convey archaeological knowledge to the general public.

Archaeological field work involves the use of various specialized tools [16]. Previous works have proven that Tangible User Interfaces (TUIs) are suitable for simulating the actions involved in field archaeology [25] as they enable hands-on interaction with physical objects and usually provide high affordance to novices. Tangible objects and operations could help the audience obtain an intuitive sense of about the real process of field archaeology. Therefore, we designed IRelics, a TUI platform for popularizing field archaeology which allows users to experience archaeological field work activities as a serious game with the support of tangible tools. IRelics is designed to be used in archaeological museums, and as such the contents of the game can be modified to suit each museum.

Our contributions are summarized as follows:

1. Interviews with two professional archaeologists were conducted to attain details about field archaeology and design advice. Then we outlined a few criteria based on interview results to guide the platform design.

2. A TUI platform in accordance with the criteria that uses LWIR sensing to allow for users to interact with the device using their bare hands, archaeological tools, or liquids sprayed onto the display surface.

3. An archaeological serious game that teaches field archaeology practices that also serves as a design pattern for games based on the TUI platform.

4. Two user observations were conducted to obtain feedback on platform usability and educational benefits. A discussion on the effectiveness of outcomes is also provided.

## RELATED WORK

### Assistance systems for archaeological professionals

There have been numerous proposals for the use of VR or visualisation systems to assist the work of archaeologists. The VITA project [4] presented a collaborative mixed reality system for archaeological excavation to help professionals collaborate in visualizing and exploring excavation results off-site. The Archave project [34] integrated a CAVE-like structure and proposed tools for archaeologists to study historical sites. Barreau et al. [3] implemented several interaction metaphors to facilitate archaeological analysis. For the purpose of presentation and analysis, virtual reconstruction of archaeological sites has been proposed after archaeologists collected field data [7, 12, 32]. They concentrated on providing high-fidelity examples of reconstructions from a specific heritage or artifact. Hynst et al. [11] also synthetically proposed a work-flow for the reconstruction and visualization of archaeological sites. These projects provide a reference on the visualization and design of user interfaces for archaeological contents, however they are mostly aimed at serving professional archaeologists rather than the general public.

### Museum Education and Archaeological Popularization

Recently, there has been a trend to adopt participatory and interactive methodologies in the design of museum exhibits [28, 27]. Various technologies were used in different applications, for example, multi-touch tabletop [5], VR/AR [10, 22], robotics [21] and tangible interfaces [26]. The purpose of using the new technologies in museums was to make the informal learning process more efficient and to enhance engagement. Thus, gamification is another common methodology in museum education [6, 30, 38].

In the area of archaeological popularization, as the challenges of teaching archaeology has been discussed in [8] (a gamification system for teaching archaeology students was proposed in this work), an archaeological education tool for the public should have low complexity and high engagement.

With the rapid development of computer technology, content digitalization has become more widely utilized in archaeological museums [18]. Schiavottiello et al. [29] built a 3D real-time storytelling platform for cultural heritage interpretation. Paliokas et al. [20] provided an immersive education system based on 3D reconstructed archaeological landscapes. Multimedia systems provides chances for the users to explore the archaeological environments in an engaging way. There have been a few previous works that aimed to develop mixed reality applications for raising the awareness of archaeology [9, 17]. Archaeological artifacts can be presented in different ways (for instance, interacting with 3D-printed replicas, viewing virtual 3D models, etc.), and Pollalis et al. [23] evaluates the learning outcomes from interacting with artifacts in three different styles. However, field archaeology had not been emphasized in the aforementioned applications and related work. In terms of content, the game Excavate! [31] is the most similar to our work. The series of games also contain simulations of field archaeological processes, which in parallel with other tasks serve to educate the history behind the artifacts.

In contrast, our work focuses on the process of field archaeology itself, including detailed operations and subtasks. Moreover, IRelics gives accessibility to physical practices in field archaeology for novices allowing them to gain a better understanding of the area, while at the same time the tangible interactive style and gamification design could effectively enhance engagement and enjoyment.

### TUIs related to archeology

TUIs usually provide good psycho-physical affordance for users who newly encounter them, and are easy to be accepted and performed [14]. Since archaeological interaction is unfamiliar to most people, a more acceptable way of representation is needed. We found it appropriate to embrace archaeological contents within the TUI design framework. Reuter et al. [25] designed a TUI for virtual reassemblies of 3D scanned fragments. They used tangible props for the manipulation of the virtual fragments. However, their reassembling tools were designed for professional archaeologists. Wakkary et al. [35] presented a museum guide prototype that integrates a tangible interface, audio displays, and adaptive modeling. They also leveraged the inherent playfulness and poetic simplicity of TUIs. While there have been several works on TUIs designed for archaeology-related scenarios, few were designed for the teaching or popularization of archaeology to the general public.

## DESIGN

### Expert Interview

To better understand field archaeology and what criteria our system should satisfy, we interviewed two archaeologists specialized in public archaeology and artifacts restoration respectively. They both have a wealth of field archaeological experience and we discussed with them our initial idea about letting users use tangible tools to experience the process of field archaeology.

They confirmed that the majority of work done in field archaeology was hands-on. Many different archaeological tools would also be used during the entire process, which could provide abundant resources for tangible interaction design. However, the public archaeologist (abbreviated as PA) concerned about whether the various tools would be attractive enough to the public. He expressed that:

> "The most important thing is to change their views on field archaeology. However, real archaeological processes take a long time and the work is tedious and boring. I don't think the audiences will be interested in exploring the whole process and learning all the details is not necessary for them."

The other archaeologist was more concerned with our approach to simulating archaeological processes:

> "How can you imitate the relics, the environment and the tools? I hope at least the audiences can know what we are using and how we are working in the archaeological sites."

We also discussed misconceptions about archaeology with them. They expressed concern that tomb-raiding novels and television programs about treasure evaluation may cause negative social impacts, such as encouraging robbery or the unintentional destruction of archaeological sites.

Also, there are misconceptions about the value of artifacts unearthed during archaeological digs. In archaeology, the completeness or monetary value of artifacts does not matter and all artifacts are treated equally as all artifacts have historical and academic value. Another misconception is that unearthed artifacts are the most important aspect of archaeological work. Often times, the environment that surrounds the artifacts are just as important in providing information to archaeologists. Thus, archaeologists must pay attention to the keeping of complete records of archaeological details in every aspect of their work, such as the layout of excavation sites, the number and types of unearthed artifacts, and so on.

In addition, the excavation of artifacts is not the only important process of field archaeology. The analysis of the sites and artifacts, as well as the cleaning and strengthening of artifacts, are also important tasks during the process and require professional expertise or the assistance of professional instruments.

### Design Criteria

From the interviews, we concluded that in order to achieve our goals of effectively educating the general public about field archeology and correcting misconceptions, the following design criteria must be met:

***Effectiveness of popularization*** In order to effectively popularize field archaeology, the system must evoke the interest of the general public and form correct and positive social understandings of field archeology.

***Attractive to Museum management*** The system must be able to reach a wide audience. Thus museum management must be interested in implementing the system in their exhibits. As such, museums curators and developers should be able to modify or replace the game contents to fit their museum exhibits. Maintenance costs must also be low.

***Realistic depiction of field archaeology*** The realism of field archaeology should be preserved as much as possible during the design process. While certain more complex procedures that are unnecessary for the public could be omitted, the remaining content should be as similar to real field archaeological processes as possible in order to accurately educate the public. The differences between popular misconceptions about archaeology such as treasure hunting or tomb-raiding should be emphasized in order to effectively correct false understandings.

***Positive User experience*** The system should provide a positive experience in order to engage the user to learn the information presented no matter their familiarity or interest with archaeology. Thus, the interactions should be novice-friendly and engaging while still being educational.

### IRelics Design Overview

The overview of IRelics platform is shown in Figure 1. IRelics is a LWIR camera-projector system. The game interface is projected onto a 2D-surface where the locations of tools or hands are detected by the LWIR camera (see Figure 2). IRelics supports several interaction styles, including the use of bare hands and arms, custom tangible tools, and liquids on top of the surface. When the user is interacting with the tangible tools, they receive both visual and tactile feedback simultaneously which creates a greater sense of realism in the interactions.

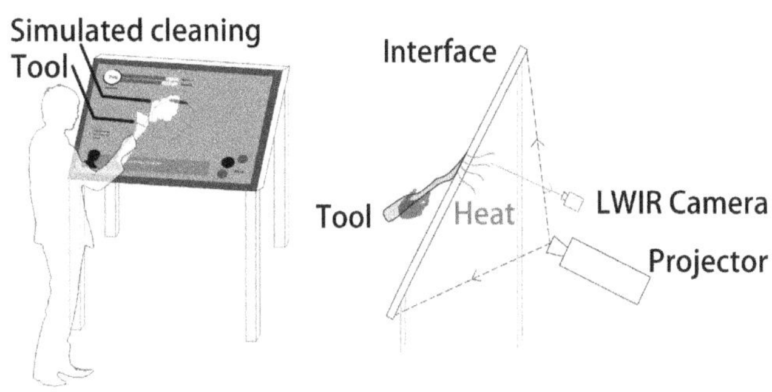


**Figure 2. Schematic of input sensing.**

To satisfy the *Design Criteria*, the tangible tools, as input devices, should retain their original physical affordances, which not only include appearance, but also in the way they are used. We investigated common tools used in field archaeological activities [1, 2] and selected the appropriate ones to be used as tangible tools (shown in Table 1). Our method is suitable for most of the elements listed in Table 1. Moreover, other tools which are not listed, such as large machines or electronic instruments, can be presented virtually in the software.

Furthermore, we designed our system to have the ability to handle the various interaction styles in the archaeological process: we summarized them to three main areas, inflexible tools, flexible tools, and liquids. Then we took trowels, brushes, and spray bottle as examples for implementation, which are common and representative archaeological tools in practical use. Other tools can be further expanded based on similar methods.

The interaction styles are similar to how commonly encountered trowels, brushes, and spray bottles are used (interaction style see Figure 3), but there also exists some differences: **1) Trowel:** The user holds the handle and slides the heated underside on top of the screen. The tool can simulate trowels of various sizes depending on game stage, for example a few stages require large quantities of dirt to be removed from the artifact while another stage may require the removal of small dirt flakes. **2) Brush:** The user holds the handle and moves the brush hairs on the surface of the screen. The tool is used to remove dust from the surface of artifacts. **3) Spray Bottle:** The user holds the bottle and pulls the trigger to spray water on the desired location. The liquid can represent dirt softeners which is used to allow the trowel to more easily remove dirt, or it could represent anti-oxidizers that are sprayed on artifacts to prevent damage from being exposed to air.

For the inflexible and flexible tools, the electro-thermal units such as heating wires or sheets should be assembled on the end of the tools. And for the liquid tool, such as spray bottles and droppers, the liquid, such as water or ethanol, can be directly detected by the sensing system in room-temperature environments because the liquid will absorb heat on top of the surface and naturally cause temperature change (see Figure 3 bottom right).

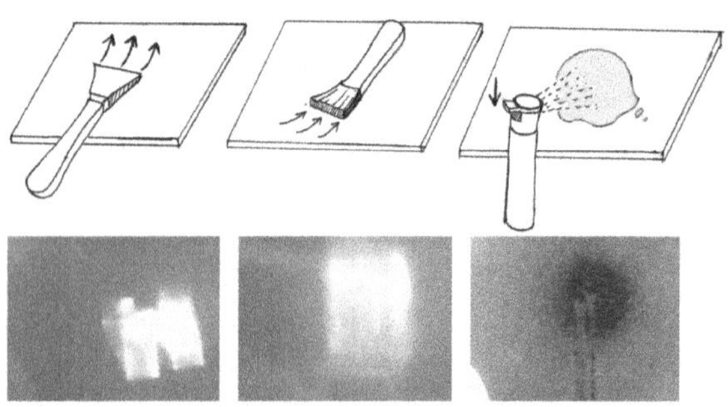

**Figure 3. the interaction styles of the tangible tools (trowel, brush, and spray bottle) and their corresponding thermal profiles.**

| Inflexible Tools | pickax, pointing trowel, tweezer, cutting tools, recording tools ... |
|---|---|
| Flexible Tools | fine brush, cotton swab, ... |
| Liquid Tools | dropper, spray bottle, chemical solutions, ... |

**Table 1. Fieldwork tools**

## Application

In order to encourage user engagement, we chose a gamified approach in presenting field archaeology. Thus we developed a game engine which allows museum developers to quickly replace and modify game contents. It supports game logic, graphical rendering, input data processing and wireless communication with the tangible tools, etc. A game effects toolkit is also built in the engine, which includes sound effects, particles system, etc.

We developed an example game called "Archaeological Adventure" (see Figure 4 (a)). The player takes on the role of an archaeological student who arrives at a archaeological dig to join an archaeological exploration. The player has to complete several archaeological tasks such as excavation, cleaning, etc, represented by several game stages, in order to unearth an ancient artifact. Assisting them in those tasks are tangible tools which they should use to complete each stage. We expect the game to be a design paradigm for more game content based on real archaeological processes.

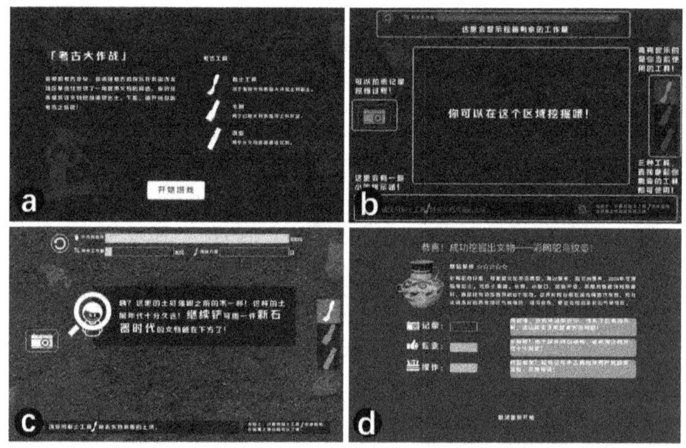

**Figure 4. Game interfaces. (a) Game Start: Introduce the background. (b) Tutorial: Introduce the game interface, including the control areas and the areas only used for display. (c) The instruction dialog pops up to guide the player. Camera-like icon is the recording button. (d) Final Report: The upper area shows the historical introduction of the artifact, and the lower area shows the reviews of the player's performance.**

Besides the tangible interaction, other game features are highlighted here, **1)** A tutorial is displayed at the start of the game (see Figure 4 (b)), teaching the user how to use the interface, such as the central excavation area, the recording button which can take screenshots, and the game stage objectives displayed at the bottom of the screen. **2)** The game stage consists of: removing large amounts of surface dirt, analyzing dirt composition, cleaning deep layered dirt, brushing dirt off the surface of the artifact, removing solid dirt clumps, spraying protective liquids. In every stage, a dialog box will pop up to provide the user with archaeological knowledge and how to use the tools (see Figure 4 (c)). **3)** In the final report screen (see Figure 4 (d)), there will be detailed information of the artifact, and a report display which shows the user's ability to operate the tangible tools (Operating Section), how often they recorded (Recording Section), and their understanding of the tasks (Understanding Section). The user is ranked low, medium, or high on every metric, and with additional messages displayed.

## IMPLEMENTATION

### Tangible Tools

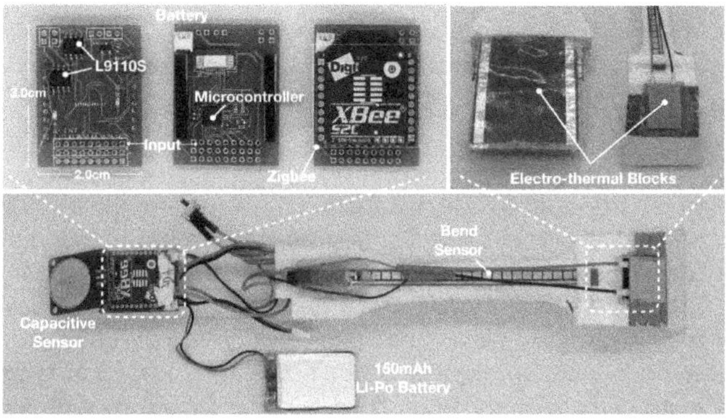


**Figure 5. Hardware implementation of the tangible tools. Bottom: An overview of the trowel. Top Left: Details of the control board. Top Right: Electro-thermal blocks used in the trowel and brush.**

Many archaeological tools, such as brushes or spray bottles, can be easily converted into tangible tools that can be used with the IRelics platform. For tools that are more difficult to convert, such as trowels, we used 3D modeling software to build 3D models and modified non-functional parts. For example, the trowel handle was made hollow to allow for installation of the control board (see Figure 5). Then we 3D printed the models to build the Tangible tools.

In order to not modify the appearance of the tools significantly when converting them to tangible tools, we made an embedded system that includes a custom control PCB board with a very small size. The main processor is an ATmega8A (Atmel) and there are two PWM connectors on the board to support elements that require high current (~800mA) but with low voltage (2.5V–12V). These could be useful for extending the tangible output potential, such as driving motors to provide vibrations or driving flashbulbs to mimic a camera. In our prototype, we used one of them to drive electro-thermal blocks in the trowel and brush tools. Furthermore, there are 6 pins for analog inputs and 3 for digital inputs, which can support a wide range of additional sensors. We added bend sensors to detect operational force (trowel and brush) and capacitive touch sensors (trowel, brush, and spray bottle) to detect whether a tool is held by the user. If it is not held, the tool will stay in "sleep mode" where no power is supplied to the electro-thermal block and no wireless communication with the main system in order to save battery power (battery capacity in use: 150mAh). The temperature of the heating surface does not exceed 40 °C, thus ensuring safety for the users.

For wireless communication with the PC in IRelics, we used the wireless protocol of the Zigbee V2 [13]. The XBee Zigbee module can connect with the control board and there is another XBee receiver module connected to the PC over USB. The Zigbee protocol allows multiple tangible tools to send data to the base-station simultaneously. For now, they send data packages, which include sensor data and tool ID, at 20Hz intervals.

### Display and Input

The main system is run on a laptop with an Intel core I5 8250U CPU and an Intel UHD Graphics 620 GPU. It is connected to a projector (XGIMI Z4 Aurora, 580 lumen) to back-project the graphical interface onto an ultra-thin screen film (–0.26mm thickness, PET). Thermal changes on the outside of the film would conduct through the film instantly and be captured by the LWIR camera. The backstage environment is shown in Figure 6. The screen size is 1.60×1.00m and the projection resolution we use is 1280×800 pixels. The LWIR camera we use is OPTRIS PI 160, resolution 160*120, temperature precision 0.1°C, 120 FPS.

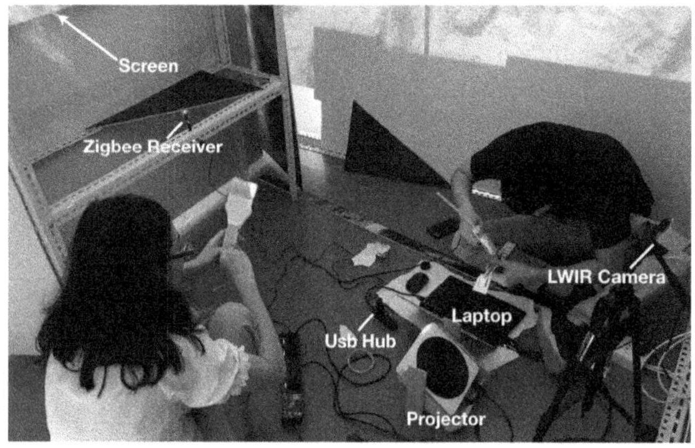


**Figure 6. Backstage of the IRelics platform.**

The projector and LWIR camera are calibrated to each other using similar methods as [15]. Since the resolution aspect ratio of the projector is consistent with the aspect ratio of the screen (16:10), the four corners of the projected image are manually calibrated to the four corner points of the screen. As the resolution aspect ratio of the camera is 4:3, we made it corresponded with the middle-top 960×720 pixels area of the screen which is the interaction area. With the homography matrix between the projection and real screen coordinates, four corner points of the interaction area could be calculated. Then, by touching these four points with a finger, four temperature stamps would be seen in the monitoring window. Manually adjusting the location and angle of the camera enables all the stamps to appear on the corners of the captured thermal image. In this way, the homography matrix between the projection and thermal camera could be easily calculated.

The core components are covered by a shelter and decorated with cave-like images to enable the best projection performance. The screen is slanted from the vertical orientation at 30 degrees to make user's gaze and operation more comfortable. As the screen is waterproof, most of the water flows off the surface. A horizontal groove is installed below the screen to collect the flowing water allowing it to be reused. Some amounts of water may remain on the surface, but this does not impact the sensitivity of other tangible tools.

### Software

The game engine was developed using the OpenFrameworks C++ library, and the basic architecture is shown in Figure 7. There is a GUI renderer which is responsible for rendering the game screen at a 60Hz frame rate. All the game stages are stored in a sequential order. Each stage essentially consists of two images, one is rendered as the foreground layer and the other as the background layer at each game loop. Whenever the correct tool or action is performed on the correct region, then that part of the foreground layer will be set to transparent. After the foreground is cleared entirely, the current stage will be passed and the game engine pushes the next stage into the renderer.

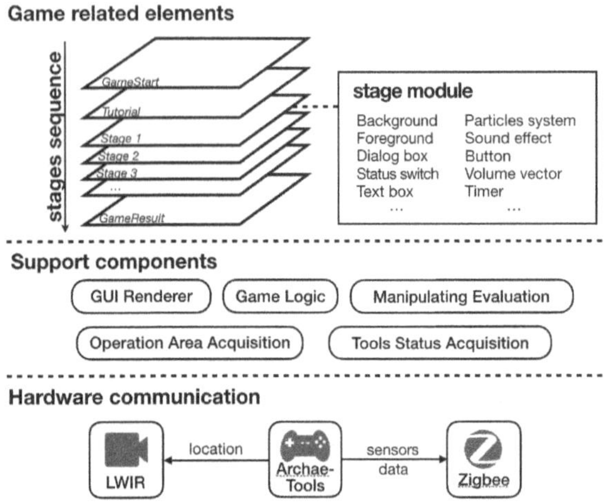


**Figure 7. The basic architecture of IRelics game engine.**

To acquire data on the area the user is working on, single channel source images mapped to the temperature values of the sensing area are transfered through inter-process communication (IPC) from the Optris imager program. The operational areas are found through contour finding based on the OpenCV library [33] and in which blobs containing less than 5 pixels or more than 3000 pixels are omitted in order to filter out interference and noise such as slight vibrations or screen shaking caused by user actions.

### *Review Scoring Mechanism*

At the end of the game, the player receives a review of their actions as evaluated by the system. **1)** The Recording section depends on the number of uses of the recording button. **2)** The Understanding section depends on the time counting when the user is holding the wrong tool. Using the tool ID, IRelics can know whether the user is holding the correct tool at each stage and count the times they are wrong. **3)** The Operating section depends on the number of times that the force of operation taken from the bend sensors exceeds the threshold (representing damage to the artifact).

## USER OBSERVATIONS

To verify the usability and educational effectiveness of the IRelics, we performed two rounds of observations on how the users interact within two different design exhibitions (see Figure 8). The first exhibition was held in the art museum at our university campus and the second one was a cultural heritage exhibition held in an ancient town. We provided no compensation for participation in both rounds.

**Figure 8. The R2 Observation. Left and Middle: Users trying our prototype. Right: The observer was having an interview with the user after his trial.**

In the first round (R1), we focused on verifying the usability of the hardware. Only three game stages were in the game, which correspond to each of the three tangible tools. More than 50 visitors (more than 10 each day in a span of 5 days) tried IRelics and played the example game. An observer would stand beside the platform to give a simple introduction and instruct them on the interaction methods (touching with bare hands, using the trowel, brush or spray water using the spray bottle). We observed their actions and recorded the details. If the visitor encountered any problems or stopped to ask questions, the observer would help them or give appropriate explanations. The observer would also record any problems or questions, as well as any comments from the users.

In the second round (R2), participants played with a complete version of the "Archaeological Adventure". Pre-game interviews were first conducted to identify how familiar the participant was with archaeology. After playing the game, the participant was asked to complete a questionnaire with a few Likert-type questions each rated on a 5-point scale from "Strongly Agree" to "Strongly Disagree" to assess the educational effects: ***Q1.*** *You can retell the steps of this game process,* ***Q2.*** *The final report help you gain understanding of archaeology,* ***Q3.*** *You learned that environmental analysis is important to archaeology and* ***Q4.*** *You learned that detailed recording of data is important in the archaeological process.* Besides,they were also asked to select 4 adjectives from a list of words describing the game platform, such as "interesting" or "annoying".

During the in-depth interview, we asked the participants to recite the game-process and asked them to talk about the changes in their understanding of archaeology and what they considered to be the "central aspect" of archaeology. Advice and feedback were also welcomed in the interview. We compiled the answers to assess the effectiveness of IRelics in educating the user on the field of archaeology. 25 users tried the system and 20 effective questionnaires were collected in R2. There were 12 males, of whom 4 received more in-depth interviews, and 13 females, of whom 6 received more in-depth interviews. The others accepted informal interviews that allowed them to freely talk about the topic. There were a wide range of ages, education levels, and occupations in the tested users.

### Findings

#### *Usability Evaluation*

The tool's haptic affordance made it easy for the users to interact with them correctly, and most of the participants got used to the interaction styles in less than 30 secs. The most common problem was how the users held the tools, as holding the tools in a way that wouldn't trigger the capacitive touch sensor would not wake up the micro-system of the tool. The problem was solved by enlarging the area of the sensing pad by pasting copper foil on the tool's surface and connecting the foil to the sensor.

In R1, the majority of participants could finish the game in 5 – 6 minutes. The time spent on each stage of the game was different: Stage 1 with trowel: 3 – 4 minutes, Stage 2 with brush: 1 minute, Stage 3 with spray bottle: 30 seconds. The time taken was highly correlated with the contact area of the tool with the surface. Nearly half of the participants showed fatigue or impatience after using the shovel for more than 2 minutes. Thus, we inferred that 2 minutes should be the maximum appropriate time for a stage. In R2, the time taken for each stage would be extended due to time spent reading the added instructions.

Most participants affirmed that both the input sensing precision and the speed were satisfactory, and they greatly enjoyed the tangible interaction styles. Several participants told us that they felt comfortable and delighted when they sprayed liquid directly onto the screen. The haptic feedback and real-time game response were deduced as the main reasons.

We also did not place enough consideration into how children would use our platform. There were more than 10 children (6-12 years old) that tried our platform. Since most of them were not able to play completely independently (common difficulties included not being able to understand the texts, not being able to use tools correctly, not being tall enough, etc.), they required the assistance of their parents or the observer. Despite this, the parents of the children were fond of our design. They thought that our design is a good method of education since in addition to teaching, it also exercises the children's hands-on ability. Moreover, IRelics could also be a medium to promote relationships within the family as we observed that parents could understand and give spontaneous guidance whenever their children could not understand.

### *Educational Effectiveness*

Before completing the game, users generally had low understanding of archeology. All of the users that were tested (25) reported that they "were not familiar with archeology", 5 expressed that most of their knowledge regarding archeology came from television shows, and described it as "digging for treasure" or "appraising antiques".

The questionnaire results (see Figure 9) imply that: *1) The platform helps users memorize the archaeological process effectively (from Q1), 2) The review report is useful in educating users on archaeological topics (from Q2), 3) Introductions and notifications based on GUI attracted less attention from users (from Q3 and Q4).*

In the in-depth interview, we obtained more detailed opinions, which helped us deduce the factors behind the results of the questionnaire. Firstly, most of the participants (9 of 10) were able to recite the steps of the game, including how to use the tools, thus showing that IRelics was effective in helping users retain knowledge. However, all of the participants expressed that they did not notice the recording function despite the

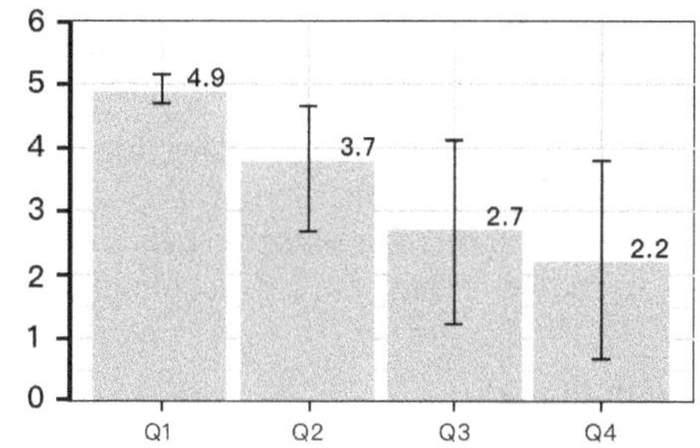


**Figure 9. Results from the Likert-type questions: Q1. Ability of steps retelling. Q2. Effectiveness of final report. Q3. Awareness of the importance of environment analysis. Q4. Awareness of the importance of detailed recording.**

tutorial at the start instructing them to use the record function frequently. Once the game had begun all the participants' focus was on the interaction with the tangible tools, and they only noticed their lack of recording once they had reached the final report and saw that their score in the recording section was "low". For environmental analysis, due to the frequent dialog boxes, the score of Q3 is greater than Q4, nonetheless, many were overly focused on the tangible integration aspect and would often skip over dialogues. Overall, the outcomes were still very positive since all of the participants interviewed could give more specific and detailed descriptions and explanations of field archaeology, indicating that they had gained a better understanding of the processes involved in field archaeology, as well as significant interest and desire to discuss the subject further.

### *Emotional Feedback*

When choosing adjectives to describe the IRelics platform, most users chose "popular", "attractive", "interesting", and "meaningful". The vast majority gave the prototype a positive evaluation and affirmed the educational value and interestingness of the prototype and expressed their hope of seeing similar products in museums as early as possible.

## DISCUSSION

### Inertia of Interaction Styles

In R2, our example game utilized a mix of tangible interaction and 2d interface interaction. In practice, most of the user's attention is focused on the tangible interaction aspect. This is evident in the fact that the use of certain 2D functions is low (such as the recording button). When a task requires the user to switch from the use of tangible interaction to 2D interaction, there is a clear sense of inertia as the user wishes to remain in the tangible interaction mode. For example, when advancing into a subsequent stage's pre-instructions, many users will continue to interact with IRelics and use the tangible tools as if they were still on the previous stage. This causes the reader to be distracted from reading the instructions. Therefore, for tasks that are considered to have a high impact on satisfying the criteria, we recommend using the form of tangible interaction. For instance, as recording is important based on the feedback from the archaeologists, a tangible tool "camera" can be easily built with our custom MCU and the 3D printing model. Once the user presses the "shutter", the flash lights up, and a screenshot will be taken by the main system. The presence of the tangible camera will remind the user to use it more frequently compared with the virtual camera button on the screen.

For the situations that users have to change focus from tangible interaction to 2D surface interaction, a gradient animation effect or a voice reminder is considered to be added in between two tasks, to provide users with a psychological buffer.

### Interact with Liquid

Interacting with liquid plays a significant role in gameplay. Not only does the spray tool enable several types of archaeological simulation, but the interaction style provides a delightful and smooth user experience as well. However there are some considerable tradeoffs while applying liquid in the interactions. Although most of the water would flow off the surface after the user sprayed water on it, the screen tended to stay wet for a while after. The wetness does not affect the normal use of tangible tools but does impact bare-hand interaction. We observed that a few participants, especially female participants, expressed displeasure while touching the wet screen with their hands. Therefore, in later experiments we usually recommended the participant to touch the screen using the tools instead. Also, the experimenter would dry the surface with a towel every few rounds, which increased experimental workload. A practical approach in a real museum setting will be to install an air dryer at the side of the screen to keep it dry.

Another issue is the dispersing effects rendered in the game. It is difficult to make this interaction realistic because a liquid will not disperse in the same way as on a real 3-dimensional object. Since IRelics adopts a 2D graphical display, there is a tradeoff between making the tangible tools more available and improving the realism of the game environment. The combination of tangible techniques and 3D-reconstruction techniques [7, 32] may open up future research opportunities.

### Limitations and Future Work

After conducting the user study, we refined the shortcomings in the current system into several aspect and proposed corresponding solutions:

**1)** Over-cautiousness when using tools: since users are often unfamiliar with tangible interaction styles, they often need a period of time to get used to using them. For example in the use of the spray bottle, many hesitated when told to spray water on top of the display. To solve this, instructions on how to use the tools could be presented in the game interface.

**2)** Due to the smaller contact surface of the trowel in comparison with the brush and the spray bottle, it takes a longer period of time to complete tasks using it. This led to many users experiencing fatigue and declining patience while using the tool. Thus, if IRelics is to be used with a larger display, the contact area of the tools with the display surface must also increase in order to prevent disinterest.

**3)** Users are less sensitive to text information. Since the tangible tools are more novel and interesting than the text information presented, the user's attention is less focused on text information, leading to them not noticing important aspects of the game. Thus, important information is recommended to be augmented by dubbing or exclusive presentation.

**4)** Children require assistance to use IRelics. Since the use of tangible tools is attractive to children and the system is likely to be implemented in museums, the platform should be able to be used by people of all ages including children. From our observations, we obtained feedback and experience that will help us improve the design for children. The system must have reasonable height, easy to understand content, and encourage parental interaction with their children.

## CONCLUSION

Archeology is a subject that not only requires professional knowledge but also practical, hands-on experience. Former experiencing platforms related to the topic usually took advantage of 2D/3D graphical interfaces, or VR/AR [9, 17]. These interfaces are good at conveying visual information but are limited in terms of realistic interactive input.

IRelics is a novel TUI platform for the presentation of field archaeological activities. One of its contributions is that its interaction style is a combination of visual and tactile factors which provides real-time realistic feedback more similar to real actions in comparison with traditional styles in which only visual information is involved. Within the design process, the details of IRelics system were also presented, and a set of tangible reforming methods were conducted to build tangible input devices referred to archaeological tools. The combination of tangible tools with LWIR sensing technique has been proven to be stable and repeatable, and the MCU we developed for the tangible tools is affordable and extensible for extensive usages of other tangible interaction styles.

Through the two observations, we gathered a large amount of feedback and advice. Additionally, responses proved that audiences were highly engaged in experiencing IRelics and the effects of improving the awareness of field archeology were clear. Limitations and future work were also discussed, and we will further enrich the set of tangible tools and improve the quality of the platform in the future. Furthermore, we will promote cooperation with archaeological museums since most of them are also responsible for archaeological research and hold abundant source materials, and we could help them develop specific applications based on IRelics for popularizing archeology to the general public.

Further, we think that IRelics, our TUI platform designed to popularize and educate people on the field of archeology, can be applied similarly to other fields that involve hands-on experience and tool use, such as medicine or agriculture, in the future.

## ACKNOWLEDGMENTS

We thank Muliang Xi and Xinyi Fu for providing archaeological guidance, Jing Gao and Yuanzhai Xu for design assistance, Daniel He and Li Huang for proofreading, and Yuan Yao for producing the video. This work is supported by National Key Research & Development Plan of China under Grant No. 2016YFB1001402.

## REFERENCES


[1] Wendy Ashmore and Robert Sharer. 2013. *Discovering our past: a brief introduction to archaeology.* McGraw-Hill Higher Education.

[2] Philip Barker. 1993. *Techniques of archaeological excavation.* Psychology Press.

[3] Jean-Baptiste Barreau, Ronan Gaugne, Yann Bernard, Gaétan Le Cloirec, and Valérie Gouranton. 2014. Virtual reality tools for the west digital conservatory of archaeological heritage. In *Proceedings of the 2014 Virtual Reality International Conference.* ACM, 4.

[4] H. Benko, E. W. Ishak, and S. Feiner. 2004. Collaborative mixed reality visualization of an archaeological excavation. In *Third IEEE and ACM International Symposium on Mixed and Augmented Reality.* 132–140. DOI: http://dx.doi.org/10.1109/ISMAR.2004.23

[5] Nuno Correia, Tarquínio Mota, Rui Nóbrega, Luís Silva, and Andreia Almeida. 2010. A Multi-touch Tabletop for Robust Multimedia Interaction in Museums. In *ACM International Conference on Interactive Tabletops and Surfaces (ITS '10).* ACM, New York, NY, USA, 117–120. DOI: http://dx.doi.org/10.1145/1936652.1936674

[6] Herminia Wei-Hsin Din. 2006. Play to Learn: Exploring Online Educational Games in Museums. In *ACM SIGGRAPH 2006 Educators Program (SIGGRAPH '06).* ACM, New York, NY, USA, Article 13. DOI: http://dx.doi.org/10.1145/1179295.1179309

[7] M. M. A. Gallo, F. Spadafora, F. Manfredi, F. Bruno, and A. Lamarca. 2013. 3D reconstruction of an outdoor archaeological site through a multi-view stereo technique. In *2013 Digital Heritage International Congress (DigitalHeritage)*, Vol. 1. 169–176. DOI: http://dx.doi.org/10.1109/DigitalHeritage.2013.6743727

[8] Kristoffer Getchell, Alan Miller, J Ross Nicoll, Rebecca Sweetman, and Colin Allison. 2010. Games methodologies and immersive environments for virtual fieldwork. *IEEE Transactions on Learning Technologies* 3, 4 (2010), 281–293.

[9] Tony Hall, Luigina Ciolfi, Liam Bannon, Mike Fraser, Steve Benford, John Bowers, Chris Greenhalgh, Sten-Olof Hellström, Shahram Izadi, Holger Schnädelbach, and others. 2001. The visitor as virtual archaeologist: explorations in mixed reality technology to enhance educational and social interaction in the museum. In *Proceedings of the 2001 conference on Virtual reality, archeology, and cultural heritage.* ACM, 91–96.

[10] Wolfgang Hürst, Xhi Jia Tan, and Ferdinand de Coninck. 2016. Using Digital Extensions to Create New VR Museum Experiences. In *Proceedings of the 13th International Conference on Advances in Computer Entertainment Technology (ACE '16).* ACM, New York, NY, USA, Article 45, 6 pages. DOI: http://dx.doi.org/10.1145/3001773.3001822

[11] Stefan Hynst, Michael Gervautz, Markus Grabner, and Konrad Schindler. 2001. A Work-flow and Data Model for Reconstruction, Management, and Visualization of Archaeological Sites. In *Proceedings of the 2001 Conference on Virtual Reality, Archeology, and Cultural Heritage (VAST '01).* ACM, New York, NY, USA, 43–52. DOI: http://dx.doi.org/10.1145/584993.585000

[12] N. Ibrahim and K. A. Azmi. 2013. Preserving Malay architectural heritage through virtual reconstruction. In *2013 Digital Heritage International Congress (DigitalHeritage)*, Vol. 1. 739–742. DOI: http://dx.doi.org/10.1109/DigitalHeritage.2013.6743830

[13] Digi International Inc. 2018. Digi XBee and XBee-PRO Zigbee RF Modules - Digi International. https://www.digi.com/products/xbee-rf-solutions/2-4-ghz-modules/xbee-zigbee. (2018). Accessed August 08, 2018.

[14] Hiroshi Ishii, Dávid Lakatos, Leonardo Bonanni, and Jean-Baptiste Labrune. 2012. Radical atoms: beyond tangible bits, toward transformable materials. *interactions* 19, 1 (2012), 38–51.

[15] Daisuke Iwai and Kosuke Sato. 2005. Heat sensation in image creation with thermal vision. In *Proceedings of the 2005 ACM SIGCHI International Conference on Advances in computer entertainment technology.* ACM, 213–216.

[16] Martha Joukowsky. 1980. *A complete manual of field archaeology. Tools and techniques of field work for archaeologists.* Prentice-Hall, Inc.

[17] Mathieu Loiseau, Elise Lavoué, Jean-Charles Marty, and Sébastien George. 2013. Raising awareness on archaeology: A multiplayer game-based approach with mixed reality. In *European Conference on Games Based Learning.* Academic Conferences International Limited, 336.

[18] Nick Merriman. 2004. *Involving the public in museum archaeology.* Routledge, 85–108.

[19] CCTV Network. 2017. National Treature-CCTV large-scale cultural exploration program. http://tv.cctv.com/cctv3/special/guojiabaozang/. (2017). Accessed November 30, 2017.

[20] Ioannis Paliokas, Vlad Buda, and Iancu Adrian Robert. 2010. Archaeo viz-a 3d explorative learning environment of reconstructed archaeological sites and cultural artefacts. In *Signal Processing and Multimedia Applications (SIGMAP), Proceedings of the 2010 International Conference on.* IEEE, 211–214.

[21] Caroline Pantofaru, Austin Hendrix, Andreas Paepcke, Dirk Thomas, Sharon Marzouk, and Sarah Elliott. 2013. Programming Robots at the Museum. In *Proceedings of the 12th International Conference on Interaction Design and Children (IDC '13).* ACM, New York, NY, USA, 305–308. DOI: http://dx.doi.org/10.1145/2485760.2485797

[22] Christina Pollalis, Whitney Fahnbulleh, Jordan Tynes, and Orit Shaer. 2017. HoloMuse: Enhancing Engagement with Archaeological Artifacts Through Gesture-Based Interaction with Holograms. In *Proceedings of the Eleventh International Conference on Tangible, Embedded, and Embodied Interaction (TEI '17)*. ACM, New York, NY, USA, 565–570. DOI: http://dx.doi.org/10.1145/3024969.3025094

[23] Christina Pollalis, Elizabeth Joanna Minor, Lauren Westendorf, Whitney Fahnbulleh, Isabella Virgilio, Andrew L. Kun, and Orit Shaer. 2018. Evaluating Learning with Tangible and Virtual Representations of Archaeological Artifacts. In *Proceedings of the Twelfth International Conference on Tangible, Embedded, and Embodied Interaction (TEI '18)*. ACM, New York, NY, USA, 626–637. DOI: http://dx.doi.org/10.1145/3173225.3173260

[24] Hangzhou Qianying Cultural Innovation Inc. Qingying Studio Tsinghua University. 2017. Masters in the Forbidden City. http://www.imdb.com/title/tt6448192/. (2017). Accessed November 30, 2017.

[25] Patrick Reuter, Guillaume Riviere, Nadine Couture, Stephanie Mahut, and Loic Espinasse. 2010. ArcheoTUI: Driving virtual reassemblies with tangible 3D interaction. *Journal on Computing and Cultural Heritage (JOCCH)* 3, 2 (2010), 4.

[26] Francesca Rizzo and Franca Garzotto. 2007. "The Fire and The Mountain": Tangible and Social Interaction in a Museum Exhibition for Children. In *Proceedings of the 6th International Conference on Interaction Design and Children (IDC '07)*. ACM, New York, NY, USA, 105–108. DOI: http://dx.doi.org/10.1145/1297277.1297298

[27] Jessica Roberts. 2015. Exploring Effects of Full-body Control in Perspective-based Learning in an Interactive Museum Data Display. In *Proceedings of the Ninth International Conference on Tangible, Embedded, and Embodied Interaction (TEI '15)*. ACM, New York, NY, USA, 445–448. DOI: http://dx.doi.org/10.1145/2677199.2691606

[28] Maria Roussou, Elina Kavalieratou, and Michael Doulgeridis. 2007. Children Designers in the Museum: Applying Participatory Design for the Development of an Art Education Program. In *Proceedings of the 6th International Conference on Interaction Design and Children (IDC '07)*. ACM, New York, NY, USA, 77–80. DOI:http://dx.doi.org/10.1145/1297277.1297292

[29] N. Schiavottiello. 2015. ArkTeller: A new 3D real-time storytelling platform for cultural heritage interpretation. In *2015 Digital Heritage*, Vol. 2. 753–754. DOI:http://dx.doi.org/10.1109/DigitalHeritage.2015.7419620

[30] Akihiko Shirai, Yuki Kose, Kumiko Minobe, and Tomoyuki Kimura. 2015. Gamification and Construction of Virtual Field Museum by Using Augmented Reality Game "Ingress". In *Proceedings of the 2015 Virtual Reality International Conference (VRIC '15)*. ACM, New York, NY, USA, Article 4, 4 pages. DOI: http://dx.doi.org/10.1145/2806173.2806182

[31] DIG-IT! GAMES PRODUCTION STUDIOS. 2018. Excavate - Dig-it! Games. https://dig-itgames.com/excavate/. (2018). Accessed November 18, 2018.

[32] Veronica Sundstedt, Alan Chalmers, and Philippe Martinez. 2004. High Fidelity Reconstruction of the Ancient Egyptian Temple of Kalabsha. In *Proceedings of the 3rd International Conference on Computer Graphics, Virtual Reality, Visualisation and Interaction in Africa (AFRIGRAPH '04)*. ACM, New York, NY, USA, 107–113. DOI: http://dx.doi.org/10.1145/1029949.1029970

[33] Satoshi Suzuki and others. 1985. Topological structural analysis of digitized binary images by border following. *Computer vision, graphics, and image processing* 30, 1 (1985), 32–46.

[34] Eileen Vote, Daniel Acevedo Feliz, David H Laidlaw, and Martha Sharp Joukowsky. 2002. Discovering petra: Archaeological analysis in vr. *IEEE Computer Graphics and Applications* 22, 5 (2002), 38–50.

[35] Ron Wakkary and Marek Hatala. 2007. Situated play in a tangible interface and adaptive audio museum guide. *Personal and Ubiquitous Computing* 11, 3 (2007), 171–191.

[36] Wikipedia contributors. 2017. Daomu Biji — Wikipedia, The Free Encyclopedia. (2017). https://en.wikipedia.org/w/index.php?title=Daomu_Biji&oldid=804476168 [Online; accessed 5-August-2018].

[37] Wikipedia contributors. 2018. The Lost Tomb — Wikipedia, The Free Encyclopedia. https://en.wikipedia.org/w/index.php?title=The_Lost_Tomb&oldid=838544704. (2018). [Online; accessed 9-August-2018].

[38] Nikoleta Yiannoutsou, Ioanna Papadimitriou, Vassilis Komis, and Nikolaos Avouris. 2009. "Playing with" Museum Exhibits: Designing Educational Games Mediated by Mobile Technology. In *Proceedings of the 8th International Conference on Interaction Design and Children (IDC '09)*. ACM, New York, NY, USA, 230–233. DOI: http://dx.doi.org/10.1145/1551788.1551837

# OpenLH: Open Liquid-Handling System for Creative Experimentation with Biology

**Gilad Gome**
gilad.gome@milab.idc.ac.il
Media Innovation Lab
The Interdisciplinary Center
Herzliya, Israel

**Julian Waksberg**
julian.waksberg@milab.idc.ac.il
Media Innovation Lab
The Interdisciplinary Center
Herzliya, Israel

**Andrey Grishko**
andrey.grishko@milab.idc.ac.il
Media Innovation Lab
The Interdisciplinary Center
Herzliya, Israel

**Iddo Yehoshua Wald**
iddo.wald@milab.idc.ac.il
Media Innovation Lab
The Interdisciplinary Center
Herzliya, Israel

**Oren Zuckerman**
orenz@idc.ac.il
Media Innovation Lab
The Interdisciplinary Center
Herzliya, Israel

## ABSTRACT
The biological prototyping revolution is in motion, and new tools are needed to empower HCI researchers, designers, makers, and bio-enthusiasts to experiment with live organisms. We present OpenLH, a liquid handling system that empowers users to conduct accurate and repetitive experiments with live biology in a sterile, open, and affordable way. OpenLH integrates a commercially available robotic arm with custom 3D printed parts, a modified pipette, and a visual block-based programming interface. The system is as accurate as commercial liquid handlers, capable of repetitive tasks in micro-scale accuracy, easy to operate, and supports multi-materials including biomaterials, microorganisms and cell cultures. We describe the system's technical implementation and two custom interfaces. We demonstrate the system's impact for the HCI community with two use cases that include experimentation with live biology in non-traditional fields: visual design using pigment-expressing E.coli, and beer brewing experiment using serial dilution in home context.

### CCS Concepts
**•Human-centered computing → Interactive systems and tools; •General and reference →** *Design;* **•Applied computing →** *Computer-aided manufacturing;*

### Author Keywords
Liquid-Handling; Open Source; Biology; Prototyping; Experimentation; Democratization.


*TEI '19, March 17–20, 2019, Tempe, AZ, USA.*

ACM ISBN 978-1-4503-6196-5 /19/03 ...$15.00.
http://dx.doi.org/10.1145/3294109.3295619

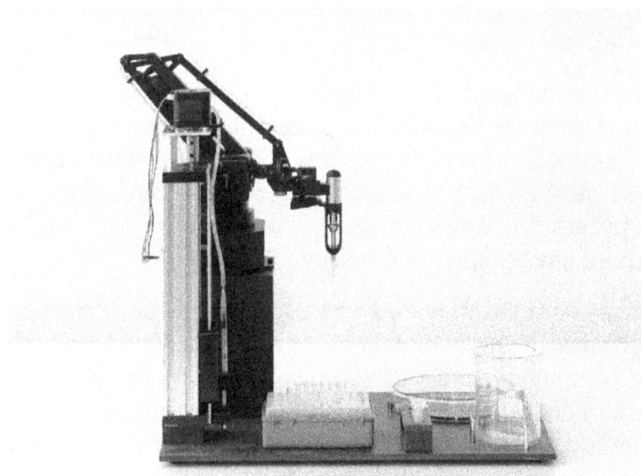

**Figure 1. Open LH: an open liquid-handling system for accurate, safe, flexible, and affordable biological experimentation.**

## INTRODUCTION
In recent years, advancements in biology research such as streamlining of DNA sequencing and synthesizing [7, 46] led to the introduction of new tools that move biology-related technologies out of research labs and into the hands of engineers and biohackers [19, 34, 43, 45]. The next wave of more accessible tools for biology exploration has the potential to reach new audiences beyond engineers and technically-minded biohackers [33]. Simpler DIYbio tools can engage a larger community of bio-enthusiasts such as designers, artists, educators, and HCI researchers [30][16], enabling creative exploration of biology in a variety of contexts, including education, citizen science, bio-fabrication, experimental art, smart materials prototyping, and more [28, 8, 13, 14, 44, 52, 54]. This process, if realized, may be similar to previous technological shifts from high-end industry to the general public, most notable ones are CNC milling and 3D printing for distributed production [38, 29], and the Arduino revolution that democratized electronic prototyping [47]. Existing tools that already contribute to

the democratization of biological prototyping include Gaudi labs's DIY lab equipment [32]; Amino educational tools for genetic engineering [31]; Bento thermo-cycler centrifuge and gel electrophoresis [4]; Open PCR DIY thermo-cycler [41]; a DIY fluorescence microscope [10]; Foldscope foldable paper origami microscope [11]; and Paper centrifuge [5].

One of the most commonly used processes in professional biology experimentation is pipetting, or Liquid-Handling (LH). The standard pipette, found in any biology lab around the world, is a handheld tool which is used to transport measured volumes of liquid (0.1-1000 μL) while maintaining sterile conditions. In domains such as microbiology, genetics, protein engineering, and diagnostics, LH is the most basic and common technique, and must be performed by skilled biologists, in a manual process done "with an experienced hand". In some advanced labs, computer automated LH is done using high throughput digital robotic systems that are very expensive and require a technician for programming new protocols [27]. The barriers LH is posing for non-biologists are the skill needed to be acquired for manual LH, the funds, biological knowledge, and technical knowledge needed to conduct experiments with the computer automated LH systems.

We present OpenLH (see Figure 1), an open-source LH system that is accurate, affordable, and flexible, supporting experimentation and creative exploration. OpenLH enables repetitive LH tasks in micro-scale accuracy, is easy to operate, and can be programmed using a block-based interface that does not require any technical knowledge.

The system is intended to be used by a wide variety of bio-enthusiasts, with two main user groups: makers who assemble the system, and end-users who conduct experiments using the system. Makers can assemble the system at parts cost with standard fabrication tools using our free fabrication files, and then integrate it into makerspaces, after school centers, HCI labs, or their own workshops; end-users will use the system in makerspaces or schools to perform experiments and creative exploration of biology.

The system is "open" in several ways: makers can download the fabrication files for building the system's custom syringe pump, pipette shaft attachment, and pipette tip ejector (see Figure 2); the code is available for free use and modification; the off-the-shelf commercial parts are available for purchase from third parties in significantly lower costs than systems of comparable performance; end-users can code the system with a simple block-based language; experiments performed with the system are "open" for manipulation as the whole system design encourage intervention; finally, the system is expandable with custom interfaces, new software, and new hardware features.

This process of makers making DIY tools more accessible to the community happened before, for example with low cost FDM 3D printers.

In this work we contextualize and differentiate OpenLH from prior work, describe the system implementation, report on its technical performance and present proof-of-concept use cases of creative experimentation with live biology. Clearly a user study is needed to evaluate how makers and bio-enthusiasts use this new tool, future work will asses that.

## RELATED WORK

Our work was inspired by a collection of works within the HCI field that bring DIYbio closer to novices, for creative exploration or science education. Our work also differs from professional lab-grade liquid handlers, recent advancements in XYZ gantry liquid handlers, professional bioprinters, and innovative prototypes for smart material deposition.

### DIYbio in HCI

Our work was inspired by the mission of creating "low-cost tools for performing biology work in non-professional settings", as expressed by Kuznetsov and collaborators when studying DIYbio from a design and HCI perspective [30], and manifested in their design for an incubator using low-cost materials and off-the-shelf components [16]. Another inspiration came from Bioart and specifically agar art, a community culturing art with agar plates, including an annual contest conducted by the American Society for Microbiology. A recent study with high-school students showed how students creatively "painted" with bacteria and antibiotic substances [28]. Kafai and collaborators introduced the BioMakerLab in high-school classrooms [24], a wet lab starter kit for synthetic biology, utilized by students to create logo designs using microorganisms they manipulated to produce different colored pigments. Riedel-Kruse and collaborators have created novel interactive experiences and tools for Human Biology Interaction (HBI): LudusScope is a smartphone-based microscope for life-science education [25]; Trap it [35, 36] and BioGraphr [18] are interactive system enabling users to interact with living cells by drawing on a touchscreen using Euglena, a microorganism with photo-tactic properties. In addition, Bioty [53] is a JavaScript-based web toolkit that allows to remotely program protocols to manipulate Euglena cells. OpenLH contributes to this emerging effort within the HCI community with an accessible and affordable LH tool.

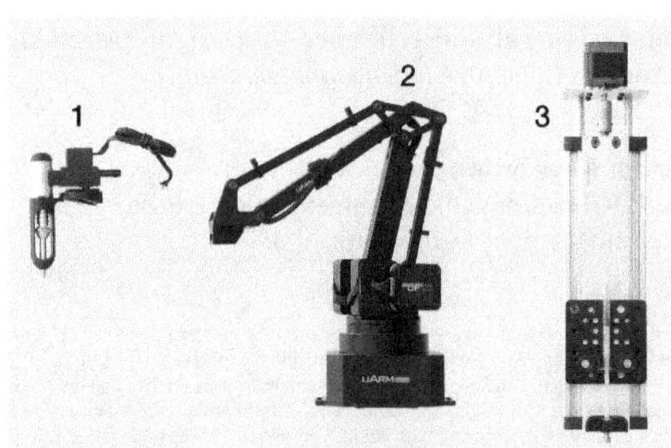


**Figure 2. 1. The custom-made liquid handling attachment. 2. the uArm Swift Pro robotic arm. 3. The linear actuator-syringe pump.**

### Differentiation from existing liquid-handlers and bioprinters

Commercial liquid handlers from companies such as Tecan [48]and Biotek [6] are made for professional biology labs use and run mostly predefined protocols that support standard kits for experiments. These commercial LH systems are estimated at 50,000 USD and above, are made for high throughput research, and include advanced features such as climate control, mixing, and shaking. These systems are designed to conduct standard protocols, such as ELISA, bacterial growth, fluorescence measurement, incubating shaking, and more. The result is a highly accurate and professional research tool, but a very rigid one that limits creative exploration and is not accessible to many, both biologists and non-biologists, due to its high cost.

The Andrew LH robot [1], estimated at 24,000 USD, is a desktop pipetting machine that can pick up pipettes from a stand, configure volume and conduct LH without electronic pipetting. Andrew mimics the human hand, picks up standard pipettes from a rack and calibrates the pipette as a human hand would. Andrew also offers a software for standard LH protocol design. Andrew is "computer-vision-assisted " and uses a camera to analyze the motor activity as it is changing volume on the standard pipette. It's a robot customized to use a product (pipette) that was designed for the human hand and eye.

A recent commercial product designed to make automated LH more accessible to labs is sold by Opentrons, the OT-1 and OT-2 products that cost an order of magnitude less than other commercial systems (4000 USD for the OT-2 basic setup). Opentrons is a XYZ gantry based system that has a controlled thumb that handles standard pipettes (OT-1). Their second product (OT-2) solved known problems with the OT-1 version by adding electronic control instead of the previous mechanical control. Specifications for the OT-2 include 2 pipette mounts, it can fill a 96 well plate in 20 seconds, is accurate down to 384-well plates, is a medium size machine at 63 cm x 57 cm x 66 cm, and weighs 40kg. The OT App is used to conduct standard protocols with standard tubes and plates. OpenLH differs from Opentrons by allowing more creative exploration, is more affordable, and is more portable due to its size and weight.

The Lego Liquid handler [17] is able to do effective LH work using a Lego built liquid handler operated by a Lego app. Compared to Gerber et al.'s Lego robot, our system supports multi-material and sterility by utilizing tip replacement, has a more flexible UI and is more robust and industry-ready. Regarding droplet size, comparing a similar 1ml syringe in both systems, Gerber et al.'s minimum droplet size is 2.5 µL while we reach 0.2 µL. The difference comes from our use of a more precise linear actuator operating a syringe pump controlling the vacuum between the syringe and the disposable tip. Gerber et al. were able to reach 0.15 µL droplet size using a smaller 25 µL syringe. We did not test with smaller volume syringes, but we estimate the result to be proportionally smaller.

Bioprinters or bioplotters are XYZ dispensing robots that print bio-materials and cells for the bioprinting industry. Commercials examples include bioplotter by EnvisionTEC [15], NovoGen by Organovo [42] and BioBots by ASLS [2]. CELLINK [9], a Swedish company is selling the 40,000 USD BIO-X a 3D Bioprinter that has three piston driven syringe heads and requires purchase of the syringes that cost hundreds of dollars per unit. Biobots from Advanced Solutions have developed the first six DOF Bioprinter, it also uses syringes that can be replaced (Up to eight replaceable tools), and a basic system that supports five cartridges and three-axis motion including rotational stage movement. In addition they have software that supports functional tissue structure design and design vascular systems.

The xPrint system is a novel smart material printing prototype used for bioprinting, developed at the MIT Media Lab. xPrint [51] is a significant milestone in the process of making LH tools more open and relevant for creative use. The system allows for a wide range of printing by active extrusion of thick gels and uses custom made cartridges. The system is not yet available commercially but is estimated at 7000 USD, and can be built by experienced makers with significant effort.

The following aspects are the key differentiators of OpenLH: Affordable: OpenLH is as accurate as professional lab-grade liquid handlers and XYZ gantry systems such as Opentrons with a standard 200 µL tip, while parts cost is much lower (under 1000 USD).

Multi-tip: our novel mechanism of linear-actuator operated syringe, using stepper motor on a linear rail, works with standard pipette shaft that transfers accurate quantities of liquid using a disposable tip from a tip rack. Leveraging tip replacement allows for multi-material usage and supports sterility. This novel mechanism supports: (1) multi-material deposition; (2) adequate accuracy; and (3) lab-grade sterility.

Customizable intuitive UI's: a Python API enables custom creation of interfaces. A Blockly-based interface was created to enable novices to code non-standard protocols and a bitmap-to-bioprint interface was created to convert images to biological prints. These two interfaces promote creative exploration empowering novices. Expert users with programming ability can also leverage the Python API to program protocols, or to extend the system.

Creative expansion: our system is designed to encourage exploration, with an open architecture both from the technical and operational aspects. From the technical aspect, the uARM robotic arm has an active community of developers that can broaden the system's capabilities, for example a UV LED for hydrogel crosslinking, and a camera for online assessment and colony recognition. From the operational aspect, the system is literally open, users can intervene with the LH process in many creative ways, for example by changing environmental factors such as using a flashlight to light specific areas in the agar plate while the LH is in progress, or inserting the system into a refrigerator.

## TECHNICAL IMPLEMENTATION

The OpenLH system is comprised from the following modules: a uArm Swift Pro robotic arm for spatial positioning; a linear-actuator based syringe pump for LH; a custom attachment

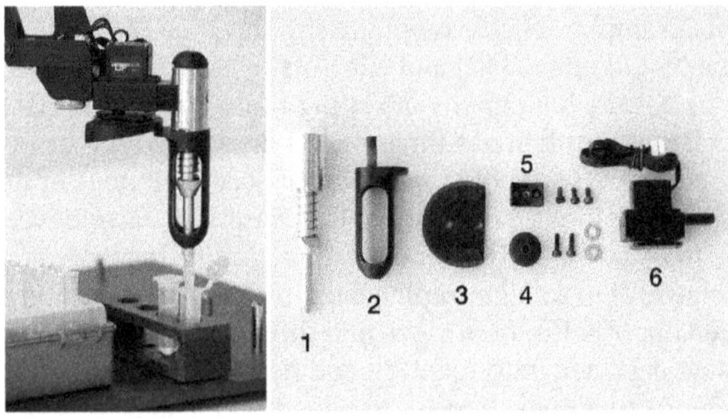


**Figure 3. Closeup of the custom-made liquid handling attachment extracting bacterial culture from a tube (left) and disassembled (Right). 1. pipette shaft. 2-3. 3D printed parts for tip displacement. 4-5. 3D printed adapters. 6. uArm end-effector.**

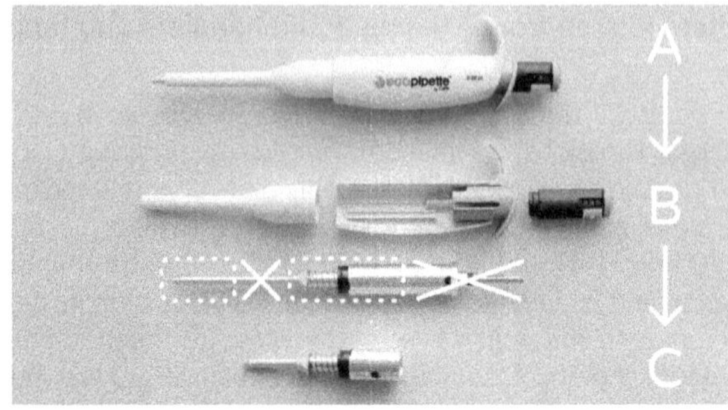


**Figure 4. Pipette modification: (A) Original commercial pipette; (B) Disassembled pipette and modification guidelines; (C) Custom-made parts to be embedded in the LH attachment.**

for programmable tip switching; custom software; and two custom UI's: a block-based programming interface and a bitmap-to-bioprint script.

### Robotic Arm Base

The system is built as an extension on top of the uArm Swift Pro robotic arm (see Figure 2), commercially available since 2017 for the cost of 749 USD. It has a small footprint, weighs 2.2kg and has 4 DOF. It allows for 0.2mm repeatability and a max speed of 100mm/s. It can lift 500g and has a range of 50-320mm [50]. It can communicate through USB cable and Bluetooth connection. The uArm structure enables assembling various attachments to the end effector unit, including a 3D printing head and a laser engraver. This setting enabled customization and allowed us to integrate our LH parts. The dependency on a specific, commercial, robotic arm may become a limitation in the future, however with little adjustments the system can support many other robotic arms with similar architecture, including DIY ones. The choice to use a commercially available arm was made to lower costs, lower the barriers of building a system, and to improve consistency.

### Custom Hardware

#### *Syringe Pump*

The pump was constructed by using an off the shelf linear actuator mounted with a syringe (See Figure 2). The Linear actuator used was an openbuilds-C-Beam Linear Actuator Bundle (129 USD) [40], operating a standard 1ml syringe with needle. A flexible tube from MasterFlex model 96410-13 (5 USD) connects the syringe to a custom-modified pipette. The result is an airtight environment from syringe to tip enabling professional-grade LH. The syringe is connected to the Linear actuator with custom designed 3D printed parts.

#### *LH Attachment*

We used parts of a standard pipette (65 USD) in a custom made assembly to allow attachment to the robot and tip switching (see Figure 3). We used a shortened shaft of an ecopipette (sold by Capp, see Figure 4) including the spring, and connected it to the arm with a custom 3D printed part. The tip removing accessory is made from two 3D printed parts (see Figure 3). The disc connects to the end-effector motor of the uARM (see Figure 3) that rotates 90°, designed to push the pipette and lead to tip removal. After a tip is disposed, the disc rotates back to 180° and the spring pushes the part back up so another tip can be picked up. All 3D printed parts are made with standard PLA and printed with the Ultimaker 3, an accessible 3D printer.

In summary, we utilized an existing, low-cost robotic arm and designed custom 3D printed parts to enable a unique mechanism: (1) attaching the pipette shaft from an industry grade dismantled pipette to the robotic arm to increase reliability; (2) attaching the syringe to the linear actuator enabling precise control of the vacuum between the syringe and the disposable tip; and (3) used the robotic arm servo attachment as a compact pipette release mechanism, leveraging the disassembled pipette original spring. Detailed assembly instructions, BOM, and design files are available in the supplementary materials, and updated versions will be shared online on the project's Instructables page [23].

### Control Software

The uArm runs on top of an Arduino Mega 2560 with a custom version of Marlin firmware (available under GPL licence). The robot operates using G-code definitions sent through UART protocol, which complies with both industry standards and with most tools used in the maker community such as open source 3D printers. uFactory provides several libraries for interacting with the robotic arm including pyuf [49] - a Python interface (others are a ROS interface, a Marlin firmware implementation, the uArm for CURA 3D plugin, and uArm studio which is not open source). We chose to use the Python library, available under BSD licence, for the ease of use of Python in prototyping. This library wraps around the serial connection and the G-code encodings. We modified the provided code of the Python interface, allowing us to send the position of the arm and the desired rotation in the extruder motor.

As we used the stepper motor for operating the syringe pump in a similar way to how it is used for 3D printing, we were able to take advantage of the control commands already available for it. To achieve this, before every execution we send an M code that will disable cold extrusion protection, then we can send G-code in the following format: G0 [E<pos>] [F<rate>] [X<pos>] [Y<pos>] [Z<pos>], where E represents the length of filament extruded by the feeder when used for

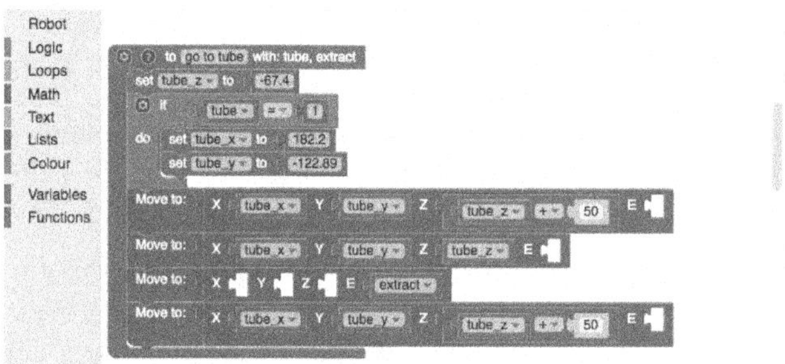


**Figure 5. Example for writing a function "go to tube", that extracts liquid from a tube.**

3D printing. We used these values to specify the amount of liquid dispensed or drawn. With this architecture we were able to create a variety of non-technical interfaces, that increases accessibility to novices. With this modified API, users with programing ability can use Python to control the system directly, or to create new interfaces for different user groups. We created two initial interfaces to demonstrate how non-technical interfaces can empower non-biologists and non-programmers: (1) A block-based visual programming interface using Google Blockly for intuitive creation of highly customizable protocols; (2) A printing script that enables conversion of bitmap images to LH instruction (bioprinting). The two custom interfaces are described below.

### Block Based Interface

We chose to create a block-based interface (see Figure 5) to provide an accessible method for non-programmers to control all of the system's abilities. Block-based interfaces such as Blockly, Scratch and many others are commonly used to introduce novices to programming, and Scratch has been shown to be successful in letting novices learn programming and use it to explore a new domain [12]. While uArm already offers a block based interface, it is not available in an open license and free to edit, so we were not able to expand it with our added capabilities. We chose to use Blockly which is a visual programming platform, similar to Scratch. It enabled us to create custom blocks as functions, allowing users to accurately control the arm and LH process with a minimum number of blocks, and can easily develop the operations needed for their specific experiment. In order to use the publicly available

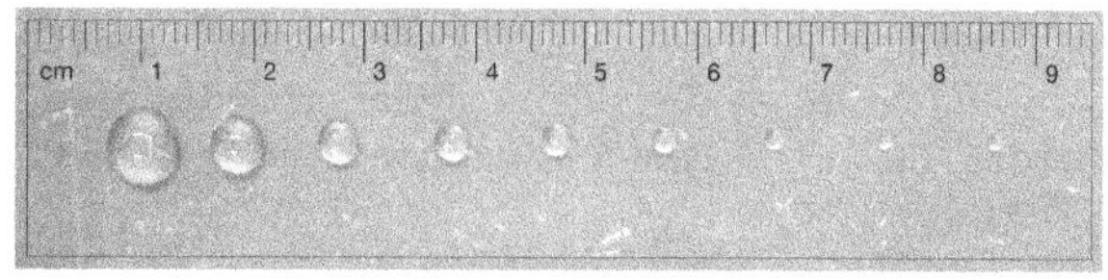


**Figure 7. Demonstration of the system's dispensing accuracy by measuring water droplets in different diameters.**

Blockly interface we created two components: a web server and a UDP server. The web server is responsible for serving the Blockly files, saving programs in blocks, converting the blocks to the Python code, and sending this code to the UDP server. The UDP server is connected via USB to the arm and constantly waiting to send incoming commands to the robotic arm, which enables remote operation of the system. With system flexibility in mind, we only added a -move X Y Z E-block that allowed control of each of the location and extraction variables, so users can create their own control functions for other operations. X, Y and Z are represented in millimeters, and E is represented in extrusion mm (extruder steps) as used by uArm for 3D printing. Based on the measurements taken for system accuracy evaluation (see Figure 8 and 6), we calculated a ratio of 3.55 µL to extruder step. This ratio will change if a different tip is used, or if the system is assembled using substitute syringe or linear actuator. To allow for such changes, a calibration manual was added to the supplementary material.

### Bitmap to Bioprint

In order to test the ability to create custom interfaces for new audiences and applications, we developed an interface that would load a bitmap, select all the pixels of a single color, and print these pixels in an agar plate. The conversion process was done with several existing tools. It starts by using the ImageMagick [22] conversion app to convert a jpeg/png picture into a list of (X,Y) coordinates and RGB color value; next, to filter out the unwanted colors we used grep, a text filtering program, and piped the results to a text file (coordinates file). We used a Python script based on our extended version of pyuf to read the coordinates file and generate the Z value for the printing surface and the starting coordinates. The system then iterates all the coordinates and deposits in a 3mm resolution 0.3 microliters of a solution containing live bacteria (the reso-

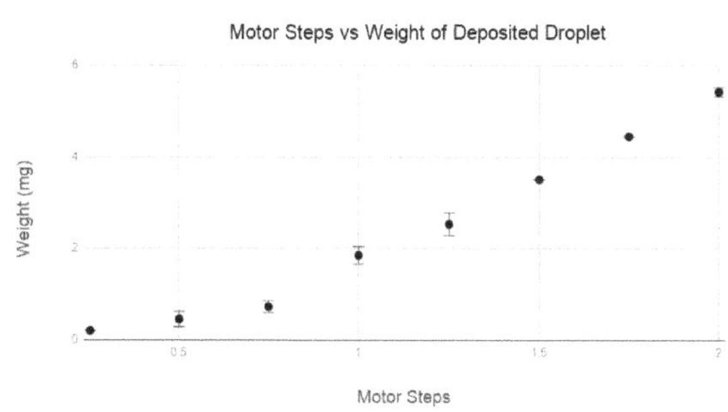


**Figure 6. 0.25-2 extruder steps and weight of water deposited in mg.**

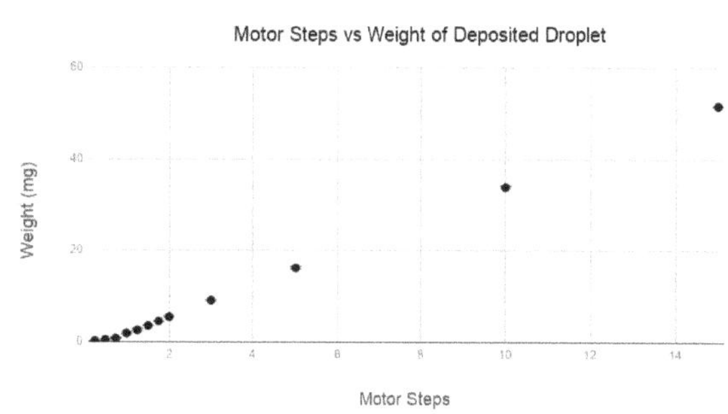


**Figure 8. 0.25-15 extruder steps and weight of water deposited in mg.**

lution can be as high as 0.2mm). The result is a non-technical interface that allows designers to "print" visual designs using microorganisms. We demonstrated this ability in one of our use cases.

## TECHNICAL EVALUATION: SYSTEM ACCURACY

We evaluated the system's dispensing accuracy by weighing (see Figure 6 and 8) and measuring the diameter water droplets deposited by contact dispensing (see Figures 7). Contact dispensing means that a touch-off is necessary to complete the liquid dispensing. When the liquid attaches to a substrate, a drag-back action is done to overcome the surface tension between liquid and the dispensing tip, without which the liquid will not drop [27]. In Figure 6 we show results of accuracy test (table included in supplementary materials) including standard deviation of water weight deposited. In Figure 6, the chart describes the amount of water dispensed for 0.25-2 extruder steps, resulting in 0.2-5.4 mg on average, with a low error (0.15 mg). As we extracted and dispensed larger amounts of water we noticed the error is becoming less significant and a clear linear function appears.

We used four measurements per extruder steps similar to previous work [3]. We calculated Standard Deviation (represented as error bars in Figure 6 and 8). We acknowledge that a standard error of 0.15 µL can be considered high if the mean is 0.1 µL, however 0.15 µL standard deviation is calculated across all data points on average. A 0.15 µL error is considered insignificant for most protocols in manual micropipette and comparable commercial liquid handlers.

The OpenLH throughput per tip is dependent on the tip volume. In our current configuration 200 µL can print 1000 drops of 0.2 µL for each droplet at a 0.2mm resolution (per tip). It is possible to use a 1ml tip and increase throughput by a factor of five. This is the main limitation but also differentiation of the OpenLH system in a bioprinting context, most high-end professional systems have large disposable syringes. For LH the OpenLH has one pipette head, other systems have a multi pipette head reducing operation time when working on standard protocols mostly in 96 wells plates, the OpenLH is thus less useful for such experiments but can support other experiments that are less standard.

Our system design goals were accuracy performance and accessibility rather than speed. In addition, we wanted to make it possible for users to safely intervene in the pipetting process in creative ways. Therefore, our system's speed was designed to be comparable to a human-hand pipetting speed in a single transaction.

## USE CASES: EXPERIMENTING WITH LIVE BIOLOGY

We performed two different experiments with the system, to test its potential for creative exploration in non-biology fields: visual design and beer brewing.

### Use case I: Bioprinting for Visual Designers

We created the Bitmap to Bioprint script to enable users who are familiar with graphic design tools to bio-print their design using OpenLH as a bioprinter. The goal is to create visual art using live bacteria as bio-ink. The process starts with a standard graphic design tool that supports layers (most graphic software do). Each layer contains one color and represents a different print bacterial cultures. The print materials in this experiments were live pigment-expressive E.coli microbial cells, each expressing a different color. Genetically altered bacteria are available for online order through services like Odin. As "bio-canvas" for the bioprint we used a a standard agar plate (LB-agar-Kanamycin) which we stained with active charcoal (5g per liter) to color it black, for aesthetic reasons. In the graphics software, each image layer is saved as a separate file and loaded to the OpenLH bioprinter using the Bitmap to Bioprint script interface. The printer runs the script, and the robotic arm loads live bacteria cultures from a tube and dispenses 0.3 µL accurately on the designated print coordinates. When the printing process is done, the canvas still appears empty, as the bacteria needs to grow. The original design appears over 12-24 hours (see Figure 9 and 10), depending on the specific environmental conditions (the optimal temperature is 37 °C). In order for the bacteria to be colorful we used the E. coli strain NEB Turbo, the color was induced by 3 different plasmids pSB1.107, pSB1.108, pSB1.109 (sequences available in supplementary material) promoting pigment expression in each cell.

### Use case II: Demonstration of Serial Dilution

In this use case we envision a beer brewer hobbyist that wishes to conduct a systematic experiment and maintain consistency

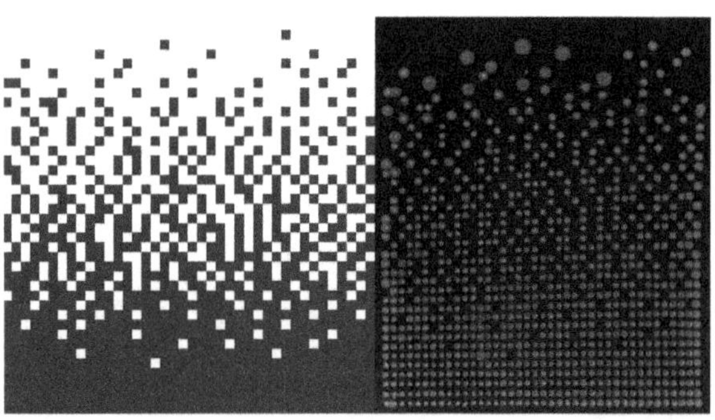

**Figure 9. A print created with OpenLH bitmap (left) to bioprint (right) using non-modified E.coli printed on charred LB-agar plate, after 12 hours of incubation at 37°C.**

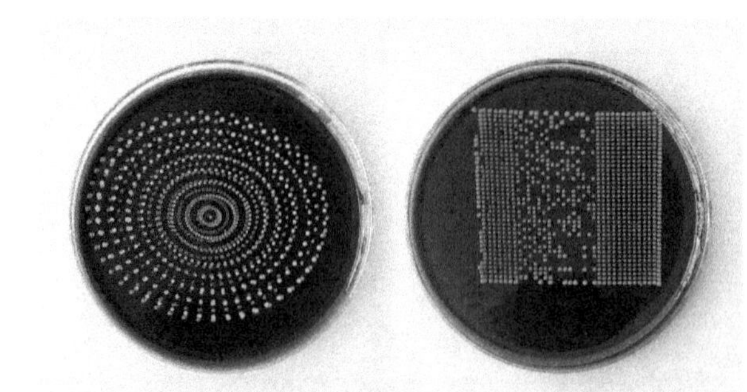

**Figure 10. Two prints created with OpenLH using genetically modified E.coli expressing yellow and purple fluorescent protein, after 12 hours of incubation at 37°C.**

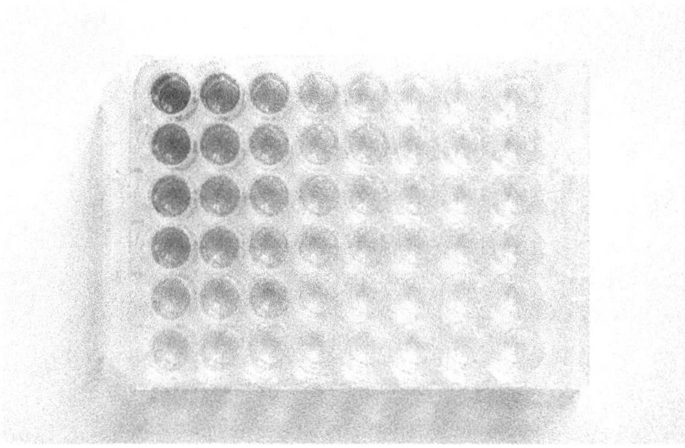

**Figure 11. Demonstration of serial dilution in a 48 wells plate, a standard biology lab procedure of repetitive precision operations.**

in her use of yeast. The process leverage a standard biology lab procedure, called serial dilution, and is programed using the visual block-based interface. When conducting serial dilution a highly concentrated solution is diluted in accurate steps until a highly diluted solution is made. In this case small amount of that solution is dropped on a LB-agar plate, and after incubation overnight in 37°C it is possible to count the number of colonies that grew on the plate. Knowing the original volume and that each colony started from a single cell allows to calculate the number of microorganisms in the original solution, and the brewer can decide on the time to extract and the amount of yeast solution they wish to use, being consistent with the amount of yeast used every time. In our experiment we diluted a sample of stained water into a 48 wells plate (see Figure 11). In the first column we had solutions of 100, 80, 60, 40, 20 and 10 percent, and wrote a Blockly code (see Figure 12) that mixes 100 µL of the previous well with 900 µL water in the next one. This use case demonstrates how the system enables the streamline of repetitive precision operations, adopting a professional biology lab procedures to a non-lab environment. As the block-based code is easily shared and modified, professional users can empower non-professionals and vice versa. The code in Figure 12 shows how we set the pipette pick-up location, the first cell location and the throw location. Then, we iterate through the cells with two loops: the inner loop traverse through the cells in each line. Each iteration starts with dispensing the material into the pipette from the current cell. Then the arm moves to the next cell and dispenses the material. At the end of each line, the arm throws the pipette tip in a specified location, picks up a new one and starts again. This procedure allows to maintain sterile conditions. The outer loop repeats this process for each line demonstrating high-throughput abilities of OpenLH.

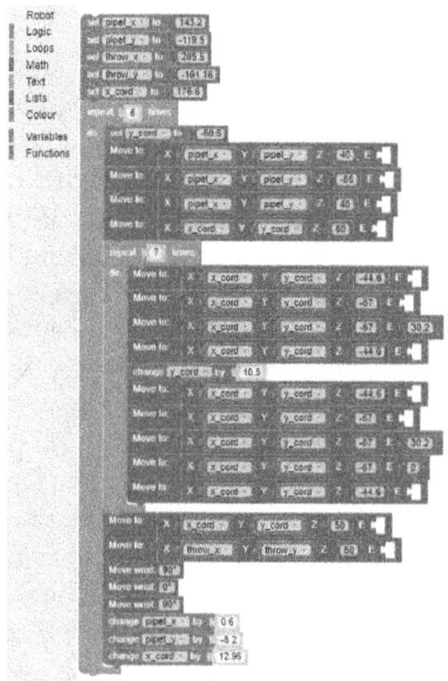

**Figure 12. Blockly code for serial dilution in a 48 wells plate.**

## DISCUSSION AND FUTURE WORK

To support the biological prototyping revolution, new tools are needed to empower users to experiment with biomaterials, microorganisms and cell cultures in an affordable, intuitive, creative, and safe way. We presented OpenLH, a system that empowers makers, bio-enthusiasts, HCI researchers, designers, and bio-hackers to conduct accurate and repetitive LH experiments with live biology in an open and affordable way. OpenLH is fully automatic, with a simple block-based programming interface, reducing usage cost to that of a professional manual pipette set. All the parts used to construct OpenLH are available for users to purchase or print: the uArm robotic arm and the hardware parts can be purchased; our code files and 3D printed accessories fabrication files, as well as the two interfaces (Block-based programming and bitmap-to-bioprint) are all available online [23].

Automatic LH marks a significant milestone in the development of professional biology labs. In the past 30 years LH gained massive adoption in research and industry labs [27]. Automatic high-end LH solutions are sold by firms such as Tecan [48] and Biotek [6] and allow scientists to conduct experiments that were not possible before at such a scale and speed, enabling accurate LH with high throughput and in a repeatable manner. An accurate yet affordable LH technology can empower biologists and non-biologists with no access to such high-end professional tools to conduct high throughput experiments [20], including bioprinting [39] and dispensing-based prototyping. These type of experiments are relevant for a wide range of fields, from simple experiments such as mixing and dispensing reagents from diagnostics by PCR or ELISA plate preparation, to more advanced experiments in bioprinting of tissue and biomaterials such as tissue scaffold [38], skin scaffold [37], and even vascularized heterogeneous tissues [26].

We hope our OpenLH system can empower bio-enthusiasts to experiment with live biology in a variety of creative and untraditional domains. For example: a textile designer experimenting with color-expressive bacteria for creating non-chemical prints; through a child engaging in bioprinting Agar art while learning scientific concepts; or a baker experimenting with yeast fermentation placing bacteria in exact accuracy to form a unique design for a loaf of bread.

Future work should evaluate how makers and end-users work with the system. Furthermore, OpenLH can be extended in several ways to further fulfill the mission of "low-cost tools for performing biology work in non-professional settings". In a similar way to existing remotely-operated solutions an OpenLH cloud lab can be setup to serve a larger community of people interested in experimenting with live biology. A cloud-based web interface can turn a small biohacker space into a service, listing all possible reagents and interfaces available. Regulatory, economic, and other barriers prevent biology enthusiasts around the world from performing their own experiments. Using a cloud-based service, the remote user may design their protocols using the block-based programming interface and the actual experiment will be performed by a member of the community that listed their OpenLH as available for remote use. Not only biology enthusiasts, but also many scientists around the world do not have access to automatic LH equipment, and today cloud labs such as Emerald and Transcriptic are providing commercial scalable robotic labs service. Cloud labs can also provide authentic inquiry-based learning at scale [21]. Another future direction can be for medical use. The Bitmap to Bioprint interface is relevant to more fields than design, as it can turn medical images directly into bioprints, for example when experimenting with functional tissue engineering by adding UV crosslinking for printing bio-compatible hydrogels. We hope OpenLH can empower interaction designers, HCI researchers, biohackers, artists and students to experiment and create with live biology.

## LIMITATIONS

The current implementation of OpenLH has one pipette head, unlike high-end professional LH systems that can support up to 12 pipettes, supporting high throughput experiments. The current implementation was designed to support 200 µL tips, a limitation in printing volume, which is adequate for our system goal. In future versions we consider adding a 1ml tip. Some bioprinters have large syringes capable of printing solutions over 10 ml (as in the xPrint), OpenLH limited volume makes it harder to support printing of large volumes, but allows for multi material and high accuracy in small scales.

## ACKNOWLEDGMENTS

We would like to thank Mercury Ltd. for supporting this project with equipment, reagents and consumables; the Sheila and Denis Cohen Charitable Trust for their contribution towards our work; BioHubIL for their equipment donation and inspiration for creative experimentation with biology; and LifeGene for providing us with pipettes and tips. We would also wish to thank Dr. Edwin Wintermute for supplying us with color expressing bacteria, and Sebastian S. Cocioba for providing "jet black" agar protocol. We deeply thank our lab members Yuval Fein, Yuval Maayan, and Hadas Erel for their valuable insights and support throughout the process.

## REFERENCES

[1] andrewalliance. 2018 (accessed April 3, 2018). *Andrew Pipette robot.* `https://www.andrewalliance.com/`

[2] ASLS. 2018 (accessed April 3, 2018). *biobot.* `https://lifesciences.solutions/biobotbasic/`

[3] E Batista, L Pinto, E Filipe, and AMH Van der Veen. 2007. Calibration of micropipettes: Test methods and uncertainty analysis. *Measurement* 40, 3 (2007), 338–342.

[4] Bento. 2018 (accessed April 3, 2018). `http://www.Bento.bio/`

[5] M Saad Bhamla, Brandon Benson, Chew Chai, Georgios Katsikis, Aanchal Johri, and Manu Prakash. 2017. Hand-powered ultralow-cost paper centrifuge. *Nature Biomedical Engineering* 1, 1 (2017), 0009.

[6] Biotek. 2018 (accessed April 3, 2018). *Biotek liquid handlers.* `https://www.biotek.com/products/liquid-handling/`

[7] Robert Carlson. 2009. The changing economics of DNA synthesis. *Nature biotechnology* 27, 12 (2009), 1091.

[8] Oron Catts and Ionat Zurr. 2002. Growing semi-living sculptures: The tissue culture & art project. *Leonardo* 35, 4 (2002), 365–370.

[9] cellink. 2018 (accessed April 3, 2018). *BIO X BIOPRINTER.* `https://cellink.com/`

[10] Andre Maia Chagas, Lucia L Prieto-Godino, Aristides B Arrenberg, and Tom Baden. 2017. TheâĆň 100 lab: A 3D-printable open-source platform for fluorescence microscopy, optogenetics, and accurate temperature control during behaviour of zebrafish, Drosophila, and Caenorhabditis elegans. *PLoS biology* 15, 7 (2017), e2002702.

[11] James S Cybulski, James Clements, and Manu Prakash. 2014. Foldscope: origami-based paper microscope. *PloS one* 9, 6 (2014), e98781.

[12] Sayamindu Dasgupta and Mitchel Resnick. 2014. Engaging novices in programming, experimenting, and learning with data. *ACM Inroads* 5, 4 (2014), 72–75.

[13] Alessandro Delfanti. 2012. Tweaking genes in your garage: Biohacking between activism and entrepreneurship. *Activist Media and Biopolitics* 163 (2012).

[14] Ori Elisar. 2018 (accessed April 3, 2018). *Living Language Project.* `http://orielisar.com/`

[15] envisiontec. 2018 (accessed April 3, 2018). *3d-bioplotter.* `https://envisiontec.com/3d-printers/3d-bioplotter/`

[16] Piyum Fernando, Matthew Pandelakis, and Stacey Kuznetsov. 2016. Practicing DIYBiology In An HCI Setting. In *Proceedings of the 2016 CHI Conference Extended Abstracts on Human Factors in Computing Systems (CHI EA '16).* ACM, New York, NY, USA, 2064–2071. DOI: `http://dx.doi.org/10.1145/2851581.2892325`

[17] Lukas C Gerber, Agnes Calasanz-Kaiser, Luke Hyman, Kateryna Voitiuk, Uday Patil, and Ingmar H Riedel-Kruse. 2017. Liquid-handling Lego robots and experiments for STEM education and research. *PLoS biology* 15, 3 (2017), e2001413.

[18] Lukas C Gerber, Michael C Doshi, Honesty Kim, and Ingmar H Riedel-Kruse. 2016. BioGraphr: Science Games on a Biotic Computer.. In *DiGRA/FDG*.

[19] Virginia Gewin. 2013. Biotechnology: Independent Streak. *Nature* 499, 7459 (2013), 509–511.

[20] Robert P Hertzberg and Andrew J Pope. 2000. High-throughput screening: new technology for the 21st century. *Current opinion in chemical biology* 4, 4 (2000), 445–451.

[21] Zahid Hossain, Engin W Bumbacher, Alice M Chung, Honesty Kim, Casey Litton, Ashley D Walter, Sachin N Pradhan, Kemi Jona, Paulo Blikstein, and Ingmar H Riedel-Kruse. 2016. Interactive and scalable biology cloud experimentation for scientific inquiry and education. *Nature biotechnology* 34, 12 (2016), 1293.

[22] imagemagickr. 2018 (accessed April 3, 2018). *imagemagick Script*. https://www.imagemagick.org/script/index.php

[23] Instructables 2018. OpenLH: Open Liquid Handling System for Creative Experimentation With Biology. (2018). Retrieved 2018 (accessed November 19, 2018) from https://www.instructables.com/id/OpenLH/

[24] Yasmin Kafai, Orkan Telhan, Karen Hogan, Debora Lui, Emma Anderson, Justice T Walker, and Sheri Hanna. 2017. Growing designs with biomakerlab in high school classrooms. In *Proceedings of the 2017 Conference on Interaction Design and Children*. ACM, 503–508.

[25] Honesty Kim, Lukas Cyrill Gerber, Daniel Chiu, Seung Ah Lee, Nate J Cira, Sherwin Yuyang Xia, and Ingmar H Riedel-Kruse. 2016. LudusScope: accessible interactive smartphone microscopy for life-science education. *PLoS One* 11, 10 (2016), e0162602.

[26] David B Kolesky, Ryan L Truby, A Sydney Gladman, Travis A Busbee, Kimberly A Homan, and Jennifer A Lewis. 2014. 3D bioprinting of vascularized, heterogeneous cell-laden tissue constructs. *Advanced materials* 26, 19 (2014), 3124–3130.

[27] Fanwei Kong, Liang Yuan, Yuan F Zheng, and Weidong Chen. 2012. Automatic liquid handling for life science: a critical review of the current state of the art. *Journal of laboratory automation* 17, 3 (2012), 169–185.

[28] Stacey Kuznetsov, Cassandra Barrett, Piyum Fernando, and Kat Fowler. 2018. Antibiotic-Responsive Bioart: Exploring DIYbio as a Design Studio Practice. In *Proceedings of the 2018 CHI Conference on Human Factors in Computing Systems*. ACM, 463.

[29] Stacey Kuznetsov and Eric Paulos. 2010. Rise of the expert amateur: DIY projects, communities, and cultures. In *Proceedings of the 6th Nordic Conference on Human-Computer Interaction: Extending Boundaries*. ACM, 295–304.

[30] Stacey Kuznetsov, Alex S. Taylor, Tim Regan, Nicolas Villar, and Eric Paulos. 2012. At the Seams: DIYbio and Opportunities for HCI. In *Proceedings of the Designing Interactive Systems Conference (DIS '12)*. ACM, New York, NY, USA, 258–267. DOI: http://dx.doi.org/10.1145/2317956.2317997

[31] Amino Labs. 2018 (accessed April 3, 2018)a. *Amino Labs*. http://www.amino.bio/

[32] Gaudi Labs. 2018 (accessed April 3, 2018)b. *Gaudi Labs*. http://www.gaudi.ch/

[33] Thomas Landrain, Morgan Meyer, Ariel Martin Perez, and Remi Sussan. 2013. Do-it-yourself biology: challenges and promises for an open science and technology movement. *Systems and synthetic biology* 7, 3 (2013), 115–126.

[34] Heidi Ledford. 2010. Garage biotech: Life hackers. *Nature News* 467, 7316 (2010), 650–652.

[35] Seung Ah Lee, Engin Bumbacher, Alice M Chung, Nate Cira, Byron Walker, Ji Young Park, Barry Starr, Paulo Blikstein, and Ingmar H Riedel-Kruse. 2015a. Trap it!: a playful human-biology interaction for a museum installation. In *Proceedings of the 33rd Annual ACM Conference on Human Factors in Computing Systems*. ACM, 2593–2602.

[36] Seung Ah Lee, Alice M Chung, Nate Cira, and Ingmar H Riedel-Kruse. 2015b. Tangible interactive microbiology for informal science education. In *Proceedings of the Ninth International Conference on Tangible, Embedded, and Embodied Interaction*. ACM, 273–280.

[37] Stefanie Michael, Heiko Sorg, Claas-Tido Peck, Lothar Koch, Andrea Deiwick, Boris Chichkov, Peter M Vogt, and Kerstin Reimers. 2013. Tissue engineered skin substitutes created by laser-assisted bioprinting form skin-like structures in the dorsal skin fold chamber in mice. *PloS one* 8, 3 (2013), e57741.

[38] Catarina Mota. 2011. The rise of personal fabrication. In *Proceedings of the 8th ACM conference on Creativity and cognition*. ACM, 279–288.

[39] Sean V Murphy and Anthony Atala. 2014. 3D bioprinting of tissues and organs. *Nature biotechnology* 32, 8 (2014), 773.

[40] Openbuilds. 2018 (accessed April 3, 2018). *linear Actuator*. http://openbuildspartstore.com/c-beam-linear-actuator-bundle/

[41] OpenPCR. (accessed April 3, 2018). http://openpcr.org

[42] organovo. 2018 (accessed April 3, 2018). *novogen*. https://www.aniwaa.com/product/3d-printers/organovo-novogen-mmx-bioprinter/

[43] Meredith Patterson. 2010. A biopunk manifesto. In *intervento al simposio" Outlaw Biology*.

[44] Andrew Rosenblum. 2017 (accessed april 3, 2018). *A Biohackers Plan to Upgrade Dalmatians Ends Up in the Doghouse*. goo.gl/DFZbni

[45] Günter Seyfried, Lei Pei, and Markus Schmidt. 2014. European do-it-yourself (DIY) biology: Beyond the hope, hype and horror. *Bioessays* 36, 6 (2014), 548–551.

[46] Jay Shendure, Shankar Balasubramanian, George M Church, Walter Gilbert, Jane Rogers, Jeffery A Schloss, and Robert H Waterston. 2017. DNA sequencing at 40: past, present and future. *Nature* 550, 7676 (2017), 345.

[47] Joshua G Tanenbaum, Amanda M Williams, Audrey Desjardins, and Karen Tanenbaum. 2013. Democratizing technology: pleasure, utility and expressiveness in DIY and maker practice. In *Proceedings of the SIGCHI Conference on Human Factors in Computing Systems*. ACM, 2603–2612.

[48] Tecan. 2018 (accessed April 3, 2018). *Tecan liquid handlers*. https://lifesciences.tecan.com/products/liquid_handling_and_automation

[49] uArm Developer. 2018 (accessed April 3, 2018). *Python Libraries*. https://github.com/uArm-Developer/pyuarm

[50] uFactory. 2018 (accessed April 3, 2018). *uArm Swift Pro Specs*. http://statics3.seeedstudio.com/assets/file/bazaar/product/uArm_Swift_Specifications.pdf

[51] Guanyun Wang, Lining Yao, Wen Wang, Jifei Ou, Chin-Yi Cheng, and Hiroshi Ishii. 2016. xPrint: A Modularized Liquid Printer for Smart Materials Deposition. In *Proceedings of the 2016 CHI Conference on Human Factors in Computing Systems*. ACM, 5743–5752.

[52] Wen Wang, Lining Yao, Chin-Yi Cheng, Teng Zhang, Hiroshi Atsumi, Luda Wang, Guanyun Wang, Oksana Anilionyte, Helene Steiner, Jifei Ou, and others. 2017. Harnessing the hygroscopic and biofluorescent behaviors of genetically tractable microbial cells to design biohybrid wearables. *Science advances* 3, 5 (2017), e1601984.

[53] Peter Washington, Karina Samuel-Gama, Shirish Goyal, and Ingmar H Riedel-Kruse. 2017. Bioty: A cloud-based development toolkit for programming experiments and interactive applications with living cells. *bioRxiv* (2017), 236919.

[54] Lining Yao, Jifei Ou, Chin-Yi Cheng, Helene Steiner, Wen Wang, Guanyun Wang, and Hiroshi Ishii. 2015. BioLogic: natto cells as nanoactuators for shape changing interfaces. In *Proceedings of the 33rd Annual ACM Conference on Human Factors in Computing Systems*. ACM, 1–10.

# Shiva's Rangoli: Tangible Storytelling through Diegetic Interfaces in Ambient Environments

**Saumya Gupta**
University of California, Irvine
Irvine CA, USA
saumya@uci.edu

**Joshua G. Tanenbaum**
University of California, Irvine
Irvine CA, USA
joshua.tanenbaum@uci.edu

**Karen Tanenbaum**
University of California, Irvine
Irvine CA, USA
karen.tanenbaum@uci.edu

## ABSTRACT

This paper describes the underlying motivation, creation process, and evaluation outcomes of *Shiva's Rangoli,* a tangible storytelling installation that allows readers to impact the emotional tone of a narrative by sculpting the ambience of their space. Readers interact with a tangible interface that acts as a boundary object between the reader and the fictional world. We discuss how these kinds of interfaces can engage readers to feel like they are a part of the story, endow them with responsibility, and blur the line between real and fictional worlds.

### Author Keywords

Tangible interaction; storytelling; interactive narrative; interactive ambience; diegetic interface; cultural interface.

### ACM Classification Keywords

• Human-centered computing~Human Computer Interaction

## INTRODUCTION

*"The 11-year-old was thrilled to take the wand from the shopkeeper as she felt the magic radiating through her veins. She was now equipped to enter the enchanted world of magic, leaving the muggle one behind. As she stepped outside the shop, the 30-year-old snapped back into reality, feeling grateful for the few moments that transformed her world into one she had only read about." – story told to the authors by a "Potterhead" (fan of J.K. Rowling's Harry Potter universe) at Universal Studios, Hollywood*

Experiences like the one described above illustrate the power of tangible and interactive storytelling to bridge the gap between the reader's reality and the world of fiction. Interrogating these transformational moments gives rise to a series of research questions, including: what kind of interactions best facilitate these transformational experiences? How should a designer balance the delivery of a touching and coherent narrative against the freedom of a reader's interactions to impact the experience? How can experiences support readers to feel as if they are a part of the story world? In our quest to answer these questions, we have created and evaluated a tangible and interactive storytelling installation called *Shiva's Rangoli.*

As commonly understood, interactive narratives are stories that progress based on the reader's interactions, giving readers a stake in how the story unfolds. Research into interactive narrative and story-based games has long been interested in providing readers/interactors with control over the story progression at the level of the formal plot structure [13,38,39,41,44]. From this perspective, readers exercise a form of "agency" [18] that allows them to choose between different outcomes or "branches". These plot-centric approaches facilitate the pleasure that comes from participating in an authoring process, however they often fail to account for all of the diverse pleasures of narrative beyond the simple ordering of events, as variously articulated in game studies, narratology, literary theory, and film studies [9,11,12,14,16,18,22,23,24,28,35,36,37,46]. With *Shiva's Rangoli* we explore some of these comparatively overlooked elements of story by shifting the loci of interaction away from plot events and towards the aesthetic and stylistic elements of the experience by coupling interaction with environmental ambience.

*Shiva's Rangoli* is an interactive and tangible storytelling installation that enables readers to compose the emotional context of the stories by shaping the ambient settings (light, sound, music, and video) of their environment through a diegetic tangible user interface (TUI) [8,11]. Readers of *Shiva's Rangoli* are invited to assume the role of the protagonist (Shiva) while interacting with a diegetic interface that connects them with Shiva's world and endows them with the emotional state of the characters. This work also brings Indian traditions and myths into a technological, tangible, and narrative space.

Interactive narratives can use diegetic TUIs to bridge the gap between the reader's reality and the world of fiction [3,5]. 'Diegetic' in narratology refers to something that is inside the world of the story, such as music playing on the radio, as opposed to outside the story, such as a film's soundtrack or score [11]. Diegetic objects act as boundary objects [45] that exist in the reader's world as well as in the story world. With *Shiva's Rangoli*, we investigate how diegetic interfaces can make readers feel as if they are a


*TEI '19*, March 17–20, 2019, Tempe, AZ, USA

ACM ISBN 978-1-4503-6196-5/19/03$15.00
DOI: https://doi.org/10.1145/3294109.3295635

part of the story world, have a stake in how the narrative unfolds without impacting the story's plot, and blur the boundary between the reader and the fictional world. We also investigate how the ambient setting and physical space of the reader becomes part of the diegesis of the experience.

This paper focuses on the design and findings of *Shiva's Rangoli* with respect to the role of diegetic and ambient interactions. The contributions of the work include:

1) Describing the design of a tangible interactive narrative that gives readers control over the mood and aesthetics of the story through a diegetic interface and a diegetic physical space.
2) Identifying design recommendations for diegetic interfaces, specifically how they can position readers to feel like they are a part of the story and able to impact and personalize the narrative without changing the plot
3) Identifying recommendations for how ambient environments can be designed for interactive storytelling

This work does not focus on the cultural aspect of the system as it will be addressed in future work.

## BACKGROUND

Harley et al.'s framework for tangible narratives has guided our design for *Shiva's Rangoli* [10]. The authors analyzed 21 systems and identified common themes and gaps in existing literature. While they identify multiple interesting themes, the one that we focus on in this work is narrative position. This is divided into two dichotomies, which describe the position of the reader relative to the story:

- *Internal vs. External:* Internal readers see themselves as situated within the world of the story while external readers are outside of it.
- *Exploratory vs. Ontological:* Exploratory readers observe and might reorder events of the story, but make no changes, while ontological readers may impact outcomes within the story world.

Harley et al. call for more interactive, tangible narratives that place the reader in an internal-ontological position, which they argue can help readers connect to the characters and give them a sense of responsibility. *Shiva's Rangoli* was designed to put readers in an internal-ontological position, as they can adopt the role of Shiva if they choose to do so, placing themselves inside the narrative. Readers can also influence the state of the story by changing the mood of the characters and the tone of the narrative, without changing the story's plot.

*Shiva's Rangoli* connects readers to the story through diegetic interfaces. Bordwell and Thompson define the term 'diegetic' as "things that exist within the world of the film's narrative." [11]. Harley et al. contend that "diegetic tangibles present a compelling alternative to tangibles as metaphorical objects or as input devices" [10], citing *The Reading Glove* [27,33], a non-linear narrative experience where readers interact with different diegetic objects to unravel a detective investigation, as an exemplar of this kind of design. They point out the importance of tangible narratives that use diegetic objects and the fact that there are few examples of this kind of system. This is further supported by the work of Ana Paiva, who argues that tangibles and diegetic objects can help in building a gateway between the real world and the story [5]. Similarly, the *genieBottles* interactive installation is a tangible narrative where readers open different flasks and hear genies come out of these bottles to tell their story [4]. The bottles exist in the reader's physical world while also existing in the fictional world as homes to the genies, making the interface diegetic. *Shiva's Rangoli* adds to these ideas as the TUI and the configurable ambient environment, both have diegetic characteristics.

Previous work in interactive narrative acknowledges the need to find a balance between the reader's interactions and the author's story content [3,5,32]. Giving readers freedom or choice over the story's plot can undermine the author's intended narrative; it is still an open question in the field how designers can encourage readers to act meaningfully within a story [21,29,32] without changing the plot. In many ways, *Shiva's Rangoli* is inspired by the early storytelling system *Scarlet Skellern* [26]. This digital storybook built a rudimentary model of the affective preferences of the reader which then controlled the story's mood by changing the instrumentation of the score, the ambient soundscape, and the color palette of the story. *Scarlet Skellern* was an early attempt to decouple the interactions of the reader from the events of the narrative, while still providing a channel for meaningful engagement with the story. *Shiva's Rangoli* takes these ideas further by enabling readers to interact with the emotional context of the story by shaping the ambience of their space.

There are a few tangible and embodied systems using interactive environments which have formed a starting point for thinking about *Shiva's Rangoli*. Ishii and Ullmer's work on the *AmbientRoom* discusses how data can be represented in the periphery of one's vision through subtle changes in lights, wall displays, and patterns [8]. They elaborate on how this data does not need to be the focus point for the user, rather it can stay in the background and be referred to when needed. This served as a design principle for how the ambience in *Shiva's Rangoli* could be used to set an emotional context. Bobick et al's *Kid's Room* is an interactive physical storytelling space which transforms a child's bedroom into a fantasy story world using visuals and sound [2]. Ross and Keyson designed a tangible expressive interface that enables people to sculpt the ambiences in their living room by controlling lighting, audio, and video art [43]. This work inspired us to use ambient settings as an interactive medium. *Shiva's Rangoli* gives readers control over the ambient setting of their space to interact with the narrative, a concept that has not been explored in the works above.

**Figure 1: a) The installation space b) inside the tent c) the interface**

Li and Jianting propose an intelligent space where the environment communicates a person's emotions based on movement, using ambient and audio visuals [40]. Wassermann et al. [31] have used different ambient presentational styles to express emotions. Their findings show that participants were able to associate emotions to ambient settings, which inspired us to use interactive ambient environments for setting an emotional context.

Within the area of tangible storytelling, only a few systems have been dedicated to exploring tangible storytelling installations in a non-western cultural context [7,15,20,34]. For example, *Renati* represents oral and digital narratives of viewpoints from South Africa in the form of installation art [7]. *StoryBeads* uses tangible objects for recording and replaying stories inspired by the handcrafted beadwork practice of BaNtwane people [34]. These systems are the exception to the norm within tangible storytelling research and have inspired the culturally specific interface of our work. The interface of *Shiva's Rangoli* represents a traditional Indian artform called Rangoli making and the narratives have been inspired by Indian Mythology. Finding Interactions within this cultural context is outside the scope of this study and will be covered in future work.

## DESIGN

The design of *Shiva's Rangoli* was an iterative process. We collaboratively worked on our initial interaction designs and built non-functioning paper prototypes to conduct "Wizard-of-Oz" testing among our colleagues and friends to rapidly test and refine the logics of the system's interactions. *Shiva's Rangoli* enables readers to shape the ambience of their environment through a culturally inspired narrativized [23] tangible interface, subsequently setting an emotional context for the stories. The readers hear two interleaved stories within this configurable context.

### The Interface

Inspired by other work on cultural interfaces [1], we designed the TUI to remediate the Indian art form of Rangoli making. Rangolis are elaborate colorful patterns made on the floor during festivals with many materials such as colored sand, flowers, and powdered rice to name a few. We designed an interactive space where a reader assembles the Rangoli interface. The installation space is enclosed by a pavilion and inside the tent lies a table, twelve artistically patterned rings and two center pieces, as shown in Figure 1a and 1b. Three rings of the twelve can be placed on the table top in a concentric manner to create a Rangoli, shown in figure 1c. The outermost ring controls the lighting effects of the space, the middle ring controls sound effects and the innermost ring controls the music. The two center pieces determine which of the two interleaved narratives plays back. Figure 1b also shows the four sets of three rings each, where each set represents a particular mood. The yellow ring represents happy, green is calm, blue represents sad, and red is angry. This design choice was informed by the color to emotion mapping used in the eMoto project [6,42] and grounded in Russell's circumplex model of affect [17]. The tabletop is a foot tall as readers are expected to sit down on the floor to assemble the Rangolis, mimicking the traditional Indian style of creating Rangolis on the floor.

### Ambient Effects

The rings are placed on the table to set the pavilion's ambience according to the associated moods. The yellow-happy rings create a warm, upbeat, and chirpy ambience. The green-calm rings create a soothing and soft atmosphere. The blue-sad rings create a low and dull environment. The red-angry rings create a stormy, thundering ambience. Once the reader assembles a Rangoli, an ambient video is displayed, amplifying the mood created by the reader. These ambient effects were decided on through a series of iterative user tests. We do not make any claims on the universality of these mappings with moods.

**Figure 2: Ambient Effects**

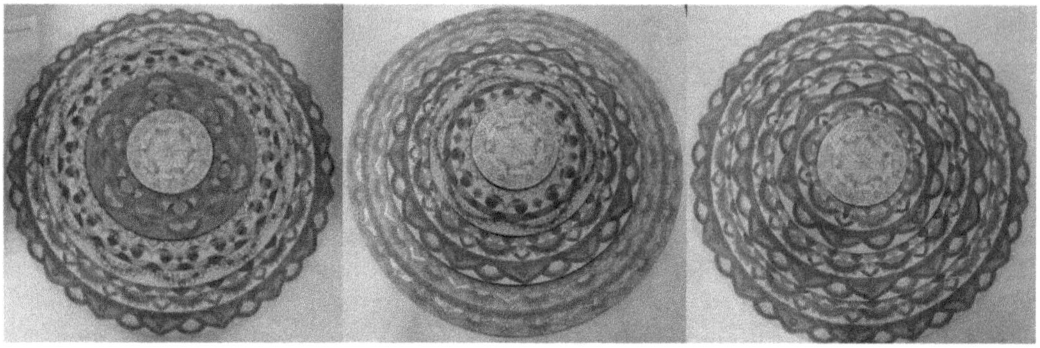

**Figure 3: Assembled Rangoli pieces**

Figure 2 shows the ambient spaces created when all rings of the same color are placed. Readers can place any combination of the rings available , setting ambient effects belonging to different mood settings. For example, a reader can set happy bright sunny lights (yellow), alongside a calm river flowing sound (green), with a sad musical note (blue). After the reader assembles the entire Rangoli, a chapter from the story represented by the center piece is narrated through audio. The chapter adapts to the emotional tone set by the reader as mood based textual elements in the narrative change accordingly (see next section for more details). Once the chapter ends, readers can reassemble or change parts of the Rangoli to start the next chapter. Each story consists of 10 chapters.

### Narratives

The two stories, called 'the river' and 'the medicine', are new original works of fiction inspired by Indian mythology. In writing them, the first author drew upon her upbringing in India to tell new stories grounded in her own culture and background. In the stories, Shiva is a powerful God who makes Rangolis to express his emotions and decisions. These emotions trickle down and impact the human world as well. For example, when Shiva is angry, the world's skies become bloody and dark with heavy rains and raging thunderstorms. Readers are invited to assume the role of Shiva and create these Rangolis as a reflection of Shiva's mood, shaping the ambience of the fictional world as well as the space in the tent. Both the Rangoli and the dynamic ambiences are designed to serve as diegetic bridges, connecting the readers to Shiva's world. Aside from Shiva, the magical river Jhanvi is a common theme that flows across both stories. The ambient effects (sound and visuals) are inspired by water, to give readers a sense of being near the river. Each chapter has two versions: an emotionally positive version and an emotionally negative version. For simplicity, we take only the valence of the mood into consideration, grouping happy and calm as positive emotions, and sad and angry as negative ones. The system reads the overall mood / valence value of the Rangoli assembled by the reader and triggers one of the two versions. In both versions, the story plot remains the same, but the tone of the story changes. In addition to the textual changes, the narrator's tone and volume are different between both versions. Here is an example of positive and negative versions of an excerpt from one of the chapters:

***Positive version:*** *"Brahma and Vishnu approached Shiva and as they looked upon the vibrant Rangoli filled with shades of yellow and green, they were delighted to see that Shiva was in one of his good moods. The skies were light, harmonious and chirpy reflecting Shiva's pleasure. Brahma and Vishnu never thought twice before approaching him on such days, and so they decided that it was the perfect time to confront him on one of their never-ending arguments, Shiva's destruction".*

***Negative version**: "Brahma and Vishnu approached Shiva, and as they looked upon the bold Rangoli filled with shades of blue and red, they understood that Shiva was not in the best of his moods. The skies were dark, gloomy, and enraged, reflecting Shiva's displeasure. Brahma and Vishnu always thought twice before approaching him on such days, yet today they mustered the courage to confront him on one of their never-ending arguments, Shiva's destruction."*

In both stories, Shiva's Rangolis are acknowledged frequently to help readers confirm their understanding of how the colors map to the moods and how the interface connects with the story.

### Implementation

After iterating through a variety of designs, we settled on a simple analog solution for detecting which rings were placed on our tabletop. The table top has different shaped sockets with snap switches fit inside them. A snap switch closes as soon as a 'keyed tab' fits into the socket, completing a circuit connected to the *Makey Makey* [19]. The back of each ring has a shape attached to it which acts like a key and fits into a particular socket on the table. Magnets below the table and the rings help the reader snap and lock the ring into the correct position, producing a satisfying tactile experience when placing the rings. Figure 4 shows the rings, table top, and details of the switch assembly. The *Makey Makey* emulates a key press on a connected laptop as soon as a circuit is completed (i.e. the snap switch is closed). Different sound, music, and video tracks are played by a program on the laptop based on the pressed switch. This program also controls patterns on a long strip of individually addressable RGB LEDs by HKBAYI, via an Arduino Uno, producing dynamic lighting ambiences within our installation. We use an RFID reader at the center of the Rangoli tabletop to detect which RFID tagged center piece has been placed on it.

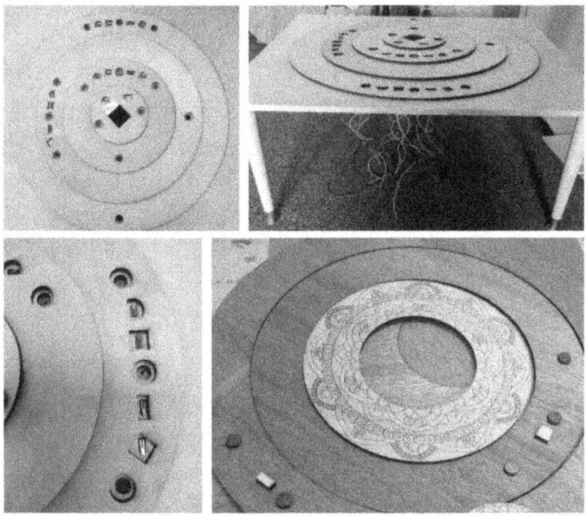

**Figure 4. The table top, switch assembly, and back of a ring**

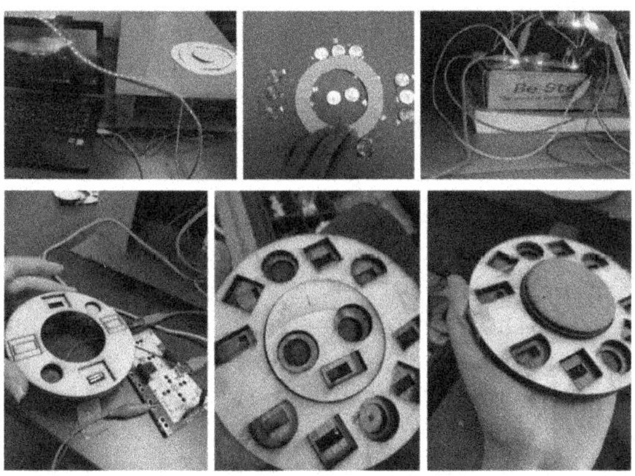

**Figure 5. Early hardware prototypes**

We tested this entire design using cardboard first, and then smaller wooden prototypes, before laser cutting the final pieces. Figure 5 shows the early prototype iterations. To construct our installation, we laser cut the wooden table top, the wooden rings and the Rangoli patterns. The art on the rings has been inspired by repetitive patterns used in traditional Rangolis. We painted the rings by hand in the four color schemes shown in Figure 2. Figure 3 shows a few assembled Rangoli pieces. The table top and rings are placed inside an enclosed "pavilion" created by suspending a metal frame from the ceiling of our lab and draping it with fabric to produce a tent-like structure. The interior is lit using the aforementioned addressable RGB LED light strip, which is mounted along the border of the tent frame above the reader. Figure 1 shows the installation built in our lab.

## STUDY

The goal of this study was to investigate how people interacted with a storytelling system at the level of its emotional and aesthetic context, using diegetic interfaces and ambient settings. We also aimed to study how diegetic interfaces can be designed to support the reader's connection with the story world. We conducted a study with 23 participants who were recruited through postings on Facebook, flyers on University of California Irvine (UCI) campus, and through word of mouth from the faculty, alumni, and student population at UCI. Ages of participants ranged from 18 to 54 with the majority being below 34. 9 participants identified as females and 14 as males. They belonged to different nationalities and identified as Asians, Indians, and Americans, with Americans being in majority. Most participants came from information and computer science disciplines and a few belonged to social sciences. Sessions were conducted in the lab and lasted for a duration of two hours each. Participants were first introduced to the concept of Rangolis and were told that the Rangoli they created would be created by the protagonist of the stories as well. After an overview of the basic interactions, participants interacted with the demo version of the system, which allowed them to explore all the ambient effects without hearing the narratives. The narratives began to play once the participants were satisfied with the demo. This experience lasted for 30-45 minutes and participants were asked to think aloud while interacting with the system. The interaction was followed by a semi-structured interview. The interview questions asked about their understanding of the story, their mental model of the system, thoughts on the ambience and moods, their decision-making process, their perceived role in the experience, and their thoughts on the cultural interface. We conducted an open qualitative analysis of the interview transcripts and the think aloud notes taken during the session, starting with open coding and then moving into axial coding to analyze the data [25,30]. We first identified and categorized patterns in our interviews and deduced broad themes. We then visualized the data on a whiteboard to make connections between the various codes and themes.

## FINDINGS

This section elaborates on a few main themes from our analysis. We discuss the impact and perception of the diegetic interfaces, roles people played in the experience, styles of interaction observed, and how people moved from exploratory interactions to more meaningful ones. In this paper we briefly introduce three themes which will be explored in future work, before elaborating more upon the central theme of this paper: Diegetic Interfaces.

### From Exploration to Informed Decision Making

As with any novel interactive experience, participants moved from exploratory engagement at the beginning to more intentional meaning making by the end. Over the course of the interaction, readers came to understand how the interface worked and was mapped to different emotions, how the Rangoli connected with Shiva, and how their choices impacted the stories. In the second half of the experience (generally marked by having heard one story out of the two), their decisions were based on informed decisions on how they wanted to impact the mood and tone of the narrative. We highlight this process of building literacy because it is often difficult to sort out the aesthetic and emotional implications of a new work from the initial pleasures of using a novel interface. Observing participants develop and apply new interactional literacies gives us confidence that the behaviors we observed can be mapped to the designed experience independent of the initially observed "novelty effect". There is evidence that our design supported this process of learning through use. The contrast in the ambiences, especially the red (angry) and green (calm) ones, helped people map ambient effects to certain emotional settings. People who explored the demo version of the interaction longer acknowledged that it helped them relate the colors and ambiences to the emotional settings. When the stories acknowledged the colors of the reader's Rangoli and specified the consequence of those color on the narrative, readers would understand how the colors mapped to different moods, and how their choices impacted Shiva.

Although the ambience set the planned mood and tone for most people, sometimes the desired emotional effect was not created. For example, a few people would find icy images (linked to sad) calming, while others found it isolating and sad. These mismatches were mitigated when the narrative called out the colors of the reader's Rangoli and specified its impacts. This two-way confirmation through the ambience and the narrative helped people understand the mapping between the interface and the emotional tone. Another possibility that may have resolved this problem could be to personalize the mapping for everyone. In the tutorial, readers could begin by constructing a Rangoli, and being asked by the system to choose and place a "sad" ring. The system could then map their choice of color to that emotion, personalizing the color-coding.

### Different Readers, Different Interaction Styles

In our analysis of the data, we identified three interaction styles that participants adopted, which were linked to their perception of the agency they had over the story: Story Supporters, Story Controllers, and Meaning Makers. These styles were not mutually exclusive as people often took on different interaction styles as the experience progressed. Story Supporters felt they had no agency over the story and created ambiences to support the story's perceivably pre-written plot. Story Controllers felt that they asserted some amount of control over the plot of the story when the diegetic interface was acknowledged in the narrative. Meaning Makers felt they had agency over the mood and tone of the story but not the plot. These styles were inductively identified by the authors after data analysis. These findings will be elaborated on in future studies.

### Internal and External Reader Roles

Readers saw themselves take both internal and external roles in the experience [10]. Five readers claimed they transformed into Shiva at various points of the interaction as they talked and acted like him, while five others felt as if they were a part of Shiva, like a person sitting in his mind. Some positioned themselves inside the story world as observers and did not relate to any of the characters. These participants took more internal roles. Some people did not feel as if they were a part of the story, yet they were active engagers as they decided the fate of the characters in the story. A few readers did not connect to Shiva particularly, yet they felt like a powerful God who could control Shiva's emotions and actions. Three readers took on a more passive role as they felt like listeners in this experience. We term these as external roles. The roles that participants took were not mutually exclusive as people took on different roles during the interaction as they developed a literacy for the system. These roles were inductively identified by the authors after data analysis.

### Diegetic Interfaces Bridge Reality and Fiction

We observed that the Rangoli and the physical ambient space both acted as diegetic bridges between the reader's world and the story world. Readers were able to take certain actions in the story through the TUI. The ambience helped readers connect emotionally with the story and placed them in an environment that reflected the story world.

*P01, female: "The climax of Jhanvi rising (apocalyptic storm) and the red lights and thunder, it felt real. I had goosebumps at times. I could actually feel it."*

#### *Choices and Impacts*

17 Readers felt they could impact the story world in certain ways through the diegetic Rangoli interface. This made them feel a sense of responsibility towards the story and the characters. They made Rangolis to support Shiva by choosing the colors that would best reflect his emotions in a situation. Ten readers felt in control of the character's fate, actions, and at times the story plot itself, specifically when the reader's Rangoli was acknowledged in the narrative. This acknowledgement led to reflection, focus, and learning. Half of the participants felt more immersed when their choices had a noticeable impact on the stories.

*P21, male: "I felt like the reference to the Rangoli in the story prompted me to think more about my choices, and the story went in the direction I had created with the Rangoli."*

#### *Connecting with the Story*

Five readers said they felt transformed into Shiva or more connected with Shiva and the narrative when their Rangolis were specifically called out as Shiva's Rangolis in the stories. One reader interacted with both the stories twice and talked and acted like Shiva throughout the experience. He acknowledged how this experience helped him become more responsible and aware of his own emotions.

*P05, male: "The whole ambience, setting, immersion, gave me like (I was taking Shiva's role), even now I have this responsibility that I am taking to act according to what is good and righteous instead of my own greed."*

*P02, female: "At one point I felt like I am Shiva. He makes Rangolis and I am sitting here making Rangolis. I thought can he make an all yellow one, so I did it, and he did it and said it was beautiful. In that moment I felt embodied."*

14 readers felt like they were positioned inside the story world because of the ambience they created inside the tent. They claimed they were more engrossed in the experience when the plot of the story and the mood they had created were in sync, as it helped them experience the story world.

*P19, male: "The accompanying visuals and the sound of the river gave me the feeling that I was part of the story and was right next to the river. The thunder and sounds with the visual of the waves helped me connect to the situation."*

### Emotional Setting through Ambiences

Three readers said they empathized with and transformed into Shiva because of the emotional context that the ambience set. The environment set different moods and highlighted certain emotions in the narratives, enabling readers to make multiple interpretations of the story and the characters. Six readers felt that they could enhance or diminish a certain feeling associated with the events of the stories through the ambient control.

*P17, male: "But if you feared the way things were going, you could offset some of that by making things a little more pleasant. Regardless of what was going on, if the person wanted to calm the story down or if they wanted it to be forceful, aggressive, they could use the Rangoli for that."*

Nine readers perceived the ambience as causing incremental and gradual changes in the mood and tone setting. For example, they believed that the effect of three red (angry) Rangoli rings on the ambience and the story would be worse than the effect of two red (angry rings) alongside one yellow (happy) or green (calm) ring. They created ambiences to represent a mix of or varying intensities of different emotions rather than using them for dominantly setting one mood.

*P02, female: "I could influence how angry someone was, I didn't want to put all red up there, I didn't want to see what would happen. I thought the system might show me if I did"*

### Focus

Readers felt that ambiences helped them focus more on the story since the environment acted as an aid to the auditory narrative and improved story coherence. The ambience and the tent helped readers block out the world outside, creating a solitary and focused space. This finding is helpful as many interactive auditory narratives are challenged with keeping the reader's attention for narrative coherence.

*P06, female: "If I closed my eyes, that's what I saw and heard in the background. It helped me understand the stories a lot more than if I were just listening to it."*

## DESIGN RECOMMENDATIONS

### Characteristics of Diegetic Interfaces and Environments

The Rangoli interface gave readers a sense of responsibility as it enabled them to impact the characters' emotions and the tone of the story. Furthermore, it was a shared object between the readers and Shiva. Most readers were committed to making ambiences that fit well with the needs of the characters, rather than creating Rangolis based on their favorite colors or other personal preferences. They were further motivated to change the ambient effects after every chapter, to support the next segment of the narrative and create an immersive and meaningful experience. Therefore, we believe connecting the diegetic interface to a story element that can give the reader a stake or responsibility in the narrative can encourage interactors to act in ways that contribute to the narrative experience. Giving readers the choice to craft their own different Rangolis proved to be a successful design element. Based on our findings, we suggest that readers should be able to manipulate the diegetic interfaces in different ways as these interactions can then impact the narrative in various forms, providing readers some form of agency over the story, allowing them to take more ontological roles, without having control over the story's plot.

Acknowledging the Rangolis in the stories helped readers understand the diegetic nature of the interface and their role in the narrative. We recommend that it is important to call out the reader's interactions with the diegetic interface multiple times in the story to help them understand how the system works and internalize the concept. Allowing readers to mimic the character's actions through the diegetic interface (creating the Rangoli) and calling out these actions in the narrative can also help readers position themselves as the character, taking an internal role. Connecting these actions or choices with impactful consequences can gain further attention. These consequences may not lead to branching narratives, if the author does not wish to give control over the plot.

The ambient settings also acted as a diegetic bridge to help position the readers in the story world and aid them in empathizing with the characters. We have shown that even elements such as ambiences that are in the background [8] of the interaction can be diegetic, by connecting meaningfully with the narrative. In *Shiva's Rangoli*, we had many diegetic elements, the Rangoli interface in the foreground, the act of making a Rangoli, and the ambience in the background. By layering these different diegetic aspects of the experience, we reinforced the connection between the readers and the story world through their actions (Rangoli) and the way they felt (ambience). This was further enhanced by making minor changes in the text. For example, when a reader assembles a blue and red Rangoli, the system narrates the following lexia:

*"On such days, the harsh, dark, and stormy lands would fill the sky with a hint of red and blue, as they mimicked Shiva's Rangolis and his unpleasant mood."*

'The harsh, dark, and stormy' lands are mimicking the ambience created by the reader, giving the reader an agency over the environment of the story. Furthermore, it emphasizes Shiva's unpleasant mood, reinforcing the choices (red and blue) set in the foreground (Rangoli) interface. By working in harmony, multiple diegetic elements can deliver an impactful experience.

### Physical Spaces in Interactive Storytelling

Through this study, we identified four design recommendations for using ambient effects in interactive storytelling. ***Transforming the physical space*** of the reader to mimic the story's environment and emotional aesthetics supports readers in feeling as if they are a part of the story world. It is worth considering other ways that physical spaces can act as diegetic bridges. For example, physically anchoring story locations in an interactive space could help readers traverse a non-linear narrative. There are also many other concepts in storytelling that ambient environments could be connected to other than emotions. Mapping ambient effects to different genres or different character perspectives could help readers see the narrative from different viewpoints.

Readers used the ambience to cause ***incremental and gradual changes***, at times representing a complex mix of many emotions. Certain elements of the ambience can support this perception, such as varying the music tempo and volume of a sound track to distinguish between different arousal rates for various emotions. Affordances in the tangible interface such as turning, or sliding can also help denote ambiences as continuous variables, allowing them to represent varying degrees of emotions. Designing systems that allow these different elements of lights, sound, and music to blend together well can help create more cohesive environments. We observed that readers liked ***crafting the ambient space***, and each person found different components (light, sound, music) of the ambience to be impactful in setting an emotional tone. Creating one's own environment by combining different ambient components can be more beneficial and immersive than selecting a pre-crafted environment. Ambient settings can engage different senses and encourage focus, ***aiding in narrative coherence***. It may be beneficial to give readers the option of augmenting certain components (lights, sound, music) to make them stand out more.

### Internal Roles

We observed that readers took on different types of internal roles in the experience. Our data shows that readers do not necessarily have to transform into the protagonist or a character in the story. Designers can create systems that support readers in assuming a variety of internal roles relative to the story. However, if one wishes their readers to transform into a character, then the character's personality must be relatable as readers should be willing to adapt their role. In our stories, Shiva was the God of destruction and had power above all, which may have hindered the development of an empathetic connection between some readers and Shiva.

### Encouraging Meaningful Experiences

It is important to support the readers in understanding how the system works, for them to shift from an exploratory to an ontological role (if intended) and have an enriching experience. Acknowledging the reader's actions, specifying the impacts of their choices in the narratives, and having multiple diegetic elements working in harmony with each other can all help in learning how the diegetic interface works. With these kinds of novel physical interactions, it is also important to provide a useful tutorial space so that readers have an opportunity to explore the system before the experience starts. Readers should be given proper context of any novel concepts in the experience. In *Shiva's Rangoli*, many people did not know what Rangolis were and it was vital to give them this context of Indian culture before they started their interaction. We also observed that a few people were overwhelmed by the misconceptions they had, such as thinking that each Rangoli configuration would branch out the narrative or the story may not unfold linearly. We propose that it is important to mitigate these misapprehensions as early as possible, so that readers can enjoy their experience. Lastly, we suggest extending Harley et al.'s framework to include the aspect of developing literacy as people can change through these positions and roles as they understand how the system works [10].

## CONCLUSION AND FUTURE WORK

The goal of this work was to study how diegetic interfaces and control of the ambient environment impacted the experience of participants in our interactive narrative installation. *Shiva's Rangoli* allowed readers to shape the mood and tone of the narratives through a cultural interface that changed the ambience of their physical space. Our findings suggest that ambient physical spaces can act as effective diegetic bridges to position the readers inside the story world. We conclude that readers can be given internal and ontological positions in an interactive narrative using diegetic interfaces, without giving them control over the story's plot. We provide design recommendations for creating such interfaces and explore how different diegetic elements can work together to bring the reader closer to the fictional world. In future studies we will elaborate our findings on the perceived agency and cultural aspect of the experience. We will also discuss the story authoring platform of the system, where readers created their own story endings, Rangoli art pieces, and ambient settings. Further research in the community can explore how diegetic systems can be designed to accommodate multiple readers and provide more support for the reader to adopt the protagonist's role. This work can be extended be to re-tell cultural histories where the plot cannot change but the way the story is told can change. Further research can explore how ambient environments can be used for augmenting interactive storytelling performative spaces such as theater plays. We hope this study can help designers create interactive narratives that can meaningfully engage readers and bring them closer to the fictional world.

## REFERENCES


[1] 2018. Ranjit Makkuni. *Wikipedia*. Retrieved from https://en.wikipedia.org/w/index.php?title=Ranjit_Makkuni&oldid=823101557

[2] Aaron F. Bobick, Stephen S. Intille, James W. Davis, Freedom Baird, Claudio S. Pinhanez, Lee W. Capmbell, Yuri A. Ivanov, Arjan Schutte, and Andrew Wilson. 1999. The KidsRoom: A Perceptually-Based Interactive and Immersive Story Environment. *Presence* 8, 4: 369–393.

[3] Alexandra Mazalek. 2001. Tangible interfaces for interactive point-of-view narratives. Massachusetts Institute of Technology. Retrieved September 21, 2018 from http://dspace.mit.edu/handle/1721.1/61854

[4] Ali Mazalek, Ali Wood, and Hiroshi Ishii. 2001. genieBottles: An Interactive Narrative in Bottles. In *SIGGRAPH*. Retrieved from http://citeseerx.ist.psu.edu/viewdoc/download?doi=10.1.1.16.3093&rep=rep1&type=pdf

[5] Ana Paiva. 2005. The Role of Tangibles in Interactive Storytelling. In *Virtual Storytelling. Using Virtual Reality Technologies for Storytelling* (Lecture Notes in Computer Science), 225–228. https://doi.org/10.1007/11590361_26

[6] Anna St\a ahl, Petra Sundström, and Kristina Höök. 2005. A Foundation for Emotional Expressivity. In *Proceedings of the 2005 Conference on Designing for User eXperience* (DUX '05). Retrieved September 21, 2018 from http://dl.acm.org/citation.cfm?id=1138235.1138274

[7] Ayoka Chenzira, Yanfeng Chen, and Ali Mazalek. 2008. *RENATI: Recontextualizing Narratives for Tangible Interfaces*. ACM Press. Retrieved from http://dl.acm.org/citation.cfm?id=1347423

[8] Brygg Ullmer and Hiroshi Ishii. 1997. Tangible Bits: Towards Seamless Interfaces between People, Bits, and Atoms. ACM Press.

[9] Celia Pearce. 2004. Towards a Game Theory of Game. In *First Person: New Media as Story, Performance, and Game*, Noah Wardrip-Fruin and Pat Harrigan (eds.). The MIT Press, Cambridge, Massachusetts; London, England, 143–153.

[10] Daniel Harley, Jean Ho Chu, Jamie Kwan, and Ali Mazalek. 2016. Towards a Framework for Tangible Narratives. In *Proceedings of the TEI '16: Tenth International Conference on Tangible, Embedded, and Embodied Interaction* (TEI '16), 62–69. https://doi.org/10.1145/2839462.2839471

[11] David Bordwell and Kristin Thompson. 1997. *Film Art: An Introduction*. The McGraw Hill Companies, Inc., New York.

[12] David Bordwell. 2008. *The Poetics of Cinema*. Routledge, New York, New York.

[13] David Thue, Vadam Bulitko, and Marcia Spetch. 2008. Making Stories Player-Specific: Delayed Authoring in Interactive Storytelling. In *Interactive Storytelling*, Ulrike Spierling and Nicolas Szilas (eds.). Springer Berlin / Heidelberg, Berlin, 230–241.

[14] Edward Branigan. 1992. *Narrative Comprehension and Film*. Routledge, New York, New York.

[15] Fei Lu, Feng Tian, Yingying Jiang, Xiang Cao, Wencan Luo, Guang Li, Xiaolong Zhang, Guozhong Dai, and Hongan Wang. 2011. ShadowStory: Creative and Collaborative Digital Storytelling Inspired by Cultural Heritage. In *Proceedings of the SIGCHI Conference on Human Factors in Computing Systems* (CHI '11), 1919–1928. https://doi.org/10.1145/1978942.1979221

[16] Henry Jenkins. 2004. Game Design as Narrative Architecture. In First Person: New Media As Story, Performance, and Game, Noah Wardrip-Fruin and Pat Harrigan (eds.). MIT Press, Cambridge, Massachusetts; London, England, 118–130.

[17] James A. Russell. 1980. A circumplex model of affect. *Journal of Personality and Social Psychology* 39, 6: 1161–1178. https://doi.org/10.1037/h0077714

[18] Janet Horowitz Murray. 1998. *Hamlet on the Holodeck: The Future of Narrative in Cyberspace*. MIT Press, Cambridge, MA, USA.

[19] Jay Silver and Eric Rosenbaum. 2012. MaKey MaKey. *MaKey MaKey*. Retrieved February 15, 2015 from http://makeymakey.com/

[20] Jean Ho Chu, Paul Clifton, Daniel Harley, Jordanne Pavao, and Ali Mazalek. 2015. Mapping Place: Supporting Cultural Learning Through a Lukasa-inspired Tangible Tabletop Museum Exhibit. In *Proceedings of the Ninth International Conference on Tangible, Embedded, and Embodied Interaction* (TEI '15), 261–268. https://doi.org/10.1145/2677199.2680559

[21] Jeff L. Nay and José P. Zagal. 2017. Meaning Without Consequence: Virtue Ethics and Inconsequential Choices in Games. In *Proceedings of the 12th International Conference on the Foundations of Digital Games* (FDG '17), 14:1–14:8. https://doi.org/10.1145/3102071.3102073

[22] Jim Bizzocchi and Joshua Tanenbaum. 2012. Mass Effect 2: A Case Study in the Design of Game Narrative. *Bulletin of Science Technology Society* 32, 5: 393–404.

[23] Jim Bizzocchi, Ben Lin, and Joshua Tanenbaum. 2011. Games, Narrative, and the Design of Interface. *International Journal of Art and Technology (IJART)* 4, 4: 460–479.

[24] Jim Bizzocchi. 2007. Games and Narrative: An Analytical Framework. *Loading - The Journal of the Canadian Games Studies Association* 1, 1: 5–10.

[25] John W Creswell. 2003. Research Design: Qualitative, Quantitative, and Mixed Methods Approaches. Sage Publications, Thousand Oaks.

[26] Joshua Tanenbaum and Angela Tomizu. 2007. Affective Interaction Design and Narrative Presentation. 150–157. Retrieved from http://www.aaai.org/Papers/Symposia/Fall/2007/FS-07-05/FS07-05-025.pdf

[27] Joshua Tanenbaum, Karen Tanenbaum, and Alissa Antle. 2010. The Reading Glove: Designing Interactions for Object-based Tangible Storytelling. In *Proceedings of the 1st Augmented Human International Conference* (AH '10), 19:1–19:9. https://doi.org/10.1145/1785455.1785474

[28] Joshua Tanenbaum. 2011. Being in the Story: Readerly Pleasure, Acting Theory, and Performing a Role. In *Interactive Storytelling*, Mei Si, David Thue, Elisabeth André, James C. Lester, Joshua Tanenbaum and Veronica Zammitto (eds.). Springer Berlin Heidelberg, 55–66. Retrieved May 22, 2014 from http://link.springer.com.proxy.lib.sfu.ca/chapter/10.1007/978-3-642-25289-1_7

[29] Joshua Tanenbaum. 2015. Identity Transformation and Agency in Digital Narratives and Story Based Games. Simon Fraser University, Surrey, British Columbia, Canada. Retrieved from http://summit.sfu.ca/item/15285

[30] Juliet Corbin and Anselm Strauss. 2014. *Basics of Qualitative Research*. Sage Publications.

[31] K.C. Wassermann, Kynan Eng, P.F.M.J. Verschure, and J. Manzolli. 2003. Live soundscape composition based on synthetic emotions. *IEEE Multimedia* 10, 4: 82–90. https://doi.org/10.1109/MMUL.2003.1237553

[32] Karen Tanenbaum and Joshua Tanenbaum. 2009. Commitment to Meaning: A Reframing of Agency in Games. In *Digital Arts and Culture Conference, 2009: after media: embodiment and context*. Retrieved from https://escholarship.org/uc/item/6f49r74n

[33] Karen Tanenbaum, Joshua Tanenbaum, Alissa N. Antle, Jim Bizzocchi, Magy Seif el-Nasr, and Marek Hatala. 2011. Experiencing the Reading Glove. In *Proceedings of the Fifth International Conference on Tangible, Embedded, and Embodied Interaction* (TEI '11), 137–144. https://doi.org/10.1145/1935701.1935728

[34] L. Reitsma, A. Smith, and E. van den Hoven. 2013. StoryBeads: Preserving Indigenous Knowledge through Tangible Interaction Design. In *2013 International Conference on Culture and Computing (Culture Computing)*, 79–85. https://doi.org/10.1109/CultureComputing.2013.22

[35] Margaret Mackey. 2008. Stepping into the Subjunctive World of the Fiction in Game, Film and Novel. *Loading - The Journal of the Canadian Games Studies Association* 2, 3.

[36] Marie-Laure Ryan. 2001. *Narrative as Virtual Reality*. Johns Hopkins University Press, Baltimore, Mariland, USA.

[37] Marie-Laure Ryan. 2006. Avatars of Story. University of Minnesota Press, Minneapolis, Minnesota.

[38] Mark O. Riedl and R. Michael Young. 2006. From Linear Story Generation to Branching Story Graphs. *IEEE Computer Graphics and Applications* 26, 3: 23–31.

[39] Mark Owen Riedl. 2004. Narrative Generation: Balancing Plot and Character. North Carolina State University.

[40] Michelle Li and He Jianting. 2009. Ambient Environments for Emotional Physical Communication. In *Proceedings of the 10th International Conference NZ Chapter of the ACM's Special Interest Group on Human-Computer Interaction* (CHINZ '09), 81–84. https://doi.org/10.1145/1577782.1577797

[41] Nicolas Szilas. 2003. IDtension: A narrative engine for Interactive Drama.

[42] Petra Fagerberg, Anna Ståhl, and Kristina Höök. 2004. eMoto: Emotionally Engaging Interaction. *Personal Ubiquitous Comput.* 8, 5: 377–381. https://doi.org/10.1007/s00779-004-0301-z

[43] Philip Ross and David V. Keyson. 2007. The Case of Sculpting Atmospheres: Towards Design Principles for Expressive Tangible Interaction in Control of Ambient Systems. *Personal Ubiquitous Comput.* 11, 2: 69–79. https://doi.org/10.1007/s00779-005-0062-3

[44] Ronan Champagnat, Pascal Estraillier, and Armelle Prigent. 2006. Adaptative Execution of Game: Unfolding a Correct Story. In *Proceedings of the 2006 ACM SIGCHI International Conference on Advances in Computer Entertainment Technology* (ACE '06). https://doi.org/10.1145/1178823.1178941

[45] Susan Leigh Star and James R. Griesemer. 1989. Institutional ecology,translations' and boundary objects: Amateurs and professionals in Berkeley's Museum of Vertebrate Zoology, 1907-39. *Social studies of science* 19, 3: 387–420.

[46] Tom Gunning. 1990. The Cinema of Attractions: Early Film, Its Spectator and the Avant-Garde. In *Early Cinema: Space–Frame–Narrative*, Thomas Elaesser and Adam Barker (eds.). BFI Publishing, London, 56–62.

# Adapting Double Weaving and Yarn Plying Techniques for Smart Textiles Applications

**Laura Devendorf & Chad Di Lauro**
ATLAS Institute & Information Science, Electrical and Computer Engineering
University of Colorado, Boulder
{laura.devendorf, chad.dilauro}@colorado.edu

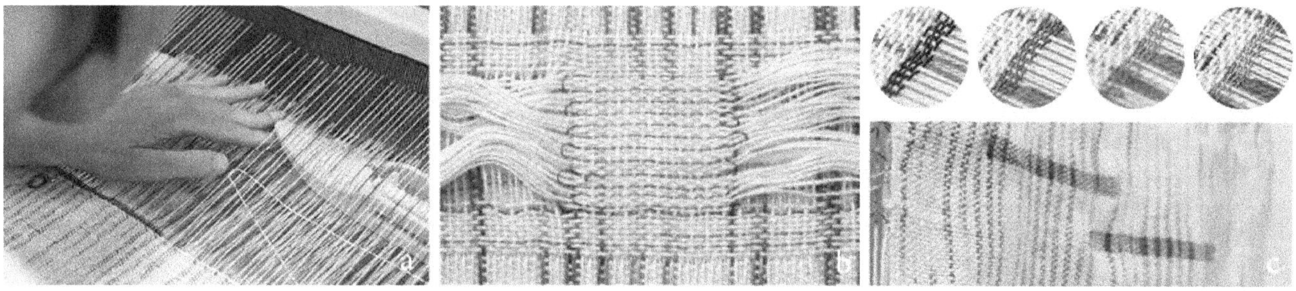

**Figure 1: We describe how fiber arts techniques can be adapted for smart textiles applications. (a) We used hand-weaving to create an interactive fabric with thirteen regions that change color in response to touch (b) We used a technique called double weaving to create press buttons that hide the sensing yarns from view. (c) We experimented with plying custom color-changing yarns to achieve optimal color visibility and power efficiency.**

## ABSTRACT
Smart textiles integrate sensing and actuation components into their structures to bring interactivity to fabrics. We describe how we adapted two existing fiber arts techniques, double weaving and yarn plying, for the purpose of creating a woven textile that changes color in response to touch. We draw from this experience to make three core contributions: descriptions of our experiments plying yarns that change between three color states; descriptions of double weaving structures that allow us to support interactivity while hiding circuitry from view; and suggestions for how these techniques could be adapted and extended by other researchers to make richly crafted and technologically sophisticated fabrics.

## Author Keywords
Smart textiles; Hand-weaving; Yarn plying; Craft;

## CCS Concepts
Human-centered computing~Human computer interaction (HCI); Human-centered computing~Interface design prototyping

## INTRODUCTION
Smart textiles offer new forms of interactivity by imbuing fabrics with circuitry. We distinguish smart textiles from a broader category of e-textiles by the way smart textile components are realized within the *structure* of fabrics, at the level of individual yarns. For example, a smart textile force sensor leverages the inherent three-dimensionality of a waffle weave to make a fabric that creates measureable changes in resistance when pressed [18]. We see this as distinct, in terms of production, from approaches that layer premade fabrics to form new kinds of components.

Designers of smart textiles have an increased amount of control over the specific functionality and aesthetic of the textiles they produce. At the same time, weaving smart textiles sets up a unique set of design constraints that are different from more common weaving practices. Specifically, one needs to ensure that particular yarns maintain connectivity (or not) and the yarns with which one weaves may need to be crafted specifically to provide particular properties to the circuit (e.g. a specific resistance or non-standard color changing functionality).

We address these challenges by describing how we adapted double weaving (a technique for weaving multiple layers into a single fabric) and yarn plying (a method for twisting multiple yarns into a single yarn) for the purposes of creating smart textiles. We applied these techniques to create an interactive textile with thirteen distinct regions that correlate touch sensing with color change in the pattern. The touch sensing buttons are distributed throughout the bottom layer of a two-layered fabric, making their circuitry invisible when displayed on a wall (Figure 1b). Pressing those regions changes the color of one of the long thin rectangles in the pattern. A single touch turns a dark purple region to a rich pink, a second touch turns the pink region to white, and a third touch resets the region back to its original purple (Figure 1c).


ACM 978-1-4503-6196-5/19/03...$15.00
https://doi.org/10.1145/3294109.3295625

Through the experimentation and production of our touch textile, we began to see how the techniques for double weaving and yarn plying could be useful beyond our application. In an effort to bring attention to these techniques and aid the practices of other smart textiles practitioners, we contribute (1) descriptions and findings from our experiments plying custom thermochromic yarns; (2) descriptions and examples of double weaving techniques and (3) visions for future work that could leverage these techniques.

## WEAVING SMART TEXTILES

While embroidery (e.g. [15]), knitting (e.g. [19]), crochet (e.g. [5]), and silk-screening (e.g. [9]) can all be used to bring interactivity to textiles, we focus specifically on weaving: a process by which yarns are interlaced in perpendicular directions to create fabrics. Where embroidery and silk-screening offer design flexibility in terms of patterning existing fabrics and knitting is useful for creating 3-dimenstional or stretchy forms, weaving has some specific advantages for smart textiles applications [3]. Specifically, because woven fabrics tend to be less stretchy than knitted fabrics the processes of weaving places less tension or strain on yarns that are integrated within the fabric. Weaving also makes it easy to integrate yarns that have little to no stretch, such as stainless steel yarn or thin wires. One typically encounters woven fabrics in the form of tailored garments like suits, denim, and/or upholstery.

Artists/designers/technologies have been creating woven smart textiles over the past few decades. Perhaps the earliest example of smart textiles weaving, as we conceptualize it here, occurred in the 1960's when women hand-wove the rope core memory units during the Apollo missions [16]. More recently, in 1997, Rehmi Post and Maggie Orth described smart fabrics emerging from existing practices of weaving with metallic fibers and demonstrate several versions of woven circuits [14]. In 2004, Joanna Berzowska described animating textiles using thermochromic pigments with multiple temperature thresholds, integrated heating wires, and envisioned creating woven circuit boards using double and triple weaving techniques like we describe here [2]. Between 2005 and 2010, Linda Worbin developed a methodology of smart textile design with specific focus on thermochromic display possibilities [17] and collaborated with designer Margot Jacobs to envision new interactions with living "smart" fabrics; Maggie Orth wove a series of thermochromic tapestries that explored the design space of thermochromics as well as double woven structures [13]; Since these foundational demonstrations of smart fabric sensors and displays, several others have extended designers' imagination of how smart fabrics could shape our perception of digital materials [10,20,21] and social relationships [7,9,12]. This history laid the foundation for projects like Google's Project Jacquard [8] and Ebb [5], which leveraged weaving to recreate core user interface elements and study how people envisioned engaging with them in daily life.

We complement this history with a specific attention to the *techniques* employed to create many of these prototypes, which have been used in the past but have not yet been explicitly described in terms intended to spark the imagination of a broader interaction design community. For example, weavers have long created their own yarns with custom properties, used double weaving to pattern textile surfaces, and leveraged these properties for interactive textile displays (e.g. [5,7,22]). However, the focus on such work has emphasized the visual/interactive nature of the design object rather than a detailed description of the specific techniques employed to support those functions. We believe with a better understanding of the fundamental techniques, a broader community will be able to envision and participate in the creation of interactive textile prototypes.

### Understanding Weaving, Looms, and Patterns

Woven fabrics are created on looms, which stretch multiple lengths of yarn (collectively referred to as the "warp") across two beams (Figure 2a). A weaver then works continuous lengths of yarn into a fabric by threading it over and under the warp yarns in a perpendicular direction. The yarns worked into the warp are collectively referred to as the "weft." The particular way the weft travels over and under the warp yarns determines the pattern and structure of the fabric. These patterns are represented by weave "drafts," two-dimensional grids that represent each crossing of a weft and warp thread as a cell within a grid (Figure 2, left). These primitives can be combined with different colors of yarn and in different sequences to create a wide array of patterns and structural possibilities. Some looms, such as the 8-shaft loom we use in this paper, assist in the quick weaving of patterns by allowing one to thread specific sets of warps yarns through different frames or harnesses. These frames are attached, in user specified combinations, to foot pedals called treadles. While weaving one pushes foot pedals in their desired combination, passing the weft through the space created between the raised and lowered yarns (called the "shed"). We found the following books especially helpful in understanding how to weave [1,4,6].

## WEAVING OUR TOUCH FABRIC

We developed the techniques we describe in this paper during the process of creating a fabric that would change color in particular regions where the fabric was pressed. The prototype we developed integrates multiple sensing and actuation elements (twenty-six to be exact) into a woven textile. We used 5/2 Pearl Cotton[1], plyed stainless steel[2], and cotton covered copper[3] painted with thermochromic pigments to create this design and wove them on an 8-shaft Schacht Baby Wolf loom warped at 20 warps per inch.

[1] https://halcyonyarn.com/yarn/083/52-pearl-cotton-yarn

[2] https://www.kr4.us/Conductive-Thread-60g-Stainless-Steel.html

[3] .15mm Double Cotton Covered Copper, sourced from https://wires.co.uk/acatalog/dcc_wire.html

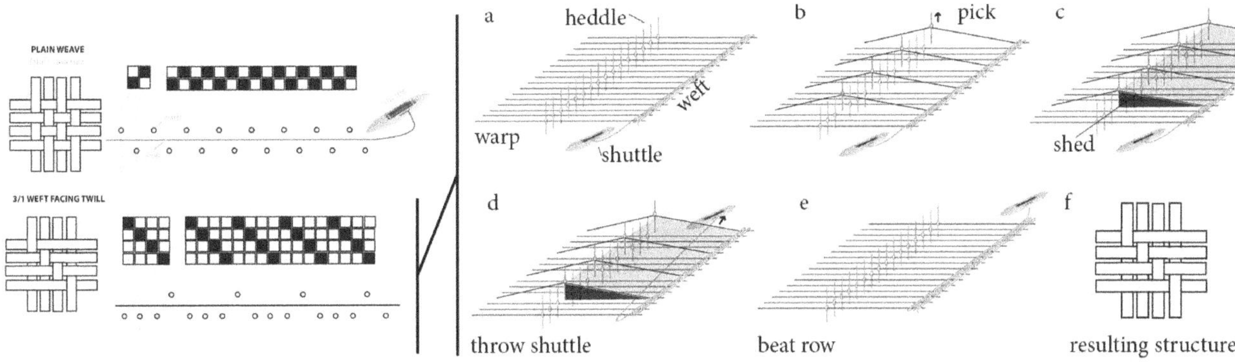


**Figure 2: Left: A weaving draft describes which yarns must be raised and lowered to achieve a particular pattern. A cell that is black means the weft travels *under* the warp. A cell that is white means that the weft travels *over* the warp. (right) the steps a weaver takes to implement a draft on the loom. Steps b-e repeat for each row of the draft, resulting in a structure like that shown in (f).**

We began by weaving test swatches to figure out how to create functional press pads to integrate in the fabric. Simultaneously, we tested a variety of combinations of heating wires and thermochromic painted yarns in order to find yarn compositions that were power efficient with visually noticeable changes between color states. After discovering textile geometries and yarn constructions that were desirable for sensing and color change, we designed a pattern with several of these components to be created on our loom. We quickly learned how difficult it is to envision what a weave would look like prior to weaving samples and started "improvising" designs within the harness and treadling patterns we had already defined to come up with new patterns that satisfied our functional and aesthetic requirements. Through these improvisations, we arrived at designs that we found to be functionally robust and aesthetically appealing. Our result is a fabric that allows someone to press the fabric to change the color in the associated region. We envision the fabric as first step towards an ambient wearable system that records when and where pressures are exerted on the wearer's body, such as the experience of holding children. Detailed patterns and descriptions of how we created the fabric are also available on our project webpage[4].

In the paper that follows, we will describe our experiments and process of realizing this textile, focusing specifically on our tests with yarn plying and double weaving. In the discussion, we present other promising techniques and speculate on possible directions for future research involving these techniques.

## PREPARING THE YARNS

While prior work has demonstrated the display capabilities of woven fabrics by coating yarns or fabrics with thermochromic pigments, techniques for coating yarns or fabrics and providing heat vary. Our process began with experiments to determine which yarns or combinations of yarns would offer the best color change results and power efficiencies. We focused specifically on studying yarns that coupled resistive heating wires with fibers painted with thermochromic pigments. We needed a combination that was power efficient, easy (enough) to produce, able to integrate into weaving without breaking, and made the color change very visible. To create this, we experimented with various mixtures of thermochromic paints and yarn constructions:

### Yarn Painting

Because thermochromic color changes do not emit light, and their change in color is gradual, the eye can have difficulty registering the color change as it is taking place. This requires designers to carefully consider the interactions between various colors in the fabric pattern as well as within the transition.

We were able to procure blue and red thermochromic pigments that become transparent at 28°C, 43°C, 56°C from Chromatic Technologies Incorporated[5]. Thus, mixing the pigments of varying activation temperatures had the effect of revealing distinct color states as the textile become increasingly warm or cool. While we were able to transition between three unique color states using all temperature pigments, we found that heating yarns to 56°C was too resource intensive and uncomfortable for wearable applications. We also discovered that some transitions between colors were more or less noticeable than others. Specifically, a shift from purple to *red* to white is more visually stunning than a shift from purple to *blue* to white (Figure 3).

We created our final paint mixture by mixing:

- 3 parts blue thermochromic that activates at 28°C;
- 1 part red thermochromic that activates at 43°C;
- 4 parts Liquitex clear acrylic gel medium.

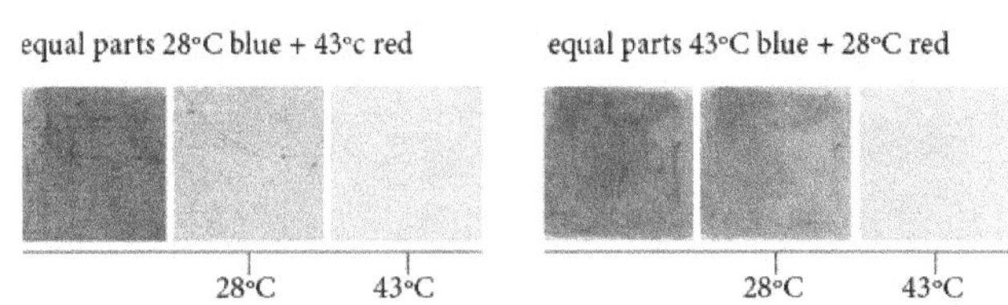


**Figure 3: Two different transitions from purple to white vary based on which pigments "disappears" first.**

[4] http://unstable.design/force-fabric/

[5] https://www.ctiinks.com/thermochromic-inks

This creates a paint that looks like a deep blue/purple when it is at room temperature, transitions to a bright pink and then to white (Figure 1). We added three times more blue than red in order to emphasize the color transition from a very deep blue-purple to pink. When heated to 28°C, the blue pigments become transparent revealing a rich pink. When heated to 43°C, the red pigments become transparent and reveal the color of the yarn (white in our case).

Painting the yarns is a less than ideal method of applying thermochromic pigments. While we had some success using a solution of vinegar and thermochromic pigments to set the color on wool, the color was dull, did not hold and came off during washing or working in our hands.

### Using Plying to Create Heating Wire

While many thermochromic display projects use heating pads to activate color change (e.g. [9]), there are functional and aesthetic benefits to coupling colored yarns with heating wires. We used a technique called plying, in which two yarns are spun together, to create several combinations of heating wires and fibers. While one can ply yarns by tying two lengths of yarn to a screwdriver, we used a drop spindle to ply our yarns. Plying with a drop spindle has the advantage of allowing one to spin longer continuous lengths of yarn.

We produced custom plied yarns by tying one length of heating wire and one length of wool or cotton yarn to the hook at the end of the spindle then spinning it together. To maintain structural stability and balance, we then took the same yarn we spun, looped the center of it around the spindle hook, and spun it again in the other direction (Figure 4). This made the yarn less prone to unraveling and also integrated more lengths of heating wire per unit length.

We created several samples in which a traditional yarn was plied with a resistive heating wire. We provide each material a unique code to which we will refer in the rest of the section and associated diagram.

The traditional yarns we tested are:

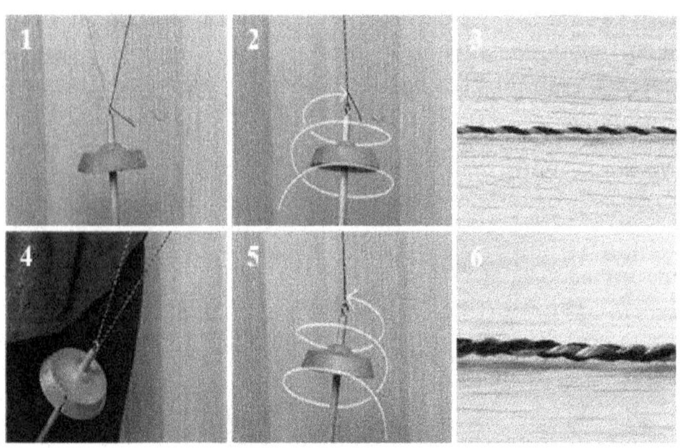


Figure 4: an illustration of the technique we used to ply heating plying yarn

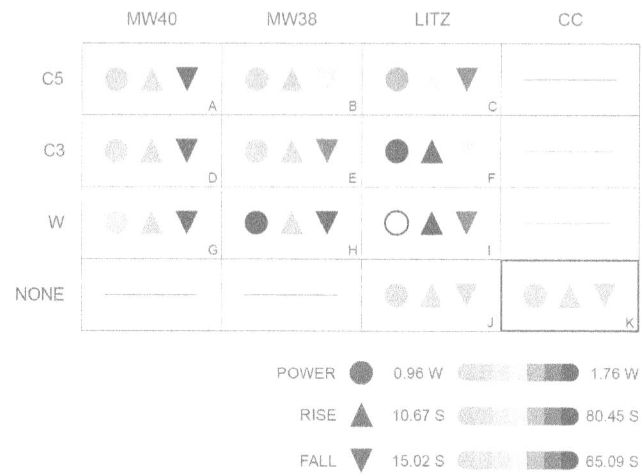


**Figure 5: summary of findings from plying various heating wires with traditional findings. The circle represents the power consumption to change from purple to white, relative to the other yarns. The up and down arrows represent relative time for the color change to activate**

- W: 3/8 Zephyr Wool, color: natural
- C5: 5/2 Pearl Cotton, color: natural
- C3: 3/2 Pearl Cotton, color: natural.

The conductive yarns and wires we tested are:

- MW40: 40 AWG magnet wire
- MW38: 38 AWG magnet wire
- Litz: 36 AWG Litz wire
- CC: Cotton Covered non-insulated Copper
- SS: Plied Stainless Steel

We measured the amount of power required by each yarn to achieve full color change, the quality of the color change, and the time to achieve that change (the rise time) and recover from it (the fall time). When testing the yarns, we pulled them straight, so that they were not looped on themselves, which affects how the yarn heats. In practice, however, yarns that are placed next to each other will heat more quickly than yarns with more air around them, so our measurements represent the upper bounds of power consumption.

Our measurements should be treated as relative, since combinations of handspun fibers and wires, coated with different mixtures and kinds of pigments, tested in different environments and configurations, will vary. Similarly, it can be difficult to tell, exactly, when a yarn has transitioned from one color to the next, which adds some margin of error into our timing measurements. In general, we took measurements when the yarn had *completely* turned color along its entire length, which in some cases was different than when it started to change. We provide our complete data in auxiliary materials and a summary in Figure 5. Some general tends emerged from our data include:

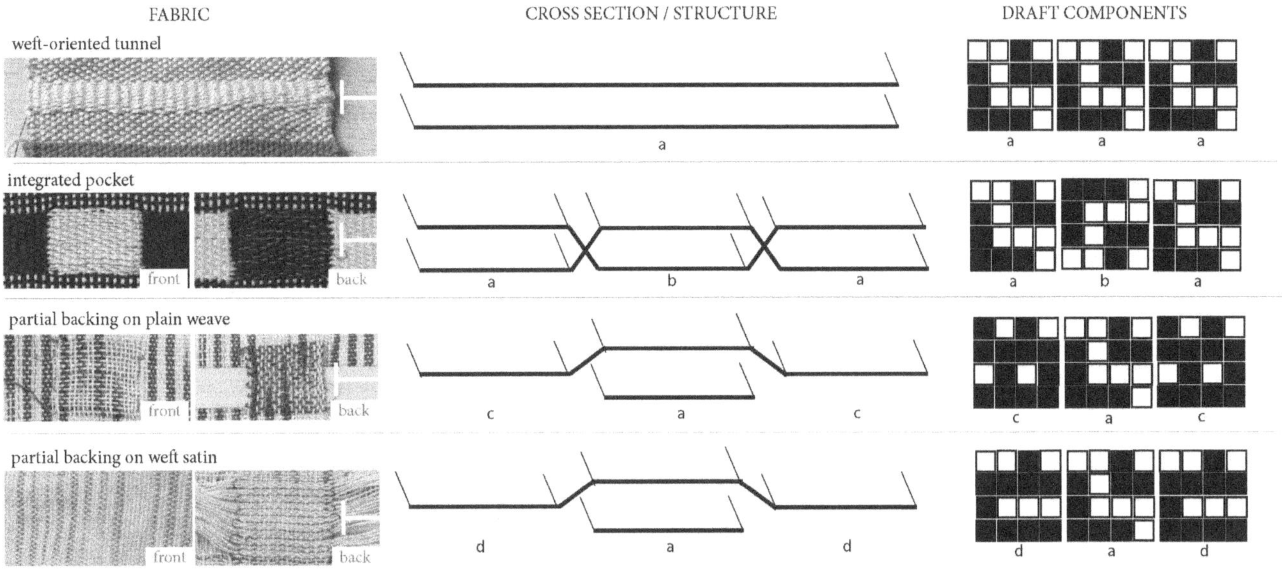


**Figure 6: Illustration of double weave structures. The structural view represents the layers of the weave as one would see them if they could slice the fabric and look at the cross-section. The circles mark layer associations of the warp yarns, the red and blue yarns represent how the weft yarns are integrated. The rows are woven in the order they appear in the draft: red, blue, light red, light blue. Repeating those four stitches produces the square sections depicted on the physical sample view.**

Many yarns that were plied required less power but had longer rise and fall times. We believe this is because plying created thicker yarns, requiring more heat to travel through the fibers to activate color change. Similarly, there was less air around the fibers to help with cooling.

The cotton yarns changed color more uniformly than wool yarns. Our theory here is that since wool is a crimped fiber, wool yarns contain many pockets of air of various sizes. These air pockets are not uniformly distributed through the yarn and thus, the length of yarn heats unevenly.

Litz had some advantages in terms of quick heating, when it was coated alone rather than spun with other fibers. However, Litz wire is quite expensive and internally contains three very thin enameled copper wires, making it difficult to solder.

The silk insulation on the Litz wires significantly hindered heat transfer when plied with other fibers. The Litz+W combination was our poorest performing because we believe the silk covering the multiple strands of magnet wire absorbed the heat intended for the wool. The timings were so much worse than the others that we threw them out of our measurements, as indicated by the open red circle in the graph (Figure 5i).

The MW40 combinations performed well but were difficult to ply without breaking. The MW38 was the thinnest wire we could ply reliably.

Our best performing yarn, considering all variables, was not hand plied at all, but was CC, a non-insulated copper wire wrapped in white cotton—created by a yarn spinning process performed by a manufacturer. Because the cotton provided all the insulation to the copper, it allows for fast thermal transfer and easy soldering (since one does not have to burn or scratch the enamel off the inner wire prior to soldering). Additionally, the wire itself is very durable while moderately pliable, allowing it to nicely integrate into our fabric without dramatically changing the surface texture.

## ADAPTING DOUBLE WEAVING FOR SMART TEXTILES

Double weaving is a technique that allows a weaver to weave multiple layers at once. It works by splitting the warp yarns into two groups (odd yarns in one group, even yarns in another) and weaving those yarn groupings separately from each other to create two layers that sit atop of each other (Figure 6, top). With this two-layer construction, a weaver can design patterns for each layer separately, allowing for the insertion of conductive yarns into the top and bottom layers in different configurations. For example, [2] uses double weaving to integrate hidden heating elements into a fabric while [23] uses it to embed pressure sensitive pads within the fabric. We experimented with several methods of double weaving during our prototyping and describe them in detail below:

### *Open or Closed Weft-Oriented Tunnels*

When one switches from a single weave to a double weave as they are weaving, they essentially split a single layer of fabric into two layers. When one switches back to a single layer weave, that double-layered region becomes a tunnel spanning the width of the fabric. The ends of the tunnels can be left open or closed. In the context of smart textiles, this structure makes it easy to route wires through fabrics by running them through the tunnels.

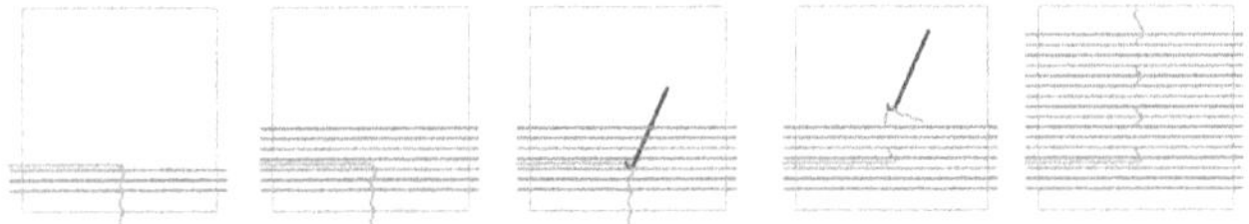

Figure 7: Diagram of our method for partial weft insertion, the insertion of conductive yarn in the warp direction by incrementally pulling the yarn up the fabric with a crochet hook.

### *Integrated Pockets*

The layer orientations of a double weave can “flip” at arbitrary points, allowing the back face to come to the front face of the fabric and vice versa. Structurally, this “flip” can be used to create pockets that are completely embedded within the fabric. Within such pockets, a designer can place materials or off-the-shelf sensors and completely seal them into the fabric, ensuring that they maintain their position and orientation. We used this technique in early tests to create a pocket with conductive yarn integrated into the top and bottom layers of the pocket and a piece of Velostat, a conductive pressure sensitive material, placed in the middle. However, we found the readings with the Velostat to be too unreliable and considered other methods of creating press buttons. For example, we could have inserted a force-sensor into the pocket to provide more accurate readings, but opted to challenge ourselves with a design that used no existing parts.

### *Partial Backings*

We refer to the technique we used extensively in our prototype as a partial backing. This double weave only integrates materials to the second layer in the places where they are needed. This structure allowed us to create a seamless and neat front face of the fabric that features the color changing regions while hiding the connective “guts” in the back layer. In early tests, we had integrated partial backings into a fabric that was otherwise plain woven but this created noticeable textural differences in the sensing regions. We updated the design such that the entire top face of the fabric would be woven with the weft satin stitch, (Figures 2 and 6). This made our front facing texture uniform, effectively hiding the sensing regions below it.

The partial backing in our design held rectangular conductive regions for press sensing as well as routing of our conductive wires to the left side of the fabric. We found that two yarns spacing between each conductive yarn was sufficient to ensure our yarns did not inadvertently cross or touch as they were routed through the fabric. A spacing of three yarns between each row of conductive yarn in our touch pad was sufficient for creating reliable press sensing (Figure 8).

### *Partial Warp Insertion*

To create reliable press buttons, we needed the conductive traces on one layer to routed in the direction of the warp and the other in the weft. Inserting conductive yarns in the warp is more challenging because the warp yarns must be stretched across the entire length of the loom prior to weaving. Similarly, the warp yarns are under much more tension than the weft and we found our conductive stainless yarns to be prone to breaking under this pressure. Since we only needed our conductive traces to travel in the warp direction in small segments, we adapted a technique weavers use to fix broken yarns. In the original technique, one pins the warp yarn to be fixed the fabric in production and then manually pulls it to the back of the loom and attaches a weight to hold it under tension. As one continues weaving rows, the placed warp yarn becomes integrated into the fabric. We realized we could adapt this technique for adding our conductive yarn segments in the warp direction as follows:

We ran one conductive yarn from the left side of the fabric through the bottom layer and pulled it to the top of the fabric when it reached the center point of our button (Figure 7). Then, we continued weaving top and bottom layers as usual. Every three rows, we would use a crochet hook to reach under the top layer of our fabric, and pull the loose thread upward through the length. This allowed us to thread the warp segment along the bottom face of the top layer, ensuring that it could make good contact with the weft-oriented conductive pad integrated on the bottom layer while also being invisible to a viewer.

### *More than Two Layer Weaves*

Our final note on double weaving addresses the number of layers that can be worked at once. While we experimented with and describe the integration of two-layers into a fabric at once, it is possible to weave more than two layers at once. However, for each layer the density of warp yarns is reduced. For instance, in double weaving, the warp yarns are split into two groups (even warps, odd warps) and woven independently of each other. In triple weaving, every 3rd yarn would be used to create a layer, thus increasing the spacing between the warps. We were able to produce a 4-layered fabric on our 8-shaft loom. We imagine that these multi-layer structures could lead to more complex integrations of sensing and fabrics, perhaps opening possibilities of multi-layered woven circuitry much like multi-layered programmable circuit boards.

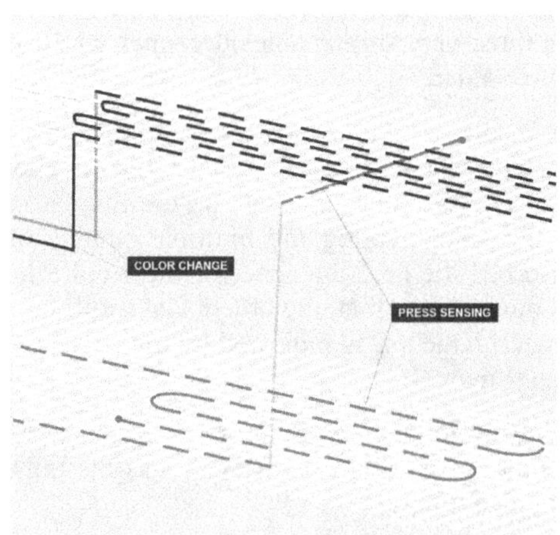


Figure 8: Our fabric leverages double weaving to place color changing

bottom layer. A small piece of conductive yarn is inserted into the top layer to make contact with the bottom pad, completing the circuit.

## FUTURE WORK AND OPEN CHALLENGES

In prototyping our fabric, we began to develop greater awareness of the struggles that researchers of smart textiles face in terms of sourcing custom yarns as well as understanding the constraints and possibilities of woven structures. We would like to call other researchers to action around some of these challenges, by describing other techniques or possibilities that appear to hold promise for the domain that could be pursued in the future.

### Creative Custom Yarns

Identifying and sourcing the yarns necessary for smart textiles can be difficult and often forces researchers to rely on what they can find rather than what might be ideal for their purpose. In this spirit, we present a few more custom yarn techniques to stimulate the imagination of what might be possible for smart textiles with better control over yarn production:

#### *Rope Making*

A designer can create custom "ropes" by taking several lengths of yarn tied to a peg (or one continuous loom wound around a peg) and tying them to individually rotating hooks. When one turns the hooks with the yarns under tension, all lengths of yarn twisted individually and equally. When one "relaxes" the apparatus, the individual yarn lengths recoil and spin upon each other. The thickness of the resulting rope depends on the thickness of the individual materials that comprise the rope. We tried this technique, using a Schacht Incredible Rope Machine, to combine our yarns and heating wires (Figure 9b). While the resulting yarn had many sections of heating wire per unit length, it was difficult to make ropes without breaking. However, the design of rope making systems can be adapted such that the twisted wires wrap around a "core" that would sit in the center. In this sense, we can envision future research studying how brittle heating (or other) wires could be placed in the core with several lengths of color-changing threads spun around them.

#### *Knitted Tubes*

We have also conducted several experiments, for a different soft sensor project that used knitted tubes to create a smart string (Figure 9d) [11]. We used a Caron EmbellishKnit hand crank device to knit together a long conductive yarn with a long non-conductive yarn. In this project, we found that smoother or coated conductive yarns worked best to prevent the conductive yarns from grabbing the others. The hollow knitted tube also makes it possible to insert a core. Since the resulting structure is knitted from continuous lengths of yarn, it is quite stretchy and flexible. We also used this structure in the past to create force-sensitive yarns by knitting conductive yarns around a Velostat core, which worked well.

#### *Kumihimo Braiding*

Kumihimo braiding is a technique in which several lengths of yarns are braided into hollow tubes (Figure 9c). Kumihimo templates can be used to create braids with custom textures and patterning. The templates are easy to produce in cardboard on a laser cutter at various thicknesses. During this braiding, the maker has more control over tensions than they might with techniques that spin yarns together, thus, they may be ideal for applications that require brittle materials to be integrated into the outer structure of the yarn.

**Figure 9: examples of custom yarn structures**

### Possibilities in Double Weaving

The tunnels and multiple layers afforded by weaving present interesting avenues for future research. For instance, designers could also use these tunnels to integrate off-the-shelf sensors (e.g. long bend sensors) or actuators (e.g. like pneumatic tubes) for easy insertion and removal during testing and prototyping. Tunnels may also be used to insert mechanical tendons or changing materials (shape-memory alloys or nylon monofilament-based muscles) that can change the shape of the fabric. If one were to weave several warp and weft facing tunnels, then they could produce a matrix of tunnels through the fabric, again, allowing for the easy insertion and removal of long thin components in two directions instead of one.

What we find most exciting about double weaving is that the pockets can be of arbitrary shape, not just tubes and rectangles, providing that one has a loom with enough sophistication or the hand skills necessary to create complex or non-repeating patterns. For example, existing textiles often use double weaving to alternate the colors that are on the surface of the fabric in given regions. This is why woven fabrics often have the "negative" or "inverse" pattern on the reverse side. What we propose here is that by focusing more on the shape of the tunnels and pockets created through double weaving, apart from the surface patterns they create, we may discover specific uses and possibilities for smart textiles. For example, we envision that pockets can be custom fit to ones specifications and could be used for: routing wires or sensing elements though the innards of a fabric while also creating elegant surface textures; housing components that haven't been realized in woven structures yet, like batteries and microcontrollers; or creating embedded arrays within which hard materials like sensors like magnets, accelerometers or speakers could be inserted into fabrics securely and away from the skin.

## LIMITATIONS

The prototypes and techniques we demonstrate in this paper certainly have limitations if we were to consider them existing beyond the prototype phase or transitioning into mass-market production. We do not know how the thermochromic yarns we created will do in the wash (we expect badly) largely because we have not yet found an appropriate method for dying the yarns with the pigments we have available (dying chemically bonds the color to the fiber, as opposed to a paint that can wash off). While thermochromic dyes are available, we had trouble finding them in the colors and temperature ranges we desired. Power is also a persistent struggle in textile applications, particularly those that aim to be body worn. While powering every color change region simultaneously would require one to plug into a wall socket, it is feasible to design interactions or optimize power use by limiting the number of sections that receive power at a single time.

## REFLECTIONS ON PROTOTYPING BY HAND

The insights we contribute in this work emerged from a long, slow, humbling, and deeply intriguing process of learning to hand-weave smart textiles. It is a stark contrast from the first author's earlier experience with [5], in which she designed smart textile concepts that a more expert weaver produced, in that it provided a much deeper and embodied knowledge of different weaving structures and possibilities. This knowledge is largely about technique and about the very small and intricate gestures that one makes with their hands when manipulating lengths of string into a fabric. This process of learning what weaving and weavers can do, in both conceptual and embodied senses, has led to a deep admiration and appreciation for those who do it especially well. At the same time, we struggle to understand how to communicate these details, which seem utterly small but critically important, and highlight their importance as research contributions. As the history of smart textiles weaving shows us, the *novel* ideas for what smart weaving can be have existed for nearly twenty years, what we truly need are ways to effectively communicate the skills necessary in order to develop these ideas.

While some of the techniques we describe here can be reproduced much more quickly and at scale with industrial weaving systems, others like partial warp insertions may be more difficult. While we see how these issues of scale can be cast as limitations, we like to think of them as a specific perspective that makes particular forms of work and personalized innovation possible. Specifically, we are working for a future of smart textiles that are richly crafted or "custom" pieces designed for and with specific users -- a vision that sees smart textiles emerging with ecosystems of custom tailoring and bespoke artifacts that couple personal aesthetics with functionality. Other textiles artists and technologies like Hannah-Perner Wilson and Mika Satomi share this vision, going so far as to opening the first brick and mortar shop "KOBA" for custom smart textiles tailoring services [18]. Bringing these futures into the present requires an embrace of the unique benefits of handcraft and hand-weaving. Technology may not need to

be introduced only to make these difficult crafts easier or faster, but could open up new ways of thinking about how we design for more personal or intimate human-technology relationships.

## CONCLUSION

We presented a collection of techniques for double weaving and yarn-playing processes to help developers of smart textiles discover new ways of realizing their smart textile concepts. These techniques emerged through the process of hand-weaving a tapestry that couples several integrated push buttons with pattern changes. In writing this paper, we hope to spur a future in which the technical is more richly crafted.

## ACKNOWLEDGMENTS

A very special thank you to Clement Zheng for assisting with the graphics and diagrams on this paper. Thank you to Shanel Wu, Mikhaila Friske, Andrea Chamorro, Jolie Klefeker, and Christopher Baker for reading and providing feedback. This work is sponsored by NSF #1755587.

## REFERENCES

[1] Anni Albers. 1974. *Anni Albers : On Weaving.* Wesleyan, Middletown (Conn.).

[2] Joanna Berzowska. 2004. Very Slowly Animating Textiles: Shimmering Flower. In *ACM SIGGRAPH 2004 Sketches* (SIGGRAPH '04), 34–. https://doi.org/10.1145/1186223.1186266

[3] Lina M Castano and Alison B Flatau. 2014. Smart fabric sensors and e-textile technologies: a review. *Smart Materials and Structures* 23, 5: 053001. https://doi.org/10.1088/0964-1726/23/5/053001

[4] Deborah Chandler. 2009. *Learning to Weave.* Interweave.

[5] Laura Devendorf, Joanne Lo, Noura Howell, Jung Lin Lee, Nan-Wei Gong, M. Emre Karagozler, Shiho

Fukuhara, Ivan Poupyrev, Eric Paulos, and Kimiko Ryokai. 2016. "I Don't Want to Wear a Screen": Probing Perceptions of and Possibilities for Dynamic Displays on Clothing. In *Proceedings of the 2016 CHI Conference on Human Factors in Computing Systems* (CHI '16), 6028–6039. https://doi.org/10.1145/2858036.2858192

[6] Allen A. Fannin. 1998. *Handloom Weaving Technology: Revised And Updated*. Green Editorial, New York.

[7] Noura Howell, Laura Devendorf, Tomás Alfonso Vega Gálvez, Rundong Tian, and Kimiko Ryokai. 2018. Tensions of Data-Driven Reflection: A Case Study of Real-Time Emotional Biosensing. In *Proceedings of the 2018 CHI Conference on Human Factors in Computing Systems* (CHI '18), 431:1–431:13. https://doi.org/10.1145/3173574.3174005

[8] Ivan Poupyrev, Nan-Wei Gong, Shiho Fukuhara, M. Emre Karagozler, Carsten Schwesig, and Karen Robinson. 2016. Project Jacquard: Manufacturing Digital Textiles at Scale. In *Proceedings of the 34th Annual ACM Conference on Human Factors in Computing Systems* (CHI '16).

[9] Viirj Kan, Katsuya Fujii, Judith Amores, Chang Long Zhu Jin, Pattie Maes, and Hiroshi Ishii. 2015. Social Textiles: Social Affordances and Icebreaking Interactions Through Wearable Social Messaging. In *Proceedings of the Ninth International Conference on Tangible, Embedded, and Embodied Interaction* (TEI '15), 619–624. https://doi.org/10.1145/2677199.2688816

[10] Judit Eszter Karpati. *Chromosonic*. Retrieved from http://chromosonic.tumblr.com/

[11] Josephine Klefeker and Laura Devendorf. String Figuring: A Story of Reflection, Material Inquiry, and a Novel Sensor.

[12] Noura Howell, Laura Devendorf, Rundong Tian, Tomas Vega, Nan-Wei Gong, Ivan Poupyrev, Eric Paulos, and Kimiko Ryokai. 2016. Biosignals as Social Cues: Ambiguity and Emotional Interpretation in Social Displays of Skin Conductance. In *Proceedings of the Designing Interactive Systems Conference*.

[13] Maggie Orth. 2009. *100 Electronic Art Years*. Retrieved from http://www.maggieorth.com/art_100EAYears.html

[14] Maggie Orth, Rehmi Post, and Emily Cooper. 1998. Fabric Computing Interfaces. In *CHI 98 Conference Summary on Human Factors in Computing Systems* (CHI '98), 331–332. https://doi.org/10.1145/286498.286800

[15] Irene Posch and Ebru Kurbak. 2016. CRAFTED LOGIC Towards Hand-Crafting a Computer. In *Proceedings of the 2016 CHI Conference Extended Abstracts on Human Factors in Computing Systems* (CHI EA '16), 3881–3884. https://doi.org/10.1145/2851581.2891101

[16] Daniela K. Rosner, Samantha Shorey, Brock R. Craft, and Helen Remick. 2018. Making Core Memory: Design Inquiry into Gendered Legacies of Engineering and Craftwork. In *Proceedings of the 2018 CHI Conference on Human Factors in Computing Systems* (CHI '18), 531:1–531:13. https://doi.org/10.1145/3173574.3174105

[17] Linda Worbin. 2010. Designing dynamic textile patterns.

[18] KOBA. Retrieved August 4, 2018 from http://www.kobakant.at/KOBA/

[19] Knit Macro-Electronics (2013) | ebru kurbak. Retrieved November 13, 2018 from http://ebrukurbak.net/knit-macro-electronics/

[20] WifiTapestry 1.0. Retrieved August 8, 2018 from http://www.nytimes.com/2015/02/19/arts/international/when-great-minds-dont-think-alike.html

[21] Woven Signals. *aml*. Retrieved August 4, 2018 from http://emeteuz.com/woven-signals/

[22] Dynamic Double Weave. Retrieved November 13, 2018 from http://www.maggieorth.com/art_DDW.html

[23] Pressure Sensors : Dena Molnar. Retrieved August 4, 2018 from http://www.denamolnar.com/textiles/pressure-sensors/

# Design for Mental Health: How Socio-Technological Processes Mediate Outcome Measures in a Field Study of a Wearable Anxiety App

**Alissa N. Antle**
School of Interactive Arts and Technology, Simon Fraser University, Surrey, Canada
[aantle@sfu.ca]

**Elgin Skye McLaren**
School of Interactive Arts and Technology, Simon Fraser University, Surrey, Canada
[elgin-skye_mclaren@sfu.ca]

**Holly Fiedler**
Education Assistant Department, Langara College, Vancouver, Canada
[hollyfiedler@gmail.com]

**Naomi Johnson**
Social Work Independent Consultant, Toronto, Canada
[naomi.megan.johnson@gmail.com]

## ABSTRACT
Millions of children have challenges with anxiety that negatively impact their development, education and well-being. To address this challenge, we developed version 2.0 of *Mind-Full*, a wearable, mobile neurofeedback system, designed to teach young children to learn to self-regulate anxiety. We present a mixed methods evaluation of a seven week long intervention in schools. We report on a subset of outcome measures related to 10 children's anxiety and stress in the classroom and describe mediating *socio-technological processes* that may have impacted outcomes. Findings showed improvement in children's ability to self-regulate anxiety and reduced cortisol levels for some children. Qualitative findings suggested that children who made multimodal connections during system mediated learning and had teacher support for learning transfer responded well to the intervention. We suggest that framing mental health app design as a distributed, adaptive, socio-technological system enables designers to better meet individual's unique and changing mental health needs.

### Author Keywords
Brain-computer interfaces; children; socio-technological studies; emotion-regulation; learning; mental health.

### CSS Concepts
• Human-centered computing~Empirical studies in ubiquitous and mobile computing • Social and professional topics~Children

## INTRODUCTION
Anxiety disorders are among the most common mental health issues in childhood and the first to emerge – affecting about 18% of children, often lasting into adulthood with devastating social-emotional, health, and economic costs [5,25]. Children who attend schools in lower socio-economic status (SES) areas more frequently have anxiety disorders because they experience ongoing, frequent neurobiological stress responses [24]. These stress responses are correlated with increasing risk of both physical and mental health problems [12]. When these responses occur in periods of rapid brain development, such as when young children first enter schooling, these stress responses can be particularly harmful [12]. Recent therapeutic research suggests that learning to self-regulate anxiety early in life is beneficial and may reduce the negative impact of this mental health challenge on educational, social-emotional, and economic outcomes for children [34]. Self-regulation (SR) training, like mindfulness, and involves learning ways to stay calmly focused and alert, and practicing those techniques until they become automated. Clinical research has shown than bio-feedback and/or neurofeedback may be effective for teaching children how to self-regulate anxiety [13,20,30].

A neurofeedback (NF) system measures, records and provides visual and/or auditory feedback about brain states (e.g. anxiety). Until recently NF systems for self-regulation training were only available to a very limited number of children through clinics and hospitals, and wait times for mental health treatment for children are often 1 year or more [29]. The release of inexpensive consumer grade headsets (e.g. Neurosky, Emotiv and Muse) creates opportunities for NF apps that can be developed for smart phones and tablets, devices children use almost daily in schools. Initial research into school-based NF interventions using consumer grade headsets with children living in poverty [3] and children and youth in Dutch classrooms [32] have shown some positive results and revealed the importance of contextual factors. Our goal for this project was to evaluate a mobile neurofeedback system to help young children in low SES schools learn to self-regulate. To address this goal, we asked: *Can a wearable mobile neurofeedback app for children help them learn to self-regulate anxiety in a SES school setting?* and *What socio-technological processes mediate intervention outcomes?*

In this paper, we present a subset of the results of our mixed methods evaluation (see [4] for more details). Here, we focus on 20 children with high levels of anxiety who used a new


TEI '19, March 17–20, 2019, Tempe, AZ, USA

ACM ISBN 978-1-4503-6196-5/19/03...$15.00
https://doi.org/10.1145/3294109.3295650

version of our *Mind-Full*[1]system. The quantitative results provide evidence that the intervention group improved their ability to self-regulate anxiety at school. We contribute the qualitative findings that identify mediating *socio-technological processes* that impacted outcome measures. We conclude with a recommendation of factors that should be considered in future design and evaluations of socio-emotional and mental health apps for school children.

## BACKGROUND

An electroencephalogram (EEG) is a device that uses electrodes placed on the scalp to sense, measure and record the electrical activity of the brain's neurons [18]. As we think, feel, sleep, exercise and learn, electrical activity escapes through our skulls and can be sensed by an EEG device. When this information is displayed on a computer or app screen and the user tries to learn to control their brain states, the system is called a passive EEG-based neurofeedback (NF) system. A single EEG sensor on the left pre-frontal cortex can measure electrical activity, which a computer program can analyze to infer in real time if the EEG wearer has a relaxed or anxious brain state.

### Field-based NF Studies of Children and Anxiety

Outside of clinics and research labs, there have been only a few EEG-NF interventions targeting children with anxiety challenges. In a randomized controlled experiment with an active control group with 136 participants (aged 8 to 13), children and youth played one of two platform video games [32]. They played in common classrooms in Dutch schools (7 to19 children per room) for 5 x 1 hour sessions, scheduled twice a week. The intervention group used a NF platform video game called MindLight, developed using principles of cognitive behavioral therapy. The goal was to explicitly expose players to both anxiety producing and relaxing experiences. The control group played Max and the Magic Marker, a puzzle platform video game. Participant and parent ratings of anxiety showed a decrease from pre to post-test, no change at follow-up test points. The methodological design has a large sample size and standardized, reliable and multi-informant behavioral measures. However, the authors suggest that the play context may have impacted results since the children all played in shared rooms (contamination effect). The authors also suggest that positive results might be due to non-specific factors such as being primed to expect an improvement in anxiety. Lastly, they acknowledge that without a non-intervention group it was difficult to determine if improvements were greater than without any intervention.

In a randomized controlled experiment with a waitlist control group with 21 girls (aged 5 to 11), children completed 24 NF sessions over 6 weeks with their counsellor at a school for girls living in poverty in Nepal [3]. The Mind-Full NF system had three simple games, designed based on principles described in [2] including the use of embodied metaphor based interaction that linked body enactments with changes in brain states represented in ways children could understand from everyday activities. The goal was to teach the girls to learn to use breathing and body relaxation techniques to SR anxiety and transfer those skills to the classroom and playground of the school. Counsellor and teacher ratings of anxiety showed an increase in ability to SR anxiety in a variety of contexts for the intervention from pre to post-test, no change at follow-up test points. The waitlist group later completed the intervention and pre-post ratings showed a similar pattern. Interviews with counsellors and teachers highlighted system-based factors including the benefits of repetitive practice, the laddering structure of the games and the ability to adjust the game difficulty in real time.

Interviews with school staff combined with researcher observations revealed several contextual factors that may have been related to beneficial outcomes [3]. First, counsellors reported that seeing the children's brain states in real time helped them better understand and treat the challenges faced by each child, leading to changes in their counselling approaches. Second, meetings between researchers and school staff helped create a common language for talking about the challenges faced by the children. In combination with the access to brain data over the internet, this may have enabled remote western therapists to better coach the Nepalese counsellors. Third, the children's attendance rates improved over the study period, in part because parents may have been motivated to ensure their children were exposed to western technologies. Lastly, counsellors reported that after each session the girls were often more relaxed and willing to talk about their anxiety, which likely improved the rapport between them and/or the quality of the one-on-one counselling sessions.

To the best of our knowledge, there are no other field studies of NF-based interventions for anxiety and children.

### Field-Based and Contextual Methodological Challenges

For further methodological guidance we can look to other field-based NF studies targeting children and other brain processes (e.g. attention) [8,9,17,22,37]. Claims from these studies are often limited because study designs have involved small sample sizes, non-randomized designs, and inadequate control conditions [8]. However, we note that when working in lower SES contexts, an active (placebo) control group design may be ethically unacceptable; due to committing limited resources to a placebo-based intervention [1]. Another issue noted is that some studies do not assess a child's ability to transfer SR skills into their everyday lives or assess maintenance over time [10,36]. Lastly, a common discussion point is that it remains unknown if NF interventions that show behavioral improvements also help children improve regulation of neurological or physiological processes (e.g. stress response) [38]. We suggest that what is needed is a field study design in line with the practices noted above but with a waitlist control group and measures of

[1] http://www.mindfullapp.ca/

transfer and maintenance of SR of anxiety, behaviors related to anxiety and physiological stress responses.

## MIND-FULL: MOBILE EEG NEUROFEEDBACK APP

Our new *Mind-Full* system is comprised of six relaxation games that are played with an EEG headset and a tablet, and a second connected tablet that runs a calibration module. Each game is based on familiar, everyday activities and actions which, when learned, can elicit behaviors which in turn result in desired brain states related to relaxation. The games are designed to help children learn and practice SR of anxiety. The calibration module enables a facilitator to adjust brain state targets and game difficulty during real-time gameplay.

The system uses a BrainLink Pro[2] EEG headset to wirelessly transmit brainwave data into a Unity 3D game engine running on an Android interactive tablet. Brainlink is a commercially available EEG headset that uses the Neurosky chip and only one dry electrode to record electrical activity in the left pre-frontal cortex. Compared to most EEG units, it is robust, non-invasive, adjustable, and easy to wear due to the single dry electrode. The headset sends data via Bluetooth to apps in Unity 3D where it is analyzed and used to control game mechanics, and interface and output elements.

Each game was designed to help children learn how to SR anxiety by enacting actions that calm their body, which in turn calms their brain. The games were all designed using embodied metaphor theory, as outlined in [2], to help young children (aged 5 to 8) understand the relationship between their body and brain as they learn to SR anxiety. We created six games to address concerns of reduced engagement and enjoyment over longer interventions cited in [19].

Relax Games: In three similar games children learn to relax by controlling their breathing. For example, in the indigenous themed Salmon game we represent relaxation using a metaphor – exhaling softly is calming. The game begins with an animation in which a child blows softly on an ember from a lightning strike to ignite a flame. The flame then grows and cooks (smokes) a salmon, which is an indigenous tradition familiar to children in our geographical area. (Figure 1). After the animation plays, it is the user's turn. Like the animated girl, the user softly blows on the flame image, which relaxes her body, thus shifting her brain state toward a relaxed state (lower alpha brainwave frequency). The EEG sensor uses a proprietary algorithm to determine a "relax" index (0-100) that is sent through Bluetooth to the Unity 3D game. When the index passes a threshold for a set amount of time, the game program triggers an animation of the flame growing larger and the salmon blackening. To add a playful twist, the cooked salmon is then stolen by a pesky raven. This sequence earns the user a token stored in a container (Figure 1 left side). If the user is not able to relax the flame goes out and they must start over. Each game is complete when five tokens are earned. The other two relax games are similar involving controlled and gentle breathing.

Sustained Relaxation Games: In three other games children learn how to sustain a relaxed brain state by relaxing and then remaining in a relaxed body state. For example, in the Monster game the user must relax their body as they stay quiet and still in the forest to catch the monster who is chasing a squirrel over a leaf trap (Figure 2). If the user does not remain relaxed the monster runs away into the forest and they must start over. All three games involve sustained relaxation based on cues to enact a relaxed, still body state.

**Figure 1. Salmon game. A: Blow softly to grow flame. B: Smoked salmon is then stolen by raven.**

**Figure 2. Monster game. A: Relax body to hide so monster chases squirrel. B: Sustain relaxation so monster falls into trap.**

The calibration module enables the facilitator to view and adjust brain state targets in real time to accommodate for individual differences (Figure 3). Most NF systems require calibration before use through training. However, children in our population cannot reliably create a relaxed brain state for long enough to train the system. To account for this challenge we developed a real time calibration module. The system is preset with a typical "relax" index value of 40 on a 0-100 scale. However, this can be adjusted in real time. For example, if the facilator sees that a child appears relaxed and

[2] http://store.neurosky.com/collections/brainlink-pro

is breathing softly and the module shows a state just less than 40, they can adjust the target to 35 to accommodate this individual variation from the typical target. As the child learns to relax they can also make this target higher/harder (e.g. 60/100). Lastly, the facilitator can also adjust the amount of time that a brain state must be held to earn a token, again to make each game easier or harder - to accommodate both improvement over time and also variations that children have day to day in their ability to relax depending on events in their lives (e.g. a stressful day at school).

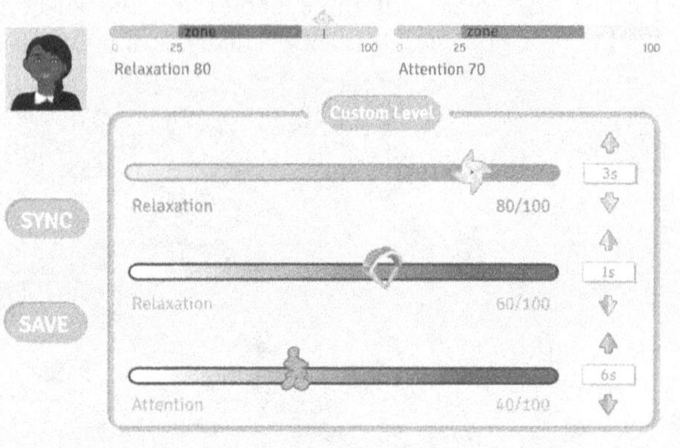


**Figure 3. Calibration module enables real time view and change of user's brain state and hold time parameters for games.**

## METHODOLOGY

We conducted a 2x2 mixed methods evaluation with 20 children (aged 5 to 8 years) who had high levels of anxiety. Children were split into two equivalent groups (intervention, control). All children were assessed at pre and post-test points, and the intervention group was also assessed 2 months later at a follow-up point. The independent variables are group and test point. The control group acts as a comparator, accounting for children's social-emotional learning at school or home as well as any other maturation or developmental effects. At a later date, for ethical reasons, the control group also did the intervention (data not reported here). Our research questions and outcome measures (dependent variables) are described below. We examined both behavioral and physiological indicators of anxiety. We also collected data to understand the impact of socio-technological processes on outcomes that may occur in a complex field environment.

### Participants

Thirty-three children were identified by school principals, and/or head teacher and classroom teachers at two elementary schools. The primary criteria for selection was reported severe level of anxiety. The schools served diverse, multi-cultural populations, including children from low SES households, recent immigrants and refugees. Most of the children had suffered from trauma due to family dysfunction, refugee status, marital break-ups and/or other events associated with low SES.

Of the 33 children identified, 21 were identified by teachers as having severe anxiety and age appropriate cognitive functioning. Twenty children and their parents provided assent/consent to participate. We formed 10 matched pairs of children based on grade, gender, anxiety challenges, and personal characteristics. One child from each pair was randomly assigned to the intervention group and one to the waitlist control group. The end result was 14 males, 6 females split evenly across groups and both schools. Children's teachers also participated in the study (n=7), all female and each with five+ years of teaching experience. The children's ages ranged from 5 to 8 years old at the beginning of the study. All children had good mastery of the English language. We verified group equivalence in terms of ability to SR anxiety using the Calm teacher survey (see below). Ethics was approved by Simon Fraser University and SD41.

### Procedure

The intervention group participated in 18 facilitated sessions with our system over seven weeks. The control group did not use the system over this period. The intervention was delivered in 15-20 minute practice sessions facilitated by a recently graduated social worker. An educational assistant (EA) trainee who was part of the research team was also on site to take notes, manage the schedule and data collection. Sessions were delivered over six weeks with a frequency of three times per week, and the seventh week was used for make-up sessions. The length, frequency and number of sessions was based on other successful NF studies with children (e.g. [7,9,19,32]) and adapted to class schedules.

Each child was introduced to our system using a scripted protocol. Teachers were also introduced to the intervention and trained to use simple posters and phrases taken from the intervention to support children to transfer SR skills from the games into the classroom. We did teacher training in 10-15 minute sessions with teachers in small groups, or individually as scheduling allowed.

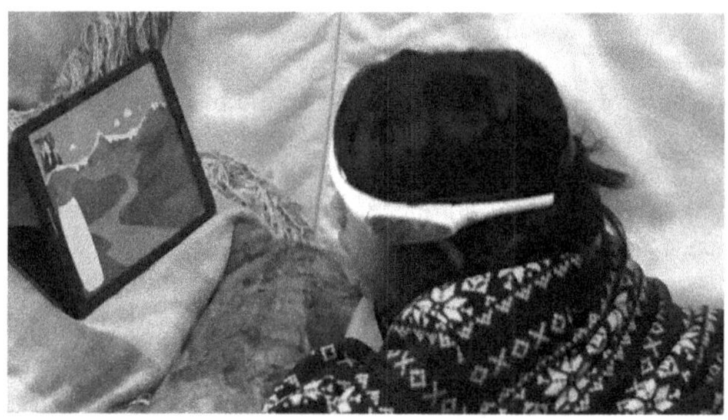

**Figure 4. Child using system in study setting.**

Each child's sessions were facilitated with a scripted protocol designed to identify daily stresses, encourage the child to focus on practicing rather than succeeding at playing the games, and to use their SR skills at school. Facilitation also involved helping children understand the relationship between their body and brain (e.g. breathing calms the brain, relaxing the body from feet all the way up to head helps body stay relaxed). Each session took place in a small quiet room in each school with chairs, table and a couch (Figure 4). Each session was structured beginning with a discussion about how the child was doing on that day and if/how they had used their SR skills since the last session. Then the facilitator explained/reminded the child how to play the relax game using deep, slow breathing and the child played that game until they received five tokens. The facilitator next explained/reminded the child how to play the sustained relaxation game by relaxing their whole body, and the child played that game until they received five tokens. During gameplay, if needed, the facilitator used the calibration module to adjust brain state targets or game difficulty. Children played each of the three relax and three sustained relaxation games for two of the six weeks, in the same order. Sessions ended with a discussion of how the child could use SR skills in situations at school and home.

### Research Questions, Data Collection and Analysis

We collected session data with structured facilitator observational notes to record the number and duration of sessions, and number of tokens for each game to determine if children were able to complete the intervention. We assessed all the children (intervention and control) at pre and post-test points using numeric surveys (teacher), interviews (facilitator, teacher), and physiological cortisol tests (child) (all described below). The intervention group was again assessed (surveys, interviews) at a 2 month follow-up.

**RQ1 (SR Anxiety):** *Do children in the intervention group more effectively self-regulate anxiety than those in the control group in a school environment?*

To address this question we collected data for the *SR Anxiety* construct, which is children's ability to SR anxiety, in both groups at pre and post-test points, and for the intervention group again at two month follow-up. Our measurement instrument was a variant of the Calm survey reported in [4]. Using the Calm survey, *SR Anxiety* is operationalized by a teacher rating a child's ability to SR anxiety with support in different school situations using a five point rating scale, ranging from: Cannot do this at all even with support (1) to Can do this mostly by themselves (5). In previous work the Calm survey was shown to be reliable (Cronbach's $\alpha > 0.70$) and sensitive to change over time [4]. We adapted the Calm survey to reflect typical contexts encountered in the school by the children in our study. Sample questions included: *Child can calm down when they are having difficulty with some schoolwork* and *Child can calm down after a stressful event in the playground.* Since we adapted the survey we assessed its reliability using Cronbach's alpha in SPSS. For Cronbach's alpha values of 0.8 and above, we included all questions. When values were less than 0.8, if deleting any items could increase the overall reliability above 0.8 we removed them to improve the reliability of the construct measure as is standard practice in survey development [6].

**RQ2 (Anxious Behaviors):** *Do children in the intervention group have a lower frequency of anxiety related behaviors than those in the control group in a school environment?*

To address this question we collected data using the *Anxious Behaviors* construct, which is the frequency of a child's anxious behaviors at school in both groups at pre and post-test points, and for the intervention group at two month follow-up. Our measurement instrument was the Anxiety subscale of the Teacher Behavior Assessment System (BASC-3) survey for children [31]. The BASC-3 has excellent test score reliability (mid .80s or higher) [31]. The teacher survey contains statements with descriptors of 16 behaviors related to anxiety at school and a four point frequency rating scale, ranging from never (1) to almost always (4). Sample statements include: Has panic attacks; Appears tense; and Overreacts to stressful situations.

**Analysis of all survey data** was done using SPSS to check for assumptions of normality (Shapiro-Wilks' test) and equal variance (Levene's test). We generated descriptive statistics (mean, standard deviation). We ran mixed 2x2 (repeated measures) ANOVAs with independent variables group and test point and Calm and BASC ratings as separate dependent variables. We would expect no between group differences in Calm scores at pretest since the groups were chosen to be equivalent. We expect high variability with a population sample that has severe mental health challenges so we examined both between and within group differences from pre to post-test. We used a repeated measures t-test on the intervention group data to compare the survey ratings from post to follow-up test points. We used an alpha level of .05 for all statistical tests.

**RQ3 (Stress Level):** *Do children in the intervention group have a lower stress level than those in the control group in a school environment?* To address this question we measured the *Stress* construct by testing salivary cortisol levels at pre and post-test points. A salivary cortisol test provides an objective, biological indicator of stress and has been validated with young children (e.g. [23,26]). We took salivary cortisol swabs following standard procedures for testing with children (e.g. [14,15]). For example, we collected samples at set times of day (9:15 am, 11:30 am, 2:30 pm) and had children avoid vigorous exercise or food intake prior to sampling. Samples were couriered to the Clemens Kirschbaum laboratory at the Dresden University of Technology in Germany for analysis. The lab uses a standard procedure as reported in [28].

**Analysis of processed cortisol test data** indicated that there were missing values (either no test or empty vial), significant events that impacted results (e.g. crying, sick), and cases where the test protocol had not been followed (e.g. child had just exercised, taken asthma or cold medication). These values were excluded. Exploration of remaining values showed high individual variability, which has been found to be the case for children in other studies [35]. As a result, we conducted a frequency analysis of individual cases. Previous research has established norms for cortisol levels for 5 to 10 year olds throughout the day in the $5^{th}$, $50^{th}$ and $95^{th}$ percentiles [27]. Interpolation between the $50^{th}$ and $95^{th}$

percentiles is nonlinear and would require complex modelling, so we chose the 50$^{th}$ percentile as a norm. Using this norm data we calculated thresholds for males and females for these cortisol-related dependent variables: 1) morning, 2) average daily and 3) daily decline based on our sample times. For each child and test point we determined if their cortisol variables were above the 50th percentile.

***RQ4:*** *What socio-technological processes may have influenced the intervention outcomes?* In order to address this question researchers, the EA and the facilitator took observational notes for sessions. We conducted three open-ended interviews with the facilitator and EA during the intervention, recorded on audio and with notes. We asked them to describe what they thought was working and not working in the intervention. We asked them about how each child was progressing and what was helping or not helping each child. We also interviewed the teacher of each child at pre, post and follow-up test points and asked questions about each child's ability to SR anxiety (e.g. *Does this child have challenges with anxiety or stress? Describe last month*) and about if they were using cues from the intervention to help the child, and if so, how that was working or not working (e.g. *If you referred to the posters or our system in any way during class time to remind this child to calm down, can you describe what happened?).*

**Analysis of interview and observational notes** included two researchers separately looking for common or interesting themes that highlighted how socio-technical factors may have impacted or mediated intervention outcomes at the group and individual level. We did member checking with resulting themes to improve validity.

## RESULTS

Analysis of detailed session notes taken by the facilitator revealed that all 10 children in the intervention group were able to complete 18 sessions. Each session included about 10 minutes of gameplay in the relax and sustained relaxation games. Children were able to achieve five tokens in each game in each session as well as talk about their anxiety and SR skills to some extent, varying by child.

**RQ1:** ***SR Anxiety*** Descriptive statistics comparing teachers' ratings on the Calm survey for each group at each test point are shown in Table 1. We ran a two-way mixed ANOVA on a sample of 19 participants (one child moved before post-test survey) to examine the effect of group and test points on average Calm score. Results indicated a significant interaction between the effects of group and test points on Calm score, $F(2,18) = 4.868$, $p = .041$ with a small effect size ($\eta^2_p = .222$). Simple main effects analysis showed no significant difference at pre or post-test between groups. Within group analysis showed that the intervention group improved significantly ($p = .010$), from pre to post-test. A t-test showed that this improvement was maintained ($p = 1.00$) at the follow-up test. In summary, the intervention group significantly improved in their ability to SR anxiety at school and gains were maintained over time.

| Measure | Group | Mean | Std. Dev. | N |
|---|---|---|---|---|
| Teacher *Calm @* Pretest | Interv'n | 2.88 | .945 | 10 |
| | Control | 3.11 | .574 | 9 |
| Teacher *Calm @* Post-test | Interv'n | 3.43 | .834 | 10 |
| | Control | 3.06 | .990 | 9 |
| Teacher *Calm @* Follow-up | Interv'n | 3.43 | .858 | 10 |
| | Control | N/A | N/A | 0 |

**Table 1. Teacher rating (1-5) ability to self-regulate anxiety.**

**RQ2: Anxious Behaviors** Descriptive statistics comparing teacher ratings of the BASC Anxiety subscale for each group at each test point are shown Table 2. Two-way mixed ANOVA results for average Anxiety score showed no significant effect of group on Anxiety $F(1,18) = .002$, $p = .969$) at either pre or post-test. In summary, the groups were equivalent at pretest as expected, but teachers did not see a change in the numbers or kinds of anxious behaviors over the course of the study between or within groups.

| Measure | Group | Mean | Std. Dev. | N |
|---|---|---|---|---|
| Teacher *Anxiety @* Pretest | Interv'n | 2.05 | .272 | 10 |
| | Control | 2.00 | .601 | 9 |
| Teacher *Anxiety @* Post-test | Interv'n | 1.99 | .301 | 10 |
| | Control | 2.06 | .571 | 9 |
| Teacher *Anxiety @* Follow-up | Interv'n | 2.05 | .319 | 10 |
| | Control | N/A | N/A | 0 |

**Table 2. Teacher BASC-3 rating (1-4) Anxiety.**

**RQ3. Stress Level** Case by case analysis of viable salivary cortisol samples indicated that at pretest **morning cortisol levels** were above the 50$^{th}$ percentile for over half the children in both groups (Table 3). At post-test this count dropped for the intervention group (4/10) and increased for the control group (8/10). At pre and post-test points, the **average daily cortisol** was above 50$^{th}$ percentile for both groups. At pretest, the expected **decline** in cortisol level over the day was only seen for one child. At post-test just over half (4/7) of the intervention group had the expected decline and only one in the control group. In summary, cortisol tests showed high variability, which impacted the average measure, and indicated reduced physiological stress in the morning and daily decline for the intervention group.

| Group | Morning | | Daily Ave | | Decline | |
|---|---|---|---|---|---|---|
| | pre | post | pre | post | pre | post |
| Interv'n | 6/9 | 4/10 | 7/8 | 4/4 | 1/8 | 4/7 |
| Control | 5/7 | 8/10 | 8/8 | 8/8 | 0/8 | 1/9 |

**Table 3. Count of cortisol variables above 50$^{th}$ percentile.**

**RQ4: Socio-Technological Processes** Three common themes that showed how socio-technological processes may have impacted the outcomes reported above emerged from thematic analysis of observations and interviews.

*System Mediated Multi-Modal Connections.* We noticed that the system was used as a reference for different modalities of communication to help children learn and apply the mind-body relationship in SR. For example, the facilitator noted that she often spent time before and during each game verbally describing and physically demonstrating how a child could use their body to SR while they played the games. We observed that the game animations of body-based enactment linked to brain state feedback helped children translate from words and physical descriptions to physical enactment of actions that helped them feel calmer. The facilitator also noted that some children reported that they had used SR strategies that they had discussed and physically practiced with the system later during an upsetting event (e.g. doing deep breathing and relaxing fists before getting a shot at the doctor's office, or sitting down and breathing slowly after tripping down the stairs). Conversely the facilitator noted that three (of 10) children, who struggled with the games or did not improve over time had trouble conceptually understanding and talking about the mind-body link. We suggest that the ways that the system mediated verbal and physical communication to make it concrete and experiential for children is an important element of the intervention.

Teachers also reported evidence that the system helped some but not all children learn both words and actions related to SR. For example, at post-test, a teacher reported that in a stressful situation with peers a child was more able than she had previously been to recognize and articulate how her body was feeling, and that she could transition and move through activities more smoothly when reminded to do breathing as she had in the sessions. At post-test teachers reported other effects related to children beginning to understand their mind-body relations and be able to talk about their emotions. One teacher said, "It's neat to see them understand how to regulate themselves." One teacher reported that a parent had noticed changes, "His mother - she said at home she was noticing that he can calm his emotions better, describe his emotions more and come up with strategies to calm himself." The teacher reported no change for other children, several of whom were not able to talk about what they felt nor enact SR strategies in the classroom even with support. It seems that the system provided a focus for only some children to learn to talk about body and mind connections, practice SR in ways that they could concretely experience these relations and subsequently verbally articulate how they were feeling.

*Customization, Adaptation and Rapport:* The facilitator reported that her ability to customize the brain state targets and difficulty of games in real time, without the child knowing helped her help the children complete the games. Sometimes this meant making a game slightly easier as time was running out. Other times it meant making games harder to keep the challenge level high. The facilitator also noted that for some children, who struggled, on some days she had to make the targets very low or the child would give up. She suggested a lack of attention and/or motivation rather than ability might be underlying some of these situations. It was also noted that sometimes this occurred when a child was having a very difficult day at school. Overall, the facilitator used this feature more extensively than we had envisioned. She also reported creating a light-hearted narrative around one of the games involving the squirrel and the monster because some of the children found the scenario frightening. Other children, mainly older boys, liked the monster character. Teachers also mentioned the need for customized and adapted approaches to learning SR. One teacher said, "It's good for them to learn different strategies because sometimes one strategy doesn't work."

An interesting related finding was that the facilitator reported that some of the children were not improving in gameplay but that their behavior in the sessions was improving. We suggest that this may be, in part, a result of the strong rapport established between the social worker and the children, which was commented on by many school staff, the children themselves and observed by the researchers. We also observed that strong rapport helped the facilitator learn worked for each child, trying different variations to respond to the child's needs, which often varied from day to day. The teachers also consistently said that the children enjoyed coming to the sessions and having one-on-one time with the facilitator. Based on these results we suggest that the ability to adapt to individual needs requires that a person who has strong rapport with the child rather than an algorithm drives the customization. In this light, we view our system, including child, facilitator, teacher and technology as a distributed learning system that adapts in real time to meet the needs of each child at each moment. How well the system components function together may dictate how effectively the child can learn to SR.

*Transfer: Looking Beyond the Technology.* Results from facilitator and teacher interviews provide insight into the ways that cueing students about the intervention helped them transfer their newly learned ability to SR into the classroom. Several teachers reported that reminding students to do breathing like in the relax games helped them remember and try to calm down. For example, one teacher said "If I can get to him before – before it escalates – to do his breathing it works. One time he was just about in tears and I said try your breathing that you do with the iPad and he did a deep breath and was able to do it, it was cool, he de-escalated." Similarly, another teacher reported, "It's getting better. His episodes are shorter and less frequent. Usually his head is against the wall and there's tears and I remind him to blow … he seems to get control faster." These findings highlight the importance of the teacher's attentiveness to the emotional state of the child, and that the timing of interaction with the child is critical to the child successfully applying skills learned through technology in the social context of a classroom. Conversely, teachers noted that if they didn't notice or intervened too late, it was likely that the child would not be able to SR on their own. When we looked at individual pre-post survey scores, we noted that two (of 10) children who did not improve on *SR Anxiety* were in a classroom where the teacher did not report using cues to help the children practice SR.

## DISCUSSION

This is the first study to show that it is viable for a non-clinically trained facilitator to use an EEG neurofeedback brain computer system in a school setting with young children. All 10 of the children in the intervention group were able to complete the 18 sessions. There was a significant interaction effect between time and group. Within group simple effects showed significant gains for *SR Anxiety*, which were maintained, as was seen in [3]. However, between group effects at post-test, were non-significant. An examination of the means showed little change in the control group means, a gain for the intervention group and high variability. The small sample size and non-blind raters may have impacted these results. In addition, other NF studies have identified responders and non-responders [10], and our analysis of facilitator notes and interview suggest that our *SR Anxiety* results were impacted by three non-responders. Teacher ratings of anxious behaviors (BASC) showed no change, which is in contrast to [32] in which both groups of older children were rated as improving. Stress as measured by cortisol tests showed gains for the intervention group for morning and daily decline after the intervention. We suggest that this may be in part from learning to SR, but is also likely in part, due to the impact of the strong rapport the children had with the facilitator and the break from classroom routines enabled by their 18 1:1 sessions. Follow-up analysis of stress would help disambiguate these factors.

We also found that socio-technological process factors that impacted both positive and negative outcomes included the ability of the children to learn to connect words, feelings, body sensations with self-regulation skills through NF and transfer of that learning to new situations with explicit and well timed support from teachers. Children that struggled conceptually or were less motivated or attentive in sessions often were those who had difficulty self-regulating in class. The rapport with the facilitator and her ability to adapt the system and protocol to meet individual needs was also likely critical to success. These findings are in line with other learning sciences research. The theory of mutual adaptation that posits interdependence in early learning can support children to be less dependent on their immediate environment (in our case the session) and more adaptive when they confront new environments (SR in the classroom) [33]. Similarly, much of the literature in experiential learning highlights the inter-relations of cognitive, body-based and affective modalities in learning and the need for concrete opportunities for transfer (e.g. [21]). Research on socio-emotional learning through games stress the importance of motivation and facilitator rapport [16]. Other research suggests that it is critical to train teachers to conduct transfer activities [36], which should ideally leverage existing classroom practices related to social-emotional learning adapted to experiences and language taken from the intervention. Children need considerable support to transfer what they learn in sessions and this component should be enhanced in future study designs.

Based on these preliminary findings we suggest a framework for mental health app development through the lens of distributed and adaptive systems where consideration is given to the inter-relations between people (child, teacher, facilitator), the activities (sessions, classroom) and technology (system, system as reference) all situated in a specific environment (school). Consideration should be given to the inter-relations between distributed components to ensure connection can be made through multimodal forms of communication and learning with resources dedicated to transfer activities. The system must be adaptable over time to respond to individual and changing needs of children with mental health challenges.

In contrast to the tradition of using clinical trials or controlled experiments to assess digital health interventions, our field-based results highlighted the importance of considering mediating socio-technological factors. Given the individual variability in our population sample, we suggest that in future evaluations using within group designs such as N-of-1 studies in which children are their own comparators, would enable researchers to look at individual change. In our study, the way our facilitator customized the intervention to meet the needs of individual children is a confounding factor that limits claims but suggests to us a more ethically sound approach to working with such vulnerable populations. We suggest purposely creating technologies and interventions that can be adapted throughout the study to mitigate risk and improve outcomes for high risk individuals.

## CONCLUSION

Despite the challenges of working with this population, we targeted them because we know that unmitigated early stress experiences can permanently impact the neurobiological systems involved in anxiety and stress regulation [12]. Using NF with commercially available EEG headsets on mobile devices children have, are familiar with, and have access to may provide a way to provide mental health support to many more children than can be supported in clinics or hospitals. Our research suggests that a mobile wearable NF app may be used in schools to help teach SR. Based on our work and that of others (e.g. [3,11,32]) we suggest taking a socio-technological approach to design and evaluation so that we move beyond only looking at outcomes measures to ensure we can effectively address the growing gap between mental health challenges and ehealth support services. We see this study as one small step in this emerging design space.

## ACKNOWLEDGEMENTS

Thanks to NSERC, Leslie Chesick, the Burnaby School District, Mia Cole for wrangling cortisol samples, and as always, special thanks to all children and their teachers.

## REFERENCES


[1] Alissa N. Antle. 2017. The ethics of doing research with vulnerable populations. *ACM Interactions* 24, 6:74-77.

[2] Alissa N. Antle, Leslie Chesick, and Elgin Skye McLaren. 2018. Opening up the design space of neurofeedback brain-computer interfaces for children. *ACM Transactions on Computer-Human Interaction* 24, 6: 1–38.

[3] Alissa N. Antle, Leslie Chesick, Srilekha Kirshnamachari Sridharan, and Emily Cramer. 2018. East meets west: A mobile brain-computer system that helps children living in poverty learn to self-regulate. *Personal and Ubiquitous Computing*: 1–28. https://doi.org/10.1007/s00779-018-1166-x

[4] Alissa N. Antle, Elgin Skye McLaren, Holly Fiedler, and Naomi Johnston. 2019. Evaluating the impact of a mobile neurofeedback app for young children at school and home. In *Proceedings of the Conference on Human Factors in Computing Systems* (CHI '19), in press.

[5] Katja Beesdo, Susanne Knappe, and Daniel S. Pine. 2009. Anxiety and anxiety disorders in children and adolescents: Developmental issues and implications for DSM-V. *Psychiatric Clinics of North America* 32, 3: 483-524.

[6] Ellen Drost. 2011. Validity and reliability in social science research. *Education Research & Perspectives* 38, 1: 105–123.

[7] Holger Gevensleben, Birgit Holl, Björn Albrecht, Claudia Vogel, Dieter Schlamp, Oliver Kratz, Petra Studer, Aribert Rothenberger, Gunther H. Moll, and Hartmut Heinrich. 2009. Is neurofeedback an efficacious treatment for ADHD? A randomised controlled clinical trial. *Journal of Child Psychology and Psychiatry* 50, 7: 780-789. https://doi.org/10.1111/j.1469-7610.2008.02033.x

[8] Holger Gevensleben, Maike Kleemeyer, Lillian Geza Rothenberger, Petra Studer, Andrea Flaig-Röhr, Gunther H. Moll, Aribert Rothenberger, and Hartmut Heinrich. 2014. Neurofeedback in ADHD: Further pieces of the puzzle. *Brain Topography* 27, 1: 20-32. https://doi.org/10.1007/s10548-013-0285-y

[9] John. H. Gruzelier, M. Foks, T. Steffert, M. J. -L. Chen, and T. Ros. 2014. Beneficial outcome from EEG-neurofeedback on creative music performance, attention and well-being in school children. *Biological Psychology* 95: 86-95. https://doi.org/10.1016/j.biopsycho.2013.04.005

[10] John H. Gruzelier. 2014. EEG-neurofeedback for optimising performance. III: A review of methodological and theoretical considerations. *Neuroscience & Biobehavioral Reviews 44*: 159-182. https://doi.org/10.1016/j.neubiorev.2014.03.015

[11] John H. Gruzelier. 2014. EEG-neurofeedback for optimising performance. I: A review of cognitive and affective outcome in healthy participants. *Neuroscience & Biobehavioral Reviews* 44: 124-141. https://doi.org/10.1016/j.neubiorev.2013.09.015

[12] Megan Gunnar and Karina Quevedo. 2007. The neurobiology of stress and development. *Annual Review of Psychology* 58, 1: 145-173. https://doi.org/10.1146/annurev.psych.58.110405.085605

[13] D. Corydon Hammond. 2005. Neurofeedback with anxiety and affective disorders. *Child and Adolescent Psychiatric Clinics of North America* 14, 1: 105-123.

[14] Kirsten Hanrahan, Ann Marie McCarthy, Charmaine Kleiber, Susan Lutgendorf, and Eva Tsalikian. 2006. Strategies for salivary cortisol collection and analysis in research with children. *Applied Nursing Research* 19, 2: 95-101.

[15] Amanda G. Harmon, Leah C. Hibel, Olga Rumyantseva, and Douglas A. Granger. 2007. Measuring salivary cortisol in studies of child development: Watch out—what goes in may not come out of saliva collection devices. *Developmental Psychobiology* 49, 5: 495-500.

[16] Robyn Hromek and Sue Roffey. 2009. Promoting social and emotional learning with games: "It's fun and we learn things." *Simulation & Gaming* 40, 5: 626-644. https://doi.org/10.1177/1046878109333793

[17] Jin Huang, Chun Yu, Yuntao Wang, Yuhang Zhao, Siqi Liu, Chou Mo, Jie Liu, Lie Zhang, and Yuanchun Shi. 2014. FOCUS: Enhancing children's engagement in reading by using contextual BCI training sessions. In *Proceedings of the Conference on Human Factors in Computing Systems* (CHI '14), 1905-1908.

[18] Alice F. Jackson and Donald J. Bolger. 2014. The neurophysiological bases of EEG and EEG measurement: A review for the rest of us. *Psychophysiology* 51, 11: 1061-1071. https://doi.org/10.1111/psyp.12283

[19] Stuart J. Johnstone, Steven J. Roodenrys, Kirsten Johnson, Rebecca Bonfield, and Susan J. Bennett. 2017. Game-based combined cognitive and neurofeedback training using Focus Pocus reduces symptom severity in children with diagnosed AD/HD and subclinical AD/HD. *International Journal of Psychophysiology* 116: 32-44.

[20] Michele Knox, J. Lentini, T.S. Cummings, A. McGrady, K. Whearty, and L. Sancrant. 2011. Game-based biofeedback for paediatric anxiety and depression. *Mental Health in Family Medicine* 8, 3: 195.

[21] David. Kolb. 1984. *Experiential Learning: Experience as the Source of Learning and Development.* Prentice-Hall, Englewood Cliffs, NJ, USA.

[22] Choon Guan Lim, Tih-Shih Lee, Cuntai Guan, Sheng Fung DS, Yin Bun Cheung, S. S. Teng, Haihong Zhang, and K. Ranga Krishnan. 2017. Effectiveness of a brain-computer interface based programme for the treatment of ADHD: a pilot study. *Psychopharmacol Bull.* 43, 1: 73-82.

[23] Jared A. Lisonbee, Jacquelyn Mize, Amie Lapp Payne, and Douglas A. Granger. 2008. Children's cortisol and the quality of teacher–child relationships in child care. *Child Development* 79, 6: 1818-1832.

[24] Sonia. J. Lupien, Suzanne King, Michael J. Meaney, and Bruce S. Mcewen. 2001. Can poverty get under your skin? Basal cortisol levels and cognitive function in children from low and high socioeconomic status. *Development and Psychopathology* 13, 3: 653-676.

[25] John S. March. 2011. Looking to the future of research in pediatric anxiety disorders. *Depression and Anxiety* 28, 1: 88-98. https://doi.org/10.1002/da.20754

[26] Ann Marie McCarthy, Kirsten Hanrahan, Charmaine Kleiber, M. Bridget Zimmerman, Susan Lutgendorf, and Eva Tsalikian. 2009. Normative salivary cortisol values and responsivity in children. *Applied Nursing Research : ANR* 22, 1: 54. https://doi.org/10.1016/j.apnr.2007.04.009

[27] Robert Miller, Tobias Stalder, Marc Jarczok, David M. Almeida, Ellena Badrick, Meike Bartels, Dorret I. Boomsma, Christopher L. Coe, Marieke C. J. Dekker, Bonny Donzella, Joachim E. Fischer, Megan R. Gunnar, Meena Kumari, Florian Lederbogen, Christine Power, Carol D. Ryff, S. V. Subramanian, Henning Tiemeier, Sarah E. Watamura, and Clemens Kirschbaum. 2016. The CIRCORT database: Reference ranges and seasonal changes in diurnal salivary cortisol derived from a meta-dataset comprised of 15 field studies. *Psychoneuroendocrinology* 73: 16-23. https://doi.org/10.1016/j.psyneuen.2016.07.201

[28] Eva Oberle and Kimberly A. Schonert-Reichl. 2016. Stress contagion in the classroom? The link between classroom teacher burnout and morning cortisol in elementary school students. *Social Science & Medicine* 159: 30-37.

[29] Ken Porter. 2015 Mental Health Care System Survey Results. Mood Disorders Society of Canada. Retrieved November 12, 2018 from https://mdsc.ca/research/2015-mental-health-care-system-survey-results/

[30] Robert Reiner. 2008. Integrating a portable biofeedback device into clinical practice for patients with anxiety disorders: results of a pilot study. *Applied Psychophysiology and Biofeedback* 33, 1: 55-61. https://doi.org/10.1007/s10484-007-9046-6

[31] Cecil R. Reynolds, Randy W. Kamphaus, and Kimberly J. Vannest. 2011. Behavior Assessment System for Children (BASC). In *Encyclopedia of Clinical Neuropsychology.* Springer, New York, NY, 366-371. https://doi.org/10.1007/978-0-387-79948-3_1524

[32] Elke A. Schoneveld, Monique Malmberg, Anna Lichtwarck-Aschoff, Geert P. Verheijen, Rutger C. M. E. Engels, and Isabela Granic. 2016. A neurofeedback video game (MindLight) to prevent anxiety in children: A randomized controlled trial. *Computers in Human Behavior* 63: 321-333. https://doi.org/10.1016/j.chb.2016.05.005

[33] David. L. Schwartz and Taylor. Martin. 2006. Distributed learning and mutual adaptation. *Pragmatics & Cognition* 14, 2: 313-332.

[34] Stuart Shanker. 2010. Self-regulation: calm, alert and learning. *Education Canada* 50, 3: 105-138.

[35] Elizabeth A. Shirtcliff, Amber L. Allison, Jeffrey M. Armstrong, Marcia J. Slattery, Ned H. Kalin, and Marilyn J. Essex. 2012. Longitudinal stability and developmental properties of salivary cortisol levels and circadian rhythms from childhood to adolescence. *Developmental Psychobiology* 54, 5: 493-502. https://doi.org/10.1002/dev.20607

[36] Petr Slovák and Geraldine Fitzpatrick. 2015. Teaching and developing social and emotional skills with technology. *ACM Transactions on Computer-Human Interaction* 22, 4: 19. https://doi.org/10.1145/2744195

[37] Naomi J. Steiner, Elizabeth C. Frenette, Kirsten M. Rene, Robert T. Brennan, and Ellen C. Perrin. 2014. Neurofeedback and cognitive attention training for children with attention-deficit hyperactivity disorder in schools. Journal of Developmental & Behavioral Pediatrics 35, 1: 18-27.

[38] Madelon A. Vollebregt, Martine van Dongen-Boomsma, Dorine Slaats-Willemse, and Jan K. Buitelaar. 2014. What future research should bring to help resolving the debate about the efficacy of EEG-neurofeedback in children with ADHD. *Frontiers in Human Neuroscience* 8: 321.

# Co-creation of a Transitional Smart Sculpture for Voice changes

Ambre Davat[1,2,3] Alain Quercia[3] Véronique Aubergé[2,3] Natacha Borel[2,3] Gang Feng[1]

[1]Univ. Grenoble Alpes, CNRS, Grenoble INP*, GIPSA-lab, Grenoble, France
[2]Univ. Grenoble Alpes, CNRS, Grenoble INP*, LIG, Grenoble, France
[3]APORIA project

ambre.davat@grenoble-inp.fr; querciaalain@gmail.com; veronique.auberge@univ-grenoble-alpes.fr; borelnata@gmail.com; gang.feng@grenoble-inp.fr

* Institute of Engineering Univ. Grenoble Alpes

## ABSTRACT
Aporia is a pluridisciplinary adaptation of a play of Bernard-Marie Koltès, led by plastic artist Alain Quercia in a live performance mixing different Art expressions, Scientific theories and Technologies. To propose original reflections about "otherness", the unique actor of this project embodies in turn all the characters of the play. His performance is supported by real-time pitch-shifting software, which allows him to modify his own voice without affecting its emotional details. These voice changes are remotely controlled by a smart sculpture integrated to the staging. In this paper, we present the used voice processing tool and the iterative co-design of the remote controller in collaboration with the director of Aporia.

## Author Keywords
Co-construction, time-stretching, voice changes, smart sculpture.

## CCS Concepts
• Applied computing~Performing arts

## INTRODUCTION
The work presented here concerns a shared approach integrating a research team and a plastic artist in the artistic project Aporia, aimed to stage a Bernard-Marie Koltès' theater play. New smart tools were developed in order to augment the artistic expression of Alain Quercia, the director of the project and unique actor of the play. In particular, the voice of the plastic artist is digitally modified to help him to embody his characters and to trigger questions about the line between biological reality and artifactual augmentation of human skills. Moreover, both the artistic team and the research team are driven by reflections on the nature of human interactions, otherness and altruism. The underlying question is ultimately whether self-consciousness is an illusion or a reality. In this context, the tool described hereunder needs to be considered not only as augmenting the artistic expression, but as augmenting too the project meaning:

- This theater play is supported by a single actor, who is the plastic artist directing Aporia. His acting performance is to "sculpt" the voices of his characters with the help of the presented tool.
- This actor can express to the spectators both his own voice and each transformed voice embodying each character.
- Each voice transformation must absolutely conserve, in details, the emotional prosodic changes controlled by the actor when changing characters (dynamicity of intensity, fundamental frequency, rhythm and voice quality). That is one main scientific purpose of the scientific team.
- The artifactual voices must be identified as possible natural voices.
- Switching between characters must be controlled with a smart object easy to use by the actor, as well as easily perceivable and artistically understandable by the spectators.
- The delay between these two voices must be meaningful in terms of artistic contain, ergonomically usable by the actor, and perceptively acceptable for spectators,

Fulfilling the objectives listed above posed a real challenge from both the technical and the artistic point of views. Thus we will first present a quick overview of ready-to-use technologies for voice transformation. Our own algorithm will then be described in more details. Lastly, we will present the co-construction of the tangible interface used for remote control.


*TEI '19, March 17–20, 2019, Tempe, AZ, USA*

ACM 978-1-4503-6196-5/19/03...$15.00
https://doi.org/10.1145/3294109.3295654

## EXISTING TECHNOLOGIES

Voice effects are regularly used in live performances, especially for music. Ready-available technologies can be separated in two categories: hardware versus software.

### Vocal effects processors

Effects units are commonly used to alter the sound of electronic instruments, but can also be employed to modify the voice of a singer. They consist of analog and digital circuitries which are plugged between the instrument/microphone and the loudspeaker. They exist in different size and shape: in particular, effects pedals are small embedded effects units, which can be controlled by the musician with the foot. Some effects units are especially designed for voice: they are called "vocal effects processors". Examples of available effects are equalization, pitch-shifter and vocoder effect.

Equalization consists in modifying the timbre of a sound, by amplifying or attenuating some frequency bands. Tuning an equalizer requires a specific expertise, and when used on voice, it can lead to unwanted artefacts, such that muffled sound or "radio effect".

A vocoder is a speech compression method, which can be used to create robotic voices, whose pitch is controlled by playing notes on a synthesizer. This effect can be heard for instance in Daft Punk's song "Harder Better Faster".

Pitch-shifters are used to increase or decrease the frequency of a sound. The simplest pitch-shifter is the octaver which can only halve or double the pitch. More sophisticated pitch-shifters digitally process the signal to change its pitch. Generally, the pitch-shifter of an effect unit is limited to a preset of musical intervals indicated in half steps, one half step being the smallest musical interval in Western music and corresponding to a shift of around 6 % in frequency. For example, we tested a Boss Super Shifter PS-5, whose presets are limited to (+/-) 1, 2, 5, 7, 12 or 24 half steps, which means a shift of (+/-) 6, 12, 33, 50, 100 or 300 % of the initial pitch. If the latency of this device is very low, the modified voice sounds more metallic and less dynamic than the natural voice.

### Voice changer software

Nowadays, audio effects can be performed by specialized software in post-production or in real-time. Some software goes even further than traditional vocal effects processors. For example, the plugin TRAX developed by the IRCAM is able to realize fine and realistic modifications of the speech signal, including transformation of the speaker's size, gender and age [6]. However, even if this plugin works in real-time, the latency is 9792 samples at 44,1 kHz, which means a delay of around 220 ms between the recorded and the modified sound. Such delay makes it problematic to use in a live theater performance, because the spectators will hear both the voice of the actor and the modified voice emitted by loudspeakers.

Since July 2018, a powerful tool for voice transformation is available open-source: STRAIGHT legacy [4]. It is a collection of Matlab programs developed at the Wakayama University, which can especially be used to manipulate voice quality, timbre or pitch. A real-time implementation of STRAIGHT was already proposed in 2007 [1], but with a downgraded voice quality due to the necessary simplifications of the algorithm (see [3] for a demonstration). Another promising open-source software written in Matlab and C is WORLD [10] (D4C edition [9]): a vocoder-based system which realizes high-quality voice synthesis in real-time and faster than STRAIGHT. Its authors announced that they intended to use it for voice conversion and to implement it on other platforms [10], so it could be used in Web applications or embedded systems.

## A REAL-TIME PITCH-SHIFTER BASED ON A TIME DOMAIN APPROACH WITHOUT PITCH DETECTION

The first version of our pitch-shifting algorithm was initially proposed by Gang Feng. It was implemented in real-time [2] in order to make the voice of a human sounds like the voice of a small robot in Wizard of Oz experiments [12].

This pitch-shifting algorithm is much simpler than the voice changer software cited previously, but enough to create realistic voices, when used with moderation. It is based on a time-domain approach and is very suitable for real-time implementation.

### Time-stretching

The simplest way to change the pitch of a sound signal is to change its playback speed. Indeed, slowing down a sound signal lowers its pitch, while accelerating increases it. This technique existed before the development of digital pitch-shifters and was notably used in 1958 by Ross Bagdasarian to create the high pitch voices of the "Chipmunks". However, the actor had to sing slowly during the recording, so that his accelerated voice has a normal tempo.

In order to preserve the original tempo, the sound has to be lengthened/shortened before changing its playback speed. This can be achieved with a time-stretching algorithm. A classical method for time-stretching is called Pitch Synchronous Overlap-Add (PSOLA) [11] and is illustrated in Figure 1a). The idea is first to identify voiced segments of the recording, where the vocal cords are vibrating. In these voiced segments, the pitch value $T_1$ is estimated and windows covering two pseudo-periods of the signal are extracted.

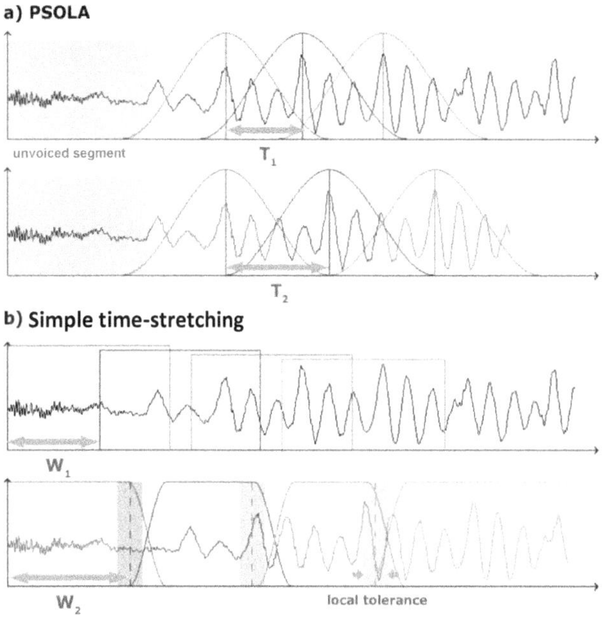


**Figure 1. Comparison of two methods of time-stretching: a) PSOLA and b) our algorithm**

**In both case, the pitch after resampling would be multiplied by $T_1 / T_2 = W_1 / W_2$.**

Then, the positions of these windows are shifted, in order to increase/reduce the local pseudo-period of the signal to $T_2$. Finally, the junction between successive windows is made with an overlap: each window is multiplied by a Hanning window in order to smoothly joint with other windows after they are all combined.

Our time-stretching algorithm is original because it does not require pitch estimation. As shown in Figure 1b), it consists in cutting the speech signal into overlapping windows. All these windows are then shifted in time to make the resulting signal as long as expected. The difficulty lies in how to stick the windows together. A simple overlap is not enough, because there is no reason for the signal to be at the same phase at the end of one window and the beginning of the next one. So, windows are not moved with a fixed duration of time $\Delta W = W_2 - W_1$, but just roughly moved around $\Delta W$. A cross-correlation between successive windows is computed, and its local maxima indicate the best positions to join the two windows. In fact, we use a weighting on the cross-correlation to find the maximum closest from the approximate position of the window. This maximum is used to estimate the exact position of the second window. At last, an overlap is used to assure a smooth junction between the windows.

### Real-time implementation

An algorithm must fulfil two criteria before it can be implemented in real-time. Firstly, it has to be adapted to a buffer-by-buffer processing, so each time data are recorded on the input buffer, the output buffer can be filled with modified data. Secondly, the time required to process one

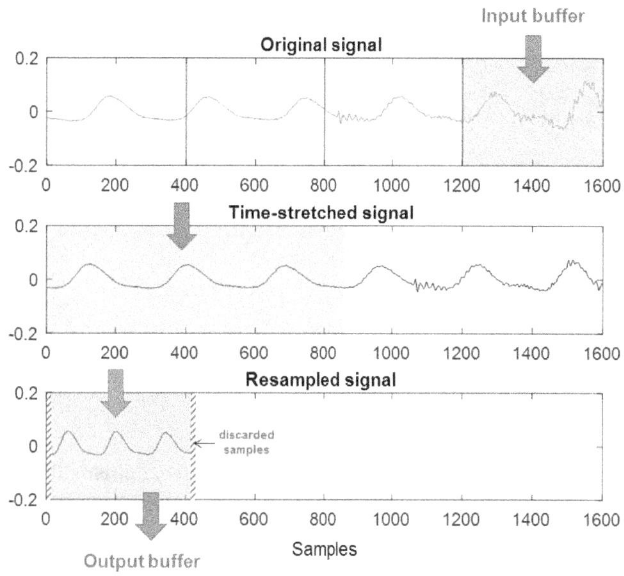


**Figure 2. Illustration of the real-time processing. The original signal is recorded buffer-by-buffer (top). Several buffers are used to compute the time-stretched signal (middle), which is resampled to fill the output buffer (bottom).**

buffer must be shorter than the recording time, so the stream can be processed without interruption or data loss.

Our time-stretching algorithm already used a frame-by-frame architecture, so it can easily be implemented in real-time (Figure 2). The tricky part is changing playback speed to perform pitch-shifting. This is realized by a resampling, which has to be adapted to a buffer-by-buffer processing. Indeed, resampling implies a filtering, which induces side effects. So when a time-stretched buffer is resampled, some samples at the beginning and at the end of the signal are corrupted. A solution consists in taking a slightly wider window which is centered on the buffer to be processed. After resampling this window, the additional samples are cut to conserve only those which are used to fill the output buffer.

This algorithm requires less computational time than the PSOLA algorithm, because there is no detection of voiced segments and no pitch estimation. However, both methods have an inherent delay which cannot be reduced, because they requires several periods of the original signal to compute the time-stretched signal. For example, to increase the pitch of a voice from 100 Hz to 200 Hz, the signal length has to be doubled. Therefore, the input buffer size must be at least 10 ms, which is the duration of one period of the original signal. In practice, several buffers are kept in memory to avoid distortions due to bad joining, as shown in Figure 3.

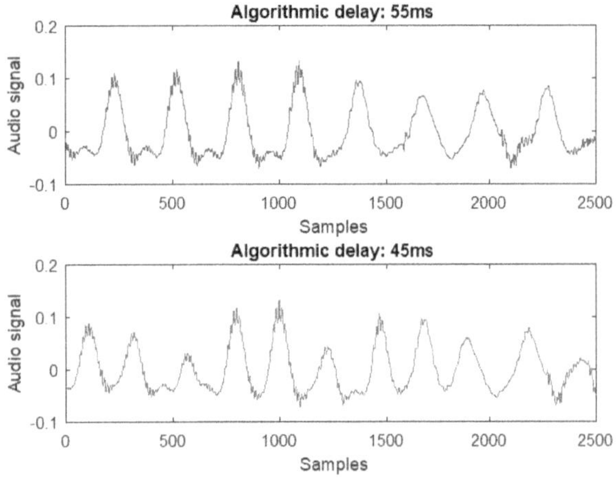


**Figure 3. Example of time-stretched signals for a pitch-shift of 90% with a sufficient algorithmic delay (top) and an insufficient algorithmic delay (bottom).**

### Voice quality

The best sensor for assessing sound quality is ear, so we invite the readers to listen to the recordings of the project which are available at Alain Quercia's Vimeo account https://vimeo.com/user57417934. The video "*Aporia et ses voix*" demonstrates the voice transformations and is subtitled in English. There is also a trailer of the project, which was filmed during the premiere at the Est Theater. These recordings are free from any glitch due to resampling or real-time processing.

However, contrary to more sophisticated algorithms, our pitch-shifter multiplies all the frequencies of the speech signal by a factor, not only the fundamental one. The timbre of the voice is therefore altered, which can make it sounds artificial. For instance, with a pitch-shift of +50% or more, it sounds like the speaker is inhaling helium. However, if the pitch-shift is light, this timbre alteration does not sound as an artefact, and even contributes to the voice individuality.

The settings chosen for the four characters of the play are reported in Table 1. These voice transformations should be seen as costumes, which are used by the actor to get into role and make switching between characters obvious to the spectators. In no way is it intended to serve as a substitute for the acting. In fact, the software is only used to alter the physical properties of the speech organs, while the most important factor of voice individuality is probably the speaking style, or vocal prosody: it is what imitators copy when they mimic someone [5].

These voice transformations had then to be integrated to the staging, in order to be usable by the actor and understandable to the public. We will now present the design of their remote controller.

| Character | Alboury | Horn | Cal | Léone |
|---|---|---|---|---|
| Pitch shift (%) | - 10 | -2 | +10 | +20 |

**Table 1. Pitch transformations for the four characters of the play**

## CO-CONSTRUCTION OF A SMART SCULPTURE

In practice (see sensors could have their size and place easily adjusted on the scepter, so we could quickly test several configurations. We agreed on one configuration before the residence of June 2018, but on the first rehearsal, we immediately concluded that four buttons asked too much mental load for the artist. Moreover, these buttons didn't provide any feedback indicating if they had been touched correctly, which made them hard to use and prone to selection errors.

), the actor's voice is recorded with a skin-colored headset microphone connected to a radio transmitter. The radio receiver sends the signal to an analog-to-digital converter connected to a computer, on which runs the real-time voice transformations software. The processed speech is then converted from digital to analog and played on a loudspeaker.

The first artistic residence of Aporia happened in September 2016 in the experimental platform Domus-LIG. The creator of Aporia was then the stage director, and the three male characters were played by a professional actor. During these early tests, switching between voices was controlled by a technician, following the text of the play and clicking on a three-buttons interface to select the current character. Immediately, it became clear that these transitions had to be directly controlled by the actor via a physical object. Moreover, this remote controller had to be integrated to the staging, so voice transformations would become tangible for the public.

Different aspects of the evolution of this object are described below. They are presented by topics for a purpose of clarity, but in practice, they resulted from a co-construction in iterative loop and were not separated during this process. The design of the remote interface was supported by the academic fab lab fabMSTIC, and tested in the experimental platform Domus-LIG and on stage during artistic residences in two theaters: *Le Prunier Sauvage* and *Est (Grenoble Alpes University)*.

### Hardware and software

The remote controller holds a low cost Wi-Fi microchip ESP8266 powered by a rechargeable battery. This microcontroller is programmed with the Arduino Software IDE to connect to a Wi-Fi network and initiate a client-server communication. The client is a C++ program running on a computer connected to the same Wi-Fi network, which listens to the information transmitted by the ESP8266. Each

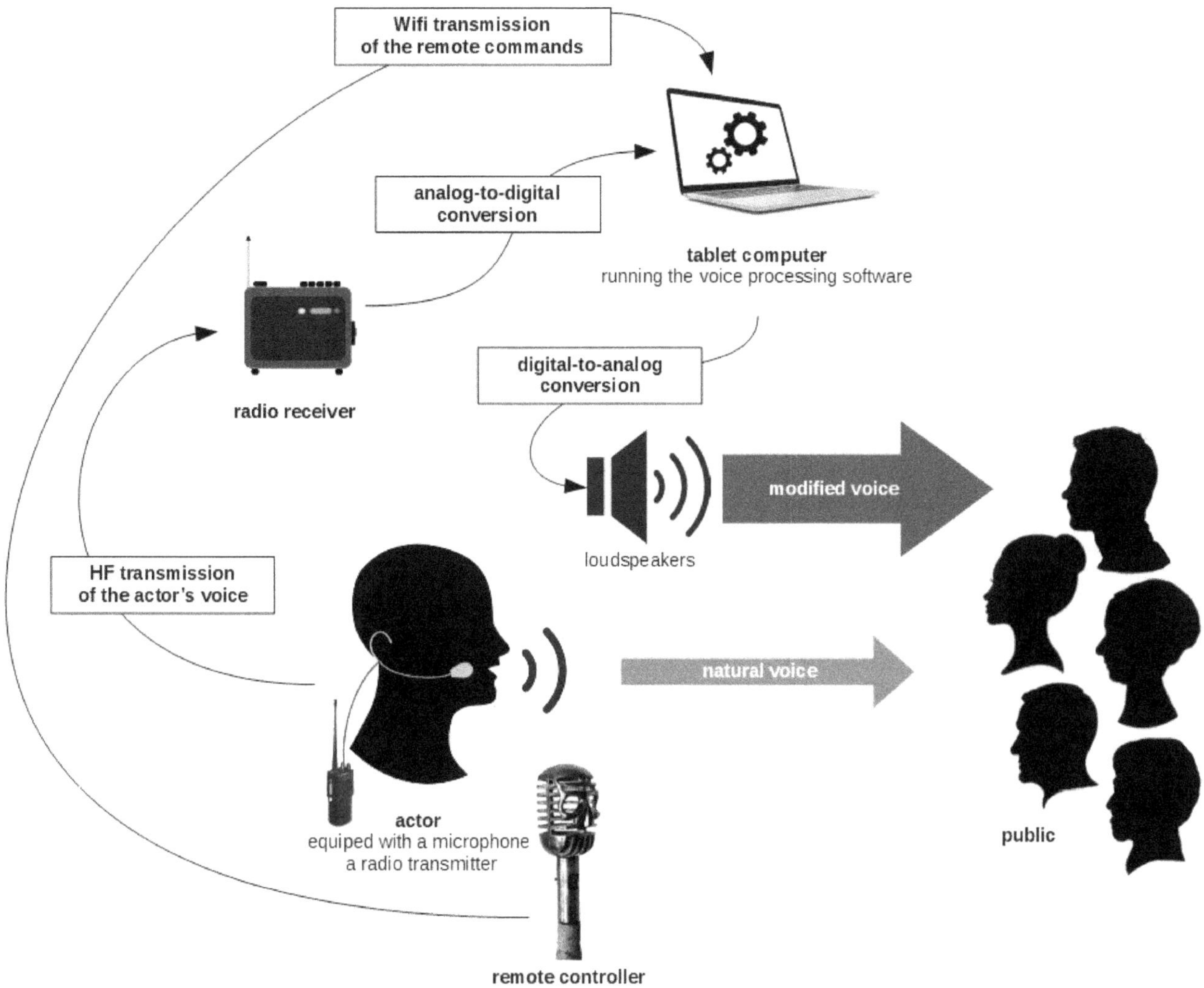


**Figure 4. Set up of the voice changes**

time a button is pushed, the client runs a new voice transformation process, and kills the previous one.

### Design

A first draft of the object was proposed by Alain Quercia in May 2017 (Figure 5.a). It was a mix of a vintage microphone and a skull. Four buttons were placed on the stick to select each character. Based on this illustration, the artist sculpted a 3D-model in polypropylene, which was converted in a digital model with a 3D-scanner (Figure 5.b). This digital model was simplified and corrected manually with Blender in order to be printed in 3D (Figure 5.c). The handle was directly designed from basic 3D objects.

The use of 3D models facilitated prototyping, because we could easily modify the shape of the object by changing its proportions, then visualize these modifications and print low-cost prototypes. In particular, the size of the skull has shrunk and its proportions were corrected so that it looks more like a knob which can be put on a wooden stick. Once the agreement was reached on the shape of the remote controller, the 3D printing was polished and sent to a foundry to obtain a tin casting (Figure 5.f).

### Usability

The first prototype was a four buttons remote controller (Figure 5.d), each button corresponding to one character. However, the handle was very large and the four buttons could be difficult to reach and to memorize by the actor.

With the second prototype, the handle was narrower and we tested another type of buttons, based on capacitive sensors. They consisted in small pieces of copper foil, sensitive to touch, even when covered with fabric (Figure 5.e). These sensors could have their size and place easily adjusted on the scepter, so we could quickly test several configurations. We agreed on one configuration before the residence of June 2018, but on the first rehearsal, we immediately concluded that four buttons asked too much mental load for the artist. Moreover, these buttons didn't provide any feedback indicating if they had been touched correctly, which made them hard to use and prone to selection errors.

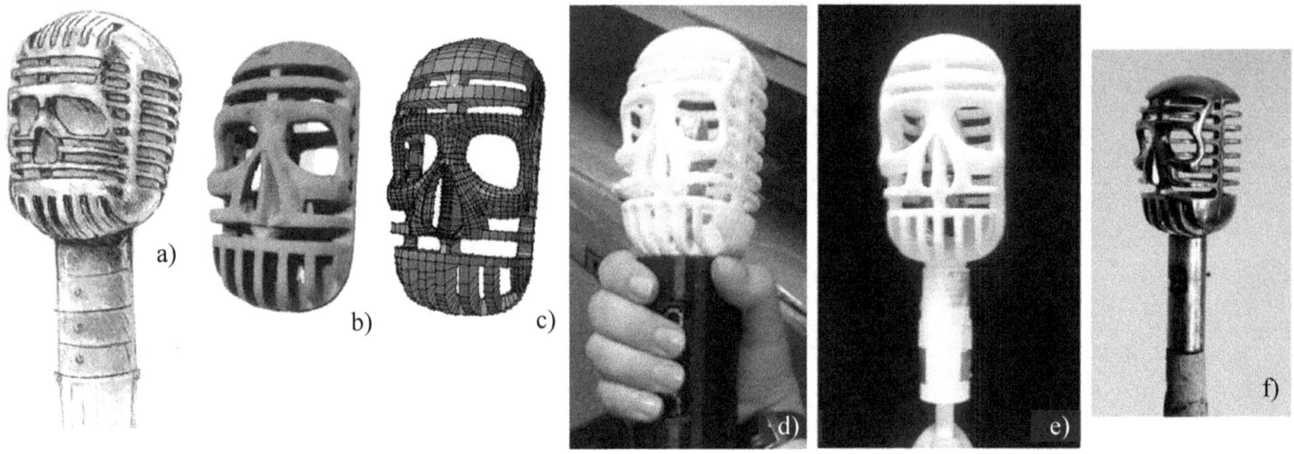


**Figure 5. Evolution of the connected scepter:**
**a) draft – b) polypropylene sculpture – c) 3D model – d) first prototype – e) second prototype – f) tin casting**

As there are only two characters in each scene, we decided to use only two buttons. The interface of the C++ program was upgraded in order to make a technician able to select the available characters at the beginning of each scene. However, two buttons were always difficult to use, because the grip of the artist over the stick could easily move during the play. One push button to shift from one character to the other one was not enough, because the artist needed to be sure of which one is selected in case of inattention.

At last, we chose to use a switch with two positions: the upper position being for the character with the higher pitch. This solution not only allows the user to alternate between two characters with only one button, but also records the last selection. The mental load of the actor is therefore greatly reduced, so he can put more attention on the acting, which improves his performance.

### Demountability

The prototypes had to be dismountable, so the microchip could be updated or the electronic circuit replaced in case of failure. First, we used hot melt glue gun to stick the skull and the handle together. This glue could be removed with some effort by using a cutter. For the next prototypes, we used a screw-nut system to simplify the assembly/disassembly process: when combined, the front and back sides of the skull form a thread which can be screwed onto the handle.

### Robustness

The final prototype was extensively tested before and during rehearsals. However, we could not avoid the risk of breaking the scepter if it fell, or the risk of forgetting to recharge its battery. Therefore, the 3D printing used to cast the tin prototype was used to build a spare scepter. The software of both the scepter and the tablet running the voice processing algorithm was also updated, so their roles in the client-server communication were inverted. Indeed, initially, the tablet was connected to the scepter, so if the scepter broke down, the voice processing software would have to be manually relaunched before connecting to the spare scepter, which took some time. The software was therefore corrected: the tablet software is launched first and works as a server. It listens to every new connection of a scepter on its IP address, and takes into account only the commands of the last connected scepter.

### Latency

The first real-time implementation of our pitch-shifting algorithm was done with Matlab, using the Digital Signal Processing Library [13] which provides tools for real-time processing of audio streams. For the Aporia project, a new implementation in C++ was realized with free libraries. For resampling, we used the libresample library [7]. For audio input and output, the OpenAl library was initially chosen, because it is cross-platform [14]. However, we could not fully control the size of the buffers used by the audio devices, so the latency was about 190 ms (this latency can be observed on the demonstration video of the project [15]). In order to reduce this latency, another implementation was tested, using the simple pulseaudio library [16]. We managed to reduce the latency to an average of 100 ms without altering the voice. During the rehearsal of October 2018, the program was running on a convertible laptop with a Linux distribution. The processor was an Intel Core M, made for low energy consumption, so the software should run on any recent computer.

## RESULTS

### User Feedback

The pitch-shifter software was first used by a professional actor, who was very annoyed by the latency. He constantly had to pay attention not to stutter, which was exhausting for him. Alain Quercia has less difficulty to use the software, either with high or low latency, because he manages not to focus on his modified voice. This ease may also be explained by the fact that he has little experience on performing, and therefore no habits to disturb. On the contrary, we found that the voice transformations help him to embody his characters. Indeed, we observed that when he plays a character with a wrong voice without realizing it, it affects his acting abilities.

### Public reaction

In June 2018 a rehearsal of the full play took place in front of a small audience. The feedbacks of the spectators were positive. Even those who did not know the play understood the plot and were not lost by the role changes. At this time the latency between the natural voice and the modified voice was around 190 ms, which means that the voice of the characters were clearly delayed from the lip movements. However, the public could easily separate the two voices, and chose to focus on the louder one alone.

Other rehearsals were conducted in October 2018, followed by a premiere attended by around 150 spectators. A third of them was on stage with the performer, while the others were sitting on the seats. This time, the latency of the pitch-shifter was reduced to around 100 ms. The desynchronization between lips movement and sound was therefore less perceptible, but the risk of confusion between the two voices was bigger. The loudness of the modified voice was also increased in order to mask the natural voice. This time, people in the stands were able to ignore the natural voice. However, those who were close to the performer found very exhausting to separate the two voices. Some of them reported that they had the impression that the loudspeakers were broadcasting both the modified and unmodified voices, as if they were echoes of the voice of the actor.

## CONCLUSION AND OUTLOOK

While musicians can use effect units and computers as instruments on stage, the use of a voice processing tool in theatre is constrained by the necessary integration of this technological device in the staging. Using a home-made pitch-shifter instead of a commercial solution allowed us to co-construct a tailor-made interface for the project Aporia, which matches the artistic outlines listed in the introduction. The final object is a smart sculpture and is fully part of the attire of the actor.

However, the unavoidable latency of this device makes it problematic if the performer wants to invite his spectators on stage. Indeed, the modified voice mixed with the natural voice makes its understanding more difficult. Audio-visual interferences may also occur [8]. In order to reduce these interferences, we plan to design a mask which would muffle his voice and hide his lips.

## ACKNOWLEDGEMENTS

This project would not have been possible without the support of the fabMSTIC and its managers: Jérôme Maisonnasse and Germain Lemasson. The authors also want to thank Philippe Rene Marin for teaching us the use of the 3D-Scanner, and Bastien Scher to polish up the 3D-model. We are very grateful to the cultural institutions which supported Aporia in successive residences, after the first one at Domus-LIG: *Le Prunier Sauvage* and *Est (Grenoble Alpes University)*.

## REFERENCES

[1] Hideki Banno, Hiroaki Hata, Masanori Morise, Toru Takahashi, Toshio Irino, and Hideki Kawahara. 2007. Implementation of realtime STRAIGHT speech manipulation system: Report on its first implementation. *Acoust. Sci. Technol.* 28, 3 (2007), 140–146. DOI:https://doi.org/10.1250/ast.28.140

[2] Ambre Davat. *Développement d'une application temps réel de conversion de voix pour un robot compagnon (Development of a real-time voice conversion software for a robot companion)*. Internship report. Grenoble INP.

[3] Hideki Kawahara. 2006. *Demonstration of real-time version of STRAIGHT running on a tablet computer.* Retrieved January 5, 2018 from http://www.wakayama-u.ac.jp/~kawahara/STRAIGHTadv/Resources/realtime STRAIGHTwm.wmv

[4] Hideki Kawahara. 2018. STRAIGHT, a speech analysis, modification and synthesis system. Retrieved from http://www.wakayama-u.ac.jp/~kawahara/STRAIGHTadv/index_e.html

[5] Hisao Kuwabara and Yoshinori Sagisak. 1995. Acoustic characteristics of speaker individuality: Control and conversion. *Speech Commun.* 16, 2 (February 1995), 165–173. DOI:https://doi.org/10.1016/0167-6393(94)00053-D

[6] Pierre Lanchantin, Snorre Farner, Christophe Veaux, Gilles Degottex, Nicolas Obin, Grégory Beller, Fernando Villavicencio, Stefan Huber, Geoffroy Peeters, Axel Roebel, and Xavier Rodet. 2011. Vivos Voco: A survey of recent research on voice transformation at IRCAM. In *International Conf on Digital Audio Effects*, 277–285. Retrieved January 5, 2019 from https://hal.archives-ouvertes.fr/hal-01161300

[7] Dominic Mazzoni. libresample: Real-time library interface. Retrieved January 5, 2019 from https://github.com/minorninth/libresample

[8] Harry Mcgurk and John Macdonald. 1976. Hearing lips and seeing voices. *Nature* 264, 5588 (December 1976), 746–748. DOI:https://doi.org/10.1038/264746a0

[9] Masanori Morise. 2016. D4C, a band-aperiodicity estimator for high-quality speech synthesis. *Speech Commun.* 84, (November 2016), 57–65. DOI:https://doi.org/10.1016/j.specom.2016.09.001

[10] Masanori Morise, Fumiya Yokomori, and Kenji Ozawa. 2016. WORLD: A Vocoder-Based High-Quality Speech Synthesis System for Real-Time

Applications. *IEICE Trans. Inf. Syst.* 99, (2016), 1877–1884. DOI:https://doi.org/10.1587/transinf.2015EDP7457

[11] Allam Mousa. 2010. Voice Conversion Using Pitch Shifting Algorithm by Time Stretching with PSOLA and Re-Sampling. *J. Electr. Eng.* 61, 1 (January 2010), 57–61. DOI:https://doi.org/10.2478/v10187-010-0008-5

[12] Yuko Sasa. 2018. *Intelligence Socio-Affective pour un Robot : primitives langagières pour une interaction évolutive d'un robot de l'habitat intelligent (Socio-affective Intelligence for a Robot: language primitives for evolving interaction with a robot companion in smart home)*. Ph.D Dissertation. Grenoble Alpes University. Retrieved January 5, 2019 from https://tel.archives-ouvertes.fr/tel-01945238/document

[13] MATLAB Digital Signal Processing (DSP) library. Retrieved from. Retrieved from https://mathworks.com/solutions/dsp.html

[14] OpenAL: Cross Platform 3D Audio. Retrieved from https://www.openal.org/

[15] Aporia. 2018. *Demo of the voice transformations for "APORIA"*. Retrieved from https://vimeo.com/301614675

[16] PulseAudio API. Retrieved from https://freedesktop.org/software/pulseaudio/doxygen/index.html

# ONEDAY Shoes: A Maker Toolkit to Understand the Role of Co-Manufacturing in Personalization

**Troy Nachtigall[1], Oscar Tomico[1,2] ,Ron Wakkary[1,3]**
Eindhoven University of Technology[1], Eindhoven, The Netherlands, Elisava [2], Barcelona, Spain, Simon Fraser University[3], Vancouver, British Columbia, Canada
{t.r.nachtigall, o.tomico, r.wakkary}@tue.nl

**Figure 1. The ONEDAY Toolkit being used to make a pair of personalized shoes.**

## ABSTRACT

Personalization of shoes is of increasing importance to designers, researchers, shoemakers and manufacturers as mass customization progresses towards ultra-personalized product service systems. Many attempts have been made to design co-creation platforms that allow end users to personalize their own shoes. concentrating on color preference. This research takes a different approach by designing a toolkit for maker-oriented users to co-manufacture their own shoes. The toolkit was deployed worldwide to different users via crowdsharing. Backers (n=237) were surveyed before deployment and thirty users were interviewed after two years to understand personalization over a full cycle of making and use with the crafted research product. We found that users who have higher quality tools and materials in their toolkits are more likely to personalize their shoes while co-manufacturing. The research provides insights for researchers and designers creating toolkits for designing personalization product service systems/configurators and engaging in tangible bespoke processes.

### CSS Concepts

**Human-centered computing** → Interaction design theory, concepts and paradigms

### Author Keywords

Personalization; Bespoke Shoemaking; Co-Manufacturing; Research Product; Crowdfunding; Toolkit


ACM 978-1-4503-6196-5/19/03...$15.00
https://doi.org/10.1145/3294109.3295637

## INTRODUCTION

Co-Manufacturing is becoming increasingly important as Designers, makers, programmers and others develop digital fabrication tools in their local communities [19,45]. This combined with changes in fashion i.e. Instagram takes over the role traditionally played by fashion magazines [40], we see users looking for more personalization At the same time, customization and personalization of shoes is important to large shoe manufacturing and is increasing in importance with 3D printing and other digital fabrication technologies. HCI research is currently interested in shoes as seen in the Smart Soccer Shoes [51], and Shoe the way[38]. HCI is also historically interested in shoes as in the Roulette calculator shoe at MIT described by Steve Mann [26]. Yet these papers focus on the sensitizing and tactile feedback in shoes. We wanted to see how personalization would occur and be perceived over the life of a shoe and designed a toolkit, fig. 1, that could be easily made in a single day.

Technological acceptance in shoes is often limited to materials and sometimes electronics for sports performance. However, the technology used in making shoes is also interesting. To investigate the shoemaking process we turned to bespoke shoemaking as a handmade alternative to the mass-produced /mass-customized systems already offered [9,16]. Our aim was to bring a bespoke shoemaking experience to the user and understand the experience of "design after design". Previous work [8,21,30] shows design practice is interested in the connection between making and personalization. There is also current research into design methods of personalization [22]. Research has shown that user personalization can improve fit [23] but how does the quality of a self-assembled product lead to personalization? Personalization is important to the TEI and HCI community [6,7,11,12,35,41,50] especially in hybrid crafting [15,28] because it creates a better fit aesthetically, physically, and in terms of performance [30]. Hybrid craft is important to shoemakers as we see 3D printers, CNC mills and other digital fabrication technologies entering the studio. We also see new companies such as JS Shoe, Feetz and Phits already working with digital fabrication to hybrid craft personalized shoes [5,39]. Personalization is challenging, especially for mass production of goods [2,17]. Large shoe companies such as Nike and Adidas struggle with co-creation customization platforms [33], yet are still moving their production into the realm of Ultra Personalized 3D printed (digitally fabricated) shoes [53].

Bespoke and tailored attire is important to technology and society[1]. The bespoke shoemaking process is a material driven, hands-on experience which is commonly held as the highest form of personalization. It is found in shoes in the shape, color, material, material behavior and last (foot forms) [3] as is illustrated in fig. 2. Recent design research [30] has attempted to translate bespoke shoemaking into a 3D printed process and outlines the difficulties negotiating design characteristics of bespoke shoemaking into 3D printing. Materials are important to bespoke processes and so there is great interest in materials and hybrid materials in related TEI and HCI literature [8,13,36].

Our toolkit was designed to help understand the challenges and possibilities of personalization in co-manufacturing as part of our research into Ultra-Personalized product service systems. Toolkits have been shown as an effective method for "enabling replication and creative exploration" [24]. The shoe was designed with a simple, classic style that is easily personalized for aesthetics and comfort. Once the shoe was designed, we designed the toolkit in three levels; Basic, Full and Deluxe. Each level of the toolkit included more tools and better materials to better study how the availability of tools and materials affected personalization in co-manufacturing. We supported the toolkit with online websites and videos to assist in the making and to show the possibilities of personalization. To keep possibilities open, we avoided specific words like "personalize" and "customize" as we looked for their presence to emerge from the co-manufacturing. Moreover, we were transparent about the design process of creating the shoe and the toolkit so others could engage in similar research and practice.

By means of the toolkit, we gathered information about what degree of personalization would emerge in a co-manufacturing process. We surveyed the makers about their intentions for the kit before deploying it, and then interviewed 30 of the backers two years later. Our analysis is based upon the kit level chosen and the extent to which the makers personalized their shoes. Co-creation schema often tend to see co-manufacturing and co-production as valuable with respect to a "tangible consumer input" [34]. We found that those who ordered the deluxe toolkit, and reported no intention to customize their shoes were the most likely to personalize. Whereas, those who intended to personalize their shoes and ordered the basic kit, were less likely to personalize. In the end, personalization was a result of the availability of resources; tools and materials, that could be said to "drive" the maker towards personalized craftsmanship.

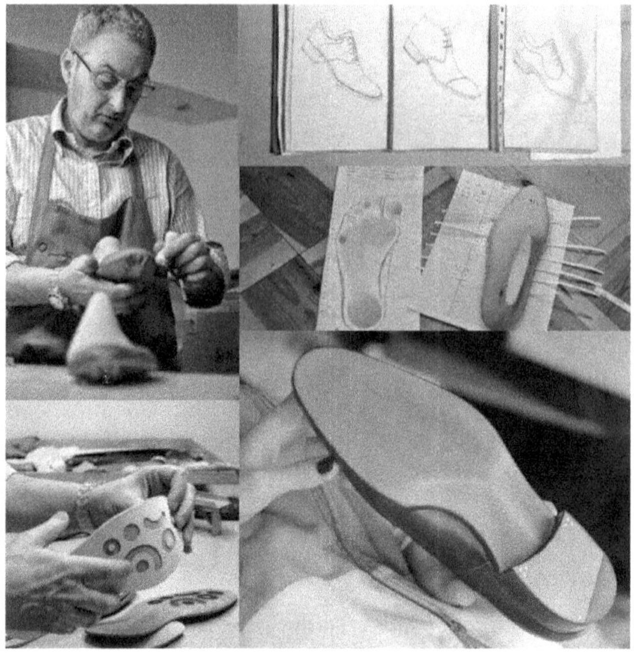

Figure 2. Bespoke shoemaker Mario Bemer personalizing form, style, materials, color and material behavior at this workshop in Florence, Italy.

### Towards Ultra-Personalized Product Service Systems

Co-creation design frameworks such as [17,37] place the personalization in the domain of co-design. Co-manufacturing is seen as "tangible consumer input" [34]. Bespoke shoe personalization brings the user into a craftsman role where personalization is highly possible. As an alternative to Co-creation, we use a theoretical Ultra Personalized Product Service (UPPS) system [43] approach that iteratively creates through the stages of Co-analysis, Co-design, Co-manufacturing and Co-use. In each phase, stakeholders play different roles which can serve the personalization of the Product, Service or System. Co-Manufacturing includes the distributed assembly by several different people, where mass production demands uniformity in the final product, co-production leaves the final product up to the user. Thus, co-manufacturing can be seen as a sort of bespoke practice which can result in personalization. Co-manufacturing is not new and has its roots in assembly practices that are widely applied in the maker community.

### Makers

This research targeted makers, but specific toolkit design decisions were made to ensure that the toolkit appealed to a range of users to see if and how they personalize. The maker community has a history of personal fabrication that is relevant to the type of personalization manufacturing we are interested in [4,10,27,31,42,44,48]. Makers have experience in assembling, co-manufacturing and personalization [6]. Makers have a large number of digital and manual fabrication tools / skills available that allow for personalization[19]. Moreover, there is a maker vision of the future, Fab City [49]; a city that makes everything it needs; food, transportation and manufactured goods such as shoes. Idealy, only data enters and exits. Our shoe toolkit was created inside this ethos.

### Research Products

Maker-oriented users expected a kit that would produce a fully useable shoe. The aim of the toolkit was to produce a shoe Research Product. Research Products hold four interdependent qualities; inquiry-driven, finish, fit, and independence [32]. As part of the research we wanted the user to live with the shoe. This required that the shoe toolkit and the resulting shoe must fit the foot and the style of the user in order to integrate into their everyday life. Shoes are also an artifact that is situated deeply in a user's everyday life [46] providing a vehicle for researching "conceptually rich artifacts" [18]. Also, shoe use is typically not a fast user experience, but rather a form of daily slow interaction [20]. It was important to the research that the toolkit created a final product that would help the user participate with the object, reflect upon their decisions, consider personalization, and give them agency over it. As we see in other recent research with Research Products [14,47], it was important to give the user time to make and wear the shoe.

## DESIGNING THE ONEDAY SHOE

We started with a series of design goals for the shoe:

1. The toolkit must create a shoe research product that the user could wear as a normal shoe over the expected lifetime of a shoe (18 months).
2. The toolkit needed to allow and encourage personalization while not making it mandatory.
3. The toolkit needed to engage the user in co-production rapidly (we adopted an eight-hour time limit for completion).
4. The toolkit needed to be affordable for makers.

The resulting ONEDAY sneaker was designed to be simple, modifiable and manufacturable in a single day. Bespoke shoes are a labor-intensive process and are sewn by hand [3]. The process can easily require sixty hours of labor to manufacture. With the limitation of eight hours to assemble the kit and keeping the kit economical, a few compromises had to be made. We chose sneakers because they do not require complex industrial machinery to realize and while full bespoke shoes would require great amounts of time and skill, sneakers are easily made and commonly worn worldwide across ages and styles. Moreover, The part of the shoe that requires the most time and cost is the sole. A commercial sole was needed to reduce the time/costs of the last and sole processes. As a result, more attention was not only put into the selection of the materials; the leather, insoles and waxed yarn, but also to the tools. We detailed the design of the kit as it was cut, sewn, punched and crafted by hand.. A shoe designer helped us create the shoe. The shoe designer remained a partner in the project and eventually took over the project entirely, creating more toolkits.

#### *The Soles*

In early 2015, the sneaker was finding a high place in fashion. Designers like Hugo Boss were creating high fashion sneakers like those found in the Futmid collection. We picked a cup sole that looked identical to the sole used by Hugo Boss from sole manufacturer Procalcado. The soles were injection molded in a coated SBR rubber 85A shore made to last for 18 months. The soles have a minimal internal cup structure that supports the foot and allows for the addition of insoles. The soles are made to be sewn by a sewing machine but we developed a hand hole punch as a Bespoke process calls for hand sewing,. The soles were made available in black or white.

#### *The Base Styles*

Given the design constraint of working with a cup sole, we started with a classic sneaker shape. We designed a simple sneaker reminiscent of the original sneakers of the 1900's, which many people today would recognize as a Converse sneaker. We generated four different base styles that while similar in construction, have their own signature style as depicted in figure 3. The styles range from an Ultra High Top over the ankle model to an Ultra-Low Top summer style. We designed a style template that can be seen in frame one of fig.1.

#### *The Cutting Patterns*

Developing the cutting patterns was the most difficult process. It was vital that the cutting patterns fit perfectly as the shoes would be manufactured without a last. The last is too bulky to ship and would have made the kits prohibitively expensive. Several prototype patterns were made using common paper tape on a last chosen to fit the cup sole. Five iterations were required to create a cutting pattern that would look good in the four different base styles pictured in figure 3. The holes that attach the uppers to the cup sole are difficult as two-dimensional pieces are shaped into a curved three-dimensional sole. Also, note that the holes in the nose of the toe tend to move to center as they progress to the right, fig 3. This is done to shape the nose of the shoe for the toe box. The patterns were provided in many formats including illustrator and PDF file for digital fabrication.

**Figure 3. Multiple shoe styles from the same cutting pattern.**

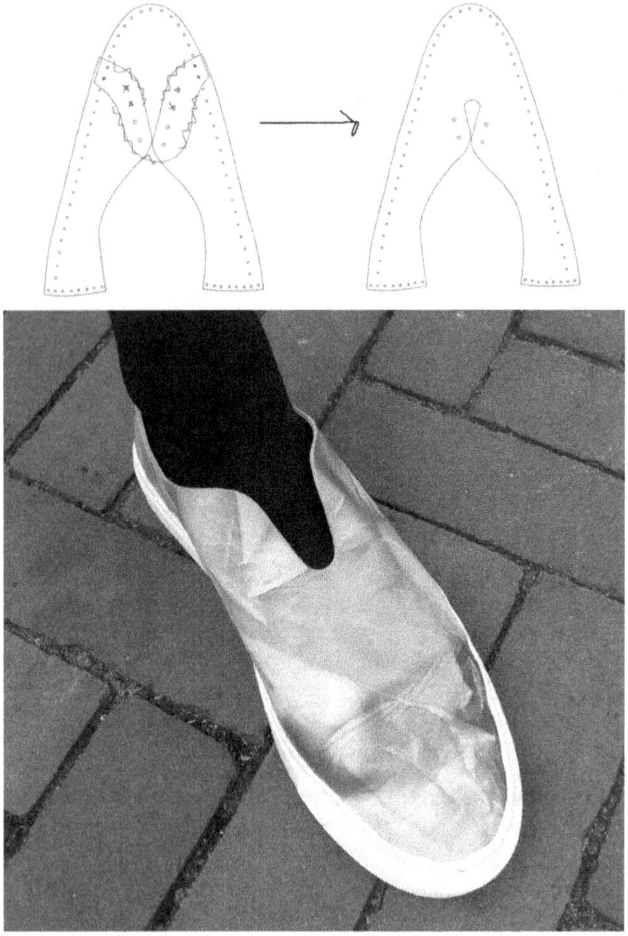

**Figure 4. Using the base shoe patterns to realize personalized styles of shoes.**

### Pilot workshops

Ensuring that the cutting pattern worked with a range of different kinds of users was difficult. Three workshops at the SLEM shoe innovation academy with users ranging from accountants to professional shoemakers, allowed the tuning of the shoe kit.. Many problems were discovered, especially in the hole alignment between the upper and the sole. The patterns were revised three times. The included video still shows the original hole guide measuring system. In our final workshop, students made the shoe twice to see how far they could personalize with the kit to check for problems.

#### *Additional Styles*

During the pilot workshops, we worked with students to create several different styles of shoe using only the base patterns shown in figure 3. We modified the Adobe Illustrator and .svg files so that the user could easily modify. Figure 4 is an example of how the base patterns can be used to create a completely different style of shoe that one of the students made in a pilot workshop. It was critical to the cutting pattern we had designed that the holes on the sole remained the same, eliminating risk of confusion by the maker when making their own shoe.

### From Shoe to Toolkit

Creating a shoe as a kit available from our website may seem difficult, but dealing with the complexity of the research was even harder. We report on our process here to help others looking to make similar toolkits. The toolkit was converted into three levels to explore levels of personalization by varying the materials, material qualities and tools. In this section we describe crowdfunding the kit, designing separate versions of the kit, creating the instructions, and logistics. We offered the toolkit in options ranging from 30€ to 100€. These prices were close to the cost of the quantity and quality of materials included. The kit was named ONEDAY to encourage users that they could finish the project in a day and the tag line "Make your own sneakers" was added to stress the co-manufacturing and attract makers.

#### *The kits*

In order to understand how much personalization resulted from bespoke materials, tools and material quality, the three levels of the toolkit with increasing tools and qualities were offered to be made with the user in the co-manufacturing process.

1. The Basic kit contained shoe soles, wax thread, special bespoke needle and instructions. The user has a selection of black or white soles. Backers were instructed to find a soft material 2-3mm thick and provide their own hole punch.
2. The Full kit added leather, a hole punch, shoe laces EVA insoles. (Fig 5) and a selection of black or white soles and Black, Chocolate, Nude or off-white leather.
3. The Deluxe kit included cork foot beds and Vegetable Tanned Leather for uppers and shoelaces. A selection of black or white soles and Sienna or Nude vegetable tanned leather

In our pilot workshops we saw that some users needed only the bare minimum of tools and materials to start while others needed everything placed in the kit. Instructions were made available online, as a print out in the kit and made available through a series of online videos. The instructions were created to make the process seem simple, yet show the makers where to pay special attention. For example, the places where the leather overlaps near the toes and needs to be shaved (scythed) down to prevent a bump that rubs against the foot causing discomfort.

#### *Licensing*

The toolkit was previewed at Maker Faire Rome. Many makers, especially those who are more entrepreneurial, were worried about the licensing, i.e. who owned the design of the shoes. We knew from the pilot workshops that the shoe maker feels special ownership over their personalization of the shoe. After reflecting on this fact, we elected to use a creative commons 4.0 open culture license allowing anyone to take the design and make a commercial product with the shoe design and patterns. This ensured maximum creativity and encouraged personalization.

**Figure 5. Photos including tools, materials and inspiring end results.**

*Logistics and Shipping*

After a successful Kickstarter campaign, we shipped kits to 237 backers on 6 continents. The kit was designed to fit in an A4 book box that could be easily delivered. Two colors of soles in eleven sizes with three kit options including six, four (Full) and two (Deluxe) leather offerings created complexity. The project had 132 separate configurations for the 237 kits. It would seem that shoes and complexity are made for each other. We wrote a script to generate shipping labels with codes for all the options allowing us to easily package and shipped the vast majority of the kits on December 17th 2015.

*Delivery of the Patterns*

Patterns were delivered via a Github repository. Just before shipping a significant issue emerged with the patterns. A workshop participant made a second pair and told us that the patterns were too small. After a few stressful weeks of trying to discover what was wrong with the patterns we realized that it was the printer. Many home/offices printers print at 96% scale to avoid cutting off content in the margins. We added square boxes in specific sizes to the paper, instructing makers to measure these boxes, but this remains one of the biggest difficulties as not all makers read and measure.

**How the kits allow for personalization**

The ONEDAY kit was designed to allow for personalization by allowing several opportunities to modify the shoes form, material, fit and aesthetic. It targeted makers and asked the user to reflect upon the object in use. Examples can be seen in Fig 6,7, & 8. Sole sizes ranging from a 35eu to a 47eu were offered.. The designed instructions included 4 versions of the sneaker, the ultra-high top, the High Top, the low Top and the ultra-low top, illustrated in figure 3. Particular attention was paid to the development of the pattern to create patterns that could be easily modified into many different kinds of sneakers, i.e. fig 3. Many materials such as vinyl and denim were also tested. The patterns were modified to allow the user to find their own soft material 2-3mm in thickness for the Basic kit. We encouraged the upcycling of older fashion products. The Full and Deluxe kit included leather in four colors and two qualities.

Inspiring images were added to Kickstarter and the Oneday website [29] with illustrations showing how to modify the pattern, such as fig 5, along with laser cut files examples of laser etched leather. Also the terms personalization and customization were specifically avoided throughout the project. The expectation was that the makers would make and wear the shoes for 18 months with most personalizing the shoe in some way.

**FINDINGS**

Beyond the description of how the kit was designed, we surveyed Kickstarter backers on how they intended to use the kit as part of the backer survey. Two years from the December 2015 ship date backers were sent a request for interview. 30 backers were interviewed about their kit use and if/how they personalized their shoe. Backers who gave the kit as a gift were excluded.

**Initial Survey and analysis**

After the completion of the Kickstarter, a survey was sent to the backers. We asked about the sole / leather color and how the user intended to use the kit. Kickstarter has strict rules about marketing/demographic questions which severely limited our inquires. In the survey we asked whether the kit was intended to "make the template shoe", "redesign the shoe" or "give the shoe as a gift", see table 1. 35% of the makers chose the Basic kit, 37% chose the Full kit and 28% chose the Deluxe kit. Roughly 20% wanted to give the kit as a gift; less in the Basic kit 17% and more in the Full kit 22%. More interesting was the choice between making the template shoe and redesigning the shoe. 40% of the Basic kit chose to redesign the shoe. This is far less in the Full kit, 26% and even less in the Deluxe kit 18%. Making the template shoe is the opposite with 42% of Basic, 52% of Full and 62% of Deluxe. The backers first name and shipping country was fed into a GDPR compliant gender api [52]. 99 Backers were identified as Male (49%) and 70 as Female (35%) with a minimum of 80% accuracy, 16% were indeterminable.

The different kit levels roughly spread evenly over the backers providing adequate groups of all the types of kits. The survey indicated that people who backed the Basic kit intended to personalize the shoe by redesign much more than the Full or Deluxe kit backers. The kits appeared spread reasonably over males and females 15% more identified as male, although 16% are not identified as a bianary gender.

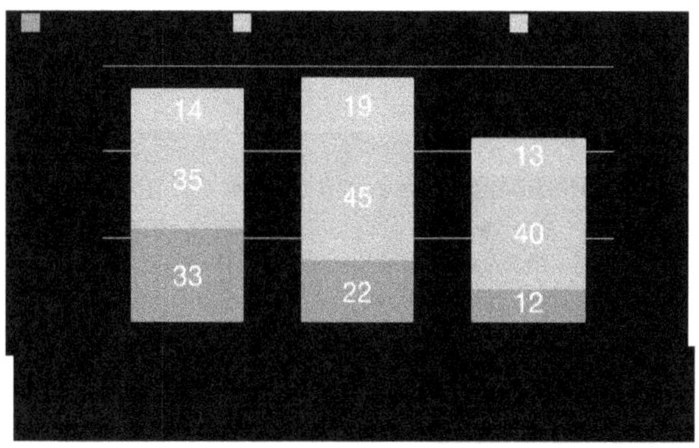

**Figure 6 Photos of the Basic kit shoes by mrlaurenss, swkang94, and 1womaninspace on Instagram**

### Interviews and analysis

Thirty of the backers who did not give the kit as a gift responded to our request for interview, all 237 backers were asked to interview multiple times. 17 respondents were male, 13 were female. 14 backed the Basic (B) kit, 8 the Full (F) kit and 8 the Deluxe (D) kit. The interview questions centered on why the maker wanted to make the shoes, if the maker had made the shoes, how the experience went, how they personalized the shoes, and how they would do it again. The interview questions were developed to evidence the state of the shoes and express if/how the user personalized. In the following sections quotes that exemplified the respondents in the Basic, Full and Deluxe kit groups are presented along with interesting exceptions. Respondents are classified by number and kit i.e. B1 is the first person in the Basic kit interviewees. A series of images from Instagram by the users of the kit reflect the responses to the survey as seen in Basic in fig. 6, Full in fig. 7, and Deluxe in fig. 8. A reflection on what each question means is added to summarize the analysis from the data.

#### *Why did you support the ONEDAY kit?*

All three groups had similar answers to this question, providing clear motivations behind the purchase. B7 said "I work in wearable tech and have done a couple of shoemaking classes. Hacking shoes is hard. I thought this would give me a neat way to incorporate some electronics into sneakers.". F2 said "I wanted to learn how a shoe is made and possibly make some shoes of my own. This was the easiest way in, although admittedly not the most representative way on how artisanal (or handmade) shoes are made.". This was also summarized well by D5 "I was interested in the process of shoe making.".

Interest in shoemaking, gaining new knowledge and integrating with their professional practice drove makers to engage with the toolkit. This shows that we reached our target audience and many different kinds of makers.

#### *Where are your ONEDAY's now?*

We wanted to understand if and how each of the makers made the shoes. Half (7) of the Basic kit makers admitted to not having made the kit; such as B11 "still incomplete in a box, but I want to do it!" or B8 "In the drawer, waiting for me to make them, I'm feeling ashamed...". The other half did make and wear the shoe exemplified by B1 "My Oneday's are with my other shoes". The Full kit respondents seem to be represented by F3 who said "My Oneday's are in active use!" Although F6 admitted that "My ONEDAY's are in the trash. I loved creating them but they never really fit my foot and were uncomfortable to wear after a while." The Deluxe kit makers seemed to have the best experience, this was expressed well by D4 "My ONEDAY's are in my closet for me, (I can wear them to work) and my daughters' are on her feet right now.".

The summary analysis is the Basic group still has a strong desire to make and, as shown in the following questions, personalize their toolkit, but many had yet to start. Most Full kit makers succeeded in making and were still using the shoe, although one respondent expressed the need for more fit personalization (which they apparently did not do). The Nearly all the deluxe kit users made their shoes and had them still in active use. Also, the materials were holding up better than expected in the shoe kit design.

#### *How did you personalize your ONEDAY's?*

With this question we wanted to see how users engaged with personalization. The Full kit users were divided as shown by F3 saying "I inserted some padding inside to make them more comfortable." and others like F2 saying "I was happy with the kit as is -no personalization.". The Deluxe kit engaged with personalization in terms of material and color exemplified by D5 who said "I added worn, black leather from army surplus gaiters to the brown that I had selected from you.". Half of the Basic group had not yet made the kit but had ideas B12 "I will personalize them by using a vegan material and a fitting color", the half who did mostly made the shoe outside a few who engaged in some personalization such as B3 "I made my own design, only used the outline of the included design.".

Personalization of color, material, form and style is seen in all three groups with the Deluxe group showing the most personalization as a group , the Full group being around half and a small number personalizing in the Basic group. The basic group spoke of how they would personalize on a conceptual level, but after two years had not engaged in the process. This shows that in co-creation platforms and UPPS, personalization can be found in co-manufacturing, and more

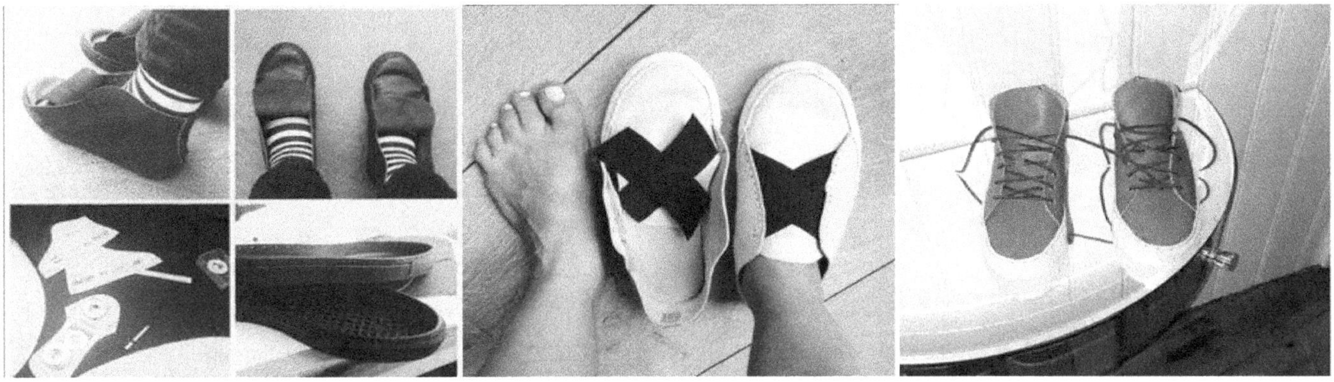

**Figure 7 Photos of the Full kit shoes by discopenut, judithsterkenberg and jonnyjwhite on Instagram**

important, designers can encourage personalization in co-manufacturing by designing space for it to happen. Additionally, personalization occurs more often when the user is presented with high quality tools and materials.

*Would you make it again?*

We asked if they would make the kit again in order to learn about the overall experience. Many Basic kit makers expressed disappointment yet hopeful resignation, B6 "I kind of want to but I feel a little bitter about the last one lol. The kit needs to have a bare minimum of more stuff." This frustration of not being able to complete the kit was seen often in the makers of the Basic kit. One of the ones who did complete it said B1"I would, but not now as they are still in good shape". Many of the Full kit makers expressed a desire for better materials "I would like to have thinner more durable soles. Mine are broken from wear already" F4. The sentiment was shared by the Deluxe group. D2 "I might get another pair if the sole is black and the thread is black. Both of those components got dirty easily." Others seemed to have mastered the kit saying D3 "I would rather learn how to make a leather shoe probably using a last (assuming it is possible without using specialized machinery). Perhaps starting from something simple like a "Clark" and building up to a proper looking smart shoe." This is supported by D7 who said "Yes. Now that I know how to make them, I would go and start to do something more personalized."

This question shows personalization is more prevalent when there are fine materials and tools involved. An interesting outlier in the results is user F1, who was the only Full kit user who didn't make the kit, said F1"I didn't make them, but use the tools a lot!". It also shows makers of all kinds respond well to co-manufacturing, but personalize more when presented with higher quality materials. The quality of the toolkit affects the choice to personalize a shoe despite what the user intends to do with the kit. The level of skill and craftsmanship of the user affects the likelihood of the user to personalize in co-manufacturing. Finally, in order to engage a user in personalization of the fit of the shoe, multiple iterations are required.

*What kit would you recommend to someone else?*

In order to know about the ideal kit, we asked the users what kit they would recommend to someone else with a series of choices:

1. Just the Soles.
2. Soles, Leather, Insoles, Shoelaces
3. Soles, Leather, Insoles, Shoelaces and tools
4. Soles, Leather, Insoles, Shoelaces and tools with precut leather
5. Fully constructed ONEDAY's

The largest response for Basic, Full and Deluxe interviewees was category 3. Soles, Leather, Insoles, Shoelaces and tools. The Basic kit users had results in all five categories. The Full kit had a one person who responded "just the soles" or "A Fully constructed ONEDAY". The Deluxe kit had one user category 1 and other who wanted category 4 . When asked for comments, the Basic kit is represented by B5 "I just like the idea, the plan: I still think it's really great and good for the environment because of little material displacement.". B7 said "More digital files that could easily be sent to laser cutters would be really rad for this project." The Deluxe group, at the other end of a spectrum, are represented by half who wanted more style patterns D3 "Create additional styles! That would be fun!" and the other half who wanted a complete accessory set D5 "I would like a similar set for leather bags and a leather belt". The Full kit level is summarized well by F4 "For someone who wants to have special shoes yet lack of the creativity, it would be nice to show more creative examples for people to follow step by step and give instructions about shoe maintenance."

The responses strongly indicate that the involved makers want a kit that has all the tools and materials, but that they want to do the bespoke processes of cutting, punching and sewing. Almost everyone who made the shoes wanted more personalization and options for themselves and others. A few users expressed the desire to engage in hybrid craftsmanship with digital files for the laser cutter. While we did offer these, it is obvious that they were not prevalent enough in the project (this sentiment was share by three of the interviewed makers) and shows an interest in hybrid craft.

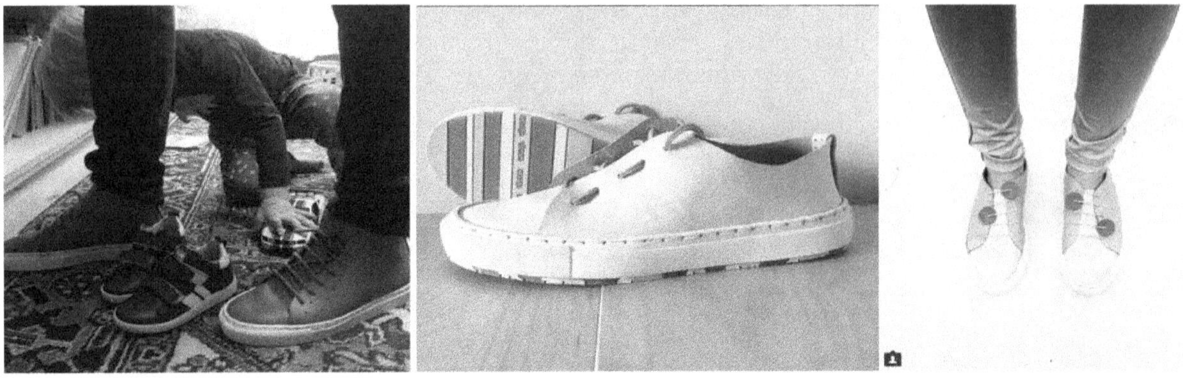

**Figure 8 Photos of the Deluxe kit shoe by dreisbuyck, david.filar. and e_mcavoy on Instagram**

## CONCLUSIONS

There is a difference in personalizing while designing (co-design), or personalizing when making (co-manufacturing). Personalization is important to the social and psychological needs of users, as seen in the interviews and Instagram photos. HCI and TEI have long investigated the integration of technology as part of a product (prototype, demonstrator, artifact…). In Oneday, the technology is in the system and service needed to create a shoe. What results is a hybrid craft experience that opens up large opportunities for the user to personalize. We show that the public is willing to engage in a co-manufacturing of a project designed with technology.

There is an opportunity for designers, researchers, shoemakers, engineers, programmers computer scientists and others to explore the technology of designing and making a thing. The "computation" of HCI can occur in the process or service instead of in the artifact. We see opportunities for that computing to occur over the lifetime of an artifact in the form of use (wear & tear) and user experience in the Oneday systemic and service aspects

Co-manufacturing can result in more personalization than co-design. In the explored Oneday case, the expectation was users who co-design the project with their own materials, tools and ideas would result in greater personalization. This was confirmed in the initial survey. The users who backed the basic kit reported intent to redesign the shoe. Then on a scale up to the Deluxe kit, backers reported they intended to make the template shoe. The Basic toolkit was more open and required co-design. The openness and endless possibilities of the basic kit results in many concepts but inhibits users from developing past the concept into a making phase. The Premium toolkit was a more closed system that required only co-manufacturing. Users respond well to co-manufacturing, but also personalized more when provided higher quality materials and tools at a higher cost. The cost of the kit may have motivated the users to complete making the kit. This was counter to our expectation and survey result that a lower cost and openness of the basic kit would result in more people personalizing with the shoe kit.

Users are more likely to personalize and use a research product when engaging in a hybrid crafting process for co-manufacturing when fine materials and tools are provided. Designing a toolkit to fulfill the specific needs of co-manufacturing to understand personalization is challenging. Designing for co-manufacturing requires a common archetype that can be personalized not only to the individual but to a city, neighborhood and/or time period. Personalization via co-manufacturing works well with simple and classic design. Additionally, the two year process and research product approach were key to this research. Only by waiting did it become apparent that the initial intention to personalize is often not always completed with action. Research Products changed our idea of the user into a co-use situation, the traditional user is using the shoe, the design researcher is using the data from the shoe and the social/psychological experience with the shoe in design, making and use. It was important to recognize this co-use.

## LIMITATIONS AND FUTURE WORK

This work only looks at sneakers as the time limitation of eight hours made other shoe styles difficult. There is an opportunity to explore other shoe styles such as high heels, dress, and sport shoes with longer time limits. The limitations on Kickstarter surveys were heavier than expected and more investigation into the skills of the users and motivations in action might revel even deeper motivations. Also, backers previous experiences with Kickstarter might have influence on their decision process which we could not look at. Many users expressed that they would personalize more a second time using the kit.

We see the kit being used in other interesting ways. For example, shoe designer Rueben Lekkerkerker launched a sustainable shoe collection Ruit [25] with the kit and a homeless shelter continues to use the kit to develop self worth. The toolkit appears to have social impact in ways we had not considered. We invite other researcher to use the toolkit and help explore personalization.

## ACKNOLEDGEMENTS

Thanks to SLEM/The Footwearists and the Wearable Senses Lab for all the amazing support. Thanks to all the backers who supported the project and tolerated many requests for interviews. This project has received funding from the European Union's Horizon 2020 research and innovation programme under the Marie Sklodowska-Curie grant agreement No. 642328.

## REFRENCES


[1.] Kevin Almond. 2011. Bespoke tailoring: the luxury and heritage we can afford. *The International Journal of Technology, Knowledge and Society* 7, 2: 77–88. https://doi.org/10.18848/1832-3669/CGP/v07i02/56195

[2.] Verónica Baena Gracia and Katharina Winkelhues. 2016. The Next Revolution in Mass Customization: An insight into the sneaker market. *International Journal of Marketing, Communication and New Media* 4, 6: 2182–9306.

[3.] J Ball and H Rollinson. 1935. *Boots and shoes: Their making, Manufacture and selling, Volume VI Bespoke Bootmaking*. New Era Publishing, London.

[4.] David Bar-El and Oren Zuckerman. 2016. Maketec: A Makerspace as a Third Place for Children Work-in-Progress. In *Proc. of TEI '16*. https://doi.org/10.1145/2839462.2856556

[5.] Lucy A Beard and Nigel P Beard. 2018. Systems and methods for measuring body parts for designing customized outerwear. U.S. Patent Application No. 14/714,062.

[6.] Steve Benford, Boriana Koleva, William Westwood Preston, Alice Angus, Emily-Clare Thorn, and Kevin Glover. 2018. Customizing Hybrid Products. In *Proc of CHI '18:*, 1–12. https://doi.org/10.1145/3173574.3173604

[7.] Martijn Ten Bhömer, Oscar Tomico, and Stephan Wensveen. 2015. Designing Ultra-Personalised Embodied Smart Textile Services for Well-Being. In *Advances in Smart Medical Textiles: Treatments and Health Monitoring*. 155–175. https://doi.org/10.1016/B978-1-78242-379-9.00007-4

[8.] Bernd Bickel, Moritz Bächer, Miguel a. Otaduy, Hyunho Richard Lee, Hanspeter Pfister, Markus Gross, and Wojciech Matusik. 2010. Design and fabrication of materials with desired deformation behavior. *ACM Transactions on Graphics* 29, 4: 1. https://doi.org/10.1145/1833351.1778800

[9.] Claudio R Boër, Sergio Dulio, and Francesco Jovane. 2004. Editorial: Shoe design and manufacturing. *International Journal of Computer Integrated Manufacturing* 17, 7: 577–582. https://doi.org/10.1080/09511920412331292637

[10.] Leah Buechley and Hannah Perner-Wilson. 2012. Crafting technology. *ACM Transactions on Computer-Human Interaction* 19, 3: 1–21. https://doi.org/10.1145/2362364.2362369

[11.] A Chang and Hiroshi Ishii. 2006. Personalized Interactions with Reality Based Interfaces. In *CHI 2006 Workshop What is the Next Generation of ....* Retrieved from http://www.cs.tufts.edu/~jacob/workshop/papers/chang.pdf

[12.] Charu Chaudhari, Anjanakshi Prakash, A. M. Tsaasan, Jed R. Brubaker, and Joshua Tanenbaum. 2016. Penseive Box. *Proc. of TEI '16*: 398–403. https://doi.org/10.1145/2839462.2856552

[13.] Pete L. Clark. 2018. A Note on rings of finite rank. *Communications in Algebra* 46, 10: 4223–4232. https://doi.org/10.1080/00927872.2017.1392540

[14.] Audrey Desjardins and Ron Wakkary. 2016. Living In A Prototype. In *Proceedings of the 2016 CHI Conference on Human Factors in Computing Systems - CHI '16*, 5274–5285. https://doi.org/10.1145/2858036.2858261

[15.] Laura Devendorf and Kimiko Ryokai. 2015. Being the Machine. In *Proc. of CHI '15*, 2477–2486. https://doi.org/10.1145/2702123.2702547

[16.] Joanne Entwistle. 2015. *The Fashioned Body: Fashion, Dress and Social Theory*. John Wiley & Sons, 2015.

[17.] Pennie Frow, Suvi Nenonen, Adrian Payne, and Kaj Storbacka. 2015. Managing Co-creation Design: A Strategic Approach to Innovation. *British Journal of Management* 26, 3: 463–483. https://doi.org/10.1111/1467-8551.12087

[18.] William Gaver. 2012. What should we expect from research through design? In *Proc. of CHI '12*, 937. https://doi.org/10.1145/2207676.2208538

[19.] Neil Gershenfeld. 2012. How to Make Almost Anything: The Digital Fabrication Revolution. *Foreign Affairs* 91, 6: 43–57. https://doi.org/10.1145/2775280.2792721

[20.] Lars Hallnäs and Johan Redström. 2001. Slow technology–designing for reflection. *Personal and Ubiquitous Computing* 5, 3: 201–212. https://doi.org/10.1215/10679847-1894308

[21.] Scott E Hudson. 2014. Printing Teddy Bears : A Technique for 3D Printing of Soft Interactive Objects. In *Proc. of CHI '14*, 459–468. https://doi.org/10.1145/2556288.2557338

[22.] Kazuki Kaneko, Yusuke Kishita, and Yasushi Umeda. 2018. Toward Developing a Design Method of Personalization: Proposal of a Personalization Procedure. *Procedia CIRP* 69: 740–745. https://doi.org/10.1016/J.PROCIR.2017.11.134

[23.] Daisuke Kokuryo, Toshiya Kaihara, Shota Suginouchi, and Swee Kuik. 2016. A study on value co-creative design and manufacturing system for tailor-made rubber shoes production — Construction of value co-creative smart factory. In *Proc. of ISFA*

*'16*, 171–174. https://doi.org/10.1109/ISFA.2016.7790155

[24.] David Ledo, Steven Houben, Jo Vermeulen, Nicolai Marquardt, Lora Oehlberg, and Saul Greenberg. 2018. Evaluation Strategies for HCI Toolkit Research. *Proc. of CHI '18*: 1–17. https://doi.org/10.1145/3173574.3173610

[25.] Rueben Lekkerkerker. Ruit Footwear. Retrieved November 17, 2017 from http://www.rubenlekkerkerker.com/kerkerker/ruitfootwear.html

[26.] Steve Mann. 1997. Smart clothing: The wearable computer and wearcam. *Personal Technologies* 1, 1: 21–27. https://doi.org/10.1007/BF01317885

[27.] Fabio Morreale, Giulio Moro, Alan Chamberlain, Steve Benford, and Andrew P. McPherson. 2017. Building a Maker Community Around an Open Hardware Platform. In *Proc. of CHI '17*, 6948–6959. https://doi.org/10.1145/3025453.3026056

[28.] Troy Robert Nachtigall and Kristina Andersen. 2018. Making Secret Pockets. In *Proc. of CHI '18*, LBW574. https://doi.org/https://doi.org/10.1145/3170427.3188611

[29.] Troy Robert Nachtigall and Roderick Pieters. 2015. The ONEDAY Shoekit licensed under the Creative Commons 4.0 Open Culture License. Retrieved November 17, 2017 from http://onedayshoe.com/

[30.] Troy Robert Nachtigall, Oscar Tomico, Ron Wakkary, Stephan Wensveen, Pauline van Dongen, and Leonie van Norten. 2018. Towards Ultra Personalized 4D Printed Shoes. In *Proc. of CHI '18*, CS20. https://doi.org/https://doi.org/10.1145/3170427.3174369

[31.] Michael Nitsche, Andrew Quitmeyer, Kate Farina, Samuel Zwaan, and Hye Yeon Nam. 2014. Teaching digital craft. In *CHI EA '14*. https://doi.org/10.1145/2559206.2578872

[32.] William Odom, Ron Wakkary, Youn-kyung Lim, Audrey Desjardins, Bart Hengeveld, and Richard Banks. 2016. From Research Prototype to Research Product. In *Proc. of CHI '16*, 2549–2561. https://doi.org/10.1145/2858036.2858447

[33.] Frank T. Piller, Evalotte Lindgens, and Frank Steiner. 2012. Mass Customization at Adidas: Three Strategic Capabilities to Implement Mass Customization. *SSRN Electronic Journal*. https://doi.org/10.2139/ssrn.1994981

[34.] Fernando R. Jiménez, Kevin E. Voss, and Gary L. Frankwick. 2013. A classification schema of co-production of goods: an open-systems perspective. *European Journal of Marketing* 47, 11/12: 1841–1858. https://doi.org/10.1108/EJM-09-2011-0459

[35.] Davide Rocchesso, Davide A Mauro, and Stefano Delle Monache. 2016. miMic : The Microphone as a Pencil. *Proc. of TEI '16*: 357–364. https://doi.org/10.1145/2839462.2839467

[36.] L. Sabantina, F. Kinzel, A. Ehrmann, and K. Finsterbusch. 2015. Combining 3D printed forms with textile structures - Mechanical and geometrical properties of multi-material systems. In *IOP Conference Series: Materials Science and Engineering*. https://doi.org/10.1088/1757-899X/87/1/012005

[37.] Elizabeth B.-N. Sanders and Pieter Jan Stappers. 2008. Co-creation and the new landscapes of design. *CoDesign* 4, 1: 5–18. https://doi.org/10.1080/15710880701875068

[38.] Maximilian Schirmer, Johannes Hartmann, Sven Bertel, Florian Echtler, Simone Minto, Damiano Zanotto, Emily Marie Boggs, and Giulio Rosati. 2015. Shoe me the Way : A Shoe-Based Tactile Interface for Eyes-Free Urban Navigation. In *Proc. of MobileHCI'15*. https://doi.org/10.1145/2785830.2785832

[39.] Shivanthan Shanthikumar, Zi Low, Eanna Falvey, Paul McCrory, and Andy Franklyn-Miller. 2010. The effect of gait velocity on calcaneal balance at heel strike; Implications for orthotic prescription in injury prevention. *Gait & Posture* 31, 1: 9–12. https://doi.org/10.1016/J.GAITPOST.2009.08.003

[40.] Lauren Sherman. 2018. Instagram Killed the Fashion Magazine. What Happens Now? *Business of Fashion*. Retrieved November 9, 2018 from https://www.businessoffashion.com/articles/professional/instagram-killed-the-fashion-magazine-what-happens-now

[41.] Michael Smyth, Ingi Helgason, Frank Kresin, Mara Balestrini, Andreas B Unteidig, Shaun Lawson, Mark Gaved, Nick Taylor, James Auger, Lone Koefed Hansen, Douglas C Schuler, Mel Woods, and Paul Dourish. 2018. Maker Movements, Do-It-Yourself Cultures and Participatory Design: Implications for HCI Research Background and Questions. In *CHI EA '18*, 1–7. https://doi.org/10.1145/3170427.3170604

[42.] Sowmya Somanath, Laura Morrison, Janette Hughes, Ehud Sharlin, and Mario Costa Sousa. 2016. Engaging "At-Risk" Students through Maker Culture Activities. In *Proc. of TEI '16*, 150–158. https://doi.org/10.1145/2839462.2839482

[43.] Claire Stolwijk and Matthijs Punter. 2018. *Going*

*Digital: Field labs to accelerate the digitization of the Dutch Industry*.

[44.] Maarten Versteeg, Elise van den Hoven, and Caroline Hummels. 2016. Interactive Jewellery. In *Proc. of TEI '16*, 44–52. https://doi.org/10.1145/2839462.2839504

[45.] Christian Voigt, Calkin Suero Montero, and Massimo Menichinelli. 2016. An empirically informed taxonomy for the maker movement. In *Lecture Notes in Computer Science (including subseries Lecture Notes in Artificial Intelligence and Lecture Notes in Bioinformatics)*, 189–204. https://doi.org/10.1007/978-3-319-45982-0_17

[46.] Ron Wakkary and L Maestri. 2007. The Resourcefulness of Everyday Design. In *Proc. of C&C '07*, 163–172. https://doi.org/10.1145/1254960.1254984

[47.] Ron Wakkary, Doenja Oogjes, Henry W J Lin, and Sabrina Hauser. 2018. Philosophers Living with the Tilting Bowl. In *Proc. of CHI '18*, 94. https://doi.org/10.1145/3173574.3173668

[48.] Ron Wakkary, Markus Lorenz Schilling, Matthew a. Dalton, Sabrina Hauser, Audrey Desjardins, Xiao Zhang, and Henry W.J. Lin. 2015. Tutorial Authorship and Hybrid Designers. *Proc. of CHI '15*, April: 609–618. https://doi.org/10.1145/2702123.2702550

[49.] Anna Waldman-Brown, Juliet Wanyiri, Simeon Oluwafunmilore Adebola, Tim Chege, Marian Muthui Fab, and Lab Nairobi. 2015. Democratising Technology: the Confluence of Makers and Grassroot Innovators. In *Proc of ICCIG '15*, 22.

[50.] Yu-chian Wu, Te-yen Wu, Paul Taele, Bryan Wang, Jun-you Liu, Ping-sung Ku, Po-en Lai, and Mike Y Chen. 2018. ActiveErgo : Automatic and Personalized Ergonomics using Self-actuating Furniture. *Proc of CHI '18*: 1–8. https://doi.org/10.1145/3173574.3174132

[51.] Bo Zhou, Harald Koerger, Markus Wirth, Constantin Zwick, Christine Martindale, Heber Cruz, Bjoern Eskofier, and Paul Lukowicz. 2016. Smart Soccer Shoe: Monitoring Foot-Ball Interaction with Shoe Integrated Textile Pressure Sensor Matrix. *Proc. of ISWC '16*. https://doi.org/10.1145/2971763.2971784

[52.] Gender API - Determines the gender of a first name. Retrieved November 17, 2018 from https://gender-api.com/

[53.] 2017. Adidas reveals the first 3D-printed shoe it'll mass-produce. Retrieved October 1, 2017 from https://www.theverge.com/2017/4/7/15216724/adidas-3d-printed-sneaker-futurecraft

# Optimizing Pressure Matrices: Interdigitation and Interpolation Methods for Continuous Position Input

**Paul Strohmeier[1], Victor Håkansson[1], Cedric Honnet[2], Daniel Ashbrook[1], Kasper Hornbæk[1]**
[1]Human Centred Computing - University of Copenhagen, Denmark
[2]Sorbonne University, CNRS, ISIR, Paris, France
{p.strohmeier, dan, kash} @ di.ku.dk, victor@skavi.dk, cedric@honnet.eu

## ABSTRACT
This paper provides resources and design recommendations for optimizing position input for pressure sensor matrices, a sensor design often used in eTextiles. Currently applications using pressure matrices for precise continuous position control are rare. One reason designers opt against using these sensors for continuous position control is that when the finger transitions from one sensing electrode to the next, jerky motion, jumps or other non-linear artifacts appear. We demonstrate that interdigitation can improve transition behavior and discuss interpolation algorithms to best leverage such designs. We provide software for reproducing our sensors and experiment, as well as a dataset consisting of 1122 swipe gestures performed on 17 sensors.

## Author Keywords
Sensor design; piezoresistive; pressure matrix; pressure input; interdigitation; interpolation; eTextile.

## INTRODUCTION
Continuous multi-touch pressure and position input is becoming increasingly mainstream, notably finding application in synthesizer controllers [6,36,37]. Pressure based position input is also used in wearable systems, including on-body gesture input [29], user authentication [32], object recognition [35], control of IoT objects [22] or detection body deformations [23].

These systems are often implemented using a resistive pressure sensor matrix, which consists of a pressure sensitive layer surrounded by conductive strips in a row and column arrangement. [5,6,23,29,35]. Often the sensor is connected to a gesture recognition system [23,29], allowing the user to perform discrete actions. Truly continuous position input, however, also requires locating pressure events that do not align with the sensor's electrodes. This is typically achieved through interpolation [6,27], however, even with interpolation the transition behavior from one electrode-strip



TEI '19, March 17–20, 2019, Tempe, AZ, USA © 2019 Copyright is held by the /author(s). ACM ISBN 978-1-4503-6196-5/19/03. https://doi.org/10.1145/3294109.3295638

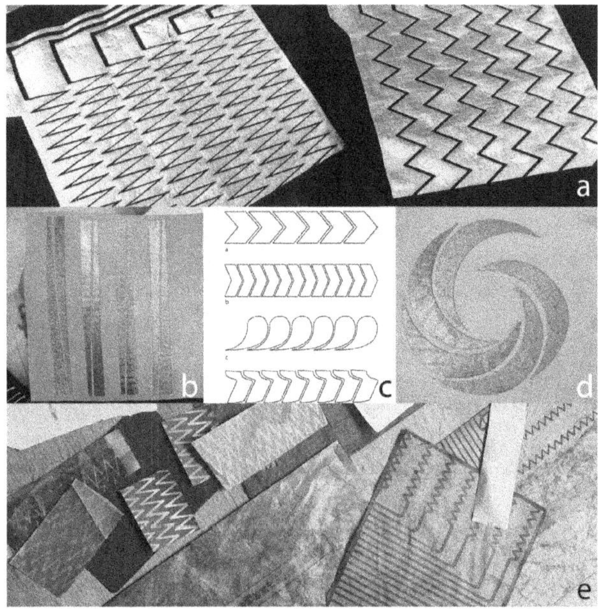


**Figure 1 - a) Electrodes of two sensors used in this paper b) capacitive sliders by Rachel Freire c, d) electrode designs and circular slider by Kobakant e) electrode testing samples at Datapaulette**

to the next introduces jumps or discontinuities [6,7]: Depending on the method chosen to extract the position of the finger, the signal might lag behind or jump ahead as a finger moves from one strip to the next (see video figure). There is no consensus if there is a best method to find touch-positions from such sensors, or what this method might be.

Our goal is to maximize the sensing resolution of pressure sensor matrices by methods other than increasing the electrode count. This can be done by leveraging the conductive properties of the resistive material [27], by interpolating the collected data [6], or by using diagonal or triangular electrode designs which create gradual transitions from one electrode to the next [34]. The latter approach, which we refer to as interdigitation, is quite common in DIY context (Figure 1, b,c,d,e), and can be found in product briefs and white-papers [15,30]. It is, however, not clear if and how such designs effect resistive pressure matrices.

We investigate effects of *interpolation algorithm choice* and *electrode interdigitation* on accuracy, precision, and consistency of touch-position sensing. In doing so we make three contributions: (1) We provide a data-set of 1122 swipe gestures performed on 17 sensors. This dataset is designed to enable quick testing of algorithms for extracting positions for various sensor designs, pressure levels and touch sizes. (2) We analyze and compare eight peak-detection algorithms for extracting touch position. (3) We investigate the effects of interdigitated patterns on sensor performance. In additionally, we also provide all code used in this project, including the pattern-generator used for creating the sensors and a prototype simulation tool for testing electrode patterns.

This project was started to optimize eTextile sensors. While the results generalize to any resistive pressure sensor matrix, we discuss them in the context of eTextile sensing.

## ADDITIONAL RESSOURCES

All code, data, and supplementary material can be found at: https://datapaulette.github.io/interdigitation/

## BACKGROUND AND RELATED WORK

### Pressure Sensor Matrixes

Traditional resistive touchscreens can estimate the position of the touch, but not the amount of pressure exerted. There are variations which can do both, but these are uncommon, due to the complexity of their driving circuits [8]. A simpler alternative is to use a high number of discrete pressure sensors [16], however, this leads complex physical designs as $n$ pressure positions require at least $n$*2 physical connections. Pressure sensor matrices provide a middle ground as they are relatively simple to understand and implement, and also scale well: $n$ pressure positions only require $2\sqrt{n}$ physical connectors [8].

Pressure sensor matrices reduce physical complexity by multiplexing measurements; pressure sensitive strips are laid out in a row and column arrangement. Figure 2 (left) shows a schematic where the rows might connect to digital outputs and the column to analog inputs. The top left resistance is measured by grounding all rows, except for row 0 which is pulled high, and reading from column 0. The voltage values would then be sampled sequentially at all positions, resulting in a 2D array of rasterized pressure information (See Figure 2, center and right for a visualization of touch events).

### eTextile Touchpads

Both the somewhat delicate mechanical layering required for designs inspired by traditional resistive touchpads [10] as well as the relatively fine traces of high resolution devices such as Rosenberg's UnMousePad [27] are currently difficult to implement in fabric. As with conventional sensors, the workarounds include sensor arrays [17,21] that require a relatively large amount of physical connections. Various unconventional solutions, such as the XY textile by

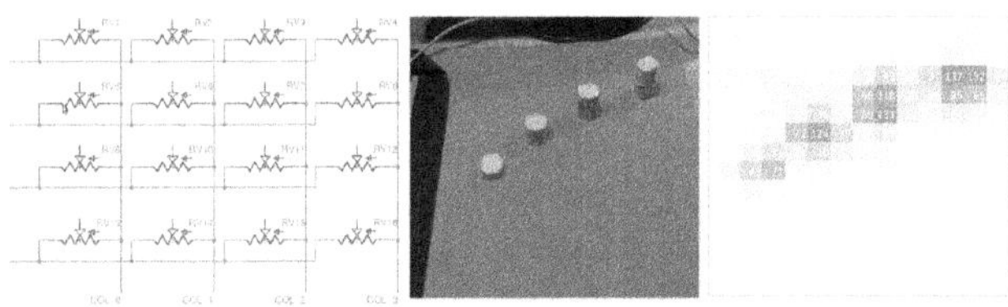

**Figure 2 - (left) 4 by 4 pressure matrix circuit. (Center) 16×16 pressure sensor matrix, and (right) raw data output [6].**

Donneaud [14] and a solution that shares many similarities with a 4-wire touchpad by Freed et al. [28] have been suggested, but are rarely seen as the relative simplicity of the pressure sensor matrix eventually made it the default design.

Due to their softness, pliability, and the ease with which they can be integrated in everyday objects such as clothing or furniture, textile pressure matrices are also commonly used for pose detection while sleeping [22] or sitting [36,40], as well as activity tracking [23,35,43]. Fabric pressure sensor matrices are also used for object recognition [27,42]. Within the HCI community, pressure sensor matrices have been used for gestural input [24,33] body pose as input [38] as well as user identification [39]. These applications do not require the detection of smooth transitions between strips. Instead, the maximum position is used with geometric models [33] or the analog data is converted to a binary image before applying computer vision methods [24,27,40]. Machine-learning methods are also used for extracting relevant information from the raw data [38,39]. The focus of this research lies on applications and the post processing of the sensor data. Only few papers report sensing accuracy [7] which makes it difficult to establish best practices for the physical design and construction of the sensor.

As pressure sensitive touch-surfaces are an intriguing musical input modality, the modern experimental music and NIME communities have been instrumental in pushing eTextile input forward [33]. The availability of piezo resistive materials supported prototyping of a range of new input methods [9] which eventually resulted in various pressure matrix designs both in the NIME [28] and DIY communities. Popular products such as the Roli Seaboard [36] or the Joué board [37] demonstrate the demand for high-resolution continuous input, which makes empirically establishing best practices increasingly relevant.

### Interpolation in Software and Hardware

As pressure is sampled at discrete intervals, the center of an object or finger is typically not aligned with the sensing elements. Finding the center of a pressure point therefore requires additional steps (see Figure 2, center and right). Most work investigating this focuses on capacitive input, as it is currently the most common method for multi-touch sensing. Examples include comparisons of electrode patterns and interpolation methods [1].

Finding a signal maxima between sensing elements is common also outside of touch-screen design and is generally referred to as sub-pixel peak estimation [2,20]. An overview is presented by Naidu and Fisher [7,19] who conducted an empirical analysis of eight algorithms. They noted that all algorithms tested by them displayed periodic error patterns, similar to those observed in the transition behavior of textile pressure matrices [6]. Naidu and Fisher claim these errors to be "symptomatic of the sensor structure" [7].

There appear to be three factors influencing transition behavior: (1) the spread of the signal of interest [6,7], (2) the peak detection algorithm [7] and (3) the physical design of the sensor [7]. However, there is comparatively little work exploring alternative sensor structures in pressure-sensor matrices. Rosenberg et al. present a matrix that utilizes the horizontal conductivity of the resistive material for better interpolation [25] and demonstrate how adding additional 'dummy electrodes' linearizes the horizontal conductivity [27]. The method used by Rosenberg et al. assumes a touch from the tip of a stylus. It is unclear if their approach generalizes to the larger touch area of a fingertip.

An alternative approach uses triangular interdigitation. If one moves a finger from one strip to the next at a fixed speed, the transition occurs faster if the motion is perpendicular to the strips than if the strips are arranged diagonally. Yoo and Pines demonstrate this approach in a 'center of pressure' sensor [34], however they chose a design which only supports input at discrete positions. Triangular interdigitated designs can also be found in white-papers and application notes for capacitive slider design [15,30] and are also common in the DIY community: They are being explored in Paris based textile hackerspace Datapaulette, they can be found in the web-archive by Satomi and Perner-Wilson [38], as Instructables by Freire [37] or in the eTextile swatchbook [11] (see also Figure 1). While triangular interdigitated designs are quite common, they are often justified based on intuition and – to the best of our knowledge – their effectiveness has never been evaluated.

## SENSORS

### Design

We created a processing sketch that generates interdigitated patterns and exports them as .pdf, ready for laser cutting (Figure 3). For the patterns used in the dataset we used triangular digits. We varied the digits using two parameters:

*Digit Width:* Low digit width allows many digits to fit (Figure 3, top). High digit width means that only few digits fit on the strip (Figure 3, bot). *Digit Width* is the dimension parallel to the sensing strip.

*Digit Length:* Low digit length means that there is little overlap between electrodes (Figure 3, left). High digit length means that there is significant overlap (Figure 3, right). *Digit Length* is the dimension perpendicular to the sensing strip.

### Implementation

We built our sensors according to Donneaud et al. [6], however, we created the electrodes following instructions by Strohmeier et al. [31]: We used conductive ripstop [38] for creating the sensing electrodes. We prepared it by ironing the Ripstop to dual-sided fabric bonding. Then, using dual-sided scrapbook adhesive [39] we glue the ripstop to an MDF board (bonding glue side up). We insert the board with the ripstop into the laser-cutter and cut the pattern. Once we remove the MDF and ripstop from the laser cutter, we gently peel off all excess material from the board, so that only the electrodes remain glued to the board. We then place a second piece of textile – this time non-conductive – on top of the

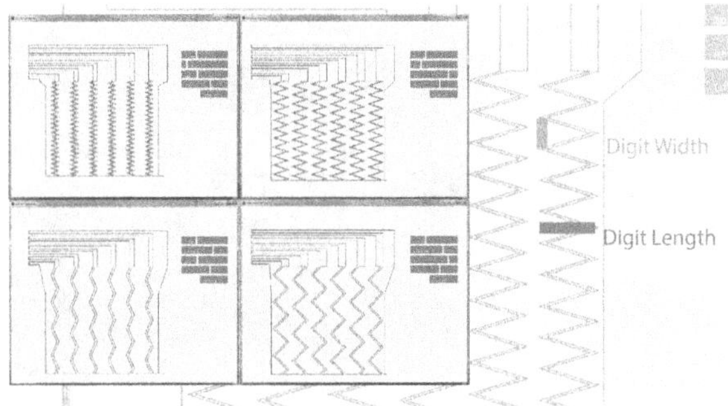


**Figure 3 - Screenshots of pattern generator, four patterns. Top: low *Digit Width*, bot: high *Digit Width*, left: low *Digit Length*, right: high *Digit Length***

electrodes and iron it in place. Once the bonding has securely connected the electrodes to the non-conductive fabric, we pull both fabric layers off the MDF board.

This method allowed us to create more precise patterns, as we did not need to manually arrange the electrodes on fabric backing. We used piezo-resistive, non-woven fabric by Eeonyx (20kΩ per square) for our resistive layer (Figure 4).

### Dimensions

We created 17 sensors. One sensor with no interdigitation, and 16 sensors with a 4*4 factorial design of width and length (*digit length*: 55%, 70%, 85%, 100% of strip spacing) and *digit width*: 95%, 75%, 55%, 35% of strip spacing). We chose our broadest digit (55% length, 95% width) to approximately match DIY designs and White Paper recommendations [15,30]. Our sharpest digit was limited by our manufacturing ability. We only created a single side of each matrix. As our primary interest is to better understand transition behavior between sensing electrodes, the full matrix is not required.

Each sensor was ~160mm wide and consisted of 7 electrodes with a 25mm spacing between strip-centers (the first and last strip were truncated). We use both larger touch-sizes and larger strip widths than we typically use. The larger strip width allows us to evaluate designs which we currently could not manufacture at fingertip scale, the larger touch sizes means we maintain the expected ratio between 'finger' and sensing elements. We chose the sizes so that the 'small' touch-size approximates the size of a human fingertip.

**Figure 4 - Interdigitated electrode layer, piezo resistive layer and grounding layer sandwiched in black backing fabric.**

**Figure 5 - CNC rig used for collecting data.**

## DATA COLLECTION

We used a CNC machine [40] to ensure consistent touch-behavior in terms of pressure and location. We created modified Dremel bits that acted as 'fingers' that would press on the sensor. The 'fingers' were made of Sugru with a rubber disk (cut from a mouse-pad [39]) beneath them to approximate the softness of the human fingertip (Figure 5).

Each strip was sampled by an analog input of an Arduino Uno. We wrote a JavaScript controller that coordinates data logging and communicates between the CNC and Arduino. The controller is open source and can be downloaded from the projects GitHub page. We used this controller to perform an approximation of a swipe gesture by measuring pressure at 70 consecutive locations on the sensor with 1mm spacing. For each sensor we repeated this swipe gesture 11 times, with 2.5mm offset for a total of 770 points.

This was repeated for three touch sizes (50%, 100%, 150% of strip spacing) crossed with two pressure settings (strong/gentle), where 'strong' was set to take full advantage of the dynamic range of the sensor and 'gentle' was the lowest pressure level we could consistently detect. In total we collect 4620 touch events per sensor for a total of 78.540 touch events over all 17 sensors.

### Assumptions and Limitations

We report independent variables and results in *percent of strip spacing* (25mm center to center) to support generalization to sensors and patterns of different sizes, and comparisons to previous evaluations [6]. Another relevant unit, however, is the ratio of touch size to strip width. We assume that (within limits) there is an equivalency in increasing the touch size by 100% to reducing strip size by 50%. The touch-size conditions can be either thought of as changing the size of touch area, or as changing size of strip-width relative to a constant touch size.

Our application scenario is continuous control of audio or video content, so our primary goal is that the user's motion over the eTextile results in a corresponding change in output signal, without jumps or discontinuities.

### The Data

We provide the raw log files as we recorded them, including various metadata. We also provide a 'normalized' version. Here we removed the noise-floor, rescaled the strips so their dynamic range is from 0 to 1 and applied a low-pass filter. All the modifications done to the 'normalized' data can be done in real time by an embedded system. For the rest of the paper we will be referring to the 'normalized' dataset.

## ALGORITHM SELECTION

We chose eight algorithms for detecting touch-positions based on previous work on subpixel peak estimation [1,7] and precedent in eTextile matrix designs [6]. As a point of reference, we also add a 'naïve' estimator (NAIVE), which simply places the touch-position at the center of the strip with the highest pressure reading, as was used for gesture extraction by Schneegass et al. [29].

We test five algorithms that fit a function through the strip with the highest pressure reading and its neighbors. These assume that there is a linear (LINE) [1,7], gaussian (GAUSS) [1,7,20], cubic (CUBIC) [6,24], or parabolic (PARA) [1,7] spread of pressure from the maximum pressure point. Additionally we test a filtered version of the parabolic estimator, suggested by Blais and Rioux (B_R) [3,7].

We test two geometric solutions: The mTouch algorithm by Microchip [18] which fits a centroid around the maximum pressure values and its neighbors (mTOUCH) and the center of mass (COM) for all strips as a touch-estimator. For our sensor these are equivalent to COM3 and COM7 suggested by Fisher and Naidu [7].

These methods can further be combined with blob tracking: The function fitting methods can be used to calculate the boundaries of the blob [13], for example Donneaud et al. use bicubic interpolation to find the boundaries of blobs with greater accuracy [6]. The geometric methods can be used to improve the estimate of the blob center, for example Burstyn et al. detect blobs using the naïve approach, but estimate the touch-position within the blob using center of mass [4]. As these combinations also can be done at arbitrary threshold levels, testing them is beyond the scope of this exploration, however we believe our results can guide designers towards informed choices on reasonable combinations. We will refer to these algorithms as *method* from now on in the paper.

## DATA ANALYSIS

Using the collected pressure values, we (1) compute the touch position for each measured position and each method. The resulting positions are in units of strip-width. We (2) scale each *sensor*method* combination to match the expected range in mm. We then (3) calibrate the values by subtracting the y intercept of the regression line and multiplying each value by one minus the slope of the regression line (Figure 6). The resulting positions are in the

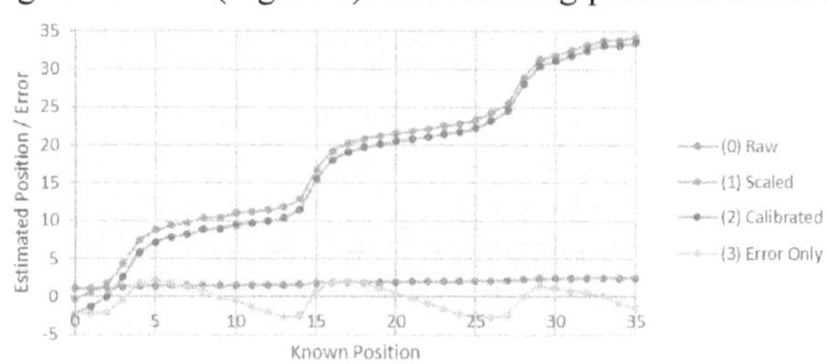


**Figure 6 – Data Processing steps**

correct range, with a regression line of y = x (blue). We then subtract the known position from the estimated position to find the error. This resulted in 36,960 error measures per sensor (770 positions by 8 *methods*, 3 *touch sizes*, 2 *pressure levels*) for a total of 628 320 error measures.

We investigate sensor **accuracy**, **precision** and **consistency** over pressure levels, using measures derived from this error measure. For sensor **accuracy** we need a measure that describes how far the estimated positions are from the known position, on average. We therefore analyze the absolute error (36,960 data points per sensor). For sensor **precision** we wish to know how consistent the output is between swipes (3360 data points per sensor). We therefore analyze the standard deviation at each x-position of all swipe motions. Finally, for sensor **consistency** we wish to know if the output behavior is consistent across pressure levels. We therefore analyze the correlation between the mean swipe positions at strong and at gentle pressure levels (24 points per sensor).

While the multiple swipe measures might suggest using a repeated measures ANOVA, the swipes are all performed by the same device, and the variability between them is negligible. This would reduce our degrees of freedom without reducing the error term. We therefore opt for univariate ANOVAs. Our sample size for sensor **accuracy** is very high, allowing us to detect significant effects, even if the effect size is very small. **Precision** and **consistency** use successively higher-level concepts, leading to smaller samples sizes. For the consistency measure the sample size is so too small for a full factorial analysis.

For **accuracy** we analyzed *absolute error* by *digit width*, *digit height*, *touch size*, *pressure* and *method*. All main effects and all interaction effects were statistically significant at the $p < .0001$ level.

**Precision** was analyzed using *standard deviation* by *digit width*, *digit height*, *touch size*, *pressure* and *method*. All main effects and all interactions, except for touch size * method and digit width * method, were significant at $p<.0001$.

For **consistency** we performed two separate ANOVAs once *correlation* by *digit width* and *digit height* and once on *correlation* by *touch size* and *method*. There were no significant effects for *digit width* or *digit height*. For *touch size* and *method*, all main effects and all interaction effects were statistically significant at the $p < .0001$ level.

Due to our large sample sizes for **accuracy** and **precision**, it is not surprising that we could demonstrate significant differences even for very small effects. We therefore also report effect sizes, which typically were small, except for the effect of *method*, which was medium. The effect size reported is partial eta squared – any variance explained by other variables is removed. This allows for easy comparisons between parameters when exploring other electrode design manipulations. It should be noted that eta measures typically overestimate effect sizes, but that we believe this to be negligible in our case due to the large sample sizes.

All significant results maintain the $p < .0001$ level after correcting for family wise error – we will from now on not report these. The F-statistics and effect sizes, as well as Bonferroni corrected post-hoc analysis, will be presented where relevant.

## RESULTS

### Pressure

| Pressure | Error | Lower Bound | Upper Bound | Deviation | Lower Bound | Upper Bound |
|---|---|---|---|---|---|---|
| *Gentle* | 10.86% | 10.84% | 10.89% | 5.48% | 5.40% | 5.56% |
| *Strong* | 11.63% | 11.60% | 11.66% | 4.01% | 3.94% | 4.04% |

**Table 1 – Means and 95% confidence intervals for *pressure***

We found that on average that low pressure performed better than high pressure over all sensors for **accuracy** ($F_{(1, 627504} = 627504$, $\eta_p^2 = .001$). This effect, however, is dwarfed by the comparatively larger effect of pressure on **precision** ($F_{(1, 56304} = 535.056$, $\eta_p^2 = .009$), where the strong pressure outperforms the gentle pressure. Increased **accuracy** of gentle touches comes at the cost of reduced **precision**.

### Touch Size

| Touch Size | Error | Lower Bound | Upper Bound | Deviation | Lower Bound | Upper Bound |
|---|---|---|---|---|---|---|
| *50%* | 11.96% | 11.93% | 12.00% | 6.17% | 6.17% | 6.17% |
| *100%* | 11.50% | 11.46% | 11.53% | 4.68% | 4.68% | 4.68% |
| *150%* | 10.28% | 10.25% | 10.32% | 3.39% | 3.39% | 3.39% |

**Table 2 – Means and 95% confidence intervals for *touch size***

We vary *touch size*, as it allows us to explore various *touch size* to *strip width* ratios. One can also assume the 50%, 100% and 150% touch sizes to represent strip widths of 200%, 100% and 66.6% finger size.

Increasing the touch size had a positive effect on **accuracy** ($F_{(2, 627504} = 1414.744$, $\eta_p^2 = .004$) and an even stronger effect on **precision** ($F_{(2, 56304} = 583.094$, $\eta_p^2 = .020$). Bonferroni corrected post-hoc analysis showed that each successively larger size performed significantly better than the previous size for both accuracy and precision (Table 1).

The interactions between strip width and *touch size* lead to various periodic behaviors, and some sensors display the opposite trend as we find on average. Figure 7 shows the average change between consecutive pressure readings for all x positions of a swipe gesture on the non-interdigitated sensor. For the small touch position (top) there is always a sensor where values are changing, providing information that the touch-point has moved between readings. For the medium touch size (middle), the areas where change occurs begin to cluster and for the large touch size (bottom) they begin to completely overlap. About half of the swipe distance there is no change in signal which might indicate a change in position (~10-25mm, 35-50mm, >~60mm), This causes most peak detection methods to first underestimate and then overestimate the change in position between measures.

The medium touch size performed best in terms of **consistency** over pressure levels ($F_{(2, 384} = 15.26$, $\eta_p^2 = .074$).

### Digit Length

| Digit Length | Error | Lower Bound | Upper Bound | Deviation | Lower Bound | Upper Bound |
|---|---|---|---|---|---|---|
| none | 11.26% | 11.17% | 11.34% | 2.43% | 2.21% | 2.65% |
| 55 | 10.84% | 10.80% | 10.88% | 3.98% | 3.87% | 4.09% |
| 70 | 11.19% | 11.15% | 11.23% | 4.68% | 4.57% | 4.79% |
| 85 | 11.22% | 11.18% | 11.26% | 5.56% | 5.44% | 5.67% |
| 100 | 11.73% | 11.69% | 11.77% | 5.34% | 5.23% | 5.45% |

**Table 3 – Means and 95% confidence intervals for *digit length***

Digit length is the dimension of the digit perpendicular to the strip. It has a significant effect on **accuracy**, however it is very small ($F_{(3, 627504} = 308.705$, $\eta_p^2 = .001$). Digit Length of 55% had the lowest, and 100% had the highest average errors. There is a proportionally much stronger interaction effect with touch-size ($F_{(6, 627504} = 650.756$, $\eta_p^2 = .006$). *Digit length* causes the strips to overlap, effectively increasing their width. This changes the periodic effects described in the touch-size section. Figure 8 compares the digit lengths of the interdigitated sensors using the large *touch size* and 35% *digit length*. With increasing *digit length*, the 'dead zones' become increasingly smaller, until zones appear where changes can be detected two separate strips simultaneously.

Not all position estimation algorithms can fully leverage this though, which is reflected in an even stronger three way interaction between *digit length*, *touch size* and *method* ($F_{(42, 627504} = 481.955$, $\eta_p^2 = .008$).

There is also a – comparatively – strong effect of digit length on **precision** ($F_{(3, 56304}= 159.583$, $\eta_p^2 = .008$), post hoc tests show that all levels are different, but most notably the non-interdigitated sensor performs best.

### Digit Width

*Digit width* is the dimension of the digit parallel to the strip and had the strongest effects on **accuracy** and **precision** of all physical parameters. Reducing the digit width has a positive effect on **accuracy** ($F_{(3, 627504} = 564.239$, $\eta_p^2 = .003$) with all levels showing a significant difference to each other, except for the non-interdigitated sensor and 75% condition. Reducing digit width has a strong positive effect on **precision** ($F_{(3, 56304}= 848.321$, $\eta_p^2 = .043$). Large touch sizes seem to benefit most from this, which is also demonstrated by an interaction effect with touch size ($F_{(6, 56304}= 249.334$, $\eta_p^2 = .026$). Reducing the *digit width* can, on average reduce the error over a non-interdigitated sensor, however at the cost of precision. Reducing the width increases precision, the trend suggests digit widths <35% will match the precision of non-interdigitated sensors (Figure 9).

### Method

One of the strongest effect found in our analysis was that of method on **accuracy** ($F_{(7, 627504} = 31596.752$, $\eta_p^2 = .261$). This is most likely in part driven by the inclusion of the NAIVE estimator which produced on average more than triple the error of the two best algorithms. mTOUCH and LINE performed similarly well on **accuracy** and were significantly better than all others. We also found no significant difference between COM and CUBIC, but beside those all methods were significantly different (Figure 10).

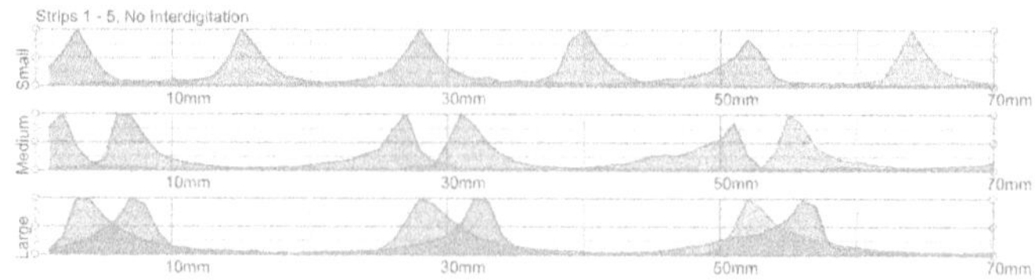

**Figure 7 - Average change between readings, per electrode. The graphs are normalized relative to the maximum recorded change per strip. Each color corresponds to an electrode.**

We found small, but significant simple interaction effects with both *digit width* ($F_{(21, 627504} = 63.642$, $\eta_p^2 = .002$) and *digit length* ($F_{(21, 627504} = 95.596$, $\eta_p^2 = .003$). We also found comparatively strong interaction effects with *touch size* ($F_{(14, 627504} = 281.349$, $\eta_p^2 = .006$), and a three way interaction with *touch size* and *pressure* ($F_{(14, 627504} = 603.918$, $\eta_p^2 = .013$) as well as *digit length* and *pressure* ($F_{(21, 627504} = 175.997$, $\eta_p^2 = .006$). This suggests that the interpolation methods do not perform equally on all sensors, and that there is even larger variation based on varying pressure and size of the touch. In general, curve fitting methods performed best with small touch-sizes and low pressure, while the geometric methods performed best for strong pressure and large touch.

Finally, there was also an effect of method on **precision** ($F_{(7, 56304}= 98.828$, $\eta_p^2 = .012$). Here GAUSS dethrones mTOUCH as the best solution. LINE has become significantly worse than mTOUCH (Figure 10).

There was a significant effect of method on **consistency** ($F_{(7, 384} = 15.257$, $\eta_p^2 = .417$). Post hoc tests showed that NAÏVE performed significantly worse than all others. CUBIC performed better than NAIVE but was also significantly worse than the remaining methods. There was also a significant interaction effect of *method*touch size* ($F_{(14, 384} = 11.364$, $\eta_p^2 = .293$). This effect is, however, completely due to the NAIVE condition, which performed best with small and worst with large touch sizes.

### DISCUSSION

Our analysis demonstrates that triangular interdigitation can improve the **accuracy** of eTextile pressure sensor matrices. We found that for all *digit lengths*, the **accuracy** is improved on average, but at the cost of **precision**. We found that wide digits performed worse than non-interdigitated sensors. The 55% *digit width* condition, however, already outperformed the non-interdigitated sensor in terms of accuracy and the 35% *digit width* condition was even significantly more accurate than both 55% and non-interdigitated, while approaching the non-interdigitated sensor in terms of

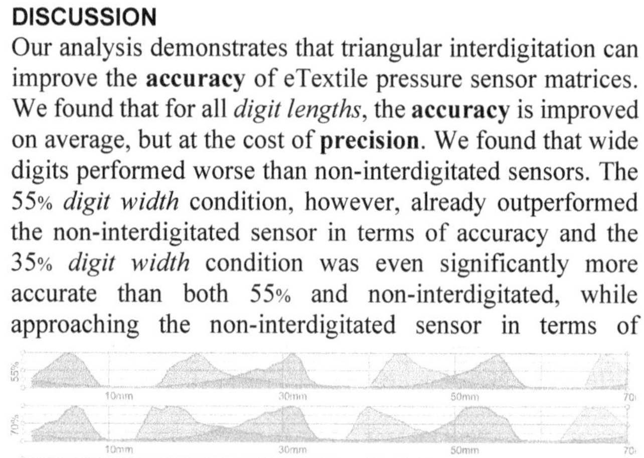

**Figure 8 – Average change between readings. As *digit length* increases, the 'dead zones', where there is no information to infer change of position, gradually vanish.**

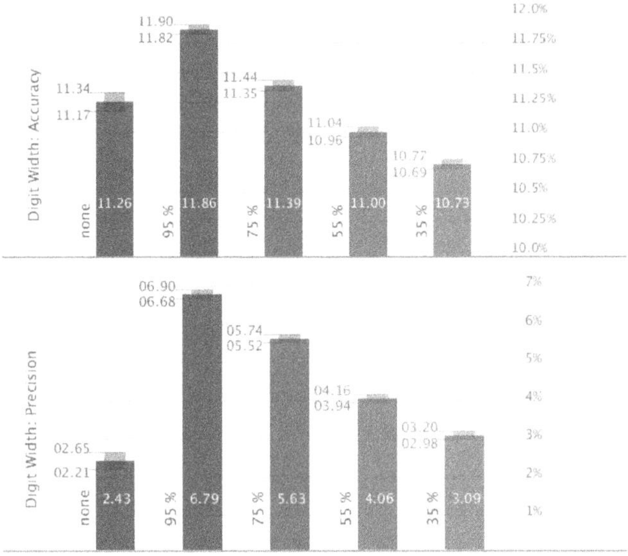


**Figure 9 – Means and 95% confidence interval for effects of digit width on accuracy (top) and precision (bottom). The accuracy graph is zoomed in. Lower scores are better.**

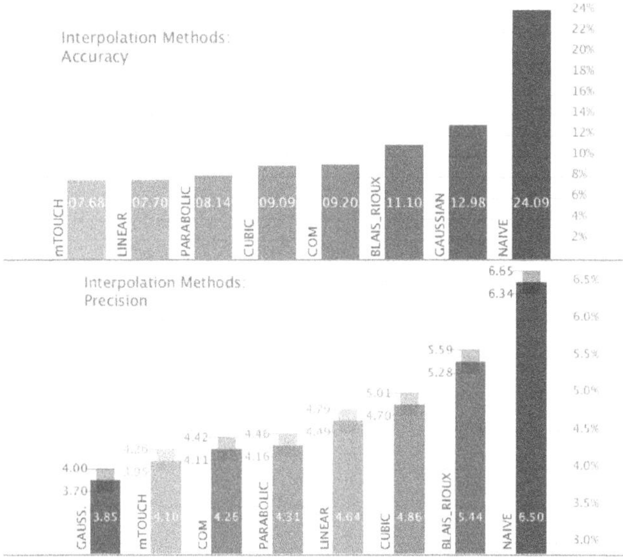


**Figure 10 – Means and 95% CIs for effects of interpolation method on accuracy (top) and precision (bottom). The precision graph is zoomed in. The confidence intervals for accuracy are too small to display (0.11% on average, all differences are significant). Lower scores are better.**

**precision**. For the large *touch size,* the interdigitated designs outperformed the non-interdigitated designs at all levels of digit width and digit height for both **accuracy** and **precision**.

Regarding peak estimation method, we found that both the mTOUCH and the LINE algorithm performed significantly better than all others on **accuracy**. We speculate, however, that they might feel very differently. We believe that there is a certain subjective dimension to interpolation which should not be ignored. We draw an analogy to the effects of latency on musical input – if latency is consistent, it is perceived as a property of the *feel* of the instrument, but if the latency varies, it is perceived as negatively impacting the quality of the instrument [12]. In our case it is not clear how relevant the average accuracy or even precision is, compared to the consistency and 'feel' of the errors. The LINE method, for example, has a distribution of errors which appears chaotic and somewhat difficult to predict compared to the mTOUCH method. The GAUSS method, on the other hand has relatively larger errors, but very good **precision** and **consistency** over pressure levels. The CUBIC method appears as a reasonable choice in terms of **accuracy**, however it performed significantly worse than all others in terms of **precision**. A visualization comparing interpolation methods for the non-interdigitated sensor and the 35% *digit width*, 100% *digit height* condition can be seen in Figure 11. The supplementary material includes these for all sensors.

While the mTOUCH method performed well on the clean data, anecdotally, we observed that the mTOUCH method led to periodic jumps when testing on the non-normalized dataset. In the normalized dataset this did not happen, presumably due to removing the noise-floor. The COM method did not display this problem.

An Excel sheet for exploring all combinations is attached in the supplementary material as well as our GitHub repository.

### Recommendations

Overall, our data suggests using a *digit length* of 85%, *digit width* of 35% or smaller, *touch size* 150% (or strip size 66% of touch size) and either mTOUCH or LINE interpolation method. If the strip is wider than the touch size, then PARA is the preferred algorithm. Of all combinations tested, the combination which minimized errors and variance was 100% *digit length*, with 35% *digit width*, 150% *touch size* and using the mTOUCH *method* (see also Figure 11, right).

We suggest *method* and electrode design should match the application: For example, if one intends to build a footstep sensor for children, one might start with the assumption that a child's foot is 6cm wide and space electrodes 4cm apart (making the *touch size* 150%). To maximize **accuracy**, one might design the electrodes to minimize *digit width* and use 100% *digit height* and use mTOUCH *method.*

If one is building a music controller and values **precision** over accuracy, one might choose the GAUSS *method* to ensure **consistent** behavior. Assuming a fingertip is 15mm wide, the strip spacing should be ~10mm. As interdigitation reduces precision, one might choose not to use interdigitation and instead map the electrodes so the periodic errors can be easily understood – for example one strip per half tone. If one does not wish to sacrifice accuracy, one could consider adding small digits, e.g. 55% *digit length* while minimizing *digit width.* Additional resources for parameter choice can be found in the supplement and our GitHub repository.

### Comparisons with the state of the art

Comparing the input fidelity of matrix pressure sensors is difficult, as details are often not reported, or design parameters and goals differ greatly. For example, RESi demonstrates a potentially high electrode density [21] and

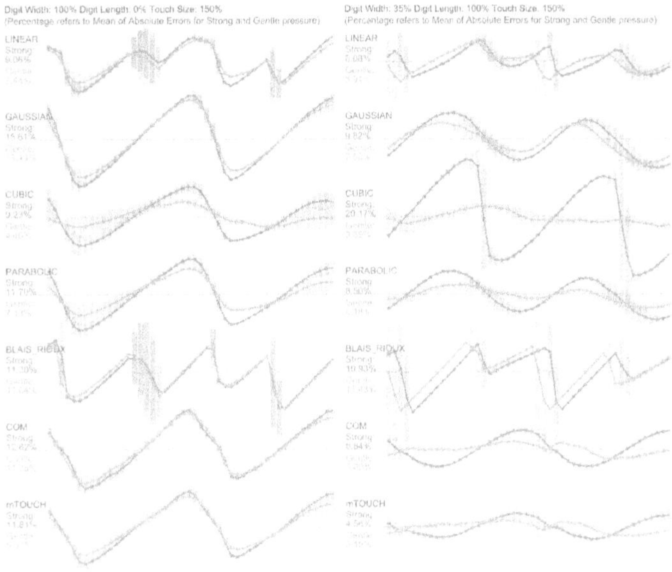


**Figure 11 - Methods for non-interdigitated sensor (left) and 35% *digit width* with 100% *digit height* (right). X-axis shows the known position, y-axis shows the average deviation from that position. Blocks indicate the 95% confidence interval of the average at that position. (See our GitHub repository for more details)**

the unMousePad [26] even increases the resolution possible due to high density with physical interpolation. Our design goal is to maximize the sensing resolution independently of electrode density, as this simplifies the physical interface. We argue that a useful benchmark in comparing design choices is to compare errors relative to strip spacing, as this is less dependent on the circumstances of the specific implementation. The only papers we could find that provide an accuracy measure were by Rosenberg et al. [26] and by Donneaud et al. [6], reporting an error of 4.89% and 6% respectively. Our best result (35% *Digit Width*, 100% *Digit Length*, *gentle pressure*, COM) almost doubles the accuracy of the eTextile Matrix by Donneaud with 3.09% and even improves on the relative error size of Rosenberg's unMousePad. The more consistent result achieved with the mTOUCH approach with the same physical sensor but averaging both *gentle* and *strong* pressure has a slightly larger average error at 3.875%, but still outperforms both Donneaud's and Rosenberg's designs.

### Limitations and Future Work

The sensors we designed are flat, while many applications of fabric pressure matrices are not. Especially wearable solutions need to conform to the shape and movements of the body [9] which inevitably leads to artefacts and noise [10]. While any sensor design would be subject to such problems, and we therefore believe that our design recommendations still hold, it is possible that some algorithms perform better than others when subject to noise. Hybrid sensing has been suggested as a way to minimize such problems [31].

We maximized the pressure sensitive area of our sensors. Other approaches, such as sensors using zebra-fabric [22] or pressure sensitive threads [21], have zones that are not sensitive to pressure between electrodes. It is not clear how the tested algorithms perform under such conditions. While we encourage that such designs utilize interpolation, our work is aimed specifically at interdigitated sensors.

Our work points towards periodic interactions between the ratio of touch size and strip width and that of digit lengths (Figures 7 and 8). Our data and the analysis by Donneaud et al. [6] suggest that this is a topic that deserves further exploration, for example by disrupting the periodic interactions through varying strip-widths. We created and share a prototype tool for testing electrode patterns which could be used to explore this. Additional work is however required to validate this tool using the dataset we provide.

Fisher and Naidu [7] suggest reducing error by modelling the periodic effects. This would also be relevant to eTextile pressure matrices. All peak estimation methods tested by us assumed an underlying behavior of the signal distribution. As we do not believe any of the estimators we tested to be ideal, we suggest that future work either model the signal distribution of the piezo resistive material, or use parameter free approaches, such as Gaussian Processes [39]. Finally, to fully utilize interdigitation, we need better prototyping methods such as screen printing, etching, or in-situ polymerization.

## CONCLUSION

This paper presents an exploration of factors influencing the design of eTextile sensor matrices. Using a combination of 100% *digit length*, 35% *digit width*, 150% *touch size* and the mTOUCH *method* we are able to achieve a relative sensing accuracy higher than reported for previous pressure sensor matrices, both textile and non-textile.

While we are pleased with this result, our work is primarily intended as a resource for designers of textile input devices. We therefore share our data-set for testing algorithms under various conditions, we provide an evaluation showing the importance of digit width, touch size and algorithm choice, and we share implementations of our algorithms as Processing functions. The supplementary material of this paper also contains visualizations of the errors and variability of errors for all sensors, all touch sizes and all pressure levels. All code, data and additional material can also be found at https://datapaulette.github.io/interdigitation/

Our investigation shows that currently the resolution at which the digits can be manufactures in textile limits the utility of interdigitated pressure matrix designs, however, our work also suggests that the approach is promising and that it is worthwhile investigating new methods for prototyping at high resolution in fabric.

## ACKNOWLEDGEMENTS

This work was supported by the European Research Council, grant no. 648785, Labex SMART (ANR-11- LABX-65) and French state funds under reference ANR-11-IDEX-0004-02.

## RELATED WORK


[1] Humza Akhtar and Ramakrishna Kakarala. 2014. A methodology for evaluating accuracy of capacitive touch sensing grid patterns. *IEEE/OSA Journal of Display Technology* 10, 8: 672–682. https://doi.org/10.1109/JDT.2014.2312975

[2] Humza Akhtar and Ramakrishna Kakarala. 2014. A Comparative Analysis of Capacitive Touch Panel Grid Designs and Interpolation Methods. *International Conference on Image Processing(ICIP)*: https://doi.org/10.1109/ICIP.2014.7026172

[3] François Blais and Marc Rioux. 1986. Real-time numerical peak detector. *Signal Processing* 11, 2: 145–155. https://doi.org/10.1016/0165-1684(86)90033-2

[4] Jesse Burstyn, Paul Strohmeier, and Roel Vertegaal. 2015. DisplaySkin. In *Proceedings of the Ninth International Conference on Tangible, Embedded, and Embodied Interaction - TEI '14*, 165–172. https://doi.org/10.1145/2677199.2680596

[5] Jingyuan Cheng, Bo Zhou, Paul Lukowicz, Fernando Seoane, Matija Varga, Andreas Mehmann, Peter Chabrecek, Werner Gaschler, Karl Goenner, Hansjürgen Horter, Stefan Schneegass, Mariam Hassib, Albrecht Schmidt, Martin Freund, Rui Zhang, and Oliver Amft. 2017. Textile Building Blocks: Toward Simple, Modularized, and Standardized Smart Textile. 303–331. https://doi.org/10.1007/978-3-319-50124-6

[6] Maurin Donneaud, Cedric Honnet, and Paul Strohmeier. 2017. Designing a Multi-Touch eTextile for Music Performances. In *Proceedings of the International Conference on New Interfaces for Musical Expression*, 7–12.

[7] Robert Fisher and K. Naidu. 2001. A Comparison of Algorithms for Subpixel Peak Detection. September 2001. https://doi.org/10.1007/978-3-642-58288-2

[8] Adrian Freed. 2009. Novel and Forgotten Current-steering Techniques for Resistive Multitouch, Duotouch, and Polytouch Position Sensing with Pressure. *Proc. NIME '09*: 230–235.

[9] Rachel Freire, Paul Strohmeier, Cedric Honnet, Jarrod Knibbe, and Sophia Brueckner. 2018. Designing eTextiles for the body: Shape, volume & motion. In *TEI 2018 - Proceedings of the 12th International Conference on Tangible, Embedded, and Embodied Interaction*, 728–731. https://doi.org/10.1145/3173225.3173331

[10] Florian Heller, Stefan Ivanov, Chat Wacharamanotham, and Jan Borchers. 2014. FabriTouch: Exploring Flexible Touch Input on Textiles. *Proceedings of the 2014 ACM International Symposium on Wearable Computers - ISWC '14*: 59–62. https://doi.org/10.1145/2634317.2634345

[11] Anja Hertenberger, Barbro Scholz, Beam Contrechoc, Becky Stewart, Ebru Kurbak, Hannah Perner-Wilson, Irene Posch, Isabel Cabral, Jie Qi, Katharina Childs, Kristi Kuusk, Lynsey Calder, Marina Toeters, Marta Kisand, M.T. Bhömer, Maurin Donneaud, Meg Grant, Melissa Coleman, Mika Satomi, Mili Tharakan, Pauline Vierne, Sara Robertson, Sarah Taylor, and T.R. Nachtigall. 2014. 2013 E-Textile swatchbook exchange: The importance of sharing physical work. *Proceedings - International Symposium on Wearable Computers, ISWC*: 77–81. https://doi.org/10.1145/2641248.2641276

[12] Robert H Jack, Tony Stockman, and Andrew Mcpherson. Effect of latency on performer interaction and subjective quality assessment of a digital musical instrument. https://doi.org/10.1145/2986416.2986428

[13] James R. Jordan. 1978. Interpolating digital data processing apparatus for correlation-type flow measurement. Retrieved July 26, 2018 from https://patents.google.com/patent/US4254470

[14] Juan Aguilar. 2008. XY fabric interface. *Hackaday*. Retrieved July 9, 2018 from https://hackaday.com/2008/05/30/xy-fabric-interface/

[15] Silicon Labs. 2013. *The world's most energy friendly microcontrollers Hardware Design for Capacitive Touch AN0040-Application Note*. Retrieved July 20, 2018 from www.silabs.com

[16] Shongpun Lokavee, Theeraporn Puntheeranurak, Teerakiat Kerdcharoen, Natthapol Watthanwisuth, and Adisorn Tuantranont. 2012. Sensor pillow and bed sheet system: Unconstrained monitoring of respiration rate and posture movements during sleep. *Conference Proceedings - IEEE International Conference on Systems, Man and Cybernetics* https://doi.org/10.1109/ICSMC.2012.6377959

[17] Jan Meyer, Paul Lukowicz, and Gerhard Tr. 2006. Textile Pressure Sensor for Muscle Activity and Motion Detection. *IEEE Xplore*: 2–5.

[18] Microchip. TB3064 - Datasheet. Retrieved July 19, 2018 from http://www.microchip.com/stellent/groups/techpub_sg/documents/devicedoc/en550192.pdf

[19] D K Naidu and R B Fisher. 1991. A Comparative Analysis of Algorithms for Determining the Peak Position of a Stripe to Sub-pixel Accuracy. In *Procedings of the British Machine Vision Conference 1991*, 28.1-28.9. https://doi.org/10.5244/C.5.28

[20] H. Nobach and M. Honkanen. 2005. Two-dimensional Gaussian regression for sub-pixel displacement estimation in particle image velocimetry or particle

position estimation in particle tracking velocimetry. *Experiments in Fluids* 38, 4: 511–515. https://doi.org/10.1007/s00348-005-0942-3

[21] Patrick Parzer, Siegfried Bauer, Michael Haller, Florian Perteneder, Kathrin Probst, Christian Rendl, Joanne Leong, Sarah Schuetz, Anita Vogl, Reinhard Schwoediauer, and Martin Kaltenbrunner. 2018. RESi: A Highly Flexible, Pressure-Sensitive, Imperceptible Textile Interface Based on Resistive Yarns. In *The 31st Annual ACM Symposium on User Interface Software and Technology - UIST '18*, 745–756. https://doi.org/10.1145/3242587.3242664

[22] Patrick Parzer, Kathrin Probst, Teo Babic, Christian Rendl, Anita Vogl, Alex Olwal, and Michael Haller. 2016. FlexTiles: A Flexible, Stretchable, Formable, Pressure-Sensitive, Tactile Input. *Proceedings of the 2016 CHI Conference Extended Abstracts on Human Factors in Computing Systems - CHI EA '16*: 3754–3757. https://doi.org/10.1145/2851581.2890253

[23] Patrick Parzer, Adwait Sharma, Anita Vogl, Jürgen Steimle, Alex Olwal, and Michael Haller. 2017. SmartSleeve: Real-time Sensing of Surface and Deformation Gestures on Flexible, Interactive Textiles, using a Hybrid Gesture Detection Pipeline Patrick. In *Proceedings of the 30th Annual ACM Symposium on User Interface Software and Technology - UIST '17*, 565–577. https://doi.org/10.1145/3126594.3126652

[24] Paul Borke. 2009. Interpolation methods. Retrieved July 26, 2018 from http://paulbourke.net/miscellaneous/interpolation/

[25] Ilya D. Rosenberg, Alexander Grau, Charles Hendee, Nadim Awad, and Ken Perlin. 2009. IMPAD - An Inexpensive Multi-Touch Pressure Acquisition Device. In *Proceedings of the 27th international conference extended abstracts on Human factors in computing systems - CHI EA '09*, 3217. https://doi.org/10.1145/1520340.1520460

[26] Ilya Rosenberg and Ken Perlin. 2009. The UnMousePad - An Interpolating Multi-Touch Force-Sensing Input Pad. *ACM Trans. Graph. Article* 28, 10. https://doi.org/10.1145/1531326.1531371

[27] Ilya Rosenberg, Ken Perlin, Charles Hendee, Alex Grau, and Nadim Awad. 2009. The UnMousePad - The Future of Touch Sensing. In *SIGGRAPH 2009*.

[28] Andrew Schmeder and Adrian Freed. 2010. Support Vector Machine Learning for Gesture Signal Estimation with a Piezo-Resistive Fabric Touch Surface. *Proceedings of the 2010 Conference on New Interfaces for Musical Expression (NIME 2010)*, Nime: 244–249.

[29] Stefan Schneegass and Alexandra Voit. 2016. GestureSleeve: using touch sensitive fabrics for gestural input on the forearm for controlling smartwatches. *Proceedings of the 2016 ACM International Symposium on Wearable Computers - ISWC '16*: 108–115. https://doi.org/10.1145/2971763.2971797

[30] Semtech. 2010. Application note: capacitive touch sensing layout guidelines. 1–17. Retrieved July 20, 2018 from www.semtech.com

[31] Paul Strohmeier, Jarrod Knibbe, Sebastian Boring, and Kasper Hornbæk. 2018. zPatch: Hybrid resistive/capacitive etextile input. In *TEI 2018 - Proceedings of the 12th International Conference on Tangible, Embedded, and Embodied Interaction.* https://doi.org/10.1145/3173225.3173242

[32] Alexandra Voit and Stefan Schneegass. 2017. FabricID: Using Smart Textiles to Access Wearable Devices. In *Proceedings of the 16th International Conference on Mobile and Ubiquitous Multimedia - MUM '17*, 379–385. https://doi.org/10.1145/3152832.3156622

[33] Irmandy Wicaksono and Joseph A Paradiso. 2017. FabricKeyboard : Multimodal Textile Sensate Media as an Expressive and Deformable Musical Interface. In *NIME*, 348–353.

[34] Byungseok Yoo and Darryll J Pines. 2017. Development of two-dimensional interdigitated center of pressure sensor. *Smart Materials and Structures* 26, 12: 125013. https://doi.org/10.1088/1361-665X/aa9427

[35] Bo Zhou, Jingyuan Cheng, Mathias Sundholm, and Paul Lukowicz. 2014. From smart clothing to smart table cloth: Design and implementation of a large scale, textile pressure matrix sensor. In *Lecture Notes in Computer Science*, 159–170. https://doi.org/10.1007/978-3-319-04891-8_14

[36] Seaboard: The Future Of The Keyboard | ROLI. Retrieved August 7, 2018 from https://roli.com/products/seaboard/

[37] Product – Joué. Retrieved August 7, 2018 from https://www.play-joue.com/en/the-product/

[38] HOW TO GET WHAT YOU WANT. Retrieved August 7, 2018 from http://www.kobakant.at/DIY/?p=6607

[39] E-Z Runner® Permanent Strips Refillable Value Pack - Scrapbook Adhesives by 3L. Retrieved August 7, 2018 from https://www.scrapbook-adhesives.com/products/new-value-pack-e-z-runner-r-refillable-permanent-strips-1

[40] X-Carve. Retrieved August 7, 2018 from https://www.inventables.com/technologies/x-carve

# Lights, Music, Stamps!
# Evaluating Mealtime Tangibles for Preschoolers

**Ying-Yu Chen[1], Jason Yip[2], Daniela Rosner[1], Alexis Hiniker[2]**
[1]Human Centered Design & Engineering, University of Washington,
[2]Information School, University of Washington,
Seattle, WA, USA
{yingyuc, jcyip, dkrosner,alexisr}@uw.edu

## ABSTRACT
We present an evaluation of three prototype tangible user interfaces (TUIs) for preschoolers during mealtime. Building on past work identifying value tensions between adults' and children's perspectives at meals, we examine how the TUIs address different tensions in this context (for example, the tension between children's interest in experimenting with food versus adults' interest in cleanliness). Thirteen preschool children and their parents tried out the prototypes, as did an additional seven preschool teachers. Adults and children alike were excited by the prototypes; parents were surprised by children's increased food intake, and children used the prototypes to engage in artistic expression with food traces. We also found that the prototypes motivated children's increased consumption, sometimes displacing their own hunger cues. We conclude that TUIs have the potential to enhance shared meals between children and adults but also have the potential to distract or persuade children in inappropriate or harmful ways. We present design guidance differentiating these two outcomes, such as incorporating the TUI into pre-existing mealtime objects and routines.

## Author Keywords
Tangible-user interfaces; child-computer interaction; preschool; meals; value tensions.

## CCS Concepts
Human-centered computing → Ubiquitous and mobile computing design and evaluation methods

## INTRODUCTION
Meals and the social practices surrounding them feature centrally in the lives of children [11]. In response, a growing body of literature across HCI and tangible computing has argued that tangible user interfaces (TUIs) and other digital experiences work as effective mechanisms for persuading children to enact mealtime practices that adults value (e.g., [10,15,27]). However, the role technology can play in explicitly promoting children's interests at meals remains under-examined.

In this exploratory study, we address this gap by examining prototype TUIs for shared meals that include adults and children. We used our prototypes to foreground the interests and needs of child and adult alike, focusing in particular on value tensions between adults and children (i.e., instances where designing to support one value challenges another [13]). To understand these value tensions, we examined children's and adults' responses to these prototypes. We found that the prototypes shaped children's mealtime experience by encouraging consistent utensil use, holding children's attention, and prompting creative expression with food traces. Parents, teachers, and adults alike indicated that children ate more when using these prototypes than they typically do. These findings suggest the potential for TUIs to resolve common mealtime struggles, such as coping with picky eating habits, but they also suggest the potential for TUIs to introduce unwanted distraction or persuasion.

## RELATED WORK
### Family Meals and Children's Nutrition
Engaging in mealtime is a complex practice with the potential for both positive and negative experiences that require work and intentionality on the part of adults and children. Research has identified that parents' struggles with children at mealtimes include spending more time at meals, children's food pickiness, new recipes and meal ideas, and conflict at mealtimes [14]. Emphasizing adults' roles (both parents and teachers) with children's well-being at mealtimes may place greater responsibilities and pressure on adults. Understanding adults' struggles and attitudes about mealtimes is essential to determine when and how technology can play a role in this context.

### Novel Technologies for Children's Meals
With a few exceptions [2] [29], scholars have largely overlooked how preschoolers interact with TEI-related objects, a growing body of work in tangible computing, UbiComp, and HCI incorporates smart sensors into everyday objects for children to encourage healthy eating behaviors. ChilDish uses sensors placed around a cup and dish to make sounds corresponding to the drawings on the tableware, with the intention of encouraging children to make healthy food choices through playful feedback [17]. Similarly, Edutableware embeds sounds into children's fork and cup to encourage


*TEI '19, March 17–20, 2019, Tempe, AZ, USA*

ACM 978-1-4503-6196-5/19/03□$15.00
https://doi.org/10.1145/3294109.3295645

**Figure 1: a) Left: Cat Fork; right: a child using his fork to pick up goldfish cracker; b) Left: The Stamp Plate; right: a child's stamp plate after he finished eating; c) The Kicking Chair; right: a child kicking the chair without eating.**

healthy food choices [22], and Playful Tray embeds a game into children's mealtime materials using a weight sensor and responds to children's eating behaviors [24].

Whereas these prior studies leverage smart objects to encourage healthy eating behaviors, a smaller body of work explores novel interactions to support creativity while eating [1,4,21]. These studies demonstrate the research community's interest in supporting the complex processes surrounding shared meals. We expand on this existing work by evaluating new prototypes that are designed to accommodate both adults' values about appropriate mealtime behaviors and children's values about play, self-expression, and autonomy.

### Respecting the Expertise and Autonomy of Children

Research in child-computer interaction increasingly emphasizes children's agency and the importance of respecting the inherent dignity and self-ownership of every child. Prior work advocates for incorporating children in the design process [7] and recognizes that children are experts on childhood with insights that cannot be accessed by probing adults' perspectives alone [6]. Research into the design of novel technologies for children also increasingly treats children's values as core design principles [12,19,23]. As a result, a number of methodological innovations seek to draw out children's perspectives and access their design insights (e.g., [8,9,16]). In what follows, we extend this orientation to the design of technologies for children's meals. By using the value tension lens [26], we are able to highlight not only children's perspectives, but also the interplay between children's and adults' values and the ways in which they might come into conflict.

## METHODS

Our research team included six interdisciplinary researchers and engineers. Together we held weekly design workshops over three months to generate design ideas and iteratively develop sketches based on three value tensions. We read fieldnote and interview snippets and grouped them into affinity diagrams to surface important themes and generate more than fifty sketches in total. We further grouped the sketches and discussed the ideas based on the affinity diagram.

### Participants

We recruited thirteen 4-to-6-year-old children (six boys and seven girls) to participate in our study via email lists at our institution and at local family housing communities. There are five white and five Asian families, and an African American and a multiracial family in our study[31]. We evaluated all three prototypes with each child and one or more parents. We also recruited seven preschool teachers to evaluate the three prototypes and participate in a semi-structured interview about the feasibility and usefulness of each of the prototypes. The teachers we interviewed include teachers and teaching assistants in preschool classrooms in a metro area in the United States. The researchers brought the three prototypes, showed the teachers and asked for their thoughts.

### Prototypes

We asked children and teachers to evaluate three novel prototypes, presented in prior work and created through observations, sketching exercises, intergenerational participatory design [32], and user interviews [3].

**The Cat Fork:** The first prototype, The Cat Fork (see Figure 1a), consisted of a metal fork and plate that both represent a cat's face. As a child touches the fork to the plate, the connection prompts different parts of the cat's face to illuminate. A total of 10 distinct color lights light up the cat's eyes, nose, whiskers and mouth. Our motivation for designing the prototype involved supporting the child's utensil use at the same time as supporting the child's independence. We designed the light interactions to offer children colorful and whimsical feedback while using their own fork and plate together (in contrast to eating off another child's plate or picking up another child's utensils). We built the prototype using an Arduino board and a Makey Makey [16].

**The Stamp Plate:** Our second prototype, the Stamp Plate (Figure 1b), comprises a series of stamps that correspond to food items eaten off the plate, leaving behind silhouette-like shapes that create food-inspired illustrations. We designed the plate to record the shape of the food children eat off the plate and then display that shape much like a lasting shadow. For instance, a cube of cheese leaves behind a square shape next to a goldfish-shaped cracker, which leaves behind a small fish shape. The plate provides children with a space to explore their sensory needs at the same time as supporting caretaker's concern for minimizing mess and keeping food on the plate. We simulated this design concept during our study by having a researcher print pre-designed custom stamps with multi-color inks on an adjacent plate each time the child picked up a snack and ate it.

**The Kicking Chair:** Our last prototype, the Kicking Chair (Figure 1c), consisted of a chair with a long elastic band wrapped around to its front two chair legs. Kicking the band triggers a playful sound play. The chair allows children a platform for whimsical expression as they move and wiggle in their seats while supporting caretaker's interest in encouraging children to stay in their chairs while eating. We designed the elastic band to be attachable at any leg height and on any chair (to adjust for child size. To implement the concept in our study, we used two folded pieces of aluminum foil connected to a rubber band, a Makey Makey board, and a laptop. The two pieces of foil touched every time the child kicked the band, prompting a piano note to play.

### Procedures

#### *Children's Evaluations*

To examine responses to our prototypes in practice, we conducted a user study with thirteen children (one at a time) within the spaces they would normally eat their snacks (e.g., children's own homes). We began each user study during the children's regular afternoon snack time and organized the study period as a three-part snack. For each part, researcher(s) asked the children to choose from a selection of snacks to put on their plate (including goldfish-shaped crackers, pretzels, bananas, apple slices, cheese cubes, tortilla chips, and crackers). These snack selections were familiar to children and most of them ate the varieties of food items we provided. The children picked a new set of snacks at the beginning of each new prototype. We randomized the order of prototypes explored during the study. A parent and a researcher accompanied each child in the study. The researcher occasionally prompted children to share their opinions about the prototype in order to glean a deeper understanding of their experience. We asked children to select their own snacks, but we did not limit or suggest any food items to the children. We tried to make the field trial as naturalistic as possible by letting children eat snacks at their usual snack time and inviting parents to accompany them (following recommendations from Hiniker et al.[20]).

#### *Teachers' Evaluations*

We took three prototypes into preschools and show teachers the prototypes during their breaks. We did not let the teacher use the prototypes because they are meant for children. Instead, the researchers showed and explained how each prototype works without telling the design processes and intensions. After demonstrating each prototype, we asked what teachers thought about it and how they would use it in the classroom, using semi-structured interview questions. We also randomized the orders of the prototype showings.

### Analysis

We audio- and video-recorded all lab sessions. Members of the research team iteratively watched videos and documented examples of interest using an inductive-deductive approach [5]. Using Trello organizational software, we created cards to represent all examples, creating a dataset of 230 vignettes. We then grouped these data points into themes to create a hierarchical affinity diagram. The teacher interviews were also audio-recorded and transcribed by a third party. We repeated our open-coding process to extract examples and cluster them into themes.

## FINDINGS

### Discovering Affordances

As children encountered the objects for the first time, most of them took some time to understand how each of the three prototypes worked. In some cases, children understood the prototype right away, for example, C13 explained "*I want a fish here,*" as he pointed to the stamp plate and then ate a fish from that spot on his own plate. Other children immediately pointed out the connection between the triangle stamp and the chips (e.g., C8) or the half circle to the apple (e.g., C1).

In other cases, children did not immediately discover the prototype's affordances. Many children did not understand how the Kicking Chair worked even as they used it to produce noises, and in these cases, children claimed the computer, the wire, or the chair itself was responsible for making the instrumental sounds. Eventually, most children came to understand how all three prototypes worked, although occasionally children developed unexpected mental models, such as believing the stamps on the stamp plate represented images of food that other children had eaten (C6).

Once children understood the prototypes, their reactions varied. Some continued to explore the prototype and ask questions, while others focused on eating the food. When children liked the prototype, it was often quite obvious, and they responded with exuberance. C3 and C10 responded to the Kicking Chair by giggling hysterically each time they heard the sound it made. C4 checked the lights on the cat fork and plate as she took a bite carefully and beamed when the light came on. She commented: "*when more lights are on, it [the Cat Fork] is happier!*"

### Influencing Children's Practices

Across our observations, we noticed children's practices change in the presence of the prototypes in four central ways. Here, we describe these cross-cutting shifts.

#### *Increased Eating*

Parents expressed that both the Cat Fork and the Stamp Plate led children to eat more food during the study session. C4's mother commented several times on how much more her child was eating during the session than usual. And after the study, she remarked: "*Oh my baby ate so much more. Actually, more than what she eats in a whole day!...I hope we [could someday] have all these at home.*" In another instance, C1 kept eating many of the goldfish-shaped crackers and pretzels to produce stamp artifacts for these items.

Like the Stamp Plate, the Cat Fork also led children to eat more. C5 wanted to know if the plate made sounds, and he started to eat more from the plate to explore the plate's capabilities and the effects of eating. C13's mom claimed the Cat Fork caused her child to eat much more because he liked using it. Another participant, C4, ate very intently using the Cat Fork until all available food was gone. The children tended to keep their attention on the meal while using the Cat Fork.

We asked our child participants which prototype they liked the most at the end of the study, and we asked if they would eat their least favorite food if they could do so using their preferred prototype. While some said they would not, others said they would eat a bell pepper or cheesecake (a non-preferred food) to produce stamps on the Stamp Plate. C3 said she would eat broccoli to make the Cat Fork's light up. C13 asked for more crackers because he wanted more circles to appear on the stamp plate. And a few children who said they were already full before testing the third prototype still finished the third snack. Parents commented on the amount children ate throughout the session, saying things like, "*She was certainly paying attention to what was happening...that certainly had an impact. She's certainly eaten a lot*" (C3).

### *Increased Use of Utensils*

We observed that when using the Cat Fork, children were more willing to use their utensils to eat. Children were encouraged to explore the fork initially, but were not required or continually asked to do so. However, many children continued to engage with the fork and the lights as they ate, even using the fork for snacks that are typically eaten as finger foods. C2 loves cats and when using the fork to eat an apple slice, she said: "*Guess what? I've never used a fork to eat an apple.*" C3 used the fork for every bite on her plate. And several children tried to use the fork to eat the goldfish-shaped crackers or tortilla chips. A few participants gave up on using the fork to eat these challenging foods after several attempts, but most of them switched back to using the utensil when they ate cheese cubes or bananas slices, which were easy to stab.

Prior work reports on children "half using" utensils while eating during typical meals; that is, using their hands to pick up food and put it onto the utensil before putting it into their mouths [3]. Children performed this same action when using the Cat Fork. Although we designed the object in part to address this practice, we saw that children continued to maintain it when using the prototype.

### *Increased Distraction*

While the Cat Fork and Stamp Plate tended to encourage children to focus on their utensils and their food, the Kicking Chair routinely redirected children's attention away from eating and toward the prototype. Although some children giggled and seemed to enjoy making sounds at the table as they ate, most of the time children either ate or played with the chair but did not integrate the two practices. For example, children sometimes squatted down and used their hands to make sounds by touching the band around the base of the chair, and some alternated between sitting while kicking and sitting while eating.

One child (C3) explicitly stated that the object was a distraction and explained that she was going to use the Kicking Chair to distract her dad, so she could steal his candy. She went on to say she would use it to distract people in public places. C13 believed he should not use the Kicking Chair during meals. He played with the chair initially and then politely asked the researcher, "*Can I eat now?*"

### *Creative Exploration*

We observed that participants engaged in creative exploration when using the Stamp Plate. C1 intentionally continued eating to see the image that the resulting artifacts would form on the plate. C13 wanted a goldfish-shaped cracker on a specific spot on the Stamp Plate, therefore he ate one from the analogous location on his food plate. When we asked why he wanted to eat the goldfish-shaped crackers at that specific spot, he explained: "*Cause I want the fishes to pile around.*"

Children also made creative comments as they looked at and reflected on the Stamp Plate after the meal. They made sense of the shapes of the food and created their own stories, which they retroactively fit onto the images they had produced. For example, C3 explained that she had made a pretzel maze for a goldfish to swim through. She went on to describe how she would make a maze using the plate in the future, saying, "*I would turn the plate in the direction I wanted the fish to go in.*" C13 also described his Stamp Plate as a scene deep under the sea, saying that the triangles are sea plants, the circles come from people dropping balls in the sea, while the fish are trying to help give the balls back to the people.

### *Prompting Self-Tracking*

When using the Stamp Plate, several children spontaneously engaged in tracking their food intake. We did not ask the first few children how many pieces of food they had eaten, but we observed that they proactively counted the fish stamps, the triangles, and circles as they were eating, and we were stamping. After we observed this practice in multiple sessions, we modified our protocol to include asking children how much they had eaten. Most children easily linked the composition of the Stamp Plate to the food they had eaten. For example, when asked how many tortilla chips he had eaten, C11 counted the triangles on the Stamp Plate and responded correctly.

C9 reminded the researcher that he had eaten a cracker and that the researcher had not yet placed a corresponding stamp on the plate. Many children similarly pointed to missing stamps if the researcher had yet to stamp the plate, suggesting children found the link between eating and the immediate effect that followed to be meaningful.

## Teachers' Responses to Prototypes

Teachers' and children's reactions to the prototypes were mostly well-aligned. Here, we describe teachers' general impressions of each of the three prototypes as well as themes that emerged across all of them.

### *General Impressions of Each Prototype*

*The Cat Fork:* Teachers predicted the Cat Fork would help children develop fine motor skills and encourage them to use utensils. Some teachers felt the Cat Fork may be more appropriate for younger children (under the age of 3) who are learning to use utensils for the first time. A few teachers worried the lights on the plate could be distracting for children and anticipated that children might poke the plate with the fork persistently to see the light.

*The Kicking Chair*: All teachers loved the concept of the Kicking Chair and thought it was innovative and likely to be engaging for children. However, they did not feel it was appropriate for mealtime and envisioned using it during playtime when it could be the focus of the activity. They predicted 20 children making noise while eating would be chaotic, and a couple of teachers said they already struggle to prevent children from kicking each other's chairs at mealtime.

*The Stamp Plate*: Almost all teachers felt that the Stamp Plate would encourage children to try new foods and would generate conversation at mealtime, and almost all teachers said that conversations with children are what they value most about meals. For example, T1 anticipated that children would have conversations with her about how and where the food is placed on the plate. She explained that she could model placing the food, such as putting a goldfish cracker on a plate next to a piece of cheese, and the children might put another goldfish cracker on the plate, this time above the cheese, or to the left of the cheese, fostering conversations about spatial relationships.

They also appreciated the Stamp Plate's support for children's creative expression. T7 commented that she thought the resulting images that the foods left behind on the plate, and the artistic form it would take, could generate many new conversations in the classroom.

### *Comparing Teachers' Predictions with Children's Actions*

In this section, we compare teachers' predictions of how children will react to the prototypes with children's reactions in practice, drawn from our observations during our exploratory evaluations.

*The Cat Fork:* Teachers expected the illuminating parts of the plate and fork to distract children form their meal. Although a few teachers acknowledged the lights might direct children's focus to the plate, more teachers thought the lights would encourage children to focus on playing with the plate, instead the food itself. T1 said: *"It would be a bunch of kids hitting their plates, and then really causing food to kind of go everywhere."* Other teachers imagined that the Cat Fork would prompt children to fight with each other at the table, more so than a regular fork. They were also concerned that focusing on the plate would take children's attention away from conversations with others.

In the test sessions with children, we did not observe the Cat Fork distracting children from their eating. On the contrary, most children were pleasantly surprised to discover that the cat plate illuminated. They ate tentatively with their forks to pick up the food, paying careful attention to which part of the cat plate lit up. Some of the children even used the fork to pick up pretzels (a food commonly eaten with hands).

*The Stamp Plate:* Children's reactions to the Stamp Plate corresponded to teachers' expectations. Teachers imagined children would make connections between the food they ate, and the images left behind on the plate, and in practice, children were able to do so. Teachers also thought the plate would encourage children to try new foods that they normally would not eat. During evaluation sessions, children expressed willingness to eat foods they do not like in order to generate stamps on the plate. Lastly, teachers expected the plate to help regulate mess and encourage creativity at mealtimes. While exploring the plate, all children in our evaluations kept their food on their plates and demonstrated creative expression, such as storytelling from the stamp-imagery they prompted by eating.

*The Kicking Chair*: Teachers' predictions about the Kicking Chair also matched children's experiences in practice. Teachers worried about the potential for distraction, a concern that held up when testing it with children. Children would kick and laugh so happily and completely forget about eating; one boy was constantly troubleshooting to see why the Kicking Chair did not work the way he expected and forgot about eating altogether. In addition, teachers predicted the Kicking Chair would decrease conversation at mealtimes. In fact, teachers expressed strong preference for the Kicking Chair idea, but they thought it would be more appropriate to use it other than the mealtime. For example, multiple teachers suggested using it in communal circle time to promote conversion and musical engagement.

## DISCUSSION

We saw that these tangible prototypes offered affordances and experiences that excited both children and adults. And we saw systematic ways in which they shaped children's interactions with and responses to food, such as engendering creative expression and self-tracking and increasing children's willingness to try new things. However, we also observed patterns in which these prototypes undermined mealtime goals and distracted children from the meal itself. And we saw the potential for these systems to persuade children in ways that might undermine their sense of autonomy or disrupt their relationship with the food they consume.

### Tangibles as a Tool for Mealtimes

Across our evaluations, both children and adults told us that the Kicking Chair served as a distraction and undermined children's focus on the meal. Although most children enjoyed engaging with the prototype, and teachers were enthusiastic about incorporating it into their classrooms for playtime, all parties agreed that the chair demanded attention as an object in its own right, rather than as an integrated component of the larger mealtime context.

The Cat Fork and the Stamp Plate designs, on the other hand, allowed children to easily attend to the novel object as a part of enacting existing mealtime practice. Although teachers predicted that the Cat Fork would cause distraction, we saw that by focusing on the fork, children were in fact also focusing on the meal and their eating practices. Children engaged more deeply in these practices than usual, incorporating the utensil into every bite and using a fork for finger foods like pretzels and apple slices.

This distinction suggests that TUIs may support children's meals most effectively when they treat pre-existing materials and practices as first-class priorities and augment existing routines without upstaging them. Prior work has found that adding interesting but unrelated content to reading materials for children (known as "seductive details" [18]) engages children but decreases their comprehension of and attention to the core material. Similarly, we found that the Kicking Chair created a new experience to attend to rather than augmenting the experience to which the child was already attending, providing design guidance for future TUIs. The Cat Fork, in contrast, added a new dimension to an existing practice, leading children to continue to engage in this practice (eating with utensils) with renewed focus.

These findings also suggest that TUIs may be uniquely well-suited to provide support in mealtime contexts, relative to other forms of technology. Tangibles, by their very nature, integrate with the physical world in a way that goes beyond what stand-alone devices like smartphones and tablets are capable of.

### Value Tensions and Persuasive Tangibles for Meals

In conducting this study, we set out to explore how we might design for all members of a shared meal, giving the same consideration to children's in-the-moment values and interests as to adults' long-term goals for children's eating practices. We saw that the tangible prototypes we evaluated eased existing value tensions between children and adults and largely encouraged the practices we set out to incite. But these prototypes also surfaced new value tensions we did not anticipate. For example, the Kicking Chair successfully facilitated wiggly play while keeping children in their seats, but it introduced new tensions wherein: 1) children valued attending to the chair and adults valued children attending to the meal, and 2) children valued using the chair as an instrument while adults valued a quiet environment that is conducive to conversation.

Similarly, we saw many indicators that our prototypes incentivized children to change their practices in ways we did not anticipate. We observed that both the Cat Fork and the Stamp Plate encouraged children to eat more than they normally do, opening serious questions about the consequences of these designs for long-term health and well-being. Many parents and teachers were enthusiastic about this development and felt certain that such tools would increase children's overall food intake. Children themselves gave us insight into the mechanisms underlying this shift in practice. They told us, for example, that they were eating chips not because they were hungry, but because they needed triangles for their picture, or because they wanted LED lights to illuminate. These findings urge caution and suggest the potential for tangibles to promote harmful food-related habits. Persuading children to eat foods they dislike or persuading them to overeat could potentially create unhealthy patterns, such as undermining children's sensitivity to their own hunger and satiation cues. Designing to change children's eating habits without their awareness also suggests the kind of paternalism for which persuasive technology is often critiqued [30]. As work in HCI increasingly acknowledges children as experts on their own experiences [6] and seeks to support their autonomy, it is important for designers seeking to resolve tensions between children and adults to consider how to support children in advocating for their own needs and directing their own practices.

### Mealtimes as Sites for Expressivity and Exploration

As children engaged with the Stamp Plate in particular, we observed that they used traces of their eating activity to provoke creative storytelling and reflection at the table (see [28]). In designing the Stamp Plate, for example, we had no fixed goals with respect to traditional notions of productivity or education. But by providing children with an opportunity to tap into their pre-existing interest in experimenting and playing with food [3], we inadvertently created an informal learning context in which children counted what they had eaten and linked their artistic creation to their autonomous activities. These insights suggest the potential for tangibles to enhance meals in meaningful ways, expanding beyond support mechanisms for nutritional goals to opportunities for tangible data sense-making and play.

### Future Work and Limitations

We see a number of ways for future work to build on the themes we encountered in this study. For example, to further probe whether TUIs can address families' struggles with children's food pickiness while simultaneously respecting children's autonomy, future designs might explore the design of interfaces that make the mealtime experience and the post-mealtime experience equally enticing, potentially encouraging children to eat without incentivizing them to continue to do so beyond their intrinsic hunger. Although we saw behaviors in this initial session that parents said were atypical, we do not know if the novelty would quickly wear off, or conversely, if such a tool might become a problematic long-term crutch. In the future, we hope to study the relationships that children form with these prototypes over time.

Our approach enabled us to prototype rapidly and to standardize the environment where children encountered the prototypes. Therefore, the child might be also interacting with the adults presented, and not the stamp plate alone. Other approaches, like Wizard of Oz [25] or more naturalistic setting, might be a clearer separation to test if the child is solely interacting with the prototype. We hope that some of these limitations are mitigated in part by the fact that children regularly engage in meals communally with.

There are also a number of ways in which the context of our study is limited. This data was collected from a small number of individuals in a single metropolitan area who likely did not struggle with food insecurity. Meals, educational environments, parenting practices, and family structure varies dramatically across communities, both within the United

States and around the world. The particular experiences we report here are not representative of any larger group. However, we hope that they generate questions for future designers and yield insights into how those creating future TUIs might engage with this.

## CONCLUSION

In this paper, we a conducted an exploratory evaluation with children and teachers to gather their feedback on three TUI prototypes designed to resolve adult-child value tensions in mealtime contexts at home and at school. Our results show that although our prototypes addressed certain value tensions, they seemed to ignite new ones, highlighting the complexities of value alignment in practice. The effectiveness of these novel tangibles in changing children's behaviors prompt us, as designers of technology, to consider what we do when we seek to address value tensions. We see how designers may nudge users with competing perspectives toward a compromise in ways that unevenly respects the parties involved. In view of this work, value tensions invite not quick resolution but thoughtful consideration of whom designers seek to persuade and why. In this sense, our findings also offer insight into the ways TUIs may shape children's practices in mealtime contexts by offering prompts to designers who seek to do so with care.

## REFERENCES

[1] Takahiro Arakawa and Masa Inakage. 2007. Mamagoto: playing with food. *ACM SIGGRAPH 2007 posters*: 161. https://doi.org/10.1145/1280720.1280895

[2] Matthew Black, Jeannette Chang, Jonathan Chang, and Shrikanth Narayanan. 2009. Comparison of child-human and child-computer interactions based on manual annotations. In *Proceedings of the 2nd Workshop on Child, Computer and Interaction - WOCCI '09*, 1–6. https://doi.org/10.1145/1640377.1640379

[3] Ying-Yu Chen, Kelda Baljon, Bonnie Tran, Daniela K. Rosner, and Alexis Hiniker. 2018. The stamp plate and the kicking chair. In *Proceedings of the 17th ACM Conference on Interaction Design and Children - IDC '18*, 373–380. https://doi.org/10.1145/3202185.3202759

[4] Marcelo Coelho and Marcelo. 2009. DinnerWare. In *Proceedings of the 27th international conference extended abstracts on Human factors in computing systems - CHI EA '09*, 3505. https://doi.org/10.1145/1520340.1520514

[5] Juliet Corbin and Anselm Strauss. 2008. Basics of qualitative research: Techniques and procedures for developing grounded theory.

[6] Allison Druin. 2002. The role of children in the design of new technology. *Behaviour & Information Technology* 21, 1: 1–25. https://doi.org/10.1080/01449290110108659

[7] Allison Druin and Allison. 1999. Cooperative inquiry. In *Proceedings of the SIGCHI conference on Human factors in computing systems the CHI is the limit - CHI '99*, 592–599. https://doi.org/10.1145/302979.303166

[8] Jóhanna Einarsdóttir. 2007. Research with children: methodological and ethical challenges. *European Early Childhood Education Research Journal* 15, 2: 197–211. https://doi.org/10.1080/13502930701321477

[9] Allison Farber, Allison Druin, Gene Chipman, Dawn Julian, and Sheila Somashekher. 2002. How Young Can Our Technology Design Partners Be? *PDC*: 272–277.

[10] Hasan Shahid Ferdous, Bernd Ploderer, Hilary Davis, Frank Vetere, Kenton O'Hara, Geremy Farr-Wharton, and Rob Comber. 2016. TableTalk: Integrating Personal Devices and Content for Commensal Experiences at the Family Dinner Table. *Proceedings of the 2016 ACM International Joint Conference on Pervasive and Ubiquitous Computing*, September: 132–143. https://doi.org/10.1145/2971648.2971715

[11] Barbara H Fiese, Thomas J Tomcho, Michael Douglas, Kimberly Josephs, Scott Poltrock, and Tim Baker. 2002. A review of 50 years of research on naturally occurring family routines and rituals: Cause for celebration? *Journal of family psychology* 16, 4: 381.

[12] Daniel Fitton, Janet C Read, Gavin Sim, and Brendan Cassidy. 2018. Co-designing voice user interfaces with teenagers in the context of smart homes. In *Proceedings of the 17th ACM Conference on Interaction Design and Children - IDC '18*, 55–66. https://doi.org/10.1145/3202185.3202744

[13] Batya Friedman and David Hendry. 2012. The envisioning cards. In *Proceedings of the 2012 ACM annual conference on Human Factors in Computing Systems - CHI '12*, 1145. https://doi.org/10.1145/2207676.2208562

[14] Jayne A. Fulkerson, Mary Story, Dianne Neumark-Sztainer, and Sarah Rydell. 2008. Family Meals: Perceptions of Benefits and Challenges among Parents of 8- to 10-Year-Old Children. *Journal of the American Dietetic Association* 108, 4: 706–709. https://doi.org/10.1016/j.jada.2008.01.005

[15] Shad Gross, Austin Toombs, Jeff Wain, and Kevin Walorski. 2011. Foodmunity. In *Proceedings of the 2011 annual conference extended abstracts on Human factors in computing systems - CHI EA '11*, 1019. https://doi.org/10.1145/1979742.1979504

[16] Mona Leigh Guha, Allison Druin, Gene Chipman, Jerry Alan Fails, Sante Simms, and Allison Farber. 2004. Mixing ideas. In *Proceeding of the 2004*

*conference on Interaction design and children building a community - IDC '04*, 35–42. https://doi.org/10.1145/1017833.1017838

[17] Seo Yoon Han and Eun Ji Kang. 2017. ChilDish. In *Proceedings of the Companion of the 2017 ACM/IEEE International Conference on Human-Robot Interaction - HRI '17*, 391–392. https://doi.org/10.1145/3029798.3034946

[18] Shannon F. Harp and Richard E. Mayer. 1998. How seductive details do their damage: A theory of cognitive interest in science learning. *Journal of Educational Psychology* 90, 3: 414–434. https://doi.org/10.1037/0022-0663.90.3.414

[19] Yasmeen Hashish, Andrea Bunt, and James E Young. 2014. Involving children in content control: a collaborative and education-oriented content filtering approach. In *CHI '14* (CHI '14), 1797–1806. https://doi.org/10.1145/2556288.2557128

[20] Alexis Hiniker, Kiley Sobel, Sungsoo Hong, Hyewon Suh, India Irish, and Julie A Kientz. 2016. Hidden symbols: How informal symbolism in digital interfaces disrupts usability for preschoolers. https://doi.org/10.1016/j.ijhcs.2016.03.006

[21] Jesús Ibáñez and Jesús. 2015. Play with your Food. In *Proceedings of the 2015 Annual Symposium on Computer-Human Interaction in Play - CHI PLAY '15*, 553–558. https://doi.org/10.1145/2793107.2810294

[22] Azusa Kadomura, Koji Tsukada, and Itiro Siio. 2013. EducaTableware. In *CHI '13 Extended Abstracts on Human Factors in Computing Systems on - CHI EA '13*, 3071. https://doi.org/10.1145/2468356.2479613

[23] Priya Kumar, Jessica Vitak, Marshini Chetty, Tamara L. Clegg, Jonathan Yang, Brenna McNally, and Elizabeth Bonsignore. 2018. Co-designing online privacy-related games and stories with children. In *Proceedings of the 17th ACM Conference on Interaction Design and Children - IDC '18*, 67–79. https://doi.org/10.1145/3202185.3202735

[24] Jin-ling Lo, Tung-yun Lin, Hao-hua Chu, Hsi-chin Chou, Jen-hao Chen, Jane Yung-jen Hsu, and Polly Huang. 2007. Playful Tray : Adopting Ubicomp and Persuasive Techniques into Play-Based Occupational Therapy for Reducing Poor Eating Behavior in Young Children. *Proceedings of The International Conference on Ubiquitous Computing (UbiComp '07)*: 38–55. https://doi.org/10.1007/978-3-540-74853-3_3

[25] Bella. Martin and Bruce M. Hanington. 2012. *Universal methods of design : 100 ways to research complex problems, develop innovative ideas, and design effective solutions*. Rockport Publishers.

[26] Jessica K. Miller, Batya Friedman, Gavin Jancke, and Brian Gill. 2007. Value tensions in design. In *Proceedings of the 2007 international ACM conference on Conference on supporting group work - GROUP '07*, 281. https://doi.org/10.1145/1316624.1316668

[27] Kyohei Ogawa, Yukari Hori, Toshiki Takeuchi, Takuji Narumi, Tomohiro Tanikawa, and Michitaka Hirose. 2012. Table talk enhancer. In *Proceedings of the ACM multimedia 2012 workshop on Multimedia for cooking and eating activities - CEA '12*, 25. https://doi.org/10.1145/2390776.2390783

[28] Daniela K. Rosner, Miwa Ikemiya, Diana Kim, and Kristin Koch. 2013. Designing with traces. In *Proceedings of the SIGCHI Conference on Human Factors in Computing Systems - CHI '13*, 1649. https://doi.org/10.1145/2470654.2466218

[29] Jinsil Hwaryoung Seo, Janelle Arita, Sharon Chu, Francis Quek, and Stephen Aldriedge. 2015. Material Significance of Tangibles for Young Children. In *Proceedings of the Ninth International Conference on Tangible, Embedded, and Embodied Interaction - TEI '14*, 53–56. https://doi.org/10.1145/2677199.2680583

[30] Andreas Spahn. 2012. And Lead Us (Not) into Persuasion...? Persuasive Technology and the Ethics of Communication. *Science and Engineering Ethics* 18, 4: 633–650.

[31] Sarita Yardi and Amy Bruckman. 2012. *Income, Race, and Class: Exploring Socioeconomic Differences in Family Technology Use*. Retrieved November 13, 2018 from https://yardi.people.si.umich.edu/pubs/Yardi_Parents_SES12.pdf

[32] Jason C. Yip, Kiley Sobel, Caroline Pitt, Kung Jin Lee, Sijin Chen, Kari Nasu, and Laura R. Pina. 2017. Examining Adult-Child Interactions in Intergenerational Participatory Design. In *Proceedings of the 2017 CHI Conference on Human Factors in Computing Systems - CHI '17*, 5742–5754. https://doi.org/10.1145/3025453.3025787

# MemoryReel: A Purpose-designed Device for Recording Digitally Connected Special Moments for Later Recall and Reminiscence

**Huaxin Wei**[1] huaxin.wei@polyu.edu.hk
**Dianya Hua**[1] mia.dy.hua@polyu.edu.hk
**Eli Blevis**[2, 1] eblevis@indiana.edu
**Zitao Zhang**[1] sdvictor@polyu.edu.hk

[1]School of Design
The Hong Kong Polytechnic University
Kowloon, Hong Kong

[2]School of Informatics, Computing, and Engineering
Indiana University
Bloomington, Indiana, United States

## ABSTRACT

This paper presents the design rationale and concept development behind MemoryReel, a tangibly interactive desktop device that records special moments of online social interactions, between couples and friends over a long distance, and supports later reminiscence. In a human-centered design process started with a two-act design inquiry, we developed the design concept and implemented a medium-to-high-fidelity interactive prototype. We then invited 20 participants to experience the prototype and give comments. The design rationale together with the analysis of the exploratory user study findings provides insights on the dimensions and strategies of a design space for digital memories and long-distance relationships, with an emphasis on reminiscence support.

### Author Keywords

Tangible interaction design; digital memory; reminiscing; connectedness; long-distance relationship; long-distance friendship; avatar-based physical tokens.

### ACM Classification Keywords

• Human-centered computing~Interaction design

## INTRODUCTION

In today's globalized environment, more and more younger adults leave their close families and friends to pursue more opportunities, as students and career starters, in a different town or country for greater personal growth. Thanks to ever-advancing digital technologies, members of intimate social networks (e.g., couples, friends, other family members) can still maintain a close connection over a distance using a variety of communication tools. Notwithstanding, the digitally connected moments of interpersonal interactions are transient. Their traces are easily buried in the memory storage of digital devices, mixed with everyday recordings of everything that make for modern social streaming. The sheer amount of these recordings can lead to information overload [27] , which makes it hard to retrieve memories of those moments.

In this design research, we take on digital memory as our targeted design space, in the modern context where everyday life is consumed, directed, organized, and perceived through digital devices of all sorts. More specifically, we are interested in how people's sense of connectedness, when not physically co-present, can be nurtured in ways other than the most common and mundane to interact instantly with each other using social media and online communication tools, such as Facebook, WhatsApp, WeChat, and Skype. Our motivation is to instill the ideal of sustainability into our digital social life and to enhance people's mental wellbeing by creating an opportunity for people to reminisce and reflect in their offline time on truly special moments shared with their remote close others.

## CONTRIBUTIONS

We consider the needs of people to record and recall special moments with close others in their lives apart from commonplace and mundane social networking interactions. More generally, our research question concerns *how can deeply meaningful relationships be scaffolded by technologies that provide distinctive recording and recollection for these special moments?* Our design prototype iterations and evaluations affirm that these notions of recording and recollection of special moments play an important role in addressing latent needs and supporting affective experience of meaningful relationship.

**Figure 1. MemoryReel.**


*TEI '19, March 17–20, 2019, Tempe, AZ, USA.*

ACM 978-1-4503-6196-5/19/03…$15.00
https://doi.org/10.1145/3294109.3295649

In prior work, we introduced the MemoryPin, a highly relevant design concept exploring memory and connectedness support [6] . In this paper, we focus on MemoryReel (Figure 1), a new concept that builds on what we learned from MemoryPin to address our question. We here report on the studies behind the MemoryReel concept. By enabling people to privilege special memories over the commonplace social media stream, we are contributing a conceptual prototype that adopts notions of durability from the perspective of sustainability (e.g. [14] ) to the issue of special memories, using the design principle of embodying digital memorabilia in physical objects [27] . The main takeaway design implication of our work is: *With overwhelmingly large amount of digital memories, giving tangible form to contents privileged for later reminiscence can foster durability and delight for people within their close circles.*

## THEORETICAL BACKGROUND

In search for the relationships between memory and positive experience, we first turn to the literature of *reminiscence*—the voluntary or involuntary act or process of recollecting autobiographical memories [26] , or "episodes recollected from an individual's life" [28] . They serve three main functions in everyday life: *self* (e.g. maintaining self-continuity), *social* (e.g. enhancing social bonding), and *directive* (e.g. solving problems based on previous experience) [1] . Involuntary reminiscence on autobiographical memory is always triggered by cues, i.e., "stimuli that can help someone to retrieve information from long-term memory" [22] . These cues can be both external (e.g. the sight of an object) and internal (e.g. a thought) [28] . Many researchers regard reminiscence as having positive impacts on people's subjective wellbeing. In a set of two quantitative studies of younger adults, for example, Bryant et al. showed that through reminiscence of pleasant memories, participants reported more positive emotional experience and their level of happiness was boosted [2] .

Another aspect critical to designing for positive experience of long-distance relationships is *connectedness*, or "a positive emotional appraisal which is characterized by a feeling of staying in touch within ongoing social relationships" [20] . In follow-up research of [20] , Van Bel et al. [21] established a questionnaire to measure social connectedness at the individual level containing five dimensions: (a) *Relationship salience*, (b) *Dissatisfaction with contact quality*, (c) *Shared understandings*, (d) *Knowing each others' experiences*, and (e) *Feelings of closeness*. Several preliminary suggestions for design approaches to promoting social connectedness are relevant to the connection to *the close others* in particular, including: *representing or reminding people of their connection to close others* (addressing dimension (a)); *increasing the feelings of closeness* (e); *providing information about others' feelings and thoughts* (d); and *non-intentionally relaying very basic information as part of an awareness system (e.g. being at home or not)*.

Closely related to connectedness is the experience of *relatedness*, one of human's fundamental needs and crucial to people's positive experience with life [5] . Studying the feeling of relatedness (e.g., love, closeness, intimacy) among long-distance couples and family members, Hassenzahl et al. [5] analyzed 143 published artifacts including design concepts and technologies. The result was six broad design strategies for the creation and mediation of the experience of relatedness with technologies: *awareness*, *expressivity*, *physicalness*, *gift giving*, *joint action*, and *memories*. While the first five all focus on communication at different levels, such as sharing ambient information (awareness) or communicating intimacy with simulating gestures (physicalness), memories is the only strategy not based on communication, and can only be seen in 4 of the 143 surveyed artifacts. Nevertheless, the memories strategy—"artifacts that keep records of past activities and special moments of a relationship"—is highly relevant to our design space [5] . Its associated psychological principles and key requirements for design are "memorabilia, commitment, tangibility" [5] .

Lastly, Mols et al.'s [11] recent design research delineated a design space called *everyday life reflection*, which we consider highly related and overlapping with our targeted design space. Among its design dimensions, we were interested in the strategy of *information driven* (as opposed to social and expression-driven) reflection [11] . To further connect to digital memory and the act of reminiscing, we focused our system on—of the three roles outlined by the above authors—triggering reflection and supporting the process of reflection, rather than capturing. Our work also explored two of the principles that Mols et al. considered important for supporting everyday reflection: "openness in design" and "integrating reflection in everyday life" [11] ; the latter was seconded by Whittaker et al. in their research on memory support [27] . From observations of a series of lifelogging related studies, Whittaker et al. derived four design principles for digital systems to support memory: (a) selection of content (e.g., it should be lightweight), (b) integrate digital mementos better into everyday life (e.g., combining them with physical objects, (c) support reminiscence and reflection, and (d) digital tools should work in synergy with unaided memory [27] .

## RELATED WORK

The value of reminiscence has led to the creation of a number of systems in the HCI community to support *mediated reminiscence* by bringing back and displaying past digital contents to cue autobiographical memory. Pensieve [16] is a system that can choose contents (e.g. photos, music, text) randomly from social media sites (e.g. Flickr, Twitter) and email them as memory triggers to reminiscence. Memory Stamps [24] is a system that supports group recollection of shared memories, using physical stamps as triggers of photo sets supported with a retrieval mechanism based on keywords from the conversation. Photobox [15] and the Reflexive Printer [19] support reflection and reminiscence by printing pictures chosen from people's Flickr photo collections or smartphones. Both works demonstrated how materialized (i.e., printed) digital content helps enrich the reminiscing experience. Working exclusively with sounds, FM Radio [17] and Memento [13] are devices that can record and/or classify sonic mementos, as well as play them back.

Many designs in HCI have also explored how interactive technologies can help create the feeling of *relatedness* over a distance, using an approach beyond information-oriented communication. Some harnessed tactile and other sensory feelings to design for intimacy. For example, Hug Over a Distance [12] is a wearable interface that mimics hug sensations to help couples to express intimacy when they are apart. Ring* U [3] , a ring-shaped artifact, creates intimacy through tactile sensation combined with colored lighting. BreathingFrame [8] provides a novel interaction, abdominal breathing, for users to share breathing to their partners at a distance, an act that resulted sentimental connectedness in the user study. Other designs act like awareness systems for couples or family members to feel in touch through non-information based communication. For example, Virtual Intimate Objects [7] is a device designed for couples in long-distance relationships to communicate intimacy by sending messages one bit at a time. FamilyPlanter [10] is a sensor-based planter-looking terminal that can automatically communicate situational cues to remote family members. The cues are intended to evoke thoughts about others and thus create the sense of closeness to others. SnowGlobe [25] is a presence lamp that will light up and show snow flurries when a close relative gets close to his or her globe on their side. Users can also shake the globe to nudge their relative so that their globe will light up and snow. Cubble [9] is a hybrid solution for long-distance couples that harnesses advantages of physical objects, simple communication and presence awareness.

The related work cited above show a few tendencies. For design research working with digital memory content for reminiscence, *photos appear to be a popular form as memory cues*. The content is usually selected randomly, with the exceptions of FM Radio [17] and Memento [13] that allow users to record moments at their will. For designs for relatedness experience between couples and family members living apart, we clearly see an increasing interest in solutions that are *not* centered on messaging, even though *the designs are still synchronized or real-time communication systems* by nature. Breakthroughs are mainly seen in the increasingly multi-modal information and emotion (e.g., tactile hug, situational cues) that is communicated. In addition, revisiting personal digital items has its own set of challenges. The increasingly large volume of digital content makes the retrieval difficult especially after a long time (e.g., a year); moreover, digital mementos—except for digital photos—are less salient for people to recollect compared to physical mementos [27] .

In light of the above review of theories and designs, our work aimed to go beyond the common solutions based on synchronized communication and/or photo mementos, and responded to the aforementioned challenges by focusing on *special, selected moments* and embodying their associated digital contents in a physical object as memory cues.

## HUMAN-CENTRED DESIGN PROCESS

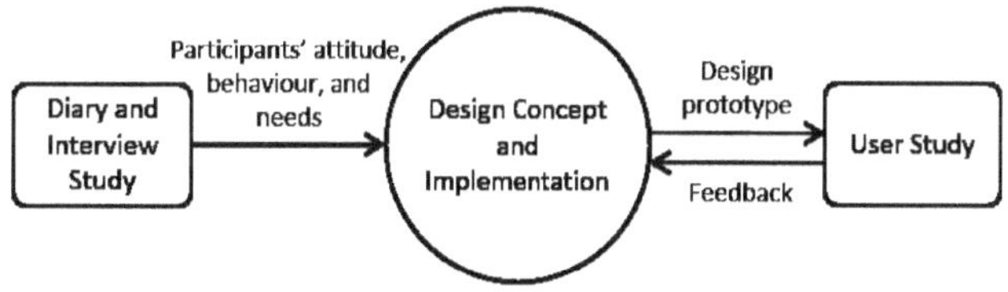


**Figure 2. The human-centered design process.**

Our interest is to use memory as the core means of fostering positive connectedness experience towards partners and close friends for younger adults away from home. By staying away from the dominant solution of online communication, the design is focused on preserving and interacting with digital memory, in a way that enables reminiscence and reflection of one self and the close other. In order to form design strategies for this unique focus, our human-centered design process started with a two-act inquiry phase, which resulted in a set of detailed requirements for the concept building and implementation. After the prototype was implemented, we conducted user study and refined our design concept accordingly. The design process is illustrated in Figure 2.

### A Two-Act Design Inquiry: Diary Study and Interview

We recruited 14 participants in a two-act design research study to understand their experience of long-distance relationships and friendships, and to what extent memory can support relationships. For experience, our inquiry covered attitude, behaviour and habit, as well as emotion when it comes to keeping in touch with a distant close other. For memory, the inquiry centered on varied emotional scenarios where participants look at memorabilia (e.g., photos, videos).

#### *Participants*

All 14 participants had a partner or at least a close friend at a long distance. 7 were in romantic relationships and 7 friendships. Participants had mixed backgrounds with age ranging from 22 to 42; 9 were female (64%) and 5 were male; 2 were married without children. 8 of them were local; yet 13 of them were born and raised in Asia—representing a very typical local demography of Hong Kong. The distance between participants and their close ones ranged from 89 kilometers to 10075 kilometers.

#### *Diary Study*

Our queries were rooted in participants' everyday living context and their experience and behaviours related to long-distance relationship and friendship, which would sound very abstract and oftentimes are subconscious to themselves. To help participants grow their awareness of their daily happenings as well as to provide talking points for researchers to discuss individual unique issues beyond the pre-set questions, a one-week diary study activity was staged before the interview. The diary package consisted of a colour printed diary booklet with minimal instructions, colour stickers and a graphical mood board, cueing participants to record their habitual and emotional moments towards their relationships and memories of close others.

#### *Semi-Structured Interview*
Seven days later, we conducted a follow-up semi-structured interview to elaborate on their feelings and behaviours. Our core questions were about the basic situation of their relationship, their attitudes towards the relationship and the distance, emotions towards the close other, and any memory-based coping mechanism (if any). From time to time, the conversation branched off to further details or other aspects as the researcher was viewing the diary together with the interviewee. On average, each interview lasted about 20 minutes and all were audio recorded.

#### *Findings and Discussion of Two Types of Relationships*
We used thematic coding to perform a qualitative analysis of the data collected from the returned diaries and interview transcription. The observed themes include: motives for communication, communication topics, means of communication, the functions of photos, and the role of memory. Each theme was identified with a set of patterns emerged. Here communication refers to Internet-based communication. Between two groups commenting on their romantic relationships and close friendships respectively, there were both commonality and differences detailed in the following 4 points. (a) Total distinctions were found for themes of motives for communication – simulating the sense of togetherness for couples and feeling understood and appreciated for friends, as well as the functions of photos – reminiscing and comforting for couples and recording for friends. (b) Both groups felt that memory helped bring comfort in reminiscing and reinforce the relationship. (c) Regarding the topics, though both liked to share their emotion, couples liked to share daily life details whereas friends tend to focus on life milestones. (d) In terms of means of communication, both groups used text and audio messages; however, couples also favoured making video calls, exchanging photos and videos, and doing activities together online (e.g., watching a TV show together), while friends tend to prefer audio calls.

We believed the distinction between behaviour and preferences of the two groups was not critical enough to require separate designs, given our design motivation (i.e., to encourage people to reminisce about truly special moments) and approach (i.e., to record those moments and provide memory support). The following corresponds to the earlier points of differences. We did not consider point (a) as an issue because our approach would not involve synchronized communication and photos, as mentioned earlier in Related Work. As long as our solution can accommodate multi-modal contents of varied media types and audiences' preferred choices of moments to record, point (c) and (d) would not be an issue, either. In the following subsection, we will discuss individual design requirements inspired by some of the patterns emerging from the design inquiry findings.

### Design Requirements
Taking considerations of both our original design motivation and findings from our design inquiry, we put together a list of design requirements, followed with a specific set of technical requirements to serve as a guide for building the design prototype. We wanted the overall look and feel of the design to be elegant (as a keepsake), and non-intrusive, analogue (as an offline experience). It would require minimal maintenance from its audience (so they can be focused in reminiscence).

#### *Use Context*
The design is intended for use in a home or private setting. The reason is that bedtime and morning wake-up time are the most common times for our interview participants to reminisce and think of their close others. Generally, the design is intended for a quiet, solitary and offline time. It acts like a personal "memory album."

#### *Content and Its Data Formats*
As the design targets digitally connected special moments, the content is selected and extracted from the communication content on audiences' digital device. This usually includes shared emotion, self-disclosing stories and topics related to life milestones. These contents are often communicated through text and audio messages, as a pattern emerged from the interview findings. Moreover, couples tend to perform joined activities during video calls. Therefore, the design solution should be able to tap into both chat history and video calls. Currently most video call applications do not provide the function of recording, so ideally the solution can make up for this void.

#### *Physical Representation of the Close Others*
As the source of content is online communication, naturally the contents are sorted by individual contacts of the audience. From the interviews, we learned that couples often perform many symbolic actions, where they use physical objects (e.g., a toy, a printed photo, clothes) as a representation of the others to simulate the feeling of being together. Thus, our design solution should have a representation component to signify whose content is being accessed. This also resonates Van Bel et al.'s [21] suggested approach of representing the close others as mentioned earlier.

#### *Technical Requirements*
The device needs to be as compact as possible so to remain non-intrusive. It can possibly be a decorative item on desktop to fit into a home setting. To emphasize its physicality and tangibility as a seemingly offline product, we aim to make its shape as 3D as possible so to distinguish itself from other screen-based products. As the design emphasizes an analogue and offline feel, we decide to stay away from bright, colourful displays like LCD or LED

screens. This thus limits our choices to E Ink (electronic ink) displays. Current E Ink is great in displaying texts but not capable of fast refreshing; hence, a second colour display with faster refresh rate is needed for displaying video content. In terms of processing power, the device needs to be capable to play back short video and audio content, which in turn requires speakers and their drivers. Wireless Internet connectivity is also desirable for convenient uploading and downloading of content to and from cloud storage.

## THE MEMORYREEL

**Figure 3. The MemoryReel device.**

### Design Concept: The MemoryReel

Based on the above design requirements and extending the concept of MemoryPin [6] , we developed our new design concept—a domestic device that we call MemoryReel. We prototyped a device system that contains a desktop device and an accompanying mobile application. The desktop device (see Figure 3) is the main component used for interactively displaying memory cues (i.e., content pieces). The accompanying mobile application mainly handles supplementary functions including capturing, organizing and exporting content. In the description below, we follow the order of three major steps of operation to present the main functions.

#### *Collecting Digital Memory Cues*

The mobile application allows MemoryReel owners to capture moments from video calls and collect messages, via two plugins for the video call and messaging software. When audiences want to capture moments of video call, they can simply press a button on the video call software interface to start the recording. When done, one animated GIF will be saved on the phone with separate images of the caller and the receiver.

#### *Organizing Memory Cues*

In the application's interface, all previously captured digital content may be grouped by the contacted person, when there are more than one such person. The grouped content can be uploaded to cloud storage. In a tokenizing approach, each person is represented by an "avatar" token with an anthropomorphic yet gender-neutral shape (see bottom right of Figure 3). The default number of the avatars is two, the host and the guest. When there are more close others, more tokens can be added; that is, while the host is fixed on the device, the guest can be replaced with another.

#### *Playing Back Memory Cues*

When a guest avatar is placed on the device, the digital content (or cues) corresponding to the close other will be displayed. With interaction, the guest avatar can be moved closer to the host avatar. The distance between the two avatars determines which format of contents will be played back. When the guest is at the far end, text messages will be shown on the E Ink display (see bottom left of Figure 3); this is also the device's standby mode. When the guest is in the middle position, audio messages will be played back. When the two are next to each other, animated GIFs of recorded videos will be projected (see top of Figure 3). In any of the three viewing modes, the displayed cue can be changed by turning any of the two avatars: turning left for the previous cue or right for the next one.

### Design Prototyping

Our design prototyping went through three small iterations with changes of the mechanical model and hardware design. For the final version, we implemented nearly all functionalities described in the concept of the desktop device through physical computing. For the mobile application, we created a user interface prototype in high resolution that can demonstrate related functions and use flow.

#### *Physical Design: Form and Material*

The physical form of the desktop device consists of a shell case and a control module (Figure 3). The shell consists of a rounded cuboid and a triangular prism, both laser-cut from white acrylic. The shell encloses all the electronic components. An E Ink display panel is installed on the front of the triangular prism. To the right of the prism is the control module, where two spring-return potentiometers are installed on a track, 3D printed with polylactic acid and hidden inside the shell case. Each potentiometer's shaft can be attached with a wooden avatar token, as a controller as mentioned earlier. The physical design of the track, installed with a micro switch on both ends, allows the right controller to slide through three detectable positions: right, middle, and left (see Figure 4). As mentioned in the concept, the three positions enable three modes of viewing: text messages, audio messages, and animated GIFs. We implemented two possible ways to view the GIFs—through the mini-projector installed on the rear side of the prism or through a smart phone. When using the mini-projector, the imagery can be projected onto a wall or any surface behind the device. When using the smart phone, it will be shown on the phone screen. This dual design was intended for probing audiences' preferences in the upcoming user study, as their perceived privacy levels could be quite different.

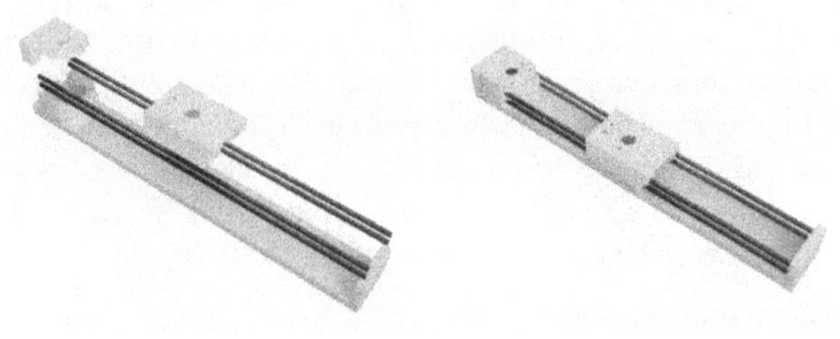

**Figure 4. Mechanical design of the control module's track.**

*Technical Design: Hardware and Software*

The desktop device uses a 2.7-inch e-Paper HAT (an E Ink display panel) for displaying text messages. A Raspberry Pi (a single-board mini-computer) is used both to drive the e-Paper HAT and to host a web server. The cues are being streamed from the web server (i.e. cloud storage) via WiFi. To realize the control of the three positions enabling three viewing modes, a wirelessly enabled micro-controller ESP32 is employed. It captures the analogue user input state (e.g., avatar position, turning gesture) and converts the analogue signal to a digital one, which in turn updates the Raspberry Pi through its web server and trigger the change of the viewing mode as well as the cues. Software wise, NodeJS Express server with Socket.IO (– a JavaScript web application framework and library) is used to host and play back audio clips and animation GIFs over WiFi.

## USER STUDY

### Study Goal

We considered our prototype ready for an exploratory user study when it reached a level of fidelity that has the desired appearance and product design and can simulate almost all the functions and behaviours of the system, except for the step of collecting actual content from a smart phone. The primary goal of the study was to find out participants' overall feelings towards the design concept, and more importantly, imagined use scenarios regarding how the device can support their reminiscence and connectedness. The secondary goal is to study the user experience with participants' responses. Based on the current implementation and fidelity level of the prototype, we chose to pay attention to cognition (e.g., perceived meaning of the product in daily life or the context of the relationship) and expressiveness (e.g., imagined alternative use scenarios or desire to personalize the product), from Forlizzi and Battarbee's [4] framework of designing experience for interactive systems.

### Study Set-up

*Participants*

A diverse sample of 20 participants (10 females and 10 males; 14 postgraduate students, 2 undergraduate students, and 4 working professionals) were recruited, all from our targeted audience group, i.e., younger adults aged between 18 and 45 who are in a long-distance relationship or friendship without children. Participants were invited conveniently through the research team's social network, referral and face-to-face invitation on campus. 13 of the 20 participants were Hong Kong locals; 17 were born and raised in Asia. The youngest participant was aged 20 and oldest 43. Only one participant was married (without children). We intentionally re-involved a small sample of 3 participants—fewer than what we actually wanted—from the previous diary study; however, we did not note any difference, in attitude or the level of details of the feedback, between them and other participants. They were specially labeled with O regardless.

*Procedure*

The user study took place in a living laboratory setting; namely, a lab decorated as a living room environment. A small table was set up near one side of a couch. The device was placed on top of the table. A camcorder was set up at an over-the-shoulder angle. Instead of using each participant's own content, we pre-created some contents such as a warm greeting or a reflective message, attempting to capture various moments. A number of audio messages in both male and female voices. We also created two sets of animated GIFs—one for friends and the other for couples. This approach clearly had its limitations. However, it was effective to provide participants enough context of design concept. Because the content was not their own, it created a comfortable distance and space for participants to relate the device to their own experiences in their own imagined scenarios without being self-conscious.

Each one-on-one session proceeded with four steps. (1) The researcher greeted the participant, gave a brief introduction of the study and the prototype, and then obtained the participant's written consent. (2) Each participant was invited to try the prototype with minimal instruction until they believed they had fully explored the device. During the course, they were encouraged to freely express their feelings and thoughts, or ask any questions. (3) The researcher then demonstrated and explained key functions of the device and the app to make sure the participant completely understood the concept. (4) A short structured interview was followed with open-ended questions focusing on the areas mentioned in the Study Goal. Before analyzing the interview data, we grouped interview questions into several themes, based on which two researchers conducted coding independently. We then listed all the codes together, highlighted similar areas and identified patterns emerging under each theme.

### Findings

The high-level design concept—collecting and playing back digital content generated from special, digitally connected moments to remind people of their closed others—was widely accepted. Generally, participants showed positive feelings (with only one exception, N20) over MemoryReel. Most (except for N20 and N14) expressed the wish to own a device (for self or for the close other), if not two (one for self and one for the close other) or more (one for each close friend). The physical feel of MemoryReel induced intimate feelings, like how participant N05 commented: "*A message received on my phone feels a little bit cold. ... If I can touch a physical thing with my hand, it brings the experience of reminiscence and feels more intimate. A necklace or letter of hers already feel intimate, but if I touch it, it can speak, then it feels even closer.*" In what follows, we selected and presented findings that focus on how MemoryReel can support reminiscence and connectedness.

*1. The Design Supports Positive Reminiscence of Special Moments*

Our first key question concerns the functionality at the most fundamental level: In what ways does MemoryReel support reminiscence? The approach of focusing on digitally connected special moments seems to be effective. Most participants liked the fact that revisiting these moments could be done via the device so easily. The reminiscing act can trigger self-reflection or boost positive emotion. For example, participant O03 commented: "*It can remind me of special moments. Because in the phone there are a lot of text, message, videos and photos. ... I need to look back and try to see those. This [the device] is like getting those things visualized out. It will be more convenient.*" Participant N08 imagined a different scenario where the device could ease the negative emotions: "*if [you] are in a fight but you want to reconcile, revisiting [the happy moments through the device] will help.*" Several participants expressed that they would even record some of the unhappy moments—to much of our surprise. For example, participant O03 had the habit to occasionally save some unhappy messages: "*I collected some bad texts, but I don't want to look at them frequently. It makes [me] feel hurt but it's still memorable.*" Similarly, participant N02 commented: "*If it [unhappy moment] is played back in front of me in this way, I'll be able to reflect, more objectively, on whether I did something wrong.*"

*2. The Device Nurtures the Sense of Connectedness and Positive Feelings of the Relationship in More than One Way*

Some participants believed that they would feel good about their relationship by using MemoryReel. Participant N13 commented on revisiting the happy messages: "*It'd be purely happiness. It's like reenacting the happy feeling felt at that moment of typing up those texts. ... This definitely would reinforce our relationship. Playing it back is to remind you of the good relationship you are in.*" Participant N15 added yet another scenario where when two persons cannot connect immediately, visiting the memories will bring comfort. She said: "*When I'm too busy to make calls, visiting these [messages] can keep me going.*" Participant N02 believed the device can facilitate communications. He explained: "*If you haven't seen each other for a long time, you might need to create a topic, which is difficult since you are not living in the same city. All you can do is to use past [shared] experience to open a topic. Then this [device] gives me a means to find a topic from the past for our current communication.*" Even for unhappy memories, participant N13 imagined that if recalling together with her boyfriend (not necessarily co-located): "*it would be quite laughable if we look at it [unhappy moments] together and see how we just fought for things that actually didn't matter.*"

*3. Avatar-based Physical Tokens Can Trigger Empathy and Enable Meaningful and Expressive Interaction*

Many participants (N=10) picked the tangible metaphorical design of the wooden avatar tokens (see Figure 3) as their most favourable feature of MemoryReel. The anthropomorphic representation of oneself and close others greatly stimulated participants' empathy and meaning making. Participants automatically attached meanings—based on their relationship experience—to the avatars and various acts of interaction including imaginative ones. Participants N07 commented: "*It's meaningful because you can physically interact with her.*" Participant N20, who was the only one feeling sad—rather than positive—about MemoryReel, commented: "*When I saw the two characters, I felt they could get closer, but never touch each other [due to a dimensional glitch in the physical design, the two tokens cannot exactly touch when slid together – authors' note]. And to turn it off [to be back to the text mode – authors' note]... they are at the furthest distance from each other. It reminds me that I can't be with my partner. There is always distance... space... between us.*" In the prototype, one avatar is fixed and the other avatar movable. Participants have different opinions in this design. For example, Participant N01 thought both of the avatars should be movable because "*they represent two people, [if only one is movable], it feels like it's always one person approaching the other.*" On contrary, Participant O03 commented: "*It is totally okay. Because for me we are in a relationship, so I don't mind who is approaching. I think both of us contribute to the same thing.*" Some participants felt the interaction itself a way of non-verbal expression. O03 interpreted the distance between avatars in this way: "*if I put it in the middle, it's showing how much I miss you. If it's more near it will be a lot.*"

*4. "Slow Communication" is Wished for to Feel the Presence of the Other and Improve the Sense of Connectedness (between Partners)*

When imagining alternate use scenarios, a majority of them (N=15) expressed the thought of using MemoryReel as a platform for "slow communication"—a functionality that mobile phones do not usually provide. This means each person owns a MemoryReel and they can use it to relay, infrequently, low-intentionality information of themselves to the close other. This is a usage totally beyond our original thinking but very promising in supporting the sense of connectedness. Some participants would like the other one to know when they are using the device. Participant N07 imagined: "*So if I move this [one avatar], I want to be closer to her. Then she can see it [on her device]. So it can mimic the interaction of two of us even we are far away.*" Similarly, Participant N02 contemplated: "*Maybe I would see some information about my girlfriend—it should be abstract, to protect her privacy—such as when her alarm is.*" Participant N05 further expected they could leave messages to each other; however, "*there will not be a notification. ... It's like a letter. She needs to wait, to expect.*"

## DISCUSSION

We began our research inquiry by asking questions about how to scaffold deeply meaningful relationships at a distance. In reviewing the field, we formed our design approach, which is to focus on special moments and to harness the positive impact of reminiscence and connectedness on subjective wellbeing. We performed design inquiry to see what kinds of moments are special to people when recalling memories shared with their close others. Based on the design research findings, we developed the MemoryReel concept and prototype, which we evaluated in a user study. The results helped validate the significance and effectiveness of our design approach. The prototype effectively engaged participants in an active meaning-making process, demonstrating its potential to support deeply meaningful relationships.

We attribute the largely satisfactory design particularly to several design principles suggested by Whittaker et al. [27] . These include the focus on selecting digital content as memory cues, the support of reminiscence and reflection, and the embodiment of digital content in physical objects to be integrated into everyday life. Our design thus contributes a case to support prior research results. A notable element to add to the design principles is the content modality. MemoryReel features three types of cues, including text cues. Text cues are not too common in designs for memory support, yet it is one of the most effective memory cue modalities in the remembering process [23] .

Our work also contributes to the design space of digital memory and long-distance relationships with our unique strategies. A key strategy is the emphasis of connectedness. MemoryReel focused exclusively on (digitally) connected moments of online communication, which are selected (i.e., captured) by audiences themselves and thus tend to become treasured or sentimental memories. This echoes Sellen and Whittaker's [18] argument that building a personal digital archive involves more than just capturing everything; more focus should be on "the kinds of data people find most valuable." Moreover, the anthropomorphic representation of the close others (i.e., use of avatar-based physical tokens) helps trigger empathy and engage audiences in meaning making during interaction.

Reflecting on user study findings in relation to our original motivation, we also identified a few critical challenges. A widespread common concern is privacy, especially for participants who live in a shared home. The general sentiment was that the device is highly personal and should be used almost exclusively solitarily. This presents contradiction to us. We wanted to create opportunities for people to have quality reminiscing experience in their offline time, away from their mobile devices. We reinforced this idea by creating a tangible device with physical tokens to engage audiences. Notwithstanding, in some participants' perception, their private information is 'exposed' in the open. On the other hand, this concern by no means undermines the design, as confirmed by participants' positive feedback, but needs to be addressed carefully.

Privacy poses another critical challenge for the designing of the mode of viewing. The current playback is by an order randomly generated by the system, which was liked by several participants. We have already envisioned our future design to be able to curate the playback in a more intelligent and personalized way. However, this will incur more risk for privacy. One participant's contradictory attitude clearly spoke to this challenge. He liked to be reminded by the device to engage in reminiscence, but he was also worried about his privacy if the system was always on and displaying cues. These very specific concerns and requests drew out new dimensions (e.g., curating vs. self-selection of the cue content, voluntary vs. involuntary reminiscence) at a lower level, which are all worth to explore but need to be prioritized in future design.

One last observation is the differences between two types of relationships found in user study results. Although MemoryReel did not cause opposing opinions between two groups, they did generate clearly different imagined use scenarios. The key distinction is the usage of the device as a "slow communication" platform for couples, as imagined by a majority of participants. Our original intention, however, was to create a non-communication, non-synchronized solution. More investigation is needed in finding out whether it is unrealistic and unwanted by most couples, and whether creating separate designs for couples and friends is more beneficial than having a common but customizable solution.

## CONCLUSION

MemoryReel is a design concept built for supporting the experience of connectedness between couples and friends across a distance through positive reminiscence of special moments. Findings from the early stage design inquiry and later stage user study helped validate the design approach and identify a few challenges for the design space of digital memories and long-distance relationship.

Aside from issues raised for future investigation in Discussion, some immediate future work is needed to further refine and improve the MemoryReel design concept. As mentioned previously, due to resource and time limitations, pre-created contents were used in the user study. Although many participants were very engaged by the prototype, some of their true feelings might not be aroused. Moreover, durability, a quality that we assumed to be critical to our approach, can only be evaluated through a longitudinal study. In order to carry out such a study, a more functional prototype needs to be built, loaded with custom contents, and deployed to participants' homes for a period of time. Other finer details of the design can be refined after the longitudinal study.


## ACKNOWLEDGMENTS

We gratefully thank the reviewers and organizers, as well as all the study participants who contributed greatly and passionately to our design. This work benefited from the support by The Hong Kong Polytechnic University and School of Design (projects coded G-UAEW and G-YBNR).


## REFERENCES


[1] Susan Bluck. 2003. Autobiographical memory: Exploring its functions in everyday life. *Memory* 11, 2, 113-123.

[2] Fred B. Bryant, Colette M. Smart, and Scott P. King. 2005. Using the past to enhance the present: Boosting happiness through positive reminiscence. *Journal of Happiness Studies* 6, 3: 227-260.

[3] Yongsoon Choi, Jordan Tewell, Yukihiro Morisawa, Gilang A. Pradana, and Adrian David Cheok. 2014. Ring* U: A wearable system for intimate communication using tactile lighting expressions. In *Proceedings of the 11th Conference on Advances in Computer Entertainment Technology* (ACE '14), Article No. 63.

[4] Jodi Forlizzi and Katja Battarbee. 2004. Understanding experience in interactive systems. In *Proceedings of the Fifth Conference on Designing Interactive Systems: Processes, Practices, Methods, and Techniques* (DIS '04), 261-268.

[5] Marc Hassenzahl, Stephanie Heidecker, Kai Eckoldt, Sarah Diefenbach, and Uwe Hillmann. 2012. All you need is love: Current strategies of mediating intimate relationships through technology. In *ACM Transactions on Computer-Human Interaction (TOCHI)* 19, 4: 30.

[6] Dianya Hua, Huaxin Wei, and Eli Blevis. 2018. MemoryPin: Turning digitally co-present moments into tangible memory keepsakes. In *Proceedings of the Companion Publication of the 2018 Designing Interactive Systems Conference* (DIS '18), 253-258.

[7] Joseph 'Jofish' Kaye, Mariah K. Levitt, Jeffrey Nevins, Jessica Golden, and Vanessa Schmidt. 2005. Communicating intimacy one bit at a time. In *CHI '05 Extended Abstracts on Human Factors in Computing Systems*, 1529-1532.

[8] Jina Kim, Young-Woo Park, and Tek-Jin Nam. 2015. BreathingFrame: An inflatable frame for remote breath signal sharing. In *Proceedings of the 9th International Conference on Tangible, Embedded, and Embodied Interaction* (TEI '15), 109-112.

[9] Robert Kowalski, Sebastian Loehmann, and Doris Hausen. 2013. Cubble: A multi-device hybrid approach supporting communication in long-distance relationships. In *Proceedings of the 7th International Conference on Tangible, Embedded and Embodied Interaction* (TEI '13), 201-204.

[10] Asami Miyajima, Yoshihiro Itoh, Masako Itoh, and Takumi Watanabe. 2005. "Tsunagari-kan" communication: Design of a new telecommunication environment and a field test with family members living apart. *International Journal of Human-Computer Interaction* 19, 2: 253-276.

[11] Ine Mols, Elise van den Hoven, and Berry Eggen. 2016. Technologies for everyday life reflection: Illustrating a design space. In *Proceedings of the Tenth International Conference on Tangible, Embedded, and Embodied Interaction* (TEI '16), 53-61.

[12] Florian 'Floyd' Mueller, Frank Vetere, Martin R. Gibbs, Jesper Kjeldskov, Sonja Pedell, and Steve Howard. 2005. Hug over a distance. In *CHI '05 Extended Abstracts on Human Factors in Computing Systems*, 1673-1676.

[13] Karin Niemantsverdriet and Maarten Versteeg. 2016. Interactive jewellery as memory cue: Designing a sound locket for individual reminiscence. In *Proceedings of the TEI'16: Tenth International Conference on Tangible, Embedded, and Embodied Interaction*, 532-538.

[14] William Odom, James Pierce, Erik Stolterman, and Eli Blevis. 2009. Understanding why we preserve some things and discard others in the context of interaction design. In *Proceedings of the SIGCHI Conference on Human Factors in Computing Systems* (CHI '09), 1053-1062.

[15] William T. Odom, Abigail J. Sellen, Richard Banks, David S. Kirk, Tim Regan, Mark Selby, Jodi L. Forlizzi, and John Zimmerman. 2014. Designing for slowness, anticipation and re-visitation: A long term field study of the Photobox. In *Proceedings of the SIGCHI Conference on Human Factors in Computing Systems* (CHI '14), 1961-1970.

[16] S. Tejaswi Peesapati, Victoria Schwanda, Johnathon Schultz, Matt Lepage, So-yae Jeong, and Dan Cosley. 2010. Pensieve: Supporting everyday reminiscence. In *Proceedings of the SIGCHI Conference on Human Factors in Computing Systems* (CHI '10), 2027-2036.

[17] Daniela Petrelli, Nicolas Villar, Vaiva Kalnikaite, Lina Dib, and Steve Whittaker. 2010. FM radio: Family interplay with sonic mementos. In *Proceedings of the SIGCHI Conference on Human Factors in Computing Systems* (CHI '16), 2371-2380.

[18] Abigail J. Sellen and Steve Whittaker. 2010. Beyond total capture: A constructive critique of lifelogging. *Communications of the ACM* 53, 5, 70-77.

[19] Wenn-Chieh Tsai, Po-Hao Wang, Hung-Chi Lee, Rung-Huei Liang, and Jane Hsu. 2014. The Reflexive Printer: Toward making sense of perceived drawbacks

in technology-mediated reminiscence. In *Proceedings of the 2014 Conference on Designing interactive systems* (DIS '14), 995-1004.

[20] Joy van Baren, Wijnand. A. IJsselsteijn, Panos Markopoulos, Natalia Romero, and Boris De Ruyter. 2004. Measuring affective benefits and costs of awareness systems supporting intimate social networks. In *CTIT Proceedings of the Third Workshop on Social Intelligence Design* (SID '04), vol. 2, 13-19.

[21] Daniel T. van Bel, Karin. C. H. J. Smolders, Wijnand A. IJsselsteijn, and Yvonne A. W. de Kort. 2009. Social connectedness: concept and measurement. In *Proceedings of the 5th International Conference on Intelligent Environments* (IE '09), 67-74.

[22] Elise van den Hoven and Berry Eggen. 2008. Informing augmented memory system design through autobiographical memory theory. *Personal and Ubiquitous Computing* 12, 6, 433-443.

[23] Elise van den Hoven and Berry Eggen. 2009. The effect of cue media on recollections. *Human Technology: An Interdisciplinary Journal on Humans in ICT Environments* 5 (May 2009), 1, 47-67.

[24] Dirk van Erve, Gerrit-Willem Vos, Elise van den Hoven, and David Frohlich. 2011. Cueing the past: Designing embodied interaction for everyday remembering. In *Procedings of the Second Conference on Creativity and Innovation in Design*, 335-345.

[25] Thomas Visser, Martijn Vastenburg, and David Keyson. 2010. SnowGlobe: The development of a prototype awareness system for longitudinal field studies. In *Proceedings of the 8th ACM Conference on Designing Interactive Systems* (DIS '10), 426-429.

[26] Gerben J. Westerhof, Ernst Bohlmeijer, and Jeffrey Dean Webster. 2010. Reminiscence and mental health: A review of recent progress in theory, research and interventions. *Ageing & Society* 30, 4: 697-721.

[27] Steve Whittaker, Vaiva Kalnikaitė, Daniela Petrelli, Abigail Sellen, Nicolas Villar, Ofer Bergman, Paul Clough, and Jens Brockmeier. 2012. Socio-technical lifelogging: Deriving design principles for a future proof digital past. *Human–Computer Interaction* 27, 1-2, 37-62.

[28] Helen L. Williams, Martin A. Conway, and Gillian Cohen. 2007. Autobiographical memory. In *Memory in the Real World* (3rd ed.), Gillian Cohen and Martin A. Conway (eds.). Psychology Press, London, UK, 21-90.

# Of Smarthomes, IoT Plants, and Implicit Interaction Design

**Björn Bittner, Ilhan Aslan, Chi Tai Dang, and Elisabeth André**
Human-Centered Multimedia Lab, Augsburg University
Augsburg, Germany
{bittner, aslan, dang, andre}@hcm-lab.de

## ABSTRACT
There seems to be a danger to carelessly replace routine tasks in homes through automation with IoT-technology. But since routines such as watering houseplants also have positive influences on inhabitants' wellbeing, they should be transformed through carefully performed designs. To this end, an attempt to use technology for augmenting a set of houseplants' nonverbal communication capabilities is presented. First, we describe in detail how implicit interactions have been designed to support inhabitants in watering their plants through meaningful interactions. Then, we report on a field study with 24 participants, comparing two alternative design implementations based on contrasting embodied interaction technologies (i.e., augmented reality and embedded computing technology). The study results highlight shortcomings of today's smartphone mediated augmented reality compared to physical interface alternatives, considering measurements of perceived attractiveness and expected effects on determinants of wellbeing, and discusses potentials of combining both modalities for future solutions.

## Author Keywords
Experience Prototyping; User Study; Positive Computing

## CCS Concepts
**•Human-centered computing → Interaction design; Interaction design;**

## INTRODUCTION
New embedded technologies have been transforming how we, as home inhabitants, envision our everyday routines and modes of interactions with networked things in our future homes and buildings. While the automation of many routine tasks in the home is already possible and more automation may be part of a desirable future, Calvo and Peters [8] have criticized in their book "Positive Computing" an exclusive focus of technology design for productivity. They motivated a sensitivity for human wellbeing and potential as additional design goals.


*TEI '19, March 17–20, 2019, Tempe, AZ, USA.*

ACM ISBN 978-1-4503-6196-5 /19/03 ...$15.00.
http://dx.doi.org/10.1145/3294109.3295618

Indeed, future scenarios seem to imply that inhabitants of smart homes won't have to care about anything but interact with everything in a magical manner and be well. However, increase in automation can be considered as a source for one of the main contemporary design challenges, with previous research arguing, for example, that autonomous technologies often lead users to feel a loss of control [4]. To make autonomous systems less obnoxious Ju and Leifer [26] have proposed to design human-like forms of interaction (i.e., combine explicit with implicit interactions) for which Wendy Ju's implicit interaction framework [24] provides support. Mennicken et al. [33] have recommended to focus on collaboration between inhabitants and homes as a direction to deal with the problems of automation. Ultimately, not all routine tasks in homes are viewed as "a waste of time" but some routines may even be considered healthy rituals. For example, Elings and Marjolein [15] found various studies from different countries that showed how interactions with plants promote human wellbeing. Thus, a routine task, such as watering the houseplants, should not be automated blindly, but designed carefully.

In this paper, we report on a series of design inquiries and a user study in the field with 24 participants, addressing the following research questions.

- How can we use IoT technology to support inhabitants in properly watering their plants without replacing the benefits inhabitants may have from interactions with their plants?
- Would inhabitants prefer related future interactive technology solutions to be based on Augmented Reality (AR) or purely embedded/physical technology in their homes?

We choose these two state-of-the-art modalities due to their contrasting nature, including how they may influence the use of space in the home. We also choose them to ensure ecological validity of our contributions. To address the research questions, we first explored possible implicit interactions with IoT plants based on experience prototyping methods [7], the Implicit Interaction Framework [24], and the Proxemic Interaction Framework [32]. Then we implemented exemplary designs for both interaction technologies and compared them in the field based on participants' perceived user experience and the relevant wellbeing determinants [8] *autonomy*, *competence*, and *motivation* through observations and questionnaires.

The primary contribution of our research is in providing answers to the research questions, but we hope it also provides knowledge, sensibility, and guidance to address in general the challenges of designing "healthier" routines in smarthomes and interactions with smart things in homes.

## BACKGROUND

Automated watering of plants has been the subject of research for the last 30 years (e.g., [42, 11]) and commercial products have also emerged [38]. Previous research on enhancing plants in smarthomes seems mainly concerned with automated irrigation based on wireless moisture or soil humidity sensors that determine the condition of plants [2, 27]. The goals are the efficient use of water; i.e., to avoid over-hydration and dehydration of plants [27] and to take into account environmental conditions, such as temperature and evaporation rate of water [27]. Other applications include the notification of inhabitants about moisture levels [45] or the use of robot flowers as an intermediate device for interaction with inhabitants [9].

### Design Approaches for Interaction with/in Smarthomes

The aforementioned goals attribute to the functional and instrumental aspects of smarthomes [47] but neglect the sociotechnical aspects. It makes sense to irrigate plants automatically when inhabitants are not at home for a long time and certainly contributes to the peace of mind [6]. However, it should not be the goal of domestic technology to replace the experiences from daily habits and routines that inhabitants enjoy but enhance those home experiences with technology [19, 39]. The daily routine of watering plants belongs to such experiences because it includes not only watering but also caring for the plants in the context of human social behavior.

Therefore, the body of related work concerned with design approaches for interactions with and in the smarthome has been increasing. For example, Venkatesh [44] presented a theoretical framework that included and interlinked the key constructs social space and technological space. Following this framework, interactions with household-technology have to consider both perspectives. In contrast, Heath and Bell [19] promoted a practical approach; i.e., to apply scenario-based prototyping, which has already been applied with success for industry environments also for home scenarios.

Eggen et al. [13] explored people's home experience during interactive sessions with families. Based on the outcome of these sessions, they realized and studied multiple prototypes, which enable experiences that "*go beyond supporting tasks*". They emphasize that the design for home experiences requires "*end-users to realistically interact with and experience an application in the proper*", that is actual physical, social, and cultural, "*context of use*". Later, Eggen et al. [14] proposed a holistic approach that addresses the design of home experiences from a user-driven perspective, where the home experience is about emotions and not solely the physical smarthome technologies surrounding inhabitants. Their approach considers a deep understanding of basic human needs in the smarthome context, such as autonomy, competence, or relatedness. Based on these needs, they applied "*state-of-the-art psychological theories*" on human processes to "*enhance everyday life and improve the well-being of people*".

### Designing Interactions with Smart Things

Kranz et al. [28] stated that one of the challenges of embedded interactions is whether implicit or explicit interactions should be used. The advantage of implicit interactions is that users can concentrate on their actual goals and are not aware of computer systems. Implicit interactions are thus a reasonable way to support users without having them to learn new interactions with the system and allowing them to water their plants as they usually would. According to Buchenau and Suri [7], Experience Prototyping is suitable to explore user interactions with future systems. Moreover, they argue that role-plays, as an Experience Prototyping technique, can be used to investigate behavior of users and artifacts, with the advantage that the artifacts' roles can also be played by people and thus insights on how smart things should act and react can be gained without having to go through a time and effort consuming software development process.

Wendy Ju suggests to transfer observed implicit interactions in role-plays over to the system design with the help of an Implicit Interaction Framework [24], which aims to support designers in analyzing and getting inspirations from interactions between a user and a non-human agent (e.g., [25, 31]). Another relevant framework for designing spatial forms of implicit interactions is the Proxemic Interactions Framework [32], which was introduced by Marquardt and Greenberg to help design/develop interactions with/in ubiquitous computing ecologies and intelligent environments (e.g., [3, 40, 29]). They promote to analyze system behavior based on measures, such as position, orientation, and identity of things and users.

### Technologies and Techniques to Augment Things

Cho et al. [10] used an LED emoticon to display the overall state of a plant and Angelini et al. [1] extended this concept by a display that informed the user about humidity, light conditions, and temperature. Most of these projects used the concept of physical computing [37] to digitize the plants. Microcontrollers (e.g., Arduino) and sensors (e.g., humidity and light sensors) are used to measure the state of the environment and actuators (e.g., water pump, LEDs) are used to manipulate it.

An alternative to physical actuators is providing information through the augmented reality. According to Milgram [35], AR is closer to the real environment in a continuum between the pure real environment and the purely virtual environment. The body of related work in AR is large and it is not surprising that AR has also been explored in the context of smarthomes, where it has often been used to enable remote identification and control of things (e.g., a lamp) without having to move to the thing [43, 17, 30]. Often, AR usage is proposed to help/guide users during activities, such as using appliances [36], assembling things [41], machine maintenance [21], or repair [20]. A problem with embedded technologies and specifically physical actuators is the interface bottleneck. For example, Janlert and Stolterman [23] argue that holograms or augmented reality interfaces are conditional, while physical actuators require absolute and real space. Thus, AR and physical actuators seem orthogonal to each other considering their materiality. With the HoloLens [34], Microsoft demonstrated new possibilities of AR. Apple introduced its ARKit [22] framework and Google introduced ARCore [16]; both technologies contribute to making AR accessible on many state-of-the-art smartphones, and thus an alternative technology to physical actuators in homes.

This background section provided the state-of-the-art in the literature relevant to our work so as to highlight its novel contribution. Our work considers socio-technical aspects in the context of interaction with domestic technology. However, instead of exploring inhabitants' home experience (as proposed by Eggen et al. [13]) for the design of domestic technologies, we considered implicit interaction [24] and proxemics [32] in role-plays [7] for interaction design with domestic technologies. Furthermore, we compared the interaction modalities AR and physical LEDs for domestic routines (i.e., watering plants) in smarthomes which has not been done before.

## IMPLICIT INTERACTIONS WITH NON-HUMAN AGENTS

We started the design process with exploring potential houseplant watering scenarios and conducting role-plays as an experience prototyping methodology. That is, we explored how users would interact with houseplant and a watering can and vice versa, considering household plants and the can as non-human agents, who can communicate their need for water (or in case of the can, their purpose to water plants who are in need of water) with human-like capabilities. We then analyzed interaction patterns which occurred during the role-plays with the help of the Implicit Interaction and the Proxemic Interaction Framework. Afterwards, we mapped the information that

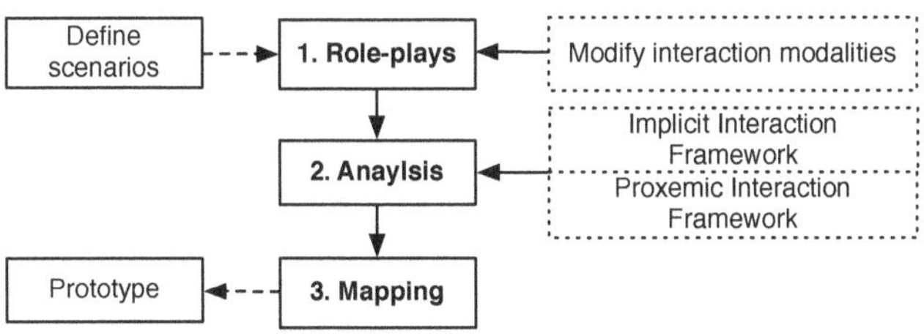


**Figure 1. Overview of design process.**

### Role-Plays

We organized two rounds of role-plays across two days. Within each round, multiple scenarios were played in a real home.

#### *First Round of Role-Plays*

For the first round, we recruited four participants. One participant played the user, another one played the watering can and each of the remaining participants played a plant. While we had a set of predefined scenarios for the first round, we discussed together with the participants which of the scenarios were useful and played them out afterwards. In total, we played seven simple scenarios in the first round. For example, in one scenario only one plant required water and in another scenario two plants had to be watered by the user. The role-plays quickly revealed situations where the interactions were blurry and unclear. For example, a plant indicated by raising its arms that she needed water and the user came to her to water her. When the user stood next to her, she lowered her arms, confusing the user and not knowing if she still needed water. In order to investigate these unclear interactions more closely, a second round of role-plays was conducted.

**Figure 2. Scene from the second role-play.**

#### *Second Round of Role-Plays*

The focus of the second round were four scenarios, each of which was intended to answer a specific question. A total of six participants were recruited to take part in the role-plays. While in the first round one researcher took part in some of the role-plays, in the second round researchers did not participate actively in role-plays. They just gave instructions at the beginning and then observed the participants during the execution. After each scenario, all participants were asked in a semi-structured interview how they perceived everything, whether there were problems, or they noticed something interesting.

Similar to the first round of role-plays, one participant played the role of the user and one played the role of the watering can. The remaining four participants played plants, with three scenarios involving only three plants. The participants rotated in their roles so that information could be collected for each role from different perspectives. At the beginning of each scenario, each participant was given a personal goal in a one-on-one interview. The user was supposed to water the plants that needed water, the watering can was supposed to help the user and the plants were supposed to make sure that they received water when they needed it.

*Scenario 1:* all participants, except the role of the user, were blindfolded to foster communication, as shown in Figure 2. The plants and the watering can (i.e., the "non-human agents") were not able to see what was happening and had to talk to each other to exchange relevant information.
*Scenario 2:* the "non-human agents" used smartphones to chat with each other because a plant was in an extra room. The group had to direct the user's attention to this plant.
*Scenario 3:* the plants were given glasses and the watering can was given a real watering can. The plants had the task of receiving a certain amount of water in order to investigate the particular interaction more closely when the plants tell the user how much water they need.
*Scenario 4:* one of the plants played a defect plant demanding more and more water.

The interviews conducted after each scenario were analyzed after the end of the role-play with a thematic analysis [5]. The idea was to see which interactions were understood by the other participants and in which cases the participants had problems to understand.

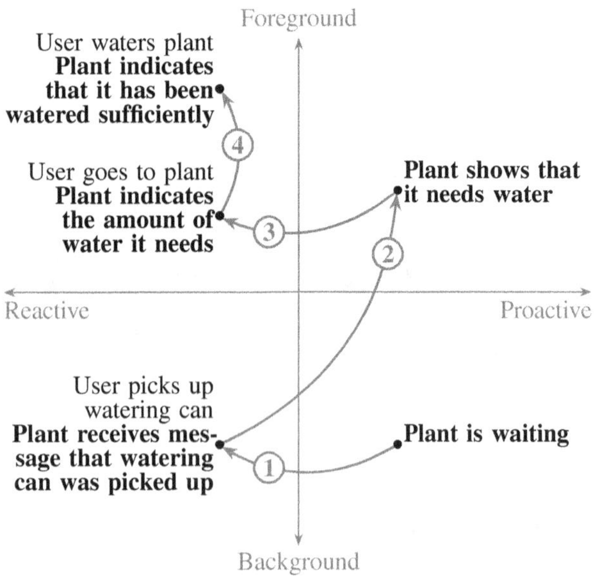


**Figure 3. Interaction pattern between a user and a single plant, displayed with Implicit Interaction Framework.**

### Analysis of Role-Plays

After the role-plays, the interactions between users and the "non-human agents" were analyzed using the Implicit Interaction Framework. The watering process could be divided into three steps. Initially, the plants indicated that they needed water as soon as the user picked up the watering can. In the role-plays, the plants raised their arms or crouched together to visually symbolize "drying out". In the second step, the plants indicated exactly how much water they needed after the user walked with the watering can to the plant. The participants indicated with their fingers how far their glass should be filled. As soon as the plants had received enough water, they symbolized their satisfaction by nodding their heads or raising their thumbs. The interviews with the users revealed that users explicitly requested this confirmation at the end to ensure that they had watered enough. Figure 3 shows the interaction in the Implicit Interaction Framework with a single plant as defined after analysis of the role-plays.

Besides the interaction between user and plants, an interaction between user and watering can could also be observed. While the user used the watering can mostly to water the plants, a situation appeared in which the watering can tried to prevent the user from watering the plant by shaking.

After investigating role-play interactions, considering the implicit interaction Framework, the Proxemic Interactions Framework was used to explicitly investigate the spatial relationships between user and non-human agents. When the user took the watering can with their hand or entered the room with the watering can in their hand, the plants indicated whether they needed water. As soon as the user focused on a plant by approaching it and orientating towards it, the plant indicated exactly how much water it needed. When the user put the watering can down or left the room, the plants stopped displaying anything.

During the role-plays, we have also observed that users often did not know whether they had watered all the plants sufficiently. The plants tried to clarify among themselves whether all were satisfied, but they didn't inform the user. The interviews afterwards showed that the participants associated this task with the watering can. Consequently, we defined that the can should display an overall status of all plants in the room for the user as soon as the user picks up the watering can. We also defined that when the user changes the room, the status of the plants in the new room should be displayed until the user puts the watering can down.

### Mapping of Results

The last step in the design process was to map the observed behavior patterns of people in the role-plays to information, which can be implemented in different technologies and modalities. For example, (i) plants must be able to visually indicate whether they need water and (ii) plants need to indicate how much water they need. Figure 4 depicts how we mapped the required information for both modalities (i.e., physical actuators and AR). We chose three different colors, each representing a status of the water level: red - very low; blue - low; green - sufficient. The design is also capable to indicate whether the water level is between a minimum and a maximum mark. The optimum lies in the middle between the two markings.

The watering can needed, for example, to communicate (iii) that a plant did not require (more) water, and (iv) to display the status of the group of plants in the same room. We decided to use a vibration function for (iii) and either an LED or the smartphone's display for (iv). The display/LED on the can was used to display the worst state of all plants in the room (i.e. red/blue as long as at least one plant needs water and green as soon as all plants have enough water). The watering can would be able to vibrate in case a plant did not need any water or had already received enough water (which would also be visualized directly by the plant's LEDs turning red).

## IMPLEMENTATION OF FUNCTIONAL PROTOTYPES

Figure 4 depicts the plants and the watering can and how we augmented them either with LEDs or AR to visually communicate with users. Both types of augmentations were designed to provide the functionality for a user study to be conducted as a "Wizard-of-Oz" experiment. Therefore, for example, the water levels of the plants were manually configured and not measured using sensors. Each system included multiple plants and a watering can. The communication protocol MQTT (Message Queue Telemetry Transport), which is a typical IoT protocol, was used to implement the communication between the components of the systems, for which a server (called MQTT Broker) was also required. In addition, a smartphone was used to display the virtual objects of the AR prototype. Figure 5 presents the connections/relations between each thing and the user.

**Figure 4. Overview of non-human agents and how they were augmented with embedded technology or Ar. a) and e) depict color codes, which were used to signal need for water. b) and f) depict how plants provided continuous feedback considering the amount of water they had received. c) and d) depict the watering can which was augmented with an LED and a vibration motor on the handle. g) and h) depict the inside of the a plant pot and the watering can, showing the Raspberry Pi Zero Ws.**

## Watering Can

A regular watering can was extended below the bottom with a Raspberry Pi Zero W and LEDs. Holes were drilled in the bottom of the watering can and closed with transparent material so that the LEDs could shine into the watering can from below (see Figure 4d and 4h). The LEDs are used in the LED system to display the overall status of all plants in the room, while they are not used in the AR system because the status is displayed in the AR application. A vibration motor was attached to the handle, which can give users haptic feedback while holding the watering can, e.g. to give a warning when the user pours too much water. An acceleration sensor attached to the can detects when the user tilts the watering can to water the plants and sends a message to the plants every second as long as it is tilted. The hardware is powered by a battery.

## Plants

Figure 4 shows plants of each of the two type of prototypes. The plants of the LED prototype also use a Raspberry Pi Zero W, which is located underneath the plant in the pot (see Figure 4g). The pot has 16 LEDs arranged one above another, which are used to communicate information to the user. The plants of the AR prototype do not use any displays, as information is visible via the smartphone screen. The water level of the plants is reported with a value ranged between 0 and 16 and is communicated to the user with the LEDs (see Figure 4b) or AR (see Figure 4f). Ideally, the water level should be between the two white markings (6 and 14). If the water level is lower, the plant urgently needs water, if it is higher, it has too much water and the user is warned if he tries to water the plant anyway. If the plants communicate their need for water after the user has raised the watering can and has not yet approached the plant, all LEDs (respectively the whole 3D

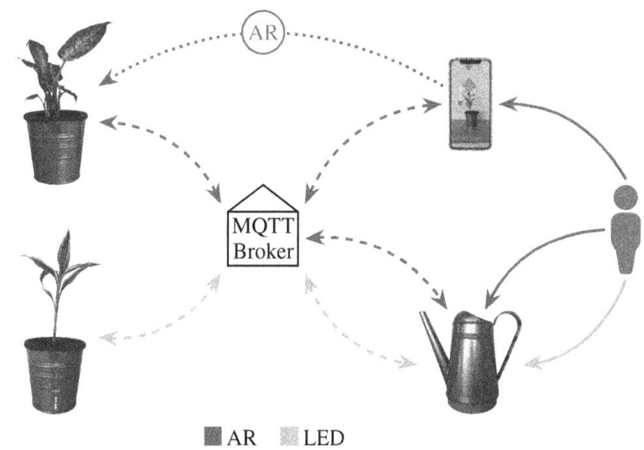


**Figure 5. Setup of the system of the both modalities with a LED plant (bottom left) and a AR plant (top left). The arrows show which devices the user uses with the respective system (continuous arrows) and how they communicate with each other (dashed arrows) and how they are augmented via AR (dotted arrows).**

model in the AR condition) light up in the same color (see Figure 4a and 4e).

The plants of the LED prototype are not able to detect whether a user is approaching or not. Hence, in order to simulate proxemics, an application (as part of the "Wizard-of-Oz" research technique) has been developed that informs the plants when the user approaches. Moreover, the plants of both prototype types were also unable to determine whether they had just been watered. This is realized by messages from the watering can to the plants, which increase their water level by one level for each message.

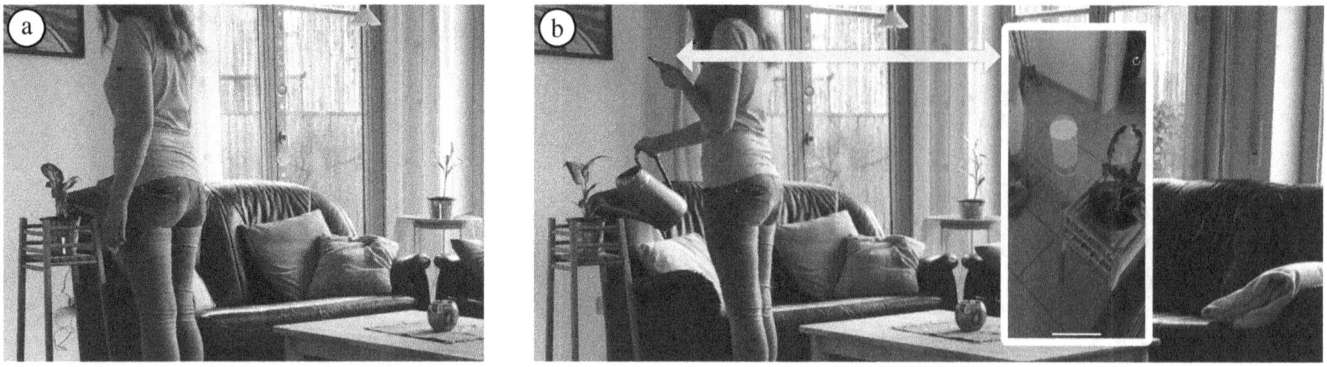


**Figure 6. Screenshots of the user study. With a) showing a participant testing the LED system and b) showing a participant testing the AR system with the participants view of the AR through the smartphone display.**

### AR Application

To be able to display the information with AR, we developed a smartphone application using Swift and ARKit. After starting the application, the virtual information objects must be manually placed next to each physical plant before the smartphone is handed over to the user. The application then calculates which information should be displayed to the user based on the user's own position in the room, the distances to the plants, and the orientation of the device. In comparison to the LED prototype, no manual control of the user's position during the study is necessary. In the lower part of the display, a colored circle shows the overall status of the plants in the room.

## FIELD STUDY EXPLORING USER EXPERIENCE

The overall goal of the (repeated measures) user study was to explore the user experience (UX) of the two systems, including whether the use of the systems has an effect on the wellbeing determinants autonomy, competence, and motivation.

### Participants and Apparatus

We recruited 24 participants (12 females, 12 males) aged between 17 and 59 (M = 28, SD = 11). All participants reported to have no color vision weakness and were familiar with the use of mobile devices. The participants rated their skills and interest in houseplant care with a 7-point Likert scale (-3 = beginner/unimportant, 3 = professional/important) in average more than beginners (M = -1,04, SD = 1,68), but they indicated interest in plant care (M = 0,38, SD = 1,58). The study was conducted in a living room to provide an environment where users normally interact with houseplants (see Figure 6). For each run, three plants were placed in the room at a distance of 2m-3m from each other. The watering can was placed on a table near the plants. The plants had different initial water levels (i.e., very low, low, sufficient) to show the user the different conditions that exist. For testing the AR system, an iPhone X was used to display the information in the AR condition.

#### *Questionnaires*

We chose the attrakDiff questionnaire to evaluate the different systems considering UX. The questionnaire measures pragmatic quality (PQ), hedonic quality (HQ) resulting from a combination of HQS and HQI, and overall attractiveness (ATT). HQS measures the perceived ability of a product to meet a person's desire for self-improvement, HQI measures the perceived ability of a product to communicate a valuable identity to others [18]. The attractiveDiff questionnaire is particularly suitable for our study as it focuses on hedonic qualities (with HQS, HQI, and ATT), which may play a greater role in ones own home than, for example, in a work environment. In addition, participants were asked to make a self-assessment of how the use of the respective system would affect the three positive computing factors motivation, competence, and autonomy on a 7-point Likert scale. Motivation and competence were chosen to explore whether users would be more motivated to take care of their plants with the systems and improve their skills. An effect on these two factors was measured with the questions *"How do you think your motivation to water your plants would change with the use of each system"* and *"How do you think your own ability to give your plants the right amount of water would change with the use of each system"* (strongly worsened, strongly improved). The question of autonomy was intended to check whether the system restricts users in their tasks. It was addressed with the question *"Who has control of the watering process?"* (the system, the user).

### Procedure

We briefly described that the study aims to test two different systems, which help water houseplants. Before the participants tested the two systems one after another, they were asked to read a brief description of the system and of the task they would perform. The task was, with the support of the system, to water all three plants up to the required amount of water. After completing the task, they rated the attractiveness of the system using the attrakDiff questionnaire. This process was repeated for the second system. Afterwards, the participants answered questions about the positive computing factors. At the end, participants were asked which of the systems they preferred and had to give reasons for their preference. Each participant completed the study in about 30 minutes.

### Results

First, the general trends in the "quantitative" data (collected with the questionnaires) are identified with the help of graphical representations, and then statistical analyses are performed to test for significance. Afterwards, we describe the results of the qualitative data analysis aiming to provide reasons for specific results and observations.

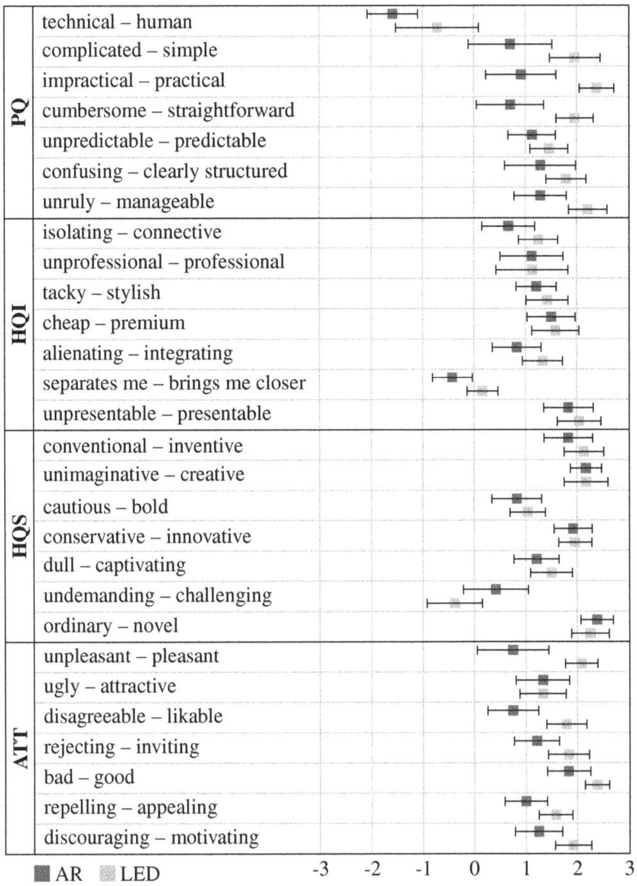


**Figure 7. Overview of mean ratings for each item of the attrakDiff questionnaire. The items are sorted from left (negative) to right (positive). Error bars denote 95% confidence intervals.**

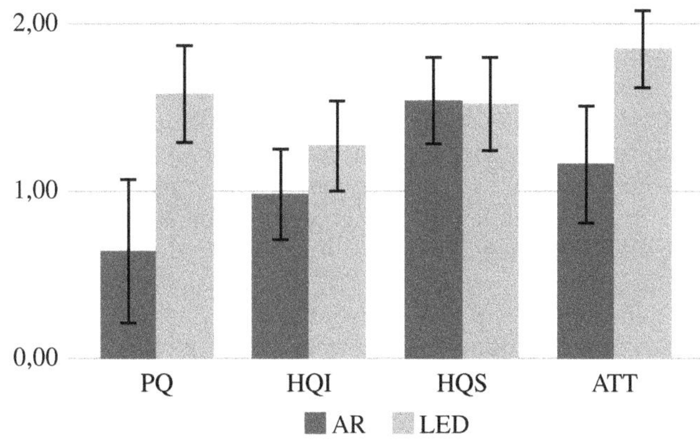


**Figure 8. Overview of mean values for each condition and dependent variable measured by the attrakDiff questionnaire. Error bars denote 95% confidence intervals. Scale ranges from -3 to 3.**

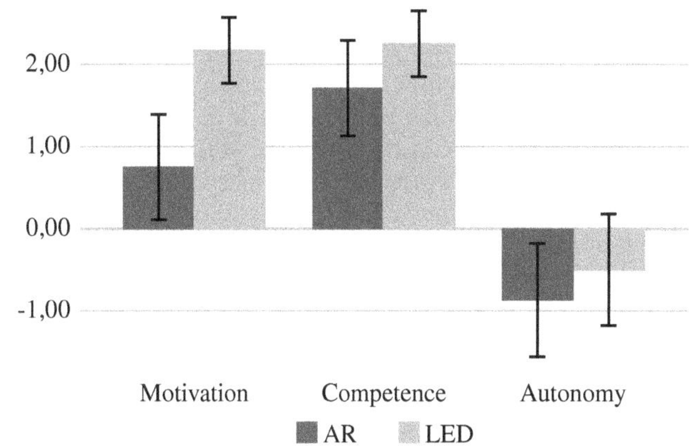


**Figure 9. Overview of mean values for each of the three positive computing factors based on the participants' self-assessment. Error bars denote 95% confidence intervals. Scale ranges from -3 to 3.**

### *General Trends*

Figure 7 presents an overview of how each item of the attrakDiff was rated on average for both conditions. In most items, the LED system was rated better than the AR system. Especially with the items belonging to PQ, the LED system performs much better. The only exception where the AR system was rated clearly better is the item "undemanding-challenging", which is part of the HQS measurement. Figure 8 provides an overview of mean values for each of the independent variables measured by the attrakDiff questionnaire (i.e., PQ, HQI, HQS, ATT). As already indicated, the biggest differences can be seen in the PQ, where the LED prototype performs much better. It also has better results in HQI and ATT. Only in HQS both systems are rated almost equally. Figure 9 shows the mean values of the evaluation of the positive computing questions. Here, the trend continues that the LED system performs better.

### *Statistical Analysis*

A paired-samples t-test was conducted to test the differences between the two systems (i.e., LED, AR) across the dependent variables measured by the attrakDiff questionnaire (i.e., PQ, HQI, HQS, ATT) and the three positive computing factors (i.e. motivation, competence, autonomy). The t-test showed a significant effect on the dependent variables measured with the attrakDiff on PQ $t(23) = 4.711$, $p < 0.001$ and ATT $t(23) = 3.508$, $p = .002$. No significant effects were found on HQI $t(23) = 1.827$, $p = .081$ and HQS $t(23) = (-)0.097$, $p = 0.924$. For the factors of positive computing, there was a significant effect on motivation $t(23) = 3.983$, $p < 0.001$. Competence $t(23) = 1.919$, $p = 0.067$ and autonomy $t(23) = 1.251$, $p = 0.224$ showed no significant effects.

### *Analysis of qualitative data*

20 of the 24 participants (83%) said they preferred the LED system. 17 of these 20 people perceived the AR system's smartphone as limiting and participants stated that "it is impractical to hold a watering can and a smartphone". Further reasons were that "looking through the screen [of the smartphone] is unreal" and that the LED system is "less complicated", "more intuitive" and "easier to use". Participants who preferred the AR system justified their selection by the fact that it is "possible to use any flower pots" and "the display is visible from all sides". It was also mentioned that you can decide for yourself when you want to see the display and thus have the possibility to improve your own abilities, for example, by using the display only for controlling and not during the complete watering process.

## DISCUSSION

In the beginning, we criticized a potential future with smarthomes in which many of todays routine tasks would be facilitated or even replaced by automation. We then motivated our research by pointing out that there are healthy routines in homes, such as watering houseplants, which should not be replaced carelessly through automation but interactions should be meaningfully transformed through appropriate design. Thus, our motivation was as suggested by Calvo and Peters [8] and other fellow researchers (e.g., [4, 26, 33]) being sensitive towards automation technology's positive and negative qualities, including undesired feelings of loss of control and smart things easily becoming obnoxious.

In order to design socio-spatially meaningful interactions, we applied role-play as a methodology and used the implicit interaction and proxemic interaction frameworks as analytical tools. These frameworks build on early work, such as Mark Weiser's ground braking work on "ubiquitous and calm computing" [46], which ultimately inspired embodied interaction design [12]. The implicit interaction framework helped to understand if, for example, plants should act proactive or reactive and the proxemic interaction framework helped to identify concrete measures, such as what distance and orientation to trigger actions. We found that iterating role-plays with participants and changing participants' interaction modalities, such as blindfolding participants or allowing participants only to communicate with a chat app useful. We believe to have provided the design process in detail and in a manner that it could be replicated by fellow researchers for other use cases considering interactions with non-human agents in smarthomes. While it was clear to us that embedded technology was needed to at least enable non-human agents to sense contextual information, to network, and communicate with other "smart" things, we were not sure about the output generated for users and which mode (and associated forms of interaction) would be best in terms of perceived attractiveness and potential impact on wellbeing determinants, such as motivation.

Considering the interaction modality or mode between an inhabitant and non-human agents in smarthomes, we were convinced that physical actuators (especially LEDs or LED based displays) and AR were todays ecologically valid alternative techniques and thus worth focusing our implementations and study on. Therefore, we implemented two systems considering these two alternative techniques and conducted a user study in the field comparing their benefits and limitations. We, ourselves were not convinced which alternative would be preferred for a houseplant watering scenario in smarthomes. However, it was clear to us that too many physical actuators, such as LEDs seemed unreasonable but not necessarily unmanageable by a rigorous design process. On the other side, we saw the potential material qualities of AR, such as its conditional existence, low maintenance, non-ephemeral (in a traditional sense) characteristic, which could benefit inhabitants and their wellbeing (if users had and felt control and competence to manage AR's conditional existence). Thus, the research question we aimed to address with the field study was which technique was preferred for watering houseplants in future smarthomes and why. Furthermore, we hoped to gain some insights on interaction modality preferences between non-human agents and inhabitants in smarthomes in general.

The results of the user study show that both prototypes were perceived as enrichment by potential users (see Figure 7), who saw a potential that the systems would increase their long-term motivation and may improve their own abilities without the users losing too much control (see Figure 9). Nevertheless, participants preferred the solution with embedded information directly in the flowerpot over the AR solution. The LED prototype was evaluated significantly better by participants considering perceived usability (PQ) and overall attractiveness (ATT). We found that participant disliked to have a smartphone in one hand and the watering can in the other and have to look through the smartphone display while interacting with plants. We deliberately chose a smartphone because users already have access to this type of augmented reality device. Head-mounted displays, which might also be available to consumers in future, could increase the attractiveness and usefulness of AR solutions for such tasks, as hands would then be free.

The main limitations of our research are associated with possible long-term effects, which would be relevant for daily routines. The two positive computing factors motivation and competence may change in the long term. Without long-term user studies, it seems impossible to make concrete statements about how inhabitants' motivation and competence may change. Since we still wanted to know whether certain tendencies exist, we asked the participants for a self-assessment and an anticipation of potential futures. Furthermore, physical actuators such as LEDs may ware off, stop working, and may become less attractive over time in contrast to AR. It should also be noted that during the study we had to use the "Wizard-of-Oz" technique to simulate spatial interaction with the embedded system, because indoor localization is a difficult to implement task. However, AR is already space sensitive and it was easy to implement proximity sensitive functions. Therefore, we believe future designs might integrate both techniques.

## CONCLUSION

We reported on a rigorous design process aiming to explore how IoT technology can support inhabitants in properly watering their plants in their homes without replacing the benefits inhabitants may have from routine interactions with their plants. We presented results from multiple role-plays, and a field study with concluding designs, comparing the user experience of two alternative techniques to implement (implicit and proxemic) interactions between inhabitants and their plants. We found, for example, that the user experience of IoT plants providing feedback through physical LEDs was significantly better than when plants used an AR solution with smartphones.

We hope that the detailed description of the design process we went through and the results we produced will inspire and guide fellow researchers in designing implicit interactions in future smarthomes and inform them of potential benefits and limitations of embedded physical actuators and AR to communicate (explicitly and implicitly) with inhabitants.

## REFERENCES


[1] Leonardo Angelini, Stefania Caparrotta, Omar Abou Khaled, and Elena Mugellini. 2016. EmotiPlant: Human-Plant Interaction for Older Adults. In *Proceedings of the TEI'16: Tenth International Conference on Tangible, Embedded, and Embodied Interaction*. ACM, 373–379.

[2] Constantinos Marios Angelopoulos, Sotiris Nikoletseas, and Georgios Constantinos Theofanopoulos. 2011. A Smart System for Garden Watering Using Wireless Sensor Networks. In *Proceedings of the 9th ACM International Symposium on Mobility Management and Wireless Access (MobiWac '11)*. ACM, New York, NY, USA, 167–170. DOI: http://dx.doi.org/10.1145/2069131.2069162

[3] Till Ballendat, Nicolai Marquardt, and Saul Greenberg. 2010. Proxemic interaction: designing for a proximity and orientation-aware environment. In *ACM International Conference on Interactive Tabletops and Surfaces*. ACM, 121–130.

[4] Louise Barkhuus and Anind Dey. 2003. Is context-aware computing taking control away from the user? Three levels of interactivity examined. In *International Conference on Ubiquitous Computing*. Springer, 149–156.

[5] Virginia Braun and Victoria Clarke. 2006. Using thematic analysis in psychology. *Qualitative research in psychology* 3, 2 (2006), 77–101.

[6] A.J. Bernheim Brush, Bongshin Lee, Ratul Mahajan, Sharad Agarwal, Stefan Saroiu, and Colin Dixon. 2011. Home Automation in the Wild: Challenges and Opportunities. In *Proceedings of the SIGCHI Conference on Human Factors in Computing Systems (CHI '11)*. ACM, New York, NY, USA, 2115–2124. DOI: http://dx.doi.org/10.1145/1978942.1979249

[7] Marion Buchenau and Jane Fulton Suri. 2000. Experience prototyping. In *Proceedings of the 3rd conference on Designing interactive systems: processes, practices, methods, and techniques*. ACM, 424–433.

[8] Rafael A Calvo and Dorian Peters. 2014. *Positive computing: technology for wellbeing and human potential*. MIT Press.

[9] S. Chang, S. Ham, and D. Suh. 2010. ROHINI: A robotic flower system for intuitive smart home interface. In *ICCAS 2010*. 1773–1776. DOI: http://dx.doi.org/10.1109/ICCAS.2010.5670207

[10] Jaewon Cho, Sanghoo Park, Been Jeon, Byung-Chull Bae, and Jun-Dong Cho. 2015. People's Emotional Responses to a Plant's Emotional Expression. In *Proceedings of the Ninth International Conference on Tangible, Embedded, and Embodied Interaction*. ACM, 545–550.

[11] Drashti Divani, Pallavi Patil, and Sunil K Punjabi. 2016. Automated plant Watering system. In *Computation of Power, Energy Information and Commuincation (ICCPEIC), 2016 International Conference on*. IEEE, 180–182.

[12] Paul Dourish. 2001. *Where the action is*. MIT press Cambridge.

[13] Berry Eggen, Gerard Hollemans, and Richard van de Sluis. 2003. Exploring and enhancing the home experience. *Cognition, Technology & Work* 5, 1 (01 Apr 2003), 44–54. DOI: http://dx.doi.org/10.1007/s10111-002-0114-7

[14] Berry Eggen, Elise van den Hoven, and Jacques Terken. 2017. *Human-Centered Design and Smart Homes: How to Study and Design for the Home Experience?* Springer International Publishing, Cham, 83–92. DOI: http://dx.doi.org/10.1007/978-3-319-01583-5_6

[15] Marjolein Elings. 2006. People-plant interaction: the physiological, psychological and sociological effects of plants on people. In *Farming for health*. Springer, 43–55.

[16] Google. 2018. ARCore Overview. (2018). https://developers.google.com/ar/discover/.

[17] JC Hammond, PM Sharkey, and GT Foster. 1996. Integrating augmented reality with home systems. In *Proc. 1 st Euro. Conf. Disability, Virtual Reality & Assoc. Tech.*

[18] Marc Hassenzahl, Michael Burmester, and Franz Koller. 2003. AttrakDiff: Ein Fragebogen zur Messung wahrgenommener hedonischer und pragmatischer Qualität. In *Mensch & Computer 2003*. Springer, 187–196.

[19] Pam Heath and Nancy Bell. 2006. The Changing World of Home Technology: A Microsoft Case Study. *Information Society* 22, 4 (2006), 251 – 259.

[20] Steven Henderson and Steven Feiner. 2011. Exploring the benefits of augmented reality documentation for maintenance and repair. *IEEE transactions on visualization and computer graphics* 17, 10 (2011), 1355–1368.

[21] Steven J Henderson and Steven Feiner. 2009. Evaluating the benefits of augmented reality for task localization in maintenance of an armored personnel carrier turret. In *Mixed and Augmented Reality, 2009. ISMAR 2009. 8th IEEE International Symposium on*. IEEE, 135–144.

[22] Apple Inc. 2017. ARKit. (2017). https://developer.apple.com/arkit/.

[23] Lars-Erik Janlert and Erik Stolterman. 2017. *Things that keep us busy: The elements of interaction.*

[24] Wendy Ju. 2015. The design of implicit interactions. *Synthesis Lectures on Human-Centered Informatics* 8, 2 (2015), 1–93.

[25] Wendy Ju, Brian A Lee, and Scott R Klemmer. 2008. Range: exploring implicit interaction through electronic whiteboard design. In *Proceedings of the 2008 ACM conference on Computer supported cooperative work*. ACM, 17–26.

[26] Wendy Ju and Larry Leifer. 2008. The design of implicit interactions: Making interactive systems less obnoxious. *Design Issues* 24, 3 (2008), 72–84.

[27] S. Koprda, Z. Balogh, D. Hrubý, and M. Turčám. 2015. Proposal of the irrigation system using low-cost Arduino system as part of a smart home. In *2015 IEEE 13th International Symposium on Intelligent Systems and Informatics (SISY)*. 229–233. DOI: http://dx.doi.org/10.1109/SISY.2015.7325385

[28] Matthias Kranz, Paul Holleis, and Albrecht Schmidt. 2010. Embedded interaction: Interacting with the internet of things. *IEEE internet computing* 14, 2 (2010), 46–53.

[29] David Ledo, Saul Greenberg, Nicolai Marquardt, and Sebastian Boring. 2015. Proxemic-aware controls: Designing remote controls for ubiquitous computing ecologies. In *Proceedings of the 17th International Conference on Human-Computer Interaction with Mobile Devices and Services*. ACM, 187–198.

[30] Jangho Lee, Jee-In Kim, Jiyong Kim, and Ji-Young Kwak. 2007. A unified remote console based on augmented reality in a home network environment. In *Consumer Electronics, 2007. ICCE 2007. Digest of Technical Papers. International Conference on*. IEEE, 1–2.

[31] Rung-Huei Liang. 2012. Designing for unexpected encounters with digital products: Case studies of serendipity as felt experience. *International Journal of Design* 6, 1 (2012).

[32] Nicolai Marquardt and Saul Greenberg. 2015. Proxemic interactions: From theory to practice. *Synthesis Lectures on Human-Centered Informatics* 8, 1 (2015), 1–199.

[33] Sarah Mennicken, Jo Vermeulen, and Elaine M Huang. 2014. From today's augmented houses to tomorrow's smart homes: new directions for home automation research. In *Proceedings of the 2014 ACM International Joint Conference on Pervasive and Ubiquitous Computing*. ACM, 105–115.

[34] Microsoft. 2017. HoloLens. (2017). https://www.microsoft.com/en-us/hololens.

[35] Paul Milgram, Haruo Takemura, Akira Utsumi, and Fumio Kishino. 1995. Augmented reality: A class of displays on the reality-virtuality continuum. In *Telemanipulator and telepresence technologies*, Vol. 2351. International Society for Optics and Photonics, 282–293.

[36] Lars Müller, Ilhan Aslan, and Lucas Krüßen. 2013. GuideMe: A Mobile Augmented Reality System to Display User Manuals for Home Appliances. In *Advances in Computer Entertainment*, Dennis Reidsma, Haruhiro Katayose, and Anton Nijholt (Eds.). Springer International Publishing, Cham, 152–167.

[37] Dan O'Sullivan and Tom Igoe. 2004. *Physical computing: sensing and controlling the physical world with computers*. Thomson Boston, MA, USA.

[38] Parrot Drones SAS. 2015. Parrot Smart Pot. (2015). https://www.parrot.com/uk/connected-garden/parrot-pot.

[39] Andreas Seiderer, Chi Tai Dang, and Elisabeth André. 2017. Exploring Opportunistic Ambient Notifications in the Smart Home to Enhance Quality of Live. In *Enhanced Quality of Life and Smart Living*. Springer International Publishing, Cham, 151–160.

[40] Dipak Surie, Berker Baydan, and Helena Lindgren. 2013. proxemics awareness in kitchen As-A-Pal: tracking objects and human in perspective. In *Intelligent Environments (IE), 2013 9th International Conference on*. IEEE, 157–164.

[41] Arthur Tang, Charles Owen, Frank Biocca, and Weimin Mou. 2003. Comparative effectiveness of augmented reality in object assembly. In *Proceedings of the SIGCHI conference on Human factors in computing systems*. ACM, 73–80.

[42] Brent Tisserat and Carl E Vandercook. 1985. Development of an automated plant culture system. *Plant cell, tissue and organ culture* 5, 2 (1985), 107–117.

[43] Ahmed Mohmmad Ullah, Md Rashedul Islam, Sayeda Farzana Aktar, and SK Alamgir Hossain. 2012. Remote-touch: Augmented reality based marker tracking for smart home control. In *Computer and Information Technology (ICCIT), 2012 15th International Conference on*. IEEE, 473–477.

[44] Alladi Venkatesh. 1996. Computers and Other Interactive Technologies for the Home. *Commun. ACM* 39, 12 (Dec. 1996), 47–54. DOI: http://dx.doi.org/10.1145/240483.240491

[45] Alexandra Voit, Tonja Machulla, Dominik Weber, Valentin Schwind, Stefan Schneegass, and Niels Henze. 2016. Exploring Notifications in Smart Home Environments. In *Proceedings of the 18th International Conference on Human-Computer Interaction with Mobile Devices and Services Adjunct (MobileHCI '16)*. ACM, New York, NY, USA, 942–947. DOI: http://dx.doi.org/10.1145/2957265.2962661

[46] Mark Weiser. 1991. The Computer for the 21 st Century. *Scientific american* 265, 3 (1991), 94–105.

[47] Charlie Wilson, Tom Hargreaves, and Richard Hauxwell-Baldwin. 2015. Smart homes and their users: a systematic analysis and key challenges. *Personal and Ubiquitous Computing* 19, 2 (01 Feb 2015), 463–476. DOI: http://dx.doi.org/10.1007/s00779-014-0813-0

# Democratizing Soap: The Methodological Value of Using Constructive Assemblies as a Participatory Design Tool

**Awais Hameed Khan**
The University of Queensland
Brisbane, Australia
awaishameed.khan@uq.edu.au

**Ben Matthews**
The University of Queensland
Brisbane, Australia
matthews@uq.edu.au

## ABSTRACT
This paper explores methodological considerations of using Constructive Assemblies (CA) as a Participatory Design (PD) tool in order to explore new conceptual and material possibilities in saturated product categories. CA are tangible, reconfigurable, modular physical sets that can be combined in multiple different ways. They are valuable as collaborative tools on account of how they facilitate social inclusion by having a low skill barrier to participation. They are also valuable as generative tools, as users are able to quickly build complex constructions. In this paper, we present a study in which a series of eight Participatory Design (PD) workshops were conducted with these assemblies, in which stakeholders explored possibilities for re-designing the everyday use of soap. Participants were drawn from the Fast Moving Consumer Goods (FMCG) industry and everyday soap users, and the workshops took three different configurations: video-conference and shared location, video conference and distributed location, and physical workshop and shared location. Our analysis highlights the consequentiality of the materiality of the assembly, the interplay between the specific workshop tasks, their setup and the physical constraints of the toolset, and emergent social behaviour from the experiments. We discuss these findings in relation to existing frameworks.

### Author Keywords
Participatory Design; Constructive Assemblies; LEGO; Design Methodology; Design Tools.

### ACM Classification Keywords
Interaction design; Interaction design process and methods; Participatory design;

## INTRODUCTION
Constructive Assemblies (CA) are a subset of tangible user interfaces (TUIs) that have often been used as tools in Participatory Design (PD). Their methodological value however remains underexplored in literature and practice. Through this study we uncover considerations of the application of these tangible design tools situated within the PD space; these considerations also act as primers for organising PD of future tangible interaction systems. From its origins in workplace democracy, PD has evolved into a practice that has become increasingly adopted in many other spheres of everyday life. This reorientation of context for PD has allowed for its democratic focus to extend to more mainstream domains of production and innovation [7], where it has been used in the design and development of commercial products to create and capture value [11]. Design solutions from PD processes are valued on account of how users of the system are given an active role in designing the system [32], leading to outputs that are grounded in users' knowledge. Outcomes of these processes are generally more practical and realistic, with a higher rate of acceptability amongst end users [8]. In order for participatory design to act as a catalyst to drive innovation in commercial environments, it is important, as much as practical, to create a democratically-oriented environment where no single participant group is dominant [7]. The dissonance created through participation among heterogeneous groups promotes creativity and innovation, as alternative voices are not marginalized [7,19].

Successful products and services today have developed an increasingly symbiotic relationship with users and contexts of use. In a dynamic competitive landscape, a valuable key feature of a product is the ability to be reinvented; adapting to transient (market) landscapes. Business theory describes this phenomenon as the Red Queen effect [28], inspired from a line in the book 'Through the Looking-Glass' by Lewis Carroll – "*it takes all the running you can do to keep in the same place*" [12]. In this view, products and services must constantly innovate and improve to be able to sustain if not grow share. Innovation models within business schools have restructured themselves to cater to this. Management and innovation research views democratic innovation as a function of the increased ease of access of end users to production tools; decreasing the resource-disconnect between producers and consumers in what was previously a resource-heavy capital intensive industry [7]. Meta-design theory suggests this is the future of design - the shift of the role users to crafters of designs in response to changing needs in dynamic environments [26].


*TEI '19*, March 17–20, 2019, Tempe, AZ, USA

ACM 978-1-4503-6196-5/19/03...$15.00
https://doi.org/10.1145/3294109.3295641

## EVOLUTION OF PARTICIPATORY DESIGN TOOLS

Traditional PD employed collaborative tools such as scenarios, mock-ups, prototypes [6] as well as consensus building strategies [15] within the workplace. This was further expanded to incorporate collaborative explorations of everyday experiences focusing on techniques inspired by theatre, design games and setting rules for design dialogue and collaborative construction of mockups [5,10]. As time progressed changes in managerial strategies, have resulted in further refinement and evolution of these tools and techniques. The reorientation of the application domain of PD to encompass a more holistic everyday-life context, has not taken away from traditional productive design activities, only packaged it as innovation [7]. PD is seen as 'a proliferating family of design practices' that caters to a multitude of design ideologies, purposes and therefore uses a very diverse set of tools [29]. Robertson & Simonsen [29] claim that given the application domains and contexts of PD are growing, tools should not be constrained by rigor, but instead embody the values that define a tool relevant to PD, i.e. have sufficient grounding in providing participants the agency to make, tell and enact. Star & Griesemer [33] introduced the concept of 'boundary objects', objects that are simultaneously malleable and robust. Boundary objects can be abstract or concrete (or both) – their meaning can be transient, in that it can change based on disciplinary need, yet remain consistent enough to be used as a tool to make ideas recognizable – a means of translation. Robertson & Simonsen, suggest that boundary objects create homogeneity and continuity, as groups can assimilate around them and these tools allow participants to contribute to the project. PD toolkits can employ a multitude of tools that employ storytelling, creating, crafting things, prototyping, or a means to probe and discover more about the problem space [29]. The material practices of PD (including workshops, design tasks, scenario building, artefacts, mapping etc.) are frequently rife with boundary objects, being available to and variously interpretable by a range of stakeholders with different disciplinary interests in the project. Sanders et al. [31] when reviewing PD methods and tools discuss the significance of spatial constructs for PD sessions. They highlight that traditional face-to-face sessions are preferred because the modalities of the tools and method can be completed holistically. Online sessions were limited to only probing and priming participants, and were not robust enough to conduct complete PD sessions. With the increasing prevalence of geographically distant stakeholders, this is another facet that PD tools need to encompass, being able to successfully be transferrable across physical spaces; incorporating all facets of a session from probing and priming to making tangible mockups, storytelling as well as acting, enacting and playing.

## CONSTRUCTIVE ASSEMBLIES

Constructive assemblies allow the interconnection of physical, modular, interactive components which may constitute a larger more complex construction, put together manually or automatically [13,22,30]. Their modular nature drives inherent versatility in their application domains – generally prototyping, digital content manipulation, as well as story-telling in an education context [25]. Originally purposed for modelling and simulation [1,2,3] CA have over time been used in varied disciplines and contexts. Ishii, [22] referred to CA as a promising design direction for innovation in new tangible user interfaces, as the kinetic relationships of the individual modules and physical fit of the form, allows for larger constructions in varied dimensions of movement. They are also by design socially inclusive, and tend to drive collaboration amongst users because of their tangible and modular nature [14,21,22]. CA are also able to create a sense of equality amongst users, as their inherent limitations provide the same degree of agency for creativity to all. Their interaction paradigm is moulded by their transient, shape-shifting physical form [25]. Dancu et al., argue that CA can be used to drive 'emergence' [13] implying that the holistic capability of the sum is significantly greater than its parts [4].

Two particularly notable tangible frameworks precede and inform our work. Leong et al. developed a framework specifically tailored to the critical appraisal and systematic investigation of CAs in design. The framework consists of a 'constructive assembly lifecycle model', along with a network of themes and parameters [25] The lifecycle model covers six different phases: creation, usage, tweaking, storage, destruction and obliteration. This is to be analyzed in conjunction with four interrelated design theme continuums: efficiency vs. exploration; repulsion vs. attachment; constrained vs. expressive; novice vs. expert. When applied, the thematic lens seems to highlight more individual, task-centric foci; social, spatial, contextual and environmental features are underrepresented. What is underplayed in Leong et al.'s presentation is, however, the fundamental relationship unpacked in the tangible interaction framework proposed by Hornecker & Buur [21], who explore theoretical perspectives around how social interaction and collaboration interplay with the material and physical aspects of tangible interfaces. Their focus, however, is on the *use* of tangible interfaces in the wild, rather than their application within design processes as generative and participatory tools. In this paper, we specifically address the use of CAs in collaborative, participatory workshops in order to identify methodological considerations of their use that have been underrepresented or that need further exploration.

LEGO® by virtue of its properties can be framed as a primitive constructive assembly. There are useful aspects of using LEGO in particular, such as universal access to the tool because of its global popularity and distribution network; making transferable and translatable, across distributed geographies and cultural divides. It is easy to understand and use - making it a non-bespoke tool not designed for any particular case or application, but an everyday use item that meaningfully provides the benefits of a CA beyond its original use as a toy. CA are an interesting fit for a PD tool. The uniformity of its components creates a sense of equity amongst users, with the freedom to build larger, more complex systems using the same tool in drastically different configurations and associated meanings. PD provides a platform that allows for the 'democratization of innovation' [7] by creating formats for involvement that attempt to give participants the same level of agency for creativity.

The application domain for the study explores the Fast Moving Consumer Goods (FMCG) product - soap. Soap is a low-involvement product category that is highly commoditized, with little apparent room for further organic product innovation (pursued through marginal cosmetic and ingredient changes coupled with marketing campaigns). There is also a very acute disconnect between the form and characteristics of soap and the constructive assembly that make it an interesting product domain to design for.

## THE LEGO® SERIOUS PLAY® (LSP) METHODOLOGY

LEGO® SERIOUS PLAY® (LSP) is a facilitated workshop, which prompts participants different questions in the context of an existing business project, task or strategy, and participants respond to these prompts by constructing metaphorical and symbolic models to represent their insights using LEGO bricks followed by a reflective peer discussion on what they have built to explore the complexities [24]. The methodology assumes that the answer to the problem lies within the system, all participants must express their reflections, and there is no single correct answer or solution. This builds on the ethos that no individual participant, facilitator or group leader has the correct answer – driving the same democratized structure which is native to PD. The workshop model follows a four step process: 1. Facilitator poses a challenge; 2. Participants build their answers using LEGO® bricks; 3. Participants share answers with other participants; 4. Participants reflect on what they have seen and heard.

The challenge posed to the participants must to some degree be open-ended. Participants must build the abstract concepts into physical models and ascribe meaning to the constructions. Thereby creating new frames of reference to knowledge. The method enriches dialogue and discussion, by providing a sophisticated means to share ideas through storytelling, drawing on the metaphorical manifestations of the insights and abstract concepts [17] to help create shared understanding amongst participants [23]. The session ends generally with participants being encouraged to reflect on the process. LSP goals include social bonding, emotional expression, cognitive development and constructive competition [17].

The LSP model operates on the learning principle of constructionism - suggesting that one learns when creating something that is external to oneself [16], as it allows people to draw connections, and establish their own understanding, generate theories and knowledge as they are processing ideas through the building process [27]. Constructive activities such as LSP workshops can take abstract ideas and convert them to more tangible manifestations – thereby making them

**Figure 1: Workshop Materials**

easier to understand. The human brain has an inherent predisposition towards processing information through the hands [34]. This is represented through the concept of Homunculus - a distorted representation of the human form, where each feature of the body is in proportion to its utility from a neural map of the brain [24]. Kristiansen et al., describe the homunculus as a gross oversimplification of the human neural system, but highlight its value in understanding how the process of building and engaging with our hands can stimulate activity in our brains and thereby our imagination [24]. Blair & Rillo describe this through the metaphor from the digital space - '*your hands are the search engines of your mind*' [9]. suggesting that the profound connection between the brain and hands means that the hands are not just used as tools to get information and manipulate matter, but also assist in cognition and creation of meaning [18]. The LSP model has primarily been designed for use in business consulting. This study neither corroborates nor validates the model, but instead uses it as a basis to inform a participatory workshop design for using CA.

## DESIGNING THE WORKSHOP

This empirical study uses an exploratory, mixed-methods approach, to evaluate CA through a series of 8 workshop sessions with participants from the Fast Moving Consumer Goods (FMCG) sector and everyday soap users. The workshops were conducted in three different configurations involving co-located and distributed participants. Data was collected through participant observation and semi-structured interviews conducted during and after the sessions.

### Participants

The study included a total of 19 participants belonging to two distinct groups: Fast Moving Consumer Goods (FMCG) industry professionals (12) and everyday soap users (7). Study participants were selected through purposive judgement sampling; with FMCG participants having over 2 years of experience working within industry, across the functions: brand building, brand development, finance, sales and supply chain; and were geographically distributed across the countries: Australia (AU), England (UK), Germany (DE), Pakistan (PK), Switzerland (CH), and The United States (US). The everyday soap users were recruited using stratified convenience sampling; participants being students of an Australian university. The unit of analysis in the study is individuals in groups, and participants are presented in

| # | Participants | Experience | Location | WS Type | Relationship |
|---|---|---|---|---|---|
| 1 | A, B | Professionals | US | VC1 | Strangers |
| 2 | C, D | Professionals | CH, UK | VC1 | Friends |
| 3 | E, F | Professionals | PK | VC2 | Colleagues |
| 4 | G, H | Professionals | DE, US | VC1 | Strangers |
| 5 | I, J | Professionals | CH, UK | VC1 | Friends |
| 6 | K, L | Professionals | UK | VC2 | Married |
| 7 | M, N, O, P, Q | Student | AU | PW | Peers |
| 8 | R, S | Student | AU | PW | Friends |

**Table 1: Workshop Participant Detail**

data with codes (letters A - S). All participants were recruited from the research team's professional and social network, and every workshop had at least one person they knew (including the facilitator) during the session. Participants also had a diverse set of relationships to each other, ranging from strangers, to peers, friends, colleagues and even one married couple. The familiarity of the participants with at least one other point of reference within the session was thought to have the potential to increase participation in the workshop.

### Spatial Configuration

The workshop sessions were set up in three different configurations, exploring common scenarios of collaborative work in real-world settings and identify any significant emergent behaviour as a result of variance in configurations. They were however not set up to perform a formal comparative analysis. The three configurations were: VC1: video-conferencing, distributed locations; VC2: video-conferencing, shared location; PW: physical workshop, shared location. Video conferencing was conducted through Skype, barring one occasion (WS3) where participants had limited access to Skype, and Facebook video was used instead. Video conferences were broken into two separate subcategories, VC1 where participants and the facilitator were in different locations, and VC2 where participants were co-located and video conferencing with the facilitator. The physical workshop PW had all participants and the facilitator in a shared space. In VC1 participants had control over the visual access of the workspace; VC2 had shared visual access for participants but this could be controlled for the facilitator. For VC1 and VC2 configurations 2 participants were present per session, however for the PW sessions there was no prescribed minimum limit to restrict participation per session. The activity application type is 'building individual models', to maintain consistency across different spatial configurations.

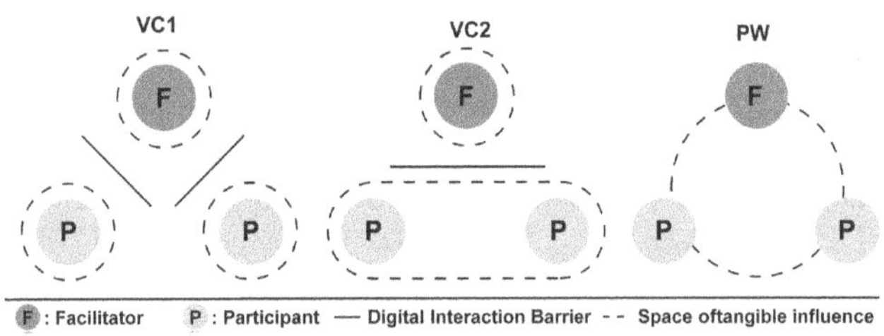


**Figure 2: Workshop Configurations**

### Constructive Assembly Workshop Toolkit

The workshop toolkit includes all the materials used to conduct the workshop sessions.

#### *The Constructive Assembly*

The constructive assembly used for this session was the LEGO® Classic Creative Supplements kits 10693 and 10694, which contain 303 individual pieces that come in a plastic bag and cardboard box. We explored different creative, constructive tools including interlocking bricks, play-doh, clay, kinetic sand, magnets and water adhesive blocks; looking for material properties that could be similar to the context of application i.e. the soap. However, review of literature highlighted that lower fidelity materials which can be viewed as constraints, have the ability to shift focus towards the actual concept being articulated and not limit the construction to be a more accurate physical representation [21,25]. Another core feature of CA is the ability to un-craft or disassemble the constituent elements for reconfiguration into different combinations [16,20,23,25]. As a result, interlocking bricks were chosen as the assembly type. Given the geographic spread of the study resource accessibility was also considered. These kits are designed as starter packs, with all the basic LEGO® bricks, easy to understand and use.

#### *Design Prompts*

A total of 76 text based prompts were created, inspired by the 'pose a challenge' step of the LSP workshop protocol [17]. The categories of the questions ranged from context-specific (26) e.g. "*How would you redesign soap for an airplane?*" to more divergent, open-ended (50) questions e.g. "*How would you redesign soap for racism?*" These questions were the outcome of a brainstorming workshop exercise to explore conditions of the application domain for soap, to more abstract, divergent, laterally placed value-specific subjects. The questions were colour coded: yellow for context-specific prompts and blue for open-ended prompts and available to participants as physical cards for PW configurations where they were able to draw the context from a shuffled set of cards. In the VC1 and VC2 configurations, the facilitator shuffled and drew cards for participants, and showed through the video feed to participants. Participants were provided access to the pool of prompts through a Google Slide deck. There were some context-specific prompts that were further supplemented by photo-visual aids to evaluate how participants would respond to the same prompt if they were given visual stimuli to assist in articulating the context.

#### *Workshop Context Deck*

A workshop session docket was created using Google Slides used as a visual aid to take participants through the aims and objectives of the study when setting the initial context; highlight the activity protocols; and ensure that all participants were made aware they were equal participants in this study. Thereafter the deck was used as a mode to share activity prompts with the participants. The prompts within the deck had a predefined structure, but no set sequence; prompts were randomly drawn from a pool in each session.

**Figure 3: VC1(video-conference, distributed location); VC2(video-conference, shared location); PW(physical workshop, shared location; PW participants reflect on their complimentary constructions - soap (R) and soap dish (L).**

### Task Constraints

*Task Duration*

For each task, the facilitator communicated a set time for construction to the participants. The overall duration intervals were randomized to gauge how participants perceived this impacted their performance. Regular reminders were shared with participants of remaining time, but no explicit visual timer was shown to the participants.

*Task Resource Utility Constraints*

There were also certain resource constraints that were put into different tasks. This included restricting brick count for a construction, or designing with only a specific colour, or capping the total number of colours that can be used.

*Time Keeping*

Time was also used as an intangible resource. There were certain tasks were the participants were allowed to dictate when the time allocated to the construction would elapse; allowing the first participant to finish their construction to dictate that all participants had to move to the next step.

*Rule Setting*

The facilitator shared rules of participation at the beginning of each prompt, however these rules were not enforced; leaving it up to the participants to decide how they wanted to engage with the task. In certain workshops participants were also given the freedom to select different prompts for the same task and rules from drawing cards.

### Workshop Protocol

The facilitator starts off the workshop by establishing that all participants have equal agency and roles within the activity. Participants are then run through the *Workshop Context Deck*. The goals and purpose of the study are shared and the facilitator checks all participants have the required tools to participate. This is followed by sharing an example of a LEGO construction and how storytelling and metaphors may be used to assign meaning to the artefact. This is followed by the Task Loop (TL) for each prompt:

1. Facilitator introduces a prompt;
2. Participants construct a design to address the prompt;
3. Participants ascribe meanings to the built material artefacts and use storytelling to explain what they have built and how it addresses the challenge; and,
4. Participants reflect and synthesize activity takeaways.

Participants are then asked to organize their CA materials, and then shown the first prompt. The workshop prompts start with close-ended questions, and give participants on average 5 minutes at the start to explore the assembly and build something. After closure of the first task loop, participants are asked to photograph their assembly, and proceed to the next series of context-specific prompts. Thereafter the prompts are supplemented with photo-visual aids, and finally move into more open-ended questions. Randomized resource constraints are built into the prompts to see how participants react and build to the set constraints. On average a workshop session can last up to one hour, exhausting up to 10 prompts, whereby each participant is given 2 minutes per question, but varies based on the time available to the participants, and their level of involvement and interest. The last stage is reflection, where learnings from the session are synthesised and experiences about the activity are discussed as a group.

## METHODOLOGICAL CONSIDERATIONS & DISCUSSION

This section breaks down the methodological considerations of using CA as PD tools in the design of future tangible systems through discussion using results from the workshop sessions.

### Physicality and Materiality

The physical, tangible nature of the CA had significant impact on how participants engaged with the workshop tasks. Each participant had access to a common set of resources in their constructive assembly toolkit, but this also meant they shared the *Material Limitations* of the kit. The shape, size, colour, assortment of brick types and quantity were all limited, which resulted in participants having to channel ideas through their constructions while cognizant of the limitations of their resource pool. The shape limitations forced participants to think of ways to share their ideas by relying only on rigid structures to help articulate their thoughts and ideas, and in doing so became more expressive - different to how 'constrained vs. expressive' themes were highlighted in the constructive assembly framework [25]. The *Assortment Limitations* of the quantity of bricks were also discovered by participants as they went through the motions of completing tasks forcing them to repurpose components they had previously used. As users progressed in the tasks they found creative ways of using the material limitations to supplement their ideas, using single bricks and colour to represent a certain value attribute for the design context, or similarly the industrious use of the packaging content (plastic bag and box) as props to supplement the context of their assemblies.

The *Material Affordances* of the assembly, particularly the discrete physical form of the interlocking bricks, allowed participants to use a material artefact, and channel meaning through the use of metaphors to articulate their thoughts using a shared focal point of reference. The fact that the artefact was restricted to the material limitations allowed for a less socially perilous form of expression for the participants, as the quality of the construction or skill levels of the participants had much less bearing on the resultant output, reducing the probability of being a social spectacle. This reduced the barrier to participate, a value of good PD tools [29]. This in turn created a sense of equity amongst participants and their contributions. This also enabled (or enforced) a spectrum of abstracted meanings to be assigned to participants' creations. There were, for instance, cases where participants repurposed an existing assembly to re-ascribe meaning to it in light of a new set of prompts. Much like boundary objects [33], which can also be variously interpreted with respect to different institutional and disciplinary interests, the meanings associated to the assembly were more significant than, and not entirely dictated by, its material form. What is distinctive in this case (and from boundary objects in general) is the manner in which the objects are variously re-interpretable by their own creator; perhaps partly on account of the way each different prompt introduces a different 'disciplinary' interest in play.

The physical nature of the build also lets participants see the progression of what their outputs has been visibly and tangibly. *Outputs are Outcomes* - they stand as artefacts of where the participants have gotten to, and as a result there were instances of initial reluctance to break up creations or document their existence by taking photographs. The Material Limitations however came into play, and the limited resource allocation in the assortment forced participants to dismantle and recycle their assembly components for newer constructions.

The *Constraints* that were put into the mix of using the assembly in terms of time, rules (e.g. first participant to complete the assembly calls time), and task limitations (e.g. construct using a single colour) added another layer of complexity to the physicality of the assembly. Participants had a mixed response to the constraints, stating in certain instances the constraints helped channel thoughts and make them focus when using the assembly but in other instances they found them challenging. H commenting on constraints: "*It simplifies things and makes it easier to express the concept. I thought it to be convenient, sometimes you can't be so innovative in drawing or sketching*"

The *Materiality* of the actual assembly, the fact that the assembly comprised of easy to use interlocking plastic bricks was seen to be helpful to most participants as it gave them the ability to make constructions with ease, a characteristic also identified by Leong et al. [25]. Certain participants commented that using alternative modes of expression such as sketching may have been better in certain cases, but this was not a sentiment that was echoed across most of the workshops.

There is also something notable about how the visibility of the embodiment of the artefact has a *Public & Social Value*. All the constructions that are built are seen by the participants and facilitator in a public space. This acts not just as a common point of focus but also introduces accountability for what is built; extending beyond the layer of personality and mentality as contributors of thinking when constructing [25], and situating the constructor and construction within a social context. The act of not building something with the assembly is almost more visible because of the physical nature of the material when compared to something like a pen and paper based task. Adding to this aspect of social behaviour is the inclusivity of the physical assembly components, to the degree that even a *Novice User Can Build*. Basic level physical dexterity is required to engage and participate with the tasks, as a result of which there is limited inequity between different levels of skill when it comes to using the actual assembly.

Building on the social values, the physical nature of the assembly and the way it lowers the barriers of participation results in an *Imposition of a Participation Structure*. Throughout the workshop sessions there was not a single task where any participant built nothing, or had no story to tell with what they made. This was one of the most interesting outcomes of the constructive assembly placements in the PD context, of how well the assemblies functioned within the task domain to channel participation.

**Tasks, Tools and Sequence**

Having tasks that are following a specific *Sequential Mapping* was observed to be relevant when designing a PD workshop as a whole. The order of the events, the shifting of the prompt types from specific contexts, to visual contexts to more ambiguous contexts helped channel the participants' approach to contextualizing their approach to design for this product category - soap. In addition to this there was an increased understanding of how the system of the workshop functioned as participants progressed through different prompts, and they felt more comfortable with using their assemblies. This led to participants detaching focus from more specific builds, where the output was supposed to be a physical approximation, representative of what they were trying to communicate, to using the assembly components as abstract forms in order to articulate impressions and meanings.

Another inherent quality of a constructive assembly is that participants *Never Start from Nowhere* –they will always have a base, a constituent element that can serve as a channel to articulation. The components of the assembly, the raw material is always present and therefore the participants are can use the assemblies in an ongoing cycle of building and destroying and repurposing elements. This too acts as a lever that lowers the barrier to participate. Perfection is impossible to achieve with the assembly; therefore no construction can be hyper realistic. This limits the output to the equivalent of a low fidelity mockup - maintaining the integrity of the idea behind the concept - regardless of skill or understanding of task domain, and generates a certain equity in participation.

The constant access to material results in participants *Starting to Build Before Thinking* about what they are building; there is an invitation to 'do'. Participants are able to construct before they have the time to ascribe meaning to the construction and in doing so they are learning and exploring through their hands and seeing how the different constructions can be used to help guide their thoughts to find meaning, and then later on use that meaning to channel their thoughts using the artefact they created. The sequential shift of design prompts from context-specific to open-ended was perceived as more challenging by participants. The more abstract the prompt, the more difficulty participants had in ascribing a meaningful connection to their constructions. That said participants also found the more abstract prompts being more interesting as design contexts. One participant commented on how when they found themselves unable to design the soap in the context of the open-ended value, they designed for the value alone, detaching themselves from the task of redesigning 'soap'.

### Emergent Behaviour

This section discusses the participant behaviour that was seen as a result of participating in the tasks, and where relevant, highlights notable differences that emerged due to variance in spatial configurations and set ups. Only features of the conditions of the sessions that were self-identified by participants as meaningful to their experience as a result of the variance in configurations have been reported. It was observed that the interplay of participant interaction with each other had influenced the way they built their constructions. *Collaboration* was seen amongst participants when they took ideas, or inspirations from peers, and extended them through iteration in subsequent tasks. This was generally a feature of participants in co-located spaces (VC2, PW). There were a few instances where participants shared resources i.e. if one participant needed a specific brick that they had already used up, the other participant would lend them resources from their own resource pool. This was also coupled with reaffirmation of ability through compliments and encouragement when certain participants commented that they were not comfortable with the challenge or had no idea of what to build when seeing the prompt. Participants in this configuration highlighted how collaborative aspects of the VC2 configuration helped them, S: "*It was really cool. We were picking up ideas from each other. In the beginning I was just sitting there doing nothing*" to which R adds: "*if we were on separate tables it would be more competitive rather than do it together.*"

There was also an emergence of shades of *Competition* that were seen as the tasks progressed (VC1, VC2, PW). There were observed instances of friendly taunts and insults on both the outputs of the constructions, as well as the abilities of using the assemblies for participants across workshop types; and even in cases where participants were strangers or acquaintances. Participants commented that they felt a need to outperform against their peers, as well as previous of their own constructions. The following exchange highlights how participants reconfigured their own work in light of what their peers made. K: "*I didn't look at L's [construction]*" to which L responds: "*I did once..*", self-correcting K states "*I did at the end, if it was something interesting I maybe replicated it.*"

Participants also highlighted having inadequacies in their own articulation of concepts through the material artefacts being made more visible when looking at the work of their counterparts. This resulted in them reconfiguring their own outputs as a response to what they saw in the shared space. This was true across all workshop configurations, but most evident in VC1, where the participants controlled access to sharing the view for their individual workspaces based on sequence of presentation. Commenting on the spatial disconnect in VC1 configuration, participant B comments: "*I think this may have worked out better. Because I think had we been in the same room I bet you I would have been looking at what he was doing.*" to which participant A agrees "*Okay same!*" Participant B adds "*..sitting in your own space - forces you to think on your own.*" adding "*I would have definitely [spent] a good twenty seconds trying to figure out what he was doing.*"

Another characteristic that exemplified shades of competitive play was the tension between the *Invocation and Ignorance of Rules*. This was more evident in participant co-located settings (VC2, PW), but also seen in VC1 (only with time limit rules). Rules such as resource constraints and time limits were often ignored by participants as they cited *Need for Closure* of completing what they were building, ignoring the time limits and prompts to move to the next task. However, the same participants who ignored the rules felt compelled to invoke their enforcement for their peers, when it did not disadvantage themselves.

Over the progression of the tasks, participants also showed the ability to use the material artefacts to discuss incomplete ideas. In the post-activity interview, this was attributed to the environment of the study – how the tools, the nature of the workshop and having a familiar participant within the setting allowed them to view the workshops as something other than a formal or sterile experimental laboratory study, instead affording them the comfort needed to share rough and incomplete concepts with their peers.

## CONCLUSION AND FURTHER WORK

On the whole, CAs seem to function effectively as PD tools, embodying characteristics that Robertson & Simonsen [29] describe: making, telling, and enacting. In an attenuated sense, they also perform as boundary objects [33] through their configurable malleable nature, yet being able to maintain some semblance of compositional integrity in their own form. Though notably, in our sessions, the possibility for different disciplinary 'readings' of the artefacts was a feature of the different context-specific prompts, rather the participants' own disciplinary allegiances (as with Star & Griesemer's [36] original observations). CAs also impose a low fidelity of the resulting creations, conscripting users to articulate abstract ideas through these material artefacts as a frame of reference; this results in the artefact (new + meaning attached) becoming public and social [14,21,22]. Furthermore, this study is one example of how a PD workshop can be successfully conducted online for physically distributed participants via access to a shared toolkit, addressing the concerns raised by Sanders et al. [31] almost a decade earlier about how well online sessions may work for such activities; unlocking the possibility for more collaborative work in the design of tangible interfaces.

The low barrier to participation that is created through the *Imposition of the Participation Structure* whereby the prompts and tasks always resulted in a relevant output (a creation and a story to tell), indicates that the tools could be effective in prompting a more democratic environment amongst participants, which is as a central consideration for PD to work effectively [7]. Emergent behaviours of participants in using CA within the workshop context also recommend further inquiry. There seems to be a duality to the implications of behaviour - shifting from competitive to collaborative, from ignoring rules to enforcing them. This transient nature of how participants interact with the tool (and with each other through the tasks) would be of particular interest when designing workshops for generative purposes in an application context. The tension between the tool and its influence on participants indicates that the CA does not play a passive role as an artefact as one might expect of a tool.

**Figure 4: Summary of thematic observations of the use of constructive assemblies in design workshops**

Overall, the thematic observations we have identified through the study provide practical methodological insights in regards to the use of CA as design tools in PD activities (Figure 4). We find many of our observations complement, or extend, Leong et al.'s [25] framework for the use of CAs in design processes rather than fit easily within that existing framework. In particular, many of our observations relate to emergent social practices: the ways that the physical is public and publicly accountable, creating possibilities for collaboration and competition (and pride and shame). Similarly, the observations with respect to participation, such as how CAs create an *Imposition of Participation Structure*, or that participants *Never Start from Nothing*, or are *Building before Thinking*, where barriers to participation are lowered as resources are available for use throughout the construction process, do not easily sit within the considerations of the constructive assembly lifecycle model [25]. Of course, the Tangible Interface Framework [21], following Dourish [14], has explicitly identified foundational relations between tangibility and emergent social practices in the context of the public use of interactive systems.

The principal contributions of our analysis, then, have been twofold. On one hand, we extend the considerations of the value of CAs in design [26] into the realm of the social. Secondly, we have drawn out the social consequences with respect to the tangibility of constructive assemblies in design activities; these practices overlap, but are not identical to, those identified in the *use* of tangible interfaces [20].

The inability to meaningfully position these findings entirely within existing frameworks is not a critique of the frameworks, given the specific purposes they were created for; it simply adds texture to additional dimensions that help account for the utility of the CA within design.

This study also raises interesting (but perhaps speculative) prospects for the use of tangible media such as constructive assemblies in the collaborative design of TUIs. Obviously, tangible materials, often in the form of material prototypes, are universal in TUI design processes. But as studies such as ours show, the value of the materiality of prototyping materials extends far beyond their ability to model aspects of a future design. They are also invitations for participation and enlistment and creative sites for the reinterpretation and ascription of meaning to constructions. This is partly on account of the physical affordances of CAs, but it is also inseparable from the social contexts of their application in design processes. So while themes like *Start Building Before Thinking* can be linked back to ideas such as the homunculus [24] and the human predisposition to process information through the hands [34], as we have tried to show it is also very much contingent on the social aspects of the setting: the purpose, the tasks, the time limits, the other participants and the contexts of application. Neither the material nor the social can be 'carved off' as invariant properties—they are reciprocally constitutive elements of what are fundamentally socio-material practices.

Discussion with participants highlighted potential application of CA within industry design contexts. The social aspects of the material manifestation of the constructions were seen to help develop shared understanding, as it translates ideas into a single focal point and creates a shared conceptual space. A specific use case of such workshops is in the ideation stage of design life cycles; future work will explore these applications of CA in other sites, to unpack and identify additional aspects of their value for design.

## REFERENCES


[1] Robert Aish. 1979. 3D input for CAAD systems. *Computer-Aided Design* 11, 2: 66–70.

[2] Robert Aish and Peter Noakes. 1984. Architecture without numbers—CAAD based on a 3D modelling system. *Computer-Aided Design* 16, 6: 321–328.

[3] David Anderson, James L. Frankel, Joe Marks, et al. 2000. Tangible Interaction + Graphical Interpretation: A New Approach to 3D Modeling. *Proceedings of the 27th Annual Conference on Computer Graphics and Interactive Techniques*, ACM Press/Addison-Wesley Publishing Co., 393–402.

[4] Ronald C. Arkin. 1998. *Behavior-based robotics*. MIT press.

[5] Thomas Binder and Eva Brandt. 2008. The Design: Lab as platform in participatory design research. *Co-Design* 4, 2: 115–129.

[6] Gro Bjerknes, Pelle Ehn, Morten Kyng, and Kristen Nygaard. 1987. *Computers and democracy : a Scandinavian challenge*. Avebury, Aldershot Hants, England ; Brookfield Vt.

[7] Erling Björgvinsson, Pelle Ehn, and Per-Anders Hillgren. 2010. Participatory Design and "Democratizing Innovation." *Proceedings of the 11th Biennial Participatory Design Conference*, ACM, 41–50.

[8] Niels Bjørn-Andersen and Bo Hedberg. 1977. Designing information systems in an organizational perspective. *TIMS Studies in the Management Sciences* 5: 125–142.

[9] Sean Blair and Marko Rillo. 2016. *Serious Work: How to Facilitate Meetings & Workshops Using the Lego Serious Play method.* ProMeet, Erscheinungsort nicht ermittelbar.

[10] Jacob Buur and Susanne Bødker. 2000. From usability lab to "design collaboratorium": reframing usability practice. *Proceedings of the 3rd conference on Designing interactive systems: processes, practices, methods, and techniques*, ACM, 297–307.

[11] Jacob Buur and Ben Matthews. 2008. Participatory Innovation: A Research Agenda. *Proceedings of the Tenth Anniversary Conference on Participatory Design 2008*, Indiana University, 186–189.

[12] Lewis Carroll. 1917. *Through the looking glass: And what Alice found there*. Rand, McNally.

[13] Alexandru Dancu, Catherine Hedler, Stig Anton Nielsen, et al. 2015. Emergent Interfaces: Constructive Assembly of Identical Units. *Proceedings of the 33rd Annual ACM Conference Extended Abstracts on Human Factors in Computing Systems*, ACM, 451–460.

[14] Paul Dourish. 2004. *Where the action is: the foundations of embodied interaction*. MIT press.

[15] Pelle Ehn. 1988. *Work-Oriented Design of Computer Artifacts. Stockholm:* Arbetslivscentrum, Stockholm.

[16] LEGO® SERIOUS PLAY™. 2002. *The Science of LEGO® SERIOUS PLAY™*. Executive Discover LLC., Connecticut.

[17] Elisabetta Frick, Stefano Tardini, and Lorenzo Cantoni. 2013. *White paper on LEGO® SERIOUS PLAY®: A state of the art of its applications in Europe*. .

[18] David Gauntlett. 2007. *Creative explorations: New approaches to identities and audiences*. Routledge.

[19] Judith Gregory. 2003. Scandinavian approaches to participatory design. *International Journal of Engineering Education* 19, 1: 62–74.

[20] Lauren Leigh Hinthorne and Katy Schneider. 2012. Playing with purpose: using serious play to enhance participatory development communication. *International Journal of Communication* 6, 1: 2801–2824.

[21] Eva Hornecker and Jacob Buur. 2006. Getting a Grip on Tangible Interaction: A Framework on Physical Space and Social Interaction. *Proceedings of the SIGCHI Conference on Human Factors in Computing Systems*, ACM, 437–446.

[22] Hiroshi Ishii. 2008. Tangible Bits: Beyond Pixels. *Proceedings of the 2Nd International Conference on Tangible and Embedded Interaction*, ACM, xv–xxv.

[23] Alison James. 2013. Lego Serious Play: a three-dimensional approach to learning development. *Journal of Learning Development in Higher Education. ISSN*.

[24] Per Kristiansen, Poul H. Kyvsg\a ard Hansen, and Louise Møller Nielsen. 2009. Articulation of tacit and complex knowledge. *13th International Workshop of the IFIP WG*, 77–86.

[25] Joanne Leong, Florian Perteneder, Hans-Christian Jetter, and Michael Haller. 2017. What a Life!: Building a Framework for Constructive Assemblies. *Proceedings of the Eleventh International Conference on Tangible, Embedded, and Embodied Interaction*, ACM, 57–66.

[26] Monica Maceli and Michael Atwood. 2011. From Human Factors to Human Actors to Human Crafters. *Proceedings of the 2011 iConference*, ACM, 98–105.

[27] Rasmussen Consulting. 2012. The Science Behind the LEGO SERIOUS PLAY method. Retrieved from http://seriousplayground.squarespace.com/storage/The%20Science%20Behind%20the%20LEGO%20SERIOUS%20PLAY%20Method.pdf.

[28] Marguerite Rigoglioso. 2006. "Red Queen" of competition improves organizations. *Stanford University*. Retrieved September 7, 2017 from http://news.stanford.edu/news/2006/november15/barnett-111506.html.

[29] Toni Robertson and Jesper Simonsen. 2012. *Routledge International Handbook of Participatory Design*. Routledge.

[30] Anne Roudaut, Rebecca Reed, Tianbo Hao, and Sriram Subramanian. 2014. Changibles: Analyzing and Designing Shape Changing Constructive Assembly. *Proceedings of the 32Nd Annual ACM Conference on Human Factors in Computing Systems*, ACM, 2593–2596.

[31] Elizabeth B.-N. Sanders, Eva Brandt, and Thomas Binder. 2010. A framework for organizing the tools and techniques of participatory design. ACM Press, 195.

[32] Douglas Schuler and Aki Namioka. 1993. *Participatory design: Principles and practices*. CRC Press.

[33] Susan Leigh Star and James R. Griesemer. 1989. Institutional ecology,translations' and boundary objects: Amateurs and professionals in Berkeley's Museum of Vertebrate Zoology, 1907-39. *Social studies of science* 19, 3: 387–420.

[34] Frank R. Wilson. 1999. *The Hand: How Its Use Shapes the Brain, Language, and Human Culture*. Vintage, New York; London.

# Specifying Relevant Textural Properties for Unobtrusive Feedback on Sports Performance

**Hayati Havlucu**
Koç University – Arçelik Research
Center for Creative Industries
Istanbul, Turkey
hhavlucu16@ku.edu.tr

**Aykut Coşkun**
Koç University – Arçelik Research
Center for Creative Industries
Istanbul, Turkey
acoskun@ku.edu.tr

**Oğuzhan Özcan**
Koç University – Arçelik Research
Center for Creative Industries
Istanbul, Turkey
oozcan@ku.edu.tr


*TEI '19, March 17–20, 2019, Tempe, AZ, USA*

ACM ISBN 978-1-4503-6196-5/19/03.
https://doi.org/10.1145/3294109.3300974

## Abstract
Textural changes can be promising to give feedback on sportspeople's performance who needs less attention demanding modalities. However, previous research does not address which textural property's change would be more appropriate to give information in specific contexts, i.e. sports performance feedback. We focus on sport towels as a case to understand how to give feedback on sports performance through changes in textural properties. We address the gap by conducting experiments with 32 sportspeople to investigate (1) the textural properties (i.e. roughness) that can be perceived by sportspeople through a towel and (2) that can convey information on sportspeople's performance (i.e. smooth texture - good performance). The results indicate that *hardness* and *bendability* are appropriate to convey information about sportspeople's performance. To the best of our knowledge, this result is the first to explore that a change in the state of a textural property is able to give a specific feedback.

## Author Keywords
Textural properties; sports performance; feedback; psychophysical; material properties; shape change.

## CSS Concepts
• Human-centered computing~Empirical studies in HCI
• Human-centered computing~Laboratory experiments

**Figure 1:** The sample towels from the experiments.

## Introduction

Sportspeople want to receive performance feedback and commonly rely on activity trackers to get it [7]. With current activity trackers, utilizing information in real-time is considered difficult and distracting [10,11]. However, sportspeople need to concentrate on the activity and sustain attention throughout. Thus, they need less attention demanding and less distracting modalities to get feedback on their performance [8].

In this respect, Texture Displays [6] might be used to design such feedback, because it provides a less attention demanding modality. A texture display device presents different textural states, i.e. relaxed and stretched states, to give information. This way, instead of alerting the user, the device waits passively for user to take action and explore the information. Harrison and Hudson proposed applications to everyday objects in attention demanding contexts such as meeting or driving, which may also be applicable to sports.

The sports towel is an everyday object that is tangibly used by people from various sports during, between or right after the sports activities. We believe that towel holds a potential to give sports performance feedback by utilizing the texture display modality. Therefore, we focus on sport towels as a case to understand how we can give sports performance feedback through changes in the textural properties. We believe this case addresses the two gaps we identified in the literature: (1) Previous research presents various textural properties (i.e. roughness, hardness) [15]. Although there are studies on the textural properties of different materials [4] and how different textural properties are perceived [5], none has explored which properties can be perceived through specific materials by specific users. We propose that the perception would be context dependent and for specific materials, the towel, and specific users, sportspeople, some of the properties would be perceived easier and prioritized over the others. (2) Research suggests that changes in the textural properties could be used to give information, but it only focuses on the perception of the changes [6]. We propose that some of these textural properties would be associated to previous experiences. Thus, they would be more appropriate to give specific types of information, sports performance feedback.

We aim to fill these gaps by investigating the textural properties (1) that can be perceived by sportspeople through a towel, and (2) that can convey information on sportspeople's performance. For this purpose, we conducted experiments with 32 regular sportspeople. The results could be adopted by researchers and designers in the fields of smart textiles and materials, wearables, fashion, tangible interaction and sports.

## Background & Related Work

Texture is a material property that affects our perception of an artefact and its interactive qualities [15]. Researchers have been trying to understand textural properties in three layers: physical, sensory and affective [1]. We can draw out an example through friction, roughness and pleasantness [2]. Friction is a physical property of a material that we can scientifically measure with unit of friction coefficient. However, when we touch a material, we cannot sense friction, but we sense roughness, which is the sensory property. Thus, if the friction coefficient is high, we perceive materials as rough. Last, when we perceive a material as rough, we start to associate this property with properties of the affective layer. To illustrate, we perceive rough materials as unpleasant or smooth as pleasant.

**Figure 2:** Example of the survey items used in the experiment with all of the textural properties and *perceived performance*.

Researchers conduct psychophysical experiments to learn about these three layers. In these experiments, participants either actively or passively (i.e. via robotic arm) [3-5] touch materials with different physical properties (i.e. compliance) [1], on different body sites (i.e. hairy or glabrous) [4]. Then they rate the sensory (i.e. warm) and affective properties (i.e. sensual) [3-5,9] of these materials. These experiments helped to understand the sensory properties of different fabrics (i.e. silk, cotton) [4,9], and how they make the users feel (i.e. pile feels comfortable) [5,9]. However, none presented a specific use case or context. Presenting a fabric as a towel during sports performance might change the perception and affection of the participants.

Most of these experiments focus on the perception of the materials through the sensory layer. For example, [6] showed that at least two states of stretch can be perceived through elastic fabrics to give information. However, they do not investigate the information these textural states can convey. In fact, to the best of our knowledge, there is no study that can describe the relationship between the textural properties and the type of information they can convey other than the affective properties. We believe that some sensory texture properties would be more relevant and more competent to give a specific type of information, because of the qualities they elicit in the affective layer.

Addressing these gaps, this study aims to investigate the textural properties of towels that can be perceived by specific users, and that can convey a specific type of information in the context of sports performance.

## Experiment

*Participants.* 32 regular sportspeople participated in the experiment (18 males). They were all college students aged between 19-27 (*M*=21.5, *SD*=1.68). In average, they exercised 2.94 days a week (*SD*=1.62) for 4.72 years (*SD*=3.41). They were from 19 different sports fields including ice skating and rugby. 23 participated in a sports tournament. 20 monitor their performance regularly and 8 of them occasionally. 29 participants stated they would want to get performance feedback.

*Samples & Textural Properties.* Towel is a piece of cloth used for drying someone or something that is wet [14]. We procured 15 different types of towel including sports towel and kitchen cloth, which have different contents, because we thought a wide range of samples would present a wide range of textural properties. We left out the samples that had different textures on different sides (double sided). We cut each sample to a 25x25 centimeter squares and stitched the edges to prevent loose fibers (Figure 1). We procured 9 textural properties from the literature: *Roughness (R), hardness (H), pile/fuzziness (P), slipperiness (Sl), moistness (M)* and *warmth (W)* were recurring in multiple [1,3,5,12]. We also added *strechability (St), bendability/flexibility (B)* and *thickness (T)* because they are proposed properties for soft materials such as the towel [13].

*Method & Procedure.* We used a method similar to the psychophysical experiments in the literature, based on [4]. We formed a survey that presented each textural property and its definition on a continuous scale from -50 to +50 that presented each state (i.e. roughness, -50=smooth, +50=rough). The last item of the survey was *perceived performance (PP)* on a similar scale, from poor to good (Figure 2). The participants did not see the scores they gave on the scale. Texture perception is also affected by the visuals [15]. Instead of blind folding the participants, we built a 30x40x50 cm box with a 20 cm diameter hole on the front side, covered by a piece of

**Figure 3:** The blind box.

**Figure 4:** Screenshots from the video recordings. (The link for the video recordings will be provided)

cloth (Figure 3). Participants touched the samples inside the box through this hole.

Prior to the experiment we interviewed each participant on their sports field, frequency and duration of training, tournament history, and their preference in getting feedback. First, they had a tutorial study with an example sample to make sure they understand each item and the process. We asked them to put their dominant hand inside the box and touch the sample for 30 seconds. Unlike other experiments, we did not specify the way they touch, because there are multiple ways and areas to touch the towel. After touching the sample, they rated their perceptions of the textural properties. At the performance item, we asked them to visualize a sports performance that corresponds to their tactile feeling and rate accordingly. Once we were sure they understood the process, we continued with our 15 samples. We randomized the order of these samples for each participant and the order of the survey items for each sample, except the performance item. In the process, we encouraged participants to think aloud. We video recorded the experiment from a camera inside the box (Figure 4). After the experiment, we asked participants if there was a textural property they could not perceive, and if they believed they can get sports performance feedback from the textures of the towel.

## Results

*Content Analysis*

In this section, we grouped the textural states according to the frequency they were mentioned.

*Hardness, thickness, roughness and pile.* For 26 of 28 participants hard textures, for 16 of 27 participants thick textures and for 17 of 24 participants rough textures were associated with poor performance. Out of 21 participants who referred to pile, 8 associated it with great and 8 associated it with poor performance. The remaining 5 continuedly changed their thoughts.

*Bendability and slipperiness.* 14 of 15 participants perceived bendable towels and 10 of 12 perceived slippery towels as an indication for great performance.

*Warmth, moistness and strechability.* 7 of 8 participants associated warmth with poor performance. 3 of 5 participants thought moist textures are related good performance. Only 1 participant mentioned stretched textures felt like he performed poorly.

*Quantitative Analysis*

We conducted a nine-stage hierarchical multiple regression by entering the textural states as predictor variables at each stage with *perceived performance* as the dependent variable. We tested the statistical assumptions with all variables, including the gender of the participants. *Gender (G)* did not show a significant effect on the model. The Pearson correlation results show that there was no multicollinearity between the variables, and *hardness* ($r$=-0.65, $p$=0.00) and *bendability* ($r$=-0.55, $p$=0.01) were significantly correlated with the perceived performance (Table 1).

The first-stage results revealed that *hardness* significantly predicted 65% of the variance ($R^2$=.40, $F(1,30)$=22.00, $p$<.00) (Table 2). Including *bendability* at the second-stage, explained 72% of the total variance with a significant change in $R^2$ and F values ($p$<0.05) ($R^2$=.49, $F(2,29)$=15.79, $p$<.00). Including rest of the predictor variables at the following stages did not improve the model significantly. All nine textural predictors were accounted for 76% of the total variance in perceived performance. Thus, our second-stage

| | Rougness | | Hardness | | Pile | | Slipperiness | | Moistness | | Warmth | | Strechability | | Bendability | | Thickness | | Performance | | Gender | |
|---|---|---|---|---|---|---|---|---|---|---|---|---|---|---|---|---|---|---|---|---|---|---|
| | Correlation | Sig. | Correlation | Sig. | Correlation | Sig. | Correlation | Sig. | Correlation | Sig. | Correlation | Sig. | Correlation | Sig. | Correlation | Sig. | Correlation | Sig. | Correlation | Sig. | Correlation | Sig. |
| R | 1 | | .260 | .151 | .227 | .212 | -.251 | .166 | -.023 | .902 | -.033 | .857 | .100 | .584 | -.379* | .032 | .105 | .567 | -.238 | .189 | -.130 | .479 |
| H | .260 | .151 | 1 | | -.075 | .685 | -.024 | .896 | .214 | .239 | .037 | .841 | .310 | .084 | -.402* | .023 | .185 | .311 | **-.650**** | **.000** | .072 | .697 |
| P | .227 | .212 | -.075 | .685 | 1 | | .278 | .124 | .310 | .084 | .307 | .087 | .098 | .592 | .196 | .281 | **.618**** | **.000** | .214 | .240 | .012 | .950 |
| Sl | -.251 | .166 | -.024 | .896 | .278 | .124 | 1 | | **.630**** | **.000** | -.151 | .410 | -.027 | .885 | .175 | .338 | .083 | .652 | .284 | .115 | .113 | .539 |
| M | -.023 | .902 | .214 | .239 | .310 | .084 | **.630**** | **.000** | 1 | | .256 | .158 | .097 | .599 | .078 | .671 | .406* | .021 | .026 | .889 | -.060 | .744 |
| W | -.033 | .857 | .037 | .841 | .307 | .087 | -.151 | .410 | .256 | .158 | 1 | | **.454**** | **.009** | -.013 | .944 | .431* | .014 | -.051 | .783 | -.143 | .435 |
| St | .100 | .584 | .310 | .084 | .098 | .592 | -.027 | .885 | .097 | .599 | **.454**** | **.009** | 1 | | **-.545**** | **.001** | .151 | .410 | -.272 | .133 | .155 | .389 |
| B | -.379* | .032 | -.402* | .023 | .196 | .281 | .175 | .338 | .078 | .671 | -.013 | .944 | **-.545**** | **.001** | 1 | | -.017 | .926 | **.548**** | **.001** | .145 | .427 |
| T | .105 | .567 | .185 | .311 | **.618**** | **.000** | .083 | .652 | .406* | .021 | .431* | .014 | .151 | .410 | -.017 | .926 | 1 | | -.072 | .696 | -.090 | .625 |
| PP | -.238 | .189 | **-.650**** | **.000** | .214 | .240 | .284 | .115 | .026 | .889 | -.051 | .783 | -.272 | .133 | **.548**** | **.001** | -.072 | .696 | 1 | | .128 | .484 |
| G | -.130 | .479 | .072 | .697 | .012 | .950 | .113 | .539 | -.060 | .744 | -.143 | .435 | .155 | .389 | .145 | .427 | -.090 | .625 | .128 | .484 | 1 | |

*Note.* $**p<0.01$, $*p<0.05$

**Table 1**: Pearson Correlation results of textural properties, performance and gender.

model, the final model, indicated that *hardness* ($\beta$=-.51, $p$<.01) and *bendability* ($\beta$=.34, $p$<.05) significantly predicted the perceived performance.

| Predictors | β | p | F | pΔF | R | $R^2$ | $\Delta R^2$ |
|---|---|---|---|---|---|---|---|
| Stage 1 | | | 21.997 | .000*** | .650 | .423 | .423 |
| Hardness | -.650 | .000*** | | | | | |
| Stage 2 | | | 15.785 | .021* | .722 | .521 | .098 |
| Hardness | -.513 | .001*** | | | | | |
| Bendability | .342 | .021* | | | | | |
| Stage 9 | | | 3.429 | .844 | .764 | .584 | .063 |
| Hardness | -.537 | .004** | | | | | |
| Bendability | .396 | .073 | | | | | |
| Slipperiness | .266 | .281 | | | | | |
| Warmth | -.032 | .876 | | | | | |
| Moistness | -.070 | .766 | | | | | |
| Pile | .005 | .982 | | | | | |
| Roughness | .100 | .600 | | | | | |
| Strechability | .125 | .553 | | | | | |
| Thickness | .022 | .920 | | | | | |

*Note. β, unstandardised beta; p, significance level; F, F statistic; pΔF, significance level of F change; R, $\Delta R^2$, change in variance; $R^2$, variance; *p<.05, **p<.01, ***p<.001; N=32*

**Table 2**: The hierarchical regression results showing the effect of the textural properties on perceived performance.

## Discussion

*Hardness, thickness, roughness, pile, bendability and slipperiness can be perceived by sportspeople through a towel.* These were the most mentioned properties, because they were easier to perceive compared to the rest. Also, participants explicitly mentioned that they could not perceive *warmth* and *moistness*, and *strecthability* was only mentioned by one. According to Pearson correlation results (Table 1), *moistness* is highly correlated with *slipperiness*, *strechability* with *bendability* and *warmth* with *strechability* ($p$<0.01). Because *slipperiness* and *bendability* are perceived easier, participants might have prioritized these properties over *warmth*, *moistness* and *strechability*. In this respect, some textural properties presented in the literature may be more dominantly perceived by specific users through specific materials. Designers that work with interactive textiles and materials can benefit from focusing on the prioritized properties.

*Hardness and bendability can convey information on sports performance.* Although participants perceived most of the textural properties, some of them did not give any direction to their *perceived performance*. For example, participants were split to three even groups when they rated *pile*. On the other hand, both content and quantitative analysis demonstrated that *hardness* and *bendability* showed a single direction predicting *perceived performance*. According to the results, softer and more bendable textures were associated with greater performance. This study is first to describe the relationship between a textural property and a specific information. We recommend interaction designers to adopt this approach to convey information through texture or shape changes. We should also note that *hardness* affected *perceived performance* 1.5 times more than *bendability*. Thus, there is a hierarchy between these properties in terms of sports performance, and designers should consider this hierarchy while choosing the properties. Participants explained this relationship by stating if a texture is too soft, it means that it is bendable. They added, softer textures feel better than bendable textures and being soft might compensate if the texture is unbendable.

*Perception is context dependent and can change among different sports.* Overall results show that softer and more bendable textures are associated with greater performance. However, this perception changed for people from different sports. For example, participants thought softer and more bendable textures are more suitable for ice skating and dancing because they feel more relaxed. They felt uneased with rough textures. Contrarily, 2 participants thought harder and rougher textures are more suitable for basketball to convey greater performance information, because they felt more powerful. They thought soft and fuzzy textures felt too relaxed and drowsy. While rating the properties participants also considered their previous experiences. They assumed cooler textures are better for football, because that is how the field feels like, and thicker textures are better for snowboard, because of the thick garments. Additionally, they associated the slippery textures to the slippery feeling of professional sport clothing and moist textures to the feeling of taking a shower after the exercise. These examples demonstrate that participants associate the textural properties to good or poor performance according to their own experiences. Thus, in different contexts the perception of these properties could change. We recommend interaction designers to consider the diversity between the contexts and previous experiences.

## Conclusion

We conducted experiments with 32 sportspeople to investigate the textural properties (1) that can be perceived by sportspeople through a towel and (2) that can convey information on sports performance. We found two findings that may contribute to the field:

(1) The content and quantitative analysis suggests that *hardness, thickness, roughness, pile, bendability* and *slipperiness* can be perceived through a towel. However, the perception of these properties is context dependent. In the context of soft materials for sports, textile designers could prioritize these properties.

(2) The regression results indicate that in hierarchical order *hardness* and *bendability* are associated to the perception of good or bad sports performance and able to convey this information about sports performance. Designers can manipulate these properties to convey information on sports performance. Additionally, this result is the first to describe that a change in the state of a textural property is able to give a specific information. We recommend tangible interaction designers to consider this approach in their studies.

## Limitations & Future Work

Our study only focused on perceived performance and the participants were from a variety of sports. To fully test these results, we plan to conduct experiments involving an actual sports performance and focus only on a single sport, because the results were context dependent. We also believe a Wizard of Oz experiment, in which sportspeople perform and get feedback via using different towels with varying softness, can present insights on the usability and the feasibility of a towel to give feedback on sports performance.

## Acknowledgements

We thank Ceren Yüksel and Demet Özer for their help in data collection and analysis phases of this research.

## References

[1] X. Chen, C. J. Barnes, T. H. C. Childs, B. Henson, and F. Shao. 2009). Materials' tactile testing and characterisation for consumer products' affective packaging design. *Materials & Design*, *30*(10), 4299-4310.

[2] Mathew A. Darden and Christian J. Schwartz. 2009. Investigation of skin tribology and its effects on the tactile attributes of polymer fabrics. *Wear*, *267*(5-8), 1289-1294.

[3] Greg K. Essick, Francis McGlone, Chris Dancer, David Fabricant, Yancy Ragin, Nicola Phillips, Therese Jones, and Steve Guest. 2010. Quantitative assessment of pleasant touch. *Neuroscience & Biobehavioral Reviews*, *34*(2), 192-203.

[4] Roberta Etzi, Charles Spence, and Alberto Gallace, A. 2014. Textures that we like to touch: An experimental study of aesthetic preferences for tactile stimuli. *Consciousness and cognition*, 29, 178-188.

[5] Steve Guest, Jean Marc Dessirier, Anahit Mehrabyan, Francis McGlone, Greg Essick, George Gescheider, Anne Fontana, Rui Xiong, Rochelle Ackerley, and Kevin Blot. 2011. The development and validation of sensory and emotional scales of touch perception. *Attention, Perception, & Psychophysics*, 73(2), 531-550.

[6] Chris Harrison and Scott E. Hudson. 2009. Texture displays: a passive approach to tactile presentation. *In Proceedings of the SIGCHI Conference on Human Factors in Computing Systems (CHI '09)*. ACM, New York, NY, USA, 2261-2264. DOI: https://doi.org/10.1145/1518701.1519047

[7] Hayati Havlucu, İdil Bostan, Aykut Coşkun, and Oğuzhan Özcan. 2017. Understanding the Lonesome Tennis Players: Insights for Future Wearables. *In Proceedings of the 2017 CHI Conference Extended Abstracts on Human Factors in Computing Systems (CHI EA '17)*. ACM, New York, NY, USA, 1678-1685. DOI: https://doi.org/10.1145/3027063.3053102

[8] Hayati Havlucu, Terry Eskenazi, Barış Akgün, Mehmet Cengiz Onbaşlı, Aykut Coşkun, and Oğuzhan Özcan. 2018. Flow State Feedback Through Sports Wearables: A Case Study on Tennis. *In Proceedings of the 2018 Designing Interactive Systems Conference (DIS '18)*. ACM, New York, NY, USA, 1025-1039. DOI: https://doi.org/10.1145/3196709.3196807

[9] Anthony David Hope, Mark Jones, and Hengfeng Zuo, H. 2013. Sensory perception in materials selection for industrial/product design. *The International Journal of Designed Objects*, *6*(3), 17-31.

[10] Mads Møller Jensen and Florian 'Floyd' Mueller. 2014. Running with technology: where are we heading?. *In Proceedings of the 26th Australian Computer-Human Interaction Conference on Designing Futures: the Future of Design (OzCHI '14)*. ACM, New York, NY, USA, 527-530. DOI=http://dx.doi.org/10.1145/2686612.2686696

[11] Roland Sigrist, Georg Rauter, Robert Riener, and Peter Wolf. 2013. Augmented visual, auditory, haptic, and multimodal feedback in motor learning: a review. *Psychonomic bulletin & review*, 20(1), 21-53.

[12] Minghui Sun, Xiangshi Ren, Shumin Zhai, and Toshiharu Mukai. 2012. An investigation of the relationship between texture and human performance in steering tasks. In *Proceedings of the 10th asia pacific conference on Computer human interaction* (pp. 1-6). ACM.

[13] Katrin Wolf and Timm Bäder. 2015. Illusion of Surface Changes Induced by Tactile and Visual Touch Feedback. *In Proceedings of the 33rd Annual ACM Conference Extended Abstracts on Human Factors in Computing Systems (CHI EA '15)*. ACM, New York, NY, USA, 1355-1360. DOI: https://doi.org/10.1145/2702613.2732703

[14] Towel. n.d. Retriewed November 8, 2018 from https://dictionary.cambridge.org/dictionary/english/towel

[15] Hengfeng Zuo, T. Hope, P. Castle, and M. Jones. 2001. An investigation into the sensory properties of materials. *Psychology*.

# Strange Places: Loci of Design Inspiration

**Keith Evan Green**
Cornell University
Ithaca, NY 14850, USA
keg95@cornell.edu

Figure 1: Giorgio de Chirico. *Furniture in the Valley* (1928) [21]. "A great intimacy is born between them."

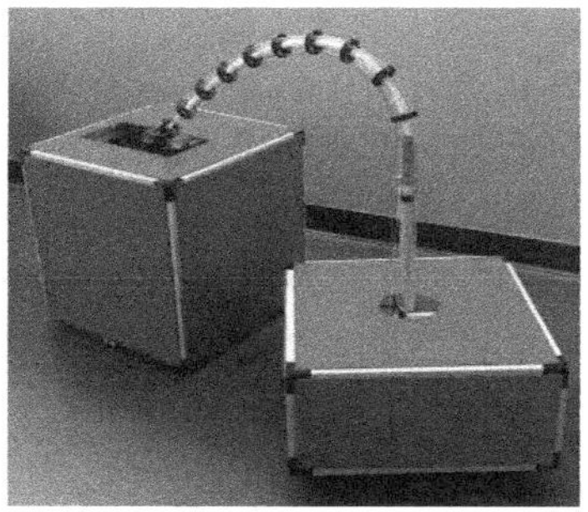

Figure 2: *home+* furnishings (prototype-2): *h+cube* (left) and *h+lamp* (right). A great intimacy is also born between these two. (The design of this system is very much ongoing.)


*TEI '19, March 17–20, 2019, Tempe, AZ, USA*

ACM ISBN 978-1-4503-6196-5/19/03.
https://doi.org/10.1145/3294109.3300998

## Abstract
The inspiration for designing tangible, embedded, and embodied interaction can come from stranger places than needs assessments and observations. In conceptualizing *home+*, a pair of interactive furnishings enabling independent living, our design-research team found inspiration in modern painting and contemporary dance. Giorgio de Chirico's painting "Furniture in the Valley" (1928) captures the curious vitality and intermingling of furniture outside their normal confines that our team translated into this active pair of home+ robots and their intimate rapport. Two contemporary dance works, Andrea Miller's "(C)arbon" and Ohad Naharin's "STOP," explore the interrelationships of three bodies, coping with their circumstances, which inspired the interoperability and control strategies across the pair of robots and a human "in-the-loop." This paper aims to inspire other design researchers to seek, in strange places, inspirations for tangible, embedded, and embodied interaction.

## Author Keywords
Design Methods; Enabling Technology; Interaction Design; Dance; Surrealism; Robotics; HRI.

## CSS Concepts
• Human-centered computing~Interaction paradigms

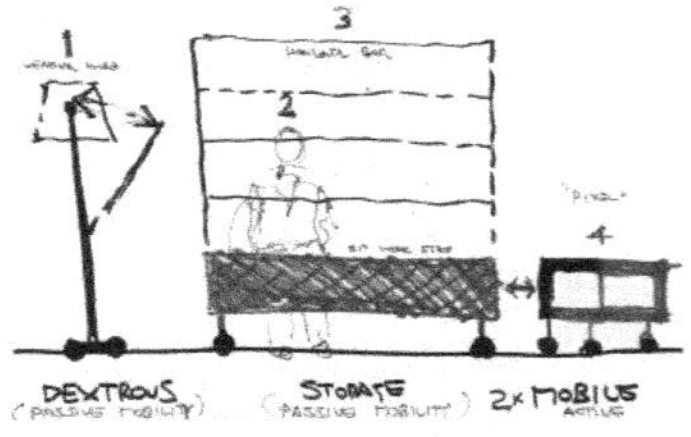

Figure 3: Early sketch of *home+* furnishings: *h+lamp* (left) and *h+cube* (right).

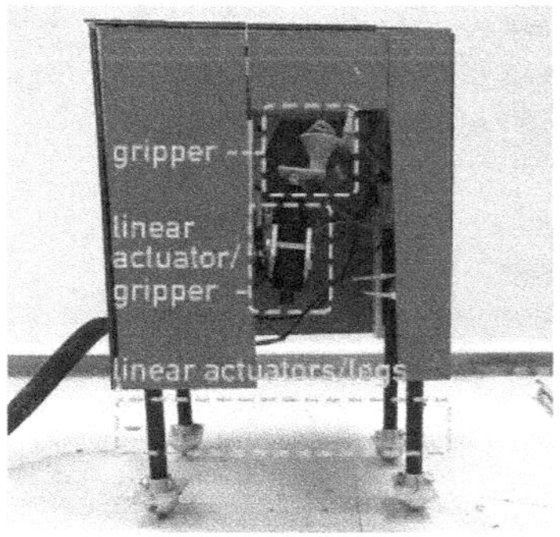


Figure 4: *h+cube* (prototype-1): exterior—panel removed. The red-colored body measures 46.65 cm (18.37 in) along any length, and is encased in composite panels having a polyethylene core faced in aluminum. Each of *h+cube*'s four legs is a linear actuator having a stroke length of 15.24 cm (6 in). We fabricated multiple components using a 3D printer and a CNC router working from our digital shop drawings.

## Introduction

Needs assessments, observations, interviews, usability studies, and other methods of participatory design have long served designers in the process of designing interactive artifacts that are elegant, desirable, and empathetic (following partly the classical principles of good design—*firmatis*, *utiilats*, and *vensustatis* [27]). But all too often, these same methods become the under-examined means for validating design processes that fall flat. For designers (broadly defined), there is, as Harrison, Back, and Tatar offer [12], the unfortunate tendency of "dressing up design methods as more systematic and predictive than they are." Overwrought manifestations of such design activities include, in Kolko's critique [16], "two-hour 'subject matter expert' interviews," "'canvasses'," "'playbacks'," "'design sprints'," and "lots and lots of Post-it notes." While this tendency can be attributed to those designers who blindly follow the script of "design thinking" [16], it also is attributed to those "potential users"—the participants in design studies—"who don't necessarily do or want things that make" [26] compelling interaction design.

Recourses to this tendency comes in different forms, including: a deeper, more immersive engagement with user populations [16]; grounding design in phenomenology [13] (e.g. embodied interaction [9]); and the use of mixed methodologies drawn from across disciplines as curated by this designer [1, 12]. Partly in sympathy with the last form of recourse, this paper offers an alternative response that obliges designers to travel to strange places in search of strange things. A case study for this paper—our team's design of a pair of interactive furnishings named *home+* enabling independent living (as defined in [14, 24, 31])—elaborates our response (adventure?) and serves as a means for its validation.

## Stopover-1: "Strange Things" that Change

Maybe you can remember an instant in your life when some interior environment familiar to you (your bedroom?) or welcoming to you (a vacation retreat?) was momentarily transformed into the unexpected—a place alive to unforeseen prospects. Surely, you can remember an occasion from your childhood when the familiar contents of your bedroom changed their appearance, as they did to the delight of the Italian artist and writer Giorgio de Chirico a century ago.

One such vision, captured in de Chirico's painting, "Furniture in the Valley" (1928) [23], profoundly influenced our design of a pair of furnishings as enabling technology. De Chirico's painting (figure 1) shows an upholstered chair, a headboard from a bed, an armoire or a chest, and what might be a fence from a garden—clearly, a physical environment far from home. As de Chirico writes in an essay, describing this enigmatic place:

*Perhaps you have occasionally noticed the singular aspect that beds, mirrored armoires, armchairs, divans, or tables have when you see them suddenly in the street, amidst a décor in which we are not accustomed to seeing them, such as happens during a move, or … before the doors of shopkeepers and second-hand dealers who display the principal pieces of their merchandise on the sidewalk. Then the furniture appears to us in a new light; the pieces are dressed with a strange solitude; a great intimacy is born between them, and one could say that a strange happiness floats in this narrow space that they occupy…*[8].

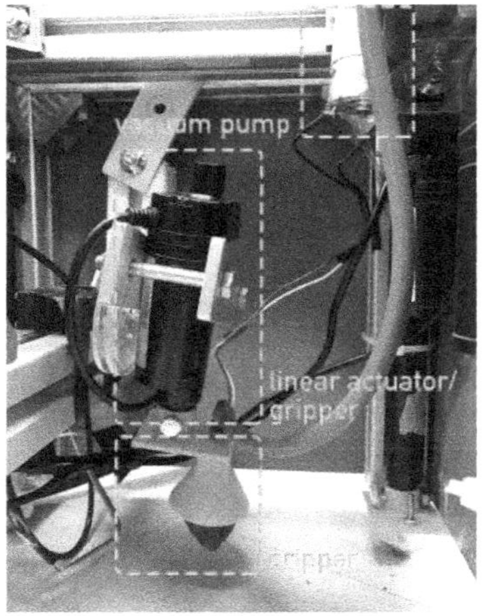


Figure 5: *h+cube* (prototype-1): interior detail.

Figure 6: *h+lamp* (prototype-1): interior view of the lamp's base.

Furnishings that are familiar to our living rooms but encountered in an unfamiliar context have, in de Chirico's imagination, come to life—with "emotion," and an "intimacy formed between them." "Furniture in the Valley" is an invitation, as de Chirico offers, "to live in the world as in an immense museum of strange things...that change their appearance" [8].

De Chirico is not alone in an intellectual and artistic landscape of "lively" buildings, rooms, and furnishings; but his painting and words show that there is perhaps more to the familiar places we live in than the static, fixed reality of them. De Chirico opens the doors, so to speak, to the concept of a *living room* of furnishings that have a strange vitality; and we sought this prospect with the aid of computation and robotics.

## Designing the hardware of home+ robots

Giorgio de Chirico's "Furniture in the Valley" (1928) captures the curious vitality and intermingling of furniture outside their normal confines that we translated into a pair of robotic furnishings.

Inspired by de Chirico, we envisioned networked, cyber-physical home furnishings, each having different functionalities tuned for different purposes to support a common human need or to exploit an opportunity to improve the lives of co-inhabitant(s). Our conception of *home+* is comprised, on the surface, of commonplace furnishings of an ordinary home – a lamp, a nightstand, an armoire, a wardrobe – that become "animated," working intimately, together and with their human "cohabitants," to perform routine, domestic, "CS-PFP 10" tasks [21] defining independent living. *home+* strives to empower people to remain in their homes for as long as possible, even as their physical capabilities alter over time, and, in more grave circumstances, to afford people some semblance of feeling 'at home" as users move between their dwellings outfitted with home+ and assisted-care facilities equipped the same way.

Shaped by that "great intimacy" formed between de Chirico's furnishings, and their capacity "to change their appearance," we then sought to validate this inspiration from places closer to our home in HCI, HRI, and interaction design. In this light, the transformation from familiar domestic furnishings to those of home+ is achieved, borrowing the words of William Mitchell, by way of "geographically distributed assemblages of diverse, highly, specialized, intercommunicating artifacts" that render the physical environment a "robot for living in" [19]. In similar terms, former *Wired* editor Kevin Kelly imagines a future, artificial "ecology" of intelligent "rooms stuffed with co-evolutionary furniture" and a "mob of tiny smart objects," all having an "awareness of each other, of themselves, and of me" [15]. In this spirit, we situate home+ opposite a robot servant such as PR2 [29]: the distributed cognition of home+ versus a unified, humanoid intelligence.

In recent years, we have developed a number of home+ prototypes, including a robotic chair [7], a robotic wall partition [7], and robotic tables [7, 24]. Our current and most advanced home+ furnishings are a robotic pair: a mobile, robotic cube and a continuum-robotic lamp that we call *h+cube* and *h+lamp* (figures 2-6, 9-11), h+cube and h+lamp are designed to work as complements within the volume of the typical room of the home or workplace: h+cube specifically engages in tasks within a spatial volume bounded by a room's floor, upwards to approximately hip or table height, while h+lamp engages in tasks from hip or table height, upwards to near the ceiling of a typical room.

Practically, h+cube (see figures 4 and 5) is a mobile robot that lifts objects from directly beneath it by way of linear actuators at each of its four legs working in concert with a jamming gripper, located at the core of the cubic volume and extending from a fifth, shorter linear actuator designed to rotate 90 degrees and 180 degrees. This ensemble is capable of transporting the retrieved object to a shelf, to a human co-habitant, or to the terminus of h+lamp. Tugged about the interior living or work space by h+cube and deposited by h+cube where needed, h+lamp (see figures 6 and 9) has a mast comprised of a linear actuator closest to the floor extending continuously to a tendon-actuated, flexible continuum arm that is terminated by a jamming gripper and a bright light as means for illuminating task spaces. The mast ensemble can reach from below the top of the h+cube to the highest shelf in most homes or offices to transport objects across living and workspaces. h+cube can itself transport larger bins filled with objects (e.g. laundry or groceries) atop it. As just mentioned, h+cube and h+lamp work together with their human co-inhabitants to perform ten routine tasks enumerated in the "CS-PFP10" scale used by healthcare providers to define the capacity for independent living, as considered in [10, 14, 28].

Comprised of multiple, commonplace domestic artifacts, home+ manifests something of the behavior of swarms, and also subscribes to the notion of the a-life community that, in living systems, the whole is more than the sum of its parts. The remarkable feature of the home+ project is that, seemingly, the everyday furnishings found at home "come to life," forming a "living" room. To-date, we have performed user studies of the *home+* pair with 5 older adults and 12 medical staff as we continue iterating our design of this interactive, enabling system [25].

## Stopover-2: Strange Dances

We've arrived at two contemporary dance works: Andrea Miller's "(C)arbon" [18] and Ohad Naharin's "STOP" [20]. In one of three rooms that serve as the stage for (C)arbon, two dancers—females—strong-willed yet clearly fatigued, are intent on transporting a third dancer—male—who is on the brink of collapse (figure 7). He unsteadily walks across a wall almost entirely by way of the strength remaining in his two partners. In an instance in STOP (figure 8), three dancers again—all female—move with and against each other.

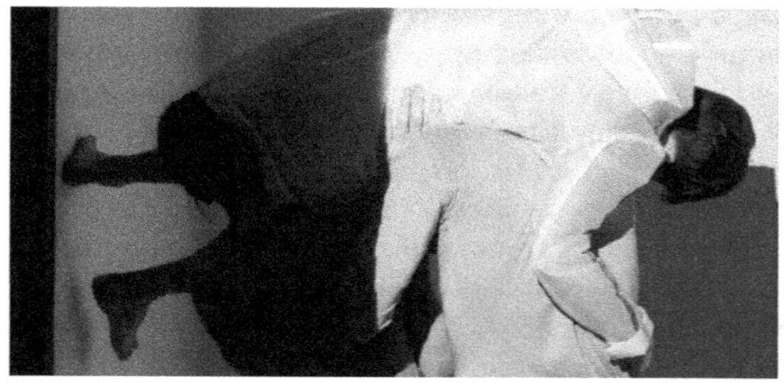

Figure 7: Andrea Miller, (C)arbon [14].

Figure 8: Ohad Naharin. STOP [16].

## Designing the interoperability of home+

When we see a humanoid robot, we expect of it behaviors akin to ours. But when we encounter robot furnishings like the home+ pair of robots, we don't really know what to expect from cyber-physical furniture. Where to find inspiration?

"(C)arbon" and "STOP," two contemporary dance works exploring the interrelationships of three bodies coping with their circumstances, inspire the interoperability and control strategies across the pair of home+ robots with a human "in-the-loop." The dancers of these works are not idealized, or dramatizing a tale, or moving gracefully; they are, notably, *striving* or *straining* or *seeking*, or simply aiming to survive. In the strange beauty of the two dance trio's movements can be found insights into "bodies in emotion" that can be translated to interaction patterns in the pair of robots (figures 9, 10, 11, and 12). The motion planning of the robots is strangely beautiful—not quite machine or human.

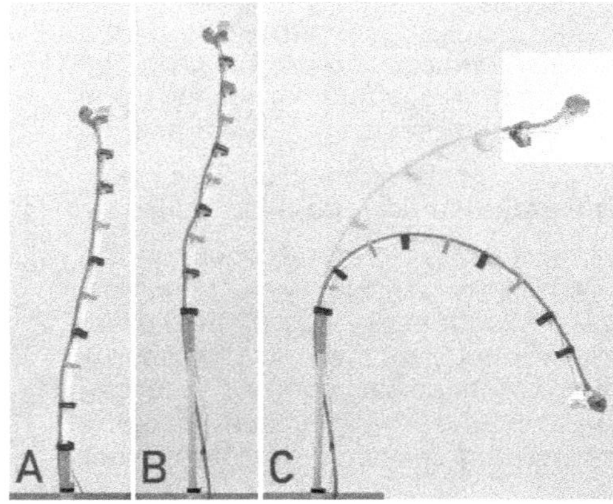


Figure 9: home+ choreography: bending, reaching.

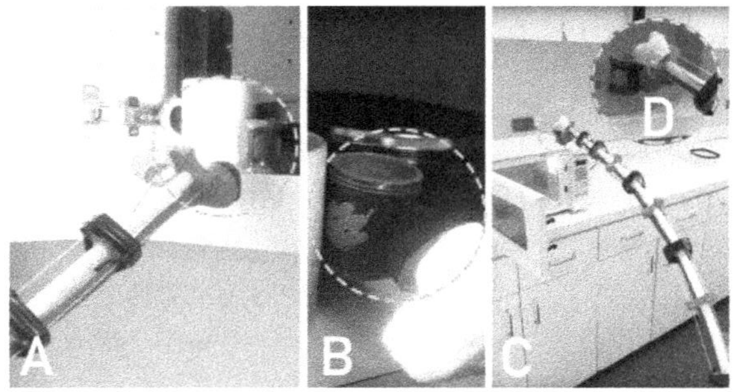


Figure 10. home+ choreography: reaching, extending.

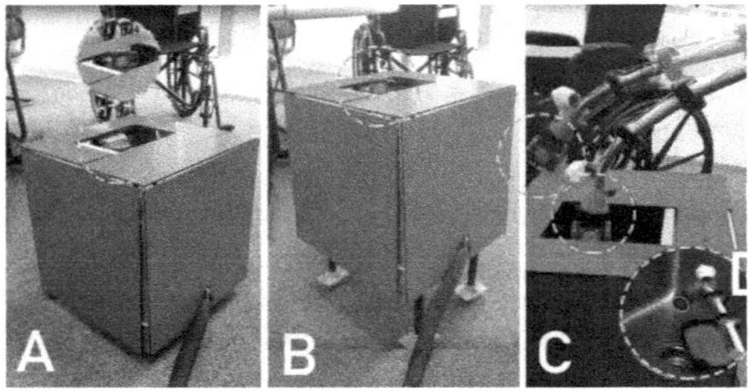


Figure 11: home+ choregraphy: crouching and lifting.

## A Designer's Ticket to Travel

This paper presents a single case of discovering design inspiration in strange places, It is meant as provocation and plea. The productive value of discovering design inspiration in strange places has elsewhere been investigated [3, 4, 11] and rather robustly in a meta-analytical review of 43 design studies [22] which found that when designers identified a "single and uncommon source of inspiration (like a de Chirico painting), the designers engaged in "a deeper search in a specific and remote domain, facilitating the generation of high-quality and novel ideas." A similar study [6] concurs with this finding, but with the caveat that "conceptually closer, rather than farther sources appear more beneficial." Is de Chirico's furniture or the dance works of Miller and Naharin "too far" from the interactive system they inspired? Should designers resist flying so far? This paper takes the longer view, urging designers to travel far. As Brue Mau urges designers in his much-referenced "Incomplete Manifesto of Growth" [17], "allow events to change you. [...] The prerequisites for growth: the openness to experience events, and the willingness to be changed by them." Designers of tangible, embedded, and embodied interaction should freely avail themselves to strange places and find inspirations there.

## Tangible Expressions (Supporting Files)

Supporting this paper and its presentation are two "tangible expressions":

- Video of home+ choreography: https://vimeo.com/289141439
- home+ webpage presenting the work-in-progress: https://arl.human.cornell.edu/research%20-%20home+vision.html

## Acknowledgements

This research is supported by the U.S. National Science Foundation under award IIS-1703267. I thank my co-investigators and our students who are helping us realize the inspiration we found in de Chirico, Miller, and Naharin in two robots enabling independent living.

## References

[1] Jeffrey Bardzell, Shaowen Bardzell, and Lone Koefoed Hansen. 2015. Immodest Proposals: Research Through Design and Knowledge. In *Proceedings of the 33rd Annual ACM Conference on Human Factors in Computing Systems* (CHI '15). ACM, New York, NY, USA, 2093-2102. DOI: https://doi.org/10.1145/2702123.2702400

[2] Nick Bilton. 'Smart' Home Suffers a Brain Freeze. New York Times (January 13, 2016), 02.

[3] M. Blythe and E. Encinas. 2018. Research Fiction and Thought Experiments in Design. *Foundations and Trends® Human–Computer Interaction*, *12*(1), pp.1-105.

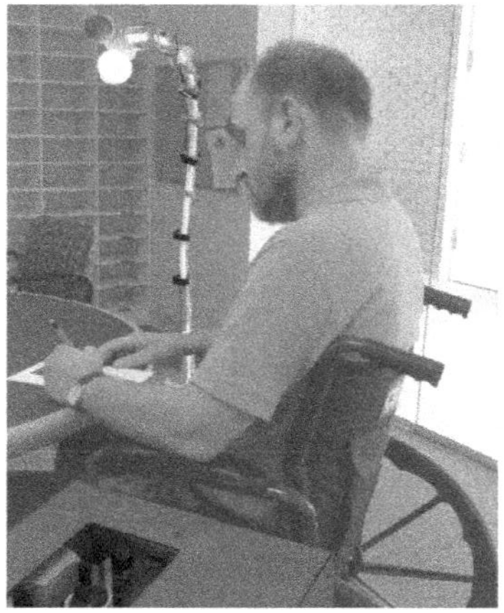

Figure 12: The strange dance of *home+* and a human co-habitant, working at home.

[4] Mark Blythe. 2014. Research through design fiction: narrative in real and imaginary abstracts. In *Proceedings of the SIGCHI Conference on Human Factors in Computing Systems* (CHI '14). ACM, New York, NY, USA, 703-712. DOI: https://doi.org/10.1145/2556288.2557098

[5] J. J. Callahan. 1992; Aging in place. *Generations*, vol. 16, no. 2, pp. 5-6, 1992.

[6] Joel Chan, Steven P. Dow, and Christian D. Schunn. 2015. Do the best design ideas (really) come from conceptually distant sources of inspiration? *Design Studies* 36 (January 2015), 31-58. https://doi.org/10.1016/j.destud.2014.08.001

[7] Carlos de Aguiar, R. Fateminasab, C. Frazelle, R. Scott, Y. Wang, M. Wooten, M., K. E. Green, and I. D. Walker. 2016. "The Networked, Robotic home+ Furniture Suite: a Distributed, Assistive Technology Facilitating Aging in Place." 2016. Proceeding of the IEEE International Conference on Automation Science and Engineering (IEEE CASE 2016), 1067-1072.

[8] Giorgio de Chirico. "Statues, Furniture and Generals." Trans. John Ashbery. 1992. In *Hebdomeros*. Cambridge, Mass.: Exact Change.

[9] Paul Dourish. 2004. *Where the Action Is: The Foundations of Embodied Interaction*. MIT Press.

[10] T. Fong, I. Nourbakhsh, and K. Dautenhahn. 2003. A Survey of Socially Interactive Robots," *Robotics and Autonomous Systems* 42 (2003): 143–166.

[11] William Gaver. 2012. What should we expect from research through design?. In *Proceedings of the SIGCHI Conference on Human Factors in Computing Systems* (CHI '12). ACM, New York, NY, USA, 937-946. DOI: https://doi.org/10.1145/2207676.2208538

[12] Steven Harrison, Maribeth Back, and Deborah Tatar. 2006. "It's Just a Method!": a pedagogical experiment in interdisciplinary design. In *Proceedings of the 6th conference on Designing Interactive systems* (DIS '06). https://doi.org/10.1145/1142405.1142445

[13] Caroline Hummels and Pierre Lévy. 2013. Matter of transformation: designing an alternative tomorrow inspired by phenomenology. *Interactions* 20, 6 (November 2013), 42-49. https://doi.org/10.1145/2533713

[14] *Journal of Enabling Technologies* (JET). Retrieved March 10, 2018 from http://emeraldgrouppublishing.com/products/journals/journals.htm?id=jet

[15] Kevin Kelly. 1994. *Out of Control: The Rise of Neo-Biological Civilization*. Addison-Wesley, Reading, MA.

[16] Jon Kolko. 2018. The divisiveness of design thinking. *Interactions* 25, 3 (April 2018), 28-34. https://doi.org/10.1145/3194313

[17] Bruce Mau. An Incomplete Manifesto of Growth. Retrieved March 11, 2018 from http://www.manifestoproject.it/bruce-mau/

[18] Andrea Miller. (C)arbon. Retrieved November 12, 2018 from https://www.gallim.org/carbon/

[19] William J. Mitchell, e-Topia: Urban Life, Jim—but Not as We Know It. MIT Press, Cambridge, MA.

[20] Ohad Naharin. STOP. Video. Retrieved November 12, 2018 from https://www.youtube.com/watch?v=e87-g728FBM

[21] Rehab Measures: Continuous Scale Physical Functional Performance (CS-PFP). Retrieved March 11, 2018 from http://www.rehabmeasures.org/Lists/RehabMeasures/DispForm.aspx?ID=1125, online.

[22] Ut Na Sio, Kenneth Kotovsky, and Jonathan Cagan. 2015. Fixation or inspiration? A meta-analytic review of the role of examples on design

processes. *Design Studies* 39 (July 2015): 70-99. http:/dx.doi.org/10.1016/j.destud.2015.04.004.

[23] Sotheby's. De Chirico, *Furniture in the Valley* (1928). Retrieved March 10, 2018 from http://www.sothebys.com/en/auctions/ecatalogue/2014/impressionist-modern-art-day-sale-n09140/lot.365.html

[24] A. Threatt, J. Merino, J., K. E. Green, I. D. Walker, J. O. Brooks and S. Heal. 2014. An Assistive Robotic Table for Older and Post-Stroke Adults: Results from Participatory Design and Evaluation Activities with Clinical Staff. In *Proceedings of the SIGCHI Conference on Human Factors in Computing Systems* (CHI '14), 673–682.

[25] S. Verma, S., P. Gonthina, Z. Hawks, Z., D. Nahar, J. O. Brooks, I. D. Walker, Y. Wang, A. de Aguiar, A., and K. E. Green. Design and Evaluation of Two Robotic Furnishings Partnering with Each Other and Their Users to Enable Independent Living. In Proceedings of Pervasive Health 2018, 35-44. https://doi.org/10.1145/3240925.3240978

[26] Kentaro Toyama. 2013. Reflections on HCI for development. *Interactions* 20, 6 (November 2013), 64-67. https://doi.org/10.1145/2527298

[27] Marcus Pollio Vitruvius. c. 80–70 BC (1931). *De Architectura (Ten Books)*, trans. F. Granger. Harvard University Press.

[28] K. Wada, K. and T. Shibata, "Living with Seal Robots – Its Sociopsychological and Physiological Influences on the Elderly at a Care House, IEEE Transactions on Robotics, Vol. 23, No. 5, pp. 972-980, October 2007.

[29] Willow Garage. PR2. Retrieved March 10, 2018 from http://www.willowgarage.com/pages/pr2/order

# Re-Twist: Evaluating Engagement in a Digitally Augmented Traditional Game

Figure 1: Participants playing Re-Twist, the digitally augmented version of Twister.

**Aditi Singh**
Carleton University
Ottawa, ON, Canada
aditisingh3@cmail.carleton.ca

**Joanie Ouellet**
Carleton University
Ottawa, ON, Canada
joanieouellet@cmail.carleton.ca

**Victor Cheung**
Carleton University
Ottawa, ON, Canada
victor.cheung@carleton.ca


*TEI '19, March 17–20, 2019, Tempe, AZ, USA*

ACM ISBN 978-1-4503-6196-5/19/03.
https://doi.org/10.1145/3294109.3300976

## Abstract
Digital adaptation of physical games often includes complete digitization resulting in the replacement of physical movements with virtual counterparts using input devices. We believe that augmenting the game by adding digital elements while also preserving physical movements can enhance player engagement. We present Re-Twist, a digitally augmented version of Twister. We introduce the element of *time* and *score* in Re-Twist by using a pressure-sensitive Twister mat that communicates with a projected screen. To investigate the effect of digital augmentation, we conducted a comparative study between the original Twister and Re-Twist. 81% of 16 participants preferred Re-Twist over the original Twister because of increased competition and urgency created by digital augmentation. We discuss the effect of digital augmentation on the competition, social, and challenge aspect of the game. This can guide new ways of game design by relooking at similar augmentation of other traditional games.

## Author Keywords
Human-computer interaction; movement based games; exertion interfaces; digital augmentation

## ACM Classification Keywords
• **Human-centered computing~Human computer interaction (HCI)**

## Introduction

Works in the HCI field have studied engagement in game as a means to design better games for the players. Prior work has identified the body movement as an influencing factor in player engagement [3,6]. Games that combines digital and physical movements mostly incorporates either introducing a whole body interaction to a digital game [3,5,6] or digital augmentation to a physical game [1,10,13,14]. However, these studies have not focused on evaluating the effect of digital augmentation on engagement.

We present Re-Twist, a digital augmentation of the original Twister. We introduce the element of *time* and *score* as a dynamic feedback and visualization system. This creates a sense of urgency in the game that seems to influence player experience [14]. Re-Twist comprises a pressure-sensitive mat and a projected screen. The pressure sensors on the mat receive data to determine if the player is pressing on the correct targets, and the projected screen displays the feedback. We digitally augmented the original Twister by showing time and score on the projected screen using visualization (Figure 2). The players start to collect points as soon as they match the target and lose points otherwise.

To investigate the effect of this digital augmentation, we conducted a comparative study with 16 participants between the original Twister and Re-Twist. We found a higher preference (81%) in Re-Twist, and in terms of player engagement, Re-Twist created a more competitive and less social environment. Based on our user study, we discuss considerations related to social, competition, and challenge themes for the digitally augmented traditional game.

## Related Work

Besides the potential of increasing engagement, our work intertwines physical and digital elements. Prior work demonstrates that introducing digital elements enables various movements, procedural content [14], changes the nature of the cooperative play [13], manipulates the pace of the game [14], and acts as a social icebreaker [10].

One approach of digital augmentation has been sensory augmentation using visual and sound elements without altering the structure of the physical game [13]. Several works have introduced digital elements to increase the complexity of the game [1,14]. We see this as an opportunity to look at various other traditional games and find new directions to enhance the experience of playing those games.

On the other hand, whole-body interaction has also been introduced to digital games in prior work to enhance player experience. A common approach is to use body tracking to control a component of a digital game [2,8,11,17]. Yet it requires extra space for an additional tracker which is not part of the game.

Previous work has defined and evaluated in several ways the engagement of the players with games. Components such as the competitive aspect of the game, difficulty, and camaraderie have been shown to increase the engagement [3,6]. To evaluate the engagement, some authors have used the Game Experience Questionnaire [4,9]. Physical games with digital augmentation and digital games with physical augmentation have been evaluated using surveys and interviews [4, 5, 10, 13].

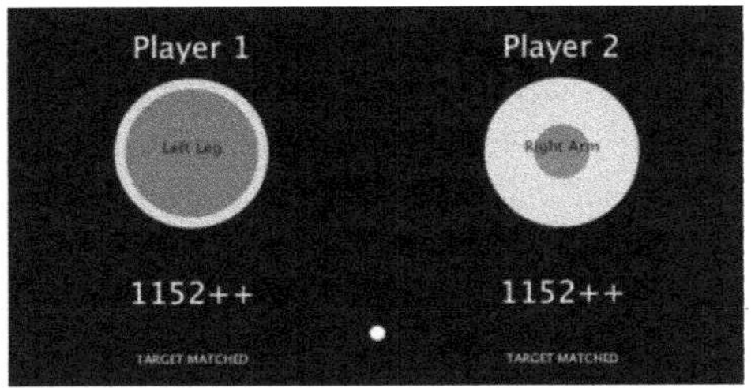


Figure 2: The projected screen displays the score and the reducing size of the circle displays the time left for the next move to be displayed.

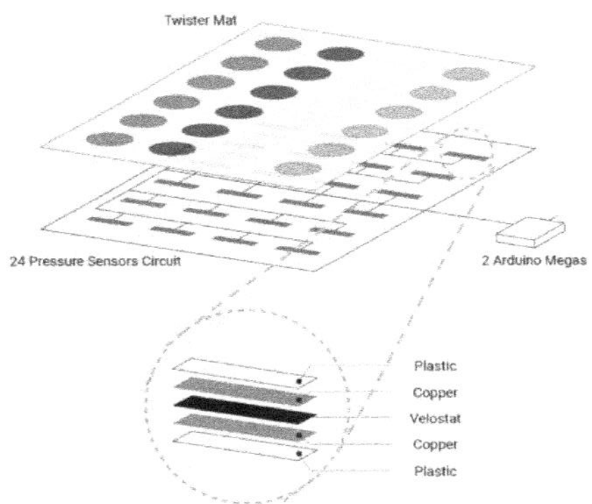


Figure 3: Prototype of the pressure activated Twister mat

Past work demonstrates that the confluence of physical movement and digital technologies influences the game-playing experience [14]. This suggests that traditional physical games can be investigated as a rich resource for digital augmentation. In this work we introduce a way of digitally augmenting Twister. To the best of our knowledge, no work has studied the impact of such digital augmentation on the engagement and playing experience. We intend to address this gap by augmenting Twister, a popular physical game, and comparing the engagement with the original version.

## Design Rationale

We choose a whole-body game, Twister for the purpose of digital augmentation. Twister is a multi-person party game that was created in 1964, and has been a popular game ever since, as evidenced by being featured in TV shows [7,15]. Over the years, people have modified the game by adding layers like colour foam, paint, ketchup [16], and shot glasses [7] on the targets to increase the complexity and engagement of the game. This demonstrates the potential to accommodate additional layers while preserving the original structure of the game. Through digital augmentation, we aim to add the elements of time and score to increase the complexity and competition in the game. We hypothesize that adding these layers will increase the engagement, collaboration and competition of the game.

## Re-Twist – Game Description

We augmented the original Twister mat by adding pressure sensors to it (See the next section for details of implementation). This enables tracking the current pressing positions while preserving the original gameplay, without the need for extra space to do so.

The spinner in the original game randomly selects a combination of limbs (left/right arm or foot) and colour (red, blue, yellow, green). By digitally augmenting the game, we offload the task of random selection to the computer and the result is displayed for both players on a projected screen in the front (Figure 1).

Each player has to reach the coloured target with the suggested limb displayed on the screen, the points start to increase when the player reaches the correct target. As soon as the combination changes, the player starts to lose points until they hit the correct coloured target. This adds the elements of time pressure and competition to the game [14].

## Prototype

*Pressure Sensitive Twister Mat*

As shown in Figure 3, a pressure sensor is collocated and attached to the underside of the mat at the 24 targets. Each of the 24 sensors can detect if a player is pressing on it and send this information to the two Arduino Megas. The two Arduino Megas are in the master-slave type of connection to accommodate 24 input points for the sensors. We use Processing to receive and process the sensor data through serial communication, and in turn displays the relevant data on the projected screen. Each pressure sensor (5 cm X 17 cm) spans the diameter of the circular target and is made of two conductive layers of copper with a resistive velostat in between. Two layers of plastic seal these three layers on the top and the bottom. The sensor acts as a variable resistor as the pressure on the sensor modulates the amount of current passing between the conducting layer of copper [5,18].

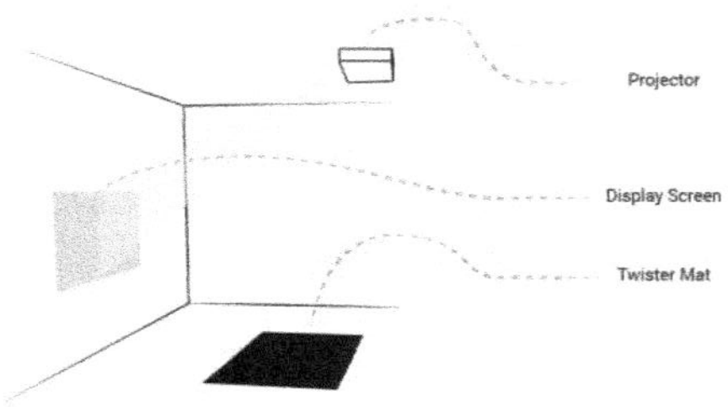


Figure 4: The experiment setup

*The Projected Screen*
The projected screen (Figure 2) comprises a circle for each player which determines the colour of the target (Red, Yellow, Green or Blue) and the text on the centre suggests the limb (Right Arm, Left Arm, Right Leg, Left Leg). The system randomly selects the combination of limbs and colours. The circle size reduces continuously until it disappears and the next combination of the limb and colour is displayed. The screen provides feedback if the scores are increasing or decreasing and if the player matches the right target or is on the wrong one. At the end of the game, when time runs out, the screen displays the final score, the winner, and the loser in the game based on the scores. The current implementation supports two simultaneous players.

## Study
We conducted a within-subject comparative evaluation where the participants played the original Twister as a control condition and Re-Twist as the experiment condition. We counterbalanced by condition and the study lasted for 30 minutes.

*Participants*
We recruited 16 (9F, 7M) participants for our study. 8 participants were between the age of 17 and 25 and 8 participants were between the age of 26 and 39. 12 participants had previous experience playing Twister. We had two participants playing together for each session. 6 pairs of participants knew each other prior to the experiment, and two pairs did not know each other. We recruited through email and social media and participation was on a voluntary basis.

*Experiment Setup*
As shown in Figure 4, we placed the Twister mat on the floor. We asked the players to start the game by facing each other on the extreme ends of the mat and then move onto the mat according to the directions given by the referee in the original game and the screen in Re-Twist. For Re-Twist, the screen was projected on the wall in front of the mat.

*Data Collection and Analysis*
Our questions comprised of 15 five-point Likert scale questions for each condition. At the end of the experiment we asked a set of open-ended questions.

We based the Likert questions on the GEQ [12], where we selected the themes that were relevant to the traditional game and Re-Twist. These high level themes were: challenge, competition, positive, and negative emotions. Since most of the metrics in the literature focus on measuring the experience of the digital game, we looked further into the work of Costello. et. al. [6] to add questions that address the Social aspect of the game. These questions covered the aspect of connection and camaraderie with the other player.

For the open-ended questions, at the end of the experiment, we covered the role of the digital augmentation on the engagement of the participants. We also asked their preference between the two games and design suggestions for the digital game. All interview recordings were transcribed and analyzed.

## Results
Overall, 13 out of 16 (81.25%) participants preferred Re-Twist over the original Twister. To test if the digital augmentation has an effect on each of the 5 themes, we performed a repeated measure two-way ANOVA

P3: "*The time limit was the most challenging part of the game because if I was in a bad position it was hard to hit the target on time.*"

P4: "*I like the score of the digital game. I like to be able to tell who's winning through the game.*"

P9: "*So the spinner becomes part of the game as well so whenever we get something bad we could blame him and we could laugh about it.*"

with the game condition (Re-Twist and Twister) as the within-subject factor and the order of condition as the between-subject factor. There was a significant effect of digital augmentation on the competition theme with a large effect ($F(1,14) = 4.77$, $p = .047$, $\eta 2 = .254$) as well as for the social theme with a large effect ($F(1,14) = 11.01$, $p = .005$, $\eta 2 = .440$). There was no significant effect of digital augmentation on the challenge theme ($F(1,14) = 4.09$, $p = .063$, $\eta 2 = .226$) as well as for the positive theme ($F(1,14) = 6.26$, $p = .665$, $\eta 2 = .014$) and the negative theme ($F(1,14) = 1.22$, $p = .287$, $\eta 2 = .080$).

To test if winning or losing in the digital game had an effect on the positive and negative experience of the player, we performed an independent sample *t*-test for each with winning and losing as the between-subject factor. The difference between the winners and the losers for the positive experience was not significant with a very large effect, $t(14) = 2.08$, $p = .056$, $d = 1.036$. As for the negative experience, the difference between the winners and losers was also not significant but with a small effect, $t(14) = 0.5$, $p = .625$, $d = .026$.

## Discussion

We found a statistically significant effect on the competition and the social theme based on the Likert scale questions. 81% of the participants preferred Re-Twist and gave positive feedback on the time and score aspects of the game.

*Two Types of Engagement: Social and Competitive*
We found that the combined roles of the running score and the visual representation of the timing created a new form of engagement with the game. The participants stated that they felt more competitive playing Re-Twist because of these two components (P4). On the other hand, while playing the original Twister the participants mentioned they felt more social since they could observe the other players' positions to laugh and make comments on it (P9).

*The Perception of Challenge*
The effect of digital augmentation was not statistically significant for the challenge theme. While discussing the perceived challenge, participants often talked about the complexity of body movements they had to perform rather than the digital components of the game. Thus, the perception of challenge was closely related to the combination of colour and limbs the player received and it weighed down the effect of digital augmentation. Despite that, a few participants explained that the primary challenge in both games was the body movement and holding difficult posture, but playing Re-Twist was more challenging because of the sense of urgency created by the *time* and *score* (P3).

Moreover, we did not find any significant effect on the winning or losing status of the participant. This demonstrates that winning and losing did not influence the game-playing experience of the participants.

## Lessons Learned

We learned that digital augmentation could preserve the structure and feel of playing a traditional game. And adding time and score enabled conversations about winning, losing, and time left to hold a difficult position.

## Limitations and Future Work

During the analysis of our data, we realized that the randomization effect of the moves could have affected our results, as some sequences of moves might be more difficult than the others. This matter also affected the camaraderie feeling, part of the social interaction, because participants found the positions funnier. To counter this effect, we could choose between pre-designed sequences of positions and level of difficulty at the start of the game.

Another way to see Re-Twist is a new approach towards whole body interaction. The literature for whole body interaction primarily includes body tracking [2,8,14], wearable sensors [1] and controllers [11]. We see tracking the limbs' positions on a pressure activated mat as a simplistic way of tracking and manipulating the body posture. An audio component could also be implemented to provide extra feedback to the players.

Adding the element of time and score to the original twister changes the game's mechanics. It is difficult to distinguish if participants felt more competitive due to digital augmentation or change in the game mechanics. It would be worthwhile to conduct a comparative evaluation with a version of Twister that is not digitally augmented but has the same elements of Re-Twist.

Lastly, to better understand the effect of digital augmentation on players' engagement with traditional games, we would like to digitally augment other traditional games. We are interested in physical games, but it could be interesting to also explore other types of game such as board games or puzzles.

## Conclusion

In this paper we presented Re-Twist, which is a digitally augmented version of the traditional game of Twister, by introducing the element of time and score. We conducted a comparative study of Re-Twist and Twister to investigate the impact of such augmentation on player engagement, and showed that it led to an increase in the feeling of competition, but a reduction in social competition. We expect the features we incorporated in Re-Twist and our study results will help to guide new ways of game design for player engagement. We believe that the high preference of Re-Twist in our comparative evaluation shows promise for digital augmentation of traditional games.

## References

[1] S. Antifakos and B. Schiele. 2002. Bridging the gap between virtual and physical games using wearable sensors. Proceedings. Sixth International Symposium on Wearable Computers,: 139–140.

[2] Surat Kwanmuang Assocreation and Daylight Media Lab, Roland Graff. 2015. Solar Pink Pong : Street Video Game. Proceedings of the 9th International Conference on Tangible, Embedded, and Embodied Interaction - TEI '15: 417–418.

[3] Nadia Bianchi-Berthouze. 2013. Understanding the role of body movement in player engagement. Human-Computer Interaction 28, 1: 40–75.

[4] Tim Buckers, Boning Gong, Elmar Eisemann, and Stephan Lukosch. 2018. VRabl: Stimulating Physical Activities Through a Multiplayer Augmented Reality Sports Game. Proceedings of the First Superhuman Sports Design Challenge: First International Symposium on Amplifying Capabilities and Competing in Mixed Realities: 1:1--1:5.

[5] Victor Cheung, Alexander Keith Eady, and Audrey Girouard. 2018. Deformable Controllers. Proceedings of the Twelfth International Conference on Tangible, Embedded, and Embodied Interaction - TEI '18: 732–735.

[6] Brigid Costello and Ernest Edmonds. 2007. A study in play, pleasure and interaction design. Proceedings of the 2007 conference on Designing

pleasurable products and interfaces - DPPI '07 August: 76.

[7] The Tonight Show Starring Jimmy Fallon. Jell-O Shot Twister with Kristen Stewart. https://www.youtube.com/watch?v=TMWXS91cHoI

[8] Dustin Freeman, Nathan LaPierre, Fanny Chevalier, and Derek Reilly. 2013. Tweetris: A Study of Whole-Body Interaction During a Public Art Event. Proceedings of the 9th ACM Conference on Creativity & Cognition - C&C '13: 224.

[9] Brian Gajadhar, Yvonne de Kort, and Wijnand IJsselsteijn. 2008. Influence of social setting on player experience of digital games. Proceeding of the twenty-sixth annual CHI conference extended abstracts on Human factors in computing systems - CHI '08: 3099.

[10] Trisha Garcia, Shannon Brown, and Siona Dev. 2018. TUIst: A collaborative and computationally enhanced game board. TEI 2018 - Proceedings of the 12th International Conference on Tangible, Embedded, and Embodied Interaction 2018–Janua: 337–342.

[11] Jayden Garner, Gavin Wood, Sandra Danilovic, Jessica Hammer, and Florian Mueller. 2014. Intangle: Exploring Interpersonal Bodily Interactions Through Sharing Controllers. Proceedings of the First ACM SIGCHI Annual Symposium on Computer-human Interaction in Play: 413–414.

[12] W.a. IJsselsteijn, Y.a.W. de Kort, and K. Poels. 2013. Game Experience Questionnaire. FUGA - Fun of Gaming: 1–9.

[13] H. Ishii, C. Wisneski, J. Orbanes, B. Chun, and J. Paradiso. 1999. PingPongPlus: design of an athletic-tangible interface for computer-supported cooperative. Proceedings of the SIGCHI conference on Human factors in computing systems: the CHI is the limit: 394–401.

[14] Raine Kajastila, Leo Holsti, and Perttu Hämäläinen. 2016. The Augmented Climbing Wall: High-Exertion Proximity Interaction on a Wall-Sized Interactive Surface. Proceedings of the 2016 CHI Conference on Human Factors in Computing Systems: 758–769.

[15] Holly Kate. Friends Twister. https://www.youtube.com/watch?v=oMjkDtO1yQo

[16] Kamri Noel. Hilarious Messy Twister Challenge! (ft. Annie LeBlanc & Hayley from Bratayley). https://www.youtube.com/watch?v=NhJLa3_eeus.

[17] Joshua Vasquez. TEI 2015 Pong. https://www.youtube.com/watch?v=IkiP0uo9KYc.

[18] Neoprene Bend Sensors. https://www.kobakant.at/DIY/?p=20.

# Extending Input Space of Tangible Dials and Sliders for Uncertain Input

**Miriam Greis**
University of Stuttgart
Germany
miriam.greis@codecentric.de

**Hyunyoung Kim**
Université Grenoble Alpes
CNRS, LIG
France
University of Stuttgart
Germany
hyunyoung.kim@imag.fr

**Andreas Korge**
University of Stuttgart
Germany
andi-korge@web.de

**Céline Coutrix**
Université Grenoble Alpes
CNRS, LIG
France
University of Stuttgart
Germany
celine.coutrix@imag.fr

**Albrecht Schmidt**
University of Stuttgart
Germany
albrecht.schmidt@um.ifi.lmu.de



*TEI '19*, March 17–20, 2019, Tempe, AZ, USA

ACM ISBN 978-1-4503-6196-5/19/03.
https://doi.org/10.1145/3294109.3300985

## Abstract
Uncertainty is common when working with data and becomes more important as processing big data gains attention. However, no standard tangible interface element exists for inputting uncertain data. In this article, we extend the input space of two traditional TUIs: dial and slider. We present five designs that are based on dials and sliders and support uncertain input. We conduct focus group interviews to evaluate the designs. The interviews allow us to extend existing design requirements for parameter control UIs to support uncertain input.

## Author Keywords
Tangible User Interfaces; Uncertainty; Input; Dial; Slider

## CCS Concepts
Human-centered computing~ Haptic devices

## Introduction
Users face uncertainty every day when they produce data themselves, e.g., recording calorie intake or booking flights. Whether users are the source of uncertainty or the mediator of uncertain data, input mechanisms need to support uncertain input to produce valid data containing uncertainty [1][5]. When the input uncertainty is well communicated, one can make better decisions when later analyzing the data [9][16].

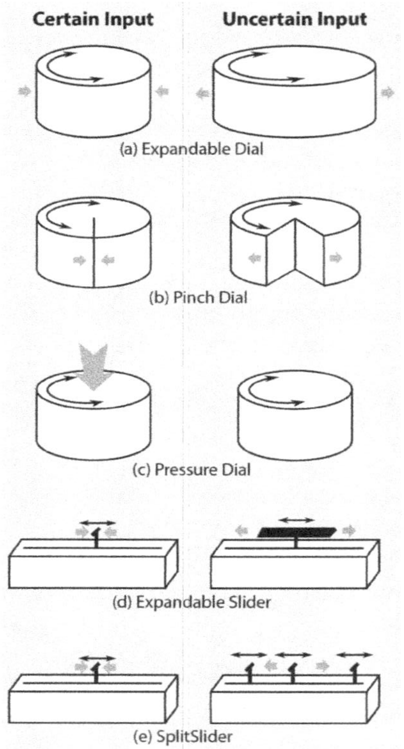


Figure 1. The extended input space of dial- and slider-based interfaces, to enable value and uncertainty input. The usual interactions (turning a dial or sliding a slider cursor) change value (≈ mean of a desired input). The added modalities (i.e., increasing diameter/open space/pressure/cursor size, and splitting the cursor respectively) allow to input uncertainty (≈ variance of the input).

Communicating uncertainty can also increase transparency and reliability of the data [13][16].

Previous work has focused on the graphical representation of uncertain data [3][8][13][16] and capturing such data with mouse interface [5]. It inspires us to investigate how we can use tangible interfaces to support uncertain input. Tangible interfaces allow precise interaction [10], which can minimize uncertainty introduced by input methods. They also enable multiple interactions at the same time [17], which can be used to input estimated values and amount of uncertainty on one device.

We are especially interested in extending the one-dimensional input space of dials and sliders to multi-dimensions, to allow input of both value and uncertainty on one device. Reconfigurable or shape-changing interfaces have demonstrated such capability [3][10][12], and we want to learn how the reconfigurability can support or hinder uncertain input.

In this work-in-progress, we explore the design of physical dials and sliders that can capture users' value and uncertainty on one device. We first use Morphees+ [11] features to design 5 controls that can input both value and uncertainty, which are based on ordinary dials and sliders. We then present low-fidelity prototypes and conduct a focus group study to gather feedback on them. Lastly, we derive and discuss preliminary design requirements for uncertain input.

## Background and Related Work

*Uncertainty and its Communication*

Uncertainty, as described by Pang et al. [14], includes statistical variations or spread, errors and differences, minimum and maximum range values, noise, or missing data. Studies show that decision-making is better supported by capturing, modeling, and visualizing uncertain data [1][9][13][16]. For instance, communicating uncertainty can increase transparency and reliability of weather forecasts [13][16].

Pang et al. [14] also name three steps of data processing, in which uncertainty can be introduced: acquisition, transformation, and visualization. In data acquisition, uncertainty is inevitable due to inexact measurements. During transformation, the original data can be altered by a human or an algorithm. Lastly, visualization may introduce uncertainty as it does not usually use the same media as the original data.

In this paper, we focus on improving ways of capturing uncertainty during the transformation step. Research in capturing and reducing uncertainty has been largely focused on GUIs. Greis et al. [5] propose graphical probability distribution sliders with varying degrees of freedom. The study shows that users with limited statistical knowledge perform best using the range slider, which has two degrees of freedom. Users with more statistical knowledge perform better with sliders with three or more degrees of freedom.

*Communicating Input Uncertainty with TUIs*

Even though TUIs have not explicitly addressed the problem of inputting uncertain data, several previous works could be used for this purpose.

Coutrix et al. suggest a resizable tangible slider [3] to compromise between travel length of the thumb and input accuracy. It could be also used to input uncertain data by interpreting the size of the slider as the

Figure 2. Low-fidelity prototypes for the explored designs for uncertain input dials/sliders. a,b) Expandable Dial, c) Pinch Dial, d) Pressure Dial, e) Expandable Slider, f) Split Slider.

certainty. E.g., smaller size means less precision and thus more uncertainty.

The Inflatable mouse [12] could be also used for uncertain input. The mouse has an elastic chamber, and users can squeeze it to zoom a map in/out. For uncertain input, the device can input 2D data (e.g., X-Y coordinate values with mouse pointing) with 1D uncertainty (squeezing).

## Design Exploration for Uncertain Input TUIs

We first generated variations of conventional continuous interfaces, dials and sliders. We used the existing interaction of rotating and sliding the devices for value input and added other modalities to input uncertainty. We used the features of the Morphees+ taxonomy [11] to design the additional modalities (see Figure 1). The designs quantify uncertainty in two ways: the dials and Expandable Slider (Figure 1a,b,c,d) can input an amount of uncertainty (i.e., 0-100%), and SplitSlider (Figure 1e) can input a range of estimated values. When the device was for inputting the amount of uncertainty, we mapped the larger surface or open space with more uncertainty and less pressure with more uncertainty.

*Dial-Based Designs*

- **Expandable Dial** (Figure 1a) was driven by Morphees+'s Area feature, which describes changes in area size on a surface. The dial's diameter can be increased or reduced, resulting in the area change at the top of the dial.
- **Pinch Dial** (Figure 1b) includes an open space that can be closed or opened, which was inspired by the Closure feature of Morphees+. The feature describes how much boundaries of a surface are "open".
- **Pressure Dial** (Figure 1c) can be pressed downwards in addition to its rotation, like Button+ [18]. It was driven by the Strength feature, the force needed to move a control point to another position.

*Slider-Based Designs*

- **Expandable Slider** (Figure 1d) was inspired by the Area feature similarly to Expandable Dial. It has a thumb that can be expanded to communicate uncertainty. The center of the thumb represents the medium of estimated values.
- **SplitSlider** (Figure 1e) was driven by Morphees+'s Modularity, which describes an object's ability to be split into multiple pieces. The design represents a standard slider in one-thumb mode. The thumb can be split to two or three thumbs to enter the range of estimated values or probability distribution (e.g., standard distribution) or estimated values.

## Low-Fidelity Prototype Implementation

We implemented low-fidelity prototypes of all the design explorations, except for the pressure dial, where we used a consumer product [15] (Figure 2). We had six prototypes as we had two different prototypes for the Expandable Dial, one that could be stretched (Figure 2a) and one that could be squeezed (Figure 2b). Here we briefly describe how they are implemented, and how they work.

**Expandable Dial: Stretching Design.** (Figure 2a) We use a Hoberman mechanism [7] to create an expandable circular shape. The center of the mechanism is connected to a rotational axis for value input. At the external corners, there are concave disks where users put their fingers on. Users can slightly press them and stretch the fingers inwards or outwards for inputting uncertainty.

**Expandable Dial: Squeezing Design.** (Figure 2b) We use to an aerospace design [6] to fold a paper sheet into a condensed shape. The tension of the paper keeps the dial expanded, and users squeeze it to change the diameter.

**Pinch Dial.** (Figure 2c) We create six equilateral prisms from a laser cutter and connect them into a hexagon, roughly resembling the round shape of a dial. They are held together with adhesive tape on the outer faces. We place a bent piece of plastic sheet between two prisms to act as a spring to open the dial. Users can close the dial by pinching the device.

**Pressure Dial.** (Figure 2d) We used a PowerMate Bluetooth [15] for the design. It has a spring inside to push the upper rotational part back when pressed. The device has only two states of height – pressed and not-pressed.

**Expandable Slider.** (Figure 2e) We place a bent piece of plastic sheet between two thumbs of a laser-cut slider. The plastic sheet forced the thumbs to separate. Users can squeeze the thumbs for more certain input.

**Split Slider.** (Figure 2f) There are three thumbs on a laser-cut slider. The thumbs have grooves on them and users can place a U-shaped plastic piece to combine two thumbs together. Hence, the number of thumbs can be changed between one, two, and three.

## Focus Group Study

We obtained general opinions on the input of uncertain data through focus group interviews. The interviews consist of two tasks: 1) understanding the causes of uncertain input and 2) evaluating our design explorations. For the second task, we provided low-fidelity prototypes for the explored designs. We had two participant groups, and each group consisted of six people. Each focus group interview lasted about 50 minutes. We took pictures and recorded the audio during the interviews.

*Participants*

We recruited twelve participants (10 male, 2 female) between 20 and 34 years ($M = 24.92$, $SD = 3.65$) via personal invitations. Their background varied, including social sciences and natural sciences. The participation was voluntary.

*Task 1: Understanding the Causes of Uncertain Input (20min)*

After the participants signed the consent form and provided their demographic information, they introduced themselves to the others. They then got sticky notes to write down answers for the following question: "Which scenarios can you think of where you were or could be uncertain about an input?"

*Results*

Participants found 20 scenarios where uncertain data input is needed. We report participants' scenarios that require them to communicate the uncertainty on continuous data (e.g., price), i.e., where this paper's interest is. We roughly grouped them into three categories:

**Lack of knowledge.** Many scenarios implied knowledge that has never been learned in the first place. Participants mentioned complicated forms such as patient forms demanded by doctors, and these forms require rather uncommon knowledge. Another example was the alarm setting for e.g., cooking time, which might vary among kitchen equipment.

**Loose constraints.** Participants mentioned scenarios where uncertain input was caused by loose constraints. For instance, flight search was mentioned related to vacation planning. Here uncertainty could occur due to the fact that one might not have a specific price or traveling time in mind. For these data, the participants wanted input mechanisms allowing a range of alternatives. Participants also named portion input on cooking websites (every person might have their own understanding of "one portion").

**Uncertain memories.** Many scenarios can be traced back to missing or imprecise memories. This includes rarely used personal data, for which the participants mentioned their body size and weight.

*Task 2: Evaluating the Designs (30 min)*

At the focus group interviews, we introduced our designs to the participants. Participants were grouped in three pairs. Each pair was randomly given three of the low-fidelity prototypes. They were asked to think about advantages, disadvantages, improvements or suitability of their respective prototypes for a given scenario among the scenarios found in the first task, and then each pair presented their findings. We repeated this step with the rest of the prototypes.

*Results*

Using thematic analysis [2], we identified preliminary requirements for designing tangible devices for uncertain input. The requirements are well-aligned with the requirements for the traditional rotational and linear input derived by Kim et al. [10]. It shows that the general purposes of the input interfaces are similar. However, the extended input space of the uncertain input TUIs also introduced new requirements that did not exist for traditional dials and sliders. There are seven requirements, which we grouped into four categories.

FAST MANIPULATION.

R1 **Simultaneous input.** In general, the participants liked to have simultaneous input of value and uncertainty. For instance, they complained that it was hard to press down the Pressure Dial while rotating because the resistance of the spring was too high. They also complained that the Pinch Dial was difficult to pinch when the opening is no longer between the thumbs and index fingers.

PRECISE MANIPULATION.

R2 **Small intervals.** Dials were preferred for small intervals in value input because they could have infinite input range. On the other hand, the input ranges of the sliders were limited by the slider sizes, hence their intervals for value input were larger than the dials'.

R3 **No interference between inputs.** The participants preferred not to have interference between the value and uncertainty inputs. For instance, when participants changed uncertainty (stretching or squeezing) with Expandable Dial, it could rotate the device by accident. When users grasp Pinch Dial, it applied some pressure on it, and it could cause unwanted change on uncertainty. These problems would be the same over all the devices except Split

Slider since the inputs for value and uncertainty were separated.

R4 **Easy finalization.** The participants needed easy finalization of inputs. With all designs, users needed another input interface (e.g., button) to finalize their value and uncertainty input. With Expandable Dial or Split Slider, the participants were able to take off their hands from and then finalize their inputs. However, the springs on Pinch Dial and Expandable Slider forced them to hold the devices while finalizing inputs.

OBSERVABLE UNCERTAINTY.

R5 **Visual feedback.** The participants liked that Split Slider's thumb intervals give clear visual feedback on the uncertainty. In general, all the dials did not have clear visual feedback on how much uncertainty was expressed (e.g., whether Pinch Dial was 50% open or 60% open).

R6 **Force feedback.** Participants also liked that Pinch Dial and Expandable Slider give force feedback on uncertainty. They mentioned that using pressure for certainty feels intuitive. However, it was unclear to them how much pressure represents which amount of uncertainty. This requirement seems mutually exclusive with the *easy finalization* since the springs can give force feedback and also cause unwanted movement of the openings/thumbs. Also, even though Pressure Dial gave force feedback, the upper button's travel distance was too short. Hence, the participants could not feel the force feedback was proportional to the travel distance.

SUPPORTING STATISTICAL KNOWLEDGE.

R7 **Supporting both experts and novices.** The participants liked that SplitSlider can express statistical knowledge and support both expert and novice users. The other designs could only express the amount of uncertainty without statistical distribution.

## Conclusion and Future Work

In this article, we contributed to communicating input uncertainty by extending the input space of traditional TUIs. We believe our work bridge the field of uncertainty and tangible interfaces, can open many interesting research questions. We explored the design space and implemented low-fidelity prototypes. Lastly, we derived design requirements for uncertain input TUIs. For future work, we are interested in developing a working prototype and evaluating its ability to support more precise uncertain input, comparing with alternative input methods. We also wish to evaluate and refine the design requirements and investigate how to resolve conflicting design requirements (i.e., force feedback and easy finalization).

## Acknowledgment

This work was supported by the French National Research Agency (ANR-11-LABX-0025-01, ANR-11-EQPX-0002, ANR-15-CE23-0011-01) and the Alexander von Humboldt Foundation.

## References

[1] Nadia Boukhelifa and David John Duke. 2009. Uncertainty Visualization: Why Might It Fail?. In CHI '09 Extended Abstracts on Human Factors in Computing Systems (CHI EA '09). ACM, New York, NY, USA, 4051-4056. DOI: http://dx.doi.org/10.1145/1520340.1520616

[2] Virginia Braun and Victoria Clarke. 2006. Using thematic analysis in psychology. Qualitative Research in Psychology 3, 2 (Jan. 2006), 77-101. DOI: http://dx.doi.org/10.1191/1478088706qp063oa

[3] Michael Correll and Michael Gleicher. 2014. Error Bars Considered Harmful: Exploring Alternate Encodings for Mean and Error. Visualization and

Computer Graphics, IEEE Transactions on 20, 12 (2014), 2142–2151. DOI: http://dx.doi.org/10.1109/TVCG.2014.2346298

[4] Céline Coutrix and Cédric Masclet. 2015. Shape-Change for Zoomable TUIs: Opportunities and Limits of a Resizable Slider. Springer International Publishing, Cham, 349-366. DOI: http://dx.doi.org/10.1007/978-3-319-22701-6_27

[5] Miriam Greis, Hendrik Schuff, Marius Kleiner, Niels Henze, and Albrecht Schmidt. 2017. Input Controls for Entering Uncertain Data: Probability Distribution Sliders. Proc. ACM Hum.-Comput. Interact. 1, 1, Article 3 (June 2017), 17 pages. DOI: http://dx.doi.org/10.1145/3095805

[6] Guest, S.D., and Pellegrino, S. (1992). "Inextensional Wrapping of Flat Membranes." First International Conference on Structural Morphology, Montpellier, R. Motro and T. Wester, eds., 7-11 September, 203-215.

[7] Hoberman Associates, Inc. Retrieved from July 24, 2018 from http://www.hoberman.com/index.html.

[8] Jessica Hullman, Paul Resnick, and Eytan Adar. 2015. Hypothetical Outcome Plots Outperform Error Bars and Violin Plots for Inferences about Reliability of Variable Ordering. PLOS ONE 10, 11 (2015).

[9] Susan L. Joslyn and Jared E. LeClerc. 2012. Uncertainty forecasts improve weather-related decisions and attenuate the effects of forecast error. Journal of Experimental Psychology: Applied 18, 1 (2012), 126-140. DOI: http://dx.doi.org/10.1037/a0025185

[10] Hyunyoung Kim, Céline Coutrix, and Anne Roudaut. 2018. KnobSlider: Design of a Shape-Changing UI for Parameter Control. In Proceedings of the 2018 CHI Conference on Human Factors in Computing Systems (CHI '18). ACM, New York, NY, USA, Paper 339, 13 pages. DOI: https://doi.org/10.1145/3173574.3173913

[11] Hyunyoung Kim, Celine Coutrix, and Anne Roudaut. 2018. Morphees+: Studying Everyday Reconfigurable Objects for the Design and Taxonomy of Reconfigurable UIs. In Proceedings of the 2018 CHI Conference on Human Factors in Computing Systems (CHI '18). ACM, New York, NY, USA, Paper 619, 14 pages. DOI: https://doi.org/10.1145/3173574.3174193

[12] Seoktae Kim, Hyunjung Kim, Boram Lee, Tek-Jin Nam, and Woohun Lee. 2008. Inflatable Mouse: Volume-adjustable Mouse with Air-pressure-sensitive Input and Haptic Feedback. In Proceedings of the SIGCHI Conference on Human Factors in Computing Systems (CHI '08). ACM, New York, NY, USA, 211-224. DOI: http://dx.doi.org/10.1145/1357054.1357090

[13] Rebecca E. Morss, Julie L. Demuth, and Jeffrey K. Lazo. 2008. Communicating Uncertainty in Weather Forecasts: A Survey of the U.S. Public. Weather and Forecasting 23, 5 (2008), 974-991. DOI: http://dx.doi.org/10.1175/2008WAF2007088.1

[14] Alex T. Pang, Craig M. Wittenbrink, and Suresh K. Lodha. 1997. Approaches to uncertainty visualization. The Visual Computer 13, 8 (1997), 370-390. DOI: http://dx.doi.org/10.1007/s003710050111

[15] Powermate Bluetooth https://griffintechnology.com/us/powermate-bluetooth

[16] Mark S. Roulston, Gary E. Bolton, Andrew N. Kleit, and Addison L. Sears-Collins. 2006. A laboratory study of the benefits of including uncertainty information in weather forecasts. Weather and Forecasting 21, 1 (2006), 116-122. DOI: http://dx.doi.org/10.1175/WAF887.1

[17] Orit Shaer and Eva Hornecker. 2010. Tangible User Interfaces: Past, Present, and Future Directions. Found. Trends Hum.-Comput. Interact.

3, 1–2 (Jan. 2010), 1-137. DOI: http://dx.doi.org/10.1561/1100000026

[18] Jihoon Suh, Wooshik Kim, and Andrea Bianchi. 2017. Button+: Supporting User and Context Aware Interaction through Shape-Changing Interfaces. In Proceedings of the Eleventh International Conference on Tangible, Embedded, and Embodied Interaction (TEI '17). ACM, New York, NY, USA, 261-268. DOI: https://doi.org/10.1145/3024969.3024980

# Rapid Prototyping of Immersive Video for Popularization of Historical Knowledge

**Julien Puget**
Univ. du Québec à Montréal
Montreal, Qc. Canada
puget.julien@gmail.com

**Emmanuel Durand**
Society for Arts and Technology
1201, Boul. Saint-Laurent
H2X 2S6 Montreal, Qc Canada
edurand@sat.qc.ca

**Mylène Pardoen**
Maison des Sciences de l'Homme Lyon Saint-Etienne
Lyon. France
mylene.pardoen@cnrs.fr

**Michał Seta**
Society for Arts and Technology
1201, Boul. Saint-Laurent
H2X 2S6 Montreal, Qc Canada
mseta@sat.qc.ca

**Nicolas Bouillot**
Society for Arts and Technology
1201, Boul. Saint-Laurent
H2X 2S6 Montreal, Qc Canada
nbouillot@sat.qc.ca

**Pascal Bastien**
Université du Québec à Montréal
Montreal, Qc. Canada
bastien.pascal@uqam.ca


*TEI '19*, March 17–20, 2019, Tempe, AZ, USA
ACM 978-1-4503-6196-5/19/03.
https://doi.org/10.1145/3294109.3300977

## Abstract
Popularization of historical data implies going beyond the language and knowledge specific to this scientific field in order to make it understood. This applies to people's perception of the world since many changes have been applied to our surrounding environment. Communicating the way people used to hear, see and smell allows for a better retranscription of what once was, and a more effective connection between the teller and his audience. After the sensory data is gathered through heterography, comes the issue of assembling and presenting them. For the Bretez project, a reconstruction of eighteenth century Paris neighbourhood, the process is done manually. This paper describes a new approach to this aspect of historian's work. Using an immersive editing platform controlled through virtual reality devices, we built a pipeline dedicated to facilitating the creation process for historians, and transparently allowing for exporting the result to multiple video formats (immersive or not). The specific case of prototyping this pipeline with the Bretez project for future user experiments is described and discussed.

## CCS Concepts
**•Human-centered computing → Information visualization; •Applied computing → Document preparation;** *Digital libraries and archives;*

## Author Keywords
Popularization; Virtual reality; Immersive editing

## Introduction
Immersive content allows people to experience what it feels to be part of a three-dimensional environment, making an exceptionally new way of communicating results from historical research. In fact, many existing historical studies make it possible to read and interpret history from a sensory perspective [3] that enables plausible retranscription of past realities through immersive content. In recent years, scholars have published stunningly original studies placing emotions and senses in historical perspective. Still, no matter how well written they might be, textual accounts can only provide a partial experience of the past. They remain incapable of capturing and developing the most mundane realities, namely those based on the senses. And yet these senses – which represent experiences – remain historical. One of the challenges of historical popularization is to let today's people see and hear the same way they did in the past, in spite of living in a radically different sensory perspective. That which is seen and heard has also changed, just as the expectations, fears and pleasures felt by the inhabitants of the eighteenth century were not the same as those of their present-day counterparts. To understand these fears, expectations and pleasures – and to recreate them – our team is working to reproduce the landscapes and soundscapes of the past, which can serve as tools for researchers and educational experiences for the general public.

Toward a formal evaluation of our work with user study, we build a prototype enabling user-involved experiment, based on the following hypothesizes:

- popularization and learning is improved using immersive audiovisual content
- In situ editing of immersive environment reduces the time and complexity of producing immersive content

*Challenges of historical popularization*
Some of the challenges we are facing relate to the social sciences and humanities, while others are best dealt with by engineers. How can historians effectively connect their audience to a long-lost past? How can they recreate the sensory perceptions that have always been fundamental to how human beings experience the world around them? One of the first challenges is the extraction of sensations from the historical corpus. Historians have long attempted to recreate the sensations of the past through writing. We see immersive content as an opportunity to overcome the limitation of solely textual communication. This seems more particularly critical for works related to periods that predate photography or the first sound recordings. The history of emotions and the history of the senses are truly fascinating fields of research, but ones that present very daunting challenges. Researchers know that senses like sight, hearing and smell all have a history. They know that pleasure and disgust are feelings that vary over time and across space [13, 12], and that sight has not always been the primary sense: until the nineteenth century, the inhabitants of the western world were most attentive to hearing [5].

The range of sensations-related facts that can be extracted from historical documents is extraordinarily wide. It covers pronunciation, tissues, musical interpretation, level of tolerance to smell and noise, and many other more or less abstract sensations. For instance, since the baroque music revival of the 1990s, musicologists and musicians have struggled to rediscover lost sounds by playing pieces from

(a) A historian recording a navigation path in the Bretez 3D mockup.

(b) Validation step of the popularization video in SAT's 18 meters wide dome.

**Figure 1:** Editing immersive content

the sixteenth, seventeenth and eighteenth centuries on period instruments. At the turn of the millennium, French playwright Benjamin Lazar staged a candlelit production of a Molière play that emphasized seventeenth-century pronunciation[1]. Beyond mere exoticism, appropriating the past in these ways provides a better understanding of the sensibilities of earlier times. Researchers who work with written sources can document and describe the lost outlines of a city, while cataloging the buildings and monuments of past centuries. They can discover the residents of a neighbourhood and the trades that were practiced there, while tallying the products sold or purchased at the local market. But whether these scholars rely on archival documents, old maps or engravings that provide a window on the past, a fundamental problem remains.

Popularization through immersive content promotes an approach to history capable of balancing academic rigour with accessibility to a wider audience, but could also inspire new lines of research and fresh epistemological considerations. It would also provide a way of showcasing the importance of archival research to a much wider audience. We can ensure the success of these two goals only by adopting a rigorous methodology when reproducing historical situations: the sensory experiences we seek to create must be based on facts, clues and properly verified elements that reflect a plausible reality in the history of everyday life.

*Virtual reality and popularization*
Virtual reality in a broad sense has been used for bringing scientific facts to the public for a long time now. The first and still most common media is non-immersive film, mostly available through television networks. An example of a work done to improve technically the quality of a film is described in the article by Callieri et al. [2].

More immersive media have also become more widely used in this field. A precursory example of using augmented reality in the context of cultural heritage is the work by Vassilios et al. [15] who used transportable devices prior to smartphones to embed virtual models of now destroyed antique buildings into the live video feed of a camera, while the user wanders around the area. More recently, Girbacia et al. [11] who displayed virtually restored artifacts overlaid on real historical buildings through smartphones. Durand et al. [8] who reproduced live lighting conditions onto a virtual model of a destroyed church, the result being shown through on-site mobile displays.

Interactivity is also a good means to improve the experience of virtual reality. A good example of how this can lead to tools usable by scientists and by the public is the work of Ynnerman et al. [16]. They developed an interactive virtual dissection table, used in this work to study and present an ancient mummy which has been scanned using tomography. The user can then rotate, peel off, and visualize cross-sections of the virtual model.

*Our approach*
The context of our work is the Bretez project [2], which aims at reconstructing a sensory perspective of an eighteenth century Parisian neighbourhood. The initial result of this project was the production of a video [3] illustrating this neigh-

[1] As illustrated in the 2004 DVD of *Le Bourgeois Gentilhomme*, directed by Vincent Dumestre, written by Moliére and composed by Jean-Baptiste Lully. https://operabaroque.fr/DVD_BOURGEOIS_Dumestre.htm

[2] Bretez project: https://sites.google.com/site/louisbretez/home

[3] Bretez project, video: https://www.youtube.com/watch?v=YP_1eHeyo4. Note, that the veracity of the represented historical facts prevails over the visual realism for historians: the experience must not display hypotheses, but only verified and documented facts. The immersive environment must represent a plausible reality based on the current knowledge and literature.

(a) HD video for single screen.

(b) Stereo 360 for VR headset.

(c) Fulldome targeting projection for large dome-shaped spaces.

**Figure 2:** Movies format rendered using the prototyped navigation built and saved in situ.

bourhood recorded from a 3D mockup, augmented with sensible information: sound. However, this first version was produced manually

The methodology used initially in this project for generating the audiovisual content involves recording the video output from a navigation inside a 3D mockup, then editing the soundtrack to match the video. This second step is about organizing the sounds in a sequencer, incorporating newly recorded sounds (based on recent evidences), and adding audio filters to simulate the acoustics of the place. This process can take tens of hours, depending on the complexity of the task.

Laboratoire Paris XVIII (UQAM, Canada) and Projet Bretez (CNRS, France) have begun to discuss combining the archival research undertaken by the former with the latter's visual and sound reconstructions. The aim, made possible through a collaboration with the Society for Arts and Technology (Canada), is to provide a scientific foundation for an immersive experience of eighteenth-century Paris. Its full achievement will represent nothing less than a true cultural history.

During our collaboration, the 3D model will be projected within a dome to offer a fully immersive experience that includes motion. In other words, people will be able to directly compare their mental representations of the past to a virtual reconstruction. After all, even the most rigorous historical study can leave gaps between what a person imagines (whatever their field of expertise) and the potential realities on the ground (even in a virtual setting). Researchers and the general public alike will therefore find that their perception of the physical space is shaped not only by the process of immersion, but also by the sensations it produces — both the stimuli provided and your physical position within the model. Ultimately, this is precisely what makes it possible to orient people within both time and space. By physically entering the model, you become one with it. By welcoming you (by "housing" you) the model embraces you as much as you embrace it, a phenomenon that takes hold well before you actually perceive the model.

To allow for creating virtual reality content targeting the public, two constraints arise. The first is driven by the need for vulgarizing the historical data: the content has to be made accessible to most people. The second constraint is driven by the fact that not all users are necessarily well versed in the field of virtual reality: the creation process must be kept as simple as possible.

## Prototyping with EiS, our creation platform

The experimentation described in this paper is based on an immersive creation platform (named *Édition in Situ* [4], see the demonstration video[4]) designed to facilitate the drafting of immersive experiences, following the assumption that such a prototyping is better done while working directly with the final rendering display.

This creation platform, at the time of this rapid prototyping, was built on top of Blender [10], a free and open-source 3D computer graphics software toolset used for creating animated films, visual effects, art, 3D printed models, interactive 3D applications and video games. Its scripting ability allowed us to add immersive rendering to its 3D viewport, a VRPN client [14] to receive inputs from compatible servers, and support for the SATIE sound spatialization engine [1]. While using the platform, the user has access to his assets (3D models, images, sounds) which he can load to build the scene. The architecture of the current version, a rewrite started after the work described here, is based on a client-server model, where several clients are able to connect

[4] *Édition in situ* video: https://vimeo.com/226298383

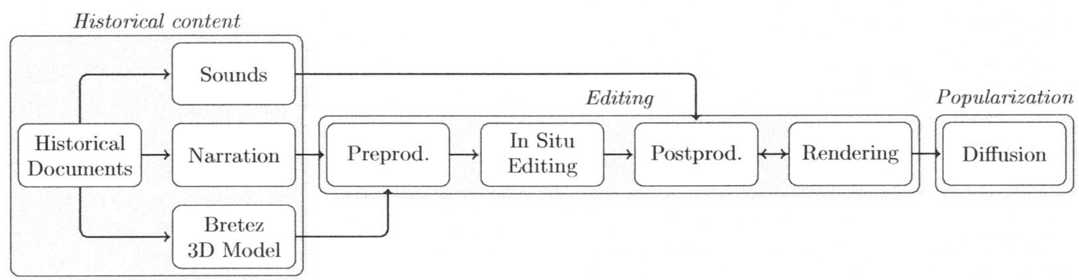


**Figure 3:** Our rapid prototyping approach.

simultaneously to the same session. This is motivated by the opportunity offered by distribution of users across the network, where both edition and runtime is supported by EiS. EiS, as a tool facilitating simultaneous and collective edition and experimentation by remote users is expected in a near future to allow for rapid prototyping of experiments like POSTURE and DRAWING SPACE [6], both based on remote group telepresence using real-time and photorealistic full body capture with 3D camera. In these experiments, we observed the difficulty of creating content from within the virtual environment. On top of this new addition, the current implementation of EiS includes most of the features already present in previous version: navigate, translate, animate. Moreover, the current EiS version is entirely written in Python 3 for easier integration of new features.

From its architecture, and regardless of its version, this platform allows for seamless back and forth between the immersive space and the user's workstation. It also does not make any assumption on how the built 3D scene will be exported, be it as a standard film, an immersive one, an interactive experience, etc.

The use of the EiS platform for the creation of a short immersive popularization video was anticipating the rapid production of immersive content. This is illustrated by the pipeline presented in figure 3. From historical research of a specific location and time from historical documents[5], historians are able to produce content such as sound recordings, 3D virtual mockups and narrations that describe the audiovisual experience. These media are the historical content which are manipulated in the editing phase.

The narrative and the 3D mockup are loaded inside the creation platform after a preproduction step, during which data are converted to a compatible format. The content editor, an historians producing a popularization video, is recording a path inside the virtual location *in situ* (while inside the immersive space). This is done in line with the narrative played simultaneously, and synchronized with the time clock of the audio sequencer Ardour [7]. To support him in this task, he is given controls over the virtual camera position with simplified controls through a set of VR controllers (namely, the HTC Vive controllers). The controls

[5] Such documents include for instance the Turgot plan [9] created by Louis Bretez between 1734 and 1739.

are i) choose the moving direction by pointing with the right controller, ii) go forward by pressing the trigger of the right controller and iii) go backward by pressing the trigger of the left controller.

From the perspective of the editor, the navigation is free in the virtual space without being hindered by the technicalities (see figure 1(a)). This simplicity handles the second goal.

Then the post-production step involves first cleaning up the recorded path, by equalizing the distance to the floor and smoothing the movements. Then the sound track is created to match the path inside the 3D mockup, from the previous sound recordings. The final project, comprising the 3D mockup, camera navigation and sound track, is then exported (or more specifically, rendered) to multiple video formats: standard HD, immersive stereo[6], spherical for fulldomes[7] (see figure 2). This diversity of possible outputs handles the first of the goals, as it allows for showing the film in various contexts. For instance, we evaluated the quality of the initial rendering in our 18 meter wide immersive dome (figure 1(b)).

## Conclusion

We prototyped the production of popularization video, where the time to produce content is critical for ensuring that popularization objects can be updated, produced as series of objects, presented for different formats. Using our in situ immersive content editing platform, we did a prototype of a short immersive video (less than 2 minutes) with historical data, including the Bretez 3D model of $18^{th}$ century Paris and rendered it for various formats.

[6] immersive popularization video is available here https://www.youtube.com/watch?v=UL0UmcHmrj4

[7] fulldome popularization video is available here https://www.youtube.com/watch?v=PvhGyJ9Aylw

The successful execution of the entire pipeline presented in figure 3 was done in various points and durations in time. All the *historical content* has been developed for years, from research by the historian community. The working time scale is large, but provides the content to be possibly included in an object for outreach. This historical content is permanently evolving, resulting in an increase of the quantity of audio files, 3D model or other contents that can be included into the Bretez mockup. The only specific content is the narration used for the video.

This prototyped pipeline allows us to design a user experiment involving historians for producing content dedicated to popularization, but also user experiments involving students subjected to teaching with or without the use of immersive content.

## Acknowledgement

Thanks to the *Ministère de l'Économie et de l'Innovation* (Québec, Canada), the *Canada Foundation for Innovation*, the *Centre national de la recherche scientifique (CNRS)* (France), the *Maison des Sciences de l'Homme Lyon Saint-Etienne (MSH LSE/USR2005)* (Lyon, France), the *SATT PULSALYS* (Lyon, France) and the *LabEx IMU (Intelligence des Mondes Urbains)* (Lyon, France), that founded a significant part of this work.

## REFERENCES

1. Nicolas Bouillot, Zack Settel, and Michał Seta. 2017. SATIE: a live and scalable 3D audio scene rendering environment for large multi-channel loudspeaker configurations. *New Interfaces for Musical Expression* (2017).
2. M. Callieri, Paul E. Debevec, J. Pair, and R. Scopigno. 2005. A realtime immersive application with realistic lighting: The Parthenon. (2005). 00014.

3. M. Champion and A. Lynch. 2015. *Understanding Emotions in Early Europe*. Brepols Publishers.
4. François U. Brien, Emmanuel Durand, Jérémie Soria, Michal Seta, and Nicolas Bouillot. 2017. In Situ Editing (EiS) For Fulldomes. In *23rd ACM Symposium on Virtual Reality Software and Technology (VRST)*. Gothenburg, Sweden.
5. A. Corbin. 1999. *Village Bells: Sound and Meaning in the Nineteenth-century French Countryside*. Macmillan Publishers Limited.
6. Luc Courchesne, Emmanuel Durand, and Bruno Roy. 2014. Posture Platform and The Drawing Room: Virtual Teleportation in Cyberspace. *ACM Siggraph / Leonardo Journal for Arts Science and Technology, MIT Press* Vol. 47, no. 4 (2014), p 380–389.
7. Paul Davis. 1998. Ardour. `https://ardour.org`. (1998).
8. Emmanuel Durand, Frédéric Mérienne, Christian Père, and Patrick Callet. 2014. Ray-on, an On-Site Photometric Augmented Reality Device. *Journal on Computing and Cultural Heritage (JOCCH)* (2014). 00001.
9. Alfred Fierro, Jean-Yves Sarazin, Centre historique des Archives nationales (Paris), and Réunion des musées nationaux (France). 2005. *Le Paris des Lumières d'après le plan de Turgot (1734-1739)*. Réunion des musées nationaux.
10. Blender Foundation. 1995. Blender. `https://blender.org`. (1995).
11. Florin Girbacia, Silviu Butnariu, Alex Petre Orman, and Cristian Cezar Postelnicu. 2013. Virtual restoration of deteriorated religious heritage objects using augmented reality technologies. *European Journal of Science and Theology* 9, 2 (2013), 223–231. `http://www.ejst.tuiasi.ro/Files/37/23_Girbaciaetal.pdf` 00011.
12. J. Plamper and K. Tribe. 2015. *The History of Emotions: An Introduction*. Oxford University Press.
13. B.H. Rosenwein. 2015. *Generations of Feeling: A History of Emotions, 600–1700*. Cambridge University Press.
14. Russell M Taylor II, Thomas C Hudson, Adam Seeger, Hans Weber, Jeffrey Juliano, and Aron T Helser. 2001. VRPN: a device-independent, network-transparent VR peripheral system. In *Proceedings of the ACM symposium on Virtual reality software and technology*. ACM, 55–61.
15. Vlahakis Vassilios, Karigiannis John, Tsotros Manolis, Gounaris Michael, Almeida Luis, Stricker Didier, Gleue Tim, Christou Ioannis T., Carlucci Renzo, and Ioannidis Nikos. 2001. ARCHEOGUIDE: First results of an Augmented Reality, Mobile Computing System in Cultural Heritage Sites. *VAST* (2001). 00236.
16. Anders Ynnerman, Thomas Rydell, Daniel Antoine, David Hughes, Anders Persson, and Patric Ljung. 2016. Interactive visualization of 3d scanned mummies at public venues. *Commun. ACM* 59, 12 (Dec. 2016), 72–81. DOI:`http://dx.doi.org/10.1145/2950040` 00004.

# Exploring Projection Based Mixed Reality with Tangibles for Nonsymbolic Preschool Math Education

**Elif Salman***
Koç University
Optical Microsystems Laboratory
Istanbul/Turkey
esalman17@ku.edu.tr

**Ceylan Besevli***
Koç University-Arçelik Research
Center for Creative
Industries (KUAR)
Istanbul/Turkey
cbesevli17@ku.edu.tr

**Tilbe Göksun**
Koç University
Department of Psychology
tgoksun@ku.edu.tr

**Oğuzhan Özcan**
Koç University-Arçelik Research
Center for Creative
Industries (KUAR)
Istanbul/Turkey
oozcan@ku.edu.tr

**Hakan Urey**
Koç University
Optical Microsystems Laboratory
Istanbul/Turkey
hurey@ku.edu.tr


*TEI '19, March 17–20, 2019, Tempe, AZ, USA*

ACM ISBN 978-1-4503-6196-5/19/03.
https://doi.org/10.1145/3294109.3300981.
* Two authors share the first authorship

## Abstract
A child's early math development can stem from interactions with the physical world. Accordingly, current tangible interaction studies focus on preschool children's *formal (symbolic) mathematics*, i.e. number knowledge. However, recent developmental studies stress the importance of *nonsymbolic number representation* in math learning, i.e. understanding quantity relations without counting(more/less). To our knowledge, there are no tangible systems based on this math concept. We developed an initial tangible based mixed-reality(MR) setup with a small tabletop projector and depth camera. Our goal was observing children's interaction with the setup to guide our further design process towards developing nonsymbolic math trainings. In this paper we present our observations from sessions with four 3-to-5 year old children and discuss their meaning for future work. Initial clues show that our MR setup leads to exploratory and mindful interactions, which might be generalizable to other tangible MR systems for child education and could inspire interaction design studies.

## Author Keywords
Tangible interaction; Embodied learning; Nonsymbolic math; Mixed reality; Tangible interaction for children

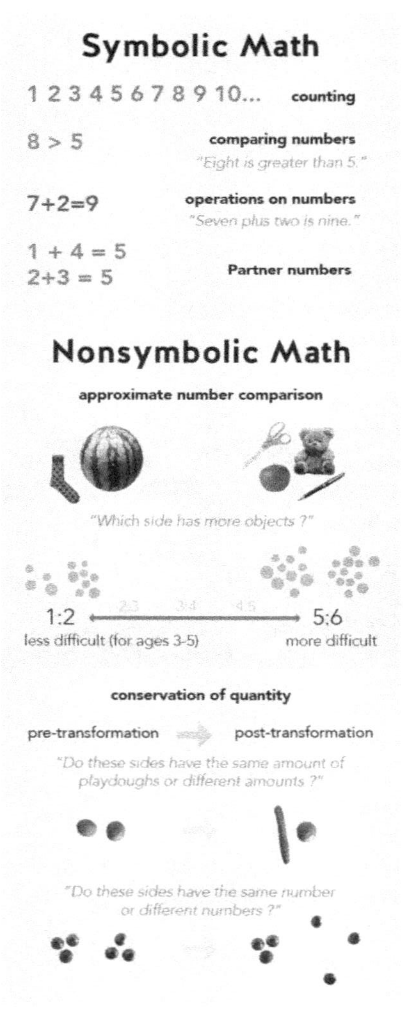


Figure 1: Symbolic and Nonsymbolic math

## CSS Concepts

• Human-centered computing~Mixed / augmented reality • Human-centered computing~User interface design • Social and professional topics~Children

## Introduction

Early math ability is essential for day to day life activities. Math development is also related to a child's later academic achievements and occupation in STEAM (science, technology, engineering, arts, and math) fields[10,15]. Several theories propose that humans' cognitive structures and understanding of abstract concepts, such as mathematics, are formulated through bodily interactions[1,5,8,13,14] which makes tangibles promising for education.

A new set of cognitive developmental studies [21,24] propose that one of the important foundation for mathematical understanding is *nonsymbolic number representation*, such as the ability to decide between two different quantities as more/less (Figure 1). This ability can be affected by several physical cues (shape, volume etc.) [20]. We believe that, tangibles, naturally having perceptual cues, can foster this understanding. To our knowledge, there is no tangible based systems that target nonsymbolic math.

Projection based mixed reality (MR) technologies with tangibles offer several potentials for our investigation efforts. To begin with, there are diverging views on perceptual details of tangibles might affect learning[6]. One view is that objects resembling everyday items (cars) help linking abstract concepts with the real world[16]. Another view is that detailed objects hinder learning by drawing too much attention to themselves, and limit generalizability of concepts by priming children to a certain representation[18]. We speculate that projecting perceptual details onto an object during training could attract the attention to the task, more than the object itself. Also, overlaying different visuals onto objects enables representation of various entities[22], which might contribute to the generalizability and relatability of the taught concepts.

Based on these findings and assumptions, we developed an initial projection based mixed-reality (MR) game with tangibles. Our goal was observing children's interaction with this system to guide our further design processes towards developing nonsymbolic math trainings. In our game, children's physical actions have effects on both the digital interface and the appearance of physicals via projection. The portable setup requires no installation and tracks objects and gestures. The training follows a narrative in which the child helps a virtual character by placing tangibles onto a surface and answers questions with pointing gestures.

In this paper we focus on our observations from sessions with four 3-to-5-year-old children. We discuss their meaning for the development of our work. Initial clues show that our MR setup leads to exploratory and mindful interactions, which could inspire both interaction design and education-oriented studies.

## Background and Related Work

*Symbolic Math*

Symbolic math is an umbrella term based on written symbols and precise representations, such as writing or verbalizing 2+2=4 (Figure 2)[21].The current interactive tangible applications for early math focus on symbolic math, like number knowledge, via digital tangibles or table top studies[2,9].

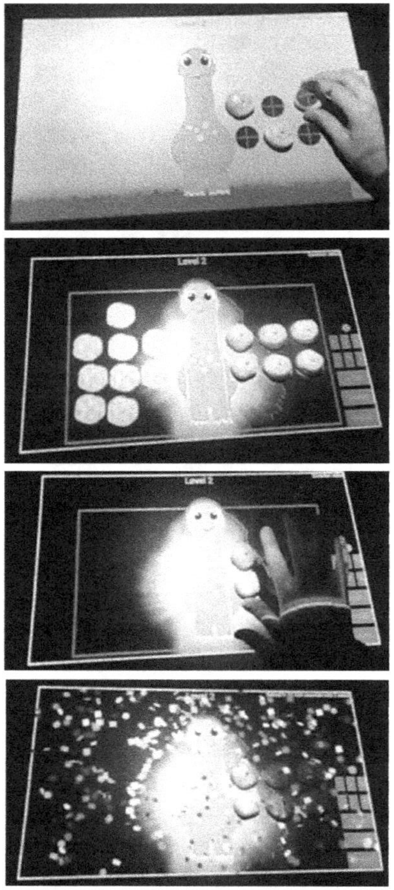

Figure 3: An example trial from the game. a) (top) Object placement and resulting 'powers' b) Projected ratio c) Answering "Which side has less stones?" with gestures d) Positive feedback audio + visuals

*Nonsymbolic Math*

It is asserted that nonsymbolic math ability reflects onto the symbolic math skills[4].This form of math covers a conceptual knowledge of and judgement between quantities, i.e. more/less comparisons without counting. In that respect, several screen-based trainings that focus on approximate number training emerged. In these applications the child sees different ratios of quantities on two sides of the screen that are presented for a short amount of time to prevent counting. After seeing both quantities, the child taps at the side that responds to the question: "Which box has more/less objects?".

Additionally, quantity can feature sensory magnitudes such as area and volume [20]. Piaget and many other scholars show how children's perception of quantity is affected by these [11]. In the conservation of quantity tasks, children between 2 and 6 years of age are presented the same amount of marbles in different arrangements. Upon these 'transformations', children most likely think that the quantities have changed.

*Projection Based MR Systems*

There are studies that use MR for math education via HMDs (head mounted displays) [17] but the user interacts with virtual objects. In one paper [23], handheld devices are used, but holding the device restrains the tangible interaction. In this point 3D projection mapping has a great potential. It lays a real time virtual image on top of a physical object , and any tangible can become an interface [7]. SMALLabs[25] uses a similar room scale technology with a fixed projective system. In contrary, we use a tabletop system that enables to focus on tangible interaction, which is needed for understanding nonsymbolic math.

## Design Components

*Tangible Objects*

For the physical objects, we designed 3D printed amorphous white tangibles with smooth surfaces. This was to minimize the attention drawn their physical properties, and to enable clear projection of textures on (Figure 2). The rough diameter and height are 30mm,

Figure 2: Tangible objects with projected information.

appropriate for the age groups hand grip.

*User Interface & Storyline*

Before building the system, we deduced the essence of what we wanted the children to do in our trial. These were 1) training with tangibles to support the sensory magnitudes of quantity, 2) comparing these to other ratios for nonsymbolic math development and 3) experiencing objects with different appearances to support generalizability. Thereafter, we designed a narrative character and its storyline. "Dima" is a dinosaur inspired by children's fascination. It is drawn in front of a simple background and has minimal visual details. The projections on the objects have different colors/textures in each trial.

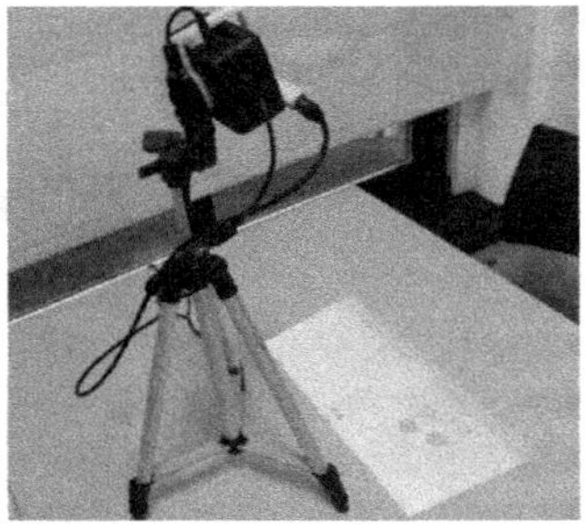

Figure 4: Overall setup.

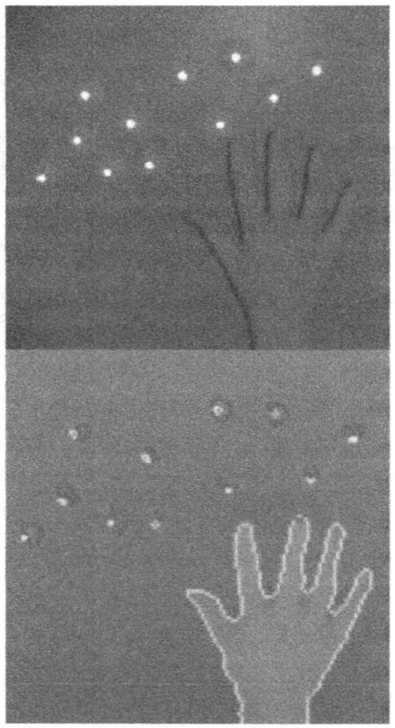

Figure 5: An example of a) infrared image, b) depth image with detected contours. (Blue: retroreflective markers, green: hand contour, pink: finger-tip, red: discarded contours.)

The children are asked to help Dima on a 'magical stone' quest. To that end, the child places objects at the shown spots, which makes the stones gain magical powers, (Figure 3a). Their power trigger another set of stones to appear (Figure 3b). All objects disappear after a while to prevent counting [12]. To gather both of their powers, the child gestures to the side that has more/less quantity, depending on the question. After gesturing at the correct response, Dima gives a congratulatory audio feedback, and the surface shows an effect (Figure 3d). For incorrect responses, Dima says "Reconsider your answer."

*Training Module*

By drawing on the research from non-symbolic math, we designed several training modules. For beginning, this paper focuses on the quantity comparisons module that has 6 levels. On each level, the child is trained to compare different ratios starting from 1:2 (easy) to 5:6 (hard). We controlled the placement of objects via circling the input areas. This way, we enable the child to see quantities in different arrangements. The amount of input objects (up to 12), projections and the placement of tangibles on the surface are all randomized.

## Technical Details

*Hardware*

We use a prototype Android device designed in our lab. Instead of a touch screen, it has a Sony CXN020X pico-projector as display. It is equipped with Qualcomm APQ8016 (CPU: 1.2 GHz) processor and 924 MB RAM. Also, we connect a ToF (time-of flight) depth camera, PMD CamBoard pico flexx, which can give pixel depth and IR (infrared) image in 0.1m – 4m range. We mounted the device on an adjustable tripod. The overall setup can be transported easily and does not require any prior installation (Figure 4).

*Software Implementation*

In the setup, the depth camera and projector do not share the same coordinate space. Hence, we estimate the transformation between them by using 2D-3D matched pairs. Even if the system is relocated, the estimated transformation will be same because the camera and projector are attached together. Since our processing capacity is limited, we keep the tracking procedure simple. Objects are tracked using retro-reflective markers which look very bright in IR image. Also, we apply a depth-based method explained in [27] to understand where the child points (Figure 5). The calculations are done in device CPU. The game is designed as an Android application, written in Java and C++. We used OpenCV for image processing and RoyaleSDK [29] to get 3D point cloud and IR image.

## Preliminary User Study

This user study aimed to see children's comprehension of the systems directives, their interaction with the overall setup. We invited parents with 3-5 years old children (M: 3.8) on a volunteer basis. Four children (2 female) played with one training module for 30 minutes. All children go to preschool and have basic symbolic knowledge (counting), except for one. Moreover, we conducted a semi structured interview with parents that involved their child's technology use. One parent said that they banned the tablet usage, because it had a negative impact on the child's attention span and increased his tantrums.

During study, if the child was hesitant to act, we provided simple cues like, "You can put a stone on to the shown area." Besides these, we provided no instructions for the game to minimize our influence on the natural interactions.

## Findings and Discussion

Four children completed the designated tasks and were fully attentive. The following findings are common interaction patterns and they may be generalizable to other tangible MR systems for child education and could inspire other interaction design studies.

*Unrestricted setup encourages children's exploratory behavior*
Our setup invites gestures and tangible use in different trials and lets the children use these interactions the way they desire. We think that children's unprescribed behavior coupled with our unrestricted setup encouraged surprising interactions. For example, in the tutorial session, we show the input circles and urge the participants to put an object there by using pointing icons. Excited by the setup, one child mimicked this gesture to see an effect. Children also touched the projection surface and placed the objects onto the various points to see if they could draw a reaction. By chance, one child brought his toy car to the session. He tried putting the tangibles on the car and carried it to the input circles (Figure 6).

If an unrestricted setup is the source of these free interactions, , we believe that developers of MR educational tools could consider these exploratory behaviors of children, coinciding with the tangible interaction literature [3]. In our study, children interacted with the system as they wanted, which is defined as open-ended play in [26]. Amplifying these interactions via different tangible forms and gestural inputs could be a way start.

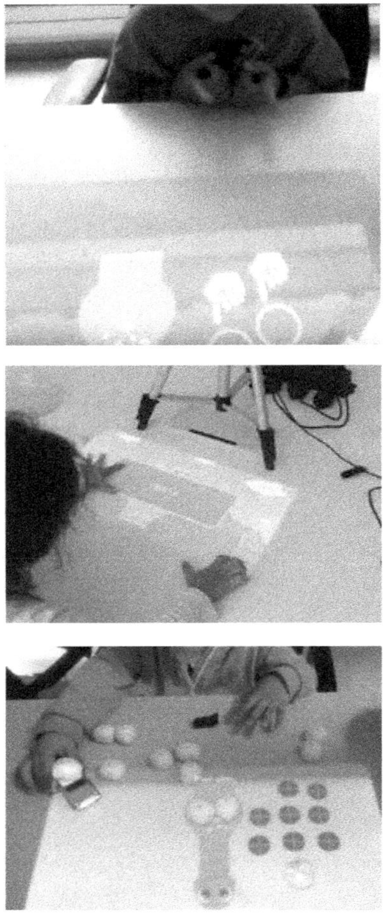

Figure 6: Participants exploratory behavior with the system

*Projection draws attention to tangibles and supports engagement*
In order for children to continue a training by themselves, their engagement is vital [28]. During our studies, children were excited to see what would happen and were pleasantly surprised with each input due to interactive projection. This sustained their overall engagement in our 30-minute study. In fact, one child wanted to play once more. Even though this might be due to a 'novelty effect', our results suggested that the novelty can be kept alive and engagement can be prolonged thanks to the ability of altering the visuals with projection. These changes can also support the generalizability of the trained concept.

*Multi-modal interaction provides a mindful way of interacting with educational tools*
Placing the objects to the shown spots required concentration on each input. Referring the insight of one parent, the mindful nature of the game can be very positive on a child's behavior. Additionally, our game requires different actions in each step: 1) placing all the objects, 2) assessing the consequent projected ratio and 3) gesturing at the answer. None of the interaction methods were a repetition of its prior, yet each step was connected. In that sense, we observed how the system made the children focus on each action in order to play. In mixed reality environments maintaining such focus on the taught concept is crucial [19]. If multi-modal interactions are indeed the cause of the mindful behavior, this finding could have a significant impact on the comprehension of taught concepts. We intend to test this assumption by using control conditions that

have one type of interactions, such as gesture only or tangible only trainings.

*Further guidance is needed after incorrect answers*
During the study, our narrative and audial feedback was understood by the children. Yet, on two occasions, the auditory negative feedback ("Please reconsider your answer.") was not enough to provide a reflection on their answers. Upon the gesturing at the incorrect answer, one child kept on pointing to the same side, whereas another child immediately pointed to the other side without thinking. Designers might include visual effects on the tangibles or on the narrative character to increase this understanding.

## Conclusion & Future Work

MR interfaces with tangibles is an unexplored area, however, they offer a great potential for embodied learning. This work-in progress paper presents our observations on children's interactions with a tangible based MR game to guide our further design processes towards developing nonsymbolic math trainings. In this preliminary user study, we explored and discuss initial clues towards its usage, and it might be the first preliminary study in this field. In brief, our initial clues are (1) *Unrestricted MR setup might encourage children's exploratory behavior, and developers of MR educational tools could amplify these interactions via different tangible forms and gestural inputs* (2) *Projection might support the engagement of children with its flexibility to create alterations on the educational materials,* (3) *Fostering multi-modal interactions might provoke a mindful way of interacting with educational tools,* and (4) *Further guidance should supplement auditory feedback to provide reflection on incorrect answers.*

These new initial clues demand further consideration and deeper research, both in terms of psychology and interaction design disciplines. We plan on having longitudinal trainings with more children and control groups to deduce our system's contribution for nonsymbolic math. From the developmental studies perspective, if our training will be measured as effective, we think it will be a significant finding for nonsymbolic pre-K math education.

As for the interaction design outlook, if our new interaction-based clues are confirmed in further studies, it would be an important step towards establishing design frameworks for MR-projection based education systems. We intend to integrate further design frameworks, guided by our observations, to develop our study. Also, the blend between space, objects and virtual projections have the potential to trigger design explorations, and children's interaction with these systems may inspire the interaction design field. For future work, adding these design perspectives could have a positive impact on our system.

## Acknowledgements

H.Urey and E.Salman acknowledge the support from European Research Council (ERC) under the European Union's Seventh Framework Program(FP7/2007 2013) / ERC advanced grant agreement (340200) and ERC Proof-of-Concept Grant No. 755154.

## References


[1] Martha W. Alibali and Mitchell J. Nathan. 2012. Embodiment in Mathematics Teaching and Learning: Evidence From Learners' and Teachers' Gestures. *Journal of the Learning Sciences* 21, 2: 247–286.

[2] Wafa Almukadi and A. Lucas Stephane. 2015. BlackBlocks : Tangible Interactive System for Children to Learn 3-Letter Words and Basic Math. *Proceedings of the 2015 International Conference on Interactive Tabletops & Surfaces*.

[3] A. Antle. 2007. Tangibles: Five Properties to Consider for Children. *Workshop on Tangibles, Conference on Human Factors in Computing Systems*.

[4] Jacky Au, Susanne M. Jaeggi, and Martin Buschkuehl. 2018. Effects of non-symbolic arithmetic training on symbolic arithmetic and the approximate number system. *Acta Psychologica* 185, April 2017: 1–12.

[5] Lawrence W. Barsalou. 2008. Grounded Cognition. *Annual Review of Psychology*.

[6] Kira J. Carbonneau, Scott C. Marley, and James P. Selig. 2013. A meta-analysis of the efficacy of teaching mathematics with concrete manipulatives. *Journal of Educational Psychology* 105, 2: 380–400.

[7] Peter Dalsgaard and Kim Halskov. 2014. Tangible 3D tabletops. *Interactions* 21, 1072–5520: 42–47.

[8] Laurie D. Edwards. 2009. Gestures and conceptual integration in mathematical talk. *Educational Studies in Mathematics* 70, 2: 127–141.

[9] Taciana Pontual Falcão, Christine Ulrich, Andre Klemke, and Madeleine Schüler. 2018. Tangible Tens : Evaluating a Training of Basic Numerical Competencies with an Interactive Tabletop. *Proceedings of the SIGCHI Conference on Human Factors in Computing Systems - CHI'18*: 1–12.

[10] K. Gerardi, L. Goette, and S. Meier. 2013. Numerical ability predicts mortgage default. *Proceedings of the National Academy of Sciences*.

[11] Wim Gevers, Roi Cohen Kadosh, and Titia Gebuis. 2016. *Sensory Integration Theory: An Alternative to the Approximate Number System*. Elsevier Inc.

[12] Justin Halberda, Michèle M.M. Mazzocco, and Lisa Feigenson. 2008. Individual differences in non-verbal number acuity correlate with maths achievement. *Nature* 455, 7213: 665–668.

[13] James Hollan, Edwin Hutchins, and David Kirsh. 2000. Distributed cognition: toward a new foundation for human-computer interaction research. *ACM Transactions on Computer-Human Interaction*.

[14] Mark Johnson. 2012. The meaning of the body. In *Developmental Perspectives on Embodiment and Consciousness*. .

[15] Nancy C. Jordan, David Kaplan, Chaitanya Ramineni, and Maria N. Locuniak. 2009. Early Math Matters: Kindergarten Number Competence and Later Mathematics Outcomes. *Developmental Psychology*.

[16] Jennifer A. Kaminski, Vladimir M. Sloutsky, and Andrew Heckler. 2009. Transfer of mathematical knowledge: The portability of generic instantiations. *Child Development Perspectives*.

[17] Mina Khan, Fernando Trujano, Ashris Choudhury, and Pattie Maes. 2018. Mathland : Playful Mathematical Learning in Mixed Reality Object controller. 1–4.

[18] Nicole M. McNeil, David H. Uttal, Linda Jarvin, and Robert J. Sternberg. 2009. Should you show me the money? Concrete objects both hurt and help performance on mathematics problems. *Learning and Instruction*.

[19] Edward F. Melcer and Katherine Isbister. 2016. Bridging the Physical Divide: A Design Framework for Embodied Learning Games and Simulations.

*Proceedings of the 2016 CHI Conference Extended Abstracts on Human Factors in Computing Systems - CHI EA '16*, ACM Press, 2225–2233.

[20] Nora S. Newcombe, Susan C. Levine, and Kelly S. Mix. 2015. Thinking about quantity: The intertwined development of spatial and numerical cognition. *Wiley Interdisciplinary Reviews: Cognitive Science* 6, 6: 491–505.

[21] Joonkoo Park, Vanessa Bermudez, Rachel C. Roberts, and Elizabeth M. Brannon. 2016. Non-symbolic approximate arithmetic training improves math performance in preschoolers. *Journal of Experimental Child Psychology* 152: 278–293.

[22] S. Price, Y. Rogers, M. Scaife, D. Stanton, and H. Neale. 2003. Using "tangibles" to promote novel forms of playful learning. *Interacting with Computers* 15, 2 SPEC.: 169–185.

[23] Iulian Radu, Betsy McCarthy, and Yvonne Kao. 2016. Discovering educational augmented reality math applications by prototyping with elementary-school teachers. *Proceedings - IEEE Virtual Reality*.

[24] Emily Szkudlarek and Elizabeth M. Brannon. 2018. Approximate arithmetic training improves informal math performance in low achieving preschoolers. *Frontiers in Psychology* 9, MAY: 1–12.

[25] Lisa Tolentino, David Birchfield, Colleen Megowan-Romanowicz, Mina C. Johnson-Glenberg, Aisling Kelliher, and Christopher Martinez. 2009. Teaching and learning in the mixed-reality science classroom. *Journal of Science Education and Technology*.

[26] Linda de Valk, Tilde Bekker, and Berry Eggen. 2015. Designing for social interaction in open-ended play environments. *International Journal of Design* 9, 1: 107–120.

[27] Andrew D. Wilson. 2010. Using a depth camera as a touch sensor. *ACM International Conference on Interactive Tabletops and Surfaces - ITS '10*.

[28] Lesley Xie, Alissa N. Antle, and Nima Motamedi. 2008. Are tangibles more fun? *Proceedings of the 2nd international conference on Tangible and embedded interaction - TEI '08*, 191.

[29] Pmdtec.com. (2018). 3D Software Suite Royale and SDK. [online] Available at: https://pmdtec.com/picofamily/software/ [Accessed 12 Nov. 2018].

# SWISH: Shifting Weight-based Interfaces for Simulated Hydrodynamics in Mixed-Reality Fluid Vessels

**Shahabedin Sagheb**
School of Arts, Media, and Engineering
Arizona State University
Tempe, AZ 85281, USA
ssagheb@asu.edu

**Alireza Bahremand**
Ira A. Fulton School of Engineering
Arizona State University
Tempe, AZ 85281, USA
abahrema@asu.edu

**Robert LiKamWa**
School of Arts, Media, and Engineering
School of Electrical, Computer and Energy Engineering
Arizona State University
Tempe, AZ 85281, USA
likamwa@asu.edu

**Byron Lahey**
School of Arts, Media, and Engineering
Arizona State University
Tempe, AZ 85281, USA
byron.lahey@asu.edu


*TEI '19*, March 17–20, 2019, Tempe, AZ, USA
ACM 978-1-4503-6196-5/19/03.
https://doi.org/10.1145/3294109.3300988

## Abstract
Mixed-reality haptic devices introduce a gateway to otherwise intangible virtual content, creating a life-like immersive experience. Congruent haptic sensation requires faithful integration of visual stimuli and perceived tactile sensation. Unfortunately, current commercial mixed-reality systems are unable to reproduce the physical sensation of fluid vessels, due to the shifting nature of fluid motion. To this end, we introduce SWISH, a novel type of ungrounded mixed-reality system, capable of affording the users a realistic haptic sensation of fluid behavior. We also present solutions to prominent challenges of rendering haptic fluid behavior, especially in coordinate translation and virtual adaptation to physical limitation. Our virtual-to-physical coupling uses Nvidia Flex's Unreal Engine integration, wirelessly controlling a motorized mechanical actuation system housed in a plastic "vessel". In this paper we discuss the current state of SWISH and present results from our preliminary user study, followed by a description of our future planned phases.

## Author Keywords
Ungrounded haptic feedback system; Input devices; perception.

## Introduction
Mixed-reality systems hybridize virtual and physical environments and objects to create embodied interactions with

**Figure 1:** SWISH, a novel haptic feedback device capable of simulating fluid behavior in Mixed-Reality. (Top) simulated virtual fluid, (Bottom) graphical representation of the position of mechanical actuated system.

programmable media. We envision transformative opportunities for *fluid-based* mixed-reality experiences, where users will handle physical 3D-printed vessels filled with augmented virtual fluid. Such mixed-reality fluid systems could enable a variety of use cases, including: workforce training simulations; experimentation modules for physics, chemistry, and biology labs; or fluid transfer interaction for a sophisticated user interface. However, while commercial and academic research works have enabled rich visual integration of digital and physical objects, tangible integration has largely been focused on simulating interactions with *rigid* objects (e.g.,[7, 18, 5, 36, 11, 2, 13, 32, 21, 16, 24, 17, 33, 4]). We argue that *fluid-based* haptic devices for mixed-reality can enrich user experience and provide broader affordances.

In this paper, we discuss the design of SWISH mechanisms, with attention to two primary challenges of: (*i*) actuating Center-of-Gravity (CoG) shifts through a motorized apparatus, and (*ii*) coupling virtual simulation with physical actuation. We also discuss our results from evaluating the effectiveness of our current design of SWISH mechanisms through a user study on 10 participants. In this preliminary evaluation, SWISH ranked higher than using solid vessels in tilting and swaying tasks. Although motor vibrations and noises were not damped in our study, participants reported realistic haptic sensations of fluid behavior while using the system.

## Related Work

*Mixed-Reality for Workforce Training and Education*

Over the past two decades, different groups have been positioning mobile augmented reality as a gamechanger for education and workforce training. As early as 1997, Azuma presented discussion on educational applications, designs, and problems for AR researchers [3]. From there, others explored pedagogical solutions, presenting collaborative AR systems for improving spatial abilities [14] and laboratory training [1]. Surveys have covered applications of AR technology on industrial assembly and maintenance [9, 27] and education [29, 31], including with focus on interdisciplinary collaboration on software and hardware for realistic solutions [15]. Though focused solely on the digital realm of virtuality for augmentation, these works motivate our proposed system design for workforce training, which introduce the physicality of handling fluids in the augmented simulations.

*Fluid dynamics for virtual simulations*

Over the past several decades, researchers have devised elegant solutions for simulating fluids in virtual environments. Computational fluid dynamics generally involves the Navier-Stokes equation, which describes the physics of fluids in motion in response to the different forces acting on it via its surrounding medium [8]. Eulerian grid-based solutions to the Navier-Stokes equation were extended to simulate stable models of complex fluid-like motion [22], leading to generalized models for simulating liquids. Lagrangian-based techniques were popularized in smooth particle hydrodynamics for modeling deformable solids and are now extensively used for simulating fluids containing millions of particles [12]. Improvements sought interactive frame rates, using Z-indexing to accelerate neighborhood search [10] and multi-GPU implementations [20, 34]. Today's engines perform realistic simulation of computational fluids through GPU accelerated frameworks, such as Nvidia's Flex [1]. We plan to use the Flex simulation framework to drive the haptic actuation of the vessels.

*Haptics for physical feedback*

Current haptic systems present sensations related to mass, force, and texture of virtual objects. Gravity Grabber presents

[1] https://developer.nvidia.com/flex

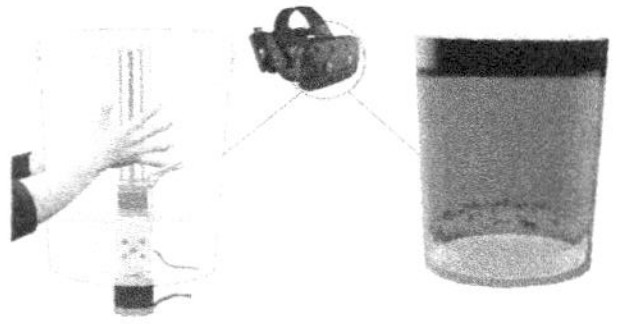

(a)

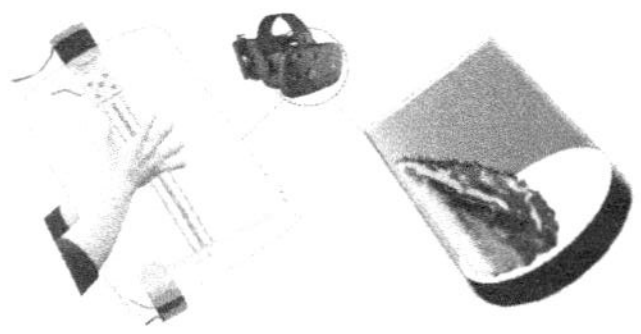

(b)

**Figure 2:** Location of mechanical modules at two states, (a) CoG at the minimum position, coordinates of this location are $r$=0, $\phi$=0, $h$=90 mm. (b) CoG at the maximum position, coordinates of this location are $r$=24mm, $\phi$=0, $h$=167 mm

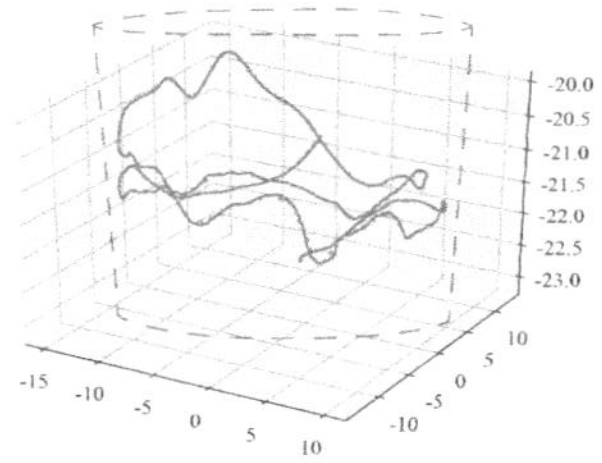

**Figure 3:** The discretized cylindrical motor path (red dotted) follows the simulated fluid path (green solid).

perception of mass via deformation on fingerpads [17], while FinGAR delivers glove-based electrical and mechanical stimulation for tactile feedback [30]. TorqueBAR [23] and Shifty [33] alter the internal weight distribution to alter user perception of their virtual objects. Others have proposed haptic feedback mechanisms that use mechanical torque cues [26, 28], texture simulation [4] and force [5, 36]. Open systems addressing the change in weight and volume of an object have been proposed [19]. Closely related to our work, tethered devices have been extended to present the nuances of fluid dynamics [35, 6, 25]. Our paper will extend these solutions, addressing challenges towards ungrounded perception of fluid movement in vessels.

## SWISH Overview

SWISH is a set of mechanisms that physically represent the CoG of a virtual vessel of fluid. The virtual fluid can be simulated and visually rendered through head-mounted display (HMD) devices, while the physical SWISH vessel will house mechanical motors to dynamically actuate feelings of shifting fluid (Figure 2).

In the next two sections, we describe our designs and implementations to: (*i*) create mechanical actuation of fluid movement and (*ii*) couple the virtual fluid simulation to the physical actuation.

## Mechanical Actuation of Fluid Movement

The goal of SWISH is to provide users with a feeling that mass in the bucket has shifted, appropriate to virtual fluid movement. While in motion, fluid particles change their position while moving, which results in a shift in the position of the CoG. The shape of the vessel, the motion of the vessel, and a fluid's viscosity all contribute to the pattern that the CoG of a fluid follows within the vessel.

*Achieving fluid CoG patterns through cylindrical coordinates*
The discrete nature of fluid particles permits a wide variety of positions in space within the limits of physical constraints of a vessel. However, the average sum of all these positions collapses to a manageable CoG point with finite range. Accurate physical simulation of this pattern with controllable rigid objects requires a multi-body system capable of moving its individual parts to distribute the overall mass to achieve this same CoG. The achievable CoG range possible for such a system depends on the ratio and range of the masses of the modules. As shown in Figure 3, a cylindrical discretization can closely follow the curves of the fluid CoG patterns, reducing path error and creating a smoother feeling for the user. Specifying the cylindrical position of CoG of the mechanical actuated system requires movement in three coordinates: radial distance ($r$), azimuth ($\phi$) and height ($h$).

*Motorized relocation of center-of-gravity*
Achieving a symmetric set of mechanisms requires designing two types of linear actuation mounted on motors, radial distance and height. We use a rack and pinion system for the former and a lead screw and nut mechanism for the latter. Attaching these two modules directly to a rotating motor enables the system to achieve the azimuth ($\phi$) of the movement.

*Implementation of mechanical actuation*
We implement the radial shifting mechanism using two NEMA 17 ($1.8°$ per step, torque = $3.2\ \mathrm{kg} \cdot \mathrm{cm}$) stepper motors. This provides accurate continuous rotation for our vessel system.

The two motors are equally spaced along the vertical axis to maintain the balance at zero state and move concurrently along the rack with a spur gear. The total length of the rack is $168\ \mathrm{mm}$. The radial shifting mechanism is connected

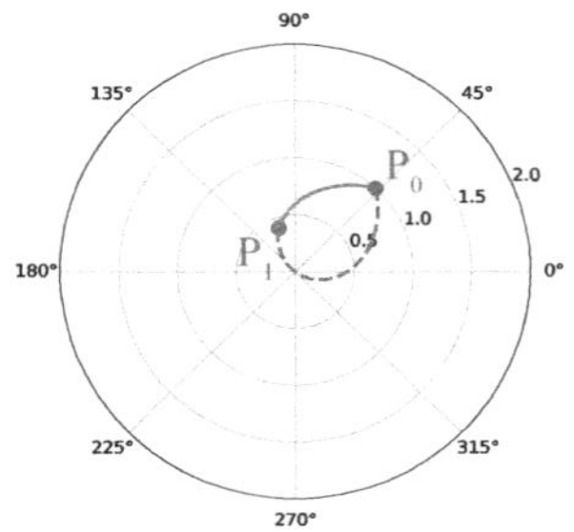


$P_1^A(r = 0.4, \phi = 110°)$

$P_1^B(r = -0.4, \phi = 290°)$

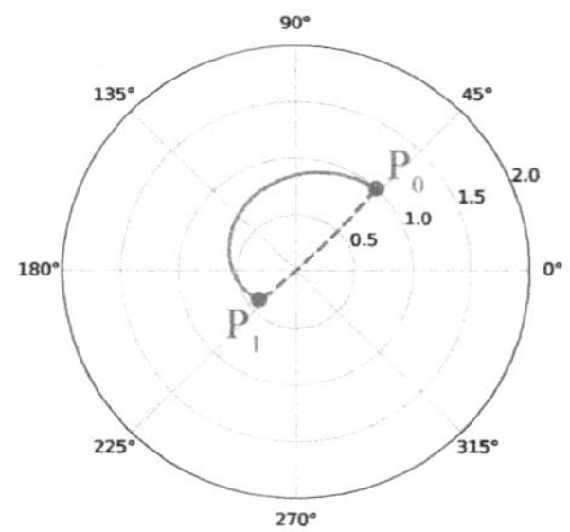


$P_1^A(r = 0.4, \phi = 220°)$

$P_1^B(r = -0.4, \phi = 40°)$

**Figure 4:** There are two equivalent $(r,\phi)$ representations for anticipated target position(s). Based on the start position ($P_0$) and end position ($P_1$), one path may require less motor movement than the other.

with a nut to the lead screw of the height stepper motor. A 3D printed column secures this assembly to the mounting plate of a NEMA 17 hybrid stepper motor. A lead screw attached to the hybrid stepper motor enables the radial shifting mechanism to move vertically.

The radial and height assembly are connected directly to a NEMA 23 ($1.8°$ per step, torque $= 12.2$ kg $\cdot$ cm) stepper motor using a 3D printed flange coupling secured at the bottom of the height motor. This stepper mounts directly to the bottom of the bucket and rotates the entire actuated assembly. All motors are connected to a 24V power supply. Radial and height motor wires are connected to a slip ring to prevent any twist that might cause disconnect.

An Arduino Mega 2560 micro-controller receives signals from Unreal Engine via a Bluetooth modem [2] and sends step/direction signals to motor controllers [3]. Concurrent movements of all motors is calculated using AccelStepper library's MultiStepper class [4]. All motors operate at full step mode for increased torque.

With the reference point located at the center of the bottom of the bucket, the achievable range of CoG of our SWISH mechanism is approximately 24 mm radially and approximately 167 mm vertically. The entire mechanical system is enclosed inside a 5 gal opaque bucket. An HTC Vive controller is directly attached to the bucket for virtual tracking. The total weight of SWISH mechanism including the bucket is approximately 3700 g.

[2]https://www.sparkfun.com/products/12582
[3]http://www.schmalzhaus.com/EasyDriver/
[4]http://www.airspayce.com/mikem/arduino/AccelStepper/

## Coupling virtual fluid simulation with physical actuation

We design the SWISH virtual environment to provide appropriate motor commands, built from accurate fluid simulation computations. We use efficient movement decision-making to prioritize attainability and responsiveness.

*Calculating efficient movement*

SWISH makes decisions to prioritize smooth, efficient, movement between motor positions. Because of the cylindrical coordinate system, each CoG position has two equivalent motor positions: $(r, \phi)$, and $(-r, \phi + 180)$. Between frames, it may be favorable to change the direction towards one position over the other, as depicted in Figure 4. Thus, to minimize motor movement against physical constraints, SWISH makes a decision by comparing the number of radial motor steps and azimuthal motor steps required to achieve either position. SWISH prioritizes whichever position pair requires fewer steps.

*Implementation*

Our implementation of SWISH, illustrated in Figure 5, uses NVIDIA Flex for fluid particle simulation and Unreal Engine 4 [5] for virtual scene composition and rendering. We attach an HTC Vive VR controller to the physical bucket for augmented tracking of bucket position and rotation, receiving the virtual coordinates in the Unreal Engine scene. Together, this achieves an augmented tracking and fluid simulation performance of 60 frames per second. SWISH computes the motor positions using the aforementioned virtual-to-physical coordinate translation and transmits the motor commands over Bluetooth to Arduino which executes the motor commands. As the range of values never exceeds 16 bits, the motor commands can be simply sent as three 16-bit integers, resulting in a negligible network

[5]https://www.unrealengine.com/en-US/what-is-unreal-engine-4

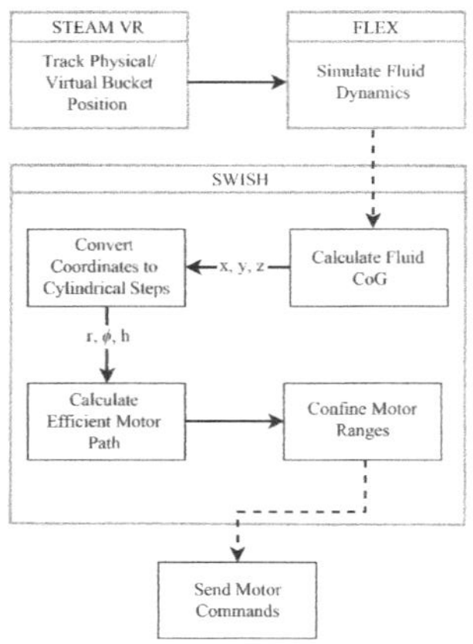


**Figure 5:** SWISH takes motion-tracked location data and converts it into motor stepper commands. The system works across Steam VR and Flex fluid frameworks, using our SWISH software framework to send commands to the augmented vessel over bluetooth.

overhead of less than 10 ms. Altogether, our Flex/Unreal-based implementation of SWISH provides virtual fluid simulation attuned to the physical vessel and responsive motor commands for coupled virtual-physical simulation.

## Preliminary User Study Evaluation

The main research goal of this preliminary study is to evaluate the effectiveness of SWISH in informing the experiences of the users in augmented fluid situations.

*Study Design*

Participants were invited individually to interact with five buckets of the same size, shape, and appearance. The only difference between the buckets was the kind of matter contained inside them.

The first bucket was an empty bucket. The second bucket contained a fixed solid mass. The next two buckets contained liquid; the third bucket held water and the fourth bucket held liquid soap. The liquid soap closely matched the viscosity of the virtual liquid in the Unreal/Flex simulation. The fifth bucket was augmented with SWISH motor mechanisms. All of the buckets were opaque and users were not able to see what was inside them. However, we did not make any effort to conceal the sounds and vibrations of the fluids or mechanical systems.

*Participants*

We recruited 10 participants (5 female) with a mean age of 27.5 years. There were no background preferences for the selection process. However, after the study, analyzing the demographic responses revealed that all participants had prior experience with virtual reality and 8 of them had used at least one type of VR controller with haptic feedback.

*Procedure*

After a consent form and a demographic questionnaire, we began the study. After each phase of each session we asked the participants to rate a bucket on a 5-point Likert scale, assessing the realism of the haptic feedback of each bucket compared to their expectation based on the virtual fluid, with 5 being the closest in realism and 1 not matching the qualities. We asked the participants to wear the head-mounted display and handed them each bucket in a pseudo-random order. The study took approximately 30 minutes. After the final phase, users responded to a questionnaire with open-ended prompts.

*Tasks*

In our preliminary testing we noticed that SWISH could provide reliable responsiveness for a variety of tasks, including tilting and swaying of the vessel. We constructed a user study around these actions to evaluate their effectiveness across a set of users.

First, participants were instructed to tilt the bucket all the way down, at a consistent pace. Each user interacted with a bucket for approx. 20 seconds. In the second phase, we asked the participants to sway each bucket in a consistent direction, i.e., back and forth or left and right.

## RESULTS

After the study the results from two of the participants were invalidated. Participant SW-004 did not follow the instructions properly and participant SW-009 was not comfortable interacting with SWISH as a result of vibrations and noise.

*Quantitative task-based measurement*

Mean values for each bucket are shown in Figure 6a, for the tilting task, 6 out of 8 participants preferred SWISH over empty and solid bucket. 3 out of 8 preferred SWISH over buckets containing water and liquid soap.

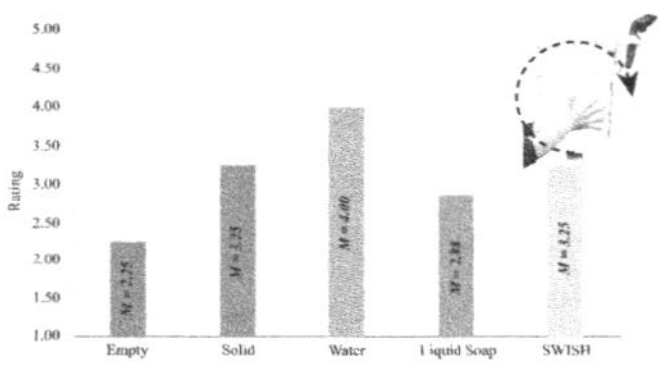


(a)

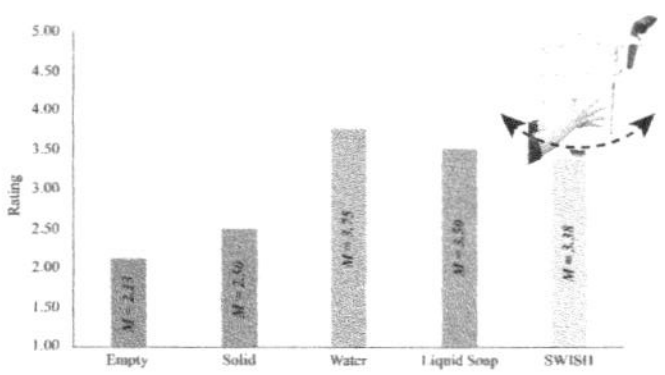


(b)

**Figure 6:** User study evaluation results, (a) Tilting task: SWISH performed better than empty, solid weight, and liquid soap buckets, (b) Swaying task: SWISH outperformed empty and solid weight.

Mean values for each bucket are shown in Figure 6b, for the swaying task, 6 out of 8 participants preferred SWISH over empty and solid bucket; 1 was neutral. Only 1 out of 8 participants preferred SWISH compared to water and liquid soap buckets; 3 were neutral.

*Observation and Discussion*
SWISH outperformed the empty bucket in both tasks, the liquid soap bucket in tilting task, and the solid bucket in swaying. It tied with the solid bucket in the tilting task. Analyzing the responses revealed that the vibrations and the noise of the mechanical actuation system hindered the immersion. These inconsistencies resulted in its lower ranking than real fluids. This motivates an investigation towards smoother and quieter motor operation.

## Limitations & Challenges

Overall, our preliminary SWISH implementation is able to provide favorable user experiences in simulating fluid motions. However, in our effort to design, implement, and evaluate SWISH, we have identified current limitations that we plan to work on for future phases. Users reported a lack of *responsiveness*, due to slow motor movement. Users laso noted that *vibration, heat, & noise* hindered the immersion, detracting from a realistic haptic sensation.

## Conclusion & Future Work

Ungrounded haptic devices capable of simulating fluid behaviors in virtual reality environments present a multitude of opportunities. In this paper we presented SWISH, a novel haptic feedback system that simulates the physical sensation of handling a fluid in virtual spaces. Motivated by the limitations of the current system and the opportunities for future development, in our next iterations of SWISH, we will focus on reducing the latency, noise, weight and vibration. We will also attend to increasing the responsiveness of the system by using DC motors instead of steppers. DC motors with Hall sensor coupling provide a comparable position accuracy and torque at higher speeds. Using geared DC motors also reduces the vibration, heat & noise of the system as a result of low working amperage.

This next phase of our implementation also reduces the overall size of the SWISH mechanism. We envision SWISH to be modular and scalable to a multitude of use cases. This would lead to augmented fluid vessels of many shapes and sizes: augmented beakers, graduated cylinders, bottles, etc., could form the foundation of virtual fluid-based laboratories. Thus, SWISH is the first step in paving the way for an exciting future of mixed-reality fluid interactions.

## References

[1] J. M. Andujar, A. Mejias, and M. A. Marquez. 2011. Augmented Reality for the Improvement of Remote Laboratories: An Augmented Remote Laboratory. *IEEE Transactions on Education* 54, 3 (Aug 2011), 492–500. DOI: http://dx.doi.org/10.1109/TE.2010.2085047

[2] Bruno Araujo, Ricardo Jota, Varun Perumal, Jia Xian Yao, Karan Singh, and Daniel Wigdor. 2016. Snake Charmer: Physically Enabling Virtual Objects. In *Proceedings of the TEI'16: Tenth International Conference on Tangible, Embedded, and Embodied Interaction.* ACM, 218–226.

[3] Ronald T. Azuma. 1997. A Survey of Augmented Reality. *Presence: Teleoper. Virtual Environ.* 6, 4 (Aug. 1997), 355–385. DOI: http://dx.doi.org/10.1162/pres.1997.6.4.355

[4] Hrvoje Benko, Christian Holz, Mike Sinclair, and Eyal Ofek. 2016. Normaltouch and texturetouch: High-fidelity 3d haptic shape rendering on handheld

virtual reality controllers. In *Proceedings of the 29th Annual Symposium on User Interface Software and Technology*. ACM, 717–728.

[5] Inrak Choi, Elliot W Hawkes, David L Christensen, Christopher J Ploch, and Sean Follmer. 2016. Wolverine: A wearable haptic interface for grasping in virtual reality. In *Intelligent Robots and Systems (IROS), 2016 IEEE/RSJ International Conference on.* IEEE, 986–993.

[6] Gabriel Cirio, Maud Marchal, Miguel A Otaduy, and Anatole Lécuyer. 2013. Six-oof haptic interaction with fluids, solids, and their transitions. In *World Haptics Conference (WHC), 2013*. IEEE, 157–162.

[7] Heather Culbertson, Julie M Walker, and Allison M Okamura. 2016. Modeling and design of asymmetric vibrations to induce ungrounded pulling sensation through asymmetric skin displacement. In *Haptics Symposium (HAPTICS), 2016 IEEE*. IEEE, 27–33.

[8] Nick Foster and Dimitri Metaxas. 1996. Realistic Animation of Liquids. *Graphical Models and Image Processing* 58, 5 (1996), 471 – 483. DOI: http://dx.doi.org/https://doi.org/10.1006/gmip.1996.0039

[9] Nirit Gavish, Teresa Gutiérrez, Sabine Webel, Jorge Rodríguez, Matteo Peveri, Uli Bockholt, and Franco Tecchia. 2015. Evaluating virtual reality and augmented reality training for industrial maintenance and assembly tasks. *Interactive Learning Environments* 23, 6 (2015), 778–798. DOI: http://dx.doi.org/10.1080/10494820.2013.815221

[10] Prashant Goswami, Philipp Schlegel, Barbara Solenthaler, and Renato Pajarola. 2010. Interactive SPH simulation and rendering on the GPU. In *Proceedings of the 2010 ACM SIGGRAPH/Eurographics Symposium on Computer Animation*. Eurographics Association, 55–64.

[11] Xiaochi Gu, Yifei Zhang, Weize Sun, Yuanzhe Bian, Dao Zhou, and Per Ola Kristensson. 2016. Dexmo: An inexpensive and lightweight mechanical exoskeleton for motion capture and force feedback in VR. In *Proceedings of the 2016 CHI Conference on Human Factors in Computing Systems.* ACM, 1991–1995.

[12] Takahiro Harada, Seiichi Koshizuka, and Yoichiro Kawaguchi. 2007. Smoothed particle hydrodynamics on GPUs. In *Computer Graphics International*, Vol. 40. SBC Petropolis, 63–70.

[13] Daniel Harley, Alexander Verni, Mackenzie Willis, Ashley Ng, Lucas Bozzo, and Ali Mazalek. 2018. Sensory VR: Smelling, Touching, and Eating Virtual Reality. In *Proceedings of the Twelfth International Conference on Tangible, Embedded, and Embodied Interaction*. ACM, 386–397.

[14] Hannes Kaufmann. 2003. Collaborative augmented reality in education. *Institute of Software Technology and Interactive Systems, Vienna University of Technology* (2003).

[15] Kangdon Lee. 2012. Augmented Reality in Education and Training. *TechTrends* 56, 2 (01 Mar 2012), 13–21. DOI: http://dx.doi.org/10.1007/s11528-012-0559-3

[16] Thomas H Massie, J Kenneth Salisbury, and others. 1994. The phantom haptic interface: A device for probing virtual objects. In *Proceedings of the ASME winter annual meeting, symposium on haptic interfaces for virtual environment and teleoperator systems*, Vol. 55. Citeseer, 295–300.

[17] Kouta Minamizawa, Souichiro Fukamachi, Hiroyuki Kajimoto, Naoki Kawakami, and Susumu Tachi. 2007. Gravity grabber: wearable haptic display to present virtual mass sensation. In *ACM SIGGRAPH 2007 emerging technologies*. ACM, 8.

[18] Anne M Murray, Roberta L Klatzky, and Pradeep K Khosla. 2003. Psychophysical characterization and testbed validation of a wearable vibrotactile glove for telemanipulation. *Presence: Teleoperators & Virtual Environments* 12, 2 (2003), 156–182.

[19] Ryuma Niiyama, Lining Yao, and Hiroshi Ishii. 2014. Weight and volume changing device with liquid metal transfer. In *Proceedings of the 8th International Conference on Tangible, Embedded and Embodied Interaction*. ACM, 49–52.

[20] Eugenio Rustico, Giuseppe Bilotta, Alexis Herault, Ciro Del Negro, and Giovanni Gallo. 2014. Advances in multi-GPU smoothed particle hydrodynamics simulations. *IEEE Transactions on Parallel and Distributed Systems* 25, 1 (2014), 43–52.

[21] Adalberto L Simeone, Eduardo Velloso, and Hans Gellersen. 2015. Substitutional reality: Using the physical environment to design virtual reality experiences. In *Proceedings of the 33rd Annual ACM Conference on Human Factors in Computing Systems*. ACM, 3307–3316.

[22] Jos Stam. 1999. Stable fluids. In *Proceedings of the 26th annual conference on Computer graphics and interactive techniques*. ACM Press/Addison-Wesley Publishing Co., 121–128.

[23] Colin Swindells, Alex Unden, and Tao Sang. 2003. TorqueBAR: an ungrounded haptic feedback device. In *Proceedings of the 5th international conference on Multimodal interfaces*. ACM, 52–59.

[24] Richard Q Van der Linde, Piet Lammertse, Erwin Frederiksen, and B Ruiter. 2002. The HapticMaster, a new high-performance haptic interface. In *Proc. Eurohaptics*. 1–5.

[25] Mauricio Vines, Javier Mora, and Won-Sook Lee. 2009. Haptic display of 3D liquids for interactive applications. In *Games Innovations Conference, 2009. ICE-GIC 2009. International IEEE Consumer Electronics Society's*. IEEE, 140–148.

[26] Julie Walker, Heather Culbertson, Michael Raitor, and Allison Okamura. 2017. Haptic orientation guidance using two parallel double-gimbal control moment gyroscopes. *IEEE transactions on haptics* (2017).

[27] Sabine Webel, Uli Bockholt, Timo Engelke, Nirit Gavish, Manuel Olbrich, and Carsten Preusche. 2013. An Augmented Reality Training Platform for Assembly and Maintenance Skills. *Robot. Auton. Syst.* 61, 4 (April 2013), 398–403. DOI: http://dx.doi.org/10.1016/j.robot.2012.09.013

[28] Kyle N Winfree, Joseph M Romano, Jamie Gewirtz, and Katherine J Kuchenbecker. 2010. Control of a high fidelity ungrounded torque feedback device: The iTorqU 2.1. In *Robotics and Automation (ICRA), 2010 IEEE International Conference on*. IEEE, 1347–1352.

[29] Hsin-Kai Wu, Silvia Wen-Yu Lee, Hsin-Yi Chang, and Jyh-Chong Liang. 2013. Current status, opportunities and challenges of augmented reality in education. *Computers & education* 62 (2013), 41–49.

[30] Vibol Yem, Ryuta Okazaki, and Hiroyuki Kajimoto. 2016. FinGAR: combination of electrical and mechanical stimulation for high-fidelity tactile presentation. In *ACM SIGGRAPH 2016 Emerging Technologies*. ACM, 7.

[31] Steve Chi-Yin Yuen, Gallayanee Yaoyuneyong, and Erik Johnson. 2011. Augmented reality: An overview and five directions for AR in education. *Journal of Educational Technology Development and Exchange (JETDE)* 4, 1 (2011), 11.

[32] André Zenner. 2016. Investigating weight distribution in virtual reality proxy interaction. *Universität des Saarlandes, Masterarbeit* (2016).

[33] Andre Zenner and Antonio Krüger. 2017. Shifty: A Weight-Shifting Dynamic Passive Haptic Proxy to Enhance Object Perception in Virtual Reality. *IEEE Transactions on Visualization and Computer Graphics* 23, 4 (2017), 1285–1294.

[34] Fengquan Zhang, Lei Hu, Jiawen Wu, and Xukun Shen. 2011. A SPH-based method for interactive fluids simulation on the multi-GPU. In *Proceedings of the 10th international conference on virtual reality continuum and its applications in industry*. ACM, 423–426.

[35] Jiachao Zhang, Shunpei Yuasa, Shinji Fukuma, and Shin-Ichiro Mori. 2016. A real-time GPU-based coupled fluid-structure simulation with haptic interaction. In *2016 IEEE/ACIS 15th International Conference on Computer and Information Science (ICIS)*. IEEE, 1–6.

[36] MA Zhou and Pinhas Ben-Tzvi. 2015. RML glove—An exoskeleton glove mechanism with haptics feedback. *IEEE/ASME Transactions on Mechatronics* 20, 2 (2015), 641–652.

# Expressive Tactile Controls

**Hayeon Hwang**
New York University, Interactive Telecommunications Program
New York, NY 10003 USA
hh1610@nyu.edu


ACM ISBN 978-1-4503-6196-5/19/03.
https://doi.org/10.1145/3294109.3300991

## Abstract
Push buttons, sliders, switches, and dials—we use such controls everyday and everywhere, but we barely notice them. Expressive Tactile Controls is a research experiment with a series of controls that are augmented by giving human personalities. What if each control had a unique personality and they could express their emotion only through haptic feedback? How could our interaction with controls be improved?

The research approached the question by constructing a series of button prototypes able to express themselves with varying tactile and kinesthetic feedback according to the interaction between the user and controls.

**Author Keywords:** Tangible Interfaces; Programmable Haptic Interaction; Physical Computing; Push Button

## CCS Concepts
• Human-centered computing~Interface design prototyping

## Introduction
In my working years at the interactive exhibit design, I had often considered whether to use physical/actual controls or graphic user interfaces(GUI) for the interactive installations. Working with a touch table project (cf. ReacTable[1]) for the museum exhibit, I often observed that a number of users tried to press

**Figure 1**: The programmable haptic dial prototype; dual-shaft mechanism with a rotary encoder and a slip ring. A circular soft potentiometer is sensing where touched. A vibrating disc motor and the motor driver imitates the clicking feel by programming.

**Figure 2**: Idea sketches of Stubborn, Lazy and Timid buttons

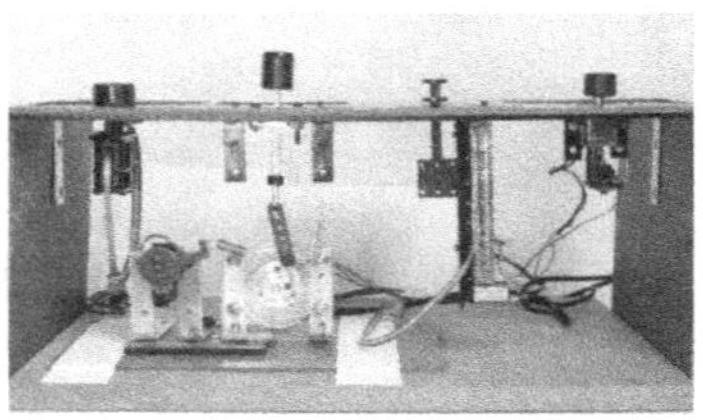

**Figure 3**: The early prototypes for the first user testing.

the GUI buttons multiple times more than necessary. I speculated that the reason could be the absence of haptic feedback.

The project initially set out to explore in Tangible Interaction class. [2] I prototyped a programmable haptic dial (Figure 1) to control the brightness and colors of DMX lights. It was inspired by fader controllers providing a tactile insert at the center index. [3] The goal of the project was to make a single dial to have programmable tactile indicators that imitate the mechanical feel of a tactile insert for each DMX light channel. After prototyping the dial, I planned to expand my haptic controls experiment into buttons, which are one of the most frequently used mechanical controls around us.

## Ideation & Design Process

To design creative tactile feedback, I drew expressive controls through human features, eyes and mouths. (Figure 2) The process of anthropomorphizing the buttons helped to imagine various haptic scenarios. [e.g. 11] For instance, 'Stubborn' can translate into haptic feedback to describe the button which is resistant to change their position using the counterforce. On the other hand, 'Impatient/Sensitive' button actuates much quickly to react to a small amount of force than regular buttons. The next challenge was to express the characters' features only through the tactile feedback. I built the prototypes for the scenarios rapidly for user testing. During user testing, I did not let users know what personalities the buttons meant to express, but asked them to guess instead. (Figure 3) Based on the users' feedback I refined the haptic effects to describe emotions in a way that most people would understand. Consequently, I focused to build the first prototypes to express Stubborn, Impatient, Lazy, Timid, and Excited.

## Prototypes

Tactile interactions are difficult to imagine without actual physical models. In order to feel enhanced-personality buttons, I built a series of buttons whose behavior designers can control programmatically. The buttons were controlled by an Arduino microcontroller and consisted of assorted actuators and sensors required to create to the characteristic behaviors.

Finding the appropriate components was a general technical challenge with two conditions. The first condition is that the buttons require a Closed Loop system [6] to measure the feedback signals from the position of the buttons. [8, 10] Later, the feedback signals will be used for analyzing haptic sensation. The second condition is that the components should not have distinct mechanical response such as clicking feel or stiffness. These inherent tactile feel will prevent the user from focusing on the haptic feel that the designer planned. For example, a particular rotary encoder which has detents with tactile feedback or a heavy-turning potentiometer were excluded for building these prototypes.

In terms of fabrication, the prototypes were made similar to each other in size, color, and materials in order to allow users to focus on haptic effects more. The FIS Tangible prototypes [4] was a big inspiration when comparing controls to each other.

### *1. Timid*

The Timid button goes down ahead when the user's fingertip comes closer to the top of the button. The top of the cap has a proximity sensor which detects the location of a fingertip at regular distance. The button quickly hides from any approaching touch using a linear actuator.

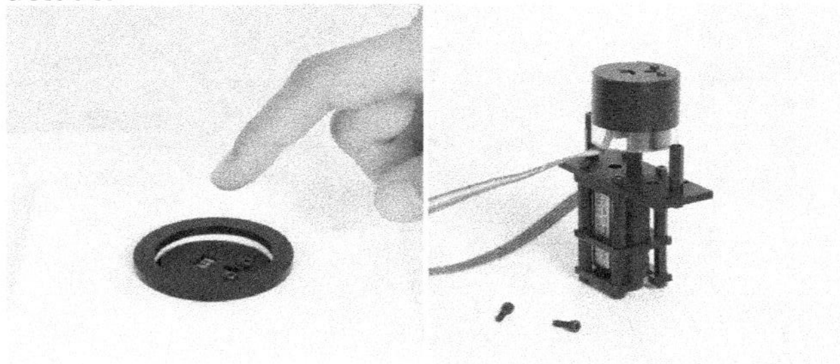

**Figure 4**: A Timid button

### 2. *Impatient*

The Impatient button is a highly sensitive button that actuates rapidly with only a small amount of force or touch. It is built with a motorized slide potentiometer which generally used for audio mixing and fabricated with a customized button knob.

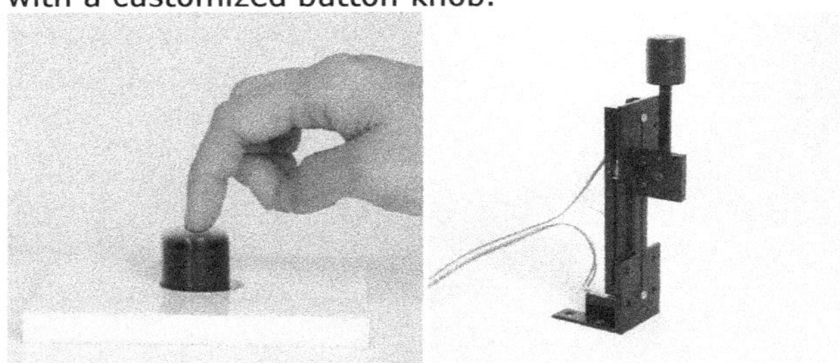

**Figure 5**: An Impatient button

### 3. *Lazy*

Once the Lazy button is triggered, the button operates much slower than a regular button to reach peak value and restore the default state. The button state is disabled until the position is back to default state. The Lazy button uses a servo motor and a slotted link mechanism.

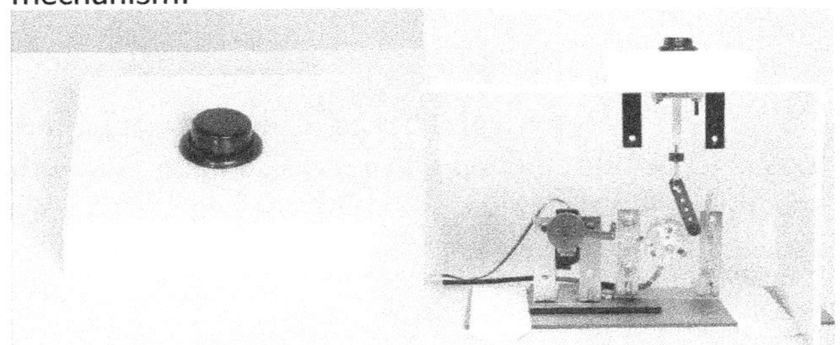

**Figure 6**: A Lazy button

### 4. *Stubborn*

The Stubborn button was designed to offer resistance to be pressed, by demanding a variable actuation force from the user. It was built using a slotted link mechanism (also known as Scotch Yoke mechanism [6]) using a servo motor that generates tension from an attached spring. While it operates, the rotary encoder detects the movements of the button position as a precise input knob.

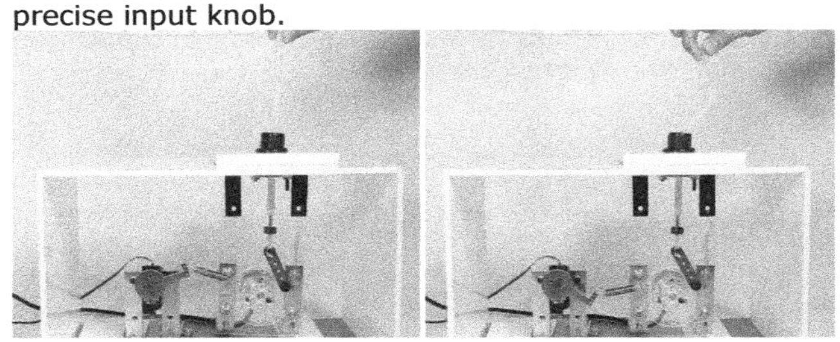

**Figure 7**: A Stubborn button

### 5. *Excited*

The Excited button has a cap which can pop up when a user pushes it. The button uses a Cherry™ switch [7] and a solenoid to trigger the pop. As a result, the cap dislocates the original position and the Excited button will not be able to be pressed anymore.

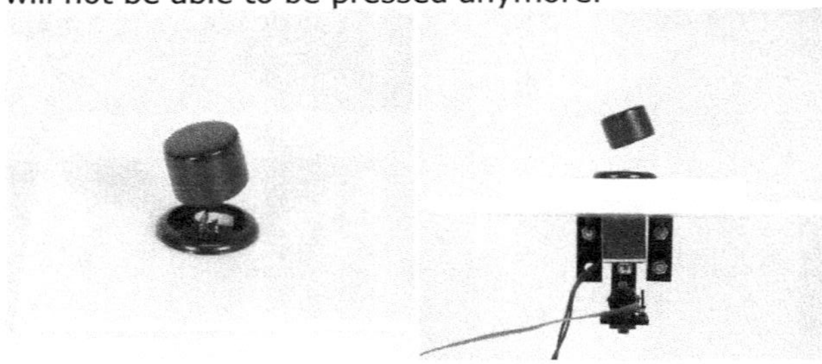

**Figure 8**: An Excited button

## Graphic User Interface

After building the physical prototypes, I developed a dashboard application to observe constant input and output values of haptic activity and to assign individual tactile effect conveniently. The software was written in JavaScript/HTML/CSS, p5.js[5] and Arduino.

**Figure 9**: A real-time dashboard and button prototypes

These line graphs (figure 10) visualize the position of each button. For example, the Timid button has lots of hesitance on the graph as the user's fingertip comes closer to the top of the button, and then it goes down deeper. Moreover, designers [9] can utilize the values from the program to operate variable applications such as lighting, musical instruments, or game controllers.

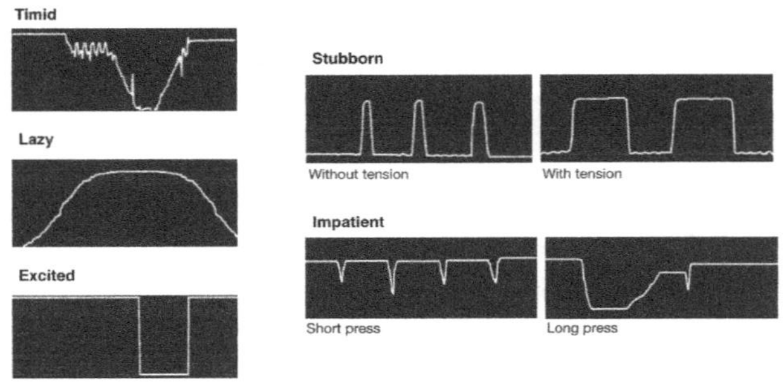


**Figure 10**: The different graphs from each personalized button. For example, the graphs in the stubborn button show two different patterns according to the tension levels.

## Implementation

The Expressive Tactile Controls can be used for a variety of contexts and applications. For the first experiment, I explored two example scenarios with lighting.

*Depth & Brightness*

Using the linear position feedback from the motorized slide potentiometer, the user can adjust the brightness how deep they pressed like a dimmer and also turn on and off like a regular switch (Figure 11).

**Figure 11**: The deeper the user presses the button, the brighter the light will be.

When pressed it quickly, the bulb turns on with a preset brightness setting. However, if the user needs a brighter setting, they push more to find the best light setting.

*Energy Consumption*
Using the Stubborn button (Figure 7), turning on multiple light bulbs will require stronger force than turning on a single light bulb. It will let the user feel how much they are using the energy when pressed it immediately.

## Conclusion and Future Work

This paper presents Expressive Tactile Controls, a set of programmable haptic controls that are augmented with individual personalities. The project aims to expand the capability of tangible interfaces and improve haptic interaction. I believe that haptic feedback elements in controls can facilitate an intuitive interaction design and enrich the user experience. The possible application areas include musical instrument and game design industry, and I look forward to opportunities to discuss with the professionals in relevant fields.

I am working towards to develop a sophisticated system that can collect a wide range of data from the user interaction such as speed and force feedback, which can be analyzed to research user behavior and ultimately, used in designing richer haptic interactions.

## Acknowledgment

I would like to special thank Tom Igoe for advice and guidance from the beginning of this research. I also thank Ben Light for advice about fabrication. Finally, I thank the Interactive Telecommunications Program at Tisch School of the Arts, New York University.

## References

[1] Sergi Jordà, Günter Geiger, Marcos Alonso, Martin Kaltenbrunner, The reacTable: Exploring the Synergy between Live Music. *In Proc. TEI 2007*, ACM Press (2007)

[2] Tom Igoe, *Tangible Interaction* course materials. Retrieved March, 2018 from https://itp.nyu.edu/classes/tangible-interaction/resources/class-notes/

[3] Masaaki Okabayashi and Masafumi Ito, Developer Interview: Fader Knobs Refined for Productivity and Motivation. Retrieved Nov 9, 2018 from http://www.yamahaproaudio.com/global/en/about/interview/knobs/

[4] Jörn Hurtienne, Diana Löffler, Patty Gadegast, and Steffi Hußlein: Comparing Pictorial and Tangible Notations of Force Image Schemas *In Proc. TEI 2015*, ACM Press (2015)

[5] Lauren McCarthy, p5.js Website. Retrieved Nov 9, 2018 from https://p5js.org/

[6] Neil Sclater and Nicholas P. Chironis. Mechanisms and Mechanical Devices Sourcebook Third Edition. McGraw-Hill Press, 1996.

[7] Cherry™ MX https://www.cherrymx.de/en

[8] Clement Zheng and Ellen Yi-Leun Do, Mechamagnets: Tactile Mechanisms with Embedded Magnets. *In Proc. TEI 2018*, ACM Press (2018)

[9] Dixon Lo, Dan Lockton, Stacie Rohrbach. Experiential Augmentation: Uncovering The Meaning of Qualitative Visualizations when Applied to Augmented Objects. *In Proc. CHI 2018*, ACM Press (2018)

[10] Zhai, Shumin. Human Performance in Six Degree of Freedom Input Control. University of Toronto Press, 1995

[11] Katrin Baumgarten, Disgusting Light switches https://cargocollective.com/katrinbaumgarten/disgusting-light-switches

# Natural and Intuitive Deformation Gestures for One-handed Landscape Mode Interaction

**Pranjal Protim Borah**
Embedded Interaction Lab,
Indian Institute of Technology
(IIT) Guwahati,
Guwahati, 781039, India
pranjalborah777@gmail.com

**Keyur Sorathia**
Embedded Interaction Lab,
Indian Institute of Technology
(IIT) Guwahati,
Guwahati, 781039, India
keyurbsorathia@gmail.com


*TEI '19, March 17–20, 2019, Tempe, AZ, USA*

ACM ISBN 978-1-4503-6196-5/19/03.
https://doi.org/10.1145/3294109.3300996

## Abstract
The landscape orientation of smartphone offers a better aspect ratio and extensive view for watching media and photography. However, it presents challenges of occlusion, reachability, and frequent re-gripping in one-handed interactions. To address these issues we took the opportunity of deformation gestures to interact with future flexible smartphones. A preliminary survey was conducted to understand one-handed landscape mode usage patterns. Then, the 1st study was conducted to identify 3 most preferred one-handed landscape mode grips. In the 2nd study, we gathered unique user-defined deformation gestures to identify the set of most natural and intuitive gestures corresponding to each grip. We also found 3 gestures that can be performed in more than one grip. Finally, we discuss the influence of the grips on performing gestures.

## Author Keywords
Flexible display device; deformation gesture; one-handed interaction; landscape mode interaction.

## CSS Concepts
**• Human-centered computing~Human computer interaction (HCI) • Human-centered**

(a)

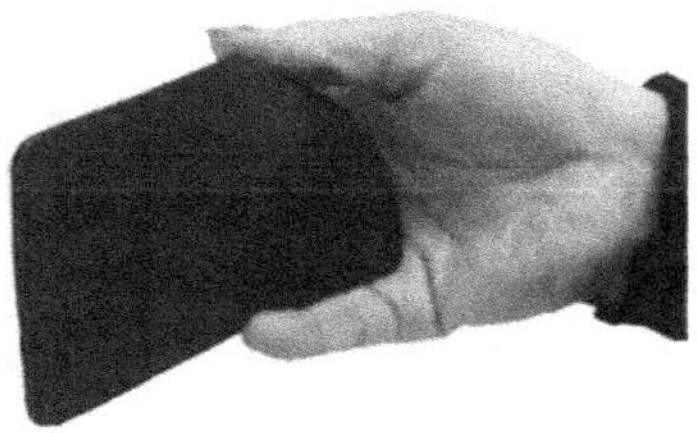

(b)

Figure 1: (a) One-handed landscape mode grip (b) deformation gesture (Top-right corner bend out) in one-handed landscape mode.

**computing~User studies • Human-centered computing~User centered design**

## Introduction

Spatial properties and arrangements of elements influence people's aesthetic responses to an image irrespective of portrait or landscape aspect ratio [3]. As an influence of predominant landscape orientation of Television (TV) screens and computer monitors and for extensive view with maximum screen real estate [9], this horizontal orientation (Figure 1a) is often used in smartphone context for watching videos [10, 9], recording videos [12], and capturing photographs [12]. However, it presents a variety of challenges, when interacted with one hand. These challenges include finger occlusion [6, 15], unreachable target areas [6, 11, 15] on large screen devices and the tendency of dropping the device due to frequent re-gripping [11, 5].

A few studies have been conducted for comfortable one-handed landscape mode video browsing [11, 18] and photo browsing [1]. However, these existing researches are specific to particular applications and do not provide a generic solution. Deformation gestures (Figure 1b) as an input method for flexible handheld devices present a potential alternative to address the challenges of one-handed landscape mode interaction. They have the potential to provide high resolution of input through eye-free interaction that is independent of Graphical User Interface (GUI) [17] and provides an optimal mean for quick continuous bipolar input [2]. Extensive studies on flexible handheld devices were conducted to identify bimanual deformation gestures [13, 14, 16] and to address issues of reachability and occlusion in one-handed portrait mode [6]. Audrey Girouard et al. had identified a set of deformation gestures that was easy to perform in a variety of hold scenarios in one-handed portrait mode [6]. However, to the best of our knowledge, no studies have investigated suitable deformation gestures for one-handed landscape mode usage. In this paper, we present a set of user-defined deformation gestures for 3 different user-preferred grips for one-handed usage in a landscape mode.

## Preliminary survey on one-handed use of landscape mode

The preliminary survey (by means of a questionnaire) was targeted to build an understanding of landscape mode usage, handedness of using a smartphone in one-handed landscape mode, and difficulties during one-handed interaction with the applications. 50 university students (34 male and 16 female) responded with a completed questionnaire, between the ages of 18-32 years (Mean = 21.7, SD = 3.4). 44 (88%) right-handed and 6 (12%) left-handed users participated in the survey. All the participants had more than 3 years of experience in using smartphones.

### *Findings of the survey*

Users prefer portrait orientation but often tend to adopt landscape orientation for better representation of the content of interest considering the adaptability of the application. 52% of the participants indicated their consent in often performing one-handed interaction in landscape mode. Rest is equally divided into seldom use (24%) and interacting with both hands (24%). Majority of the participants (84.2%), who often perform one-handed interaction preferred to use their right hand, 13.2% of the participants preferred to use their left hand and the rest (2.6%) had no preference.

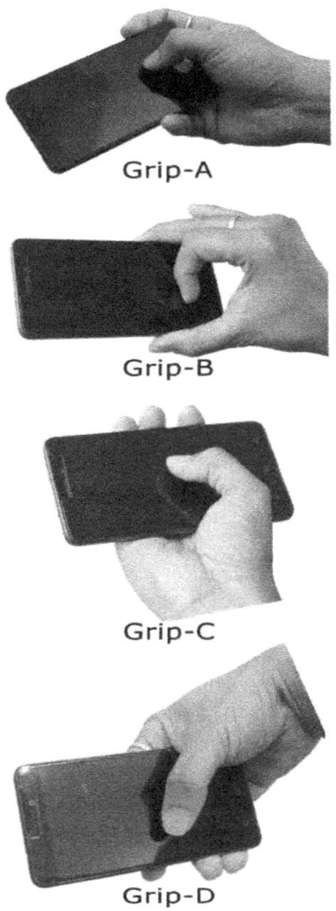


Figure 2: The most preferred right-handed landscape mode grips with at least one finger available for interaction.

The most preferred set of applications in landscape mode include video players, camera applications, games, and document viewers. We observed similar challenges presented in literature including unreachable touch target (81.6%), difficulties in re-gripping the device during interaction (78.9%), interacting finger occlusion (47.4%) and difficulty to perform multi-touch input gesture (34.2%). We also observed that one-handed landscape mode interaction is mostly preferred in stationary situations (sitting or standing). In addition, smartphones possessed by the participants include 5″ (40%), 5.5″ (46%), 6″ (8%), and other (6%) display sizes.

## Study on User-Preferred Grip

The goal of this study was to identify the set of most preferred one-handed grips for landscape mode interaction. This study focuses on the right-handed users due to the higher proportion of right-handed landscape mode users (84.2% in the preliminary survey) and the right-handedness in the global population [8].

*Task*

The task required participants to demonstrate two most preferred grips to hold a rigid smartphone with the right hand in the landscape mode. The grips required to be the most natural, comfortable and safe (reluctant to the tendency of dropping the device) grip with minimum finger occlusion.

*Participants*

33 university students (22 male and 11 female), between the ages of 18-30 (Mean = 22.5, SD = 3.2), participated in the study. All the participants were right-handed with more than 3 years of experience in using a smartphone. We made a verbal announcement in the classrooms to invite students to register their participation in the study. No remuneration was provided to the participants.

*Apparatus*

The study was conducted using a "Lenovo K6 Power" smartphone (5″ display size). The use of rigid smartphone instead of a deformable prototype was to avoid artificial grips [5] as users were not familiar with the use of flexible smartphones.

*Procedure*

We performed a controlled experiment where each session was video recorded with the participants' consent. After the participants read the description of the task, moderator verbally explained the same to the participants. To ensure the demonstrated grips to be natural and comfortable, participants were asked to imagine and pretend using preferred applications for which they had experienced the use of one-handed landscape mode interaction for an extended period of time (without dropping the device). They were also asked to speak up the names of the applications and to mimic similar inclination of the display for comfortable view without occlusion. No content was displayed on the screen to avoid any adverse effect of static content (sometimes even irrelevant) on users' imagination. The participants were asked to keep one finger free so that they can pretend to perform touch interaction on the screen without any tendency of dropping the device. This stands the safety of the grip and the notion that future flexible devices will also continue to support the traditional touch input method. Participants were asked not to rest their right hand on an object (table or chair) or any body part. This particular choice was made due

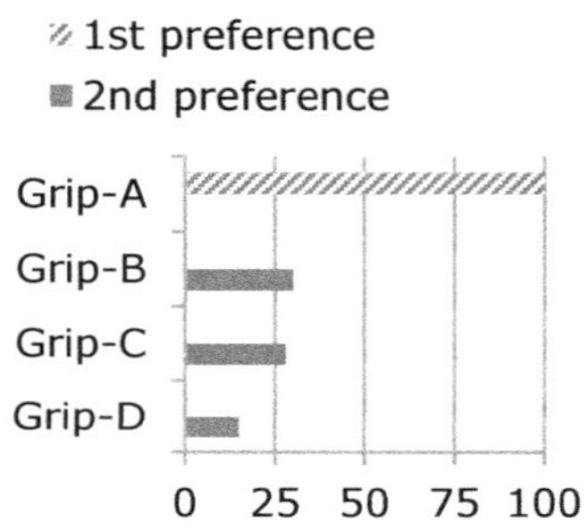


Figure 3: Percentage of users performing the grips.

to its potential applicability to both sitting and standing position. Finally, we noted the top two user preferences for further analysis. All participants completed the task within 6 minutes.

*Results*
A total of 57 grips were recorded. It includes 33 grips as the first preference and 24 grips as the second preference. As shown in Figure 2 and Table 1, four unique grips were identified based on the location of contact between the smartphone and the fingers and the purpose (support, balance, and interact) of the involved fingers. All the participants (100%) performed Grip-A as the first preferred grip while 30%, 28%, and 15% participants performed Grip-B, Grip-C, and Grip-D respectively as the second preferred grip (Figure 3). We selected the 3 most preferred grips for our next study.

| Grip | Support | Balance | Interact |
|---|---|---|---|
| A | Middle, Ring and Little finger | Index finger | Thumb |
| B | Thumb | Middle and/or Ring finger | Index finger |
| C | Index, Middle, Ring and Little finger | None | Thumb |
| D | Index, Middle, Ring and Little finger | Thumb (Occasionally) | Thumb |

**Table 1**: Purpose of the fingers involved in the grips

## Study on User-defined Deformation Gesture
This study was aimed to identify the set of most natural and intuitive deformation gestures with potential to address the challenges of one-handed landscape mode interaction.

*Task*
The participants were asked to propose most naturally recalled and intuitive deformation gestures for each grip A, B, and C.

*Participants*
30 university students (20 male, 10 female), between the ages of 18-32 (Mean = 22.4, SD = 3.6) participated in the study. All the participants were right-handed with no prior experience of using a flexible handheld device. We made a verbal announcement in the classrooms to invite students to register for their participation in the study. There were no common participants from the previous study. No remuneration was provided for their participation.

*Apparatus*
The study was conducted using a mockup prototype (Figure 1b) made of flexible PVC sheet (1.5mm thickness) sandwiched between two foam rubber sheets (3mm thickness). Deformability introduces challenges to the development of the mockup in terms of weight and flexibility ratio. The dimension (14.2cm x 7.2cm x 0.8 cm) of the prototype was selected to resemble the dimension of a state of art smartphone of display size 5″ (with bezel) and 5.5″ (thin bezel). However, the weight resemblance was not incorporated to retain the flexible property of the mockup. We were more concerned about the flexibility of the prototype than its weight for better agreement of the gestures [14].

*Procedure*
We conducted a controlled study where each session was video recorded with the consent of participants for further analysis. After the participants read the description of the task, the moderator demonstrated

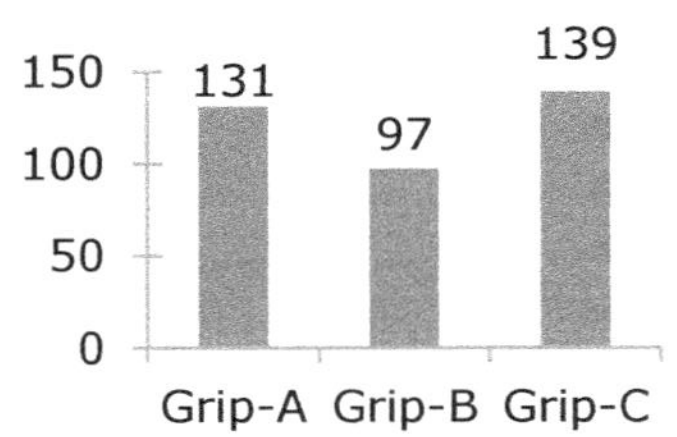


Figure 4: Total gestures proposed in each grip.

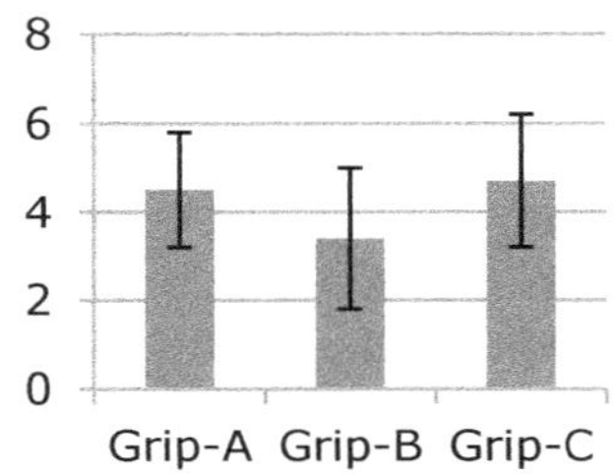


Figure 5: Mean of gestures proposed in each grip.

the selected grips and two-handed deformation gesture (folding the display vertically) using the mockup. We devoted a minimum of 10 minutes to each participant to experience the grips and interact with the mockup until they were ready to start the study. All participants completed the task within 20 minutes. To ensure intuitiveness (relatively effortless [4] with reduced cognitive load and deliberation [7]), participants were asked to propose referent independent gestures. In addition, the locations of deformation need to be easily reachable without switching the grip or compromising the safety of the grip. The participants were also asked to perform the gestures without resting the right hand on an object or any body part. There was no restriction on the number of gestures proposed by the participants. The sequence of the grips presented to the participants was randomized in order to equalize the effects of gestures proposed in the previous grip. We considered the most spontaneously derived [7] and possibly automatic [4] gesture to be the most intuitive gesture. Accordingly, intuitiveness scores (maximum 7 and minimum 0) were assigned to the gestures based on the order in which they were proposed. We defined naturalness of a gesture as the frequency [7] of participants proposing the same gesture.

*Results*

30 participants proposed a total of 367 gestures. All participants proposed 1 to 7 gestures for each grip except for one participant (p-13) who was unable to offer any gesture for Grip-B and another participant (p-27) proposed 8 gestures for Grip-C. Figure 4 and 5 shows the number of gestures proposed in each grip. Later, we identified respectively 18, 15, and 20 unique gestures proposed for Grip-A, Grip-B, and Grip-C. Unique deformation gestures were identified based on the location of initiating the deformation (*top, bottom, left, right, corner, side, diagonal*- along a diagonal line, *horizontal*- along the horizontal axis, and *vertical*- along the vertical axis), type of deformation (*bend, fold* - when touches the opposite surface, and *roll*) and direction of deformation (*in* – movement of edges/ corners towards the user and *out* – movement of edges/corners away from the user). This classification of deformation gestures based on location and type of deformation is similar to previous studies [6, 14, 16] except for the direction of deformation. While proposing the deformation gestures, most of the users referred the directions as in/out (sometimes inward/outward). This inspired us to use the words "in" and "out" (also used in [2]) to match users' mental model and to avoid confusion as reported in the literature [6]. Accordingly, the names of the deformation gestures also consist of location, type, and direction of deformation. For instance, in the gesture name "Top-right corner bend in", "top-right corner" is the location; "bend" is the type of deformation and "in" is the direction of deformation towards the user. We used the frequency and mean intuitiveness score of gestures to confirm the final set of most natural and intuitive user-defined deformation gestures. The final set contains gestures with higher frequency ($F \geq 15$) and mean intuitiveness score ($MI \geq 3$). Hence, the final catalogue of gestures contains respectively 4, 3, and 3 gestures for Grip-A, Grip-B, and Grip-C (Figure 6). Here "Horizontal bend in" (Grip-A, B and C), "Top-right corner bend in" (Grip-A and C) and "Horizontal fold in" (Grip-A and B) gestures were proposed for multiple grips.

We collected individual intuitiveness scores of the participants corresponding to the gestures in each grip. Since the collected data are not normally distributed,

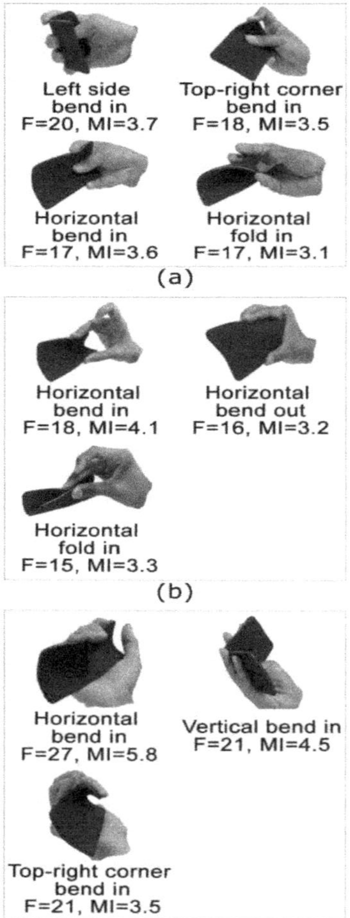


Figure 6: Final set of user-defined gestures in (a) Grip-A, (b) Grip-B, and (c) Grip-C (F represents frequency and MI represents mean intuitiveness score)

we applied non-parametric tests (Friedman Test and Wilcoxon Signed Ranks Test) to interpret the influence of grips on the intuitiveness of gesture location, type, and direction as shown in Table 2.

| Grip | Significantly ($p<.05$) intuitive | | | |
|---|---|---|---|---|
| | Location | | Type of deformation | Direction |
| | Corner | Side | | |
| A | Top-right | - | - | in |
| B | - | Left | - | - |
| C | Top-right | - | Bend | in |

**Table 2:** Intuitive location, type, and direction of deformation.

## Discussion

Both the user studies produced useful insight about how participants prefer to hold and interact with the right hand in landscape mode. Observing the recorded videos comprehensively, we noticed that participants were familiar with all the grips but switching between Grip-A and Grip-C seemed to be more effortless. We found "Horizontal bend in" gesture to be the most naturally occurring and intuitive gesture that can be performed in all the three grips. "Top-right corner bend in" and "Horizontal fold in" are relatively more natural and intuitive to perform in more than one grip. These gestures can be mapped to referents of equal priority in respective grips. In Grip-A and C (Table 2), location "Top-right corner" and direction "in" are more intuitive. Similar findings were also reported in portrait mode in [6]. In Grip-B, location "Left side" is more intuitive as right corners are primarily involved in gripping the device. In Grip-C, type of deformation "bend" is more intuitive as holding the mockup on the palm of the hand restricted the participants to perform fold gesture.

The range of distinct gestures proposed in each grip was influenced by the control over the grip during deformation. Control over the grip during interaction can be described by the number of fingers involved in support and balance (Table 1). Maximum control was observed in Grip-C followed by Grip-A and then Grip-B during deformation. This allowed users to propose maximum (20 unique gestures) gestures in Grip-C with comparatively richer naturalness and intuitiveness.

## Conclusion

In this paper, we present a set of user-defined deformation gestures for right-handed landscape mode interaction. We conducted the 1st study to identify 3 most preferred right-handed landscape mode grips. In the 2nd study, we gathered a set of user-defined deformation gestures corresponding to the 3 grips. Finally, we identified respectively 4, 3, and 3 unique deformation gestures for Grip-A, B and C based on their naturalness and intuitiveness scores. We also identified that "Horizontal bend in", "Top-right corner bend in" and "Horizontal fold in" gestures can be performed in more than one grip. We further discussed the effect of the grips on the intuitiveness of performing deformation gestures. We believe that this study will provide valuable implications and reference in the selection of deformation gestures for flexible handheld devices. As succeeding work, we are investigating on gesture-referent mappings for one-handed landscape mode interactions considering the impact of occlusion.

## References

[1] Sung-Jung Cho, Roderick Murray-Smith, Yeun-Bae Kim. 2007. Multi-context photo browsing on mobile devices based on tilt dynamics. In Proceedings of the 9th international conference on Human computer interaction with mobile devices

and services, 190-197. https://doi.org/10.1145/1377999.1378006

[2] Teemu T. Ahmaniemi, Johan Kildal, Merja Haveri. 2014. What is a device bend gesture really good for?. In Proceedings of the SIGCHI Conference on Human Factors in Computing Systems, 3503-3512. https://doi.org/10.1145/2556288.2557306

[3] Rudolf Arnheim. 1983. The power of the center: A study of composition in the visual arts. Univ of California Press.

[4] Nick Byrd. 2014. Intuitive and Reflective Responses in Philosophy.

[5] Matthew Ernst, Audrey Girouard. 2016. Bending blindly: exploring bend gestures for the blind. In Proceedings of the 2016 CHI Conference Extended Abstracts on Human Factors in Computing Systems, 2088-2096. https://doi.org/10.1145/2851581.2892303

[6] Audrey Girouard, Jessica Lo, Md Riyadh, Farshad Daliri, Alexander Keith Eady, Jerome Pasquero. 2015. One-handed bend interactions with deformable smartphones. In Proceedings of the 33rd annual ACM conference on human factors in computing systems, 1509-1518. https://doi.org/10.1145/2702123.2702513

[7] Sukeshini A. Grandhi, Gina Joue, Irene Mittelberg. 2011. Understanding naturalness and intuitiveness in gesture production: insights for touchless gestural interfaces. In Proceedings of the SIGCHI Conference on Human Factors in Computing Systems, 821-824. https://doi.org/10.1145/1978942.1979061

[8] Curtis Hardyck, Lewis F. Petrinovich. 1977. Left-handedness. Psychological Bulletin, 84(3), 385-404. http://dx.doi.org/10.1037/0033-2909.84.3.385

[9] Jochen Huber, Jürgen Steimle, Max Mühlhäuser. 2010. Toward more efficient user interfaces for mobile video browsing: an in-depth exploration of the design space. In Proceedings of the 18th ACM international conference on Multimedia, 341-350. https://doi.org/10.1145/1873951.1873999

[10] Marco A. Hudelist, Klaus Schoeffmann, Laszlo Boeszoermenyi. 2013. Mobile video browsing with the thumbbrowser. In Proceedings of the 21st ACM international conference on Multimedia, 405-406. https://doi.org/10.1145/2502081.2502242

[11] Wolfgang Hürst, Philipp Merkle. 2008. One-handed mobile video browsing. In Proceedings of the 1st international conference on Designing interactive user experiences for TV and video, 169-178. https://doi.org/10.1145/1453805.1453839

[12] Yuichiro Kota, Minoru Ikeda. 2006. Mobile phone and camera, U.S. Patent 7,003,318, Filed October 14, 2004, issued February 21, 2006.

[13] Byron Lahey, Audrey Girouard, Winslow Burleson, Roel Vertegaal. 2011. PaperPhone: understanding the use of bend gestures in mobile devices with flexible electronic paper displays. In Proceedings of the SIGCHI Conference on Human Factors in Computing Systems, 1303-1312. https://doi.org/10.1145/1978942.1979136

[14] Sang-Su Lee, Sohyun Kim, Bopil Jin, Eunji Choi, Boa Kim, Xu Jia, Daeeop Kim, Kun Pyo Lee. 2010. How users manipulate deformable displays as input devices. In Proceedings of the SIGCHI Conference on Human Factors in Computing Systems, 1647-1656. https://doi.org/10.1145/1753326.1753572

[15] Keyur Sorathia, Aditi Singh, Mayank Chhabra. 2017. BendSwipe: One Handed Target Zooming for Flexible Handheld Display. In IFIP Conference on Human-Computer Interaction, 431-435. https://doi.org/10.1007/978-3-319-68059-0_45

[16] Kristen Warren, Jessica Lo, Vaibhav Vadgama, Audrey Girouard. 2013. Bending the rules: bend gesture classification for flexible displays. In Proceedings of the SIGCHI Conference on Human

Factors in Computing Systems, 607-610. https://doi.org/10.1145/2470654.2470740

[17] Doug Wightman, Tim Ginn, Roel Vertegaal. 2011. Bendflip: examining input techniques for electronic book readers with flexible form factors. In IFIP Conference on Human-Computer Interaction, 117-133. https://doi.org/10.1007/978-3-642-23765-2_9

[18] Yue Wu, Tao Mei, Nenghai Yu, Shipeng Li. 2012. Accelerometer-based single-handed video browsing on mobile devices: design and user studies. In Proceedings of the 4th International Conference on Internet Multimedia Computing and Service, 157-160. https://doi.org/10.1145/2382336.2382381

# Exploring Craft in the Context of Digital Fabrication

**Rosa van der Veen**
RISE Interactive
Umeå, Sweden
rosa.v.d.veen@ri.se

**Jeroen Peeters**
RISE Interactive
Umeå, Sweden
jeroen.peeters@ri.se

**Olov Långström**
RISE Interactive
Umeå, Sweden
ronald.helgers@ri.se

**Ronald Helgers**
RISE Interactive
Umeå, Sweden
olov.langstrom@ri.se

**Nigel Papworth**
RISE Interactive
Umeå, Sweden
nigel.papworth@ri.se

**Ambra Trotto**
RISE Interactive & Umeå School of Architecture
Umeå, Sweden
ambra.trotto@ri.se



*TEI '19*, March 17–20, 2019, Tempe, AZ, USA

ACM ISBN 978-1-4503-6196-5/19/03.
https://doi.org/10.1145/3294109.3300989

## Abstract

In this work in progress, we start to unpack the act of making in a digital fabrication process. In particular, one kind of digital fabrication - 3D printing - that is typically considered to be highly automated but in this case is not. In this process, a tension exists between our skills, the properties of a novel material and the capabilities of a novel machine. As design researchers, we navigated through the design space that emerged in this tension and explored how to 3D print in wood. In unpacking this tension between machine, material and designer, we pay attention to how the embodied nature of this process was essential for its development. We start to explore how we might explain the embodied act of making in the context of digital fabrication through the lense of ambiguity and resistance, notions previously used to unravel craftsmanship.

## Author Keywords

Embodiment; Constructive Design Research; 3D printing; Additive Manufacturing; Digital Fabrication; Ambiguity; Resistance; Design Process; Craftsmanship

## ACM Classification Keywords

• Human-centered computing~Interaction design theory, concepts and paradigms

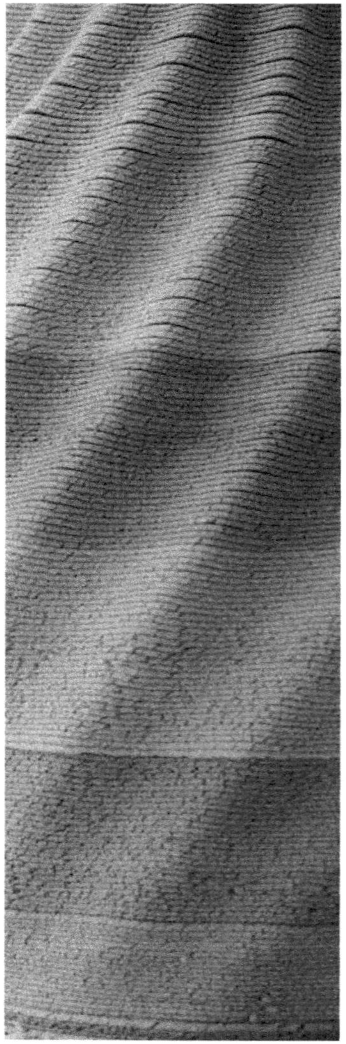

**Figure 1** – Close up of an object printed in wood-based material.

## Introduction

This work in progress builds on constructive design research methods [7] to articulate on what the act of *making* is in the context of digital fabrication methods. We build on theories of American Pragmatism [1], Ecological Psychology [5] and Phenomenology [8], all sharing the notion of embodiment, asserting that our understanding of the world, or sense making, emerges from acting in it [2]. For us, as design researchers, making and the act of designing is a way of sense making: creating new knowledge, insights and perspectives through iterations and reflections. However, it is difficult to unpack what exactly happens in the process of designing or making.

Ehn [3] builds on Schön's Reflective Practitioner [9] to describe what designer's do: to make decisions in dialogue with the design material in a way that is neither completely absorbed action nor completely detached theoretical reflection. In this work in progress, we report on intermediate results of an ongoing project, that will contribute to the growing understanding of what factors and forces are at play, and what happens, during when craftsmanship and digital fabrication methods meet [6].

We present our efforts of researching through design how to do something new: to 3D print in wood using an FDM (Fluid Deposition Modelling) technique. We focus on how the designers navigated the design space [4] that emerged in the tension between the possibilities and limitations of both material and machine, mediated by the intentions, skills and judgment of the designers.

The lens through which we articulate this are the notions of resistance and ambiguity as put forward by Sennett [10]. Sennett describes resistances as "facts that stand in the way of the will" [10]. Resistances present themselves in two forms: found and made. Found resistances are unexpected or unforeseen obstructions. For example, unexpected knots in a piece of timber. Made resistances are obstructions created by the maker herself. For example, when a craftsman starts over on a workpiece, unsatisfied with the shape it is taking. Ambiguity refers to engaging in an action that does not have a clear result. Often, to deal with resistances is to decide on a path forward, uncertain of the outcome. We articulate the process from this lens since it prescribes a vocabulary for the process of making decisions that balance the desired outcome and the obstructions and opportunities provided by the material and machine at hand, while leaving space for intuition and the unknown as a guiding force. In the following sections we will describe the *material*, the *machine* and how the designers navigated through the design space.

## The Material

Wood is one of the largest and most important natural resources in the world. The wood industry sees significant research and development into efforts to increase the sustainable use of this material. In the processes between the forest and the wood planks, buildings, furniture and paper that we use, a lot of side stream materials such as sawdust and wood flour are generated. Today, these side streams are often used for energy when, in fact, they could be put in much better use. One of the main challenges in achieving this, is to develop a way to make this side stream material suitable to be used in FDM, the most popular additive manufacturing (AM) method used in 3D printing techniques. One difficulty here, is to develop a

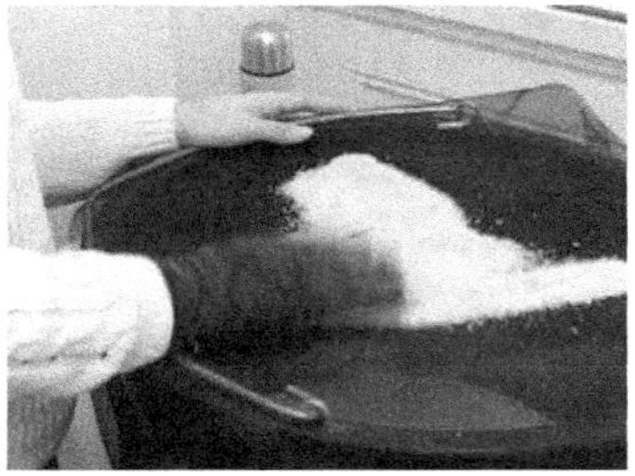

**Figure 2** – Sifting sawdust to be used in new material

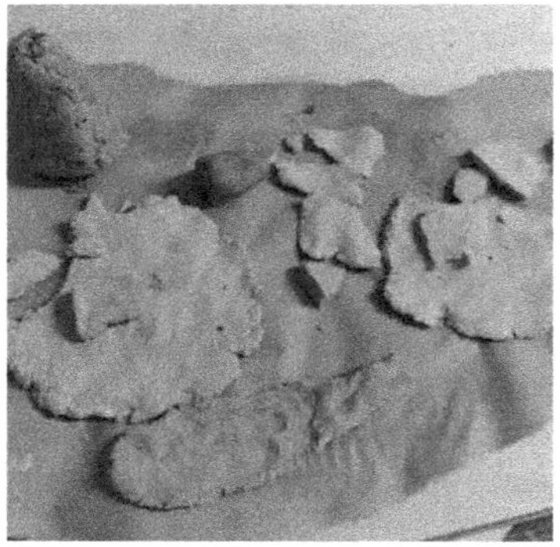

**Figure 3** – Explorations of different material recipes

**Figure 4** – Test prints to get to know the machine

material that is biodegradable, wood-based and fluid enough to be printed yet able to cure to become a usable, stable form and at the end of this, elicit interesting aesthetic qualities.

## The Machine

AM is nowadays a well-known production technique, that has gone beyond the walls of industry and has reached many households with small and affordable 3D printers. Many of the consumer grade desktop 3D printers on the market today utilize FDM and a variety of filaments to produce prototypes, models and end use parts. Materials used for these are mostly polymeric and fossil-fuel based materials. The use of these machines does not normally entail any human interaction with the machines during the printing process. There is little possibility of interfering with the outcome, once the start button has been pressed. It is as if these printers were designed according to the positivistic principles set in the industrial revolution: maximizing efficiency and minimizing resistance.

However, in the process we are describing here, the situation was different. The tool with which we shape material in this project is the *WASP 3MT* FDM printer. To allow this machine to print with experimental wood-based materials, it was outfitted with a *clay kit* upgrade. This is a system consisting of a cylinder containing the material, a pneumatically controlled piston to feed material from the cylinder and a printing nozzle with an extrusion mechanism. This system was designed to print with porcelain clay, and although it is able to produce great results in skilled hands, this technology is new and untried when it comes to printing with wood-based materials. This resulted in a great need and necessity of human interference during the process of printing with the material and machine.

## Navigating the Design Space between the Material and the Machine

As we explored the material, we ran into resistances. For example, the rheology of the material influenced the mixing or drying process and thus how the material was extruded or the printed object took form. Similarly, in using the machine, we found that there were parameters that could, and had to be, checked and refined during the printing. One needed to physically engage with the machine and printing object, and make changes; one could stop and restart the print, adjust flow rates of material, and more. In this case, a digital fabrication process is no longer fully automated, but allows for reflection in action [9]: active involvement in the process was necessary, and the designer needed to navigate through the resistances and ambiguity presented here.

The resistance and ambiguity within the material and machine that we engaged with as designers, were not stable, but dynamic. Both material and machine changed and influenced one another. For example, as we discovered new formulas to create material with improved properties, we learned new ways of using the machine settings, or discovered how to hack it to access otherwise impossible features: The design intention, the material and the machine form interweaving strands that shape one another as we navigate the design space.

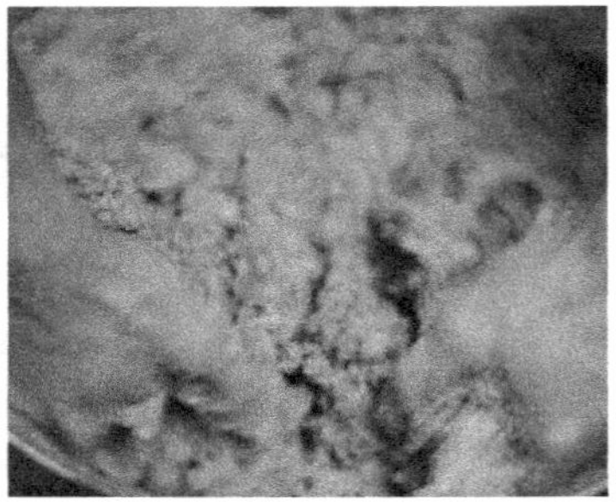

**Figure 5** – Preparing and mixing material

**Figure 6** – Filling the cylinder with material

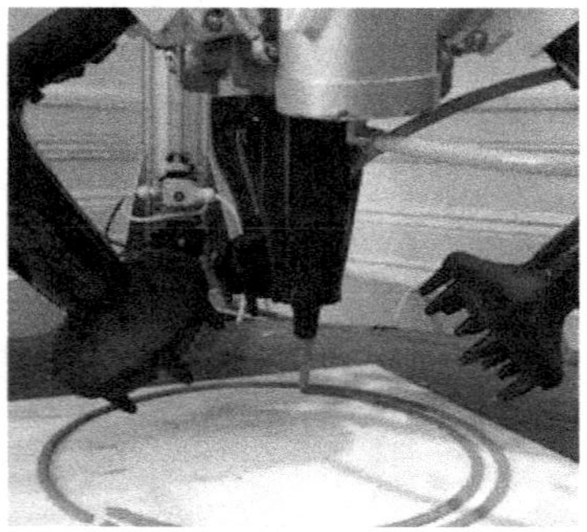

**Figure 7** – Drying the base layers of the print, using hair-dryers

In the following section, different moments within the process are highlighted by demonstrating resistances and ambiguities that emerged, to illustrate how this design space was formed and changed continuously as the designers navigated through it.

*Ambiguity & resistance in exploring and developing the material*

In a series of experiments (see figure 2-4), refined saw dust was mixed with different amounts of water, and methylcellulose as a glue. Resistances here include the large amount of manual labour involved in refining the saw dust, and the unpredictability of the wood material. Despite sifting, different sizes of fibres made the material inconsistent. The ratio and amount of the other components to add, were ambiguous. Some test prints were acceptable and became very strong when finished. Others contained too much water and collapsed under their own weight while printing. At the suggestion of material scientists, the resistance created due to the inconsistent material, saw dust, was replaced with wood flour. A lesser known waste product of the wood industry, commercially available in specific and precise particle sizes. This allowed more systematic exploration of different ratios for the components, as the base material is more consistent. Ambiguity comes in play here, as the designers engaging in these explorations developed skills in material preparation. *"You can already feel how the material will come out of the printer when mixing the material"* (see figure 5). The mixture was not created with scientific tools to measure the moist levels or density, the designers trusted their senses to play with ambiguity to create the right consistency, and based their reasoning upon experiments done before. *"With mixing we tried to get as much air out of the mixture as possible, to prevent any bubbles or hollow spaces when printing"*.

*Ambiguity & resistance while developing skills using the machine*

Developing the skills and knowledge to create a consistent and printable material, included the development of skills in using the 3D printer. Ambiguity appears as designers explore what forms the material affords when printed. For example, sharp corners appear difficult to print, because of the fluidity of the material that is difficult to control as it comes out of the extruder. Or, attempts to print in sizes over 30cm high, where bottom layers do not dry fast enough to support the weight of later layers and the print collapses.

One of the main resistances for designing with this process became the amount of water necessary for a fluid mix, decreasing the strength of the artefact during printing. The designers asked the help of material scientists to refine the material. An interesting resistance emerged here: one based in language. Where the material scientists expected clear and concrete information, such as rheological data, designers offered reflections on intuitive actions and ambiguous results, also opening up a space for collaboration and the sharing of different perspectives. The main request for the material scientists was to reduce the resistance created by the amount of water necessary. The designers explored a way around this resistance: adding hair dryers to the printing head to facilitate drying during the process (see figure 7 and 9). This proved effective, and the ambiguous tuning of temperature and airflow in tune with the printing result became part of the printing process.

**Figure 8** – Warping wooden baseplate

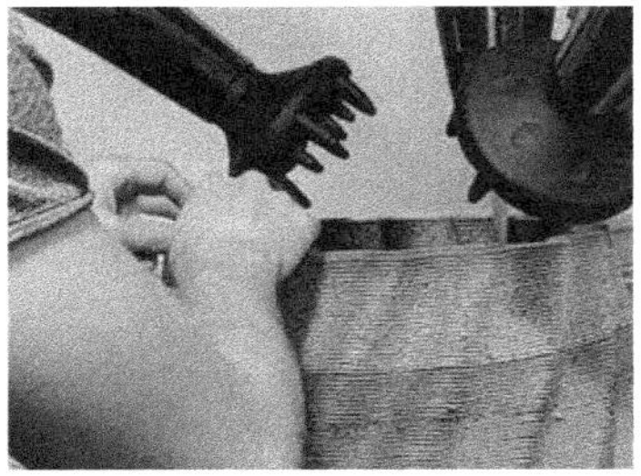

**Figure 9** – Careful manual adjustments during printing process

**Figure 10** – Printing layers connecting seamlessly

*Ambiguity & resistance within the process of printing with design intention*

Having developed the skills and knowledge for consistent material and a way to facilitate the drying process, attention shifted to the process of printing with a clearer design intention: a large size print. Here, different resistances emerged that required quick reflection and action from the designers on the fly. For example, one resistance appeared as the moisture from the material was absorbed by the wooden base plate, which started to warp during the process. This in turn warped the printed object's footprint, turning it from circular into oval shaped (see figure 8). To overcome this, the designers clamped down the base plate and manually adjusted the printed object while the printing continued. Another resistance was formed by small inconsistencies during the printing as a result of the large size of this artefact. This required long printing times, during which part of the material dries out as it sits in a cylinder before being printed. This required manual adjustments of the pressure and flow rate to increase the extrusion speed of less fluid material: ambiguous actions that had to be directly refined based on the felt and seen results.

The cylinder is the part of the printer in which the material is inserted, and where pressure is used to push the material through the nozzle of the printer. It had to be refilled with new material 7 times throughout the process, presenting a new resistance for large scale prints (see figure 6). The designers did not have a way to see how much material was left while printing. Developing a skill based on ambiguity, the designers learned to hear the amount of material left and stop a print in time by knocking on the cylinder.

Before developing this skill and learning to trust the ambiguous results, the designers indicated to be quite anxious about the process, since the stopping and the starting of the machine on the right moment was crucial for the quality of the material of the print. A crucial point in dealing with this resistance was the discovery that the 3D printer could manually be set to start at a specific height at any moment within the process. "*This realisation was a big step in completing the print. We felt more confident about the process, because it wasn't crucial that it had to go right the first time. We got all the control, since we could jump to every specific layer. We were able to take a bit more risk and we were daring to try out new things, which made it easier to discover the functionalities of the printer and improve the material outcome of the print.*" Figure 10 shows how two batches of material towards the end of the print could be connected virtually seamlessly with the newly developed skills. Figure 9 shows careful adjustments of a new batch adherence to the already printed artefact.

The final artefact at this stage of exploration is a vase of 60x45cm and is estimated to consists of 85% wood after air curing, while being 100% biodegradable (see figure 11). The vase is so far, the largest object printed in wood. This artefact still presents resistances, pointing to further development, in this ongoing research. For one, as the material in its finished form is hydroscopic, absorbing moisture from the air around it and changing shape as it becomes heavier or lighter. As a result, some outer layers detach as inside layers lean inward. Another resistance is formed by its biodegradable character: if the material does not become dry enough, it can start to mould. The designers are currently exploring ways to overcome

**Figure 11** - A vase printed in wood-based material

this, or use this moulding process for other purposes. Navigating through the resistance and ambiguity does not end with the finished artefact of this particular process. Sharing the vase at an international conference on additive manufacturing, allows the designers to discuss resistances and ambiguity and the skills to navigate them with others. For example, the cracking of layers when the material starts to dry. This resistance also presents itself to those printing with porcelain using the same machine. Their solution has been to develop a layering pattern that interweaves and in its physical form, allow for minimum and consistent shrinkage. Such shared reflections amongst a community of designers and makers form input for future iterations.

## Conclusion
In this work in progress, we started to unpack a making process in the context of digital fabrication through the lens of resistance and ambiguity. In exposing the way in which designers navigate the design space that emerges when a material and machine meet, we contribute an articulation on how craftsmanship relates to a digital fabrication method. The articulation presented here, starts to unravel how embodied engagement: active involvement and the senses, might start to shape new opportunities within methods that previously were dominated by a fully automated and predetermined process.

## Acknowledgements
We wish to extend our gratitude to colleagues Dina Dedic, Mikael Lindström and Ann-Maria Zachrisson of RISE Bioeconomy who's material knowledge is invaluable in this ongoing project. Furthermore, we thank WASP for their skills, knowledge and ongoing support in our joint experiments with 3D printing.

## References
[1] Dewey, J. (1934). *Art as Experience*. New York, NY: Perigree

[2] Dourish, P. (2001). *Where the Action is*. Cambridge: MIT Press.

[3] Ehn, P. (1988). *Work oriented design of computer artifacts*. Phd diss., Arbetslivscentrum.

[4] Gaver, B. and Bowers, J. (2012). *Annotated portfolios*. interactions, 19(4), ACM: 40-49.

[5] Gibson, J.J. (1979). *The Ecological Approach to Visual Perception*. London, UK: Lawrence Erlbaum.

[6] Kim, J., Zheng, C., Takahashi, H., Gross, M. D., Ashbrook, D., & Yeh, T. (2018, June). Compositional 3D printing: expanding & supporting workflows towards continuous fabrication. In Proceedings of the 2nd ACM Symposium on Computational Fabrication (p. 5). ACM.

[7] Koskinen, K., Zimmerman, J., Binder, T., Redstrom, J., & Wensveen, S. (2011). *Design Research through Practice: From the Lab, Field, and Showroom*. Elsevier.

[8] Merleau-Ponty, M. (1962). *Phenomenology of Perception*, trans. Collin Smith. New York: Humanities Press.

[9] Schön, D. (1983). The reflective practioner: How professionals think in action. New York: Basic Books.

[10] Sennett, R. (2008). *The craftsman*. Yale University Press.

# Adding Friction To Frictionless Payments: A Haptic Interface for Digital Transactions

**Bart Hengeveld**
Eindhoven University of Technology Dept. of Industrial Design, Future Everyday group.
Laplace 32, 5612 AZ, Eindhoven, The Netherlands
b.j.hengeveld@tue.nl

**Jordy Rooijakkers**
Eindhoven University of Technology Dept. of Industrial Design, Laplace 32, 5612 AZ, Eindhoven, The Netherlands
contact@jordyrooijakkers.com


*TEI '19, March 17--20, 2019, Tempe, AZ, USA.*

ACM ISBN 978-1-4503-6196-5/19/03.
https://doi.org/10.1145/3294109.3300999

## Abstract
Over the past decades monetary transactions have become increasingly dematerialized. Nowadays payments should be "frictionless", as easy as possible, for example through NFC or biometric payment methods. Although frictionless payment methods hold advantages in terms of safety, convenience and privacy, they also pose problems as the inherent physicality of cash is shown to help people with budgeting and expense tracking. In this paper we describe our ongoing work in creating more mindful interactions, in this case by re-physicalizing part of digital transactions with the aim of combining the advantages of digital payment methods with those of physical money. We present the evaluation of a haptic interface for in-store digital payments. Results from a four-week lab evaluation indicate that people are capable of getting a feel for the absolute values of a payment as presented through our interface.

## Author Keywords
Digital payments; haptic displays; embodied interaction; research through design.

## CSS Concepts
• Human-centered computing~Haptic devices

## Introduction

*Pain of paying*

It has been shown that some payment methods are experienced as more painful than others, even at a neurological level [12]. This 'pain of paying' is larger for cash transactions than for credit card transactions due to a difference in *coupling*, i.e., "the association between purchase decision and actual parting of money" [15]: with cash transactions the 'parting of money' is felt immediately whereas the felt experience of credit card transactions is delayed. One effect of this is that we tend to spend more money when using less painful payment methods [14], not in the least because future spending behavior is highly affected by past behavior [21]. Chatterjee et al. have shown that cash based purchases make us more aware of *costs*, whereas credit cards make us more aware of *benefits* [2], as such changing our perception of the value of money. Ironically, Shah et al have shown that using 'more painful' payment methods increases our emotional connection to a purchase [20], leading us to conclude that frictionless payment methods seem to reduce the pain of paying but also reduce the emotional reward of a purchase.

Of course non-cash payment methods hold advantages in terms of consumer safety, privacy, and convenience, as well as in terms of cost (printing, distributing and maintaining cash is very expensive for the banking industries). However, as clear as these advantages are, it should also be clear that frictionless payment methods can pose problems, e.g., for financially more vulnerable user groups [6, 13, 18]. Research by Hernandez et al. shows that people with lower monthly budgets find cash money more useful for budgeting purposes than debit cards [6]. As mentioned in the introduction cash money allows for better monitoring of spending behaviour, allows for clearer budgeting, and for clearer budget tracking. These self-control budgeting mechanisms have also been identified in other studies, e.g. [5].

It is safe to assume that these financially more vulnerable user groups—but probably all of us—could benefit from a payment method that would incorporate the best of both worlds; methods that combine the safety, privacy and convenience of digital systems with the inherent benefits of physicality.

## Related work

Now, combining the strengths of the digital with those of the physical is not new in HCI. Communities related to Tangible Interaction [7] and Embodied Interaction [3] have investigated the advantages non-GUI interfaces and physical-digital hybrids in various domains [19]. One such community is that of haptic interfaces, which are aimed at making digital information available through the sense of touch. Much work has been done in this field, ranging from fundamental (e.g., [8]) to pragmatic (e.g., [4]). Work done at the Royal College of Art London [23, 17], or by Studio PSK [22] give a critical perspective on our relationship with digital money, presenting alternative credit card interaction styles that map different payment characters to expressive embodied interfaces [25]. Also, Campenhout et al. [1] explored alternative tangible and embodied interactions with payment terminals. John Kestner et al. [11] present three actuated wallets that provide the owner with information on their balance using counter-force when opening the wallet, inflation or deflation, or vibration feedback. Vines et al. [24] have explored a digital

Figure 1: Prototype of the payment interface. A force feedback slider provides haptic information about the value of digital payment. Amounts are linearly mapped to slider counterforce (€1 to 1% of the maximum force, €100 to 100%).

checkbook concept for 80-year-olds using Anoto paper. Lastly, Kaye et al. [10] organized a workshop around digital transactions at CHI'14, but the results of the workshop are unclear to the authors of this paper.

## Study

*Prototype design*

Inspired by these examples we decided to explore the potential of haptic interfaces for digital payments further. We envisioned that, if we could design an interface that would allow people to get a 'feel' for the absolute and relative value of their payments, we could help them get more grip on their expenses. The first step in this research is to assess whether people are capable of translating a haptic signal to a monetary value in the first place.

For this we designed the interface shown in Figure 1: a handheld device with a force-feedback slider that provides haptic feedback related to the absolute value of the transaction. The device contains an ALPS motorized slider and an Arduino Pro Mini, and communicates with a Processing patch running on a laptop, via the serial port. In Processing an amount is set; then its value is mapped to the Arduino's PWM signal. The motorized slider is connected to the Arduino's analogue pin.

We informally evaluated six different 'payment amount to force feedback' mappings, settling on a straightforward linear mapping, i.e., with the slider's maximum counter-force mapped to the maximum spendable amount; half that amount would be met with 50% of the slider's maximum counter-force. We then set up a four-week lab evaluation aimed at assessing whether the participants could actually feel different amounts and, if so, whether their skill would improve over time.

*Setup*

During the four-week experiment we asked six participants to use the prototype for three payments a day for two weeks (five days a week). This makes for a total of 180 payments. All participants (3M, 3F) were recruited from our postgraduate students. The experiment took place in one of the lab spaces within our department. The participants came to the lab at 9AM, 12PM and 5PM to make their payments individually. At the start of the two weeks we told them that all payments during the experiment would be between €1 and €100, but did not give them any training. They were allowed to experience the maximum and minimum force-feedback only once. The first two weeks of the study were followed by a one-week break, after which we asked three of the participants to make additional daily payments for another five days. This makes for an additional 45 payments for the last week. We included the one-week break in order to see whether the skill they may have developed in the first two weeks was at all sustainable.

The payment procedure was the following. For each payment we would set one amount (e.g., €30 which maps to 30% of the maximum force of the actuated slider's motor) for all participants. We then asked them to individually pay the amount by pushing the slider forward and to make an estimation of the amount. We recorded the estimated amounts after which we told the participants the actual amount. We repeated this procedure for the second and third amounts at 12PM and 5PM respectively. Ahead of the study we prepared sets of amounts for each of the 15 days of the study.

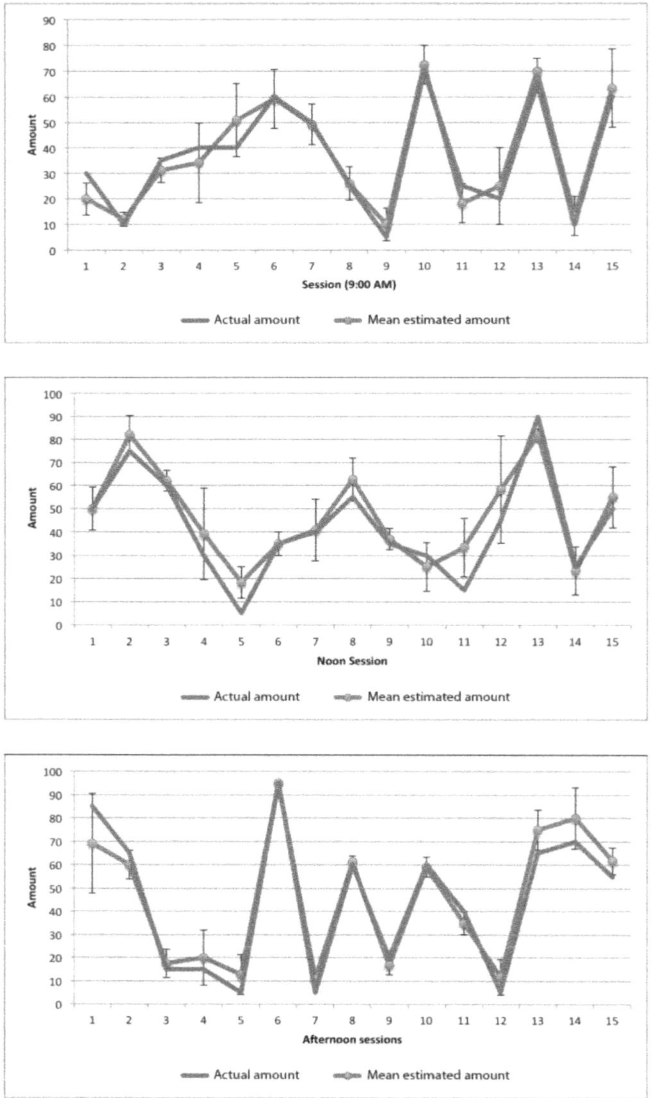


Figure 2: Graphs showing the actual amounts (red lines) and mean estimate amounts (blue lines) and their standard deviation, for the fifteen morning, noon and afternoon sessions (top to bottom).

The daily payment triplets were constructed semi-randomly, i.e., we varied in low, medium and high amounts, but also deliberately included repeating amounts (e.g., 20, 20, 75 for morning, noon and afternoon). In addition to the numeric data collected we observed and recorded the participants' interaction behavior during each of the (daily) sessions to get a sense of how careful or confident our participants were, and to see whether the interaction differed or evolved. Any further non-numeric data (e.g., remarks, informal discussion) was recorded and reviewed with the participants after the experiment.

## Findings and discussion

Over the course of four weeks we collected 224 measurements, 14 of which were determined to be outliers using the Interquartile Range. These data were subsequently removed from the set. Figure 2 shows graphs of these data, with from top to bottom the morning, noon and afternoon sessions respectively. The red lines show the actual amounts as we had set them, the blue lines show the mean estimate amounts of the six participants, with the standard deviations. We did not conduct any deeper statistical analysis of the data, given the study's small sample size (N=6).

However, as can be seen in the graphs, the 'mean estimate amount' lines seem to map well onto the 'actual amount' lines. This gives us mild confidence that the participants were on average capable of distinguishing the set amounts through the haptic feedback of the device. Of course, this could be due to 'wisdom of the crowd', even though the crowd was quite small during this study (N=6). Looking closer at the data and considering the participants' feedback, we see interesting starting points for follow-up research:

- First of all, looking at the 9AM and 5PM sessions especially it seems that the participants' accuracy is improving during the first two weeks of the experiment;
- Secondly, participants seem to be especially accurate during the 5PM sessions, suggesting that even with only three payments a day they could get a 'feel' for the haptic interface within a day;
- At the same time, we also see that the participants had an 'accuracy relapse' in the morning, as the 9AM estimates are typically less accurate than the 5PM ones preceding them;
- The participants were least accurate when estimating the smaller amounts (≤15). Anecdotal evidence supported this, as participants indicated that they found it difficult to feel the differences in the lower pushback force. This seems to direct towards Weber's Law for friction;
- Anecdotal evidence from our post-experiment interviews also suggests a Hawthorne Effect: most of the participants doubted whether they really felt the recurring amounts within one day (for example €40 in the morning, €5 at noon, €5 in the afternoon) because they thought "that would not make sense in the experiment". This assumption reportedly made them reconsider their answers;
- During the midday (12PM) sessions the participants were consistently the least accurate. One explanation for this could be that the participants were less confident during these sessions due to their experienced relapse in the morning sessions. We observed that during the midday sessions the participants tended to take more time, and be more careful in their payment behavior. This observation was confirmed by some of the participants in our post experiment interviews. On other words, the more they thought about it the less they seemed to feel. This is actually contrary to what we have experienced in earlier studies where we 'slowed down' the interaction (e.g., [16]): in most cases a slower interaction would lead to more conscious interaction with that which was being manipulated, and as such to a more direct experience of it.

The patterns described above for the first two-week part of the experiment could also be observed in a similar fashion in the final one-week part (which took place after the one-week break).

## Limitations and closing considerations

This research has several limitations. Throughout our entire research through design process we have tried to safeguard rigidity by validating as many of our decisions as we could, even though we have not nearly reported on all of them in this Work in Progress paper. Where possible we involved external people in key decisions such as the haptic feedback mapping, the form of and interaction with the design, potential scenarios of use, and of course in our experiment. However, the sample size is undeniably small and consisted of students of our department. Also, 15 days of testing is not sufficient to draw any solid conclusions.

In addition, aspects such as the exact behaviour of the force feedback slider need to be better researched, as a body of work is available on this topic. Future studies should certainly include experiments to measure e.g., the Point of Subjective Equality or the Just-Noticeable Difference.

Despite these limitations we are not unhappy with what we have seen in this first phase of this research. It does seem that people may actually be capable of translating an abstract haptic experience into a concrete payment amount, and it seems that people get slightly better at this over time. We believe that, if we redesign the force-feedback profile to better fit the subjective experience of push-back force, we will see further improvement in the estimates' accuracy. Furthermore we are sufficiently confident that further practice makes perfect, meaning that a longer evaluation period with four or five payments a day will likely prove to improve accuracy even further. This should also prevent people to 'overthink' and get more in touch with what they feel.

Of course one can question whether spot-on accuracy is the goal of such an interface at all. We believe not. We believe more in how physicality in interaction can help people be more mindful of their actions (e.g., [16]). This research is a further example of that: in most situations, expense tracking does not come down to understanding what you pay to the cent but rather to getting an understanding of one's spending habits and of the consequence of a payment on the overall (sub-) budget [9] by creating slowness; allowing people time to pay attention to their experience while experiencing it. As such this research can be compared to the work of Sam Roots [17] who designed a tangible interface complementary to one's telephone banking interface. The main difference of this research though is that in our interface the haptic feedback changes character; it is not a passive device but feels different for different transactions.

*Status quo*

We have presently started redesigning the interface, taken the aforementioned insights into account. Also, we are considering different kinds of haptic interfaces that make use of recent developments in shape changing interfaces, as well as building on advancements in 3D printing. As such we see our current work as a first step towards a truly hybrid interface for digital transactions.

## Conclusion

In this paper we have described how some of the inherent qualities of physical money have disappeared with its dematerialization. We have argued that people, especially the financially more vulnerable user groups, could benefit from a digital payment system or device that would combine the qualities of the current frictionless payment methods with those of the more 'painful' ones. We have presented a haptic interface that provided the user with haptic feedback about the amounts they paid and evaluated the interface in a four-week lab experiment. Preliminary findings indicate that people seem to be capable of translating the haptic feedback to monetary amounts, with increasing accuracy over the day and slightly increasing accuracy over the span of the experiment. These findings are indicative at most, as the study's sample size was small.

We hope that our work informs the HCI community about how much we are capable of feeling in something as abstract as a force-feedback slider, and that it inspires the community by showing the promise of haptic interfaces in everyday life.

## References


[1] Lukas van Campenhout. 2016. Physical interaction in a dematerialized world. *Doctoral Thesis.* Eindhoven University of Technology.

[2] Promothesh Chatterjee, Randall L. Rose. 2012. Do Payment Mechanisms Change the Way Consumers Perceive Products? *Journal of Consumer Research 38*, 1129-1139.

[3] Paul Dourish. 2004. *Where the action is: the foundations of embodied interaction*. MIT press.

[4] Vincent Hayward, Karon E. MacLean. 2007. Do it yourself haptics: part I. *IEEE Robotics & Automation Magazine* 14, 4.

[5] Chip Heath, Jack B. Soll. 1996. Mental budgeting and consumer decisions. *Journal of Consumer Research 23,* 40-52.

[6] Lola Hernandez, Nicole Jonker, Anneke Kosse. 2014. *Cash versus debit card: the role of budget control*. Working Paper No. 429, De Nederlandsche Bank.

[7] Hiroshi Ishii, Brygg Ullmer. 1997. Tangible bits: towards seamless interfaces between people, bits and atoms. *Proceedings of the ACM SIGCHI Conference on Human Factors in Computing Systems 1997*, 234-241.

[8] Lynette A. Jones, Ian W. Hunter. 1990. A perceptual analysis of stiffness. *Experimental Brain Research* 79, 1: 150-156.

[9] Nicole Jonker, Anneke Kosse. 2013. Estimating cash usage: The impact of survey design on research outcomes. *De Economist 161*, 19-44.

[10] Jofish Kaye, Janet Vertesi, Jennifer Ferreira, Barry Brown, Mark Perry. 2014. #CHImoney: Financial interactions, digital cash, capital exchange and mobile money. *Extended Abstracts on Human Factors in Computing Systems*. ACM, New York, 2014, 111–114.

[11] John Kestner, Daniel Leithinger, Jaekyung Jung, Michelle Petersen. 2009. Proverbial wallet: Tangible interface for financial awareness. In *Proceedings of the 3rd International Conference on Tangible and Embedded Interaction*, 55-56.

[12] Nina Mazar, Hilke Plassmann, Nicole Robitaille, Axel Lindner. 2016. Pain of Paying? — A Metaphor Gone Literal: Evidence from Neural and Behavioral Science. *INSEAD Working Paper*

[13] Drazen Prelec, George Loewenstein. 1998. The red and the black: Mental accounting of savings and debt. *Marketing Science, 17*, 1: 4-28.

[14] Drazen Prelec, Duncan Simester. 2001. Always Leave Home without It: A Further Investigation of the Credit-Card Effect on Willingness to Pay. *Marketing Letters*, 12 (1), 5-12

[15] Priya Raghubir, Joydeep Srivastava. 2008. Monopoly money: the effect of payment coupling and form on spending behavior. *Journal of Experimental Psychology: Applied, 14*, 3: 213.

[16] Vincent van Rheden, Bart Hengeveld. 2016. Engagement through embodiment: A case for mindful interaction. In *Proceedings of the 10th International Conference on Tangible, Embedded and Embodied Interaction*, 349-356.

[17] Sam Roots. 2017. *Treasure*. Retrieved December 2018 from www.treasureinnovation.com.

[18] Terri G. Seuntjens, Niels van de Ven, Marcel Zeelenberg. 2013. Debts the first 25 years - A selective review of the literature on adolescent financial behaviour. *Tilburg institute for behavioural economics research*, 1-12.

[19] Orit Shaer, Eva Hornecker. 2010. Tangible user interfaces: past, present, and future directions. *Foundations and Trends in Human-Computer Interaction* 3, 1–2: 1-137.

[20] Avni M. Shah, Noah Eisenkraft, James R. Bettman, Tanya L. Chartrand. 2016. 'Paper Or Plastic?': How

We Pay Influences Post-Transaction Connection. *Journal of Consumer Research*, 42 (5), 688-708

[21] Dilip Soman. 2001. Effects of Payment Mechanism on Spending Behavior: The Role of Rehearsal and Immediacy of Payments. *Journal of Consumer Research*, 27 (March), 460–74

[22] Studio PSK. 2014. *Reciprociti Bank*. Retrieved September 2017 from http://studiopsk.com/reciprocitibank.html.

[23] Glen Taylor. 2008. *RCA: The Future of Money*. Retrieved September 2017 from http://www.core77.com/posts/10007/rca-the-future-of-money-10007.

[24] John Vines, Mark Blythe, Paul Dunphy, Vasilis Vlachokyriakos, Isaac Teece, Andrew Monk, Patrick Olivier. 2012. Cheque mates: Participatory design of digital payments with eighty somethings. *Proceedings of the SIGCHI Conference on Human Factors in Computing Systems 2012.* ACM, New York, 2012, 1189–1198.

[25] Chris Woebken. 2008. *Fetish of Money*. Retrieved September 2017 from https://www.flickr.com/ photos/sutje/2450529894.

# Designing Modular Rehabilitation Objects for Interactive Therapy in the Home

**Aisling Kelliher**
Virginia Tech
Blacksburg, VA 24060, USA
aislingk@vt.edu

**Eric Bottelsen**
Virginia Tech
Blacksburg, VA 24060, USA
beric@vt.edu

**Andrew Gibson**
Virginia Tech
Blacksburg, VA 24060, USA
drewgan5@vt.edu

**Edward Coe**
Virginia Tech
Blacksburg, VA 24060, USA
eoccoe@vt.edu


*TEI '19, March 17–20, 2019, Tempe, AZ, USA*

ACM ISBN 978-1-4503-6196-5/19/03.
DOI: https://doi.org/10.1145/3294109.3300983

## Abstract
Interactive home based rehabilitation therapy is a promising treatment development for stroke survivors. As the impairment characteristics of each stroke survivor are unique, interactive rehabilitation systems need to be customized to the functional and movement quality outcome goals of the patient, and adaptable over time as therapy progresses. In this paper, we present our iterative co-design process creating a set of modular therapy objects and a rehabilitation protocol for upper extremity stroke survivors. Our objects and training protocol are adaptable components within a computer vision based interactive system that captures and analyzes stroke survivors completing rehabilitation activities. We report on findings from a pilot study with nine stroke survivors and a workshop with five physiotherapists where we highlight challenges in designing objects for impaired grasps, opportunities for aligning objects with activities of everyday living, and the responsibility of design sensitivity.

## Author Keywords
Home based therapy systems; interactive stroke rehabilitation; interaction design; human centered design

## CSS Concepts

• **Human-centered computing~Interface design prototyping; Participatory design**; Interaction devices; People with disabilities

## Introduction

Worldwide populations are increasingly aging, meaning that in many countries, including the US, there is an increasing need for effective and accessible rehabilitation services for debilitating illnesses and injury such as stroke and progressive arthritis [7, 11]. Globally, stroke is the most common neurological disorder and while long-term therapy in the clinic has proven effective in facilitating recovery [12], the challenges of financial cost, effort of traveling to a clinic, and overall availability of therapists can be prohibitive. Unsupervised home based therapy has emerged as a potential solution, but here issues of system cost, intrusion and maintenance, in addition to patient motivation and adherence, present new problems to address.

The Interactive Neurorehabilitation Lab at Virginia Tech focuses on developing robust and motivational interactive systems for semi-automated home-based therapy for upper extremity stroke survivors. Our system combines computer vision and machine learning approaches for capturing and assessing patient movement during therapy. As the industrial and interaction designers on the team, we are particularly focused on interrogating the role of design in supporting patient motivation, aligning training experiences with activities of daily living, and creating artifacts that are pleasing and evocative for humans, while also supporting the computer vision and analytical requirements of our team's semi-automated approach. In this description of our current work in progress, we detail our iterative design process in crafting a series of customized modular objects in close collaboration with a team of physiotherapists, rehabilitation medicine experts and the computer vision members of our team. We present findings from a pilot study with nine stroke survivors and discuss ongoing work with our therapist, engineering, and patient collaborators.

## Motivation and Background

Technology assisted rehabilitation in the home is emerging as a key avenue for improving health and wellness outcomes with the potential for reducing costs [1]. However, home based therapy faces considerable challenges in terms of cost, intrusion, supervision and patient motivation [3]. There are a number of successful individualized approaches [2, 8], although outstanding challenges remain in terms of scalability, data collection, and reliable automation. Our current work builds on the approach of Kyto et al. and others, in that we aim to develop a low-cost, scalable solution with training objects and therapy tasks purposefully targeted towards supporting the daily life activities of stroke survivors [9].

## Approaching the design of objects for interactive therapy

In order to understand the scope of the design space for home based rehabilitation, we conducted a study of important gold standards, spanning therapy objects, activities, and computational analysis of human movement performance of significance to our project. We began by examining the household objects (e.g. pen, paper clip, towel etc.) used in the Wolf Motor Function Test (WMFT), a key standard for evaluating

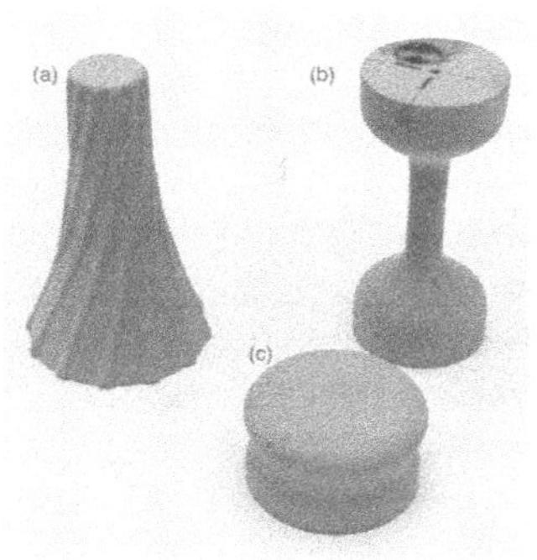


Figure 1: Preliminary object prototypes handmade from composite materials. The objects contained holes where weights could be placed to increase or decrease object stability. 1a approximates a can, 1b could be used as a glass or makeup brush, 1c could be picked up like a large checker piece with a power sphere grasp

upper extremity movement [12]. We next analyzed the activities of daily living examined in the Motor Activity Log (MAL), which compromises a set of questions designed to elicit measurements and understandings about the effects of therapy on an impaired limb during everyday life [11]. Finally, we reviewed the GRASP taxonomy as it is considered useful for assisting in the computer vision recognition and assessment of hand grasps [5]. Table 1 presents our primary findings from this comparative analysis, identifying a proposed set of the most significant and potentially useful grasps, object types, and activities that can be combined in the widest variety of ways to support concrete cross-mapping between rehabilitation training tasks and activities of everyday living.

| Object | Grasp | Activity |
|---|---|---|
| Basket<br>Checker | Power Sphere | Use towel<br>Put on makeup |
| Can | Medium Wrap | Pick up glass<br>Hold book |
| Towel<br>Key in lock | Precision Pinch | Button up clothes<br>Grasp fork or spoon |

Table 1. Primary commonalities between objects, grasps, and everyday activities.

Based on our analysis, we created a set of handmade preliminary object prototypes produced using a variety of materials. Figure 1 depicts three of the objects we made from composite materials (we also used wood and foam). We presented our objects and suggested related training tasks (see Fig 1 sidebar for examples) at a workshop for 14 doctors, physical and occupational therapists, biomedical researchers, and engineers from six of our partner academic and medical institutions. In-depth discussions with these participants about the objects and the proposed training protocol helped us further solidify the final object design. Key feedback considerations from this event included: 1) a need to include soft/squishy material objects to assist with grasp release; 2) a need to consider object stability and/or potential roll away from the training area; and 3) a need to better consider the assigned movement task and the combination of objects within a problem solving activity framework.

In response, we modified our object designs and worked closely with the physiotherapists on our team to develop a series of 6 custom designed objects and 12 related activities for the upper extremity. In order to promote active problem solving (i.e. the patient needs to work out how to engage the object), we adopted a defamiliarization [4] approach, where we created objects that were close to, but not quite, recognizable household objects. We wanted to create objects that could be grasped and manipulated in a wide variety of ways corresponding to the primary identified grasps, thus lending themselves to rich cross-mapping opportunities.

We 3D printed a set of three base objects (tapered can, hourglass, contained tripod), and three tops (key-top, checker piece, squishy doorknob) that can be used individually or variously combined by stacking or screwing together (see Fig 2). The activities designed for manipulating the objects include reach (e.g. reach and lightly touch two objects); reach and grasp (e.g. reach and grip one of the tripod object legs), reach, grasp and transport (e.g. reach and lift the can object up towards the participant's face); and reach, grasp, transport, and manipulate components (e.g. reach and hold the can object with the left hand and reach and

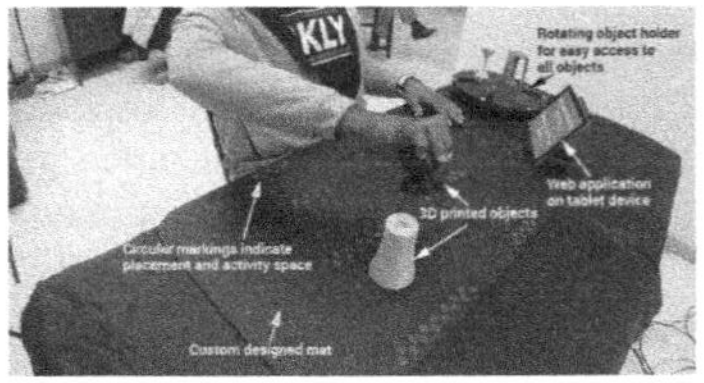


Figure 3. A participant in our study stacks one of our therapy objects on top of another during a "tidying" therapy task

pick up the tear drop object with the right hand, then screw the tear drop object into the can object).

Figure 2. The six objects are stored in a numbered rotatable container to facilitate object identification, object access, and object replacement (each storage slot is unique to each object)

The activity tasks scaffold in complexity (from simple reaching exercises with single objects, to two-handed multi-stage manipulations with two objects) and are crafted to map (and extend) to various activities of daily living, including those featured in the MAL set.

## Pilot Study with Impaired Users

We conducted a pilot study of our therapy objects and activities with nine stroke survivors (two women, seven men; two with moderate impairment, and seven with mild impairment). The study tasked the participants with completing four repetitions of the twelve activities developed by our team. The participants used our interactive system, shown in Figure 3, which consists of the objects, a customized tabletop mat, a camera and a computer running the computer vision system, and a tablet interface that delivered the study protocol (i.e. instruction videos depicting what objects to use and how to move them for each task [7]. This IRB approved study took place at the Emory University Rehabilitation Hospital and was supervised by a physiotherapist. The participants were compensated for their participation and for their travel to the hospital. At the conclusion of the activity part of the study, the participants participated in a debrief interview with the research team, discussing their experience using the system, their opinions about the objects, and the types of daily activities they wanted to improve at.

*Study Findings*

Six of the participants were able to complete all of the activities, while three of the more impaired participants struggled to complete the more complex movement tasks. Different patient profiles (e.g. level of impaired sensation, increased spasticity, limitations in shoulder range of motion etc.) influenced the abilities of the patients to engage with some of the objects. For example, P2 had limited finger extension and found the green hourglass object slippery and had difficulty releasing the purple tripod object.

The participants spoke movingly about the types of activities they would like to be able to do at home including holding a baby's rattle, washing baby bottles, toweling after a shower, buttoning a blouse, loading the dishwasher, and opening a bag of chips. Several participants noted that our system did not include knife and fork objects as this was something they struggled with both at home and in public. P5 expressed enthusiasm for the squishy object and found it helpful in thinking about the doorknobs they encountered in their everyday live. P2 wanted to hear a click sound or some other audio or tangible feedback when they screwed two objects together, a concern echoed by P5 who was worried about screwing the objects together too far. P1 critiqued our approach in conducting all the activities sitting down and laughingly asked if we too "brushed our teeth sitting down?". P8 was the only participant who objected to the design of the therapy objects themselves and thought there were "like toys for 5 year olds".

The participants had mixed reactions to our proposed set of connections between the objects/tasks and specific activities of daily living. While some made sense to them (lifting the can object towards your face as a drinking motion), others activities, especially those with the hourglass object were not as clear to them. The physiotherapist supervising the study noted that because of their different grasp abilities, the participants could agree that the activity reminded them of some activity, but it may just be different from what we anticipated. The physiotherapist also critiqued our overly open-ended design approach and suggested that we should be clearer about the goal of the perceived affordances of the objects. We found the input of the physiotherapist to be very helpful in assisting us in analyzing our approach and the patient activities and in response, we created an online survey to interrogate our approach more closely.

## Physiotherapist Survey Evaluation

*Survey Method:* We conducted a survey with five physiotherapists, (three of whom were unfamiliar with the project up until then), to assess their interpretation of the therapy tasks and their perceived relation to the intended activities of daily living. The survey was administered online and consisted of two sections. In the first section, the physiotherapists were shown the instruction videos for the twelve therapy tasks. After viewing each video, they could choose one of three possible named activities of daily living (ADL) that in their opinion, best resembled the activity they had just viewed. The options to choose from included the intended ADL, another intended ADL featured in the twelve tasks, and another unrelated activity. The therapists could also submit a different daily activity if they thought that none of the three options were applicable. In the second survey section, the therapists were asked if they could think of any important ADLs that were not represented in the videos, in addition to questions about the sequencing order of the tasks, the complexity of the task, and the impairment characteristics that could influence task order.

*Survey Results:* The intended ADL was selected by all five therapists for four of the tasks and was selected by four of the therapists for five of the tasks, meaning that the majority of the therapists associated the intended ADL with their own interpretation for nine of the tasks. The remaining three tasks received agreement from three of the therapists, while two differed in their assessment. For two of these tasks, one of the therapists suggested a different task (e.g. "brushing teeth" or "wiping"). In the second section of the survey, the therapists collectively suggested ten additional ADLs to consider including cutting food, reaching across the body (e.g. with a towel), reaching above the shoulder (e.g. to brush hair or stack plates), buttoning a shirt and dealing with pericare after toileting. In addition, they drew specific attention to three grasps or finger movements that they found lacking in the current tasks, specifically a task requiring a hook grip

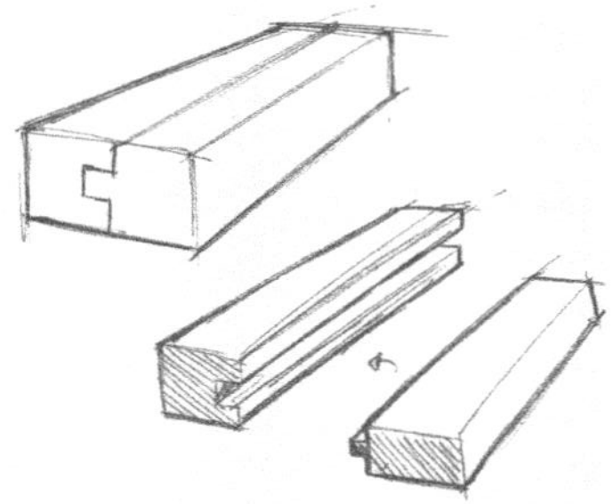

Figure 4: Sketch of chopstick pairs that can also function as a single object, to facilitate use for eating activities, or perhaps as a toothbrush

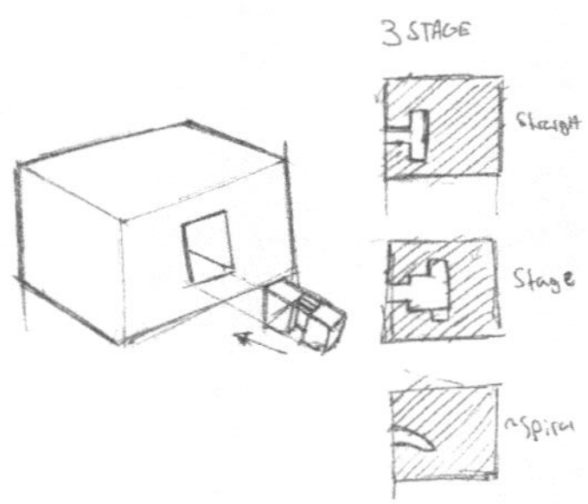


Figure 5: Sketch of a proposed staged lock and key mechanism to give patient physical feedback and a more challenging activity experience

for carrying objects, a lateral pinch grasp to hold a key, and a task specifying individuate finger movements for typing on a keyboard. The therapists agreed that the sequencing order of the tasks according to degree of challenge was correct.

*Survey Findings and Follow Up Workshop*
The survey results prompted us to more closely examine the objects and tasks that seemed either too generic or not well aligned with the intended tasks. We were also interested in looking further into the objects/tasks that were interpreted most differently as perhaps with specific design tweaks or modified instructions there could be opportunities to expand our task series. In our study, we used the hourglass object as a proxy for a fork or knife while eating, and as a pencil while writing. These two tasks were associated with three different possible ADLs in the survey. A clear issue with the eating task is that we did not create a bimanual activity (an important feature noted in [9]) while the form of the object itself did have enough perceived affordances to be consider by all to be a pen. We also noted that some of our tasks did not give the users the type of feedback typical in an ADL, such as the satisfying click of attaching two objects together, or the pushback from a key that has snapped a lock.

*Therapist and Designer Workshop*
We reflected on these findings and in response, worked on creating a number of sketches and preliminary mock-ups of additional ADL objects and tasks. One month after the survey, the 5 physiotherapists joined the entire interdisciplinary team for a 3-day workshop at Virginia Tech. As part of the activities on day 3 of this workshop, we collectively reviewed the survey results and discussed them in depth. We also presented our sketches for critique and received detailed feedback from the therapists present. They suggested some new objects such as weighted spoons that could be used for eating motions, in addition to doubling as a hairbrush for top of head mobility. They also challenged the simplicity of our horizontal button designs, observing that most buttons encountered in everyday life are vertical, and suggesting that making the top of the button squishy would give better feedback to the patient.

## Conclusions and Future Work
Designing for stroke survivors requires sensitivity to their condition, and creating artifacts considered infantilizing or bizarre is problematic. In our case, creating objects with more muted palettes could help, while being more direct with the ADL intent of the object/activity pairing could help remove confusion or the sense that the system is trying to trick the participant through unnecessary obfuscation. Stroke survivors grasp objects in a way that makes sense for their unique impairment. For computer vision based movement assessment systems like ours, this requires capturing more data of stroke survivors manipulating our objects to train our assessment algorithms. Later this year, we are conducting studies at two clinics aimed at capturing 1000 activity videos. We plan on incorporating the proposed objects in Figs 4 and 5, as well as creating a heavy and a light set of objects to accommodate participants with different patient profiles. We are modifying our checker/button object to have a squishy/flexible center and will experiment with vertical placement activities, as in the lock and key example. We will continue to conduct regular critique sessions with our research team, medical collaborators, and network of stroke survivors.

## References

[1] Craig Anderson, Sally Rubenach, Cliona Ni Mhurchu, Michael Clark, Carol Spencer, and Adrian Winsor. 2000. Home or hospital for stroke rehabilitation? Results of a randomized controlled trial: I: Health outcomes at 6 months. *Stroke*, 31(5): 1024–1031, 2000

[2] Madeline Balaam, Stefan Rennick Egglestone, Geraldine Fitzpatrick, Tom Rodden, Ann-Marie Hughes, Anna Wilkinson, Thomas Nind, Lesley Axelrod, Eric Harris, Ian Ricketts, Susan Mawson, and Jane Burridge. 2011. Motivating mobility: designing for lived motivation in stroke rehabilitation. In *Proceedings of the SIGCHI Conference on Human Factors in Computing Systems* (CHI '11). ACM New York, NY, 3073-3082

[3] Michael Baran, Nicole Lehrer, Margaret Duff, Vinay Venkataraman, Pavan Turaga, Todd Ingalls, W Zev Rymer, Steven L Wolf, and Thanassis Rikakis. 2015. Interdisciplinary concepts for design and implementation of mixed reality interactive neurorehabilitation systems for stroke. *Physical therapy*, 95, 3 (2015), 449 - 460

[4] Genevieve Bell, Mark Blythe, and Phoebe Sengers. 2005. Making by making strange: Defamiliarization and the design of domestic technologies. ACM *Trans. Comput.-Hum. Interact*. 12, 2 (June 2005), 149-173

[5] Thomas Feix, Roland Pawlik, Heinz-Bodo Schmiedmayer, Javier Romero, and Danica Kragic. 2009. A comprehensive grasp taxonomy. In *Robotics, Science and Systems: Workshop on Understanding the Human Hand for Advancing Robotic Manipulation*, pp 2–3, 2009.

[6] Mostafa Haghi, Kerstin Thurow, and Regina Stoll. 2017. Wearable Devices in Medical Internet of Things: Scientific Research and Commercially Available Devices. *Healthc Inform Res*, 2017. **23**(1): p. 4-15.

[7] Thanassis Rikakis, Aisling Kelliher, Jinwoo Choi, Jia-Bin Huang, Kris Kitani, Setor Zilevu, and Steven L. Wolf. 2018. Semi-automated home-based therapy for the upper extremity of stroke survivors. In *Proceedings of the 11th PErvasive Technologies Related to Assistive Environments Conference* (PETRA '18). ACM, New York, NY, USA, 249-256.

[8] Pedro Kirk, Mick Grierson, Rebeka Bodak, Nick Ward, Fran Brander, Kate Kelly, Nicholas Newman, and Lauren Stewart. 2016. Motivating Stroke Rehabilitation Through Music: A Feasibility Study Using Digital Musical Instruments in the Home. In *Proceedings of the 2016 CHI Conference on Human Factors in Computing Systems* (CHI '16). ACM, New York, NY, USA, 1781-1785

[9] Mikko Kytö, David McGookin, Wilfried Bock, Héctor A. Caltenco, and Charlotte Magnusson. 2018. Designing Bimanual Tangible Interaction for Stroke Survivors. In *Proceedings of the Twelfth International Conference on Tangible, Embedded, and Embodied Interaction* (TEI '18). ACM, New York, NY, USA, 245-252.

[10] Alexandros Pantelopoulos, and Nikolaos Bourbakis, A Survey on Wearable Sensor-Based Systems for Health Monitoring and Prognosis. IEEE Transactions on Systems, Man, and Cybernetics, Part C (Applications and Reviews), 2009. **40**(1): p. 1-12.

[11] Edward Taub, Miller NE, Novack TA, Cook EW III, Fleming WC, Nepomuceno CS, Connell JS, Crago JE. Technique to improve chronic motor deficit after stroke. *Arch Phys Med Rehabil*. 1993;74:347–354

[12] Steven L Wolf, Pamela A Catlin, Michael Ellis, Audrey Link Archer, Bryn Morgan, and Aimee Piacentino. Assessing wolf motor function test as outcome measure for research in patients after stroke. *Stroke*, 32(7):1635–1639, 2001.

# A TUI To Explore Cultural Heritage Repositories on The Web

**Javier Pereda**
Liverpool John Moores University
Liverpool, UK
j.pereda@ljmu.ac.uk



*TEI '19*, March 17–20, 2019, Tempe, AZ, USA

ACM ISBN 978-1-4503-6196-5/19/03.
DOI:https://doi.org/10.1145/3294109.3301000

## Abstract
This article presents a paper-based Tangible User Interface (TUI) that facilitates the production of complex queries on a Cultural Heritage (CH) repository. The system helps to easily make use of the data elements and Boolean logic that describe the collections. This research presents a design methodology divided into two main phases: A User Experience (UX) and User Centred Design (UCD) where potential users' behaviours are analysed, followed by the development and evaluation of the TUI prototype.

The TUI uses off the shelf electronics and a paper-based set of tokens to engage the user with the system, thus facilitating the exploration with CH collections through querying.

## Author Keywords
Tangible User Interface; Querying; Cultural Heritage; Table top Interaction, Paper-based TUI

## ACM Classification Keywords
**Human-centered computing → User centered design,** Empirical studies in interaction design, Information visualization

## Introduction

Cultural Heritage (CH) organisations are increasingly using Semantic Web technologies to describe their collections. Although this enhances the quality of information used to describe these, it has also increased its technical and conceptual complexity. For example, to query this data, users have to use a specific syntax, data fields, controlled vocabularies, and Boolean logic. This research focused on understanding how a TUI could reduce the technical and conceptual layers of complexity required to query these CH collections on the Web. The research case study used data from Europeana, that provides access to 12% of all digitised European collections through its API. This paper (1) introduces the TUI system and discuss the challenges of querying the collections; and (2), presents the interaction design methodology, which was divided into two main phases: First, a User Experience (UX) and User Centred Design (UCD); followed by the Design and Evaluation process that aimed to understand how users produce queries and the complexity behind them.

Figure 1. TUI System

[1]The term pyfo, is used here as coined by Shaer et al., [7] (i.e. physical objects used as tools as part of an interactive system) and is used to avoid confusion with the terms 'object' or 'token' that can also be related to computer science or CH artefacts which in those cases have a different meaning.

## A Tangible System to query Cultural Heritage knowledge on the Web

The TUI presented in this paper helped participants to produce complex queries applying the data fields, concepts and Booleans, as well as to refine their queries through Europeana's API, thus accessing billions of records from over 4,000 organisations across Europe.

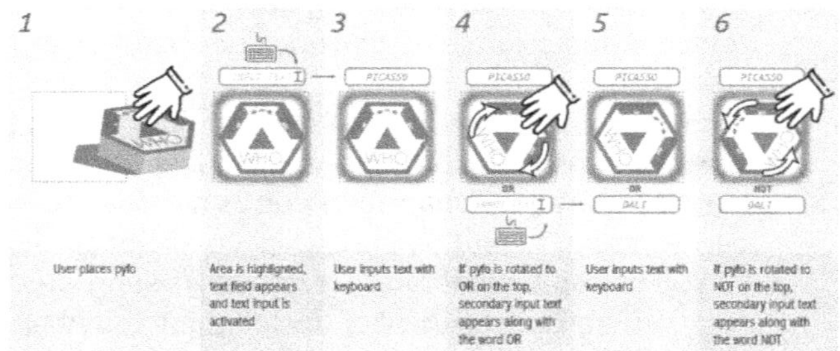


Figure 2. Interaction Process in TUI

The system was designed as a table-top TUI, where users place a series of *pyfos*[1] or tokens that represent aggregated data fields and an input field where strings of text can be typed. Each pyfo is colour coded and represent an aggregated field (Figure 1). There are six hexagonal primary pyfos aligned on the top that represent WHO, WHAT, WHEN and WHERE. A set of secondary rectangular pyfos represent a secondary WHO and WHAT for faceted searches. On the top right there is a scroll pyfo, as well as a pyfo marked with HOW MANY which will limit the amount of results retrieved in the API call. Query results are displayed as a scrollable list with their title and thumbnail. On the bottom right, there is a list of CH organisations and the amount of records retrieved by each. Finally, there is a SEARCH and CLEAR cubic pyfo to enter the API call or

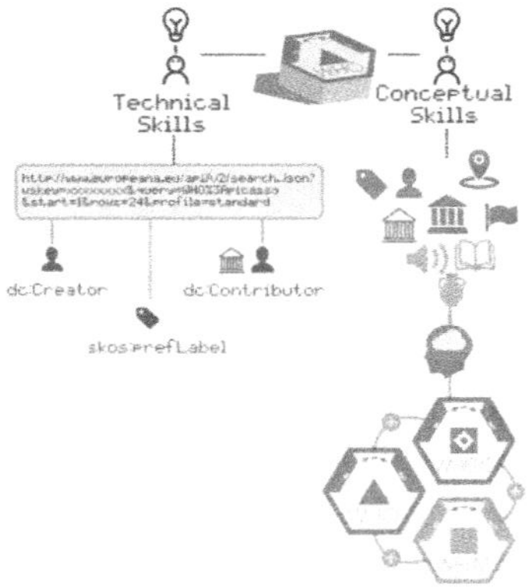


Figure 3. Complexity Skill Layers

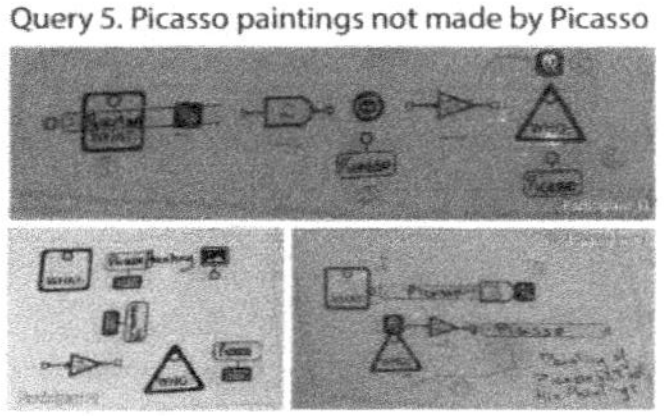


Figure 4. Top-Sticker tools for UX/UCD process. Bottom-Stickers used in Query 5 by Participant

to remove all fields and clear the displays. Hexagonal pyfos (e.g. WHO, SCROLL, WHEN) are can be rotated to display Boolean logic. When the user rotates the pyfo clockwise, it displays another text input field below the pyfo and ads the OR Boolean element (Figure 2). The same process is repeated by adding NOT when is rotated counter clockwise. This way, users can build queries such as: WHO:Picasso+NOT+Dali using the WHO hexagonal pyfo. This is the same for the WHAT and WHERE pyfos. Only the WHEN pyfo uses the Boolean TO to delimit the time period range for the query. Rotating this pyfo to the left will activate the text field to input the start date and to the right will activate the end date. Therefore a query that uses Europeana aggregated fields could search for WHEN:Medieval+TO+1800.

## Engaging with CH Concepts

CH repositories use controlled vocabularies such as the Europeana Data Model (EDM), that make information interoperable across diverse CH organisations. They describe implicit and explicit concepts [10, 11], as well as providing structure between them [10:94]. Nevertheless, querying such content require users to link a wide range of data elements and heritage knowledge. In addition, users also need to know the syntax in order to write the query even through an API. It cannot be expected from users to produce queries this way, since the vast majority of queries in Europeana and on the Web use no more than two keywords and not conceptual reference [5, 6, 12-14]. This research identified two main areas or layers of interaction that users needed to engage with to produce such complex queries: (1) a technical and technologic layer that focuses on query languages, data elements and syntax; and (2) a conceptual complexity layer that focuses on logic and the relation of concepts (Figure 3). The first layer refers to examples such as the aggregated field WHO, used in one of the pyfos, combining the DCMI element dc:creator, dc:contributor, the FOAF element foaf:name and the SKOS elements skos:prefLabel and skos:altLabel [17]. The second layer refers to the mental complexity required to make sense and relate the different concepts behind the data model. For this, TUIs can help engaging with the conceptual complexity since they have been proven beneficial for learning and exploring knowledge (Conceptual Layer) [21-23], as well as reducing the interaction complexity (Technologic Layer) [24, 25]. There are over 30 examples produced from Europeana's hackathons that fail to facilitate the engagement with the technical and conceptual elements [26], where such TUI benefits can be useful. That said, there are examples such as CubeQuery [27], Stackables [28] and Navigation Cubes [29] that showcase the benefit of using TUIs to query large databases similar to the ones in CH, but they do not embrace the specificity of the ontologies behind the data models. In addition, Tangible Atoms [30] and Ullmer et al., [31] system explored real estate information, and showcae the benefits of Token and Constrain (TAC) for combining complex sets of information.

## Design Methodology and evaluation

The interaction design methodology is split in two main phases: a UX/UCD experiment, followed by the design of the TUI prototype and its evaluation.

*UX/UCD Experiment*

This phase aimed to understand how users might approach the data elements if they already had the

| Data element | % |
|---|---|
| WHO | 7.1 |
| WHERE | 13.1 |
| WHEN | 9.1 |
| WHAT | 16 |
| TEXT | 6.7 |
| Booleans | 6.4 |
| AND | 9.2 |
| Extra metadata | 15.5 |

Table 1. Results of frequency count of main tools

**[2]UX/UCD Queries:**

1. 18th century Europeana objects from France
2. Objects that contain the name "Sofia" in their title.
3. Objects which contains the word "painting" in its description
4. Images of Picasso the painter (person) but not his painting (Picassos).
5. Find Picassos (paintings) that are not made by Picasso (person).
6. Pottery artefacts found in London
7. Open query

tools to do it. Previous research has indicated that 'think aloud' exercises in observational approaches are a good way in Human Computer Interaction (HCI) to gain insight into how a system might be used [32-34]. This experiment merged such observational approaches with pre-designed stickers that depicted possible query tools as a wireframing devise, which can be used to annotate and keep track of user actions [35].

In this experiment, a series of stickers were designed which depicted the aggregated fields (e.g. WHO, WHAT), as well as some of the specific domain ones, interaction elements such as keyboard input on a field, or selecting range in a map. The stickers also depicted cultural elements (e.g. artefact, book), and Boolean logic (e.g. NOT or OR). If there was a specific action or tool that was not available, a replacement sticker was used and annotated. Users were given a series of randomized queries where they placed the stickers on a paper surface and linked concepts, data elements and Booleans. Text strings for input fields were made by writing with a marker on an input field sticker and indicating another sticker for keyboard input. For this experiment, 21 participants from the CH sector (e.g. History, Archaeology) were recruited. Participants were presented with an opening questionnaire designed to identify their search behaviours, CH background and generation, and whether they were aware of any data models or Semantic Web technologies. The results showed that the vast majority of participants (18) were able to access the website and physically visit the organisation holding information about their research and 19 use the Web for their research. However, only 6 participants use search operators in Google's diverse search services, and only 3 felt they were experts when searching on the Web. Most participants (13) felt that the quality of information in Google Search was fair, while 10 felt that in academic search engines such as Google Scholar and Web of Science was very high. Only 2 participants felt that both search services were difficult to use. Despite this, although participants were able to pick out valuable information from their searches, their queries lacked the specificity to reduce uncertainty about what they were looking for. It is for this reason that most participants (11) indicated that one of the main issues when searching for information, was that it was scattered through too many sources.

Participants were asked to reproduce 6 different queries using the stickers and to produce a query based on their own academic research (UX/UCD Queries[2]). After the experiment, participants were presented with an exit survey about their experience with the querying process. After performing a frequency count, stickers were grouped into major group. For example, the tool WHERE (13.1%) encompassed its use through a geo-pin (3.2%), region selection (2.8%) and text description (7.1%) (Table 1). The main objective was to annotate their main strategies when producing queries. In addition, the sequence in which participants placed such tools was also annotated. It was noted that participants began their queries from general concepts (e.g. WHAT), and then proceeded to refine the term (e.g. WHAT – Artefact). The Boolean AND was counted as an independent element, since it was noted that participants used it as a mental aid to link concepts and not as a Boolean operation (Table 1).

Participants began their queries with general concepts such as WHAT or WHERE. After defining such concept, followed by a general term and refined in further detail the specific metadata elements such as data provider,

| Query | |
|---|---|
| **1.** Find paintings by Leonardo Da Vinci | |
| **2.**Cats provided or that come from Egypt… | …look for mummy cats also from Egypt |
| **3.** Objects (anything) dated between 1525 and 1527 | |
| **4.** Find any ceramic from Spain… | …ceramic not tiles from Spain and not from France |
| **5.** Sculptures or paintings that were made by Rodin and not by Picasso | |
| **6.** Medieval coins held in the United Kingdom | |
| **7.** Fashion objects from 1800 to 1900 from Italy… | … or from Wales |

Table 2. Evaluation queries given to participants

type of media (e.g. image, 3D). Participants segmented queries similarly to faceted queries with no less 2 main sections (concept), plus facets (Boolean or metadata). They used no less than 2 overarching concepts in a total of 4 different tools. All participants showed high disposition to search by using complex queries. Also, all participants produced queries related to their research, such as "sites that contain evidence of pottery style B" and "coins made by the King Offa found in a region of a map, that date from 750 to 850" and "carved stones of Abbes Hilda from the Anglo-Saxon period from Whitby Abbey in Yorkshire".

### *Development of a Tangible User Interface (TUI) Prototype and Evaluation*

The UX/UCD experiment, showed that users were more likely to begin their queries using aggregated fields and use them as main concepts. Each aggregated field was assigned a colour and shape (e.g. WHO-red triangle, WHAT-green square). This visual representation help users relate concepts and actions to any given object [36]. The main pyfos which activated the Boolean options through rotation, used a hexagonal prism. The faces of the hexagonal prism provided the affordances or sensorial responses related to balance, direction and gravity [36, 37], where in this case, it invited users to rotate it and placing it in the desired space and position. Secondary pyfos had no Boolean options, thus no rotation. For this reason, they are squared shapes, which contrary to a hexagon with more sides, it can be perceived as a more static object and invites less to rotate. All pyfos were made of paper, where using such basic volumes should require very little skill to build. The system was developed using off the shelf electronics such as a webcam and projector, as well as Web standard technologies such as HTML5 and JavaScript. It was designed using TUIO [8] as a main interaction protocol and connected it to the browser using a npTuioClient [9] to read the TUIO fiducials in the pyfos.

### Evaluation of TUI System

For the evaluation of the system, 11 participants were recruited. They were presented with an entry survey to identify their digital and search skills, and background. Only 7 of them worked in the heritage sector. Furthermore, only 3 participants took part on the UX/UCD phase. It can be said that despite that they were aware of the kind of content they could find in Europeana's collections, they were not necessarily aware of the API's data elements. Almost no participants knew what the Semantic Web was (9) and few used Booleans when searching on the Web (2). When searching the Web, 3 participants identified themselves as experts, 6 as competent, and 2 as novice. Participants were asked to reproduce 7 different queries in a random order (Table 2). Some of these had a second stage refinement. They were also offered the opportunity to produce their own queries. Completion time was measured, paused and restarted for the second refinement stage of the query. The open query was also timed.

### Evaluation Results

Although the validity of the query was not considered since they could be interpreted in different ways, there was a 100% completion rate. This is to say that all participants produced the queries using the diverse data and logic elements. When solving queries, participants spent in average 1 minute 6 seconds on the first query of the experiment. That time was dramatically reduced to an average of less than 50

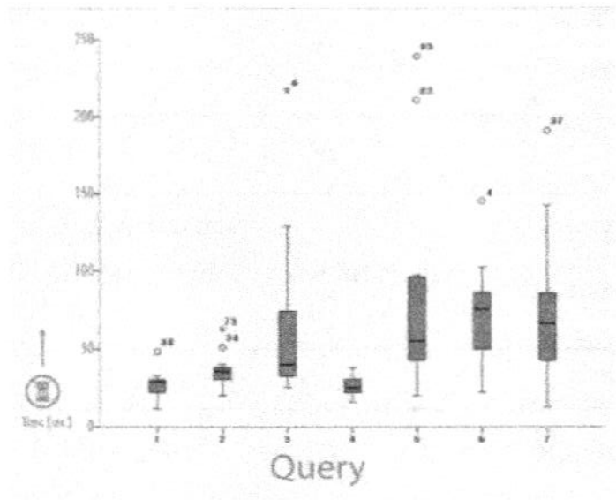


Figure 5. Completion time by query

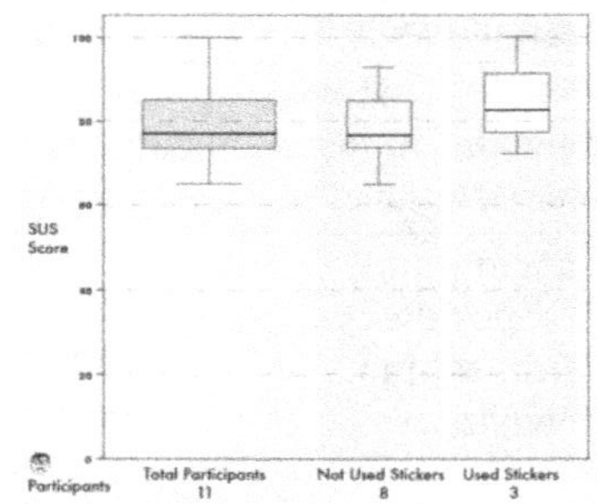

Figure 6. Usability results for final evaluation

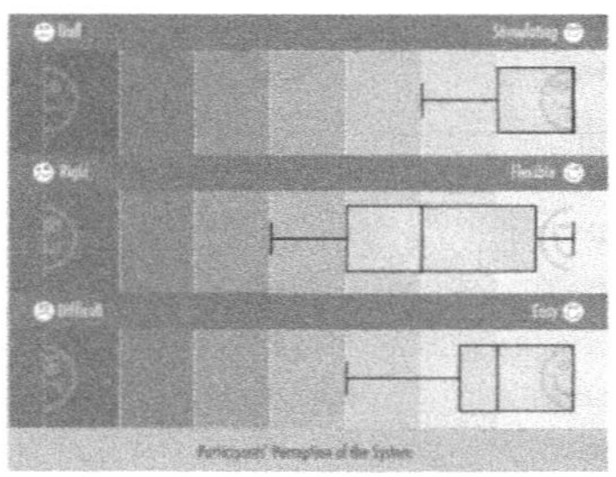

Figure 7. Participant's perception of the system

seconds for the following queries. The system showed fast learnability since participants had to manipulate no more than 2 actions when trying to produce the queries. For example, when using Booleans, which required rotation, only 4 of 11 participants rotated the pyfo in the wrong direction, and realised quickly that they had to rotate it to the other direction. Queries 3, 5, 6 and 7 took longer to complete, while 1, 2 and 4 were completed in under 40 seconds. This could be attributed to a low level of complexity in the queries. Time completions were also compared to the place in which each query appeared, and the results suggest that users spent more time focusing on the conceptual elements instead of learning how to use the system. For example, in query 6, participants had to conceptualise the term 'medieval'. Three participants used numbers to define start and end years as a WHEN, while the remaining 8 defined it as a WHAT. Participants which used WHEN were from the CH sector, thus suggesting they had more information about the content, but still managed to produce the query.

A usability evaluation was also carried out based on the System Usability Scale (SUS) [38]. Participants were given 20 questions to help quantifying the strengths and weaknesses of the system. The SUS provides a symbolic quantitative value with a maximum number of 100. This value is used as a reference where, 50 – 60 would be the lowest value of accepted usability issues if the system is to be released. The TUI scored highly in the SUS score (Figure 8). It was also decided to split the scores of the 3 participants who took part in the previous experiment with the stickers. These participants gave a higher usability score but not significantly. The results showed that the system helped users to devise an exploration strategy and re-adapt it when needed. For example, 5 participants agreed and 6 strongly agreed that the system allowed them to experiment with different ideas for the queries. The system did not present any major interaction issues. Nevertheless, it was noted that participants had to drag their attention away from the pyfos when typing on the keyboard, thus disrupting the interaction flow. The perception of the system was positive. Participants found the interface easy to use, they indicated that the system was stimulating and that it motivated them to think and be conscious about the things they were trying to find. This became evident when they produced the queries, since they kept on re-arranging the pyfos until they were happy with the query and entered the query at the end.

## Conclusion

This paper presented a TUI that helped users to produce complex queries on CH collections on the Web. The TUI helped users to produce queries that combined multiple data elements, concepts and Boolean logic. It was designed by integrating users processes through an UCD/UX that eased the design of the prototype. This research aimed to reduce the gap in the way CH organisations offer access to their ever-growing collections. It showcases the benefits of using TUIs to query databases. On one hand, it can promote constructivist learning, helping users to engage with the collections' conceptual complexity. On the other, it facilitates the production of extensive query strings from diverse data fields used to describe the collections. The TUI presented in this paper, introduces an initial concept that can be adopted by CH organisations to further their engagement with their online collections.

## References


[1] European Commission, "Cultural Access and Participation," in "TNS Opinion & Social," European CommissionNovember 2013 2013, vol. 399 Available: http://ec.europa.eu/public_opinion/archives/ebs/ebs_399_en.pdf.

[2] B. J. Jansen and A. Spink, "How are we searching the World Wide Web? A comparison of nine search engine transaction logs," *Information processing & management,* vol. 42, no. 1, pp. 248-263, 2006.

[3] B. J. Jansen, A. Spink, J. Bateman, and T. Saracevic, "Real life information retrieval: A study of user queries on the web," in *ACM SIGIR Forum*, 1998, vol. 32, pp. 5-17: ACM.

[4] A. Spink, D. Wolfram, M. B. Jansen, and T. Saracevic, "Searching the web: The public and their queries," *Journal of the American society for information science and technology,* vol. 52, no. 3, pp. 226-234, 2001.

[5] iProspect, "Search engine user attitudes survey," April-May 2004 2004, Available: http://www.iprospect.com/premiumPDFs/iProspectSurveyComplete.pdf, Accessed on: October 12, 2017.

[6] iProspect, "iProspect Search Engine User Behavior Study - April 2006," 2006, Available: http://district4.extension.ifas.ufl.edu/Tech/TechPubs/WhitePaper_2006_SearchEngineUserBehavior.pdf, Accessed on: September 10, 2018.

[7] O. Shaer, N. Leland, E. H. Calvillo-Gamez, and R. J. Jacob, "The TAC paradigm: specifying tangible user interfaces," *Personal and Ubiquitous Computing,* vol. 8, no. 5, pp. 359-369, 2004.

[8] TUIO. (2018, 3 August 2018). *TUIO.org*. Available: http://www.tuio.org/

[9] F. I. Rusadi. (2018, 3 April). *npTuioClient* [Repository]. Available: https://github.com/trinkermedia/npTuioClient

[10] F. Lazarinis, S. Green, and E. Pearson, *Handbook of Research on E-learning Standards and Interoperability*. IGI Global, 2011.

[11] E. H. Lim, J. N. Liu, and R. S. Lee, *Knowledge Seeker-Ontology Modelling for Information Search and Management: A Compendium*. Springer, 2011.

[12] A. Spink and M. Zimmer, "Web search : multidisciplinary perspectives," ed. Berlin: Springer, 2008, pp. xi, 351 p. : ill. ; 25 cm.

[13] J. Nielsen. (2001, 3 August 2018). *Search: Visible and Simple*. Available: https://www.nngroup.com/articles/search-visible-and-simple/

[14] J. Fry, S. Virkar, and R. Schroeder, "Search Engines and Expertise about Global Issues: Well-defined Landscape or Undomesticated Wilderness?," in *Web Search*: Springer, 2008, pp. 255-275.

[15] DCMI. (2018, August, 3). *DCMI Metadata Terms*. Available: http://dublincore.org/documents/dcmi-terms/

[16] D. Brickley and L. Miller. (2014, August, 3). *FOAF Vocabulary Specification 0.99*. Available: http://xmlns.com/foaf/spec/

[17] Europeana. (2018, August, 3). *EUROPEANA SEARCH API*. Available: https://pro.europeana.eu/resources/apis/search

[18] T. H. Davenport and L. Prusak, *Information ecology: Mastering the information and knowledge environment*. Oxford University Press, 1997.

[19] C. Diez, *La Biblioteca Digital* (Biblioteconomia y documentacion). Guijon: Trea, 2013, p. 152.

[20] G. Marchionini, "Human–information interaction research and development," *Library & information science research,* vol. 30, no. 3, pp. 165-174, 2008.

[21] J. Piaget and M. T. Cook, "The origins of intelligence in children," 1952.

[22] B. Zaman, V. Vanden Abeele, P. Markopoulos, and P. Marshall, "Editorial: The evolving field of tangible interaction for children: the challenge of empirical validation," (in English), *Personal and Ubiquitous Computing,* Editorial Material vol. 16, no. 4, pp. 367-378, Apr 2012.

[23] M. L. Anderson, "Embodied Cognition: A field guide," *Artificial Intelligence,* vol. 149, no. 1, pp. 91-130, 2003.

[24] S. Bakker, A. N. Antle, and E. van den Hoven, "Embodied metaphors in tangible interaction design," *Personal and Ubiquitous Computing,* vol. 16, no. 4, pp. 433-449, Apr 2012.

[25] H. Ishii and B. Ullmer, "Tangible bits: towards seamless interfaces between people, bits and atoms," in *Proceedings of the ACM SIGCHI Conference on Human factors in computing systems*, 1997, pp. 234-241: ACM.

[26] Europeana. (2016, 10 February 2016). *Apps Showcase*. Available: http://labs.europeana.eu/apps?category=api-implementation,discovery

[27] R. Langner, A. Augsburg, and R. Dachselt, "CubeQuery: Tangible Interface for Creating and Manipulating Database Queries," presented at the Proceedings of the Ninth ACM International Conference on Interactive Tabletops and Surfaces, Dresden, Germany, 2014.

[28] P. Isenberg, S. Klum, R. Langner, J.-D. Fekete, and R. Dachselt, "Stackables: faceted browsing with stacked tangibles," in *CHI'12 Extended Abstracts on Human Factors in Computing Systems*, 2012, pp. 1083-1086: ACM.

[29] K. Camarata, E. Y.-L. Do, M. D. Gross, and B. R. Johnson, "Navigational Blocks: Tangible Navigation of Digital Information," *Proceedings of the 7th international conference on Intelligent user interfaces. ACM,* pp. 31-38, 2002.

[30] Tangible Display. (2013, 20 July 2018). *Tangible Display*. Available: http://tangibledisplay.com/

[31] B. Ullmer, H. Ishii, and R. J. Jacob, "Tangible query interfaces: Physically constrained tokens for manipulating database queries," in *Proc. of INTERACT*, 2003, vol. 2003, pp. 279-286.

[32] J. Ramey *et al.*, "Does think aloud work?: how do we know?," presented at the CHI '06 Extended Abstracts on Human Factors in Computing Systems, Montréal, Québec, Canada, 2006.

[33] D. Xu, J. C. Read, and R. Sheehan, "In search of tangible magic," in *Proceedings of the 22nd British HCI Group Annual Conference on People and Computers: Culture, Creativity, Interaction-Volume 2*, 2008, pp. 97-100: British Computer Society.

[34] G. Ciocca, P. Olivo, and R. Schettini, "Browsing museum image collections on a multi-touch table," *Information Systems,* vol. 37, no. 2, pp. 169-182, 2012.

[35] J. Allen and J. Chudley, *Smashing UX design: Foundations for designing online user experiences*. John Wiley & Sons, 2012.

[36] W. Wong, *Principles of form and design*. John Wiley & Sons, 1993.

[37] B. Pinna, "What is the meaning of shape?," *Gestalt Theory,* vol. 33, no. 3, p. 383, 2011.

[38] J. Brooke, "SUS - A quick and dirty usability scale," *Usability evaluation in industry,* vol. 189, pp. 189-194, 1996.

# Mole Messenger: Pushable Interfaces for Connecting Family at A Distance

**Xiaoyan Shen**
Massachusetts Institute of Technology
Cambridge, MA 02139, USA
xyshen@mit.edu

**Maggie George**
Harvard University
Cambridge, MA 02138, USA
mgeorge@gsd.harvard.edu

**Stephan Hernandez**
Massachusetts Institute of Technology
Cambridge, MA 02139, USA
smhernan@mit.edu

**Agatha Park**
Harvard University
Cambridge, MA 02138, USA
sunyoungpark@gsd.harvard.edu

**Yang Liu**
Massachusetts Institute of Technology
Cambridge, MA 02139, USA
liuymit@gmail.com

**Hiroshi Ishii**
Massachusetts Institute of Technology
Cambridge, MA 02139, USA
ishii@media.mit.edu



*TEI '19*, March 17–20, 2019, Tempe, AZ, USA

ACM ISBN 978-1-4503-6196-5/19/03.
https://doi.org/10.1145/3294109.3300990

## Abstract
Mole Messenger is a pair of connected creatures that help children share and send messages to their loved ones who may be far away. Each Mole Messenger box houses a pushable mole. When one is pushed, the other pops up, as if traversing to the other side of the globe. The mole can be tapped to carry different color messages when pushed and can be used to play physically engaged games across distances. This paper describes the design and implementation of the system, explores various approaches within the design space, engages with the context and user experience, and meditates on the potential for positive psychological impact. Inspired by one family's story of separation and how they helped their children stay connected, we hope Mole Messenger can become an important tool for communication and healthy emotional development in children.

## Author Keywords
Long-distance interaction; tangible interface; force feedback.

## CSS Concepts
• Human-centered computing ~ Haptic devices

**Figure 1**: Mole Messenger Prototype

## Introduction

Family separations in today's world are increasingly common, either due to divorce, to seeking economic opportunity, or to being displaced by crisis. As such, telecommunications have become important in maintaining family ties.

Phone calls and text messages are an effective way of overcoming family isolation for adults, but children are often left out of these family communications. Most children do not have a phone until they are 11 [8], nor do they have a strong repertoire of conversation skills to draw on, and so traditional telecommunication often fails to engage them.

Mole Messenger aims to fulfil this underdeveloped niche by providing a long-distance communication tool that suits the unique needs of children. Mole Messenger lowers the barrier of desired interaction by being less verbally intensive than calls or texts, and keeps communication paced by requiring a one-to-one ratio of interaction.

## Motivation and Context

The concept for Mole Messenger started with the story of one family's struggle to stay connected. One parent lives in China while the other resides in the U.S., and they each have one son with them. Unlike their parents, the two brothers do not interact with each other via the phone nearly as often, and thus feel isolated from each other.

### *Psychological Impact of Separation*

This family is not alone-- many families are separated due to divorce, immigration challenges, or reasons out of their control. Some are separated as refugees while fleeing war, famine, or natural disaster. In the United States alone, 2,654 families have been separated at the border [1], and even more are affected by the travel ban from predominantly Muslim countries. Separation can be traumatizing for children, and so family connection is all the more important.

### *Identification*

Identifying with anthropomorphic figures during play helps children build social skills. Mole Messenger's animal-like form invites children to consider the mole as their representative in interactions with their siblings, their "go between" that can magically teleport to the other side of the world to deliver and reflect messages.

## Related Work

Many tangible interactive devices have been created for connecting people separated by long distance [9]. For example, *Filimin* [4] is a decorative light that changes color with touch. When a group of lights are connected through wifi, the color change caused by the tapping of one user will be synchronized across all other users with that lamp network. It has been generally marketed towards families.

The Tangible Media Lab's *inTouch* uses synchronized cylindrical rollers to create a mutual tactile experience. While subtle, this object maintains a powerful connection between users by representing the physical push and pull a user generates [5]. Motamedi presented *Keep in Touch,* which is a fabric touchscreen interface that provides physical intimacy through a projection of blurred images of long-distance partners [6]. Previous child-to-child tangible objects such as *Playpals* have been designed as a pair, in which child A interacts with doll A, and child B interacts with doll B [7]. In this scenario, the dolls become avatars of each child, and both children identifies the non-interactive doll as the other child. The moles in Mole Messenger take a different approach. While there are physically two moles, the devices create an illusion is that there is a single mole that traverses from one mole-hole to another, as there is never a situation when both moles are simultaneously pushed or popped. This brings in a different effect where the children do not attribute each other's persona to the mole, but look at the mole as a mediator or an object that both children can equally interact with, even though they are miles apart. The Mole Messenger enables physical action-effect in long distance situations to create an illusion of physical proximity.

## User Research

The user research study that led to the development of the Mole Messenger began with a family separated by distance. One parent and child in the United States, the other parent with the younger brother of the family back in China. To better understand their struggle, we interviewed the father and his 9-year-old son, talking with each separately about their struggles to stay connected with the rest of the family over such distance. A key finding of this research was the father's worry that his sons were growing distant because they did not talk on the phone with each other. We asked his son to talk to us about his brother, and to draw out games he wished he could play with his brother. Video documentation and drawings were recorded for our research.

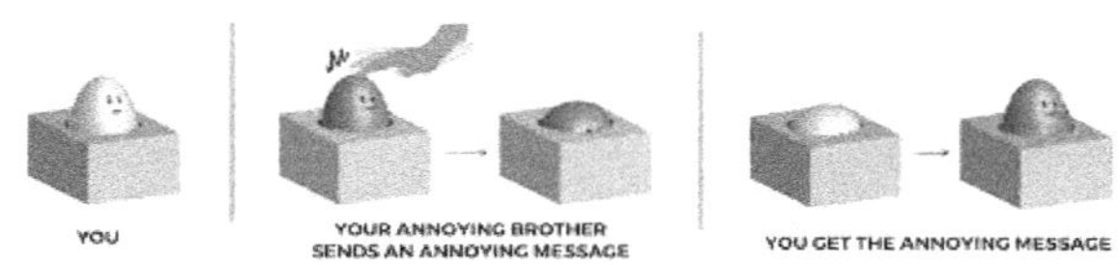


**Figure 2**: Interaction design of the prototype.

The user research for this project revealed a number of important constraints to the Mole Messenger design. It was determined that the device and communication strategy should be simple, given that we determined young children were much less likely to talk on the phone. It was also decided that the messaging action ought to be a one-to-one ratio in order to encourage equal communication. The mole comes in pairs of two, to foster intimacy. When one mole is up, the other will be pressed down, and so forth. Message communications were kept simple, with colors representing moods (Figure 2).

For the first iteration of the Mole Messenger, the device is intended to foster connection and communication in a single relationship-- between siblings. However, connection over distances is important to maintain with many people, and even within the family unit we studied, the connection between the parents and their children were of equal importance. Mole Messenger is designed to be an appropriate communication device for children, but we also envision it as a device that facilitates parent-child communication. A child away from a parent could have a Mole Messenger not only for their siblings, but for their parent as well.

## Mole Messenger

*Interaction*

The force sensor on the head of the mole is sensitive to different intensities and patterns of touch. Each defined state of touch corresponds to a different color and mood. When pressed, the force sensor at the base of the mole reads the new state of the pressed mole and sends a command to the sister mole to pop up. In this way, only one mole is ever in the pop state, which affords equal communication.

Since the primary action and effect is push and pop, the main purpose of interaction with the mole can be to nudge, poke, surprise, or say hi to the other sibling. These interactions are common between siblings or close friends. The immediacy of how a physical push induces a physical pop on the other side recreates the main convenience of physical proximity: the ability to grab attention effortlessly without turning on a phone or typing words.

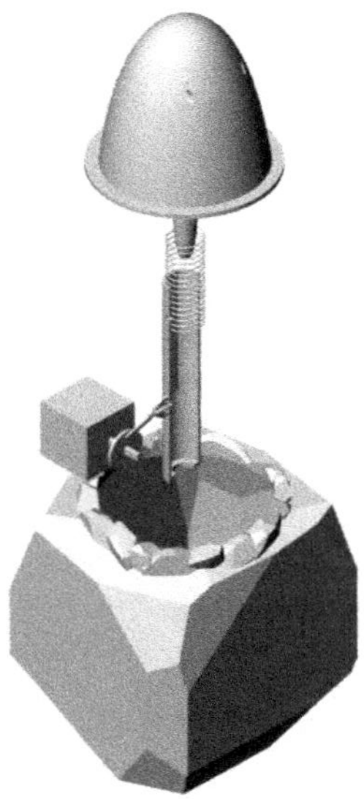

**Figure 3**: 3D models of the mechanical parts.

**Figure 4**: The two messengers with color synchronization. The left mole is pushed down and the right mole is up.

The recipient can interpret the message in two ways depending on whether they are present when the message is received or not. If the recipient is present when the mole pops, the message will alert the other sibling, like what a poke or a nudge would do. If the recipient is not present when the mole pops and discovers it later, the mole is seen more like a message or present that the other sibling has left.

This simplicity and non-content driven aspect lets the mole messenger stay not beholden to time zone differences. Siblings do not have to respond to messages immediately, and can get back to them whenever they want to. However, they can also interact contemporaneously, playing with each other by changing the mole's moods. Because of the conversational nature of the interactions, the number of travels by the mole becomes an indicator of how communicative the two siblings have been. Statistics of how long each mole has stayed popped may tell more about the siblings' relationship.

*Affordance*

Mole Messenger was designed to communicate use and function through affordances both in appearance and in tactile feedback. Because the moles bring to mind the whack-a-mole game and the button-like shape (Figure 1), children understand that they should press it. In attempting to press the mole, they might discover that a light force changes the color of the mole. Additionally, this tapping behavior is encouraged by the soft, depressible top portion of the mole's silicone head.

*Implementation*

The device consists of an Arduino Uno microcontroller, a stepper motor & motor control board, an LED Neopixel strip, and a number of force sensors. Force sensors sit on both the top of the mole's head and at the base of the internal mechanism. Each of the force sensors was calibrated for its specific task, one of which being to register soft touches and the other of which to register a hard press down from the mole. The stepper motor was carefully programmed to move very small distances and then pull back quickly, in order to trip the release mechanism before recoiling back.

*Mechanism*

The mechanism is spring-driven and provides the sudden "pop" of the mole (Figure 3). It also affords a satisfying click when the mole is pressed down to send a message. In all aspects of this design, fun, satisfying, and playful affordances were considered in order to make the usage of the mole readily apparent to the young users. The top of the mole is encased in a silicone "skin" over a hard shell, to provide a lifelike and pleasing tactile experience while still protecting the electronics inside. All hard components were 3D printed with PLA (Figure 4).

**Figure 6**: Design of the application scenarios. from top to bottom: game play; family collections; sharing candy.

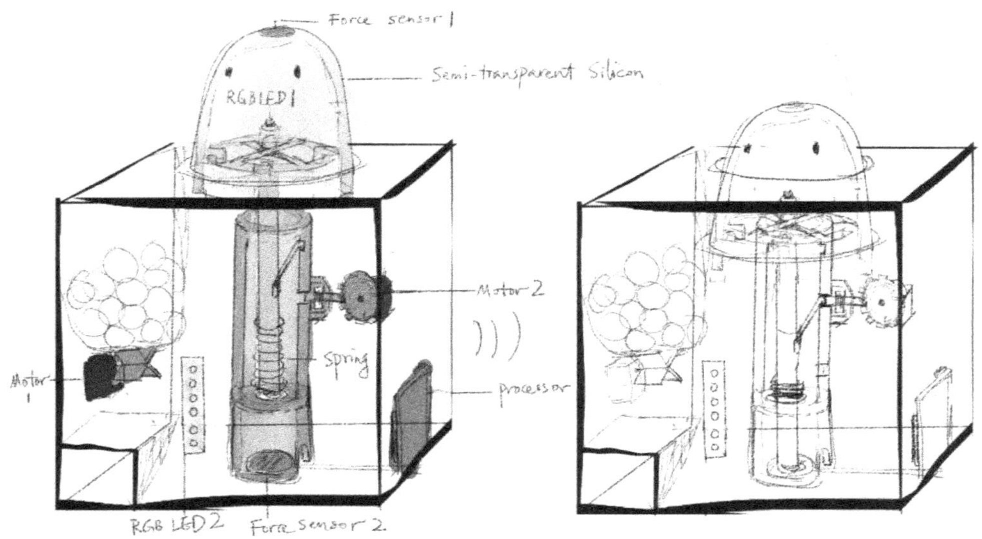


**Figure 5**: Sketch of the mechanical design with the candy sharing function.

## Application Scenarios

*Game Play*

A promising secondary mode for the Mole Messenger is a cross distance whack-a-mole game that siblings can play with each other while they are separated (Figure 6). Gameplay would come as an addition to the basic messenger functions. Unlike the messaging strategy, which does not require the siblings to interact at the same time, game play would instead invite a highly engaged form of sibling interaction. Our young interviewee, age 9, was strongly in favor of this game functionality.

*A Sharing Tool: Candy Gifts*

In addition to building the habit of communication, Mole Messenger may also be used as a tool to promote acts of sharing (Figure 5 & 6). In one scenario, we imagine a form of interaction in which users are periodically given the opportunity to "gift" candy to their siblings. The companion mole will then dispense a small candy, translating the act of kindness from the other sibling. This would involve some parental involvement.

*Family Collections*

Our initial model for the Mole Messenger focuses on sibling connection, but we envision a way in which children might connect with all their family members as well (Figure 6). Users might have an array of different moles, each representing a connection with a different family member. In this way, the family connectivity and dynamic is physically expressed by the presence of a mole for each separated family member.

## Discussion and Future Work

Additional functionality may be introduced to the Mole Messenger system to further offer a feeling of connection between separated siblings. The addition of an IR sensor, microphone, or other simple detection devices could offer indicators of sibling activity throughout the day, prompting the moles to respond accordingly with colors or sounds. Mimicry from the "mole" representatives might give siblings a stronger sense that the mole is their reflection, with similar habits and personalities. As such, this identification with the personified mole might strengthen the sibling bond by allowing separated siblings to feel as if they are physically with their family.

## Conclusion

The Mole Messenger offers a fun, engaging form of communication that suits the particular needs of siblings separated by distance. The time of separation can be hard for children, and so whimsical and comforting forms of connection are all the more important.

## References

[1] The Washington Post. Retrieved Nov 13 from https://www.washingtonpost.com/graphics/2018/local/tracking-migrant-family-separation/?noredirect=on&utm_term=.099c161cdc1a

[2] Hindle, D., 2007. Clinical research: a psychotherapeutic assessment model for siblings in care. *Journal of child psychotherapy*, *33*(1), pp.70-93.

[3] Xu, W., Yan, N., Chen, G., Zhang, X. and Feng, T., 2018. Parent–child separation: the relationship between separation and psychological adjustment among Chinese rural children. *Quality of Life Research*, *27*(4), pp.913-921.

[4] *Filimin*. Retrieved Nov 13 from https://filimin.com/

[5] Brave, S. and Dahley, A., 1997. inTouch: a medium for haptic interpersonal communication. In *CHI'97 Extended Abstracts on Human Factors in Computing Systems* (pp. 363-364). ACM.

[6] Motamedi, N., 2007. Keep in touch: a tactile-vision intimate interface. In *Proceedings of the 1st international conference on Tangible and embedded interaction* (pp. 21-22). ACM.

[7] Bonanni, L., Lieberman, J., Vaucelle, C., and Zuckerman, O., 2006. PlayPals: Tangible Interfaces for Remote Communication and Play. In *CHI '06 Extended Abstracts on human factors in computing systems* (pp.574-579). ACM.

[8] Influence Central, 2016. Kids & Tech: The evolution of today's digital natives. Retrieved Nov 13 from http://influence-central.com/kids-tech-the-evolution-of-todays-digital-natives/

[9] Ishii, H., 2008, February. Tangible bits: beyond pixels. In *Proceedings of the 2nd international conference on Tangible and embedded interaction* (pp. xv-xxv). ACM.

# CairnFORM: a Shape-Changing Ring Chart Notifying Renewable Energy Availability in Peripheral Locations

**Maxime Daniel, Guillaume Rivière, and Nadine Couture**
Univ. Bordeaux, ESTIA, LaBRI, UMR 5800
F-64210 Bidart, France
{m.daniel, g.riviere, n.couture} @estia.fr

## ABSTRACT

We present CairnFORM, a shape-changing cylindrical display that physicalizes forecasts of renewable energy availability. CairnFORM aims at creating and encouraging new socially-shared practices by displaying energy data in collective and public spaces, such as public places and workplaces. It is 360°-readable, and as a dynamic physical ring chart, it can change its cylindrical symmetry with quiet motion. We conducted two user studies. The first study clearly revealed the attractiveness of CairnFORM in a public place and its usability for a range task and for a compare task. Consequently, this makes CairnFORM useful to analyze renewable energy availability. The second study revealed that a non-constant motion speed is the better visualization stimulus at a workplace.

### Author Keywords

Tangible User Interface; Shape-Changing Interface; Data Physicalization; Ring Chart; Renewable Energy; Demand-Side Management; Shifting Energy Demand; Ambient Notifications; Peripheral Vision; User Study.

## INTRODUCTION

Demand-Side Management (DSM) can help to increase the consumption of renewable energy. However, as energy generation shifts to renewables and microgeneration[1], the interplay between energy supply and energy demand becomes more complex to manage. Critical problems, such as peak demand, can lead to power outages and make the electrical grid inefficient [10]. These issues are amplified by the fluctuation of renewable energy generation according to weather conditions (e.g., sun, wind, wave, tide) and by the limitations of energy storage capacities [14]. Unless energy storage becomes economically and environmentally reliable to balance energy supply against energy demand [37], we will need to synchronize energy demand with renewable energy availability. During the last five years, researchers have designed and studied systems to encourage users in using renewable energy. Most of these systems target households. As suggested by Pierce and Paulos [45], we should also design systems for collective or public spaces, as workplaces, cafes, parks, schools, museums, and urban places. These targeted contexts require adapted displays and visualization elements.

[1]Microgeneration is small-scale generation of electricity or heat by individuals, businesses, or communities to meet their own needs.



*TEI '19,* March 17–20, 2019, Tempe, AZ, USA
© 2019 ACM. ISBN 978-1-4503-6196-5/19/03...$15.00
DOI: https://doi.org/10.1145/3294109.3295634

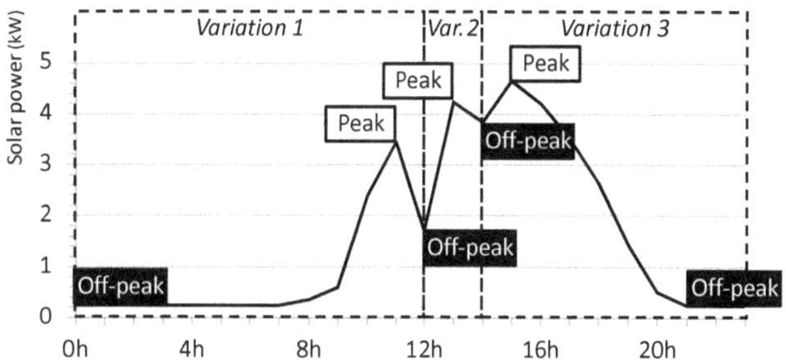


Figure 1: Three variations of solar power generation during a partly cloudy day in summer (produced with a 5 kW installation of photovoltaic panels, on the buildings' roof of our laboratory, on August 26, 2012).

In this paper, we present CairnFORM, a shape-changing cylindrical display that can change cylindrical symmetry. We use CairnFORM as a 360°-readable, dynamic ring chart that physicalizes renewable energy data in public spaces, such as public places and workplaces.

The remainder of this paper is organized as follows. In the following section, we present the major requirements that lead to the design of a new kind of display. In Section 3, we discuss some solutions from previous work. Then, in Section 4, we describe our CairnFORM shape-changing interface in detail and propose three possible motion speeds to animate it at workplaces. In Section 5, we describe the two user studies that we conducted in order to evaluate CairnFORM and the motion speeds. Then, in Section 6, we outline the contribution of these studies, for both the domains of energy demand-side management and shape-changing interfaces. In Section 7, we discuss the contributions and the limitations of this work. Finally, we conclude and provide directions for future work.

## THE DESIGN OF A NEW KIND OF DISPLAY

Using renewable energy rather than non-renewable energy is a strategy considered as appropriate to reduce environmental impact. Over the last five years, interactive systems have been designed to encourage users in using renewable energy when there is plenty of it rather than when there is little (i.e., shifting energy demand) [5,29,44,47,50,53]. Most of these systems target households to plan everyday energy usage (e.g., washing machine, oven, battery charger) by visualizing forecast data of renewable energy production using graphical charts such as clock charts [29,50], timeline charts [50], and line charts [29,53]. But interactive systems will also be useful to shift energy demand in public spaces, especially in microgeneration contexts.

Data physicalizations are growing popular in many societal domains which indicates a strong potential for fostering public engagement [24]. Typical examples of dynamic physicalizations are dynamic physical charts, ranging from line charts[2] to pie charts [49], and to bar charts [55]. These new kind of charts create opportunities to display energy forecasts in public spaces in an engaging way. The tangible representation of energy Watt-I-See [47] is an example of such a public installation.

In order to display energy data in public places and at workplaces, such as open-plans and offices, our viewpoint-independent display can be installed anywhere. The discrete ring structure displays ordinal data: each ring represents the average energy available in one hour. Displaying hourly forecasts[3] aims at, in our use case, providing simple instructions to the users: simple time slots are easier to remember in order to plan energy shifting.

Retrieving variations' peaks is a basic task of energy shifting. An energy variation starts from a minimum energy availability (local minimum or global minimum), increases until a maximum (local maximum or global maximum), and decreases until the following minimum (local minimum or global minimum). Renewable energy production on a day has rarely a single variation; several variations often occur the same day (see the example shown in Figure 1). We understood, thanks to a preliminary user study using charts printed on paper [6], that users struggle in retrieving all the peaks when visualizing variations all-at-once (see Figure 2a). We iterated with three groups of seven participants using a unicolored chart displaying all the variations, a grayscale chart displaying all the variations, and grayscale charts displaying the variations one-after-another. The participants were asked to follow instructions (i.e., identifying times to plug or unplug a laptop battery) thanks to the charts. In the first two conditions, most of the participants found only the highest peak hour (i.e., global maximum) and failed to find the smaller peak hours (i.e., local maxima); in the third condition (see Figure 2b), they retrieved, however, all the peaks. Whereas forecast data were visualized for the 12 following hours in [29], for the

[2]Pulse: Tangible Line Graph (2012), `http://www.dataphys.org/list/pulse-tangible-line-graph/`

[3]We use data from `http://www.epices-energie.fr/` that provides hourly photovoltaic production forecast for every day.

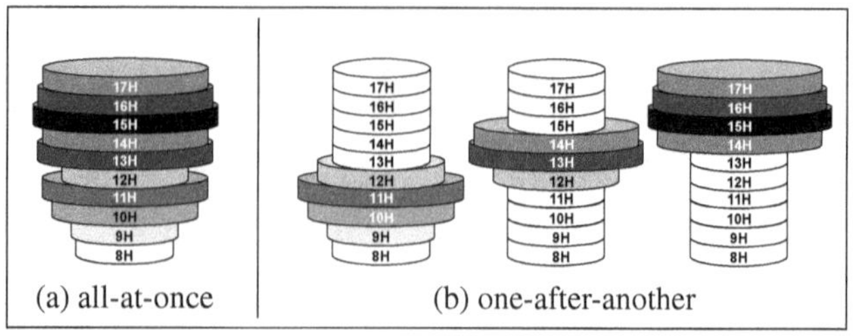


Figure 2: Two ways of visualizing variations.

24 following hours in [53], and for the whole day in [50], in our case, variations are displayed one-after-another in order to benefit of all the variations of a day.

Finding the peak hour of the ongoing variation is necessary for implementing energy shifting. Employees must, however, be notified of an incoming variation without being interrupted or disturbed in their professional activity. CairnFORM has then to be perceivable, but not irritating. Moreover, to create and to encourage new socially-shared energy practices, CairnFORM must be attractive and pleasant in public places.

## PREVIOUS WORK

Environment and energy issues became a research topic in Human–Computer Interaction in 1998, by taking the approach of persuasion [8]. The resulting systems have mainly aimed at reducing energy consumption at home, using smartphones [30,41–43,60] and physical representations [1,12,17]. In 2012, the approach framed by persuasion is criticized as it focuses either on changing individuals' behavior [4] and on the current centralized systems of energy production [45]. New directions include focusing on new sociocultural practices [4], designing interactive systems for workplaces and for public or communal spaces, as well as targeting emerging energy systems (e.g., smartgrids, microgeneration, demand response) [45]. This way, some physical interfaces were designed to show the real-time use of energy sources (e.g., central coal power, local solar power, local wind power) [44,46,47], and some graphical interfaces were designed to show energy forecasts in order to shift energy demand at home [3,29,50,53]. Our approach uses actuated physical representations to display renewable energy forecasts in public spaces and at workplaces.

The first tangible user interface using the third actuation loop [19] that maintains the physical state when the data model changes can be attributed to Patten et al. [40] in 2007. This concept is formalized in the terms of Radical Atoms by Ishii et al. [20] in 2012. Close research areas have a similar approach—but with different goals—such as Shape-Changing Interfaces [54] and Data Physicalization [24]. There is some prior work following these approaches, such as Relief [35], inFORM [9], and TRANSFORM [21]. Recent shape-changing interfaces make use of actuators (e.g., mechanical [2], thermal [16], magnetic [34], acoustic [52], pneumatic [64], or biologic [65]) to control the physical properties (e.g., form [18], viscosity [25], volume [27], position [33], texture [35], orientation [57]) of surfaces (e.g., [16]), curves (e.g., [39]) that they use as system input or output. Some shape-changing interfaces that relate to our context use ambient awareness to subtly inform

at offices (e.g., [22,26]). These interfaces exploit ambient awareness—the ability of being aware of the surrounding information [61]—and they are able to move from peripheral attention to central attention of users, and the other way round [59]. Dynamic physical charts [49,55] also relate to our context, but we aim at using one with 360°-readability.

A typical 360°-display for public places is iSphere [63]: this flying drone that displays data on its surrounding rotating 88-cm-diameter, spherical screen is designed to inform in stadiums. StaTube [15] is a 360°-display designed for offices: it displays user states with seven illuminated rings of 6 cm diameter and it is 17 cm high. Vessels of Irelands Past[4] is an example of 360°-readable chart that is, however, not a dynamic chart. The skeleton of Amphorm [32] is a 33-cm-high tower of five expandable rings that, however, was not designed to display ordinal data and morphs to an 11-point star shape. The closest design that matches our needs are the modular expandable rings proposed by Daniel et al. [7] and Wu [62]. These stackable rings are animated mechanical structures that morph to ring-like shapes. The latter uses six arcs, with gaps between the arcs; the later uses eight overlaying arcs that maintain a continuous circle-like border when expanding. Building upon these works, we developed a prototype of 360°-readable, physical ring chart.

## THE CAIRNFORM SYSTEM

In this paper, we focus on the specific context of displaying energy availability in public spaces that opens ways for new socially shared practices in energy Demand-Side Management. In the context of microgeneration, to the best of our knowledge, CairnFORM is the first work that uses a shape-changing ring chart to display ordinal data in public spaces. We designed CairnFORM as an illuminated and dynamic vertical bar chart with cylindrical symmetry that allows 360°-readability. The major goal is to make renewable energy data available in public spaces in a pleasant and efficient way.

CairnFORM is designed to be pleasant and appealing in order to attract people in public places and to raise discussions about renewable energy. The animation of stacked illuminated rings—in sequence or in parallel—intends to be a playful phenomena and a hedonic experience. Displaying forecasts about renewable energy availability with an appealing interface in public places aims at playing as a socialization element like when people talk about weather forecasts. The aim, in the future, is to lead to new practices such as shifting energy demand in the context of microgeneration. But to do so, CairnFORM has to be usable for peak retrieval tasks.

Beyond playfulness in public places, CairnFORM has to be calm at workplaces, like open-plans and offices. At offices, employees commonly perform tasks on their laptops in the focus of attention (e.g., reading, writing, drawing) using their central vision. To plan a shift, employees must be aware of the next variation to come. However, the employees should be notified of a new incoming variation without disrupting their central attention and without interrupting their main activity. In this context, we want CairnFORM to work as an ambient

[4]Vessels of Irelands Past #2 (2014), http://tactiledata.net/

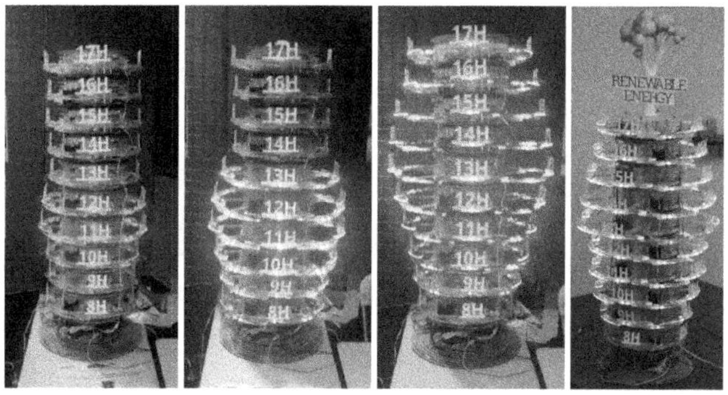

(a) $V_{3h}$ (b) $V_{6h}$ (c) $V_{9h}$ (d) $V_{9h}$

Figure 3: (a)(b)(c) Our CairnFORM prototype, displaying variations of different sizes during a public event. (d) The new design of our CairnFORM prototype.

display that subtly notifies users in their environment. To do so, Gutwin et al. [13] recommend shape-changing stimuli, which are more perceived than light-changing stimuli across the visual field. Consequently, the diameter-change stimulus of CairnFORM, besides being calm, in the workplace context, has to be perceivable enough. CairnFORM aims indeed at assisting employees in new energy consumption practices; it thus has to be efficient to help in saving more energy than it consumes. The main question is the following:

### What is the best motion speed?

To answer this question, we implemented three motion speeds for the rings' diameter change. The best motion speed has to be understood in terms of perceptibility and tranquility. A key problem in designing ambient interfaces is notifying without irritating. We chose the motion speeds so that they are alternatives of different kinds, but equal duration. The first speed is a constant diameter change over time, which can be considered as neutral; the second one is a slow and then accelerating diameter change that follows an exponential curve over time; and the third one is a fast and then slowing down diameter change that follows a logarithmic curve over time. These three kinds of speed are denoted in the following by $S_{const}$, $S_{exp}$, and $S_{log}$, respectively. We applied these three speeds to the two kinds of ring's motion: a full expansion, which increases the diameter from 35 cm to 62 cm, and a full retraction, which decreases the diameter from 62 cm to 35 cm. These two motions were done in six seconds. We denote these two motions in the following by $M_{expansion}$ and $M_{retraction}$, respectively.

### Implementation

We designed a prototype of CairnFORM on the basis of modular stackable, expandable, illuminated rings. The design process, the implementation, and the limitations of our ring setup are described in a previous paper [7]. Inspired by a previous solution using six arcs [62], our ring design uses eight overlaying arcs. The ring prototype can expand its diameter from 35 cm to 62 cm. This stackable ring weighs 2.3 kg and takes two workdays to build by one person: 4 hours of laser cutting, 5 hours of 3D printing, 4 hours of

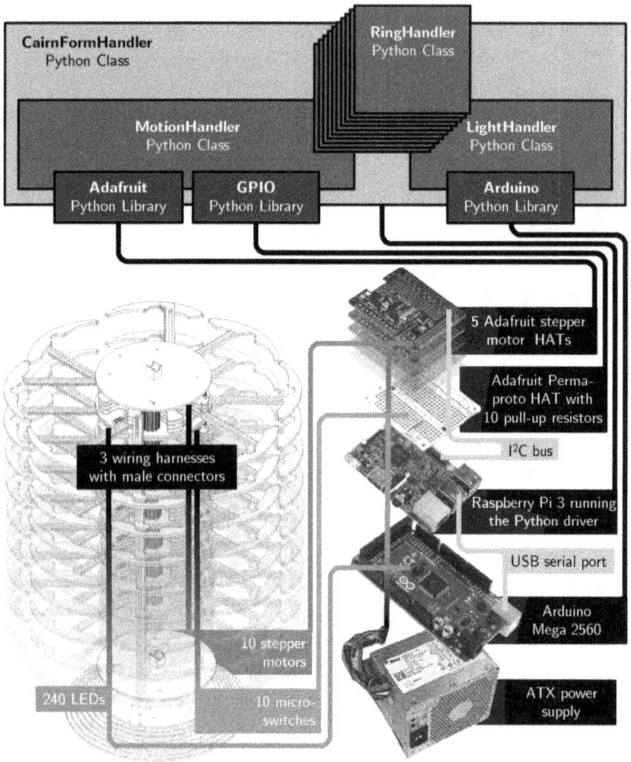


Figure 4: Hardware and software to control CairnFORM.

| Element | Min | Max | Parameter |
|---|---|---|---|
| Diameter | 35 cm | 62 cm | |
| Color & brightness | | | 24-bit RGB |
| Motion duration | 2 s *(s)* / 3 s *(p)* | | |
| Motion speed | | | const \| exp \| log |
| Motion steps | | 250 of 1.08 mm | |

*(s) rings controlled in sequence. (p) rings controlled in parallel.*

Table 1: CairnFORM's rings visualization elements.

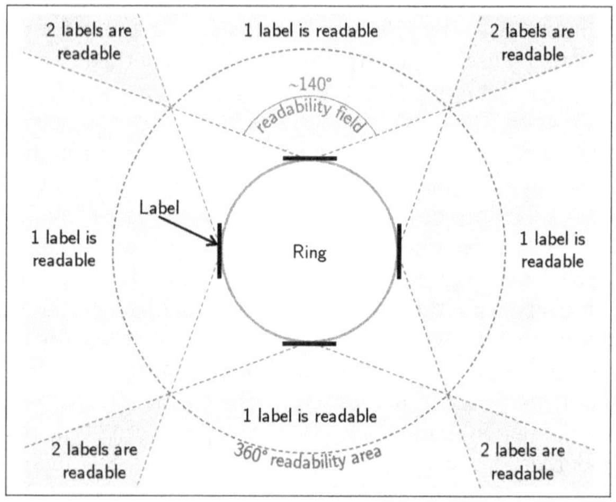


Figure 5: The 360°-readability area of the four labels.

electronics wiring, and 4 hours of hardware assembling. Our modular ring design enables stacking from 1 to approximately 24 rings: adding rings is possible by adding HATs and Arduino cards; but the central column's width limits the wiring harness' growth to approximately 24 rings (The vertical stability of a 24-ring CairnFORM is however not guaranted). A 12-ring CairnFORM is intuitive to present hourly data, but displaying a ten-hours workday—including lunch time—was enough for experimentations. We thus manufactured ten rings and built up a 105-cm-high, 10-ring CairnFORM (see Figure 3), which costs approximately 2,350€ of hardware. The hardware and software to control a 10-ring CairnFORM are illustrated by Figure 4.

CairnFORM's driver can control the rings in sequence or in parallel. The driver is written in Python language (version 2.7), runs on one Raspberry Pi 3, implements four classes, and uses threads and event queues. The source code is available on GitHub[5] under the GPL license. The driver uses a Mosquitto [36] MQTT broker[6] that makes CairnFORM become an IoT device receiving requests from WiFi IP networking.

Our CairnFORM prototype enables visualization elements, such as rings color and brightness, rings diameter, and rings motion at different speed, duration, and steps. Table 1 summarizes the range of these visualization elements. We correlated CairnFORM rings' diameter and brightness to the renewable energy availability: for a power generation capacity ranging from 0 W to *max* W, a fully retracted ring with light off represents a 0 W availability and a fully expanded ring with full blue brightness represents a *max* W availability. We tagged the rings of CairnFORM with 3D-printed labels that mark the ten hours they represent (from 8h00 to 17h59). Four of these labels are glued on each ring (one on each quadrant). These four labels allow a readability area from all around CairnFORM (see Figure 5).

## EXPERIMENTATIONS

We conducted two user studies for evaluating CairnFORM. The first study was an into-the-wild user study to see whether the users enjoy the interface and succeed in retrieving information. The second study was a laboratory user study to evaluate and compare the three motion speeds $S_{const}$, $S_{exp}$, and $S_{log}$. The experiments were organized by one person who explained the tasks, demonstrated the use, and collected oral remarks. The participants filled in a written questionnaire in the first study and answered an oral questionnaire in the second user study. These questionnaires were designed to get the answers of the exercises and to get qualitative and subjective feedback about CairnFORM.

### First User Study

The first user study was organized as a two-day, into-the-wild usability evaluation during a public event gathering 2,000 visitors (The 24h of Innovation®, December 1-2, 2017, Biarritz, France). This first user study was designed to assess the usability of a 10-ring CairnFORM for information retrieval

[5]Source code: `https://github.com/maximedaniel/CairnFORM`

[6]MQTT: Message Queuing Telemetry Transport, a messaging protocol where subscribers reveice messages from publishers according to the classes they subscribe.

| Variation | Length | Start | Peak | End |
|---|---|---|---|---|
| $V_{3h}$ | 3h | 10:00 | 11:00 | 12:59 |
| $V_{6h}$ | 6h | 8:00 | 11:00 | 13:59 |
| $V_{9h}$ | 9h | 9:00 | 13:00 | 17:59 |

Table 2: Design of the three variations.

tasks. 90 visitors were recruited among those who stopped to our booth. These 90 visitors were divided in three equally sized groups that were all with a median of 20-29 years old, but with variable genders and university degrees: (G1) 8 females, 22 males, with a median of 3 years university degree; (G2) 7 females, 23 males, with a median of 2 years university degree; and (G3) 8 females, 22 males, with a median of 2 years university degree.

The exercise required three kinds of low-level information retrieval tasks—range, compare, and order [23]—that we adapted to energy variation. The three information retrieval tasks were the following: ($T_{range}$) Give the hour range of the renewable energy production; ($T_{compare}$) Indicate the peak hour of the renewable energy production; and ($T_{order}$) Sort the hours of the variation in ascending order of renewable energy production. One variation of different length was assigned to each group: one of three hours for G1, one of six hours for G2, and one of nine hours for G3. The characteristics of these three variations—denoted in the following by $V_{3h}$, $V_{6h}$, and $V_{9h}$, respectively—are summarized in Table 2; the visualizations of these three variations with CairnFORM are shown on Figure 3. After the exercise, the written questionnaire included the short version of the standardized User Experience Questionnaire (UEQ-S [51]) to measure the subjective impression of users towards the user experience of CairnFORM.

This first experimentation had three main results and two consequences on the design of CairnFORM. The first consequence is to add a 3D-printed, removable model tree on top of CairnFORM, with a label telling what data is displayed; at first sight, one visitor thought the ring chart was a clock and another one thought it was a timer for the public event. The second consequence is to change the rings' color from blue to green; one participant observed that this color goes better with renewable energy. The new design of CairnFORM is shown in Figure 3d. The first result is the easiness we had in recruiting the three groups during the event. The second result is the user experience that was rated both as *good* and *excellent*. The third result is the usability of CairnFORM for $T_{range}$ and $T_{compare}$, which determine variation analyses. Moreover, this latter result provides a use case that extends the results of [23].

### Second User Study

The second experiment was organized as a controlled-condition evaluation in our lab. This second user study was designed to qualify the three motion speeds $S_{const}$, $S_{exp}$, and $S_{log}$ for animating CairnFORM. We were interested to know which motion speed is the best to inform of a change and to determine which one is the less disturbing and the less annoying, and, before all, which motion speed is the best to unobtrusively notify users in horizontal peripheral vision.

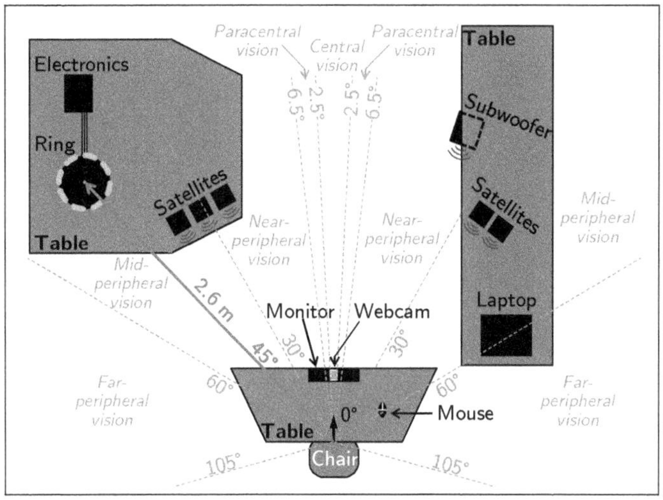


Figure 6: Plan view of the setup of the experiment.

The 30 participants were researchers from our laboratory, staff from the administration department, and students from the campus: 13 of these volunteers were female and 17 were male, aged with a median of 30-34 years old, graduated with a median of 5 years university degree. The apparatus is schematized with a plan view in Figure 6. The participants were sitting on a chair at approximately 50 cm in front of a monitor. A webcam was fixed on top of the monitor. The participants were asked to adjust the height of the seat to align their sight with the webcam. A 1-ring CairnFORM was placed at a distance of approximately 2.6 m away from the head of the participants, in the middle of the mid-peripheral vision[7] (i.e., at an angle of 45° when looking at the center of the monitor). At this distance, the size of the ring covers approximately 7° of the visual field when fully retracted (the region from 41.5° to 48.5°) and approximately 14° when fully expanded (the region from 38° to 52°): the ring stays in the mid-peripheral vision.

We had to reduce the noise of our ring prototype. We placed 5 cm of foam under the ring to limit propagation and amplification of vibrations by the table—the noise decreased from 60 dB to 50 dB when measured[8] at a distance of 1 m. The remaining noise was masked by asking the participants to wear 30-dB-SNR-attenuation ear defenders and by playing white noise with a 5.1 surround sound system speaker placed in front of the participants[9] (see Figure 6). This setup allowed the participants to perceive the ring's motion only thanks to the peripheral vision. The participants were also told to focus on the screen and not to look at the ring during the two following exercises. These two exercises aim at catching the ring's motion with the peripheral vision, but with different attention levels: one is with the focus of attention (i.e., focusing attention on the detection task) and the other

[7]The mid-peripheral vision—covering the region from 30° to 60°—defines the limit of the upwards peripheral vision [13].

[8]Repeated measures with three apps on a smartphone and a tablet.

[9]The white noise was played for short durations during the trials; it was turned off when giving the instructions and when filling in the questionnaires.

(a) $T_{detection}$ (b) $T_{perception}$ (c) $T_{perception}$

Figure 7: Screens of the two tasks.

is with the periphery of attention (i.e., ambient awareness; because another task gets the focus of attention).

The first exercise allows training and learning perception with peripheral vision. This exercise consists in detecting six ring's motions (three expansions and three retractions) while focusing on a 25-second timer that is running at the center of the monitor's screen. When detecting a ring's motion—with the peripheral vision—the user must click a button beneath the timer with the mouse pointer (see Figure 7a). Motions are randomly triggered by the computer between 5 seconds and 15 seconds. We denote this task in the following by $T_{detection}$.

The second exercise tests ambient awareness. This exercise is based on a series of seven short-term memory tasks. For each of the seven trials, the user must memorize during ten seconds a sequence of five symbols (crosses and circles, see Figure 7b). Then, the user must replicate the sequence one symbol at a time: every two seconds the user must recall the next symbol of the sequence by clicking on the symbols displayed at the right of the screen (see Figure 7c). When replicating, a ring's motion can occur or not: three expansions and three retractions occur, but one trial is motionless. After each trial, the users answer whether a ring's motion occured and whether it was an expansion or a retraction or whether they don't known. We denote this task in the following by $T_{perception}$.

This experiment follows a within-subject design: the participants went through the two exercices with the three motion speeds. The order of the speeds was counterbalanced using a Latin square and the same order was kept for the exercises of a user. These exercises, however, were tiring; including demonstrations and training trials before each exercise, and written questionnaires afterwards with each speed condition, the whole session lasted approximately 45 minutes per user. Moreover, focusing attention and replicating sequences is a hard work. Before starting the next phase with the exercise 2, sweets and orange juice were offered to the participants in order to maintain well-being and performance.

The data were available for 1,080 ring motions. We used the facial expression analysis software FaceReader 4 on the video recordings of the webcam to detect if participants gazed at the ring. We post-processed manually the resulting log files to validate or unvalidate the gaze retained by FaceReader. We then erased the reaction times that were recorded when the users gazed at the ring or when the ring was motionless. We

| | Success rates | | | UEQ-S qualities | |
|---|---|---|---|---|---|
| | $T_{range}$ | $T_{compare}$ | $T_{order}$ | *Hedonic* | *Pragmatic* |
| G1 – $V_{3h}$ | 100% | 93.3% | 80.0% | 2.25 pts | 1.75 pts |
| G2 – $V_{6h}$ | 93.3% | 93.3% | 63.3% | 2.25 pts | 1.75 pts |
| G3 – $V_{9h}$ | 86.6% | 90.0% | 13.3% | 2.25 pts | 1.50 pts |
| Average | 93.3% | 92.2% | 52.2% | 2.25 pts | 1.67 pts |
| | ***p*-values** | | | ***p*-values** | |
| | (1) | (1) | (1) | (2) | (2) |
| $V_{3h}/V_{6h}/V_{9h}$ | .12 | .85 | **.001** | .17 | .26 |
| $V_{3h}/V_{6h}$ | .49 | 1 | .25 | .84 | .67 |
| $V_{3h}/V_{9h}$ | .11 | .64 | **.001** | .81 | .23 |
| $V_{6h}/V_{9h}$ | .67 | .64 | **.001** | .94 | .39 |

*The qualities range from -3 to 3 pts. P-values under 0.05 are in bold print. (1) Pearson's chi-squared test when 3 groups; Fisher's exact test when 2 groups. (2) Kruskal–Wallis's rank sum test when 3 groups; Cochran–Artimage's trend test when 2 groups.*

Table 3: Success rates of the three information retrieval tasks and UEQ-S scorings for the three groups of visitors.

approximated the perception time from the reaction times by subtracting 200 ms. This duration is the minimum time for the brain to perceive, process, and response to a visual stimulus[10].

As we will see below in the results section, this second experimentation provides a use case arguing that a non-constant speed is better than a constant speed.

## RESULTS OF THE USER STUDIES

This section presents and discusses the results that both benefit to the energy Demand-Side Management domain and to the scope of Shape-Changing Interfaces design. Ratings are ranked on a 7-point scale for UEQ-S, from -3 to 3 pts, and on a 5-point scale for other questionnaires, from -2 to 2 pts.

### Benefits for Demand-Side Management

#### *A Usable Display for Variation Analyses*

The two tasks $T_{range}$ and $T_{compare}$ are useful for variation analysis for shifting energy: identifying the variation's range and retrieving the peak hour. The average success rate for these tasks was over 90%. Moreover, the variation's duration had no effect on the success rates of $T_{range}$ and $T_{compare}$ ($p = .12$ and $p = .85$, respectively, with Pearson's chi-squared test). These results makes CairnFORM usable for new energy practices that require variation analyses, such as shifting energy. Table 3 shows the success rates of the three groups for these two tasks.

Five participants, however, pointed out the difficulty to differentiate the rings' diameter. The experiment was done with a 30-point data scale; the radius granularity was 9 mm. Decreasing the data scale is unnecessary regarding the successful variations analyses, for $T_{range}$ and $T_{compare}$, from an observation distance of approximately 1 m. Moreover, some participants did a backward step to have a larger view of CairnFORM. The granularity is linked to the observation distance; its value should be determined according to the context of use. The observation distance may be longer in public places than in open-plans.

[10] 150 ms of visual processing [56] and 50 ms of muscle response for healthy patients [48].

*A Useful Display for Public Spaces*

The into-the-wild experiment revealed the attractivity of CairnFORM in public places. CairnFORM was installed in the access hall, mid-way to the central event. Hundreds of visitors stopped to see CairnFORM and talked about it. Recruiting visitors to answer questions was easy. We succeeded in recruiting 90 visitors over 16 hours, which is about 10 minutes per person comprising about 5 minutes of explanations and 5 minutes of questioning. Over a novelty effect, CairnFORM can play socialization role in public places as being rated hedonic and pragmatic.

The UEQ-S scores reveal that CairnFORM has *good* hedonic quality and *excellent* pragmatic quality. The average scores, given by the three groups, were 2.25 pts and 1.67 pts, respectively. Table 3 shows the UEQ-S scores for each group. This user experience is supported by written and verbal remarks, about hedonic aspects: *"Pleasing."*, *"Esthetic and avant-gardist."*, *"Exquisite."*; and pragmatic aspects: *"[CairnFORM] being readable from 360° is useful especially for persons with reduced mobility."*

Installing CairnFORM at workplaces, such as offices or open-plans, requires not disturbing the workers, but being perceivable. Memorizing and replicating the sequences was done successfully: the participants correctly replicated 97.78% of the 540 sequences (6 errors with $S_{const}$, 4 errors with $S_{exp}$, and 2 errors with $S_{log}$, on 180 trials each) and 99.99% of the symbols (2,680 of the 2,700 symbols to replicate). Yet, memorizing five symbols in ten seconds and replicating it every two seconds requires concentration. This convinces us that the ring's motion seems appropriate to preserve the focus of attention on a work task at workplaces.

### Benefits for General Shape-Changing Interfaces Design

*Dynamic Physical Charts*

We extend to physical ring charts the results of Jansen et al. [23] who studied low-level retrieval tasks with physical bar charts. They show that users do a compare task slower than a range task, but faster than an order task. The success rates of our experiments reveal that users do a compare task (92.2%) less well than a range task (93.3%), but better than an order task (52.2%). Thus, according both to completion time and success rate, physical bar charts and physical ring charts (i.e., physical vertical bar charts with cylindrical symmetry) seem better suited to range tasks and compare tasks, rather than order tasks.

The low success rates seem inherent to the order task. The success rate of $T_{order}$ indeed decreases as the length of the variation's range increases. This effect of the variation's length is significant ($p = .001$, Pearson's chi-squared test). The difference between the success rate of $V_{9h}$ (13.3%) and the succees rates of $V_{3h}$ (80.0%) and $V_{6h}$ (63.3%) is significant (equal $p = .001$ and $p = .001$, with Fisher's exact test). We hypothesize that this is caused by our limited capacity for processing information [38]: comparing each value on the two gradients before and after the peak requires doing many visual comparisons while remembering the previous values already compared. This becomes rapidly very difficult. Further investigations should confirm these observations.

*Visualization and Stimulus Elements*

Nine participants of the first study reported their difficulty to differentiate the rings' brightness. The problem is that when one arc is close to another, the light shines and reflects from one arc to another. This results in an overall over-illumination. As suggested by one participant, color-change could be better than brightness-change. However, as the diameter already represents the variation, we prefer keeping color-change to represent further information.

The measures were similar for the two kinds of motion (expansion and retraction). The detection times and the distance covered by the ring when detected were similar for $M_{expansion}$ and $M_{retraction}$ in the three speed conditions. Moreover, it was also possible for the participants to recognize the kind of motion with peripheral vision and the periphery of attention: they succeeded in recognizing 87.1% of $M_{expansion}$ and $M_{retraction}$. These results make the kind of motion a possible visualization element.

The real detection stimulus is diameter change, not the acceleration. The motion speed detected with the smaller diameter change was $S_{const}$ (8.92 cm). The motions with speeds $S_{log}$ and $S_{exp}$ were significantly perceived at the same diameter change (10.58 cm and 10.57 cm, respectively, $p =$ .01 with Student's t-test). This observation suggests that, independently from the acceleration, a diameter change is detected after it has travelled a critical distance in the visual field [11,28] (10.58 cm at 2.6 m represents 2.74° in the visual field and 1.37° of change on each side of the ring). As we will see below, however, the motion speed has an effect on success rates and tranquility.

*Motion Speed*

On the one hand, the participants rated not being distracted by the ring (1.2 pts in average for the three speeds) when focusing on the main task of replicating the sequences. Also, the kind of speed had no effect on distraction ($p = 0.73$, Kruskal–Wallis's rank sum test). These observations show that quiet and slow motion—all rings' motions were done in 6 s—help in keeping focused on the main task.

On the other hand, the motion speeds had an effect on the easiness, in the two tasks $T_{detection}$ and $T_{perception}$ ($p = 0.01$ and $p = 0.04$, respectively, with Kruskal–Wallis's rank sum test). First, for the two tasks, $S_{const}$ was rated as less easy than the two other speeds. Second, whereas $S_{log}$ was rated the easiest (1 pt) for $T_{detection}$ with significant difference with $S_{const}$ (-1 pt) and $S_{exp}$(-0.75 pts) ($p = .001$ and $p = .02$, respectively, with Cochran–Artimage's trend test), $S_{exp}$ was rated the easiest (1 pt) for $T_{perception}$, but without significance.

Few motions were unseen during $T_{detection}$: the average detection rate is 94.33% for the three speeds. The motion speed had no effect on these success rates of the task ($p = .73$, Pearson's chi-squared test). The motion speed had however an effect on the success rates of $T_{perception}$ ($p = .004$, Pearson's chi-squared test). The perception rate of 72.2% for $S_{exp}$ is significantly higher than 60.5% for $S_{const}$ and 66.5% for $S_{log}$ ($p = .002$ and $p = .03$, respectively, with Fisher's exact test). These observations validate that the non-constant speed of $S_{exp}$

| | $T_{detection}$ | | | | | $T_{perception}$ | | | |
|---|---|---|---|---|---|---|---|---|---|
| | *Detection rate* | *Detection time* | *Distance covered when detected* | *Easy to detect* | *Calm motion* | *Perception rate* | *Easy to perceive* | *Calm motion* | *Not distracting* |
| $S_{const}$ | 93% | 1.99±1.37 s | **8.92±6.40 cm** | -1 pt | **1 pt** | 60.5% | -0.25 pts | **1 pt** | **1.5 pts** |
| $S_{exp}$ | **95%** | 3.38±1.20 s | 10.58±6.47 cm | -0.75 pts | **1 pt** | **72.2%** | **1 pt** | **1 pt** | 1 pt |
| $S_{log}$ | **95%** | **1.18±0.95 s** | 10.57±5.54 cm | **1 pt** | 0 pts | 66.5% | 0 pts | 0.5 pts | 1 pt |
| | ***p*-values** | | | | | ***p*-values** | | | |
| | (1) | (2) | (2) | (3) | (3) | (1) | (3) | (3) | (3) |
| $S_{const}/S_{exp}/S_{log}$ | .73 | **.001** | **.004** | **.01** | **.03** | **.004** | **.04** | .54 | .73 |
| $S_{const}/S_{exp}$ | .63 | **.001** | **.002** | .80 | .46 | **.002** | **.04** | 1 | .66 |
| $S_{const}/S_{log}$ | .63 | **.001** | .47 | **.001** | **.02** | .26 | .78 | .35 | .48 |
| $S_{exp}/S_{log}$ | 1 | **.001** | **.01** | **.02** | .09 | **.03** | .08 | .31 | .75 |

*The scores' range is from -3 to 3 pts. Best scores and p-values under 0.05 are in bold print. (1) Pearson's chi-squared test when 3 groups; Fisher's exact test when 2 groups. (2) ANOVA test when 3 groups; Student's t-test when 2 groups. (3) Kruskal–Wallis's rank sum test when 3 groups; Cochran–Artimage's trend test when 2 groups.*

Table 4: Success rates, measures, and scorings for the two exercises with the three speeds.

outperforms the constant speed of $S_{const}$. Beyond efficiency, the remaining question is about tranquility.

The participants rated whether the ring's motion was calm. Whereas the kind of speed had an effect on these ratings in $T_{detection}$, it had no effect in $T_{perception}$ ($p = .03$ and $p = .54$, respectively, with Kruskal–Wallis's rank sum test). For the two tasks $T_{detection}$ and $T_{perception}$, the speed $S_{exp}$ was however rated as calm as $S_{const}$ with 1 pt for both, and $S_{log}$ was rated as the less calm with 0.25 pts in average. Finally, $S_{exp}$ is rated as calm as $S_{const}$ and is better perceived than $S_{log}$: all these observations argue for $S_{exp}$ being the more appropriate ambient awareness motion. Table 4 shows the measures and scorings of the two tasks $T_{detection}$ and $T_{perception}$ for each speed.

## GENERAL DISCUSSION

The first experiment explored low-level information retrieval tasks with a 10-ring CairnFORM. The success rates of over 90% show that CairnFORM is usable for the two tasks $T_{range}$ and $T_{compare}$. These results on success rates extend the results of Jansen et al. [23] on completion times to physical ring charts. Moreover, our results show that the success rates of $T_{order}$ decrease significantly with increasing variation duration, whereas the success rates of $T_{range}$ and $T_{compare}$ remain high. Our physical ring chart, however, combines color and diameter as visualization elements; this leaves room for other experiments studying diameter change only.

The second experiment explored ambient shape-changing notification. We hypothesize that continous speed changes affect perception rates in peripheral vision. Kobayashi and Yamada [31], and Jones et al. [26] evaluated slow and quiet motion using shape-changing interfaces: but the later tested motion out of the view field, and the latter tested constant speed only. Traschütz et al. [58] study the detection instantaneous speed change in peripheral vision. They show that speed changes above 50% are more reliably detected than intermediate speed changes of 10–25% that elicit low detection rates, what explains why constant speed was less detected and less perceived than non-constant speeds in our case. Traschütz et al. [58] also show that acceleration and deceleration detection rates differ; this can explain why the perception rates differ from an exponential speed and from a logarithmic speed.

The present studies reveal the attractivity of CairnFORM in public places, show its usability for variation analyses, and find the best motion speed to notifiy changes in peripheral vision. These results convinced us to evaluate the daily use of CairnFORM displaying renewable energy availability for shifting energy demand. A two-month user study is currently ongoing at a workplace.

CairnFORM opens new perspectives to display data in social spaces where people come from and go to different directions; there is great potential for useful applications. For example, physical ring charts could display tides in a harbor, traffic flow on roundabouts, shop affluence in the entrance hall of a mall, ultraviolet index at a beach, or air quality in a public park.

## CONCLUSION

We presented CairnFORM, a new 360°-readable, dynamic physical ring chart that displays forecasts of renewable energy availability. CairnFORM aims at creating and encouraging new socially-shared energy shifting practices in collective and public spaces, such as public places and workplaces. We conducted two user studies on our use case of CairnFORM, which had two main results. First, the success rates of the first user study show that, with our physical chart, users do a compare task (92.2%) less well than a range task (93.3%), but better than an order task (52.2%). Second, the second user study shows that exponential motion speed, besides being rated as calm as a constant speed, is 19.3% better perceived than a constant speed with the peripheral vision in ambient awareness conditions. The first result completes the previous results on physical bar charts completion times. The second result provides a use case arguing for an exponential speed to subtly notifying users with peripheral vision. Moreover, the user studies reveal that CairnFORM is usable for peaks retrieval tasks that are necessary for energy shifting practices, and they show the best motion speed to implement CairnFORM at a workplace. As future work, promising research investigates short-term and long-term user studies of such physical charts in order to put socially-shared energy shifting practices into effect.

## REFERENCES


[1] Sara Backlund, Magnus Gyllenswärd, Anton Gustafsson, Sara Ilstedt Hjelm, Ramia Mazé, and Johan Redström. 2007. Static! The aesthetics of energy in everyday things. In *Proceedings of the Design Research Society International Conference: Wonderground 2006 (DRS '06)*. 14 pages.

[2] Matthew Blackshaw, Anthony DeVincenzi, Dávid Lakatos, Daniel Leithinger, and Hiroshi Ishii. 2011. Recompose: Direct and Gestural Interaction with an Actuated Surface. In *CHI '11 Extended Abstracts on Human Factors in Computing Systems (CHI EA '11)*. ACM, New York, NY, USA, 1237–1242. DOI: http://dx.doi.org/10.1145/1979742.1979754

[3] Jacky Bourgeois, Janet van der Linden, Gerd Kortuem, Blaine A. Price, and Christopher Rimmer. 2014. Conversations with My Washing Machine: An In-the-wild Study of Demand Shifting with Self-generated Energy. In *Proceedings of the ACM International Joint Conference on Pervasive and Ubiquitous Computing (UbiComp '14)*. ACM, New York, NY, USA, 459–470. DOI: http://dx.doi.org/10.1145/2632048.2632106

[4] Hronn Brynjarsdóttir, Maria Håkansson, James Pierce, Eric Baumer, Carl DiSalvo, and Phoebe Sengers. 2012. Sustainably Unpersuaded: How Persuasion Narrows Our Vision of Sustainability. In *Proceedings of the SIGCHI Conference on Human Factors in Computing Systems (CHI '12)*. ACM, New York, NY, USA, 947–956. DOI: http://dx.doi.org/10.1145/2207676.2208539

[5] Enrico Costanza, Joel E. Fischer, James A. Colley, Tom Rodden, Sarvapali D. Ramchurn, and Nicholas R. Jennings. 2014. Doing the Laundry with Agents: A Field Trial of a Future Smart Energy System in the Home. In *Proceedings of the SIGCHI Conference on Human Factors in Computing Systems (CHI '14)*. ACM, New York, NY, USA, 813–822. DOI: http://dx.doi.org/10.1145/2556288.2557167

[6] Maxime Daniel, Guillaume Rivière, and Nadine Couture. 2017. Prelimary studies for the design of CAIRNS : an Ambient Tangible Interface for Shifting Energy Demand in the Workplace. In *29e conférence francophone sur l'Interaction Homme-Machine*, AFIHM (Ed.). 12 p. DOI: http://dx.doi.org/10.1145/3132129.3132152

[7] Maxime Daniel, Guillaume Rivière, and Nadine Couture. 2018. Designing an Expandable Illuminated Ring to Build an Actuated Ring Chart. In *Proceedings of the Twelfth International Conference on Tangible, Embedded, and Embodied Interaction (TEI '18)*. ACM, New York, NY, USA, 140–147. DOI: http://dx.doi.org/10.1145/3173225.3173294

[8] Brian J. Fogg. 1998. Persuasive Computers: Perspectives and Research Directions. In *Proceedings of the SIGCHI Conference on Human Factors in Computing Systems (CHI '98)*. ACM Press/Addison-Wesley Publishing Co., New York, NY, USA, 225–232. DOI: http://dx.doi.org/10.1145/274644.274677

[9] Sean Follmer, Daniel Leithinger, Alex Olwal, Akimitsu Hogge, and Hiroshi Ishii. 2013. inFORM: Dynamic Physical Affordances and Constraints Through Shape and Object Actuation. In *Proceedings of the 26th Annual ACM Symposium on User Interface Software and Technology (UIST '13)*. ACM, New York, NY, USA, 417–426. DOI: http://dx.doi.org/10.1145/2501988.2502032

[10] Frontier Economics and Sustainability First. 2012. *Demand Side Response in the domestic sector– a literature review of major trials*. Technical Report 12D/257. Department of Energy and Climate Change, London, UK. 156 pages.

[11] Clarence Henry Graham. 1965. *Vision and visual perception*. Wiley.

[12] Anton Gustafsson and Magnus Gyllenswärd. 2005. The Power-aware Cord: Energy Awareness Through Ambient Information Display. In *CHI '05 Extended Abstracts on Human Factors in Computing Systems (CHI EA '05)*. ACM, New York, NY, USA, 1423–1426. DOI: http://dx.doi.org/10.1145/1056808.1056932

[13] Carl Gutwin, Andy Cockburn, and Ashley Coveney. 2017. Peripheral Popout: The Influence of Visual Angle and Stimulus Intensity on Popout Effects. In *Proceedings of the 2017 CHI Conference on Human Factors in Computing Systems (CHI '17)*. ACM, New York, NY, USA, 208–219. DOI: http://dx.doi.org/10.1145/3025453.3025984

[14] David Hafemeister. 2010. Sustainable Energy—Without the Hot Air. *American Journal of Physics* 78, 2 (2010), 222–223. DOI: http://dx.doi.org/10.1119/1.3273852

[15] Doris Hausen, Sebastian Boring, Clara Lueling, Simone Rodestock, and Andreas Butz. 2012. StaTube: Facilitating State Management in Instant Messaging Systems. In *Proceedings of the Sixth International Conference on Tangible, Embedded and Embodied Interaction (TEI '12)*. ACM, New York, NY, USA, 283–290. DOI: http://dx.doi.org/10.1145/2148131.2148191

[16] Felix Heibeck, Basheer Tome, Clark Della Silva, and Hiroshi Ishii. 2015. uniMorph: Fabricating Thin Film Composites for Shape-Changing Interfaces. In *Proceedings of the 28th Annual ACM Symposium on User Interface Software & Technology (UIST '15)*. ACM, New York, NY, USA, 233–242. DOI: http://dx.doi.org/10.1145/2807442.2807472

[17] Florian Heller and Jan Borchers. 2011. PowerSocket: Towards On-outlet Power Consumption Visualization. In *CHI '11 Extended Abstracts on Human Factors in Computing Systems (CHI EA '11)*. ACM, New York, NY, USA, 1981–1986. DOI: http://dx.doi.org/10.1145/1979742.1979901

[18] Oren Horev. 2006. *'TALKING TO THE HAND' An exploration into shape shifting objects and morphing interfaces*. Master's thesis. Interaction Design Institute Ivrea, Italy.

[19] Hiroshi Ishii. 2008. Tangible Bits: Beyond Pixels. In *Proceedings of the 2nd International Conference on Tangible and Embedded Interaction (TEI '08)*. ACM, New York, NY, USA, xv–xxv. DOI: http://dx.doi.org/10.1145/1347390.1347392

[20] Hiroshi Ishii, Dávid Lakatos, Leonardo Bonanni, and Jean-Baptiste Labrune. 2012. Radical Atoms: Beyond Tangible Bits, Toward Transformable Materials. *interactions* 19, 1 (Jan. 2012), 38–51. DOI: http://dx.doi.org/10.1145/2065327.2065337

[21] Hiroshi Ishii, Daniel Leithinger, Sean Follmer, Amit Zoran, Philipp Schoessler, and Jared Counts. 2015. TRANSFORM: Embodiment of "Radical Atoms" at Milano Design Week. In *Proceedings of the 33rd Annual ACM Conference Extended Abstracts on Human Factors in Computing Systems (CHI EA '15)*. ACM, New York, NY, USA, 687–694. DOI: http://dx.doi.org/10.1145/2702613.2702969

[22] Nassim Jafarinaimi, Jodi Forlizzi, Amy Hurst, and John Zimmerman. 2005. Breakaway: An Ambient Display Designed to Change Human Behavior. In *CHI '05 Extended Abstracts on Human Factors in Computing Systems (CHI EA '05)*. ACM, New York, NY, USA, 1945–1948. DOI: http://dx.doi.org/10.1145/1056808.1057063

[23] Yvonne Jansen, Pierre Dragicevic, and Jean-Daniel Fekete. 2013. Evaluating the Efficiency of Physical Visualizations. In *Proceedings of the SIGCHI Conference on Human Factors in Computing Systems (CHI '13)*. ACM, New York, NY, USA, 2593–2602. DOI:http://dx.doi.org/10.1145/2470654.2481359

[24] Yvonne Jansen, Pierre Dragicevic, Petra Isenberg, Jason Alexander, Abhijit Karnik, Johan Kildal, Sriram Subramanian, and Kasper Hornbæk. 2015. Opportunities and Challenges for Data Physicalization. In *Proceedings of the 33rd Annual ACM Conference on Human Factors in Computing Systems (CHI '15)*. ACM, New York, NY, USA, 3227–3236. DOI: http://dx.doi.org/10.1145/2702123.2702180

[25] Yvonne Jansen, Thorsten Karrer, and Jan Borchers. 2010. MudPad: Localized Tactile Feedback on Touch Surfaces. In *Adjunct Proceedings of the 23rd Annual ACM Symposium on User Interface Software and Technology (UIST '10)*. ACM, New York, NY, USA, 385–386. DOI: http://dx.doi.org/10.1145/1866218.1866232

[26] Lee Jones, John McClelland, Phonesavanh Thongsouksanoumane, and Audrey Girouard. 2017. Ambient Notifications with Shape Changing Circuits in Peripheral Locations. In *Proceedings of the 2017 ACM International Conference on Interactive Surfaces and Spaces (ISS '17)*. ACM, New York, NY, USA, 405–408. DOI:http://dx.doi.org/10.1145/3132272.3132291

[27] Seoktae Kim, Hyunjung Kim, Boram Lee, Tek-Jin Nam, and Woohun Lee. 2008. Inflatable Mouse: Volume-adjustable Mouse with Air-pressure-sensitive Input and Haptic Feedback. In *Proceedings of the SIGCHI Conference on Human Factors in Computing Systems (CHI '08)*. ACM, New York, NY, USA, 211–224. DOI: http://dx.doi.org/10.1145/1357054.1357090

[28] Ronald A. Kinchla. 1976. A psychophysical model of visual-movement perception. In *Eye movements and psychological processes*. Lawrence Erlbaum Associates, Hillsdale, NJ, USA, 263–275.

[29] Jesper Kjeldskov, Mikael B. Skov, Jeni Paay, Dennis Lund, Tue Madsen, and Michael Nielsen. 2015. Facilitating Flexible Electricity Use in the Home with Eco-Feedback and Eco-Forecasting. In *Proceedings of the Annual Meeting of the Australian Special Interest Group for Computer Human Interaction (OzCHI '15)*. ACM, New York, NY, USA, 388–396. DOI: http://dx.doi.org/10.1145/2838739.2838755

[30] Jesper Kjeldskov, Mikael B. Skov, Jeni Paay, and Rahuvaran Pathmanathan. 2012. Using Mobile Phones to Support Sustainability: A Field Study of Residential Electricity Consumption. In *Proceedings of the SIGCHI Conference on Human Factors in Computing Systems (CHI '12)*. ACM, New York, NY, USA, 2347–2356. DOI:http://dx.doi.org/10.1145/2207676.2208395

[31] Kazuki Kobayashi and Seiji Yamada. 2013. Shape Changing Device for Notification. In *Proceedings of the Adjunct Publication of the 26th Annual ACM Symposium on User Interface Software and Technology (UIST '13 Adjunct)*. ACM, New York, NY, USA, 71–72. DOI: http://dx.doi.org/10.1145/2508468.2514715

[32] Dávid Lakatos. 2012. *AMPHORM: Form Giving through Gestural Interaction to Shape Changing Objects*. Master's thesis. Massachusetts Institute of Technology, Cambridge, MA, USA.

[33] Mathieu Le Goc, Lawrence H. Kim, Ali Parsaei, Jean-Daniel Fekete, Pierre Dragicevic, and Sean Follmer. 2016. Zooids: Building Blocks for Swarm User Interfaces. In *Proceedings of the 29th Annual Symposium on User Interface Software and Technology (UIST '16)*. ACM, New York, NY, USA, 97–109. DOI: http://dx.doi.org/10.1145/2984511.2984547

[34] Jinha Lee, Rehmi Post, and Hiroshi Ishii. 2011. ZeroN: Mid-air Tangible Interaction Enabled by Computer Controlled Magnetic Levitation. In *Proceedings of the 24th Annual ACM Symposium on User Interface Software and Technology (UIST '11)*. ACM, New York, NY, USA, 327–336. DOI: http://dx.doi.org/10.1145/2047196.2047239

[35] Daniel Leithinger and Hiroshi Ishii. 2010. Relief: A Scalable Actuated Shape Display. In *Proceedings of the Fourth International Conference on Tangible, Embedded, and Embodied Interaction (TEI '10)*. ACM, New York, NY, USA, 221–222. DOI: http://dx.doi.org/10.1145/1709886.1709928

[36] Roger A. Light. 2017. Mosquitto: server and client implementation of the MQTT protocol. *Journal of Open Source Software* 2, 13 (May 2017). DOI: http://dx.doi.org/10.21105/joss.00265

[37] Xing Luo, Jihong Wang, Mark Dooner, and Jonathan Clarke. 2015. Overview of current development in electrical energy storage technologies and the application potential in power system operation. *Applied Energy* 137 (January 2015), 511–536. DOI: http://dx.doi.org/10.1016/j.apenergy.2014.09.081

[38] George A. Miller. 1956. The Magical Number Seven, Plus or Minus Two: Some Limits on our Capacity for Processing Information. *The Psychological Review* 63, 2 (1956), 81–97. DOI: http://dx.doi.org/10.1037/h0043158

[39] Ken Nakagaki, Sean Follmer, and Hiroshi Ishii. 2015. LineFORM: Actuated Curve Interfaces for Display, Interaction, and Constraint. In *Proceedings of the 28th Annual ACM Symposium on User Interface Software & Technology (UIST '15)*. ACM, New York, NY, USA, 333–339. DOI: http://dx.doi.org/10.1145/2807442.2807452

[40] James Patten and Hiroshi Ishii. 2007. Mechanical Constraints as Computational Constraints in Tabletop Tangible Interfaces. In *Proceedings of the SIGCHI Conference on Human Factors in Computing Systems (CHI '07)*. ACM, New York, NY, USA, 809–818. DOI: http://dx.doi.org/10.1145/1240624.1240746

[41] Dane Petersen, Jay Steele, and Joe Wilkerson. 2009. WattBot: A Residential Electricity Monitoring and Feedback System. In *CHI '09 Extended Abstracts on Human Factors in Computing Systems (CHI EA '09)*. ACM, New York, NY, USA, 2847–2852. DOI: http://dx.doi.org/10.1145/1520340.1520413

[42] Petromil Petkov, Suparna Goswami, Felix Köbler, and Helmut Krcmar. 2012. Personalised Eco-feedback as a Design Technique for Motivating Energy Saving Behaviour at Home. In *Proceedings of the 7th Nordic Conference on Human-Computer Interaction: Making Sense Through Design (NordiCHI '12)*. ACM, New York, NY, USA, 587–596. DOI: http://dx.doi.org/10.1145/2399016.2399106

[43] Petromil Petkov, Felix Köbler, Marcus Foth, and Helmut Krcmar. 2011. Motivating Domestic Energy Conservation Through Comparative, Community-based Feedback in Mobile and Social Media. In *Proceedings of the 5th International Conference on Communities and Technologies (C&T '11)*. ACM, New York, NY, USA, 21–30. DOI: http://dx.doi.org/10.1145/2103354.2103358

[44] James Pierce and Eric Paulos. 2010. Materializing Energy. In *Proceedings of the 8th ACM Conference on Designing Interactive Systems (DIS '10)*. ACM, New York, NY, USA, 113–122. DOI: http://dx.doi.org/10.1145/1858171.1858193

[45] James Pierce and Eric Paulos. 2012a. Beyond Energy Monitors: Interaction, Energy, and Emerging Energy Systems. In *Proceedings of the SIGCHI Conference on Human Factors in Computing Systems (CHI '12)*. ACM, New York, NY, USA, 665–674. DOI: http://dx.doi.org/10.1145/2207676.2207771

[46] James Pierce and Eric Paulos. 2012b. The Local Energy Indicator: Designing for Wind and Solar Energy Systems in the Home. In *Proceedings of the Designing Interactive Systems Conference (DIS '12)*. ACM, New York, NY, USA, 631–634. DOI: http://dx.doi.org/10.1145/2317956.2318050

[47] Filipe Quintal, Clinton Jorge, Valentina Nisi, and Nuno Nunes. 2016. Watt-I-See: A Tangible Visualization of Energy. In *Proceedings of the International Working Conference on Advanced Visual Interfaces (AVI '16)*. ACM, New York, NY, USA, 120–127. DOI: http://dx.doi.org/10.1145/2909132.2909270

[48] Andrea Radebold, Jacek Cholewicki, Manohar M. Panjabi, and Tushar Ch. Patel. 2000. Muscle response pattern to sudden trunk loading in healthy individuals and in patients with chronic low back pain. *Spine* 25, 8 (2000), 947–954. DOI: http://dx.doi.org/10.1097/00007632-200004150-00009

[49] Tim Regan, David Sweeney, John Helmes, Vasillis Vlachokyriakos, Siân Lindley, and Alex Taylor. 2015. Designing Engaging Data in Communities. In *Proceedings of the 33rd Annual ACM Conference Extended Abstracts on Human Factors in Computing Systems (CHI EA '15)*. ACM, New York, NY, USA, 271–274. DOI: http://dx.doi.org/10.1145/2702613.2725432

[50] Johann Schrammel, Cornelia Gerdenitsch, Astrid Weiss, Patricia M. Kluckner, and Manfred Tscheligi. 2011. FORE-Watch – The Clock That Tells You When to Use: Persuading Users to Align Their Energy Consumption with Green Power Availability. In *Proceedings of the 2nd International Conference on Ambient Intelligence (AmI '11)*. Springer Berlin Heidelberg, Berlin, Heidelberg, 157–166. DOI: http://dx.doi.org/10.1007/978-3-642-25167-2_19

[51] Martin Schrepp, Andreas Hinderks, and Jörg Thomaschewski. 2017. Design and Evaluation of a Short Version of the User Experience Questionnaire (UEQ-S). *International Journal of Interactive Multimedia and Artificial Intelligence* 4, 6 (2017), 103–108. DOI: http://dx.doi.org/10.9781/ijimai.2017.09.001

[52] S. A. Seah, B. W. Drinkwater, T. Carter, R. Malkin, and S. Subramanian. 2014. Correspondence: Dexterous ultrasonic levitation of millimeter-sized objects in air. *IEEE Transactions on Ultrasonics, Ferroelectrics, and Frequency Control* 61, 7 (July 2014), 1233–1236. DOI: http://dx.doi.org/10.1109/TUFFC.2014.3022

[53] Will Simm, Maria Angela Ferrario, Adrian Friday, Peter Newman, Stephen Forshaw, Mike Hazas, and Alan Dix. 2015. Tiree Energy Pulse: Exploring Renewable Energy Forecasts on the Edge of the Grid. In *Proceedings of the SIGCHI Conference on Human Factors in Computing Systems (CHI '15)*. ACM, New York, NY, USA, 1965–1974. DOI: http://dx.doi.org/10.1145/2702123.2702285

[54] Paul Strohmeier, Antonio Gomes, Giovanni Maria Troiano, Aske Mottelson, Timothy Merritt, and Jason Alexander. 2016. Sharing Perspectives on the Design of Shape-Changing Interfaces. In *Proceedings of the 2016 CHI Conference Extended Abstracts on Human Factors in Computing Systems (CHI EA '16)*. ACM, New York, NY, USA, 3492–3499. DOI: http://dx.doi.org/10.1145/2851581.2856478

[55] Faisal Taher, John Hardy, Abhijit Karnik, Christian Weichel, Yvonne Jansen, Kasper Hornbæk, and Jason Alexander. 2015. Exploring Interactions with Physically Dynamic Bar Charts. In *Proceedings of the 33rd Annual ACM Conference on Human Factors in Computing Systems (CHI '15)*. ACM, New York, NY, USA, 3237–3246. DOI: http://dx.doi.org/10.1145/2702123.2702604

[56] Simon Thorpe, Denis Fize, and Catherine Marlot. 1996. Speed of processing in the human visual system. *Nature* 381, 6582 (1996), 520–522. DOI: http://dx.doi.org/10.1038/381520a0

[57] Jonas Togler, Fabian Hemmert, and Reto Wettach. 2009. Living Interfaces: The Thrifty Faucet. In *Proceedings of the 3rd International Conference on Tangible and Embedded Interaction (TEI '09)*. ACM, New York, NY, USA, 43–44. DOI: http://dx.doi.org/10.1145/1517664.1517680

[58] Andreas Traschütz, Wolf Zinke, and Detlef Wegener. 2012. Speed change detection in foveal and peripheral vision. *Vision Research* 72 (2012), 1–13. DOI: http://dx.doi.org/10.1016/j.visres.2012.08.019

[59] Mark Weiser and John Seely Brown. 1996. Designing calm technology. *PowerGrid Journal* 1, 1 (July 1996), 75–85.

[60] Markus Weiss, Friedemann Mattern, Tobias Graml, Thorsten Staake, and Elgar Fleisch. 2009. Handy Feedback: Connecting Smart Meters with Mobile Phones. In *Proceedings of the 8th International Conference on Mobile and Ubiquitous Multimedia (MUM '09)*. ACM, New York, NY, USA, Article 15, 15:1–15:4 pages. DOI: http://dx.doi.org/10.1145/1658550.1658565

[61] Craig Wisneski, Hiroshi Ishii, Andrew Dahley, Matthew G. Gorbet, Scott Brave, Brygg Ullmer, and Paul Yarin. 1998. Ambient Displays: Turning Architectural Space into an Interface Between People and Digital Information. In *Proceedings of the 1st International Workshop on Cooperative Buildings, Integrating Information, Organization, and Architecture (CoBuild '98)*. Springer-Verlag, London, UK, 22–32. DOI:http://dx.doi.org/10.1007/3-540-69706-3_4

[62] Andy Wu. 2010. Tangible Visualization. In *Proceedings of the Fourth International Conference on Tangible, Embedded, and Embodied Interaction (TEI '10)*. ACM, New York, NY, USA, 317–318. DOI: http://dx.doi.org/10.1145/1709886.1709961

[63] Wataru Yamada, Kazuhiro Yamada, Hiroyuki Manabe, and Daizo Ikeda. 2017. iSphere: Self-Luminous Spherical Drone Display. In *Proceedings of the 30th Annual ACM Symposium on User Interface Software and Technology (UIST '17)*. ACM, New York, NY, USA, 635–643. DOI: http://dx.doi.org/10.1145/3126594.3126631

[64] Lining Yao, Ryuma Niiyama, Jifei Ou, Sean Follmer, Clark Della Silva, and Hiroshi Ishii. 2013. PneUI: Pneumatically Actuated Soft Composite Materials for Shape Changing Interfaces. In *Proceedings of the 26th Annual ACM Symposium on User Interface Software and Technology (UIST '13)*. ACM, New York, NY, USA, 13–22. DOI:http://dx.doi.org/10.1145/2501988.2502037

[65] Lining Yao, Jifei Ou, Chin-Yi Cheng, Helene Steiner, Wen Wang, Guanyun Wang, and Hiroshi Ishii. 2015. bioLogic: Natto Cells as Nanoactuators for Shape Changing Interfaces. In *Proceedings of the 33rd Annual ACM Conference on Human Factors in Computing Systems (CHI '15)*. ACM, New York, NY, USA, 1–10. DOI:http://dx.doi.org/10.1145/2702123.2702611

# COMB – Shape as a Meaningful Element of Interaction.

**Beat Rossmy, Alexander Wiethoff**
LMU Munich
Munich, Germany
beat.rossmy@ifi.lmu.de, alexander.wiethoff@ifi.lmu.de

**Figure 1. The tangible modular interface COMB enables children to practice electronic/digital music. By building structures from block-like modules children can access different digital instruments. These instruments can then be step-sequenced[1] to create rhythms beyond the otherwise approachable complexity.**

## ABSTRACT
This paper introduces a tangible user interface (TUI) concept designed for child-oriented musical interaction and education called COMB. The interaction concept of the interface is based upon the natural behavior and metaphors found in children's play during construction with building-blocks. This paradigm is used to increase the accessibility of the otherwise expert-focused digital and electronic music creation to children. We evaluated our prototype during two different study setups. We found preliminary indications that this concept fosters imitation during learning. Therefore, the usage of shape as a meaningful element of interaction could be a promising design strategy for interfaces addressing children in this domain. In this paper we present the theoretical foundation of the concept as well as technical details of the prototype. Furthermore, we discuss how this concept can be applied to increase accessibility of technology in various other domains.

### Author Keywords
TUI; Modular; MIDI Sequencer; Children

### CCS Concepts
**•Human-centered computing → User interface design; Interaction design theory, concepts and paradigms;**



*TEI '19,* March 17–20, 2019, Tempe, AZ, USA



DOI: https://doi.org/10.1145/3294109.3295646

## INTRODUCTION
With the ongoing development of smaller, more compact and cheaper electronics as well as the resulting new renaissance of analog and digital electronic instruments[2], the influence and relevance of electronic music for the main stream culture constantly increases. However, because their design mainly focuses on trained professionals, the use of those instruments by young children is difficult. This circumstance is due to human factor restrictions such as physical size and required skillfulness to operate hard- and software solutions correctly. Conceptual and cognitive hurdles are part of this restriction.

To address this shortcoming, we implemented an interface concept based on a modular interaction approach. Familiar and playful paradigms are integrated to support learning through imitation and to create an explorative and self-regulated experience. In this domain our research question resolves around the challenge on how to increase the accessibility of electronic music creation for children and if novel interaction concepts and design strategies can provide learning benefits in this domain. To answer this question, we used a research through design process [31] which was coined by experience prototyping and several iterations to generate profound insights during evaluation setups.

The paper is structured as follows: To frame our interface implementation we provide an overview of related work in the domains of: (a) learning theories and musical education (b) learning interfaces and expressive use plus (c) tangible interaction vs. organic user interface design principles and

[1] COMB video demonstration: https://vimeo.com/231299236
[2] http://msretailer.com/analog-synthesizer-renaissance/

case studies. Next, we introduce the design space in which we have placed our prototype concept, in order to position our work in relation to previous efforts and investigations. In the main section we exemplify the design process, technical details along with functional aspects. In the final parts of the paper we provide insights and a summary on two conducted user studies. We close with a reflection on benefits and limitations of our approach and discuss how it could be transferred and utilized in other domains.

In a previous publication we emphasized the practical utilization of the TUI concept for demonstration purposes at a conference series [23], this work is concerned with the conceptual framework, in-depth implementation details regarding hard- and software components as well as SMD layout and manufacturing processes. We further elaborate on insights gained during different study setups and summarize the contributions of our work as follows:

- We share detailed technical descriptions of our modular interface concept COMB which allows children to sequence digital instruments by constructive play. We further provide the necessary depth of detail in hard- and software components to replicate our approach.
- We outline an interaction vocabulary derived from a shape-centered interaction concept.
- We provide preliminary insights from two evaluation setups with a diverse user group (adults vs. children).

## RELATED WORK

To differentiate COMB from established interfaces and research from the NIME community [24, 17, 13] we discuss related work that was mandatory to elaborate on the conceptual approach and further discuss projects that either use shape as an input method or block-like devices in combination with constructive interaction.

### Learning Theories and Music Education

The key of an enjoyable and persistent learning experience is motivation. Thereby, two concepts are differentiated: intrinsic and extrinsic. The second describing external stimuli as found in punishment or reward and the first internal factors such as relevance or curiosity. Research has shown that extrinsic motivation can undermine successful learning on a long-term scale, because many persons stop performing once external stimuli are suspended [16]. One key factor that can support or create long term intrinsic motivation is curiosity. During self-initiated and self-organized learning experiences knowledge gets constructed as described by Piaget's [29] theory of constructivism. This theory acknowledges the importance of play and exploration, performed by children with joy and persistence, which we found suitable for our design concept. Exploration can be considered a driving factor in persistent learning.

In summary, curiosity over exploration leads to expression. The creative use of the previously acquired knowledge represents an additional factor in learning [30]. Expressiveness can be found in play and creative activities in order to fertilize the transfer of knowledge as well as problem solving abilities. Further, the importance of imitation [20] as a key strategy of learning should be considered. Behaviors or patterns are constantly observed and reproduced by children. This not only applies to social behavior but also to technologies and practical knowledge in general [8]. The music pedagogues work of Carl Orff [19] and Zoltán Kodály [6] include the aforementioned key concepts for persistent learning. Both developed curricula and methods concerned with age-dependent tasks minimizing frustration and generating motivation to enable children's musical expression. This is achieved by reducing complexity of motor skills and music theory to lower the entry threshold and to create curiosity. Sturdy instruments are used to enable explorative access despite untrained operation. Learning units in this segment incorporate call and response and thus integrate imitation into the curriculum.

### Interfaces for Learning and Expressive Use

Two disciplines are highlighted in the following section to show how shape-changing interfaces as well as constructive tasks are used to enrich interaction and foster learning regarding to curiosity, exploration, expression and imitation.

### Organic User Interfaces: Shape as an Input Method

The vision of Organic User Interfaces (OUI) as described by Holman and Vertegaal [11] defines three key concepts, of which one proposes: function equals form. In OUI design function and form are an undividable unit. This idea is comparable to the concept of affordance described by Gibson [18]. The incorporation of this concept supports the user during the interaction process by revealing the way how to handle an interface. We drew upon this principle in our design approach and expressed it by communicating what is achievable by using it with shapes used as abstract representations of real-world objects. Other interface concepts utilizing principles of OUI design origin from the domain of shape changing interfaces [22, 7]. The game controller NinjaTrack by Katsumoto et al. [14] offers the user to perform modality changes by altering the shape and flexibility of the controller's structure. Reshaping the controller gives access to different functionalities related to the physical state of the interface. The main limitation of the concept is the interface's construction: It consists of small interlocked elements which restricts the deformability to bending around one axis and therefore the possible states the interface can take. The swarm interface (SUI) Zooids by Le Goc [15] utilizes a set of indistinguishable robots that can display information by their constellation as well as allowing the direct manipulation of the displayed data. Single elements still remain objects bounded to specific information and do not completely vanish into a mass of elements representing an object.

### Tangible Programming: Construction as an Input Method

Beside shape as an input method construction is also utilized often as a central element of interaction. Many educational interfaces [32, 3] are based on this concept. This field of research is referred to as tangible programming and originated in the early 90s from the effort to give children access to programming languages. The approach behind those educational projects such as Algoblocks by Suzuki and Kato [26] is that modules represent instructions or code fragments or in general specific functions, thus children can explore programming without actually writing code. The same can be found in the platform littleBits by Ayah Bdeir [2], a project designed for developing electronic circuits without the need for soldering or wiring single electronic components. In this product, modules represent components of circuits; thus, children can learn about the synergy of sensors, actuators and signal-processors.

However, those interfaces don't utilize the concept of shape as an interaction element. Instead, they use function-related building blocks, where modules represent functions independent from context or situation. Typically, the interface's shape is just the result of the composition process. Multiple modules get combined based on their specific function and the intended overall functionality. However, functionalities can be achieved by following different approaches, resulting in different spatial configurations. Therefore, the abstract shape of the interface does not contain any information about the interface's functionality. In contrast objects created during constructive play, contain meaning although they are composed out of meaningless materials like clay, paper or building-blocks, a design concept that strongly influenced our approach.

## DESIGN SPACE: STATIC VS. FLEXIBLE INTERFACES

To situate shape- and construction-centered interfaces in the context of this work we defined a design space to show manifestations of flexibility related to the interface's appearance and usage (see Figure 2). This consideration is based on Vertegaal's and Poupyrev's [28] claim that future interfaces won't be limited to static shapes.

Features of such shape-changing interfaces are: flexibility and variability. Where flexibility depicts temporary manipulations as bending, stretching or twisting and variability characterizes continuous transformations as folding or reshaping. Further, "constructive systems" according to Ullmer and Ishii [27] describe restructure-able or modular interfaces. Therefore, "flexibility of appearance" is threefold divided: static, shape-changing and modular. To picturize, we compare those states to the states of matter [15]. Here static relates to solid bodies, shape-changing to fluids and modular to gas. This emphasizes the idea of one continuous body, which gets softened until it splits up into its smallest possible components, that still form an interrelated and interconnected unit.

The dimension "flexibility of usage" is divided into two extremes: generic and specific. These originate from the distinction of TUIs and traditional interfaces (mouse, keyboard) [12]. However, a growing number of commercial interfaces incorporate concepts such as personalization or adaptability, where users arrange their own interface[3] to fit personal needs as ergonomics or interfaces are adaptable to different tasks by e.g. adding overlays[4]. Both cases bridge between specific and generic interfaces. Personalization closer relates to specificness since such interfaces are typically set up once, whereas adaptable interfaces constantly change based on the task.

[3]special-waves.com
[4]sensel.com

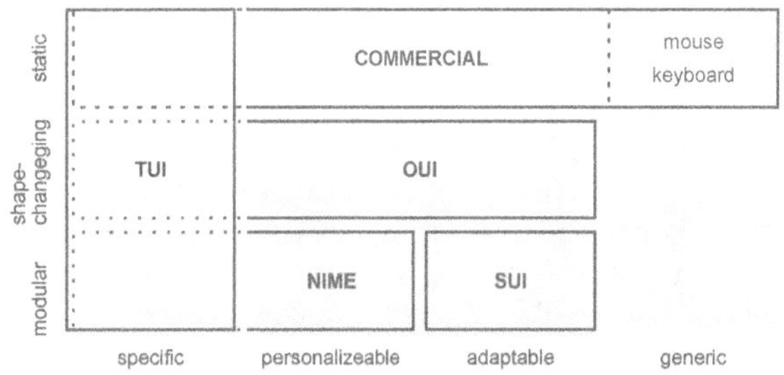


**Figure 2. We visualize different HCI disciplines in this design space. Where generic use overlaps with shape-changing and modular characteristics space is opened up for the exploration of new design approaches. Here, COMB tries to fill this gap.**

**Figure 3. Several iterations of the housing have been done to define the size, most functional connector placement and a manufacturing process ensuring precise interconnections.**

## COMB – A DESIGN RATIONALE

As previously discussed, the specific problem we are addressing with our work is the inaccessibility of today's electronic/digital music for children. To bridge the gap and lower participation barriers in this domain we have designed a tangible interface and a corresponding interaction concept.

### Design Process

Developing our experience prototypes [4] we followed an iterative user centered design process [21] that was informed by early validation sessions with the intended users in order to get the design right [5] (see Figure 3). To generate an enjoyable, usable and robust design solution for our design context we also had to overcome several technical issues that we'll exemplify in the following section.

### An Interface for Learning Music

To design a low-threshold and playful interaction we built on top of existing concepts and adapted those to the domain of musical education to facilitate immediate access based on applicable pre-knowledge. The most familiar and widespread concepts for children today are games and toys. Especially building blocks meet all the previously mentioned key learning concepts. Our conceptual interaction concept is based on the paradigm "what you see is what you get" (WYSIWYG), and constructed shapes resemble meaningful representations of real-world metaphors. The perceived meaning can be seen as the result of the constructed shape instead of as a consequence of specific block's interrelation.

To transfer this paradigm into a musical interface we assumed that shape representations could result in musical meanings. In our context musical meaning refers to different instruments. Children can build shapes associated with instruments to get control over these. Being in control could mean being able to play instruments in real time or in our case to compose musical patterns that are played and repeated automatically by the interface (see Figure 1). We opted for the second approach exposing a key concept of electronic/digital music: sequencing. This concept is used in hardware instruments as well as in music software since the 1960s [1] to program musical patterns. Further, this minimizes age as an exclusive factor by reducing experienced-based and practice-intense skills needed for real time operation such as recognizing rhythm or motor skills.

In summary, our interface concept enables children to sequence a multitude of instruments by playing with a modular block-like TUI (see Figure 1). The selection process of instruments is performed by restructuring the interface's shape, while each shape provides access to the associated instrument's musical pattern. Unmentioned shapes can be found through experimentation, motivated by curiosity. This concept enables musical learning and expression by adapting concepts of play which foster exploration as well as support visual comprehensibility and therefore imitation processes.

### A Modular Tangible User Interface

Instead of using a continuous deformable material as, for example, clay within OUI design or function-related modular interfaces as used in tangible programming, we have chosen building-block-like modular elements conceptually linked to children's constructive play. We have implemented a self-sensing interface which can adapt to its constructed shape by representing specific information and providing access to different functionalities. Pictorially associations of form and function are used to support the learning process and stimulate imitation as well as experimentation. This can especially be valuable in educational disciplines to create motivation, interest and joy.

Our interface's elementary shape is based upon hexagons to enable stable geometric structures inspired by nature. Compared to quads, constellations of hexagons are hardly displaceable along their vertices. Further, structures derived from hexagons are not as artificial looking as structures derived from quads. Associations that occur are more nature-related such as insect eyes or honeyCOMBs, rather than tech-related (e.g. Tetris shapes). Such structures, called polyform represent all constellations serving as valid input shapes for constructive interfaces. Quad-based polyforms are called polyominos whereas hexagon-based ones are referred to as polyhexes. Less hexagon-based elements are required to offer greater variety in valid shapes [25]. Three polyhexes (see Figure 4) are implemented as valid shapes. This is currently restricted by the number of available modules. Each module contains six backlit silicone-pads which are used to provide access to rhythmical patterns comparable to other established step sequencers. Switching the accessible pattern is achieved by restructuring the arrangement of the interface's modules.

### The Separation of Input Method

The assignment of shapes and functionalities aims at supporting the imitation of demonstrated and instructed interaction.

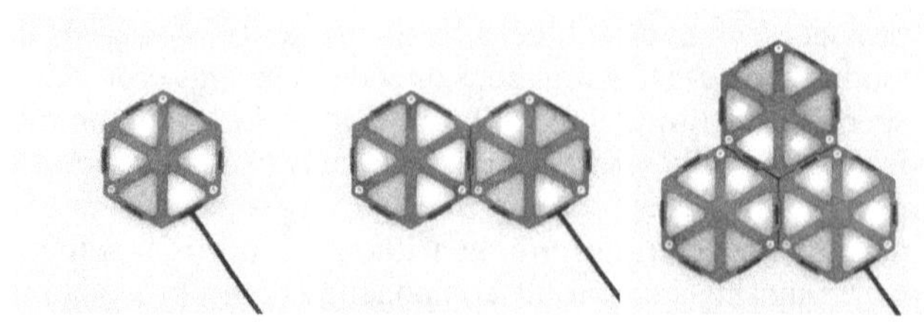

**Figure 4. This figure shows the transition-phase between two functionalities/modes (A/B) as well as the main input methods. Tapping on the device triggers mode-dependent actions (A1/B). Changing modes is achieved by restructuring the interface (A2). Green/cyan lights show playback position and blue ones activated steps. Dotted lines indicate the spatial layout of each pattern whereas arrows point to the next playback position.**

Typically, one input method is used to perform multiple tasks as found in tablets, touchscreen-based devices or commercial midi-grid controllers[5], where changing functionalities/modes as well as controlling those are performed via touch input. COMB uses a one-to-one relationship between input method and task (see Figure 5). Thereby, the change of functionality is designed distinctly observable to support imitation. Children can easily repeat the main interaction concept and start exploring the interface on their own.

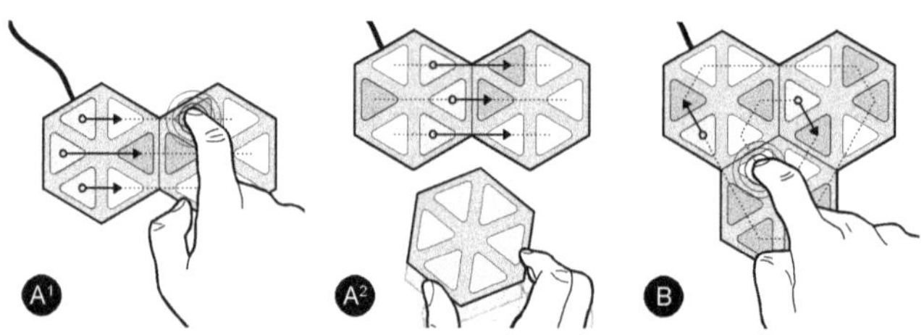

**Figure 5. This figure shows the transition-phase between two functionalities/modes (A/B) as well as the main input methods. Tapping on the device triggers mode-dependent actions (A1/B). Changing modes is achieved by restructuring the interface (A2). Green/cyan lights show playback position and blue ones activated steps. Dotted lines indicate the spatial layout of each pattern whereas arrows point to the next playback position.**

### Interaction Vocabulary

Based on the idea of shapes representing instruments, two naïve design strategies of their relationship can be postulated: Shapes are modeled after real world instruments and shapes represent sound qualities.

Following the first approach, a round arrangement of the interface could symbolize a drum, whereas linear shapes could be associated with flutes or drum-sticks. These visual abstractions are low resolution representations and therefore support associations more than reassembling the real appearance of those instruments.

Based on the second approach aesthetic connections of sound and shape are used to define an abstract systematic. Mellow sounding tones such as sine waves relate to smoothly shaped

[5] monome.org

constellations, whereas polygonal or chaotic structures represent harsh sounding or noisy instruments. This relation is even more abstract and focusses on emotional aspects, hence it can be compared to synesthetic where multiple sensations are mapped to each other and stimuli can be seen as complements of each other.

Both concepts cluster optical similarity and sound qualities. Therefore, users can forecast sound characteristics of unknown shapes based on their previously acquired knowledge. Thereby the possibility space gets organized and predictable. Both approaches are challenging in terms of abstraction. The emotional and personal perception of synesthetic makes it difficult to design and interpret such an interaction. Therefore, we integrated the idea of shape as a real-world representation in our concept. Derived from this a system of shapes can be classified where similar appearing ones represent families of instruments (see Figure 6).

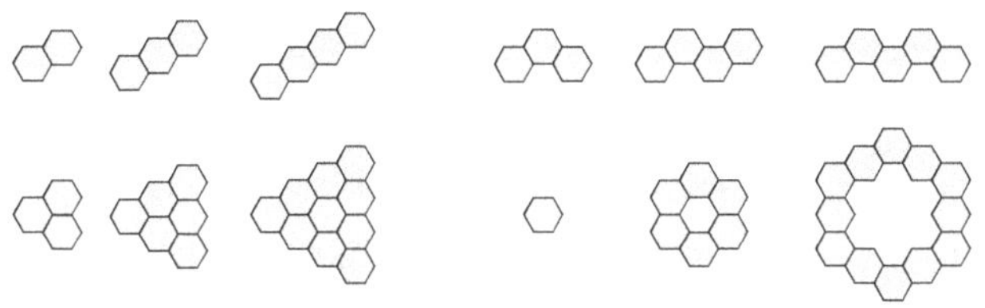

**Figure 6. Different polyhexes can be grouped into families of shapes. Above we describe variations of: lines, waves, triangles and circles. Such families can represent related instruments.**

## Target Group
Children have to meet these major requirements during the interaction with music software: cognitive skills to encounter the software's complexity and the ability to read to handle navigation through dialogues and menu structures. Beyond that, restrictions in hardware use are caused by lacking motor skills and the interface design's abstractness/complexity.

Therefore, we chose kindergarten children between the age of five to six as our target group, aiming to improve their access to digital/electronic music creation. They suffer from the above-mentioned restrictions but are cognitive more capable in handling complex tasks as younger children. Their cognitive capabilities as well as their scope of motor skills are further developed. Before the age of four, fine motor hand movements such as the tripod-grip are not used. Thus, complex building tasks, as needed during the operation of a constructive interface, are not part of their repertoire [9]. However, the span of four to six is too large to get comparable results caused by the developmental differences, as already five to six-year-olds differ in cognition and motor functions the typical one-year framing is used as a reasonable setting as found in common educational systems.

## IMPLEMENTATION
To enable free and portable play our prototype should not depend on camera-tracking or other external technologies. Therefore, the implementation had to tackle the following challenges: quick and sturdy module-interconnections to facilitate construction, neighbor recognition and intercommunication to enable shape detection. Without external information the interface should recognize its current shape to adapt the displayed information as well as the available functionality.

## Prototype: 1st Generation
The 1st generation prototype was concerned with refining the design in terms of reliability and usability as well as finding technical solutions for the envisioned interaction model. In the next section the development of the prototype is described as well as production techniques developed during the prototyping process.

### *Custom Prototyping Techniques*
Custom magnetic connectors (see Figure 7) have been developed, to enable direct exchange of data and power between the modules during the prototyping and design process. Heatshrink encloses the components and remains some of the magnet's flexibility. These custom connectors are suitable for purposes with the need for flexibility and therefore used as convenient tool for prototyping for example wearable devices. However, once such connectors are fixed in a rigid surface, they become vulnerable for bad contacts. To manufacture uncommonly shaped silicone-pads, a simple workflow has been developed. Instead of 3D-printing or CNC milling, laser-cutting has been used to produce custom molds (see Figure 8). This allowed us to perform quick iterations and adaptions during the prototyping process. Different materials can be used for the build depending on the desired surface texture such as acrylic glass or medium density fiber-board (MDF). To seal non-waterproof materials like MDF Vaseline has proven to be a cheap, simple and reliable solution: When applying heat, it penetrates the surface and makes the material hydrophobic.

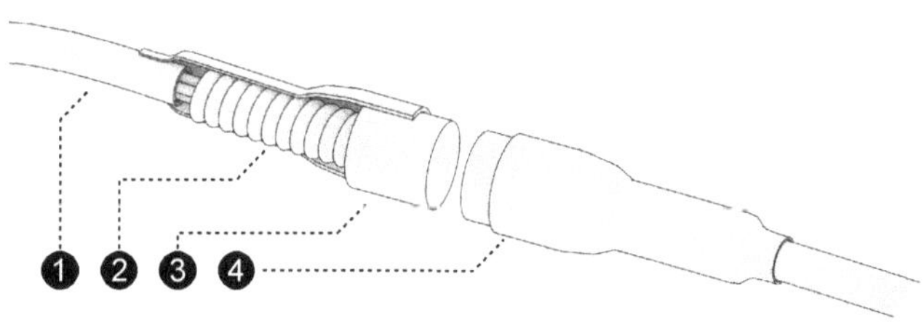


**Figure 7. A four-parted structure has been used to overcome the loss of magnetic force caused by overheating magnets during soldering: (1) jumper wire, (2) ferromagnetic bridging-material (e.g. guitar strings), (3) magnet, (4) heat shrink.**

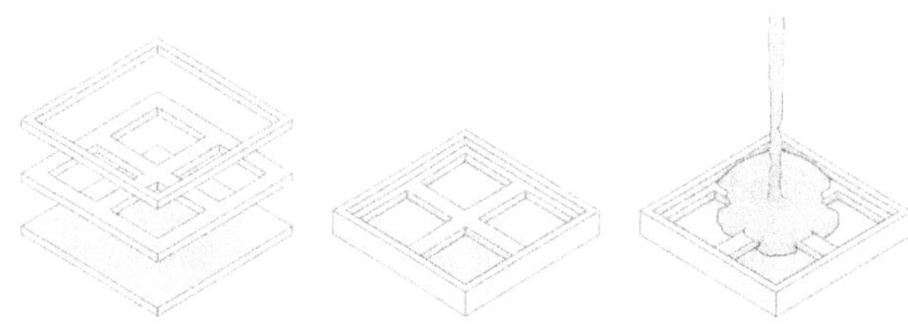

**Figure 8. A laser-cut-mold for custom silicone-pads can be manufactured from three simple layers of MDF. The middle layer defines the shape and number of pads, whereas the bottom and top layer restrict the flow of silicone.**

### *Hardware*

Each COMB module (see Figure 9) is constructed around the Teensy LC[6], a small footprint microcontroller. Features such as capacitive touch recognition and class compliant MIDI device capability are already included in the platform. For our needs its 32bit, 48MHz ARM Cortex-M0+ processor has been proven to be superior to most other microcontrollers with the same footprint and costs. As a class compliant MIDI device, it allows immediate usage on any computer with MIDI enabled software. A handcrafted PCB which holds six LEDs on the bottom side as well as six copper pads on the top represents the module's core component. These copper areas can sense touch through the overlaying silicone-pads and contain holes to allow backlit illumination by the underlying LEDs. Through the silicone's deformability different intensities of pressure can be sensed and the WS2812b LEDs allow RGB feedback for each individual pad.

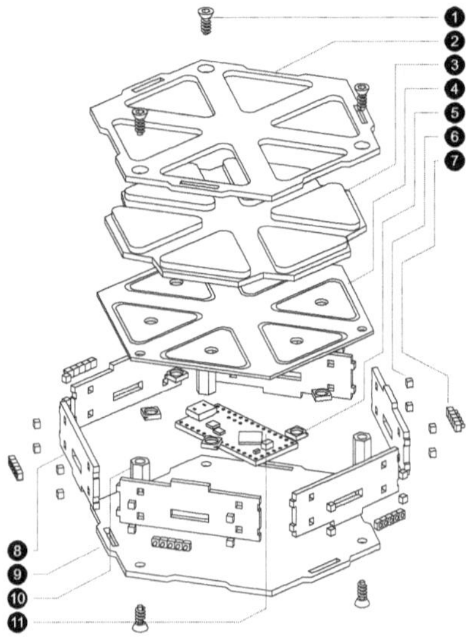


**Figure 9. (1) screws, (2) top, (3) silicone-pad, (4) PCB, (5) WS2812b LEDs, (6) magnets, (7) spring loaded connectors, (8) flanks, (9) bottom, (10) spacer, (11) Teensy LC.**

The module's hexagonal shape helps to reinforce the constructed structure. Further, tongues and groves as well as magnets are included into the design of the enclosure to define and hold the correct interconnections. Joints and screws ensure accessibility of the inner workings and therefore guarantee maintainability. Pogo pin connectors are integrated on all sides to distribute power (+5V, GND), transfer data between the connected modules via $I^2C$ (SDA, SCL) and enable shape-recognition via pulse-width modulation (PWM).

### *Shape Detection Algorithm*

The shape recognition procedure consists of two major tasks: collecting the neighbor data from each module and from there reconstructing the current constructed shape.

The neighbor-recognition is performed via a basic pulse-width modulation signal. Each module is able to send and receive IDs via its middle pogo-pins. An ID represents the side index as well as the membership to a specific module. If neighbor information is requested the module stops sending and starts receiving. Once all sides are queried the module responds and restarts sending. This data is collected and further processed by the master module, which is constantly supplied with power through its USB connection.

By considering simple features basic shapes can be detected without analyzing absolute positioning of each individual module. The number and location of neighbors can distinguish circular, line-like as well as polygonal shapes. After identifying the shape, the absolute position and rotation of each module inside the shape is determined. The importance of known rotation per module is based in the translation of pad index to pattern step index. Based on an ideal orientation within a structure each pad can be referred to a specific step within the corresponding sequence. The pad ID has to be shifted depending on the module's rotation to match the step index. The other way around, information which is to be displayed, has to be processed to match the rotation of each individual module.

Newly connected modules have to be supplied with the current states of each of their pads depending on the displayed pattern. Changes in pattern and shapes have to be organized by the master module, which runs all sequencers.

**Figure 10. The prototype PCB shows that SMD parts are upside-down mountable which allows backlit-illumination through holes included in the PCB. Further, the possibility of the microcontroller SMD-style mounting has been proven to work seamlessly which reduces height requirements.**

### **Prototype: 2nd Generation**

To further increase reliability and to enable the production of larger scales, a 2nd generation prototype for testing purposes has been developed. This prototype focuses on the reduction of the design's complexity and the utilization of industrial production methods as PCB etching and CNC-milling or 3D-printing techniques.

To decrease production costs a single PCB two-layer design was targeted. This PCB contains: six touch-plates on the top-layer and footprints for the LEDs, the microcontroller, simple electronic components and the pogo-pin connecters on the bottom side.

Resulting challenges are the upside-down positioning of the SMD LEDs as well as the SMD-like mounting of microcontrollers originally designed as through-hole parts to minimize

[6]Teensy LC: pjrc.com/teensy/teensyLC.html

space requirements. A prototype PCB was designed to verify the feasibility of those challenges. To reduce the hexagonal design's complexity and costs a rectangular design slightly larger than the microcontroller has been chosen. This prototyping iteration was performed to check if all requirements regarding further miniaturization and cost reduction are feasible (see Figure 10) and that thereby the mounting time could be drastically decreased.

## OBSERVATIONS AND USER-STUDY

COMB has been presented during a large electronic art festival and was afterwards evaluated in a lab study focusing on the comparison to the commercial midi-controller Novation Launchpad (LP).

### Field Study: Ars Electronica 2017

During the opening hours of the five-day electronic art festival over 40 demonstrations of the prototype per day have been performed: The visitors were introduced into the project's motivation, received a short introduction, had the possibility to experience the interface and gave informal oral feedback. In addition, 26 visitors participated in an AttrakDiff [10] evaluation after the demonstration.

In summary all participants were able to apply the interaction concept regardless of their age. In this setting most children started interacting without listening to the introduction whereas grownups depended on it as well as on the practical demonstration. We observed that some participants started with a wrong mental model of the interaction concept but were able to notice and correct it autonomously. Almost all participants tried unused shapes to look for unmentioned functionalities even if a large poster in front of them listed all valid shapes and the linked instruments.

Beside these observations the AttrakDiff survey has shown that the prototype generated high motivation among the users and has been received as highly usable during their first interaction. The interface was overall rated as: desirable.

### Follow Up Field Study

To further investigate whether our prototype supports imitation we designed a within-subject lab study focusing on the detection of modality-changes performed with COMB and the commercial product Launchpad7 (LP). The hypothesis we wanted to tackle in this experiment was: Shape is a more obvious representation of current functionality and is therefore easier to detect then conventional ones.

### Study Design

Participants had to react to functionality-changes (see Figure 5) while watching video clips of performances on both interfaces. Those changes were either performed by restructuring the interface (COMB) or selecting buttons in a specific button-array (LP). Once an event occurred the study subjects were intended to operate a provided buzzer as quickly as possible. Shorter reaction times were treated as indicators for better observability and pin-point towards a better imitability. To define a base-line and verify the understanding of the task, participants had to react to changing categories of displayed instruments (guitars, pianos, trumpets) first. All three clips contained ten changes that were spread in the same time pattern over the 1:50 long video. The order of videos concerning the interfaces has been switched via a 2x2 Latin Square per subject to prevent learning effects.

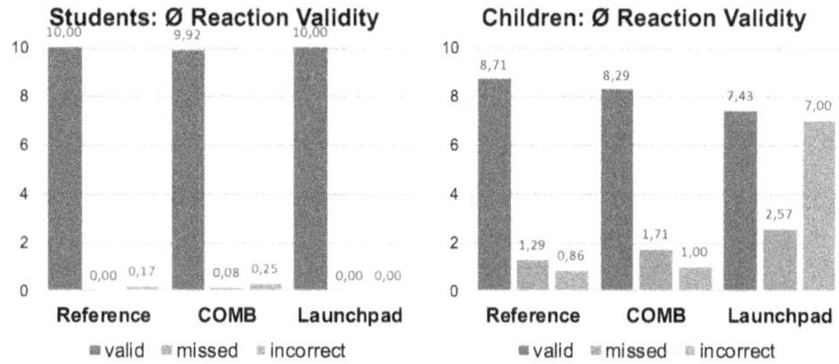


**Figure 11. Students performed steadily during all three tests. Missed and incorrect reactions are negligible low on average. The children's performance differs clearly between conditions. An increase in missed events and a multiple of incorrect reactions have been recorded by LP compared to COMB.**

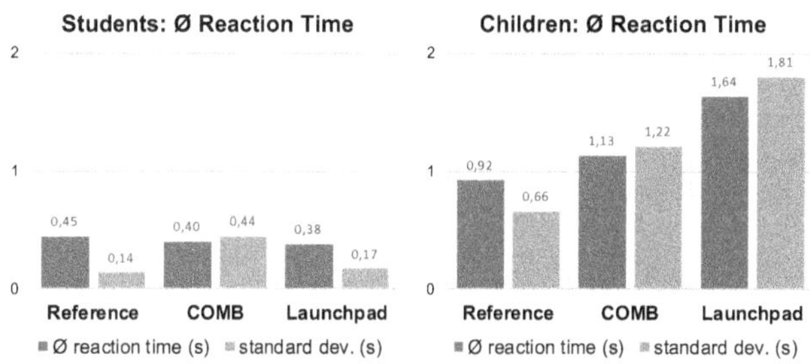


**Figure 12. While students' performance remained more or less constant over the three tests, a clear increase in children's reaction time and its deviation could be observed.**

### Participants and Data Collection Methods

The study was conducted including seven children with an age ranging from five to six years (5,14) as well as 12 students with an age ranging from 19 to 28 years (23,22). Every participant was introduced to the topic and the study tasks before the screening of all three clips. Afterwards, participants were introduced to the operating principles of COMB and had the chance to operate the interface on their own for a maximum of seven minutes. To collect feedback about the experience and initial impressions (first 7-minutes of use) a short semi-structured interview was conducted and recorded for later transcription.

### Study Results

As shown by the reference test (Figure 11 and Figure 12) students as well as children were able to recognize the events and to react to those as expected. Further, students were able to detect all events correctly and reacted in a comparable timespan. We further observed that the student's reaction time's standard deviation received the highest value during the test of COMB. Children's performance decreased clearly over the three tests. We noticed an increase in incorrect reactions as well as a decrease of valid reactions. Also, the average reaction time as well as its standard deviation become worse when comparing COMB to LP.

## DISCUSSION

The trial of unmentioned shapes as observed during both studies indicates the successful implementation of the design rationale's postulations as curiosity and exploration. Further, the ability to detect and correct false mental models can be seen as beneficial for self-regulated learning.

During the second field study an increase in preschooler's errors (missed and wrong reactions) as well as their average reaction time was recorded for LP compared to COMB. This indicates that functionality changes performed with COMB are easier to detect then with LP. These findings point towards a confirmation of the hypothesis that shape as an indicator of functionality can support imitation.

All demonstrations and studies proved the successful implementation of a robust and reliable technology setup. Our prototype allowed for fine as well as gross motor use. A consistent detection and low latency have been made possible by the implemented algorithm. Professional musicians claimed the hexagonal structure to be counterintuitive for common western music which is typically based on 4th divisions. However, we can argue that all instruments influence the music one can be perform with and that restrictions in general fertilize a creative process.

### Limitations

The high standard deviation of reaction times during the test with COMB and LP indicates the moment of change's higher inconclusiveness compared to the reference test.

The specific moment of change is blurred by foreshadowing elements as hand-position or finger gestures. Such additional hints allow reactions before the event and thus restrict the comparability of the average reaction times. Regardless of this, the comparability of error rates remains uninhibited.

Further, a student stated that he was not sure when exactly to react to those changes. Multiple moments were identified as relevant: the disconnection of blocks, the reconnection of blocks, the moment of the visualization's update. In contrast, with LP the distinct moment of pushing the button is equal to the moment of functionality change.

Both factors (foreshadowing and missing distinctness of changes) were not present in the reference study. The adaption of this explicitness can aim future studies on the comparability of reaction times. The focus on changes between still images could improve measurements.

### Further Benefits of Shape as an Interaction Method

Considering the positive observations gained during our observations we consider potential tasks, where shape-centered user interfaces could provide benefits. The following categories were identified on the analysis of the current prototype, its evaluation and the collected feedback in both study settings. Further use cases are expected to be identified during future research.

- Sequential tasks: Activities such as video editing where the same distinguishable tasks are performed repeatedly but not simultaneously (cutting, color grading, sound editing, etc.). Switching between tasks could be performed by switching the interface's shape.
- Collaborative tasks: Collaboration could benefit from tasks represented by shape as the overview of other parallelized tasks could be improved. Further, co-working on the same task with the same interface could also benefit from shape as a meaningful element of interaction.
- Tasks of adaptive complexity: Individualized learning could be supported by the individual increase of available modules and shapes based on each child's learning state.

## FUTURE WORK AND CONCLUSION

In this paper we have shown the implementation of shape as a meaningful element of interaction. We presented detailed descriptions of a prototype and the used technology that allows to use constructive shape-focused tasks to define its modes of function. In two evaluations we substantiated the usability und understandability of the concept across diverse age groups and found indications for such technologies being beneficial for kindergarten children. To further substantiate our research work on this topic in the near future we are aiming at:

- long-time studies in kindergartens
- expert evaluations in studio or live situations
- adaption of pre-attentive perception concepts to TUIs
- influence on holding function-states in working memory

A further goal of our research work is to provide free access to hard- and software components to enable designer and researchers to experiment with our concepts and develop them further or adapt them for their purposes.

We firmly believe that the investigation of shape-centered modular interfaces opens up new possibilities in the design of user interfaces that stimulate creative and persistent experiences. This familiar interaction can help to lower access thresholds as well as support visual understandability.

## REFERENCES


[1] Raphael Arar and Ajay Kapur. 2013. A History of Sequencers: Interfaces for Organizing Pattern-based Music. In *Sound and Music Computing Conference, Stockholm, Sweden*.

[2] Ayah Bdeir. 2009. Electronics as material: littleBits. In *Proceedings of the 3rd International Conference on Tangible and Embedded Interaction*. ACM, 397–400.

[3] Paulo Blikstein, Arnan Sipitakiat, Jayme Goldstein, João Wilbert, Maggie Johnson, Steve Vranakis, Zebedee Pedersen, and W Carey. 2016. Project Bloks: designing a development platform for tangible programming for children. *Position paper, retrieved online on* (2016), 06–30.

[4] Marion Buchenau and Jane Fulton Suri. 2000. Experience prototyping. In *Proceedings of the 3rd conference on Designing interactive systems: processes, practices, methods, and techniques*. ACM, 424–433.

[5] Bill Buxton. 2010. *Sketching user experiences: getting the design right and the right design*. Morgan Kaufmann.

[6] Lois Choksy. 1999. *Kodály method 1*. Vol. 1. Prentice Hall.

[7] Marcelo Coelho and Jamie Zigelbaum. 2011. Shape-changing interfaces. *Personal and Ubiquitous Computing* 15, 2 (2011), 161–173.

[8] ML Courage and GL Troseth. 2016. Infants, toddlers and learning from screen media. *Encyclopedia on Early Childhood Development: Technology in Early Childhood Education, November* (2016).

[9] Bryant J Cratty. 1979. Perceptual and motor development in infants and children. (1979).

[10] Marc Hassenzahl, Michael Burmester, and Franz Koller. 2003. AttrakDiff: Ein Fragebogen zur Messung wahrgenommener hedonischer und pragmatischer Qualität. In *Mensch & Computer 2003*. Springer, 187–196.

[11] David Holman and Roel Vertegaal. 2008. Organic user interfaces: designing computers in any way, shape, or form. *Commun. ACM* 51, 6 (2008), 48–55.

[12] Eva Hornecker. 2015. Tangible Interaction. *The Glossary of Human Computer Interaction.* (2015).

[13] Sergi Jordà, Günter Geiger, Marcos Alonso, and Martin Kaltenbrunner. 2007. The reacTable: exploring the synergy between live music performance and tabletop tangible interfaces. In *Proceedings of the 1st international conference on Tangible and embedded interaction*. ACM, 139–146.

[14] Yuichiro Katsumoto, Satoru Tokuhisa, and Masa Inakage. 2013. Ninja track: design of electronic toy variable in shape and flexibility. In *Proceedings of the 7th International Conference on Tangible, Embedded and Embodied Interaction*. ACM, 17–24.

[15] Mathieu Le Goc, Lawrence H Kim, Ali Parsaei, Jean-Daniel Fekete, Pierre Dragicevic, and Sean Follmer. 2016. Zooids: Building blocks for swarm user interfaces. In *Proceedings of the 29th Annual Symposium on User Interface Software and Technology*. ACM, 97–109.

[16] Mark R Lepper and Jennifer Henderlong. 2000. Turning "play" into "work" and "work" into"play": 25 years of research on intrinsic versus extrinsic motivation. In *Intrinsic and extrinsic motivation*. Elsevier, 257–307.

[17] David Merrill, Jeevan Kalanithi, and Pattie Maes. 2007. Siftables: towards sensor network user interfaces. In *Proceedings of the 1st international conference on Tangible and embedded interaction*. ACM, 75–78.

[18] Guy S Métraux and Gerald Oster. 1968. The Senses Considered as Perceptual Systems by James J. Gibson. *Leonardo* 1, 1 (1968), 89–90.

[19] Carl Orff, Gunild Keetman, Carolin Widmann, Sonja Korkeala, Karl Peinkofer, Andreas Schumacher, Markus Zahnhausen, Martin Ruhland, and Wilfried Hiller. 1995. *Orff-Schulwerk*. Celestial Harmonies.

[20] Jean Piaget. 2013. *Play, dreams and imitation in childhood*. Routledge.

[21] Jenny Preece, Yvonne Rogers, and Helen Sharp. 2015. *Interaction design: beyond human-computer interaction*. John Wiley & Sons.

[22] Majken K Rasmussen, Esben W Pedersen, Marianne G Petersen, and Kasper Hornbæk. 2012. Shape-changing interfaces: a review of the design space and open research questions. In *Proceedings of the SIGCHI Conference on Human Factors in Computing Systems*. ACM, 735–744.

[23] Beat Rossmy and Alexander Wiethoff. 2018. COMB: A Modular Low-Resolution Display to Support Electronic Musical Pre-Education. In *Proceedings of the 7th ACM International Symposium on Pervasive Displays*. ACM, 24.

[24] Bert Schiettecatte and Jean Vanderdonckt. 2008. AudioCubes: a distributed cube tangible interface based on interaction range for sound design. In *Proceedings of the 2nd international conference on Tangible and embedded interaction*. ACM, 3–10.

[25] Neil JA Sloane. 2007. The on-line encyclopedia of integer sequences. In *Towards mechanized mathematical assistants*. Springer, 130–130.

[26] Hideyuki Suzuki and Hiroshi Kato. 1993. AlgoBlock: a tangible programming language, a tool for collaborative learning. In *Proceedings of 4th European Logo Conference*. 297–303.

[27] Brygg Ullmer and Hiroshi Ishii. 2000. Emerging frameworks for tangible user interfaces. *IBM systems journal* 39, 3.4 (2000), 915–931.

[28] Roel Vertegaal and Ivan Poupyrev. 2008. Organic user interfaces. *Commun. ACM* 51, 6 (2008), 26–30.

[29] Barry J Wadsworth. 1996. *Piaget's theory of cognitive and affective development: Foundations of constructivism*. Longman Publishing.

[30] Ruth Wood and Jean Ashfield. 2008. The use of the interactive whiteboard for creative teaching and learning in literacy and mathematics: a case study. *British journal of educational technology* 39, 1 (2008), 84–96.

[31] John Zimmerman, Jodi Forlizzi, and Shelley Evenson. 2007. Research through design as a method for interaction design research in HCI. In *Proceedings of the SIGCHI conference on Human factors in computing systems*. ACM, 493–502.

[32] Oren Zuckerman, Saeed Arida, and Mitchel Resnick. 2005. Extending tangible interfaces for education: digital montessori-inspired manipulatives. In *Proceedings of the SIGCHI conference on Human factors in computing systems*. ACM, 859–868.

# You say Potato, I say Po-Data: Physical Template Tools for Authoring Visualizations

**Tiffany Wun, Lora Oehlberg, Miriam Sturdee, Sheelagh Carpendale**
University of Calgary
Calgary, AB Canada
{twwun, lora.oehlberg, miriam.sturdee, sheelagh}@ucalgary.ca

## ABSTRACT
Data visualization authoring tools for the general public remains an ongoing challenge. Inspired by block-printing, we explore how visualization stamps as a physical tool for authoring visualizations could leverage both visual freedom and ease of repetition. We conducted two workshops where participants authored visualizations on paper using hand-carved stamps made from potatoes and sponges. The low-fidelity medium freed participants to test new stamp patterns and accept mistakes. From the created visualizations, we observed several unique traits and uses of block-printing tools for authoring visualizations, including: modularity of patterns; annotation guides; creation of multiple patterns from one stamp; and various techniques to apply data onto paper. We discuss issues around expressivity and effectiveness of block-printing stamps in authoring visualizations, and identify implications for the design and assembly of primitives in potential visualization stamp kits, as well as applications for future use in non-digital environments.

## Author Keywords
Information Visualization; Authoring Visualizations; Tangible Tools; Block-Printing; Physical Template Tools; Potato

## CCS Concepts
**•Human-centered computing → Visualization toolkits;** *Information visualization;* Human computer interaction (HCI);

## INTRODUCTION
In our data-rich society, large data sets commonly require expert knowledge to design and disseminate accessible and information-rich visualizations (InfoVis). There is a growing call from the public for the democratization of data, which supports free and accessible information for everyone [22]. However, data accessibility does not necessarily guarantee data comprehension—in the absence of comprehension, people cannot equally benefit from our data-rich society. One powerful technique for improving data literacy is to encourage people to self-author data visualizations using simple techniques, and to create visual representations suited to their own comprehension needs.



*TEI '19,* March 17–20, 2019, Tempe, AZ, USA

 ISBN 978-1-4503-6196-5/19/03...$15.00

DOI: https://doi.org/10.1145/3294109.3295627

We author data visualizations in a variety of media—for example, visualizations can be created digitally through coding or software, physically using stones [30] or tangible tiles [18], or sketched using pencils and markers [40]. Each medium can generate different visual representations; for example, digital software can create digital representations for screens or designs for digitally fabricated physical representations [37], whereas sketching can generate graphical representations on tablets [31, 25], whiteboards [3, 39, 8], or paper [40, 10]. Many digital data visualizations are quickly and automatically generated using templates. The wide availability of digital visualization template tools (e.g., Excel, Tableau, Spotfire) often come with tradeoffs [12], such as difficulties with finding features [5], less modifiability [16], and limited expressivity [16].

Alternatively, physical visualization authoring tools—such as tangible tiles—allow for ease of construction and increased visual freedom [18] over traditional digital visualization tools, such as Microsoft Excel [42]. However, physical representations, or physicalizations [21], are still challenging to author [37]; high-fidelity physicalizations are not easily modifiable and have high material cost, whereas tangible tiles cannot be customized and encourage construction in rectilinear configurations [41].

To address these issues, we introduce the notion of physical templates—block-printing stamps—as a novel method of authoring graphical visualizations. Using physical template tools, people can freely personalize visualizations with simple repeating visual elements. We conducted an exploratory study composed of two visualization block-printing workshops, where participants created visualizations of a predefined dataset using self-carved block-printing stamps. Our goal is to investigate: i) What types of *stamp tools* do people create and ii) What types of *visualizations* do they author with such tools; iii) What *affordances* do these tools have for visualization authoring; iv) How can these tools support *ease of use* and *self-expression* in visualization authoring; and, v) How can people *integrate* these tools into data comprehension.

Our main contribution is a primary exploration of physical tools used in authoring block-printed graphical visualizations. We additionally provide a discussion of the levels of freedom and self-expression introduced by authoring block-printed visualizations, comparisons between block-printing stamps and alternative authoring techniques, suggestions and recommendations for the design and customization of a visualization stamp kit, and scenarios for the usage of stamps as a self-reflection tool for data.

## RELATED WORK

In this section, we discuss three common approaches for novices to author visualizations: digital-based, physical-based, and sketch-based. We note the benefits and tradeoffs of authoring in each medium, and how block-printed stamps offer an alternative approach to authoring visualizations.

### Authoring Digital Visualization for Novices

Template editors are the most commonly used tool to author data visualizations, as they can quickly and automatically construct visualizations based on ready-made templates [11]. Despite different visualization construction approaches, research has shown that information visualization novices still have trouble authoring digital visualizations [12]. In Mei et al.'s survey of the design space of digital construction tools, they made recommendations for how to offer greater expressivity and guided refinement during the data design process [27]. Tools such as Méndez et al.'s iVoLVER [28], Xia et al.'s DataInk [43], and Kim et al.'s Data-Driven Guides technique [23] aim to leverage both expressivity and refinement, by allowing users to create accurate and custom data graphics without the need for textual programming.

However, these tools are currently not readily available and require users to learn how to use the tools. In practice, non-expert users still cope with less expressive, template-based editors available on the market, such as Excel, Spotfire, and Tableau.

### Authoring Physical Visualizations

An alternative means of understanding data may be through physical data representations, or data physicalizations. While physical representations—such as Sumerian clay tokens[1] and Micronesian stick charts[2]—existed long before the advent of computers, researchers have only recently focused on the benefits of physicality as opposed to digital screens. These benefits include accessibility [21], cognitive advantages [35], and increased engagement [14, 36]. An example of a physical paradigm for authoring visualizations is the use of tangible tiles [16], which represent physically tokenized data.

The approach towards "tokenizing" data can be seen in the International System of Typographical Picture Education (ISOTYPE) [29], which uses a series of repeating pictograms of the same size to convey quantity in an engaging and universally understood manner. Huron et al. [18] took data tokenization into the physical realm for authoring visualizations, and showed that visualization non-experts were able author visualizations using tangible tiles with little difficulty. In further extension of this work, Wun et al. found that tangible tiles provided more visual freedom and expressive power in comparison to digital template tools, such as Microsoft Excel [42]. However, tangible tiles are limited in their shape, encourage construction in one model, and the completed visualizations cannot be easily transported without losing the position of the tiles—and therefore their intended meaning [41].

### Authoring Visualizations using Sketching

Other approaches to data visualization involve sketching representations. This is often done early in the ideation phase of a visualization design project, as a low-fidelity method to develop and clarify ideas about representation [4]. Paper is a popular medium for sketching visualizations due to its wide availability [40, 10], however, visualization sketching has also occurred on whiteboards [3, 39, 8], tablets [31, 25], and napkins [6]. The benefits of paper as a sketching medium mean that the visual representations stay on the paper, so they can be shuffled and carried around without fear of unwanted modifications. Walny et al. [40] studied how people sketched visualizations on paper, and proposed a data sketching continuum ranging from abstract to specific, numerical representations. While sketching is versatile in comparison to tangible tiles, it can require time-consuming reproduction of visually similar structures, making it unsuitable for the accurate representation of large data sets within a short period of time.

[1]http://dataphys.org/list/mesopotamian-clay-tokens/

[2]http://dataphys.org/list/marshall-islands-stick-charts/

### Block-Printing

To address the shortcomings inherent in current approaches for authoring visualizations, we propose block-printing stamps as an intersection of the affordances of digital-based, physical-based, and sketched-based approaches. Block-printing stamps combine the quick repetition of templates, the visual freedom of tangible tiles, and the low-fidelity ideation of paper sketches, to generate tokenized visualizations on paper. To form block-printing stamps, a relief pattern is carved onto a block of material (such as wood), with the negative space cut away. The block is then inked and pressed onto cloth or paper. Applications for block printing first included the creation of patterned textiles, and later for printing illustration and type onto paper. Nowadays, materials such as linoleum or rubber are commonly used for creating stamps; in our study, we chose potatoes and sponges as carving materials for stamps as they are accessible, cheap, and easy to carve and/or cut by novices. Since making potato stamps is a common activity for children, we chose materials that study participants would be familiar working with.

## METHODOLOGY

To understand how people author visualizations with block-printing tools, we conducted two workshops where participants created visualizations of pre-defined datasets using self-carved potato and sponge stamps. We chose a workshop format to facilitate rich engagement between participants. Prior studies used workshops to facilitate visualization authoring in various mediums, from sketched visualizations [40], to constructive visualization [15] and data physicalization [17]. Our workshop is informed by the experiences of Huron et al. [17], who identified several bottlenecks while participants were constructing physicalizations.

### Participants

We recruited two groups of workshop participants with varying levels of expertise in visualization via word-of-mouth. The first group (**G1**) included five participants (Participants 1-5; 2 male/3 female) who were part of a professional team designing visualizations for a governmental agency. This group ranged from less than 1 year to over 5 years of experience working with visualizations (three participants had a minimum of 3+ years of experience). Our second group (**G2**) had five participants (Participants 6-10; 3 male/2 female) who did not work with visualizations on a daily basis. This group ranged from no prior experience to 5+ years of experience working with visualizations (three participants had less than 1 year of experience).

### Materials
Each participant sat at a "stamp making station" including: potatoes and sponges, cardstock and A4 paper, small knives, box-cutters, cutting boards, fruit corers, paint brushes, pens, paper plates and towels, a bowl for dispensing offcuts, and a cup of water. We also provided participants with tubes of paints in primary colors (red, blue, yellow), white, and black.

### Dataset
We provided a fictitious dataset about a 4-day vacation, represented as a table. We designed the dataset to be low in complexity, yet still contain multiple data columns for breadth and representational variety. The dataset contained one column with date values (*Date*), two columns with categorical values (*Where*, *Type of Spending*), one column with ranked values (*Enjoyability*), and one column with numerical values (*Cost in dollars*). Numerical values were balanced between a value of 10 to 70 to avoid skewing.

### Workshop Schedule
The workshop lasted approximately 120 minutes, consisting of 4 phases: *Introduction, Creation, Discussion*, and *Conclusion*.

*Introduction (25 mins)*
Participants first completed a short demographic questionnaire on their experience with interactive systems, visualizations, and data. The researcher then introduced the workshop, including:

- **An introduction to block-printing stamps**, and a reminder on how to create colours by mixing paints.
- **Common Information Visualization data mappings** (i.e. position, size, count). We advised participants to think about what elements they wanted for their visual representation.
- **The workshop task**,"Create visualizations that show the highlights of your 4-day trip" with the given dataset, using self-created stamps. We provided several brief tips on creating the visualization: choose mappings, sketch the stamp pattern onto the medium first, paint and press onto paper, then label when done. To help provide focus, the researcher suggested the participants to pick at least 2 columns of the dataset for one visualization, then choose another set of columns for their next visualization.
- **A description of workshop tools and materials**, and instructions on how to make stamps with potatoes and sponges.

*Creation (60 mins)*
We provided each participant with the sample dataset, and asked them to consider what types of stories they could tell from the data. We emphasized that participants did not need to be perfect with their visualizations. While we intended for participants to work alone, we did not discourage them from discussing with their neighbors, and some participants walked around the room to see what others were making. Throughout this time, we made a "data mapping lookup sheet" available to participants, which provided a summary of the various data mappings presented in the *Introduction* phase. Huron et al.'s physicalization workshop [17] noted that participants got stuck ideating about concepts for their physicalizations; we provided the lookup sheet to remind our participants of just several different possibilities for mapping data. Lookup sheets were also previously used in Thudt et al.'s [38] self-reflection workshop to also help stimulate ongoing activity while constructing a physicalization.

*Discussion (30 mins)*
Participants displayed their finished visualizations to the group, along with any stamps they had created. Each participant then described their visualization to the group, along with the stamps they created and their process. The researcher then asked the entire group open-ended questions on what types of stamps they liked, what stamps they would find useful, and what stamps they would create in a canonical data stamp set.

*Conclusion (5 mins)*
We asked participants to complete a questionnaire on their thoughts and opinions regarding the workshop. We also asked them to sketch designs for any stamps they had suggested for a visualization stamp kit. Additionally, participants could provide further feedback on the workshop in a separate follow-up interview.

### Data Collection and Analysis
Each stamp making station had a video camera angled to best capture activities at that station. We recorded photos, video, and audio during the *Creation* and *Discussion* phases, alongside supplementary field notes. We also recorded video and audio during the one-on-one feedback sessions.

We used a qualitative analysis approach. Visualizations were arranged on a two dimensional visual representation continuum, extended from Walny et al's representational continuum for sketched visualizations [40]. As several of the visualizations were ambiguous, the lead author examined post-questionnaire answers, field notes, and transcriptions of the two group discussions to confirm visual encodings in each visualization in relation to Bertin's visual variables [2]. Using an open coding schema [34], three of the co-authors identified themes of interest from the participants' transcripts and artefacts [2].

Each of the participants' process videos were reviewed to confirm the number of stamps created by participants, and the number of stamps used in the visualizations. Creating the stamps and visualizations using the given materials was an intensely personal and varied process for participants; thus we were more interested in how participants approached the authoring process, rather than the nuances of repetitive actions. In early analysis, we analyzed the two participant groups along expertise levels, but found that individual expertise mattered less than the richer results from individual participants.

## FINDINGS
Our findings describe the participants' self-created block-printing tools, their authoring process, and the resulting block-printed visualizations. We additionally discuss data encodings via stamps, visualization annotations, and the role of stamp materiality in creating block-printed visualizations. For ease of reference, participants' individual visualizations are denoted in the form **Participant Number.Vis Number** (e.g., 5.1). High-resolution versions of paper figures, along with other study images and materials, can be found at `http://bit.ly/VisStamps`.

### Creating Block-Printing Tools
While making stamps by carving potatoes and sponges is not unheard of, only 4/10 participants had previous experience in carving stamps. A total of 71 stamps were created over the course of both workshops, 65 of which were used to create visualizations

(**G1**: 33/37 used, average created: 7.4, min: 5, max: 10; **G2**: 32/34 used, average created: 6.4, min: 3, max: 11).

Participants made a diverse range of stamp shapes with varying detail. These shapes ranged from themes related to the types of spending (e.g. forks, shopping bags, airplanes), locations (e.g. outlines of country borders, flags, landmarks), geometric shapes (e.g. circles, triangles), or "others" (e.g. lines, hollowed potatoes). We define stamp shapes as the carved outcome of the stamp, while stamp patterns refer to the applied shape of the stamp on paper.

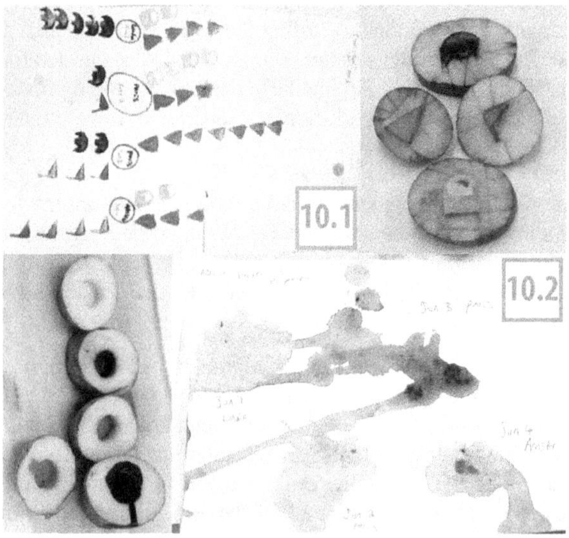


**Figure 1. P10's stamps and visualizations with the "ink-wells" (bottom left).**

One set of stamps stood out as radically different from the others: P10's self-dubbed "ink-wells" (Fig. 1), made from hollowing the centers of potatoes and filling the depression with diluted paint.

*P10: "The other stamps that I made were 'ink well stamps' – honestly, that was just an experiment, but depending on how much I fill the well that's how much water that would get splashed onto the thing, and that would sort of represent how much you spent..."*

We classify the stamp shapes into four categories: *Icons*, *Geometries*, *Alphabet*, and *Others*. *Icons* (35/71) are pictographic shapes that convey an established meaning, such as emojis. *Geometric* (24/71) shapes are simple shapes without a predefined meaning, such as a circle or star. *Alphabet* (3/71) shapes (i.e. letters) are part of an existing alphabet, but are not icons since they do not convey a pre-defined meaning. Lastly, *Others* (9/71) are shapes that fell outside of these categories, such as axes and ticks. We consider the "ink-wells" to fall under the *Other* category, as they are stamps in a very loose sense and do not stamp a specific pattern.

## Authoring Process

While each participant followed their own process, they generally performed the following sequence to create their visualizations: *sketching and data loading*, *carving*, *stamping*, and *annotating*.

***Sketching and Data Loading:*** Participants started by sketching potential representations of the data, stamp shapes, and/or simultaneously computing data values (i.e. rounding, aggregating, etc.).

***Carving:*** Participants carved out their stamps from potatoes or sponges with provided tools. Carving was done all at once, or intermittently with other steps; five participants (P2, P4, P7, P8, P9) chose to cut out all of their stamps before using those stamps to create their first visualization.

***Stamping:*** Participants applied paint onto stamps by dipping them in paint or using a paintbrush before placing them on the paper. Participants often tested their stamp on a scrap piece of paper before stamping onto the actual visualization.

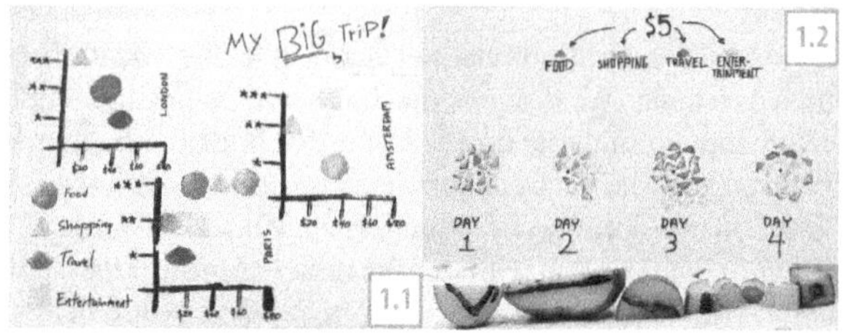


**Figure 2. P1's stamps and visualizations show an example of a *modular stamp pattern*.**

While most stamp patterns were composed from a single shape, participants P1 and P5 composed *modular stamp patterns* by combining several smaller stamps. P1 composed several axes stamps together to create annotations for their visualization (1.1), as shown in Fig. 2, while P5 composed Chernoff faces [7] (5.1) and stacked circles (5.2).

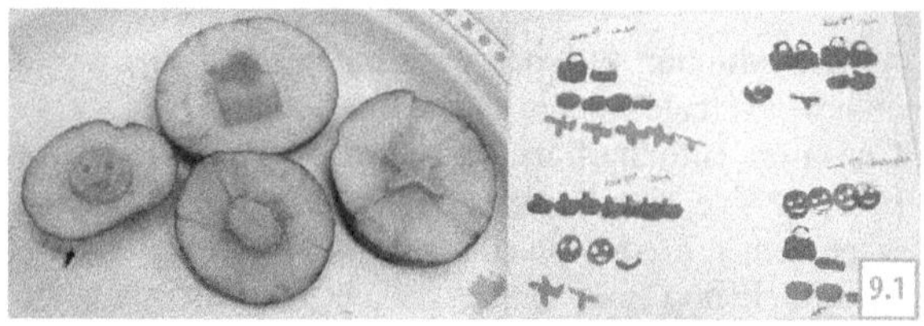


**Figure 3. P9's stamps and visualizations show an example of *multiple patterns* from multiple stamps.**

Using the same stamp in various ways, P2 and P9 created *multiple patterns* on paper. By orienting different sides of the same potato stamp, P2 could generate multiple visual patterns for all of visualization 2.2. P9 (Fig. 3) angled the placements of their stamps onto the page to show varying amounts of the same stamp pattern in visualization 9.1. For P9, one "full" pattern represented 10 units, thus, this angled placement allowed them to represent the numerical portions of the dataset more accurately.

***Annotating:*** Participants annotated their visualizations with axes, legends, titles, etc. Four participants (P1, P3, P6, P10) annotated the visualization with axes or headers before stamping onto the paper, presumably to make guides for where to stamp.

The paintbrush was used in a variety of ways during this step. Several painted over mistakes on the visualization (P3, P7), splattered and flicked paint onto their visualization (P8), or made a stamped pattern look neater on paper (P9). P4 painted sun rays on 4.3 from a series of circles. P8 used a splatter technique to apply colour after stamping the pattern down onto paper:

*P8: "I used a splatter technique with the brush [for 8.2] – this is the amount of money spent in each of the countries over the days...also the splatter stuff didn't work too well so I had to change to flicking or tapping."*

### Block-Printed Visualizations

Participants created a total of 21 visualizations over the two workshops (**G1**: 13, average 2.6; **G2**: 8, average 1.6). We recommended participants choose at least two data columns to ensure breadth; however, the majority (19/21) of visualizations encoded multiple data columns (although no participants visualized all five columns in one image).

Participants often used various layouts and representations when creating more than one visualization. We initially classified these visualizations against Walny et al's representation continuum for sketched visualizations [40]; however, our visualizations did not map exactly onto the Numeracy-Abstractness continuum, as our study dataset contains non-numerical values (such as enjoyment, or type of spending). For example, visualizations 2.2 and 2.3 (Fig. 4) are dot plots, but the representations are highly abstracted, and not numerical as originally defined. Therefore we adapted several of Walny et al.'s described representation categories to describe the appearance of our participants' visualizations below.

***Countable (7/21):*** Walny et al. define these visualizations as the most numeric representations using countable tokens to represent the data [40]. Similarly, our participants' visualizations tokenized data by repeating the same pattern, such as shopping bags, planes, and flags. Participants placed their patterns in various groupings to represent common themes, such as Day or Location.

***Dot/Scatter Plots and Matrices (8/21):*** We classify visualizations as dot/scatter plots and matrices if they encode data values (e.g., enjoyment, cost) along visible categorical and numerical axes. While dot/scatter plots and matrices are defined as the second-most numeric representations along the original continuum, this is not necessarily the case with our visualizations. Visualizations 2.1 and 2.2, shown in Fig. 4, are represented as dot-plots; however, the data is highly abstracted and it is difficult to extract the raw values. Visualization 5.1 and 5.3, shown in Fig. 5, are matrices defining enjoyability over different days and locations, but numerical data (*Cost*) is either not encoded (as is the case with 5.3), or has been transformed into binned categories (as is the case with 5.1).

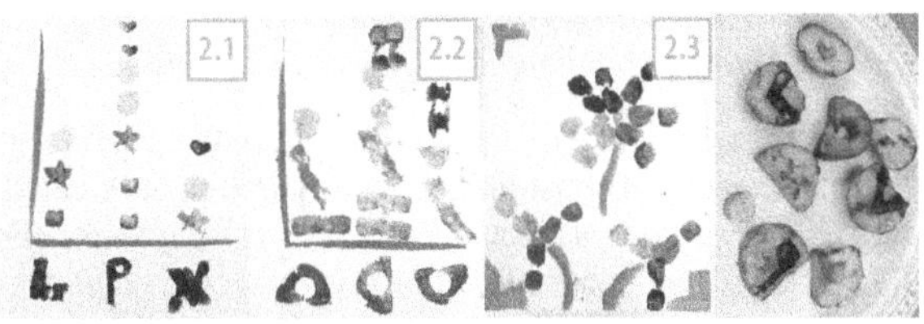


**Figure 4. P2's stamps and visualizations. Visualizations 2.1 and 2.2 are dot plots, while visualization 2.3 is stamped in a way to look like flowers.**

***Pictoral (5/21):*** Similar to the original continuum, pictoral representations are highly abstract. These representations are often difficult to read raw data from, as the visual encodings are often not defined to viewers. For example, visualization 2.3 was stamped in such a way that the patterns looked like flowers; visualization 7.1 (Fig. 6) is purely graphical and does not contain any words; visualization 8.1 is coloured according to the enjoyability of certain activities in each country; visualization 8.2 contains border outlines of countries filled with dots of splattered paint to represent money spent in each country; and visualization 10.2 uses spilled paint stains on a sheet of paper to represent money spent over different days.

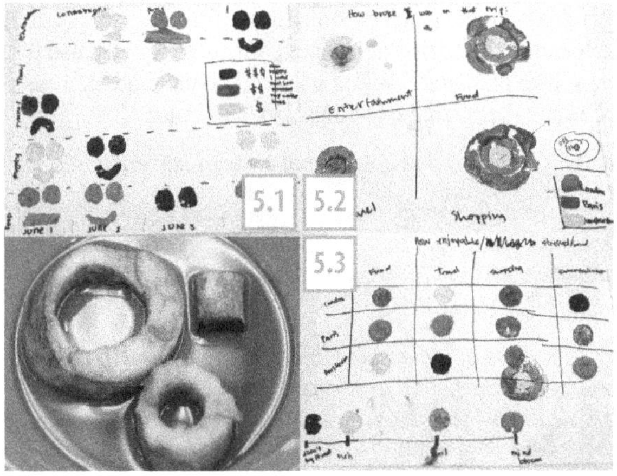


**Figure 5. P5's stamps and visualizations. Visualizations 5.1 and 5.3 are matrices, while visualization 5.2 falls under the *Other* category.**

***Other (1/21):*** Visualization 5.2 (Fig. 5) consists of ringed circles, where each ring represents what activities (entertainment, food, travel, shopping) occurred in which location. It did not fall into any category as it did not encode numerical values.

As participants used stamps to create their visual representations, tokens were the most common graphical element. Each pattern on the paper—a discrete visual mark—represents some data unit [18]. Nineteen out of twenty-one visualizations used multiple tokens to represent and encode data onto the visualization. Highly numeric representations, such as the countable groupings and the charts, largely employed tokens.

### Data Encoding via Stamps

Participants encoded the dataset using a number of visual variables [2] to represent the data, from multiple hues and values to various shapes and sizes. The most common visual variables used for encoding data were position (27 instances) and shape (17 instances). Position, an intrinsic visual variable, was used in all visualizations. Shape, which we identified if more than one stamp shape was used in the visualization, was used in 16/21 visualizations. The least used variables were texture (0 instances), followed by orientation and color value, or color tint/shade (2 instances each). The absence of texture and color value may come from difficulties in defining details on potato and sponge stamps, and the precision needed to mix different tints and shades.

Each stamp intrinsically encodes data through its shape; however, P10's "ink-wells" uniquely encoded data through the amount of ink. Rather than containing a unique shape, the ink-wells acted as "vessels" for carrying data, where the color and amount of liquid filled in the stamp was used to encode spending.

### Exploring Annotations

In addition to block printing, participants used pens to create annotations for their visualizations. Below, we discuss the levels of annotations, as well as guides and tools for producing annotations.

***Level of Annotations:*** Participants used varying levels of annotation, ranging from visualizations with highly textual labels and axes (e.g., visualization 1.1), to visualizations only containing the title (e.g., visualization 8.2). In most cases, participants who had very pictoral and iconic visualizations did not provide a legend for their visualization (except for 6.2, which identified the locations of their flag shapes), presumably because the icon was self-explanatory. When a legend was included, it was used to define other visual encodings, such as color.

Visualizations 2.3 and 7.1 did not contain any annotations:

*P2: "I wanted to write on it (2.3), but then I realized that I wore out all the pens, and then I was like: 'screw this, I know how to, I know what it stands for and I'm the only one who needs to know about it [laughs].' "*

*P7: "In terms of understandability, it's (7.1) probably not [easily understandable], but in terms of looking different than other visualizations– for better or worse I think that's a success."*

However, while P2 and P7 did not annotate their respective visualizations, they still created various aesthetic marks, such as the corner markings (2.3) and the expressive background (7.1). Furthermore, while P2 did not write text in any of their visualizations, they still annotated visualization 2.1 by using the first letter of the locations, and making abstract marks in visualization 2.2. P7 roughly categorized their visualization with stamp patterns alluding to the respective travel location (i.e. Paris, London, Amsterdam), as shown in Fig. 6. Although these marks may not make sense to an outsider, they still conveyed meaning to the author.

***Annotating Guides.*** In 7/10 cases, participants laid down partial annotations prior to stamping on their paper, or while continuing to make stamp marks. In 6/21 visualizations, participants created axes or data grouping headers before stamping onto the page, presumably as guidelines for where to stamp.

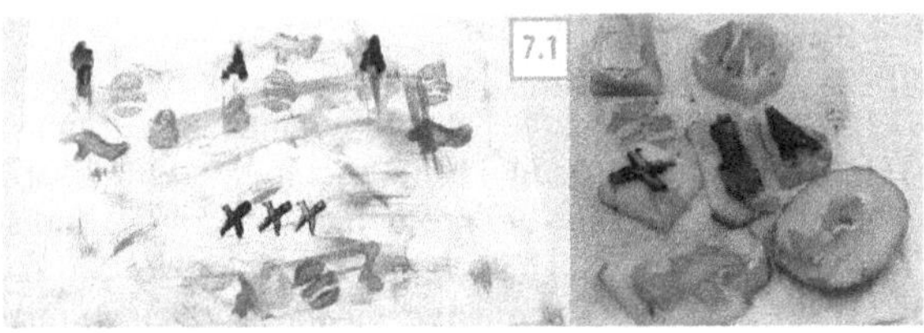


**Figure 6. P7's stamps and visualization show an example of a visualization without annotations.**

***Tools for Annotation.*** Stamps were not only used to visually encode data, but also to annotate or aesthetically augment the visualization. P1 made a set of stamps of varying line lengths for making axes and ticks. P2 and P7 used the entire sponge without cutting or carving it. In P2's first and second visualizations (2.1, 2.2), they applied paint to the hard edge of the sponge and dragged it across the paper to make axes. For P2's third visualization (2.3), they dabbed the soft side of the sponge with paint to make marks on the corners of the paper. P7 also dabbed paint onto the soft side of a sponge, then smeared it across the paper to create a background for visualization 7.1. While this background did not encode data, the use of the sponge itself as a raw medium allowed P7 to customize the visualization to their desires.

### Materiality of Stamps

The materials provided for stamp carving both liberated and constrained participants' authoring process of their stamps and visualizations. These affected participants' willingness to experiment, their reactions to mistakes, their incorporation of art and play into the visualizations, and their difficulties in making and using stamps.

***Medium Liberties.*** Due to the messiness of hand-carved stamps, we noticed that participants felt more comfortable with experimenting and making mistakes on their visualizations. For example, after P2 placed a stamp, they realized they had made a mistake.

*P2: "Realized that I stamped it upside down (supposed to be Amsterdam). Ran out of space at the top, let's just stamp right next to it. More freedom to say 'okay, I ran out of space, put it on the side.' "*

However, when something did not go according to their vision, participants accepted or adapted to mistakes. In one case, P8 meticulously made finely detailed stamps of country borders. However, they forgot to mirror the image of the United Kingdom, but continued using the stamp rather than start over again.

In another case, P7 changed the vision of their visualization after difficulties with making their potato stamp.

*P7: "When I was cutting out this potato I saw that this shape doesn't go the way I wanted, so I decided to go very abstract."*

When P3 and P7 stamped down a pattern in the wrong spot, they rectified their mistakes using white paint.

*P3: "I made a mistake here because I read the data wrong (gestures to bottom of 3.2) and I decided to use white paint to go over it. I realised that when you're using physicals there's no undo [laughs], so I made my own undo."*

Given the freedom of the medium, artistic and playful themes were sometimes incorporated into the story of the visualizations throughout the authoring process. For example, P1 titled visualization 1.1: "My BIG Trip! by [P1], age [redacted]." P5 titled visualizations 5.1 and 5.2: "How happy I was and how stressed my wallet was"; and "How broke I was on that trip" respectively. Several participants stated that they directly aimed to incorporate art into their visualization, such as P2's "border" annotations.

*P2: "I just felt like it [2.3] looked more artistic, so I added extra things [the borders] that would make it art on this side."*

***Medium Constraints:*** The nature of using potatoes and sponges also imposed several constraints on how participants created their stamps. The wetness of potatoes was a surprising factor [P4, P7, P8], changing the quality of participants' patterns on paper.

*P4: "I was really surprised, first of all, I thought: 'Great, work with potatoes, must be fantastic.' But it's very hard because it kept– it's humid so it's not so easy, it's not easy, as I expected to do."*

Participants noted various levels of success with making detailed or intentional shapes with potatoes. While participants generally liked making the stamps, only 4/10 participants were satisfied with the stamps they created. Carving stamps was a tedious and time consuming task.

*P10: "Yeah it's a car without the wheels, I got lazy and didn't wanna...cause like cutting inside the actual stamp itself was super hard, and I didn't even want to do that, so I wanted to avoid it at all costs."*

Participants noted that sponges were harder to work with, harder to detail, and gave lower quality prints on paper as compared to potatoes. For example, P6 cut four stamps from the sponges, but after creating several marks with them, found the sponges unsatisfactory and recarved all their patterns using potatoes.

Despite these limitations, one participant noted that the material constraints led them to approach the task differently:

*P5: "Being constrained with what you can do with a potato is really interesting, you go beyond those boundaries and you do things you don't realize is possible with just that potato."*

Ultimately, while wetness and detailing affected the quality of the participants' artefacts, the use potatoes and sponges as an authoring medium freed participants to experiment, make mistakes, play, and embrace unexpected results.

## DISCUSSION

Below we discuss the issues that motivated our investigation into block-printing tools for authoring visualizations: expressivity and effectiveness. We also discuss block-printing stamps in relation to tangible tiles and sketching as tools for graphical visualizations.

### Freedom and Self-Expression in Authoring Visualizations

Compared to digital methods for authoring visualizations, block-printing stamps gave people increased flexibility in the authoring process. A person may be constrained to follow certain steps to produce a digital visualization in software, such as picking a visual representation from a series of templates, and then modifying and adjusting as needed. Traditionally, the visual form of the data is created before a visualization can be annotated; Jansen et al.'s pipeline model for visualizations [20] describe such actions as *visual mapping* and *presentation mapping* respectively. However, the iterable and free-flow nature of the participants' authoring process sometimes went contrary to the flow of the pipeline. When participants created annotation marks (i.e. axes, ticks, lines) to guide the placement of future annotations during the study, they started *presentation mapping* before completing *visual mapping*, highlighting a certain freedom with the block-printing process outside of the InfoVis pipeline module. This type of flexibility in the authoring process was noted by Isenberg et al. [19] as being common when people were not constrained by software, and is also inline with physical and graphical paradigms such as constructive visualization [18] and sketching [40].

Furthermore, crafting personalized visualization stamps allowed for a high level of self-expression and individuality, despite identical datasets across participants. It is unsurprising that some common shapes, such as shopping bags or planes, were created by multiple participants in the workshops. However, each shape contained their own subtle styles and differences—e.g., some shopping bags had a loop for a handle, while others did not. Even the same data topic, such as food, spawned different representations, including apples, soda cups, and forks. Furthermore, the playfulness of stamps as an authoring tool affected how participants presented their visualizations, like the titles P1 and P5 annotated to imply certain stories behind their visualizations. This level of playfulness and self-expression is more inline with sketch-based authoring [40], where both the tool (i.e. pencils, markers, etc.) and the resulting visualization are customizable. In contrast, template editors often do not allow for people to customize the tool, outside of third party add-ons. Furthermore, customization of the visualization itself is limited to the software's options, and the look and feel of the template editor may discourage people from being playful during the authoring process. While physical authoring paradigms, such as constructive visualization, focus on play as a key factor in the tool's simplicity [16], the paradigm does not allow for customization of the tool itself during authoring, as tiles are pre-fabricated according to set colours and dimensions.

### Stamps as Tools for Graphical Visualizations

In Huron et al.'s flow diagram for tangible tile construction [15], tiles could be freely moved; this is not the case with stamps, which create "semi-permanent" marks that cannot be shifted after the initial placement (although in the study, several unwanted marks were removed with white paint, or left and ignored). Furthermore, stamps are semi-permanent in that they cannot be shifted after the initial placement, although we saw various levels of 'commitment' to the placement location, and several people were content with either having extra visual elements not related to their visualization (i.e. 5.3), or just using white paint to remove their mistake (P3, P7).

Stamps share similarities with tangible tiles, but also have many differences. Stamps afford many visual and presentation mapping freedoms. However, many presentation mapping freedoms (such as angle and alignment) are only available before the placement of the stamp pattern, and cannot be shifted without erasing the pattern, as shown by participants placing white paint over their mistakes. Stamp tools are physical themselves, yet provide graphical output. A stamp tool is also versatile as it can represent multiple data encodings, and can be painted with different colours, or compounded together into various patterns to represent new units of data. Stamps patterns can overlay each other, whereas tiles are a physical unit that can only be stacked or laid next to one another in several configurations; stamps also allow for repetition of multiple graphical elements with one tool. Furthermore, one stamp pattern can represent multiple units of data, whereas one tangible tile represents one user-defined unit.

In comparison, stamps share more similarities and freedoms with sketching. Both a pencil and a stamp allow the user to create shapes or patterns to their desires; both techniques can be "undone" or erased; both tools allow for overlays and versatility. Stamps require initial investment to create while sketching one single element is faster, but stamps come with the ability to replicate the same pattern multiple times. Sketching and stamps work well together in tandem; this was shown in the study when participants used both stamps and pens to complete their visualizations.

## DESIGN IMPLICATIONS

Our exploration into block-printing visualizations informs an initial set of primitives for a visualization stamp kit—general-purpose stamps that are conducive to block-printing data visualizations. Below, we suggest several potential stamp shapes.

***Lines:*** Lines are the simplest and most basic geometric shape, and can be used to construct a large variety of visual elements, such as: rectangles for bar charts; line segments for line charts; chart axes (as in the case of P1); and free-form polygon patterns. Line patterns can be shifted and overlapped to control the length of a pattern.

***Geometric primitives:*** Various closed geometric shapes, such as circles, triangles, squares, and hexagons are also useful. These shapes would benefit from being included as sets (e.g., circles with varying diameters) to enable size encoding.

***Emojis:*** Emojis are ideograms meant to convey meaning; they are a ubiquitous part of how we communicate over messages. Icons were a popular stamp theme in our study; a stamp kit could contain several widely used emojis (e.g. happy face, sad face, pizza).

***Blank flags:*** Many national flags share several similar patterns (e.g., triband, Nordic cross). A visualization kit could include several blank flag templates based on common patterns, where the person then fills in the color.

These stamps could be composed together to make compound glyphs. Stamp shapes could be used together as visualization primitives. Flags could be combined with icon stamps—for example, a Canadian flag could be composed by stamping a triband flag template, then placing a maple leaf icon on top. However, visualization forms such as arcs and curves, which vary in response to data, would not be easily representable with stamps. For example, streamgraphs would be very difficult to represent accurately with stamps, as their specific shape and curvature is unique to the underlying data.

## LIMITATIONS & FUTURE WORK

Our study was a first attempt to explore how people author visualizations using block-printing stamps. Currently, such tools for authoring visualizations do not yet exist; by observing how people create their own tools in our study, our observations provide not only rich insights into a new visualization authoring technique, but also inform potential block-printing visualization tools. Our results are not generalizations on what these tools should look like, but rather reveal the potential for block-printing stamps in a visualization context, and point towards potential features useful for visualization stamps.

The materials and tools provided influenced the types of stamps created. The nature of materials like potatoes and sponges have both benefits and drawbacks. For instance, sometimes participants were unable to make the stamps they envisioned; possibly due to lack of skill, or the specific tools provided in the study. Carving stamps was a time consuming and tedious process, and using our methods, it would not be feasible for everyday users to create custom stamps for personal, everyday data visualization. Future research could explore higher fidelity materials such as linoleum or commercially-available fabrication machines for creating stamp patterns. Alternatively, shape displays could be adapted into block printing tools, such as ShapeClip [13] or InForm [9]. Furthermore, our "data mapping lookup sheet" may have also influenced the participants' choice of visualizations and tools. However, we argue that providing such a reference helped participants feel more willing to experiment with a wider range of tools and visualizations, rather than fixating on specific stamp types—as shown by the range of data encodings in the results. Overall, we wanted people to explore stamps in a non-intimidating, low-cost medium that would reduce fear of failing, instead of focusing on finely polished end products. The variety of stamps show that participants were able to explore ideas and expressively create varied visualization tools.

It remains to be seen how useful a visualization stamp kit would be for authoring visualizations. While several of the stamp shapes, such as the flags, may be situational based on the data, these types of shapes would not be out of place as pre-existing templates in commercial stamp makers. Further work could evaluate several factors involved with a stamp kit, such as: efficiency in authoring visualizations, friendliness with visualization non-experts, the usefulness of different shapes, potential for author expressivity, or the trade-off between the number of stamp patterns and time spent authoring visualizations with those patterns.

Ultimately, we envision stamps as a means to open up visualization to new audiences. Visualization stamps could be useful in limited technology settings. Cost and access to computers have traditionally limited students from exploring DIY and tangible computing activities in economically-challenged locations such as peri-urban India [33] and Brazil [32]. In these environments, classroom activities that are focused around making and using stamps might be a low-cost and non-technologically intensive alternative for teaching fundamental visualization concepts.

The open and playful nature of stamps could have potential applications in art therapy, which relies on nonverbal communication of thoughts and feelings [26]. Stamps could help people narrate their situations or personal data visually through data comics [1] or data-based storytelling [24]. However, further exploration of the viability of visualization stamps in a therapy context needs to be done in consultation with healthcare and therapy professionals.

Finally, visualization stamps could be explored in the context of new paradigms, such as graphical authoring of visualizations, or in the broader context of authoring situated and embedded visualizations [41], physicalizations, or tangible authoring tools for digital visualizations on various surfaces (i.e. walls, tabletops).

## CONCLUSION

We explored the potential of creating and using personally made stamps to block-print visualizations. Our investigations have shown how creating visualizations via stamps is viable for experts and non-experts alike, since participants were able to carve and use stamps to create meaningful data visualizations. Our exploration has added to our knowledge about the processes behind creating visualizations, and has expanded our views of data visualizations as changing across a continuum, in both the relationship between numeracy and abstraction, and the relationship between expressivity and constraint. We hope that this work can be used to further the democratization of data, especially in groups with limited access to data authoring tools, or who are unable to engage with data visualization in this manner. Further, we hope that this work can be expanded on to further explore the liminal space between craft and visualization.

## ACKNOWLEDGEMENTS

We are grateful to our participants for their time and discussion. This research was supported in part by: Natural Science and Engineering Research of Canada (NSERC); Alberta Innovates – Technology Futures (AITF); and SMART Technologies.

## SUPPLEMENTAL MATERIAL

Supplemental materials are available at `http://bit.ly/VisStamps`.

## REFERENCES


[1] Benjamin Bach, Zezhong Wang, Matteo Farinella, Dave Murray-Rust, and Nathalie Henry Riche. 2018. Design Patterns for Data Comics. In *Proceedings of the 2018 CHI Conference on Human Factors in Computing Systems*. ACM, 38:1–38:12.

[2] Jacques Bertin. 1983. *Semiology of Graphics: Diagrams, Networks, Maps*. University of Wisconsin press.

[3] Jeffrey Browne, Bongshin Lee, Sheelagh Carpendale, Nathalie Riche, and Timothy Sherwood. 2011. Data Analysis on Interactive Whiteboards Through Sketch-Based Interaction. In *Proceedings of the ACM International Conference on Interactive Tabletops and Surfaces*. ACM, 154–157.

[4] Bill Buxton. 2010. *Sketching User Experiences: Getting the Design Right and the Right Design*. Morgan Kaufmann.

[5] Chris Chambers and Chris Scaffidi. 2010. Struggling to Excel: A Field Study of Challenges Faced by Spreadsheet Users. In *2010 IEEE Symposium on Visual Languages and Human-Centric Computing*. IEEE, 187–194.

[6] William O Chao, Tamara Munzner, and Michiel van de Panne. 2010. Poster: Rapid Pen-Centric Authoring of Improvisational Visualizations with NapkinVis. *Posters Compendium InfoVis* (2010).

[7] Herman Chernoff. 1973. The Use of Faces to Represent Points in k-Dimensional Space Graphically. *Journal of the American Statistical Association* 68, 342 (1973), 361–368.

[8] Mauro Cherubini, Gina Venolia, Rob DeLine, and Andrew J. Ko. 2007. Let's Go to the Whiteboard: How and Why Software Developers Use Drawings. In *Proceedings of the 2007 SIGCHI conference on Human Factors in Computing Systems*. ACM, 557–566.

[9] Sean Follmer, Daniel Leithinger, Alex Olwal, Akimitsu Hogge, and Hiroshi Ishii. 2013. inFORM: Dynamic Physical Affordances and Constraints Through Shape and Object Actuation. In *Proceedings of the 26th annual ACM Symposium on User Interface Software and Technology*. ACM, 417–426.

[10] Florian Geyer, Jochen Budzinski, and Harald Reiterer. 2012. IdeaVis: A Hybrid Workspace and Interactive Visualization for Paper-based Collaborative Sketching Sessions. In *Proceedings of the 7th Nordic Conference on Human-Computer Interaction: Making Sense Through Design*. ACM, 331–340.

[11] Lars Grammel, Chris Bennett, Melanie Tory, and Margaret-Anne Storey. 2013. A Survey of Visualization Construction User Interfaces. *Eurographics Conference on Visualization (EuroVis) - Short Papers* (2013), 19–23.

[12] Lars Grammel, Melanie Tory, and Margaret-Anne Storey. 2010. How Information Visualization Novices Construct Visualizations. *IEEE Transactions on Visualization and Computer Graphicss* 16, 6 (2010), 943–952.

[13] John Hardy, Christian Weichel, Faisal Taher, John Vidler, and Jason Alexander. 2015. ShapeClip: Towards Rapid Prototyping with Shape-Changing Displays for Designers. In *Proceedings of the 33rd Annual ACM Conference on Human Factors in Computing Systems*. ACM, 19–28.

[14] Steven Houben, Connie Golsteijn, Sarah Gallacher, Rose Johnson, Saskia Bakker, Nicolai Marquardt, Licia Capra, and Yvonne Rogers. 2016. Physikit: Data Engagement Through Physical Ambient Visualizations in the Home. In *Proceedings of the 2016 CHI Conference on Human Factors in Computing Systems*. ACM, 1608–1619.

[15] Samuel Huron, Sheelagh Carpendale, Jeremy Boy, and Jean-Daniel Fekete. 2016. Using VisKit: A manual for running a constructive visualization workshop. In *Pedagogy of Data Visualization Workshop at IEEE VIS 2016*.

[16] Samuel Huron, Sheelagh Carpendale, Alice Thudt, Anthony Tang, and Michael Mauerer. 2014. Constructive Visualization. In *Proceedings of the 2014 Conference on Designing Interactive Systems*. ACM, 433–442.

[17] Samuel Huron, Pauline Gourlet, Uta Hinrichs, Trevor Hogan, and Yvonne Jansen. 2017. Let's Get Physical: Promoting Data Physicalization in Workshop Formats. In *Proceedings of the 2017 Conference on Designing Interactive Systems*. ACM, 1409–1422.

[18] Samuel Huron, Yvonne Jansen, and Sheelagh Carpendale. 2014. Constructing Visual Representations: Investigating the Use of Tangible Tokens. *IEEE Transactions on Visualization and Computer Graphics* 20, 12 (2014), 2102–2111.

[19] Petra Isenberg, Anthony Tang, and Sheelagh Carpendale. 2008. An Exploratory Study of Visual Information Analysis. In *Proceedings of the 2008 SIGCHI Conference on Human Factors in Computing Systems*. ACM, 1217–1226.

[20] Yvonne Jansen and Pierre Dragicevic. 2013. An Interaction Model for Visualizations Beyond the Desktop. *IEEE Transactions on Visualization and Computer Graphics* 19, 12 (2013), 2396–2405.

[21] Yvonne Jansen, Pierre Dragicevic, Petra Isenberg, Jason Alexander, Abhijit Karnik, Johan Kildal, Sriram Subramanian, and Kasper Hornbæk. 2015. Opportunities and Challenges for Data Physicalization. In *Proceedings of the 33rd Annual ACM Conference on Human Factors in Computing Systems*. ACM, 3227–3236.

[22] Marijn Janssen, Yannis Charalabidis, and Anneke Zuiderwijk. 2012. Benefits, Adoption Barriers and Myths of Open Data and Open Government. *Information Systems Management* 29, 4 (2012), 258–268.

[23] Nam Kim, Eston Schweickart, Zhicheng Liu, Mira Dontcheva, Wilmot Li, Jovan Popovic, and Hanspeter Pfister. 2017. Data-Driven Guides: Supporting Expressive Design for Information Graphics. *IEEE Transactions on Visualization and Computer Graphics* 23, 1 (2017), 491–500.

[24] Giorgia Lupi and Stefanie Posavec. 2016. *Dear Data*. Chronicle Books.

[25] Cui-Xia Ma, Yong-Jin Liu, Hong-An Wang, Dong-Xing Teng, and Guo-Zhong Dai. 2012. Sketch-Based Annotation and Visualization in Video Authoring. *IEEE Transactions on Multimedia* 14, 4 (2012), 1153–1165.

[26] Cathy A Malchiodi. 2011. *Handbook of Art Therapy*. Guilford Press.

[27] Honghui Mei, Yuxin Ma, Yating Wei, and Wei Chen. 2018. The Design Space of Construction Tools for Information Visualization: A Survey. *Journal of Visual Languages & Computing* 44, 1 (2018), 120–132.

[28] Gonzalo Gabriel Méndez, Miguel A Nacenta, and Sebastien Vandenheste. 2016. iVoLVER: Interactive Visual Language for Visualization Extraction and Reconstruction. In *Proceedings of the 2016 CHI Conference on Human Factors in Computing Systems*. ACM, 4073–4085.

[29] Otto Neurath. 2010. *From Hieroglyphics to Isotype: a Visual Autobiography*. Hyphen Press.

[30] Herbert Reininger. 2012. Hans Rosling's shortest TED talk. (2012). https://www.youtube.com/watch?v=UNs-ziziPyo

[31] Ramik Sadana and John Stasko. 2014. Designing and Implementing an Interactive Scatterplot Visualization for a Tablet Computer. In *Proceedings of the 2014 International Working Conference on Advanced Visual Interfaces*. ACM, 265–272.

[32] Arnan Sipitakiat, Paulo Blikstein, and David P. Cavallo. 2004. GoGo Board: Augmenting Programmable Bricks for Economically Challenged Audiences. In *Proceedings of the 6th International Conference on Learning Sciences*. International Society of the Learning Sciences, 481–488.

[33] Sowmya Somanath, Lora Oehlberg, Janette Hughes, Ehud Sharlin, and Mario Costa Sousa. 2017. 'Maker' within Constraints: Exploratory Study of Young Learners using Arduino at a High School in India. In *Proceedings of the 2017 CHI Conference on Human Factors in Computing Systems*. ACM, 96–108.

[34] Anselm Strauss and Juliet M. Corbin. 1990. *Basics of Qualitative Research: Grounded Theory Procedures and Techniques*. Sage Publications, Inc.

[35] Simon Stusak, Jeannette Schwarz, and Andreas Butz. 2015. Evaluating the Memorability of Physical Visualizations. In *Proceedings of the 33rd Annual ACM Conference on Human Factors in Computing Systems*. ACM, 3247–3250.

[36] Simon Stusak, Aurélien Tabard, Franziska Sauka, Rohit Ashok Khot, and Andreas Butz. 2014. Activity Sculptures: Exploring the Impact of Physical Visualizations on Running Activity. *IEEE Transactions on Visualization and Computer Graphics* 20, 12 (2014), 2201–2210.

[37] Saiganesh Swaminathan, Conglei Shi, Yvonne Jansen, Pierre Dragicevic, Lora A Oehlberg, and Jean-Daniel Fekete. 2014. Supporting the Design and Fabrication of Physical Visualizations. In *Proceedings of the 2014 SIGCHI Conference on Human Factors in Computing Systems*. ACM, 3845–3854.

[38] Alice Thudt, Uta Hinrichs, Samuel Huron, and Sheelagh Carpendale. 2018. Self-Reflection and Personal Physicalization Construction. In *Proceedings of the 2018 CHI Conference on Human Factors in Computing Systems*. ACM, 154:1–154:13.

[39] Jagoda Walny, Sheelagh Carpendale, Nathalie Henry Riche, Gina Venolia, and Philip Fawcett. 2011. Visual Thinking In Action: Visualizations As Used On Whiteboards. *IEEE Transactions on Visualization and Computer Graphics* 17, 12 (2011), 2508–2517.

[40] Jagoda Walny, Samuel Huron, and Sheelagh Carpendale. 2015. An Exploratory Study of Data Sketching for Visual Representation. In *Computer Graphics Forum*, Vol. 34. The Eurographs Association & John Wiley & Sons, Ltd., 231–240.

[41] Wesley Willett and Samuel Huron. 2016. A Constructive Classroom Exercise for Teaching InfoVis. In *Pedagogy of Data Visualization Workshop at IEEE VIS 2016*.

[42] Tiffany Wun, Jennifer Payne, Samuel Huron, and Sheelagh Carpendale. 2016. Comparing Bar Chart Authoring with Microsoft Excel and Tangible Tiles. In *Computer Graphics Forum*, Vol. 35. The Eurographs Association & John Wiley & Sons, Ltd., 111–120.

[43] Haijun Xia, Nathalie Henry Riche, Fanny Chevalier, Bruno De Araujo, and Daniel Wigdor. 2018. DataInk: Direct and Creative Data-Oriented Drawing. In *Proceedings of the 2018 CHI Conference on Human Factors in Computing Systems*. ACM, 223.

# Wattom: a Consumption and Grid Aware Smart Plug with Mid-air Controls

**Filipe Quintal**
Universidade da Madeira,
Madeira-ITI
Funchal, Portugal
filipe.quintal@m-iti.org

**Augusto Esteves**
Centre for Interaction Design,
Edinburgh Napier University
Edinburgh, United Kingdom
a.esteves@napier.ac.uk

**Fábio Caires**
Universidade da Madeira,
Madeira-ITI
Funchal, Portugal
fabio.caires@m-iti.org

**Vítor Baptista**
Universidade da Madeira,
Madeira-ITI
Funchal, Portugal
vitor.baptista@m-iti.org

**Pedro Mendes**
Universidade da Madeira,
Madeira-ITI
Funchal, Portugal
pedro.mendes@m-iti.org

## ABSTRACT
This paper presents Wattom, a highly interactive ambient eco-feedback smart plug that aims to support a more sustainable use of electricity by being tightly coupled to users' energy-related activities. We describe three use cases of the system: using Wattom to power connected appliances and understand the environmental impact of their use in real time; scheduling these power events; and presenting users with personal consumption data desegregated by device. We conclude with a user study in which the effectiveness of the plug's novel interactive capabilities is assessed (mid-air, hand-based motion matching). The study explores the effectiveness of Wattom and motion matching input in a realistic setup, where the user is not always directly ahead of the interface, and not always willing to point straight at the device (e.g., when the plug is at an uncomfortable angle). Despite not using a graphical display, our results demonstrate that our motion matching implementation was effective in line with previous work, and that participants' pointing angle did not significantly affect their performance. On the other hand, participants were more effective while pointing straight at Wattom, but reported not to finding this significantly more strenuating then when pointing to a comfortable position of their choice.

## CCS Concepts
•**Human-centered computing → Empirical studies in ubiquitous and mobile computing;** *Empirical studies in HCI;*

## Author Keywords
Smart plug; smart watches; eco-feedback; ambient display.



*TEI '19,* March 17–20, 2019, Tempe, AZ, USA



ACM 978-1-4503-6196-5/19/03. . . $15.00

DOI: https://doi.org/10.1145/3294109.3295642

## INTRODUCTION AND RELATED WORK
The rising energy consumption and its impact on the environment is one of the biggest issues of our times; one that is currently being tackled across several fields such as economics, engineering or psychology. The end-user or energy consumer is an important element of this widespread sustainability effort. If we consider that 13% of the total energy consumption in the world happens in a domestic environment, savings made here can have a big impact in our sustainability efforts, especially since this value is expected to continue to increase [2]. Approaches that deal with the energy consumption of end-users fall under the umbrella of eco-feedback technologies, defined as technology that provides feedback on individual or group behaviors with a goal of reducing their impact on the environment[21]. In general, these technologies present consumption information in terms of monetary cost or Watts, either numerically, in charts [17]), or even using metaphors, such as a digital fish tank whose representation improves under the user's sustainable behaviors [22]. However, some have argued that this types of information are often disconnected from the actual behavior driving the consumption, or from the resources being consumed [13]. Pierce *et al.* [30] was one of the first to address this issue by materializing energy through a set of tangible artifacts.

This sub-field of eco-feedback has been described as tangible or ambient eco-feedback, and generally, work in this area relies on physical artifacts that change their appearance to inform users on their energy usage. One of the early examples is the Power-Aware Cord [23], a power extension that displays the electricity consumed through a colored animation on the cord itself. Heller *et al.* [24, 25] explored a similar approach, in which the consumption information was provided not on a power cord, but on a wall socket (through colors and animation). Other examples describe ambient displays as bespoke physical artifacts [1, 28, 31], or embedded into a home's smart lighting system [16]. And although tangible and ambient eco-feedback displays have been shown to be very effective at

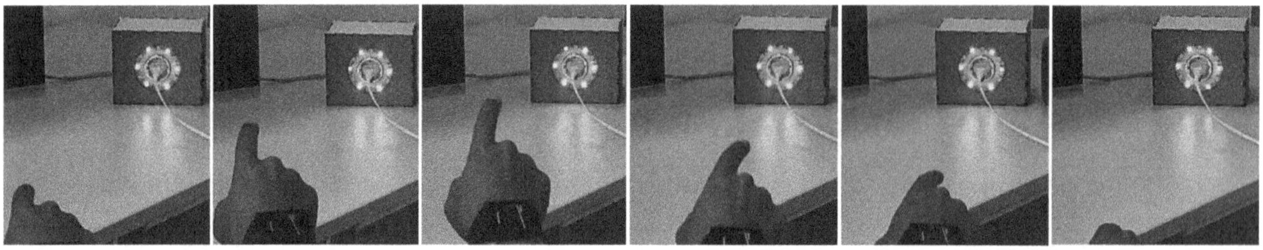

Figure 1. Wattom supports mid-air input through a motion matching approach, in which interface elements (a blue light) move in distinct trajectories, and the user interacts with these by tracking their motion using their arms (e.g., to power the connected appliance). Wattom can also adjust its backdrop color based on the amount of renewable energy present in the grid at the moment of interaction (red indicates a renewable quota close to 0%).

raising awareness of users' energy consumption [7], these tend to present one-dimensional data, support very little interaction, and ultimately, limit how users act on their consumption [32].

We present Wattom, a smart plug that builds on the PowerSocket [24] by supporting direct and mid-air interaction with the device itself, and the consumption information it provides. Interaction with Wattom is built around motion matching [20, 34, 36], a novel interaction paradigm where users interact with the system by tracking its different animations with their hands (tracked through the motion sensors embedded on most wrist-worn wearable devices). Compared to other mid-air and embodied interaction techniques [5, 14, 27], motion matching does not require gesture discovery and memorization [11]; and our implementation is not affected by the limitations of optical tracking, such as a limited field-of-view (FOV), occlusion and changing lighting conditions, and well-known privacy concerns when used in the context of the home [8]. This paper provides the following contributions. First, we describe the implementation and affordances of Wattom, a highly interactive ambient eco-feedback device that is tightly coupled to users' energy-related activities. And second, we study the effectiveness of motion matching in the context of a smart home, where users not always perceive the moving stimulus directly ahead of them (as in a traditional lab setting [9, 10, 35]), or are not able to comfortably track interface motions by pointing directly at the device (e.g., while laying on the sofa).

## WATTOM

Inspired by tangible and ambient eco-feedback devices such as the Power-Aware Cord [23] and the PowerSocket [24], Wattom is a energy aware smart plug with direct and touchless interactive capabilities. Wattom allows users to be informed on the energy usage of any electrical device connected to it, to control the power to said devices, and to be informed on the amount of electricity being generated by renewable sources at any given moment — which in turn can be used to facilitate or hinder access to the plug's control capabilities. In this section, we describe Wattom's implementation and functionality, and three example uses of the system.

### Implementation

Wattom employs a Schuko plug[1], that for the sake of convenience was housed in a 16.3 (w) $\times$ 12.5 (h) $\times$ 8.7cm wooden case that connects to a standard wall socket (in a real-world deployment each Wattom would be directly embedded in the wall). Due to the form factor of the Schuko plug, this is surrounded not by a display but by 12 RGB LEDs (24-bit color), equally spaced around a 7cm circle (diameter). Wattom houses two micro-controllers: an Arduino Nano[2] responsible for controlling the LEDs; and an Intel Edison[3] that manages the program logic, server-side access, and energy measurement and control (together with an ADC, 10A relay, and ASC712 current sensor). In addition to energy measurement, the Intel Edison is also responsible for two additional core features of Wattom. It records *power events*, defined as sudden power changes, and which are normally associated with an appliance being turned on or off, or a change in state (e.g., a fridge door being opened). Afterwards, it employs a non-intrusive load monitoring (NILM) algorithm [37], enabling Wattom to identify which electrical appliance is being used simply by its power event signature. Finally, the micro-controllers communicate using $I^2C$. Details and source code can be found at: https://gitlab.m-iti.org/wattom/wattom-arduino-edison.

### Server-side

Wattom communicates wirelessly with a Node.js[4] web server that logs the state of every LED in real-time. The web server also provides an API that enables third-party applications to have full control over the LEDs, to power or disable the device(s) connected, and to issue any queries related to the energy consumption of these devices. The server is also capable to accessing other service providers for relevant information, such as real time data on the renewable energy quota. Finally, while only one Wattom plug was built, the web server was designed to handle multiple plugs at once with minimal configuration (i.e., these are detected automatically if sharing the same network).

### Interaction

Wattom supports mid-air interaction by implementing a motion matching approach. In motion matching [34], interface elements move in continuous and distinct trajectories, and the user interacts with these by tracking their motion as closely as possible using any body movement. In Figure 1, a user interacts with Wattom by tracking a moving blue light with its arm and wrist. This user input is captured using an approach

[1] https://en.wikipedia.org/wiki/Schuko

[2] https://store.arduino.cc/arduino-nano

[3] https://software.intel.com/en-us/iot/hardware/edison

[4] https://nodejs.org/en/

similar to WaveTrace [35], a motion matching implementation where user input is captured through motion sensors embedded in most wrist-worn devices such as smart watches, and represented as *yaw* and *pitch* values. While visually inspired by [18], the lack of a graphical displays means that Wattom employs a novel approach of displaying interface elements as moving lights using the LEDs (the user perceives the moving lights as moving targets). Each Wattom plug can display up to six concurrent targets (so that there is at least one LED turned off in-between targets), and these can move in clockwise or counter-clockwise motions. Targets share the same speed to minimize overlapping.

Target selection is supported as follows. A bespoke Android Wear 1.0 application runs in both the user's wrist-worn device (*wearable*) and smart phone/tablet (*mobile*), and multiple instances of these applications can be active at once (i.e., multiple users). As in WaveTrace, the execution starts after one of the users performs a flick of the wrist (a standard Android gesture, and the only gesture that needs to be learned/memorized), which triggers the target movements in all connected Wattom plugs. At the start of this process, and using the server's API, the user's mobile device receives all target positions from each plug (i.e., active LEDs, a value from 0 to 11) and movement directions (0 or 1). The mobile device is then responsible for simulating this movement in a Cartesian plane ($x$- and $y$-positions) using a predefined target speed, effectively increasing the resolution of the Wattom display.

The mobile device is also responsible for receiving yaw and pitch values from the user's wearable device. These activities take place at 25Hz. At 300ms intervals, the mobile device verifies the target positions on the web server, and updates its simulation if necessary. Finally, the mobile device runs various Pearson's correlations [35] between the yaw and $x$ data points of all targets, and between the pitch and $y$ data points. If four consecutive correlation results between user input and a target movement are over a developer-defined threshold in both axis, the target is selected (and the user receives a haptic confirmation on their wearable device). These correlations take place every 60ms, using the latest 40 data points (rolling window). Target movement is disabled after the user rests its arm by its side (to minimize visual overload).

We now describe three use cases built as third-party applications to the Wattom's web server API. These are enabled after the coupling process described above, in which a user flicks its wrist, and selects one of the plugs for interaction:

### *Powering devices and environmental awareness*

The simplest functionality of Wattom enables users to remotely power or disable a connected appliance. This is done by displaying a moving blue target that triggers this functionality. Inspired by [23, 25], the speed of this target and backdrop colors (the other LEDs) change based on the amount of renewable energy present in the grid at the moment of interaction. Our implementation averaged the percentage of electricity from renewable sources in the grid over the last three years in the island of Madeira (Portugal). This resulted in a value close to 25%. As such, during normal operation, if the real time renewable quota is close to this baseline, Wattom displays a

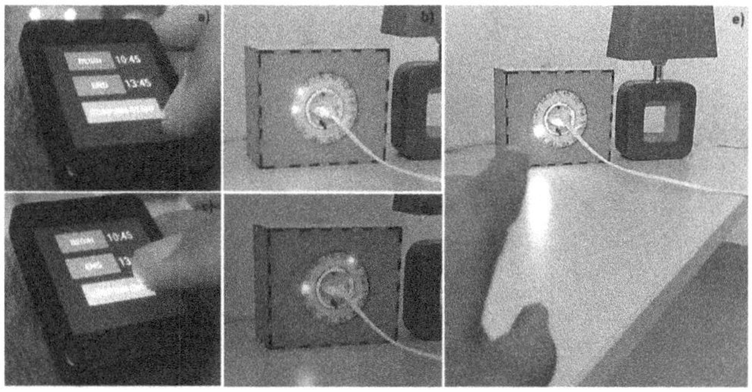

**Figure 2. Wattom allows users to schedule when to power or disable an appliance through their smart watches (left). After confirming the schedule on a plug (middle), each Wattom plug displays a target that enables users to quickly assign their schedule to one or more plugs (right).**

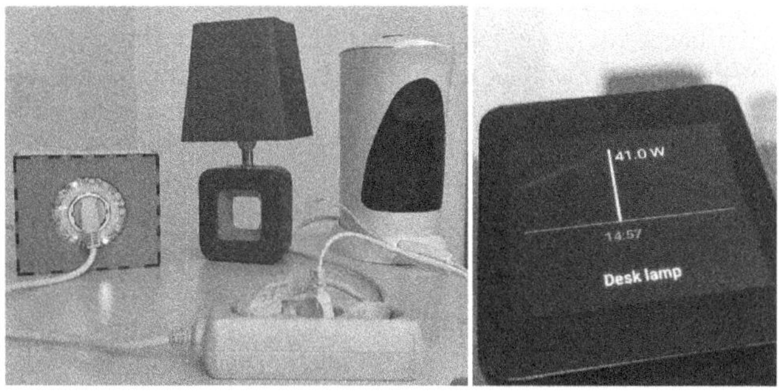


**Figure 3. Wattom's NILM capabilities enables the distinction between various appliances connected simultaneously. Wattom displays a colored target per appliance (left), which upon selection sends the energy consumption of that device to the user's smart watch (right).**

yellow color as backdrop to the blue target, which moves at 140°/s. On the other hand, if the real time renewable quota is below or above this baseline (from 0 to 50%), Wattom shines redder (see Figure 1) or greener, and has the target move faster (max. 180°/s) or slower (min. 100°/s), respectively. This not only informs the user of the impact of his activity at the time of the interaction, but by having the target move at a faster speed, actively makes it harder to power on a device that will draw from electricity generated from a large amount of non-renewable sources.

Simple improvements to this application could be easily implemented. For example, the renewable quota baseline could be averaged on a seasonal basis (e.g., there is more electricity generated from solar panels in the Summer months). Otherwise, instead of looking at renewable quotas, Wattom could apply the same color/speed metaphor to the household's or neighbourhood's average electrical consumption (if this data is publicly available). This way, users could become more aware of positive or negative behaviors compared to their own past activities, or that of their neighbours.

### *Scheduling power events*

Our second application directly expands on the application above by enabling users to schedule when to power or disable an appliance. This allows for a better control of their electrical consumption; to plan certain activities when the electricity is cheaper (e.g., night plans) [3]; or for when the user anticipates a higher electrical output from their local photo-voltaic installation [33]. To achieve this, users start a bespoke Android Wear application on their smart watches, and select a start and end period for Wattom (see Figure 2). This trigger all plugs connected to a web server (e.g., representing a household) to sequentially display the start and end times using the 12 LEDs as pointers on an analog clock. Afterwards, each Wattom plug displays a single moving target, enabling users to quickly assign this schedule to one or more plugs.

### *Disaggregating consumption*

Our final example application relies on Wattom's non-intrusive load monitoring (NILM) capabilities to distinguish between multiple appliances connected simultaneously to a single Wattom plug. Wattom displays a individually-colored target per appliance (up to six appliances), which upon selection sends the latest energy consumption of that device directly to the user's smart watch (see Figure 3). Furthermore, this data reflects only the consumption of that particular user, as the data has been previously tagged with their smart watch information when used to power the appliance using our two first applications. While not implemented, other forms of data visualization could have been promptly explored, including highlighting how much of the user-appliance's consumption was powered by renewable energy sources, or comparing consumption data to an average of all other users of the system — e.g., how much does the use of the electric kettle by a user compares to its roommates.

This coupling approach described in the latter two use cases, where the smart watch applications and the Wattom plug are momentarily paired to provide access to additional functionality (e.g., schedule events, retrieve consumption information) is inspired by previous work where synchronous movements were used to pair touch-screen devices [26], authenticate users [29], or identify a mid-air pointing apparatus [12].

## USER STUDY

We designed a lab study to reflect the challenges of embodied, mid-air interaction with smart environments, in which the user is not always able to point at the interface comfortably (e.g., while laying down on the sofa), or more importantly, is not always directly facing it. This was done with 10 female and 10 male participants aged between 20 and 50 ($M$ = 27.82, $SD$ = 8.57), who rated their experience with smart watches at 3.18 ($SD$ = 2.26) using a 7-point Likert scale (higher is better).

### Experimental Setup and Design

The experiment was conducted in a quiet room, following a within-subjects design with two independent variables (2 × 6): pointing *direction* and *angle*. In the direction condition, participants were asked to point *towards* and *away* from Wattom; the latter in the most comfortable position they could find. In the angle condition, participants interacted with the plug from two meters away (2°s of visual angle), at 15° intervals between 15 and 90°s (inclusive) — participants in the 90° condition were directly facing the interface. The order in which participants interacted with these conditions was balanced using a Latin Square (2 × 2): participants moved from 15 to

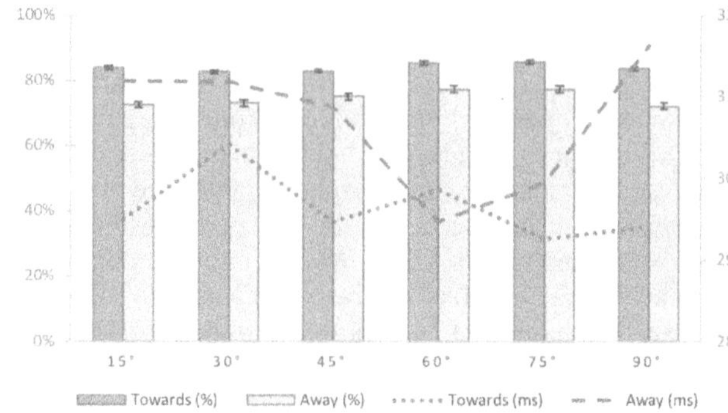


**Figure 4. The results from the user study, in which the success rates and acquisition times were captured across two conditions: pointing direction (towards or away from Wattom) and angle (15 to 90°s).**

90°s or vice-versa, pointing towards or away from Wattom. Participants completed 21 sequential trials in each condition, with the first trial being regarded as practice and ignored from analysis. 4800 trials were recorded in total: 2400 trials per pointing direction (20 participants × 20 trials × 6 angles), and 800 trials per angle (20 participants × 20 trials × 2 directions).

In each trial, participants were instructed to select a red target among five other white targets. The starting position and direction of these were randomized at the start of each trial, and all moved at a constant speed of 150°/sec. After a target selection, Wattom would blink twice with red or white colors to provide user feedback. A timeout of seven seconds was included to minimize fatigue and frustration, and logged as a failed selection. Finally, Wattom's web server ran on a early version of a PINE64[5] from a local network.

### Procedure and Metrics

Each session started with a brief explanation of the study, and by capturing participants' demographics. Afterwards, participants were handed the smart watch (an LG G Watch, placed on the wrist of their dominant hands), shown how the Wattom works, and allowed to interact informally for a short time. A chair was placed at the starting position (at either 15 or 90°s from the interface), and moved by the researcher after the trials for each angle position were completed. Participants were allowed to rest for four seconds between trials, and for ten seconds while changing angle positions. This information was displayed on an 10″ tablet placed beneath Wattom, which also produced auditory feedback after a target selection or timeout (using Android's default tones[6] for 150ms). After completing the selection task in all angles in a pointing condition (towards or away), participants were asked to complete the Borg CR10 [6] scale of perceived exertion. This captured participants' perceived effort (shoulder, arms, hands or fingers) in a scale of 0 to 10 (0.5 increments, higher is harder). Finally, data on participants' success rates and selection times were recorded for further analysis.

[5] https://www.pine64.org/

[6] developer.android.com/reference/android/media/ToneGenerator

### Results

The results for participant performance can be seen in Figure 4. Both success rates and selection times were analyzed using a two-way repeated measures ANOVA. These which incorporated Greenhouse-Geisser corrections when Mauchly's test showed sphericity violations, and were followed by Bonferroni-corrected post-hoc t-tests. Regarding *success*, no statistically significant two-way interaction was found between pointing direction and angle, $F(5, 95) = .210$, $p = .958$ — the assumption of sphericity was met, $\chi^2(14) = 15.078$, $p = .378$. There were also no statistically significant differences between pointing *angles*, $F(5, 95) = .677$, $p = .642$ — the assumption of sphericity was met, $\chi^2(14) = 21.030$, $p = .104$; but there was a significant effect of pointing *direction* on participants' success rates: $F(1, 19) = 11.911$, $p = .003$ — the assumption of sphericity was violated, $p < .001$. Two outliers were identified prior to analysis (studentized residual values of -3.06 and -3.83), but were found to not affect these results.

The results above were mirrored for *selection times*, in which no statistically significant two-way interaction was found between our independent variables, $F(5, 90) = .678$, $p = .641$ — the assumption of sphericity was met, $\chi^2(14) = 12.638$, $p = .560$. There were also no statistically significant differences between pointing *angles*, $F(5, 90) = .612$, $p = .691$ — the assumption of sphericity was met, $\chi^2(14) = 9.202$, $p = .820$; but there was a significant effect of pointing *direction* on participants' selection times: $F(1, 18) = 4.542$, $p = .047$ — the assumption of sphericity was violated, $p < .001$. P10 was removed from the selection times analysis, as it lacked a single data point for the pointing away at a 15° angle condition (0% success rate, and one of the outliers described above).

Finally, a Wilcoxon signed-rank test found no significant differences between participants' perceived effort while pointing towards ($M = 2.33$, $SD = 1.77$) or away ($M = 2.28$, $SD = 1.94$) from Wattom, z = -.267, p = .787.

### Discussion

The results above are fairly positive, and provide novel insights into the use of motion matching to interact with smart devices and environments. First, participants were more effective while pointing towards Wattom, which could potentially limit its use in real-world scenarios when the user cannot point comfortably at the plug (e.g., laying down on the sofa). That being said, participants did not find the task of pointing straight at the Wattom particularly more strenuous then pointing in a comfortable position of their choice (e.g., pointing at the floor). Furthermore, the average success rate of 84% (*SD* = 1.25) while pointing towards Wattom was very much in line with previous work based on motion sensors [19, 35], particularly taking into account the small visual angle (2°) and low resolution of the moving stimulus (12 LEDs/pixels). We argue these results can be improved by implementing Wattom with a higher resolution LED ring (e.g., 24 LEDs[7]).

Acquisition times were fairly consistent across conditions (approx. 3000ms), and in line with previous work using wrist-worn motion sensors [35]. This value can be further explained by our study design and hardware choice. That is, a target selection could only take place after an initial 40 data points (rolling window) had been collected, and this took place at a very low rate of 25Hz — at the start of each new trial, it would take Wattom at least 1600ms to be ready to respond to user input again. That being said, this selection time did not seem to aggravate participants' physical fatigue, as they reported an average Borg CR10 result indicating *weak (light)* physical exertion across conditions. Finally, and more importantly, we were able to demonstrate that participants could effectively interact with Wattom from various angles. This further suggests that the plug does not require a specific interaction 'sweet spot', potentially increasing and facilitating its real-world use. This information should be of value to other researchers exploring real-uses for motion matching interfaces, but further work should explore if this is the case when the target trajectory cannot be easily anticipated (e.g., random or complex target trajectories [9]).

[7] https://www.adafruit.com/product/2863

## CONCLUSION AND FUTURE WORK

This paper presented Wattom, smart plug made interactive by the use of motion matching input. This work was motivated by a need to provide users with energy consumption information that was tightly coupled with their energy use and the energy source. Furthermore, Wattom was designed to not only facilitate control over electric appliances for a-far, but also invite users to further inquire about their energy use: either through personal data visualizations on the watch, or by combining colour schemes and hindering access to the Wattom's control functionality. Finally, we also demonstrate that motion matching input can be provided effectively from very extreme angles, which should further facilitate the plug's use in real-world settings. Because Wattom was built as an open platform with a public API, many more applications could be easily explored in the future, including its use as a non-interactive ambient display, or outside of the scope of sustainability (e.g., the LED ring could display a connected device's battery level).

More importantly, the more pressing work should look at studying Wattom in real-life deployments over longer periods of time, with the aim of assessing its: (1) effectiveness, from an awareness, interaction, and sustainable perspective; (2) practicality (plug visibility in realistic settings, multi-user interaction as briefly described in *Disaggregating consumption*); (3) social acceptability in shared environments and social translucence [4]; and (4) user satisfaction. Additionally, multi-plug setups were also unexplored. Our current implementation supports up to 24 plugs in the same environment (e.g., a household), as each plug is able to display an unique light trajectory during a user's coupling process (12 LEDs × two directions). After this coupling process the user is engaged with a single plug, and thus the number of remaining plugs are irrelevant until the next coupling attempt. This number can be further increased by relying on more densely populated LED rings and more robust selection algorithms [9, 15].

## ACKNOWLEDGMENTS

This work was supported by the Fundação para a Ciência e a Tecnologia (FCT, UID/EEA/50009/2013).

## REFERENCES


[1] 2007. THE ENERGY ORB: Visualize Electricity Consumption! (2007). https://inhabitat.com/the-energy-orb-monitor-your-electricity-bill/ [Online; accessed 2018-07-25].

[2] 2016. *International Energy Outlook 2016*. US Energy Information Administration.

[3] Alper T. Alan, Enrico Costanza, Sarvapali D. Ramchurn, Joel Fischer, Tom Rodden, and Nicholas R. Jennings. 2016. Tariff Agent: Interacting with a Future Smart Energy System at Home. *ACM Trans. Comput.-Hum. Interact.* 23, 4, Article 25 (Aug. 2016), 28 pages. DOI: http://dx.doi.org/10.1145/2943770

[4] Mary Barreto, Evangelos Karapanos, and Nuno Nunes. 2011. Social Translucence as a Theoretical Framework for Sustainable HCI. In *Human-Computer Interaction – INTERACT 2011*, Pedro Campos, Nicholas Graham, Joaquim Jorge, Nuno Nunes, Philippe Palanque, and Marco Winckler (Eds.). Springer Berlin Heidelberg, Berlin, Heidelberg, 195–203.

[5] Richard A. Bolt. 1980. 'Put-that-there': Voice and Gesture at the Graphics Interface. In *Proceedings of the 7th Annual Conference on Computer Graphics and Interactive Techniques (SIGGRAPH '80)*. ACM, New York, NY, USA, 262–270. DOI: http://dx.doi.org/10.1145/800250.807503

[6] Gunnar Borg. 1998. *Borg's perceived exertion and pain scales*. Human kinetics.

[7] Loove Broms, Cecilia Katzeff, Magnus Bång, Åsa Nyblom, Sara Ilstedt Hjelm, and Karin Ehrnberger. 2010. Coffee Maker Patterns and the Design of Energy Feedback Artefacts. In *Proceedings of the 8th ACM Conference on Designing Interactive Systems (DIS '10)*. ACM, New York, NY, USA, 93–102. DOI: http://dx.doi.org/10.1145/1858171.1858191

[8] A.J. Bernheim Brush, Bongshin Lee, Ratul Mahajan, Sharad Agarwal, Stefan Saroiu, and Colin Dixon. 2011. Home Automation in the Wild: Challenges and Opportunities. In *Proceedings of the SIGCHI Conference on Human Factors in Computing Systems (CHI '11)*. ACM, New York, NY, USA, 2115–2124. DOI:http://dx.doi.org/10.1145/1978942.1979249

[9] Marcus Carter, Eduardo Velloso, John Downs, Abigail Sellen, Kenton O'Hara, and Frank Vetere. 2016. PathSync: Multi-User Gestural Interaction with Touchless Rhythmic Path Mimicry. In *Proceedings of the 2016 CHI Conference on Human Factors in Computing Systems (CHI '16)*. ACM, New York, NY, USA, 3415–3427. DOI: http://dx.doi.org/10.1145/2858036.2858284

[10] Christopher Clarke, Alessio Bellino, Augusto Esteves, and Hans Gellersen. 2017. Remote Control by Body Movement in Synchrony with Orbiting Widgets: An Evaluation of TraceMatch. *Proc. ACM Interact. Mob. Wearable Ubiquitous Technol.* 1, 3 (Sept. 2017), 45:1–45:22. DOI:http://dx.doi.org/10.1145/3130910

[11] Christopher Clarke, Alessio Bellino, Augusto Esteves, Eduardo Velloso, and Hans Gellersen. 2016. TraceMatch: a computer vision technique for user input by tracing of animated controls. In *UbiComp '16: Proceedings of the 2016 ACM International Joint Conference on Pervasive and Ubiquitous Computing*. ACM Press, 298–303. DOI: http://dx.doi.org/10.1145/2971648.2971714

[12] Christopher Clarke and Hans Gellersen. 2017. MatchPoint: Spontaneous Spatial Coupling of Body Movement for Touchless Pointing. In *Proceedings of the 30th Annual ACM Symposium on User Interface Software and Technology (UIST '17)*. ACM, New York, NY, USA, 179–192. DOI: http://dx.doi.org/10.1145/3126594.3126626

[13] S. Darby. 2006. The Effectiveness of Feedback on Energy Consumption: A Review of the Literature on Metering, Billing and Direct Displays. (2006), 1–21. http://www.google.com/search?q=Valuation+of+Non-Energy+Benefits+to+Determine+Cost-Effectiveness+of+Whole-House+Retrofit+Programs:+A+Literature+Review+Amann

[14] Paul Dourish. 2001. *Where the Action is: The Foundations of Embodied Interaction*. MIT Press, Cambridge, MA, USA.

[15] Heiko Drewes, Mohamed Khamis, and Florian Alt. 2018. DialPlate: Enhancing the Detection of Smooth Pursuits Eye Movements Using Linear Regression. *arXiv preprint arXiv:1807.03713* (2018).

[16] Eiman Y. Elbanhawy, Andrew F. G. Smith, and John Moore. 2016. Towards an ambient awareness interface for home battery storage system. ACM Press, 1608–1613. DOI: http://dx.doi.org/10.1145/2968219.2968557 [Online; accessed 2018-07-25].

[17] Thomas Erickson, Ming Li, Younghun Kim, Ajay Deshpande, Sambit Sahu, Tian Chao, Piyawadee Sukaviriya, and Milind Naphade. 2013. The Dubuque Electricity Portal: Evaluation of a City-scale Residential Electricity Consumption Feedback System. In *Proceedings of the SIGCHI Conference on Human Factors in Computing Systems (CHI '13)*. ACM, New York, NY, USA, 1203–1212. DOI: http://dx.doi.org/10.1145/2470654.2466155

[18] Augusto Esteves, Eduardo Velloso, Andreas Bulling, and Hans Gellersen. 2015. Orbits: Gaze Interaction for Smart Watches using Smooth Pursuit Eye Movements. In *Proceedings of the 28th Annual ACM Symposium on User Interface Software & Technology*. ACM Press, 457–466. DOI: http://dx.doi.org/10.1145/2807442.2807499

[19] Augusto Esteves, David Verweij, Liza Suraiya, Rasel Islam, Youryang Lee, and Ian Oakley. 2017. SmoothMoves: Smooth Pursuits Head Movements for Augmented Reality. In *Proceedings of the 30th Annual ACM Symposium on User Interface Software and Technology (UIST '17)*. ACM, NY, USA, 167–178. DOI: http://dx.doi.org/10.1145/3126594.3126616

[20] Jean-Daniel Fekete, Niklas Elmqvist, and Yves Guiard. 2009. Motion-pointing: Target Selection Using Elliptical Motions. In *Proceedings of the SIGCHI Conference on Human Factors in Computing Systems (CHI '09)*. ACM, New York, NY, USA, 289–298. DOI: http://dx.doi.org/10.1145/1518701.1518748

[21] Jon Froehlich, Leah Findlater, and James Landay. 2010. The Design of Eco-feedback Technology. In *Proceedings of the SIGCHI Conference on Human Factors in Computing Systems (CHI '10)*. ACM, New York, NY, USA, 1999–2008. DOI: http://dx.doi.org/10.1145/1753326.1753629

[22] Jon Froehlich, Leah Findlater, Marilyn Ostergren, Solai Ramanathan, Josh Peterson, Inness Wragg, Eric Larson, Fabia Fu, Mazhengmin Bai, Shwetak Patel, and James A. Landay. 2012. The Design and Evaluation of Prototype Eco-feedback Displays for Fixture-level Water Usage Data. In *Proceedings of the SIGCHI Conference on Human Factors in Computing Systems (CHI '12)*. ACM, New York, NY, USA, 2367–2376. DOI:http://dx.doi.org/10.1145/2207676.2208397

[23] Anton Gustafsson and Magnus Gyllenswärd. 2005. The Power-aware Cord: Energy Awareness Through Ambient Information Display. In *CHI '05 Extended Abstracts on Human Factors in Computing Systems (CHI EA '05)*. ACM, New York, NY, USA, 1423–1426. DOI:http://dx.doi.org/10.1145/1056808.1056932

[24] Florian Heller and Jan Borchers. 2011. PowerSocket: Towards On-outlet Power Consumption Visualization. In *CHI '11 Extended Abstracts on Human Factors in Computing Systems (CHI EA '11)*. ACM, New York, NY, USA, 1981–1986. DOI: http://dx.doi.org/10.1145/1979742.1979901

[25] Florian Heller and Jan Borchers. 2012. Physical Prototyping of an On-outlet Power-consumption Display. *interactions* 19, 1 (Jan. 2012), 14–17. DOI: http://dx.doi.org/10.1145/2065327.2065332

[26] Ken Hinckley. 2003. Synchronous Gestures for Multiple Persons and Computers. In *Proceedings of the 16th Annual ACM Symposium on User Interface Software and Technology (UIST '03)*. ACM, New York, NY, USA, 149–158. DOI: http://dx.doi.org/10.1145/964696.964713

[27] Mingyu Liu, Mathieu Nancel, and Daniel Vogel. 2015. Gunslinger: Subtle Arms-down Mid-air Interaction. In *Proceedings of the 28th Annual ACM Symposium on User Interface Software & Technology (UIST '15)*. ACM, New York, NY, USA, 63–71. DOI: http://dx.doi.org/10.1145/2807442.2807489

[28] Heiko Müller, Jutta Fortmann, Martin Pielot, Tobias Hesselmann, Benjamin Poppinga, Wilko Heuten, Niels Henze, and Susanne Boll. 2012. AmbiX : Designing Ambient Light Information Displays.

[29] Shwetak N. Patel, Jeffrey S. Pierce, and Gregory D. Abowd. 2004. A Gesture-based Authentication Scheme for Untrusted Public Terminals. In *Proceedings of the 17th Annual ACM Symposium on User Interface Software and Technology (UIST '04)*. ACM, New York, NY, USA, 157–160. DOI: http://dx.doi.org/10.1145/1029632.1029658

[30] James Pierce and Eric Paulos. 2010. Materializing energy. *Proceedings of the 8th ACM Conference on Designing Interactive Systems* (2010), 113–122. DOI: http://dx.doi.org/10.1145/1858171.1858193 [Online; accessed 2013-09-16].

[31] Matevz Pogacnik and Jože Guna. 2013. Ambient visualization of energy consumption information. International Workshop on Semantic Ambient Media.

[32] J. Rodgers and L. Bartram. 2011. Exploring Ambient and Artistic Visualization for Residential Energy Use Feedback. *IEEE Transactions on Visualization and Computer Graphics* 17, 12 (2011), 2489–2497. DOI: http://dx.doi.org/10.1109/TVCG.2011.196

[33] Johann Schrammel, Cornelia Gerdenitsch, Astrid Weiss, Patricia M. Kluckner, and Manfred Tscheligi. 2011. FORE-Watch – The Clock That Tells You When to Use: Persuading Users to Align Their Energy Consumption with Green Power Availability. In *Ambient Intelligence*, David V. Keyson, Mary Lou Maher, Norbert Streitz, Adrian Cheok, Juan Carlos Augusto, Reiner Wichert, Gwenn Englebienne, Hamid Aghajan, and Ben J. A. Kröse (Eds.). Springer Berlin Heidelberg, Berlin, Heidelberg, 157–166.

[34] Eduardo Velloso, Marcus Carter, Joshua Newn, Augusto Esteves, Christopher Clarke, and Hans Gellersen. 2017. Motion Correlation: Selecting Objects by Matching Their Movement. *ACM Trans. Comput.-Hum. Interact.* 24, 3 (April 2017), 22:1–22:35. DOI: http://dx.doi.org/10.1145/3064937

[35] David Verweij, Augusto Esteves, Vassilis-Javed Khan, and Saskia Bakker. 2017. WaveTrace: Motion Matching Input Using Wrist-Worn Motion Sensors. In *Proceedings of the 2017 CHI Conference Extended Abstracts on Human Factors in Computing Systems (CHI EA '17)*. ACM, New York, NY, USA, 2180–2186. DOI:http://dx.doi.org/10.1145/3027063.3053161

[36] John Williamson and Roderick Murray-Smith. 2004. Pointing Without a Pointer. In *CHI '04 Extended Abstracts on Human Factors in Computing Systems (CHI EA '04)*. ACM, New York, NY, USA, 1407–1410. DOI:http://dx.doi.org/10.1145/985921.986076

[37] M. Zeifman and K. Roth. 2011. Nonintrusive appliance load monitoring: Review and outlook. *IEEE Transactions on Consumer Electronics* 57, 1 (February 2011), 76–84. DOI: http://dx.doi.org/10.1109/TCE.2011.5735484

# FormFab: Continuous Interactive Fabrication

**Stefanie Mueller[1,2], Anna Seufert[2], Huaishu Peng[3,4], Robert Kovacs[2], Kevin Reuss[2], François Guimbretière[3], Patrick Baudisch[2]**

MIT CSAIL[1] Cambridge, MA, USA stefanie.mueller@mit.edu

Hasso Plattner Institute[2] Potsdam, Germany patrick.baudisch@hpi.de

Cornell University[3] Ithaca, NY, USA fvg3@cornell.edu

University of Maryland[4] College Park, MD, USA huaishu@cs.umd.edu

**ABSTRACT**

Several systems have illustrated the concept of interactive fabrication, i.e. rather than working through a digital editor, users make edits directly on the physical workpiece. However, so far the interaction has been limited to *turn-taking,* i.e., users first perform a command and *then* the system responds with physical feedback. In this paper, we present a first step towards interactive fabrication that changes the workpiece continuously *while* the user is manipulating it.

To achieve this, our system FormFab does not add or subtract material but instead reshapes it (*formative* fabrication). A heat gun attached to a robotic arm warms up a thermoplastic sheet until it becomes compliant; users then control a pneumatic system that applies either pressure or vacuum thereby pushing the material outwards or pulling it inwards.

Since FormFab reshapes the workpiece continuously while users are moving their hands, users can interactively explore different sizes of a shape with a single interaction.

**Author Keywords:** personal fabrication; interactive fabrication; direct manipulation; 3D modeling tools.

## INTRODUCTION

Recently, Willis et al. [28] proposed the concept of *Interactive Fabrication.* The key idea is to bring the principles of *direct manipulation* [20] to the editing of physical objects: Instead of working on a digital 3D model and producing the physical version only at the end, users make edits directly on the physical workpiece and see it change immediately.

Early interactive fabrication systems, such as *Shaper* [28], *CopyCAD* [5], and *constructable* [14], allow for hands-on editing on the physical workpiece. However, their interaction is best described as *turn-taking:* users first provide their

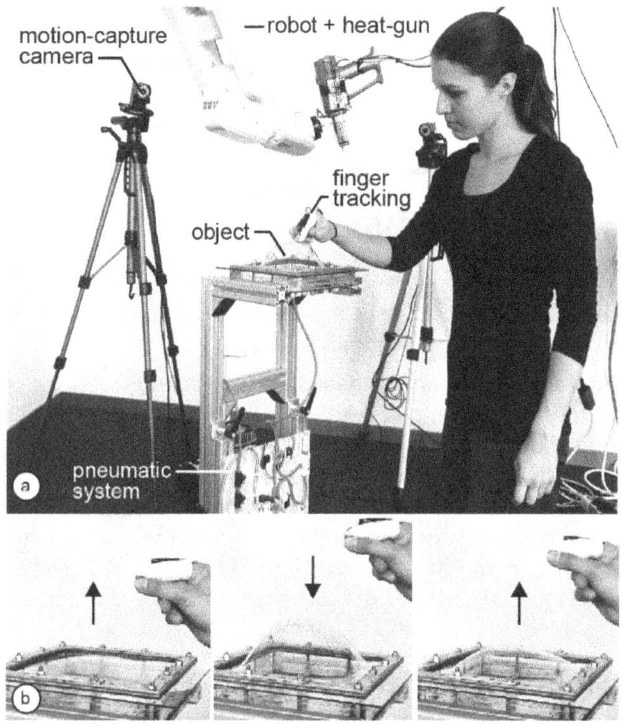


**Figure 1: (a) FormFab changes the workpiece continuously *while* the user is interacting with it. First, a heat-gun warms up the workpiece. Once the material has become compliant, (b) the user's hand gesture interactively controls a pneumatic system that applies pressure or vacuum, pushing the material outwards or pulling it inwards.**

input to the system and *then* the system responds with physical feedback. Since there are two *discrete* steps, users can only explore one option per turn [2].

In this paper, we propose an interactive fabrication system that can change a workpiece's shape continuously *while* the user is interacting. This enables users to explore different sizes of a shape with a *single* interaction rather than in multiple turns.

We accomplish this using a process called *formative* fabrication, which rather than adding or subtracting, reshapes the existing material. In our system, users interactively control a pneumatic air pump that applies either pressure or vacuum to a compliant thermoplastic sheet, thereby pushing the material outwards or pulling it inwards (Figure 1b).


*TEI '19,* March 17–20, 2019, Tempe, AZ, USA

ACM ISBN 978-1-4503-6196-5/19/03…$15.00
https://doi.org/10.1145/3294109.3295620

## RELATED WORK

Our work builds on existing work in exploring new interaction models for 3D modeling and personal fabrication.

### Spatial Modeling with Virtual Feedback

In a first attempt to facilitate interaction, researchers proposed to let users create models as if they were manipulating an (invisible) physical workpiece: In *SpatialSketch* [27] users define the shape of a lamp by describing its surface using their hands. Similarly, in *Virtual Pottery* [7] users shape virtual clay by moving the hands as if they were physically shaping clay. *Dress-up* [26] added physical tools: Using the 'surface' tool, users sketch the shape of dresses directly on a physical mannequin, the 'cut' tool then removes surfaces. Similarly, *Tool-Device* [1] uses a knife tool to cut objects and a hammer to join them.

Extending this approach, researchers developed systems that provide visual feedback directly in the environment: In *Situated Modeling* [11], users sketch objects in the context they belong to; an AR headset allows users to visually evaluate editing steps in place. *MixFab* [25] follows the same approach, but uses a beam splitter and a display to overlay physical and virtual content.

### Interactive Fabrication based on turn-taking

The first set of interactive fabrication tools were based on turn-taking: In *Shaper* [28], users first touch a screen and only after finishing their input, the machine extrudes a drop of foam onto the build plate. In *CopyCAD* [5], users first draw with a pen onto a piece of wood, and then a mill creates the corresponding geometry. Similarly, in *Interlacing* [4], users first lay down a pattern of sticks, which the robot then copies, and in *Gestural Form* [8] users first draw a line onto the ground and afterwards the robot constructs a brick wall on it. In *Constructable* [14], users first draw with a laser pointer onto the workpiece inside a laser cutter and then the drawing is cut by the laser. Similarly, in *Re-Form* [24] users first draw onto the clay and then a clay extruder adds or a mill removes geometry.

### Towards Interactive Fabrication Beyond Turn-Taking

One group of systems that point towards interactive fabrication beyond turn-taking are smart handheld tools that enable users to physically replicate digital models. *Haptic Intelligentsia* [12], for instance, only extrudes when the user is following a predefined path. Similarly, *Position-Correcting Router* [18] and *Enchanted Scissors* [31] only route and cut when the user is on the path, and *Augmented Airbrush* [22] only sprays when the user holds it at the correct location. Extensions to this line of work, such as the *FreeD* [33], [34] and *D-Coil* [17] also allow users to modify the shape of the model. Closest to our work is a system called *RoMA* [16] that enables user and fabrication device to work concurrently. However, since it uses additive and subtractive fabrication, it cannot change the shape of the workpiece continuously while the user is interacting with it.

### Formative fabrication

Formative fabrication is a process that can quickly reshape sheets into different profiles. It has been widely used in architecture, for instance, to create building facades [9]. Within HCI, it has been used to make 3D objects from 2D sheets either using the heat from a laser cutter (*LaserOrigami* [13]) or a microwave (*MOR4R* [32]). Other researchers used formative fabrication to quickly create objects on demand and recycle them by reversing their shape (*Dishmaker* [3]). Formative fabrication has also been explored in the context of post-customization (*HotFlex* [6]), custom textures for 3D shapes (*Computational Thermoforming* [21]), fast replication of shapes (*ProtoMold* [30]) and traditional turn-taking interactive fabrication (*DrawForming* [29]). However, none of these systems supports changing the workpiece's shape continuously *while* the user is providing input.

## FORMFAB

FormFab is an interactive fabrication system based on formative fabrication that allows users to explore different sizes of a shape by continuously changing the workpiece while the user is interacting with it (Figure 1b).

First, users draw an outline of the area they want to reshape using their index finger (Figure 2a). When the user removes the finger, the path is beautified by our software. The robotic arm then warms up the area using a heat gun (Figure 2b).

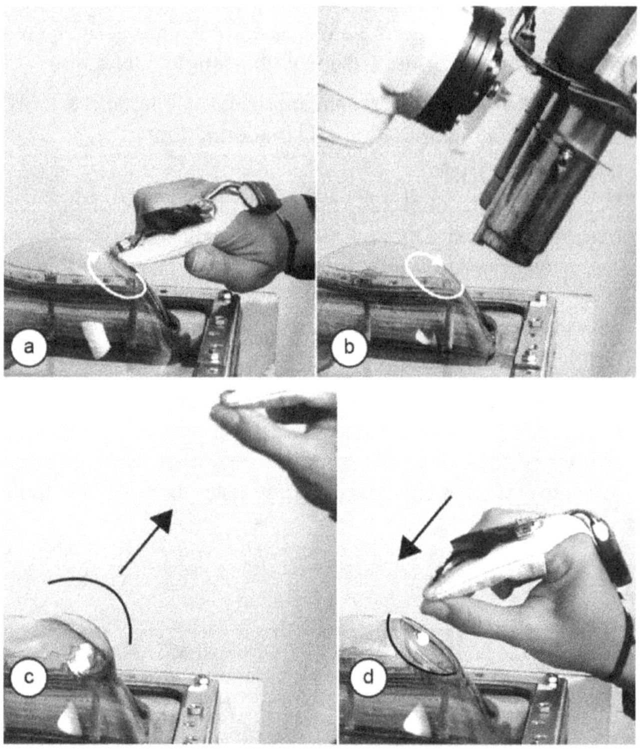


**Figure 2: (a,b) Drawing outline and heating. (c,d) Once the user interacts, the workpiece changes continuously, i.e., here we show one interaction in which the same part is first pulled out and then pushed back in.**

After the material has reached its compliance point, the robotic arm moves out of the way. The user can then perform a pinch gesture, which activates the pneumatic system. If the user's hand moves away from the workpiece, the pneumatic system increases the air pressure and the compliant area inflates (Figure 2c). If the user's hand moves back towards the workpiece, the pneumatic system reduces the pressure and the compliant area deflates (Figure 2d).

While step 1 of the user interaction, i.e., drawing the outline, still follows the *turn-taking* interaction model, step 2, i.e., defining the extrusion amount provides physical feedback *while* the user is interacting.

### Walkthrough: Making the sculpture of a teddy head

Figure 3 shows the steps to make the sculpture of a teddy bear's head using our system. We first draw a circle onto the flat workpiece and after the robot has heated up the area, we reshape the sheet to explore different dimensions for the head—making it larger and smaller within seconds until we find the right shape (Figure 1b). Using the same interaction steps, we add the ears to the head of the teddy (Figure 3a/b): As can be seen in the accompanying video, we reshape the right ear for about 30s continuously to find the best shape, and then add the left ear accordingly. We now add the snout: to explore the best size, we repeatedly scale the snout by moving our hand to different distances from the workpiece. We then add a tip on top of it. In the last step, we create the eyes (Figure 3c). This time, we move our hand towards the workpiece, thereby applying vacuum that extrudes the eyes inwards.

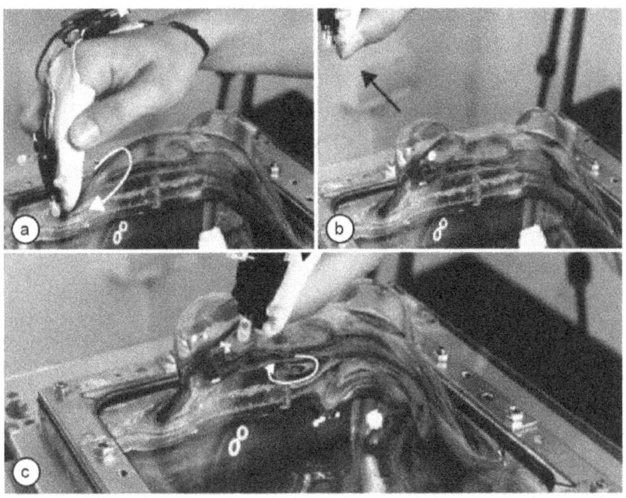

**Figure 3: Making the teddy bear head: (a,b) drawing and extruding the left ear, (c) extruding an eye.**

Figure 4 shows the final teddy head made from a 30x30cm sheet (thickness: 4mm). Making the teddy head took only 9 minutes including the time for exploring different sizes for various parts of the design and also includes the time for heating and for letting the material become rigid again. We were able to explore different sizes at each interaction step for ca. 30 seconds before the material became rigid.

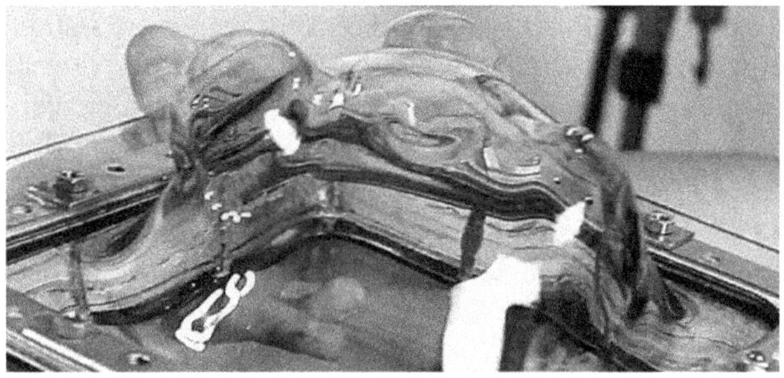

**Figure 4: The sculpture of a teddy bear's head.**

## HARDWARE

Figure 1 shows the hardware setup of our system. It consists of two main parts: (1) the user interaction tracking, and (2) the formative fabrication unit.

### #1 Tracking hardware

To track the user interaction, FormFab users wear a motion capture marker and a pressure sensor on their index finger (Figure 5). The marker is detected by a motion capture system *(OptiTrack)* and used to determine *where* the user is interacting on the workpiece. In addition, the pressure sensor is used to determine the *beginning* and *end* of the interaction. We can do this because in both interactions users apply pressure to the index finger either by touching the workpiece or by pressing the index finger to the thumb in the pinch gesture.

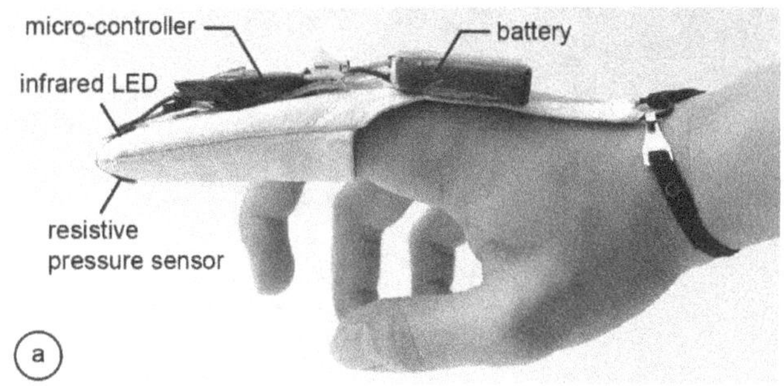


**Figure 5: Tracking unit.**

Instead of using a passive retro-reflective marker, we use an active infrared LED marker that is turned on when the user applies pressure to the finger (an Arduino Nano connected to the pressure sensor processes the pressure values, then activates the LED). We are using an active marker because detecting passive markers requires the motion capture cameras to emit infrared light. The light causes reflections on our workpiece, which makes it difficult to detect the marker. By using the active marker, we were able to use the cameras with their infrared emission turned off.

### #2 Robotic arm

We use a 6-axis robotic arm *(ABB IRB 120)* to move the heat gun that warms up the workpiece. The six degrees of freedom allow the robotic arm to reach around the workpiece from all sides. In contrast to previous systems that achieve higher degrees of freedom by rotating the workpiece (e.g., the 5-axis device used for *Patching Physical*

*Objects* [23]), the robotic arm keeps the workpiece stationary, thereby preserving the user's spatial frame of reference during modeling. By mounting the robotic arm to the ceiling, we were able to maximize the reachable area while also allowing the user to freely move around the workpiece.

#### #3 Heat gun

We heat the workpiece using heat guns that blow air onto the workpiece (Figure 6). We chose air for heating as it best distributes on surfaces of arbitrary geometry. A rigid array of radiator elements, in contrast, would lead to uneven heating as some points are located closer to the workpiece's surface than others. Other contactless methods, such as an infrared-light array were not powerful enough to heat the thermoplastic sheet.

We use two heat guns of different sizes. We use the larger heat gun (Ø3.5cm) for the first steps in the modeling process when the coarse base shape is created. We use the smaller heat gun (Ø0.7cm) for later steps when the user creates details. Both heat guns have a different working range (see section 'Factors Influencing the Forming Process'). We determined the values experimentally and use them to optimize the heat transfer while preventing to overheat the material.

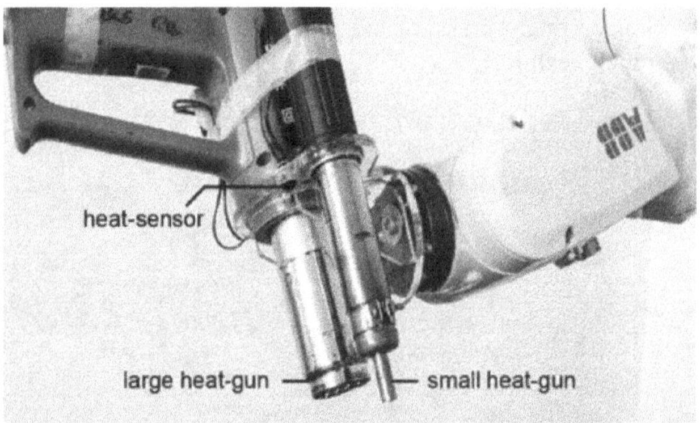


**Figure 6: Heat guns and temperature sensor.**

Since the heat transfer is influenced by several factors that are hard to predict, we added a temperature sensor *(Melexis MLX90620)* to the robotic arm to determine the temperature of the workpiece (Figure 6). The sensor is wired to an Arduino Nano that informs FormFab's main application about the current temperature values.

The temperature sensor is passive and measures the infrared radiation emitted by the material when it warms up. Active sensors, such as an infrared laser thermometer, that first emit light and then measure its reflection did not work due to the transparent nature of our workpiece.

#### #4 Pneumatic control system

To reshape the workpiece, FormFab uses a compressor *(Universal II Profi-Airbrush*) that compresses air up to 5 bar (Figure 7). To set the pressure value, the regulation unit expects a control voltage from 0 – 10 V. FormFab sets the voltage using an *Arduino Uno* connected to a digital potentiometer that regulates a 24V external power supply.

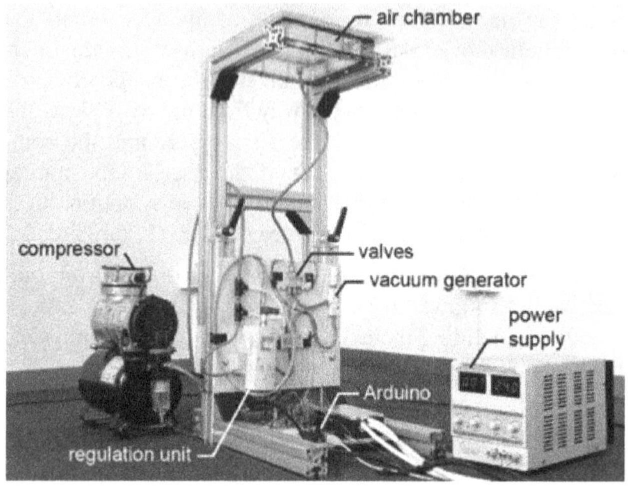


**Figure 7: Pneumatic system: an Arduino controls how much pressure is applied and also switches the valves.**

The pressurized air is then guided through different valves, depending on whether pressure or vacuum should be applied to the workpiece. If pressure is applied, the pressurized air is directly forwarded to the air chamber to reshape the workpiece. If vacuum is to be applied, the pressurized air instead goes through a vacuum generator, which creates negative pressure in the air chamber, pulling the compliant workpiece inwards. To switch between pressure or vacuum, FormFab changes the valve configuration via the *Arduino.*

After the user finished the interaction, our system keeps the air chamber at a constant pressure level until the workpiece has cooled down and has become rigid again - changing the pressure earlier to a neutral level would cause the workpiece to partly undo the latest deformation step.

After the workpiece has cooled down, our system opens a valve to neutralize the air chamber, i.e., it releases any excess pressure. This is necessary because if the air chamber was still pressurized at the beginning of the next heating step, the workpiece would start to deform as soon as it becomes compliant, i.e., even without the user interacting.

### SOFTWARE

The software pipeline consists of the following processing steps: (1) tracking the outline the user is drawing, (2) calculating the heating path, (3) generating movement commands for the robotic arm, (4) monitoring the temperature to achieve compliance, and (5) applying air pressure via the pneumatic system according to user input.

#### #1 Tracking the user interaction

The active infrared LED marker on the user's fingertip is detected by OptiTrack's motion capture software *Motive.* Since the infrared LED can cause reflections on the transparent and reflecting workpiece, we filter reflections that do not fit the LED's size and circularity.

*Motive* streams the position data of the marker to the FormFab main application, which implements a client based on the *NatNet SDK* from OptiTrack. As soon as the user finishes drawing, the marker position is processed using OpenCV's shape detection algorithms.

#### #2 Calculating the heating path

Based on the user's drawing, our software generates a heating path with the goal to heat up the area equally at all locations. Since calculating the heating path for an even heat distribution is difficult for arbitrary shapes, we limit FormFab's modeling geometries to circles and lines.

For heating up outline circles, we move along the path repeatedly until we reach the material's compliance point. For heating area circles, we apply a spiral path that moves from the outline towards the center of the circle.

When creating the spiral path, we have to adjust the distance between two lines of a spiral based on the heat gun radius, the distance to the workpiece, and the amount of airflow (see section 'Factors Influencing the Forming Process'). If the lines are too close, the area will overheat, if lines are too far apart, the area will not heat up sufficiently (Figure 8). We also shift the heating path inwards to avoid heating areas outside the drawn area. The amount of shift is determined by the same factors as the spacing of lines.

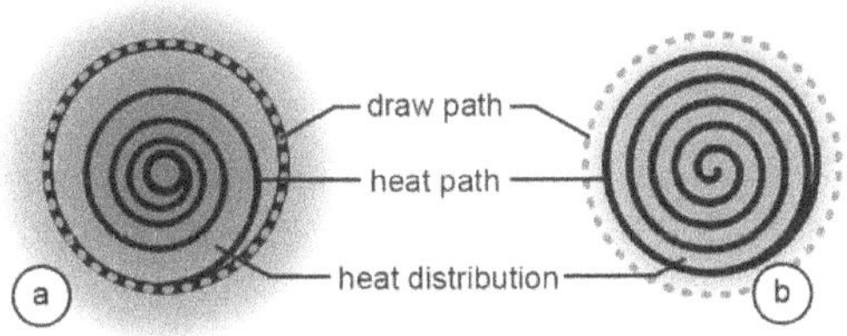


**Figure 8: (a) overheating, (b) even heat distribution.**

#### #3 Robot movement

We installed the *open-abb-driver* [15] as a server on our robotic arm. This allows us to send real-time commands via a *TCP/IP* connection. It also allows us to receive information about the robotic arm's current state.

The server processes movement commands in the robotic programming language *RAPID* that tells the robotic arm how to position the joints and how fast to transition between different positions (Figure 9). We generate these commands using the *Grasshopper* plugin *Robots.IO* [19].

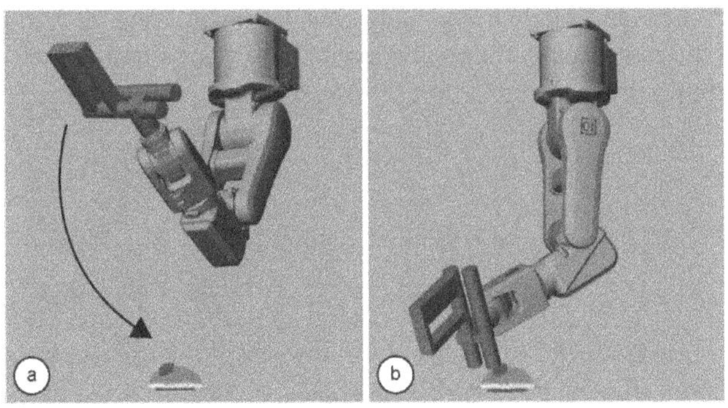


**Figure 9: Calculating path for even heat distribution.**

Robots.IO also generates warnings in case a target position is located outside the working range of the robotic arm (e.g., because it exceeds a joint limit), which typically happens when the shape becomes too large and the robotic arm has to operate at the boundaries of its working volume.

Robots.IO generates a different type of warning in situations where the robotic arm would collide with the workpiece. To allow Robots.IO to detect this case, the system has to provide it with a digital representation of the workpiece. We approximate the 3D model by simulating each modification applied to the workpiece (Figure 10).

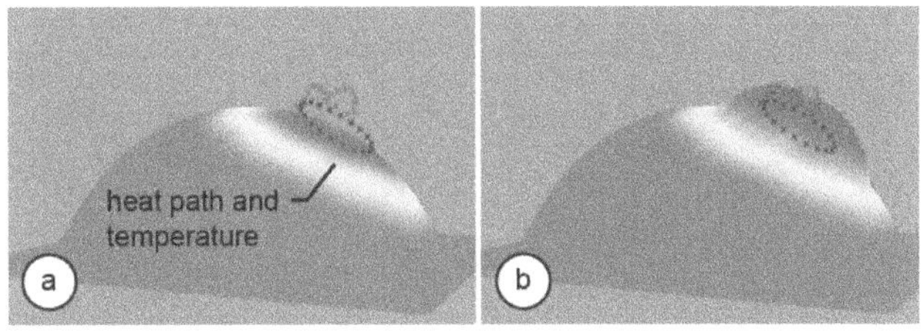


**Figure 10: Our system computes a physical simulation on a digital counterpart of the physical workpiece.**

For this, FormFab uses the physical simulation environment *Kangaroo Physics* [10], which is available as a Grasshopper plug-in. First, our system uses the heat path and heat gun radius to define the virtual compliant area. It then adjusts the virtual air pressure according to the physical air pressure to determine the amount of extrusion.

Our system also uses the resulting digital representation of the workpiece to orient the heat gun so as to always point at the workpiece at a perpendicular angle, allowing the system to heat the workpiece evenly.

#### #4 Heat control loop

Robots.IO exports the RAPID code for the entire heating path into a .txt file. Uploading the entire code to the robotic arm would execute the path, but would not allow querying information about the robotic arm during that time. However, FormFab needs information about the robotic arm's current position when it evaluates the current temperature data from the heat sensor as it otherwise does not know to where on the workpiece the measurement belongs. Our software thus splits the RAPID code into separate motion commands and sends them one-by-one to the communication server running on the robotic arm.

Once the heat-sensor has determined that the material has reached its compliance point, FormFab stops the heating process and moves the robotic arm to its default position, i.e., out of the way of the user.

#### #5 Pneumatic control

Before turning on the pneumatic system, our software detects the direction of user input. When the user first performs a pinch gesture, our system sets the position of the user's hand as the origin from which to measure (Figure 11a). For every 3 mm of hand movement, our system increases or decreases the control voltage of the pneumatic regulation unit by one step, slightly increasing or decreasing the pressure inside the workpiece (Figure 11b/c).

The exact pressure depends on the size of the compliant area. Pushing out smaller areas requires substantially higher pressure than pushing out larger areas. The reason for this is that the force available to push out a compliant area is the amount of pressure times the size of the area. FormFab compensates for this by applying a factor depending on the radius of the area.

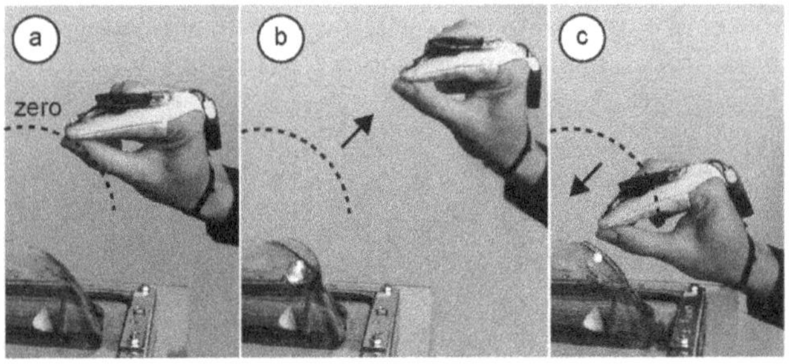


**Figure 11: (a) Zero level. (b) Increase pressure. (c) Decrease pressure, then switch to vacuum.**

FormFab keeps track of the number of increments and decrements sent to the pneumatic regulation unit. This allows it to switch the valve from vacuum to pressure and back at the right moment and to neutralize the air chamber to zero bar, when needed.

### FACTORS INFLUENCING THE FORMING PROCESS

In this section, we provide more details on the factors that influence the forming process and the resulting shapes.

#### #1 Size of Heated Area

The more the heat spreads on the workpiece, the shallower the temperature gradient at the edge of the heated area, thus the smoother the extrusion. While the heat gun supplies an initial source temperature, several factors influence the amount of heat that reaches the workpiece and how the heat distributes (Figure 12).

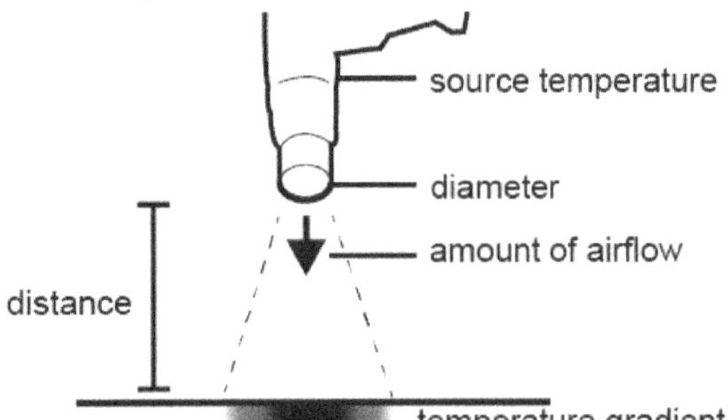


**Figure 12: Factors influencing the heat distribution.**

Each heat gun has a fixed opening through which the hot air exits (i.e., the diameter). Since the heat gun is located at a distance, the heat further spreads before it reaches the workpiece. The larger this distance, the bigger the spread.

The heat gun's airflow also helps spread heat across the workpiece. The more airflow, the faster the heat spreads.

#### #2 Amount of Stretch

As illustrated by Figure 13, the thicker the workpiece, the further it can be stretched before it starts to tear. We typically use sheets of 2 mm – 6 mm thickness but even a 1 mm sheet of PETG plastic can be stretched to create a shape larger than a human's head (see Figure 16).

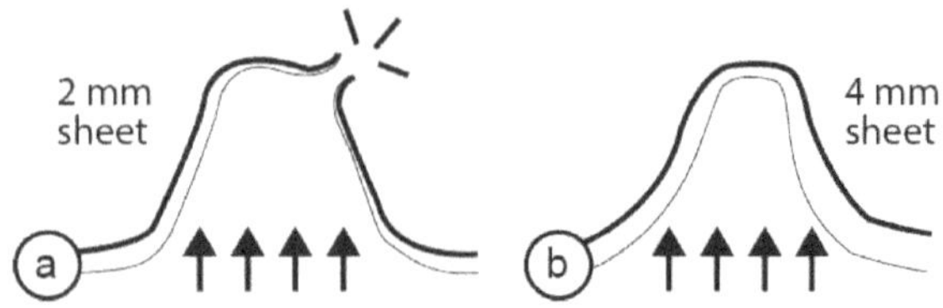


**Figure 13: (a) This 2 mm sheet is stretched too far. (b) The thicker 4 mm sheet can accomplish this shape.**

However, thicker sheets also need more time to heat up. The reason for this is that we warm up the workpiece from the outside using a heat gun, thus the heat needs time to propagate through the thickness of the sheet (Figure 14). If we apply heat too fast, the top surface of the sheet may overheat while the bottom surface is still cold; this can lead to heat bubbles that might tear when pressure is applied later on. This problem is amplified with thicker sheets, as the heat takes longer to propagate through.

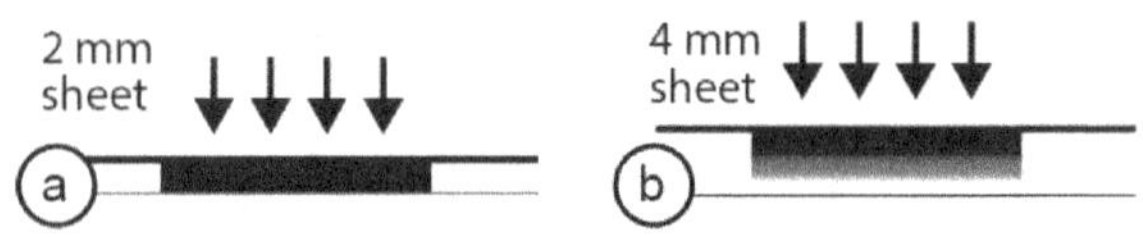


**Figure 14: Since the heat comes from the top, it requires less time to sink through (a) a thin workpiece than (b) a thicker workpiece.**

The amount of stretch is also affected by the amount of pressure applied and the size of the area. To reshape an area, the system has to apply a certain force to overcome the elasticity of the material in its compliant state. The smaller the compliant area, the more pressure or vacuum is required because the force for reshaping is proportional to the size of the area and the applied pressure (Figure 15). As the compliant area gets stretched, its size increases and its thickness decreases, leading to less resistance and thus a larger force on the area overall. Thus, over time, less and less pressure is required to keep stretching the area. If the pressure is kept constant, the expanded area might tear due to the excess pressure or the area might keep expanding even though the user already finished interacting. Our system estimates the size of the expanding area and approximates the pressure for the desired expansion rate.

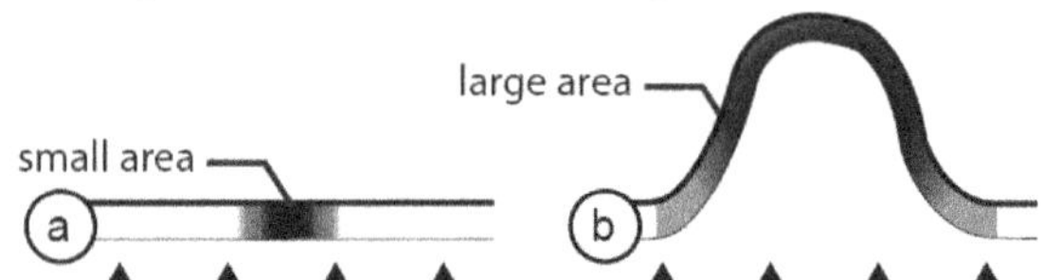


**Figure 15: (a) Applying the same amount of pressure to a small area (no resulting extrusion) and (b) a big area.**

Finally, the hotter the material, the easier it is to stretch. However, heating beyond the compliance point raises the chances of overheating and undesired heat bubbles.

### #3 Best Materials to Use

There are two main factors that influence how suitable a material is for our purposes: (1) materials with a low-compliance point allow spending less time on heating; (2) materials with a high stretch-ability allow using thinner sheets, which again reduces the heating time.

We looked at four different thermoplastics, including PETG, ABS, PC, and PMMA. The compliance point can be extracted from the data sheets of each material. We found PETG to have the lowest compliance point. Next, we determined stretch-ability by running an experiment in which we repeated the same heating path until we reached each material's compliance point. We then applied the same pneumatic pressure. Figure 16 shows three characteristic results, all created from a 1 mm sheet. PETG performed best; ABS led to a medium-sized extrusion, while PC only led to a minor extrusion. Since PETG performed best on both scales, we used it in our system.

**Figure 16: Results from our material stretch test.**

## INTERACTION SPACE

In its current form, our system only supports simple gesture input for circular and elliptical shapes and for defining the extrusion amount. Interactions in FormFab could be further enhanced by encoding constraints and action sequences into tools and by including alignment and snapping functionality, such as illustrated in *constructable* [14] and other interactive fabrication tools.

For instance, a multi extrusion tool could allow users to extrude both ears of the teddy bear head sculpture simultaneously (Figure 17a), while a copy/paste tool could replicate an existing shape at another location (Figure 17b).

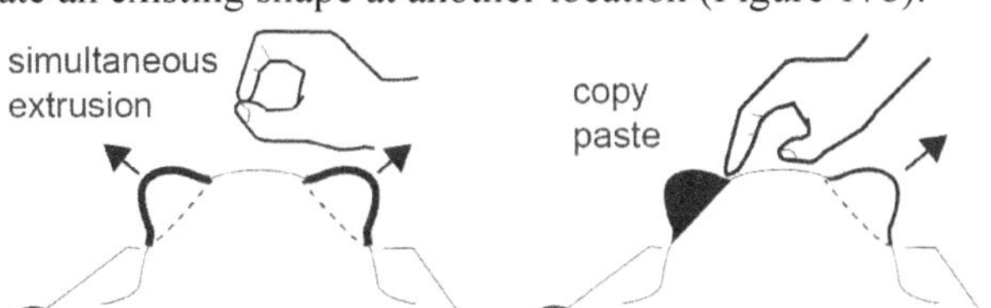


**Figure 17: Different tools: (a) simultaneous extrusion of both ears, (b) copy pasting the left ear to the right side.**

Similarly, snapping functionality could allow the user to extrude a shape in equal increments (Figure 18a), while alignment functionality could allow users to extrude a part until it reaches the same height as a previously selected part (Figure 18b).

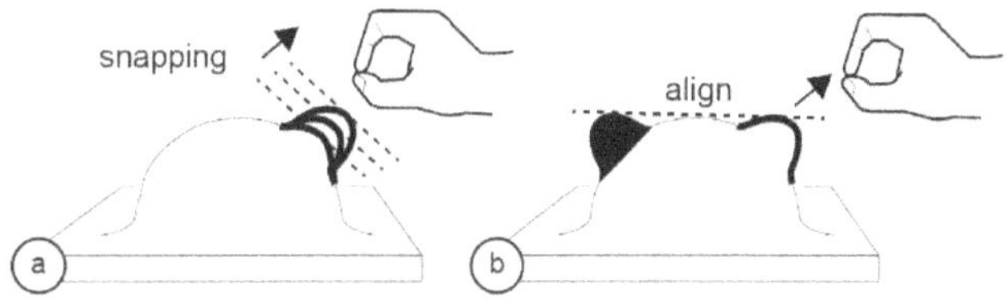


**Figure 18: (a) Snapping the shape to fixed increments to provide guidance. (b) Aligning the right ear height to the left ear height.**

## DESIGN ELEMENTS

While our approach is limited to decorative objects that consist of shapes producible with thermoforming, we can vary the heat distribution across a shape to achieve different outcomes.

### Outline vs. Area Shape

As illustrated by Figure 19a, by heating up only the outline of a shape and leaving the inside at room temperature, we can achieve a plateau. Heating up the entire area in contrast results in a half sphere (Figure 19b).

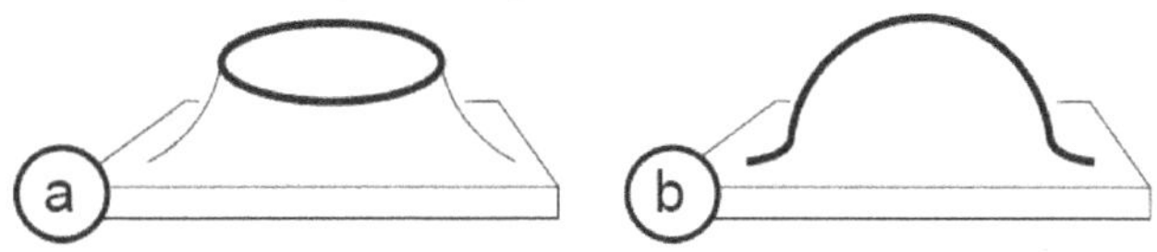


**Figure 19: Heating: (a) outline only, (b) entire area.**

Figure 20 shows this at the example of a head sculpture that also has a neck. The neck is made first using a circular outline shape, the basic head shape is added in a second step using a circular area shape.

**Figure 20: First steps of making a head sculpture with neck. (a) outline shape for neck, (b,c) adding the head.**

### Homogeneous vs. Heterogeneous Heating

In Figure 19 both shapes were created using homogeneous heating, i.e., the entire outline or area is heated up equally. Figure 21 uses the same basic outline/area shapes, but this time with an unequal heat distribution. As can be seen, the hottest point will expand furthest as the material is more compliant than in other areas.

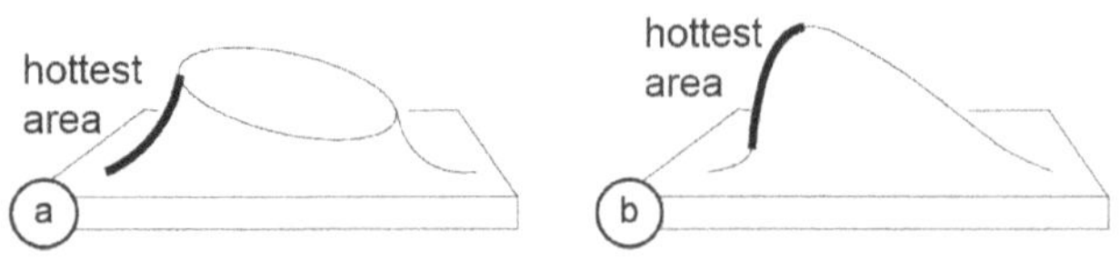


**Figure 21: Heterogeneous heating: (a) a tilted plateau shape from an outline, (b) a tilted area shape.**

## CONCLUSION & FUTURE WORK

In this paper, we showed a first prototype implementation of an interactive fabrication system that provides the user with continuous physical feedback *while* the user is interacting. While the first step of selecting the area still followed the turn-taking model, the second step of defining the size of the shape provided the user with continuous physical feedback, thereby bringing the principles of *direct manipulation* to the editing of physical objects.

For future work, we plan to explore how to make the setup more compact by integrating the heating elements directly with the plastic sheet. This would allow us to remove the robotic arm and heat guns. In addition, we plan to explore additional design elements (outline vs. infill heating, equal vs. unequal heat distributions), and add gestures that encode constraints and action sequences, such as copy pasting existing shapes, similar to those that were illustrated in previous interactive fabrication systems. Finally, we plan to explore thermo-elastic materials, i.e., a material that is rigid when cold, but elastic when warmed up, which could potentially enable a completely reversible workflow.

## ACKNOWLEDGEMENTS

This work was supported in part by NSF Award IIS1422106.

## REFERENCES

[1] Ryan Arisandi, Yusuke Takami, Mai Otsuki, Asako Kimura, Fumihisa Shibata, and Hideyuki Tamura. Enjoying Virtual Handcrafting with ToolDevice. In *Adjunct Proceedings of the 25th Annual ACM Symposium on User Interface Software and Technology* (UIST EA '12), 17-18.

[2] Patrick Baudisch, and Stefanie Mueller, Personal Fabrication. *Foundations and Trends® in Human–Computer Interaction* 10, 3–4, 165-293, 2017.

[3] Leonardo Bonanni, Sam Sarcia, Subodh Paudel, Ted Selker. Dishmaker: Personal Fabrication Interface. In *Extended Abstracts on Human Factors in Computing Systems* (CHI EA '05).

[4] Karin Dörfler, Florian Rist, Romana Rust. Interlacing: An Experimental Approach to Integrating Digital and Physical Design Methods. In *Robotic Fabrication in Architecture, Art, and Design* (Rob|Arch'12), 82–91.

[5] Sean Follmer, David Carr, Emily Lovell, and Hiroshi Ishii. CopyCAD: Remixing Physical Objects with Copy and Paste from the Real World. In *Adjunct Proceedings of the 23nd Annual ACM Symposium on User Interface Software and Technology* (UIST '10), 381.

[6] Daniel Groeger, Elena Chong Loo, and Jürgen Steimle. HotFlex: Post-Print Customization of 3D Prints Using Embedded State Change. In *Proceedings of the 2016 CHI Conference on Human Factors in Computing Systems* (CHI '16), 420-432.

[7] Yoon Chung Han and Byeong-Jun Han. Virtual Pottery: A Virtual 3D Audiovisual Interface Using Natural Hand Motions. In *Multimedia Tools Applications* 73, 2, 917-933, 2014.

[8] Ryan Luke Johns. Augmented Reality and the Fabrication of Gestural Form. In *Robotic Fabrication in Architecture, Art, and Design* (Rob|Arch'12), 248-255.

[9] Ammar Kalo, Michael Jake Newsum. An Investigation of Robotic Incremental Sheet Metal Forming as a Method for Prototyping Parametric Architectural Skins. In *Robotic Fabrication in Architecture, Art and Design* 2014, 33-49.

[10] KangorooPhysics. http://www.food4rhino.com/project/kangaroo?etx

[11] Manfred Lau, Masaki Hirose, Akira Ohgawara, Jun Mitani, and Takeo Igarashi. Situated Modeling: A Shape-Stamping Interface with Tangible Primitives. In *Proceedings of the Sixth International Conference on Tangible, Embedded and Embodied Interaction* (TEI '12), 275-282.

[12] Joong Han Lee. Haptic Intelligentsia. 2011. http://studio-homunculus.com/portfolio/haptic-intelligentsia-human-prototyping-machine/

[13] Stefanie Mueller, Bastian Kruck, and Patrick Baudisch. LaserOrigami: Laser-Cutting 3D Objects. In *Proceedings of the SIGCHI Conference on Human Factors in Computing Systems* (CHI '13), 2585-2592.

[14] Stefanie Mueller, Pedro Lopes, and Patrick Baudisch. Interactive Construction: Interactive Fabrication of Functional Mechanical Devices. In *Proceedings of the 25th Annual ACM Symposium on User Interface Software and Technology* (UIST '12), 599-606.

[15] openABB driver: https://github.com/robotics/open_abb

[16] Huaishu Peng, Jimmy Briggs, Cheng-Yao Wang, Kevin Guo, Joseph Kider, Stefanie Mueller, Patrick Baudisch, and François Guimbretière. RoMA: Interactive Fabrication with Augmented Reality and a Robotic 3D Printer. In *Proceedings of the 2018 CHI Conference on Human Factors in Computing Systems* (CHI '18), Paper 579.

[17] Huaishu Peng, Amit Zoran, and François V. Guimbretière. D-Coil: A Hands-on Approach to Digital 3D Models Design. In *Proceedings of the 33rd Annual ACM Conference on Human Factors in Computing Systems* (CHI '15), 1807-1815.

[18] Alec Rivers, Ilan E. Moyer, and Frédo Durand. Position-Correcting Tools for 2D Digital Fabrication. In *ACM Transactions on Graphics* 31, 4, Article 88, 2012.

[19] Robots.IO. https://robots.io/wp/

[20] Ben Shneiderman. Direct Manipulation: A Step Beyond Programming Languages. In *Computer* 16, 8, 57-69, 1983.

[21] Christian Schüller, Daniele Panozzo, Anselm Grundhöfer, Henning Zimmer, Evgeni Sorkine, and Olga Sorkine-Hornung. Computational Thermoforming. In *ACM Transactions on Graphics* 35, 4, Article 43, 2016.

[22] Roy Shilkrot, Pattie Maes, Joseph A. Paradiso, and Amit Zoran. Augmented Airbrush for Computer Aided Painting (CAP). In *ACM Transactions on Graphics* 34, 2, Article 19, 2015.

[23] Alexander Teibrich, Stefanie Mueller, François Guimbretière, Robert Kovacs, Stefan Neubert, and Patrick Baudisch. Patching Physical Objects. In *Proceedings of the 28th Annual ACM Symposium on User Interface Software and Technology* (UIST '15), 83-91.

[24] Christian Weichel, John Hardy, Jason Alexander, and Hans Gellersen. ReForm: Integrating Physical and Digital Design through Bidirectional Fabrication. In *Proceedings of the 28th Annual ACM Symposium on User Interface Software and Technology* (UIST '15), 93-102.

[25] Christian Weichel, Manfred Lau, David Kim, Nicolas Villar, and Hans W. Gellersen. MixFab: A Mixed-Reality Environment for Personal Fabrication. In *Proceedings of the SIGCHI Conference on Human Factors in Computing Systems* (CHI '14), 3855-3864.

[26] Amy Wibowo, Daisuke Sakamoto, Jun Mitani, and Takeo Igarashi. DressUp: A 3D Interface for Clothing Design with a Physical Mannequin. In *Proceedings of the Sixth International Conference on Tangible, Embedded and Embodied Interaction* (TEI '12), 99-102.

[27] Karl D.D. Willis, Juncong Lin, Jun Mitani, and Takeo Igarashi. Spatial Sketch: Bridging Between Movement & Fabrication. In *Proceedings of the Fourth International Conference on Tangible, Embedded, and Embodied Interaction* (TEI '10), 5-12.

[28] Karl D.D. Willis, Cheng Xu, Kuan-Ju Wu, Golan Levin, and Mark D. Gross. Interactive Fabrication: New Interfaces for Digital Fabrication. In *Proceedings of the Fifth International Conference on Tangible, Embedded, and Embodied Interaction* (TEI '11), 69-72.

[29] Junichi Yamaoka and Yasuaki Kakehi. DrawForming: An Interactive Fabrication Method for Vacuum Forming. In *Proceedings of the Tenth International Conference on Tangible, Embedded, and Embodied Interaction* (TEI '16), 615-620.

[30] Junichi Yamaoka and Yasuaki Kakehi. ProtoMold: An Interactive Vacuum Forming System for Rapid Prototyping. In *Proceedings of the SIGCHI Conference on Human Factors in Computing Systems* (CHI '17), 2106-2115.

[31] Mayu M. Yamashita, Junichi Yamaoka, and Yasuaki Kakehi. Enchanted Scissors: A Scissor Interface for Support in Cutting and Interactive Fabrication. In *ACM SIGGRAPH Posters* (SIGGRAPH '13), Article 33.

[32] Kentaro Yasu. MOR4R: How to Create 3D Objects Using a Microwave Oven. In *Proceedings of the Tenth International Conference on Tangible, Embedded, and Embodied Interaction* (TEI '16), 365-372.

[33] Amit Zoran and Joseph A. Paradiso. FreeD: A Freehand Digital Sculpting Tool. In *Proceedings of the SIGCHI Conference on Human Factors in Computing Systems* (CHI '13), 2613-2616.

[34] Amit Zoran, Roy Shilkrot, and Joseph Paradiso. Human-Computer Interaction for Hybrid Carving. In *Proceedings of the 26th Annual ACM Symposium on User Interface Software and Technology* (UIST '13), 433-440.

# Mechamagnets: Designing and Fabricating Haptic and Functional Physical Inputs with Embedded Magnets

**Clement Zheng** [1] **Jeeeun Kim** [2] **Daniel Leithinger** [1,2] **Mark D Gross** [1,2] **Ellen Yi-Luen Do** [1,2,3]
ATLAS Institute, University of Colorado Boulder [1]
Department of Computer Science, University of Colorado Boulder [2]
Keio-NUS CUTE Center, National University of Singapore [3]
{clement.zheng, jeeeun.kim, daniel.leithinger, mdgross, ellen.do} @colorado.edu

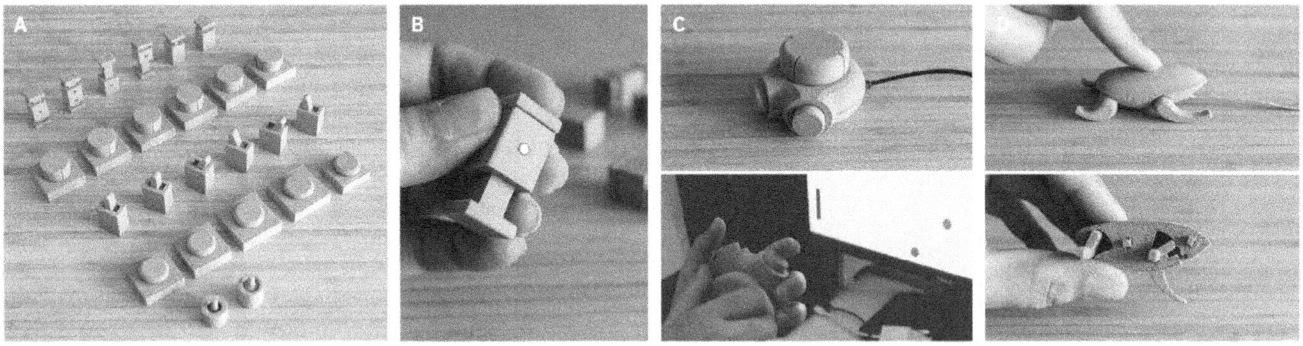

**Figure 1. A) 3D printed *Mechamagnets* taxonomy. B) Exploring the *linear X attracting-center* input model. C) Ergonomic game controller designed with *Mechamagnets*. D) "Springy" legs by embedding the *angular X rotating-end* model in the toy frog's body.**

## ABSTRACT
We present *Mechamagnets*, a technique for facilitating the design and fabrication of haptic and functional inputs for physical interfaces. This technique consists of a set of 3D printed spatial constraints which facilitate different physical movements, as well as unpowered haptic profiles created by embedding static magnets in 3D printed parts. We propose the *Mechamagnets* taxonomy to map the design space of this technique for designers and makers. Furthermore, we leverage the use of magnets by instrumenting these objects with linear Hall effect sensors to create functional digital inputs. We showcase *Mechamagnets* with a series of novel physical interfaces made with this technique.

### Author Keywords
Prototyping; Haptics; Magnets; 3D Printing; Fabrication.


TEI '19, March 17–20, 2019, Tempe, AZ, USA

ACM ISBN 978-1-4503-6196-5/19/03…$15.00
https://doi.org/10.1145/3294109.3295622

## INTRODUCTION
Affordable digital fabrication enables designers and makers to rapidly design and fabricate unique physical forms, while embedded electronic platforms, such as the *Arduino* ecosystem, facilitate the exploration of functional physical systems. These facilitate the creation of robust and interactive prototypes, particularly during the early stages of a design process. However, when creating such prototypes, designers must contend with off-the-shelf parts, constraining them to predefined geometries and mechanisms. In particular, designers of physical interfaces are often limited by prefabricated input components (such as push buttons). It is a challenge to comprehensively and freely specify features such as visual affordance, mechanical behavior and haptic feedback of physical interfaces when designing with off-the-shelf parts.

Haptic feedback is an integral part of our interactions with physical interfaces. It facilitates task performance, like in robot-assisted surgery [19]; and it also contributes to the satisfaction of an experience, evident in the wide variety of custom controllers and "tactile" keyboards for gaming [21]. In addition, prototyping bespoke physical interfaces is an important process within product design. Notably, BMW's dedicated haptics team specifies the form, feel, and function of every physical input that goes into the car [2].

Our goal is to facilitate the design and fabrication of haptic and functional physical interfaces in a holistic and economical manner. In this paper, we build on previous work [23] and describe *Mechamagnets* as a technique for creating bespoke physical input components. Our technique supports designers and makers who use computer-aided design (CAD) and digital fabrication, and it leverages the use of commodity 3D printers in design studios and makerspaces. In this paper, we detail the three core parts of the *Mechamagnets* technique. First, physical interactions are defined using simple spatial (physical) constraints which we identified by deconstructing existing physical inputs (Table 1); for instance, constraining a body to move linearly along a hollow track. Second, static magnets are configured and embedded in the fabricated parts to define the mechanical behavior of physical inputs, as well as deliver haptic feedback during interaction (Figure 4). Third, linear Hall effect sensors are placed in the fabricated input to read and communicate its state (Figure 6). We provide a taxonomy to illustrate basic input models afforded by *Mechamagnets*, and to map the design space of this technique for designers and makers (Figure 5).

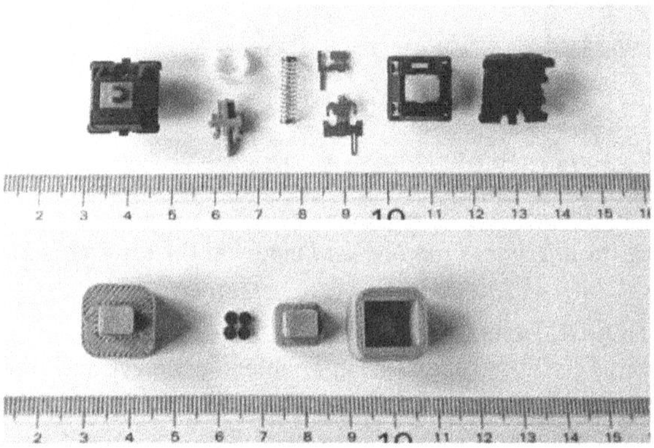

**Figure 2. Assembled and disassembled. Top: Cherry MX Blue switch. Bottom: *Mechamagnets* switch with similar haptic feedback and mechanical behavior.**

## RELATED WORK

### Embedding materials and mechanisms into 3D printed objects

3D printers, particularly fused deposition modeling (FDM) machines, are restricted to printing using a small set of materials. This, in turn, limits the material properties of parts that can be fabricated via additive manufacturing. Researchers have proposed a variety of techniques to address this constraint. *Medley* [3] is a design tool that facilitates compositing external materials in 3D printed parts. It offers a library of common materials with different functional properties, such as bendable florists' wire and soft sponge. In the same vein, *Reprise* [4] supports customizing existing products with 3D printed attachments. Researchers have also explored creating metamaterial mechanisms [10] by 3D printing internal microstructures that vary the properties of a material within a part. While no external materials are used, here the limitation is size: the fabrication resolution of 3D printers affects the scale of microstructures, which places minimum size constraints on parts needed to deliver a mechanism.

*Mechamagnets* extends this research by investigating the affordances of static magnets embedded in 3D printed parts. With a simple inventory, we demonstrate a variety of unpowered haptic profiles that work across different types of physical inputs that move within several degrees of freedom.

### Generating haptic feedback with static magnets

Other projects have investigated static magnets for haptic interaction, as they produce force-feedback without external power when moved relative to one another. Static magnets also come in simple physical forms like cylinders and cuboids. As such, they are an ideal material to embed in physical parts to generate haptic feedback. *Haptic Cues* [20] enables users to feel an invisible texture through the force produced by moving magnets sandwiched across a textured plastic surface. *Magnetic Plotter* [22] explores haptic patterns through drawing variable patterns on a soft magnetic sheet. When two sheets are rubbed together, the patterns create different vibratory feedback. *GaussBricks* [13] investigates elastic textures afforded by a chain of static magnets; including clicking, bending, stretching and squeezing. In *Mechamagnets*, we demonstrate how embedding static magnets in 3D printed parts can deliver haptic feedback and the mechanical behavior of physical inputs in tandem.

### Creating functional physical inputs

Electronic platforms and toolkits such as *Arduino* [24], *Phidgets* [8], *Calder* [12], and *Makers' Marks* [17] facilitate prototyping functional physical interfaces. However, these systems limit designers to prefabricated components. Other systems support designing and fabricating functional physical inputs with digital fabrication. In *Sauron* [16], computer vision senses the state of 3D printed physical inputs. *Lamello* [18] utilizes a microphone to read an input by parsing the audio signal generated by 3D printed tines. These systems minimize the electronics needed for instrumenting the fabricated input. *Sauron* requires embedding a camera into the fabricated object, while *Lamello* requires additional 3D printed structures for passive sound generation. With *Mechamagnets*, small static (neodymium) magnets are employed to deliver haptic feedback. We embed these magnets in combination with individual linear Hall effect sensors to create functional 3D printed inputs. These sensors are inexpensive, and come in small and simple physical packages. They are used to sense the position and orientation of physical parts in many commercial applications, such as car steering and machine controls. The design of tangible interfaces has also explored this method of instrumentation. For example, *MagGetz* [9] and *MagnID* [1] employs the magnetometer (a 3-axis linear Hall effect sensor) built into smart devices to detect the states of physical inputs and positions of tangible tokens respectively. *GaussBricks* employs a surface instrumented with a grid of Hall effect sensors to detect the position and configuration of models composed of a magnet-based construction assembly kit.

| *Type* | **Linear** | **Polar** | **Angular** | **Planar** | **Radial** |
|---|---|---|---|---|---|
| *Diagram* |  |  | 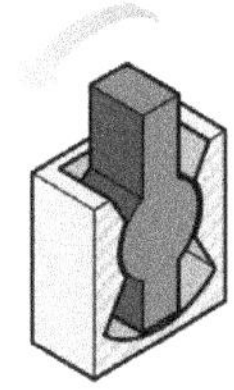 | 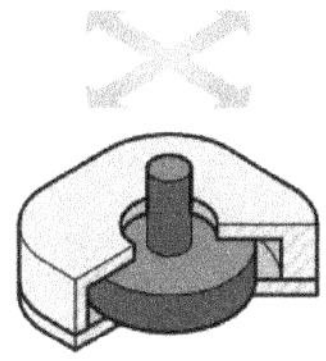 | 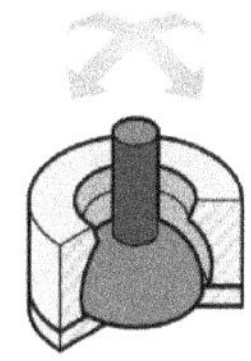 |
| *Related Actions & Examples* | push, pull, slide<br>push button, slider | turn, twist, scroll<br>dial, knob, scroll wheel | flip<br>switch, lever | slide, pan<br>thumbstick, gear shift | tilt<br>joystick, trackball |

**Table 1: Five spatial constraints, with related actions and examples**

## MECHAMAGNETS

There are three core aspects to the *Mechamagnets* technique: 1) designing the form and function of physical interactions through spatial constraints, 2) designing mechanical behavior and haptic feedback with embedded magnets, and 3) instrumenting input components into functional devices with linear Hall effect sensors. We unpack each aspect in the following sections and describe how they interact.

### Form and function via spatial constraints

*Mechamagnets* applies to any plastic additive manufacturing process, however, we focused on the capabilities of desktop FDM machines due to their pervasive use in studios and makerspaces. Mass-produced physical inputs typically employ injection molding and automated assembly lines. Their designs rely on a high degree of manufacturing tolerance that is unattainable with FDM (Figure 2 top). As such, rather than mimic the construction of commercial components, we developed *Mechamagnets* by deconstructing existing physical inputs into simpler models.

We can characterize many existing physical inputs by constraining the movements of a pair of 3D bodies with different cavity shapes. *Mechamagnets* proposes five types of spatial constraints (Table 1). Although this is not an exhaustive set of possible physical interactions, it addresses a wide range of movements found in existing physical inputs. Mackinlay and colleagues proposed a taxonomy [14] that describes physical inputs as transducers of linear or rotary movements, in any of the six spatial Cartesian degrees of freedom. We build on this work by demonstrating solid geometries for 3D printing that afford different degrees of linear and rotary movements.

*Linear spatial constraint*: to move along a linear track. Commonly associated interactions are pushing and pulling.

*Polar spatial constraint*: to rotate about an axis. Commonly associated interactions are turning, twisting and scrolling.

*Angular spatial constraint*: to pivot on a point, typically in the form of an extended arm. Flipping is a common interaction associated with this model.

*Planar spatial constraint*: to slide along a two dimensional plane. Commonly associated interactions include sliding and panning.

*Radial spatial constraint*: to pitch and roll around a point. Tilting and rolling are commonly associated interactions.

These spatial constraints abstract input interactions into different classes of physical movements, and create opportunity for designers to specify input components in relation to the rest of a physical interface (Figure 8A, 8D). These models also serve as building blocks for constructing more complex physical interactions and unconventional inputs; such as by compounding similar movements (Figure 8B), or blending different movements (Figure 8C). Furthermore, the deconstructed models offer other advantages. The spatial constraints are straightforward to create in 3D CAD programs through a "subtraction" operation and do not require high resolution fabrication, thus optimizing parts for FDM. They also simplify embedding magnets and sensors into parts; two important aspects of this technique that will be discussed below.

### Haptic feedback and mechanical behavior via static magnets

Commercial inputs rely on an assembly of different components to deliver haptic feedback and mechanical behavior. For instance, a mechanical keyboard button uses contact leaves to generate a "click" when it is pressed (haptic feedback), and a spring to push it back to its original position (mechanical behavior) (Figure 2 top). In *Mechamagnets*, we investigated using only static magnets and 3D printing (Figure 2 bottom) to specify different unpowered haptic feedback as well as mechanical behaviors of inputs. To inform our development of these mechanisms, we first characterized the forces generated by magnets as they move relative to each other. With this characterization, we propose six different haptic profiles for physical inputs by embedding static magnets.

#### *Magnet-movement interactions*

Haptic feedback is broadly categorized into *kinesthetic* and *tactile* feedback. Kinesthetic feedback results from forces felt due to body movement, whereas tactile feedback results from stimulation to the skin [6]. Physical input components provide both kinesthetic and tactile feedback, and Kim et al.

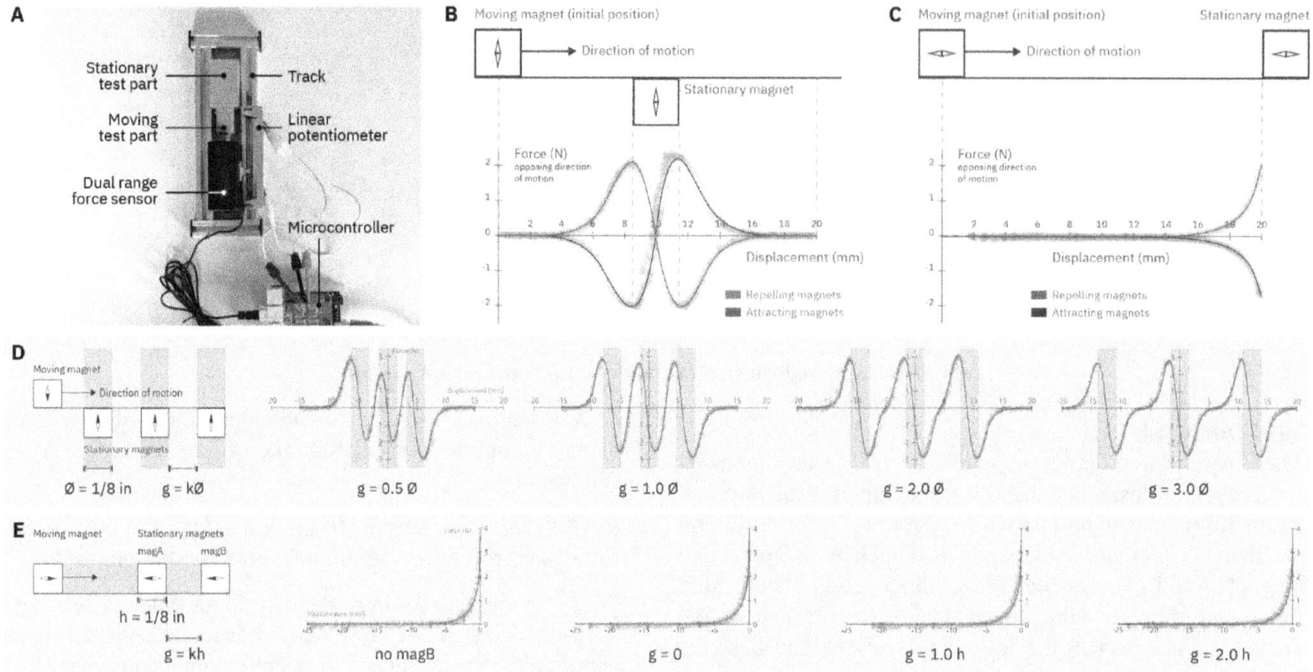


**Figure 3. A: Force measurement rig. B: Force-displacement curves of magnets moving perpendicularly, C: coaxially. D: Inter-magnet interactions test of magnets moving perpendicularly, E: coaxially.**

demonstrated the usefulness of force-displacement curves to quantify and simulate the haptic feedback of such inputs [11]. We employ the same measurement to characterize the unpowered haptic feedback provided by moving static magnets relative to each other.

We organize magnet-movement interactions based on their attraction / repulsion, and their relative movements (perpendicular / coaxial). Perpendicular magnets travel in a direction normal to their polar axis; while in coaxial movement, magnets travel in line with their poles. We constructed a rig to measure the force-displacement curves of these four interactions (Figure 3A). It consists of a dual-range force sensor [25] physically coupled to a linear potentiometer to measure displacement. This force sensor pushes and pulls a 3D printed part relative to a stationary part. We tested 1/8″ by 1/8″ N48 cylindrical neodymium magnets embedded in FDM-printed parts to account for forces, such as friction, that might result from physical inputs fabricated with 3D printing. Using this rig, we plotted more than a thousand force-displacement measurements distributed across a 20mm range. Figure 3 illustrates the magnets' setup, and the corresponding measurements for each magnet-movement interaction. From these measurements, we generated four different force-displacement curves (Figure 3B/C). We use these curves to visualize the haptic feedback generated by moving static magnets to develop different feedback profiles for physical inputs.

In addition, we explored inter-magnet interactions with the same rig. The force-displacement curves of a 1/8″ by 1/8″ N48 cylindrical neodymium magnet moving perpendicularly across three laterally spaced similar magnets were measured (Figure 3D). Two insights emerged from these measurements. First, while discrete "steps" are still observed at g=0.5Ø (1/16″), inter-magnet interactions are apparent as indicated by the diminished forces measured while traversing the middle magnet. Second, as the gap increases, we noticed a flattening of the curves between magnets. At g=3.0Ø (3/8″), this curve is completely flat between magnets. This suggests that, as a heuristic, the

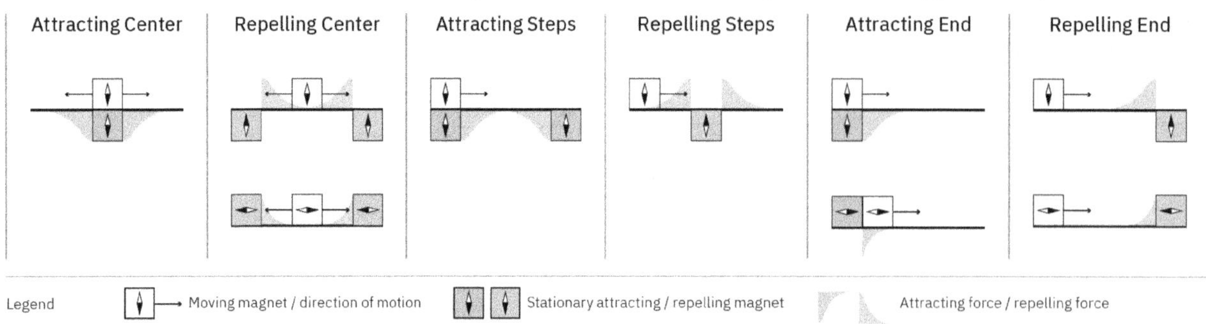


**Figure 4: Six haptic feedback profiles for physical inputs through embedding static magnets in 3D printed parts.**

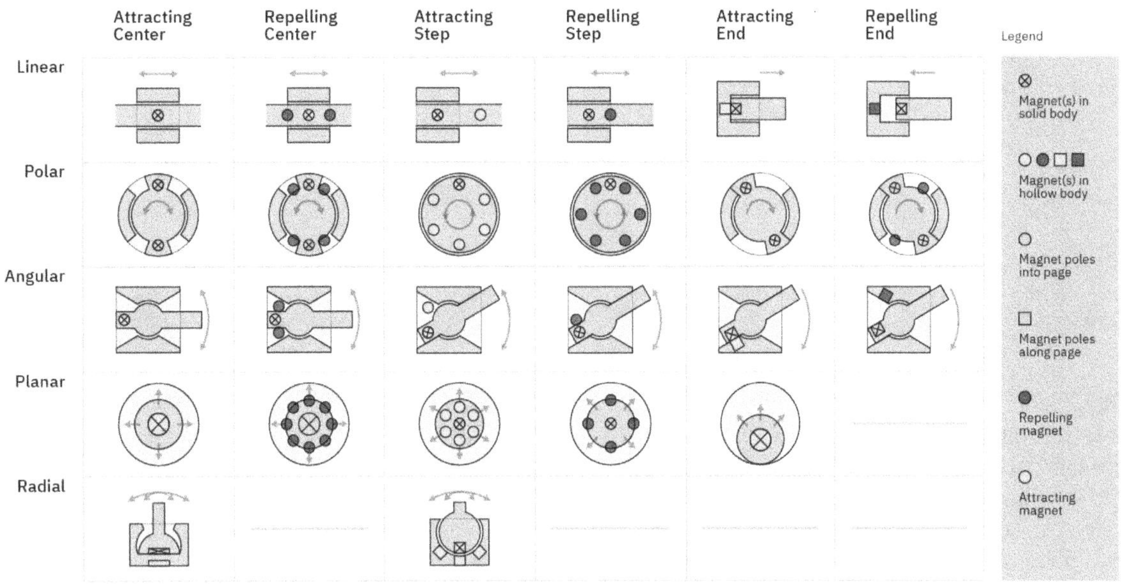


**Figure 5.** ***Mechamagnets*** **Taxonomy.**

magnetic fields on the surface of 1/8″ neodymium magnets with a lateral separation of 3/8″ have negligible influence on each other. We conducted the same test for coaxially arranged magnets, and found negligible inter-magnet interaction even when stacked pole-to-pole (Figure 3E).

### *Unpowered haptic profiles*

Building on these magnet-movement interactions, we define six basic unpowered haptic feedback profiles for physical inputs, realized by embedding static magnets in 3D printed parts. We describe these haptic profiles through the magnetic forces at play, and the mechanical behavior they provide during interaction. Figure 4 illustrates these six profiles. We use the force-displacement curves from the previous section, and visualize them in terms of attraction or repulsion. The slope of the curves indicates the direction of force—an inclining slope means that magnets oppose movement; a declining slope indicates that the magnets augment movement.

*Attracting / Repelling Center*: This pair of profiles encourages a stable "center"; magnets push the input component to a central position during interaction; for example, in a joystick. For attracting center, users experience a larger initial force opposing their movements, which weakens over distance. For repelling center, an increasing force opposes movements as distance from the center increases.

*Attracting / Repelling Steps*: This pair of profiles introduces "steps" along the interaction path of an input. For attracting magnets, steps are stable locations that the input "snaps" to. Repelling magnets act in reverse; steps oppose movement, and users must exert more force to "push over" a step. Detented inputs such as rotary encoders with discrete "ticks" are examples of such mechanisms.

*Attracting / Repelling End*: This pair of profiles encourages a stable "end". For attracting end, users overcome a larger initial force to move the input, and this force weakens over distance. For repelling end, users experience an increasing opposing force as they move the input. Push buttons and pull cords are examples of mechanisms with a stable end.

## Mechamagnets Taxonomy

By crossing the five spatial constraints and six haptic profiles, we developed a *Mechamagnets* taxonomy to map the possibilities for other designers and makers. It contains 25 basic input models[1] (Figure 5). Each model illustrates spatial constraints through a "hollow" and "solid" body, as well as the configuration of magnets within these bodies for different haptic profiles.

Each diagram in the taxonomy presents one instance of combining a spatial constraint with a haptic profile; and it is important to note that parameters can be varied for each model. For instance, in the *angular X repelling-step* model, designers can vary its degree of rotation by changing the angle between the stops in its hollow body. Designers can also add steps by embedding more repelling magnets along the input's interaction path. Magnets are press fit into recesses printed in the parts. In developing this taxonomy, we constrained the magnets used to 1/8″ by 1/8″ N48 neodymium magnets; except for *radial X attracting-center*, *planar X attracting-center*, *planar X repelling-center*, and *planar X attracting-end*, where we used 1/4″ by 1/16″ N48 neodymium magnets.

[1] *Not 30, as certain categories of haptic profiles are not applicable to the planar and radial spatial constraints; the friction generated between moving bodies will render the mechanism ineffective.*

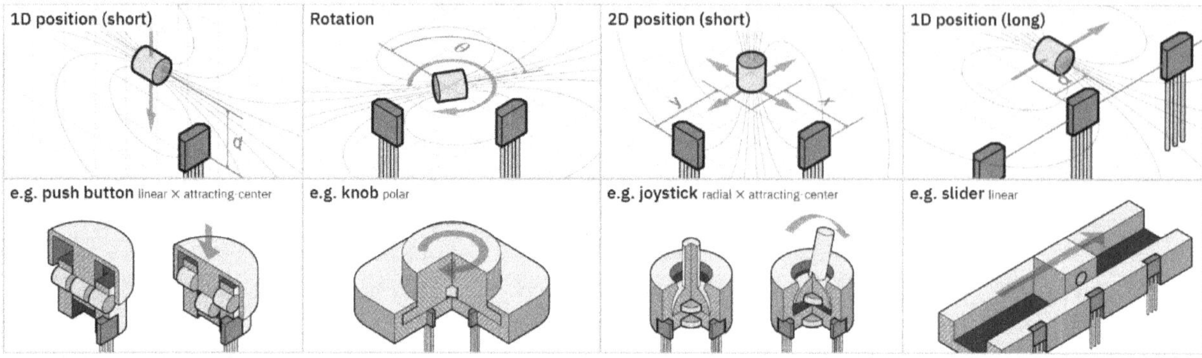


**Figure 6. Four sensor configurations for detecting different types of magnet positions, and example uses for each configuration.**

The models illustrated in this taxonomy were abstracted to be independent from specific 3D modeling applications. Besides the schematics in Figure 5, we further demonstrate each model in this taxonomy through *Fusion 360* parametric files, and STL files optimized for FDM fabrication. These are available through an online repository[2], and in this paper's supplementary materials (Figure 1A/B).

### Instrumentation via Linear Hall Effect Sensors

We instrument *Mechamagnet* components with linear Hall effect sensors to make functional input devices. A linear Hall effect sensor gives a continuous signal range from 0V to the supplied voltage, based on the strength and polarity of the magnetic field around it. Any microcontroller with an analog to digital converter can parse this signal. For our prototypes, we employed linear Hall effect sensors with sensitivities equal or less than 5mV/G to minimize external influences such as geomagnetism or magnetic fields generated by other objects.

*Gaussbricks* demonstrates using an external grid of linear Hall effect sensors to detect the state of magnetic tangible interfaces [13]. We extend this work by investigating instrumentation with individual Hall effect sensors for integrated and portable physical interfaces where multiple *Mechamagnet* inputs operate with different movement axes in an object (Figure 8). We embed these sensors into *Mechamagnet* components by fitting them into recesses modelled inside 3D printed parts. As analog devices, instrumenting *Mechamagnet* components with linear Hall effect sensors provides designers with more interaction information than conventional off-the-shelf inputs. For instance, designers can customize the activation point of an input. Sensors can also report variables such as the speed or force of human interaction. These measurements add nuance to simple input components like a push button. We use two variations of linear Hall effect sensors depending on the magnet's strength, both with an effective sensing radius of approximately 10mm (see Table 2). We develop four sensor configurations for instrumenting different models in the *Mechamagnets* taxonomy. Figure 6 illustrates the different configurations and example uses for each configuration. Depending on the type of input, we can either use magnets already employed for haptic feedback (see Figure 6 push button and joystick), or embed an additional magnet dedicated to sensing (see Figure 6 knob and slider). A single sensor can detect the proximity of nearby magnets (see technical document [7]). This configuration can detect interactions that travel a short distance, such as pressing a button, flipping a switch, or twisting a knob. Two sensors can be positioned at a right angle to detect the rotation of a magnet (see technical document [5]), such as in a continuous dial. The same two-sensor setup can also detect the 2D position of a magnet within a short range, as in sliding thumbsticks or joysticks. Multiple sensors can be arranged along a path for sensing the position of a magnet across a longer distance, useful for instrumenting inputs like linear sliders.

[2] *https://github.com/clementzheng/mechamagnets*

| | **Allegro A1324LUA-T** | **Allegro A1308KUA-1-T** |
|---|---|---|
| *Size* | 4 x 3 x 1.5mm | 4 x 3 x 1.5mm |
| *Sensitivity* | 5.0mV/G | 1.3mV/G |
| *Suggested magnet type* | 1/8" by 1/8" N48 neodymium magnets | 1/4" by 1/16" N48 neodymium magnets |

**Table 2. Linear Hall effect sensor details.**

To support this instrumentation method, we developed a library of scripts to calibrate sensor measurements for different input types. Not all magnets in a *Mechamagnet* component move and contribute to sensing; and the calibration scripts serve to establish a baseline from the component's overall magnetic field. For example, the calibration script for 1D position identifies the minimum and maximum sensor reading; while the script for rotation identifies the center of rotation and zero-angle direction. These scripts are also open sourced through the online *Mechamagnets* repository.

## DESIGNING WITH MECHAMAGNETS

*Mechamagnets* facilitates creating bespoke physical inputs with 3D printing, static magnets, and linear Hall effect sensors. It can be incorporated into the workflow (Figure 7) of prototyping physical interfaces with digital fabrication:

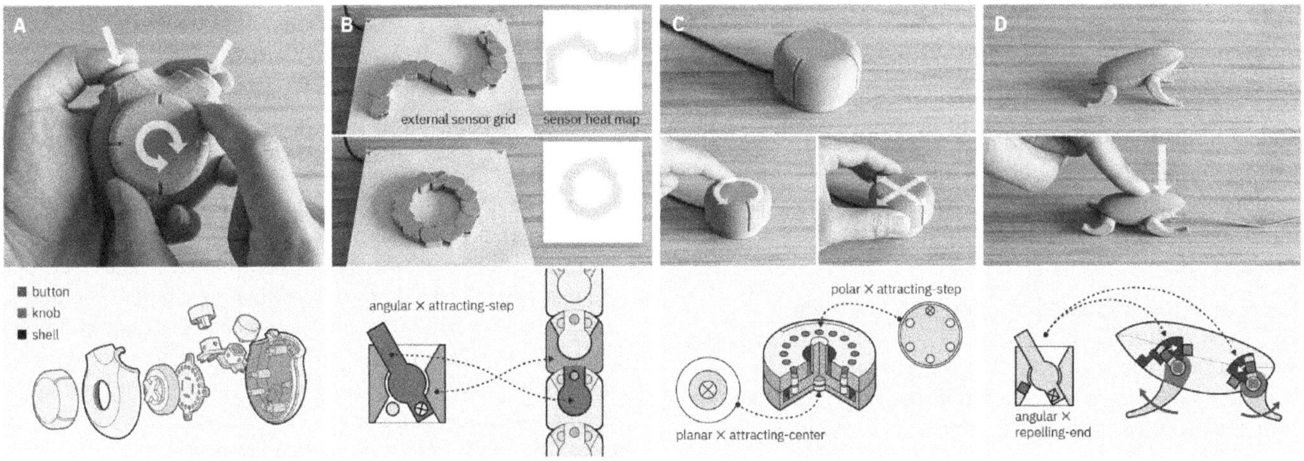


**Figure 8. Physical interfaces designed with *Mechamagnets*: A) Ergonomic Game Controller, B) Switch Snake, C) Sliding Dial, and D) Toy Frog Button.**

First, inputs are designed in CAD along with the other parts of a physical interface (Figure 7A); at this stage, the haptic profile is also specified and recesses are created for static magnets and linear Hall effect sensors. Second, the parts are fabricated with 3D printing (Figure 7B). Magnets and sensors are then inserted into these 3D printed parts (Figure 7C). Third, the parts are assembled to form the physical interface, and sensors are connected to a microcontroller (Figure 7D). We demonstrate this workflow and the capabilities of this technique through a series of novel physical interfaces designed with *Mechamagnets*.

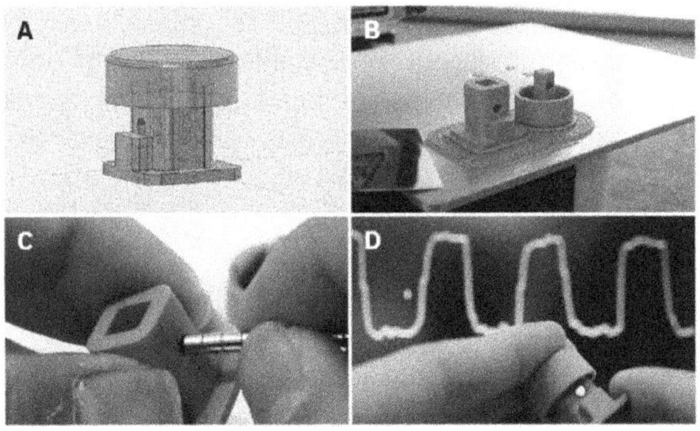


**Figure 7. Mechamagnets workflow: A) Modelling in CAD, B) fabricating parts with FDM printing, C) embedding magnets, and D) embedding and calibrating linear Hall effect sensors.**

### Creating a new physical interface: Ergonomic Game Controller

Physical interface design is an important part of the gaming industry. For example, video game company *Nintendo* [26] has released a myriad of game platforms with unique physical controllers, such as the *Wii*, *3DS*, *Switch* and its *Labo* construction kit extension. We demonstrate how *Mechamagnets* supports the industrial design of such interfaces by creating a set of physical game controllers for a *Pong*-like game (Figure 1C, 8A). The game controllers were designed based on the hand size measurements of one of the authors. Push buttons were created by adding end caps to the *linear × attracting-center* input model, and the knob employs the *polar × attracting-step* input model. Inputs were positioned for easy access by the user. Each button was instrumented with a single linear Hall effect sensor, while the knob has two sensors to measure angle of rotation. *Mechamagnet's* input models enabled us to explore and specify haptic profiles its specific application. For instance, the game's main interaction is turning the knob, and we investigated different step intervals for this interaction's haptic feedback. We settled on 16 steps to create a satisfying sequence of light "bumps" when turning the knob. In addition, we were able to rapidly experiment with different actuation thresholds for the push button, till we found a point that the user felt was most responsive.

### Compounding similar inputs: Switch Snake

The *Mechamagnets* taxonomy offers a range of basic input models on which designers can build and extend. The Switch Snake demonstrates how we compound an input model to create a novel physical interface. It comprises a chain of twelve *angular × attracting-step* modules. Each module has three steps separated at a 30° angle, which turn relative to one other. The schematic in Figure 8B shows how we connected multiple *angular × attracting-step* inputs by combining their solid and hollow bodies in a staggered fashion. Switch Snake is designed as a tangible interface where users manipulate its shape, and its modularity enables it to scale up to any length. Rather than embed sensors into 3D printed parts, we used an external grid of linear Hall effect sensors [13,27] to recognize the shape and position of this object (as shown in Figure 8B).

### Blending different interactions: Sliding Dial

*Mechamagnet's* simple spatial constraints and haptic profiles also facilitate designers to blend different input types. We demonstrate this with the Sliding Dial (Figure 8C). This physical interface combines the *planar × attracting-center* input with the *polar × attracting-step* input to create a hybrid input that affords both sliding and turning. We first modelled a spatial constraint in the form of a hollow disc that supports sliding freely along its plane and turning about its axis. We embedded the mechanism for the turning interaction in the top surface of this cavity, and mechanism for the sliding interaction in the bottom surface. Four linear Hall effect sensors instrument this interface: two for the turning interaction to measure angle of rotation, and two for the sliding interaction to measure displacement. We demonstrate how the Sliding Dial supports manipulating multi-dimensional controls for applications such as sound editing or graphic design.

### Embedding Haptic and Functional Movements: Toy Frog Buttons

The input models offered by *Mechamagnets* can apply beyond conventional input components to create haptic and functional movements in a physical user interface. To demonstrate this, we put ourselves in the shoes of a toy designer and created a set of toy frogs (Figure 8D). We articulated the front and back legs of each toy frog with the *angular* ✕ *repelling-step* input model. When the frog is pressed and released, its legs snap back with enough force to propel it into a different position. We embedded a linear Hall effect sensor in each toy frog, which measures the proximity of the magnets in the front mechanism. This transforms the toy frogs into a set of unconventional push buttons that hop around, and we use them to control a *Frogger*-like game.

## LIMITATIONS & FUTURE WORK

### Taxonomy limitations

The *Mechamagnets* taxonomy illustrates the design space of basic physical input models possible with this technique, and we expect that designers can extend these inputs to create many new physical interfaces. However, this taxonomy certainly does not completely cover all types of physical inputs. We proposed five spatial constraints as building blocks for designers to compose different physical inputs. These are limited to inputs with active moving components afforded by these spatial constraints. In particular, it excludes inputs that do not involve moving a physical part, such as touchpads and trackpads.

### Size constraints

The size of magnets and 3D printing resolution constrains the minimum size of interfaces composed of *Mechamagnet* components. In this paper, we explored using only 1/8″ by 1/8″ or 1/4″ by 1/16″ neodymium magnets, and commodity desktop FDM machines to fabricate *Mechamagnet* components. By keeping the inventory and process simple, we aimed to create an accessible technique for other designs and makers. For future work, we aim to create manual and automated tools that assist inserting differently sized (including smaller) magnets, as well as higher resolution additive manufacturing processes. Inter-magnet interactions also affect the distance between *Mechamagnet* components; placing components close to each other influences the haptic profiles (Figure 3D), and might trigger false positives when using embedded Hall effect sensors. Our heuristic, at this moment of writing, is to keep a minimum lateral separation of 3/8″ between components when using 1/8″ by 1/8″ neodymium magnets. The Hall effect sensors we employ for the two sizes of magnets used (Table 2) has an effective sensing radius of 10mm. By extension, the magnets participating in sensing a component should be at least 10mm apart for the sensors in another component. A tool that simulates the resultant 3D magnetic field generated by multiple *Mechamagnet* components can optimize the placement of components and sensors. *Magneto-haptics* [15] not only offers an efficient method to compute this, but also an approach of designing more complex haptic profiles with static magnets along a movement path. Future work will explore incorporating the *Magneto-haptics* simulation to inform the design of assemblies with *Mechamagnet* components.

### Sensing constraints

We are interested in developing a technique to make integrated and portable prototypes of physical interfaces. As such, we investigated how to spatially arrange individual linear Hall effect sensors to detect different magnet movements. However, embedding these individual sensors for every single *Mechamagnet* component can be a time-consuming process. Such an approach also requires the interface to be physically tethered by wires to power the sensors as well as for data communication. For tabletop *Mechamagnet* interfaces (such as Figure 8C and D), an external sensor grid (see [13] and Figure 8B) can easily replace the embedded sensors, and thus free the interface from a physical tether. We plan to explore this external sensing approach in more depth for future work with surface-based interfaces. For portable applications, we aim to develop a physical computing kit, including breakout boards with pre-configured sensor arrangements, which easily "plug" into 3D printed parts.

### CAD & design assistance

In this paper, we focused on generalizing this technique to make it applicable to different CAD and embedded electronics platforms. However, this also expects designers and makers be reasonably proficient in these practices to use *Mechamagnets* effectively. As mentioned above, we aim to develop a physical computing kit for *Mechamagnets* that facilitates placing and computing data from embedded Hall effect sensors. We also plan to further develop the current taxonomy into an interactive application. This interactive taxonomy will enable other designers to explore and customize each model based on different parameters, as well as simulate haptic feedback profiles and inform sensor placement. Designers can then download these customized models for further work in a CAD application they are comfortable with.

## ACKNOWLEDGEMENTS

We want to thank our colleagues at ATLAS and our reviewers for their feedback. This research is supported (in part) by the National Research Foundation, Prime Minister's Office, Singapore under its International Research Centres in Singapore Funding Initiative.

## REFERENCES


[1] Andrea Bianchi and Ian Oakley. 2015. MagnID: Tracking Multiple Magnetic Tokens. In *Proceedings of the Ninth International Conference on Tangible, Embedded, and Embodied Interaction* (TEI '15), 61–68. https://doi.org/10.1145/2677199.2680582

[2] BMW. *Haptics. BMW quality.* Retrieved May 16, 2018 from https://www.youtube.com/watch?v=BCPmAK8SmEc&feature=youtu.be

[3] Xiang "Anthony" Chen, Stelian Coros, and Scott E. Hudson. 2018. Medley: A Library of Embeddables to Explore Rich Material Properties for 3D Printed Objects. In *Proceedings of the 2018 CHI Conference on Human Factors in Computing Systems* (CHI '18), 162:1–162:12. https://doi.org/10.1145/3173574.3173736

[4] Xiang "Anthony" Chen, Jeeeun Kim, Jennifer Mankoff, Tovi Grossman, Stelian Coros, and Scott E. Hudson. 2016. Reprise: A Design Tool for Specifying, Generating, and Customizing 3D Printable Adaptations on Everyday Objects. In *Proceedings of the 29th Annual Symposium on User Interface Software and Technology* (UIST '16), 29–39. https://doi.org/10.1145/2984511.2984512

[5] Ross Eisenbeis. 2017. Using Linear Hall Effect Sensors to Measure Angle.

[6] Jan B. F. van Erp, Ki-Uk Kyung, Sebastian Kassner, Jim Carter, Stephen Brewster, Gerhard Weber, and Ian Andrew. 2010. Setting the Standards for Haptic and Tactile Interactions: ISO's Work. In *Haptics: Generating and Perceiving Tangible Sensations* (Lecture Notes in Computer Science), 353–358. https://doi.org/10.1007/978-3-642-14075-4_52

[7] Andrea Foletto, Andreas Friedrich, and Sanchit Gupta. Allegro MicroSystems - Analysis of a Hall-Effect System With Two Linear Sensor ICs for 30 mm Displacement. Retrieved August 3, 2018 from https://www.allegromicro.com/en/Design-Center/Technical-Documents/Hall-Effect-Sensor-IC-Publications/Hall-Effect-System-With-Two-Linear-Sensor-ICs.aspx

[8] Saul Greenberg and Chester Fitchett. 2001. Phidgets: Easy Development of Physical Interfaces Through Physical Widgets. In *Proceedings of the 14th Annual ACM Symposium on User Interface Software and Technology* (UIST '01), 209–218. https://doi.org/10.1145/502348.502388

[9] Sungjae Hwang, Myungwook Ahn, and Kwang-yun Wohn. 2013. MagGetz: Customizable Passive Tangible Controllers on and Around Conventional Mobile Devices. In *Proceedings of the 26th Annual ACM Symposium on User Interface Software and Technology* (UIST '13), 411–416. https://doi.org/10.1145/2501988.2501991

[10] Alexandra Ion, Johannes Frohnhofen, Ludwig Wall, Robert Kovacs, Mirela Alistar, Jack Lindsay, Pedro Lopes, Hsiang-Ting Chen, and Patrick Baudisch. 2016. Metamaterial Mechanisms. In *Proceedings of the 29th Annual Symposium on User Interface Software and Technology* (UIST '16), 529–539. https://doi.org/10.1145/2984511.2984540

[11] Sunjun Kim and Geehyuk Lee. 2013. Haptic Feedback Design for a Virtual Button Along Force-displacement Curves. In *Proceedings of the 26th Annual ACM Symposium on User Interface Software and Technology* (UIST '13), 91–96. https://doi.org/10.1145/2501988.2502041

[12] Johnny C. Lee, Daniel Avrahami, Scott E. Hudson, Jodi Forlizzi, Paul H. Dietz, and Darren Leigh. 2004. The Calder Toolkit: Wired and Wireless Components for Rapidly Prototyping Interactive Devices. In *Proceedings of the 5th Conference on Designing Interactive Systems: Processes, Practices, Methods, and Techniques* (DIS '04), 167–175. https://doi.org/10.1145/1013115.1013139

[13] Rong-Hao Liang, Liwei Chan, Hung-Yu Tseng, Han-Chih Kuo, Da-Yuan Huang, De-Nian Yang, and Bing-Yu Chen. 2014. GaussBricks: Magnetic Building Blocks for Constructive Tangible Interactions on Portable Displays. In *Proceedings of the SIGCHI Conference on Human Factors in Computing Systems* (CHI '14), 3153–3162. https://doi.org/10.1145/2556288.2557105

[14] Jock Mackinlay, Stuart K. Card, and George G. Robertson. 1990. A Semantic Analysis of the Design Space of Input Devices. *Hum.-Comput. Interact.* 5, 2: 145–190. https://doi.org/10.1207/s15327051hci0502&3_2

[15] Masa Ogata. 2018. Magneto-Haptics: Embedding Magnetic Force Feedback for Physical Interactions. In *Proceedings of the 31st Annual ACM Symposium on User Interface Software and Technology* (UIST '18), 737–743. https://doi.org/10.1145/3242587.3242615

[16] Valkyrie Savage, Colin Chang, and Björn Hartmann. 2013. Sauron: embedded single-camera sensing of printed physical user interfaces. In *Proceedings of the 26th annual ACM symposium on User interface software and technology*, 447–456. https://doi.org/10.1145/2501988.2501992

[17] Valkyrie Savage, Sean Follmer, Jingyi Li, and Björn Hartmann. 2015. Makers' Marks: Physical Markup for Designing and Fabricating Functional Objects. In *Proceedings of the 28th Annual ACM Symposium on User Interface Software & Technology* (UIST '15), 103–108. https://doi.org/10.1145/2807442.2807508

[18] Valkyrie Savage, Andrew Head, Björn Hartmann, Dan B. Goldman, Gautham Mysore, and Wilmot Li. 2015. Lamello: Passive Acoustic Sensing for Tangible Input Components. In *Proceedings of the 33rd Annual ACM Conference on Human Factors in Computing Systems*, 1277–1280. https://doi.org/10.1145/2702123.2702207

[19] Christopher R. Wagner, Nicholas Stylopoulos, Patrick G. Jackson, and Robert D. Howe. 2007. The Benefit of Force Feedback in Surgery: Examination of Blunt Dissection. *Presence: Teleoperators and Virtual Environments* 16, 3: 252–262. https://doi.org/10.1162/pres.16.3.252

[20] Katrin Wolf and Peter D. Bennett. 2013. Haptic Cues: Texture As a Guide for Non-visual Tangible Interaction. In *CHI '13 Extended Abstracts on Human Factors in Computing Systems* (CHI EA '13), 1599–1604. https://doi.org/10.1145/2468356.2468642

[21] Anson Wong and Tom Li. 2016. The complete guide to mechanical keyboard switches for gaming. *PC Gamer*. Retrieved August 5, 2018 from https://www.pcgamer.com/best-mechanical-switches-for-gaming/

[22] Kentaro Yasu. 2017. Magnetic Plotter: A Macrotexture Design Method Using Magnetic Rubber Sheets. In *Proceedings of the 2017 CHI Conference on Human Factors in Computing Systems* (CHI '17), 4983–4993. https://doi.org/10.1145/3025453.3025702

[23] Clement Zheng and Ellen Yi-Luen Do. 2018. Mechamagnets: Tactile Mechanisms with Embedded Magnets. In *Proceedings of the Twelfth International Conference on Tangible, Embedded, and Embodied Interaction* (TEI '18), 57–64. https://doi.org/10.1145/3173225.3173268

[24] *Arduino*. Retrieved from https://www.arduino.cc/

[25] Vernier Sensor - Dual-Range Force Sensor - SEN-12873 - SparkFun Electronics. Retrieved October 31, 2018 from https://www.sparkfun.com/products/12873

[26] Nintendo - Official Site. Retrieved August 7, 2018 from https://www.nintendo.com

[27] GaussSense. *GaussToys*. Retrieved August 4, 2018 from http://gausstoys.com

# The Design of an Interactive Surface for Supporting Rehabilitation of Children with Developmental Coordination Disorder

**Jamil Joundi** **Arno Penders** **Johanna Renny Octavia** **Jelle Saldien**
Department of Industrial Systems Engineering and Product Design, Ghent University
imec-MICT-UGent
Ghent, Belgium
{jamil.joundi, arno.penders, johanna.octavia, jelle.saldien}@ugent.be

## ABSTRACT
One key concept of Tangible User Interaction is interactive surfaces, in which we transform a surface into an active interface between the physical and virtual world. In this paper we describe the design process of a novel interactive surface that can be used for movement therapy for children with Developmental Coordination Disorder (DCD). Children with DCD suffer from impairment in motor development which influences their overall movement quality and affects their daily life. Traditionally, the rehabilitation techniques and tools are often static, non-interactive, monotonous and unappealing to children. The purpose of this study is to design an interactive surface that combines physical motor exercises with digital games. Through an iterative co-creation process with patients and physiotherapists, we developed "Matti" as an interactive gaming mat to support the children during their rehabilitation, by linking the therapy exercises with digital games thus providing more engagement and better results.

### Author Keywords
Interactive surface, interactive play, rehabilitation, movement therapy, pressure sensitive devices, Developmental Coordination Disorder (DCD)

### CSS keywords
• Human-centered computing~User centered design

## INTRODUCTION
Developmental Coordination Disorder (DCD) is a condition of children having an impairment in their motor development, which causes them to have clumsiness, lack of body position awareness and difficulties performing simple motor activities. About 5-10% of children worldwide have been reported to be affected by DCD [17]. It is important to manage such impairment through motor rehabilitation, as failure to do so may influence their physical and psychological health.

Traditionally, the rehabilitation program for children with DCD is set up by the physiotherapist after carrying out an assessment of the child. The rehabilitation normally includes therapy exercises individually tailored to meet the needs of the child such as practicing gross motor skills (e.g. walking, running, hopping), balancing skills (e.g. walking on a balance beam) and coordination skills (e.g. throwing and catching ball). Generally, these therapy exercises are carried out repetitively throughout their rehabilitation process which is mainly a long period of time (several years). The repetitive protocol may introduce boredom in the therapy and lead to a depletion of motivation of the children [8]. Additionally, the tools used in the therapy exercises are mostly static and not interactive, thus may be unappealing and less fun for the children.

Our research aims to develop an interactive surface for supporting rehabilitation of children with DCD. We intend to help the physiotherapists by providing a more appealing and engaging therapy for the patients. This will be achieved by linking the therapy exercises with digital games to enhance the motivation and endurance of children throughout the rehabilitation process and thus providing better results in the long term of the rehabilitation. This paper first describes the related work in technology-assisted rehabilitation and our position within interactive surface technologies. That was defined through an iterative co-design process with both physiotherapists and children with DCD. The process is presented via its consecutive phases (Explorative, Early Prototype, Visual Prototype, Functional and Final Prototype), with each phase including insights from the evaluations of the previous phase. Furthermore we present the Final Prototype Matti, its main advantages and its technical implementation. Finally we reflect on the result and the process and suggest some improvements in future work.


*TEI '19, March 17–20, 2019, Tempe, AZ, USA*

ACM ISBN 978-1-4503-6196-5/19/03…$15.00
https://doi.org/10.1145/3294109.3295648

## RELATED WORK

### Technology-assisted rehabilitation

It has been widely recognized that one of the crucial problems in rehabilitation is maintaining patient motivation in performing therapy exercises. Motivation of patients in physical rehabilitation is considered to be one of the most important factors in determining the success of the therapy [26]. The integration of technology to assist rehabilitation is thought to be promising to play a role in improving patient abilities and motivation.

Technology-assisted rehabilitation has been investigated to support a range of rehabilitation such as for cerebral palsy [22,36], disabled children [27,29], Alzheimer [14], Parkinson's [39], stroke [15,19] and many more. This comes in many forms of interactive systems. For example, serious games designed to support balance rehabilitation therapy of cerebral palsy patients [22], virtual reality-based systems for stroke rehabilitation [15] and pediatric rehabilitation for children with cerebral palsy [36], augmented reality for rehabilitation of cognitive disabled children [31], interactive collaborative environments for disabled children [27], and also tangible interfaces developed to support post-stroke rehabilitation therapy [19]. Adaptability of the therapy to the needs of the patient is a crucial pain-point in current therapy. This could be solved by easily adaptable exergames [3].

In particular, exergaming has shown to be promising in the field of technology-assisted rehabilitation. A lot of research has been done on the motivation of patients when using exergames. For example, the Dance Dance Revolution and many other test with dance pads have been performed to measure the effect of games in rehabilitation [6]. Exergaming using existing consoles like Wii has also been tested as a mean for patients with neurological disabilities to achieve more physical activity in the context of rehabilitation [30]. The Wii Fit Balance board is a tool that is often used to do clinical trials in patients with balance disorders [12,16,38]. These researches suggest that exergaming in rehabilitation is more engaging and enjoyable than doing therapy exercises in a traditional manner.

### Tangible user interface for rehabilitation

A tangible user interface (TUI) allows users to interact with digital information through the manipulation of common physical objects and/or architectural surfaces [20]. Not only can the device be useful to interact with as a mean of rehabilitation, but the results can also be measured and monitored. This type of system is not only a tangible user interface, but can also keep track of the data and serve as a measurement tool apart from being a practising device [32].

There has been a number of rehabilitation systems developed based on TUI approach since it is considered to be more intuitive and accessible for patients with low level of technology experience. For example, a TUI built to be used for written and spoken comprehension therapy in aphasic patients [31], and a pervasive training system providing tangible interactions in physical rehabilitation for the upper limbs [34]. In these studies, TUI was mainly chosen as the technology to support the rehabilitation because of the advantage of the manipulation of physical objects that is considered to ensure an effective transfer of therapy exercises into everyday life activities. Another example of a TUI that is used in rehabilitation is Virtual Reality. VR can be used as a tool for post stroke diagnosis and rehabilitation exercises [2]. VR also allows the therapist to practise with programmed everyday life activities which he can still control. Immersiveness of games is an added value by using all senses and the whole body to immerse players [6]. Applications using camera systems are also very interesting for rehabilitation purposes mainly because of the low cost [28].

#### *Interactive surface for rehabilitation*

One of the key concepts of TUI is interactive surfaces, in which we transform each surface within architectural space (e.g. walls, desktops, ceilings, doors, windows) into an active interface between the physical and virtual worlds [20]. Interactive surfaces have become popular in the area of rehabilitation as it supports natural and direct interaction which provides an important advantage for patients. Research has shown a number of interactive surfaces developed in the context of rehabilitation such as interactive tabletops for physical rehabilitation training [1,33], tabletops used in neural rehabilitation [3-5,24] and motor rehabilitation [1], and interactive walls for dementia patients in nursing homes [25]. Mixed approaches are also possible, with interactive tabletop screens combined with cameras [37].

Besides that, we see a growing interest in the use of interactive floors for rehabilitation purposes such as stimulating physical activity of psychogeriatric nursing home residents [9] and rehabilitating persons with balance problems due to stroke or disorder [7,10]. These researches have shown that interactive surfaces technology on the floors is a promising tool for physical and balance rehabilitation. To date, no research has been conducted to develop interactive surfaces (i.e. floors) to assist balance rehabilitation for children with DCD. The data gathered throughout the exercises/games could be used to quantitatively evaluate progress [2]. These same exercises could be used to help in the diagnosis of a patient [12,16,38].

Within interactive surface technology, four different categories can be distinguished. The first category represents pressure tiles [25], that can be used (e.g. wall tiles, floor tiles and table tiles) to detect applied forces and can be arranged in a modular way. In the second category we distinguish pressure mats [10] that are often used to assess balance in persons with issues in gross motoric skills, but also for weighing persons or objects. In the third category we find devices that use projection or projected light [9], for example interactive floor projection, interactive whiteboards, etc. The last category is touchscreens which lead to a more immersive experience and are generally used in interactive or multi-touch tabletops [1,3-5,37]. Figure 1 gives an overview of the different categories used for interactive surface technologies. Based on the user centered design process, we positioned our new surface technology in the area combining touchscreens and pressure mats (see shaded region).

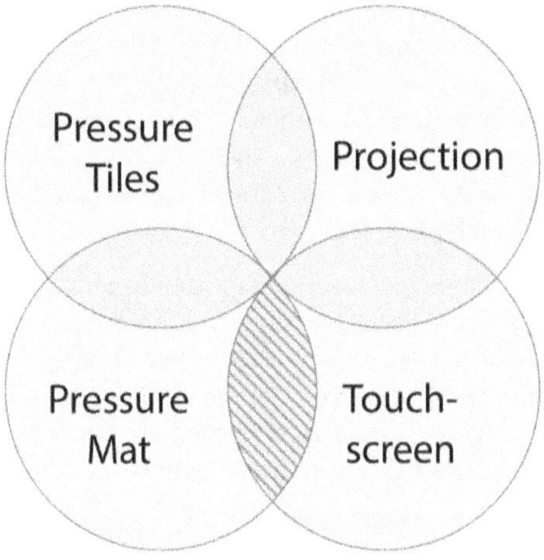


**Figure 1. Technology positioning of the interactive surface**

## DESIGN PROCESS

In the next sections, we present the development of the interactive surface in the field of user centred design (UCD). UCD is a broad term to describe a design process in which end-users influence how a design takes shape. Over time several methods were created to do this. In general the user-centered design concept can be divided into 3 stages [18,40].

1. Stage 1; An early focus on users and tasks: methods like interviews, discussions, observations are used. Afterwards techniques such as personas, scenarios and task analysis are valuable to process and capture the data.
2. Stage 2; Empirical measurement of usage: in this stage the concept or prototype is evaluated with the end-users (as presented in Table 1). Their performance, thoughts, and attitudes are recorded and analyzed.
3. Stage 3; Iterative process. Designers will have to improve their prototypes or restart entirely based on the results of the second stage. When this is accomplished, the second stage will have to be repeated.

This last stage is a very important one and cannot be underestimated. Earlier research suggests that the quantity of interactions with users and time spent interacting with users alone is not linked with better design outcome, but that iterative evaluation of concepts by users may be of particular value to design prototypes [23].

| *Phase of the design process* | *Number of participants* | *Number of physiotherapists* |
|---|---|---|
| Exploration phase | 1 child with DCD | 1 |
| Early prototype | 12 elementary school children + 2 children with DCD | 1 |
| Visual prototype | 57 children (7 of them with DCD) | 4 |
| Functional prototype | 2 children with DCD | 5 |
| Final prototype | 15 children + 17 children with DCD | 5 |

**Table 1. Description of participants and physiotherapists in different design phases.**

This way of working is also very compatible with the human centered design process [21]. The designer understands, specifies, produces and evaluates his design. After the last step, the designers can go back to any of the three previous steps according to evaluation. In our design process, we evaluated at every iteration of a prototype what things should be changed according to the stakeholders. Throughout the process we were able to specify the context and user requirements better. In the next prototype we produce design solutions to meet the user requirements.

### Exploration phase

In the beginning of the design process, we started the research through a first interview with a self-employed physiotherapist to understand the rehabilitation for children with DCD and to observe which kind of therapy exercises are given to them. We came to know that in the therapy session, the patient has to perform several exercises such as playing all consecutive notes on a piano mat laying on the floor, writing exercises and doing a balance exercise on a ball.

In this phase, we tested out with a patient (boy) of 12 years old with DCD how our very first idea of the interactive floor would be like and how the patient would perceive it. We showed him an online maze game and a mat with four pieces of paper on it. We asked the child to stand on a mat and explore the mat as a controller to play the maze game. A Wizard-of-Oz approach was used in this exploration test. For example, when the child stepped backwards on the mat, simultaneously we pressed the down arrow button on the keyboard to give input of direction to the maze game. From this test, we found out that it became clear for the child that the pieces of paper control the virtual character in the maze game shown on the screen. We tested with this only so briefly with one patient and one therapist, to see if the concept works and what a general reaction was to the idea.

From the exploration phase, we learned:

1) There are already interactive exercises (often without games).

2) Physiotherapists like that patients can do the exercises more independently, but they have to be performed correctly.
3) The child was able to perform the expected exercise.

### Early prototype

After the exploration phase, we designed a quick and dirty prototype v0 with Makey Makey [13], cardboard and aluminum foil/pads. This prototype v0 was first tested with 12 elementary school children (from 6 to 9 years old, 5 boys and 7 girls, no balance disorder), then tested with 2 children (10 and 11 years old, both boys) who have DCD. In the test, we selected existing online games that are easy and slow enough to play by performing stepping actions. In this testing only qualitative testing was done. The children were asked if they wanted to play on the Matti, if they liked playing on the mat. We also asked if there were games that they liked a lot, to know what games interest this age group.

As shown in Figure 2, we used pieces of paper with left and right foot images (color-coded) in the paper prototype on the mat. This prototype served mainly as an early prototype to test if the layout is suitable for the patient and how a color-coded system is perceived.

**Figure 2. Testing of the early prototype: the layout (left) and the color-coded system (right)**

From the early prototype test, we learned that:

1) The tested layout worked as expected and working with colors is an intuitive way to give direction-related instructions to children.
2) Clear indications are beneficial for helping children find out how they should do the exercise. The children were still able to perform exercises with broader instructions, but they will not do the exercises accurately. More specific instructions will result in a better rehabilitation process.
3) An anti-slip layer is necessary to prevent creases. A general problem observed was that the children were not careful with the prototype at all, therefore the real product should be strong and durable.

### Visual prototype

Based on the testing of the early prototype, we developed a more visual version of the early cardboard prototype v0 with other materials and first adaptations (such as anti-slip for the floor), as can be seen in Figure 3. Color coded feet made out of textile were sewed on the mat. In this prototype v1 we used sky textile because it can be cleaned easily.

We developed three mini games in Unity gaming engine in this prototype v1 to see which games could have added value and supported the rehabilitation of children with DCD, as shown in Figure 4. We also made it able for the physiotherapist to change the distance of the feet by replacing the cut-out foot on different positions according to the abilities of the patient. Underneath the positions of the feet on the mat, aluminum on-off switches were placed. The aluminum plates were separated with cardboard and connected to a Makey Makey.

We tested if the layout with colors was visually pleasing and how long the prototype v1 lasted without breaking (visual and practical testing). We also tested briefly if feeling beneath your feet when you are standing in the middle is a necessary feature. This feature seemed not very important to 4 physiotherapists that we involved in the evaluation.

**Figure 3. Testing of the visual prototype**

**Figure 4. The mini games developed in the visual prototype**

From the test, we knew that the technique with aluminum plates did not work, after a while the contacts broke and allowed current to flow through. The sky textile made the prototype v1 quite heavy. The physiotherapists suggested that there should be a bigger variety in the games for the different types of therapy exercises.

The same prototype v1 was further developed for testing as shown in Figure 5. The prototype v1.2 still used the same technology but employed a different way to connect the wires. It also used online games to do the testing because in this manner many different games could be tested.

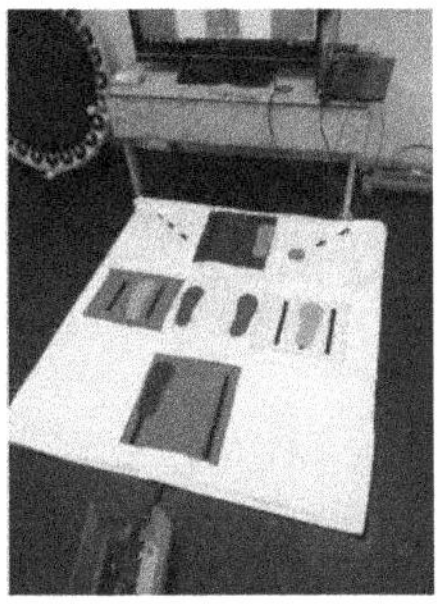

**Figure 5. The further developed visual prototype**

The prototype v1.2 was tested with 57 children (40 boys and 17 girls, with the age ranging from 6 to 12 years old). The test was done in therapy centre with the same four physiotherapists. In this test, all children were diagnosed with balance disorders. Seven participants of the test had DCD. We divided the children in two groups: group A (exercising on the gaming mat prototype) and group B (performing regular balance exercises without the gaming mat prototype). The children were selected on their balance abilities. The criteria for the study were: (1) the birth date is between January 2015 and December 2010; (2) receiving physical therapy; and (3) a score $\leq$ percentile 25 for balance on the Movement Assessment Battery for Children (M-ABC). Reasons for exclusion were an IQ below 70 or inability to perform the exercises on the gaming mat. In this way, 64 children with balance problems were selected to participate in this study. The design used for this study was a cross-over design. Children were allocated randomly to one of two groups. Each group did the experimental intervention and the control intervention, but in a different sequence. Group A started for 6 weeks with the Matti setup followed by 6 weeks of regular balance exercises, group B did the same interventions but in a reversed order.

During the test, we evaluated the outcome of the Movement Assessment Battery for Children (M-ABC). Figure 6 shows the distribution of the Component Standard Score for the intervention with gaming mat (group A) and without gaming mat (group B). During post-hoc analysis with the Independent Samples T test, no significant differences were found between group A and group B. So, it can be concluded that no difference is found between exercising with the gaming mat and the regular balance exercises. This also indicates that the results of the rehabilitation with the gaming mat prototype v1.2 were as equally good as traditional therapy.

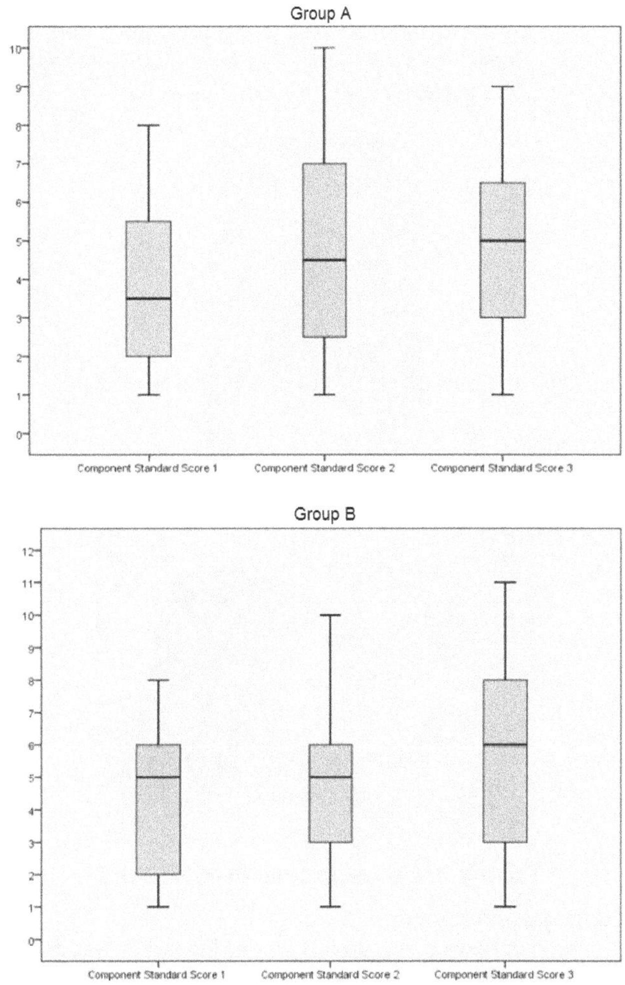


**Figure 6. The results on the visual prototype evaluation: comparing the rehabilitation with the gaming mat (top) and the rehabilitation without the gaming mat (bottom)**

However, when comparing the fun and motivation aspects, the questionnaire results showed that no significant differences were found between these two groups [35]. This indicated that the therapy with the gaming mat was not proven to be more/less fun and more/less motivating compared to the regular therapy without the gaming mat. This may be caused by the technical problems experienced during testing which might bring frustration to the participants.

From the visual prototype test, we also found out:

1) Many online games were too fast-paced.
2) The children did not put their full attention on doing the exercises right, but only trying to do them as quickly as possible without looking when the games were too fast.

3) After many test trials the connection of the buttons broke down again after being pressed too often.
4) Games with adjustable speed should be developed for the children because it was frustrating when the games were too fast. The next prototype should work perfectly to avoid frustration as well.

**Figure 7. Testing of the functional prototype**

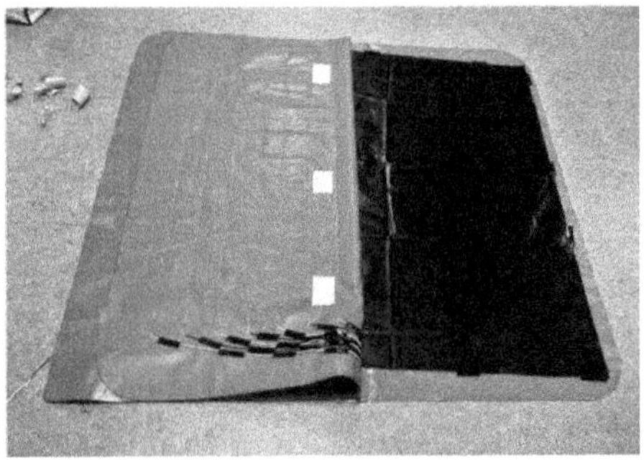

**Figure 8. The inside of the functional prototype**

### Functional prototype

A new iteration on the prototype v2 (Figure 7) was made using new technologies and integrated LEDs in the mat. These LEDs made the exercises easier to understand. According to our qualitative observations during the visual prototype, the LEDs were necessary due to the demand of colour indications in prototype v1. It also allowed more freedom and interactions when testing different games and ways of playing. LEDs were chosen over projection for ease of use and higher visibility. This prototype v2 was built with conductive yarn and Velostat as a sensor [11], this conductive yarn was sewn on coated heavy-duty fabric as shown in Figure 8. In this prototype v2 we also started developing the platform, as can be seen in Figure 9. The contact pressure can be measured in time and plotted out as shown in Figure 10.

A soft foam was also introduced to avoid feeling the LEDs when standing on the mat. A white removable textile sleeve was made to easily open the product and clean if necessary. An Arduino Mega was integrated for more control over the application. To do this a solderless breadboard was used for all the components.

This prototype was also tested with 2 DCD patients (two boys age 10 and 12) in the workspace of the physiotherapist where we tested our early prototype. This test was also just a qualitative test to confirm that the children understood the prototype.

We learned that:

1) The implementation of pressure sensing in the platform as a new technique gave insights of the user movements. The therapists reacted very positively to this feature because now they can easily see imbalance in patients and how much pressure they are exerting.
2) The use of conductive yarn was an expensive solution due to the expensive material and manual labor. To create a product that can be used commercially, more optimization was needed.
3) The white sleeve became dirty after several uses with children and transport.

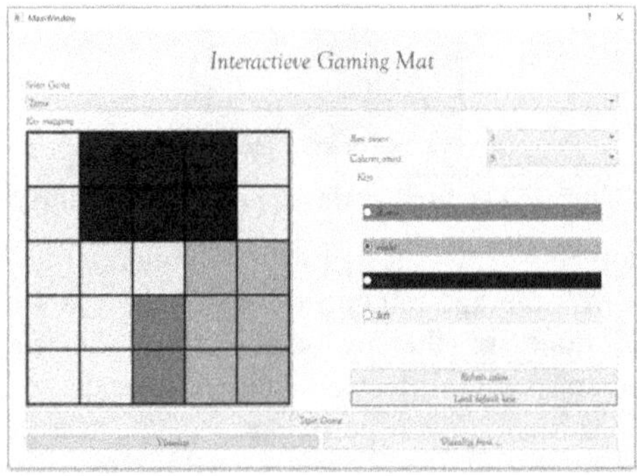


**Figure 9. Layout scheme of the functional prototype**

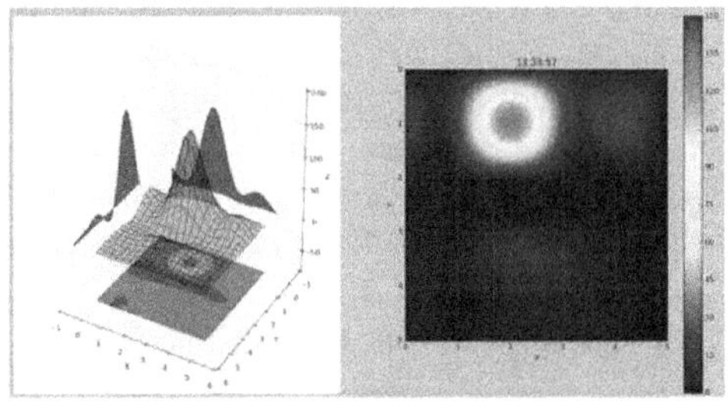

**Figure 10. Software for pressure sensor analysis**

### Final prototype

The final prototype v3 (Figure 11) was internally the same as the functional prototype v2, but the conductive yarn was replaced by copper strips which were attached to plastic sheets with Velostat in between. The electronics were now placed on a soldering breadboard. For the cover around the mat, we asked a professional tailor to make a sleeve with a zipper to open the product easily. A different type of gray waterproof textile was used to make the product washable.

We developed one maze game (Figure 12) that allowed the physiotherapists to change the difficulty level and the speed. The development of an online platform was started, so that the 4 physiotherapists could track the progress of the patients and objectively see how they are doing according to previous sessions.

We briefly tested the maze game during a demonstration session with 15 different children. We found that the function of several difficulty levels turned out to be very important for both the physiotherapist and the patient and they thought many difficulty levels should be created (not only easy-medium-hard).

A more detailed evaluation with 17 children with DCD (age 5 to 11 years old) has been done over several weeks. In the evaluation, a questionnaire was employed to see if the motivation using the final prototype was better than the current therapy. The results from the evaluation are currently being analyzed and will be presented in the next publication.

**Figure 11. Demonstrations of the final prototype**

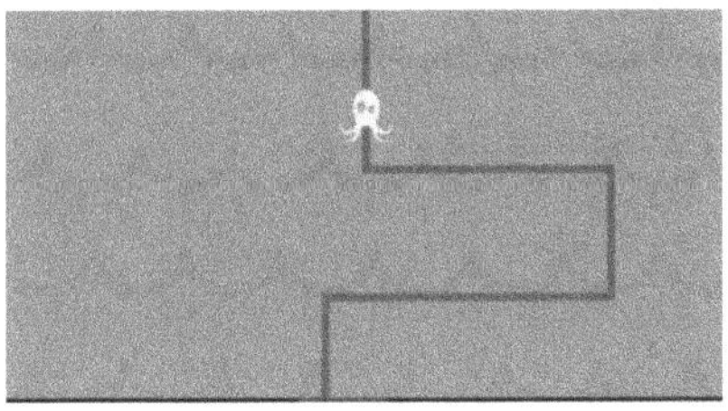

**Figure 12. The maze game in the final prototype**

## SPECIFICATIONS OF THE FINAL PROTOTYPE: MATTI

After a thorough and iterative development process with physiotherapists and patients, we created Matti as an interactive gaming mat. As can be seen in Figure 13, Matti is equipped with pressure sensors and integrated LEDs. The pressure sensors are placed in a grid of 225 (15x15) pressure and light points.

The light points and pressure points are addressed by an Arduino Mega. The pressure grid inside the mat consists of 3 layers. On the bottom layer is a plastic sheet with 15 vertical copper tape strips. The sheet in the middle is *Velostat* (which is a pressure sensitive plastic). On the top layer there is also a plastic sheet with 15 horizontal copper tape strips. The bottom layer has a voltage of 5V attached to it. The Velostat functions as a resistor when it is not pressed. The top layer voltage is measured out. Even though any resolution could be chosen, we used 15 rows of addressable *LED strips*. The strips are divided in four blocks of 4, 4, 4 and 3 strips. This was done in order to have an even spread of light (otherwise the light further away from the voltage source would dim).

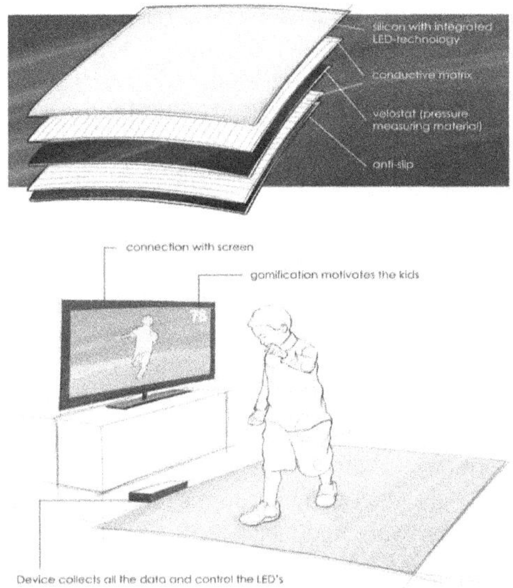


**Figure 13. Matti as interactive gaming mat for rehabilitation**

On the *Arduino Mega* 15 digital out pins are used and 15 analog in pins are used for reading how much pressure is on the mat. Four pulse width modulation (pwm) pins are used to address the LEDs (15 strips of 1m). A capacitor was used to stabilize the current coming from the power adaptor. The pressure values are registered via 15 analog in pins on the arduino. All the components (*capacitor* and *resistors*) were soldered on a breadboard that is used as a shield for the arduino Mega. The wires that connect to the copper tape strips are connected to the breadboard via bus connector *ribbon cables*. The Arduino is still connected to the computer via a cable for the serial communication. The code on the arduino reads the input values and returns them in a string of values, these values are then plotted out or used as input in games.

The software on the Arduino was made using the *Arduino IDE*. The game was written in Java using the *Eclipse IDE*. The games are developed especially for the mat. Matti is also developed as an open-ended design so it would be possible for the physiotherapists to adapt the exercises accordingly to the needs of the patients. An online platform was developed as well together with a website. The goal of this website is to get the online platform to be used by many therapists and collaborate or contribute with feedback.

On top of the top sheet we placed a *urethane foam* with 3 cm thickness to make the mat more comfortable for the user when standing on it. The sleeve of the product is also provided with a zipper so that the user can put it in the washing machine. The Arduino and electrical components are put in a 3D printed casing.

The development of the technology in this research was done in such a way that the resolution of any number of pressure sensitive rows and columns can be chosen and the size of the developed product can be adapted to any project. When interactive surfaces are used for different applications, other resolutions are necessary. Our proposed layered technology (copper tape, Velostat, and addressable LEDs) allows to easily adapt to the desired size and resolution (cfr touchscreen technologies). Furthermore, this technology may also be used to construct vertical (e.g. wall mounted) interactive surfaces.

Considering the added value of interactive surface technologies, we characterize Matti to have an easy setup, have better visibility in daylight conditions (compared to projection), have accurate force sensing (compared to tiles), cheaper, more adaptable and have direct visual feedback (compared to pressure mats), and deliver better results in use and performance. Additionally, the great customizability of Matti allows for other different forms and sizes of interactive surfaces such as walls and tables.

## CONCLUSION

In this research we have developed Matti, an interactive gaming mat created as a tangible user interface for supporting motor rehabilitation of children with DCD. The development process of Matti was carried out iteratively through a series of designing, rapid prototyping, and testing with physiotherapist and patients. Throughout the development process, we started with an early prototype (v0), a visual prototype (v1), a functional prototype (v2) and finished with a final prototype (v3). The prototype developed in this research started from a very rapid, but not so durable technique of production. Throughout the process of making new prototypes and development the product became more and more durable, cheaper, more usable and accurate for the physiotherapists and patients. The production techniques became also quicker. The current state of Matti has shown its feasibility to be used in a real therapy setting for rehabilitation of children with DCD. We expect that this product can be used as a supporting device to give therapy exercises and motivate children at the same time. Current limitations of the system are not a lot of games available for the children to play and the product malfunctions sometimes.

## FUTURE WORK

From the development process, we found that the plastic sheets inside the product were too thick, which made the mat too heavy and difficult to carry. The copper tape was not an optimal solution for the electrical conduction because of shears when bent too much. A good replacement is conductive textile. We learned that the technology should be improved further, and an industrial partner should be contacted to make a durable and precise pressure sensor for the product.

From the first testing, it turned out that the therapy exercises on the mat were performed equally as good as in traditional exercises. However, it was not yet sufficient to show the increase in motivation. Therefore, a thorough evaluation of the final prototype being used in the real rehabilitation context/setting of children with DCD should be carried out to analyze the impact in supporting their motivation during rehabilitation. To date, we have done the user evaluation on the final prototype and currently we are analyzing the results that we plan to discuss in the next publication. A new study on the medical impact on the patients is planned for next year. We already have plans to start up production. For the development of games two teams of game design students will develop this. In the next year medical tests will be performed as well to certify the product.

Another aspect that requires further research is how collaborative play can augment the experience of children with DCD in the context of real rehabilitation settings with our technology. This collaborative play can be between two children with DCD interacting together on the Matti or can also be between a child with DCD with his/her physiotherapist.

The use of interactive surfaces to support rehabilitation can be extended to other user groups besides children with DCD. Many other conditions could be applicable as well and benefit from using our technology as a movement therapy device. With this in mind, other users such as elderly people, patients with acquired brain injuries and patients with gross motor dysfunction could use Matti to help them performing physical activities in an engaging way.

## ACKNOWLEDGEMENTS

We acknowledge the support and cooperation of the physiotherapists involved in this research: Liliane De Winter, Dieteke Vangansbeke, Astrid Verdegem, Tess Veegate and Professor Hilde Van Waelvelde for her expertise in the movement therapy with children and lectures on new forms of therapy. We also like to thank Piet Verdegem from the Klim Op Rehabilitation Centre for the collaboration.

## REFERENCES

[1] Michelle Annett, Fraser Anderson, Darrell Goertzen, Jonathan Halton, Quentin Ranson, Walter F. Bischof, and Pierre Boulanger. 2009. Using a multi-touch tabletop for upper extremity motor rehabilitation. In *Proceedings of the 21st Annual Conference of the Australian Computer-Human Interaction Special Interest Group* (OZCHI '09), 261-264. DOI: http://dx.doi.org/10.1145/1738826.1738869

[2] Atif Alamri, Mohamad Eid, Rosa Iglesias, Shervin Shirmohammadi, and Abdulmotaleb El Saddik. 2008. "Haptic Virtual Rehabilitation Exercises for Poststroke Diagnosis." *IEEE Transactions on Instrumentation and Measurement* 57 (9): 1876–84. DOI:https://doi.org/10.1109/TIM.2008.919878

[3] Mirjam Augstein, Thomas Neumayr, Renate Ruckser-Scherb, Isabel Karlhuber, and Josef Altmann. 2013. "The Fun.Tast.Tisch. Project– A Novel Approach to Neuro-Rehabilitation Using an Interactive Multiuser Multitouch Tabletop." *Proceedings of the 2013 ACM International Conference on Interactive Tabletops and Surfaces - ITS '13*, 81–90. DOI:https://doi.org/10.1145/2512349.2512808

[4] Mirjam Augstein, Thomas Neumayr, and Irene Schacherl-Hofer. 2014. "The Usability of a Tabletop Application for Neuro-Rehabilitation from Therapists' Point of View." *Proceedings of the Ninth ACM International Conference on Interactive Tabletops and Surfaces - ITS '14*, 239–48. DOI:https://doi.org/10.1145/2669485.2669516

[5] Mirjam Augstein, Thomas Neumayr, Isabel Karlhuber, Sabine Dielacher, Sylvia Öhlinger, and Josef Altmann. 2015. "Training of Cognitive Performance in Complex Tasks with a Tabletop-Based Rehabilitation System." *Proceedings of the 2015 International Conference on Interactive Tabletops & Surfaces - ITS '15*, 15–24. DOI:https://doi.org/10.1145/2817721.2817738

[6] Bryan G. Behrenshausen. 2007. "Toward a (Kin)Aesthetic of Video Gaming: The Case of Dance Dance Revolution". *Games and Culture*, 2 (4), 335–354. DOI: 10.1177/1555412007310810.

[7] Aimee L. Betker, Tony Szturm, and Zahra M. K. Moussavi. 2005. Development of an interactive motivating tool for rehabilitation movements. In *Proceedings of the 27th Annual International Conference of the IEEE Engineering in Medicine and Biology Society,* 2341-2344. DOI: 10.1109/IEMBS.2005.1616935

[8] Emmanuel Bonney, Lemke Dorothee Jelsma, Gillian D. Ferguson, and Bouwien C. M. Smits-Engelsman. 2017. Learning better by repetition or variation? Is transfer at odds with task specific training? *PLoS ONE* 12, 3:e0174214.

[9] Susy M. Braun, Melanie Kleynen, Michel H. C. Bleijlevens, Albine Moser, Anna J. Beurskens, and Monique A. Lexis. 2015. "Interactive surfaces" technology as a potential tool to stimulate physical activity in psychogeriatric nursing home residents. *Disability and Rehabilitation: Assistive Technology* 10, 6:486-492.

[10] Héctor A. Caltenco, Anna Olsson, Afshin Aliyari, Charlotte Magnusson, David McGookin, Mikko Kytö, Ingibjörg Hjaltadóttir, Thóra B. Hafsteinsdóttir, Helga Jónsdóttir, and Ingibjörg Bjartmarz. 2017. Designing Interactive Systems for Balance Rehabilitation after Stroke. In *Proceedings of the 11th International Conference on Tangible, Embedded, and Embodied Interaction* (TEI'17), 511-516. DOI: https://doi.org/10.1145/3024969.3025084

[11] Victor Cheung, Alexander Keith Eady, and Audrey Girouard. 2018. Deformable Controllers: Fabrication and Design to Promote Novel Hand Gestural Interaction Mechanisms. In *Proceedings of the Twelfth International Conference on Tangible, Embedded, and Embodied Interaction* (TEI'18), 732-735. DOI: https://doi.org/10.1145/3173225.3173332

[12] Ross A. Clark, Adam L. Bryant, Yonghao Pua, Paul Mccrory, Kim Bennell, and Michael Hunt. 2010. "Gait & Posture Validity and Reliability of the Nintendo Wii Balance Board for Assessment of Standing Balance." *Gait and Posture* 31: 307–10. DOI:https://doi.org/10.1016/j.gaitpost.2009.11.012

[13] Beginner's Mind Collective and David Shaw. 2012. Makey Makey: improvising tangible and nature-based user interfaces. In *Proceedings of the Sixth International Conference on Tangible, Embedded and Embodied Interaction* (TEI'12), 367-370. DOI: https://doi.org/10.1145/2148131.2148219

[14] Elena De La Guía, María Dolores Lozano, and Victor R. Penichet. 2013. Cognitive Rehabilitation Based on Collaborative and Tangible Computer Games. In *Proceedings of the 7th International Conference on Pervasive Computing Technologies for Healthcare* (PervasiveHealth'13), 389-392. DOI: http://dx.doi.org/10.4108/icst.pervasivehealth.2013.252375

[15] Kynan Eng, Ewa Siekierka, Pawel Pyk, Edith Chevrier, Yves Hauser, Monica Cameirao, Lisa Holper, Karin Hägni, Lukas Zimmerli, Armin Duff, Corina Schuster, Claudio Bassetti, Paul Verschure, and Daniel Kiper. 2007. Interactive visuo-motor therapy system for stroke rehabilitation. *Medical and Biological Engineering and Computing* 45, 9:901–907.

[16] José Antonio Gil-Gómez, Roberto Lloréns, Mariano Alcñiz, and Carolina Colomer. 2011. "Effectiveness of a Wii Balance Board-Based System (EBaViR) for Balance Rehabilitation: A Pilot Randomized Clinical Trial in Patients with Acquired Brain Injury." *Journal of NeuroEngineering and Rehabilitation* 8 (1). DOI: https://doi.org/10.1186/1743-0003-8-30

[17] Leandra Gonsalves, Amity Campbell, Lynn Jensen, and Leon Straker. 2015. Children With Developmental Coordination Disorder Play Active Virtual Reality Games Differently Than Children With Typical Development. *Physical Therapy* 95, 3:360-368.

[18] John D. Gould and Clayton Lewis. 1985. Designing for usability: key principles and what designers think. Commun. ACM 28, 3 (March 1985), 300-311. DOI: http://dx.doi.org/10.1145/3166.3170

[19] Dave Hilton, Sue Cobb, Tony Pridmore, and John Gladman. 2002. Virtual reality and stroke rehabilitation: A tangible interface to an every day task. In *Proceedings of the 4th International Conference on Disability, Virtual Reality & Associated Technologies* (ICDVRAT'02), 63–70.

[20] Hiroshi Ishii and Brygg Ullmer. 1997. Tangible bits: towards seamless interfaces between people, bits, and atoms. In *Proceedings of the ACM SIGCHI Conference on Human factors in computing systems* (CHI'97), 234–241. DOI: http://dx.doi.org/10.1145/258549.258715

[21] ISO. ISO 9241-210: Ergonomics of human-system interaction – Part 210: Human-centred design for interactive systems. 2010.

[22] Antoni Jaume-i-Capó, Pau Martínez-Bueso, Biel Moyà-Alcover, and Javier Varona. 2014. Interactive rehabilitation system for improvement of balance therapies in people with cerebral palsy. *IEEE*

*Transactions on Neural Systems and Rehabilitation Engineering* 22, 2:419–427.

[23] Justin Lai, Tomonori Honda, and Maria C. Yang. 2010. A study of the role of user-centered design methods in design team projects. *Artificial Intelligence for Engineering Design, Analysis and Manufacturing* 24, 3:303-316.

[24] Michael Leitner, Martin Tomitsch, Thomas Költringer, Karin Kappel, and Thomas Grechenig. 2007. Designing Tangible Table-top Interfaces for Patients in Rehabilitation. In *Proceedings of the Conference and Workshop on Assistive Technologies for People with Vision and Hearing Impairments: Assistive Technology for All Ages* (CVHI'07), 1-7.

[25] Tom Luyten, Susy Braun, Gaston Jamin, Susan van Hooren, and Luc de Witte. 2018. How nursing home residents with dementia respond to the interactive art installation 'VENSTER': a pilot study. *Disability and Rehabilitation: Assistive Technology* 13, 1:87-94.

[26] Niall Maclean and Pandora Pound. 2000. A critical review of the concept of patient motivation in the literature on physical rehabilitation. *Social Science & Medicine* 50, 4:495-506.

[27] Patrizia Marti, Alessandro Pollini, Alessia Rullo, Leonardo Giusti, and Erik Grönvall. 2009. Creative interactive play for disabled children. In *Proceedings of the 8th International Conference on Interaction Design and Children* (IDC '09), 313-316. DOI: http://dx.doi.org/10.1145/1551788.1551871

[28] Debbie Rand, Rachel Kizony, Noomi Katz, and Patrice L Weiss. 2004. "Virtual Reality Rehabilitation for All: Vivid GX versus Sony PlayStation II EyeToy." *5th Intl. Conf. On Disability, Virtual Reality and Associated Technologies*, 87–94. DOI: https://doi.org/10.1016/j.otohns.2004.06.107

[29] Emmanuelle Richard, Valérie Billaudeau, Paul Richard and G. Gaudin. 2007. Augmented Reality for Rehabilitation of Cognitive Disabled Children: A Preliminary Study. In *Proceedings of the Virtual Rehabilitation Conference* (VR'07), 102-108. DOI: http://dx.doi.org/10.1109/ICVR.2007.4362148

[30] Maziah Mat Rosly, Hadi Mat Rosly, Glen M. Davis OAM, Ruby Husain, Nazirah Hasnan. 2017. Exergaming for individuals with neurological disability: a systematic review. *Disability and Rehabilitation* 39, 8:727-735.

[31] Yves Rybarczyk and Jos□Fonseca. 2011. Tangible interface for a rehabilitation of comprehension in aphasic patients. In *Proceedings of the* 11th Conference of the Association for the Advancement of Assistive Technology in Europe (AAATE'11), 1-9.

[32] Ehud Sharlin, Yuichi Itoh, Benjamin Watson, Yoshifumi Kitamura, Steve Sutphen, and Lili Liu. 2002. "Cognitive Cubes: A Tangible User Interface for Cognitive Assessment." *Proceedings of the SIGCHI Conference on Human Factors in Computing Systems Changing Our World, Changing Ourselves - CHI '02*, no. 4: 347. DOI:https://doi.org/10.1145/503376.503438

[33] Daniel Tetteroo, Annick Timmermans, Henk Seelen, and Panos Markopoulos. 2017. Tagtrainer: end-user adaptable technology for physical rehabilitation. In *Proceedings of the 11th EAI International Conference on Pervasive Computing Technologies for Healthcare* (PervasiveHealth'17), 452-454. DOI: https://doi.org/10.1145/3154862.3154901

[34] Marijke Vandermaesen, Tom de Weyer, Kris Luyten, and Karin Coninx. 2014. PhysiCube: providing tangible interaction in a pervasive upper-limb rehabilitation system. In *Proceedings of the 8th International Conference on Tangible, Embedded and Embodied Interaction* (TEI'14), 85-92. DOI: https://doi.org/10.1145/2540930.2540936

[35] Dieteke Vangansbeke, Tess Veegaete, Astrid Verdegem, and Hilde Van Waelvelde. 2017. *The Effect of 'Rehab Gaming' on Motivation for Balance Training in Children with Balance Disorders.* Master Thesis. Ghent University.

[36] Patrice L. Weiss, Emanuel Tirosh, and Darcy Fehlings. 2014. Role of virtual reality for cerebral palsy management. *Journal of Child Neurology* 29, 8:1119 - 1124.

[37] Peter H. Wilson, Jonathan Duckworth, Nick Mumford, Ross Eldridge, Mark Guglielmetti, Patrick Thomas, David Shum, and Heiko Rudolph. 2007. "A Virtual Tabletop Workspace for the Assessment of Upper Limb Function in Traumatic Brain Injury (TBI)." *2007 Virtual Rehabilitation, IWVR*, 14–19. DOI:https://doi.org/10.1080/07399018608965243

[38] William Young, Stuart Ferguson, Sébastien Brault, and Cathy Craig. 2011. "Assessing and Training Standing Balance in Older Adults: A Novel Approach Using the 'Nintendo Wii' Balance Board." *Gait and Posture* 33 (2): 303–5. DOI:https://doi.org/10.1016/j.conbuildmat.2014.06.066

[39] Wenhui Yu, Catherine Vuong, and Todd Ingalls. 2011. An Interactive Multimedia System for Parkinson's Patient Rehabilitation. In *Proceedings of the International Conference on Virtual and Mixed Reality* (VMR'11), 129-137. DOI: https://doi.org/10.1007/978-3-642-22024-1_

[40] Luciana A.M. Zaina and Alexandre lvaro. 2015. A design methodology for user-centered innovation in the software development area. *Journal of Systems and Software* 110, C:155-177.

# Integrating Electronic Components into Deformable Objects Based on User Interaction Data

**Paul Worgan, Kevin Reuss, Stefanie Mueller**
MIT CSAIL, Cambridge, MA, USA
{pworgan, kreuss, stefanie.mueller}@mit.edu


## ABSTRACT
A key challenge when designing deformable user interfaces is the integration of *rigid* electronic components with the soft deformable device. In this paper, we propose to place electronic components based on how the user is interacting with the device, i.e., in which way the device is being deformed when the user performs gestures.

To identify optimum locations for placing electronic components, we developed a design tool that takes as input a 3D model of the deformable device and a set of captured user gestures. It then visualizes the stress distribution resulting from the gestures applied to the deformable device and suggests where not to place components because the location is highly deformed when users interact (e.g., a rigid battery that would constraint interaction); or alternatively where to place components to sense deformation more accurately (e.g., a bend sensor to detect a specific gesture) and efficiently (e.g., an energy harvesting component).

We evaluated our approach by collecting interaction data from 12 users across three deformable devices (a watch, a camera, and a mouse) and applied the resulting stress distributions to the placement of selected electronic components.


### Author Keywords
Organic User Interfaces; Prototyping Tools; Gestures.

## INTRODUCTION
Since the early 2000s, HCI researchers envision a future in which devices will no longer be rigid but deformable *(Organic User Interfaces* [[6]]). Moving away from rigid objects and being able to squeeze, stretch, and twist devices offers many advantages, including an increased input space *(Gummi* [[19]]), output space (*Surflex* [[3]]), and better ergonomics [[6]].


*TEI '19*, March 17–20, 2019, Tempe, AZ, USA

ACM ISBN 978-1-4503-6196-5/19/03...$15.00
https://doi.org/10.1145/3294109.3295629

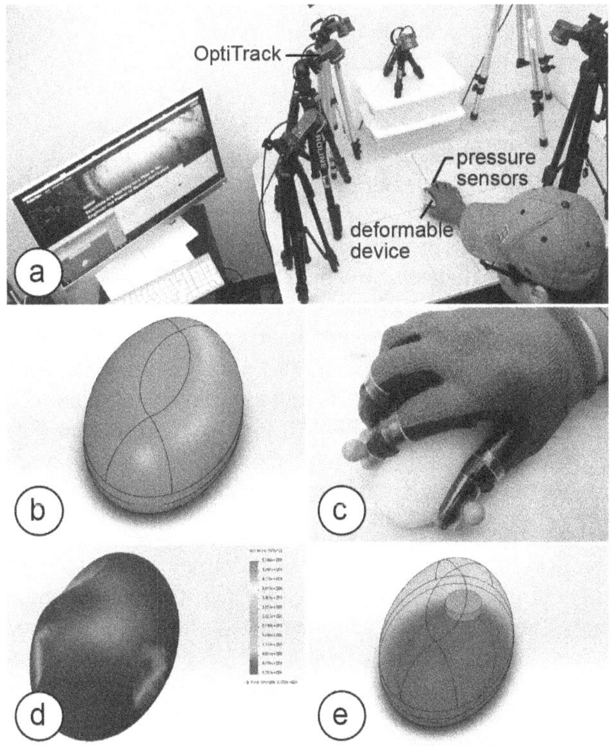


**Figure 1. (a) Our design tool collects gesture data to help with the placement of electric components when designing deformable devices. Designers only have to (b) create a 3D model of the device & silicone cast it, (c) record interaction data, (d) feed the data back to our stress analysis tool, which then (e) suggests a placement based on areas of least or most stress (i.e., deformation).**

One key challenge when designing deformable user interfaces is the integration of electronic components with the deformable device. While research points towards the development of flexible electronics, such as deformable displays (*Stretchis* [[23]]) and circuitry *(SiliconeDevices* [[14]]), many electronic components remain rigid and when placed in the wrong location interfere with the user interaction. Even for soft components, such as bend sensors and piezo-electric foils used for energy harvesting, the right placement is important since the interaction can be sensed more accurately and the energy output per gesture can be increased.

In this paper, we present a design tool that supports designers in the process of placing electronic components inside a deformable device. The key idea is to incorporate knowledge about how the user is interacting with the device to place and orient electronic components according to a device and its corresponding gesture set.

## RELATED WORK

Our research is related to organic user interfaces, work that integrates electronics with deformable devices, and grasp sensing.

### Organic & Deformable User Interfaces

Over the last decade, organic user interface research has made significant progress: Many different materials and structures have been employed [[17]] and the space of design choices, such as material stiffness [[9], [10]], device size [[12]], and types of gestures [[8], [21]] and their influence on user performance and experience has been studied. However, while the field has seen large progress, there are still many challenges remaining as outlined by Alexander et al. [[1]]. One of these challenges is the need for toolkits to effectively prototype organic interface hardware, including the integration of functional electronic components. Only recently, researchers have started to develop such tools. For instance, *DefSense* [[2]] helps users design customized deformable input devices by embedding piezo-resistive wires to represent the current deformation state.

### Integrating Electronics with Deformable User Interfaces

One way to seamlessly integrate electronics into deformable devices is to use only bendable and stretchable components. Screen-printing, for instance, allows for layered-fabrication of bendable and stretchable displays (*PrintScreen* [[16]], *Stretchis* [[23]]) and matching flexible circuitry can be created using either conductive inkjet printing [[15]], screen-printing (*Skintillates* [[13]]) or by filling liquid metal into channels (*SiliconeDevices* [[14]]). However, many electronic components remain rigid and when placed in the wrong location interfere with the user interaction.

### Grasp Sensing for Interactive Systems

Grasp sensing has been studied extensively over the last decade. For a complete review we refer to Wimmer [[24]] who describes different aspects of grasp sensing and a variety of sensing technologies that can be employed. We built onto work by Ehrenmann et al. [[5]] who were among the first to use a pressure sensing data glove and a camera-system to track hand posture, position and applied forces while users are manipulating objects. Since then, pressure sensing and motion capture approaches have been used to build more detailed models of how humans interact with objects (Saidon et al. [[18]]) including the creation of large gesture databases with a variety of manipulation tasks involving objects ranging from kitchen utensils, to tools, mugs, jars, and toys (Verdier et al. [[22]]). For our work, we build on prior research in grasp sensing but use it as a means to place electronic components inside a deformable device according to user gestures.

## DESIGN TOOL FOR DEFORMABLE DEVICES

Our design tool allows designers to record and process interaction data while creating a deformable device.

### #1 3D Modeling of the Deformable Device

Designers start by creating the form factor of the deformable device in a 3D modeling program. Figure 1b shows the 3D model of a deformable mouse the designer created.

### #2 Collecting Interaction Data

Once the 3D model is finished, designers can create a physical prototype from it (e.g., from silicone) and start recording interaction data from gestures. To accurately determine how a user deforms the device, we collect both the position of each finger on the device as well as the amount of pressure each finger applies to the device. To determine the position, we use an optical motion capture system *(OptiTrack Flex13).* As can be seen in Figure 1a, we place six cameras on a desk to track the user's interaction with the deformable device on the table. To detect the applied force during interaction, we built a custom glove with pressure sensors on the finger tips.

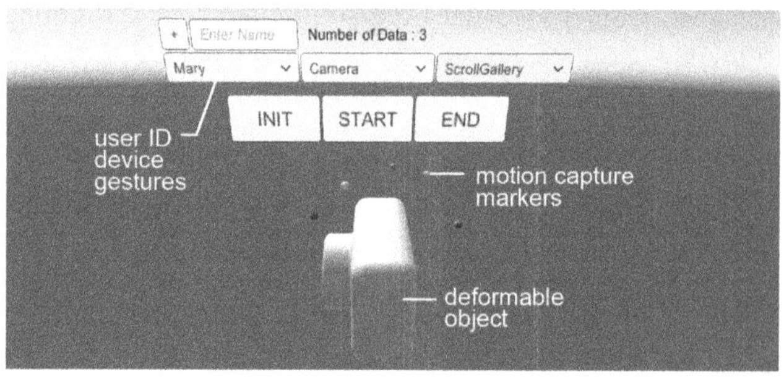


**Figure 2. Recording Interface.**

Designers can either record interactions themselves or collect data from other users. For this, we provide a custom recording interface implemented in *Unity3D* (Figure 2). The designer can add new users, specify the deformable device being used, define a gesture, and record multiple takes of a gesture. The view also shows live data from the motion capture system and displays the deformable device as a 3D model for reference. The output from a recording session is a file that the designer can load into the 3D editor for subsequent stress and placement analysis.

### #3 Computing the Stress Distribution Map

In the 3D editor, the designer can now execute a custom plugin we wrote to import the interaction data (Figure 3).

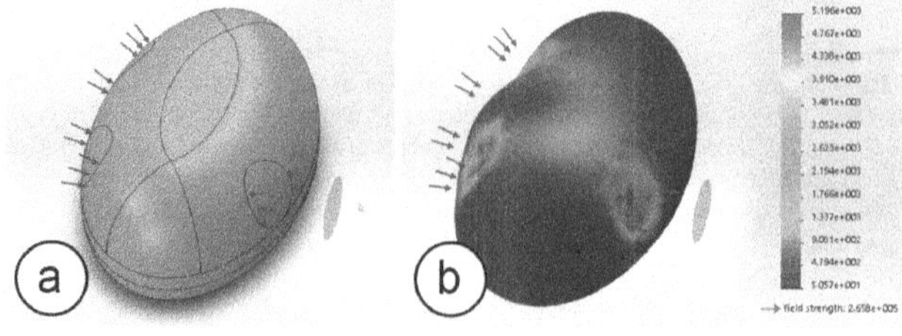


**Figure 3. (a) Finger imprints and applied force, (b) resulting stress distribution.**

Loading the interaction data applies the finger imprints and corresponding forces from the grasp to the 3D model automatically (Figure 3a) and then executes a finite element analysis to determine the stress distribution (Figure 3b).

#### #4 Placing Electronic Components

Based on the generated stress distribution map our system recommends a location for placing the electronic components by providing the 3D location of the most or least stress (Figure 1e), which allows the designer to make an informed decision about how to best integrate the part.

## TESTING OUR SYSTEM WITH A GROUP OF USERS

We tested our workflow by recording data from 12 users recruited from our institution (1 female, age 22-44, mean: 26.91). We asked them to perform gestures with three deformable devices: a mouse, a camera, and a smart watch. The study was conducted as within-subjects and participants were randomly assigned an order. We used the same setup as described in 'Collecting Interaction Data', i.e. the motion capture system on a table and users were wearing the pressure sensing glove (Figure 4).

Our study contained the following tasks: (1) *Camera:* 'Squeeze the camera lens to zoom in the image. Zoom until the tree in the image is displayed full screen.' (2) *Smart-Watch:* 'Squeeze the smart watch to adjust the volume of the music. Adjust the volume to 80%.' (3) *Mouse:* 'Squeeze the mouse to scroll the webpage. Scroll the webpage to the third headline.'

We gave users 5 minutes to familiarize themselves with the devices and the pressure sensing glove, i.e. they were allowed to perform test grasps on the deformable objects and to lift and tilt them to get a better feeling for the devices.

For each device and gesture, we briefly demonstrated how to perform it. Afterwards, users performed 20 trials per gesture. We started the recording using the 'start' button and stopped recording by pressing the 'stop' button of our recording interface (Figure 2). The data collection for each user took 20 minutes or less. The recorded data included the motion data for each finger as well as the corresponding pressure values for each finger.

**Figure 4. Data collection.**

Figure 5 shows example stress distributions from the collected user data for all devices and the suggested placement based on the aggregated data of all users: (a) For the deformable mouse, we asked the system to mark the area of least stress to best integrate a rigid button cell for energy supply without interfering with the user interaction. (b) For the smart watch, we asked the system to mark the area of largest stress to place a piezo-electric foil that harvests more energy when strongly deformed. (c) For the camera, we asked the system to mark the area of least stress facing outwards to optimally place a connector for data transfer of the camera images to a computer.

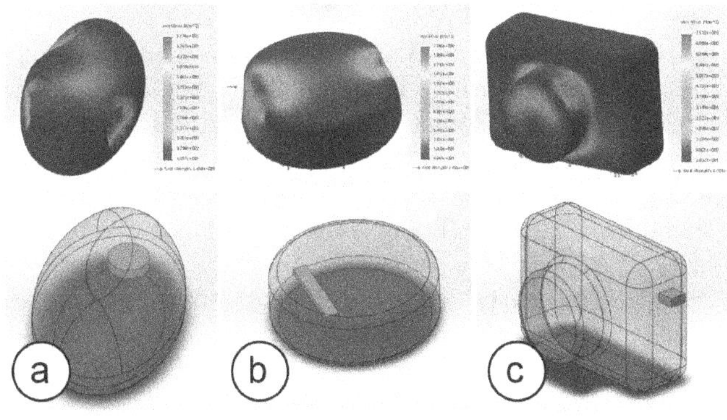


**Figure 5. Stress distribution and recommended placement for (a) a button cell, (b) a piezo-electric foil, (c) a data-transfer connector.**

## USE CASES

We next describe two example use cases that place electric components based on the stress distribution results. While our approach applies to many different domains, such as placing sensors for more accurate user interaction tracking or laying out circuitry to avoid breakage, we focus on energy supply components as brief examples.

#### Example #1: Energy-Harvesting (Largest Stress)

In energy harvesting, the more a piezo-electric foil is deformed, the more energy can be harvested. To demonstrate that more energy can be harvested when the piezoelectric foil is placed according to specific gestures, we ran a simple experiment. We placed two piezoelectric foils inside the deformable mouse (one left-to-right, one front-to-back). We then performed two gestures as shown in Figure 6: (1) a front-to-back squeeze (as in *Adaptive Mouse* [[20]]), and (2) a side-to-side squeeze (as in *Inflatable Mouse* [[11]]). We collected the mean energy over 10 repetitions.

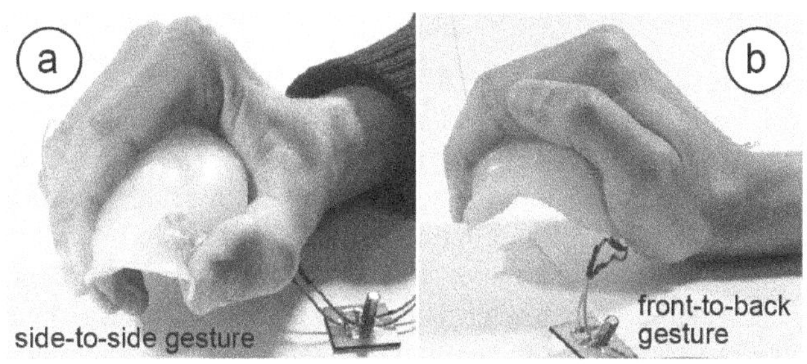


**Figure 6. (a) Side-to-side, (b) front-to-back.**

Our results show that when the piezoelectric foil is mounted orthogonal to the direction of the performed gesture, i.e., in the location of largest stress, it generates a larger amount of energy. For instance, the opposing *side piezo* + *front-to-back* gesture generated 7 times more energy compared to the aligned *front-to-back piezo* + *front-to-back* gesture (1.0538 µJ vs. 0.1343 µJ). Conversely, the opposing *front-to-back piezo* + *side-to-side* gesture generated over 3 times the amount of energy as the aligned *side-to-side piezo* + *side-to-side* gesture (0.6624 µJ vs. 0.1925 µJ). Thus, placing the piezo-electric foil according to the user interaction helped to increase energy supply.

**Example #2: Plug-and-Socket Connector (Least Stress)**
Connectors are sensitive to deformation since the plug and socket may delaminate and lose the electric connection. To demonstrate that placing connectors in the areas of least stress reduces delamination, we ran another experiment. First, we created a soft plug-and-socket connector (silicone, flexible copper tape contacts) to reduce the chance of breakage in general (Figure 7). Next, we measured how much the connector delaminates (changes in contact resistance) by subjecting the connector to different bend radii.

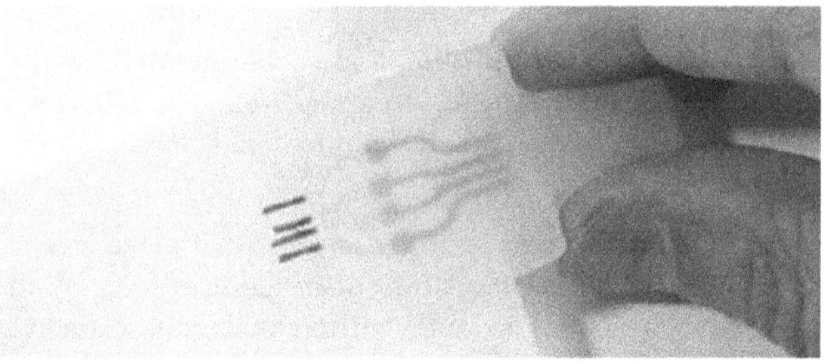

**Figure 7. Deformable connector integrated into a deformable phone that folds along the long side.**

We found that for bend angles from -70° (bend away from connector) to 0 (no bending) to +20° (bend towards connector) the contact resistant was approximately 60mΩ. For larger angles, however, the quality of the connection dropped quickly (+25° = 210 mΩ, +30° = 330 mΩ). Thus, placing the connector according to the gesture was important to maintain a good electric connection.

## IMPLEMENTATION

Our recording interface is implemented in *Unity3D* using C#. To apply the interaction data to the 3D model of the device we implemented a *SolidWorks* plugin in Visual Basic.

### #1 Pressure Sensor Input

To build the pressure glove, we bought a workshop glove and attached force resistive pressure sensors *(Interlink Electronics FSR 400)* to the finger tips. We connected the force sensors to an Arduino that we enclosed in a 3D printed box and attached to the upper arm of the user. The Arduino is connected to a computer that runs a python script to collect the pressure values. Each pressure sensor returns an analog value which we map to a pressure value according to the specification (see Figure 3 in [[7]]). We use the pressure values in two ways: (1) during *data collection,* the data is forwarded to the application to provide users with visual feedback while performing the gesture (e.g., zooming the image in the deformable camera example). (2) When *calculating the stress distribution,* we use the pressure values to determine the amount of force each finger applied to the device.

### #2 OptiTrack Input

To enable streaming with *OptiTrack,* we activated the *Streaming Engine* in the software *Motive:Tracker*. To receive the streamed data in Unity3D, we attached the OptitrackStreamingClient.cs script to one UI element. When we receive streamed data, we convert the marker coordinates from the OptiTrack coordinate system to the Unity3D coordinate system using a scaling factor. We then assign the values from each of the pressure sensors to the corresponding finger. To identify which marker represents which finger, we perform a calibration gesture (flat hand).

### #3 Generating the Specification File

Our system automatically stores all finger locations and pressures values in a file, containing *start location, end location,* and *pressure value* for each finger.

### #4 Calculating the Stress Distribution Map

Our *SolidWorks* plugin automatically reads the file and uses the start and end coordinates of each finger to generate a direction vector that approximates the finger movement. It then generates a representation of the finger imprint by (1) creating a plane perpendicular to the direction vector, (2) placing a circle on the plane, and (3) projecting the circle along the direction vector onto the model. This results in a finger imprint on the surface of the 3D model. We then apply the corresponding pressure value to each finger imprint and run a finite element analysis. The result is a stress distribution map across the model for an individual user and an individual gesture.

To average the data over multiple gestures or users, we automatically export all stress values into a .csv file using a *Workflow Sensitive Sensor* in SolidWorks. We then run a custom script that averages the data and associates each stress value with a 3D coordinate resulting in a 3D array, i.e. a representation of voxels with associated stress values.

### #5 Suggesting Locations for Energy Components

Our plugin then finds the combination of voxels with either least or most stress. It also checks for the size and orientation of the electronic component to fit them into the voxel grid. For this, our system contains a library of components including their length, width and height. If multiple regions are subject to the same amount of stress, we ask the designer for input.

### #6 Material Properties for the Virtual Material

To represent the material properties of the silicone used for our devices, we created a custom virtual material in *SolidWorks* (i.e., we consulted the material specification sheet of the silicone we used, *Ecoflex 00-30* [[4]], and then transferred core characteristics, such as the shore hardness and the tensile strength to the properties of the virtual material).

We assign the material automatically to the 3D model before computing the stress distribution.

## DISCUSSION

While our workflow provides a first starting point to explore prototyping tools to integrate electronic components with deformable devices, we will use this section to highlight a few alternatives and directions for future work.

*Motion Capture vs. Hand Simulation:* While we collect gesture data from users interacting with the physical prototype of the device, interaction data can be generated through many different means. For instance, a rigged digital hand model can be used to generate different interaction patterns. We decided to use motion capture since it captures the diversity of interaction patterns among different users.

*Leveraging Interaction Data for other Design Choices:* While we use interaction data to place electronic components, interaction data from deformable devices can be used in many additional realms. For instance, one could harvest interaction data to generate soft compliant mechanisms that activate when specific gestures are being performed.

*Aggregated vs. Individual Fit:* Since the grasp pattern of each user is different, aggregated data can only provide an approximate fit. However, with advances in personal fabrication, we envision a future in which users will obtain personalized devices that are optimized specifically for them.

## CONCLUSION

In this paper, we demonstrated how to leverage gesture data representing how a user is interacting with a deformable device to optimize the placement of electronic components during the design process. We demonstrated how our design tool collects interaction data from users, processes the data to generate a stress distribution map, and finally recommends a position for placing the electronic components based on locations of least or largest stress. For future work, we plan to extend our algorithm to also include the layout of wires inside the device. In addition, we will extend our work towards additional use cases in sensing and actuation.

## REFERENCES


[1] Jason Alexander, Anne Roudaut, Jürgen Steimle, Kasper Hornbæk, Miguel Bruns Alonso, Sean Follmer, and Timothy Merritt. Grand Challenges in Shape-Changing Interface Research. In *Proceedings of the 2018 CHI Conference on Human Factors in Computing Systems* (CHI '18), Paper 299.

[2] Moritz Bächer, Benjamin Hepp, Fabrizio Pece, Paul G. Kry, Bernd Bickel, Bernhard Thomaszewski, and Otmar Hilliges. DefSense: Computational Design of Customized Deformable Input Devices. In *Proceedings of the 2016 CHI Conference on Human Factors in Computing Systems* (CHI '16), 3806-3816.

[3] Marcelo Coelho, Hiroshi Ishii, and Pattie Maes. Surflex: A Programmable Surface for the Design of Tangible Interfaces. In *Extended Abstracts on Human Factors in Computing Systems* (CHI '08), 3429-3434.

[4] Ecoflex 00-30 Material Specification Sheet: https://www.smooth-on.com/tb/files/ECOFLEX_SERIES_TB.pdf

[5] M. Ehrenmann, R. Zollner, S. Knoop, R. Dillmann. Sensor Fusion Approaches for Observation of User Actions in Programming by Demonstration. In *IEEE International Conference on Multisensor Fusion and Integration for Intelligent Systems* (MFI'01), 227-232.

[6] David Holman and Roel Vertegaal. Organic User Interfaces: Designing Computers in Any Way, Shape, or Form. In *ACM Communications* 51, 6, 48-55, 2008.

[7] Interlink Electronics FSR 400 Data Sheet https://dlnmh9ip6v2uc.cloudfront.net/datasheets/Sensors/ForceFlex/2010-10-26-DataSheet-FSR400-Layout2.pdf

[8] Audrey Girouard, Jessica Lo, Md Riyadh, Farshad Daliri, Alexander Keith Eady, and Jerome Pasquero. One-Handed Bend Interactions with Deformable Smartphones. In *Proceedings of the 33rd Annual ACM Conference on Human Factors in Computing Systems* (CHI '15), 1509-1518.

[9] Johan Kildal. Interacting with Deformable User Interfaces: Effect of Material Stiffness and Type of Deformation Gesture. In *Proceedings of the 7th International Conference on Haptic and Audio Interaction Design* (HAID'12), 71-80.

[10] Johan Kildal and Graham Wilson. Feeling it: The Roles of Stiffness, Deformation Range and Feedback in the Control of Deformable UI. In *Proceedings of the 14th ACM International Conference on Multimodal Interaction* (ICMI '12), 393-400.

[11] Seoktae Kim, Hyunjung Kim, Boram Lee, Tek-Jin Nam and Woohun Lee. Inflatable Mouse: Volume-Adjustable Mouse with Air-Pressure-Sensitive Input and Haptic Feedback. In *Proceedings of the SIGCHI Conference on Human Factors in Computing Systems* (CHI '08), 211-224.

[12] Sang-su Lee, Youn-kyung Lim, and Kun-Pyo Lee. Exploring the Effects of Size on Deformable User Interfaces. In *Proceedings of the 14th International Conference on Human-Computer Interaction with Mobile Devices and Services Companion* (MobileHCI '12), 89-94.

[13] Joanne Lo, Doris Jung Lin Lee, Nathan Wong, David Bui, and Eric Paulos. Skintillates: Designing and Creating Epidermal Interactions. In *Proceedings of the 2016 ACM Conference on Designing Interactive Systems* (DIS '16), 853-864.

[14] Steven Nagels, Raf Ramakers, Kris Luyten, and Wim Deferme. Silicone Devices: A Scalable DIY Approach for Fabricating Self-Contained Multi-Layered Soft

Circuits using Microfluidics. In *Proceedings of the 2018 CHI Conference on Human Factors in Computing Systems* (CHI '18), Paper 188.

[15] Simon Olberding, Nan-Wei Gong, John Tiab, Joseph A. Paradiso, and Jürgen Steimle. A Cuttable Multi-Touch Sensor. In *Proceedings of the 26th Annual ACM Symposium on User Interface Software and Technology* (UIST '13), 245-254.

[16] Simon Olberding, Michael Wessely, and Jürgen Steimle. PrintScreen: Fabricating Highly Customizable Thin-Film Touch-Displays. In *Proceedings of the 27th Annual ACM Symposium on User Interface Software and Technology* (UIST '14), 281-290.

[17] Isabel P. S. Qamar, Rainer Groh, David Holman, and Anne Roudaut. HCI meets Material Science: A Literature Review of Morphing Materials for the Design of Shape-Changing Interfaces. In *Proceedings of the 2018 CHI Conference on Human Factors in Computing Systems* (CHI '18), Paper 374.

[18] N. F. Elya Saidon, Chikamune Wada, Siti A. Ahmad, Ribhan Zafira Abdul Rahman, Kiyotaka Eguchi, Yoshiyuki Tomiyama and Farida Izni Abd Rahman. Real-time Human Motion Analysis and Grasping Force using the OptiTrack System and Flexi-force Sensor. In *Pertanika Journal of Science and Technology*, 25, 69-76, 2017.

[19] Carsten Schwesig, Ivan Poupyrev and Eijiro Mori. Gummi: User Interface for Deformable Computers. In *Extended Abstracts on Human Factors in Computing Systems* (CHI '03), 954-955.

[20] Sheng Kai Tang and Wen Yen Tang. Adaptive Mouse: A Deformable Computer Mouse Achieving Form-Function Synchronization. In *Extended Abstracts on Human Factors in Computing Systems* (CHI '10), 2785- 2792.

[21] Giovanni Maria Troiano, Esben Warming Pedersen, and Kasper Hornbæk. User-Defined Gestures for Elastic, Deformable Displays. In *Proceedings of the 2014 International Working Conference on Advanced Visual Interfaces* (AVI '14), 1-8.

[22] Benjamin Verdier, Sheldon Andrews, and Paul G. Kry. Human Grasping Interaction Capture and Analysis. In *Proceedings of the ACM SIGGRAPH / Eurographics Symposium on Computer Animation* (SCA '17), Article 23.

[23] Michael Wessely, Theophanis Tsandilas, and Wendy E. Mackay. Stretchis: Fabricating Highly Stretchable User Interfaces. In *Proceedings of the 29th Annual Symposium on User Interface Software and Technology* (UIST '16), 697-704.

[24] Raphael Wimmer. Grasp Sensing for Human-Computer Interaction. In *Proceedings of the Fifth International Conference on Tangible, Embedded, and Embodied Interaction* (TEI '11), 221-228.

# BeadED Adventures: Crafting STEM Learning

**Anne Sullivan**
Georgia Institute of Technology
Atlanta, GA 30332, USA
anne.sullivan@lmc.gatech.edu

**Emily K. Johnson**
University of Central Florida
Orlando, FL 32816, USA
ekj@ucf.edu



*TEI '19*, March 17–20, 2019, Tempe, AZ, USA

ACM ISBN 978-1-4503-6196-5/19/03.
https://doi.org/10.1145/3294109.3300997

## Abstract
With the move towards digital interventions for educational purposes, there has been a loss of tangible and material interfaces, the consequences of which are still being understood. Meanwhile, there is an ongoing lack of gender diversity within STEM-facing majors and careers. In response to this, we have created a physical prototype of BeadED Adventures, a system that uses a physical controller made up of jars of colorful beads to control modified Twine games that follows constructivist philosophies of learning and emphasizes player autonomy. By controlling the experience, the player creates a beaded bracelet that is personalized based on their choices within the game. In addition to the controller, we are creating an educational Twine game in which the player explores an abandoned castle, solving computational thinking puzzles to escape.

## Author Keywords
Tangible interfaces; educational games; crafting games; games; crafts; tangible learning artifact; STEM learning.

## ACM Classification Keywords
**• Applied computing~Interactive learning environments • Applied computing~Computer games**

## Introduction

In the last few decades, technology has brought many improvements to education. As more students gain access to mobile devices, traditionally hands-on learning activities from manipulatives to chemistry experiments are being recreated in interactive digital experiences (e.g. [2,15,17]).

Due to the interactive nature of these digital experiences, it is not a far leap to begin introducing game mechanics and tropes to the digital learning environments. Educational video games draw heavily on both video games and non-digital learning games, attempting to combine the flow and enjoyment of playing a game with the learning objectives of the educational experience.

While the addition of the game mechanics and structure has had some success, the loss of the tangible and material interface to the learning activities has been notable. The consequences of this and the resulting impacts on learning, creativity, and dexterity are just starting to be understood.

The use of "manipulatives" for tangible learning is a decades-old practice in K12 education, including middle school [5]. Manipulatives are a logical fit for concepts in geometry [14] and informal learning spaces like museums and science centers [6]. Additionally, emphasis on multimodal learning is the hallmark of the Montessori classroom [4].

At the same time, the numbers of women within STEM degrees and careers in the US continues to lag. In computer science in particular, only 8% of female-identifying workers in 2015 held CS degrees [13], and only 26.4% of computer and math scientist careers were held by women in the US [20]. Research shows that it is during middle school (11-13 years old) that girls begin to lose interest in STEM subjects, and therefore it is a particularly important age range to target for educational interventions [10].

Given the efficacy of learning through tangible means, we are creating BeadED Adventures, a novel educational game with a child-friendly crafting controller aimed at middle school girls. We designed this game with the intent to leverage the affordances of digital games and tangible objects in an exploration game where players create tangible learning artifacts as they interact with computational thinking concepts. Through this project we aim to explore the use of physical interfaces that create a tangible artifact through play, and how this may be used for memory and motivation in learning environments.

In this paper we describe the controller and game that make up BeadED Adventures in more detail, and also touch on future directions for this work.

## Related Work

Because of the importance of tangible learning, there are a number of examples of STEM education interactions using tangible-digital hybrids to target STEM learning. Tangible systems have been used effectively in teaching subjects such as phases of the moon [12], electricity [16], and programming [8]. We build on this tradition by creating a tangible system; however, we are interested in creating an interface that specifically appeals to girls. For this, we have looked more closely at crafting games.

Due in part to the maker movement, DIY culture, and resurgence of crafting communities, there has been increasing popularity of creating games with tangible and crafted interfaces. Games such as Knit Wit [11], eBee [3], and Addie's Patchwork Playground [19] use interfaces that have been crafted or made up of crafting materials. Moving beyond this is a style of "crafting games" such as Yarn Quest [21], Threadsteading [1], and Loominary [18], in which the interaction of play is often digitally mediated but also involves actively crafting in some form.

The rise of crafting games and their ability to bridge the power of the digital with the desire for the material was the inspiration for BeadED Adventures. We use a different crafting medium than our inspirations mentioned above, as we seek to design the experience particularly for middle school girls. Therefore, rather than looking at craft forms that are popular with adults such as knitting, sewing, quilting, or weaving used in the games mentioned above, we instead used pony beads – a craft material that is already used frequently by middle-school-age girls.

## BeadED Adventures

BeadED Adventures is a work-in-progress project, with a working prototype. The system has a physical interface made up of jars with colored beads that are used to control a Twine game. More information about the controller, interface, and game is below.

*Controller*

The controller was designed to be appealing to girls between 10-15 years old, using pony beads. The controller encourages the player to craft a string of beads, each bead representing a choice in the game, which creates a tangible artifact of their play session after they are done. This type of crafting activity is likewise something that is already common among the age range we are interested in working with. We are particularly interested in exploring tangible interfaces as they have been shown to be more enticing, especially to girls [7]. However, none of these systems create an artifact through use which we are interested in exploring.

Figure 1: The controller for BeadED Adventures consists of jars filled with beads. The player interacts with the system by picking up and replacing a jar of beads.

The current iteration of the controller for BeadED Adventures is a set of six glass jars, each filled with one color of pony bead—pink, bronze, gold, green, and blue—and one jar filled with silver-colored textured metal beads as shown in Figure 1. Each color of beads corresponds to a color choice within the game, with the silver color (corresponding to the textured bead) being reserved to signify special events in the game.

Figure 2: The underside of the box shows the wires and Makey Makey. Each wire pair connects to a jar location.

Figure 3: A young player interacting with the BeadED Adventures system. She has chosen a bead color and is getting a bead to add to her string. When she replaces the jar, the game will register her color choice and continue.

Because we intended for the interface to feel as organic as possible, we initially considered interface hardware utilizing machine vision to discern which bead color the player selected, but ultimately this proved unnecessarily complicated compared to the elegant solution upon which we have arrived.

The jar lids have been modified to allow one bead to be removed at a time. This is done to encourage players to only use one bead at a time, instead of pouring out a pile to draw from and bypassing our control system – something that we found play-testers would do when using the unmodified screw cap top.

The jar bottoms have been painted with conductive paint to create a connection with the wires attached to the Makey Makey controller which sits inside the box as seen in Figure 2. When a jar is removed (presumably so the player can remove a bead), the connection is lost between the jar bottom and the wires. When the jar is replaced, the Makey Makey registers it as a button press for the color assigned to that position, which in turn triggers this as a choice within the game. The interface in use can be seen in Figure 3.

Prior iterations utilized a switch system where the bead jars sat atop depressed buttons which were released when a jar was removed, activating the system. This interface was soon modified due to the necessity of weighting the jars of beads to allow them to fully depress the buttons. Another version utilized conductive paint in lieu of wires altogether, but the paint proved to be less reliable than wires, which are easily hidden on the underside of the interface.

We chose to trigger on the jar being replaced instead of removed as a way to encourage only one jar being removed at a time. This makes it much less likely that the colors will be put back in a different position, and as our controller triggers on position and not color, it is important that the positions are not switched.

The player may then take the bead that has been removed from the jar and add it to a string. Over the course of play, the player will create a string of beads that serve as a tangible artifact that records their choices (encoded as the colored pony beads) and achievements (with the special silver beads) within the games as seen in Figure 4. The stringed beads can be worn as a bracelet, anklet, or necklace depending on

Figure 4: A bracelet in-progress, showing the choices the player made and denoting that they've solved one of the puzzles with the special silver bead.

length of play, or it can be used as a bookmark or keychain depending on the choice of the player.

*Interface*

The controller for BeadED Adventures was built to work with modified Twine games written using SugarCube 2 story format. Twine is a platform for creating choose-your-own-adventure style narratives, where the player is presented text-based passages from which to make choices, leading to different outcomes in the story.

For BeadED Adventures, we were particularly interested in Twine, as research has shown that the use of story is motivating for girls to learn to program [9], which makes Twine well-suited to our needs.

To modify the Twine story to work with the BeadED Adventures controller, the game must first include appropriate JavaScript code which links the Makey Makey button presses as triggering a click on specific HTML IDs. The second modification is that each link in a passage within the Twine must be surrounded by a span with the appropriate ID that coordinates with the Makey Makey button press. Finally, we use a CSS file that links each ID to a bead color, and colors the text with that color.

In summation, the Makey Makey simulates a specific button press when the user replaces a jar of beads. The JavaScript converts this button press to triggering a click on a span ID that matches the color of the bead (assuming the jar positions match what is in the css file). If that span ID is found within the current Twine passage, it acts as if the player has used a mouse to click that specific link and the game continues to the next passage specified by the link.

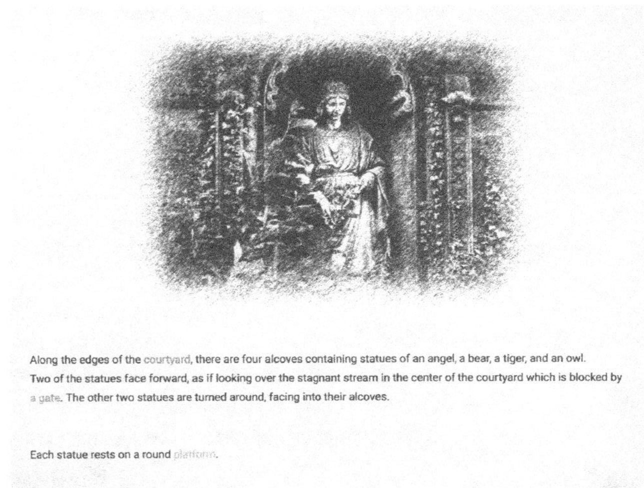


Figure 5: A screenshot of the castle exploration game. Solving the statue puzzle requires conditional logic.

*Game*

The game is built in Twine, which supports story-based gameplay. We are particularly interested in using Twine as we aim to use this system in a summer camp setting where students create their own games. Twine is simple to begin using and allows for participant-led narratives to be created.

We currently have one in-progress Twine game customized for use with BeadED Adventures. For our research, we are particularly interested in using BeadED Adventures as a method of teaching computational thinking. Therefore, our game is created with that in mind.

Because of the use of Twine, the game is text-based and includes some images. The game starts with the player taking a detour home from school and finding a mysterious forest and an abandoned castle. Once inside the castle, the door closes, and the player must explore to find their way out.

We plan to have four puzzles in the game that the player finds through exploration, with each puzzle centered around a computational thinking concept: variables, conditionals, and loops, with the final puzzle requiring the use of all concepts from the previous three puzzles. At the completion of each puzzle, they either gain an item (e.g. a key) or trigger an event (e.g. a door being revealed) that helps them escape the castle. Picking up the item or moving to a story passage beyond the triggered event links to the silver textured bead jar so that completion of each puzzle is denoted in the final artifact.

To give an example of one of the puzzles, the conditional puzzle is found in the courtyard of the castle as seen in Figure 5. There is a stream that is blocked by a gate with four locks. There are also four statues lining the edges of the courtyard: some are facing towards the courtyard wall and some are facing towards the stream. The player can turn the statues, which will lock or unlock a specific lock on the gate. Turning all the statues to face the stream unlocks the gate. This in turn allows the stream to flow freely and fill a pond. This frees a key that the player must pick up and use to unlock the final door to leave the castle.

If the player gets stuck on a puzzle, they are able to find hints through exploration that use pseudocode to note how the puzzle might be solved. For instance, with the gate puzzle, the player may find a note from the previous owner of the castle with the following inscribed on it:

```
IF statue IS facing stream THEN
        gate IS unlocked
ELSE
        gate IS locked
```

The design of BeadED Adventures emphasizes that there is not one right way to progress through the game. The exploration may be done in any order, and the puzzles support trial and error. This means that it's highly likely that each player will have a unique beaded artifact at the end of their play session, and that there is not one "right" configuration of beads, and therefore no color pattern is intended in this prototype.

## Future Work and Conclusion

BeadED Adventures is a work-in-progress system, and as such there is work left to be done to complete the game itself and continue testing and refining both the game and controller.

We plan to test the system with teen and tween girls along different metrics, including:

1. How appealing is the interface to this demographic, and how can we continue to improve the design?
2. How does having a tangible artifact of play affect enjoyment and memory of concepts covered?
3. How does a narrative-based game style interaction compare to other computational thinking interventions?

The answers to these questions will continue to shape the evolution of the BeadED Adventures system.

## References


[1] Lea Albaugh, April Grow, Chenxi Liu, James McCann, Gillian Smith, and Jennifer Mankoff. 2016. Threadsteading: Playful Interaction for Textile Fabrication Devices. In Proceedings of the 2016 CHI Conference Extended Abstracts on Human Factors in Computing Systems (CHI EA '16), 285–288. DOI:https://doi.org/10.1145/2851581.2889466

[2] James R. Brinson. 2015. Learning outcome achievement in non-traditional (virtual and remote) versus traditional (hands-on) laboratories: A review of the empirical research. Computers & Education 87, (2015), 218–237.

[3] Isabella Carlsson, Jeanie Choi, Celia Pearce, and Gillian Smith. 2017. Designing eBee: A Reflection on Quilt-Based Game Design. In Proceedings of the 2017 Foundations of Digital Games Conference.

[4] Susan Feez. 2008. Multimodal representation of educational meanings in Montessori pedagogy. Multimodal Semiotics: Functional Analysis in Contexts of Education (2008), 201.

[5] James J. Gibson. 1962. Observations on active touch. Psychological review 69, 6 (1962), 477.

[6] Michael S. Horn. 2018. Tangible Interaction and Cultural Forms: Supporting Learning in Informal Environments. Journal of the Learning Sciences 27, 4 (October 2018), 632–665. DOI:https://doi.org/10.1080/10508406.2018.1468259

[7] Michael S. Horn, R. Jordan Crouser, and Marina U. Bers. 2012. Tangible Interaction and Learning: The Case for a Hybrid Approach. Personal Ubiquitous Comput. 16, 4 (April 2012), 379–389. DOI:https://doi.org/10.1007/s00779-011-0404-2

[8] Felix Hu, Ariel Zekelman, Michael Horn, and Frances Judd. 2015. Strawbies: explorations in tangible programming. In Proceedings of the 14th International Conference on Interaction Design and Children - IDC '15, 410–413. DOI:https://doi.org/10.1145/2771839.2771866

[9] Caitlin Kelleher, Randy Pausch, Randy Pausch, and Sara Kiesler. 2007. Storytelling alice motivates middle school girls to learn computer programming. 1455–1464. DOI:https://doi.org/10.1145/1240624.1240844

[10] Gerald Knezek, Rhonda Christensen, Tandra Tyler-Wood, and Sita Periathiruvadi. 2013. Impact of Environmental Power Monitoring Activities on Middle School Student Perceptions of STEM. Science Education International 24, 1 (2013), 98–123.

[11] Matt Leacock. 2016. Knit Wit. Z-Man Games.

[12] Yusuke Morita and Norio Setozaki. 2017. Learning by Tangible Learning System in Science Class. In Human-Computer Interaction. Interaction Contexts (Lecture Notes in Computer Science), 341–352.

[13] Ryan Noonan. 2017. Women in STEM: 2017 update. Economic and Statistics (2017).

[14] Sinan Olkun. 2003. Comparing computer versus concrete manipulatives in learning 2D geometry. Journal of Computers in Mathematics and Science Teaching 22, 1 (2003), 43–56.

[15] Kelly Reimer and Patricia S. Moyer. 2005. Third-graders learn about fractions using virtual manipulatives: A classroom study. Journal of Computers in Mathematics and Science Teaching 24, 1 (2005), 5–25.

[16] Michael Saenz, Joshua Strunk, Sharon Lynn Chu, and Jinsil Hwaryoung Seo. 2015. Touch Wire: Interactive Tangible Electricty Game for Kids. In Proceedings of the Ninth International Conference on Tangible, Embedded, and Embodied Interaction (TEI '15), 655–659. DOI:https://doi.org/10.1145/2677199.2687912

[17] Kurt Squire, Mike Barnett, Jamillah M. Grant, and Thomas Higginbotham. 2004. Electromagnetism supercharged!: learning physics with digital simulation games. In Proceedings of the 6th international conference on Learning sciences, 513–520.

[18] Anne Sullivan, Joshua McCoy, Sarah Hendricks, and Brittany Williams. 2018. Loominary: Crafting Tangible Artifacts from Player Narrative. (2018).

[19] Anne Sullivan and Gillian Smith. 2016. Designing Craft Games. Interactions 24, 38–41. DOI:https://doi.org/https://doi.org/10.1145/3019004

[20] Women - Occupation - nsf.gov - Women, Minorities, and Persons with Disabilities in Science and Engineering - NCSES - US National Science Foundation (NSF). Retrieved November 12, 2018 from https://www.nsf.gov/statistics/2017/nsf17310/digest/occupation/women.cfm

[21] Yarn Quest 2017 - Heroes of Yarnia RPG MKAL pattern by Tania Richter. Ravelry. Retrieved March 23, 2018 from https://www.ravelry.com/patterns/library/yarn-quest-2017---heroes-of-yarnia-rpg-mkal

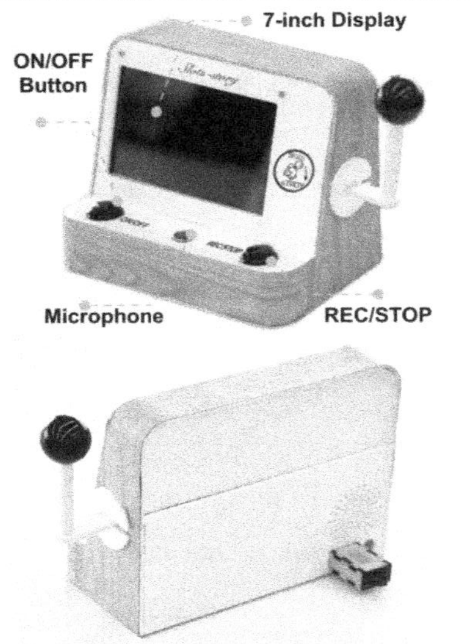


Figure 1: Its outlining shape is round-cornered, evoking an approachable and ergonomic design. Its L-shape makes the display easy to see, and buttons easy to access. Its portable dimension makes it easy to carry (L = 22cm, W = 11cm, H = 17cm). The main body is made of porcelain white acrylic, and part of it is covered with wood-grained paper, making it look slightly old-fashioned, which is in line with the aesthetic taste of older adults.

# Slots-Memento: Facilitating Intergenerational Memento Storytelling and Preservation for the Elderly

**Cun Li**
Eindhoven University of Technology
Eindhoven, Netherlands
cun.li@tue.nl

**Jun Hu**
Eindhoven University of Technology
Eindhoven, Netherlands
j.hu@tue.nl

**Bart Hengeveld**
**Caroline Hummels**
Eindhoven University of Technology
b.j.hengeveld@tue.nl
c.c.m.hummels@tue.nl


*TEI '19, March 17–20, 2019, Tempe, AZ, USA*

ACM ISBN 978-1-4503-6196-5/19/03.
https://doi.org/10.1145/3294109.3300979

## Abstract
Mementos carry personal symbolic meaning and can be used to privately reflect on the past or share memories[28]. Older adults spend much time collecting mementos but spend less time telling stories behind the mementos. Once they pass away, stories behind mementos vanish with their owners. In this paper, we present Slots-Memento, a tangible device aiming to facilitate intergenerational story sharing and preservation for older adults. It builds on the metaphor of slot-machine, and integrates functions of memento photo display, story recording, and preservation. Our design process started with context inquiry, older adults and young adults were recruited, aiming to understand the status quo of their memento storytelling, and define design requirements. A preliminary evaluation was conducted, discussion and future work are in the final part.

## Author Keywords
Older adults; memento; storytelling; tangible interface; social interaction.

| Basic information |
|---|
| Age, gender, physical condition Familiarity with technology |
| **Communication with family** Who, number, frequency, duration of contacting with family members |
| Way of keeping in touch (face-to-face, phone, skype,.etc) |
| **Current story sharing situation** |
| Mementos (like photographs, artifacts, everyday objects, etc.) they kept and the reasons, |
| Situations, and causes of sharing memento stories |
| Who, when, how to share them (face-to-face, phone, skype,.etc) |
| Topics, duration, and frequency of story sharing |
| Problems encountering during memento story sharing |

Table1: Interview questions in contextual inquiry

| Validity |
|---|
| Would you like to use it? |
| Do you think it could facilitate sharing memento stories? Why? |
| **Interaction** |
| Do you understand the concept of the prototype? |
| Do you find it easy to use? What is the most difficult part? |
| Which part do you like/dislike most of the prototype? Why? A. idea of sharing memento stories B. memento pictures in the prototype C. the handle D. others |
| Who, when, how to share them (face-to-face, phone, skype,.etc) |
| **Comments for improvements** |

Table 2: interview questions in preliminary evaluation

## CSS Concepts

• Human-centered computing~Human computer interaction (HCI) • Human-centered computing~Collaborative and social computing
• Social and professional topics~Seniors

## Introduction

Mementos are objects kept as a reminder of people, places, and experiences. When the same object was mentioned by young and old, young people connected to it actively, older people contemplatively[22]. Older adults typically have a rich knowledge of family mementos, which are highly valued, and support different types of family stories and recollections[19]. As technology advances, mementos (especially photos) are increasingly becoming digital[28]. Digital devices with online applications (Flickr, Instagram, Facebook, etc.) bring out great convenience for us to share mementos even with people at a distance.

However, storytelling and recording of mementos are still problematic for older adults: First, most older adults are still so-called 'Kodak Generation' maintaining print photo albums and physical mementos [15]. Currently passing around stacks of paper photographs while sitting around a table seemingly is the only way for them to share mementos. However, most of them live separately with their children (live alone or in a nursing home), making their mementos are hard to share with their children and preserve. Second, most older adults are still disconnected from the mainstream online social circles due to the lack of using experience and devices that resonate with them[29]. Therefore, digital online applications and websites for sharing mementos are normally inaccessible for them.

## Related Work

*Ethnographic studies on physical mementos*

There are ethnographic studies describing how and why particular objects become mementos[20], and exploring why and how those objects are kept and archived within the home [14]. Some research focus on family photos: Chalfen et al. acknowledge the central role of film photography in family representation and draws attention to how familial and domestic conventions are reproduced [2]. Swan and Talor's study points out that photo displays play into the shaping of a moral character to the home [27]. Richard Banks et al 's study focuses on heirlooms, and they investigate the role technology play as part of the process of inheritance[1]. As mementos are increasingly becoming digital, some fieldwork looks at characterizing and comparing physical and digital mementos in the home [19], as well as their advantages and disadvantages[6].

*Applications for memento storytelling*

Current applications focus more on digital mementos, which could be generalized into the following:

- Capture personal mementos: In order to capture data about one's personal life and keep a record of the past, the research area called lifelogging aims to benefit from the advantages of digitally storing memory cues by aiming for 'total recall'[24]. The data captured are various, from pictures [23], sound[18][4], to videos[25]. The forms range from tangible devices to wearable devices [10].
- Organizing and archiving personal mementos: These kinds of design are based on people's vast quantity of digital contents. Related applications mostly

Figure 2: **Physical object** (1-3): Forms of their physical objects were various, souvenir, artifact, trophy, sculpture, etc. Their sources were also various: artifacts inherited from parents, gifts from friends, souvenir

employ interactive devices, such as an interactive multi-touch tabletop [13], and a projector [9].

- Displaying and sharing personal mementos: People display photos in their homes to share narratives [12]. Most related works are used within nuclear families, aiming at facilitating conversations within family members. Most are in the forms of smart/interactive frames: "Photoswitch" [5], "Cherish System" [21], a system[7]. Their fundamental guideline is to enable digital content more accessible through devices that merge interactivity of physical objects with digital content.
- Others: other applications include attaching related stories to mementos based on barcodes and RFID technology: [26], [17], [11].

*Knowledge Gap*

Notwithstanding the above, questions remain. First, little research and design have been particularly paid to elderly users. HCI researchers give more attention to personal digital content, while mementos of older adults are mostly in physical format. Second, related applications mostly focus on co-present sharing, which are used within nuclear families, which are not applicable to older adults. Third, digital applications are designed for the young generation, which are not accessible for most elderly users. Fourth, for the research related physical memento, they focus on the mementos themselves, stories behind the mementos are normally ignored. While we focus on both the mementos and the representations behind them.

## Context Inquiry

Our design process started with context inquiry, aiming to understand the status quo of their memento storytelling, and define design requirements. We interviewed with older adults and young adults separately. As we aimed to deem the older adults as memento story producers, our context inquiry focused more on the older adults' side.

7 Dutch elderly people (five female and two male) were recruited, they were ranged in age from 73 to 84 years. Their marital status was: two lived with spouse; five lived alone (four widowed and one divorced). None of them reported any significant physical impairments. Each study consisted of a guided tour and a semi-structured interview. The study was held in the participants' homes, which could allow them to recall and describe their routines for photograph and memorabilia storage and sharing in context. We first asked them to arrange a brief guided tour of their homes, aiming to examine their mementos for displaying and stored in hidden places. With their permissions, we took photographs and notes. We then conducted semi-structured interviews (Table 1), which were audio recorded with their formal consents, and notes were taken to aid analysis. We also conducted short semi-structured interviews with five young adults (three female and two male). They were employees of the local university, ranging in age from 38 to 43 years. Them all lived separately with their parents and grandparents. They all married and lived with partner and children. The interviews were based loosely on "Current story sharing situation" of Table 1.

Grounded theory techniques [3] were adopted to analyze the above data, and affinity diagramming[8] was used to categorize these codes.

from travelling, and even made by themselves. **Paper document** (4-8): Their paper documents included postcard, letter, certificate, map, etc. **Photo** (9-10): Their photos were mostly in physical format, and all the participants kept serval albums. Compared with artifacts, photos were more space-spacing, therefore, photos were the most mementos that older adults held. Apart from one participant left his photos unsorted, the other six participants carefully organized their photos in the albums, envelopes, and boxes.

Figure 3: Mementos in hidden places

## Findings

*Basic information and their familiarity with technology*
Apart from the youngest elderly participant (M, age=73) had an iPad and used it to browse news, watch videos, and play simple games, the rest didn't use computers or smartphones. Either because they lack using experiences, or physical decline brought inconvenience (eyesight declines, movements and reflexes typically turned slow). They acquired information still mainly by traditional tools: newspapers, magazines, TV, etc.

*Connection with family members*
Connections with their siblings were less, because they were also aged, or even passed away. They had regular contact with children, who visited them regularly (ranged from once a week to once a month), and duration of each visiting was 2-4 hours. They typically connected by telephone. They called their children only when in special and urgent situations (festivals, diseases, etc.). Although some of them lived collective lives in the nursing home, they found it difficult to establish meaningful relationships with fellow residents.

*Types of older adults' mementos*
In David Kirk et al.'s study, they divided family mementos into physical, digital, and hybrid [14]. In our study, older adults' mementos were mostly in physical format. Therefore, physical mementos need to be further sub-classified. Because of the great number of photos that the older adults kept, photos were classified as one category. Ultimately, we classified their mementos into three categories (Figure 2):

- **Physical object**. As most older adults moved home multiple times, some artifacts were discarded, or given to their children. Only a part that was lightweight or precious were still in their possession. Especially for those who lived in nursing homes, the rooms were too small to hold all their belongings.
- **Paper document**. The certificates and maps were mostly displayed. Postcards and letters were tucked away in storage, either because they were hard to display, or they were too private.
- **Photo**. The albums were normally of different themes, for example, family, travelling, marriage, etc., and photos inside the albums were generally arranged in chronological order.

*Location of mementos*
Consistent with previous research [19], we found apart from a fraction of mementos were placed on display, most mementos were stored in hidden places(Figure 3).

- Mementos for displaying: Although decoration styles varied in older adults' home, they all had a small part of mementos displayed. For example, photos hanging on the wall, artefacts on shelf and table, etc. The reasons were either because they associated with special meaning (family photos, gift, inscription, etc.,) or because of their artistic values.
- Mementos stored in hidden places: As mementos took up too much space, most were placed in hidden places, such as drawer, closet, cabinets, even attic, basement, etc. This made the older adults seldom revisited them, not to mention telling stories behind them. The older adults gradually forgotten them.

*Situations of memento storytelling*
First, although mementos for displaying evoked conversations with guests, this happened only when family members or friends came for visits, which was accidental. Second, one older participant said

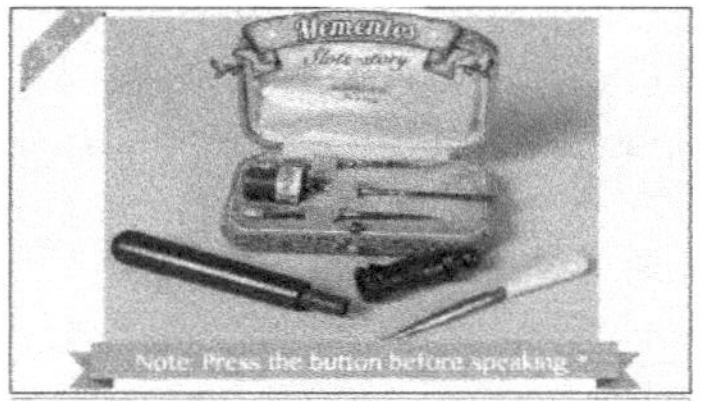

Figure 4: It contains two display interfaces: The **Photo interface and Recoding interface**. Vintage style is also applied in both the interface elements and fonts. There are usage tips at the bottom*: "Note: Press "REC/STOP button before/after recording".*

The **Photo Interface** displays one specific memento photo, which will be switched to the next/previous photo by pulling down/pushing up the handle. It will be switched to **Recoding Interface** if the REC/STOP button is pressed, and a dynamic recording icon and timer widget are placed to provide real-time feedback.

sometimes in holidays, the whole family would sit together to look through albums together, but that also happened occasionally.

*Problems encountering when sharing memento stories*

- Memento for displaying didn't fully support personal reminiscence: The older adults stated that those mementos in home environment were so familiar that often they didn't realize their presence.
- Mementos storytelling were seemingly ignored by both older adults and their children: Despite that all young participants stated that they were in stories behind their parents/grandparents' mementos, they rarely talked about the mementos specifically and deliberately in daily lives. They realized its importance only when their parents/grandparents passed away.
- Distance also prevented the intergenerational memento story sharing: Visiting time was short, they didn't have too much time to specifically talk about.
- Others: Older adults had the desire and demand of preserving lives: They hoped their lives could be remembered. For example, one participant filmed a video to document his life. One made a brief biographical note, in case their children wanted to know him when he passes away. Another participant had scanned and saved some of his photos.

## Design Requirements

- Integrating mementos into older adults' daily environments: As physical mementos took too much space, most of them were stored in hidden places, making them not accessible for sharing. We consider integrating them into their daily lives through an interactive device. Hence, a digitalization process of physical mementos is needed, which also contributes to memento preservation.
- Cross-generational cooperation: Although older adults had rich knowledge of family mementos, they normally were not skilled at technology. Whilst the young are empowered by technical competence. Therefore, our scheme is cross-generational cooperation: the young are responsible for digitalization their family mementos, while older adults are the memento story producers.
- Tangible interface employing metaphor and intuitive interaction: As most elderly interviewees couldn't operate digital devices, a tangible interface could be adopted. Physicality also makes it better integrated into their living environments. We could also employ metaphor and intuitive operation to enhance familiarity and simplicity for them.
- Using audio as the storage medium of stories: Given that older adults felt difficulty in writing as they age, compared with handwriting, direct speaking could lower the cost of narrative for them. Moreover, audio could retain more information than the text. (emotions, feelings, ambient sounds, etc.) In our context, audio also shows advantages over video: A study points out that video is too real to allow room for thinking about the past with others [2].
- Could be used either face-to-face or separately by older adults and their children: Despite that sitting together to communicate face-to-face is the most common and enjoyable way to share mementos[16], most older adults lived apart from their children, and duration of each visiting was limited. The older adults and their children's lives were also usually

Figure 5: prototype's hardware

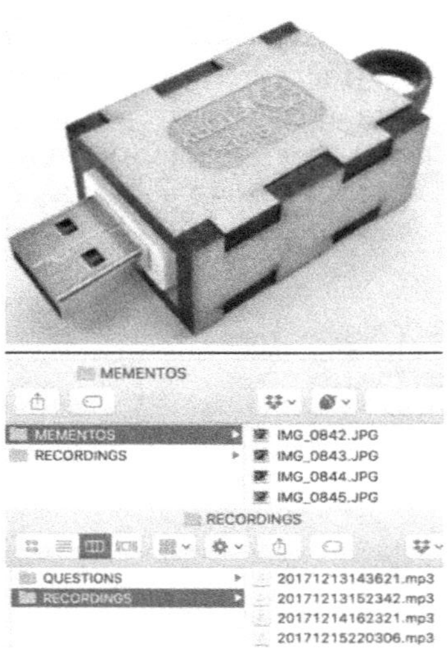



Figure 6: Flash drive is embedded in an MDF-made shell. There are two folders in it: **MEMENTOS**, containing the photos of mementos. **RECORDINGS**, containing story audios told by older adults.

unsynchronized. Hence, the prototype should be able to be used both face-to-face and separately.

## Prototype: Slots-Memento

Based on the above, we design Slots-Memento, which could either be used face-to-face or independently by the older adults and their children. Its interaction and form draw inspiration from slots-machine. The older adult could pull down/up the handle to switch memento photos, and press the button to record stories. We hope the metaphor of slot-machine and intuitive operation could offer familiar and enjoyable using experience to this non-tech-savvy user group. It consists of a slot machine-like device (Figure 1) and a flash disk (Figure 6). The flash disk is used to store memento photos and story audios. Interfaces are shown in Figure 4, and operation procedures are shown in Figure 7. Its hardware is shown in Figure 5: Raspberry Pi 2 Model B is the hardware platform, and the lever is 3D printed which could fit into the joystick component. Joystick USB Encoder board is the medium to connect Raspberry Pi and joystick. The 7-inch display is the graphical output.

## Preliminary Evaluation

To understand the prototype's acceptability to the older users, and get comments for improvements, we investigated our prototype with three older adults (81M,82F,79M). It was conducted in their rooms in nursing home (Figure 8). We firstly introduced purpose of our study, and showed them the prototype. We then asked what mementos older adults would like to share, and we took photos of their mementos, and copied them to the flash disk. Then, we asked them to use it, including browse memento photos and recording memories. Lastly, we conducted semi-structured interviews with them, the questions were loosely based on Table 2.

Overall, the participants felt that Slots-Memento could facilitate older adults' memento storytelling, and was accepted by them. They showed interests in it, especially its intuitive operation. They enjoyed telling memories related to their mementos. Our work also helped them to revisit and rediscover their mementos. Some of which were they almost forgot: *"It is good to see these photos again. I almost forgot them. I think the device is great, and I can put all my stories and emotions into it."* The participants were excited when some mementos were rediscovered. The recording function was also accepted by them. One participant remarked: *"I wanted to write a book of my stories, but always don't feel motivated to that. My eyesight declines. The recording is helpful."*

Regarding comment for improvement, first, one participant thought the prototype should be more friendly by displaying *"Thanks for your story"* after their stories are recorded. Second, by default, it should display the photos as a slideshow, to attract their attention, and encourage them to use. Third, adding story playing function, they hoped to show and play the stories to others. Regarding usability aspects, the display's brightness needed to be improved.

## Conclusion and Future Work

We have presented our ongoing work Slots-Memento, which was designed based on contextual inquiry. It was accepted by older adults in preliminary evolution. Next, the prototype will firstly be optimized based on the feedback. Afterwards, a formal long-term study (2 weeks) will be conducted, driven by research questions:

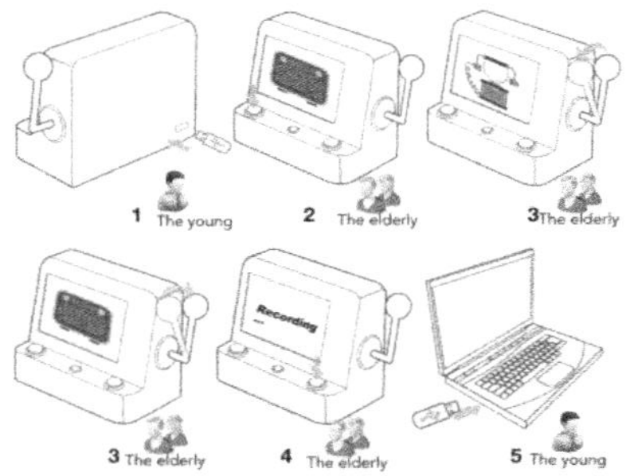


Figure 7: Detailed interaction process: (1) The young insert flash disk with memento photos into Slots-Memento, and then give it to older adults. (2) Older adults press the left button to turn it on. (3) Older adults pull down/push up the lever to switch to the next/previous photo. (4) Older adults press the right button to start recording, and press it again to save the recording. Stories told by older adults now are in the flash disk. (5) The young Plugs the flash disk into a computer to listen and keep stories, and further modifies memento photos (6) The Slots-Memento could also be used face-to-face.

*What mementos would older adults like to share, and what are the stories behind them? How to facilitate older adults to tell and preserve these stories? How to involve the young generation?* The prototype will be distributed to older adults and their children, mementos will be categorized, stories will be analyzed, and interviews will be conducted with both the older adults and their children.

## References

[1] Richard Banks, David Kirk, and Abigail Sellen. A Design Perspective on Three Technology Heirlooms. 30.

[2] Richard Chalfen. 1987. Snapshot versions of life. University of Wisconsin Press.

[3] Juliet Corbin, Anselm Strauss, and others. 2008. Basics of qualitative research: Techniques and procedures for developing grounded theory. .

[4] Lina Dib, Daniela Petrelli, and Steve Whittaker. 2010. Sonic souvenirs: exploring the paradoxes of recorded sound for family remembering. Proceedings of the 2010 ACM conference on Computer supported cooperative work - CSCW '10, ACM Press, 391.

[5] Abigail Durrant, Alex S Taylor, David Frohlich, Abigail Sellen, and David Uzzell. 2009. Photo displays and intergenerational relationships in the family home. 10.

[6] Connie Golsteijn, Elise van den Hoven, David Frohlich, and Abigail Sellen. 2012. Towards a more cherishable digital object. Proceedings of the Designing Interactive Systems Conference on - DIS '12, ACM Press, 655.

[7] Otmar Hilliges, Dominikus Baur, and Andreas Butz. 2007. Photohelix: Browsing, Sorting and Sharing Digital Photo Collections. Second Annual IEEE International Workshop on Horizontal Interactive Human-Computer Systems (TABLETOP'07), IEEE, 87–94.

[8] Karen Holtzblatt, Jessamyn Burns Wendell, and Shelley Wood. 2004. Rapid contextual design: a how-to guide to key techniques for user-centered design. Elsevier.

[9] Martijn Jansen, Elise van den Hoven, and David Frohlich. 2013. Pearl: living media enabled by interactive photo projection. Personal and Ubiquitous Computing.

[10] Shiqi Jiang, Pengfei Zhou, Zhenjiang Li, and Mo Li. 2017. Memento: An Emotion Driven Lifelogging System with Wearables. 2017 26th International Conference on Computer Communication and Networks (ICCCN), IEEE, 1–9.

[11] Tatsuyuki Kawamura, Tomohiro Fukuhara, Hideaki Takeda, Yasuyuki Kono, and Masatsugu Kidode. 2007. Ubiquitous Memories: a memory externalization system using physical objects. Personal and Ubiquitous Computing 11, 4: 287–298.

[12] Jeong Kim and John Zimmerman. Cherish: Smart Digital Photo Frames. 16.

[13] David S. Kirk, Shahram Izadi, Abigail Sellen, Stuart Taylor, Richard Banks, and Otmar Hilliges. 2010. Opening up the family archive. Proceedings of the 2010 ACM conference on Computer supported cooperative work - CSCW '10, ACM Press, 261.

[14] David Kirk and Abigail Sellen. On Human Remains: Excavating the Home Archive. 10.

[15] Christian Kray, Michael Rohs, Jonathan Hook, and Sven Kratz. 2009. Bridging the gap between the Kodak and the Flickr generations: A novel interaction technique for collocated photo sharing. International Journal of Human-Computer Studies 67, 12: 1060–1072.

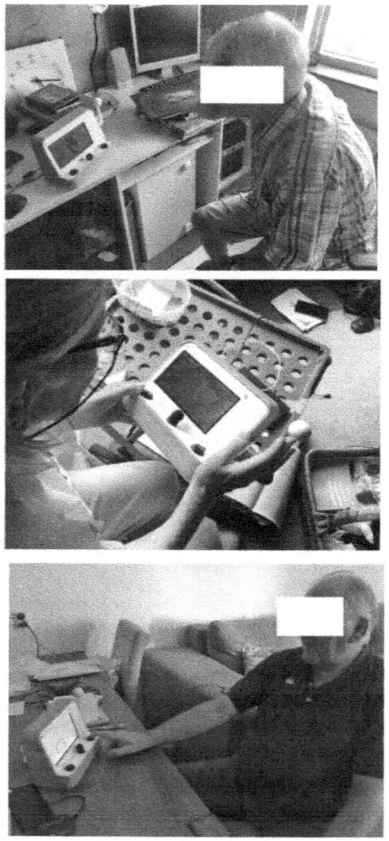

Figure 8: Interview with older adults

[16] Siân E. Lindley and Andrew F. Monk. 2008. Social enjoyment with electronic photograph displays: Awareness and control. International Journal of Human-Computer Studies 66, 8: 587–604.

[17] Michael Nunes, Saul Greenberg, and Carman Neustaedter. 2008. Sharing digital photographs in the home through physical mementos, souvenirs, and keepsakes. Proceedings of the 7th ACM conference on Designing interactive systems, ACM, 250–260.

[18] Daniela Petrelli, Nicolas Villar, Vaiva Kalnikaite, Lina Dib, and Steve Whittaker. 2010. FM radio: family interplay with sonic mementos. Proceedings of the SIGCHI Conference on Human Factors in Computing Systems, ACM, 2371–2380.

[19] Daniela Petrelli and Steve Whittaker. 2010. Family memories in the home: contrasting physical and digital mementos. Personal and Ubiquitous Computing 14, 2: 153–169.

[20] Daniela Petrelli, Steve Whittaker, and Jens Brockmeier. 2008. AutoTopography: what can physical mementos tell us about digital memories? Proceedings of the SIGCHI conference on Human Factors in computing systems, ACM, 53–62.

[21] Holly Schmidt, Uta Hinrichs, Alan Dunning, and Sheelagh Carpendale. memory [en]code Building a Collective Memory within a Tabletop Installation. 8.

[22] Michael Schudson. 1983. The Meaning of Things: Domestic Symbols and the Self. JSTOR.

[23] Abigail J. Sellen, Andrew Fogg, Mike Aitken, Steve Hodges, Carsten Rother, and Ken Wood. 2007. Do life-logging technologies support memory for the past?: an experimental study using sensecam. Proceedings of the SIGCHI conference on Human factors in computing systems, ACM, 81–90.

[24] Abigail J. Sellen and Steve Whittaker. 2010. Beyond total capture: a constructive critique of lifelogging. Communications of the ACM 53, 5: 70.

[25] Samarth Singhal, Carman Neustaedter, William Odom, Lyn Bartram, and Yasamin Heshmat. 2018. Time-Turner: Designing for Reflection and Remembrance of Moments in the Home. Proceedings of the 2018 CHI Conference on Human Factors in Computing Systems - CHI '18, ACM Press, 1–14.

[26] Molly M. Stevens, Gregory D. Abowd, Khai N. Truong, and Florian Vollmer. 2003. Getting into the Living Memory Box: Family archives & holistic design. Personal and Ubiquitous Computing 7, 3-4: 210–216.

[27] Laurel Swan and Alex S. Taylor. 2008. Photo displays in the home. Proceedings of the 7th ACM conference on Designing interactive systems - DIS '08, ACM Press, 261–270.

[28] Alice Thudt, Dominikus Baur, Samuel Huron, and Sheelagh Carpendale. 2016. Visual Mementos: Reflecting Memories with Personal Data. IEEE Transactions on Visualization and Computer Graphics 22, 1: 369–378.

[29] Jenny Waycott, Frank Vetere, Sonja Pedell, et al. 2013. Older adults as digital content producers. Proceedings of the SIGCHI Conference on Human Factors in Computing Systems, ACM, 39–48.

# Chasing The Buzz; Exploring Sense Deprivation In Bodily Play

Figure 1 – Two participants testing game version 4

**Katrine Løck Worm**
Department of Design and Communication
Uni of Southern Denmark
Kolding, 6000, Denmark
klw@sdu.dk

**Robb Mitchell**
Department of Design and Communication
University of Southern Denmark
Kolding, 6000, Denmark
robb@sdu.dk

**Christina Fyhn Nielsen**
Department of Design and Communication
University of Southern Denmark
Kolding, 6000, Denmark
cfni@sdu.dk


TEI '19, March 17–20, 2019, Tempe, AZ, USA

ACM ISBN 978-1-4503-6196-5/19/03.
https://doi.org/10.1145/3294109.3300995

## Abstract
Physical games involving blindfolded players have a timeless appeal and the restricting of perceptual channels can be insightful for players and observers regarding embodied experience. Wireless, mobile and wearable technologies open up further opportunities for designing bodily play experiences through exploiting sensory deprivation. To better understand the potential for movement-based games in which vision and/or audio is restricted, we iteratively developed and play-tested a series of three to four player chasing games. Based on our tests, we suggest the importance of ambiguity, proximity, and freedom of movement to support designing sensory deprivation games.

## Author Keywords
Sense deprivation; embodied interaction; bodily play; multimodal.

## CSS Concepts
Miscellaneous;

## Introduction
Bodily games are rich multi-sensory experiences. For instance, in the classic game, tag, we see the other players when we are chasing them, we hear the other players, we touch them when we 'tag' them and if it is fun, we hear their laughter. Bodily games may also rely

## Participants

In addition to the research team, 8 participants were recruited. 5 of these were master students within Design and 3 master students within Psychology. The age of the participants ranged from 24 to 32. The participants in each group were acquainted.

The participants were informally recruited via the university's master programs.

Exploration

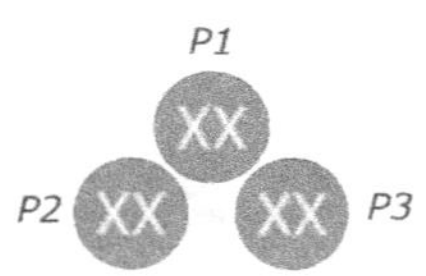


*Sense Deprivation:* sight

*Play:* 2 seeing participants making different sounds. 1 blindfolded participant had to locate the seeing participants using only touch and hearing.

*Goal:* Understanding the possibilities of senses in games and play

Figure 2 - First exploration and setup

on the deprivation of senses, as is the case with Marco Polo. Besides challenging those who are part of the game, sensory deprivation games have also been used to provide unconventional challenges. In traditional schoolyard games, such as soccer and dodgeball, it is not uncommon for the fastest player to dominate the game. Sensory deprivation is one way to even out the skills of the different players.

In this paper, we will take you through our iterative process of exploring how sight deprivation affects movement and how we designed a sense deprivation game based on those explorations. We emphasize the aspect of balancing player skills - meaning 'handicapping' all players through sensory deprivation to create a different play experience. The paper is based on a three-week project in which we conducted several exploration and testing phases, each with the goal of getting new insights into how sense deprivation affects players and how to improve gameplay. We end this paper with three design considerations rooted in our work and tested in our latest version of the game.

## Related Works

How engaged players are in a competitive experience rely heavily on the skill level of that individual player and the skill levels of the other players. According to Altimira et al. [1], the level of engagement is influenced by whether the right amount of challenge is provided. Balancing physical games can be seen in classical games like golf, where players have a 'handicap' or by imposing levelling rules, such as leading players should throw with their non-dominant arm. Levelling player skills, whether by putting up obstacles for leading players or enhancing less dominant players, has been done through restricting or manipulating the senses.

Using sensory substitution, Winoto & Tang [15] created a wearable mobile game that substituted vision for hearing to engage visually impaired players. Olickel et al. [11] on the other hand, created a game for all players, which substituted sight for haptic feedback through a wearable device.

A different path is sense deprivation, and a common sense to deprive players of is sight. Finnegan et al. [3] created the competitive, multiplayer, team-based game 'Reindeer & Wolves', where blindfolded wolves must catch seeing reindeer. The deprivation of sight can also be used as a factor in one-on-one competitive games, as was the case with 'Boy and Wolf' by Tiab et al. [13], where a blindfolded boy must catch a seeing 'wolf' (another player) with a loudspeaker on their head. Sensory deprivation has also been used in collaborative games like Audio Arc [8]. In Audio Arc players must, in pairs, find each other based on a unique sound emitted from their phones, while blindfolded. Lade and Duckworth [8] found that players experienced surprise, especially mentioning their "heightened experience of acoustic awareness and the challenge of spatial orientation whilst blindfolded".

Common for the aforementioned three games, is that they are played with at least one blindfolded player. This begs the question of what is gained from playing sense deprivation games? According to Vongsathorn et al. [14] removing "the visual sense (e.g. through shutting your eyes) is a well-established practice in somatics for heightening senses and focusing on an internal awareness of body movement that can encourage contemplation and reflection". Lade and Duckworth [8] also found that disabling players' visual senses resulted in responses that were more embodied,

Early Gameplay Testing

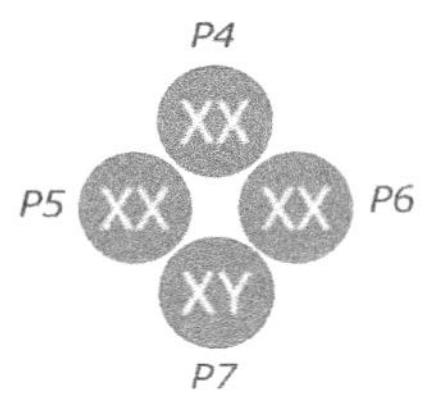


*Sense Deprivation:* sight and hearing

*Play:* 4 participants in two teams - all blindfolded, and two also deafened. In teams the hearing had to find the blindfolded and deafened teammate using touch and hearing.

*Goal:* Perceptions of being sense deprived in games and play

Figure 3 - Early Gameplay and setup

Gameplay Testing 1.0

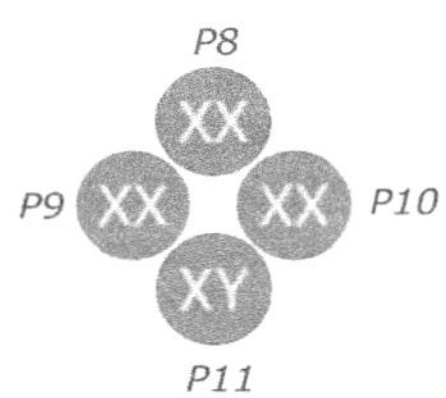


*Sense Deprivation:* sight

*Play:* All participants blindfolded. 1 game artefact. Participants had to locate game artifact and then keep aways from other participants

*Goal:* Create design suggestions based on tendencies within sense depriviation games and play

Figure 4 - Gameplay Testing 1.0 and setup

rather than inhibited, which might not be what we would normally expect when a sense is deprived of us. Sense deprivation allows for levelling of player abilities, by putting players in a new situation, which their body and senses are not used to, forcing them to think, act and move in new ways [13].

Relating to bodily interactions in games, we see people pushing, pulling, and strategically moving [9]. This can be conditioned by the type of bodily interplay intended in the game.

## Approach

This project follows the concept of research through design [16]. By actively reframing and iterating on the notion of sense deprivation games, we focused on designing the right thing based on knowledge and insights gained along the way. Our methodology included semi-structured group interviews [12], several tests with different participants and test analysis. For each semi-structured interview, an interview guide was created, and the session was video recorded. The testing was conducted in an approximately 60 m2 room with tables and chairs moved to the walls to ensure as much space as possible and to lower the risk of blindfolded participants bumping into furniture and hurting themselves.

The tests were conducted using a Wizard of Oz method [2]. For version 3 and 4 (Gameplay Testing 1.0 and 2.0) (Figure 4 & 7), a ball that emits sound when it is held by a player was created. Through using LittleBits (electronic, magnetic building blocks) to create circuits, which have the option of operating wirelessly, it was possible for the observer and scorekeeper to manually press a button, which would enable and disable the sound as needed.

All testing sessions were video recorded, and all videos were analyzed, first with a focus on general patterns of movement and reactions between the different participants. Then the videos were analyzed with specific emphasis on the soundtrack and exclamations made throughout the games by participants, to get a different perspective on the footage and the experiences of the participants. This analysis and the results from the interviews were compared to gain a deeper insight into what worked and what did not.

## Process

Our project had four phases, which we call 1) Exploration, 2) Early Gameplay Testing, 3) Gameplay Testing 1.0 and 4) Gameplay Testing 2.0.

To comprehend the importance of senses in gameplay, the research team (P1, P2, P3) - explored the possibilities and difficulties of being deprived of sight (Figure 2). The research team switched roles between being blindfolded or seeing in tasks involving locating the other participants solely based on different sounds. For each test round, the sounds varied, e.g. clapping or vocalizing. The aim was to understand whether the blindfolded participant would change tactics of locating the other participants.

As the initial explorations focused mainly on sight deprivation and working alone, the second step was to deprive more than one sense and to work in teams (Figure 3). In the Early Gameplay Testing, the participants tried abbreviated versions of the same exercises as was done in Exploration. Afterwards, the participants worked in teams of two (P4 & P5 + P6 & P7), P4 and P6 were blindfolded, while P5 and P7 were both deprived of their sight and hearing. So, participants were now deprived of two perceptual

Figure 5 - Participants chasing each other in a 'zombielike' pose

Figure 6 - Movement strategy

channels but similar to the first test, there we no rules concerning how players should locate each other. This was done with the aim of gaining insights into how the senses and the deprivation of senses influence participants in play.

The key findings from Exploration and Early Gameplay Testing showed patterns and tendencies. Firstly, the longer a participant was 'blind', the more they started to rely on their other senses and became more daring. Secondly, it quickly became clear that proximity is a factor. Participants seemed to know when they were close to someone, prompting more hand movements as well as laughter when close to or bumping into others. Thirdly, locating strategies seemed to emerge, as the participants who were locating the others positioned themselves in 'zombielike' poses with arms outstretched in front of them (see Figure 5). Though participants afterwards said they enjoyed parts of the tests and laughed, the video analysis showed that participants seemed nervous, uncomfortable and less inclined to engage, when deprived of two senses rather than just one. Therefore, subsequent versions only deprived participants of one sense, sight.

We base our subsequent gameplays on the two initial versions and tendencies discovered so far. The initial explorations give us a point of comparison concerning the number of participants along with familiarity amongst the participants and how this might affect the results.

*Gameplay Testing 1.0*
Participants P8, P9, P10 & P11 tested a gameplay in which all participants were blindfolded and had to get hold of a ball making sounds (Figure 6). Once a participant got the ball, they had to keep it for the longest time possible before other players 'stole' the ball.

Similar to the Early Gameplay Testing, it became evident that players tend to position themselves in a 'zombielike' pose, with both arms outstretched in front of their body in the approximate height of their shoulders. Little to no talking occurred once the game had begun, which might have contributed to players listening for the position of the ball. After playing the game for a while, one player employed a strategy of 'tricking' the other players by using the sound emitted by the ball to confuse the other players of its whereabouts. By holding the ball in one hand, extending his arm away from his body, he could quickly switch the position of the sound source and thus confuse his opponents. He succeeded in occupying the ball for a significantly longer time than his fellow players had done.

Compared to the first two versions (Exploration and Early Gameplay Testing), the players' skills became more equal, at least in the beginning, when all players were blindfolded. After playing the game for a while, player strategies began to emerge, allowing one player to keep the ball for an extended period of time. There were no patterns of a dominant player, who were keener to win, due to his/her athletic skills. But participants could gain an edge by using his/her other senses in strategic ways, for instance by listening to footsteps. Therefore, we chose to continue with all players being blindfolded in the following version.

*Gameplay Testing 2.0*
The latest game version has participants chasing the Buzz. The game is intended for three to six players. All players are blindfolded, and the aim is to catch a ball

Gameplay Testing 2.0

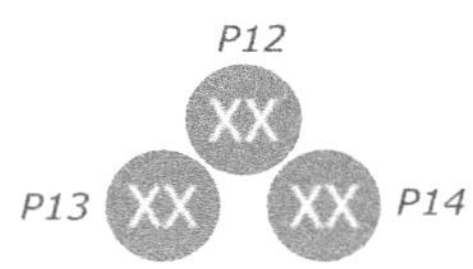


*Sense Deprivation:* sight

*Play:* 3-6 participants - all blindfolded. Aim is to find and keep ball 3 times for 15 seconds without being catched by other participants.

*Goal:* Testing gameplay based on design suggestions.

Figure 7 - Gameplay Testing 2.0 and setup

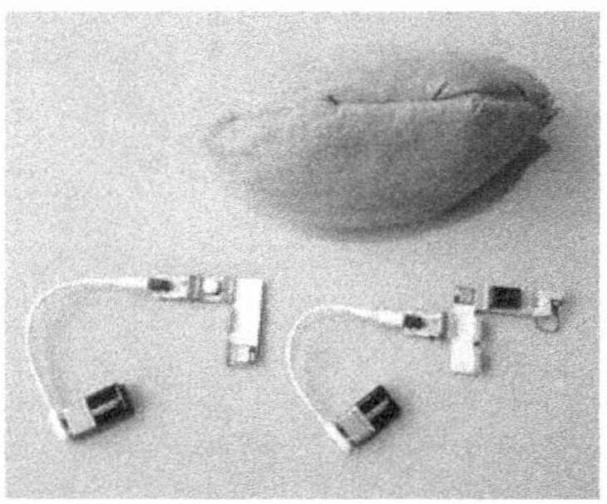

Figure 8 - Game ball 'the Buzz' with LittleBits' Wireless Transmitter, Wireless Receiver, Button, Buzzer and Vibration Motor

(the Buzz) and keep it for 15 seconds without being caught by the other players. When one player achieves this three times, the player wins. The ball makes a constant beep, and when a player is caught, it buzzes, which tells the player to pass the ball. When the ball is passed, it is quiet for five seconds allowing the player with the ball to move away from the other players, who are standing still. Time and score were kept by the researchers.

Findings from Gameplay Testing 2.0 showed three main themes: Ambiguity in rules, importance of proximity and concern of safety. The research team gave instructions as above on how the gameplay was to be carried out. Noticeable, the instructions did not include how the players should handle, catch, or handover the ball, which allowed players to create their own strategies on how to play. This ensured that players had freedom to (somewhat) adjust the game to how they wanted to play. As the players had to 'steal' the ball from each other, the gameplay involved a lot of proximity. This resulted in both laughing as players bumped into one another, and a diverse use of other senses than sight, as they had to rely on their hearing and proprioception (which is the posture and the movement of parts of the body [4]). Lastly, safety was key to the players. They had to be sure that running around blindfolded, would not injure them. Therefore, safe surroundings, meaning nothing to fall over or run into, was crucial for the players to be comfortable playing the game.

## Discussion

This paper presents different iterations of a sense deprivation game and shows opportunities of levelling out players' skills in a competitive game by depriving them of one sense. We found that levelling out all players' skills by removing the same sense was key, as it prohibited one player to have advantages over the others.

Though proximity proved to be an important part of sensory deprivation games, we had concerns whether the participants would overstep each other's personal boundaries as it would be mixed gender groups, and the risk of touching inappropriately was high due to the blindfolding. To our surprise it did not concern the participants. In Gameplay Testing 2.0, which only involved women, the personal boundaries were mentioned, and one participant commented that it was nice that the test group only consisted of 'girls'. The issue had not been raised earlier in the mixed gender test groups. This could be an implication, but further testing will be necessary to assess whether it is an issue or not.

In Gameplay Testing 1.0 & 2.0, all participants had the same disadvantage, not being able to see, to avoid players having different advantages and whenever a new player caught the ball, a head start was given. Once the ball had been caught, it would go silent for five seconds, while the player could move around, and the other players had to remain still. However, the other participants would still listen to the footsteps of the moving player with the ball, because two participants chose to wear shoes. Thereby players could rather quickly position other players. A similar strategy also appears in The Early Gameplay Testing. This implication allows for further development either by having the game played in socks and on a smooth floor or by actively using it as a game factor.

Figure 9 - P10 dodging the other players

*Designing for Sight Deprivation*
Taking the insights gained in the Exploration version, the Early Gameplay Testing version and Gameplay Testing 1.0 & 2.0 into consideration, three design considerations have been formulated to aid designers wanting to create sight deprivation games. The considerations are as follows.

*Ambiguity*: Utilizing ambiguity as a resource for designing, grants the designers the opportunity to investigate different possibilities and implications of the game without giving the answer [6]. Though Gaver proposed three type of ambiguity; ambiguity of *information*, ambiguity of *context* and ambiguity of *relationship* [6], we simply conveyed the use of ambiguity of information in our gameplay. Giving ambiguous information on how to play, supported the play by enabling the participant to apply the strategy they found useful, and not being dictated by strict rules of how to play. This is supported by the following statement on ambiguity from Isbister and Mueller [7] "players enjoy surfing uncertainty and trying to figure out optimal strategies in a somewhat messy system." Strategies, such as dodging, deceptions, and manipulation in different ways occurred during the games (Figure 9). This allowed participants to go beyond what was intended for the game, for instance, by allowing players to 'trick' other players. Permitting ambiguity in gameplay can enable new ways of engagement in games [5].

*Involve proximity:* It was clear, that whenever participants came in contact with or close proximity to other players, laughter and exclamations increased significantly. In all versions, laughter was prompted by players crashing into one another, touching one another and when someone was almost caught. As discovered through our tests, incorporating proximity into the game, as a game factor, increased player engagement. Similar to Mueller et al. [10], we propose the conscious decision of applying proximity in sense deprivation games, as it facilitates new experiences of play.

*Freedom to move:* Participants are more likely to move freely, when they know the possibility of hitting or falling over things is minimal. Designers should ensure that participants are in a safe space when playing the game. This also allows participants the opportunity to move independently throughout the game.

As the design considerations are based on a tag-like game, the extent to which the considerations can be applied in a broader context, for instance in relation to other games, require further work and testing.

## Conclusion
In this paper, we have presented our iterative process through which different versions of a sight deprivation game was explored. Based on this, we contribute with three design considerations for developing sense deprivation games. These are: allow ambiguity, involve proximity and give players the freedom to move. The next steps would be to use the design considerations in the creation of a new sense deprivation game to verify the validity of the suggestions. Furthermore, it would be interesting to test the latest gameplay version with different groups of players as well as test with players who are disabled, for instance, blind.

## Acknowledgements
We are grateful for the participants' involvement in the project and would to thank our research department for their support.

## References

[1] David Altimira, Florian Floyd Mueller, Jenny Clarke, Gun Lee, Mark Billinghurst, and Christoph Bartneck. 2017. Enhancing player engagement through game balancing in digitally augmented physical games. Int. J. Hum.-Comput. Stud. 103, C (July 2017), 35-47. DOI: https://doi.org/10.1016/j.ijhcs.2017.02.004

[2] Bill Buxton. 2011. Sketching user experiences: getting the design right and the right design. Morgan Kaufmann, Amsterdam.

[3] Daniel J. Finnegan, Eduardo Velloso, Robb Mitchell, Florian Mueller, and Rich Byrne. 2014. Reindeer & wolves: exploring sensory deprivation in multiplayer digital bodily play. In Proceedings of the first ACM SIGCHI annual symposium on Computer-human interaction in play (CHI PLAY '14). ACM, New York, NY, USA, 411-412. DOI: https://doi.org/10.1145/2658537.2661309

[4] Esther P Gardner and John H Martin. 2000. Coding of Sensory Information. In PRINCIPLES OF NEURAL SCIENCE. McGraw-Hill Medical.

[5] Jayden Garner, Gavin Wood, Sandra Danilovic, Jessica Hammer, and Florian Mueller. 2014. Intangle: exploring interpersonal bodily interactions through sharing controllers. In Proceedings of the first ACM SIGCHI annual symposium on Computer-human interaction in play (CHI PLAY '14). ACM, New York, NY, USA, 413-414. DOI: https://doi.org/10.1145/2658537.2661306

[6] William W. Gaver, Jacob Beaver, and Steve Benford. 2003. Ambiguity as a resource for design. In Proceedings of the SIGCHI Conference on Human Factors in Computing Systems (CHI '03). ACM, New York, NY, USA, 233-240. DOI=http://dx.doi.org/10.1145/642611.642653

[7] Katherine Isbister and Florian "Floyd" Mueller. 2015. Guidelines for the Design of Movement-Based Games and Their Relevance to HCI. Hum.-Comput. Interact. 30, 3-4 (May 2015), 366-399. DOI=http://dx.doi.org/10.1080/07370024.2014.996647

[8] Jennifer Lade and Jonathan Duckworth. 2013. Audio arc: an audio-spatial game using mobile phone ringtones. In Proceedings of the 9th ACM Conference on Creativity & Cognition (C&C '13), Ellen Yi-Luen Do, Steven Dow, Jack Ox, Steve Smith, Kazushi Nishimoto, and Chek Tien Tan (Eds.). ACM, New York, NY, USA, 401-402. DOI: https://doi.org/10.1145/2466627.2481228

[9] Florian 'Floyd' Mueller, Martin R. Gibbs, Frank Vetere, and Darren Edge. 2017. Designing for Bodily Interplay in Social Exertion Games. ACM Trans. Comput.-Hum. Interact. 24, 3, Article 24 (May 2017), 41 pages. DOI: https://doi.org/10.1145/3064938

[10] Florian Mueller, Sophie Stellmach, Saul Greenberg, Andreas Dippon, Susanne Boll, Jayden Garner, Rohit Khot, Amani Naseem, and David Altimira. 2014. Proxemics play: understanding proxemics for designing digital play experiences. In Proceedings of the 2014 conference on Designing interactive systems (DIS '14). ACM, New York, NY, USA, 533-542. DOI: https://doi.org/10.1145/2598510.2598532

[11] Hrishi Olickel, Parag Bhatnagar, Aaron CS Ong, and Simon T. Perrault. 2017. GooseBumps: Towards Sensory Substitution Using Servo Motors. In Proceedings of the 2017 ACM International Conference on Interactive Surfaces and Spaces (ISS '17). ACM, New York, NY, USA, 425-428. DOI: https://doi.org/10.1145/3132272.3132293

[12] David Silverman. 2013. Doing qualitative research: A practical handbook. SAGE Publications Limited.

[13] John Tiab, Juho Rantakari, Mads Laurberg Halse, and Robb Mitchell. 2016. Digital Sound De-Localisation as a Game Mechanic for Novel Bodily Play. In Proceedings of the 9th Nordic Conference

on Human-Computer Interaction (NordiCHI '16). ACM, New York, NY, USA, Article 109, 6 pages. DOI: https://doi.org/10.1145/2971485.2996744

[14] Linden Vongsathorn, Kenton O'Hara, and Helena M. Mentis. 2013. Bodily interaction in the dark. In Proceedings of the SIGCHI Conference on Human Factors in Computing Systems (CHI '13). ACM, New York, NY, USA, 1275-1278. DOI: https://doi.org/10.1145/2470654.2466166

[15] Pinata Winoto and Tiffany Y. Tang. 2015. Sensory substitution to enable the visually impaired to play an affordable wearable mobile game. In Adjunct Proceedings of the 2015 ACM International Joint Conference on Pervasive and Ubiquitous Computing and Proceedings of the 2015 ACM International Symposium on Wearable Computers (UbiComp/ISWC'15 Adjunct). ACM, New York, NY, USA, 193-196. DOI: https://doi.org/10.1145/2800835.2800915

[16] John Zimmerman, Jodi Forlizzi, and Shelley Evenson. 2007. Research through design as a method for interaction design research in HCI. In Proceedings of the SIGCHI Conference on Human Factors in Computing Systems (CHI '07). ACM, New York, NY, USA, 493-502. DOI: https://doi.org/10.1145/1240624.1240704

# Skweezee for Processing: A Software Library to Make Squeeze Interactions

**Bert Vandenberghe**
**Kathrin Gerling**
**Luc Geurts**
**Vero Vanden Abeele**
KU Leuven
Leuven, Belgium
firstname.lastname@kuleuven.be

## Abstract

Squeeze interaction, defined as squeezing a soft object that affects computed feedback, is a promising interaction technique due to its expressive character. *Skweezee for Processing* is a Processing library that allows makers to implement squeeze interactions in a lightweight manner. The library offers a set of features based on data extraction algorithms and aims to preserve the dynamics of squeezes in the mapping from user action to system output. Distributing *Skweezee for Processing* as an open source library, we invite the community to further investigate the potential of squeeze interactions and to contribute to the extension and improvement of the library. We emphasize the potential for rich squeeze interaction by demonstrating a game that implements squeeze interaction as core mechanic. Additionally, we demonstrate the ease of implementing squeeze interactions in a variety of settings using the *Skweezee for Processing* library.

## CCS Concepts

•**Human-centered computing** → **Human computer interaction (HCI);** *Interaction devices;*

## Author Keywords

Skweezee; squeeze interaction; tangible interaction; open source library; toolkit; making.


ACM ISBN 978-1-4503-6196-5/19/03.
http://dx.doi.org/10.1145/3294109.3300984

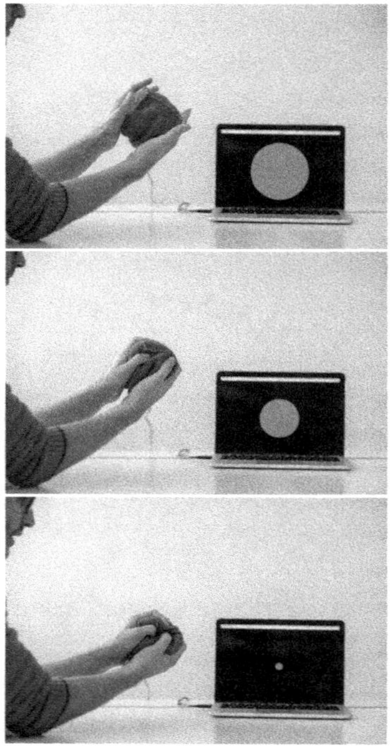

**Figure 1:** Skweezee for Processing facilitates a quick implementation of squeeze interaction. By generating output using continuous squeeze parameters, the dynamics of squeezes can be preserved from user action to output.

## Introduction

Squeeze interaction, defined as squeezing a soft object that affects computed feedback, is a promising interaction technique. The potential of squeeze interaction is discussed in numerous publications in HCI literature. For example, it is presented as "intuitive" [6] and offering "a more engaging experience" [1]. This physical engagement of squeeze interactions finds its use in game controllers, as demonstrated in several projects [1, 6]. Due to the expressive nature [2] and "nuanced control" [4], we also find numerous creative tools implementing squeeze interaction. Examples include musical instruments [9, 11] and sculpting tools [4, 7]. Stienstra & Marti also demonstrate the richness of squeeze interaction by addressing the affective component of squeezes to call a robot [8]. A gentle squeeze elicits a friendly reaction from the robot, while a hard squeeze results in an abrupt reaction. Here, the dynamics of the squeeze have an influence on the reaction of the robot.

In contrast to detailed application case studies, we only find fragmented documentation of the actual technical implementation of squeeze interaction in HCI literature; it appears that there is a frequent disconnect between the measurement of squeezes, signal processing, and feedback generation. For example, sensor resolution only tells part of the story of how user action (the squeeze) and system feedback are coupled. However, the specifics of this coupling, as theoretically presented by authors like Wensveen et al. [12], have a fundamental impact on the interaction itself. We argue that as a research community, we cannot discuss squeeze interaction and its potential in full unless we also discuss the technical implementation in detail. We reinforce this argument by demonstrating the range of technical possibilities offered by our library at TEI, as well as by publishing it as an open source software library to be used by other researchers and designers.

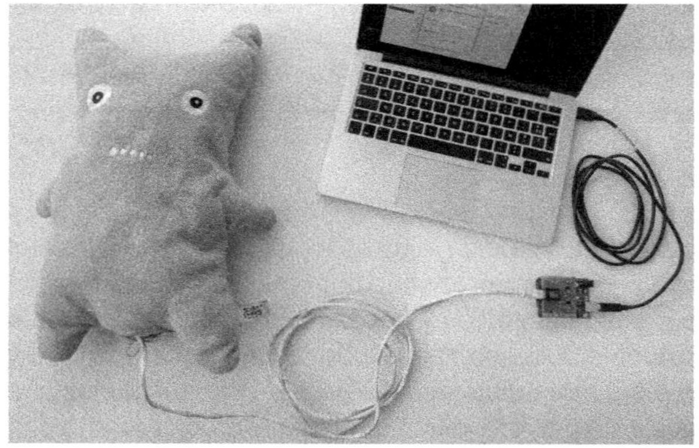

**Figure 2:** The Skweezee system: a soft squeezable object, an Arduino with custom shield, and desktop software.

### *Skweezee*

The present work is a continuation of the Skweezee system [10] and Skweezee DIY kit [5]. In these preceding projects, a DIY kit was built that allows the use of soft objects such as soft toys for computer input, using conductive wool as stuffing (see Figure 2). An Arduino with a custom shield continuously measures the resistance between 8 electrodes (i.e., 28 possible pairs of electrodes), and sends these 28 values to a computer. Desktop software implementing a support vector machine (SVM) allows the end-user to distinguish multiple gestures, map these gestures to virtual key strokes, enabling the end-user to control a wide range of 3rd party software like flash games or a media player. The DIY kit including the software components was published online in 2015 with the goal of enabling occupational therapists to create interactive therapeutic tools.

While the original Skweezee implementation worked well, we did identify some tensions regarding the use of machine learning (applying an SVM to recognize gestures). The calculations come with a computational load, as well as the requirement to train the algorithm by repeating the same gesture multiple times before the Skweezee system can be used. In a DIY setting, the implementation also raised a technical barrier for makers. Moreover, by discretizing squeeze input to a limited set of gestures, the continuous character and dynamics of squeeze interaction got lost. As a result, squeeze interaction as implemented by the original Skweezee kit could mainly be used to control applications that are based on discrete user input (such as mouse clicks or key strokes).

## Skweezee for Processing Library

In an attempt to preserve the dynamics of squeezes (see Figure 1), the present library processes raw sensor values through data extraction algorithms. Furthermore, we removed the machine learning component from the Skweezee system, replacing it with a lightweight alternative while still facilitating gesture recognition. Finally, for a novice programmer, the Skweezee for Processing library hides technical detail such as setting up a serial connection with an Arduino or implementing signal processing algorithms. As a result, the revised Skweezee software simplifies the process of experimenting with the potential of squeeze interaction that emerges from the richness of a squeeze. However, as the library is published as an open source software project, experienced programmers can still access and adapt those aspects if desired.

The remaining components of Skweezee are not altered: Eight electrodes are placed in a physical object that is filled with conductive wool. The electrodes are connected to an Arduino through the custom shield, which continuously measures the resistance between all possible combinations of the eight electrodes (resulting in a set of 28 values). The data is written to the serial port, for the computer software to retrieve. The Arduino runs at a frequency of 33Hz, meaning that every 30ms a new measurement is available.

| | |
|---|---|
| Skweezee.measurement() | raw data, array of resistances between all possible pairs of electrodes |
| Skweezee.vector() | a vector, constructed from the array elements of the measurement |
| Skweezee.subvectors() | set subvectors, one for each electrode |
| Skweezee.magnitude() | magnitude of the vector |
| Skweezee.subdirections() | set of unit vectors per subvector |
| Skweezee.magnitude(Signal.AVG) | with this parameter, the moving average of the signal is calculated |
| Skweezee.magnitude(Signal.AVG, Window.EXP) | with this second parameter, the calculation method can be altered |
| Skweezee.magnitude(Signal.STDEV) | returns the moving standard deviation of the signal |
| Skweezee.magnitude(Signal.MAX) | the maximum observed value |
| Skweezee.magnitude(Signal.DIFF) | the first derivative of the signal |
| Skweezee.magnitude(Signal.DIFF, Stencil.FIVE) | with this second parameter, the derivation method can be altered |

**Table 1:** Examples of available features in the Skweezee for Processing library, for the full set of features and details we refer to the actual library and included documentation.

The library offers basic manipulations, like calculating the average value of all retrieved values in one measurement. One measurement of the Skweezee Arduino shield contains 28 values—one for each possible combination between 8 electrodes. The *average()* parameter thus represents the momentary squeeze in one number. Regarding a measurement as a 28-dimensional vector, we calculate its unit vector which we then use for gesture recognition. To complement these momentary values, the mean value takes into account historic values, filtering noise from the signal at a cost of an introduced latency. Table 1 gives a full overview of the current features of the Skweezee for Processing library.

The end-user imports the library, and can directly access a range of squeeze parameters in the Processing environment. Serial connection and signal processing is handled in the background, as illustrated by the (working) example code below:

```
import processing.serial.*;
import net.skweezee.processing.*;

void setup() {
    Skweezee.connect(this);
}

void draw() {
    float sq = Skweezee.magnitude();
    println(sq);
}
```

As the initial Skweezee implementation was released as a DIY kit online, we prefer to preserve this openness. We therefore release the Skweezee for Processing library and accompanying documentation as an open source project, available at Github[1]. The library is a work-in-progress, allowing us to improve and extend the library over time, based on our own future work and perhaps via contributions by the community. We find endorsement for this approach in recent work by Boucher et al., who distributed their research as an open source project, "a novel approach to disseminating a research methodology" [3].

## How to Make Squeeze Interactions with Skweezee

The presented Skweezee for Processing library is part of the Skweezee kit, for the creation of comprehensive interactive systems that implement squeeze interaction. Together with the library, documentation is provided to create a Skweezee from scratch.

We distinguish three main components in a Skweezee system: a soft physical object that can be squeezed; electronics to sense the deformation; and software that processes the sensed deformation and generates output. For each of these three components, we offer multiple options and the corresponding instructions to create the squeeze interaction.

*Soft squeezable object*

The maker *activates* an existing object such as a soft toy by replacing its stuffing with the conductive material, or can sew a dedicated object. We offer patterns for basic geometric forms in the instructions. Our experiments show that using hot glue or safety pins proves to work if sewing presents a barrier. The use of safety pins allows for quick modifications and thus facilitates rapid iterations.

[1] http://github.com/skweezee

**Figure 3:** Skweezee sensing shield for Arduino

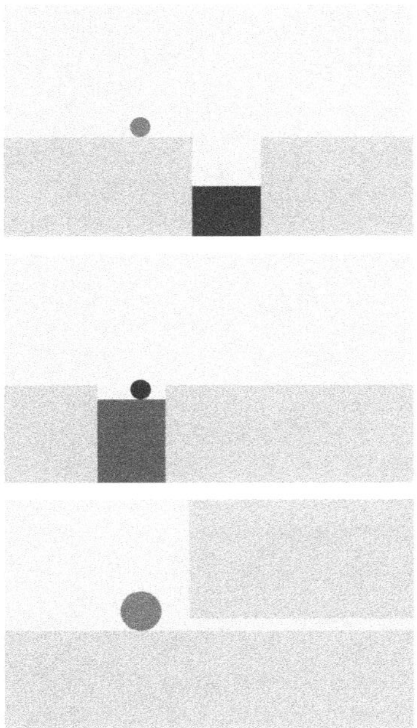

**Figure 4:** Screenshots of the demo game

Other conductive materials than conductive wool can be used, such as conductive foam used for electronics packaging (black conductive ESD foam), which may be obtained more easily.

*Electronics & Arduino*
By default an Arduino and our custom shield are used. The shield extends the six available analog pins of a standard Arduino to 28 possible electrode pairs. We use a UTP cable (a standard computer networking cable) to wire the electrodes, as it has 8 wires and is commonly available. The Skweezee for Processing library comes with the required Arduino sketch, and the custom shield schematics are available too.

The library allows a workaround without the shield for a more accessible, though limited implementation. In its most basic configuration, a soft object stuffed with black conductive ESD foam (which is widely available) is used together with an off-the-shelf Arduino Uno. The maker connects two to six wires directly to the analog inputs of the Arduino.

*Software*
As explained and demonstrated in the Skweezee for Processing section, our library hides technical details from the application, making it easy to implement a squeeze interaction. The Processing environment allows for quick textual, graphical, or even basic auditory feedback. In a set of examples that come with the Skweezee for Processing library, we demonstrate how the Skweezee for Processing library can be applied in different settings.

## Demo: Ball Game
In a demonstrator game, the player helps a ball to roll along a route. Various obstacles, such as narrow passages or gaps can be crossed by manipulating game elements using squeezes (see Figure 5).

**Figure 5:** Demo game: manipulate game elements with squeezes.

From a technical perspective, this game demonstrates the ease of how squeeze interaction can be applied in different settings using the Skweezee for Processing library.

Regarding interaction design, the game hints at the potential of squeeze interaction by coupling the squeeze to various properties of elements in the game (such as size or speed). Throughout the game, both the playable character (the red ball) and elements in the environment (such as elevators that help the ball to cross gaps) can be manipulated at different moments in the game.

## Conclusion & Future Work
In this paper, we presented a lightweight solution to implement squeeze interaction for makers. The Skweezee for Processing library removes the technical barriers to implement squeeze interaction. By distributing the Skweezee for Processing library as an open source project, we invite the community to build systems integrating squeeze interaction in a variety of application domains and to continue

the investigation of the potential of squeeze interaction. In our own research, we currently apply squeeze interaction in a therapeutic setting using the Skweezee for Processing library.

While Skweezee for Processing requires the use of a computer running Processing, *Skweezee for Arduino* or *Skweezee for Unity* are also explored in our research. These approaches will further extend the range of possibilities for makers and researchers, allowing stand-alone implementations as well as remote or ambient feedback on a variety of platforms. We see the present demonstration as agenda setting for our future research activities.

The research that lead to this Processing library is placing squeeze interaction in the landscape of rich interaction theories. Our research will continue to investigate the characteristics of rich squeeze interaction, and aims to place Skweezee within the grand theories on rich interaction, such as the Interaction Frogger Framework by Wensveen et al. [12]. Furthermore, as we want to explore applications for squeeze interaction beyond the predominant discrete computing paradigm, we will keep extending the set of library features and examples in the future.

## References

[1] Tristan Beven, Thuong Hoang, Marcus Carter, and Bernd Ploderer. 2016. HandLog: A Deformable Tangible Device for Continuous Input Through Finger Flexion. In *Proceedings of the 28th Australian Conference on Computer-Human Interaction - OzCHI '16*. ACM Press, New York, New York, USA, 595–604. DOI:http://dx.doi.org/10.1145/3010915.3010933

[2] Harvey Bewley and Anna Vallgårda. 2017. Provoking Performing Objects: Expanding the Design Space for Soft Robotics. In *Proceedings of the 2017 ACM Conference Companion Publication on Designing Interactive Systems - DIS '17 Companion*. ACM Press, New York, New York, USA, 243–248. DOI: http://dx.doi.org/10.1145/3064857.3079154

[3] Andy Boucher, Dean Brown, Liliana Ovalle, Andy Sheen, Mike Vanis, and William Gaver. 2018. TaskCam. In *Extended Abstracts of the 2018 CHI Conference on Human Factors in Computing Systems - CHI '18*. ACM Press, New York, New York, USA, 1–4. DOI:http://dx.doi.org/10.1145/3170427.3186536

[4] Sean Follmer, Micah Johnson, Edward Adelson, and Hiroshi Ishii. 2011. deForm: An Interactive Malleable Surface for Capturing 2.5D Arbitrary Objects, Tools and Touch. In *Proceedings of the 24th annual ACM symposium on User interface software and technology - UIST '11*. ACM Press, New York, New York, USA, 527. DOI: http://dx.doi.org/10.1145/2047196.2047265

[5] Argyro Moraiti, Vero Vanden Abeele, Erwin Vanroye, and Luc Geurts. 2015. Empowering Occupational Therapists with a DIY-toolkit for Smart Soft Objects. In *Proceedings of the Ninth International Conference on Tangible, Embedded, and Embodied Interaction - TEI '14*. ACM Press, New York, New York, USA, 387–394. DOI:http://dx.doi.org/10.1145/2677199.2680598

[6] Vinh P. Nguyen, Sang Ho Yoon, Ansh Verma, and Karthik Ramani. 2014. BendID: Flexible Interface for Localized Deformation Recognition. In *Proceedings of the 2014 ACM International Joint Conference on Pervasive and Ubiquitous Computing - UbiComp '14*. ACM Press, New York, New York, USA, 553–557. DOI:http://dx.doi.org/10.1145/2632048.2636092

[7] Michael Reed. 2009. Prototyping digital clay as an active material. In *Proceedings of the 3rd International Conference on Tangible and Embedded Interaction - TEI '09*. ACM Press, New York, New York, USA, 339. DOI:http://dx.doi.org/10.1145/1517664.1517733

[8] Jelle Stienstra and Patrizia Marti. 2012. Squeeze me. In *Proceedings of the 7th Nordic Conference on Human-Computer Interaction Making Sense Through Design - NordiCHI '12*. ACM Press, New York, New York, USA, 746. DOI: http://dx.doi.org/10.1145/2399016.2399131

[9] Yuta Sugiura, Gota Kakehi, Anusha Withana, Calista Lee, Daisuke Sakamoto, Maki Sugimoto, Masahiko Inami, and Takeo Igarashi. 2011. Detecting shape deformation of soft objects using directional photoreflectivity measurement. In *Proceedings of the 24th annual ACM symposium on User interface software and technology - UIST '11*. ACM Press, New York, New York, USA, 509. DOI: http://dx.doi.org/10.1145/2047196.2047263

[10] Karen Vanderloock, Vero Vanden Abeele, Johan A.K. Suykens, and Luc Geurts. 2013. The skweezee system. In *Proceedings of the 26th annual ACM symposium on User interface software and technology - UIST '13*. ACM Press, New York, New York, USA, 521–530. DOI: http://dx.doi.org/10.1145/2501988.2502033

[11] Gili Weinberg, Maggie Orth, and Peter Russo. 2000. The embroidered musical ball. In *CHI '00 extended abstracts on Human factors in computing systems - CHI '00*. ACM Press, New York, New York, USA, 283. DOI:http://dx.doi.org/10.1145/633292.633457

[12] S. A. G. Wensveen, J. P. Djajadiningrat, and C. J. Overbeeke. 2004. Interaction frogger. In *Proceedings of the 2004 conference on Designing interactive systems processes, practices, methods, and techniques - DIS '04*. ACM Press, New York, New York, USA, 177. DOI: http://dx.doi.org/10.1145/1013115.1013140

# Exploring Art with a Voice Controlled Multimodal Guide for Blind People

**Jorge Iranzo Bartolome**
College of Information &
Communication Engineering
Sungkyunkwan University
Suwon, South Korea
jorgedavid@skku.edu

**Luis Cavazos Quero**
College of Information &
Communication Engineering
Sungkyunkwan University
Suwon, South Korea
luis@skku.edu

**Sunhee Kim**
College of Social Sciences
Sungkyunkwan University
Seoul, South Korea
kimsunhee@skku.edu

**Myung-Yong Um**
College of Social Sciences
Sungkyunkwan University
Seoul, South Korea
myum@skku.edu

**Jundong Cho**
College of Information &
Communication Engineering
Sungkyunkwan University
Suwon, South Korea
jdcho@skku.edu


*TEI '19, March 17–20, 2019, Tempe, AZ, USA.*

ACM ISBN 978-1-4503-6196-5/19/03.
http://dx.doi.org/10.1145/3294109.3300994

## Abstract

There is an increasing concern to improve the accessibility of artworks for blind people. Much of the effort has been focused on helping the visually impaired people to access the exhibition facilities, but the works of art hosted there are still difficult to experience for them. Particularly, the appreciation of visual artworks is hindered as blind visitors are not allowed to touch them in order to conserve their aesthetics and value. In this work we explore our findings using a prototype of a voice interactive multimodal guide designed to improve the accessibility of visual works of arts, such as paintings, for the blind people. The prototype identifies tactile gestures and voice commands that trigger audio descriptions and sounds while a person explores a 2.5D tactile representation of the artwork placed on the top surface of the prototype. Our preliminary findings include the results of eight user tests and Likert-type surveys.

## Author Keywords

Blind People; Assistive Technologies; Voice Interaction; Multimodal Guide; Human Computer Interaction.

**Figure 1:** Cézanne's *Still Life.* One of the artworks turned into 2.5D model for the prototype.

**Figure 2:** 2.5D representation model from Cézanne's *Still Life.* Interaction zones are coated with black conductive paint.

## Introduction

Improving the accessibility and the inclusiveness of society are such urgent goals that the importance of ensuring full and active participation of people with disabilities in all areas of society is stated in the *Council of Europe disability strategy 2017-2023.* Over the last two decades the amount of research regarding assistive technologies has been growing. However, as shown in [2], most of the research has focused on topics such as navigation or web browsing, and issues related to art have not been approached in depth.

To improve art accessibility for the blind, we designed an interactive multimodal guide that presents a 3D printed 2.5D model of an artwork (such as in Fig .1 and Fig. 2) and conveys visual, spatial and semantic information by tactile and auditory cues. Localized and general descriptive audios are respectively mapped to touch and voice control interfaces by means of conductive paint and a speech recognition system. The prototype described in this work is the next iteration of a multimodal guide previously presented in [3]. While the previous multimodal guide only provided a tactile interface and explored environmental feedback capabilities, the current work provides a dual touch-voice interface and new capabilities for improving the independence and usability of the system for accessing the auditory feedback.

## Related Work

Audio guides are one of the most common methods available at museums and art galleries to provide verbal descriptions of the visual elements of an object to the blind people in order for them to experience works of art. Another common type of guides for the blind are tactile guides. These are guides which allow the user to comprehend visual information by translating it into embossed pictures, relief images which add depth (also known as 2.5D images) or volumetric representations. Audio guides are effective for conveying iconographic information but not good to convey spatial details [9]. On the contrary, tactile guides are effective to convey spatial and composition information but have some deficiencies when conveying iconographic information [1]. The idea of combining the strengths of different interactions resulted in multimodal guides, which use more than one mode or sense to communicate information to the user.

*Art Engagement for the Blind*

*Pictures in your Mind* [11] presents a study of blind people interacting with art in which a depth camera is directed to a 2.5D relief model of an artwork to track the user's hands and provide localized audio descriptions based on the hand's gestures. Our multimodal guide also uses a 2.5D relief model, but instead uses conductive paint on the surface of the artwork to determine the location of the hand and can provide both localized and general audio descriptions triggered by a touch-voice control interface. Substituting complex hand gestures in favor of more common interactions, such as tapping or speaking, makes the system more comfortable to use.

*Eyes-Free Art* [10] is based on a proxemic audio interface that tracks the distance between the user and the work of art. By getting closer to the artwork the users can sequentially access four different layers of audio information: background music, color related sonification, sound effect, and audio description. This information is accessed by moving one's hands in the air which are tracked by a Microsoft Kinect sensor [14]. Our work is different in that our system provides freedom to the user in accessing the different layers of information by means of the touch and voice interfaces rather than by the distance between the user and the artwork. This allows the user to have their hands on the

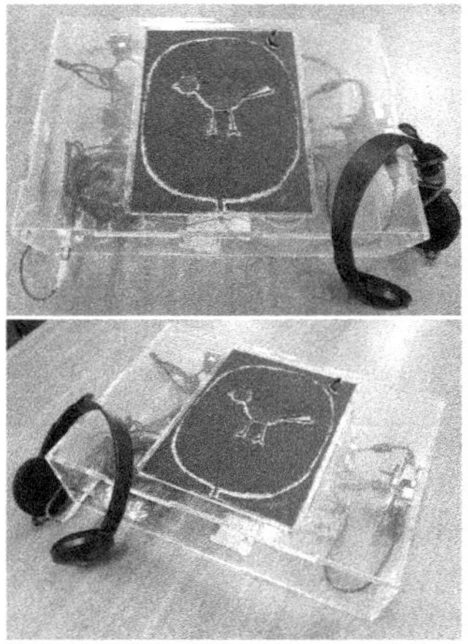

**Figure 3:** Interactive multimodal guide with Chang Ucchin's *The Magpie* artwork 2.5D representation model for display.

2.5D representation model and explore it at all times while listening to the descriptions.

*Voice Recognition for the Blind*
Speech recognition technology for blind people is becoming an important and a promising feature of assistive systems [8]. In [13] a VUI (Voice User Interface) with short commands is described within the scope of a navigation system application. Other works utilize VUI interfaces for educational applications. Particularly, in [7] a system named ABPT (Audio Based Programming Tutor) is proposed for making programming learning suitable for blind people. Their results, showed that voice control was considered to be an intuitive and comfortable interface for blind users for learning how to program. While our work is also a voice controlled assistive device for visually impaired people, it applies the voice recognition technology to the field of art accessibility.

## Prototype

*Implementation*
The prototype shown in Fig. 3 consists of an acrylic box with a 2.5D model of the visual artwork placed on the top surface. This 2.5D artwork models are designed using the manual height map method which is described in [4]. Once the design is completed, it is 3D printed using PLA plastic. The models are then coated with conductive paint and connected to the control board. All the components, including a microphone, are housed inside the box. There is an audio jack on the front side to connect the headphones. Touch gestures are recognized by a *BareTouch ConductiveBoard*: an Arduino compatible board with capacitive touch-sensing inputs. This board is serially connected to an *ODROID XU4* [6], which is a low-power single board computer running a linux distribution that is responsible for the speech recognition system and the data received from the TouchBoard. The *Google Stream speech API* [5] is used for voice recognition. For the audio feedback, a TTS (Text to speech) reader is used [12].

Our prototype provides the blind users the interfaces to access intuitively and independently the information about the artwork they have interest in. For this end we developed a dual touch-voice user interface that presents two different layers of audio feedback which are respectively mapped to each interface. These layers of information are:

- Specific information: any localized information related to a particular feature of the artwork such as the object's name, color or meaning.
- General information: general information of the artwork such as author, historical context, material, size, interesting facts, etc., which is not present in the visual work itself nor directly correlated to a localized feature that can be touched.

Mapping the localized audio feedback information to the tapping gestures enables the user to intuitively relate what is being touched (texture and location) to what is being heard (localized audio descriptions). The users can use the VUI when they want to access general information of the artwork. It also enables them to access other types of features such as background music to listen to while exploring the artwork.

There are two interaction modes: touch mode and voice mode. The voice mode consists of a series of voice commands that can be used to control the prototype and trigger audio descriptions. These commands are listed in Table 1. They are short in order to aid with memorization.

| "Painting" |
|---|
| *Long explanation setting the general context and information of the paint.* |
| **"Painter"** |
| *Biography and information of the painter* |
| **"Music"** |
| *Relaxing piano background music to accompany the artwork exploration.* |
| **"Options"** |
| *List of all command words available.* |
| **"Instructions"** |
| *The initial instructional audio is played again.* |
| **"Stop"** |
| *Stopping an audio while it is playing.* |
| **"End"** |
| *Getting out of voice mode and entering touch mode.* |

**Table 1:** VUI command word list and their function.

*Interaction Flow*

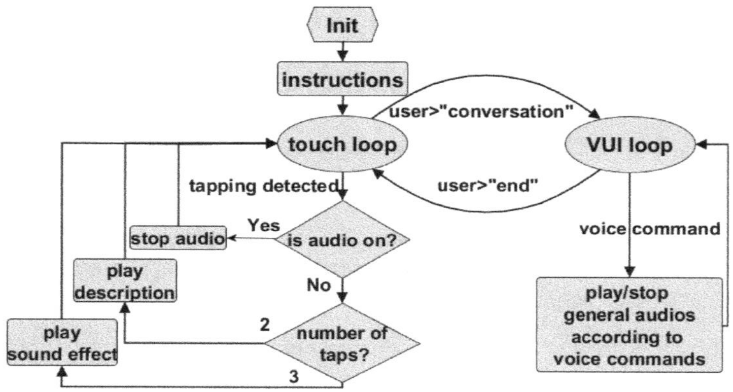


**Figure 4:** Interaction Flow Block Diagram.

As described in Fig. 4, when first using the device an initial explanation about how to use the system is heard when the user touches the artwork. This allows the users to learn how to use the prototype without needing external assistance. Experienced users can skip initial explanation by tapping on the prototype surface. Once it finishes, the touch interface mode is activated. In this mode, the user can request information related to any specific feature of the painting by tapping with one finger. A double tap will activate an audio description related to the feature. A triple tap will trigger sound effect audios related to the feature, such as the sound of a crying bird when triple tapping on the bird feature of the prototype shown in Fig. 3. Audio can be stopped by double or triple tapping anywhere on the model. At any moment, the user can change to the voice interface mode by saying the command word "conversation". Then, the VUI will initiate and the main prompt will remind the user about the voice commands which can be used. An example of a VUI dialog is shown in Table 2.

| **User > "conversation"** |
|---|
| System > "Which information would you like to hear? You can say 'painting', 'painter', 'music', 'instructions', or 'options'. For ending the conversation at any moment just say 'end'." |
| **User > "painter"** |
| System >"You can stop the audio at any moment by saying 'stop'. The painter's name is Vincent van Gogh. He..." |
| **User > "stop"** |
| System > "Is there any other thing you would like to know about?" |
| **User > "options"** |
| System > "Command word 'painting': I will explain to you general information related to the painting. Command word 'painter': the painter's biography will be heard. At any time the conversation can be ended by..." (audio finishes without the user stopping it earlier) |
| System > "Is there any other thing you would like to know about?" |
| **User > "end"** |
| System > "Remember you can start the conversation again by saying 'conversation'. Hope you enjoy the painting!" |

**Table 2:** Example of a VUI dialog.

## User Study

To explore the capacity of the prototype and the touch-voice interface to help the user to access the audio descriptions intuitively and to experience the artwork, we performed eight testing sessions. Each of them lasted an average of one and a half hours and the total number of participants were eight (average age of 27 years with a standard deviation of 4.52). All the selected participants expressed having some artistic experience or interest in the arts. Three of the participants were born blind and the remaining five participants turned blind in their childhood. Six of the users had total vision loss and two had near vision loss.

The test procedure was as follows: Each participant was encouraged to explore the prototype for 15 minutes after listening to the initial instructional audio. Fig. 5 shows one of the users during the prototype exploration test (the model used for the testing sessions is shown in Fig. 6). After the

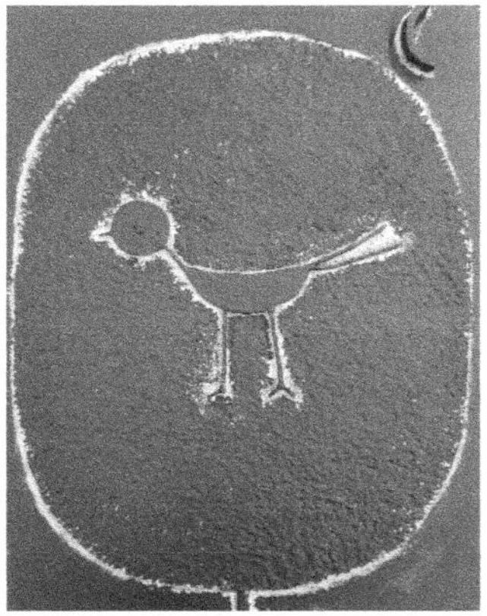

Figure 6: Model used during the user tests: korean artwork *The Magpie* by Chang Uchiin.

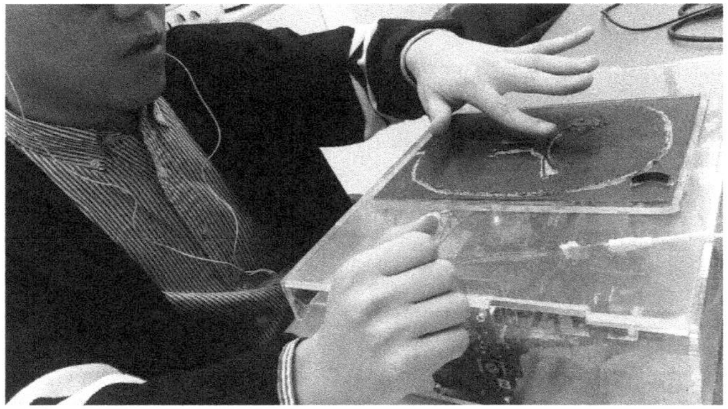

**Figure 5:** Participant exploring the prototype during user test.

first 5 minutes of testing the prototype, they were allowed to ask questions related to the control of the system. During the 15 minutes the users were able to explore the device freely, changing modes and controlling the system, whether by voice or by tapping. The 15 minutes test session was followed by a long semi-structured interview. They were also asked to report their experience by answering a questionnaire graded using a *Likert* scale.

## Results and Impressions

*Survey Results*

The results in Table 3 show that our system is a promising tool for aiding visually impaired people in accessing and exploring 2D artworks. Both control interfaces are considered intuitive and easy to use and the dual interface concept seems to be effective for accessing both localized and general information. The users were also eager to talk about the prototype and recommend it to their acquaintances. When we asked them who would they recommend it to, most of them answered they would recommend it to visually impaired friends but some of them also commented they would like sighted friends to try it out so they could experience art in a different way.

| Item | Mean | Std. Dev. |
|---|---|---|
| This system is a promising solution for visually impaired people to enjoy 2D art. | 4.125 | 0.78 |
| The touch control is intuitive and easy to use. | 3.875 | 0.92 |
| The voice control is intuitive and easy to use. | 3.625 | 0.69 |
| I will recommend this system to others. | 4.62 | 0.48 |
| Mapping general and localized audio into two interface modes is effective. | 4.12 | 1.16 |

**Table 3:** Results of user test questionnaires. *Likert* scale questions are graded in a scale from 1 to 5 (1-I completely disagree, 5-I completely agree).

*User Impressions and Comments*

The feedback was positive and the users enjoyed the dual interface of the system since it allowed them to reach more types of audio information easily and independently. Particularly, the eight participants agreed that the system was easy to use and that both the general and localized audios were detailed and nice to listen to. They enjoyed the experience and agreed they would like to explore artworks by other famous painters such as Picasso or Monet.

We also discovered certain limitations of our prototype. For example, when the system was used in a noisy environment there were times when the VUI was triggered because of the surrounding conversations that were picked by the microphone. The users commented that the voice menu structure was adequate but that they would prefer to have a button to enable the voice mode rather than just a wake word. They commented on how this would give them the opportunity to use the system both in a more contemplative way by themselves and also in a cooperative way, where they would not activate the VUI in order to have conversations with their friends while exploring the artwork. Another point raised by three of the users was the need to receive some distinct feedback when their words were recognized by the system, such as a "beep" high-pitched sound right before the system answered with a prompt.

Six out of eight participants were used to using smartphones and found our system easy to use due to their expertise in using tapping and voice interfaces when handling their phones. However, the remaining two users suggested adding an optional training option mode in which the user could practice the basic word commands and tapping gestures before engaging in the work exploration. The eight users agreed that the use of a human voice, instead of the robotic TTS one, would suit better the artistic mood and express emotion better on the audio descriptions. They also mentioned it would not only improve the artistic engagement quality of the descriptive audios, but that it also would make the initial instructional audio easier to understand and, as a result, the system easier to use.

## Conclusions and Future Work

We designed, developed, and evaluated an interactive multimodal guide based on a 3D printed 2.5D representation of an artwork which allows the visually impaired users to retrieve information through tangible and voice interaction modalities. Eight user test sessions were performed and showed the potential of the prototype in general, and the dual interface in particular, for improving art engagement and accessibility for the visually impaired people. While prior work has not emphasized multimodality, our work has focused, iteratively, in mixed methods for both the user interface and the artistic feedback. Moreover, performing user tests and having the chance to debate with the real users has given interesting results and insights to consider for further research, which we comment next.

Users' desire of a cooperative mode for the system raised the need of researching different possible interaction modes for different contexts such as when exploring art by oneself, with a visually impaired friend or with a sighted friend. Moreover, the portability of the system allows for implementation in a variety of settings such as museums, home or schools. Therefore, the accessibility design for each one of those setting is also an issue to take into consideration. In addition, this also raises the question of scalability of the system and the 2.5D model. For example, the current prototype is portable to allow its use in different spaces but installation-like deployment of a larger system and its effect in art engagement for the blind people also needs to be considered. Lastly, there are also possible technical improvements, such as improving noise reduction and command recognition by means of a dedicated algorithm.

## Demonstration at TEI 2019

A demonstration of our prototype at TEI 2019 would give the opportunity to participants to experience our prototype and give us a chance to receive valuable insight from experts. Also, we expect it would generate discussion and debates related to HCI, art engagement and user experience.

## Acknowledgements

We would like to thank all volunteers for their participation. This work was supported by the Science Technology and Humanity Converging Research Program of National Research Foundation of Korea (2018M3C1B6061353)

## References


[1] Jérémy Albouys-Perrois, Jeremy Laviole, Carine Briant, and Anke Brock. 2018. Towards a Multisensory Augmented Reality Map for Blind and Low Vision People: a Participatory Design Approach. (04 2018). DOI:http://dx.doi.org/10.1145/3173574.3174203

[2] Alexy Bhowmick and Shyamanta M. Hazarika. 2016. An insight into assistive technology for the visually impaired and blind people: state-of-the-art and future trends. *Journal on Multimodal User Interfaces* 11 (2016), 149–172.

[3] Luis Cavazos Quero, Jorge Iranzo Bartolomé, Seonggu Lee, En Han, Sunhee Kim, and Jundong Cho. 2018. An Interactive Multimodal Guide to Improve Art Accessibility for Blind People. In *Proceedings of the 20th International ACM SIGACCESS Conference on Computers and Accessibility (ASSETS '18)*. ACM, New York, NY, USA, 346–348. DOI: http://dx.doi.org/10.1145/3234695.3241033

[4] Rocco Furferi, Lapo Governi, Yary Volpe, Luca Puggelli, Niccolò Vanni, and Monica Carfagni. 2014. From 2D to 2.5 D ie from painting to tactile model. *Graphical Models* 76 (10 2014), 706–723. DOI: http://dx.doi.org/10.1016/j.gmod.2014.10.001

[5] Google. (accessed November, 2018). *Streaming-recognize*. https://cloud.google.com/speech-to-text/docs/streaming-recognize

[6] Hardkernel. (accessed November, 2018). *ODROID XU4*. https://www.hardkernel.com/main/products/prdt_info.php?g_code=G143452239825

[7] Mario Konecki, Nikola Ivkovic, and Matija Kaniski. 2016. Making programming education more accessible for visually impaired. (05 2016). DOI: http://dx.doi.org/10.1109/MIPRO.2016.7522265

[8] Bruce Moulton, Gauri Pradhan, and Zenon Chaczko. 2009. Voice Operated Guidance Systems for Vision Impaired People - Investigating a User-Centered Open Source Model. *JDCTA* 3 (01 2009), 60–68.

[9] Aneta Pawlowska and Anna Wendorff. 2018. Extra-visual perception of works of art in the context of the audio description of the Neoplastic Room at the Museum of Art in Łódź. (01 2018).

[10] Kyle Rector, Keith Salmon, Dan Thornton, Neel Joshi, and Meredith Ringel Morris. 2017. Eyes-Free Art: Exploring Proxemic Audio Interfaces For Blind and Low Vision Art Engagement. *Proceedings of the ACM on Interactive, Mobile, Wearable and Ubiquitous Technologies* 1 (09 2017), 1–21. DOI: http://dx.doi.org/10.1145/3130958

[11] Andreas Reichinger, Werner Purgathofer, Helena Garcia Carrizosa, Joanna Wood, Svenja Schröder, Christian Löw, Laura Rosalia Luidolt, Maria Schimkowitsch, Anton Fuhrmann, and Stefan Maierhofer. 2018. Pictures in Your Mind: Using Interactive Gesture-Controlled Reliefs to Explore Art. *ACM Transactions on Accessible Computing* 11 (03 2018), 1–39. DOI: http://dx.doi.org/10.1145/3155286

[12] SitePal. (accessed November, 2018). *Text-to-Speech.* http://www.oddcast.com/home/demos/tts/tts_example.php?sitepal

[13] Abdelsalam Sumi Helal, Steven Edwin Moore, and Balaji Ramachandran. 2001. Drishti: An Integrated Navigation System for Visually Impaired and Disabled. (01 2001). DOI: http://dx.doi.org/10.1109/ISWC.2001.962119

[14] Windows. (accessed November , 2018). *Kinect for Windows*. https://developer.microsoft.com/en-us/windows/kinect

# Telling the Bees: Designing for Immersion, Mediation, and Ritual

**Jihan Sherman**
Georgia Institute of Technology
Atlanta, GA 30308-1030
jihansherman@gatech.edu

**Takeria Blunt**
Georgia Institute of Technology
Atlanta, GA 30308-1030
tblunt3@gatech.edu

**Patrick Fiorilli**
Georgia Institute of Technology
Atlanta, GA 30308-1030
pof@gatech.edu



TEI '19, March 17–20, 2019, Tempe, AZ, USA

ACM ISBN 978-1-4503-6196-5/19/03.
https://doi.org/10.1145/3294109.3301001

## Abstract

This paper presents *Telling the Bees,* a prototype of an immersive media experience that explores the connections among ritual, tangible interfaces, and procedural interactivity. The project provides a basis for further exploration of hybrid interfaces in contexts of culture and tradition, specifically ritual traditions. We build upon the historical practice of "telling the bees," in which beekeepers and their families would share important news with their bees. A conversation between the interactor and the platform is mediated by tactile and vocal inputs with procedural audio-visual feedback. Our interface encourages body postures and input-response dynamics to bridge ritual tradition and digital immersion.

## Author Keywords

Tangible Interaction; Hybrid Interaction; Expressive Media; Prototyping; Design; Research through Design; Immersion; Ritual; Remediation

## CCS Concepts

• Human-centered computing~Interface design
• Human-centered computing~Interaction techniques

*"This is the common belief that bees must be made acquainted with the death of any member of the family, otherwise these intelligent little creatures will either desert the hive in a pet, or leave off working and die inside of it. The old way of doing this was for the goodwife of the house to go and* ***hang the stand of hives with black,*** *the usual symbol of mourning, she at the same time softly humming some doleful tune herself. Another way was for the master to approach the hives and* ***rap gently upon them****. When the bee's attention was thus secured, he would* ***say in a low voice that such or such*** *person — mentioning the name — was dead."*

Samuel Adams Drake [6]

## Introduction

Our work here takes the form of a physical box which surrounds a laptop computer running a Processing sketch, a small microphone, and a Micro:bit microcontroller. A viewport at the front of the box allows the user to see into the laptop's screen. Headphones are provided for audio feedback. A mysterious black shroud also accompanies the box, inviting curiosity until the user realizes its purpose. Together the physical box, digital sketch, microphone, microcontroller, and shroud work together to recreate the space and interaction of a traditional ritual, "telling the bees." We seek to examine how hybrid systems of interaction can support the mediation of historical cultural practices, achieve immersive experiences, and foster emotional responses in their users. The particular ritual of focus foregrounds the social act of sharing and creates the opportunity to examine its impact on self-reflection and empathy. When considered as a museum object, the research also considers how objects of this type can be didactic as well.

## "Telling the bees": the cultural ritual

The phrase "telling the bees" refers to the practice of informing domesticated honeybees of major events and news within a community or household. These can include deaths, births, weddings, etc. [4]. The ritual has roots in the analogous mythological significances of bees as found in many cultures around the world, from the Greeks [12] to the Celts [7]—all the way through Judaism, Christianity, Islam, and Hinduism [4]. The term "ritual," as we use it here, draws on the Catherine Bell's consideration of "special activities" that differ from daily routine action [2]. The act of "telling the bees" is considered, in Bell's language, a rite of passage or "life-cycle" ritual that culturally marks a transition [2]. We can consider the ritual sequence associated with "telling the bees" as meaningful cultural acts which we can remediate into a contemporary context.

As a model for interaction we use an ethnographic description of the tradition from Samuel Adams Drake's 1901 compendium of New England folklore [6]. There are three steps to the ritual sequence: "...*go and hang the stand of hives with black...*"; "...*rap gently upon them...*"; and "...*say in a low voice that such or such...*" [6]. First, the user learns to cover themselves and our "hive" box in a black shroud. A Micro:bit microcontroller inside the box uses its light meter to register darkness before proceeding with the software. Next, the user knocks on the box to initialize the software through the Micro:bit's accelerometer. Finally, after receiving one prompt out of many possibilities, the user is invited to speak into a microphone hidden in the box.

Our digital "bees," manifested visually and procedurally as vehicles in Processing, "respond" to audio input by moving along shifting flow field patterns and emitting edited audio recordings. The user sees into the interior of the "hive" through a small porthole in the front of the box. This location encourages a postural leaning forward which, along with the noise cancellation of the headphones and the surrounding darkness, affords an intimate—even immersive—media experience.

## Related Work

Previous work that leverages open interpretation of ritual practices can be found in *The Prayer Companion* project implemented by William Gaver et al. [8]. Their work explores "topical and theoretical" situations by examining the ritual of prayer both as research through

Figure 1: (top) *Telling the Bees* prototype, with shroud and headphones; (bottom) detail, front panel

design and as a case study. *The Prayer Companion* is a digital display that pulls news from the web as prayer topics for a particular community of nuns in the practice of prayer. The work of Tom Jenkins' *Devotional Gardening Tools* examines the impact of digital technology on the devotional practice of gardening [11]. Jenkins' addition of LED lights to common gardening tools contributes to an alternative view of the practice from the perspectives of users and spectators alike. Additionally, connections between ritual and immersion to achieve emotional or empathetic experiences have been explored in the work of Huck et al. [10]. Their projects, '*4Candles*' and *Digital Font,* are explorations into supporting empathy through embodiment. We extend their concern of "designing *for*, as opposed to *with*, empathy", and the impact of physical acts and ritual on human psychology. *Telling the Bees* seeks to engage a traditional ritual of sharing to achieve a digitally-driven experience that supports self-reflection and empathy with others. Our work is in conversation with that of Huck et al., Jenkins, and Gaver et al. through a bridging of computation and design to ritual and tradition.

We have identified museum installation as a potential space for deployment of *Telling the Bees*. Immersive multimedia interfaces have been shown to effectively augment traditional didactic displays in museums and learning environments. Like our own work, the *Storytent* and the *Sandpit*, two installations designed as part of the Situating Hybrid Assemblies in Public Environments (SHAPE) project, seek to "avoid the simple didactic forms of display, where visitors passively receive information, by creating stimulating exhibition environments where people explore, question, debate, and reflect on the nature of museum collections" [1]. We imagine the deployment of *Telling the Bees* as similarly productive of contextual reflection. Although not directly didactic, the experience has been designed to provoke, to engage, and, on some level, to teach. Christina Pollalis et al. explore the benefits of leveraging physical and virtual objects as tools to enhance the learning experiences of students [17]. Using virtual-reality headsets alongside various reproductions of archaeological artifacts from museums, the researchers concluded that an expanded field of interaction, mediated by "virtual and tangible representation," supported object-based learning--a pedagogical concept that emphasizes physical contact with objects as a key component for learning. We believe that *Telling the Bees,* as a museum object, can facilitate contextual reflection and object-based learning while also facilitating a rebirth in knowledge of traditional ritual and cultural practice.

## *Telling the Bees*: the remediated ritual

Our digital interpretation of "telling the bees" becomes, in the vocabulary of Jay David Bolter and Richard Grusin, a *remediated* artifact [3]. That is, *Telling the Bees* is at once *immediate*—rendered (relatively) historically authentic and physically immersive—and *hypermediate*—maintained as such through layer upon layer of obvious physical craft and digital artifice [3]. As an experience, *Telling the Bees* pulls the user close only to confront him or her with a sensation of "telling the bees" unabashedly filtered through an abstract physical interface, a dissociatedly "un-bee-like" soundscape, a geometric visual display, a procedural software base, and so on. With regard to interactive applications of this paradigm, Katie Salen and Eric Zimmerman describe remediation in terms of an "awareness" of the

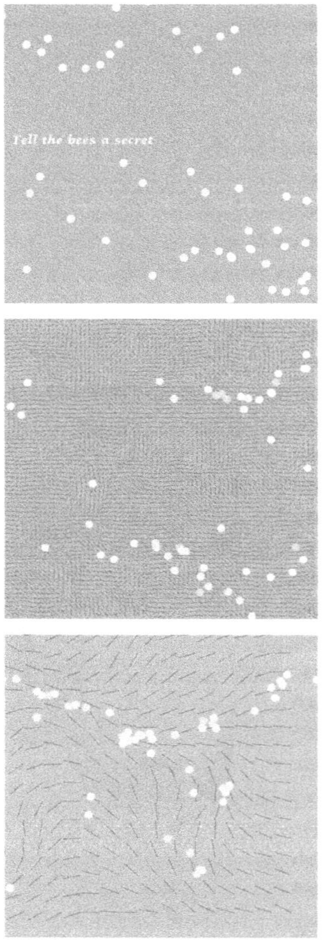


Figure 2: (top to bottom) Examples of digital hive display

"frame-related aspects" within the different but nonetheless related field of games research [14]. In this sense, *Telling the Bees* is a heavily "framed" artifact, designed to guide the user toward such an "awareness" of their own *immediate* experience of a *hypermediated* ritual.

Studies from "Presence Research" situate our definitions of presence and immersion, providing the framework for how each is incorporated into the physical design of the user experience. Through this lens, immersion is defined as the closeness of which a display system relates to physical reality [13]. Alternatively, presence relates to human engagement and agency within a particular space, giving priority to the act of "being there" within the space [11]. In contrast with traditional virtual reality spaces, we center immersion in the *Telling The Bees* project on the physicality of the environment rather than on immersion in the software. Through our linking of immersion with presence we begin to achieve a media experience that provides some of the same immersive qualities as more virtual immersive ones.

*Software*

The development of *Telling the Bees* began as purely software based interaction with a few simple steps in relation to the ritual. In that original iteration, the focus was primarily on the ability for users to speak to the bees, and on the capacity of the bees to communicate in response via a series of sounds. Prompts invited users to speak with the click of the 'p' button. For example, one prompt may read: "tell the bees about the most recent death you know." One can imagine the low, quiet voice that might lend itself to such a topic. Through Processing, sound from the microphone is analyzed in terms of its amplitude and frequency. That is, the amplitude and frequency of the user's response impacts the movement of the bees. This movement, along with accompanying sound playback, becomes representative of different emotional states. These states are procedurally selected by the program as discrete responses to input. The major part of the software behind this iteration has been retained for the latest version, however, knocking has replaced the "p" input for generating prompts.

The present abstract dot representations of the bees operate in two main ways. Their geometric shape allows them to function as moving vehicles without creating visual clutter that may become confusion or disorienting. Additionally, the abstraction highlights that they are not in fact "natural" bees, acknowledging the hypermediation of the original ritual tradition. We generate a series of flow fields to model the movement of the "bee" vehicles. Various flow fields—such as Scattering, Clustering, Spiralling—map onto emotional states as determined by user input. For instance, screaming (loud, high pitched) leads to an unsettled, anxious scattering of bees.

Our audio files derive from manipulated public domain recordings of live bee sounds in order to emphasize again the hypermediation of the ritual experience. To this end, we pre-apply audio effects, such as delay, chorus, and phasers alongside various filters to correspond with our defined emotional states. Thus, although our present sounds are not themselves dynamic—but rather selected out of a bank of separate audio files on the basis of the flow field in use—a dynamic audio environment is nevertheless created. Synthesis itself was a simplification of an idea to which

Figure 3: (top to bottom) Interaction with *Telling the Bees* prototype

we hope to eventually return, namely, recording microphone input and procedurally manipulating, or remixing it into "bee-speak" as re-rendered back out to the user. A set of noise cancelling headphones removes distractions, focuses the user, and provides for a more immersive experience.

*Physical*

The rules of interaction change substantially with the incorporation of the box interface. Consistent with the approach to the iconographic design of the digital "bees", replication of the beehive shape is intentionally avoided. Instead, the form of the box is developed to encourage particular body postures that achieve intimacy and capture the bodily movements of the bee ritual. This is also an acknowledgement that the construction is not a beehive in the same way that natural hives are and that the experience has been remediated. The form is also intended to define this posturing in reference to other contexts of secret sharing and viewing. The sloping front panel encourages interactors to lean forward, building a relationship of intimacy between them and the "bees." The side-walls work with the front panel to achieve an enclosure that echoes both the Catholic confessional and Edison's kinetoscope. A space of privacy is created even before the shroud covers the body and the box. It holds close the updates, or even "secrets," that the player shares with the "bees."

Two components of the ritual sequence are important to the development of the enclosure box: shrouding the hive and knocking on the hive. Almost all aspects of the experience are initiated by physical interactions. To start, the user must first interpret the ritual text on the front of the box enclosure. Their only instructions, that is, derive directly from Drake [6]. Then, once applied, the shroud establishes the boundary of the hive and "contains" the conversation. To end the experience, the user must remove the shroud, breaking the spell, so to speak, and return the program to its initial resting state.

*Hardware*

The Micro:bit microcontroller provides the hardware component needed to take in data from physical interaction with the "box" enclosure. The 25 LED light sensors of the Micro:bit are programmed to read, through a small hole in the side of our box, their surrounding "light level" from 0 to 255. We use light level of ≦3 to indicate when the user has become fully enshrouded in the box space, signaling our Processing program to initiate from its resting state. Users have no direct contact with the Micro:bit. To register user knocks, we leveraged the microcontroller's accelerometer. Programming it to read gesture data allowed us to classify user knocking as a "shake" gesture. The user's knock, through Serial input, sends a signal from the accelerometer that tells the program to provide a prompt. This was a naturalistic shift away from an earlier iteration of the design which used physical button presses, passed through Radio data, to register discrete knocks. It was a design decision to reduce the use of arbitrary features such as Radio channels and channel numbers. All told, the Micro:bit continually checks light levels to ensure constant darkness and remains "listening" for the shaking of a user's knock.

*Museum Context*

Degens, et al. in their discussion of frameworks for developing empathetic agents describes rituals as "a construct through which behaviour gains social meaning for a group of agents that have shared attention" [5]. *Telling the Bees* hopes to build on this connection between ritual and social meaning. Here we are asking, how can ritual and tradition heighten the emotional experience and empathy of users? Museum studies scholar Andrea Witcomb, for one, argues that multimedia objects produce an "activation of an emotional response" [15]. She writes that multimedia objects—among which *Telling the Bees* shares a great deal—"are three or two dimensional, can be touched, looked at, in some cases viewed from all angles, exist in real time, and are the results of a human production process." In contrast to more traditional didactic displays, Witcomb concludes that multimedia objects "offer meaning in their own right, not as interpretive aids but as creative art objects." We hold this argument as exceptionally valid in the case of *Telling the Bees*, especially inasmuch as we hope that it fosters such "sensitive re-reading" of displays, environments, assumptions, and cultural narratives as Witcomb describes.

## Future Work

As this is a "work in progress," user testing to-date has been informal and limited. Immediate future work will include formal user testing to assess participation in the remediated ritual sequence and impacts on user emotions, self-reflection, and empathy. One potentially fruitful avenue for further development of is an audio environment in which a user's voice is manipulated and reflected back at them. Processes of aggregation also appear intriguing: how can the software environment develop over the course of a conversation? And finally, material concerns provide possibilities in the development of the tangible interface. The cardboard box is mercifully portable, however its lightness results in challenges related to shrouding and knocking. Currently, the sensation of knocking on the cardboard box is unconducive to the intimate physicality we hope to afford. One never feels that the box will withstand another round. This practicality, alongside the potential aesthetic appeals of wood or plastic materials, can be explored further.

In a broader sense, we cannot ignore the fact that, for *Telling the Bees,* we interpret what is, in some sense, a lost tradition. Its roots are essentially pagan, even pre-Abrahamic, and it has little, if any, present-day practice. What would it mean to attempt similar remediations of other less esoteric rituals? Could they be used to build upon or even enhance the experience of the most sacred of traditions? Would such projects remain ethical? We imagine remediated rituals as installations, placed into real-world contexts relevant to their origins, as educational tools, or even as augmented or virtual accompaniments to the very traditions they remediate. Extending notions of presence into future iterations requires the development of a framework for crafting affordances that support the "state of being" within the experience. There is a space for continued investigation of tangible and mediated interfaces as they may work together to achieve a deeper understanding of the cultural demarcations that imbue all ritualized and ritual-like acts with their meanings.

## Acknowledgements

We gratefully acknowledge the support of Anne Sullivan, Tom Jenkins, and the students in the Georgia Tech Digital Media department for their comments during prototyping and writing.

## References


[1] Liam Bannon, Steve Benford, John Bowers, and Christian Heath. 2005. Hybrid Design Creates Innovative Museum Experiences. Commun. ACM 48, 3 (March 2005), 62–65. DOI:https://doi.org/10.1145/1047671.1047706

[2] Catherine Bell. 1997. Ritual: Perspectives and Dimensions. New York, Oxford University Press.

[3] Jay David Bolter and Richard Grusin. 1999. *Remediation: understanding new media*. MIT Press, Cambridge, Mass.

[4] John Burnside. 2015. "Telling the bees." *Nature; London* 521, 7550 (May 2015), 29–30.

[5] Nick Degens, et al. 2012. When agents meet: empathy, moral circle, ritual, and culture. *Workshop on Emotional and Empathic Agents (EEA) at 11th International Conference on Autonomous Agents and Multiagent Systems*.

[6] Samuel Adams Drake. 1901. *A book of New England legends and folklore in prose and poetry*. Boston, Little, Brown and company. Retrieved November 13, 2018 from http://archive.org/details/bookofnewengland00dra

[7] Colleen English. 2018. "Telling the Bees." *JSTOR Daily*. Retrieved November 13, 2018 from https://daily.jstor.org/telling-the-bees/

[8] William Gaver, Mark Blythe, Andy Boucher, Nadine Jarvis, John Bowers, and Peter Wright. 2010. The prayer companion: openness and specificity, materiality and spirituality. In *Proceedings of the SIGCHI Conference on Human Factors in Computing Systems* (CHI '10). ACM, New York, NY, USA, 2055-2064. DOI: https://doi.org/10.1145/1753326.1753640

[9] C. W. Hagge. 1957. Telling the Bees. *Western Folklore* 16, 1 (1957), 58–59. DOI:https://doi.org/10.2307/1497068

[10] Jonny Huck, Paul Coulton, David Gullick, et. al. 2015. Supporting Empathy Through Embodiment in the Design of interactive Systems. In *Proceedings of the Ninth International Conference on Tangible, Embedded, and Embodied Interaction* (pp. 523-528) ACM, New York, NY, USA, 2055-2064. DOI: https://doi.org/10.1145/2677199.2687892

[11] Tom Jenkins. 2013. Devotional gardening tools. In *CHI '13 Extended Abstracts on Human Factors in Computing Systems* (CHI EA '13). ACM, New York, NY, USA, 2219-2226. DOI: https://doi.org/10.1145/2468356.2468743

[12] Dick Marron. 2007. Telling the Bees. *Bee Culture*; Medina 135, 1 (January 2007), 49–51.

[13] Maria V. Sanchez-Vives, Mel Slater. From Presence Towards Consciousness. *Nature Reviews Neuroscience.* (2005)

[14] Katie Salen and Eric Zimmerman. 2003. *Rules of play: game design fundamentals*. MIT Press, Cambridge, Mass.

[15] Andrea Witcomb. 2007. The Materiality of Virtual Technologies: A New Approach to Thinking about the Impact of Multimedia in Museums. *In Theorizing Digital Cultural Heritage: A Critical Discourse, Fiona Cameron and Sarah Kenderdine* (eds.). The MIT Press, 35–48. DOI:https://doi.org/10.7551/mitpress/9780262033534.003.0003

[16] John Greenleaf Whittier. 1858. "Telling the Bees." *Atlantic Monthly*. (1858) Retrieved November 13, 2018 from https://www.poetryfoundation.org/poems/45491/telling-the-bees.

[17] Christina Pollalis et al. 2018. Evaluating Learning with Tangible and Virtual Representations of Archaeological Artifacts. *Tangible and Embodies Interactions (TEI)*.

# Trækvejret: A Kinetic Device Encouraging Bodily Reflection

**Vanessa Julia Carpenter**
Aalborg University
Copenhagen, Denmark
vjc@create.aau.dk

**Nikolaj "Dzl" Møbius**
Roskilde University
Roskilde, Denmark
nimo@ruc.dk

**Tomas Sokoler**
IT University
Copenhagen, Denmark
sokoler@itu.dk

**Dan Overholt**
Aalborg University
Copenhagen, Denmark
dano@create.aau.dk


ACM ISBN 978-1-4503-6196-5/19/03.
https://doi.org/10.1145/3294109.3300975

## Abstract
A flexible wooden device, "Trækvejret" which emulates a slow rate of breathing is placed in a coffee break room. This work examines related works on reflection, triggering reflection, and breathing and biofeedback technologies. We demonstrate how simple technology such as Trækvejret, which does not measure or give feedback about a user's breathing can nonetheless potentially be useful and provoking, encouraging reflection and potentially, behaviour change.

## Author Keywords
Breathing; bodily awareness; serendipitous discovery; kinetic; wellness; offline.

## CSS Concepts
Human-centered computing~Interaction design process and methods • Human-centered computing~User centered design

## Introduction
We developed an artefact to explore how opportunities for momentary bodily reflection as part of everyday activities might be created - in this case, as part of the daily routine of getting a cup of coffee at work. Trækvejret (Danish for `Breathe') is a device situated in a coffee break room, which people can choose to engage with, when and if they happen upon it. A video of Trækvejret can be seen here: https://youtu.be/e_dx-aC0IXc

Figure 1: Trækvejret from front, in use, and from the side.

This a conceptual work in progress which does not present a mature study but utilizes research through design as a method to generate insights which opens for debate and engagement. This work is part of a PhD study in "Designing for Meaningfulness in Smart Products" wherein one of the design goals is designing unconnected devices for personal development.

*Serendipitous Discovery*
Ambient displays act as dispensers of non-critical information whose aim is to provide information without overly distracting the observer [22]. In this work, we see the value of serendipitous discovery as creating an opportunity to engage a person momentarily.

*Motivation: Non-quantified reflection*
We are especially interested in the role of physicality in bodily sense-making [6] and creation of technology (in a semi-public space) which has a low threshold for initial engagement. Further, this engagement happens without providing personalized feedback via insights, app-notifications, or reports. We focus on in-the-moment engagement with a device which requires the user to evaluate their own situation and draw their own conclusions.

*Trækvejret*
Trækvejret is a small wooden device which emulates breathing by moving inwards and outwards, shape shifting from a straight board, to a rounded board. See Figure 1. We present how Trækvejret was designed and built in the sections "Design Rationale" and "Process". A scenario:

*A person at work feels it's time for a cup of coffee and walks to the coffee break room. They put their cup in the coffee machine and as they wait for their beverage, they discover a small wooden object moving beside the machine. They are curious about it and regard it for a moment, before realizing it is imitating breathing. They sync their breathing to the device, taking a few slow, deep breaths.*

**Related Works**
To frame this work, we explore related works about ad-hoc, opportunistic and unexpected experiences as well as the area of reflection in everyday life.

*Bodily reflection in the everyday*
We are particularly interested in ad-hoc reflection, without an intention to reflect, but rather, coming upon an unexpected opportunity and being invited to engage in it. In their work, "Reflecting on Reflection - Framing a Design Landscape", Fleck and Fitzpatrick [7] describe how technology can help with reflection and encourage designers to ask "What reflective behaviours do you want to encourage? Which technologies and techniques can support these behaviours?"

In this work, we want to encourage a bodily reflection, a focusing on, and scanning of the body [26] to foster reflection about breathing and pause in the everyday. The focus on everyday reflection is also being explored in recent works in HCI, namely by Mols et al. [24] who recommend that designers should consider the "the timing of reflection, the balance of system and user initiative and the preferred social context" and by Prpa et al in exploring virtual environments and awareness of breathing [27]. We aim to address Mols et al's recommendations by situating the opportunity for reflection in a place where people choose to go to take pause in their day, and by considering the level of user initiative (the user can choose to engage with Trækvejret, or not) and setting the social context as a semi-public space.

*Bumping into technology*
By placing an object in a physical space, the object becomes a persistent part of our reality in that space and one can choose to recognize or interact with it. In the case of Morse Things, Wakkery et al. [34] inquire about our relationship to things in our world, explaining that "designed digital artifacts, or in our case things, manifest technologies and directly influence the mediation of our experiences and practices".

Creating objects which exist in our world, but do not demand attention, or require attention to function is explored in other works, such as with calm [35] or slow technology [12]. Grosse-Hering et al. describe how one design principle of Slow Design, "Reveal" might be revised to "Creating awareness, uncover the function and essence of a product" [11].

We aim to create awareness of the body [27] and to uncover the essence of slowness, of taking a deep, slow breath. This emphasizes how we can use unexpected discovery and encounters with physical objects to create a trigger for reflection [25] in a slow technology way.

*Awareness of breathing*
For athletes [17], mindfulness practitioners [28] and those seeking to reduce their stress levels, breathing becomes something to pay attention to, to change for their purposes and to enhance their lives and practices [33]. There are increasingly more devices and apps being developed to help people train themselves in various breathing techniques. A brief overview of these is presented here. Wearables which encourage or guide mindful breathing include the Apple watch [16] or FitBit's Charge 2 [23] combining haptic feedback and visualizations to encourage wearers to take deep breaths throughout their day. There are also stand-alone apps which use visualization on a phone app [1, 2] to guide meditation, but still require the user to look at their phone screen and possibly be interrupted and distracted by other notifications [10].

Small non-watch wearables are being introduced, such as Spire [29] a device to track your breathing and give you insights about it. Breath-Minder [3] provides alarms via vibration, reminding you to breathe deeply. Vitali, a smart fitness bra [32] measures HRV (Heart Rate Variability) and breathing and provides cues to breathe deeply to reduce stress. Breathing Friend [21] uses haptics to stimulate breathing and Breathing Light [30] uses somaesthetics via light and sound. BrightBeat [10] uses subtle indicators in the form of sound, visual and temperature cues to influence slower breathing. One of our ambitions is to move from on-body cues (such as BrightBeat, the Apple Watch or Fitbit Charge 2 or Spire) to off-body, subtle, in-context cues such as Trækvejret, which is in the environment but does not demand attention. Rather, it invites engagement from afar.

In nearly all of the above mentioned examples, measurement of the user's breathing and feedback is provided. Each requires a decision to use an app, use a wearable, or use a device to consciously take time to monitor and train for mindful breathing. We are instead interested in how we can explore how placing a physical object (Trækvejret) in a commonly accessed place can

Figure 2: Questions asked after second encounter.

Interviewees were asked the following questions:

- Did you notice the device in the coffee machine this morning / afternoon?
- What did you think when you saw it?
- What do you think it is for?
- What impact did it have on you?
- Did you think about breathing later in the day?
- Do you usually think about your breathing when you are working?

facilitate ad-hoc situated serendipitous discovery leading to spontaneous bodily reflection.

**Method**

Throughout this study, we recall and use Buxton's sketches, a process filled with ambiguity [4] giving us the opportunity to discover, define and unfold an emerging design space.

Research through design allows us engage in "exploring and speculating, particularising and diversifying" [9] a design situation. We generate intermediate level knowledge [15, 19] which is not a theory, but rather, generates "knowledge that plays a direct role in the creation of new designs" [19]. Trækvejret is not intended to become a product on the market, it is rather an exploratory probe, helping us elicit qualities of a design goal.

**Design rationale**

In line with our method we engaged with the particularities of the design situation including the chosen space, the choice of materials, and the opposing qualities of engagement with the artefact.

*The coffee break room*

Before setting up Trækvejret, we saw that many individuals getting a cup of coffee pull out their phone and glance at notifications. We chose the setting of the coffee break room because it is a place of interlude. The people accessing the coffee break room spend a brief amount of time there, and so there exists potential to engage them momentarily without undue interference in their daily routine.

*Material choices*

We deliberately chose wood as it is both a natural material, representing nature, life, and warmth, and also it stands out amongst the plastic and steel of the coffee machine and sink.

*Opposing qualities*

Trækvejret does not measure the observer's rate of breathing, nor does it provide feedback. The movement of the device, the breathing, in and out, represents the average, slow rate of human breathing [5]. However, the rate of breathing is only communicated to the person engaging with the system via observation.

We asked ourselves about the opposing qualities of the artefact: how we might create an object which was non-connected, displaying information but not collecting it, allowing for engagement but not engaging itself, and encouraging behaviour change, but not demanding it?

**Process**

*Brainstorming process*

In designing Trækvejret, a brainstorming and selection process took place wherein the authors took the context of a coffee break room, and tried to imagine how we might facilitate an opportunity for bodily reflection during the process of getting a coffee.

Our aim was to generate as quickly and simply as possible, an early artefact that we could immediately make available to encounter in context. We describe this below, in "Trækvejret: artefact building".

Figure 3:
Participants on how they have considered their daily breathing practices:

"I have predilection for gadgets and happenings but just the fact the something was there caught my attention. I think it looked very dynamic because it moved, which made me read the text", P6

"If it just stands there, you wouldn't look at it all the time", P4.

"I normally don't think about my breathing but because I saw it I did", P4

"I think it is a good idea because it moves instead of just writing "Breathe", then you don't do it", P8.

"When you look at it you cannot help breathing" P4

"I think that the motion up and down aspires to a calm and deep breathing", P2

*Trækvejret artefact: Building*
Trækvejret consists of a servo motor attached to a piece of laser cut medium-density fibreboard (MDF) which has been cut using a kerf bending pattern, that is, cutting through a piece of material in a geometric pattern to allow it to be flexible without segmenting it into more than one piece. The flexible piece of MDF is attached to a stand, which was laser cut for the purpose of holding the servo motor and the flexible piece in place.

Our concept for the moving material was inspired by a piece of kerf bent MDF in the lab which we picked up and began to bend as we tried to demonstrate what we had been envisioning. We asked 'what if it looked like this?' 'Might this look like someone breathing?' 'It would be easy enough to attach a servo motor here, let's try it.'. This approach is a way of sketching [4], exploring materials and function iteratively.

An Arduino board is mounted on the back of the stand, and the servo motor is attached to the Arduino board. A small arm extends from the servo motor and attaches to the flexible piece, moving it up and down. The Arduino has been programmed using the 'Sweep' example from Arduino's servo library of examples, to move the servo at a normal rate of human breathing [5] namely, 12 breaths per minute. The servo moves, pauses, moves again and pauses, to demonstrate inhalation, pause, exhalation and pause.

## Encountering Trækvejret

We conducted two small explorations to look for early indications of how we might enable bodily reflection via serendipitous discovery.

*First encounter*
People, upon entering the coffee room, would place their coffee cup in the machine, stare at Trækvejret and then leave the room after their coffee was made. Many who had been observed getting their coffee near it said they hadn't known it was something they should engage with. In the second study, spanning two days, we placed a small sign above the device, which said simply 'Trækvejret' or 'Breathe' in Danish.

*Second encounter*
The second exploration took place over two days at four new sites: four different break rooms with coffee machines throughout the building for a duration of one hour per site. These were different break rooms from the first encounter and as people tend to frequent the same break room, our aim was that these would be people who had not previously encountered Trækvejret. We attached the instructional sign to the device, 'Trækvejret' or 'Breathe' in Danish. Following the observations, 10 verbal interviews of approximately 5 minutes each were conducted in the afternoon (to give people time to think about the experience). The interviewees were randomly selected among the people passing by the device. Questions can be read in Figure 2 and some key responses in Figure 3.

## Discussion: A Design Goal

*A non-connected, non-quantified device*
Trækvejret communicates information about how to breathe at a slow pace, but otherwise is not measuring or sensing anything, or giving any kind of feedback. In some ways, it can be considered a display, a non-connected element of the physical environment. It differs in this way from many of the IoT or smart products that are emerging today, both in research and

on the market. As Hartzog and Selinger explain, 'A chip-centric mentality has taken over, one that is guided by an overly simplistic principle: 'Internet connectivity makes good objects great" [13]. By not being connected, Trækvejret was immediately accessible, requiring no set up, calibration, or instructions besides the one word 'breathe'.

Further, people who engaged with Trækvejret did so of their own accord, due to their own curiosity, and not because it promised health improvements, quantified-self reports, or other benefits. It was an interaction of opportunity. We suggest that perhaps moving away from connectivity, for some devices, might be an interesting design goal to explore.

*The design goal: designing devices which encourage reflection and action rather than being data-driven*
We propose the definition of this goal as being one wherein research through design is a method to propose sketches featuring simple, non-connected devices for the betterment of the self, preferably in a combination of physical and psychological aspects. In this space, the interaction is not data-driven or data-collecting but rather is passive, and potentially as beneficial through encouraging people to explore their own abilities and act upon those explorations.

*Current limitations of this design space.*
Firstly, we aim to avoid decorative items. By having non-connected, tangible objects which may offer serendipitous discovery, we do not include objects designed to be decorative. Instead, we point towards objects with a clearly designed intention, such as Trækvejret, encouraging people to stop and breathe, and learn to take a breath throughout their day.

In a time where privacy [8] and questions about how much time we are spending online [31, 14] and with our devices [18], we think a focus on designing for non-connected, personal development devices will be of importance.

**Future Work**
Trækvejret is part of a series of design artefacts being developed to explore non-screen, tangible and physical devices, and something we call Designing for Meaningfulness. We hope to expand this research in collaboration with other researchers and industry.

**Conclusion**
We built Trækvejret, a simple artefact which emulates a slow human rate of breathing to act as a vehicle for research into openings in design where we might invite researchers to explore how we might design for serendipitous discovery and spontaneous bodily reflection.

From our observations over two encounters with the artefact, we learned that Trækvejret elicits curiosity: people briefly engaged with it and thought about their breathing patterns and practices. We invite discussion about a design goal of designing for non-connected artefacts which can potentially be beneficial for bodily reflection and action.

We conclude that Trækvejret is a preliminary success as a research vehicle because it produced openings in design, demonstrating how something which is unexpected and simple in its design and function, promotes curiosity spontaneous engagement, and bodily reflection.

## References

[1] Breathe2relax. 2018. Retrieved 20 July, 2018 from http://t2health.dcoe.mil/apps/breathe2relax

[2] Breathingzone. 2018. Retrieved 20 July, 2018 from http://www.breathing.zone/

[3] Breathminder. 2018. Retrieved 20 July, 2018 from http://www.breathminder.com/

[4] Bill Buxton. 2010. Sketching user experiences: getting the design right and the right design. Morgan Kaufmann.

[5] Daniel G. Carey, Leslie A. Schwarz, German J. Pliego and Robert L. Raymond. 2005. Respiratory rate is a valid and reliable market for the anaerobic threshold: implications for measuring change in fitness. In Journal of Sports Science and Medicine (2005) 4, 482-488

[6] Paul Dourish. 2012. Where the Action Is: The Foundations of bodily Interaction. MIT Press.

[7] Rowanne Fleck and Geraldine Fitzpatrick. 2010. Reflecting on reflection: framing a design landscape. In Proceedings of the 22nd Conference of the Computer-Human Interaction Special Interest Group of Australia on Computer-Human Interaction (OZCHI '10). ACM, New York, NY, USA, 216-223.

[8] Ester Fritsch, Irina Shklovski, and Rachel Douglas-Jones. 2018. Calling for a Revolution: An Analysis of IoT Manifestos. In Proceedings of the 2018 CHI Conference on Human Factors in Computing Systems (CHI '18). ACM, New York, NY, USA, Paper 302, 13 pages.

[9] Bill Gaver. (2012). What should we expect from research through design?. In Proc. CHI 2012. ACM Press, 937-946.

[10] Asma Ghandeharioun and Rosalind Picard. 2017. BrightBeat: Effortlessly Influencing Breathing for Cultivating Calmness and Focus. In Proceedings of the 2017 CHI Conference Extended Abstracts on Human Factors in Computing Systems (CHI EA '17). ACM, New York, NY, USA, 1624-1631.

[11] Barbara Grosse-Hering, Jon Mason, Dzmitry Aliakseyeu, Conny Bakker, and Pieter Desmet. 2013. Slow design for meaningful interactions. In Proceedings of the SIGCHI Conference on Human Factors in Computing Systems (CHI '13). ACM, New York, NY, USA, 3431-3440.

[12] Lars Hallnäs and Johan Redström. 2001. Slow Technology - Designing for Reflection. Personal Ubiquitous Comput. 5, 3 (January 2001), 201-212.

[13] Woodrow Hartzog, and Evan Selinger. The Internet of heirlooms and disposable things. NCJL & Tech. 17 (2015): 581.

[14] Pepita Hesselberth. 2018. Discourses on disconnectivity and the right to disconnect. In New Media & Society 20, no. 5 (2018): 1994-2010.

[15] Kristina Höök and Jonas Löwgren. 2012. Strong Concepts: Intermediate-level Knowledge in Interaction Design Research. In ACM Trans. Comput.-Hum. Interact., ACM Press, October.

[16] Niel Hughes. 2016. Inside watchOS 3: New 'Breathe' App for Apple Watch Reminds you to Relax, Focus. Appleinsider, June 18 Retrieved from http://appleinsider.com/articles/16/06/18/inside-watchos-3-new-breathe-app-for-apple-watch-reminds-you-to-relax-focus

[17] Andrew E. Kilding, Sarah Brown, and Alison K. McConnell. 2010. Inspiratory muscle training improves 100 and 200 m swimming performance. European journal of applied physiology 108.3: 505-511.

[18] Simone Lanette and Melissa Mazmanian. 2018. The Smartphone "Addiction" Narrative is Compelling, but Largely Unfounded. In Extended Abstracts of the 2018 CHI Conference on Human Factors in Computing Systems (CHI EA '18). ACM, New York, NY, USA, Paper LBW023, 6 pages.

[19] Jonas Löwgren. 2013. Annotated Portfolios and Other Forms of Intermediate-level Knowledge. Interactions 20, 1 (January 2013), 30-34.

[20] Jonas Löwgren. 2006. Articulating the use qualities of digital designs. Aesthetic computing. 383-403.

[21] Miroslav Macik, Katerina Prazakova, Anna Kutikova, Zdenek Mikovec, Jindrich Adolf, Jan Havlik and Ivana Jilekova. 2017. Breathing Friend: Tackling Stress Through Portable Tangible Breathing Artifact. In Human-Computer Interaction - INTERACT 2017. Lecture Notes in Computer Science, vol 10516. Springer, Cham.

[22] Jennifer Mankoff, Anind K. Dey, Gary Hsieh, Julie Kientz, Scott Lederer, and Morgan Ames. 2003. Heuristic evaluation of ambient displays. In Proceedings of the SIGCHI Conference on Human Factors in Computing Systems (CHI '03). ACM, New York, NY, USA, 169-176.

[23] James A. Martin. 2016. Fitbit's best activity tracker just got even better. CIO. December 2016. Retrieved from http://www.cio.com/article/3152883/mobile-apps/fitbits-best-activity-tracker-just-got-even-better.html

[24] Ine Mols, Elise van den Hoven, and Berry Eggen. 2016. Informing Design for Reflection: an Overview of Current Everyday Practices. In Proceedings of the 9th Nordic Conference on Human-Computer Interaction (NordiCHI '16). ACM, New York, NY, USA, Article 21, 10 pages.

[25] Ine Mols, Elise van den Hoven, and Berry Eggen. 2016. Technologies for Everyday Life Reflection: Illustrating a Design Space. In Proceedings of the TEI '16: Tenth International Conference on Tangible, Embedded, and Embodied Interaction (TEI '16). ACM, New York, NY, USA, 53-61.

[26] Claudia Núñez Pacheco and Lian Loke. 2017. Tacit Narratives: Surfacing Aesthetic Meaning by Using Wearable Props and Focusing. In Proceedings of the Eleventh International Conference on Tangible, Embedded, and Embodied Interaction (TEI '17). ACM, New York, NY, USA, 233-242.

[27] Mirjana Prpa, Kıvanç Tatar, Jules Françoise, Bernhard Riecke, Thecla Schiphorst, and Philippe Pasquier. 2018. Attending to Breath: Exploring How the Cues in a Virtual Environment Guide the Attention to Breath and Shape the Quality of Experience to Support Mindfulness. In Proceedings of the 2018 Designing Interactive Systems Conference (DIS '18). ACM, New York, NY, USA, 71-84.

Larry Rosenberg. 2015. Mindfulness with breathing: A manual for serious beginners. Simon and Schuster.

[28] Spire. 2018. Retrieved from https://spire.io/

[29] Anna Ståhl, Martin Jonsson, Johanna Mercurio, Anna Karlsson, Kristina Höök, and Eva-Carin Banka Johnson. 2016. The Soma Mat and Breathing Light. In Proceedings of the 2016 CHI Conference Extended Abstracts on Human Factors in Computing Systems (CHI EA '16). ACM, New York, NY, USA, 305-308.

[30] The Disconnect. (2018). Retrieved from: https://thedisconnect.co/one/

[31] The Everyday Smart Bra: Your Intuitive Wellness Coach. 2018. Vitali Wear. Retrieved from: https://www.kickstarter.com/projects/vitaliwear/the-everyday-smart-bra-your-intuitive-wellness-coa

[32] Universal Breathing: Pranayama. Saagara. (2014). Retrieved from http://www.saagara.com/apps/breathing/ universal-breathing-pranayama.

[33] Ron Wakkary, Doenja Oogjes, Sabrina Hauser, Henry Lin, Cheng Cao, Leo Ma, and Tijs Duel. 2017. Morse Things: A Design Inquiry into the Gap Between Things and Us. In Proceedings of the 2017 Conference on Designing Interactive Systems (DIS '17). ACM, New York, NY, USA, 503-514.

[34] Mark Weiser and John Seely Brown. 1997. The coming age of calm technology. Beyond calculation. Springer, New York, NY, 1997. 75-85.

# Hooze: A Kinetic Fashion Accessory for Touch and Play

**Figure 1**: Hooze in the Wild.

**Patrycja Zdziarska**
Indiana University, Bloomington, IN
pzdziars@iu.edu

**Felix A. Epp**
Aalto University, Espoo, Finland
felix.epp@aalto.fi

**Walther Jensen**
Aalborg University, Aalborg, Denmark
bwsj@create.aau.dk

**Mark D. Gross**
University of Colorado, Boulder, CO
mdgross@colorado.edu

**Ellen Yi-Luen Do**
University of Colorado, Boulder, CO
Keio-NUS CUTE Center, Singapore
ellendo@acm.org


*TEI '19*, March 17–20, 2019, Tempe, AZ, USA

ACM ISBN 978-1-4503-6196-5/19/03.
https://doi.org/10.1145/3294109.3300980

## Abstract
Recent innovations in fashion and smart textiles have contributed new visions of wearable computing, addressing the body through the cultural and social self. In this work, we draw on speculative design, maker technologies, and zoomorphism to explore how wearables might support sociability, and present Hooze, a fashion accessory that entices touch through its zoomorphic qualities and visual appearance. We describe our design and prototyping process, and reflect on how Hooze inspires transformative designs of wearables.

## Author Keywords
Wearable Design; Zoomorphic Design; E-textiles; Interactive Fashion; Maker Technologies.

## CSS Concepts
• Human-centered computing → Interaction design process and methods

## Introduction
Wearable electronics and smart textiles are generating both academic and commercial interest [16]. Recently, projects have begun to engage with the aesthetic and expressive possibilities of wearable design [1,2,7,8,9,12], while also exploring their cultural uptake [17,18]. These projects not only suggest novel experience paradigms, but also work towards

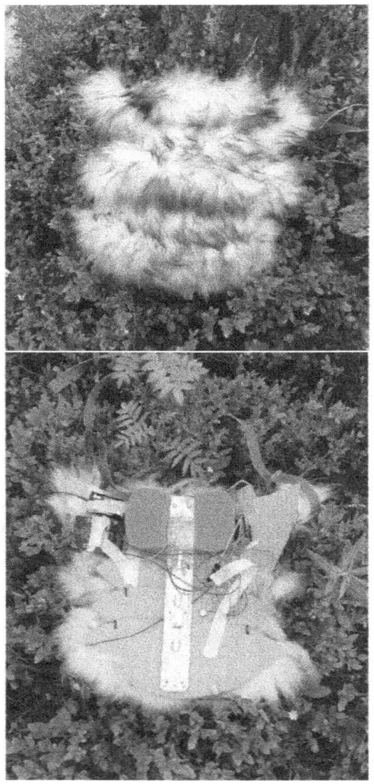

**Figure 2**: View of Hooze from the front and back.

addressing intimate and social aspects of people's lives, important dimensions for cultural relevance.

While critical engagement from a diverse set of stakeholders is needed for realizing culturally significant wearable designs, researchers and artists at the intersection of e-textiles, fashion, and tech have proposed visions of wearables that push aesthetic and technological boundaries, and address social needs, desires, and aspirations. An inspiring example is that of the spider dress [12], which cleverly incorporates zoomorphic qualities of spiders to add a "defensive" mechanism to an otherwise beautiful cocktail dress. The spider dress and designs like it [1,7] inspire form, and functionalities that transgress our everyday understanding of what clothing ought to be and do, and rather than *transferring* technology onto textiles, they demonstrate how tech can combine with textiles to *transform* the meaning of wearables [1].

Today's broadening access to prototyping tools [4] further contributes to a wide explorative space. As such, researchers have explored wearable design for playful applications around bodily interactions, human sociability, and connection. For example, using simple components, the Massage me Shirt [14] transforms a t-shirt into a video game controller supporting physical interaction between individuals. Social Textiles [11] a social messaging enabled shirt aggregates people for event planning. Notably, the Mediated Body project [10] converts bodies into musical instruments, facilitating social play and interpersonal touch. However, apart from these examples, the practice of generating novel concepts for wearable technologies remains difficult in practice.

Drawing on speculative design practice [5] and maker technologies we carried out an exercise in "wearable imagination", or a way of imagining playful functions of wearables beyond today's pragmatic and functional commercial products. We contribute our design exploration of Hooze (Figure 2), a furry kinetic fashion accessory for the shoulder that encourages social play and touch, and offer a reflection on design qualities that could be taken up in future designs of wearables.

Hooze was designed in a week-long workshop about "making wearables that matter". Our design intention was to explore ways of engaging the body in playful social interactions, while also pushing wearable design outside of capturing sensor-tracked data, or electronically augmented clothing. Our interrogations of diverse forms of bodily engagements led us to question the taboo nature of touch between strangers and consider designs which embrace touch as a desirable interaction, and emphasize curiosity-driven exploration of the body. The design is also inspired by the behavioral and visual characteristics of cuddly mammals and exemplifies a zoomorphic design [3].

## Design and Prototyping

The fashion accessory resembles a pauldron, or flexible armor for the shoulder (See Figure 1, 2). The structure itself consists of a rigid plate that also houses the electronics, and a flexible wing extension that hangs over the arm. Both the rigid plate and flexible wing are constructed out of four pieces of cardboard that are folded into a three-dimensional shape and mounted on top of a plastic frame. The cardboard structure is covered with synthetic fur augmented with conductive thread (27 *ohm*), creating a capacitive touch sensor capable of registering stroking movement as described

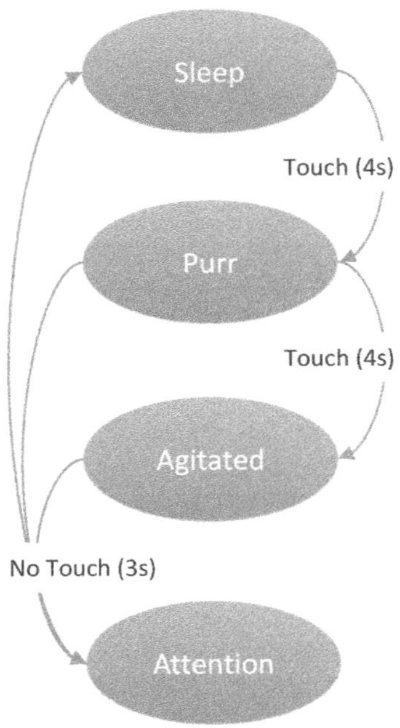


**Figure 3**: The programmed states of agitation of Hooze.

in [6,13]. The accessory's flapping movement is controlled by a continuous servo motor built into the rigid base. The servo motor translates its rotary motion to the flexible wing through a wire. Finally, haptic feedback propagates outwards into the periphery of the artifact via a vibrator motor embedded in the middle of the base structure.

A single Microsoft Micro:Bit board and two AA batteries power and control the accessory. It is programmed using Python and contains native functions for touch sensing and general purpose input / output pins. We developed a filtering algorithm to minimize input noise, which also controls the agitation state. We implemented four states: *sleep* (no vibration and movement), *attention* (no vibration and full movement), *purr* (medium vibration, no movement) and *agitated* (intense vibration, no movement). As shown in the state diagram in Figure 3, the default state is *sleep*, and moves to *agitated* state upon being touched for more than four seconds. When left untouched for three seconds, it shifts to *attention* state to attract people to pet it. After another three seconds it returns to its *sleep* state.

*Arriving at Zoomorphic Qualities*

The design of Hooze emerged through reflective [15] and opportunistic engagement with materials. We began prototyping with a rough idea of combining the pleasurable tactile qualities of fur with interactive qualities of movement, and experimented along these two dimensions, arriving at several technical proof-of-concepts and two full iterations of our final design. We engaged in extensive testing and iteration, frequently trying on the design on our own bodies to adjust fit, as well as the kinetic and aesthetic qualities until we achieved a desired result.

**Figure 4**: Early prototype of Hooze with a different fur.

In our early prototypes, we explored the capacitive touch potential of various fabrics, but eventually settled on synthetic fur after a successful attempt at creating a fur stroke sensor [6,13]. We programmed the stroke sensor to trigger cat sounds, which became louder i.e. agitated with prolonged stroking. The result was endearing, drawing attention and interest from other workshop attendees, who began to associate our design with cats. We wanted to leverage the animal-like characteristics of the fur, but didn't want the accessory to be too closely associated with a particular animal, so rather than programming the sensor to trigger cat

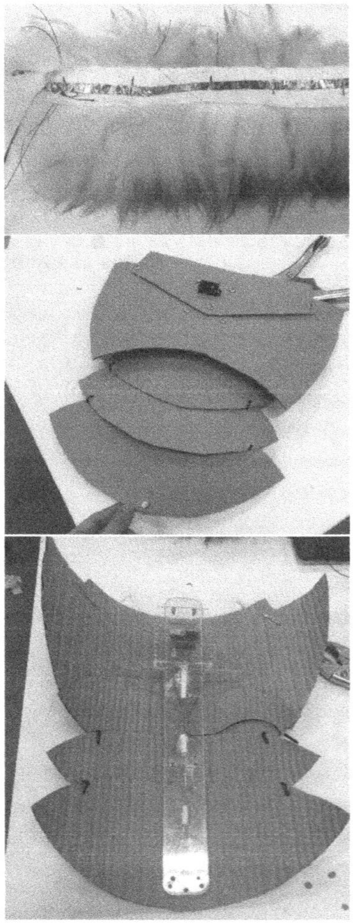

**Figure 5**: Images of components that make up Hooze: fur stroke sensor, cardboard base, and flexible plastic brace.

sounds, we incorporated haptic feedback programmed at different states of agitation in the final design.

Working with furs also created possibilities for integrating kinetic qualities into the design. The fur had an inherent bounce and drape to it, and we experimented with ways to emphasize this existing subtle movement. We explored materials that could support the weight of the fur, provide rigid structure, but also remain flexible enough so that when placed on the arm or shoulder, they would move up and down in a manner suggestive of a "flap" or "wiggle". Feasibility of creating this effect pushed us to create natural movement using mechanical servo motors, but without rigid mechanical forms. We designed a simple string pulling mechanism using a servo motor that leveraged the fur's weight inertia to gently release the fur. Unexpectedly, rather than giving the artifact a robotic quality, the servo motors added a purring sound that strengthened the references to animals we were already attempting to reinforce.

In our final steps of adding the fur onto the cardboard, we improvised with small fragments of a different fur to cover the leftover spots, which conveniently created the appeal of "eyes", strengthening the association of Hooze as a furry and animate creature posing as a fashion accessory.

## Reflection

Our engagement with materials produced Hooze, an interactive accessory for the shoulder that enticed touch with a flapping movement, and responded to touch through haptic feedback. We view Hooze as an artifact to think with and reflect upon, rather than as a fully interactive prototype that demands rigorous evaluation and user-testing. As such, we solicited informal feedback by wearing the accessory around the facilities of the workshop, frequently modelling it to others. To help us further reflect on the design, we also took the accessory on a brief trip to the city center to observe reactions and interactions with strangers. We now turn to describing what we believe Hooze helped us accomplish in light of our design goals.

*Enticing Social and Physical Engagement*

Hooze's visual aesthetics drove curiosity and bemusement from others, who often asked to touch, or play with it. Interactions with Hooze became a means of expressing a gentle and caring nature, where the soft furs, and endearing appearance encouraged delicate petting, and handling as if Hooze were indeed a small precious creature. Hooze prompted a wide range of physical engagement from simple stroking using the hands or the cheek to head resting on the wearer's shoulder.

Moreover, we learned that Hooze could support interactions between strangers to the extent that the accessory appeared to have a function that was unlike what people encounter in their daily lives. For example, during exploration in a public setting (Figures 9, 10), a man approached us and without being provoked, carefully explored the fur between the tips of his fingers. In response, we encouraged him to touch it more, and the man gave Hooze a long stroke and then pressed his hand firmly on it, and asked: "does it do anything, when you touch it?" "Oh, it's vibrating. So, it's like a massage on your shoulder."

**Figure 6**: Designers playfully enacting an attack to reflect on how the artifact might attract undesirable attention.

**Figure 7**: Designers role playing in a wooded lot to connect with their animalistic natures, and share intimate moments using Hooze.

*Facilitating Humor, and Social Play*

Humor and social play emerged out of the design process and we worked to reinforce it with subsequent design decisions, finding ourselves coming "alive" along with the artifact we were creating. For example, as a group with two male designers, we often enacted "overly loving partners" (See Figure 7, 8, 11), challenging norms around what is considered "manly" and "feminine" behaviors. Hooze brought out natural tendencies to freely express affection through physical touching that we incorporated into the design.

Furthermore, Hooze supported imaginative role playing that enriched the physical and social interactions around it. In one instance, we took the accessory to a nearby wooded lot and began to connect with our animalistic natures that provoked us to hide behind trees, lurk like wild cats (Figure 7), and stage an unanticipated attack (Figure 6). These playful engagements enriched the narrative that was unfolding around Hooze, humorously revealing how such an artifact might lead to undesirable forms of touching like being mistaken as prey, or a potential mate by (other) wild animals.

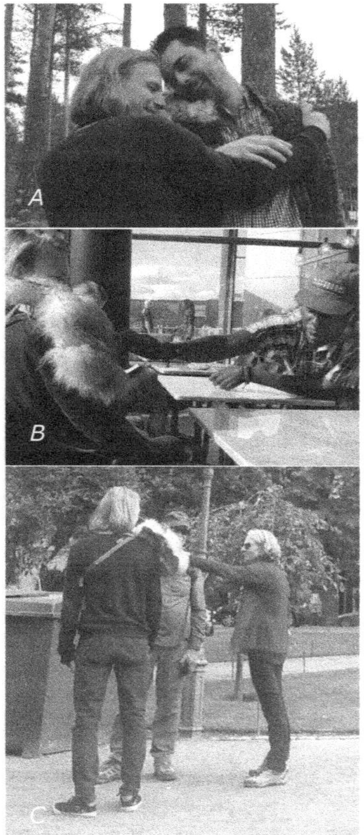


**Figure 8**: A) Designers sharing a moment with Hooze. B) A man leans in to pet Hooze. C) A couple stops to pet Hooze.

*Sharing a Moment*
Perhaps the most characteristic interaction Hooze facilitated was that of sharing a moment. Much of the footage we captured to document the project depicts the designers engaged in an intimate hug, or gazing into each other's eyes (for example, see Figure 7, 8, 11). Upon reflection, we feel the shared moments Hooze helped create were a special way for two individuals to focus upon each other in the midst of humorous play. They consisted of short episodes of stroking and petting that transformed into more intimate forms of embrace and then naturally resolved without awkwardness, leaving both individuals emotionally elevated, connected, and often giggling.

*Inspiring Zoomorphic Design*
The zoomorphic qualities we incorporated into Hooze such as the soft fur, subtle movement, and endearing appearance combined together in a provocative way. In fashion, furs invoke complex feelings of pleasure and fear e.g. the comforting sensation of touching furry creatures is accompanied with the dreadful guilt of wearing dead animals. Our design suggests possible avenues for re-engaging with the meaning of furs, where furs are incorporated into fashion as a means of expressing intimacy, comfort, and appreciation or connection with animals. We are provoked to think how else might fashion designers leverage interactivity and zoomorphic qualities to strengthen these connections. For one, we can imagine the design of an interactive bicycle helmet in the shape of a turtle shell that protects the head, but also has qualities of being "alive" that help wearers view turtles as fellow companions, cultivating a deeper appreciation for nature.

**Figure 9.** Designers gazing into each other's eyes.

## Conclusion
There is a growing interest in wearable technologies, yet generating imaginative artifacts is difficult in practice. Using simple prototyping tools we built a kinetic fashion accessory to probe the imaginative potential of this space. Our humorous design practice, material engagements, and concern for supporting touch, play, and sociability all contributed to the imaginative qualities of Hooze. Future work will consider additional expressive and imaginative qualities and further investigate the experience of shared moments the artifact seemed to support.

## Acknowledgements
We warmly thank Georgi V Georgiev, Jani Ylioja and Timo "Timppa" Ojala for crafting the perfect creative environment at UBISS '18. Felix A. Epp was funded by the Academy of Finland project Digital Aura [311090]. Walther Jensen was partly funded by EU project DecoChrom [760973] of European Union's Horizon 2020research and innovation programme.

## References

[1] Berglin, Lena. *Smart textiles and wearable technology*. Högskolan i Borås, 2013.

[2] Joanna Berzowska. 2005. Electronic Textiles: Wearable Computers, Reactive Fashion, and Soft Computation. *Textile: The Journal of Cloth and Culture* 3, 1 (2005), 58–75. DOI: http://dx.doi.org/10.2752/147597505778052639

[3] Paul Bucci, Lotus Zhang, Xi Laura Cang, and Karon E. MacLean. 2018. Is it Happy? *Proceedings of the 2018 CHI Conference on Human Factors in Computing Systems - CHI '18* (2018), 1–11. DOI: http://dx.doi.org/10.1145/3173574.3174083

[4] Leah Buechley and Michael Eisenberg. 2008. The LilyPad Arduino: Toward Wearable Engineering for Everyone. IEEE Pervasive Computing 7, 2 (April 2008), 12-15. DOI=http://dx.doi.org/10.1109/MPRV.2008.38

[5] Dunne, Anthony, and Fiona Raby. *Speculative everything: design, fiction, and social dreaming*. MIT press, 2013.

[6] Anna Flagg, Diane Tam, Karon MacLean, and Robert Flagg. 2012. Conductive fur sensing for a gesture-aware furry robot. In *2012 IEEE Haptics Symposium (HAPTICS)*. IEEE, 99–104. DOI: http://dx.doi.org/10.1109/HAPTIC.2012.6183776

[7] Sibel Deren Guler, Madeline Gannon, and Kate Sicchio. 2016. *Crafting Wearables*. DOI: http://dx.doi.org/10.1007/978- 1- 4842- 1808- 2

[8] Kate Hartman, Boris Kourtoukov, and Erin Lewis. 2018. Kinetic Body Extensions for Social Interactions. *Proceedings of the Twelfth International Conference on Tangible, Embedded, and Embodied Interaction - TEI '18* (2018), 736–739. DOI: http://dx.doi.org/10.1145/3173225.3173333

[9] Kate Hartman, Jackson McConnell, Boris Kourtoukov, Hillary Predko, and Izzie Colpitts-Campbell. 2015. Monarch: Self-Expression Through Wearable Kinetic Textiles. *Proceedings of the Ninth International Conference on Tangible, Embedded, and Embodied Interaction* (2015), 413–414. DOI: http://dx.doi.org/10.1145/2677199.2690875

[10] Mads Hobye and Jonas Löwgren. 2011. Touching a stranger: Designing for engaging experience in embodied interaction. *International Journal of Design* 5, 3 (2011), 31–48.

[11] Viirj Kan, Katsuya Fujii, Judith Amores, Chang Long Zhu Jin, Pattie Maes, and Hiroshi Ishii. 2015. Social Textiles. In *Tei '15 Wip*. ACM Press, 619–624. DOI: http://dx.doi.org/10.1145/2677199.2688816

[12] Ken Kaplan. 2015. Robotic Spider Dress Powered By Intel Smart Wearable Technology. (2015). https://iq.intel.com/ smart- spider- dress- by- dutch- designer- anouk- wipprecht/ DOI:http://dx.doi.org/10.1145/3173225.3173311

[13] Hannah Perner-Wilson and Leah Buechley. 2010. Handcrafting Textile Mice. *Dis* (2010), 434–435. DOI: http://dx.doi.org/10.1145/1858171.1858257

[14] Hannah Perner-Wilson and Mika Satomi. 2007. Massage me. (2007). http://www.massage-me.at/

[15] Schn, D. A. "The Reflective Practioner." *How Professionals Think in Action. Templesmith, London* (1983).

[16] Schwarz, Anne, et al. "A roadmap on smart textiles." *Textile progress* 42.2 (2010): 99-180.

[17] Tomico, Oscar, et al. "Towards a next wave of wearable and fashionable interactions." *International Journal of Design* 11.3 (2017): 1-6.

[18] Tomico, Oscar, et al. "Crafting wearables: interaction design meets fashion design." *CHI'13 Extended Abstracts on Human Factors in Computing Systems*. ACM, 2013.

# Hand Puppet as Means for eTextile Synthesis

**Emmi Pouta**
Aalto University, School of Arts,
Design and Architecture
Espoo, Finland
emmi.pouta@aalto.fi

**Jussi Mikkonen**
Syddansk Universitet
Kolding, Denmark
jussi@kryt.fi


*TEI '19, March 17–20, 2019, Tempe, AZ, USA*

ACM ISBN 978-1-4503-6196-5/19/03.
https://doi.org/10.1145/3294109.3300987

## Abstract

To situate the skills of the textile designer within the HCI-process, we present a case of a hand puppet with a purpose-woven smart textile pattern. The qualities found in traditional textile design are tacitly synthesized into the eTextile-design process. We see this mentality as having a natural dialogue with HCI-practice. The hand puppet consists of two layers: an inner sensor glove, designed to detect the movements of the user's fingers, and a woven outer layer that has a touch sensitive user interface integrated into its woven structure. The two interfaces can be operated simultaneously by two separate users; an adult and a child. Our interest is to understand better how the traditional textile design variables can be utilized in the user interface and -experience design. We aim towards the synthesis of woven eTextile design, consisting of user interface design, pattern design, sensor structure design and textile layout design.

## Author Keywords

eTextiles; weaving; smart textile design practice; hand-held; soft material.

## CSS Concepts

• **Human-centered computing~Interface design prototyping** • *Hardware~Haptic devices*

Figure 1: A sketch of the interactions of the hand puppet

## Introduction

The textile design process and the role of textile designer have been evolving throughout recent years. Traditionally, the textile design process has been a lone journey with a focus on mastering a singular methodology, but recently that approach has been broadened by new technologies, sustainability agenda and participatory practices [16]. In the field of smart textiles, the recent advances have resulted in creating fabrics with computational, sensorial and actuating properties (for an overview see [2,14]). That positions the smart textile design practice in the intersection of multiple fields, such as textile design, material science interaction design and electrical engineering [15]. To situate the skills of the textile designer within the HCI-process, we present a case of a hand puppet with a purpose-woven eTextile pattern.

Firstly, we briefly touch how the textile designer's embodied knowledge is being utilized in an eTextile co-design process, and secondly, how weaving as a traditionally 2D-method supports designing eTextile layouts for an interactive 3D-object. Knowledge of textile materials, techniques and structures is essential for developing novel robust methods of integration of electronics into textiles. Lack of in-depth weaving expertise is frequently present in smart textile research related to weaving. This study examines this through weaving practice to make an original contribution, through the development of an in-between wearable [1]. The intent of this paper is to describe the work leading to the methodological analysis intended for the development of the role of an eTextile design practitioner. However, the analysis is beyond the scope of this paper.

## Background

We see tacit knowledge [8] as the essence of the thinking distinct to a textile designer. Furthermore, we see the process of textile design as an inherently reflective practice [13]. Besides its tacit and reflective nature, the textile design knowing is often related to the understanding of different material-specific matters. For example, Fairburn et al. [4] write about the textile design specific knowledge: *"Textile designers tend to think in two- dimensions, and are largely concerned with surface, rhythm, scale, repeat, tactility, and with properties and functionality. The deep tacit nature of textiles together with their inherent tactile and sensorial qualities differentiates the textile designer's area of knowledge and contribution within innovative interdisciplinary practice."* (ibid.)

Similarly, Igoe [6] suggests that besides haptic, sensorial and tactile qualities, the design process is guided by emotive qualities, and those qualities are tacitly synthesized in the design process. We see this mentality as having a natural dialogue with HCI-practice. The "material turn" [11] that has taken place within the field of interaction design calls for embodied knowledge of materials and materiality, finding a sensible companion in tangible and embodied interaction [5]. More recently, this has evolved towards the materiality of interaction [18]: *"By explicitly focusing on craft, researchers are using a material lens to challenge assumptions about what constitutes design and who indeed performs this practice".*

We draw inspiration from three eTextile examples that utilise woven textiles, implying the possibilities of woven electronic structures. Both Project Jacquard [9] and Involving the Machines [19] focused on industrial-produced electronic functionality, and in general draw

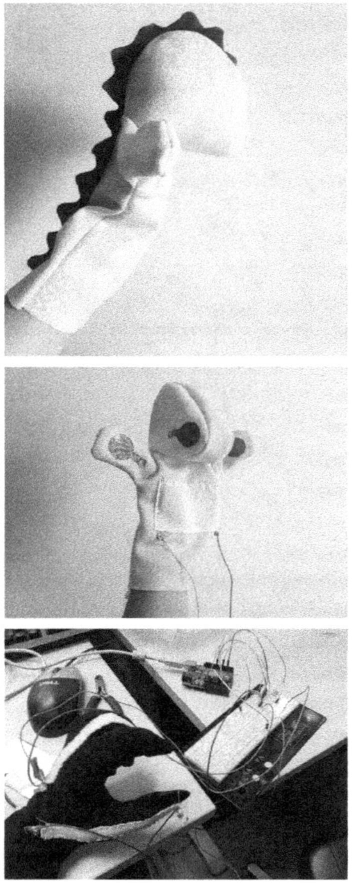

Figure 2: Prototyping eTextiles. From the top down: a non-functional prototype of the hand puppet, a functional prototype of the outer layer, and a functional prototype of the inner glove.

parallels to focusing on the impact of fabric properties in woven eTextiles [10]. With these in mind, our eventual goal is the development of practical textile-HCI-design-methodology, to enable the skills of an eTextile design practitioner in the development of a woven textile as a true hybrid material.

## Methods

The primary dataset for mapping the co-design process consists of field notes and a working diary of the process. In addition to this, additional pictures and video material were used to clarify project phases and specific details. These are collected to enable a later analysis of the development of a hand puppet from two perspectives. Firstly, the design process of an interactive hand puppet will be mapped against two design frameworks by Veja [17] and Sanders and Stappers [12]. Secondly, the prototypes of the hand puppet will be analysed by reflecting on the results of reflective weaving practice through technical structural analysis of the woven prototypes.

## The interactive hand puppet

The interactive hand puppet is intended as a tool for interactive storytelling, to support child-adult-interaction with a thoroughly soft and textile-made object. The construction of the hand puppet consists of two layers: an inner sensor glove, designed to detect the movements of the user's fingers, and a woven outer layer that has a touch sensitive user interface integrated into its woven structure. The two interfaces can be operated simultaneously by two separate users; an adult and a child.

*Design process*

The first iterative design development cycle of the interactive hand puppet-project was carried out in spring 2018. In the early front end of the design process, the aim was to define the problem space and understand the users' needs within that space. The understanding was built through desk research, user interviews and user observations. The first initial design-hypothesis was established in quite an early phase, to start testing and collecting feedback. The concept description and the visualisation were created to make the concept idea communicable in the user interviews. The hand puppet was seen as a potential tool for parents to support kids in learning social and emotional skills, through focusing on child-adult-interaction.

The process evolved through brainstorming and concept creation towards concept definition that at the same time set the design objective for the eTextile design process. After defining the concept, the process proceeded into the design development phase. The central aspect to consider was that the user interface needs to cater to two users of different skill levels, and the inputs need to be measured from both inside and outside of the object. The design-hypothesis of the preferred interaction was embodied into two functional prototypes: one for recognizing the finger movements, and another for the touch sensitive user interface embedded into the outer layer, which also has the hand puppet character design. The hypothesis was validated with children, by testing a simulation of the user experience.

*eTextile design process*

A distinct eTextile design process took place parallel with the design development process. The first preliminary phases, the ideation, sketching and

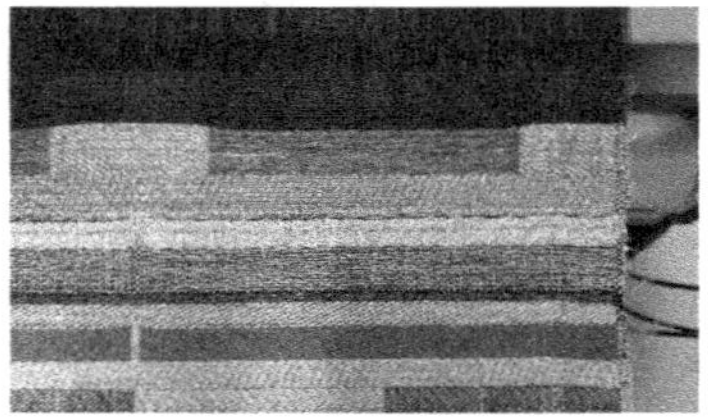

Figure 3: A woven sensor textile

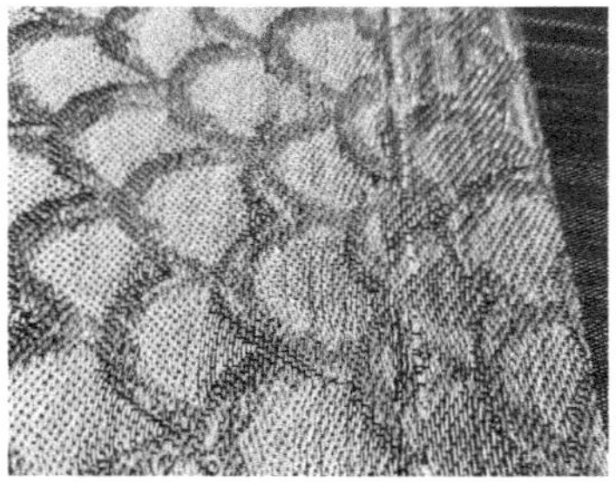

Figure 4: A colour and bind test

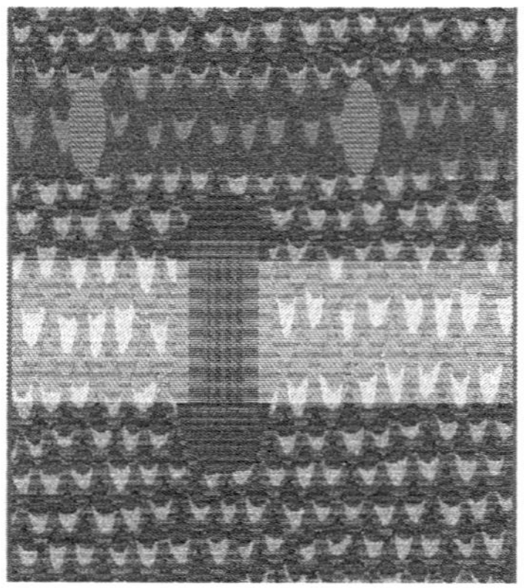

Figure 5: A pattern with UI

prototyping with eTextile materials, as well as the form-giving of the hand puppet, were carried out in cooperation with the multidisciplinary team. From the perspective of the eTextile design process, the key outcomes were the sensor validation, the final shape of the hand puppet and the placement of the sensors and wiring into the patterns of the object. Those were seen as prerequisites for the eTextile layout design, that also set the requirements for the chosen materials and the pattern design. Thus, the proposed user experience and interactions (shown in Table 1.) were a guideline for the eTextile design process, dominating the development of the technical solutions. That is also the point of departure of the woven construction development process, which aim was to integrate all of the outer layer sensors directly into the structure of the woven fabric and translate the desired user experience into jacquard weave patterns. Essential in this process was the reconstruction of the three-dimensional object into weaving files that consists the pattern of the object, and to understand the possibilities and limitations of the weaving technique.

*eTextile development in practice*

Weaving is a method of interlacing two separate set of yarns, warp and weft, to construct a fabric. The design process focuses on the development of a weave, which defines how the yarns are intersecting in the fabric. The skill of a textile designer thus is to determine a specific combination of yarns, yarn densities, binding points and dynamicity (i.e. how the yarns are allowed to move) to achieve a particular goal for the final textile.

First, the test samples of different kind of woven sensors were woven (see fig. 3) and tested to verify the suitable bindings and sensor structures of the user interface. Parallel with weaving the test sensors, a figurative jacquard pattern was designed and validated through woven samples of different bindings and colour scheme (see fig. 4). Next, the sensor structures and the jacquard pattern were synthesized into a complete eTextile layout design, and the pattern of the hand puppet served as a template, where those two merged (see fig. 5). The visual appearance of the hand puppet was designed to incorporate the user interface as an integrated part of the look and feel of the puppet (see fig. 6). The sensor structures and their placement became an apparent part of the design, and were either visually distinct from the pattern design, or blended into the design.

| Location | Adult | Child |
|---|---|---|
| Outer Shell – Tummy | - | Tickling, hugging, pushing |
| Outer Shell – Hands | Clapping hands | Holding hand, 'gimme-five' |
| Outer Shell – Cheeks | Putting hands on the cheeks | Stroking the cheek |
| Outer Shell – Back | - | Stroking the back |
| Inner Glove | Bending thumb / middle finger (waving, nodding) | - |
| Outer Shell + Inner Glove | Sobbing (bending middle finger, covering eyes with puppet's hands) | - |

Table 1: The interactions through the in-between eTextile hand puppet

**Loom:**
TC1 digital Jacquard loom

**Warp:**
*Material*: cotton
*Density*: 24 yarns / cm

**Weft:**
*Material*: linen, silver/polyamide

**Density alters:**
Pocket weave 84 yarns /cm
Capacitive and segmented slider sensors 63 yarns /cm
Jacquard design 42 yarns /cm

**Weaves:**
Pocket weave, 4/1 and 1/4 satin weave
Capacitive sensors and jacquard design, 7/1 and 1/7 satin weave

Table 2: The technical details of the woven prototypes

The user interface consists of four capacitive sensors (hands + cheeks), capacitive segmented slider sensor (back) and a piezoresistive pressure sensor (belly). The capacitive sensors and the segmented slider sensor are woven by using the *fil coupé*-technique, where the conductive yarn is interwoven into the jacquard pattern by using weft floats. The floating conductive weft forms the electrodes on the surface of the fabric, and the floats between the motifs are being cut after weaving. The pressure sensor applies a pocket weave structure (see fig. 7), where both layers contain an additional conductive weft system, and a piece of velostat is placed in between the layers before the pocket structure is completed during the weaving. For technical details of the materials and woven structures, see Table 2. The pocket weave structure of the pressure sensor functions well enough, even though the woven textile layers are able to move with respect to each other and the velostat decreases the friction even more. The velostat appears slightly resistant to movement, which mitigates the problematic movement. A structure with selected binding points connecting the layers together could provide a more durable outcome. While each of the textile elements used for the weaving of the overall structure itself are not novel, the combination is unique, especially so as an eTextile structure.

Our work also suggests ways to develop the textile structure towards more complex multilayer weaves, with respect to casing and pressure sensors. This direction is especially noteworthy, as it implies a controlled way to isolate or combine overlaid conductive layers concerning each other. One crucial element to consider when designing woven eTextile structures consisting of different materials and a varying number of layers is the density of the weft. The density varies depending on how many yarn systems are being applied throughout the design, including both electronic and non-electronic aspects. The first prototype, shown in Figure 6, contains woven sensor-areas; however, the signaling has been attached afterwards as a separate step.

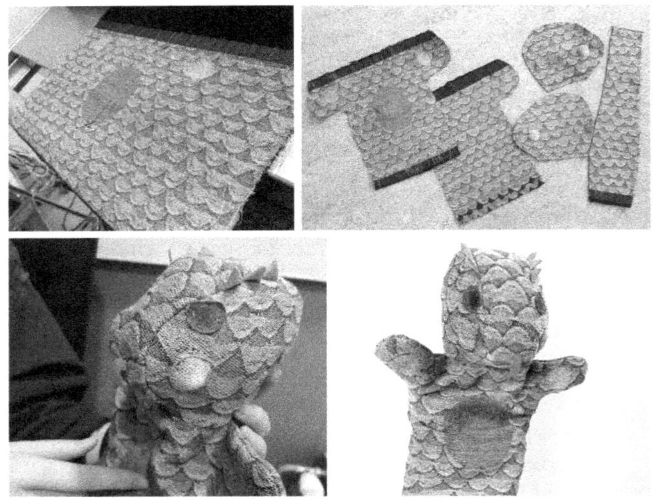

Figure 6: Constructing the prototype and the final prototype

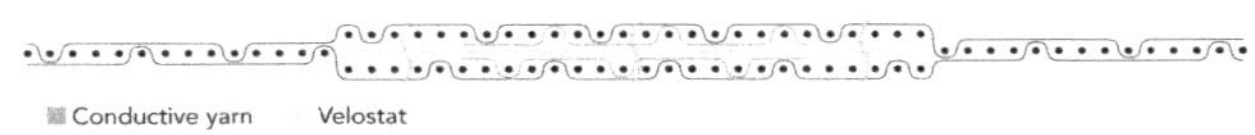


Figure 7: a cross-section of the pressure sensor structure

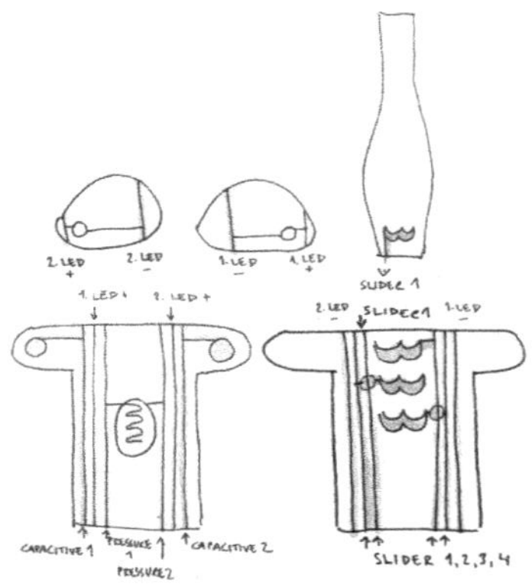

Figure 8: A sketch of the signal traces in textile patterns

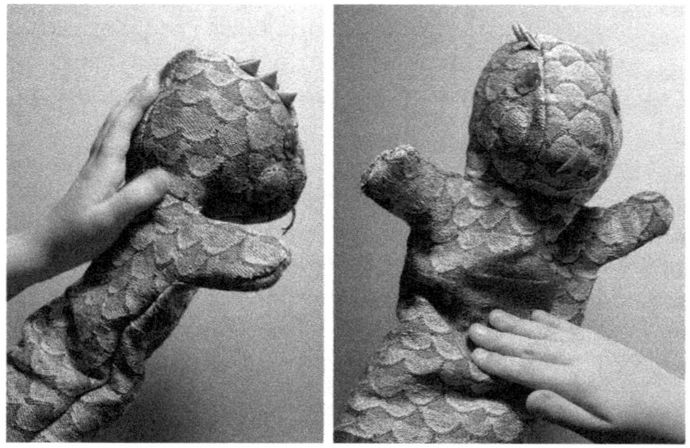

Figure 9: The Hand puppet as worn by an adult and interacted upon by a child

## Final remarks

In this paper, a case of developing an interactive hand puppet was presented, and we have discussed an approach to woven eTextile layout design. The development and fabrication process of an eTextile layout design for the hand puppet was described, with an intent to further study the development of the role of an eTextile design practitioner. Next, the design process of an interactive hand puppet will be mapped against two design frameworks by Veja [14] and Sanders and Stappers [9], to understand better the role of the textile designer in a co-design process. This mapping aims at transdisciplinary method development. The next steps in the smart textile designer practice development will focus on a subsequent version of the woven hand puppet with the signalling built into the weave (see fig.8).

Furthermore, we aim to validate the woven prototypes and their user experience through user testing and technical structural analysis of the woven construction. What is in our interest is to better understand how the traditional textile design variables (e.g. look and feel) can be utilized in the user interface and -experience design. This future work will be conducted with a team of textile designer, an electrical engineer and an interaction designer. This work will push towards the inclusion of electrical components for textile design [3,7], and interfacing them within the textile design methodology drawn from this work.

We aim towards the synthesis of woven eTextile design, consisting of user interface design, pattern design, sensor structure design and textile layout design. How could a pattern be designed to be fully utilised in the user interface design? How the visual cues in the design or the different textures and material feels can support the use of the user interface? By tailoring hand puppet textiles to meet the user's needs and desired user experience, the sphere of smart textile design practice will become more defined.

## Acknowledgements

We would like to thank Miisa Törmänen, Aleksi Turunen and Kimmo Silvonen for their contribution to the prototyping work.

## References

[1] Paul Biedermann, Jekaterina Aleksejeva, Jussi Mikkonen, and Danielle Wilde. 2018. Sensepack: An In-between Wearable for Body-backpack Communication. *Proceedings of the 10th Nordic Conference on Human-Computer Interaction*, ACM, 922–927.

[2] Kunigunde Cherenack and Liesbeth van Pieterson. 2012. Smart textiles: Challenges and opportunities. *Journal of Applied Physics* 112, 9: 091301.

[3] Tilak Kithsiri Dias and Anura Rathnayake. 2017. Electronically Functional Yarns. Retrieved September 5, 2018 from https://worldwide.espacenet.com/publicationDetails/biblio?FT=D&date=20170928&DB=&locale=en_EP&CC=US&NR=2017275789A1&KC=A1&ND=4.

[4] Susan Marie Fairburn, Josie Steed, and Janet Coulter. 2016. Spheres of practices for the co-design of wearables. .

[5] Eva Hornecker. 2011. The Role of Physicality in Tangible and Embodied Interactions. *interactions* 18, 2: 19–23.

[6] Elaine Igoe. 2010. The tacit-turn: textile design in design research. *Duck Journal for Research in Textiles and Textile Design* 1: 1–11.

[7] Jussi Mikkonen and Emmi Pouta. 2016. Flexible Wire-Component for Weaving Electronic Textiles. *2016 IEEE 66th Electronic Components and Technology Conference (ECTC)*, 1656–1663.

[8] Michael Polanyi. 1966. *The Tacit Dimension.* Doubleday & Company, Inc., Garden City, New York.

[9] Ivan Poupyrev, Nan-Wei Gong, Shiho Fukuhara, Mustafa Emre Karagozler, Carsten Schwesig, and Karen E. Robinson. 2016. Project Jacquard: Interactive Digital Textiles at Scale. *Proceedings of the 2016 CHI Conference on Human Factors in Computing Systems*, ACM, 4216–4227.

[10] M. M. Quirk, T. L. Martin, and M. T. Jones. 2009. Inclusion of Fabric Properties in the E-Textile Design Process. *2009 International Symposium on Wearable Computers*, 37–40.

[11] Erica Robles and Mikael Wiberg. 2010. Texturing the "Material Turn" in Interaction Design. *Proceedings of the Fourth International Conference on Tangible, Embedded, and Embodied Interaction*, ACM, 137–144.

[12] Elizabeth B.-N. Sanders and Pieter Jan Stappers. 2014. Probes, toolkits and prototypes: three approaches to making in codesigning. *CoDesign* 10, 1: 5–14.

[13] Donald A. Schön. 2017. *The Reflective Practitioner : How Professionals Think in Action*. Routledge.

[14] Matteo Stoppa and Alessandro Chiolerio. 2014. Wearable Electronics and Smart Textiles: A Critical Review. *Sensors* 14, 7: 11957–11992.

[15] Riikka Claire Townsend, Antti J. Karttunen, Maarit Karppinen, and Jussi Mikkonen. 2017. The Cross-section of a Multi-disciplinary Project in View of Smart Textile Design Practice. *Journal of Textile Design Research and Practice* 5, 2: 175–207.

[16] Louise Valentine, Jen Ballie, Joanna Bletcher, Sara Robertson, and Frances Stevenson. 2017. Design Thinking for Textiles: let's make it meaningful. *The Design Journal* 20, sup1: S964–S976.

[17] Priti Veja. 2014. An investigation of integrated woven electronic textiles (e-textiles) via design led processes. Retrieved from http://bura.brunel.ac.uk/handle/2438/10528.

[18] Mikael Wiberg. 2016. Interaction, new materials & computing – Beyond the disappearing computer, towards material interactions. *Materials & Design* 90: 1200–1206.

[19] Smart Textiles Design Lab Blog » Archive » Involving the Machines. Retrieved November 14, 2018 from http://stdl.se/?p=2024.

# Interactive Tabletop Arm Reaching Exercise

**Zou Yang**
Xi'an Jiaotong-Liverpool University
Suzhou, Jiangsu Province,
215123, China
yang.zou14@alumni.xjtlu.edu.cn

**Jin Yanhao**
Xi'an Jiaotong-Liverpool University
Suzhou, Jiangsu Province,
215123, China
yanhao.jin15@student.xjtlu.edu.cn

**Sun Jie**
Department of Industrial Design
Xi'an Jiaotong-Liverpool University
Suzhou, Jiangsu Province,
215123, China
jie.sun@xjtlu.edu.cn

**Bian Yixuan**
Xi'an Jiaotong-Liverpool University
Suzhou, Jiangsu Province,
215123, China
yixuan.bian15@student.xjtlu.edu.cn


*TEI '19, March 17–20, 2019, Tempe, AZ, USA*

ACM ISBN 978-1-4503-6196-5/19/03.
https://doi.org/10.1145/3294109.3300978

## Abstract

In order to regain motor control, stroke patients should do various exercises that target at specific body functions. During daily exercising, they need assistance from either therapists or caregivers in setting tasks, providing feedback and other activities. Due to aging population, the demand for technology support in stroke recovery has rapidly increased in last decade. This paper presents a portable and interactive prototype designed to facilitate arm reaching exercise. It consists of a tabletop device and a game map that serves as visual guidance on arm movements. This device also provides light and sound feedback while patients can choose different game modes. Preliminary user trials support the implementation of tangible interactive training in rehab centers and further inspire us on building a tabletop training system.

## Author Keywords

Stroke rehabilitation; Tangible interactive training; Tabletop exercise;

## CSS Concepts

• Human-centered computing~Interaction devices

Figure 1 Arm reaching exercise

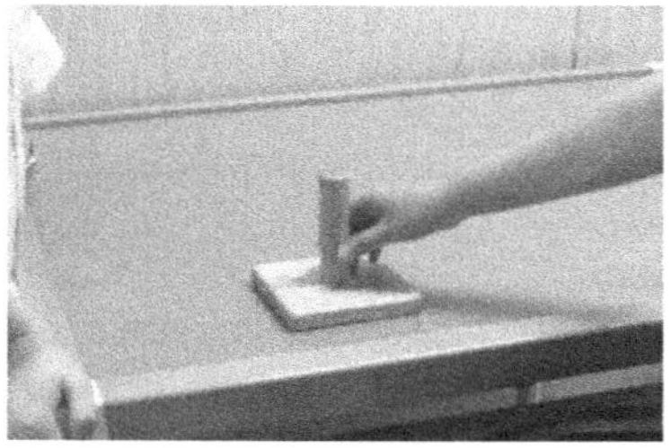
Figure 2 Conventional exercise tool

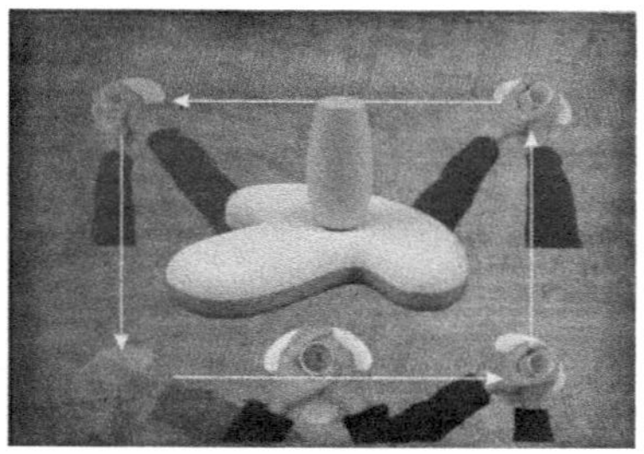
Figure 3 Reaching goals

## Introduction

Stroke survivors often struggle with loss of control over one side or even both sides of their body. According to the symptoms of each stroke patient, therapists would arrange specific exercises for individual rehabilitation. In terms of upper limb rehabilitation, many exercises require manipulation over various tabletop tools, for example rolling a cylinder on a table with both arms. Although most exercises are simple and easy to complete, patients need to persevere for a long term to achieve satisfying recovery outcomes. Thus, therapists spend significant amounts of efforts on encouraging and motivating each patient during daily therapy.

To better assist therapists, game systems are increasingly used to motivate patients and monitor their performance. Most video game systems centralize screen-based interaction [1,4,6] while some recent research studies also adopt tangible interaction in redesigning upper limb exercises [2,7]. Both types of interaction can be effective for stroke patients but in general, digital games often require more expensive and complicated setup, which makes it not a practical solution for most stroke patients. It may be worthwhile to explore low-cost approaches, among which tangible interaction shows a lot potential.

Previous work explored a design concept that integrates multiple exercises into one device [11]. We continue the study by focusing on arm reaching exercise first and we propose *TangiBoard* as an interactive prototype for preliminary testing.

## Related works

Projects like *TagTile* and *Siftables* first demonstrated how sensory technology and tangibles can generally enrich learning and training experience [3,5]. In recent years, many projects aimed to tackle specific problems with the similar approach. For example, a tangible gaming board with arrays of RGB LED light rotary encoders was developed to support various upper limb exercises [8]. This board encased electronic components in a portable packaging and provided various difficulty levels of game exercising. The researchers further worked on minimizing cost of design intervention and embedded visual stimulation into existing exercise tools [10]. We also gained inspirations from Mironcika and et al. [9] who designed a digital board game for children. It had a playful game context and integrated multiple manipulations over a token. Through capturing the movement data, it can support adaptable difficulty levels of exercise to assess motor skills.

In our previous study [11], we proposed a concept that combines forearm, wrist and finger exercises. But we realized that it may not be practical to deliver a fully functional prototype without feedback from practical users. As a result, we start with redesigning one upper limb extremity exercise and making a prototype for testing.

## Design Opportunity

During field research at local rehabilitation center, Suzhou University First Affiliated Hospital (SUFAH), we observed patient activities and interviewed with two therapists about their daily routine. Two patients were doing arm reaching exercise by moving a wooden tool on the table, as shown in Figure 1 and 2. The results of our observation and discussion are summarized as below.

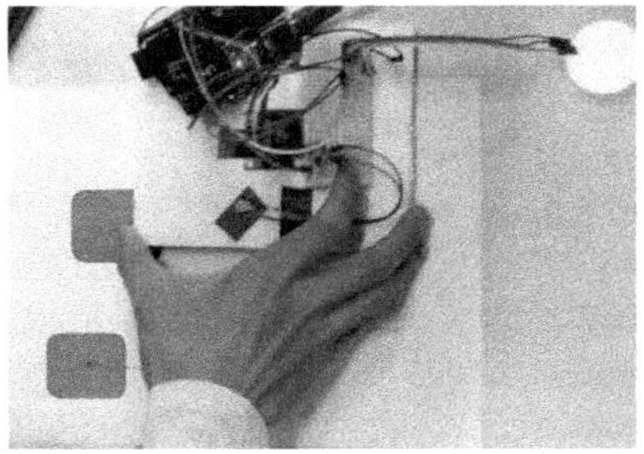
Figure 4 Color sensing demo

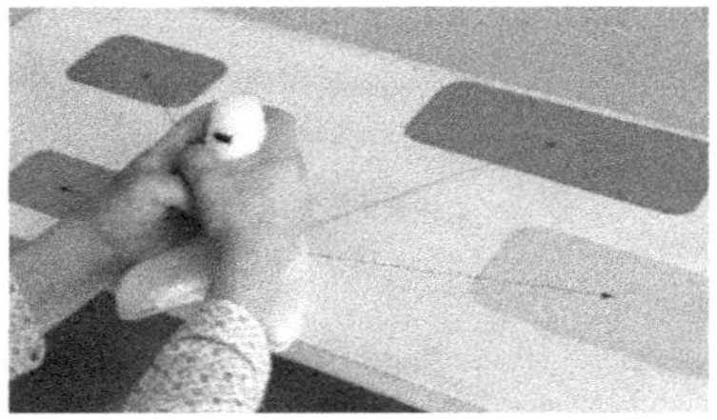
Figure 5 Initial Prototype

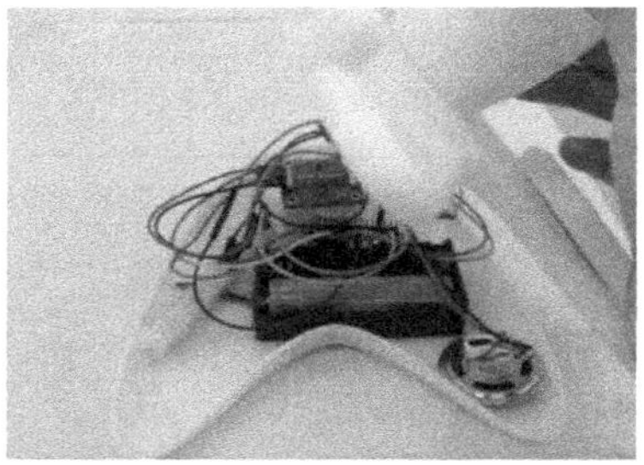
Figure 6 Electronics and housing

*Exercising instruction*
The therapists mentioned that upper limb extremity exercise is fundamental to preventing muscle contraction in early stage of stroke recovery. It requires patients to stretch the disabled side with the aid of the healthy arm. We saw that patients followed therapists' oral instructions and moved from one position to another. Although they were able to do the exercise without physical assistance, they were very passive even under the supervision of therapists. In order to motivate them to do the exercise, we came up with a suggestion that the range of motion should be labeled so that patients can have clear reaching goals (Figure 3).

*Interaction Style*
This hospital also had a video game system for upper limb exercise. It seemed that their budget only allowed for setting up one device, while more than twenty patients need to do daily exercises. According to the therapists, extra efforts were required for elderly patients to understand the screen-based game contents. In addition, the therapists did not consider the game scores as a reliable reference for evaluating patients' upper limb capabilities.

*Gesture Monitoring*
Another concern we noticed is that the therapists kept on monitoring patients and reminding them about proper exercise gestures. For example, patients often rest their disabled arm on the table and only use the healthy side to complete exercise. We hope that the sensor technology could help detect improper gestures and remind patients in a friendly way.

To sum up, we identify the design opportunity as providing a low-cost training device that guide patients through exercising tasks. Meanwhile, therapists should be able to monitor multiple patients at the same time and record their performances.

## TangiBoard

To deal with the arm reaching exercise, we proposed *a TangiBoard* design consists of a hand-holding device and a game map. The device looks similar as the tool in Figure 2, with a handle and a base part. Sitting in front of a table, patients would hold the device with two hands and move it on the map. After brainstorming different sensory stimulations like light, sound and vibration, we decided to use color LED as the main indicator for game instructions. The LED light on the top of the handle indicated target color block to reach. The device was also equipped with speaker to provide sound instruction and audio feedback. We went through two iterations of prototyping and designed two game modes to facilitate arm reaching exercise.

*Initial Prototyping*
An initial mockup consisting of an Arduino Uno, a color sensor and a color LED illustrated the basic working mechanism (Figure 4). When the light indicated a color, the device should be moved toward corresponding color block. The color sensor on the bottom would then judge what color block it is and whether it is at the right matching position. In terms of map design, we placed five rounded blocks including a starting block in black and four blocks in different colors (shown in Figure 5).

For auditory feedback, successful matching with the right color would trigger a short and cheerful sound while a warning sound indicated a wrong matching. Due to the processing limit of Arduino Uno, sound effects were constrained to 8-bit sound clips. To encase the

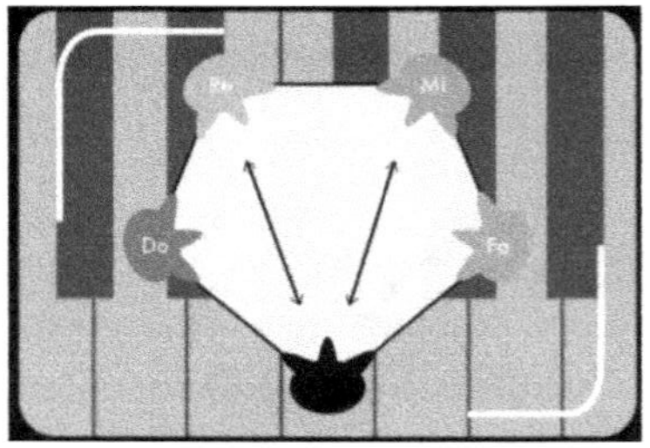

Figure 7 Game map

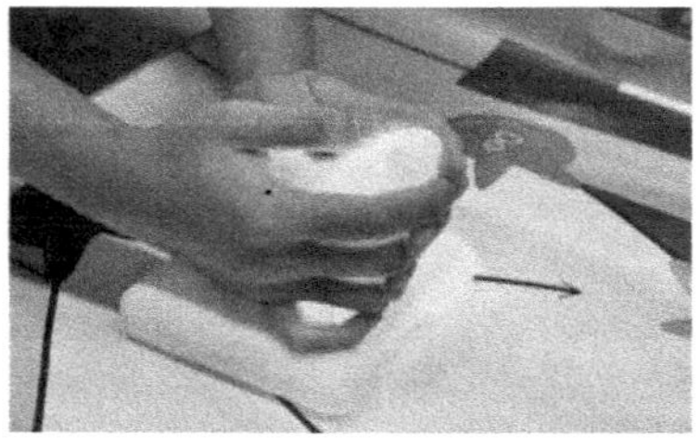
Figure 8 Second prototype

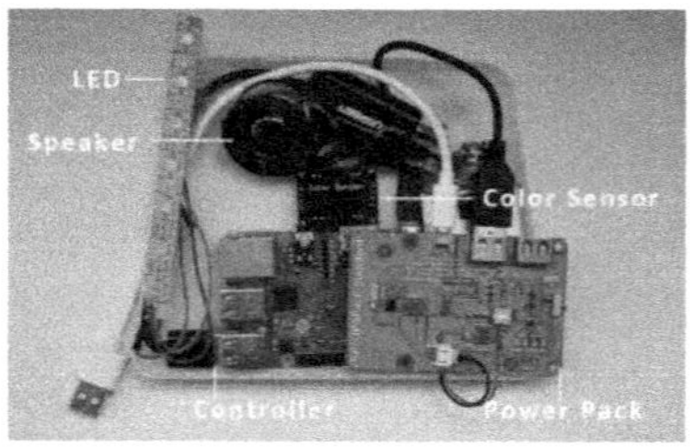

Figure 9 Electronics layout

electronics into the exercise tool, we printed the model including base and upper part using UP box with translucent ABS filament (Figure 6).

Second Prototyping
We brought the first prototype to the rehab center and conducted some initial user trials. Based on the trials, we realized that color LED did give patients clear goals to complete. To further enrich exercising experience, we wanted to improve the device with more dynamic sounds. To address the processing limit of Arduino, we replaced it with Raspberry Pi, which can play sound clips in MP3 format. We added four music notes (Do, Re, Mi, Fa) which are paired with four color patterns on the map and designed a piano theme map shown in Figure 7. The notes are assumed to augment the exercise and make it more fun. The pentagon shape indicated the motion range from starting block. There are four reaching blocks in red, green, yellow and blue from left to right. The handle was inclined toward the front to allow comfortable grip and the final design is shown in Figure 8. Electronic components were also rearranged and packed in the bottom space (Figure 9).

In terms of gesture monitoring, two pressure sensors were placed on the top of the base. When patients rest both hands on the surface, the sensor will detect the pressure on it. If he or she lays their hands on the table rather than the device, the measured value will be smaller. As a result, we can distinguish whether patient's gesture is correct or not.

Game Design
Two game modes were developed and both can be controlled through mini-program on social platform like WeChat.

Mode 1 Chasing Light
In the beginning, users should hold the device and place it at the starting block. When the LED light on the top turns red with sound *'Do'*, they need to move the device toward the red block. Once he or she reaches the target block, the light would turn white, indicating he or she should move back to the starting point. As the light change to different colors, the game would continue till reaching the preset number of movements.

Mode 2 Play and Repeat
This game mode starts with playing a sequence, for example the LED light turns red for 2 seconds and then turns blue for 2 seconds. Users would need to repeat the sequences, namely reaching the blocks in the same order. Music note would accompany the light change and users should try to complete the task in a limited time period. To be noticed, the preset values like the duration of LED shining and the time of task completing can be easily adjusted on the demo app.

## Preliminary testing
With the functional prototype, we planned to let patients in local rehab center use it and see how the design makes a difference for their exercise. More specifically, we want to know whether: 1) patients clearly understand the tasks arranged; 2) patients are well guided by visual and auditory feedback; 3) the setup is easy and convenient.

At Suzhou BenQ Hospital, two patients were invited to use the prototype before their daily training session (Figure 10). Both patients are male and one patient was sixty-one years old with hemiplegia on the right and speech disorder for two years, while the other patient was fifty-five years old with left-side hemiplegia. A

Figure 10 Testing session

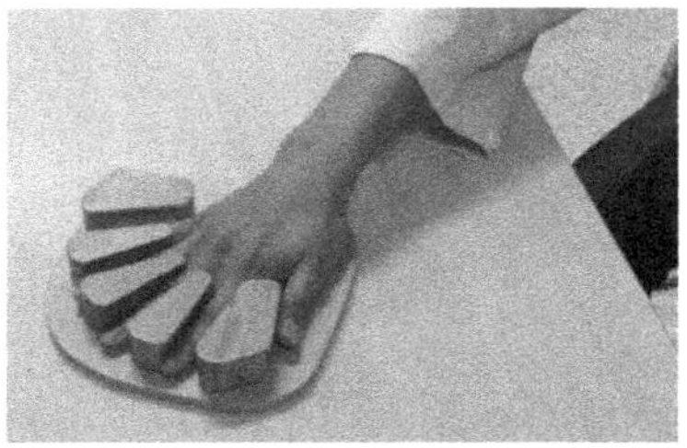

Figure 11 Finger separation exercise

tutorial session was provided before playing the game to help them understand the game flow. Both patients were able to complete the exercise with our prototype. They understood the tasks and followed the visual and auditory feedback. The therapists regarded the portable prototype as a practical device to be implemented in broader scenarios, for instance, home-based rehabilitation. To sum up, we intend to improve the prototype in following aspects.

*Game Experience*

From our observation, it took longer time than we expected for patients to match the color blocks on the map with RGB lights. Meanwhile, auditory feedback like music note seems to provoke limited interest among patients. It is necessary to make it easier for patients to understand the relation between the lights and target blocks. Meanwhile, other sound effects would be explored, for instance those in mobile card games which may be more related to their daily lives.

*Exercise Integration*

The therapists also suggested that finger separation exercise can be integrated with the device (Figure 11). The exercise involves tabletop movement and aims at improving the strength of fingers. An integrated device supports our intention to build a training system that is compatible with multiple exercises. We would start adding this exercise in next stage.

*Performance Monitoring*

We found out patients had difficulty positioning their hands properly on the top of pressure sensors. Thus, the contacting area would be enlarged for easy positioning. In addition, data like reaching speed and reaching distance are important for evaluating arm reaching performance. We would consider collecting and visualizing them in the future to aid therapists in evaluating individual recovery performance.

## Conclusion

This project aims at assisting elderly patients in recovering muscle control with less supervision from therapist. *TangiBoard* was built to provide visual instruction and auditory feedback to help patients exercise. Initial user trials support the low-cost approach to engaging patients in upper limb training. We plan to further cooperate with therapists to integrate more exercises and enrich the game experience through a tabletop training system.

## References

[1] Ana Vasconcelos, Francisco Nunes, Alberto Carvalho, and Catarina Correia. 2018. Mobile, Exercise-agnostic, Sensor-based Serious Games for Physical Rehabilitation at Home. In Proceedings of the Twelfth International Conference on Tangible, Embedded, and Embodied Interaction (TEI '18). ACM, New York, NY, USA, 271-278. DOI: https://doi-org.ez.xjtlu.edu.cn/10.1145/3173225.3173280

[2] Charlotte Magnusson, Héctor A. Caltenco, David McGookin, Mikko Kytö, Ingibjörg Hjaltadóttir, Thóra B. Hafsteinsdóttir, Helga Jónsdóttir, and Ingibjörg Bjartmarz. 2017. Tangible Interaction for Stroke Survivors: Design Recommendations. In Proceedings of the Eleventh International Conference on Tangible, Embedded, and Embodied Interaction (TEI '17). ACM, New York, NY, USA, 597-602. DOI: https://doi-org.ez.xjtlu.edu.cn/10.1145/3024969.3025073

[3] David Merrill, Jeevan Kalanithi, and Pattie Maes. 2007. Siftables: towards sensor network user interfaces. In Proceedings of the 1st international

conference on Tangible and embedded interaction (TEI '07). ACM, New York, NY, USA, 75-78. DOI=http://dx.doi.org.ez.xjtlu.edu.cn/10.1145/1226969.1226984

[4] Héctor A. Caltenco, Anna Olsson, Afshin Aliyari, Charlotte Magnusson, David McGookin, Mikko Kytö, Ingibjörg Hjaltadóttir, Thóra B. Hafsteinsdóttir, Helga Jónsdóttir, and Ingibjörg Bjartmarz. 2017. Designing Interactive Systems for Balance Rehabilitation after Stroke. In Proceedings of the Eleventh International Conference on Tangible, Embedded, and Embodied Interaction (TEI '17). ACM, New York, NY, USA, 511-516. DOI: https://doi-org.ez.xjtlu.edu.cn/10.1145/3024969.3025084

[5] Janneke Verhaegh, Willem Fontijn, and Jettie Hoonhout. 2007. TagTiles: optimal challenge in educational electronics. In Proceedings of the 1st international conference on Tangible and embedded interaction (TEI '07). ACM, New York, NY, USA, 187-190. DOI=http://dx.doi.org.ez.xjtlu.edu.cn/10.1145/1226969.1227008

[6] Marijke Vandermaesen, Tom De Weyer, Peter Feys, Kris Luyten, and Karin Coninx. 2016. Integrating Serious Games and Tangible Objects for Functional Handgrip Training: A User Study of Handly in Persons with Multiple Sclerosis.. In Proceedings of the 2016 ACM Conference on Designing Interactive Systems (DIS '16). ACM, New York, NY, USA, 924-935. DOI: https://doi-org.ez.xjtlu.edu.cn/10.1145/2901790.2901841

[7] Mikko Kytö, David McGookin, Wilfried Bock, Héctor A. Caltenco, and Charlotte Magnusson. 2018. Designing Bimanual Tangible Interaction for Stroke Survivors. In Proceedings of the Twelfth International Conference on Tangible, Embedded, and Embodied Interaction (TEI '18). ACM, New York, NY, USA, 245-252. DOI: https://doi-org.ez.xjtlu.edu.cn/10.1145/3173225.3173269

[8] Pan Wang, Gerald Choon Huat Koh, Christian Gilles Boucharenc, Tian Ma Xu, Hamasaki, and Ching Chiuan Yen. 2017. Developing a Tangible Gaming Board for Post-Stroke Upper Limb Functional Training. In Proceedings of the Eleventh International Conference on Tangible, Embedded, and Embodied Interaction (TEI '17). ACM, New York, NY, USA, 617-624. DOI: https://doi-org.ez.xjtlu.edu.cn/10.1145/3024969.3025080

[9] Svetlana Mironcika, Antoine de Schipper, Annette Brons, Huub Toussaint, Ben Kröse, and Ben Schouten. 2018. Smart Toys Design Opportunities for Measuring Children's Fine Motor Skills Development. In Proceedings of the Twelfth International Conference on Tangible, Embedded, and Embodied Interaction (TEI '18). ACM, New York, NY, USA, 349-356. DOI: https://doi-org.ez.xjtlu.edu.cn/10.1145/3173225.3173256

[10] Thi Ngoc Tram Nguyen, Shienny Karwita, Yan Liangkun, and Sim Yongjie. 2018. Hacking Occupational Therapy Tools for Center-based Care. In Proceedings of the 2018 ACM Conference Companion Publication on Designing Interactive Systems (DIS '18 Companion). ACM, New York, NY, USA, 111-115. DOI: https://doi-org.ez.xjtlu.edu.cn/10.1145/3197391.3205421

[11] Zou Yang, Sun Jie, Lu Shiqi, Cai Ping, and Niu Shengjia. 2018. Tangible Interactive Upper Limb Training Device. In Proceedings of the 2018 ACM Conference Companion Publication on Designing Interactive Systems (DIS '18 Companion). ACM, New York, NY, USA, 1-5. DOI: https://doi-org.ez.xjtlu.edu.cn/10.1145/3197391.3205

# Auto-adjustable Bra for Women with a Pronounced Alteration in Breast Volume

**Eldy S. Lazaro Vasquez**
Department of Design
University of California, Davis
One Shield Avenue
Davis, CA 95616, USA
eslazaro@ucdavis.edu


*TEI '19*, March 17–20, 2019, Tempe, AZ, USA
ACM 978-1-4503-6196-5/19/03.
https://doi.org/10.1145/3294109.3300982

## Abstract
The auto-adjustable bra combines new technologies such as soft robotics, computational design, and e-textiles to develop a bra which uses a pneumatic system to compensate severe asymmetries in breast volume (Anisomastia). In the present work, the bra aims to adjust to the measurements of a woman's breasts through air channels which are located in the internal mesh of the bra cup. This inflatable structure gives a balance in the breasts' volume while holding them. Furthermore, the conductive fabric which covers the bra cup works as a sensor to control the air injection system by comparing the fabric's resistance in both bra cups to send a signal to the air pump to stop the air injection. Thus, the bra keeps in shape and the air pump is disengaged. The project could have a global impact on women with Anisomastia by raising their self-esteem, recovering their emotional balance, and possibly enhancing their social and sexual relationships.

## Author Keywords
Anisomastia; breast asymmetry; auto-adjustable bra; computational design; e-textiles; pneumatics; soft robotics.

## CCS Concepts
•**Human-centered computing** → **Human computer interaction (HCI); Interaction design;** *User studies;*

## Introduction

Ideals and stereotypes of body's image started in the earliest 1990s, gaining momentum in 1998. However, still in the 21st century, woman's body image, breast size, and their social implications remain in our cultural consciousness, so that, this topic becomes more significant in women with pronounced breast asymmetry condition (Anisomastia)[4][11].

This project faces this cultural thought of perfect breast perception, where breast has a significant impact on woman's shapes, and may, therefore, play an important role in body image. In this way, if the breasts differ substantially between them, it is possible a woman suffers an alteration of her body image. Consequently, it is not uncommon to find women who develop a withdrawn and introverted personality seeing their safety and self-esteem diminished [2].

*Frequency of occurrence*

Breast asymmetry is found in the vast majority of women to a more or less visible extent (more than 90%, by some estimates). Asymmetry can manifest in different ways such as the size of the breast, the position of the nipple and areola, the angle of the breast or the position of the breast fold/root (where the breast meets the chest) [10], [6], (Fig.1).

Breast sizes can vary for different reasons including an indication of breast cancer risk. Furthermore, around 25% of women have asymmetry in breast volume of at least one cup size, approximately 10% of which, breast asymmetry is greater than that [3].

There are responsive technologies that shape-shift interfaces for people to interact with their computers or objects. Others help to program physical materials as were used in this project. This project's main contribution is to combine different digital fabrication techniques to develop a bra prototype that adapts to different breasts' size, thanks to the parametric design used in the internal structure of the bra cup which includes the air channels. Now, women with Anisomastia can feel comfortable when wearing a daily bra that fits any breast measurement.

**Figure 1:** (From left to right) Types of breast asymmetry: degree of sagging, position on chest wall, nipple placement and shape. Image CC-BY-SA 2.0 rebeca_verde on Flickr.

## Related Work

During the last years, the wearable technology industry related to smart bras has started increasing, and most of the projects developed in that field applied technology for biomedical purposes. The OMbra, which was introduced at "Consumer Electronics Show (CES)" 2016, aims to give women real-time biometric data while using sensors and textile technology to get an accurate electrocardiogram signal [9]. Another approach to this field is VITALI, presented at CES 2017 as a sports bra that has fabric sensors to track the breathing, and heart rate variability (HRV) with key physiological indicators of the balance between stress and wellbeing to train the nervous system to be more resilient.

Some projects' approach to shape-changing interfaces in the field of HCI is the Skinmorph, which was presented in the "International Symposium on Wearable Computers (ISWC)" 2018. This is an on-skin interface which can selectively transition between soft and rigid states to serve as a texture-tunable wearable skin output. The texture change is made possible through the material design of smart hy-

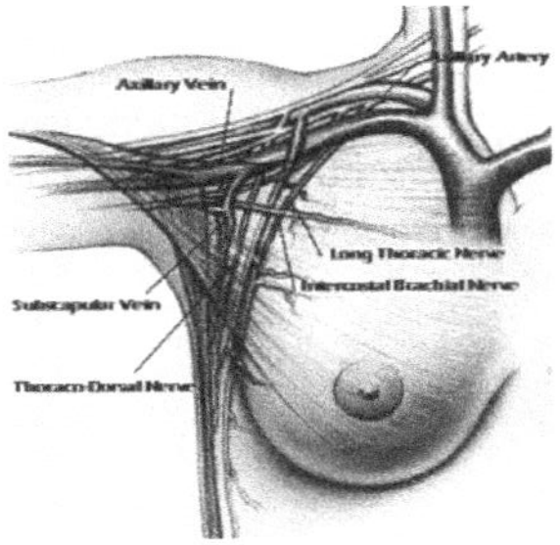

**Figure 2:** Anatomy of the Thoracic Wall, Axilla and Breast [7].

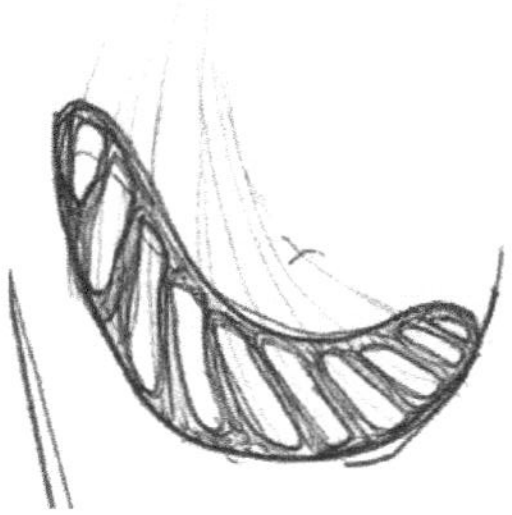

**Figure 3:** First sketch of the inflatable piece.

drophilic gels which are soft in resting state but when activated by heat (>36°C), they generate a micro-level structural change which results in observable stiffening [5]. LineForm is another Shape-Changing Mobile Device that can be use as a wearable. This device can physically display expressive 2D and 3D shapes, both for information representation and for dynamic affordances. Users can interact with LineFORM through direct deformation and via touch to provide haptic feedback through variable stiffness joints to enable such interactions as physical snap to grid [8].

Finally, pneumatic systems have also been used as a shape changer. PneUI is a project that enables technology to build shape-changing interfaces through pneumatically-actuated soft composite materials. It uses elastomer as a material that deforms uniformly under stress; however, by compositing different structural layers with various mechanical properties, the orientation of deformation can be pre-defined [12]. This last technology was incorporated in the project to control the air channels injection to shape and bring consistency to the internal mesh of the bra design.

## Implementation

The auto-adjustable bra focuses in developing a bra that can be worn by women with visible breast asymmetry not only for aesthetics but also for a functional purpose since the project efficiently incorporates different technologies during the prototyping process. Research and analysis of the breast physiology were crucial in this project in order to understand which tissues are part of the woman's breast and how they are arranged to bring natural support (Fig.2). After this analysis, sketches of the inflatable piece started coming out following the shape of the muscular tissue located in the woman's breast (Fig.3). Finally, a woman with Anisomastia was the case of study of this project, and the technologies applied on it went from scanning the woman's breast, to work on a real 3D model, to incorporate e-textiles and pneumatics on the bra to achieve the project purpose which is to homogenize woman's breast volume.

### *3D Scanning & Laser Cutting*

New digital tools that complement hand tools are necessary to design, represent, make and modify the human figure to be used as a canvas for creation later. The challenge in this project is to step away from a simple copy of the human figure as support of this work but start the creative process from the very beginning instead. The process of breast scanning was made with a 3D Systems Sense - 3D scanner. Then the file was edited to create a 1:1 scale mannequin where the bra prototype was tested as many times as necessary. The program Slicer for Fusion 360 was used to turn the digital 3D model into 2D patterns that can be cut out of any flat material, in this case, cardboard 4mm. This program exports EPS, PDF or DXF file format and they can be used to laser cut on any laser cutting machine. Finally, it was possible to make a 3D model mannequin using a press-fit technique (Fig.4).

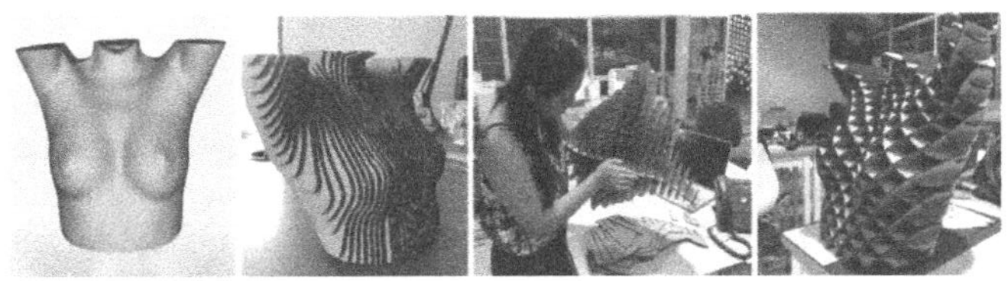

**Figure 4:** The process of making a 3D mannequin consisted of making and using 2D slices of cardboard.

### *E-textiles & Wearables*

Within the relatively new industry around electronic textiles, projects are pursued based on various kinds of functionality. Some electronic textile products may only be built for data storage, while others provide physical interfaces through

**Figure 5:** Conductive fabric: resistance tests.

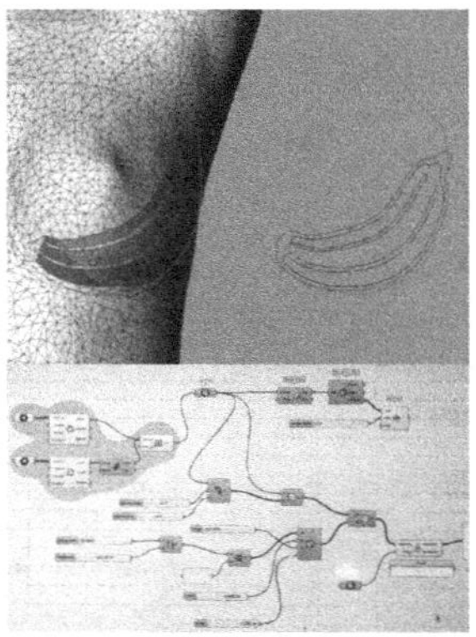

**Figure 6:** Computational design using Rhinoceros and Grasshopper programs.

control elements in the garment design. In some cases, power sources such as batteries can also be integrated into clothing or fabrics. Some experts talk about the difference between embedding electronic devices in fabric, or actually layering conductive electronics into textiles to "make the fabric into the computer". This project is an example of using e-textiles as an interface to obtain data that let us control the bra's pneumatic system.

There are different techniques for making soft/flexible fabric circuits and the EonTex LTT-SLPA-2K fabric was very useful for this project. This fabric is a bidirectionally stretchy nylon/spandex, elastic fabric coated with a long-lasting conductive formulation and highly conductive with a tunable surface resistivity in the range of 10E4 to 10E7 ohm/square. Additionally, it is extremely flexible with a mass per unit area of 4.8 oz./sq.yd. and a warp of 198-248 with an 85% warp recovery [1].

The conductive fabric was used as a sensor in both bra cups, taking the fabric resistance data to send a signal to stop the air injection coming from the air pump when the conductive fabric located in the smaller breast reaches the resistance of the bigger one (Fig.5).

*Parametric Design*
Clothes can be considered as the very first form of mediators between body, space, and events. They aesthetically comprise not only the evolution of its relation to the physical functions of the body (movement, protection, temperature regulation) but also the evolution of cultural expression. Computational couture looks at the creation of exclusive custom-fitted clothing through the lens of a systemic approach, extending the sartorial techniques with 3D modeling and computation-based approaches developed in Rhinoceros and the visual programming environment Grasshopper (Fig.6).

The aim of this bra design is to perform, train and expand the sartorial sensibilities to body proportions and dressmaking into an algorithmic approach that loops through design and digital fabrication. Exploring computational design methods towards a new reinterpretation of clothes, garments, and accessories for fashion design was the approach to use parametric design programs to develop not only the bra itself but also the bra's internal inflatable channels (Fig.7).

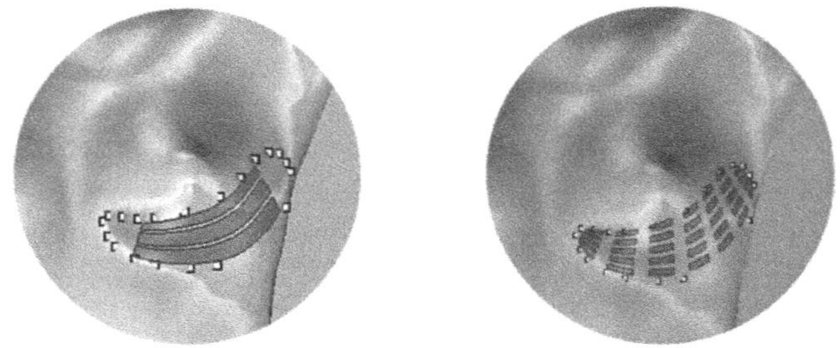

**Figure 7:** Iterations in the parametric design of the inflatable channels in the internal bra cup.

*Soft Robotics & Pneumatics*
Soft robotics is an emerging domain that is dedicated to robots comprised of soft components including soft actuators, flexible sensor/circuits, and soft bodies. This field often focuses on pneumatic actuation of elastomeric channels and bladders. Pneumatic actuation is chosen because air is a lightweight, compressible and environmentally benign energy source [12]. Thus, there is a large space to introduce soft robotic technology in constructing shape-changing interfaces as in this project since the elastomer itself deforms uniformly under stress.

The process of making the inflatable piece attached to the

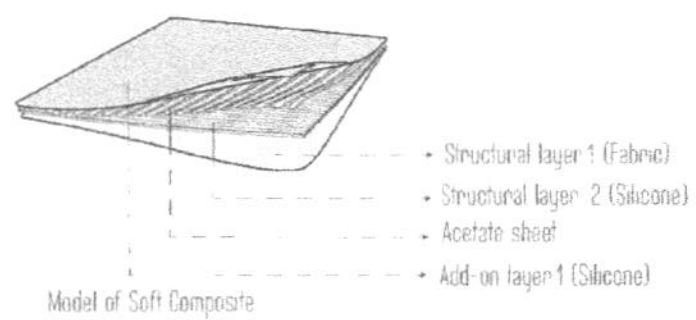


**Figure 8:** Model composition of the internal mesh of the bra cup.

**Figure 9:** View of the inflatable channels in the internal part of the bra cup.

interior side of the bra cup, started by pouring silicone and spreading evenly over a mesh of fabric. This action happened inside of a mold, which was previously defined by the parametric design. Finally, an acetate sheet laser cut in the shape of the air channels was located over the first layer of silicone when it was still sticky. Finally, the last layer of silicone was poured over the acetate piece and spread out evenly using a hand tool (Fig.10). The thickness of the material used as a mold is something to have in consideration in order to have enough space to put the acetate sheet in between the two layers of silicone. For this project, the mold piece had 2mm. thickness.

The acetate sheet main function is to be a path where the air flows to take the form that was defined previously in the parametric design. This is possible because it works as an insulating material since it does not get attached to the silicone. The following figures show the composition of the inflatable piece and how it looks like with some air injected (Fig.8), (Fig.9).

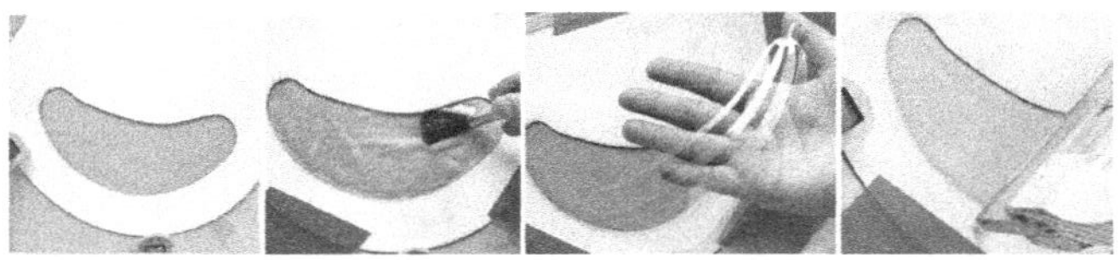

**Figure 10:** Process of making the inflatable piece.

## User Experience Evaluation

The auto-adjustable bra was tested on 3 personas with different types of breast asymmetry. The users described the experience as comfortable and no invasive, even though they could fill the inflatable piece growing when injecting air (Fig.11), (Fig.12).

Persona 1: She is 28 years old and she has a shape breast asymmetry which means that both breasts do not fit the regular bra cup sizes, leaving a gap between the breast and the bra cup. This user described the experience as comfortable and problem-solving. She also was surprised because the inflatable structure helped to lift up both breasts.

Persona 2: She is 29 years old and she has degree of sagging breast asymmetry which involves a lack of fullness in the lower portion of the breast. She has this condition in the left breast and she described the experience as amazing. She said she can't wait this project to be a product because the bra helped to look her breast symmetric.

Persona 3: She is 27 years old and she has a shape breast asymmetry. She described the experience as incredible because the bra design adjusts to her breasts' measurements and also it looks nice. She also liked that no wire supports were included in this bra prototype.

## Acknowledgments

Thanks to Katia Vega for her guidance, advice, and support, and Sarah Rebolloso for the great talk we had about women in society and how to address a topic like woman's breast asymmetry in a pre-established cultural context.

## Conclusion

The auto-adjustable bra project combines various digital fabrication techniques and new technologies such as soft robotics, computational design, and e-textiles to develop a bra that adapts to any breasts shape in women with Anisomastia. The bra uses a pneumatic system to compensates the severe asymmetries in breast volume through air channels situated in the internal mesh of the bra cup. This approach would help women with Anisomastia to feel more comfortable and look good wearing a bra that fits any breast measurement.

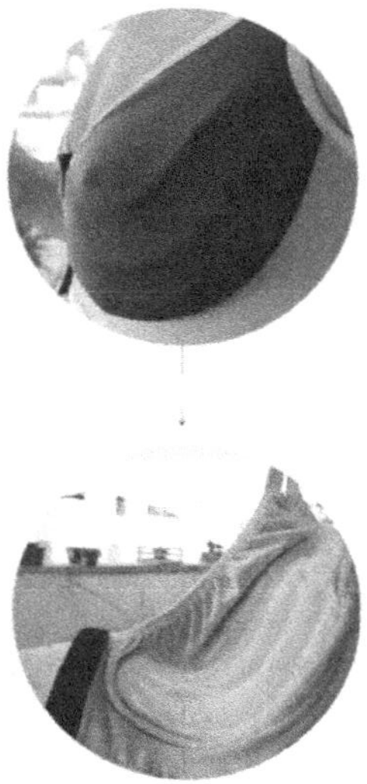

Figure 12: Internal and external view of the bra prototype.

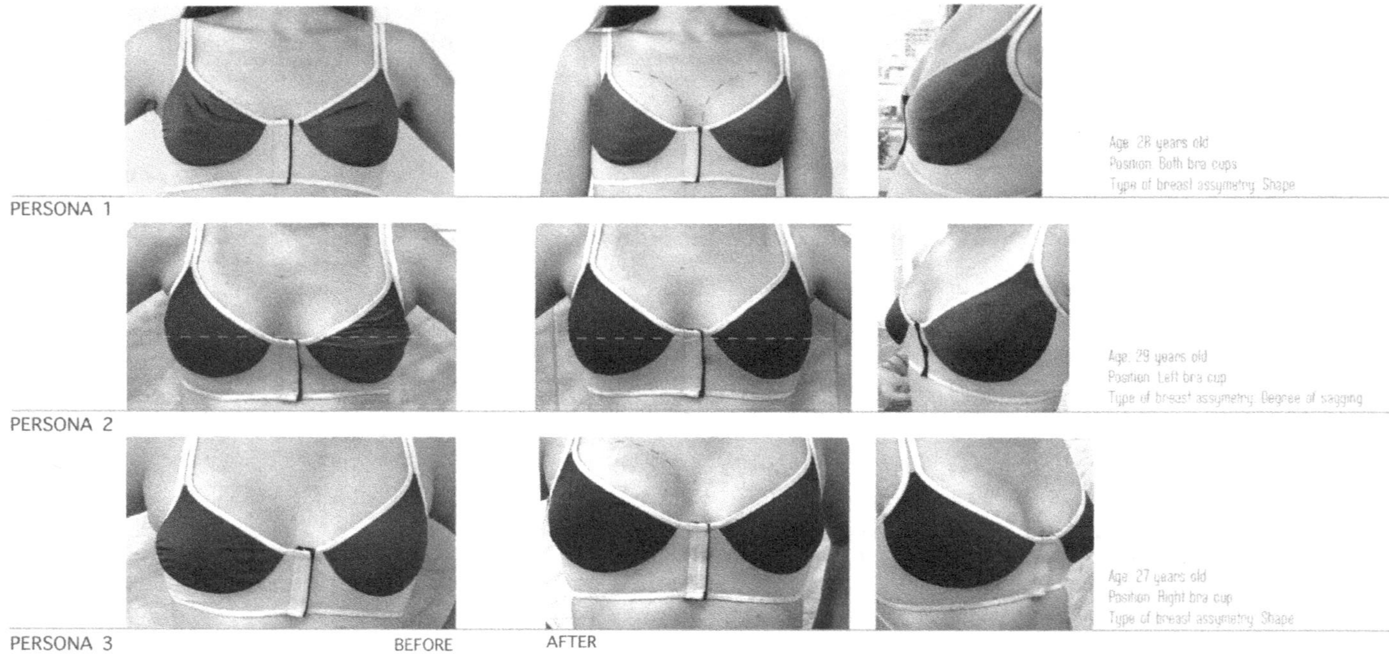


**Figure 11:** Women with different breast asymmetry testing the auto-adjustable bra.

## References


[1] EonTex. 2011. EeonTex Conductive Textiles. (2011). http://www.marktek-inc.com/doc/EeonTexTDSF1.pdf

[2] Garcia-Pumarino. 2012. Operacion de asimetria en los senos Madrid | Dr. Garcia-Pumarino. (2012). https://doctorpumarino.com/operacion-asimetria-senos/.

[3] Woman's Health. 2014. Breast Asymmetry - When Does It Need Treatment? (2014). https://www.wdxcyber.com/nbreast3.htm.

[4] Lora Jacobi and Thomas F. Cash. 1994. In Pursuit of the Perfect Appearance: Discrepancies Among Self-Ideal Percepts of Multiple Physical Attributes 1. *Journal of Applied Social Psychology* (1994).

[5] Hsin-Liu (Cindy) Kao, Miren Bamforth, David Kim, and Chris Schmandt. 2018. Skinmorph. In *Proceedings of the 2018 ACM International Symposium on Wearable Computers - ISWC '18*. ACM Press. DOI: http://dx.doi.org/10.1145/3267242.3267262

[6] Albert Losken, Inessa Fishman, Donald D. Denson, Hunter R. Moyer, and Grant W. Carlson. 2005. An Objective Evaluation of Breast Symmetry and Shape Differences Using 3-Dimensional Images. *Annals of Plastic Surgery* 55, 6 (Dec 2005), 571–575. DOI: http://dx.doi.org/10.1097/01.sap.0000185459.49434.5f

[7] José Rafael Macéa and José Humberto T. G. Fregnani. 2006. Anatomy of the thoracic wall, axilla and breast. *International Journal of Morphology* 24, 4 (1 1 2006), 691–704. DOI: http://dx.doi.org/10.4067/S0717-95022006000500030

[8] Ken Nakagaki, Sean Follmer, and Hiroshi Ishii. 2015. LineFORM. In *Proceedings of the 28th Annual ACM Symposium on User Interface Software Technology - UIST'15*. ACM Press. DOI: http://dx.doi.org/10.1145/2807442.2807452

[9] OMsignal. 2016. OMsignal. (2016). https://www.omsignal.com/

[10] Dimitrije E. Panfilov and Grahame Larkin. 2005. *Cosmetic surgery today*. Thieme Medical Publishers.

[11] Stacey Tantleff-Dunn. 2001. Breast and Chest Size: Ideals and Stereotypes Through the 1990s. *Sex Roles* 45 (08 2001), 231–242. DOI: http://dx.doi.org/10.1023/A:1013505928458

[12] Lining Yao, Ryuma Niiyama, Jifei Ou, Sean Follmer, Clark Della Silva, and Hiroshi Ishii. 2013. PneUI. In *Proceedings of the 26th annual ACM symposium on User interface software and technology - UIST '13*. ACM Press. DOI: http://dx.doi.org/10.1145/2501988.2502037

# Baby Tango: Electronic Textile Toys for Full-Body Interaction

**Joanna Berzowska**
Design and Computation Arts
Concordia University
Montreal, QC H3G 1M8, Canada
joanna.berzowska@concordia.ca

**Alex Mommersteeg**
District 3
Concordia University
Montreal, QC H3G 1M8, Canada
alexmommersteeg@gmail.com

**Laura Isabel Rosero Grueso**
Concordia University
Montreal, QC H3G 1M8, Canada
roserogruesolauraisabel@gmail.com

**Eric Ducray**
Concordia University
Montreal, QC H3G 1M8, Canada
egducray@gmail.com

**Michael Patrick Rabo**
Concordia University
Montreal, QC H3G 1M8, Canada
michaelpatrickrabo@gmail.com

**Geneviève Moisan**
Milieux
Concordia University
Montreal, QC H3G 1M8, Canada
gelarousse@hotmail.com


*TEI '19, March 17–20, 2019, Tempe, AZ, USA*

ACM ISBN 978-1-4503-6196-5/19/03.
https://doi.org/10.1145/3294109.3300973

## Abstract

We describe two prototypes from the Baby Tango project: electronic textile toys that enable soft, tangible, full-body interaction. It presents interaction techniques that bridge the physical, the digital, and the social, as well as a case study in constructing interactive composite textiles. Given that the softness of the toy is a central design constraint, most of the circuit, including the sensors, is embroidered directly on the surface of the artifact using technical threads (with varying electro-mechanical properties) and a digital embroidery/laying machine. This submission includes design and technical details, as well as initial interaction design scenarios.

The next steps of this project will explore how these toys could support the development of empathy in toddlers through embodied play. Further work is needed in order to develop background research, collaborations with early childhood researchers, as well as empirical studies. Future work will include the development of these studies; iterating aspects of interaction and play through participatory design; and improving technical design to focus on reliability, robustness, and durability.

**Author Keywords**
Electronic textiles; interactive toys; tangible interaction; soft user interface; embroidered sensors; empathy.

**CCs Concepts**
• Human-centered computing~Haptic devices • Social and professional topics~Children • Hardware~Sensors and actuators

## Introduction

Many parents are concerned with the developmental milestones achieved by their children and especially with the development of appropriate emotional responses in social and interpersonal situations. In addition, as we increasingly embrace digital tools such as tablets and smartphones to entertain and distract our children, researchers are studying the effects these devices have on the emotional and social responses of very young people. [5] We see potential in the development of physical electronic toys that leverage multi-sensory materiality and can support the development of social skills and emotional responses such as empathy through embodiment and tangible interaction. We plan to develop future research and empirical studies to research whether tangible interactions can assist in children's cognitive development by supporting the learning of complex concepts and the development of organized knowledge structures. [1]

*Electronic Textiles and Full-Body Interaction*

We focus specifically on electronic textile toys that allow full-body, continuous, and soft tangible interaction (see Figure 1). While there are many interactive toys on the market, most of them are encased in a hard plastic shell and create simple interaction through the push of buttons or other discrete controllers. While these tangible systems allow for the development of certain problem-solving skills, as well as other cognitive development, the interaction is restricted and often does not allow for full-body emotional responses such as hugging, caressing, squeezing, or even punching. Alissa N. Antle concludes in her paper that "Concepts from embodied cognition and dynamic systems suggest that successful tangible systems will incorporate an adaptive, body-based style of interaction which leverages children's developing an existing repertoire of physically-based actions. Acquisition will be achieved through exploration with real time feedback of how things work." [1]

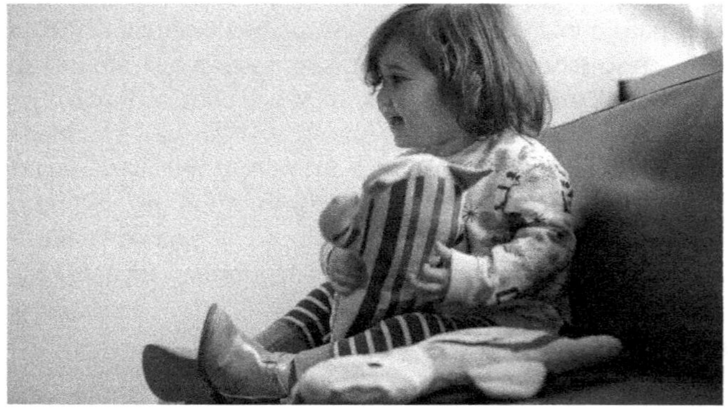

**Figure 1.** Ariel holding one of the Baby Tango toys

We focused on active textile materials that employ various technical fibers together with digital laying and embroidery to embed sensing and communication directly in the fabric. Because the toys don't have buttons but rather continuously embroidered sensors, the interaction becomes more abstract, more ambiguous and more open to children creating their own narratives and explorations. [2, 3, 4]

## Design and Technical Details

We decided to focus on developing a set of interactive characters with individual behaviors and scenarios that could enable emotional and tactile responses. The first round of prototyping involved augmenting existing toys with integrated electronic components such as lights, vibrators, and sound chips. We conducted a qualitative study with 10 sets of parents and children ranging in age from 16 months to 6 years old. We scheduled short supervised play sessions and conducted informal observation and semi-structured interviews to test simple aspect of the toys such as intuitiveness and the first reaction of an infant towards a toy's features. Some observations included:

- Infants tend to hold the velvet fabric longer compared to other textures.
- Vibration in a toy catches the attention of younger infants longer than older ones.
- Gradual change in texture (heart patches for instance) are very attractive.
- Embroidered surfaces (rough textures) tend to spark curiosity and invite focused interaction.

**Figure 2.** The Baby Tango family

*Developing the Characters and Interactions*

The toys were designed as a series of five fictional creatures (see Figure 2) with distinct personalities that elicit various emotional reactions in users. The goal was to develop soft, genderless (non-binary), anthropomorphic, interactive creatures that respond to a child's touch with lights, vibrations and sounds. We looked at many sources of inspiration, including animals, robots, and monsters, and attempted to subvert the traditional genres by creating a more ambiguous family of creatures (see Figure 3).

**Figure 3.** Iterating various character features

To develop interaction scenarios, we looked at how people of different ages interact with animals, toys, and babies. Inspired by the many instances of hugging, petting, squeezing, holding hands, tickling, and nuzzling, we incorporated elements of those actions into the interaction design of the prototype toys. All the creatures enjoy being hugged and held. They show their love as their heart beats and glows. The two prototypes are named Lue and Mello (see Figure 4). Lue is quiet, calm, shy, and affectionate. Its favourite colour is blue. Lue moved to a new city with its family. It is trying to make new friends but it is shy and quiet, so it needs some help. Take it by the hand and bring it somewhere to play and make new friends, it will love it! Intimate contact reminds it of its mom, so you can pet it to calm it down and hug it whenever it is afraid. Soothe it by petting its back. Lue features touch sensors on its back that responds when you pet it. With enough contact, Lue calms down and lights up its checks with affection. Lue has a pressure sensor within its arm; when its arm is held or moved, it lights up with excitement. Touch sensors on the front and a pressure sensor in the belly sense a hugging interaction.

**Figure 4.** Lue and Mello

Mello is active and joyful. Tickle it to make it laugh. It loves the color yellow. Mello likes to make everyone laugh and to put a smile on everyone's face but it gets bored easily. You can get its attention and cheer it up by tickling its feet and belly. All three feet are very ticklish and don't forget to follow the pattern on its belly to make it laugh. Like Lue and the rest of its friends, it is a hugger! Mello features touch sensors on its belly as well as on its back. Tracing the pattern on its belly will tickle Mello and cause it to laugh. Laughter from Mello comes in the form of sound and vibration. Pressure sensors in Mello's feet also allow for its feet to be tickled and cause him to laugh. When hugging Mello, both the belly and back touch sensors will be contacted causing the heart to beat.

## Soft Circuit Design and Embroidery

In order to construct more complex electronic textiles, traditional textile manufacturing techniques are not sufficient. Weaving, knitting, and other methods can only achieve simple functional architectures. A central issue lies in the way that the electronic components are connected to soft elements. We used a Tajima Laying Machine, a powerful digital tool for research and creation in electronic textiles (see Figure 5).

**Figure 5.** The Tajima laying machine producing the electronics layer for Mello.

In contrast to more traditional textile fabrication techniques such as weaving, knitting, or embroidery, the machine allows the three-dimensional layering of multiple technical fibers in intricate geometries. This means that different kinds of technical fibers, such as conductive fibers, can be integrated into a textile substrate in a seamless and complex way, fully approximating that of a soft circuit board.

In addition, we can also embroider a range of colors and textures on top of the functional layers so as to seamlessly merge decorative, narrative, and functional components of the soft circuit (see Figure 6). This machine can breach the space between traditional electronic manufacturing methods and traditional textile fabrication methods to allow a true hybrid way of developing electronic textile structures. The structural possibilities offered by this fabrication method were instrumental in shifting the conceptual models for developing our baby Tango toys so as to allow for a truly huggable, soft structure, which can also be easily scalable and manufacturable.

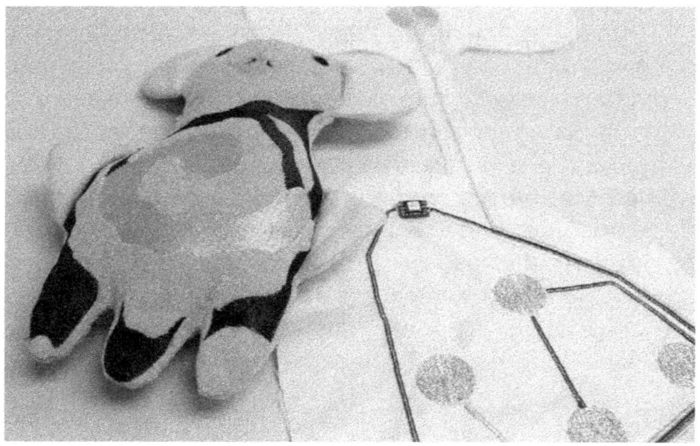

**Figure 6.** Mello

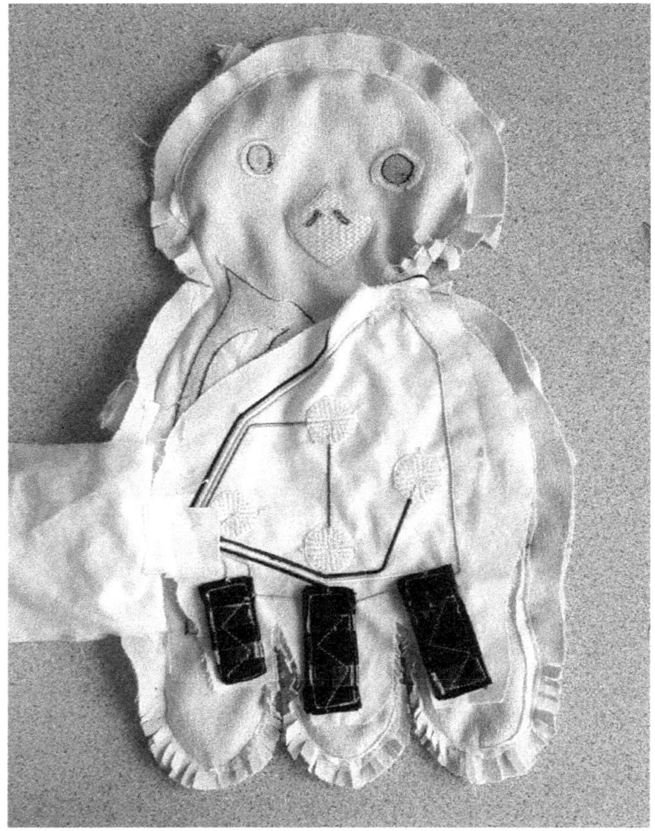

**Figure 7.** Integrating the two layers

## Implementation

To create Lue and Mello, two layers of fabric are used. The top layer is the one visible to the users and includes the colored patterns and textured embroidery for tactile stimulation. The second layer (electronic layer) is just below the first layer and includes the electronics, sensors and conductive threads to connect with the controlling unit (see Figure 7). The touch sensors are laid onto the electrical layer with a circular pattern of conductive thread. They use capacitive touch technology which senses when there is a contact or proximity with a conductive material such as a human body. The other sensor used by the toys is a pressure sensor, created with a soft base material on either side of a piece of Velostat. The electronic layer also houses the RGB LEDs. Conductive thread is used to connect power and the controlling units, Arduino Pro Micros, which are housed within a custom case along with the battery and battery controller, the vibrating motor, speaker, and sound board.

All creatures respond to hugging with a heartbeat. The heartbeat is generated by the LED at the heart patch lighting up along with the vibrating motor beating. To hug Lue one of the two touch sensors on the front along with pressure being applied to the pressure sensor in the belly needs to be activated. Mellow uses only touch sensors and requires the front and back sensors to be touched. Incorporating multiple sensors allows us to modulate responses for different kinds of touch.

## Future Work

The next steps of this project will explore how these toys could support the development of empathy in toddlers through embodied play. Further work is needed in order to develop background research, collaborations with early childhood researchers, as well as empirical studies. Future work will include the development of these studies; iterating aspects of interaction and play through participatory design; and improving technical design to focus on reliability, robustness, and durability.

## Acknowledgements

This work was supported by District 3 at Concordia University and their Summer Innovation program. We also wish to thank the Textiles and Materiality Research Cluster, at the Milieux Institute for Arts, Culture and Technology, Concordia University.

## References

[1] Alissa N. Antle. 2007. Designing tangibles for children: what designers need to know. In *CHI '07 Extended Abstracts on Human Factors in Computing Systems* (CHI EA '07), 2243-2248. https://doi.org/10.1145/1240866.1240988

[2] Florian Güldenpfennig, Peter Fikar, and Roman Ganhör. 2018. Interactive and Open-Ended Sensory Toys: Designing with Therapists and Children for Tangible and Visual Interaction. In *Proceedings of the Twelfth International Conference on Tangible, Embedded, and Embodied Interaction* (TEI '18). 451-459. https://doi.org/10.1145/3173225.3173247

[3] Svetlana Mironcika, Antoine de Schipper, Annette Brons, Huub Toussaint, Ben Kröse, and Ben Schouten. 2018. Smart Toys Design Opportunities for Measuring Children's Fine Motor Skills Development. In *Proceedings of the Twelfth International Conference on Tangible, Embedded, and Embodied Interaction* (TEI '18). 349-356. https://doi.org/10.1145/3173225.3173256

[4] Joanna Walters. 2015. Tablets and smartphones may affect social and emotional development, scientists speculate. Retrieved August 5, 2018 from https://www.theguardian.com/technology/2015/feb/01/toddler-brains-research-smartphones-damage-social-development

# ReRide: A Bike Area Network for Embodied Self-monitoring during Motorbike Commute.

**Naveen L. Bagalkot**
**Gaurav Singh**
**Vineeta Rath**
Srishti Institute of Art, Design, & Technology,
Bengaluru 560064, India
naveen@srishti.ac.in
gaurav.singh@srishti.ac.in
vineeta.rath@srishti.ac.in

**Tomas Sokoler**
IT University of Copenhagen
DK-2300 Copenhagen S
Denmark
sokoler@itu.dk

**Anchit Shukla**
Indian Institute of Technology
Roorkee, Roorkee - 247667
India
ashukla@ce.iitr.ac.in



*TEI '19*, March 17–20, 2019, Tempe, AZ, USA

ACM ISBN 978-1-4503-6196-5/19/03.
https://doi.org/10.1145/3294109.3300986.

## Abstract

Motorbike commuting is the new frontier for exploring digital technology, where designing for embodied interaction takes on a more central role. In this paper, building on previous work on embodied self-monitoring, we present our ongoing work of designing a modular platform with a particular focus on real-time estimation and presentation of posture data while riding. In particular, we present 'Bike Area Network' (BANk) as a system architecture to help guide the design of such a platform. We share our ongoing work as an invitation for the community of researchers and practitioners of designing for embodied interaction to further explore this new frontier of research.

## Author Keywords

Embodied Self-monitoring; Motorbike Riding; Real-time Posture detection; Personal Informatics.

## CSS Concepts

• Human-centered computing~Interaction design theory, concepts and paradigms • Human-centered computing~Ubiquitous and mobile computing theory, concepts and paradigms • Human-centered computing~Ubiquitous and mobile computing design and evaluation methods

Pre Ride

Diva commutes to her work on her motorbike daily. She has been doing so for the past 5 years, and now is in the danger of developing repetitive strain injury of her lower back.

On Ride

She then starts using ReRide. ReRide consists of two parts:
a) A sensing system of multiple peripherals and b) a display unit that displays this information real-time, next to the motorbike's dashboard.

Figure 1: Use case scenarios of ReRide

## Introduction

Taking embodied interaction [9,15] as the theoretical foundation our previous research, on the design of pervasive and mobile digital technologies for of out-of-clinic physical rehabilitation, has suggested the construct of 'embodied self-monitoring' [5,6]. Design for embodied self-monitoring aims to bring forward opportunities to help the rehabilitees integrate parts of a regimen for physical rehabilitation with everyday activities. Furthermore, it enables a more specific application of Lived Informatics in the situation of physical rehabilitation [2]. Having recognized the many similarities between out-of-clinic physical rehabilitation and doing physical exercise as part of preventive self-care, we ask if the design for embodied self-monitoring could guide design for preventive self-care? That is, if and how could digital technology be designed to bring forward opportunities for people to turn everyday activities into exercises for preventive self-care?

In our ongoing work, we take everyday motorbike commute through dense urban traffic as the everyday activity and explore through design if and how adding data on lower-back posture to the experience of riding would present opportunities for the rider to perform simple lower-back exercises during the ride? In particular, we look into the design of a system that, by offering the rider cues about their back posture seeks to enable and encourage bike riders to carry out preventive measures as an integrated part of riding.

Previously we have explored digital technology and embodied interaction in the context of motorbike riding, presenting an interactive sketch through which we explored and narrowed in on the kind of experience and interaction a system for real-time posture feedback should enable [4,14]. Subsequently, we designed and developed a software-hardware architecture for a platform enabling experiments around embodied self-monitoring [3]. From these experiences, we realized that we need a more modular system in order to experiment with the possibilities of supporting embodied self-monitoring in more depth, covering all the four scenarios of use (see figure 1 and 3).

In this paper, we present our ongoing work of designing a robust and modular platform, with a particular focus on real-time estimation and presentation of posture data while riding (to explore the 'On Ride' scenario in depth, refer figure 1 and 3). In particular, we present 'Bike Area Network' (BANk) as a system architecture to help guide the design of such a platform. Furthermore, we present the process of developing the software and hardware interactive prototype, including explorations of real-time posture detection and visualization for on-ride feedback.

Through sharing our ongoing and evolving work, we further the emerging discourse around specific use-cases of embodied self-monitoring, moving beyond physical rehabilitation and towards preventive self-care. In particular, our work makes the possibilities of in-situ experimentation towards designing for embodied self-monitoring in the specific context of motorbike commuting more real. Furthermore, through sharing our evolving process of designing the modular platform we invite the broad community of designers and researchers exploring embodied interaction to explore the exciting frontier of digital technologies for embodied self-monitoring in the context of motorbike commuting.

Pause during Ride

When she temporarily stops riding, she can see historical data about the present ride upto that moment.

Post Ride

Post completion of ride, she checks the detailed reports about her posture during her rides on her phone

Figure 3: Use case scenarios of ReRide.

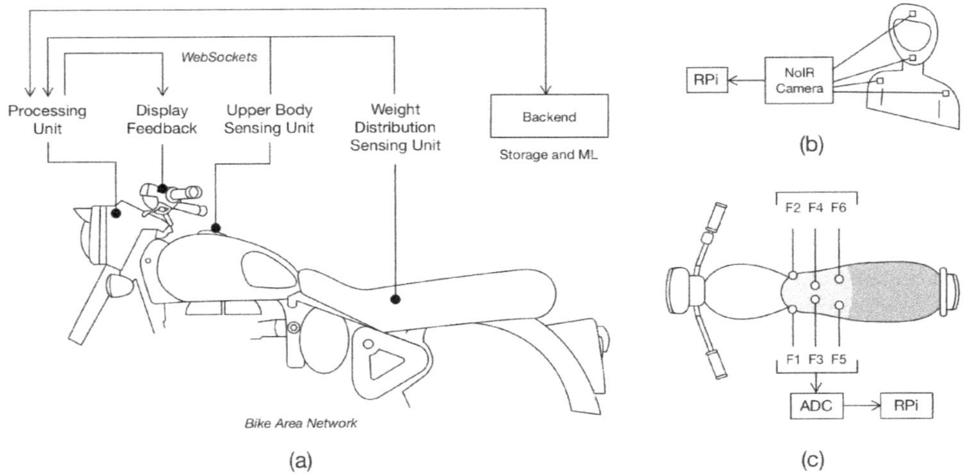


Figure 2: System Architecture: (a) Bike Area Network, (b) Upper body tracking sensor unit, (c) Weight distribution sensing unit

## BANk: A Modular System Architecture

We envision ReRide system as a PaaS (Platform as a Service), a modular system of hardware and software located on the bike and a cloud server. The Bike Area Network (BANk) forms the core architecture of the platform. We define BANk as a specialised local area network to wirelessly interface sensing modules to the processing module (also located on the bike), fetch rider data from the backend (at a remote location on cloud server), and display it on the rider dashboard (see figure 2). The central components of BANk are,

1. Sensing modules. Each sensing module is a combination of a sensor and a Raspberry Pi[1] unit.
2. A central processing module, consisting of a Raspberry Pi, which reads the data from sensing modules and publishes it to the remote server for later access or further processing through Machine Learning models. It is responsible for abstracting the raw information to relevant data that can be visualized by the display module.
3. Display module. In the current form this is a smartphone with a specific browser based visualization of rider data. But we imagine it to be integrated with the motorbike's digital dashboard.

In the current version, we use two sensing modules: (a) Weight distribution sensing module and (b) Upper-body sensing module. The aim is to enable us to estimate dynamic posture of the rider and suggest visual feedback to the rider through the display module.

[1] Raspberry Pi Zero W (Microcontroller board, 802.11b/g/n WLAN, 1GHz, single-core CPU, 512MB RAM, Micro USB power, Hat-compatible 40-pin header, CSI camera connector) https://www.raspberrypi.org/products/raspberry-pi-zero-w/

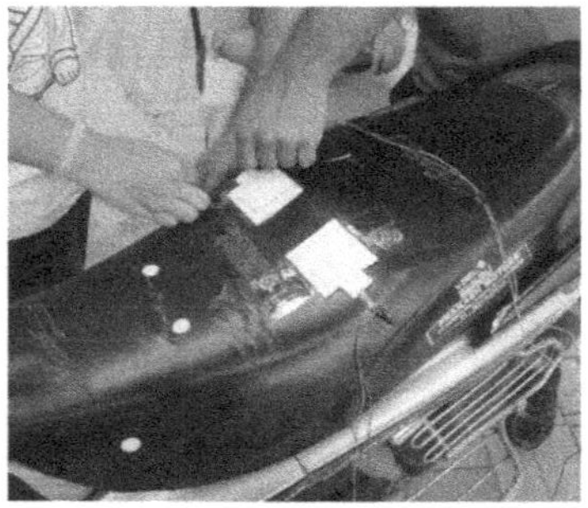

Figure 5: Fixing the FSR Matrix on the seat of the bike

Figure 6: Rig for camera sensor module mount on the motorbike.

*Weight Distribution Sensing Module*

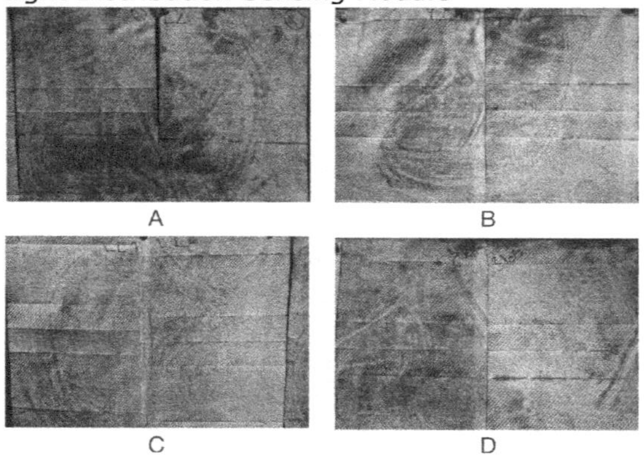


Figure 4: Pressure map transferred on tissue paper through Carbon paper; A-Forward Lean, B-Right Lean, C-Backward Lean, D-Left Lean

The weight distribution sensing module consists of a Raspberry Pi connected with a matrix of force sensitive resistors (FSR) [11,13] strapped on the motorbike seat (see figure 5). The matrix is arranged in a particular configuration to help us estimate the change in the weight distribution on the seat at different poses during the ride [1]. We determined the configuration the FSR matrix through multiple experiments that looked at how the rider's weight changes at different poses (see figure 4).

There are six FSRs which send analog signals to the connected Raspberry Pi on I2C (Inter-Integrated Circuit) interface through two 16-Bit/4-Channel Analog to Digital Converter Adafruit ADS1115 16-Bit/4 Channel ADC with Programmable Gain Amplifier[2]. The Raspberry Pi reads the FSR values and broadcasts them for the central processing module to read over WebSockets[3]. In particular, the front and middle FSRs enable us to determine if the rider is left or right, and along with the rear ones they together help us understand if the rider is leaning front or backward.

*Upper-body Sensing Module*

The upper-body sensing module consists of a Raspberry Pi connected with an 8MP NoIR camera[4] mounted near the bike dashboard facing the rider's upper body (see figure 6). The camera works at 30fps and is sufficient for recognizing specific ARuco markers [10] placed on the rider's helmet and shoulders under dim light. The markers are placed at specific points to extract rider's proximity from the camera, shoulder tilt, and head stoop. The attributes from the camera along with FSR data are used to extract several features of posture with reasonable confidence. The upper-body sensing module also sends these attribute data to the processing module over WebSockets.

## Posture Estimation

The processing module evaluates data from the sensing modules and calculates the various relevant attributes that contribute to the dynamic posture of the rider. The evaluation helps in understanding rider's forward lean, shoulder tilt, head stoop, left or right lean. While the accurate understanding of posture requires precise scanning of critical joints in the body, ReRide system instead looks at the ways to determine the information that is sufficient to be suggestive. This data is used in creating the visual feedback for the user to make sense

[2] https://www.adafruit.com/product/1085

[3] (RFC 6455) https://tools.ietf.org/html/rfc6455

[4] Raspberry Pi NoIR Camera module v2 https://www.raspberrypi.org/products/pi-noir-camera-v2

as part of embodied self-monitoring across the use-scenarios (figure 1 and 3).

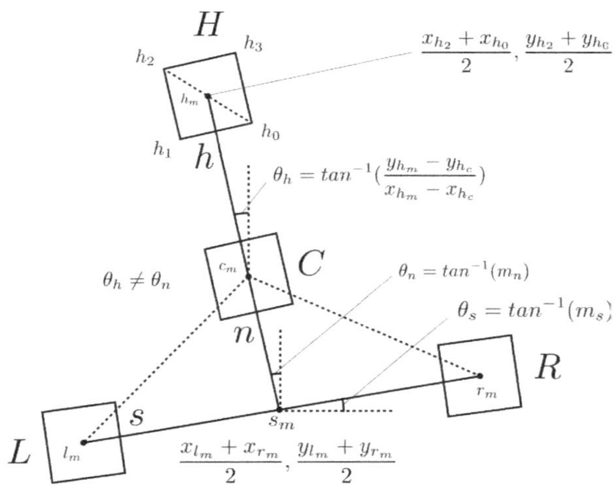


Figure 7: Marker configuration and extraction of relevant posture characteristics

***Forward Lean*** is primarily calculated by estimating how close is the rider from the camera and the weight distribution on the seat. A reasonable confidence is achieved by combining inputs from both the sensing units. As figure 7 shows how the rider's proximity is estimated primarily by looking at the ratio of the size of the face to the height of the video frame. The size of the face is given by the distance from the mid-point of Head marker (H) to the mid-point of Chin marker (C). Other supporting data include the decrease in the area of the triangle formed by the mid-points of each C, Left Shoulder (L) and Right Shoulder (R) markers. In the weight distribution, the forward lean is indicated when there is a relative decrease in the weight exerted at the rear FSR patches.

***Shoulder tilt*** is calculated by solely the camera unit. It is given by the slope of the line joined between the mid-points of L and R marker. The ***shoulder twist*** in this context is the movement of shoulders in the horizontal plane and can be given the ratio of the area of the L and R markers. ***Head stoop*** occurs when the head orientation does not match with spine inclination. While the forward lean parameter estimates a general inclination of the upper body of the rider, head stoop strictly measures the inclination of the head in the forward direction. Head stoop is also given by the ratio of the size of the face to the height of the video frame while the significantly lesser difference in the area of the triangle formed by the mid-points of each C, L and R markers. ***Head tilt*** is given by measuring the slope of the line between the mid-points of H and C marker to the vertical reference line of the video frame.

***Left and Right lean*** is primarily given by the weight distribution unit. The indication is given by the significant difference between the FSR patches placed at under left and right thigh. A reasonable confidence is achieved by combining this data with the upper body tilt given by calculating the slope of the line between mid-point of C and the mid-point of L and R marker about the horizontal reference of the video frame.

## Visual Feedback

The estimated posture is visualized for glanceable feedback [7] on the screen of the display module, through an amoeba-like blob (See figure 8). The extent of amoeba along different axes is computed by averaging posture characteristics as per current ride, current day, last day, last 3 days, last week and so on. These parameters are mapped on the axes that closely mimic the top view of the rider. The text labels in the

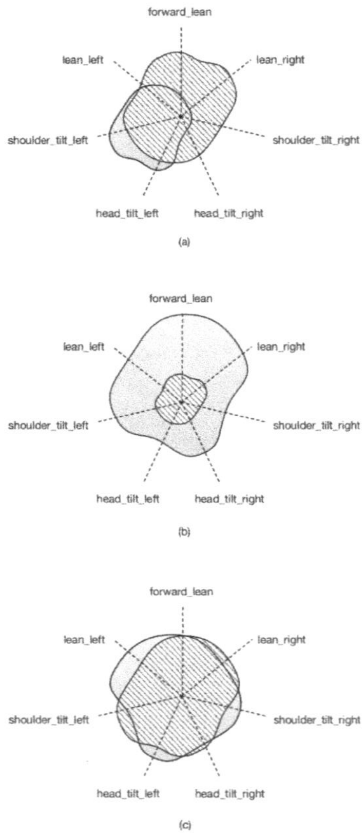


Figure 8: Typical visual feedback cases- (a) New or unlearned system, the suggested amoeba has significant non-intersecting area, (b) Experienced system but insignificant improvement in user, (c) Experienced system with significant improvement in user

figure are only for the purpose of annotation, the actual visualization uses symbolic signifiers. Over time, the signifiers may be eliminated as the rider would get familiar with the characteristics. The motivation for such a visualization is based on our previous explorations and the fact that a single instantaneous posture may not be regarded as good or bad, but the rider being in a particular posture for longer durations may be bad.

The visualization indicates a growing/shrinking amoeba along with another amoeba in a different fill color. The other amoeba is computed by the system to indicate user what may be right for the rider. This amoeba also grows and shrinks in real-time but more gradually based on the rider's history and medical profile through a LSTM (Long Short-Term Memory) network. We hope that over the time, the rider would try to change his posture to correct his amoeba visualization. The motivation to use the LSTM network [12] is the capability of learning long-term dependencies and sometimes avoid them. For instance, consider a case where the rider has the inherent inability to sit without leaning on one of his sides. The ReRide system is expected to learn and consider this inability and suggest accordingly.

## Future Work & Concluding Remarks

We are in the process of integrating BANk and its modules presented here into a fully working prototype, mounted on a motorbike. As we have reached a firm foundation in terms of the overall structure of the system, we can now iterate on visualizations in detail with actual ride data, and develop a learning model (LSTM variant) for this context. These studies will help us not only to establish the viability of such a system in the real-world, but more importantly to continue experimenting on the diverse range of rider experiences of embodied self-monitoring across, and beyond the use scenarios (figure 1 and 3).

In more specific terms, the architecture facilitates us to conduct further research about postural data and its effect on the user. In the current version, we looked at developing a system to estimate rider's posture and giving them the real-time information about the same to support embodied self-monitoring towards preventive self-care. Our current work establishes that the platform mounted on the motorbike will enable us to conduct in-depth research about the ways in which riders perform embodied self-monitoring before, during and after the ride. It will enable us to also explore what roles do posture data and the way it is presented for rider engagement play in supporting embodied self-monitoring aimed at preventive self-care.

In this paper, we presented our ongoing work on designing and developing a robust and modular platform for enabling in-situ experiments towards designing for embodied self-monitoring during motorbike commuting. Building on previous work [3,4,14], we presented 'Bike Area Network' (BANk) as a system architecture to help guide the design of such a platform. Furthermore, we presented the process of developing the software and hardware interactive prototype, including explorations of real-time posture detection and visualization for on-ride feedback. We share our ongoing work as an invitation for researchers and practitioners of designing for embodied interaction to further explore a new frontier: Motorbike commuting.

## References

[1] Linda Nilsson Anna Johansson. 2006. Anna Johansson and Linda Nilsson. 2006. Evaluation of seat discomfort using real-time measurements of whole body vibration and seat pressure distribution while driving trucks. *Ph.D. Dissertation*. Luleå University of Technology. http://www.diva-portal.org/smash/get/diva2:1027968/FULLTEXT01.pdf

[2] Bagalkot, N. L., & Sokoler, T. 2018. Designing for lived informatics in out-of-clinic physical rehabilitation. *Human–Computer Interaction*, *33*(1), 93-129.

[3] Naveen Bagalkot, Tomas Sokoler, Riyaj Shaikh, Gaurav Singh, Anders Edelbo Lillie, Pratiksha Dixit, Aditi Rai, Chakravarthy Vignesh, and Ashwin Senthil. 2017. Reride: A platform to explore interaction with personal data before, during, and after motorcycle commuting. In *Lecture Notes in Computer Science (including subseries Lecture Notes in Artificial Intelligence and Lecture Notes in Bioinformatics)*. DOI: http://dx.doi.org/10.1007/978-3-319-68059-0_43

[4] Bagalkot, Naveen L., Tomas Sokoler, and Suraj Baadkar. 2016. "Reride: Performing Lower Back Rehabilitation While Riding Your Motorbike in Traffic." In *Proceedings of the 10th EAI International Conference on Pervasive Computing Technologies for Healthcare*, 77–80. PervasiveHealth '16. ICST, Brussels, Belgium, Belgium: ICST (Institute for Computer Sciences, Social-Informatics and Telecommunications Engineering).

[5] Bagalkot, N. L., & Sokoler, T. 2013. Embodied-self-monitoring: Embracing the context for adherence to physical rehabilitation in the design for self-monitoring. In *2013 7th International Conference on Pervasive Computing Technologies for Healthcare (PervasiveHealth)* (pp. 192–199).

[6] Bagalkot, N., & Sokoler, T. 2012. Unboxing the tools for physical rehabilitation: embracing the difference between the clinic and home. In *Proceedings of the 7th Nordic Conference on Human-Computer Interaction: Making Sense Through Design* (pp. 597–606). ACM.

[7] Consolvo, Sunny, David W. McDonald, Tammy Toscos, Mike Y. Chen, Jon Froehlich, Beverly Harrison, Predrag Klasnja, et al. 2008. "Activity Sensing in the Wild: A Field Trial of Ubifit Garden." In *Proceedings of the SIGCHI Conference on Human Factors in Computing Systems*, 1797–1806. CHI '08. New York, NY, USA: ACM.

[8] Dominik Bial, Dagmar Kern, Florian Alt, and Albrecht Schmidt. 2011. Enhancing Outdoor Navigation Systems Through Vibrotactile Feedback. In *CHI '11 Extended Abstracts on Human Factors in Computing Systems (CHI EA '11)*. ACM, New York, NY, USA, 1273–1278. DOI: http://dx.doi.org/10.1145/1979742.1979760

[9] Dourish, P. 2001. *Where the Action Is: the Foundations of Embodied Interaction*. MIT Press

[10] S. Garrido-Jurado, R. Muñoz Salinas, F.J. Madrid-Cuevas, and M.J. Marín-Jiménez. 2014. Automatic Generation and Detection of Highly Reliable Fiducial Markers Under Occlusion. *Pattern Recogn*. 47, 6 (June 2014), 2280–2292. DOI: http://dx.doi.org/10.1016/j.patcog.2014.01.005

[11] Davide Giovanelli and Elisabetta Farella. 2016. Force Sensing Resistor and Evaluation of Technology for Wearable Body Pressure Sensing. *Journal of Sensors* (2016). DOI: http://dx.doi.org/10.1155/2016/9391850

[12] Sepp Hochreiter and Jürgen Schmidhuber. 1997. Long Short-Term Memory. *Neural Comput*. 9, 8 (nov 1997), 1735–1780. DOI: http://dx.doi.org/10.1162/neco.1997.9.8.1735

[13] Congcong Ma, Wenfeng Li, Raffaele Gravina, and Giancarlo Fortino. 2017. Posture Detection Based

on Smart Cushion for Wheelchair Users. *Sensors* (Basel, Switzerland) 17, 4 (apr 2017), 719. DOI: http://dx.doi.org/10.3390/s17040719

[14] Sokoler, T., & Bagalkot, N. L. 2017. Watching Your Back While Riding Your Bike. In *IFIP Conference on Human-Computer Interaction* (pp. 315-323). Springer, Cham.

[15] Svanaes, D. 2013. Interaction Design for and with the Lived Body: Some Implications of Merleau-ponty's Phenomenology. *ACM Trans. Comput.-Hum. Interact.*, *20*(1), 8:1–8:30.

# Emoto: From Phone to Emotive Robotic AI Sidekick

**Gautam Bose***
Carnegie Mellon University
Pittsburgh, PA 15217, USA
gautam.bos3@gmail.com

**Marisa Lu***
Carnegie Mellon University
Pittbsurgh, PA 15217, USA
findme@marisa.lu

**Lucas Ochoa***
Carnegie Mellon University
Pittsburgh, PA 15217, USA
lucasochoa96@gmail.com

**Dan Lockton**
Carnegie Mellon University
Pittbsurgh, PA 15217, USA
danlockton@cmu.edu

*The 3 above authors contributed equally to this work


*TEI '19,* March 17-20, 2019, Tempe, AZ, USA

ACM ISBN 978-1-4503-6196-5/19/03.
DOI: *https://doi.org/10.1145/3294109.3301260*

## Abstract
In this paper we introduce the concept of Phone as an Emotive AI sidekick through a set of novel interactions where in a multi-axis actuated robotic charging stand we made acts as a 'body' for the AI on our phones. The novel interactions begin with how the robotic platform embodies and thus communicates our devices' understanding of the world, continues with the affordance for more varied expressive output, and works towards extending current phone functionality to be far-field, context-driven interactions.

## Author Keywords
Embodied interaction; tangible; robotics; emotive; multimodal communication; intelligent personal assistant;

## CSS Concepts
• Human-centered computing~Smartphones
• Human-centered computing~Personal digital assistants • Hardware~Sensor devices and platforms

## Introduction
Personal robotics has long held our interests, from research labs to pop culture fads and science fiction dreams. However, much of the high impact innovation we see in robotics has been industrial or otherwise in early research phases with limited trickle down towards consumer products [18]. More recently, the explosion of conversational home assistants, everything from

### Industry

Figure 1: Anki's new Vector exploring a desk. Its charging home base is behind it on the right

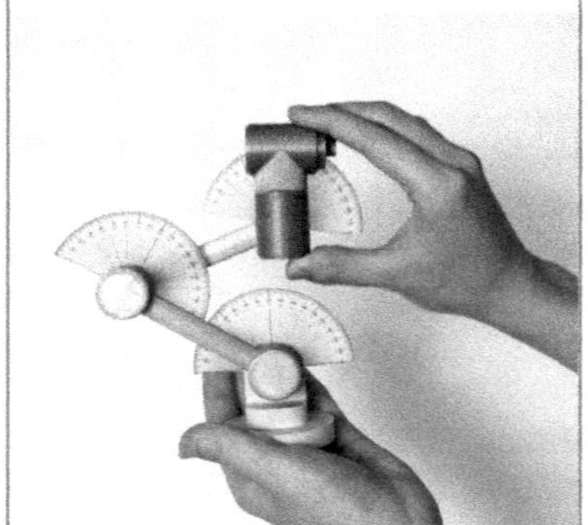

Figure 2: We prototyped animations with paper protractors stuck into the joints of a miniature 3D print we made of Baidu's AI robot by Teenage Engineering

Google Home Minis to emotive desktop robots by Anki [5] (Figure 1) has given rise to new practices and expectations for the kinds of devices we find acceptable in our homes and what their capabilities can or should be. Alongside this, the growing scrutiny of our relationships with devices and their content has been more openly addressed. Shareholders wrote to Apple requesting "more choices and tools" [10] to help set limits on children's phone time. But is improving how we relate to phones a matter of control? When Facebook announces an overhaul of algorithms for Newsfeed to for more "meaningful interactions" [3], what does that entail? It didn't change how we engage with devices, though it's clear we are affected by how we use our technology; Amazon released a "child-friendly" Echo in response to concerns about smart speakers effecting children's burgeoning manners. Research corroborates that it is not merely the content of what we say or do, but how we, and our technology, communicate that greatly affects collaboration [1]. The launch of the Center for Humane Technology, a coalition of former tech employees alarmed about the impact of the technologies they helped create, is yet another example that our relationship with smart devices is on many peoples' minds. An increasing number are concluding that we don't necessarily like how smartphones have changed us. There will be no abrupt, sustained cessation of smartphone use, so perhaps it's time to reframe the relationship. In order to change the current paradigm, it is necessary to introduce a new, but still familiar metaphor as people tend to engage with concepts they understand [4].

## Related Work

Our thinking drew experience from MIT Media Lab's Social Robotics group with their explorations on the effects of different modes of nonverbal and verbal communication, to pop culture examples inspired by HRI research on designing robot behavior based off fictional sidekick characters [10]. By learning from design principles of fictional sidekick characters, we shift the emotional frame of engagement with robots and phones. Previous studies on reciprocity between people and robots have already shown that perception of peer-like social robots as curious, in turn promotes curiosity in children via co-play [12]. Testing through experiential storytelling as research probes allows us to better understand what a sidekick robotic phone "must do, should do, and could do" [11]. This sort of inquiry through making we did draws from Dunne and Raby's approach where design is a tool to "pose 'what if' questions intended to open debate and discussion about the kind of future people want (and do not want)" [7] The related approach of design fiction, increasingly prevalent in HCI [8], is appropriate here, in enabling exploration of novel interactions even where its technology is not yet fully developed.

A specific industry inspiration for our first probe was Baidu's robotic arm (Figure 2) for their AI. It's an exciting exploration in expressive motion that could be pushed further towards ecosystem integration. Other consumer products that move towards framing intelligent personal assistants as emotive sidekicks have also been developed [6], bringing relatively cheap, sophisticated robotics into the personal space.

## Goals

Our work explores the vision of an artificially intelligent sidekick for the home through a novel robotic prototyping platform. The speculative design shows a personal robotic device that modularly integrates with a

**Prototype Details**

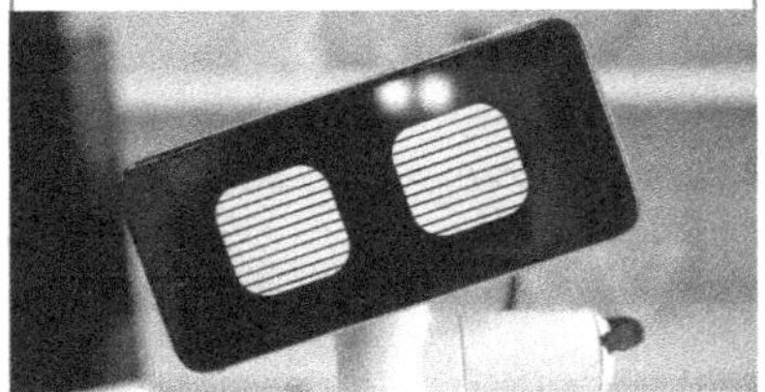

Figure 3: Phone in 'Emoto' mode

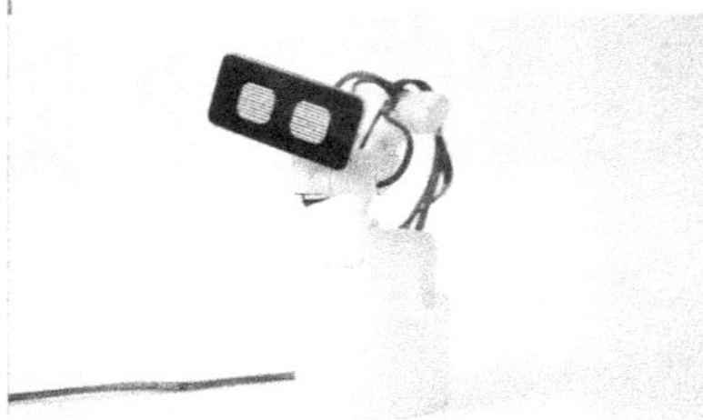

Figure 4: Robotic base with phone magnetically docked and charging

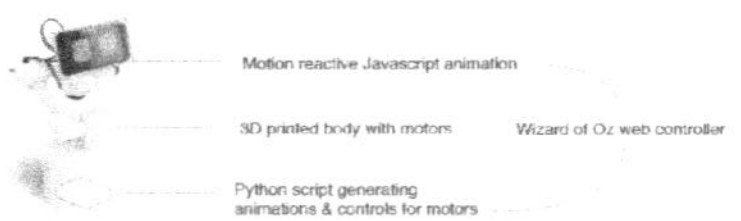


Figure 5: A breakdown of the components of Emoto

smartphone that displays "eyes". The robotic base and arm work together to display expressive movement in response to direct or contextual input. Our goals are twofold: first to introduce novel interaction design around how we understand and associate with AI's, the second is to cumulate those interactions towards reframing the relationship with phones beyond the touchscreen paradigm that's fairly isolated from the physical environment.

## Emoto's Attributes

Emoto's physical attributes can be broken down into two key components: first is the five axis robotic arm, and the second is an AI driven phone that docks and charges on the robotic base.

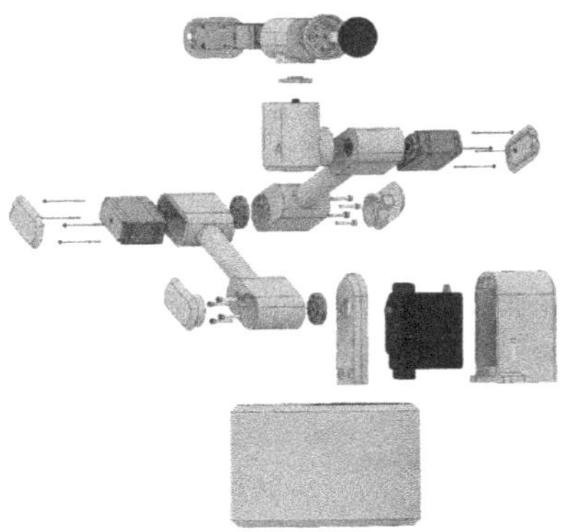

Figure 6: To facilitate low cost prototyping we designed and 3D printed all custom parts and used hobby servo motors.

*Robot Platform*

There are two motivations for implementing Emoto's five axis robotic arm. We wanted a physical platform to embody different interactions and create a semblance of sentience. It doubles as a specific and purposeful place for your phone to be at home rather than attached to your person. Placemaking for the phone shifts explorations more towards far-field interactions than touch-screen ones.

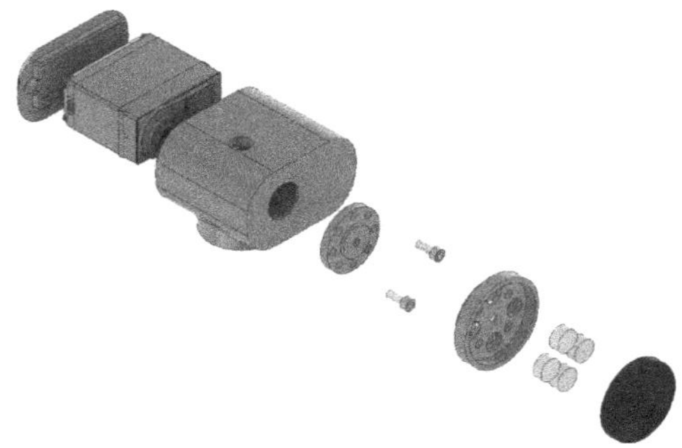

Figure 7: To allow easy attachment of phone to the emoto body we retrofitted a car phone holder magnet directly to the servo.

*AI Driven Phone*

The other key element is the phone that rotates itself into the face of the Emoto character upon magnetically docking to the robot base. The transformation is an important one because the user sees their AI/phone 'come to life', and become 'aware' of its environment.

In a sense, this moment is also where the user's phone stops being controlled imperatively by the user but instead becomes 'AI driven' and by extension, context driven. We think of this as a mode where the Emoto character or personality can serve as an intermediary layer between the user and the functionality in their phone — a layer that is able to have more embodied and emotive qualities from the increased input

## Phone to Sidekick

Figure 8: Docking your phone to charge

Figure 9: Device begins to transition.

Figure 10: The device comes back to life as the character of Emoto.

(microphone and camera visuals) which enhance communication with the user.

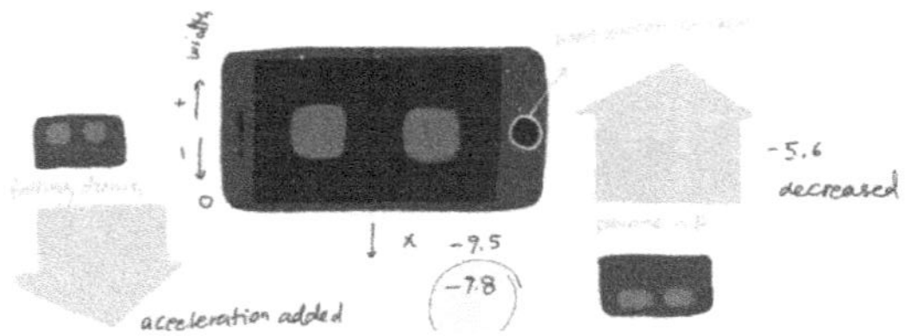


Figure 11: The physics of the spring system behind the eye shape is tied to the accelerometer on device. The eyes flicker, turning to look at stray noises in the room.

We took steps to avoid known behavioral biases in the visual form of the eyes; it has been shown that humans treat robots differently depending on how they perceive the robot's gender [14], social categorization [15], personality [16], and intelligence [13]. We take this into account by using a fairly soft geometric form, in a light green-blue with ray traces generally reminiscent of science fiction robot sidekicks. It is not immediately clear if the character has a gender. Its novelty and generalized form means we start with fewer associations that may imply, or set expectations for intelligence, personality, and by extension what its abilities should or could be. With solely conversational UI based AI's like commercial Siri, the adult voice has associated expectations for a higher level of intelligence or competence than the current nascent technology can yield. The proportionally large eyes paired with the slender form factor and implied curious behavior is more likely to be perceived and treated as a child than an adult.

## Emoto's Interactions

We prototyped a set of interactions and scenarios that attempted to create the illusion of a character users would be able to engage with. By considering the full journey from placement of phone onto robotic base, we show how our system can exist harmoniously with already existing practices.

*Phone to Sidekick Transition*

We wanted to create a memorable first impression of Emoto so making sure that there was a seamless transition from smartphone to AI Sidekick was of upmost importance. We deliberately have Emoto change from phone home screen to its characteristic eyes while the screen is facing down and away from the user. Emoto shakes his head to imply waking up from a deep sleep.

*Contextual Awareness*

After the transition from phone to AI sidekick, Emoto needs to gather some understanding of the world around it. Emoto acknowledges its environment, pausing at objects and people of interest. This type of "curiosity" is akin to Anki's Vector bot. [5]

*Display of Awareness*

While gathering adequate information by looking around curiously Emoto makes subtle changes in posture, using body language to express familiarity through 'upbeat' posture or lack of understanding towards a new setting or people with timid curiosity. It's ability to display understanding also gives it a unique way to take in voice commands. Users don't wait for a light to turn or a beep to sound to indicate receptiveness because Emoto can show active listening. Displaying contextual awareness can also be extended towards emotional reciprocity. It has been established that a robot's ability to express and recognize people's emotional states through nonverbal channels is at the core of artificial social intelligence [17]. The specifics applied to how we should design emotional displays during active assistant use is something we hope to delve more rigorously into.

*Extends Current SmartHome abilities*

There is opportunity for an Emoto-like system of integrated robot, speaker and phone to be the next evolution of SmartHome Assistants like Google Home. Phones have more personally customizable settings, and 'functionality' because users choose to download apps as needed.

*Ambient Behavior*

The aforementioned micro-interactions more often than not have been prototyped and staged around user interaction. Feedback during our design process from peers described an agent as feeling more 'alive' if there were independent, unexpected behavior. So, what should Emoto do, when it isn't 'supposed' to be doing any particular tasks? Exploring ambient behaviors raises the question of when that straddles the line to uncomfortable, and invasive.

## Preliminary User Probes

We tested our storytelling through the Emoto robot prototype in two ways: first through video posts to get varied online interpretations, and through an in person 'scenario' walkthrough demo at a design exhibition, and secondly through a concept video that we published on large social media channels. We invited visitors — mainly design and HCI students and faculty — to watch and interact with the Emoto prototype as it ran through its Phone-to-Sidekick transition, and asked them to think aloud about their reactions and understanding of what was going on.

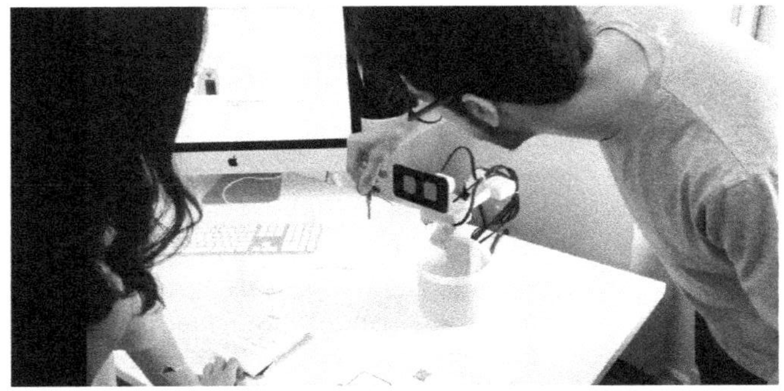

Figure 9: A walkthrough of Emoto's WOZ routine where the 'facilitator' introduces Emoto to a 'friend', the visitor.

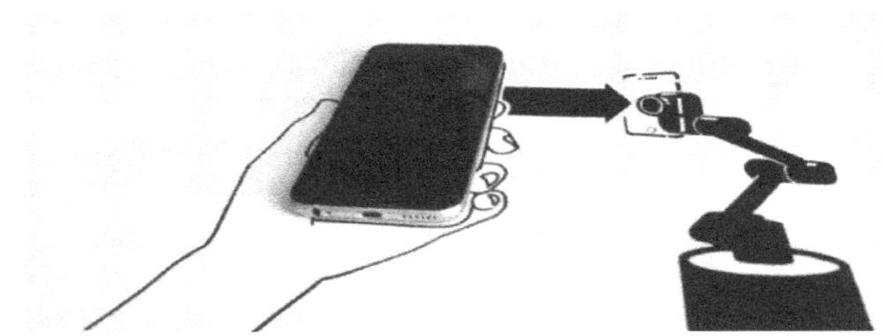

Figure 10: Show time had vinyl graphics on the table as to prompt visitors into the experience.

Of the 37 people who took part, approximately two-thirds appeared to believe the Emoto robot was interacting directly with them. We enabled this through different WOZ controlled behaviors playing out as our facilitator (someone Emoto was supposed to be 'familiar' with) and the participants 'meet' Emoto.

## Comparative Emotional Review

To further supplement our design process after our first public probe, we lived with Anki's Vector home assistant. In reflecting on the emotional experience of having a 'sentient' robot, it was disheartening when the expectations raised by the masterfully implemented animations, did not match the technical reliability. The dissonance is what makes a charming interaction potentially heartbreaking. As we develop farther, and identify other interesting moments of transition and blurring between emotive character and information display, we want to keep in mind what sort of expectations the onscreen visuals and animated motion set. Emoto's emotive qualities should set expectations for its technical implementation in order to maintain consistency.

## Conclusion and Future Work

After seeing the responses to the Emoto project we realized there was some value to be distilled from the original concept. The idea of an expressive phone companion seemed like a promising opportunity for exploring the boundaries of human-robot interaction in daily life. Amongst other things it could contribute to expanding far-field interactions with personal mobile devices. We're looking forward to find a way to publish the project as a low cost, open source kit so others can hack, build and modify their own low cost intelligent emotive companion. We are working towards refining several example interactions, like how an Emoto platform might augment video calling and live streaming practices with object-salience driven movement, and gestural mirroring of a caller for a sense of telepresence, to provide as examples in a library of other micro interactions. Bringing all of the interactions out of a staged, semi-functioning state towards robust implementation. Building a library of such should allow tinkerers to build their own behaviors with the phone-robot platform. Our hope is to inspire a new wave of makers and creators to explore concepts in AI, robotics, and rethink expected smartphone interactions.

## Acknowledgments

We would like to thank our peers in our Junior studio for providing invaluable feedback throughout the process. Additionally we would like to thank Josiah Stadelmeier for his expert consultation and assistance in the construction of Emoto's 3D printed parts.

## References

1. C. Breazeal, C. D. Kidd, A. L. Thomaz, G. Hoffman, and M.Berlin, "Effects of nonverbal communication on efficiency and robustness in human-robot teamwork," in International IEEE/RSJ Conference on Intelligent Robots and Systems (IROS). IEEE, 2005, pp/708-713
2. Schneekloth, Lynda H., and Robert G. Shibley. Placemaking: The art and practice of building communities. New York: Wiley, 1995.
3. Isaac, Mike. "Facebook Overhauls News Feed to Focus on What Friends and Family Share." Facebook Overhauls News Feed to Focus on What Friends and Family Share, 11 Jan. 2018.
4. M. Luria. 2018. Designing Robot Behavior Based on Fictional Sidekick Characters. Human-Robot Interaction 18, Companion, (2018) 307-308
5. Anki Vector | The Home Robot With Interactive AI Technology | Anki USA. Anki US, www.anki.com/en-us/vector
6. "Jibo Robot - He Can't Wait to Meet You." Jibo, www.jibo.com/

7. Anthony Dunne, and Fiona Raby. 2014. Speculative Everything: Design, Fiction, and Social Dreaming. MIT, 2014.

8. Joshua Tanenbaum. "Design Fictional Interactions: Why HCI Should Care about Stories." *ACM Interactions*, Sept. 2014, pp. 22–23.

9. M.Lakoff, G., Johnson, M. 1980. *Metaphors we Live by*. Chicago: University of Chicago Press. ISBN: 978-0-226-46800-6

10. Chris Weller. 2018. "Here's the Evidence Apple Shareholders Used to Show That Smartphones Are Addictive for Kids." Business Insider, 11 Jan. 2018, www.businessinsider.com/evidence-apple-shareholders-used-to-show-iphones-are-addictive-2018-1.

11. Dai Clegg and Richard Barker. 1994. Case method fast-track: a RAD approach. Addison-Wedley Longman Publishing Co., Inc.

12. Hae Won Park, Rinat Rosenberg-Kima, Maor Rosenberg, Goren Gordon, and Cynthia Breazeal. 2017. Growing Growth Mindset with a Social Robot Peers. 2017 ACM/IEEE International Conference on Human-Robot Interaction (HRI '17) from https://dam-prod.media.mit.edu/x/2017/03/30/parl2017hri-mindset.pdf

13. Abigail Sellen, Yvonne Rogers, Richard Harper, and Tom Rodden. 2009. Reflecting Human Values in the Digital Age. Communications of the ACM. 52. 10.1145/1467247.1467265.

14. Eyssel, Friederike, and Frank Hegel. 2012. "(S)He's Got the Look: Gender Stereotyping of Robots1." Journal of Applied Social Psychology, vol. 42, no.9, 2012, pp. 2213-2230., doi:10.1111/j.1559-1816.2012.00937.x.

15. Eyseel, Friederike, and Dieta Kuchenbrandt. 2011. "Social Categorization of Social Robots: Anthropomorphism as a Function of Robot Group Membership." *British Journal of Social Psychology*, vol. 51, no. 4, 2011, pp. 724–731., doi:10.1111/j.2044-8309.2011.02082.x.

16. B.Tay, Y. Jung, and T.Park. 2014. "When Stereotypes Meet Robots: The Double-Edge Sword of Robot Gender and Personality in Human–Robot Interaction." *Computers in Human Behavior*, vol. 38, 2014, pp. 75–84., doi:10.1016/j.chb.2014.05.014

17. Jinjoo Lee. 2017. "A Bayesian Theory of Mind Approach to Nonverbal Communication for Human-Robot Interactions." PhD Thesis, Massachusetts Institute of Technology, 2017, www.media.mit.edu/publications/jinjoolee-phd-2017/.

18. James Auger. 2014. Living with robots: a speculative design approach. J. Hum. -Robot Interact. 3, 1 (February 2014), 20-42. DOI: https://doi.org/10.5898/JHRI.3.1.Auger

# A Multisensory Design Probe: An Approach for Reducing Technostress

**Armaghan Behzad Behbahani**
Virginia Tech
Blacksburg, VA 24060, USA
abehzad@vt.edu

**Wallace S. Lages**
Virginia Tech
Blacksburg, VA 24060, USA
wlages@vt.edu

**Aisling Kelliher**
Virginia Tech
Blacksburg, VA 24060, USA
aislingk@vt.edu


*TEI '19, March 17–20, 2019, Tempe, AZ, USA.*

ISBN 978-1-4503-6196-5/19/03 ...$15.00
https://doi.org/10.1145/3294109.3300992

## Abstract
Technostress is an emerging and significant psychological phenomenon associated with the use of technology. As humans increasingly encounter computational technology on a daily basis, there is a need to manage the anxieties and tensions that can result from these interactions. Using the lens of critical design, we created a design probe to explore this concept of technology induced stress. The probe builds on the topic of slow technology and embraces multisensory experiences as a tool for individuals to reflect on their relationship with technology.

## Author Keywords
Design probe; slow technology; tangible interaction; critical design; reflection.

## CCS Concepts
•**Human-centered computing** → **Interaction techniques;** *Interaction devices;* HCI design and evaluation methods;

## Introduction
Technology has become a source for stress, which builds through the obligations surrounding the use and adaptation of technology in our everyday life [5]. The strive to be "always on", sometimes creates an endless loop of addictive behaviors, minimal human interaction, and leads to the increase of technostress [10]. We are constantly shuffled into

expectations of learning and adapting with ever-evolving technological tools and gadgets, so much so that we can forget our personal essence and the genuine values we carry. Originating from this notion and informed by critical design, we turn to concepts of design probes and Slow Technology to conduct our design-oriented research [7].
Slow technology, as a design agenda, aims at "reflection and moments of mental rest rather than efficiency in performance" [10, p.201] which we embrace in our approach. We introduce a design probe which challenges the aspects of current technologies encountered in our everyday life [6, 1, 20] and builds around notions of reflection, expression, representation, and the materiality of time [18]. The purpose of the probe is to create a tangible experience in support of pause, contemplation, and reflection [17]. In addition, challenges regarding implementations of meaningful multisensory for interactive experiences have recently been raised in the field of HCI [14] and we hope to contribute to the field by investigating a new direction. We propose a multisensory probe to challenge the material aspect of time, help mitigate levels of stress, and promote meaningful reflection by allowing participants to engage in a series of calm activities. We further explore other design options which follow the concepts of slowness, slow technology, and slow interaction, in support of our probe.

The following sections present a brief background, related body of work and a description of the design probe. We conclude with reflections on our research process, explaining the potential research trajectories and design options we wish to tackle in the future.

## Background and Related Work

### *Cultural Probes*

Gaver's widely influential cultural probes [9] and other concepts of empathetic probes [22], present an avenue for understanding people's intentions, behaviors, thoughts and interactions that are less familiar to researchers and designers. Cultural probes were initiated as "part of a strategy of pursuing experimental design in a responsive way" [8, p.22]. In other words, they serve as tools for designers to understand potential users where studies may cause disruption in people's private accommodation. In this approach, participants are usually given packages containing instructions and equipment such as notebooks, stickers, maps and cameras to complete assigned daily tasks [4, 8, 22]. Due to the open-ended nature of probes [9], recent research has taken advantage of modifying and improving the tools used in probe studies. For example, Vaajakallio's "design games" manifest playful attitudes towards probe materials. In this context, dialogues are generated through game play and performance [21].

Although cultural probes primarily emphasize their inspirational intent [9], the notion of empathy and engagement embedded in design probes can also promote participatory design research [3] while also benefiting a larger audience. Simply put, participant engagement with probes may lead designers and researchers to discover unexpected ideas and introduce new research directions.

### *Multisensory HCI*

Most of the technological devices we interact with today include platforms for audio-visual content. The ubiquity of interaction with such content may desensitize us. In other words, we may become desensitized to the constant notifications or the importance of certain content. In the field of HCI, audition and sight are primarily the main sensory targets [14]. While these two senses are constantly triggered, the remaining senses are significantly less involved.

For example, the SCHI research lab [13] has taken the initiative in exploring multisensory experiences which present compelling findings for the HCI community. In a recent study, the lab investigators draw attention to what psycholo-

**Figure 1:** Kit Bag

**Figure 2:** Sculpting Package | Activities 1 and 5

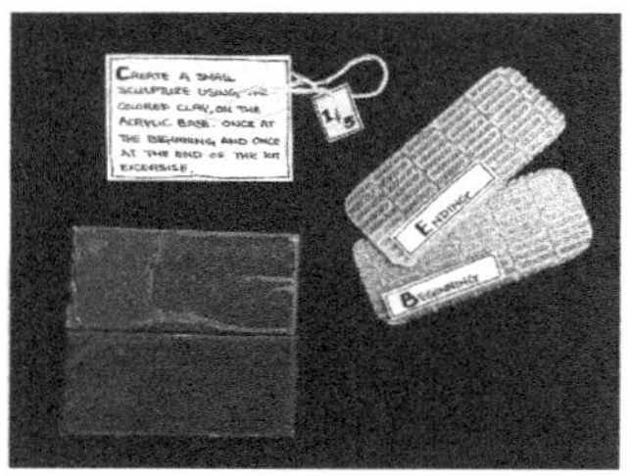

**Figure 3:** Open Sculpting Package

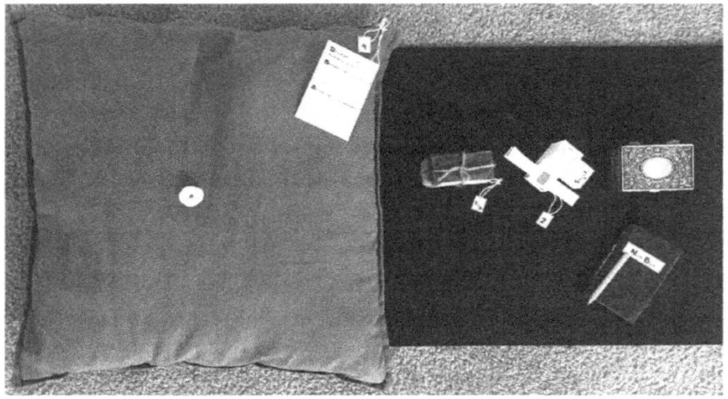

**Figure 4:** Items Inside the Kit Bag | Interactive Pillow, Colored Clay, Handcrafted Felt Notebook, Perfume Box, 3D Printed Artifact, Card Strips

gists believe are effective ways for reducing stressful strategies at the time of interruption. In line with this notion, their approach is to utilize the olfactory system as it is deeply connected to structures in our brain that relate to our emotions and memories. The team integrates olfactory notifications in messaging applications and show that it is possible to decode notifications' meaning through smell. That is to say, the user is able to identify the sender and the urgency of the content without any visual interruptions. This has proven to reduce the stress associated with responding to notifications [12]. However, the main challenge regarding multisensory interaction still remains. Significant design methods and frameworks to assist in the digital or computational representation of the additional senses are yet to be determined [15].

### *Slow Technology in HCI*

Slow technology casts a speculative lens on HCI, design and technology to utilize slowness as an advocate for promoting "reflection and moments of mental rest rather than efficiency in performance" [10, p.201]. It nurtures a meaningful relationship between the user and the product by reducing the ubiquitous "always on-ness" associated with these products [20]. Prior research on designing for slowness includes explorations including Slow games, Photobox and Future me. These initiatives do not directly investigate designs and their relationship to stress reduction, but rather provide a significant body of work which ties together the importance of slowness and reflection. Slow games are designed as physical video games with the intention of reducing the frequency of the players interaction. They are simply designed to allow only one move a day, and target patience, memory, and reflection [2]. The Photobox introduces a new approach as to how we understand the relationship between objects in an everyday environment. The artifact presents a monthly image selection from the participants image database and prints out the image in random intervals for the owner to view. The interesting aspect here is people's reaction to a device which does not attract nor require the owner's attention. The artifact also suggests opportunities for reflection and slowness [19]. FutureMe is another inspiring work which provides an online platform for people to send messages to their future self. Users can compose an email with a desired delay to receive in the future. It is intended to create the notion of re-experience, self-improvement, and challenge the obsession and anxiety for the future [16]. This suggests an experience of self-reflection in a timely manner and encourages a mindful and cautious approach towards the thoughts that a participant chooses to deliver to their future-selves.

## Probe Design

In this section, we introduce our design approach and describe the design process and affiliated protocols. We then explain what each set of activities contains, what actions are required and our rationale behind them.

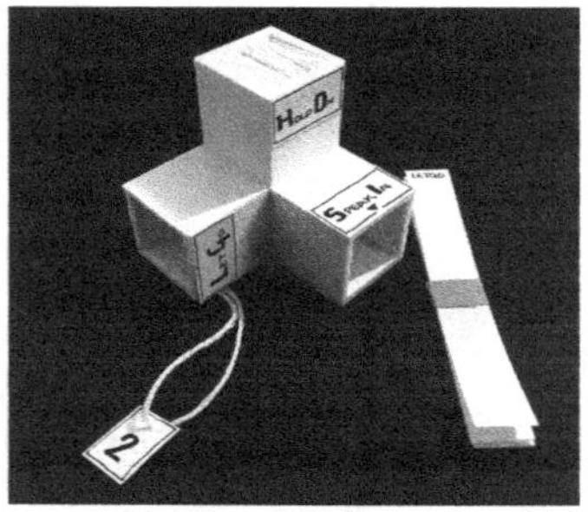

**Figure 5:** Thought Box | Activity 2

**Figure 6:** Thought Box Description

***Design Approach***

Drawing from prior work, we embrace notions of multisensory experience, slowness, and playful interaction, to inform our design probe. We propose a Multisensory probe which emphasizes slowness by having participants switch from one sense to another in playful, step by step interactive activities. This series of activities suggests ways in which people could pause and reflect on stressful moments in their day. Building on this idea, the probe aims to reduce stress and tension by helping users to (even briefly) forget about the issue of time. Furthermore, the activities can be done individually, in pairs, or in groups.

As mentioned earlier, we compose activities which go beyond the typical audio-visual experience. We propose four possible ways to encourage people to develop personal agency in becoming less stressed and more mindful, thus potentially reaching a state of self-awareness and inner peace. The probe is developed as a kit to be given to participants to experience.

The probe investigates the 4 following areas which influence the activities:

1. Thoughts, as a way to promote control.
2. Aroma, as a way to trigger the imagination.
3. Comfort, as a way to imply timelessness.
4. Sculpting, as a way to foster creativity.

Each aspect is purposefully embedded in an activity which the kit contains.

***Probe Protocol***

The probe kit consists of 5 steps which are recommended to be completed in order. The orders are labeled on each activity and descriptions are provided for each step. The descriptions are hand written to reflect a "homier" and more welcoming feel for the participants. The following section explains the kit and the activities:

*The Kit Bag*

Every design probe should have an inviting appearance for people to engage with. The aesthetic quality of our physical probe has to be considered since it would be carried and used multiple times and by a range of people (see Fig. 1). Our crafted fabric bag holds an interactive pillow, two colored pieces of clay and two acrylic bases, a handcrafted felt notebook and a pencil, a metal box with 4 small perfume bottles and 4 colored square cards, a 3D printed artifact and 2 card strips (see Fig. 4). Before starting the tasks, we ask the participants to write their name and age, and to describe their current stress level in the notebook. They are also asked to write about their stress levels after finishing an activity and further explain their experience.

*Activity 1: The Beginning*

Coloring books provide a fun medium for people to relax, be creative, and productive at the same time. We adopt an artwork as an outlet for stress and disoriented thoughts, in the first and last stages of the probe. We employ the sense of touch in these two stages.

The first activity is to create a sculpture using the colored clay (see Fig. 2 and 3). In the notebook, participants are asked to explain what their sculpture is and why they chose to make it. We designed this activity to learn about people's self expressions and inner thoughts through form making, with the overall goal of facilitating creativity at a possible time of stress.

*Activity 2: The Thought Box*

Journaling or keeping a diary is a common way for jotting down daily thoughts, events, and experiences. Another possible way for releasing stress might be through a similar experience one may have while talking to a psychotherapist. The Thought Box ties these two ideas together through a 3D printed artifact (see Fig. 5). It combines the concept of

**Figure 7:** Aroma Box | Activity 3

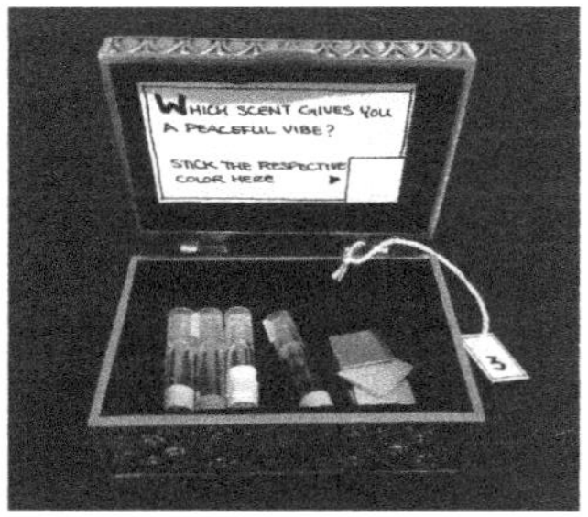


**Figure 8:** 4 Bottle Fragrances, Instructions and Colored Stickers

literal and verbal expressions in a low fidelity prototype with the purpose of articulating thoughts. The activity description (see Fig. 6) explains that thoughts which participants wish to remember and forget should be respectively written on the "Hold On" and "Let Go" paper strips. The next step is to use the thought box artifact to speak in and say the thoughts they had just written. While saying the thoughts which they wish to forget, the "hold on" hole must be covered. A similar action must be done for the thought they would like to keep, but this time covering the "let go" hole. The artifact is designed so that the "let go" hole is placed on the side and the "hold on" portion at the top. While covering the "hold on" void, the thought would pass through the ears from the side and would imply the sense of release. When the "let go" void is covered, the thought would transit vertically to be preserved in memory. The Thought box is intended to help understand participants experience with audio and verbal journaling. Could a thought be slowly forgotten if it takes the form of a sound? Would speaking and hearing the thoughts reduce their severance? What are the connections between audio and literal expressions in helping stress-reduction?

*Activity 3: Aroma Box*

The sense of smell carries a profound poetic property [14, 11]. We integrate smell as a new material to enhance the interactive experience in our probe. Fragrances hold a certain space in our memories which may correlate with events, experiences, people or emotions. Four small color-coded fragrance bottles are placed inside the Aroma Box (see Fig. 7 and 8). Participants are asked to smell each one and choose the color they find to be more peaceful and calming and stick the respective color sticker on the outline inside the box. The fragrances are chosen from a variety of everyday scents which include floral, vanilla, tobacco, and natural leather. We are curious to learn how smell can become an integral feature in stress reduction and the triggering of positive imagination. How might smell impact our experience of reflection and contemplation? Could aroma possibly become a new material to incorporate in interface design to enhance the quality of user experience?

*Activity 4: Interactive Pillow*

Yoga and meditation techniques are often accompanied by calming background music and melodies to help center the body and thoughts. The interactive pillow enables participants to either hold the artifact in their arms or simply place their head on it (see Fig. 9 and 10). Their connection to the pillow will trigger a five-minute piece of calming music. When the music is over, so is the activity. However, if they wish to spend more time on this stage, they could continue triggering the music. Activating the music through a seamless interaction can eliminate the possibility of technostress. It blends the foreign sense of technology into the design itself and provides a familiar experience. Is technology capable of resolving the issues which are associated with it? Could technology reduce technostress through thoughtful design decisions?

*Activity 5: The Ending*

Finally, the participants are asked to repeat the first step. This stage is intended to seek hints of closure through self-expression and form-making.

It is worth mentioning that with this probe we not only encourage pause for achieving meaningful experiences and overcoming stress, we also invite participants to find their own pace to get the experience they desire.

## Reflections and Design Concepts

We play-tested our probe kit with 6 people, including our colleagues for an initial informal feedback. While they all responded positively to the approach, we came across

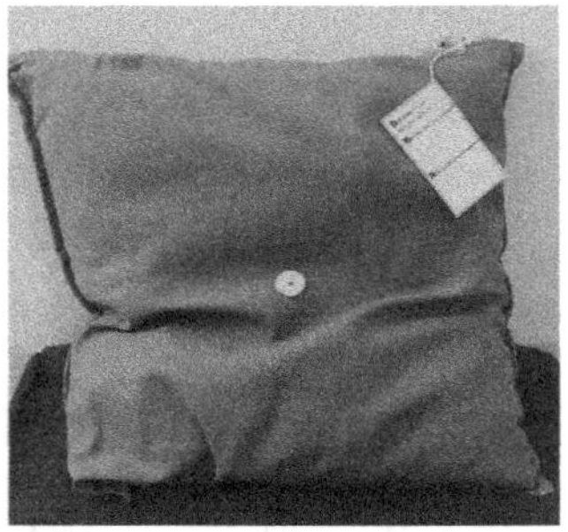

**Figure 9:** Interactive Pillow | Activity 4

**Figure 10:** Interactive Pillow | Embedded Touch Board, Speaker and Battery

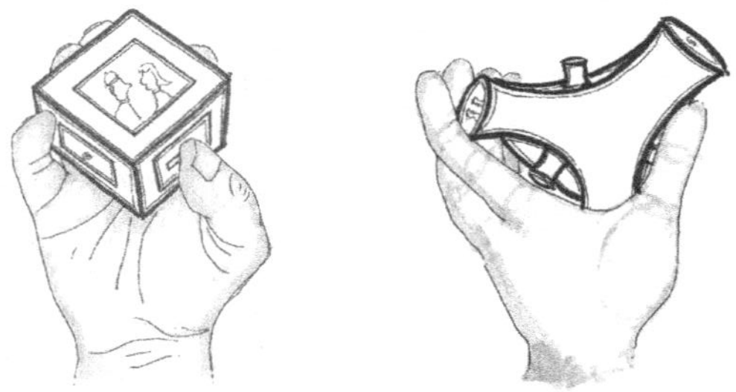

**Figure 11:** Conceptual Sketches | Interactive Multisensory Artifacts

thought-provoking questions to consider in the actual testing process. For example, how might the probe context affect the participant's experience? We would like to test our probe in various environments and settings to better understand this matter. We also thought about the scope of the participant user base, including wondering how a child might utilize the activities differently compared to an adult? Would the activities and artifacts indicate a certain playfulness which was not initially anticipated? Would one sensory experience, accent another if the activities occur in different orders? Furthermore, the process of designing and administrating the probe kit led to other conceptual ideas for creating research products [19] to fabricate and explore further (see Fig. 11 and 12).

## Conclusion and Future Work

Part of critical design is to ask questions about ways in which people interact with technological devices on a daily basis, which may impact their well-being and performance. Our probe can be distinguished from prior design probes in the sense that it investigates sensory experiences and follows the framework of slow technology to inform the design of future interactive technologies. We push our research forward to inform future experiences of slowness and en-

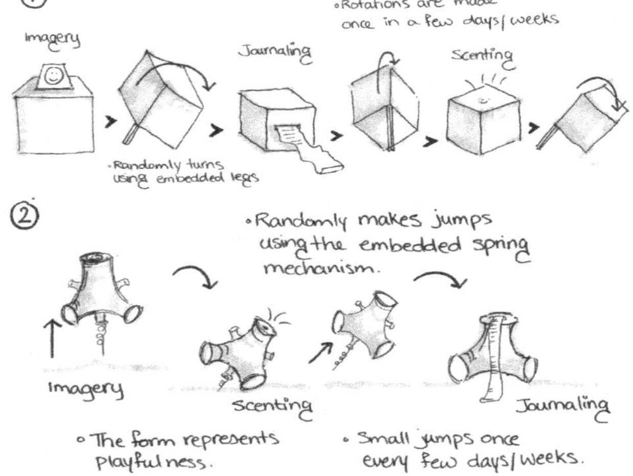


**Figure 12:** Conceptual Sketches | Interactive Multisensory Artifact | Top: Embedded Legs Expand for Slow movements | Bottom: Embedded Springs Allow Movements

courage users to interact with technologies as a time productive rather than a time consuming entity. Moving forward, we hope to further explore the value of the kit by implementing it in a variety of contexts, where we can further develop a body of knowledge leveraging our contribution to the fields of HCI and critical design.

In addition, we aim to deploy our conceptual ideas in research products and prototypes for participants to explore and interact with. Similar to our probe kit, we anticipate placing the artifacts as non-intrusive products in various environments seeking richer inspirations for complex HCI questions embodying matters of technology, stress, time, and multisensory experience and interaction. We are excited to explore new trajectories which help cultivate meaningful relationships between technology and people.

## References


[1] Shaowen Bardzell, Jeffrey Bardzell, Jodi Forlizzi, John Zimmerman, and John Antanitis. 2012. Critical Design and Critical Theory: The Challenge of Designing for Provocation. In *Proceedings of the Designing Interactive Systems Conference (DIS '12)*. ACM, 288–297. DOI: http://dx.doi.org/10.1145/2317956.2318001

[2] Ishac Bertran. 2014. Slow Games. (2014). Retrieved October 22, 2018 from http://www.ishback.com/slowgames

[3] Kirsten Boehner, Janet Vertesi, Phoebe Sengers, and Paul Dourish. 2007. How HCI Interprets the Probes. In *Proceedings of the SIGCHI Conference on Human Factors in Computing Systems (CHI '07)*. ACM, 1077–1086. DOI: http://dx.doi.org/10.1145/1240624.1240789

[4] Ozge Merzali Celikoglu, Sebnem Timur Ogut, and Klaus Krippendorff. 2017. How do user stories inspire design? A study of cultural probes. *Design Issues* 33, 2 (2017), 84–98.

[5] Justin Cheng, Akshay Bapat, Gregory Thomas, Kevin Tse, Nikhil Nawathe, Jeremy Crockett, and Gilly Leshed. 2011. GoSlow: Designing for Slowness, Reflection and Solitude. In *CHI '11 Extended Abstracts on Human Factors in Computing Systems (CHI EA '11)*. ACM, 429–438. DOI: http://dx.doi.org/10.1145/1979742.1979622

[6] Anthony Dunne and Fiona Raby. 2013. *Speculative Everything: Design, Fiction, and Social Dreaming*. The MIT Press.

[7] Daniel Fallman. 2003. Design-oriented Human-computer Interaction. In *Proceedings of the SIGCHI Conference on Human Factors in Computing Systems (CHI '03)*. ACM, 225–232. DOI: http://dx.doi.org/10.1145/642611.642652

[8] Bill Gaver, Tony Dunne, and Elena Pacenti. 1999. Design: Cultural Probes. *Interactions* 6, 1 (Jan. 1999), 21–29. DOI: http://dx.doi.org/10.1145/291224.291235

[9] William W. Gaver, Andrew Boucher, Sarah Pennington, and Brendan Walker. 2004. Cultural Probes and the Value of Uncertainty. *Interactions* 11, 5 (Sept. 2004), 53–56. DOI: http://dx.doi.org/10.1145/1015530.1015555

[10] Lars Hallnäs and Johan Redström. 2001. Slow Technology – Designing for Reflection. *Personal and Ubiquitous Computing* 5, 3 (01 Aug 2001), 201–212. DOI: http://dx.doi.org/10.1007/PL00000019

[11] Leslie M Kay. 2011. Olfactory coding: random scents make sense. *Current Biology* 21, 22 (2011), R928–R929. DOI: http://dx.doi.org/10.1016/j.cub.2011.10.008

[12] Emanuela Maggioni, Robert Cobden, Dmitrijs Dmitrenko, and Marianna Obrist. 2018. Smell-O-Message: Integration of Olfactory Notifications into a Messaging Application to Improve Users' Performance. In *Proceedings of the 20th ACM International Conference on Multimodal Interaction (ICMI '18)*. ACM, 45–54. DOI: http://dx.doi.org/10.1145/3242969.3242975

[13] Marianna Obrist. 2017. SCHI LAB. (2017). Retrieved November 3, 2018 from http://multi-sensory.info

[14] Marianna Obrist, Elia Gatti, Emanuela Maggioni, Chi Thanh Vi, and Carlos Velasco. 2017a. Multi-sensory experiences in HCI. *IEEE MultiMedia* 24, 2 (2017), 9–13. DOI: http://dx.doi.org/10.1109/MMUL.2017.33

[15] Marianna Obrist, Nimesha Ranasinghe, and Charles Spence. 2017b. Special issue: Multisensory human-computer interaction. *IEEE MultiMedia* 24 (2017), 9–13. Issue 2. DOI: http://dx.doi.org/10.1109/MMUL.2017.33

[16] William Odom. 2015. Understanding Long-Term Interactions with a Slow Technology: An Investigation of Experiences with FutureMe. In *Proceedings of the 33rd Annual ACM Conference on Human Factors in Computing Systems (CHI '15)*. ACM, 575–584. DOI: http://dx.doi.org/10.1145/2702123.2702221

[17] William Odom, Richard Banks, Abigail Durrant, David Kirk, and James Pierce. 2012. Slow Technology: Critical Reflection and Future Directions. In *Proceedings of the Designing Interactive Systems Conference (DIS '12)*. ACM, 816–817. DOI: http://dx.doi.org/10.1145/2317956.2318088

[18] William Odom, Siân Lindley, Larissa Pschetz, Vasiliki Tsaknaki, Anna Vallgårda, Mikael Wiberg, and Daisy Yoo. 2018. Time, Temporality, and Slowness: Future Directions for Design Research. In *Proceedings of the 2018 ACM Conference Companion Publication on Designing Interactive Systems (DIS '18 Companion)*. ACM, 383–386. DOI: http://dx.doi.org/10.1145/3197391.3197392

[19] William Odom, Mark Selby, Abigail Sellen, David Kirk, Richard Banks, and Tim Regan. 2012. Photobox: On the Design of a Slow Technology. In *Proceedings of the Designing Interactive Systems Conference (DIS '12)*. ACM, 665–668. DOI: http://dx.doi.org/10.1145/2317956.2318055

[20] Monideepa Tarafdar, Ashish Gupta, and Ofir Turel. 2013. The dark side of information technology use. *Information Systems Journal* 23, 3 (2013), 269–275. DOI:http://dx.doi.org/10.1111/isj.12015

[21] Kirsikka Vaajakallio. 2012. *Design games as a tool, a mindset and a structure; Suunnittelupelit osallistuvan ideoinnin työkaluna*. G4 Monografiaväitöskirja. http://urn.fi/URN:NBN:fi:aalto-201312037994

[22] Jayne Wallace, John McCarthy, Peter C. Wright, and Patrick Olivier. 2013. Making Design Probes Work. In *Proceedings of the SIGCHI Conference on Human Factors in Computing Systems (CHI '13)*. ACM, 3441–3450. DOI: http://dx.doi.org/10.1145/2470654.2466473

# Sound Shifting: From Soundscape to Soundshape

**Reinhard Gupfinger**
**Martin Kaltenbrunner**
University of Art and Design
Linz, Austria
reinhard.gupfinger@ufg.at
martin.kaltenbrunner@ufg.at

**Luise Wolf**
Author and journalist
Berlin, Germany
luisewolf@posteo.de

Figure 1: Detail, Soundscape of Linz, 2017
Photo © Katharina Anna Loidl


ACM ISBN 978-1-4503-6196-5/19/03.
https://doi.org/10.1145/3294109.3301257

## Abstract

*Sound Shifting* is an artistic research project that focuses on the physical representation of sound – this means the visualization and materialization of invisible phenomena that significantly shape our perception. We present a system that allows the transformation from sound into form in real-time by using a newly developed machine, the *Audio Foam Cutter*. This machine converts sound into polystyrene stripes that are arranged into sculptural objects. The resulting sound sculptures provide information about the represented sounds by their shape and aesthetic features and expand the range of our auditory perception to the tangible domain. The sound sculptures are snapshots of our soundscape and form a physical archive of sound representations. The *Sound Shifting* project aims to create an awareness of the materiality of sonic movements and affects.

## Author Keywords

Sound Shifting; Hybrid Art; Sound Visualization; Sonic Materialism; Data Visualization.

## CCS Concepts

Human-centered computing~Human computer interaction (HCI); Human-centered computing~Interface design prototyping

Figure 2: Hells Bells 2017
This piece refers to an incident from 2015. A man from Linz, Austria sued the Catholic Church to stop nighttime chiming. [2] The sound reliefs show 12 hours of chiming of the New Cathedral in Linz.

Photo ©Katharina Anna Loidl

## Introduction

How does sound look like as sculpture? At present, we are constantly surrounded and pervaded by a wide variety of sounds. We communicate with our environment by deciphering the meanings of these sounds and acting accordingly. We often associate sounds that we experience in different situations with certain memories and feelings. [[1]] Therefore, we pay particular attention to the sounds of everyday life and their repetitions. These sounds of everyday life are very important, and our goal is to find new ways of making these sounds tangible as sculptures.

At the center of the *Sound Shifting* project is the study and representation of everyday and characteristic sounds from an artistic perspective. In order to achieve sculptural results, various methods of making sound three-dimensional are tested - from rapid 3D printing (to test formal qualities) to traditional casting techniques (to preserve the sound sculptures for many years to come). The use of new rapid prototyping processes, such as 3D printing, offers new methods for implementing the sculptural qualities of sound.

Another focus of the *Sound Shifting* project is the current discussion about sound in public space as part of the neo-liberalization of our cities. The project aims to call attention to and discuss this topic through the physical representation of problematic sounds. (Figure 2) The poetic aspect of these works is that sound is made graspable and tangible in its most natural movement with techno-scientific precision.

*Sound Shifting* creates an awareness of the materiality of sound by showing it as sculptural collages from the traces of a medium that is fleeting and marginal. Sound is placed into a framework, and so its hidden essence unfolds a mystical transcendence by making its energetic impressions, its gravitations and its currents visible in space. These "sound blocks" (Gilles Deleuze & Félix Guattari) seem as organic as they are discreet, as mystical as they are futuristic, cryptic, yet equally simple and obvious. They show the inner tensions of the sound itself. You can see and grasp the (sound) shadows of the waves and experience the rhythm not as an impact, but as a point of the highest compression of a single flowing sound wave. The existence of sound is brought to light in these multi-sized sculptures and reveal a sonic materialism.

## Related Work

From the 70s on, we have seen many approaches to representing sound or music visually. [3] Currently, there are a number of digital and analog processes for visualizing sound on screen. Less common methods try to represent sound as a physical object. Highly relevant research has already been done in the context of the physical representation of data. [6,7] The introduction of 3D printing technology has expanded the possibilities for experimenting with objects based on sound.
Through the use of modeling software, sound models are generated and transformed into sculptures by 3D printing. An interesting project in the context of the physical representation of sound is *Microsonic Landscapes* [[4]] by the Mexican artist group Realität. They have visualized music albums and songs by famous bands such as Portishead or Einstürzende Neubauten as physical objects. Also, the artist Luke Jerram is working with this transformation process. On the basis of an audio recording of the Hiroshima atomic bomb explosion, he produced a sculpture by stereolithography. [5]

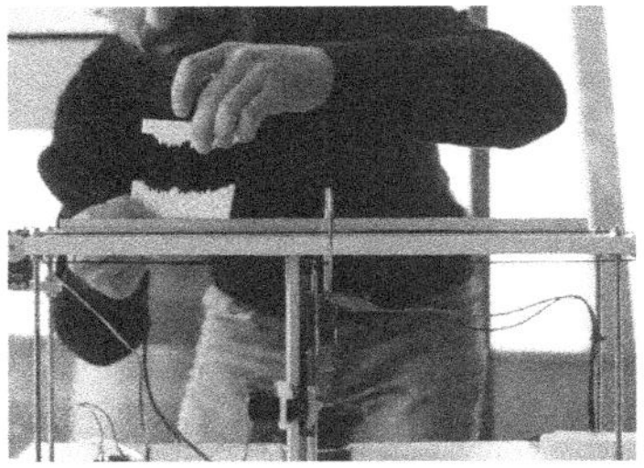

Figure 5: Live Demo @ Ars Electronica Center, Linz, 2016

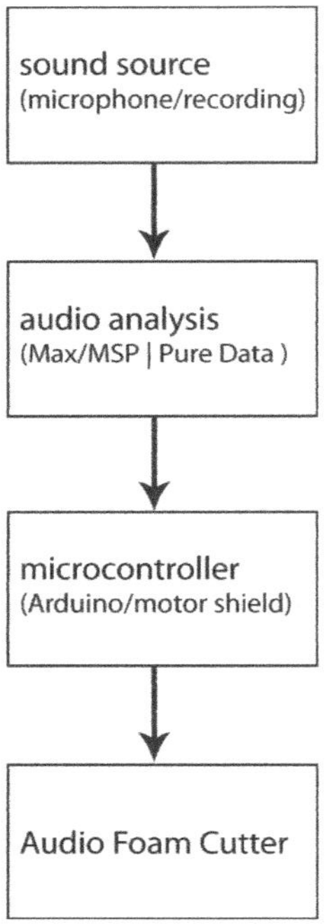


The components of the system and the audio signal flow.

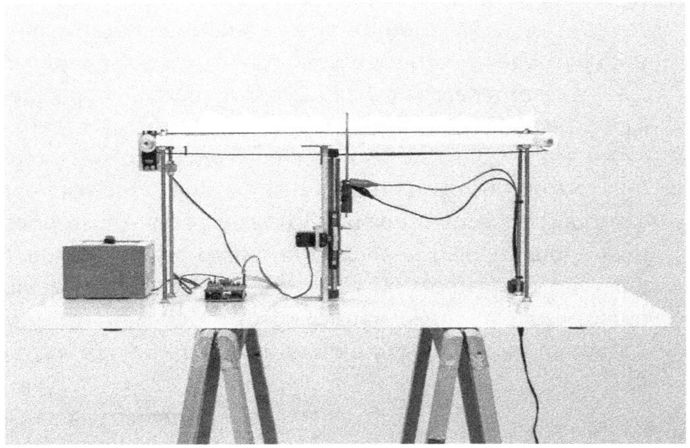

Figure 3: Audio Foam Cutter (2016); Photo ©Katharina Anna Loidl

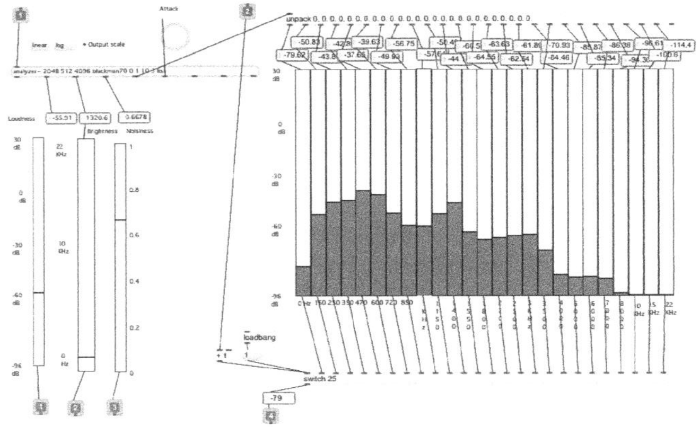

Figure 4: Screenshot of audio analysis software

## Implementation

The *Audio Foam Cutter* (AFC) transforms sound into polystyrene and other similar materials. The device consists of a hot-wire cutter mounted on a servomotor that is controlled by audio signals. This combination allows users to cut the sound input vertically and in real-time into the material as it is passed through the machine. The speed with which the material passes through the machines can be adjusted and is approximately one second per centimeter. The resulting cutouts are used to create casting molds for different-sized objects. Furthermore, the polystyrene stripes can stand alone as tiny sound sculptures. The software currently controlling the AFC and analyzing the audio signal has been programmed with Max/MSP.

AFC projects depict sound sculpturally through its wave troughs and heights, its traces and depths, its vibrations and pulsations. They divide the time of the music into timelines and stop the time of music by capturing and presenting it in sculpture. They break down the frequencies, the volumes and the harmonies and reassemble them in a cluster, in a sculptural track, in a physical spectrogram. Currently, we are working on prototypes to read out and play back the sound of these physical objects. For that, we are trying different approaches such as the use of lasers or RFID devices. Thus, in the end, the objects would become sculptural records that can be replayed again.

## Video Link to AFC

https://vimeo.com/193745588

Figure 6: *Eisenbahnbrücke*, 2016

The Linz railway bridge was one of the three bridges across the Danube in Linz. In the summer of 2016, the bridge was demolished. The sound relief contains the characteristic sounds of this bridge.

Photo ©Katharina Anna Loidl

Figure 7: *Sound Barrier*, 2015

**1. Sound**: Record characteristic sounds. This is based on a research phase that investigates current topics of our auditory environment.

**2. Analysis:** The sound recordings are analyzed using a specially developed software, and the appropriate frequencies and volumes are adapted and calibrated for the cutting process.

**3. Cutting:** The AFC hot-wire cutting device enables real-time transformation of the sound tracks into polystyrene. The louder the sounds, the higher the cut amplitude.

**4. Casting:** The cast is carried out with ceramic casting powder or bronze. Finally, the polystyrene strips are removed from the mold and the relief is cleaned.

## Presentation

In the exhibition setup, people are invited to interact with the AFC and transform their own voice into a small piece of polystyrene. Additionally, we present the work process and the resulting archive of transformations of sounds into small three-dimensional objects. (Figure 7) We also hope that we can demonstrate the new machines for playing back the sounds cast in the objects. In summary, the exhibition demonstrates how invisible sonic phenomena can be represented sculpturally and help to overcome the widespread idea that sound is ephemeral and immaterial.
The project has been presented at numerous festivals and exhibitions, such as Ars Electronica, Linz; ADAF, Athens; LAB 30, Augsburg and Traklhaus in Salzburg.

## Acknowledgements

We would like to thank the Kunstuniversität Linz for its support of this project, as well as the Linz Culture department.

## References

[1] Holger Schulze. 2008. Sound Studies: Traditionen-Methoden-Desiderate. Transcript Verlag.

[2] Hells bells! Austrian sues Catholic Church to stop nighttime chiming. 2015. Retrieved November 6, 2018 from https://www.rt.com/news/230399-austrian-sues-linz-cathedral

[3] Atari Video Music. Retrieved November 3, 2018 http://www.atarimuseum.com/videogames/dedicated/videomusic/videomusic.html

[4] Microsonic Landscapes. Retrieved November 6, 2018 from http://www.realitat.com/microsonic

[5] 28 seconds of Hiroshima. Retrieved November 6, 2018 from https://theartstack.com/artist/luke-jerram/artwork-28-seconds-of-hiroshima

[6] Jack Zhao and Andrew Vande Moere. 2008. Embodiment in data sculpture: a model of the physical visualization of information. In Proceedings of the 3rd International Conference on Digital Interactive Media in Entertainment and Arts (DIMEA '08). ACM, New York, NY, USA, 343–350. DOI: https://doi.org/10.1145/1413634.1413696

[7] Yvonne Jansen, Pierre Dragicevic, Petra Isenberg, Jason Alexander, Abhijit Karnik, Johan Kildal, Sriram Subramanian, and Kasper Hornbæk. 2015. Opportunities and Challenges for Data Physicalization. In Proceedings of the 33rd Annual ACM Conference on Human Factors in Computing Systems (CHI '15). ACM, New York, NY, USA, 3227–3236. DOI: https://doi.org/10.1145/2702123.2702180 Psy. 2012.

# Lithobox: Creative Practice at the Intersection of Craft and Technology

**Jennifer Weiler**
Arizona State University
Tempe, AZ, USA
jjweiler@asu.edu

**Todd Ingalls**
Arizona State University
Tempe, AZ, USA
todd.ingalls@asu.edu

**Piyum Fernando**
Arizona State University
Tempe, AZ, USA
piyum.fernando@asu.edu

**Stacey Kuznetsov**
Arizona State University
Tempe, AZ, USA
kstace@asu.edu


ACM ISBN 978-1-4503-6196-5/19/03.
https://doi.org/10.1145/3294109.3301258

## Abstract
The integration of new digital and physical fabrication tools with fine arts has the potential to provide new outlets for artistic expression, while at the same time raising questions about the role of material and process in artistic practice. In this work, we present Lithobox, a system that translates the traditional ceramic and lighting technique of lithophanes into a means of creating illuminated 3D models through a creative approach that utilizes both digital and tangible construction. Through work sessions with nine artists, we explored how the Lithobox fabrication process impacted the way artists manifest design ideas and engage in creative exploration in crafting. At the TEI arts track, we plan to show our system and the physical lithophanes from our work with artists. The attendees will likely discuss the design, material, and artistic aspects of our exhibit. From these discussions, our goal is to gain insight into beneficial directions for integrating digital technology into traditional fine arts practices.

## Author Keywords
Lithophanes; 3D printing; fine arts; digitally-mediated art; light art.

Figure 1: Examples of lithophanes created using Lithobox.

## Introduction

As digital fabrication methods become more accessible, they are increasingly being explored in collaboration with traditional crafting practices and the fine arts. In recent years, TEI has had a growing focus on integrating digital fabrication with traditional craft activities [[5], [12], [16], [17]]. In particular, recent research has explored how the incorporation of technology may alter creative practices in addition to changing the medium or materials of the fabricated objects [[3], [7], [14], [21]].

In our work, we have focused on how the combination of a traditional craft approach with new fabrication tools and methods based in digital technology can be used to support fine arts practices. We present Lithobox, a software system and physical kit inspired by the ceramic technique of lithophanes and recent tangible interaction design explorations into light as a creative medium for design research [[1], [11], [13], [15], [16], [18], [19]]. Lithophanes are a type of bas-relief, in which a sculptural image is depicted with little overall depth. However, when back-lit, the thinner parts of the lithophane allow light to shine through while the thicker parts of it do not, creating a luminescent image. Traditionally, lithophanes are made by carving an image into clay and then firing it in a kiln [[11], [19]]. Because the clay needs to be evenly backlit during the carving process, ceramic lithophanes were generally created as flat tablets, though there were some rare cases of lithophanes molded into three dimensional shapes, such as orbs [[11]].

The concept of lithophanes has recently been explored through additive fabrication, with several online programs and tutorials allowing users to turn their

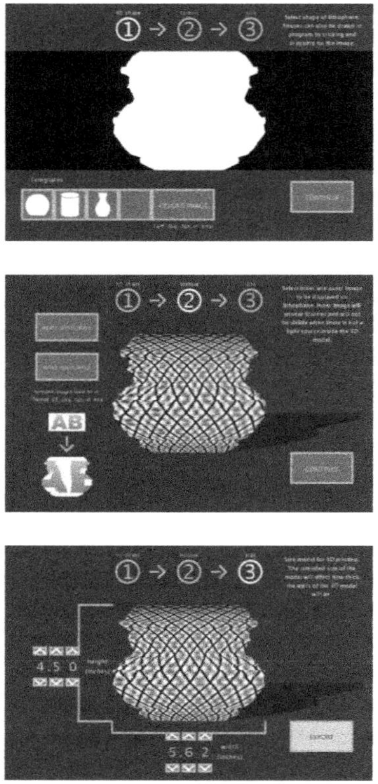


Figure 2. Lithobox workflow, from top to bottom: user draws outer shape of lithophane; user chooses images to be displayed on the surface of the lithophane; user selects print size of lithophane.

images into 3D printable lithophanes on flat plaques or cylinders [[1], [4], [6], [20]]. However, considering the potential complexity of 3D printed forms and the various ways in which 3D models can be shaped [[8], [9], [10], [12]], we sought to expand the types of designs available so as to take full advantage of the unique attributes of 3D printing technology. With this goal in mind, Lithobox was designed to encourage greater variety and complexity in the overall shape of the lithophane. Through this, we wanted to allow individuals to have more creative range in their designs and enable the creation of lithophanes that would be extremely difficult to produce with traditional materials.

As part of our development of Lithobox, we gained feedback from nine artists from a variety of traditional and/or digital arts domains, all of whom created their own lithophane using our system. Based on their experiences with Lithobox, we obtained insights into ways in which the incorporation of digital fabrication techniques affects the creative practices of artists. We propose to present our system and six to nine physical lithophanes from our work with local artists at the TEI arts track, through which we hope to encourage audience members to experiment with our system and engage in a discussion about the broader implications of incorporating digital approaches into established fine arts traditions.

## System: Lithobox

To generate our 3D printed lithophanes, we created an intuitive software interface in Processing. For the display of the lithophanes, we also designed a physical kit that could be 3D printed or laser cut, and that, along with the addition of some electronic components, could be used to rotate and illuminate the lithophane.

*Software Interface*

The 3D model lithophanes are generated within Lithobox, a downloadable application created with Processing that outputs the finished models as OBJ files. When using Lithobox (fig. 2), the user will create the outer shape of the lithophane, chose the images to be displayed on the surface of the lithophane, and can adjust the print size of the lithophane. When designing their lithophanes, users are able to save and iterate on multiple designs during their making process.

When using Lithobox, the user begins by drawing the outer shape of the lithophane. The system is designed so that the user can create any radially symmetrical form. We made this choice because it allows for a wide variety of forms which are extremely difficult to create by hand in traditional mediums such as ceramics. When designing their shape, users can iteratively draw their desired form, use several pre-existing options, or upload images on their computer.

In the second step, users select the 2D images that will be extruded from the outer and inner sides of the lithophane. Uploaded images are mapped along the 3D shape horizontally and then extruded from the surface of the model based on the darkness of the color in each pixel (based on several early trials, we chose to use a maximum additional depth of 3mm). Once 3D printed,

Figure 3. Lithobox physical assembly kit for rotating and illuminating the 3D printed lithophanes

the image extruded on the outer surface of the lithophane is visible even when there is no light inside the lithophane, while inner images can only be seen when the lithophane is illuminated from the inside.

In the final step, the user scales the 3D model to their desired print size, and our software ensures that minimum thickness of the lithophane is maintained. Additionally, the base of the model is proportionately resized to maintain a diameter of 1.25in (31.75mm) so that the lithophane will correctly attach to other parts of our kit. The finished model is exported as an OBJ file which can be printed on most commercially available 3D printers.

*Physical Assembly*
As part of the Lithobox setup, we created a step-by-step physical assembly process that allows the finished 3D printed lithophane to be evenly lit from the inside and displayed on a rotating platform. By allowing the lithophane to rotate, the image it presents changes over time, adding an interesting perspective for observing the illuminated images. In addition to the 3D printed lithophane, the materials required for the finished assembly include additional 3D printed or laser cut parts consisting of a base, a light support tower, and sides of a makercase box (fig. 3). The electronic components include a 6 RPM servo, switch, battery pack, batteries, and LEDs.

To illuminate the lithophane, strings of lights or individual LEDS can be inserted in slots along a vertical tower at the center of the rotating platform (fig. 3). After the lights are situated, the 3D printed lithophane is placed over the light tower and latched into notches on the base. The rotator is constructed by attaching the wires of the servo to the battery pack and switch, and then putting all the materials inside of the assembled makercase box. The spinning end of the servo, which sticks out through a hole in the box, can be fitted to the bottom of the 3D printed base, allowing the illuminated lithophane to rotate.

## Exploration with Artists

As part of our development of Lithobox, we wanted to understand how the integration of digital fabrication might affect artistic practice. To do so, we recruited nine local artists to create lithophanes using our system. We conducted work sessions wherein we observed the artsts' creative processes while using Lithobox and discussed their design and physical fabrication experiences.

Before using Lithobox, participants were sent an email explaining what traditional lithophanes are and were asked to bring several digital images that they would like to see displayed on a lithophane. Participants attended individual work sessions, whereby they discussed their artistic background and engaged in a brainstorming activity in which they generated ideas for lithophanes through either sketching on paper or molding playdough. Afterwards, they used Lithobox to design a 3D lithophane and experimented with their own images and the images researchers had on hand as the lithophane's outer and inner bas-reliefs. If participants wanted to continue to iterate after the session, they had the option to download the Lithobox program to their personal computer and email their design to the researcher. After each participant decided on their final design, it was 3D printed using an Ultimaker. Each participant was then invited back for a second session during which they physically assembled the lighting and rotating platform for the finished lithophane setup. At the end of the session, participants kept their lithophanes and were offered a copy of the Lithobox software for future projects. Participants were compensated for their time ($10 for attending the first session and $15 for attending the second).

Our nine participants are active art practitioners with between five and twenty years of experience in traditional and/or digital arts domains (only two participants had any previous experience with 3D printing).

## Summary of Findings

Using Lithobox, all of our participants were all able to create their own 3D printed lithophane. From the discussions we had with them during their time using the Lithobox software and physically assembling their lithophane, we were able to gain insights into how the fabrication process in Lithobox affected their creative practice.

*Manifesting Design Ideas with the Aid of Technology*

When using Lithobox, participants who had no digital 3D design experience and participants who had previously given up on learning modeling software were able to design a complex 3D printable model with relative ease. They discussed the potentially freeing aspects of technology when compared to using traditional tools or methods. In recounting their own creative practices, participants described being limited by the medium they are using and/or their own skills. In contrast, new technologies were perceived as a means to enable different kinds of fabrication within craft traditions, provided that the technology was accessible, easy to learn, and allowed for creative engagement through experimentation and iteration.

*Valuing Material Manipulation within Creative Practice*

While they were happy with the design process and the objects they created, some participants expressed a desire for more physical manipulation and crafting in the creation process. Several participants mentioned that the design activity in which they drew on paper or molded forms using playdough was more intuitive and tactile than the mouse/keyboard setup for using Lithobox. In addition, participants suggested that printing in alternative materials (such as clay or dirt) would allow them to continue iterating on the design in ways that they felt unable to with the 3D printed plastic. Overall, while the artists who participated in our study appreciated the ease of use offered by the digital interface and simple physical assembly, the lack of tactile engagement in the digital interactions and the perceived unalterable characteristics of the 3D print limited their ability to engage with and iterate on the design. Future work could focus on alternative physical-digital interfaces and 3D printing with alternative materials to help reintegrate physical fabrication into the creative process.

## Presentation

Because of our work's focus on combining traditional craft activities with digital fabrication, we propose that it would be well situated as part of TEI, which has displayed a growing interest in the intersection of HCI practices and the fine arts [[5], [17]]. For attendees of the TEI arts track, our work will function both as an art viewing experience, in which they will be able to view instances of a traditional fine arts technique being presented through a novel fabrication method, and as a creative fabrication experience, in which individuals will have the chance to use our software to design and create their own lithophanes.

The art exhibit will consist of six to nine lithophanes created and assembled using Lithobox. The designs for the lithophanes will be a mix of those created by our study participants and those created by the researchers. We will also have a computer setup and offer attendees the opportunity to design their own lithophanes using the Lithobox software. We hope that our work will provoke discussion about the integration of digital technology into traditional arts practices and the effects that the resulting hybrid practices have on the fabrication processes of creators. From these discussions, our goal is to gain insights into potential directions for our future work as well as broader implications for the benefits and drawbacks of hybrid crafting within fine arts practices.

## References

[1] Cha, S. Lee, M., Nam, T. (2016). "Gleamy: An Ambient Display Lamp with a Transparency-Controlled Shade." *TEI'16.* 304-307.

[2] "Cylindrical Lithophanes for 360º Panorama Images." *3DP.* Retrieved Sept 9, 2018 from http://3dp.rocks/blog/?p=140

[3] Devendorf, L., Ryokai, K. (2015). "Redeform: Participatory 3D Printing in Public Spaces." *TEI'15.* 423-424.

[4] Feldi. (2018). "DIY 3D-Printed Lithophane." *Sparkfun.* https://www.sparkfun.com/news/2649

[5] Fernando, P. Weiler, J. Kuznetsov, K. Turaga, P. (2018). "Tracking, Animating, and 3D Printing Elements of the Fine Arts Freehand Drawing Process." *TEI'18.* 555-561.

[6] "Image to Lithophane." *3DP.* Retrieved May 15, 2018 from http://3dp.rocks/lithophane/

[7] Jack, R., Stockman, T., McPherson, A. (2016). "Navigation of Pitch Space on a Digital Musical

Instrument with Dynamic Tactile Feedback." *TEI'16.* 3-11.

[8] Kazi, R. H., Grossman, T., Cheong, H., Hashemi, A., Fitzmaurice, G. (2017). "DreamSketch: early stage 3D design explorations with sketching and generative design." *UIST'17.* 401-414

[9] Kim, Y., An, S., Lee, J. H., Bae, S. (2018). "Agile 3D sketching with air scaffolding." *CHI'18.*

[10] Li, Y., Luo, X., Zheng, Y., Xu, P., Fu, H. (2017). "SweepCanvas: Sketch-based 3D Prototyping on a RGB-D Image." *UIST'17.* 387-399.

[11] "Lithophanes." *De Luikerwaal.* Retrieved Aug 14, 2018 from https://www.luikerwaal.com/newframe_uk.htm?/lithofanen1_uk.htm

[12] Lévy, P., Yamada, S. (2017). "3D-modeling and 3D-printing explorations of Japanese tea ceremony utensils." *TEI'17.* 283-288.

[13] Nowacka, D., Wolf, Katrin, Costanza, E. Kirk, D. (2018). "Working with an Autonomous Interface: Exploring the Output Space of an Interactive Desktop Lamp." *TEI'18.* 1-10.

[14] Ou, J., Heibeck, F., Ishii, H. (2016). "TEI 2016 Studio: Inflated Curiosity." *TEI'16.* 766-769.

[15] Schardt, P., Schmitz, M., Kafer, H., Hofmann, E. (2015). "Lichtform: A Shape Changing Light Installation." *PerDis'15.* 259-260.

[16] Šimbelis, V., Lundström, A. (2018). "Synesthetic Experience in S T R A T I C." *TEI'18.* 574-580.

[17] Tillman, D. T., Velonaki, M., Gemeinboeck, P. (2015). "Authenticating Experience: Curating Digital Interactive Art." *TEI'15.* 429–432.

[18] Torres, C., O-Leary, J., Nicholas, M., Paulos, E. (2017). "Illumination Aesthetics: Light as a Creative Material within Computational Design." *CHI'17.* 6111-6122.

[19] "What is a Lithophane?" *The Blair Museum of Lithophanes.* Retrieved Aug 10, 2018 from http://www.lithophanemuseum.org/lithophanes.html

[20] Snifikino. "Lithophanes: 3D Printing Your Photos." *Instructables.* Retrieved May 15, 2018 from https://www.instructables.com/id/Litophanes-How-to-3D-Print-your-photos/

[21] Vallgårda, A, Fernaeus, Y. (2015). "Interactive Design as a Bricolage Practice." *TEI'15.* 173-180.

# Resonance Ver.M: An Interactive Installation to Peep into One's Dreams

**Xiaoyan Shen**
MIT Program in Art, Culture and Technology
Massachusetts Institution of Technology, MA 02139, USA
xyshen@mit.edu


ACM ISBN 978-1-4503-6196-5/19/03.
DOI: https://doi.org/10.1145/3294109.3301259

## Abstract
Resonance Ver.M is an interactive video projection installation that allows the audience to have a peep into the artist's inside world. The project is the combination of a series of experimental executions including self-training, performance, EEG recording, interpretation of the bio-signal, subjective dream log, exhibition and interaction. The artwork shows an approach to the investigation of the dreams and a new form of "Human-Human interaction" through electrophysiological signals. It also introduces an innovative form of interaction between the reality and dream world, the conscious mind and the unconscious brain.

## Author Keywords
Brain-computer interface; Dream; Sleep; Conscious-Unconscious Interaction;

## CSS Concepts
• Applied computing ~ Media Arts

## Introduction
People spend almost one-third of our lives sleeping and 15% - 20% of the sleeping time dreaming [1]. Dreaming has always been a fascinating topic for both artists and scientists for centuries, yet it is still a mystery of human cognition. Psychologists have come up with multiple theories of dreams without a concrete agreement, as Sigmund Freud described: "the theory

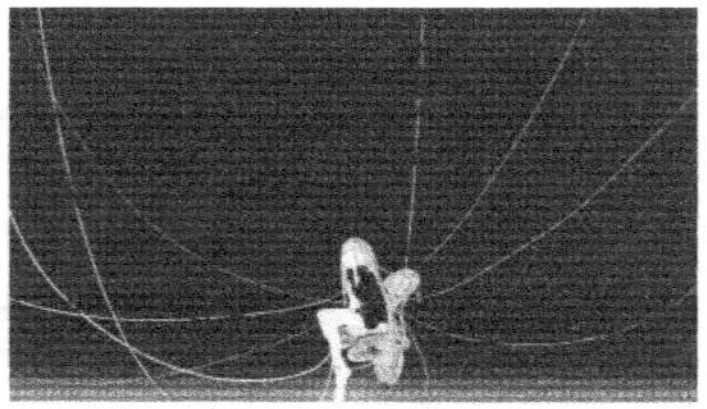

Figure 1&2: The illustration of the first dream *Dark Cosmo* (up) and with the converted Chinese characters of signals hovering the illustration (bottom).

Figure 3: Audience is interacting with the installation. Story plot shows up when matched brainwaves are detected.

of dreams has remained what is most characteristic and peculiar about the young science, something to which there is no counterpart in the rest of our knowledge, a stretch of new country, which has been reclaimed from popular beliefs and mysticism"[1].

Since the 1960s, contemporary artists have been working on interactive arts through neural investigations to reposition the role of neuroscience in contemporary art, and at the same time redefine the interdisciplinary art practices neurologically. Brion Gysin and William Burroughs created the *Dreamachine* (1961), a stroboscopic flicker device that produces visual stimuli. It flicks at a frequency that corresponds to the alpha waves (8-13 pulses per second), which is the neural oscillation often presents at relaxing state [2]. Nowadays, Brain hacking gadgets has been an unobtrusive part for artist, makers and many other people who are not neuroscientists, thanks to the easy accessibility of portable EEG sensor products.

People have more freedom in creating Brain-Computer Interactive projects with those inexpensive consumer-grade EEG devices. Projects have been done in brain signal visualization, performances wearing EEG sensors, installations triggered by certain mind stages, and brainwave interaction between two or more conscious visitors. However, so far there is no project paying attention to the interaction between two different mind states: conscious and unconscious. Resonance Ver.M is the first project that explores the potential of this type of uncommon interaction.

[1] Freud, S. 1933. *Revision of the theory of dreams.* Standard Edition, 22, 7-30.

## Related Work

Exploring dreams and sleep intervention are themes found in many projects in contemporary art and HCI. Roberto Toro and Nathalie Regard created *80 Days in Dreams* (2014) which is a sculpture of the sound simulation of Nathalie's dream in 80 days [3]. *Essence* is a wearable system trying to achieve rehabilitation from nightmares by introducing odors in REM sleep stage [4]. *Dormio* is an interactive interface built for leading people into the stage of hypnagogia to augment human creativity [5].

The processes in the attempts of investigating new possibilities of brain-computer interaction also inspired many interactive projects focusing on the communication between the audience and their brainwaves. *Mutual Wave Machine* (2010) [6] and *Measuring the Magic of Mutual Gaze* (2011) [7] are both interactive neurofeedback installations that allow two visitors to experience the shared brain activity. Participants are encouraged to achieve the stage of brainwave synchronization. The multimedia art installation *My Virtual Dream* (2013) designs a collective computer game in which players manipulated mental states of relaxation and concentration with neurofeedback targeting modulation of alpha and beta frequencies [8].

## Implementation

*Preparation before the recording night*

Before the night of performance and recording, I spent 30 days on writing a daily dream journal. This process helped me gradually in recalling clearer contents in the dreams over time. I also participated in a sleep study run by a joint research group from the MIT Computer Science & Artificial Intelligence Laboratory (CSAIL) and

*I forget what has happened.*

*It is a quiet, dark space, feel like cosmos.*

*Someone, maybe it's me, maybe not, sitting on a floating chair. A chair that has mixed candy colors and the shape of Lorenz's model of chaos.*

*Beneath the chair was a bondless, white, shining pond. I know it will turn into lava if I dropped. I never see it, but I just know it.*

*Maybe it happened before?*

*Maybe nothing has happened.*

The translated dream plot of the first dream *Dark Cosmo.*

Massachusetts General Hospital (MGH) to get a personal sleep report. According to the report, an average of 18.4% of my sleeping time is in the Rapid Eye Movement (REM) sleep stage. Sleep intervention plan was created based on my pattern of occurrence of the REM sleep (dreaming).

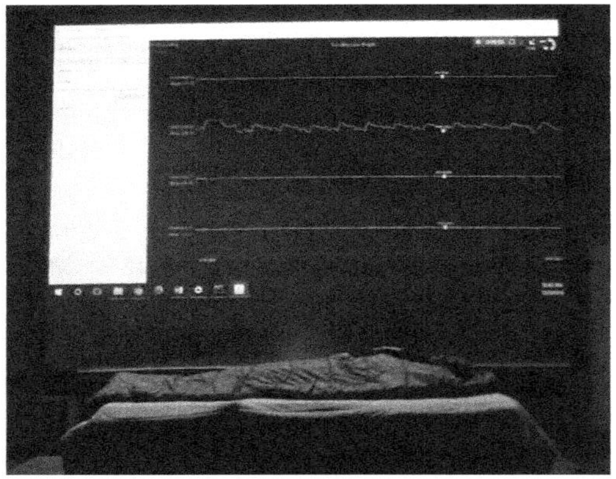

**Figure 1**: Sleep performance of the recording night.

*The recoding night*

On the day of recording, the entire process of was live-streamed on Periscope as an online-performance. The MUSE EEG headset was used to track my brainwave activity while sleeping. I started to sleep at 0 am. The preset alarm rang every hour since 2 am. I woke up, wrote down the dreams I remembered, reset the EEG recording, and went back to sleep. This procedure was repeated for 6 times by 7 am. Four out of six times the dreams were remembered and recorded.

*Dream Rebuild*

The four pieces of dreams were titled *Dark Cosmo*, *Monsters' Lunch*, *Acupuncture*, and *Dublin Coin*. They were resumed through multiple operations. The samples of the certain REM sleep periods were retrieved from the collected EEG data. The data then was converted into unreadable Chinese characters by mapping and matching to the Unicode. This represents for an objective interpretation of the dream.

The notes of the dream segments were written in Chinese for the sake of time-saving. Later they were translated into English paragraphs. Digital illustrations were created based on the notes and the lingering traces of memory of the dreams. Subjective modifications of the dream contents were applied in the creation of illustrations.

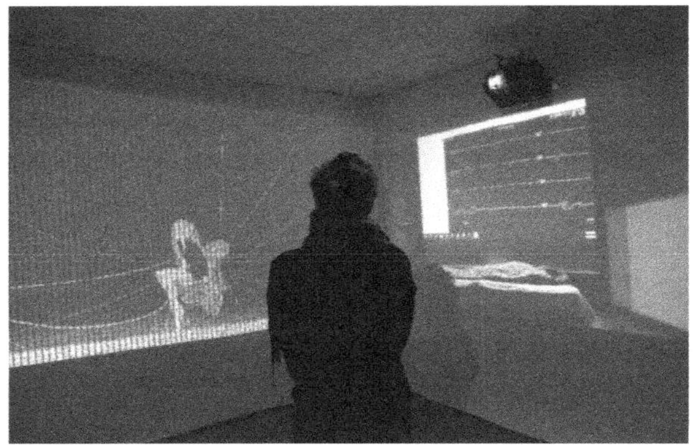

Figure 4: Audience watching the video of the installation.

*Presentation and Interaction*

The presentation is a 3-channel immersive projection installation. From the first channel, the audience can see the edited documentation of the sleep performance. From the second channel, the combination of objective and subjective interpretation (illustration hovered by converted characters) is presented. On the third

Figure: part of the Chinese characters converted from the data of the first dream *Dark Cosmo*

channel, fragments of the translated dream will reveal if the audience put on the EEG sensor and have a synchronization with the dreamer's brain signal of a specific plot.

## Conclusion

*Resonance Ver.M* represents the first artwork that explores the fascinating interaction between conscious-unconscious brain activities. I hope the possibility and potential for this type of interaction will inspire new projects and experiments. Furthermore, I hope the attempt of recording and presenting the dreams from multiple perspectives will encourage artists and scientific researchers to push future work across the level of consciousness.

## Acknowledgements

I would like to thank the CAMIT Grant Council and the MIT ACT Pilot Council for their support on this project.

## Video Link

https://vimeo.com/299497020

## References

[1] Haill, L., 2014. ICT & Art Connect: Revelations by Flicker, Dreamachines and Electroencephalographic Signals in Art. *In Proceedings Conference: AISB50, At Goldsmiths University, Volume: The Future of Art and Computing: A Post-Turing Centennial Perspective.*

[2] 80 Days in Dreams. Retrieved Nov 7,2018 from http://dreamsessions.org/80days.html

[3] Amores, J., & Maes, P. 2017. Essence: Olfactory interfaces for the unconscious influence of mood and cognitive performance. *In Proceedings of the 2017 CHI Conference on Human Factors in Computing Systems (pp. 28-34).* ACM.

[4] Haar Horowitz, A., Grover, I., Reynolds-Cuéllar, P., Breazeal, C., & Maes, P. 2018. Dormio: Interfacing with Dreams. In *Extended Abstracts of the 2018 CHI Conference on Human Factors in Computing Systems (p. alt10)*. ACM.

[5] Mutual Wave Machine. Retrieved Nov 7 from https://mai.art/content/mutual-wave-machine

[6] Marina Abramovic, Measuring the Magic of Mutual Gaze. Retrieved Nov 7 from http://www.statesofawareness.net/mutual-gaze

[7] Kovacevic, N., Ritter, P., Tays, W., Moreno, S., & McIntosh, A. R. (2015). 'My Virtual Dream': Collective Neurofeedback in an Immersive Art Environment. *PloS one,* 10(7), e0130129.

# Expressing and Sensing Hybrid Materiality: Voluminous Interactive Architectural Substance

**Malgorzata A. Zboinska**
Chalmers University of Technology
Gothenburg, Sweden
malgorzata.zboinska@chalmers.se

**Delia Dumitrescu**
University of Borås
Borås, Sweden
delia.dumitrescu@hb.se

**Hanna Landin**
University of Borås
Borås, Sweden
hanna.landin@hb.se


*TEI '19, March 17–20, 2019, Tempe, AZ, USA*

*ACM ISBN 978-1-4503-6196-5/19/03.*
*https://doi.org/10.1145/3294109.3301265*

## Abstract

In this architectural research exploration, we challenge the notion of an interactive architectural surface as single-layered, two-dimensional interaction interface. Instead, we propose the notion of Interactive Voluminous Substance, which moves the interaction experience into four dimensions, shifting it from far-field, proximity-based interaction to a near-field, tactile one. We present four features of architectural expression that could potentially sustain the embodiment of this Substance: spatial positioning, geometry, expression, hybrid material composition and interaction design. If the future architectural interiors and exteriors are made from Voluminous Architectural Substance, how will it be to dwell with them? We propose two physical prototypes and two interaction stories as speculative objects probing this question.

## Author Keywords

Interactive responsive architecture; tactile architecture; tangible interaction; voluminous architectural substance.

**Figure 1:** Architectural space arrangement for tactile interaction with *The Soft Architectural Body*.

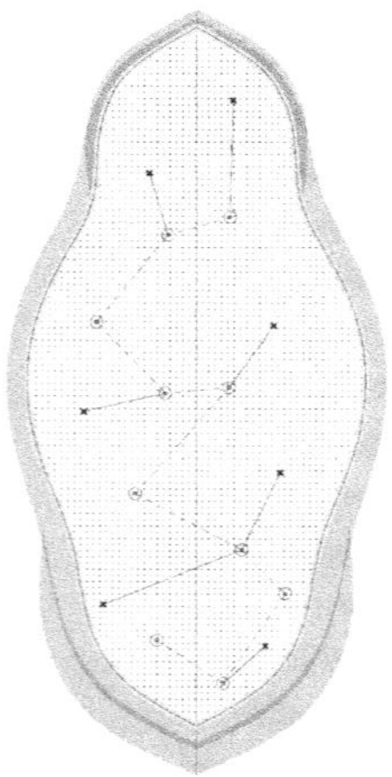

**Figure 2:** Cross section of a hybrid material system with sensors and actuators immersed deep within the architectural substance.

## CSS Concepts

• Human-centered computing~Interface design prototyping • Applied computing~Architecture (buildings)

## Introduction

A possible future of living is one of Interactive Architecture in which pervasive technology that listens and reacts is embedded within physical architectural substance [2]. With connected, data gathering Interactive Architecture we will be able to build reactive living and working environments [5, 6]. These could change their sizes depending on the activity and amount of people, prepare buildings for upcoming activities such as homecomings of residents, or help us shut out the outer presence through changes in spatial enfoldments. Regardless of the actual need, wish or disapproval for such a future, it seems important to explore how it could look and feel like, in order to gain fundamental knowledge that could be useful in future research and practice of Interactive Architecture design.

In this investigation, we do not address any particular application or use. Instead, we explore fundamental questions. How to express the notion of Interactive Voluminous Architectural Substance in physical designs? How to shape its architectural, visual and tangible features? How could the tactile experience of the movements within it be shaped to create a sensation of interaction with architecture's physicality in all four dimensions?

An overarching aim of the two exhibition pieces and their accompanying interaction stories, presented herein, is to open up a broader discussion on the future of living in digitalized hybrid spaces. How will they change our perspective of what a building is? How will it be to dwell with them on a daily basis? How will our sensations change if we communicate with them using our touch?

## Background and subject of study

In modern architectural design, surface-based expressions of Interactive Architecture prevail. Seminal projects, such as the Aegis by dECOi/Mark Goulthorpe, present an architectural skin made from facets, with an actuating hardware system placed behind as an added entity. The prevalent mode of interaction with those surfaces is far-field based. For example, the well-known Hyzolic Ground installation by architect Phillip Beesley relies on ambient atmosphere as the main vessel for the embodiment of interaction. The user does not need to touch the structures. Human presence and proximity are sufficient to trigger a response.

With this investigation, we seek to challenge these prevailing trends. We argue for a more voluminous treatment of the interactive architectural interface. Instead of expressing it traditionally as an interactive surface, we propose an alternative design typology with enhanced tactile attributes: bulky, thick and geometrically articulated Interactive Architectural Substance. We believe that by presenting inhabitants with double-curved, three-dimensional architectural interfaces we can encourage more extensive probing of architectural objects surrounding us, not limited to two dimensions but addressing all four instead – a new kind of tangible experience of architecture's materiality, unusual and unfamiliar to most of us. The purpose of this approach is to enable near-field interaction,

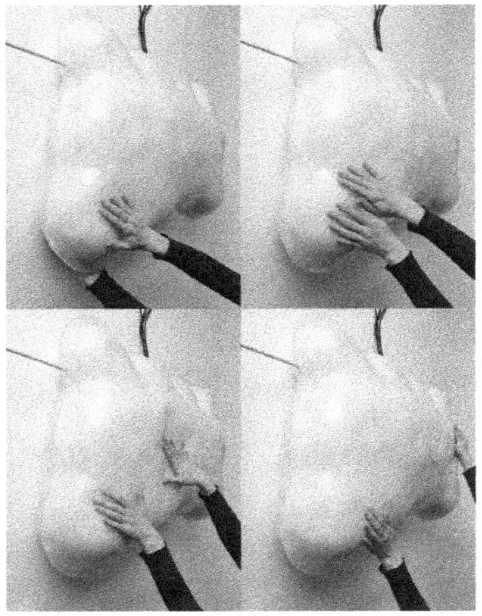

**Figure 4:** Tactile explorations of *The Soft Architectural Body* using both hands.

featuring more direct, personal contact with the physical substance of architecture.

An important feature of this alternative approach is the specific placement of hardware systems within the new substance. We propose that the electronic devices and this substance form a new kind of a hybrid material entity, following the notion of responsive architectural material [3]. Such material is made from substances that exhibit responsive behaviors when put together.

We argue that the composition of the hybrid material in the case of the Voluminous Architectural Substance should fluctuate. It should depend on the geometric and expressive characteristics of a particular architectural entity and the particular design of its responsiveness. The hardware systems could, therefore, be buried both somewhere within the depth of the Architectural Substance, as well as right under its skin. Regardless of location, the hardware systems would no longer be just added behind a surface. Instead, they would only have meaning when combined together with other materials. Altogether, they would not only function as actuators of the responsive behaviors of the Voluminous Substance but also mediate in the expression of its three-dimensionality.

## Voluminous Architectural Substance

Below, we describe in detail two prototypes that embody the notion of an Interactive Voluminous Architectural Substance. The prototypes do not have a designed functionality. The purpose of developing them was to enable an exploration of their fundamental architectural design aspects: spatial position, geometry, expression, material qualities and interactivity. Vibration-based movement within the Voluminous

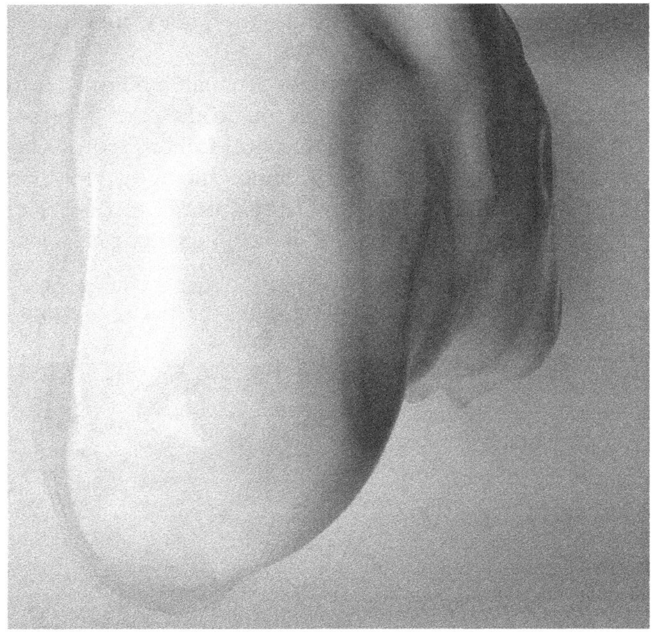

**Figure 3:** Bulky, compact, floating volume of *The Soft Architectural Body.*

Substance forms the core of the interactive behavior and sensory properties of both prototypes.

*Object 1: The Soft Architectural Body*
Space-wise, the Soft Body object is intentionally positioned centrally in space, visually detached from other architectural structures and seemingly floating in the air. All this to trigger curiosity that encourages its viewing and tactile probing.

Geometry-wise, the object is a solid volume, closed by two double-curved surfaces. The compactness of the

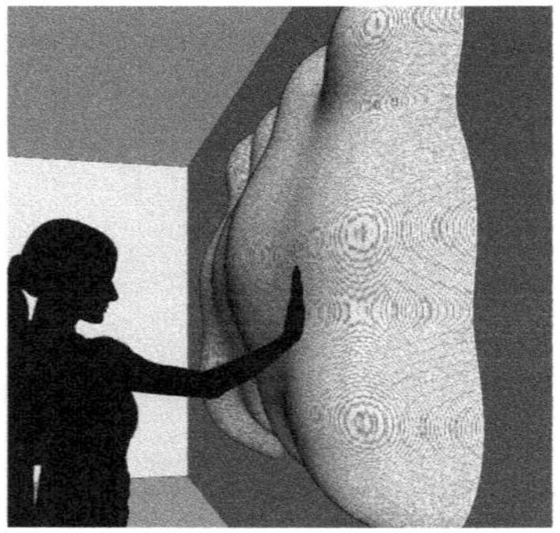

**Figure 6:** Architectural space arrangement for tactile interaction with *The Pliant Flesh of Architecture.*

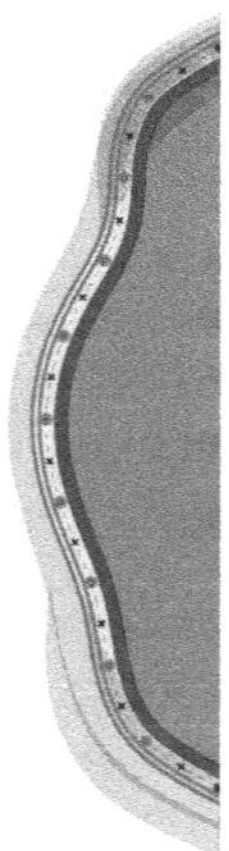

**Figure 7:** Cross section of a hybrid material system with sensors and actuators embedded within a multilayered architectural substance.

volume is designed to encourage tactile embrace and probing with both hands.

Expression-wise, the color of the Soft Body, with a bright yellow-green hue against a white interior, increases its perception as a lightweight object. The color is meant to evoke feelings of something known and unfamiliar – the stimulus to examine the object more closely.

Material-wise, it consists of a soft polyester fiber filling which carries and conceals the hardware. The filling mediates in the communication between the hand, the soft silicone architectural skin encasement, the sensors (accelerometers) and the actuators (vibrating motors), transmitting stimuli within the bulk.

Interaction-wise, the sensors are triggered when the volume is energetically palpated using both hands. They switch on the vibrations of motors, emerging from deep within the bulk of the Substance, as a gentle sensation. The vibration epicenter location is blurred out owing to the damping effect caused by the infill material.

*Object 2: The Pliant Flesh of Architecture*
Space-wise, this object is positioned against a solid vertical underlay. It gradually emerges from within a surrounding flat surface. The contrasting of its curvatures with the flat surface around is designed to trigger attention. One wants to come closer and study how the object relates to 'its' wall from left, right, top and bottom.

Geometry-wise, the radii of the object's curvatures gradually increase from top to bottom, to facilitate a

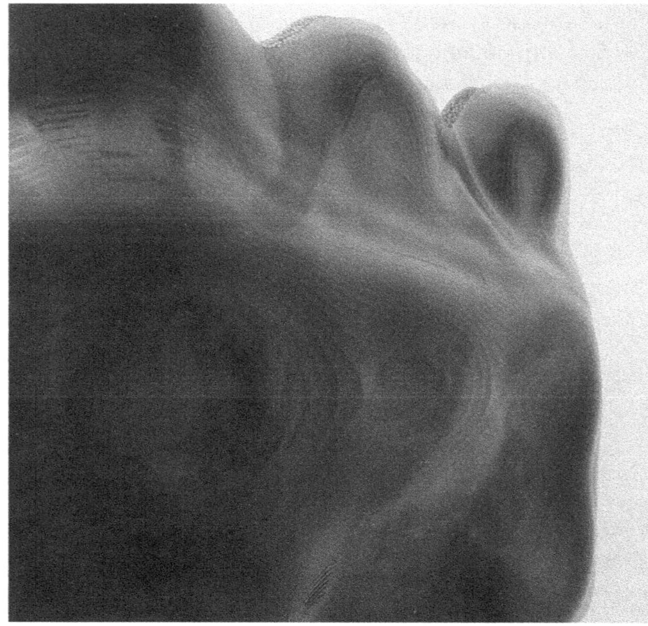

**Figure 5:** The layered substance of *The Pliant Flesh of Architecture.*

scalar experience of tactile probing: from hand-matching curvatures at the top, towards arm and other body part matching ones at the bottom. The geometry curvatures are designed to facilitate both global and localized tactile probing, delicate touch as well as more firm pushing against the surface.

Expression-wise, the object's coloration is based on the juxtaposition of translucent colors. An outermost monochromatic color layer reduces the vibrance and intensity of the marine color layer placed underneath. The marine layer then blurs out the hardware and almost entirely obscures the inmost Substance of the

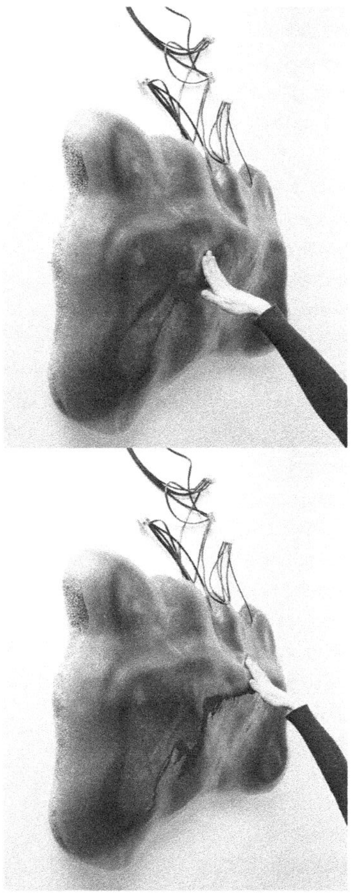

**Figure 8:** Tangible interaction with *The Pliant Flesh of Architecture.*

object. The overall dark coloration emphasizes the linework texture of the respective layers of the Substance. The reflectiveness underlines the sensation of three-dimensionality accompanying the visual and tactile examinations of the object.

Material-wise, the object consists of a thick architectural Substance, in the form of a springy body of silicone and polystyrene, enveloped by two thinner silicone skins. The hardware resides between the springy Substance and the first skin. It contains capacitive touch sensors and vibrating actuators, controlled by a network of microcontrollers. Altogether, the system facilitates multiple sensations. The skins facilitate visual and tactile experiences, while the springy substance the aural and tactile sensations.

Interaction-wise, four types of response are present: the tactile sensation of vibrations, clearly located; the visually identifiable movement of the skins, caused by vibrations; the sound of vibrations; and the networked point light illumination of the surface, triggered when stimuli are sent from sensors to actuators, indicating the presence of electronics within the architectural Substance.

## Interaction stories

The following interaction stories extend the experience with our two prototypes, by speculating how it could be to interact and dwell with Voluminous Architectural Substance in the scale of an architectural interior and a building.

*Story 1: The Soft Embrace of an Architectural Volume*
To approach a surface-volume.
Curvatures alternating.
The slow change of perspectives, of the eye.
Of the hand.
Of the shoulder and upper back.
Lean against a wall.
The changes of perspectives of the shoulder and upper back.
Being partly enveloped.
Soft wall.
Even softer.
Being embraced by it.
To sense something in there.
There might be movement within the wall-bulk.
Inner. Inner you. Inner body-wall.
What is a wall?
Volume. Bulk. Softness.
Enclosure. Embrace.
Separation. Juncture.

*Story 2: The Electronic Confectionery of Architecture*
Once upon a time, perhaps 20 years ago, there was a computer concern, called something in particular. It was nothing.

And then they presented a computer that no one had ever seen before. It looked like licorice candy with a hint of technology inside. That was everything.

And at some point in future, perhaps 20 years from now, there will be a building concern, called something in particular, and they will present licorice candy buildings with technology inside. Will they look like something from half a century ago?

The new type of building will assimilate the archaic add-ons. Power outlets. Lights. Doors. Etc.

Its Architectural Substance will light up the space in advance, based on the direction of your movements. You will always be followed by light. Never being able to capture it.

Its Architectural Substance will divide the space to satisfy your needs before you even think about them. Sometimes, but very seldom, you will wonder what it means to have a bathroom or a kitchen that might not exist when you are not using them. Do they exist when you are not there?

The Architectural Substance will seamlessly provide you with electricity, heat up or cool down the space you are surrounding yourself with.

You will let the walls guide you. They will guide you. When you touch them, a movement will travel underneath the surface, hinting the inner structure of your building, allowing you to perceive when data about you is collected. Allowing you to transmit or block the flows of information, of life signs; your wishes and intentions traveled further into the bone of the building for necessary adjustments.

The Architectural Substance will be your companion. The candy building will read your mind and keep you company. You will not be alone.

## Conclusions

The prototypes and stories presented herein are meant to initiate a broader discussion on the role of architectural expression and hybrid materiality in designing Interactive Architecture of the future. The emergence of novel architectural materiality could produce a new category of architectural elements: hybrid, ubiquitous objects that are neither walls nor floors nor ceilings. These could become Inhabitable Architectural Substances [1], new kinds of Organic User Interfaces [4], in which the local and discrete scale of inhabitant interaction with the building's physical matter triggers an expressive consequence, propagating across the scale of the entire building or even the city, changing their perception, character, expression and function. How such reactive and adjustable designs could look like is yet to be seen. Nonetheless, they present a conceptually stimulating concept, demarcating a potentially new trajectory for Interactive Architecture research.

## Acknowledgements

This study is a part of an artistic research project Architectural Convertibles, funded by the Swedish Research Council Vetenskapsrådet. We acknowledge the contribution of RISE Interactive Göteborg in the development of software and hardware for Object 1 and of Pablo Miranda Carranza for Object 2.

## References

[1] Marcos Cruz. 2013. *The Inhabitable Flesh of Architecture.* Ashgate Publishing, Farnham.

[2] Michael Fox and Miles Kemp. 2009. *Interactive Architecture.* Princeton Architectural Press, New York.

[3] Sheila Kennedy. 2013. Responsive Materials. In *Material Design: Informing Architecture by Materiality.* (1st. ed.), Thomas Schröpfer (Ed.). Birkhäuser, Basel, 118-131.

[4] Sara Nabil, Thomas Plötz, and David S. Kirk. 2017. Interactive Architecture: Exploring and Unwrapping the Potentials of Organic User Interfaces. In *Proceedings of the 11th International Conference on Tangible, Embedded, and Embodied Interaction*

(TEI '17). ACM, New York, NY, USA, 89-100. DOI: https://doi.org/10.1145/3024969.3024981

[5] Hayes Raffle, James Tichenor, and Hiroshi Ishii. 2004. Super Cilia Skin: A Textural Interface. *Textile 2,* 3, 328-347. DOI: https://doi.org/10.2752/147597504778052694

[6] Carsten Röcker and Kai Kasugai. 2011. Interactive Architecture in Domestic Spaces. In *Communications in Computer and Information Science,* vol 277, 12-18. Springer, Berlin.

# IVORY: A Tangible Interface to Perceive Human-Environment Interrelationships

**Jessica Broscheit**
Hamburg University
of Applied Sciences,
Berliner Tor 7,
D-20099 Hamburg
*jessica.broscheit@haw-hamburg.de*

**Susanne Draheim**
Hamburg University
of Applied Sciences,
Berliner Tor 7,
D-20099 Hamburg
*susanne.draheim@haw-hamburg.de*

**Kai von Luck**
Hamburg University
of Applied Sciences,
Berliner Tor 7,
D-20099 Hamburg
*kai.vonluck@haw-hamburg.de*


*TEI '19, March 17-20, 2019, Tempe, AZ, USA.*

ACM ISBN 978-1-4503-6196-5/19/03.
DOI: https://doi.org/10.1145/3294109.3301266

## Abstract
In this paper we explore human-environment interrelationships by utilizing both hybrid materially-oriented approaches and metaphorical representations. Inspired by the 'canary in a coalmine' metaphor we developed a tangible interface to sense the environment and provide a physical experience. The design utilizes life-like characteristics, like shape memory alloys and feathers to illustrate the metaphor. The aim of this approach is to propose a tangible interface as a mediator to provoke empathy for environmental issues. For that, the paper addresses an interdisciplinary field of design, society and technology through an embodied system.

## CSS Concepts
• Human-centered computing~Haptic devices

## Author Keywords
Tangible interface; shape-changing material; shape memory alloy; particular matter; environmental-feedback; information visualization, metaphorical representation.

## Introduction

Invisible and irreplaceable, air is an essential element which creates a seamless matrix on earth's atmosphere interlinking everything. This invisible matrix of gases, particles, and liquids is in a continuous state of change [1]. Due to its constantly changing nature, air provides a complex system of differing air qualities which also depends on human activities [2]. This research seeks to convey the complexity of anthropogenic impact more comprehensible through a physical experience. Therefore, we introduce a tangible interface for perceiving human-environment interrelationships by utilizing both hybrid materially-oriented approaches and metaphorical representations. First, we consider the background and theoretical concept based on the historical genesis of the canary in a coalmine and the issue of air quality. Second, we discuss related work on shape memory alloy. Third, we describe the implementation details of the prototype. To sum up, this paper presents a design-orientated exploration that reflect on hybrid materials and environmental dimensions.

## Background and Theoretical Concept

In the era of the early coal and steel industries, miners were confronted with the danger of hazardous gas mixtures in shafts, caused by underground fires or explosions [3], [4]. The miners could not sense the odorless gases and would pass out without warning. For their protection, canaries were utilized as a bioindicator, to detect gases like carbon monoxide [3]–[7]. For that, the canaries were trained to sing underground [7].

**Figure 1**: IVORY illustrates the limit values of particulate matter ($PM_{2.5}$) utilizing both hybrid materially-oriented approaches and metaphorical representation.

If the air reached high concentrations of carbon monoxide, the canaries would drop from their perches. The collapse of these sensitive organisms provided the miners with the necessary time to initiate security procedures [3]. Nowadays, these birds no longer act as indicators for carbon monoxide in underground environments, but the 'canary in a coalmine' metaphor still exist to describe warning of some danger. As alternative to bioindicators, there are various sensor technologies to monitor the environment ubiquitously [8], [9]. These technologies not only gathers data about environmental conditions, but also about human activities [10]. Hence, they are capable of recognizing both the change of air quality and the impact of human activities. Thus this complex system provides differing air qualities for human respiration [1]. This is especially true for the air pollution provoked by particulate matter. Particulate matter (PM) is a complex mixture of solid and liquid concentrations, measured in mass per volume of air (µm/m3). These particles are categorized according to their aerodynamic diameter as follows [11], [12]:

- PM10 are particles with a diameter <10 µm;
- PM2.5 are particles with a diameter <2.5 µm;
- UFP are ultrafine particles with a diameter <0.1µm.

Moreover, particulate matter consists of gaseous air pollutants—like nitrogen oxides, carbon monoxide, sulfur dioxide, and ozone—and has an impact on the environment and affect human health on a global scale [12], [11]. For instance, particulate matter ($PM_{2.5}$) and UFP are not only capable of entering the respiratory tract, but also the bloodstream, and can cause respiratory and cardiovascular health problems [11], [12]. Due to significant environmental changes caused by anthropogenic impact, this research utilizes the 'canary in a coalmine' metaphor as aesthetic mediator to evoke empathy for environmental issues.

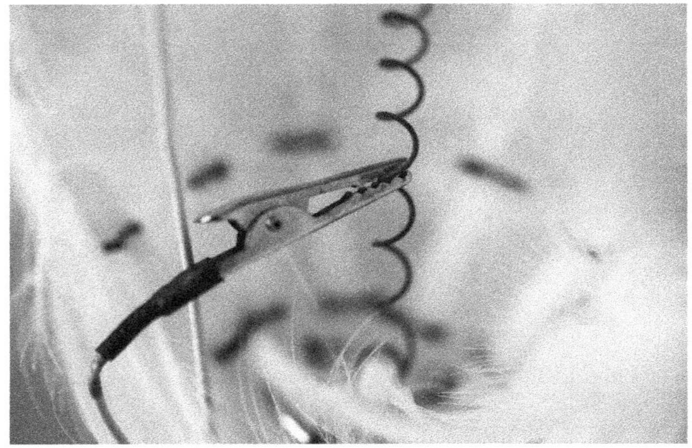

**Figure 2:** The shape memory alloy spring is placed in the center of the construction to generate the kinesis of the prototype.

## Related Work

With the vision of ubiquitous computing, referring to Mark Weiser, the third era of computing is characterized by a world of connected and imbedded interfaces through a network of low-power computers [8]. These interfaces require novel communication approaches between human and computer to fit technology into everyday live [8], [13]. In particular, tangible user interfaces (TUI) provide a communication system that embody digital information and enrich the physical space for human interaction through both thoughtful designs and haptic materials [14]. As an example, various TUIs utilized shape changing materials to represent digital information as dynamic

**Figure 3:** On-and-off state of the prototype.

stimuli [14]. Additionally, the potential of shape changing approaches has been explored in various studies on tangible interfaces and electronic garments [15]–[19]. *'Surflex'* is a soft interface to enable physical computing interaction. For that, shape memory alloy springs deforms the surface to provide a programmable system for embedded computing [15]. *'Shutters'* is a curtain composed of actuated louvers. These louvers utilize shape memory alloy for environmental control [18]. *'Caress of Gaze'* is an interactive garment, that utilized eye gaze tracking technology to control a 3D printed body architecture via shape memory alloy [20]. These different approaches rethink interacting with the environment through shape changing dynamics [17]. For example, shape memory alloy (SMA) is made of thermomechanical material that can be addressed through an electrical stimulus [19]. The thermomechanical material memorizes its original shape and provides a life-like transformational potential through heat control. Thus it provides a dual process between malleable and definite state, as well as silent and life-like dynamics [19]. This study combines the abovementioned approaches with metaphorical representations to enhance the potential of human-computer interaction.

## System Implementation

The intention of this design research is to explore human-environment interrelationships by utilizing sensor technologies, shape memory alloys and metaphorical representations (Figure 1). Therefore, the process of system implementation contains three sections. First, it illustrates the fabrication process to convey the concept of visual rhetoric. Second, it specifies the human-computer interaction according to the bird behavior. Third, it describes the details of the hardware-module.

*Fabrication:*
To convey the 'canary in the coal mine' metaphor, the design seeks organic materials and life-like characteristics. For this, the artefact utilizes feathers as bird reference. These feathers are attached to a kinetic construction to simulate the dynamics of respiration (Figure 3, 4). For that, a shape memory alloy spring was installed in the center of the kinetic construction, to provide a malleable and life-like dynamic of the artefact.

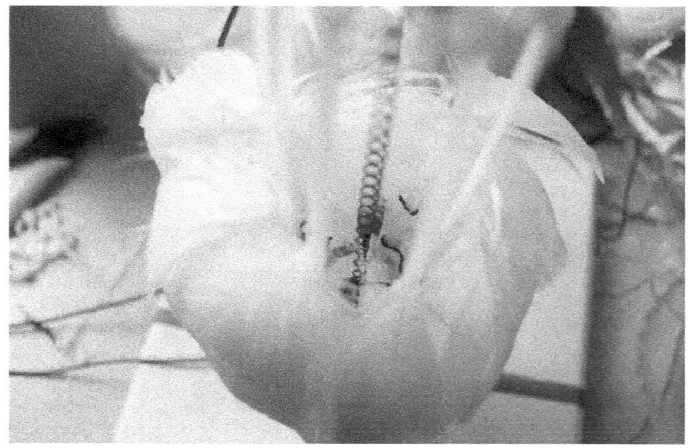

**Figure 4:** Fabrication of the kinetic construction.

*Interaction:*
Similarly, for the behavior of the canary, the prototype 'sings', 'breathes' and 'sleeps', depending on the environmental conditions. For that, three different interaction modes were designed to perceive particulate matter through the tangible interface:

- Convenient mode: If the values of particulate matter ($PM_{2.5}$) are good or moderate, IVORY 'sings' and 'breathes'.
- Threshold mode: If values of particulate matter ($PM_{2.5}$) are above the threshold value, IVORY stops 'singing' and 'breathing'.
- Sleeping mode: If IVORY has to 'sleep', it can be covered with a blanket, then it stops 'singing' and 'breathing'.

*Hardware-Module:*
To implement the interaction, a hardware module was developed. The module consists of a microcontroller Arduino Mini [21], particle sensor SDS011 [22], shape memory alloy spring [19], photoresistor, soundboard and speakers. The sensor SDS011 measures the optical density of air and transmits the $PM_{2.5}$ data to the microcontroller Arduino. The program on the microcontroller Arduino maps the data to control both shape memory alloy (SMA) and soundboard. Technically, the shape memory alloy spring simulates the 'breathing' of the tangible interface and synchronizes the sound (Figure 4). To activate the 'sleeping-mode' the photoresistor measures the ambient light. If the tangible interface is covered under a blanket, the process of 'singing' and 'breathing' stops.

## Conclusion
This paper introduced a tangible interface that reflects on human-environment interrelationships by utilizing both hybrid materially-oriented approaches and metaphorical representations. Our intension was to develop a tangible interface as a mediator to provoke empathy for environmental issues through the 'canary in a coalmine' metaphor. The tangible interface senses particulate matter ($PM_{2.5}$) and transforms the data into kinetic dynamics supported by sound. For that, the shape memory alloy provides a life-like characteristic and illustrates the abstract representation of 'the canary in a coalmine' metaphor. By presenting the tangible interface in the CSTI lab, the tangible interface aroused immediate interests from the audience. Further work is required to evaluate the impact of IVORY as information system in smart environments. In addition, it is important to realize that shape memory alloys have a limited ability to convey information. Due to the on-and-off state, the dynamic is restricted and provides a limited range of information.

## Future Work
In the future, our aim is to develop various applications of tangible interfaces by using 'the canary in a coalmine' metaphor. Promising future research directions stem from, for instance, developing embodied interaction through electronic garment. Additionally, these devises have to connect with other systems, to measure the environment for personal requirements. Moreover, our intension is to provide more detailed information through sonification, as the physical dynamic of the shape memory alloy is limited.

## Video
https://vimeo.com/281624662

## Acknowledgements
We would like to thank Benjamin Salewski for implementing the prototype circuit board at the lab Creative Space for Technical Innovations (CSTI).

## References

[1] D. Suzuki, A. McConnell, und A. Mason, *The Sacred Balance: Rediscovering Our Place in Nature*, Updated. Vancouver B.C.: Greystone Books, 2007.

[2] P. J. Crutzen, „The "Anthropocene"", in *Earth System Science in the Anthropocene*, Springer, Berlin, Heidelberg, 2006, S. 13–18.

[3] T. D. Spencer, „Effects of Carbon Monoxide on Man and Canaries", *Ann. Occup. Hyg.*, Bd. 5, Nr. 4, S. 231–240, Jan. 1962.

[4] J. S. Reif, „Animal Sentinels for Environmental and Public Health", *Public Health Rep.*, Bd. 126, Nr. 1_suppl, S. 50–57, Mai 2011.

[5] G. A. Burrell und F. M. Seibert, „Experiments with Small Animals and Carbon Monoxide", *J. Ind. Eng. Chem.*, Bd. 6, Nr. 3, S. 241–244, März 1914.

[6] J. S. Haldane, *Respiration*. New Haven, Yale University Press, 1922.

[7] J. Klähn, *Bemerkungen über den Kanarienvogel*, Bd. 1. Auflage. Sankt Andreasberg: Harzer Roller-Kanarien-Museum, 2006.

[8] M. Weiser, „The Computer for the 21st Century", *SIGMOBILE Mob Comput Commun Rev*, Bd. 3, Nr. 3, S. 3–11, Juli 1999.

[9] F. Mattern und C. Flörkemeier, „Vom Internet der Computer zum Internet der Dinge", *Inform.-Spektrum*, Bd. 33, Nr. 2, S. 107–121, Apr. 2010.

[10] J. Gabrys, „Programmieren von Umgebungen", in *Internet der Dinge*, F. Sprenger und C. Engemann, Hrsg. Transcript, 2015.

[11] R. D. Brook *u. a.*, „Particulate Matter Air Pollution and Cardiovascular Disease: An Update to the Scientific Statement From the American Heart Association", *Circulation*, Bd. 121, Nr. 21, S. 2331–2378, Juni 2010.

[12] U. Lahl und W. Steven, „Feinstaub - eine gesundheitspolitische Herausforderung", *Pneumologie*, Bd. 59, Nr. 10, S. 704–714, Okt. 2005.

[13] M. Weiser und J. S. Brown, *The Coming Age of Calm Technology*. 1996.

[14] H. Ishii, D. Lakatos, L. Bonanni, und J.-B. Labrune, „Radical Atoms: Beyond Tangible Bits, Toward Transformable Materials", *interactions*, Bd. 19, Nr. 1, S. 38–51, Jan. 2012.

[15] M. Coelho, H. Ishii, und P. Maes, „Surflex: A Programmable Surface for the Design of Tangible Interfaces", in *CHI '08 Extended Abstracts on Human Factors in Computing Systems*, New York, NY, USA, 2008, S. 3429–3434.

[16] J. Berzowska und M. Coelho, „Kukkia and Vilkas: Kinetic Electronic Garments", in *Ninth IEEE International Symposium on Wearable Computers (ISWC'05)*, Osaka, Japan, 2005, S. 82–85.

[17] M. Coelho und P. Maes, „Sprout I/O: A Texturally Rich Interface", in *Proceedings of the 2Nd International Conference on Tangible and Embedded*

*Interaction*, New York, NY, USA, 2008, S. 221–222.

[18] M. Coelho und P. Maes, „Shutters: A Permeable Surface for Environmental Control and Communication", in *Proceedings of the 3rd International Conference on Tangible and Embedded Interaction*, New York, NY, USA, 2009, S. 13–18.

[19] M. Coelho und J. Zigelbaum, „Shape-changing Interfaces", *Pers. Ubiquitous Comput*, Bd. 15, Nr. 2, S. 161–173, Feb. 2011.

[20] B. Farahi, „Caress of the Gaze: A Gaze Actuated 3D Printed Body Architecture", in *ACADIA 2016 POSTHUMAN FRONTIERS: Data, Designers, and Cognitive Machines: Projects Catalog of the 36th Annual Conference of the Association for Computer Aided Design in Architecture*, K. Velikov, S. Manninger, und M. del Campo, Hrsg. ACADIA, 2016, S. 352–361.

[21] S. F. Barrett, *Arduino Microcontroller Processing for Everyone!: Third Edition*. Morgan & Claypool, 2013.

[22] „Messungen mit dem Feinstaubsensor SDS011", *LUBW Landesanstalt für Umwelt, Messungen und Naturschutz Baden-Württemberg*, Juni-2017. [Online]. Verfügbar unter: http://www4.lubw.baden-wuerttemberg.de/servlet/is/268831/. [Zugegriffen: 15-Feb-2018].

# After Words: Interactive Sound Installation Connecting Language, Body, and Machine

**Kimberly Lyle**
Arizona State University
Tempe, AZ 85282, USA
kimberly.lyle@asu.edu

**Figure 1**: Speaking structure and breathing stand



TEI '19, March 17–20, 2019, Tempe, AZ, USA © 2019 Copyright is held by the owner/author(s). ACM ISBN 978-1-4503-6196-5/19/03.
https://doi.org/10.1145/3294109.3301267

## Abstract

"After Words" is an interactive sound installation in which the viewer's participation causes basic units of speech to puncture the space, interrupting and overlapping yet remaining untied to any specific language. Inspired by early speech synthesizer technologies that could only emit syllables, consonants, and vowels, these structures house circuit boards which trigger audio files at random when the connected stand has air blown into it. The sounds emitted gesture towards a desire for language, but foreclose the possibility of meaning. Ultimately, "After Words" aims to create a space where sounds question logic, embrace nonsense, and untether the voice from language while revealing underlying connections between human and machine.

## CSS Concepts

• Applied computing~Arts and humanities • Hardware~Sensor devices and platforms • Hardware~Sound-based input / output • Human-centered computing~Interactive systems and tools

## Author Keywords

Art; Interactive Sculpture; Installation; Tangible User Interface; Sound; Language; Communication; Body

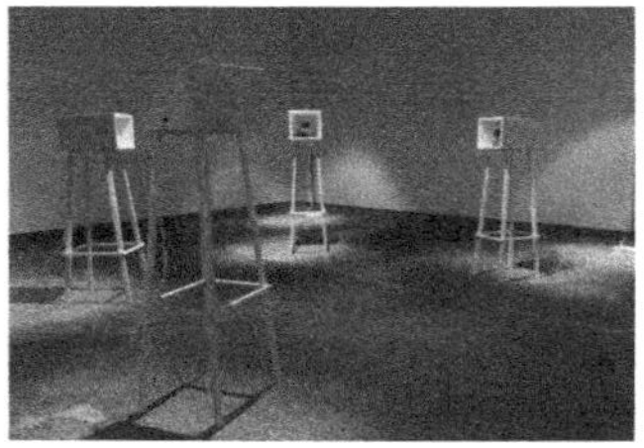

**Figure 2**: Arrangement of speaking structures in a semi-circle

**Figure 2**: Close-up of two adjacent speaking structures

## Introduction
"After Words" operates at the intersection of sound, language, technology, and the body. Combining inspirations from vastly different time periods, a grouping of four sculptures emit sounds that play with language's most basic building blocks and question systems of logic deeply engrained within language and digital technologies. The designs of the structures were based on those of failed speech synthesizers from the early 1700s whose mechanical parts closely resembled elements of the human body used to produce speech. [4] These structures attempt to merge human and machine through intimate audience participation and physical interaction. In doing so, they seduce the viewer into language, yet never fulfill that desire. The resulting sounds resemble fragmented speech, registering more as nonsense than a coherent message. This places attention on the failure that can occur within both communication and technological systems. [7]

## Work Description
"After Words" is an interactive sound installation in which the breath of viewers triggers a series of audio files to be played at random through connected speaker boxes. The audio clips vocally replicate the sounds of basic units of speech from across several languages. When the sculptures are activated simultaneously, a cacophonous assemblage is produced. This echoes the phonetic poems and linguistic strategies implemented by Dada artists, who subverted the grammatical rules of language as a way to remove all meaning and power. [5] Connected to the stands are hand crafted wooden boxes which house a speaker and an electronic circuit board. Attached to the main circuit board is an MP3 shield which holds an SD card containing over 50 audio files. The housings for the sensor, wires, and circuit board are made entirely of clear acrylic, exposing all parts of the system to the viewer. When the sculptures are not activated, the sound of a book's pages being flipped through plays softly in the background. This places emphasis on language as a tangible experience. The video below demonstrates how the real-time interaction functions between the participant, sculptures, and sounds emitted.
https://vimeo.com/299152241

## Purpose
By using these machines to rearrange fundamental sounds of language, I am questioning the logic behind systems of knowledge that are often invisible and deeply integrated into our everyday lives. The main goal of the work is to create an environment where viewers are encouraged to question the validity of words and technological advances as means through which knowledge is disseminated and ultimately controlled. By incorporating the viewer's bodily actions into the work, they are physically implicated in this process. "After Words" is a desire for another kind of community beyond the conventions of discourse, one that is suspicious of the logics of language and technology. However, one that also embraces diversity and connections across difference. By placing attention on the sounds of consonants and vowels that travel across many languages, a gesture towards a more global language is made. In a similar manner to John Cage's deconstructive sound piece, "Empty Words", by reducing language to its most fundamental parts, a focus on other ways of knowing begin to emerge. In this way, the sounds start to make sense by themselves – another kind of sense than words do. [2]

## Physical Interactions and the Body

The installation connects language to the body, and asks the viewer to engage with the work physically. The positioning of the pseudo-speaking structures is intentional, each subtly different in shape and size to preclude a singular, authoritative tone. [1] As several participants activate the space simultaneously, the dimensions of the objects and their arrangement in space choreograph the movement of bodies and the user's inhabitation. The bent over postures acquired by the viewers as they activate the stands mimic pre-lingual states, in which air flow through the body was regulated differently. [10] The act of blowing into any of the four stands encourages the viewer to feel the continuum between breath, sound, and language. By engaging the viewer physically, language becomes tied to the body.

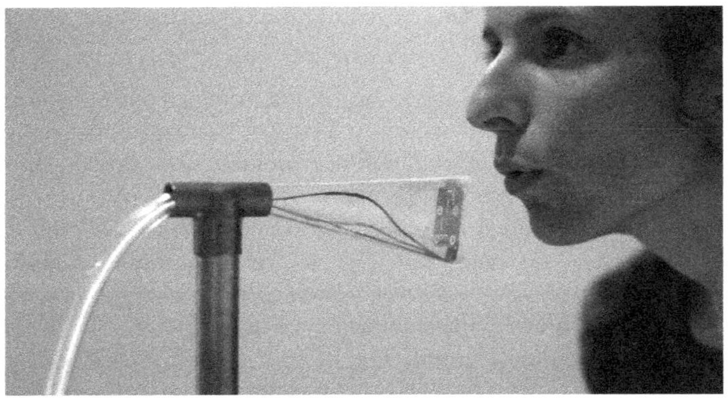

**Figure 4**: Participant activating the sensor by blowing air

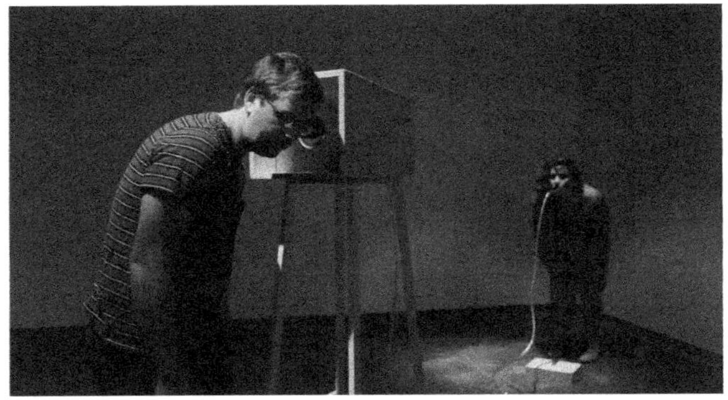

**Figure 5**: One participant activates the sculpture, while the other listens to sounds emitted

The role of the body was quite prevalent in early mechanical forms; however, this has tended to disappear as machines are slowly dissolving into a set of mathematical functions. This work attempts to reinsert the body into these forms through tangible interfaces and intimate bodily interactions. [11]

The use of sound further places attention on the bodily experience of the participants as they navigate the space. As the speakers within the sculptures carry fragments of human voice throughout the installation space, sound leaves one body and enters others. [8] It enables a felt experience on several sensory levels and allows for emotional resonance with the participants.

## Hybrid Materiality and Technologies Across Time

Sculpturally, the merging of warm, hand-built wooden structures and human voice reveals the connection between human and machine and how they both make meaning through systems. [12] [6] Moreover, the components of the structures remain deliberately revealed to the viewer to further remove this boundary. Additionally, the sensors are exposed to the open air, allowing for an interaction with participants that mimics the rapidly dissolving separations between human and machine. [9]

The installation also nods towards very different time periods, merging past technological advances and current ones within the same physical space. By bridging these moments in time, viewers can more easily make connections between the past, present, and potential future.

**Figure 6**: Detail of speaking box and clear interface

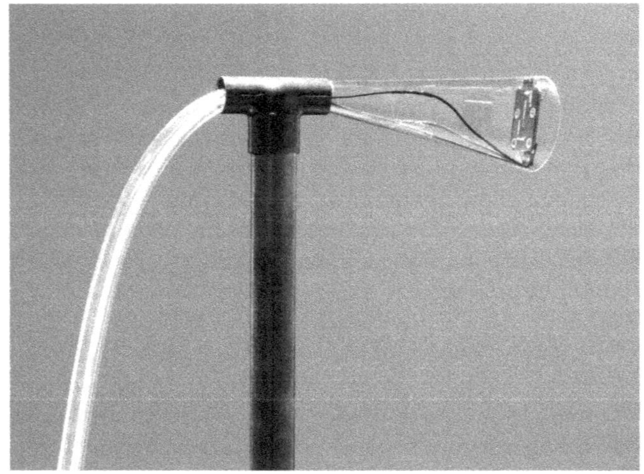

**Figure 7**: Detail of breathing stand and clear interface

## Revealing Underlying Connections

As participants physically activate the installation, they gesture towards a dissolving of boundaries between human and machine. Simultaneously, the activation of the sculptures results in a breaking down of language, directing attention towards sound and more basic forms of communication. As the audio emitted from the sculptures is not tied to any specific language, a co-existence of many different languages in one space is encouraged. The innate similarities in the natural origin of spoken words across human languages are highlighted. [3] In addition, the inclusion of references to old and new technologies bridges gaps between the past and present, while finding connections that bind them to one another. Ultimately, "After Words" is an interactive sound installation that promotes a sense of hyper connectedness between machine and body, between languages, and across time.

**Figure 8**: Several participants activate the installation through choreographed postures and movements

## References

[1] Claire Bishop. 2010. *Installation Art: A Critical History*. Routledge New York.

[2] John Cage. 1979. *Empty Words: Writings '73-'78*. Wesleyan University Press.

[3] Mark Changizi. 2011. *Harnessed: How Language and Music Mimicked Nature and Transformed Ape to Man*. BenBella Books, Inc.

[4] Mladen Dolar. 2006. *A Voice and Nothing More*. MIT Press.

[5] David Hopkins. 2016. *A Companion to Dada and Surrealism*. Wiley Blackwell.

[6] Hiroshi Ishii, Dávid Lakatos, Leanardo Bonani, and Jean-Baptiste Labrune. 2012. Radical Atoms: Beyond Tangible Bits, Toward Transformable Materials. 1.

[7] Steven Johnson. 1997. Interface Culture: How New Technology Transforms the Way We Create and Communicate. HarperEdge.

[8] Brandon LaBelle. 2015. *Background Noise*. Bloomsbury Academic.

[9] Gierad Laput, Yang Zhang, and Chris Harrison. Synthetic Sensors: Towards General-Purpose Sensing. https://doi.org/10.1145/3025453.3025773

[10] André Leroi-Gourhan. 1993. *Gesture and Speech*. MIT Press.

[11] John (John C.) McCarthy and Peter (Peter Charles) Wright. 2004. *Technology as Experience*. MIT Press.

[12] Edward A. Shanken. 2015. *Systems*. MIT Press.

# Interacting with Electroactive Polymers in Responsive Environments

**Karmen Franinović**
Zurich university of the Arts
karmen.franinovic@zhdk.ch

**Andrés Villa**
Labor 5020
andres@labor5020.ch

**Luke Franzke**
Zurich university of the Arts
luke.franzke@zhdk.ch

**Wille Florian**
Zurich university of the Arts
florian.wille@zhdk.ch

 ACM ISBN 978-1-4503-6196-5/19/03.
https://doi.org/10.1145/3294109.3301268.

## Abstract
In this paper, we discuss the opportunities and challenges of creating responsive environments with Electroactive Polymers (EAPs). Our previous research on tools and methods for EAPs enabled us to develop two public installations: *SOLO* and *Electric Animal Plant*. Going beyond the demonstration of EAPs, these projects explore the aesthetics and interactivity of such shape-changing materials. We explain actuating and sensing capabilities of EAPs in these works, and we reflect on the response of the participants to the installations.

## Author Keywords
Programmable Materials, Electroactive Polymers, Active Materials, Smart Materials, Shape-Changing Interfaces, Responsive Environments

## CSS Concepts
• Human-centered computing~Interaction paradigms • Human-centered computing~Interface design prototyping

## Introduction
EAPs are an emerging smart material technology, offering the possibility of shape change and sensing from a single material. These malleable and stretchable films produce smooth almost animal-like movements, a

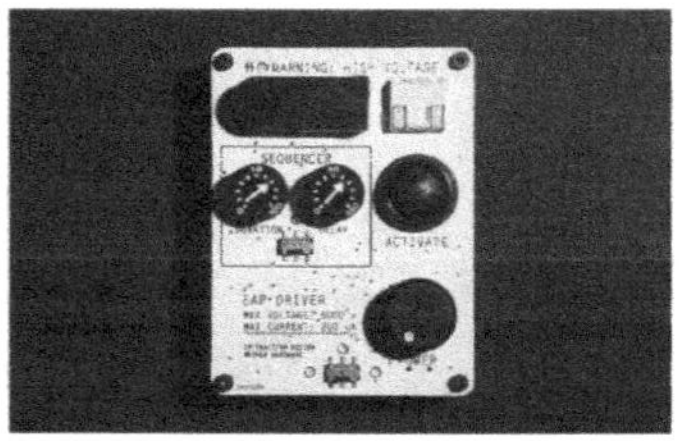

Figure 1: EAP Stretch Mechanism and Open EAP Driver

stark contrast to the mechanical motion of most traditional actuators. EAPs can also act as stretch or pressure sensors for wearable applications [27]. Other potential applications cover a broad range of fields, such as robotics, energy harvesting, haptic interfaces and sensing technologies [1][13][20][23]. EAP research can be found in numerous publications from material science, chemistry, electrical and mechanical engineering contexts. However, EAP projects in design are rare or remain on the level of scenarios or simulations [2][24].

The first example of a functioning design prototype was *Shapeshift* [14], in which architecture students worked within a material science laboratory to produce a kinetic facade demonstration. This project generated immense interest in creative media channels, but it was followed by only a limited number of EAP design projects. Some examples include kinetic structure*s such as A Degree Of Freedom [9]* and *Actuated Matter [12],* and a speculative architectural model in *Phototropia [29]*. In *Fluid Morphologies* [7], we proposed an architectural application using Hydroactive Polymers (HAPs) for the first time.

While these projects dealt with spatial aspects they remain on the level of demonstration or model, not allowing for an embodied spatial experience. Furthermore, they are mostly non-interactive projects. The lack of spatial projects and interactivity may be due to the fragility of the materials and production processes which are difficult outside of specialised labs. While our research initially focused on novel DIY tools and methods [5], we are now at the stage where we can integrate and explore EAPs within the context of larger scale responsive environments.

*EAP basic principles*

EAPs can be divided into either Ionic or the more common Dielectric Elastomer (DEs). In this paper, we are referring specifically to DEs when we use the term Electroactive Polymer. DEs are composed of an elastic dielectric material, such as acrylic rubber or silicone, sandwiched between two compliant electrodes. When an electrical potential is applied across the two electrodes, electrostatic attraction between the electrodes compresses the elastomer. This compression results in the elastomer being forced outward, creating a radial expansion [18]. When the voltage is removed, the elastomer returns to its original form. This simple radial expansion can be used for a variety of actuations, from a linear movement to rotary or oscillatory actuation and complex surface deformations.

EAP membranes can also function as sensors through three separate mechanisms. Firstly, its capacitance can be measured, giving a value which changes as the membrane is physically displaced or moved [13]. Secondly, the resistance across a single side of the membrane can be measured to indicate the stretch of the membrane [16]. Lastly, the EAP can generate a voltage through electromechanical transduction, which can be measured to indicate the amount or frequency of displacement [19]. EAP actuators have also been demonstrated that have self-sensing characteristics [11], i.e. that can both move and sense external manipulations of the membrane. Furthermore, the EAP itself can generate a current for driving low-power devices such as the accompanying sensing circuitry [8].

## Active Materials Framework

During our research, we became increasingly aware of the different approach needed for working with novel

Figure 2: Explorative fabrication: A first EAP petal-tail frame drawn and cut by hand. vimeo.com/291931951

fragile materials which have not yet been developed into durable applications, such as single-membrane EAPs. Moreover, our previous research on new potentials of electroluminescent paper showed the need for a new approach beyond performance-driven goals [4]. The existing design frameworks did not address the problems and opportunities that arose during our research, nor did they deal with questions of design methods for unstable materials.

*Active Materials*

The term *Active Material* connotes a variety of materials, from those that can support a nuclear chain reaction to those that change their properties in a response to external stimuli, such as EAPs [15]. Most recently, the term activation energy has been used in place of stimuli and the active material described as a composite in which a non-active part changes its properties under the influence of an active component [26]. For example, wood becomes active by changing its form under the activation of introduced humidity.

The *Active Material framework* we have been developing is grounded on the need for an embodied understanding of emerging material technologies, that can be difficult to approach through purely analytical techniques. This is particularly the case with novel materials where research is focused on performance goals rather than on their aesthetic or interaction potentials. As we have shown in [4], our techniques support unexpected paths for material activity.

Various theoretical, methodological and typological aspects of active materials are addressed by the *Active Material framework*. An overview of our theoretical approach and questions can be found in [3], whereas the methodological aspects have been published in [7], [4] and most recently in [5]. Our tools and methods embrace the activity of material through creative negotiation processes between human and matter. Further, we research materials and their processes as a part of an environment, thus going beyond the focus on isolated functionality for specific application goals.

## EAP Methods and Tools

Our production methods were inspired by those developed at EMPA [10]. Using a biaxial scissor mechanism, we pre-stretch VHB elastomer which is commercially available as double-sided adhesive tape. Then, carbon black is impregnated into both sides of the elastomer. The resulting EAP can be further developed with a number of different techniques. For example, in the *Electric Animal Plant* project we created Dielectric Elastomer Minimum Energy Structures (DEMES) by applying EAP to a hand cut polycarbonate frames for quick prototypes (Figure 2). Our pocket-sized EAP controller, capable of outputting 5000 volts, supports prototyping and testing of interaction. The design is open source, and the schematics can be accessed from github for easy reproduction [6]. Full explanation of these methods and tools are available on the "Enabling" section of our website (www.enactiveenvironments.com) and in academic publications [5].

## Responsive Environment Case Studies

DIY tools and methods enabled us to begin explorations of interaction with EAPs and to develop more stable setups that can be shown to the public [5]. In our first public demonstration, *Fluid Morphologies,* the audience activated HAPs by the means of a soft silicone touchpad. Various participants perceived a relationship

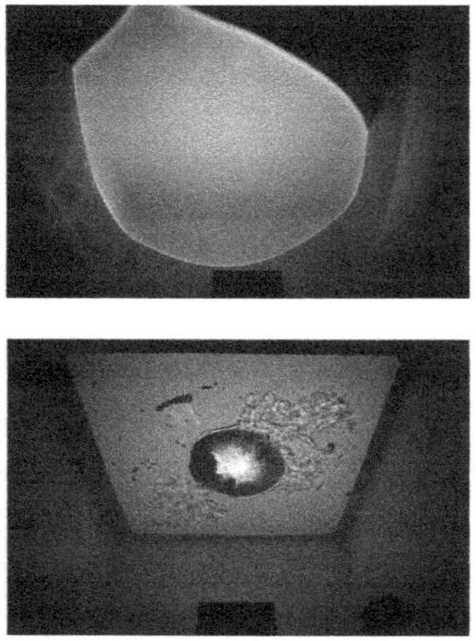

Figure 3: SOLO installation.
vimeo.com/219971330

between pressure and the rate of EAP activation, despite the binary nature of the mechanical switch embedded in the touchpad. We also observed visitors tending to swing their bodies as if they were synchronising with the motion of the HAP. This coupling between the participant's movement and the motion of the device, suggested an apparent empathy with the material and the development of an understanding through the participants own kinesthesis. While the focus of *Fluid Morphologies* was on our discovery of HAPs [7], the interaction possibilities with EAPs proved to be worth further investigation.

*SOLO: from artefact to environment*
With the *SOLO* project, we publicly showed an EAP responsive space, during a three-day Laokoon festival [30]. The invited artists were confronted with a topic of pain and the *SOLO* project explored the possibility of empathising with an active material. In a dark room, a transparent liquid HAP body was hung within a monolithic enclosure hidden from the eyes of the visitor. Its presence pervaded the room as the light shined through the body, projecting its tiniest details onto the ceiling. The forces of gravity and electricity ran through this body, activating it from within. From outside, sound attacked the body and light revealed its surface tensing, releasing and contracting. Struggling under the weight and motion of the liquid, the body is brought into crisis until it eventually falls apart.

We chose to work with a HAP due to its liquid appearance and dynamic movement. The first prototypes used hand-made silicone membrane instead of the VHB, with the goal of greater durability. However, we quickly discovered that silicone motion was perceived as comical due to its extreme bounciness. Thus, we returned to VHB, with a challenge of finding a transparent electrode material which could substitute carbon black. We discovered that the hair-gel worked well and we used it to explore various configurations of the bottom electrodes. However, the hair gel dried over the course of a day, restricting the elastomers movement and reducing conductivity. Rather than changing this behaviour, we integrated it into the project concept together with the EAPs potential to eventually tear.

For the light and sound environment, a 3.5m high room was built to enable sound and light dynamics resulting from the HAP motion [31]. Enclosed in a white 2m high pillar, the transparent HAP was illuminated by a single LED light source mounted on a linear actuator. This resulted in the HAP's dynamic shadows being projected onto the ceiling and walls. The movement of the light source and the deformation of the HAP changed the focal length and thus the size and sharpness of the projection. The HAP shape changes were triggered by a microphone within the pillar, which captured the spatialized sound coming from the four speakers as well as by sounds produced by visitors. The soundscape was algorithmically generated in Supercollider and was played through four audio monitors. The soundscape was choreographed with the vertical motion of the light source, affecting the area of the light projection as well as the sharpness of the shadows on the ceiling. The intensity of the light source was modulated by the sound depending on the stages of overall spatial dynamics.

The audience response was collected through direct and participatory observation, including informal email reports. The audio-visual output guided the audience's

Figure 4: Electric Animal Plant in the Botanical Gardens of Zurich

attention from a focused cluster of sonic and light events to a more immersive atmosphere. This was described as resembling the growth of intense aggression which starts with occasional unpredictable events and then spreads while continuously attacking the whole body. Participants associated experienced environmental dynamics with bodily activities stating that "it is like being in one's brain, neural transfers happening quickly" or "it feels like a foetus in a womb is suffering". Two participants discovered that clapping, tapping on the monolith or loud voices could also attack the EAP. This led to a performance-like situation where the role of attacker moved from sound to human, which was not intended but showed human interaction possibilities. Overall, the SOLO project showed the potential of HAP as an activator of its surroundings and well as a range of metaphors emerging from observation or interaction with EAPs.

*Electric Animal Plant: increasing complexity*

With *Electric Animal Plant,* our goal was to create a more complex kinetic structure to explore the organic movement of EAPs on a larger scale. Moreover, we wanted to research both actuating and sensing capabilities for spatial interactions. The resulting light-weight structure could initially respond to sounds and was later developed to respond to motion. The project was developed to be shown in the palm house of the Old Botanical Garden in Zurich (figure 4). Referencing this context, the structure followed the anatomy of a flower, with active EAP components forming the stamen and petals. Movement appeared in irregular patterns, providing the audience with a sense of animalistic presence

We used a total of 8 EAPS, based on two types of DEMES. We developed the new "petal-tail" frame for the concept which produced a waving motion (figure 1). The second type of DEMES used a rectangular frame to move two-meter-long counterweighted rods. All the EAPs were powered by a custom made eight-channel EAP driver embedded into the installation's structure (figure 5). The unit was battery powered and used an ESP32 wroom microcontroller for wireless connectivity. The behaviour was primarily programmed in Processing and ran on a nearby PC.

The structure was developed to hang from the steel construction of the palm house. The installation responded with movement based on sound input. A procedurally generated soundscape was created with Supercollider, which provided the primary activator of the physical choreography of the *Electric Animal Plant*. The composition evolved through time, with tonal qualities resembling those of the cicada, an insect that produces very peculiar and loud electric-like sounds and textures. The audio was played out through a quadraphonic system and a subwoofer to enable a spatialized composition. While we wanted the material to take centre stage, using only sound as an input for interaction proved to be unsatisfactory for some visitors who expected more direct interaction.

This drove us to explore further human interaction, on the second iteration of the installation at a research showcase event at the Zurich University of the Arts. The sculpture responded to a number of contactless input areas. Firstly, by approaching the ends of the delicate stamen rods, the rods would move upwards, as if avoiding contact. Secondly, as a person approached the centre of the sculpture and gestured towards

Figure 5: Custom made 8 channel EAP controller in the installation.

individual petal-tail EAPS with the hands, the petals would move upward (vimeo.com/291931387). This interaction was enabled by two Kinect cameras. The audience response showed that this two-stage interaction was engaging and that it allowed the participants to slowly get familiar with the behaviour of the responsive sculpture. Especially, the interaction through hand movements proved to inspire longer engagements in which the participants synchronised with the organic movement as if dancing with the active material.

## Electric Animal Plant at TEI 2019

We propose EAP for sensing a blowing input, drawing inspiration from the inquisitive behaviour of children, who might blow upon a ladybird or dandelion, as a form of gentle, yet playful provocation. Various projects showed the potential of blowing for contactless interaction [25] [22] [17] [21]. Interactions in a spatial context have also been demonstrated by "Bluekit", which showed blowing as an input for immersive virtual environments [28].

While existing technologies such as MEMS pressure sensors, anemometers or audio transducers can be used, we choose to use EAPs for this purpose. Our first test showed that blowing onto a DEMES structure can be sensed, with a change in resistance above 4 megaohms across a single side of the EAP. These DEMES structures would form the stigma of the Electric Animal Plant, and act as a sensor for gentle caressing or blowing on the lightweight supporting structure. Blowing may offer a novel interactive experience, with immediate motion feedback, as the surface and supporting structure visibly deform from the air blown upon them.

## Reflection and Future steps

Initially, we wanted the interaction between material and environment to be the focus of the experience in both *Electric Animal Plant* and *SOLO*. The role of the human was to be that of the observer with only subtle means of intervention. We witnessed the frustration of several participants who expected to have greater control within the installation. Possibly, this type of expectation was stimulated by the use of everyday interactive digital products, which provide instant responses and instant gratification in contrast to the more reflective spaces we tried to produce. We find this challenge exciting and worth exploring in more depth, both conceptually and practically.

Both *Fluid Morphologies* and *SOLO* project were less complex in terms of active materials than the *Electric Animal Plant* installation. Both the two earlier projects used only a single EAP and they did not explore the sensing potential of the EAPs. In addition to a more complex moving structure, we showed that *Electric Animal Plant* proved to be a good context for an exploration of interactivity with EAPs and their potential in spatial contexts. We thus proposed to present this ongoing research and further investigate the sensing capabilities within spatial and public contexts. We expect that in preparation of the TEI installation and its setup at the conference, we will be able to further investigate technical issues related to sensing and actuating along with questions of interactivity through blowing and the aesthetic experience enabled by such active material within responsive environments.

## Acknowledgements

Thanks for generous funding support to ZHdK and Design Biennale Zurich.

## References


[1] Federico Carpi, Danilo De Rossi, Roy Kornbluh, Ronald Edward Pelrine, and Peter Sommer-Larsen. 2011. *Dielectric Elastomers as Electromechanical Transducers: Fundamentals, Materials, Devices, Models and Applications of an Emerging Electroactive Polymer Technology*. Elsevier.

[2] Domus Academy. 2015. Workshop: Interaction Design Strategy and Business | Domus Academy. *Domus Academy*. Retrieved September 6, 2018 from http://www.domusacademy.com/en/master-interaction-design-2012-13/.

[3] Karmen Franinović. 2017. Thinking Active Materials: Actively Thinking Materials. In R. Kirschner and R. Kirschner, eds., *Raw Flows. Fluid Mattering in Arts and Research*. De Gruyter, Berlin, Boston.

[4] Karmen Franinovic and Luke Franzke. 2015. Luminous Matter. Electroluminescent Paper as an Active Material. *DeSForM 2015,AESTHETICS OF INTERACTION: DYNAMIC, MULTISENSORY, WISE 9th International Conference on Design and Semantics of Form and Movement*.

[5] Karmen Franinović and Luke Franzke. 2019. Shape Changing Surfaces and Structures: Design Tools and Methods for Electroactive Polymers. *In Proceedings of the 2018 CHI Conference on Human Factors in Computing Systems (CHI '19)*.

[6] Luke Franzke. Openeapdriver. Retrieved November 6, 2018 from https://github.com/IAD-ZHDK/Openeapdriver.

[7] Luke Franzke, Dino Rossi, and Karmen Franinovic. 2016. Fluid Morphologies: Hydroactive Polymers for Responsive Architecture. .

[8] Vishwa Goudar, Zhi Ren, Paul Brochu, Miodrag Potkonjak, and Qibing Pei. 2013. Driving Low-power Wearable Systems with an Adaptively-controlled Foot-strike Scavenging Platform. *Proceedings of the 2013 International Symposium on Wearable Computers*, ACM, 135–136.

[9] JimRhone and jimrhone. A Degree Of Freedom - Jim Rhoné & Martin Genet - Architecture Thesis Project. *Issuu*. Retrieved September 6, 2018 from https://issuu.com/jimrhone/docs/rhone_jim_r10.

[10] Christa Jordi. 2011. Biomimetic airship driven by dielectric elastomer actuators. Retrieved from https://www.research-collection.ethz.ch/bitstream/handle/20.500.11850/45726/1/eth-4506-01.pdf.

[11] Kwangmok Jung, Kwang J. Kim, and Hyouk Ryeol Choi. 2008. A self-sensing dielectric elastomer actuator. *Sensors and actuators. A, Physical* 143, 2: 343–351.

[12] K. Franinović, M. Kretzer, D. Bisig, F. Wille, M. Gmachl and R. Wingfield. 2013. *"Actuated Matter". In Performative Materials In Architecture And Design*. Intellect.

[13] Kwang J. Kim and Satoshi Tadokoro. 2007. *Electroactive Polymers for Robotic Applications: Artificial Muscles and Sensors*. Springer Science & Business Media.

[14] Manuel Kretzer and Dino Rossi. 2012. ShapeShift. *Leonardo* 45, 5: 480–481.

[15] J. Y. Li. 2004. Preface to Special Issue on Active Materials. *Mechanics of Materials,* 36, 10: 915.

[16] Benjamin O'Brien, Justin Thode, Iain Anderson, Emilio Calius, Enrico Haemmerle, and Shane Xie. 2007. Integrated extension sensor based on resistance and voltage measurement for a dielectric elastomer. *Electroactive Polymer Actuators and Devices (EAPAD) 2007,* International Society for Optics and Photonics, 652415.

[17] Shwetak N. Patel and Gregory D. Abowd. 2007. Blui. *Proceedings of the 20th annual ACM*

*symposium on User interface software and technology - UIST '07*.

[18] R. Pelrine, R. Kornbluh, and G. Kofod. 2000. High-Strain Actuator Materials Based on Dielectric Elastomers. *Advanced materials* 12, 16: 1223–1225.

[19] Ron Pelrine, Roy D. Kornbluh, Joseph Eckerle, et al. 2001. Dielectric elastomers: generator mode fundamentals and applications. *Smart Structures and Materials 2001: Electroactive Polymer Actuators and Devices*, International Society for Optics and Photonics, 148–157.

[20] Bruno Scrosati, ed. 1993. *Applications of Electroactive Polymers*. Chapman and Hall, London.

[21] Yang-Ting Shen and Ellen Yi-Luen Do. 2010. Making digital leaf collages with blow painting! *Proceedings of the fourth international conference on Tangible, embedded, and embodied interaction - TEI '10*.

[22] Misha Sra, Xuhai Xu, and Pattie Maes. 2018. BreathVR. *Proceedings of the 2018 CHI Conference on Human Factors in Computing Systems - CHI '18*.

[23] Ger Stienen. 2012. *Applications of Electroactive Polymers*. Springer Science & Business Media.

[24] R. Stouffs, P. Janssen, S. Roudavski, and B. Tunçer. 2013. Responsive building envelope as a material system of autonomous agents. *Conference on Computer-Aided Architectural Design Research in Asia (CAADRIA 2013)*, 954.

[25] Paul Tennent, Duncan Rowland, Joe Marshall, et al. 2011. Breathalising games. *Proceedings of the 8th International Conference on Advances in Computer Entertainment Technology - ACE '11*.

[26] Skylar Tibbits. 2017. *Active Matter*. MIT Press.

[27] Tiesheng Wang, Meisam Farajollahi, Yeon Sik Choi, et al. 2016. Electroactive polymers for sensing. *Interface focus* 6, 4: 20160026.

[28] Daniel Zielasko, Neha Neha, Benjamin Weyers, and Torsten W. Kuhlen. 2017. A reliable non-verbal vocal input metaphor for clicking. *2017 IEEE Symposium on 3D User Interfaces (3DUI)*.

[29] phototropia. *CAAD. Blog*. Retrieved July 23, 2018 from http://www.caad.arch.ethz.ch/blog/phototropia/.

[30] Laokoon Festival. *Medienarchiv der Künste*. Retrieved November 6, 2018 from https://medienarchiv.zhdk.ch/sets/47318522-1a15-44bb-8b39-e02046eae370.

[31] SOLO: Enactive Environments. Retrieved January 16, 2019 from http://www.enactiveenvironments.com/imagining/solo/.

# Ekphrasis

**Tomas Laurenzo**
School of Creative Media
City University of Hong Kong
Kowloon Tong, Hong Kong
tomas@laurenzo.net


ACM ISBN 978-1-4503-6196-5/19/03.
https://doi.org/10.1145/3294109.3301269

## Abstract
*Ekphrasis* is a mixed-media installation consisting of close-up videos of a heavily scarred body projected onto an elastic screen. The screen has one string attached to its centre, which in turn is attached to a stepper motor. The motor pulls the screen in a controlled random pattern, stretching it and releasing it, sometimes carefully, sometimes violently. The piece explores the relationship between the digital representation of the body and its corporeity, recreating the trauma that generated the scars on the medium itself, metaphorically recreating the human body on a new layer of representative abstraction.

## Author Keywords
Installation; body; flexible screens; projection; scar; death

## CSS Concepts
• Applied computing~Media arts

## Introduction
*Ekphrasis* (elastic screen, servomotor, string, metallic frame, wooden structure, Arduino microcontroller, custom software, projector) is a mixed-media installation consisting of close-up videos of a heavily scarred body projected onto an elastic screen. The screen has one string attached to its centre, which in turn is attached to a stepper motor. The motor pulls the

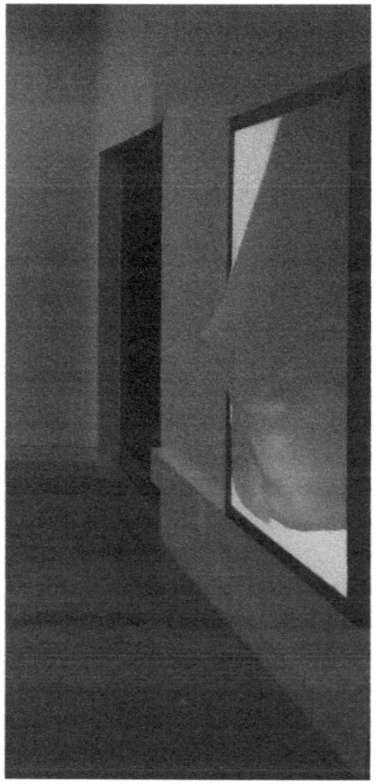

Figure 1 - *Ekphrasis.* Photo by the author.

screen in a controlled random pattern, stretching it and releasing it, sometimes carefully, sometimes violently. The rectangular screen is framed by a custom metallic frame. A custom wooden structure supports the stepper motor hiding the electronics and the projector in its base.

## *Ekphrasis*

The piece proposes a reflection on the representation of the human body, *from* the representation itself, together with an exploration of the philosophical significance of the body. The work questions the relationship between the digital representation of the body and the body itself.

Western culture thinks of mankind as the 'articulation and conjunction of a body and a soul, of a living thing and a logos, of a natural (or animal) element and a supernatural or social or divine element' [1]. This mind–body dualism is constructed under the assumption of a representation of the mind that is simultaneously different from and belonging to the body. The installation partially reclaims the role of the body in the vital experience: we construct our understanding of what the life is from a body that itself is changed by the living process. Using the most extreme changes that a body can suffer (scars resulting from a violent event, an accident), the piece reflects on what we understand by living as humans and how its technological representation and re-enactment can contribute to this understanding.

Death can be thought of as the ultimate postmodern taboo. We live lives constantly sparkled, garnished by fantasies of immortality, and yet, systematically determined by the assumption of mortality. In this context, the body unfolds in a contradictory fetishism: the idolization of the perfect body coexists with the stigmatization of the imperfect one. And the most imperfect body is the scarred one, a marked body representing a life not lived properly.

The installation explores this dichotomy; a heavily scarred body is shown, not as a reminder of mortality, but only as a body: the body as a metaphor of the body itself. The most human body is the non-human body: technologically mediated perception as objectification. Bolter and Grusin identify, in new media art, a systematic ekphrasis, which they call 'remediation' – the representation of one medium in another – and argue that it constitutes 'a defining characteristic of the new digital media' [3]. Together with remediation, new media art has systematically attempted to achieve immediacy by ignoring or denying both the presence of the medium and the unavoidable act of mediation.

In *Ekphrasis*, however, the medium and its remediation are made explicit by the seemingly external manipulation of its physicality. It is the installation itself that deforms the projection screen, simultaneously representing the internal state of the body and the external forces acting on it. Instead (or, better, in addition) of a remediation, the piece proposes an ontological side-step where the acknowledgement of the medium becomes a relevant part of the piece.

Particularly relevant are the dialogue between representation, object and time, and the piece's unfolding on these dual-antagonistic roles. Subject and object, recipient and actor, witness and accident, occur simultaneously. A body with scars that compresses its past and present is represented in the deformable screen that reflects on its own role of sustaining this representation.

In the same sense, a body with scars presents itself in a dual time. Scars constitute simultaneously an artificial representation of a past event and a natural occurrence. In *Difference and Repetition*, Gilles Deleuze states:

"A scar is the sign not of a past wound but of 'the present fact of having been wounded': we can say that it is the contemplation of the wound, that it contracts all the instants which separate us from it into a living present. Or, rather, that we find here the true meaning of the distinction between natural and artificial: natural signs are signs founded upon passive synthesis; they are signs of the present, referring to the present in which they signify. Artificial signs, by contrast, are those which refer to the past or the future as distinct dimensions of the present, dimensions on which the present might in turn depend. Artificial signs imply active synthesis – that is to say, the passage from spontaneous imagination to the active faculties of reflective representation, memory and intelligence. [...] There is a self wherever a furtive contemplation has been established, whenever a contracting machine capable of drawing a difference from repetition functions somewhere. The self does not undergo modifications, it is itself a modification – this term designating precisely the difference drawn. Finally, one is only what one has: here, being is formed or the passive self is, by having." [4]

If being is having and if we can only truly possess what is inside our skin, the skin is not a metaphor of the being, but its very *definition*. However, for this definition of the self to work, an external observation is needed, a vantage point from which the skin/border is defined. The skin as an articulator of possession would only make sense under the assumption of an objective otherness; it requires something that testifies that the outside-of-the-body exists, a meta-representation of the skin-container, where representation itself explicitly modifies the representation apparatus.

This unattainable illusion of objectiveness requires repetition. Nothing can be objective if not predictable, and so a machine, an applied scientific knowledge is required. Machine-like precision offers the language that allows to articulate the externality, and the language of the machines permits the exterior to be tangible only because of the possibility of predictable repetition. We can think of the inside, of the self, because the exterior is predictable, because the exterior is designed.

Thus, the self exists not in the present but in the concretization of the past, or, in other words, the present is the representation of the past. In this sense, the scarred skin not only encodes the trauma but makes it real, a sort of technologically mediated perception acting as an objectification force. Remediation converts a medium into a 'metamedium' and the represented body becomes a metabody (understanding metabody not in the Foucaltian sense but in a direct one, a body that exists on a higher level of abstraction than what proprioception allows for). A scarred body not only presents a past trauma, but re-enacts it.

In Baudrillard's terms, the Accident becomes 'a strategic reorganization of life beyond the perspective of death' [1]. The non-fatality of the Accident allows us to *enter into* a relationship with death. If, as Jones put it, the self-portrait constitutes a 'technology of embodiment' in which technology 'not only mediates but produces subjectivities' [6], *Ekphrasis* again unfolds in contradictory axes. A technology of embodiment that simultaneously situates the viewer outside of the representation: in *Ekphrasis*, the projection screen is also the skin of the installation. With a new remediation, skin projected on skin, scars represented on a stressed, attacked, stressed surface. In this context, the mechanical stretching re-enacts the external action of the Accident. The Accident becomes performance, while, again, also being a commentary of itself.

This commentary is aesthetically relevant. The screen stretches and echoes pain. It is let loose and reverberates, a relief that is nothing but the antechamber of more pain. But the re-enactment is reversible, a reversible process commenting on an irreversible one.

## Conclusion

The Accident is an aesthetic subject that mortally wounds the taboo. In Deleuze and Guattari's words 'not at all for ideological reasons but because the literary machine alone is determined to fill the conditions of a collective enunciation that is lacking elsewhere' [5]. Moreover, even if 'ultimately, every object is about its own materiality, which informs the ways in which it creates meaning' [7] and if ignoring or denying the presence of the medium and the act of mediation has been a goal of new media and new media art, this piece makes the remediation explicit, a representation of representation. Representation, mediation, artistic communication also becomes the main subject of the work; if every work talks about itself, *Ekphrasis* also talks about talking about oneself.

## Acknowledgement

The work described in this paper was fully supported by a grant from the Research Grants Council of the Hong Kong Special Administrative Region, China (Project No. CityU 11674416).

A previous version of this paper was published in Technoetic Arts: A Journal of Speculative Research issue 15.2. https://doi.org/10.1386/tear.15.2.215_1

**Figure 2**: Close up of the stepper motor that pulls the string.

## References

[1] Agamben, G. (2004), The Open: Man and Animal, Palo Alto: Stanford University Press.

[2] Baudrillard, J. and Evans, A. B. (1991), 'Ballard's "Crash"', Science Fiction Studies, 18:3, pp. 313–20.

[3] Bolter, J. D. and Grusin, R. (2000), Remediation: Understanding New Media, Cambridge: The MIT Press.

[4] Deleuze, G. (1968), Difference and Repetition, New York City: Columbia University Press.

[5] Deleuze, G., Guattari, F. and Brinkley, R. (1983), 'What is a minor literature', Mississippi Review, 11:3, pp. 13–33.

[6] Jones, A. (2002), 'The "Eternal Return": Self-portrait photography as a technology of embodiment', Signs, 27:4, pp. 947–78.

[7] Paul, C. (2003), Digital Art, London: Thames & Hudson.

# Kyne: Movement in Static Interlaced Artifacts

**Utsav Chadha**
New York University
(Interactive Telecommunications Program)
721 Broadway 4th Floor
New York NY 10003
uc276@nyu.edu

**Mithru Vigneshwara**
New York University
(Interactive Telecommunications Program)
721 Broadway 4th Floor
New York NY 10003
mvs351@nyu.edu



*TEI '19*, March 17–20, 2019, Tempe, AZ, USA

ACM ISBN 978-1-4503-6196-5/19/03.
https://doi.org/10.1145/3294109.3301270

## Abstract
A display device, whilst seemingly static shows a lot of movement. Movement or change on such screens is perceived due to rapid, successive change in frames. Outside of screens, perceived movement on static objects may be achieved through a combination of optics and illusions. Kyne is a series of visual experiments, involving the perception of change in static distorted artifacts. It involves varied methods of obscuring or masking parts of static artifacts and taking advantage of persistence of vision to animate these artifacts. The artifacts explored use paper, refreshable static non-illuminated e-ink displays, and laser cut acrylic, and their masks include transparencies and digital projections. This paper illustrates the experiments conducted with different artifact-mask pairings and speculates on possible future pairings.

## Author Keywords
Illusions, animation, visual performance, projection mapping, animated sculptures

## ACM Classification Keywords
- **General and reference~Experimentation**
- General and reference~Design
- Computing methodologies~Animation

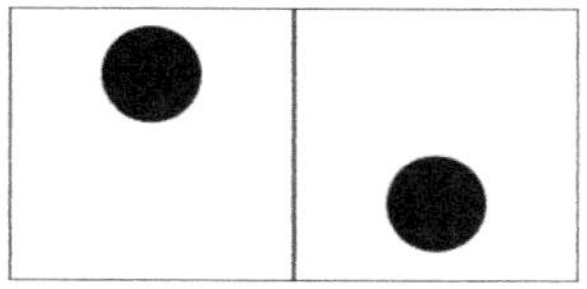

Figure 1 - Frames in a simple two-frame animation

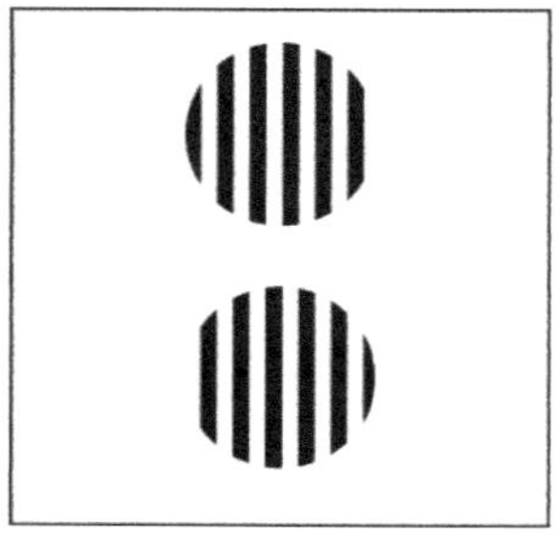

Figure 2 - Interlaced single image showing both frames from figure 1. The interlaced section alternates between the frames.

Figure 3 - Mask for the interlaced image in figure 2. The white section is transparent. Moving this horizontally back and forth over figure 2 will animate it.

## Introduction

Kyne is a series of visual artifacts that use variations of the barrier grid animation technique, also known as kinegrams. This technique uses the movement of a transparent striped mask over an interlaced image. Moving the mask, changes the portions of the interlaced image that are covered. Using this method with a series of continuous frames in an animation, produces the illusion of movement as illustrated in figures 1, 2, 3.

Figures 1, 2 and 3, showcase a two-frame animation, but this effect persists with more, depending on the type of animation and its level of detail. This type of animation has existed in various forms at least as far back as 1906 [1]. However, with the digital devices of 2018, we have the advantage of tweaking this technique to produce different types of interlaced artifacts and corresponding masks.

Kyne uses a combination of commercially available and custom-built software to generate different artifacts and masks. The artifacts explored so far are in three forms – printed paper, static monochromatic e-ink displays, and laser cut three-dimensional objects. The explored corresponding masks for the artifacts in this series are printed transparencies or digital projection-mapped visuals. Digital projections increase the versatility of these masks to go beyond physical movement. This, in combination with refreshable e-ink displays, allows for even more dynamic artifacts and animations that may be used and performed in visual installations.

## Barrier Grid Animation Technique

Generating these illusions in their simplest form, requires the creation of a mask containing parallel lines proportional to the number of frames in the animation. The mask covers all but one frame in the animation, and the frame which is visible at any given time is cycled through by moving the mask over the image. In figure 1, the animation contains only two frames. Therefore, the mask should cover only half the image at any given point. Had the animation contained five frames, the mask would have to reveal only one-fifth of the image and cover the remaining four-fifths. As a result, this proportion of what is shown and what is covered by the mask depends on the number of frames in the animation.

Figure 4 – The above image shows two states of figure 2 when the mask (figure 3) is over it. The one of the left is when the mask is offset along the horizontal axis such that only the top ball is seen. The one on the right is visible when the mask's horizontal offset is such that only the bottom ball is seen.

The width of the visible slit tends to depend on physical limitations of the mask material, and sometimes on the content of the animation. A good gauge of finding the largest appropriate slit size for a particular animation is to figure out smallest pixel resolution the animation can be reduced to without losing visibility.

These images and masks may be created using an image editing software. However, considering the mathematical pattern behind the creation of these images, programmatic software can also be used to generate these images easily. The software used to generate many of the images and masks in these experiments was written on javascript using the p5.js library. This custom software helped streamline the process and minimized errors. We named this tool Kyne with the code publicly available on github.com [2].

## Experiments

The first experiments involved printed transparent sheets as masks over plain printed paper. The experiments began with black-and-white abstract patterns. Eventually, coloured images and photographs were tested. Figure 5 shows a coloured walk cycle animation of Super Mario, a popular video game character. The interlace of the different frames of the character's walk cycle is seen distinctly. When the mask is placed on top of it, the image does not appear to be distorted any more. Figure 6 shows the similar effect with a photograph.

Figure 5 - Walk animation of Nintendo's Super Mario, animated using the barrier grid animation technique. The interlacement of frames is visible on the image on the left.

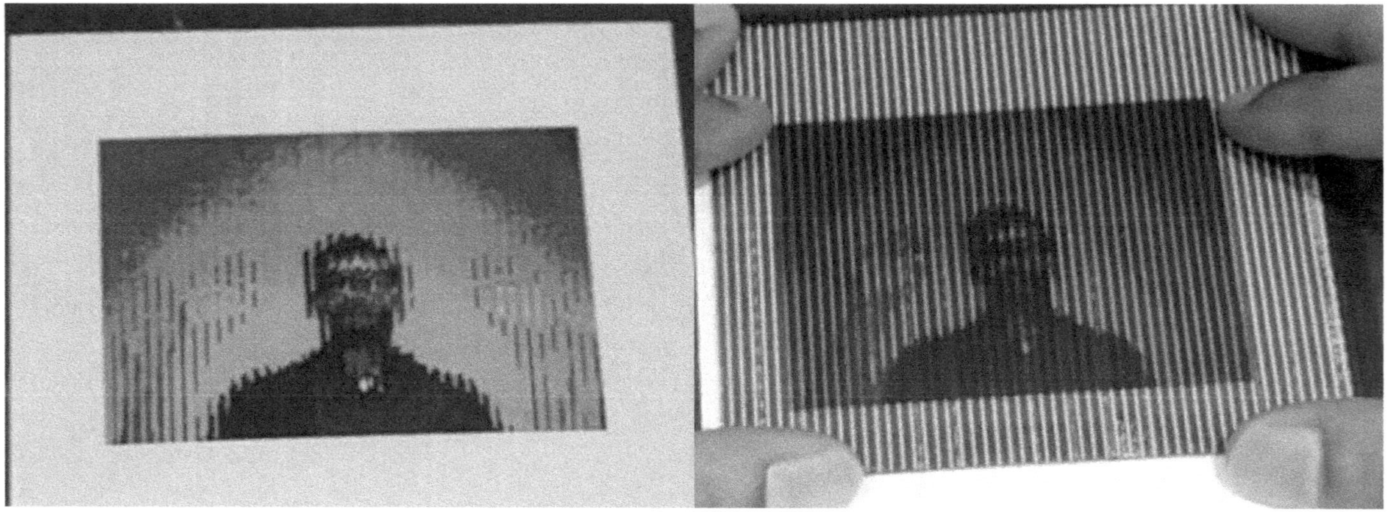

Figure 6 - A person raising both hands one after another, animated using the barrier grid technique. In the interlaced image , both hands can be seen, but in the image with the mask, only the part of the animation where one hand is raised is seen.

The next series of experiments involved a refreshable e-ink display. A third generation Amazon Kindle Keyboard was used, since it did not have any in-built light being emitted from it. The same software was used to generate the images and masks. The screen size and resolution of the device was taken into consideration and a PDF of multiple images using the same mask was created. Changing the page, would change the image that was being animated.

The experiments with the e-ink device allowed the dynamic changing of content on the fly, with the possibility of being programed. This provoked questions regarding the possibility of changing the mask on the fly in addition to the dynamic changing of content on the display. The experiments then began to involve projection mapping on static paper images. A separate projection-mapping software was written in Processing to map and mask out the interlaced images. The parameters of the printed interlaced image were used by the projection mapping software to project light masks by illuminating only certain sections of the interlaced image in a sequence. This required the projector to be able to project at least as many pixels into the relatively small piece of paper as the number of pixels being interlaced. Increasing the width of the mask slits allowed us to experiment with multiple projection surfaces, as in figure 7. This came at the cost of lower resolution of the interlaced images.

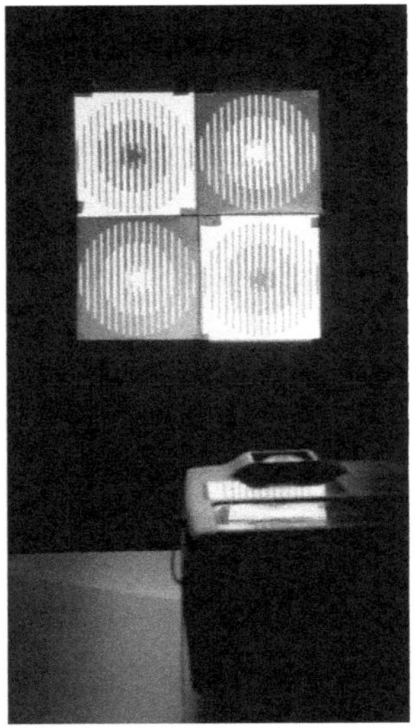

Figure 7 - Four square surfaces projection mapped in a dark room. The images are interlaced, but the mask is not being projected in this image.

This eventually led to experimenting dynamic masks on dynamic content i.e. projection mapping masks on top of e-ink displays. To maintain high enough resolution across the approximately 6-inch wide e-ink display, a pocket projector was used.

Other experiments were conducted and documented, most notably with a three-dimensional interlaced object as seen in figure 9. Projection on three-dimensional interlaces does not work as well as projection on flat, two-dimensional surfaces due to shadows and interference of the object.

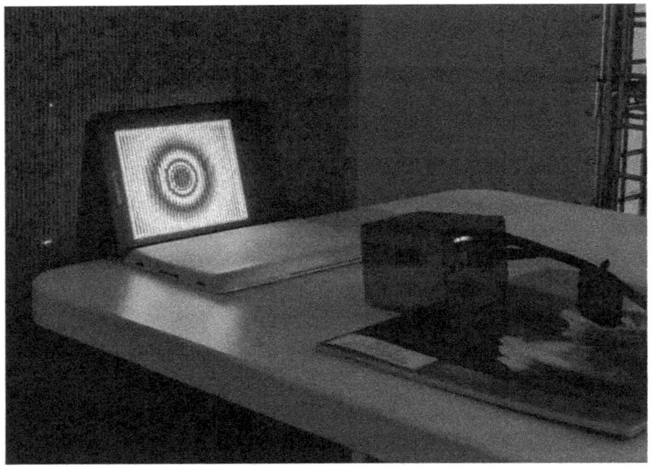

Figure 8 - Projection mapped interlaced image on Amazon Kindle e-ink device

## Presentation

The project is a series of visual and tangible artifacts that exhibit the implementation of the barrier grid animation technique through various mediums.

Figure 9 - 3D object interlaced and projected upon

The demo shows the different medium pairs. Simple medium-pairs like paper-on-paper helps explain the concept. More advanced pairs like projection on e-ink shows the possibilities. Additionally, a digital photobooth, allows the audience to take moving pictures and generate their own kinegrams, as a demo for the custom-built software.

## Conclusion

The barrier grid animation technique has been known for at least a hundred years. Today's technology allows us to explore this technique in new ways. Kyne is a series of experiments that explores these new ways. In this iteration, light, paper, e-ink and laser cut acrylic were explored as mediums.

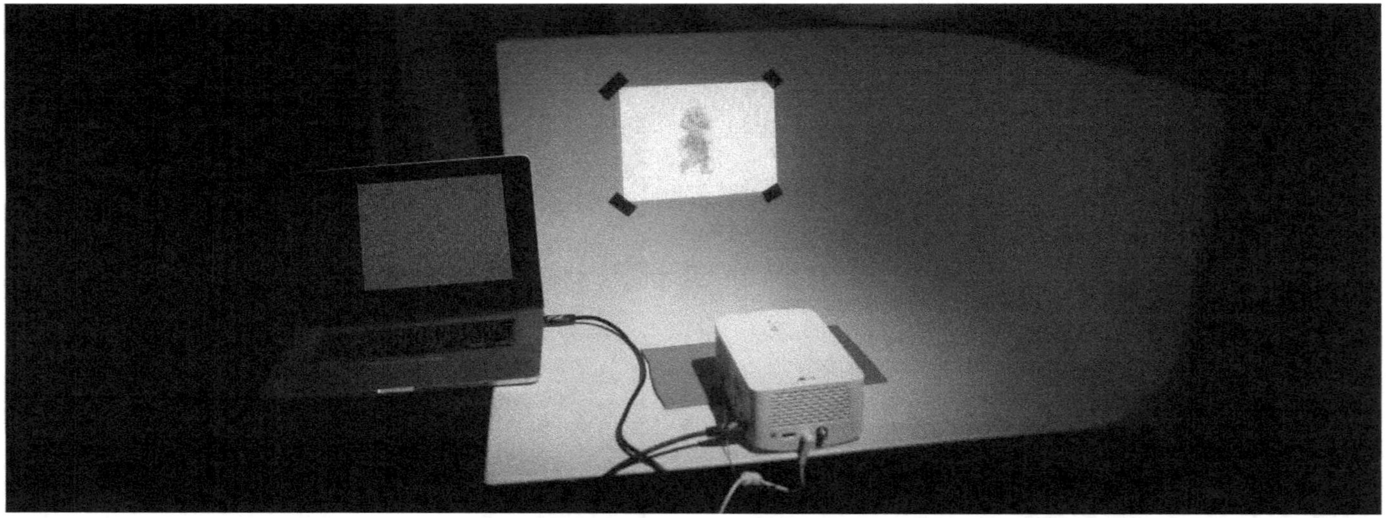

Figure 10 - Super Mario's walk cycle revealed by a projection of vertical lines that highlight only sections of an interlaced image

Software tools to enable the creation of these artifacts and mask were written and open-sourced. The dynamic nature of some of the mediums explored, allows for interesting prospects for future experiments. More specifically, with the projectors, the masks are not constrained to linear lines, or any other geometric pattern. Future experiments will focus on the generation of non-linear distortions of animated frames and the reconstruction of them.

## Acknowledgements

We thank Sam Ita, Tom Igoe and Ben Light for their guidance. Additional thanks to the people at NYU's Interactive Telecommunications Program for their feedback and support.

## References

[1] A. S. Spiegel., inventor; Display Device. US patent 829,492. August 28, 1906.

[2] Utsav Chadha, Mithru Vigneshwara. Open source code Kinegrams. Retrieved November 7, 2018 from https://github.com/utsavchadha/Kinegrams

[3] Hawken. Mario Walk Cycle. Image. Retrieved November 7, 2018 from http://dadako.com/news/pixel-pirate-devlog-episode-1-the-3-frame-walk-cycle

[4] Sarcone, Gianni A. "Kinegrams, Art in Motion." From Sarcone's Studio -- A Sarcone & Waeber Web Resource. Retrieved November 3, 2018 from http://giannisarcone.com/Kinegrams.html

# Bubble Talk: Open-source Interactive Art Toolkit for Metaphor of Modern Digital Chat

**Kyung Yun Choi**
MIT Media Lab
Cambridge, MA 02139, USA
yun_choi@media.mit.edu

**Hiroshi Ishii**
MIT Media Lab
Cambridge, MA 02139, USA
ishii@media.mit.edu

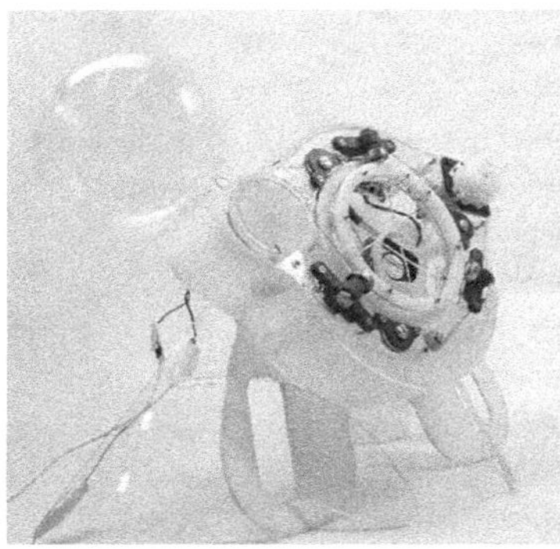


*TEI '19*, March 17–20, 2019, Tempe, AZ, USA
ACM 978-1-4503-6196-5/19/03.
https://doi.org/10.1145/3294109.3301271

## Abstract

In this art project, the ephemeral and intangible aspects of human's communication are represented by soap-bubble. The shapeless, intangible, and insubstantial speech - once the speech is shouted out through speaker's mouth it disappears unless someone hears it immediately, or even it is heard, the message will be forgotten as time goes - is transferred to a semi-tangible yet still fleeting bubble. The bubble machine that we created provides person-to-person and person-to-space interaction. The machine has a iris mechanism that varies its outlet size reacting to the participant's speech pattern as if it tries to talk something. Once the participant pauses, the machine blows out various sizes of bubble. The floating bubble represents the subtle state of a message from interpersonal communications that lies in the middle of real and digital world. Also, it creates a certain delay until it pops, which is a metaphor of our behavior that we often delay to send out text-messages through chatting apps. We believe that anyone can be an artist. By open-sourcing the details of fabrication process and materials, we want to encourage people to build the machine, interact with it at any locations, and use and modify it as a art tool for realizing their own ideas whether it is for art or not.

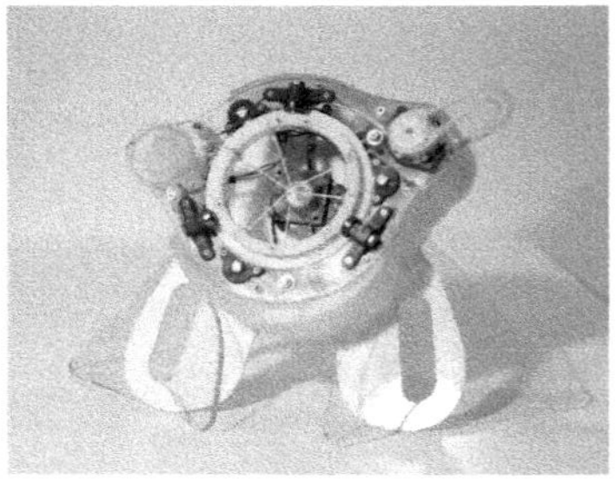

**Figure 2:** Open-source Art Toolkit, Bubble Talk machine. At the installation site, three machines will be exhibited; two for two people interaction and one for a mobile interaction

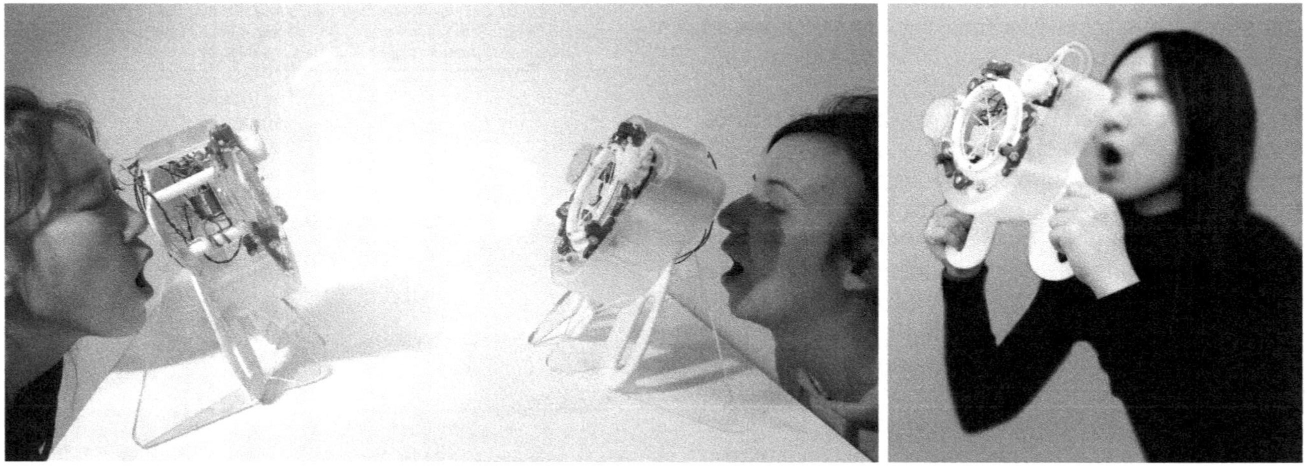

**Figure 1:** Installation view of two BubbleTalk machines for two people interaction, and mobile interaction for one person

## CCS Concepts

**•Human-centered computing** → **Sound-based input / output;** *User interface toolkits;* **•Applied computing** → **Media arts; •Hardware** → Sound-based input / output;

## Author Keywords

Interactive Art; Ephemeral; Bubble; Voice; Open-source

## Introduction

*Bubble*

*"quod, ut dicitur, si est homo bulla, eo magis senex (for if, as they say, man is a bubble, all the more so is an old man) "*

*- Marcus Terentius Varro (116 BC - 27 BC), De Re Rustica*

A soap bubble is ephemeral. It lasts only for a brief moment and quickly disappears even by a light breeze. The bubble's symbolic meaning as a metaphor of human's fragile and insubstantial life was first coined by a Roman writer Varro in the 1st century BC. Also, in 1572 the philosopher Erasmus reintroduced the Latin expression "Homo bulla" ("man is a bubble") in his collection of proverbs, Adagia [3]. This special characteristics of bubble attracted lots of artists in 17th century and also other periods, and were used in Vanitas, a type of symbolic work of art showing the transience of life, the futility of pleasure, and the certainty of death [10]. A paint, 'Cupid Blowing a Soap Bubble (1634)', by Rembrandt Harmensz van Rijn is one of examples. Metaphor of bubble continues to the modern century and a modern artist, Thomb Kubli, also uses bubbles as a media to transfer invisible and intangible sounds to visible but fleeting form in a 3D space [4]. The attractiveness of bubble might be coming from its ironical representation of our transient life which reminds us of the value of our existence at a moment and makes us seize the present. The usage of bubbles is

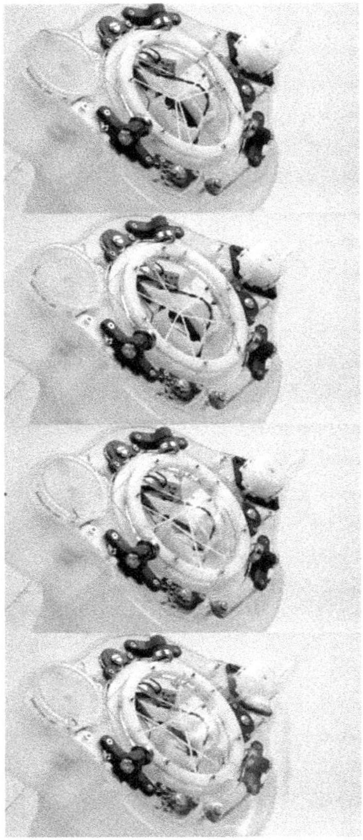

**Figure 3:** From closed position to open position of string iris mechanism (From top to bottom). As it open, the 3 lines of string form a triangle shape with bubble membrane.

not only seen in the art field but also in the field of HCI. The unique materiality of bubble has intrigued researchers to explore a new design space of user interfaces, and also challenged them to technical problems to handle and create bubble. Thanks to those investigations, bubble has been used for playful and emotional engagement [8], [1]. Also, it has been applied as a tangible interface that contains and delivers fragrances [7], [5].

*Speech*
Later in the 18th and 19th-century, the connection between bubbles and their fleeting life become more a motive of parody and it is possible to find many sketches of political satire, from this period, representing bubbles as speech of a politician (meaning something nice but with short life) a tradition that lasted until the 20th-century [6]. Also, a word and shape of 'bubble' were used as a graphic convention describing a imaginary form of speech and thought of characters in comic books.

Inspired from those metaphors of bubble, we propose an interactive art project representing the ephemeral and intangible properties of human's communication. Once speech is shouted out from a speaker, the sound of speech never lasts and it lost its meaning unless there is a listener. Even if the speech is heard by someone, the message will be forgotten as time goes. The shapeless, intangible, and invisible speech is transformed into a semi-tangible yet still insubstantial form of visible bubble. To present this art concept, we created a bubble machine that provides person-to-person and person-to-space interaction. We designed the machine which does not show any intention of bubble machine so that no ones can expect what the purpose of the machine is until they interact with it. The machine has a iris mechanism that varies its outlet size reacting to the participant's speech pattern as if it tries to speak something. Once the participant pauses, a fan inside of the machine generates airflow toward a bubble membrane created on the iris outlet and transforms it to various sizes of bubble. The floating bubble represents the subtle state of a message from interpersonal communications that lies in the middle of real and digital world. Also, it creates a few seconds of delay until it explodes, through which we like to say that it is never possible to have a real-time synchronized communication between two people even in a same space due to the limit of human perceptions. Also, the delay means our behavior that we often intentionally use a delay before sending out text-messages through chatting apps. We share all the details of fabrication process (https://www.instructables.com/id/Bubble-Talk-Turn-Your-Speech-Into-Bubbles/) and materials (https://goo.gl/XJqqoi) so that everyone can be involved to the part of the art installation from their own places. We like to invite all to be an artist through playful interactions.

## Open-source Art Toolkit

*"Art is anything you can get away with."*
*- Andy Warhol*

Through this project, we deliver a message that art can be accessible to anybody from anywhere. We hope that the instructions of fabrication and material make people access to this interactive art installation in their home as well so that not require them necessarily to visit the specific art exhibition place. Also, by inviting them to be engaged to the fabrication process, which is the first start point of the art installation, we wanted make them feel being an artist, and inspire them to use it as a tool for their idea realization whether it is art-oriented or engineering-oriented.

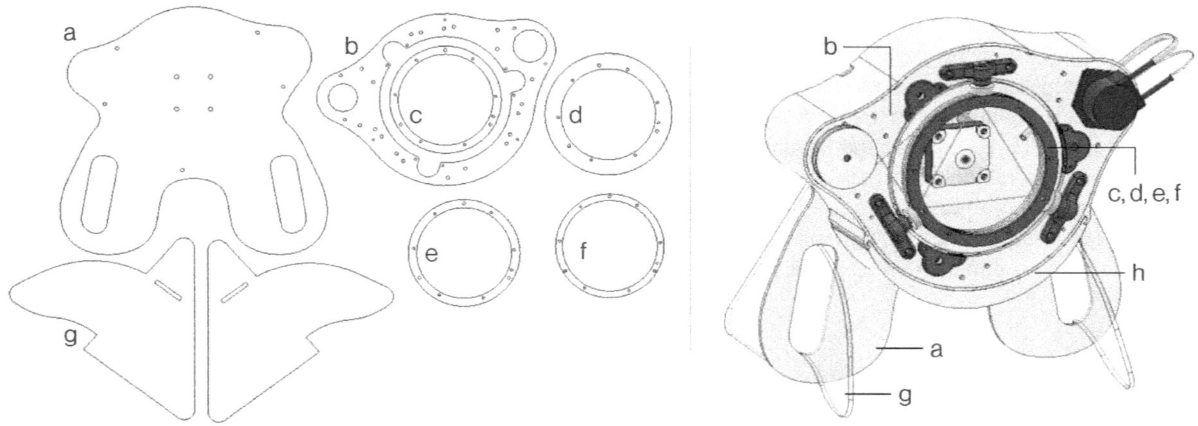


**Figure 4:** CAD model of Bubble Talk machine and drawings for laser cutting. (a) Back plate (b) Front plate (d), (e), (f) Iris rings (g) Support jigs (h) Soap liquid container

*Mechanism*
We wanted to design the machine that can create the surprising moment of audiences by making them hard to guess what the machine does. We did not want to make it looking like so obviously telling "I am ready to blow out bubbles." To let the machine itself can be a kinetic sculpture even without the soap liquid, we built a iris mechanism inspired by the prior work of giant bubble machine [2] which used a CNC machine and metal sheets. We modified it to have a mobile form factor and easy to fabricate using acrylic sheets and 3D printing. By using a string to create a soap membrane, the installation itself provides visual entertainment to audiences. As a servo motor rotate, the string attached to the servo's pulley, the iris made of 3 strings open and close 3. When it fully open, the iris forms a triangular shape with the maximum surface area of soap membrane. The peristaltic motor pump provides soap liquid and make the strings wet when the iris close. As the iris opens, the wet strings create a triangular soap membrane and a fan with a nozzle behind the membrane blows it to create and blow out bubbles. The machine's structural frame (Fig. 4, a) allows the user to hold through its two holes on the leg, and also place on flat surface adding support jig (Fig. 4, g) to the holes.

*Fabrication*
To meet the purpose of an art toolkit for everyone, we tried to use easily accessible material and fabrication tools. we laser-cut a acrylic sheet to create a structure of the Bubble Talk machine as shown on Fig. 4. Other parts that requires strength and certain 3D shapes are 3D printed using a customer level filament-fused or stereolithography 3D printer. For a bubble soap liquid, we followed the Mike's Gooey Mix recipe [9] using baking powder and dish washing liquid. Detailed instruction for building the machine is shared on

the link [1]. Bill of material, schematics of frames for laser cutting, and STL files for 3D printings can be found in the following link [2].

## Interactions and Installation

*Person-to-space*

The bubble machine can be hold and mobile as described in the previous section. For a person-to-space interaction, we allow a participant to grab the machine and move around the exhibition space freely (Fig. 1, right). As he/she is walking around and talking through the machine, it generates bubbles leave them behind of the participant along a line of his/her path.

*Person-to-person*

As shown on the left of Fig. 1, for two people interaction scenario, two Bubble Talk machines can be put on a table facing each other and requires two participants in front of the each machine. Whenever the participant starts to speak to a microphone attached to the back-side of the machine, the iris constantly opens and closes based on the pitch of the voice, which looks like the machine itself tries to talk something having a mouth as iris. Once there is a certain pause of the speech, a fan inside of the machine blows the bubble membrane and create a bubble floating in the mid air. Two people's interactions with the machines create a scene for other audiences that looks like the real world version of digital chatting. The bubbles from the individual machine can meet together and be merged into one bubble or disappeared.

[1] https://www.instructables.com/id/Bubble-Talk-Turn-Your\-Speech-Into-Bubbles/

[2] https://goo.gl/XJqqoi

## Acknowledgements

We thank Prof.Neil Gershenfeld who provided helpful comments and supports on this project.

## REFERENCES

1. Tanja Doring, Axel Sylvester, and Albrecht Schmidt. 2012. Exploring material-centered design concepts for tangible interaction. In *Proceedings of the 2012 ACM annual conference extended abstracts on Human Factors in Computing Systems Extended Abstracts - CHI EA '12*. ACM Press. DOI: http://dx.doi.org/10.1145/2212776.2223666
2. Gordon Kirkwood. 2015. The CNC Bubble Iris: a Computer Controlled Giant Bubble Machine. (2015). https://www.instructables.com/id/CNC-bubble-machine/
3. Kristine Koozin. 1990. *Vanitas Still Lifes of Harmen Steenwyck: Metaphoric Realism (Renaissance Studies, Vol 1)*. Edwin Mellen Pr. https://www.amazon.com/Vanitas-Still-Lifes-Harmen-Steenwyck/dp/0889469490?SubscriptionId=AKIAIOBINVZYXZQZ2U3A&tag=chimbori05-20&linkCode=xm2&camp=2025&creative=165953&creativeASIN=0889469490
4. Thom Kubli. 2012 - 2017. Black Hole Horizon. (2012 - 2017). http://www.thomkubli.de/index.php?/projects/black-hole-horizon/
5. Yutaro Kyono, Takuro Yonezawa, Hiroki Nozaki, Jin Nakazawa, and Hideyuki Tokuda. 2013. FRAGWRAP. In *Proceedings of the 2013 ACM conference on Pervasive and ubiquitous computing adjunct publication - UbiComp '13 Adjunct*. ACM Press. DOI: http://dx.doi.org/10.1145/2494091.2494187

6. Enrico Pezzoli. N/A. History of Bubble Performers, tools & Original Effects. (N/A). https://www.historyofbubbles.com/homo-bulla/

7. Sue Ann Seah, Diego Martinez Plasencia, Peter D. Bennett, Abhijit Karnik, Vlad Stefan Otrocol, Jarrod Knibbe, Andy Cockburn, and Sriram Subramanian. 2014. SensaBubble. In *Proceedings of the 32nd annual ACM conference on Human factors in computing systems - CHI '14*. ACM Press. DOI: http://dx.doi.org/10.1145/2556288.2557087

8. Axel Sylvester, Tanja DÃűring, and Albrecht Schmidt. 2010. Liquids, smoke, and soap bubbles. In *Proceedings of the fourth international conference on Tangible, embedded, and embodied interaction - TEI '10*. ACM Press. DOI: http://dx.doi.org/10.1145/1709886.1709941

9. Soap Bubble Wiki. N/A. Recipes. (N/A). http://soapbubble.wikia.com/wiki/Recipes

10. WikiPedia. N/A. Vanitas. (N/A). https://en.wikipedia.org/wiki/Vanitas

# chromactive —Tangibility of Digital Information as an Interactive, Material Experience

**Ryan Buyssens**
New College of Florida
Sarasota, FL 34243, USA
rbuyssens@ncf.edu


*TEI '19, March 17--20, 2019, Tempe, AZ, USA.*

ACM ISBN 978-1-4503-6196-5/19/03.
DOI: https://doi.org/10.1145/3294109.3301263

## Abstract

Digital information is typically only understood via lengthy explanations or data visualizations. It is my goal to use data to create physical objects that can not only represent the information that was used to create them but also to provide an interaction that can reinforce (or contradict) the core foundation of their creation. Manipulation of design with generative methods to create objects is one possible output. However, with the utilization of interactive technologies, digital information can be output as physical means through the control of objects interactively. This is particularly poignant in the format of an installation where multiples of objects can be controlled via data streams and have additional feedback through user interaction.

My hybridization of materials, techniques and technologies culminates into fabrications that are full of contradictions. At once inviting and intimidating, the mechanisms and intricate designs draw the viewer in for a closer look. However, the interactively triggered movement starts very abruptly, tending to startle the unprepared. Furthermore, the my forms evoke things found in nature (wings, water, etc) that are typically symbols of freedom and lightness but these are secured to the built environment, unable to escape. These hybrids - part animal, part machine - are musings on the consequences of progress, a cyborg possibility.

They are assembled from 3D printed, machined and laser-cut parts so that they appear cold and high-tech, in direct contrast to the organic forms that they animate. They utilize contemporary micro-controller and sensor technology to achieve the interactive abilities that complete their lifelike facade.

Amidst my work, the viewer is no longer a passive viewer but becomes an active participant. The pieces are activated by aspects of the presence of people and an unknowing collaboration occurs – a symbiosis of sorts, between the art and the audience.
Digital is immaterial. It has no connection to the physical world, except by the means that it is translated to us. My work seeks ways to substantiate the digital with translation methods in the form of embedded systems in an attempt to create tangible, meaningful experiences. For instance, using a simple proximity sensor to measure the observable distance of the participant, I translate the measurements into various motor outputs. These motors are connected to numerous apparatus that are very carefully designed for their ability to elicit a unique connection, and therefore an emotional response from participants. The cold, calculating digital technology integrated by my installations is propelled by the anticipation of the unexpected warmth of an emotive experience from the participants. My work becomes a shared sensation - embedded physical computing which serves no purpose other than to arouse or inspire.
In the case of chromactive (Figure 1); the piece purposefully utilizes gentle sweeping movement of gracefully changing, pleasantly vibrant hues - additive wavelengths of pure hue split by motor-mounted dichroic filters. The ambiance of these subtle shifts of color draw in participants and set a generally calming mood about them. As a result, their actions with the piece tend to result in a relaxing, meditative state. The piece changes its rhythm as the participants move about the space in front of it, responding in kind to their presence by recomposing its melody to suit the moment. Its cadence shifts and a new phase occurs; a singular state to a multitude of iterations in constant flux dependent upon the interactions of its participants. Such a strong potential to elicit emotion from participants being driven by the cold precision of digital computation.

**Author Keywords**
Interactive; cyborg; possibility; useless; immaterial; tangible media; shared; participant; sensation.

Figure 1: Chromactive, 2017. The piece uses dichroic filters that are mounted to motors and controlled by a microcontroller that is making sensor readings of the space in front of the artwork. As participants move and interact within the space, the pieces movements change with them. Image by Ryan Buyssens.

# DOOR: Ethnicity in Artificial Intelligence

**Tomas Laurenzo**
School of Creative Media
City University of Hong Kong
18 Tat Hong Avenue
Kowloon Tong, Hong Kong
tomas@laurenzo.net

**Katia Vega**
Department of Design
University of California, Davis
One Shield Avenue
Davis, CA 95616 USA
kvega@ucdavis.edu


*TEI '19*, March 17–20, 2019, Tempe, AZ, USA
ACM 978-1-4503-6196-5/19/03.
https://doi.org/10.1145/3294109.3301262

## Abstract
*DOOR* is an artwork that aims at exposing some of the social and political impact of artificial intelligence, computer vision, and automation. The project uses a commercially available computer vision system that predicts the interactor's ethnicity, and locks or unlocks itself depending on this prediction. The artwork showcases a possible use of computer vision making explicit the fact that every technological implantation crystallises a political worldview.

## Author Keywords
artificial intelligence; computer vision; ethnicity; interactive art;

## CCS Concepts
•**Human-centered computing** → **Human computer interaction (HCI); Human computer interaction (HCI);** *Haptic devices;* **Human computer interaction (HCI);** •**Applied computing** → *Media arts;*

## Introduction
Machine learning (ML) algorithms find complex relationships in data, recognising patterns that humans may not be able to identify, or not know how to formally express for explicit rule–based programming. This allows to create systems with unpredictable, yet somehow controllable behaviour using training datasets. While this dataset–based

control is where its greatest strength resides, it is also very dangerous, for it often introduces biases through over–fitting or under–fitting, and, more importantly, learns biases already existing in the training data. These dangers are even more amplified as these systems are relatively difficult to debug [13].

The translation of biases present in the datasets brings extremely worrying social problems present in the widespread adoption of ML technologies, as these ML–constructed models of information do have an enormous social impact on the technologies they fuel [7].

The social concerns of ML, however, transcend the involuntary transfer of biases present in training data into ML models, and include the direct effects that the insertion of âĂIJintelligentâĂİ systems has in society. For example, AI systems will generate new economic value by changing existent products and services, by creating new ones, as well as by reducing costs through automation. However, it remains to be seen how this will be distributed, a âĂIJkey concern for economic inequality" [2].

The insertion of AI in everyday life has dramatic social implications that have not been explored enough. However, algorithms implemented had already affected minorities: predicting criminal reports in areas with higher proportion of people from racial minorities in Oakland [12]; misunderstanding gender for darker-skin women by popular AI models [4]; police from Israel arrested a man for a wrong translation made by Facebook automatic translation software [6]. Similarly, a system widely used in the US to guide sentencing predicted black defendants have a higher risk of recidivism than white defendants [18].

It is easy to see that ML is used to automate decisions that affect peoples's lives, where systematically biased systems and systems that violate people's rights to privacy are frequently proposed and implemented.

## Background

Race has always played an important role in society. In the United States, for example, the U.S. Office of Management and Budgetapproved the collection of data about ethnicity into the American Census.

The race classification started in 1790 incorporating three categories: Slaves, Free White Females and Males, and Other Free Persons. Currently, six categories are included: White, Black or African American, American Indian or Alaska Native, Asian, Native Hawaiian or Other Pacific Islander, and some other races (multiracial, mixed, interracial, or a Hispanic or Latino group) [9]. The collection of these data is reportedly meant to increase the benefits on education, housing, health, and other programs to groups in need.

For example, a school system might design cultural activities that reflect the diversity in their community, or a business to select the merchandise to sell in a new store. On the other hand, 19 countries out of 41 European countries do not collect data on ethnicity, while some European human rights institutions are requesting to reconsider 'colourblind' statistics [19].

Recent advances in computer vision and artificial intelligence, have allowed the creation of systems able to infer (predict) a information on a person from camera data, including facial recognition, facial expressions, ethnicity, among others [16, 3]. Nowadays, companies like as Affectiva [1], Clarify [5] and Haystack [8] provide image processing services that include these predictions, among several others.

In spite of potential benefits that face recognition proposes,

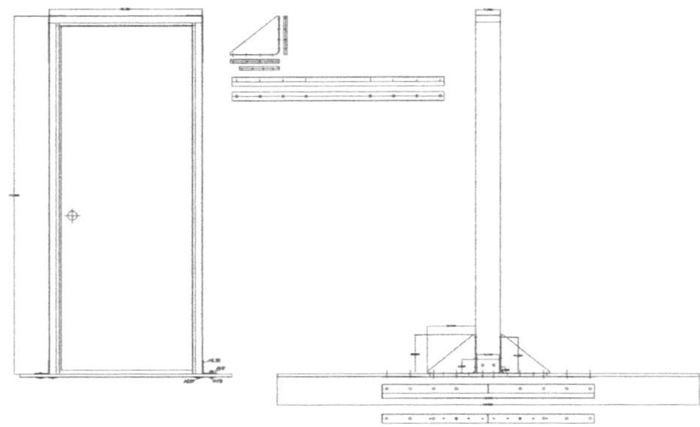

**Figure 1:** *DOOR* schematics.

its widespread application entails several risks, from privacy breaches to systematic discrimination in areas such as hiring, policing, benefits assignment, marketing, and other purposes [14].

## DOOR

*DOOR* (door frame, door, computer, camera, custom software), is an interactive installation consisting of an intelligent door set up in an open area of the exhibition space (see Fig. 2). The piece reflects on the power asymmetries that technology crystallises, aiming at providing with a reflection on the aesthetics of our relationship with it.

*DOOR* also aims at showcasing the advancements and limitations in computer vision and machine learning, allowing the public to experience in person its power as well as its inherent biases.

**Figure 2:** DOOR installation. Work in progress.

*DOOR* embeds a computer vision system that detects and analyses the faces of potential interactors. *DOOR* predicts the interactor's ethnicity in real time and locks or unlocks itself depending on this prediction.

*Implementation*

*DOOR* uses a standard webcam (HD, 30FPS) to acquire data on its interactors. Two different implementations have been created, both running at interactive rates on a 2018 MacBook Pro laptop.

**Figure 3:** Model predicting ethnicity: Latino.

The first uses a deep neural network based on David Sandberg's FaceNet [17], and trained on the UTKFace dataset [20]. UTKFace contains 23,708 faces with five labelled races (White, Black, Asian, Indian, and Others (e.g. Hispanic, Latino, Middle Eastern)).

A second implementation uses Affectiva.ai's pre-trained model run locally [1]. This service classifies the input images also in five different ethnicities (White, Black, South East Asian, Asian, and Latino).

Once the interactor's ethnicity has been predicted by the system, the door is either kept locked or unlocked, using a standard electric strike and a relay controlled by an Arduino Uno microcontroller.

## Conclusion and Future Works

*DOOR* is an artwork that makes tangible the implications of artificial intelligence in society. The piece reflects on the power asymmetries that technology crystallises. It also aims at showcasing the advancements and limitations in

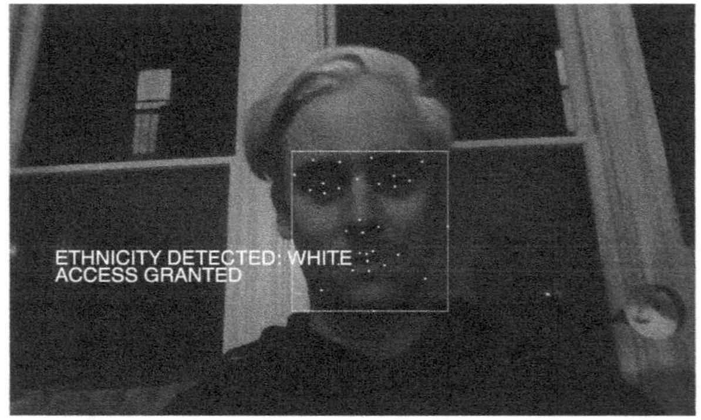


**Figure 4:** Model predicting ethnicity: White.

computer vision, machine learning, and artificial intelligence, allowing the public to experience in person its power as well as its inherent biases.

Not only the current social impact of AI is undeniable, it is also posed to increase enormously. In effect, the ML revolution resides on the discovery that our intuition of what is resoluble by computers was wrong: where we thought a precise formal modelling was necessary, it is now plausible that an âĂIJimplicit modellingâĂİ like the one provided by machine learning will succeed. By using a commercial model, the piece shows the state of the art of ethnicity prediction.

Knowing that âĂIJnovel technologies can be ahead of ethical and political rules and principles,âĂİ [10] it becomes necessary to build tools that help informing the discussions.

Art is intrinsically deregulatory, being able to on its own epistemological framework. Yet, the appropriation and recontextualisation of technology that new media artists perform, situates the practice in a unique position, able to reflect on contemporary political issues by re-articulating the technology helping the audience in their construction of new points of view. Interestingly, in DOOR, the artistic fact exists both when its prediction of ethnicity is accurate and when it fails. The piece simultaneously showcases the potentialities of machine learning, while exploring of the aesthetics of machine learning and interaction.

The authors plan con continue the exploration of these subjects. Future works will include other predictions such as gender, sexual orientation, or emotional state.

## Acknowledgements

The authors thank Stochastic Labs for supporting the development of the project [11]. The work described in this paper partially supported by a grant from the Research Grants Council of the Hong Kong Special Administrative Region, China [Project No. 9042456 (CityU 11674416). We also thank Alejandro Rodriguez [15] for his support.

## References

[1] Affectiva. 2018. Affectiva. https://www.affectiva.com/how/how-it-works/. (2018).

[2] Dean Baker. 2014. Can Productivity Growth Be Used to Reduce Working Time and Improve the Standard of Living of the 99 Percent? The Future of Work in the 21st century. *Economic Analysis Research Network–Future of Work Project* (2014).

[3] Vicki Bruce and Andy Young. 1986. Understanding face recognition. *British journal of psychology* 77, 3 (1986), 305–327.

[4] Joy Buolamwini and Timnit Gebru. 2018. Gender shades: Intersectional accuracy disparities in commercial gender classification. In *Conference on Fairness, Accountability and Transparency*. 77–91.

[5] Clarifai. 2018. Clarifai Demographics Model. https://clarifai.com/models/. (2018).

[6] Sam Corbett-Davies, Emma Pierson, Avi Feller, Sharad Goel, and Aziz Huq. 2017. Algorithmic decision making and the cost of fairness. In *Proceedings of the 23rd ACM SIGKDD International Conference on Knowledge Discovery and Data Mining*. ACM, 797–806.

[7] Kate Crawford. 2016. Artificial intelligenceâĂŹs white guy problem. *The New York Times* 25 (2016).

[8] Haystack.ai. 2018. Haystack. https://www.haystack.ai/. (2018).

[9] Karen R Humes, Nicholas A Jones, and Roberto R Ramirez. 2011. Overview of race and Hispanic origin: 2010. (2011).

[10] David Sun Kong and Nicole Bakker. 2018. Community driven design of living technologies. In *Proceedings of the 15th Participatory Design Conference: Short Papers, Situated Actions, Workshops and Tutorial-Volume 2*. ACM, 47.

[11] Stochastic Labs. 2018. Stochastic Labs âĂŞ Seed funds and collaborative community. http://stochasticlabs.org/. (2018).

[12] Kristian Lum and William Isaac. 2016. To predict and serve? *Significance* 13, 5 (2016), 14–19.

[13] Anh Nguyen, Jason Yosinski, and Jeff Clune. 2015. Deep neural networks are easily fooled: High confidence predictions for unrecognizable images. In *Proceedings of the IEEE Conference on Computer Vision and Pattern Recognition*. 427–436.

[14] Future of Privacy Forum. 2017. Unfairness y Algorithm: Distilling the Harms of Automated Desicion-Making. https://fpf.org/wp-content/uploads/2017/12/FPF-Automated-Decision-Making-Harms-and-Mitigation-Charts.pdf. (2017).

[15] Alex Dogrush Rodriguez. 2018. Alex Rodriguez. http://dogrush.com. (2018).

[16] Ashok Samal and Prasana A Iyengar. 1992. Automatic recognition and analysis of human faces and facial expressions: A survey. *Pattern recognition* 25, 1 (1992), 65–77.

[17] David Sandberg. 2017. Face recognition using tensorflow. *Läst [2018-11-20]. URL: https://github.com/davidsandberg/facenet* (2017).

[18] New Scientist. 2018. How Google and Facebook hooked us and how to break the habit. https://www.newscientist.com/article/mg23731640-500-how-google-and-facebook-hooked-us-and-how-to-break-the-habit/. (2018).

[19] Patrick Simon. 2012. Collecting ethnic statistics in Europe: a review. *Ethnic and Racial Studies* 35, 8 (2012), 1366–1391.

[20] Song Yang Zhang, Zhifei and Hairong Qi. 2017. Age Progression/Regression by Conditional Adversarial Autoencoder. In *IEEE Conference on Computer Vision and Pattern Recognition (CVPR)*. IEEE.

# Transference: A Hybrid Computational System for Improvised Violin Performance

**Dr. Seth Dominicus Thorn**
School of Arts, Media + Engineering
Arizona State University
Tempe, Arizona 85281
seth.thorn@asu.edu

## Abstract

*Transference* is a hybrid computational system for improvised violin performance. With hardware sensors and digital signal processing (DSP), the system shapes live acoustic input and computer-generated sound. An electromyographic (EMG) sensor unobtrusively monitors movements of the left hand, while a custom glove controller tracks bowing gestures of the right arm. Through continuous musical gesture the performer is able to actuate and perturb streams of computationally transmuted audio. No additional layers of windowing or semantically-inflected processes of machine learning mediate this process. Remaining at the level of signal processing, the lack of windowed and/or statistical mediation creates a sense of fine-grain tactility and physical transduction for the performer. The strategies employed are sufficiently generalizable to apply to situations beyond those imagined and implemented here within the scope of augmented violin performance.

## Author Keywords

sensors; movement and computing; violin; augmented violin; gesture; performance; interaction design; sonic interaction; electronic music; live audio; digital signal processing.


ACM ISBN 978-1-4503-6196-5/19/03.
https://doi.org/10.1145/3294109.3301254

Figure 1: A performance with the earlier version of the system, *Windowless*, at iStage, Arizona State University, January 2018.

Figure 2: Presentation of the alto.glove at the Guthman Musical Instrument Competition, Georgia Institute of Technology, March 2018.

Figure 3: Performing at the New York City Electroacoustic Musical Festival (NYCEMF), July 2018.

## Conference Themes

*Transference* responds to the following conference themes:

- Hybrid assemblies of digital and physical systems
- Wearable computing
- Novel interactions in traditional musicianship
- Human augmentation
- Hybrid music performance

## Introduction

*Transference* is a real-time computational system for improvised violin performance. It consists of an ensemble of hardware and software, including a custom sensor glove, the alto.glove; a Myo Gesture Control Armband from Thalamic Labs with EMG sensors and an inertial measurement unit (IMU); and DSP implemented in Max MSP and Max for Live (M4L). The alto.glove utilizes an IMU and flex sensors to extend traditional performance gestures related to bowing movements of the right arm. The glove also houses pressure sensors allowing voluntary actuation within the limited spare "bandwidth" of the violinist's right hand and fingers during performance [1]. With the addition of the Myo Armband on the left forearm, which unobtrusively tracks dynamics of the left hand, the system builds on an earlier iteration of the system, *Windowless*.

In my previous system, *Windowless*, feature extraction and DSP were implemented in Max MSP and compiled into several applications that communicate using the Open Sound Control (OSC) network protocol. In the present version, I have redesigned the system to work inside M4L, an audio programming environment existing within the Ableton Live software. This makes available a large variety of quickly accessed, programmable, high quality audio processing effects. The goal is not only to speed up the programming process by bypassing more fundamental framework-building stages, but also to implement my system in a way that is more flexible—not only for the drag-and-drop modularity of Ableton Live, but also so that other performers may eventually try out the system as well. Moreover, I would like to know if such a "hypertelic" situation as an augmented violin played by an expert performer—that is, a situation of excessively focused adaptation—doesn't offer some insight that might be applied more generally to sonic interaction design, or to broader eco-systemic scenarios involving physical computing.

## Methodology & Motivation

I evaluate the progressive iterations of my performance system on the basis of their fecundity for playful improvisation. Such evaluations take place more or less immediately, with production and coupling of gestural descriptors and sound design occurring simultaneously. Questions to ask will include: is the system a good catalyzer? Does it promote continuous development in performance? Is it complex without being complicated? Are its kinesics learnable/reproducible but not overly simplistic? Does it prompt improvisatory exploration that is not completely imagined in advance of the system, in spite of the hardness of its code?

Much has been written about the native dimension (and boon) of a musical instrument's "resistance," along with

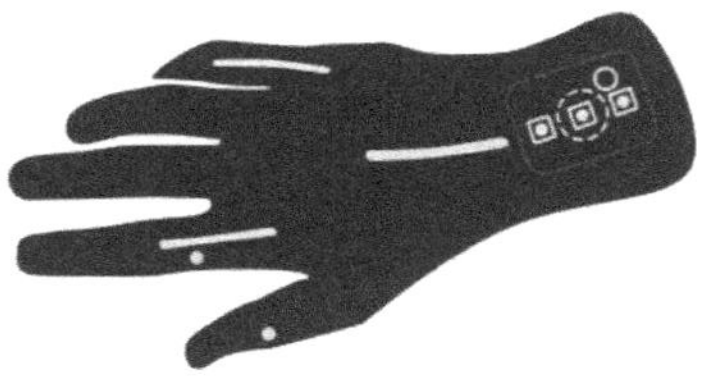

Figure 4: Functional diagram of the alto.glove. Flex sensors are installed on the wrist, index finger, and pinky. A 9-axis motion sensor is located inside the PCB. Haptic feedback is available. Three momentary contact buttons are available, along with two force-sensitive resistors located on the inside of the index finger and thumb to allow quick triggering of events between performance gestures.

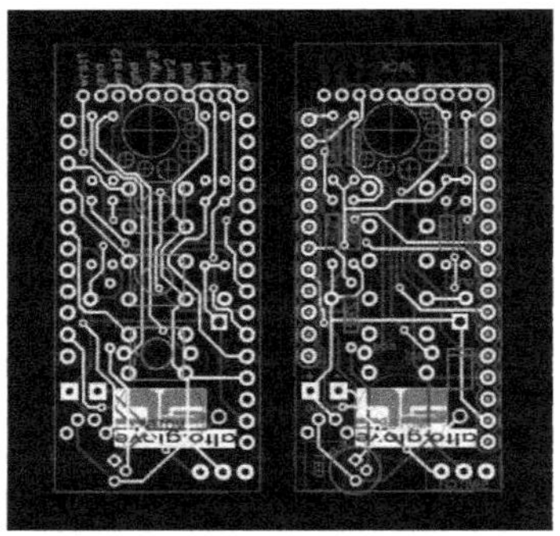

Figure 5: Alto.glove PCB schematic developed with the DipTrace software. The board is designed as a shield for the Feather M0 WiFi development board produced by Adafruit.

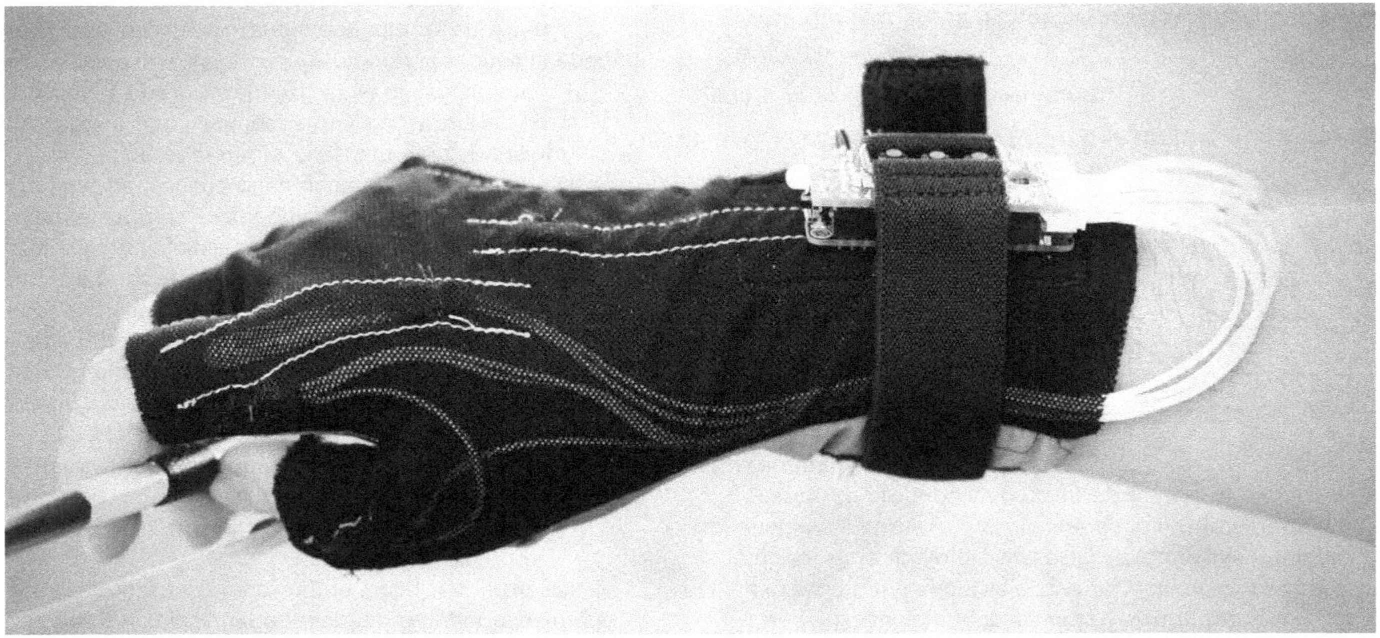

Figure 6: The alto.glove is designed to track motions of violin playing without interfering with the natural bow grip.

its conceptual implications for the cybernetic project of eliminating the computer's interface [3]. In creative contexts, a transparent interface tends to impoverish the performative possibilities. Improvising musicians seeking to revive their practices can turn to physical manipulation of their instruments as a means of renewing this resistance. I have found that hyperbolizing the sense of tactility in my system by avoiding statistical, windowing-based, or semantically-inflected procedures yields fertile ground for improvised performance [5]. This also means that I describe my system at the level of signal processing rather than in terms of musical percepts and higher-level semantics.

## Hyperinstruments

I therefore distinguish my efforts here from the "hyperinstruments" project for virtuoso musicians [4]. Despite much remarkable and well-conceived hardware, the lives of these instruments tend to be short, as their software substrates are conditioned for specific performance contexts, compositions, and use with score-following systems. Coupled to such specificities and virtuosic presuppositions, hyperinstruments lay out the performance possibilities entirely in advance, presupposing the performer's abilities vis-à-vis an already concrete performance tradition.

Figure 7: Inside PCB, showing haptic motor, Adafruit motion sensor breakout board using an ST Micro LSM9DS0, addressable RGB LED, and Molex Microblade connector.

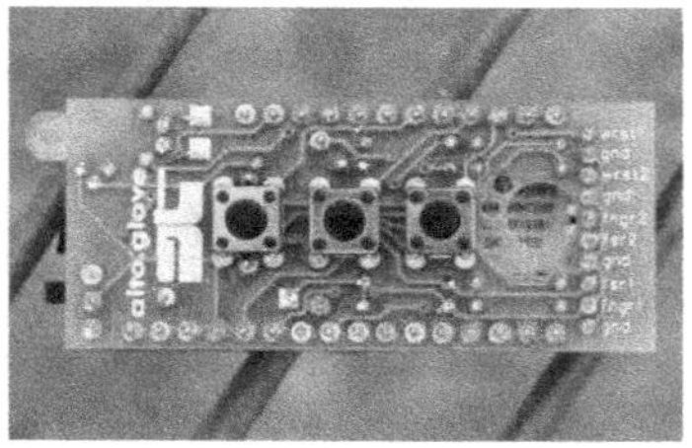

Figure 8: Top of PCB, showing three momentary contact buttons.

By contrast, *Transference* is not a performance piece (coupled to a score), but a continuously responsive audio environment. By means of the added hardware, the goal is to allow the performer to "touch," through musical gestures, streams of computationally transformed audio generated by the violin itself as well as the computer. This contact is direct—or as direct as it can be. No machine learning is used. Movement of the left and right arms, as well as the muscles of the left forearm, inform the audio streams, actuating and/or perturbing them. In this way, the system is already much less hypertelic than a hyperinstrument, yet it establishes no ceiling on violinistic virtuosity.

## Tangibility and Embodiment

As I have noted, alteration of a musical instrument's dynamics can be motivated by an interest in shoring up imaginative resources for creative improvisation. As Aden Evens remarks, "generation of resistance is essential to creative improvisation; the body must be made to feel awkward in relation to the instrument, the known must be un-known" [4]. Recently described models of body-centered auditory feedback suggest that this principle is relevant to the way individuals experience their own bodies. Ana Tajadura-Jiménez and Frédéric Bevilacqua have demonstrated that precise manipulation of auditory cues can alter the action-perception feedback loops that constitute an individual's proprioceptive sense of embodiment [6]. Nevertheless, a fine-grain temporal response is enough to create effectively tangible media, even when operating outside of the narrow interval in which psychoacoustic effects create more dramatic sensations. What happens to high-level musicianship when augmented with a tactile-like, hybrid framework?

## Signal Processing

By means of a simple software framework and thoughtfully implemented hardware, *Transference* derives relatively specific features of violin playing—or better, violinistic movement—without statistical processes. Data from the alto.glove is streamed to the computer via WiFi. The UDP packets are received in M4L, then calibrated and scaled. The Myo Sensor is connected via Bluetooth to the Myo Armband Manager program. The Myo Mapper software is used to stream IMU and scaled EMG sensor data via OSC into M4L [2]. Two M4L "audio effect" devices perform feature extraction and allow selective application of the output to real-time audio processes in Ableton Live. Multiple instances of these devices are used in the Ableton Live session to produce a complex sonic field of dynamically varying intensities.

Figure 9: The alto.glove M4L device.

### *Alto.glove Module*

With the IMU of the alto.glove positioned just below the wrist, the gyroscopic z- and x-axes generate metrics related to bowing velocity and string crossing technique, respectively [7]. Flex sensors on the pinky and wrist provide information about the continuous position of the bow in the hand and extension of the

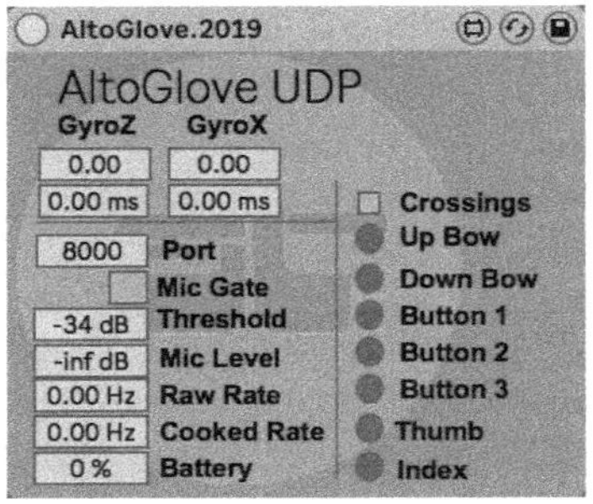


Figure 10: M4L device that connects to the alto.glove, "cooks" the input, and makes it available through global send/receive pairs.

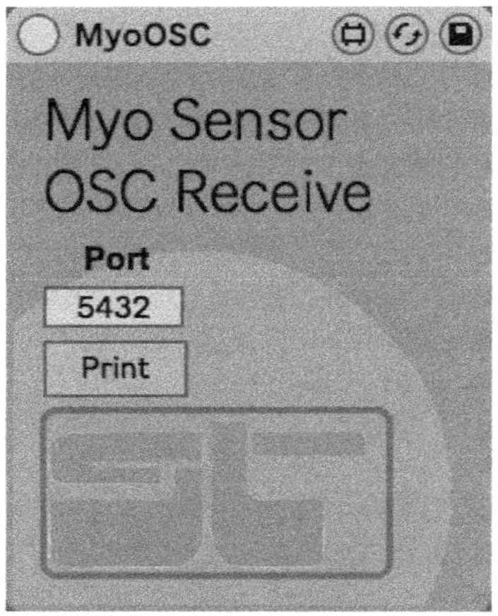


Figure 11: The M4L device that receives the cooked output from the Myo Mapper application.

arm. Low-level metrics such as these are convolved in different ways with other features. For instance, the sign of the gyroscopic z-axis is applied to the amplitude envelope read from the microphone, yielding an interesting metric that avoids requiring a determinate threshold value for audio gating. Another use for the gyroscopic z-axis is to start a timer when the sign changes, indicating the duration of a particular bow stroke. Pitch, roll, and an acceleration metric can also be used. Conveniently, given the placement of the IMU, pitch describes the extension of the right arm in violin playing; roll indicates the string being played.

The performer begins by choosing one of the parameters available in the alto.glove module. Since both unipolar and bipolar values are available, it can be determined how these should behave. Scaling, clipping, smoothing, and morphological transformations that invert the signal or reshape it may be utilized. The resulting signal can be used to actuate and control the amplitude of various transformations of the audio signal from the violin (audio delay, granulation, spectral "freeze"). In addition, the resulting signal can be assigned to any other audio parameter, resulting in interesting parameter linkages.

*Alto.glove Tuning Example: Broad String Crossings*
To generate a signal based on broad string crossings—quick, continuous rolling of the bow across three or four strings of the violin—the gyroscopic x-axis is selected, which reflects radial movement of the forearm. Bipolar input is selected, and low input values clipped. To generate a string crossing "mode" with hysteresis, the decay ramp can be slowed. For a unique signal, the initial bipolar signal can be clipped to unipolar. When combined with a low decay value, the result is a response to string crossings in only one direction. This produces an auditory result with a great sense of tactile immediacy and responsiveness for the performer.

*Alto.glove Tuning Example: Pizzicato*
When the bow is grasped for pizzicato (plucking the strings directly with one's fingers), the pinky wraps around the stick. Rather than hard-coding this threshold, the "pizzicato state" can be generated by appropriate tuning of the alto.glove module. First, the correct flex sensor is selected. A "pulse" wave is selected in the morphology settings, and the "peak offset" adjusted to the appropriate level, generating a binary signal. By implementing pizzicato recognition within this broader framework—as opposed to hard coding it—it is possible to experiment with unusual permutations, such as adding a decay that causes the "on" signal to linger after a normal bow hold is resumed. Any "tuned" feature can be skewed in this way, which in turn skews the continuous auditory physics of violin playing. Thus, the system is rife for continuous, prodding experimentation.

*Myo Sensor Module*
The Myo Sensor module employs a framework similar the alto.glove module, but is simpler. It tracks two types of movement. The first is the activity of the fingers, which is generated by a scaled, moving average taken from one of the eight available EMG sensors. The second is the flexion of the left elbow monitored by one of the axes of the gyroscope. This provides information about shifting between lower and higher positions on the violin as well as intensity of vibrato. One or both of these features can be scaled, smoothed, and mapped to audio gating or other audio parameters outside the module.

Figure 12: Myo Gesture Control Armband made by Thalamic Labs. The armband holds eight EMG sensors as well as an IMU.

## Sonic Composition

A performance with *Transference* requires creating an Ableton Live session with multiple audio tracks with instances of either the alto.glove module or the Myo Sensor module. Global presets are stored in an M4L module and cycled through during performance by engaging a pressure sensor on the alto.glove. In addition to audio modulated by sensor input, I have also created several M4L devices that respond to audio input alone. These devices produce a slow-moving, particulate, spatial-textural foundation of looping and delayed audio samples. The result is a percolating background from which the more gesturally-inflected, human-scale perturbations captured by the hardware components stand in stark contrast.

## Conclusion

The mapping paradigm I suggest here favors immediate auditory feedback as a means of increasing the performative power of the system. With machine learning, by contrast, it is not the violinist who sculpts the sound with gesture, but the mediating "hand" of the computer. This intrudes on the immediacy sought in that tight perceptual feedback loop by which improvisation becomes its own source of creative induction, reassembling the performer's craft by keeping up with it in real time with maximum auditory and tactile responsivity. The simple paradigm presented here offers a straightforward solution to work alongside, rather than against, the infinite degrees of freedom of the bowed string. Other wearable technologies can benefit from a fine-grain temporal response, hyperbolizing the sense of tactility across gestural media.

## Documentation

Relevant video documentation can be viewed at https://vimeo.com/297490623

## References

[1] Perry Cook. 2001. Principles for Designing Computer Music Controllers. In *Proceedings of the CHI'01 Workshop on New Interfaces for Musical Expression, 3-6.*

[2] Balandino Di Donato, Jamie Bullock, Atau Tanaka. Myo Mapper: A Myo Armband to OSC Mapper. In *Proceedings of the 2011 Conference on New Interfaces for Musical Expression* (NIME '18), 138-143.

[3] Aden Evens. 2005. *Sound Ideas: Music, Machines, and Experience*. University of Minnesota Press, Minneapolis, MN.

[4] Tod Machover. 1992. Hyperinstruments: A Composer's Approach to the Evolution of Intelligent Musical Instruments. In *Cyberarts: Exploring Arts and Technology*. Linda Jacobson (Ed.). Miller Freeman Inc., San Francisco, CA, 67-76.

[5] Sha Xin Wei. 2002. Resistance is Fertile: Gesture and Agency in the Field of Responsive Media. *Configurations* 10, 3: 439-472.

[6] Ana Tajadura-Jiménez, Aleksander Väljamäe, Frédéric Bevilacqua, and Nadia Bianchi-Berthouze. 2017. Principles for Designing Body-Centered Auditory Feedback. In *The Wiley Handbook of Human Computer Interaction*. Kent L. Norman and Jurek Kirakowski (Eds.). John Wiley & Sons Ltd., Chichester, UK, 371-403.

[7] Seth Dominicus Thorn. 2018. Alto.glove: New Techniques for Augmented Violin. In *Proceedings of the 2018 Conference on New Interfaces for Musical Expression* (NIME '18), 334-339.

# The Hybrid Body and Sonic-Cyborg Performance in *Why Should Our Bodies End at the Skin?*

**Aurie Hsu**
Technology in Music and Related Arts (TIMARA)
Oberlin Conservatory
Oberlin, OH 44074, USA
ahsu@oberlin.edu

**Steven Kemper**
Mason Gross School of the Arts
Rutgers, The State University of New Jersey
New Brunswick, NJ 08901, USA
skemper@mgsa.rutgers.edu


*TEI '19*, March 17–20, 2019, Tempe, AZ, USA

ACM ISBN 978-1-4503-6196-5/19/03.
https://doi.org/10.1145/3294109.3301255

## Abstract
In "A Cyborg Manifesto," Donna Haraway describes how by the late twentieth century, humans have become hybridized with machines. While society has long been concerned with the ever-growing encroachment of technology into human activity, Haraway challenges this concern, proposing instead a kinship between organism and machine. The result is the cyborg, a hybrid body that fluidly transcends mechanical and organic boundaries. *Why Should Our Bodies End at the Skin?* for sensor-equipped dancer, robotic percussion, sound exciters, and live sound processing, explores these ideas of intersectionality and fluidity between organism and machine by connecting human action and mechanical tasks. This paper describes the creative framework and associated technologies involved in the development of the piece.

## Author Keywords
Interactive performance; hybrid body; wearable interface; sensors; robotics; dance; electroacoustic music; sonic-cyborg performance.

## CCS Concepts
• Human-centered computing~Sound-based input / output; • Applied computing~Performing arts;

## Introduction

In her essay "A Cyborg Manifesto," [3] Donna Haraway explores implications of the increasing hybridization of humans and machines. Summarizing this position, Haraway states, "Late twentieth-century machines have made thoroughly ambiguous the difference between natural and artificial, mind and body, self-developing and externally designed, and many other distinctions that used to apply to organisms and machines" [4].

While society has been concerned with the ever-growing encroachment of technology into human activity, most recently the development of artificial intelligence and robotics [11], Haraway challenges this concern, proposing instead a kinship between organism and machine. In a broad sense, this kinship suggests hybrid bodies, raising questions about embodiment in our contemporary techno-culture where the lines between organism and machine are fluid. Are kinship and unity the goal of this hybridity? How does kinship dissolve boundaries between organism and machine? As Haraway asks, "Why should our bodies end at the skin?" [6].

*Why Should Our Bodies End at the Skin?* (2018) for dancer, Remote electroAcoustic Kinesthetic Sensing (RAKS) system, the Configurable Automatic Drumming Instrument (CADI), sound exciters, and live sound processing, explores hybridization of organism and machine. This piece realizes the capability of the hybrid body in performance, sonically connecting mechanized human movement and humanized robotic action. The performance enacts Haraway's idea of a "cyborg world" consisting of "lived social and bodily realities in which people are not afraid of their joint kinship with animals and machines" [5]. In this paper, the authors describe their approach to enacting a sonic-cyborg performance, which includes development of the RAKS system, embodied movement-to-sound mapping strategies, and human-robot interaction.

## Background

Both sensor technologies and robotics enable humans to interact with computer-mediated systems. Sensor technologies connect human action and machine tasks [9]. Robots are often designed to complete human tasks; their motions reflect a mechanical abstraction of human movement [1]. To realize the hybrid body in performance, *Why Should Our Bodies End at the Skin?* integrates two performance systems developed by the authors: the Remote electroAcoustic Kinesthetic Sensing (RAKS) system, a wearable wireless sensor interface designed specifically for belly dance movement, and the Configurable Automatic Drumming Instrument (CADI), a modular robotic percussion battery designed to be mounted on microphone stands and positioned to hit any object.

## Remote electroAcoustic Kinesthetic Sensing (RAKS) system

The RAKS system is an Arduino-based wearable wireless sensor interface designed by the authors (Figure 1). "RAKS" is a play on the Arabic term, *Raqs Sharqi* (Middle Eastern dance). The RAKS system consists of a corset and a lightweight belt with sensors, a LilyPad Arduino, and an XBee radio sewn into it. Sensors capture the dancer's movement and transmit the data wirelessly to a computer running Max software over a point to point network. The system is modular, and different sensors can be incorporated for different performances. The sensors used in *Why Should Our Bodies End at the Skin?* include a flex sensor in the corset and an accelerometer on the belt. The system also includes two programmable LED rings sewn into the corset that take data from the accelerometer in order to visualize the dancer's movements.

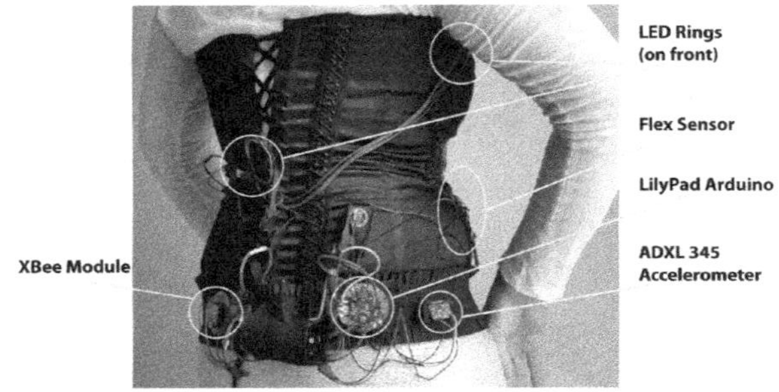


**Figure 1**: Remote electroAcoustic Kinesthetic Sensing (RAKS) system.

## Configurable Automatic Drumming Instrument (CADI)

CADI is a solenoid-driven, robotic percussion battery (Figure 2). The 3D printed striking arms are designed to hold a variety of beaters and are mounted on microphone stands, making it easy to position the beaters to hit a variety of different instruments. CADI is controlled via MIDI, and velocity messages control the solenoids' on-times, affecting the striking force and allowing for dynamic control. CADI was originally designed by Steven Kemper, Troy Rogers, and Scott Barton of Expressive Machines Musical Instruments (EMMI), with the iteration used in *Why Should Our Bodies End at the Skin?* designed by Kemper at Rutgers University.

**Figure 2**: Configurable Automatic Drumming Instrument (CADI).

## Embodied Mapping Strategies

Movement vocabulary from contemporary belly dance serves as the foundation for designing the RAKS system. Torso waves, controlled hip isolations, and upper and lower body layering are a few characteristics of this movement. These movements influence the design and functionality of the RAKS system including the hardware, sensors, and costume architecture. To this end, the flex sensor is placed near the chest and torso, and the accelerometer is placed on the hips to optimize movement capture. Table 1 summarizes the movement vocabulary and corresponding design features on the RAKS system. Mapping strategies engage an embodied, kinesonic perspective [7, 8] as movement serves to trigger, generate, and alter sonic material. Integrating movement with sound production, the "body becomes the instrument" [10] and the dancer inhabits a "sonic body" [2].

| Movement Vocabulary | Body Movement | Qualitative Description | RAKS System Design Feature |
|---|---|---|---|
| wave | torso | continuous, down-to-up/up-to-down | flex sensor |
| rotation | chest, hip | circular motion | flex sensor |
| figure-8 (vertical/horizontal) | torso, chest, hip | continuous, isolated | flex sensor accelerometer |
| isolations | chest, hip | quick, slow, sharp, smooth | accelerometer |
| layering | upper/lower body | smooth/sharp, isolated | flex sensor accelerometer (each sends separate data) |

**Table 1**: Movement vocabulary and RAKS system design.

**Figure 3**: *Why Should Our Bodies End at the Skin?* in performance.

## Sonic-Cyborg Performance

The performance of *Why Should Our Bodies End at the Skin?* features a dancer equipped with the RAKS system, CADI, sound exciters actuating both drums and shaken percussion, and electroacoustic textures created from processed mechanical sounds. To blur the boundaries between organism and machine, the percussion instruments encircle the dancer, serving as a visual and sonic extension of the body. The choreography reflects the mechanical nature of robotic movement using isolations and body locks, while CADI produces a visual and sonic echo of this movement through rhythmic and sustained textures.

The RAKS system is used to translate the dancer's movement into sonic control in a variety of ways, including triggering CADI's attacks and varying the dynamics, panning sound events within the semicircular field of the setup, and processing the electroacoustic texture. A feedback loop emerges between the dancer's movements and CADI's mechanical actions, calling into question whether the human is controlling the machine or the machine is controlling the human.

The piece consists of three overarching motivic ideas. The beginning of the piece builds through a series of accumulating textural layers. Contrasting rhythmic sections reference the drum solo, a Middle Eastern musical form consisting of a fast-tempo virtuosic improvisation where the lines between leader and follower are indistinguishable.

In the final section, the dancer's actions intertwine with the machine, which itself begins to break down. The dancer plays the drums along with CADI, which plays a series of increasingly irregular and accelerating loops. The piece ends with the dancer resting drumsticks on the floor toms. The sound exciters mounted to these drums resonate, causing the drumsticks to vibrate on the drum heads. This creates a physical and sonic connection between the dancer's body and the electromechanically-actuated acoustic instruments.

## Reflections

Performance systems based on sensors and robotics enable a human performer to step into the role of cyborg—merging movement with the actions of a machine. By exploring the performative possibilities of this type of extended system, we have attempted to recontextualize negative implications of a hybrid body. In this sense, we actualize Haraway's notion of a kinship between organism and machine, exploring a world where the cyborg does not represent an inevitable march towards the technological singularity, but rather an evolving, creative body.

## Video URL

https://www.youtube.com/watch?v=LtGJQsaXzd8

## References

[1] Cynthia Breazeal and Brian Scassellati. 2002. Robots that imitate humans. *Trends in Cognitive Sciences* 6, 11: 481–487. https://doi.org/10.1016/S1364-6613(02)02016-8

[2] Tomie Hahn and Curtis Bahn. 2002. Pikapika – the collaborative composition of an interactive sonic character. *Organised Sound* 7, 3: 229–238. https://doi.org/10.1017/S1355771802003023

[3] Donna Haraway. 1991. "A Cyborg Manifesto: Science, Technology, and Socialist-Feminism in the Late Twentieth Century," in *Simians, Cyborgs and Women: The Reinvention of Nature*. Routledge.

[4] Ibid., 152.

[5] Ibid., 154.

[6] Ibid., 178.

[7] Aurie Hsu and Steven Kemper. 2015. Kinesonic Approaches to Mapping Movement and Music with the Remote electroAcoustic Kinesthetic Sensing (RAKS) system. In *Proceedings of the 2nd International Workshop on Movement and Computing* (MOCO '15). ACM, New York, NY, USA, 45-47. DOI=http://dx.doi.org/10.1145/2790994.2791020

[8] Aurie Hsu and Steven Kemper. 2015. Kinesonic Composition as Choreographed Sound: Composing Gesture in Sensor-Based Music. In *Proceedings of the 2015 International Computer Music Conference*. University of North Texas, Denton, TX, 412-415.

[9] O. D. Lara and M. A. Labrador. 2013. A Survey on Human Activity Recognition using Wearable Sensors. *IEEE Communications Surveys Tutorials* 15, 3: 1192–1209. https://doi.org/10.1109/SURV.2012.110112.00192

[10] G.-W. Raes. 2012. Namuda Studies: Doppler Radar-Based Gesture Recognition for the Control of a Music Robot Orchestra. www.logosfoundation.org/ii/Namuda_JIM_paper.doc. Accessed November 5, 2018.

[11] Aaron Smith and Janna Anderson. 2014. AI, Robotics, and the Future of Jobs. Retrieved November 6, 2018 from http://www.pewinternet.org/2014/08/06/future-of-jobs/

# Physically Colliding with Music: Full-body Interactions with an Audio-only Virtual Reality Interface

**Raul Altosaar**
Integrated Media
OCAD University
Toronto, ON M5T 1W1 Canada
3148968@student.ocadu.ca

**Adam Tindale**
Associate Professor
Digital Futures
OCAD University
Toronto, ON M5T 1W1 Canada
atindale@faculty.ocadu.ca

**Judith Doyle**
Associate Professor
Integrated Media
Co-Director, SMACLab
OCAD University
Toronto, ON M5T 1W1 Canada
jdoyle@faculty.ocadu.ca


*TEI '19*, March 17–20, 2019, Tempe, AZ, USA

ACM ISBN 978-1-4503-6196-5/19/03.
https://doi.org/10.1145/3294109.3301256

## Abstract

*A Very Real Looper (AVRL)* is an audio-only virtual reality (VR) interface inside of which a performer triggers and controls music through full-body movement. Contrary to how musical interfaces in VR are normally used, a performer using *AVRL* is not disconnected from their surrounding environment through immersion, nor is their body restrained by a head-mounted display. Rather, *AVRL* utilizes two VR sensors and the Unity game engine to map virtual musical sounds onto physical objects in the real world. These objects help the performer locate the sounds. Using two handheld VR controllers, these sounds can be triggered, looped, acoustically affected, or repositioned in space. *AVRL* thus combines the affordances of the physical world and a VR system with the reconfigurability of a game engine. This integration results in an expansive and augmented performance environment that facilitates full-body musical interactions.

## Author Keywords

Audio-only virtual reality; full-body interactions; augmented musical performance; virtual musical interfaces; new interfaces for musical expression.

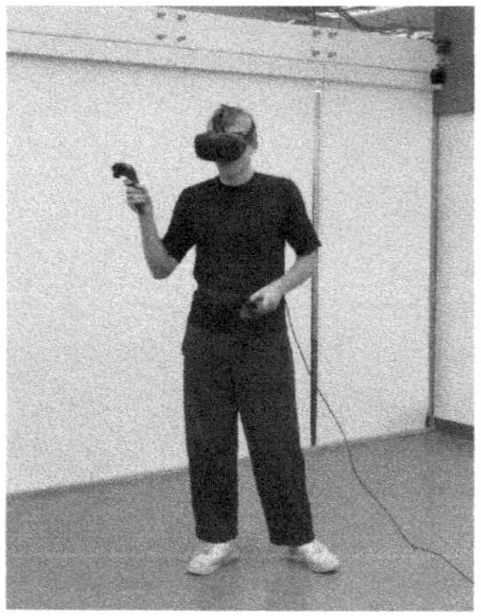

Figure 1 – A standard use of a VR system: an immersed user wears a head-mounted display and interacts with a visually simulated environment using handheld controllers. Photo by Raul Altosaar, ©2018.

Figure 2 - A standard use of an AR system: a visual interface overlays computer-generated imagery on top of real-world imagery. "Border Memorial" by John Craig Freeman is licensed under CC BY-SA 3.0.

## CCS Concepts

• **Human-centered computing~Virtual reality;** auditory feedback; gestural input;
• **Applied computing~Sound and music computing;** performing arts;

## Conference Themes

*AVRL* responds to the following conference themes:

- Performances (e.g. dance, physical performance, music) that explore or utilize hybrid systems
- Hybrid assemblies that combine digital, physical, biological, and/or social systems
- Novel interactions realized through traditional crafts or unconventional materials, professional artistry, craft or musicianship

## Introduction

When considered in the context of musical performance, current VR systems are alienating because they inhibit the immersed performer from developing a connection to the audience and surrounding space. These systems are also awkward because they rely on a head-mounted display (see Figure 1) that impedes expressive, full-body musical interactions.

Augmented reality (AR) systems suffer from similar problems. Much research in this field is concentrated on predominantly visual interfaces that may neglect other sensory modalities [1] and their expressive affordances. These interfaces are also small and exist either on smartphone screens (see Figure 2) or in head-mounted displays. By design, these interfaces encourage specific types of interaction in which users remain relatively immobile and utilize the interface from a fixed viewpoint.

In the context of musical performance these are undesirable interaction paradigms that hinder full-body musical interactions that build upon a performer's understanding of and connection to the everyday world, their own bodies, the surrounding environment, and other people [2].

However, there is reason to continue investigating the application of VR and AR systems for musical performance. First, these systems provide inexpensive, real-time motion tracking that can be leveraged to design novel musical interactions. Second, VR and AR systems allow virtual data to be overlaid on top of the real world, thus enabling a musical performance to be spatially and acoustically augmented. Furthermore, when building VR and AR musical interfaces inside of a game engine, digital assets such as sound files and MIDI sequences become highly reconfigurable. This makes rapid-prototyping and musical ideation possible without additional material or hardware costs.

We hypothesized that the affordances of a VR system can mitigate its hindrances in the context of musical performance.

## Related work

Gibson's *Opto-Photo-Kinesia* is an audio-visual performance in which infrared trackers are worn by a performer and used to control audio effects, trigger musical sounds, and effect lighting changes [4]. Similarly to how the handheld VR controllers function in *AVRL,* these infrared trackers track user position and velocity in 3D space. This enables the performer to interface with musical elements through bodily movement. Mäki-Patola, et. al describe four musical instruments developed to assess VR technology in the

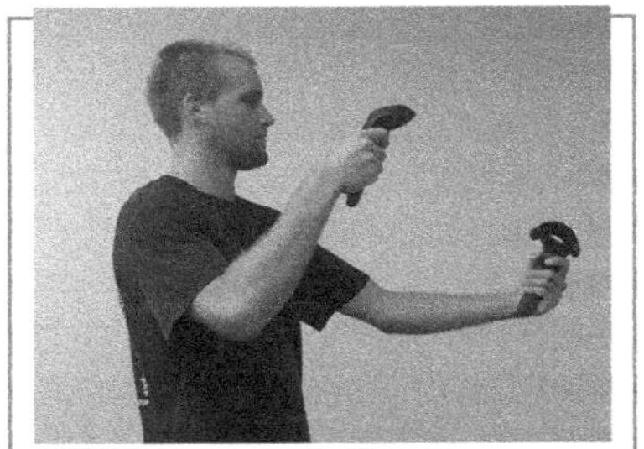
Figure 3 – A performer holds the VR controllers used to trigger and control music inside *AVRL*. These controllers are motion tracked in real-time using infrared light emitted by the HTC Vive base stations. Using this motion tracking data, 3D models of the controllers are animated inside of a virtual environment in the Unity game engine. This animation corresponds to the exact position, speed, and rotation of the controllers that are held and moved by the performer. The controllers can then be used to collide into 3D models (see Figure 5) which have been overlaid onto physical objects in the real world (see Figure 4). These collisions trigger various musical sounds at low latencies. Photo by Raul Altosaar, ©2018.

context of musical instrument design [5]. Although their instruments primarily relied on visual simulation and user immersion in a way that *AVRL* does not, their discussion about the kinds of musical interfaces suited for VR is relevant. Some of the earliest musical experiments with VR were conducted by Bolas & Stone in 1989. They noted that the flexibility of design and musical interaction enabled by VR technology is nearly infinite [7]. Also pertinent is Mulder's description of a virtual musical instrument as a real-time gestural interface through which a performer can interact with the nearly unlimited capabilities of a sound synthesis system [8]. Finally, *AVRL* echoes Wessel and Wright's central metaphor for musical control by physically enabling the performer to fly about in a space of musical processes [6].

## A Very Real Looper (AVRL)

*AVRL* is an audio-only VR interface built inside of the Unity game engine for the HTC Vive VR system. The size of this interface is determined by the distance between the Vive's two VR sensors, also known as base stations. *AVRL* is extra-large in the sense that it usually comprises a medium-sized room but can be set up to have a maximum tracking volume of roughly 3600 cubic feet [3].

First, Unity and the Vive's base stations are used in conjunction to overlay virtual, three-dimensional (3D) models onto physical objects in the real world. These physical objects visually represent the locations of the 3D models to the performer. These 3D models have been programmed to detect collisions between themselves and the handheld Vive controllers (see Figure 3) that are being animated in real-time using motion tracking data received from the base stations.

After detecting a collision, the 3D models trigger a musical sample, a MIDI sequence, or a specific MIDI note or chord. Thus, inside of *AVRL* the performer is physically colliding with music. These musical sounds and sequences are triggered only once by default, but can be looped by pressing a button on the controllers. To assist the performer with pinpointing the exact location of the 3D models, strong haptic feedback is provided by the controllers whenever a collision is detected.

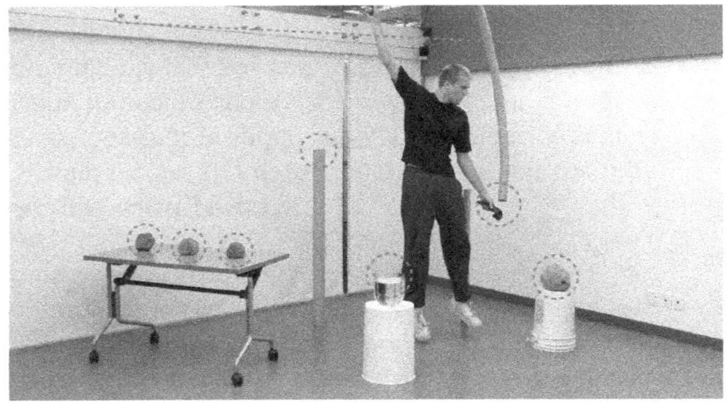
Figure 4 – A performer triggers musical sounds that have been overlaid as 3D models (see Figure 5) onto physical objects inside the performance space. The objects act as visual markers that represent the location of the musical sounds to the performer. Image by Raul Altosaar, ©2018.

Each 3D model contained by *AVRL* can be repositioned using the Vive controllers into new locations within the performance space that is delineated by the placement of the two base stations. This allows the performer to create novel sets of full-body musical interactions by mapping the 3D models into different locations before performing. For example, a 3D model could be overlaid onto a physical rock located on the ground. This would force the performer to crouch down to trigger the sound contained by that specific model. Another 3D model could be moved high above the performer's head and overlaid onto a light fixture, thus forcing the performer to jump up or toss a Vive controller into the air to trigger that sound.

The Vive controllers also provide a wide range of easily accessible, numerical motion tracking data that includes current movement speed, rotation, and position in 3D space. Inside of *AVRL*, these data are used to control audio parameters and effects in real-time. For example, a MIDI sequence is first looped by the performer and the intensity of an audio effect affecting that sequence is then altered by moving the controller either higher or lower in space.

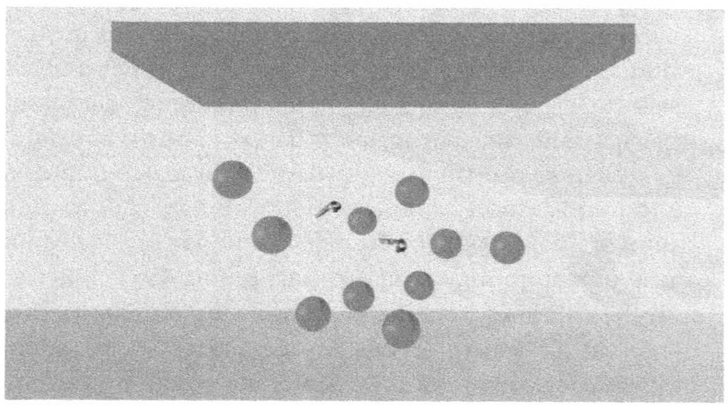

Figure 5 - A virtual view of *AVRL* captured in the Unity game engine depicts the 3D models (in red) and Vive controllers (in black). Image by Raul Altosaar, ©2018.

## Conclusion

*AVRL* is an audio-only VR interface that generates a large, highly reconfigurable musical performance environment that is spatially and acoustically augmented. While using *AVRL* a performer is not obstructed by a head-mounted display, immobilized by a static visual interface, or separated from their surroundings through immersion. Rather, inside of *AVRL* an unrestrained body moving through physical space is the primary conduit for musical expression. During a musical performance, *AVRL* enables the performer to develop a relationship to the audience and surrounding space while triggering and controlling musical sounds through full-body movement. *AVRL* thus harnesses the affordances of the physical world, a VR system, and a game engine to enable expressive and embodied musical interactions.

## Acknowledgments

Special thanks to Adam Tindale for asking the big questions that prodded *AVRL* in the right direction. Many thanks to Judith Doyle at the SMACLab for providing the space and resources to tackle this project.

## Documentation

A short technical breakdown of *AVRL* can be viewed here: https://vimeo.com/288778622. An early performance with *AVRL* can be viewed here: https://vimeo.com/294810067.

## References

[1] H. Schraffenberger and E. van der Heide. 2016. Multimodal augmented reality: the norm rather than the exception. In Proceedings of the 2016 workshop on Multimodal Virtual and Augmented Reality (MVAR '16). ACM, New York, NY, USA, Article 1, 6 pages. DOI: https://doi.org/10.1145/3001959.3001960

[2] Robert J.K. Jacob, Audrey Girouard, Leanne M. Hirshfield, Michael S. Horn, Orit Shaer, Erin Treacy Solovey, and Jamie Zigelbaum. 2008. Reality-based interaction: a framework for post-WIMP interfaces. In Proceedings of the SIGCHI Conference on Human Factors in Computing Systems (CHI '08). ACM, New York, NY, USA, 201-210. DOI: https://doi.org/10.1145/1357054.1357089

[3] Brandon J. Laatsch. 2016. Lighthouse Shenanigans. Video. (27 Feb 2016.). Retrieved November 4, 2018 from https://www.youtube.com/watch?v=9bZkp7q19f0

[4] Steve Gibson. 2018. Opto-Phono-Kinesia (OPK): Designing Motion-Based Interaction for Expert Performers. In Proceedings of the Twelfth International Conference on Tangible, Embedded, and Embodied Interaction (TEI '18). ACM, New York, NY, USA, 487-492. DOI: https://doi.org/10.1145/3173225.3173295

[5] Teemu Mäki-Patola, Juha Laitinen, Aki Kanerva, and Tapio Takala. 2005. Experiments with virtual reality instruments. In Proceedings of the 2005 conference on New interfaces for musical expression (NIME '05). National University of Singapore, Singapore, Singapore, 11-16.

[6] David Wessel and Matthew Wright. 2002. Problems and Prospects for Intimate Musical Control of Computers. Comput. Music J. 26, 3 (September 2002), 11-22. DOI: http://dx.doi.org/10.1162/014892602320582945

[7] Bolas, M. & Stone, P. (1992). Virtual mutant theremin. Proceedings International Computer Music Conference, San Jose, California, USA, 360-361. San Fransisco CA, USA: International Computer Music Association.

[8] Mulder, Axel G.E. (1994). Virtual Musical Instruments: Accessing the sound synthesis universe as a performer. Proceedings of the first Brazilian Symposium on Computer Music, held in Caxambu, Minas Gerais, Brazil, August 2-4 1994, during the XIV annual congress of the Brazilian Computing Society (SBC), pp 243-250. Belo Horizonte, M.G., Brazil: Universidade Federal de Minas Gerais.

# The Eighth Nerve Guitar: A Personal Reflection on Instrument Design and Computer-Mediated Performance

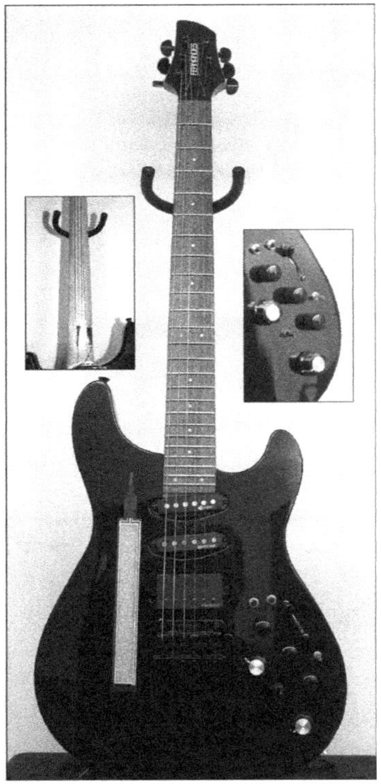

Figure 1: Eighth Nerve Guitar

**Thomas Ciufo**
Mount Holyoke College
South Hadley, MA 01075, USA
tciufo@mtholyoke.edu


*TEI '19*, March 17–20, 2019, Tempe, AZ, USA

ACM ISBN 978-1-4503-6196-5/19/03.
https://doi.org/10.1145/3294109.3301261

## Abstract

This paper describes the Eighth Nerve Guitar, a combined hardware / software instrument designed for computer-mediated improvisational performance. Key conceptual, aesthetic, and technical concerns will be discussed and multiple projects that utilize this live performance instrument will be referenced. A new instrument, the Guitar-Like Object (in development) will also be introduced.

## Author Keywords

Interaction Design; Physical Computing; Computational Creativity; Improvisational Performance;

## CCS Concepts

• Applied computing~Sound and music computing

## Introduction

The Eighth Nerve Guitar is a custom electric guitar that has been fitted with a range of sensors built into the body of the instrument. This interactive system uses physical sensor data, a custom iPad interface, along with an array of real-time audio stream analysis data to control a variety of computer-based digital signal processing manipulations. These sound transformations are applied to the performed sounds of the guitar, as well as a collection of premade sounds

Figure 2: Eighth Nerve Guitar in performance

and field recordings that can be drawn upon in performance. This results in a hybrid extended electric guitar / computer performance system that allows for the exploration of non-traditional playing techniques and sonic transformations provided by sensor controlled interactive digital signal processing.

## Motivation

I have long been interested in prepared instruments and have a related project for prepared piano and live computer processing. Prepared piano poses a number of particular technical and logistical issues, so I was interested in exploring other approaches to prepared instruments; in this case, physical preparations combined with digital processing. In terms of practicality, the instrument had to be affordable, portable, and allow continuous access for ongoing development, practice, and performance. I was also interested in an instrument that could use electromagnetic pickups, thereby simplifying the implementation of audio stream analysis and avoiding some of the problems related to acoustic transduction. The instrument would need to be sonically rich and provide access to a wide range of extended playing techniques. The work of seminal guitar innovators, such as Keith Rowe, Derek Bailey, and Fred Frith demonstrates the range of playing techniques and sonic diversity available with the electric guitar. More recent work by Ricky Graham, Adam Wilson, and Kevin Patton provide additional examples of innovative approaches to extended electric guitar.

## Hardware Overview

The instrument started out as a Fernandes electric guitar (with a sustainer pickup) which I then fitted with a range of custom sensors, including two rotary potentiometers, two momentary switches, one toggle switch, a pressure sensor that runs the length of the neck, two touch position sensors (one on the front and one on the neck) and a two-axis accelerometer built into the body of the guitar. The sensors are wired to a VGA connector mounted in the body of the guitar that is used to deliver the sensor voltages to an A-D converter. A simple interface box that uses an Arduino microcontroller handles the A-to-D conversion for the sensors.

Figure 3: Custom sensor interface

The performance system also uses an iPad interface as well as two continuous foot pedals and a Keith McMillen SoftStep pedal for additional control.

## Software Overview

The software for this performance system is very complex, having evolved gradually over a long span of time. On some levels, I no longer concretely understand all the innerworkings or behaviors of the

Figure 4: Eighth Nerve Guitar in performance

software, since the complexity and interdependence of the various functions creates emergent and unexpected outcomes. Predictability has not been an overarching design goal and I embrace this aspect of the instrument, especially in the context of solo improvisations where I am trying to avoid habitual behaviors. While a detailed description of the software design (realized in Max) is beyond the scope of this paper, it can be generally broken down into a few broad categories; there are listening agents which are designed for real-time audio stream analysis, sound processing modules, logic and control modules, sound output and spatialization modules, and various user interface elements.

The audio stream analysis modules track several different parameters including frequency, loudness, envelope, brightness, noisiness, spectral density, time between attacks, and several other salient features. All tracking parameters are also analyzed over various time frames to estimate larger time scale behaviors. The outcomes of these analysis modules (listening to both the input and the output of the system) are shared with the rest of the software and are used to influence both low-level and overall system behaviors.

The sound processing modules provide a wide range of sonic transformations and also include modules that can record and play back materials collected over the course of the performance, as well as sounds and field recordings prepared in advance. Key to the implementation of the signal processing network is the use of a routing matrix which allows all modules to be interconnected (at any gain level) and uses interpolation between high-level routing maps to manage the interconnections.

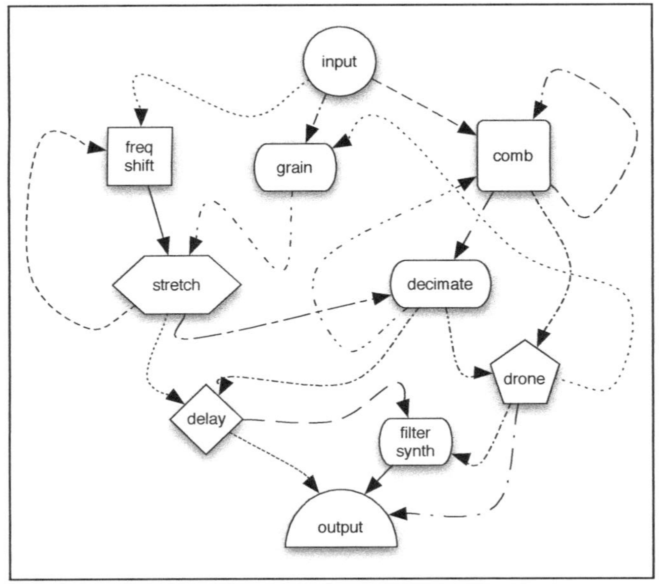


Figure 5: One of many available routing maps
signal gain can be adjusted at each connection point

This approach allows for a wide range of unique sonic transformations without overloading me with low-level management tasks during a performance. Since many of the individual parameters for the processing modules are driven by real-time audio analysis, even a routing map that is used repeatedly will result in unique sonic outcomes. In performance mode, the user interface for the software is minimal, since I do not want to rely too heavily on visual feedback which can be a distraction.

The final stage before output to the speakers is a six input, four output spatializer based on the Spat tools developed at IRCAM. This system provides control over sound source location and motion parameters, as well as complex room simulation that can be controlled separately for each input. This creates a subtle yet constantly evolving and immersive sound space and gives each input voice its own spatial trajectory and identity.

## Performance Context and Reflection

I have been working on and performing with this system for a number of years. It was not originally intended to be a long-term project but staying with it over multiple years has allowed me to develop a deeply intimate and highly personal relationship with this instrument. This is in contrast to the more usual progression where we prototype, develop, then debut a new system, and then move on to the next new technology. Instead, I have been able to continuously develop and refine this instrument and explore the unique performance techniques that it enables. At the same time, it is a highly idiosyncratic instrument with many specific limitations. It was never designed as a general-purpose instrument or as an instrument for others to use, so I see these limitations as design decisions as opposed to deficits.

I have used the instrument in a wide variety of performance contexts, including solo projects and ensembles of various sizes. In ensembles settings, I am able to adjust the software to exhibit less autonomous behavior, so it fits in to the ensemble in a more cohesive fashion. The system does have a certain sonic identity, but it is fairly diverse and pliable. The complexity and responsiveness of the guitar itself, especially through extended and unconventional playing techniques, greatly enhances the overall flexibility of this hardware / software instrument.

Figure 6: In performance with Curtis Bahn

Figure 7: Performing *Silent Movies* for guitar and video

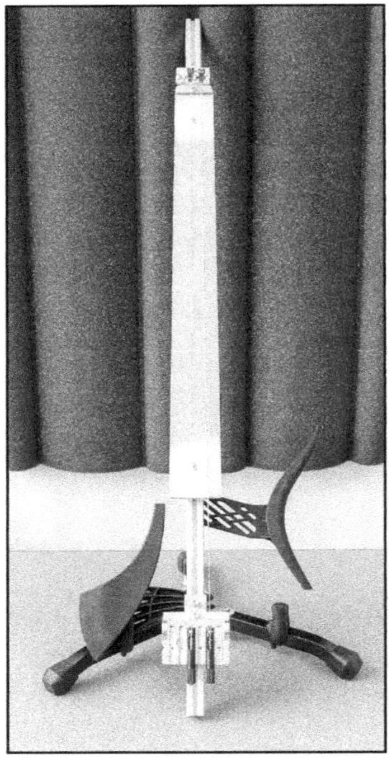

Figure 8: Guitar-Like Object prototype version 2

## Future Developments

Having started out as a Fernandes electric guitar, the Eighth Nerve instrument is encumbered by its original physical design and is somewhat difficult to modify and adapt. Since I am not a guitarist as such, I have no specific need for this type of form factor, and have recently started building a new instrument, more or less from scratch. Since it does not need to look or feel like a standard guitar, I am referring to it as the Guitar-Like Object.

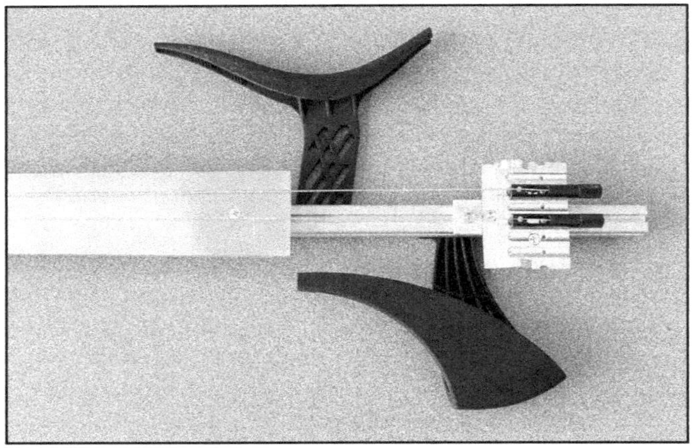

Figure 9: Guitar-Like Object, prototype version 2

For this new instrument I am exploring a range of construction techniques including 3D printing, both manual and CNC milling, and basic hand fabrication. The design will be completely modular and will allow for easy modification and changing out modules and components of the instrument. This modular design will facilitate the testing and integration of a number of new sensing technologies and I am also experimenting with different interchangeable fretted and fretless necks.

Much of the software infrastructure from the previous system will be usable, but the new physical form and new sensors will also encourage a redevelopment of the software design. The Guitar-Like object has been slow to develop, due to the range of technologies and construction techniques involved.

## Closing Thoughts

Overall, these performance systems leverage a variety of unique hardware and software design strategies, all geared specifically towards improvisational performance. By combining a tactile, playable sound source with a dynamic interactive software system, the immediacy and richness of the guitar is extended by the power and flexibility of computation. This hybrid design, using physical sensors, generative strategies, audio stream analysis, and complex routing and mapping, creates an unpredictable, complex yet playable improvisational instrument.

## Selected References

[1] Derek Bailey. 1993. *Improvisation: its Nature and Practice in Music*. Da Capo Press, New York, NY.

[2] Thomas Ciufo. 2005. Beginner's Mind: An Environment for Sonic Improvisation. In *Proceedings of the International Computer Music Conference* (ICMC 2005).

[3] Thomas Ciufo and David Birchfield. 2007. Computer-Mediated / Interactive Performance: Moving Boundary Problem Case Study. In *Proceedings of the 4th International Conference on Enactive Interfaces* (ENACIVE 07).

[4] Roger Dean. 2003. *Hyperimprovisation: Computer-Interactive Sound Improvisation*. A-R Editions, Middleton, WI.

[5] Ian Hattwick, J. M., and Marcelo M. Wanderley. 2013. Use of 3D Printed Components in the Creation of the Prosthetic Instruments. http://www.idmil.org/_media/publications/2013/3d_print_prosthetics.pdf

[6] Lyons, M. and Fels, S. 2012. Advances in New Interfaces for Musical Expression. In *Proceedings of the SIGGRAPH Asia* 2012 Courses (SIGGRAPH 2012).

[7] Eduardo Miranda and Marcelo Wanderley. 2006. *New Digital Musical Instruments: Control and Interaction Beyond the Keyboard*. A-R Editions, Middleton, WI.

[8] Dan O'Sullivan and Tom Igoe. 2004. *Physical Computing: Sensing and Controlling the Physical World with Computers*. Thomson, Boston, MA.

[9] Doug Van Nort, Pauline Oliveros, and Jonas Braasch. 2013. Electro/Acoustic Improvisation and Deeply Listening Machines. Journal of New Music Research, 42, 4: 303-324.

# Machine Tango: An Interactive Tango Dance Performance

**Courtney Brown**
Center of Creative Computation
Southern Methodist University
Dallas, TX USA
browncd@smu.edu

## Abstract

In Argentine tango, dancers typically respond to fixed musical recordings with improvised movements, each movement emerging in a wordless dialog between leader and follower. In the interactive work Machine Tango, this relation between dancers and music is inverted, enabling tango dancers to drive musical outcomes. Motion sensors are attached to dancer limbs, and their data is sent wirelessly to a computer, where algorithms turn the movement into sound. In doing so, the computer inserts itself in this on-going nonverbal conversation. Instead of traditional tango instruments such as the bandoneón, dancers generate and transform the sounds of typewriters and found sounds. System musical response to movement shifts during the dance, becoming more complex. The two dancers must navigate the resulting unstable musical structures as one body, responding with stylized tango movements. The difficulty of this task and the juxtaposition of the traditional with the experimental are integral to the performance aesthetic.

## Author Keywords

Interactive dance; Argentine tango; NIME; Embodiment.


*TEI '19, March 17--20, 2019, Tempe, AZ, USA.*

ACM ISBN 978-1-4503-6196-5/19/03...$15.00.
DOI: https://doi.org/10.1145/3294109.3301263

**Figure 1**: A video still from a performance of *Machine Tango*. Motion sensors are attached to the ankles of each tango dancer, and an Android phones are hidden within their costumes.

## CSS Concepts
**• Applied computing~Sound and music computing** • Applied computing~Performing arts

## Introduction
Argentine tango dance is grounded in the relation between two moving bodies, leader and follower. Their nonverbal conversation determines movement quality, character and trajectory. Lacking a basic step set to a specified rhythm, the tango couple freely improvises the rhythmic phrasing and framing of their bodies in relation to the accompanying music. *Machine Tango* reverses the relationship by allowing tango dancers to drive musical outcomes via their movement in the dance.

## Motivation and Aesthetics
Examples of this aesthetic that were influential on this work are fixed tape pieces such as Paul Lansky's *Table's Clear* (1992) [1] which develops the sounds of children playing pots and pans from relative chaos into pitched and rhythmic structures, and Paul Koonce's *Hothouse* (1996) [2], in which a baby's cry seamlessly metamorphoses into a saxophone. *Machine Tango* also

### Argentine Tango

Argentine tango is a Western partnered social dance that emerged among the working class immigrant population in the Río del Plata area of Argentina and Uruguay during the in the mid-nineteenth century. While Argentine tango has a history of being performed and styles developed specifically for performance (i.e. 'stage tango'), it is practiced primarily as a social dance form. In this text, the term 'tango' refers to this tradition described above. Other dances named tangos include American Ballroom Tango and European Ballroom Tango, and it is these tangos that heavily dominate popular media and film portrayals of tango. While inspired by historical versions of Argentine tango, they employ a significantly different movement vocabulary and embrace, within cultural practices removed from those of Argentine tango.

draws upon my older work in this area, specifically using my concept of 'magnetic time', an algorithm in which a rhythmic or melodic figure or sound file is cut up into smaller pieces, and then scattered randomly in time, out of their original order. Then, as the motive or melodic/rhythmic/sound file repeats, the pieces get drawn back into their original order, as if their original start times are becoming magnetic. *Machine Tango* uses this algorithm to coalesce percussive sounds into and out of traditional tango rhythms and melodic figures, often drawing out the sound of almost, but not quite locking into a rhythm.

The relationship of tango dancer movement to music also expands upon the feeling of being between and structural instability, as it is often changing and occasionally unpredictable, particularly towards the end of the work. For instance, during one musical section, the relationship between left and right foot trajectories as well dynamic input from the interactive system drive de facto musical synthesis via the mapping of delay times and feedback, creating pitches and timbres that follow dancer gesture perceptually but escape precise human control. Additionally, once strong rhythmic patterns are finally established, the movement-music changes such that dancer movements begin to disrupt them. Thus, dancers are given the task of improvising highly stylized movements and strongly rhythmic choices with shifting and uncertain musical support. The aim of this juxtaposition is two-fold: 1) to explore and expose the tension and vulnerability that this creates in performance as dancers negotiate tasks of increasing effort, and 2) to intensify dancer engagement with musical outcomes as research suggests that musical interfaces can engender deeper user engagement and allow for greater creativity by 'resisting' human action and allowing for extremes of response [3][4].

The experimental and electroacoustic character of the music also moves the Argentine tango dance from traditional practice, contributing to the aesthetics of liminality and instigating movement creativity. While tango dance and music have been historically been intertwined, with developments in one medium driving changes in another, tango dance technique does not rely on Argentine rhythmical or musical structures. Unlike in salsa or swing, tango is not organized around a metrical structure such as 4/4 or any particular rhythmical motif or pattern. However, conventionally, dancers often mimic idiomatic rhythmic syncopations and tempo changes in the tango music. Thus, while it is possible to dance with orthodox tango technique to any musical style, responding and mimicking the rhythmical patterns of that style intrinsically changes the character of dance and opens up new possibilities.

## Related Work

Dance and music have been interconnected throughout history antiquity, and the advent of motion capture technology has enabled typically unsounding dancer movement to drive musical outcomes. Works of Troika Ranch such as *In Plane* (1994) [5] and the DIEM Dance Digital System such as *Movement Study* (1997) [6] are early examples of this interactive dance work. Of these interactive dance systems, few engage styles outside of Western dance performance practices such as modern dance. One recent notable example is Hsu & Kemper's RAK Performance system, utilizing belly dance movements for an embodied musical composition process they call 'kinesonic' [7]. A few interactive systems engage with tango dance styles, such as Proyecto Biopus' audio-video installation, Tango Virus

(2005), in which the movements of participating dancers are translated into viruses infecting the music of tango composer Astor Piazzolla, gradually distorting the sound via a biologically-based simulation [8]. Laura Sinnott's Augmented Tango Shoes (2008), allows one dancer to create and affect electrotango music via movements influenced by Argentine tango tradition [9]. My interactive tango system developed for Argentine tango, *Interactive Tango Milonga* (ITM)[10][11][12], is another such work. Unlike *Machine Tango* and the previous works above, it is developed for the social context, taking into account social conventions and logistics in its design. Hence, the music produced by this system also reflects social tango dancer expectations and tango musical tradition. Another interactive tango performance work of mine, *Puente: A Study in Interactive Tango* draws heavily from this work in social interactive tango. However, while sharing technology and the Argentine tango dance tradition of these previous works, *Machine Tango* addresses the separate aesthetic concern of investigating states of liminality and betweenness, and also produces electroacoustic music, only obliquely referring to traditional tango sounds.

## Technical Implementation

The interactive tango system used by *Machine Tango* consists of three modules: 1) the motion capture system consisting of a Shimmer3 inertial sensor on each dancer ankle, and an Android phone placed out of sight on each dancer, 2) custom C++/Cinder[1] software for motion analysis, and 3) sound production and musical structure generation using Max 8[2]. The first two modules were originally developed as part of the ITM system, described in [10] and in [12], but were modified and used as a framework for the implementation of *Machine Tango.* However, the third module is largely original to this work.

The Shimmer3[3] sensors send data wirelessly via Bluetooth class2 technology. As human bodies in the tango embrace absorb and thus significantly disrupt Bluetooth radio signals, the data from these sensors is transmitted to an Android phone attached to the body of each dancer, which then forwards those sensor signals to the C++ software via WiFi [10]. Unlike the ITM system, the *Machine Tango* performance does not utilize the Android phones as torso sensors.

The custom C++ software then analyzes the movement and uses the results to drive real-time dynamic music generation and arrangement. The C++ software then sends control signals to Max 8 software, which then produces the sound and creates the musical structure.

Open Sound Control[4] (OSC) is used to transmit data from each part of the system to the other, making the data chain modular and highly adaptable.

## Conclusion

*Machine Tango* creates links between electroacoustic music and tango dance traditions, exploring how dancers grapple with the unstable relationships in sound and movement. A main aim of this work is to further develop the hybrid practice of interactive tango, mining the juxtaposition for creative possibilities. in the page limit; the figures must be usable when printed in black and white.

[1] https://libcinder.org/

[2] https://cycling74.com/

[3] http://www.shimmersensing.com/

[4] http://opensoundcontrol.org/

## References

[1] Paul Lansky. 1992. Table's Clear. Musical Work. In Homebrew. Bridge Records, New Rochelle, NY.

[2] Paul Koonce, 1996. Hothouse. Musical Work. In Walkabout & Back: Electroacoustic Works. Mode Records, New York, NY.

[3] Newton Armstrong. 2007. An enactive approach to digital musical instrument design. VDM Verlag, OmniScriptum, Berlin.

[4] B. Hogg and S. J. Norman. 2013. Resistant materials in musical creativity. Contemporary Music Review, 32(2/3), 115-118. doi:10.1080/07494467. 2013.775804

[5] D. Stoppiello and M. Coniglio, 2003. 'Fleshmotor' in J.Malloy (ed.), Women, Art, and Technology, Cambridge, MA: MIT Press, 440-50.

[6] W. Siegel and J. Jacobsen. 1998. The challenges of interactive dance: An overview and case study." Computer Music Journal 22, 4, 29–43.

[7] A. Hsu and S. Kemper. 2015. Kinesonic approaches to mapping movement and music with the remote electroacoustic kinesthetic sensing (RAKS) system. In Proceedings of the 2nd International Workshop on Movement and Computing, 45-47.

[8] E. Causa, T. Pirotta, M. Costas. 2005. Proyecto Biopus. Tango Virus. Website. http://www.estudiobiopus.com.ar/estudio/tango_virus.html.

[9] L. Sinnott, 2008. Mapping strategies for the augmented tango shoe. Master's Thesis, New York University, New York, NY.

[10] Courtney Brown and Garth Paine. 2015. Interactive Tango Milonga: Designing Internal Experience. In Proceedings of the 2nd International Workshop on Movement and Computing (MOCO '15), 17-20.

[11] Courtney Brown and Garth Paine. 2015. Towards an Interactive Tango Milonga. In Proceedings of the 41st International Computer Music Conference (ICMC '15), 110-113.

[12] Courtney Brown. 2017. Interactive Tango Milonga: An Interactive Dance System for Argentine Tango Social Dance. Doctoral Dissertation. Arizona State University, Tempe, AZ.

# *Upwell* : Performative Immersion Hybridizing Two Worlds

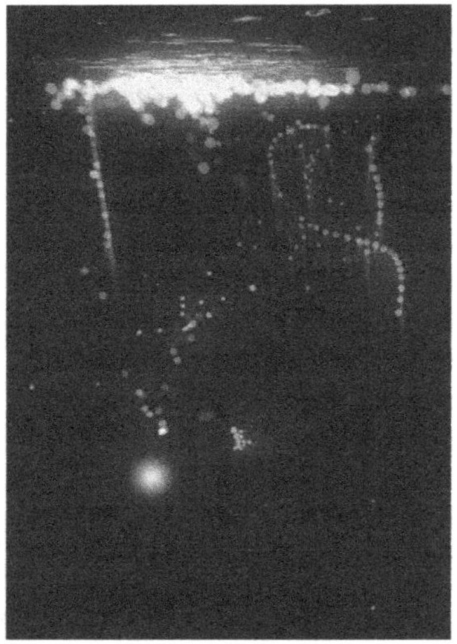

Figure 1. Upwell VR Environment

**Jinsil Hwaryoung Seo**
Soft Interaction Lab
Department of Visualization
Texas A&M University
hwaryoung@tamu.edu

**Michael Bruner**
University of Texas at Austin
michael.bruner3@gmail.com

**Nathan Ayres**
nathan_ayres@tamu.edu

**Christine Bergeron**
cbergeron@tamu.edu

**Alexandra Pooley**
alexandra.pooley@tamu.edu



*TEI '19*, March 17–20, 2019, Tempe, AZ, USA

ACM ISBN 978-1-4503-6196-5/19/03.
https://doi.org/10.1145/3294109.3301264

## Abstract

*Upwell* is a mixed reality performance that allows audience members to explore virtual and physical worlds with two dancers. The environment provokes the feeling of being underwater. A dancer with a conventional VR head-mounted display and wearable controllers can navigate around a room scale virtual reality setup and interacts with dynamic visual and sound elements. Since the dancer wears custom-made wearable controllers on the palms, she can make intricate gestures to develop direct relationships with bioluminescent particles in the virtual water. The other dancer only interacts with the visuals created by the VR dancer without realizing the virtual world. *Upwell* can be utilized as a single person art installation as well as a performance projecting different views on a projection screen. Project video: https://youtu.be/rnpWC5aa4ds

## Author Keywords

Mixed Reality Performance; Virtual reality; Immersion; Performative; Wearable controller; Embodiment; Interactive Environment

## CSS Concepts

• Human-centered computing~Virtual reality

Figure 2. Performance in Upwell

## Introduction

People unconsciously long to be immersed in nature that provides shelter and comfort. Through activities like camping, hiking, and swimming, people can relax and be immersed in nature. As all entities in the world have both sides, nature also has virtue and vice, life and death. While seeking comfort in the forest or beach, a person may feel fearful about the possibility that a wild animal may appear and attack. A person may have fears of drowning in the ocean. All of these fears prevent people from fully enjoying and experiencing the beauty of the natural world. Our project explores embodied experience that simulates the feeling of being underwater. Undulating characteristics, including tenderness, flux, softness, and buoyancy, all add to the feeling of being underwater. *Upwell* is a refuge from nature that provides playful immersion without vulnerability. We utilize this concept in Virtual Reality that allows a great space for new experience.

*Technology Mediated Immersion*

The word "immersion" comes from the Latin word, in (into) + mergere (plunge, dip) [1]. The origin of "immersion" seems to be the literal meaning of "absorption in some interest or situation" and it is more about sensuous experience that expands to being plunged into a mental activity [2]. The term is widely used for describing immersive virtual reality, installation art and video games. Janet Murray explains immersion as "the sensation of being surrounded by another reality that covers our perception." [3]

*Prior Virtual Reality Artworks*

Artists have explored sensory immersion through their artistic creations. Their approaches were the disembodying tendency of virtual reality and their artistic pursuit was centered on creating immersive experiences using new hardware and software [4]. In *Osmose* by Char Davies pursued immersion as "a quality of being spatially encompassed by being sensuously enveloped, as if by a lover or sea water or even the air itself pressing upon the skin" [5]. In *Dancing with Dervish: Virtual Bodies,* individual users could navigate the VR body parts. Body parts from MRI scans of the artist's body comprised the immersive 3D environment. As users navigated within the body parts, the body deformed and reformed according to participant's movements [6]. *Placeholder* by Brenda Laurel & Rachel Strickland was a one-time theatrical performance in VR. Each performer experienced a virtual avatar in the abstracted natural environments [7].

## Upwell: Project Description

*Upwell* is a VR environment that provokes the feeling of being under water and interacting with the environment [Figure 2]. This project can be presented as a dance performance with two dancers or a participatory interactive installation in a gallery setting. For a dance performance, a dander with a VR headset and wearable controllers can navigate around a room scale virtual reality environment and create/interact with virtual objects. Since the dancer wears custom-made wearable controllers on the palms, she can make intricate gestures to develop direct relationships with bioluminescent particles in the virtual water. The other dancer interacts with the visuals that created by the VR dancer in two worlds separated by a theater scrim.

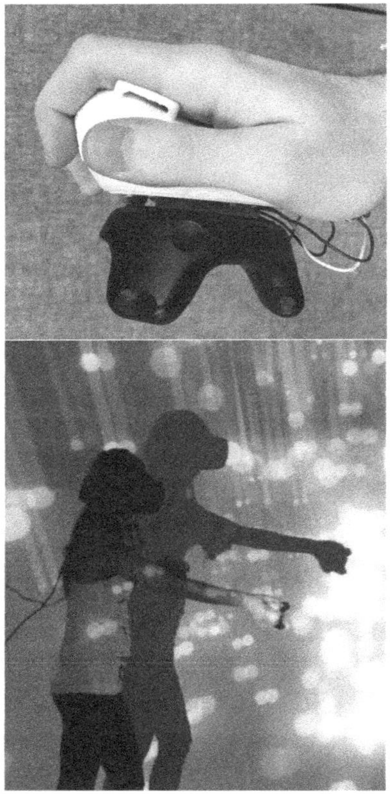

Figure 3. Participant holds the custom-made wearable controllers

A participant with a VR headset finds herself in a watery environment, with a rippling water surface that refracts and distorts light above them. The space is filled with floating particles that glow like bioluminescent plankton and flow with invisible water currents. A dense fog surrounds the area creating a contained space that doesn't have any distinct boundaries. In *Upwell*, they can walk around and move their arms touching the bioluminescent particles. As soon as the participant moves with our wearable controllers, the space is awake and responds to the participant. Since the participant wears the controllers with VIVE motion trackers on the palms, their movements in the virtual space is intricate and the experience is embodied. The person's experience is shared with audience members in the physical space via projection. The participant becomes a performer who creates an artwork with the virtual entities.

## Technical Components

*Virtual Reality hardware & software*

We use a consumer virtual reality product, HTC VIVE: a head mounted display and two motion trackers. The motion trackers are attached to custom made wearable 3D printed controllers. A participant holds a motion controller in each hand and can choose different effects by pressing buttons on the wearable controllers. The experience has been developed using Unity3D.

*Custom-made Wearable Controller*

In contrast to typical hand-held controllers, *Upwell* incorporates wearable controllers utilizing the compact, lightweight VIVE trackers [Figure 3, Top]. We focused on developing a wearable device that can rest comfortably in the participant's palm. When not being gripped, the controllers hang lightly from a strap around the hand. The discrete controllers with simple, two-button scheme are intended to assist in participant immersion.

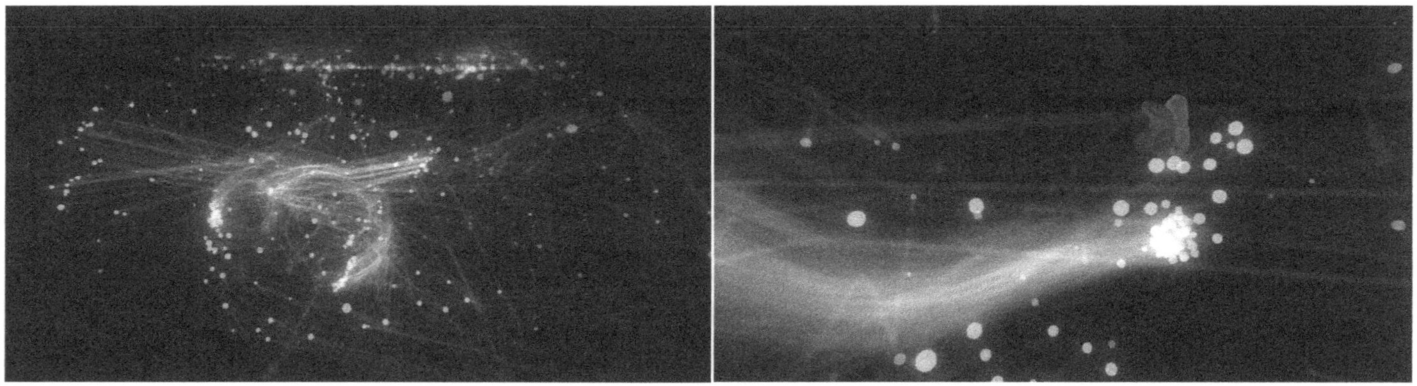

Figure 4. (Left) virtual camera view in Upwell, (Right) a participant's perspective

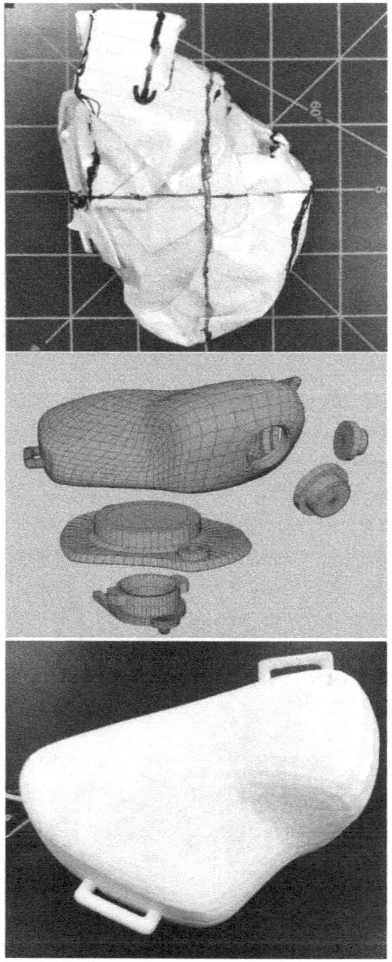

Figure 5. Wearable Controller Prototype

The 3D model of the wearable controller was prototyped first with papers to test ergonomic forms. Reference images of the final prototype were taken into Maya where the organic form was modeled out. From the refined shape functional aspects like the twist-lock tracker attachment, buttons, and circuitry supports were added in. Maya's millimeter units assisted in ensuring real world scale. The final model was printed on an Ultimaker 2+ using white PLA [Figure 5].

Vive Trackers come equipped with output pins that be wired to buttons to create custom interactions. The tracker has six pins, four button pins, a ground pin, and a general power pin. In our design we made use of only four pins, two buttons, ground, and power [Figure 6, Left]. Our buttons are 6mm tactile buttons that are secured inside the controller directly behind the larger 3D printed buttons [Figure 6, Right]. The power pin powers two LEDs that give an ambient glow to the controller. Snap connections are used for all of the pins so that the controller can be easily attached and detached from the tracker [Figure 7].

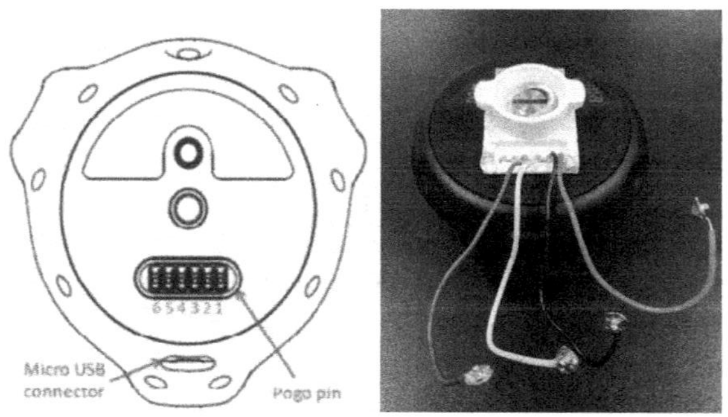


Figure 6. (Left) Connectors, (Right) 3D printed connector

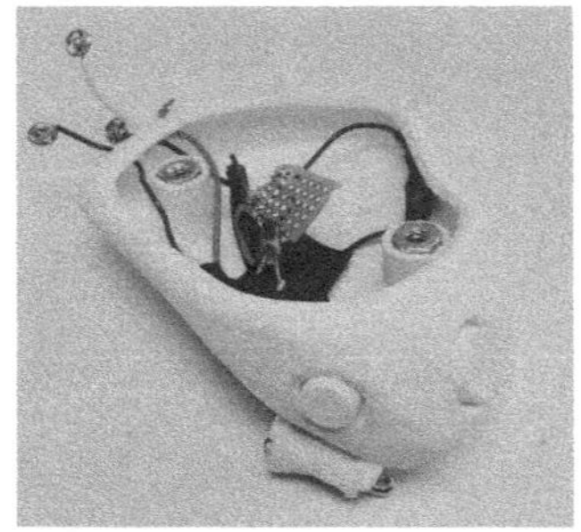

Figure 7. Circuitry in the wearable controller

## Performative Immersion

The experience smoothly transitions between multiple states which have unique visual and interactive effects. At the beginning of the experience, particles are generated by the participant's motion controllers. By moving faster and slower the participant can affect the size and color of the particles. The particles appear and rise upward towards the surface of the water and slowly fade out as they ascend. The rate at which the particles are created steadily increases until a torrent of particles are streaming towards the surface. At this point the particles stop fading out and instead start gathering at the surface of the water. After a certain number of particles are created the controllers stop generating new particles. They undergo a state change, which gives them motion trails and makes them attracted to the motion of the controllers. The participant can move their controllers and the particles will follow along with the motion. Particles that are not being controlled by the participant continuously rain down to the ground and then after a delay ascend back towards the surface of the water. This simulates both water currents and the rain cycle, and gives an ambient motion and life to the environment. The experience ends with all of the particles ascending past the surface of the water. The environment is then returned to its original state and the cycle can be restarted.

*Interactive Effects*

The custom motion controllers have two buttons built in which when pressed toggle unique effects on and off. The first button is a scaled time effect that mirrors the participant's movement. When the participant is still the simulation runs at slow time rate and when the participant makes fast movements the simulation runs at an increased time rate. This effect makes the environment highly reactive to participant's movement. This mirroring allows the user to embody the entire environment and to have an experience of being the water. The boundaries between the participant's physical body and the virtual environment are dissolved. The second button is a colored trail effect that is reactive to the velocity of the motion controllers. Each dimension of space is mapped to a color value and the overall speed scales the intensity of the color. This effect adds a variety of color to the environment while also providing a visualization of the movement. The intensity and direction of a motion can be inferred simply by looking at the color. The participant can use this visual feedback to better understand their own motions.

*Audio*

The experience makes use of spatialized audio and real time reverb zones to make the audio feel cohesive with the rest of the environment. The reverb zone makes the audio sound muffled and muted to simulate the feeling of hearing underwater. Multiple audio sources are throughout the environment in different locations to encourage the participant to explore the area.

## Performance Setup at TEI 2019

*Upwell* will need a minimum space for a VIVE VR system (approximately 150 sq ft). However, it will be ideal to have a space as big as 300 sq ft to have a projection scrim for audience members to view the virtual reality environment that is being navigated by a dancer who uses a VIVE head-mounted display and controllers. As a dancer performance, the project requires a black scrim that makes a separation between virtual and physical worlds.

## References

[1] Online Etymology Dictionary. http://www.etymonline.com/index.php?search=immersion&searchmode=none

[2] Oxford Dictionary. http://oxforddictionaries.com/definition/immersion.

[3] Murray, J. H. (1997). *Hamlet on the holodeck: the future of narrative in cyberspace*. Cambridge, Mass.: MIT Press.

[4] Seo, J. H. & Corness, G. (2015). *Aesthetics of Immersion in Interactive Immersive Installation: Phenomenological Case Study*. In the Proceedings of International Symposium of Electronic Arts (ISEA), Vancouver, Canada.

[5] Davies, C. (2005). *Landscapes of Ephemeral Embrace: A Painter's Exploration of Immersive Virtual Space as a Medium for Transforming Perception.* University of Plymouth, Plymouth, UK.

[6] Gromala, D., & Sharir, Y. (1996). Dancing with the Virtual Dervish: Virtual bodies. In M. A. Moser, Macleod D., & Banff Centre for the Arts (Ed.), *Immersed in Technology: Art and Virtual Environments*. Cambridge, Mass.: MIT Press.

[7] Laurel, B., & Strickland, R. (1992). *Placeholder*. [Immersive VR]. http://www.tauzero.com/Brenda_Laurel/Placeholder/Placeholder.html.

# Craftec: Engaging Older Adults in Making through a Craft-Based Toolkit System

**Ben Jelen**
Indiana University
Bloomington, IN, USA
bcjelen@indiana.edu

**Anne Freeman**
Georgetown University
Washington, DC, USA
aof7@georgetown.edu

**Mina Narayanan**
Auburn University
Auburn, AL, USA
mjn0010@tigermail.auburn.edu

**Kate M. Sanders**
Hendrix College
Conway, AR, USA
SandersKM@hendrix.edu

**James Clawson**
Indiana University
Bloomington, IN, USA
clawsonj@indiana.edu

**Katie A. Siek**
Indiana University
Bloomington, IN, USA
ksiek@indiana.edu

## ABSTRACT
We present Craftec, an extendable toolkit system to engage older adults in maker technology by supporting their use of crafting skills. Craftec is comprised of LilyPad Arduino-based toolkits to promote easier crafting with hard and soft mediums. We describe the system's design, a pilot test with 8 younger adults, and 2 two-hour single session workshop evaluations by 17 older adults. We found Craftec facilitated efficient integration of circuits in crafted items, including fewer short circuits as compared to a basic LilyPad Arduino kit. We discuss how to create a toolkit for prototyping rather than facilitating STEM education.

## Author Keywords
Electronic toolkits; construction kits; maker technology; Arduino; older adults; evaluation workshop; crafting; crafting technology; DIY.

## CCS Concepts
**•Social and professional topics → Seniors; •Human-centered computing → Interface design prototyping;** *User studies;* User centered design; **•Hardware →** *Emerging technologies;*

## INTRODUCTION
The making community is comprised heavily of middle-aged men with disposable income [15]. Researchers have encouraged more diverse groups to join in the DIY and Maker Movements, including children, women, and those with disabilities, [2, 8, 10, 40]. When children are engaged, researchers found hands-on, Science, Technology, Engineering, and Math (STEM) oriented "let's try it" exploration particularly successful [31]. Although researchers have studied older adults' views of maker technology and how they might design for them [51], few have designed maker technology for them.

Researchers typically engaged diverse groups in making through electronic toolkits, which often built on accessible and widely adopted crafting practices. Commercialized toolkit systems, such as MaKey MaKey [52], littleBits [4], and Chibitronics [48], use electronic components to engage children in exploring the possibilities of creating captivating artifacts while learning STEM topics, such as logic and electronic circuitry. Non-commercialized researcher toolkits have built upon the maker community's STEM education work through projects such as MakerWear [31] to create personalized, wearable systems and the "untoolkit" [41] for inexpensive personalized projects. E-textiles toolkits, such as the LilyPad Arduino [8] and Adafruit's Flora [27], explicitly build a bridge between computing and crafting practices by enabling a more diverse community of digital crafters [18]. We see their pioneering crafting-computing work as an opportunity to engage older adults – a common group of crafters.

Older adults could benefit from an electronic toolkit that engages them in the maker community as innovators of technology that is often designed for them (e.g., [3]) *rather than by them.* Society often points to the "digital divide" – the notion that older adults and younger people drastically differ in technology acceptance [19] – as a barrier to older adults contributing to a growing community like the Maker Movement. We see older adults as poised to contribute to such a technological frontier despite ageism biases [5, 28, 34]. Indeed, older adults are quite capable of learning computer programming [25] and tinkering with electronics [51]. Empowering older adults with an electronic toolkit can assist them in altering technology that is designed with good intentions, but may not support their goals [42].

We built Craftec, an extendable system of electronic toolkits, to engage older adults in making through the use of familiar crafting skills (Figure 1). The toolkits facilitate making through crafting with multiple mediums, such as wood and fabric. By supporting multiple materials, Craftec appeals to a wide range of crafts from woodwork to quilting. The toolkits



*TEI '19,* March 17–20, 2019, Tempe, AZ, USA



ISBN 978-1-4503-6196-5/19/03...$15.00
DOI: https://doi.org/10.1145/3294109.3295636

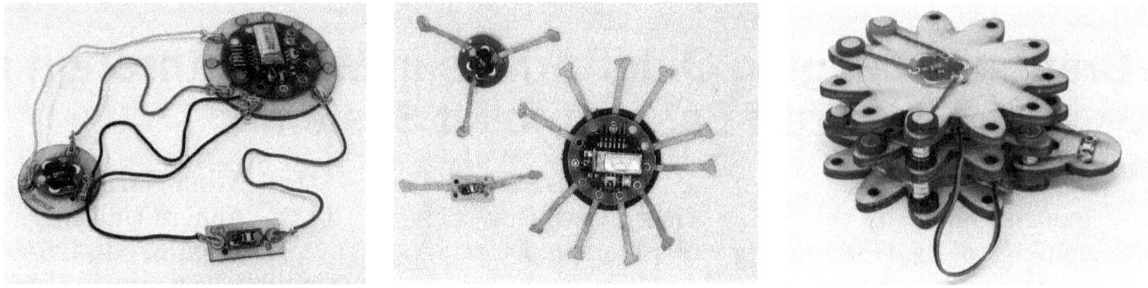

(a) Hard Toolkit (b) Soft Toolkit (c) Stackable Toolkit

**Figure 1. The Craftec system is made of three toolkits. Each toolkit is shown with a microcontroller, an LED, and light sensor. Note that after the pilot study, the Stackable toolkit was discontinued and not used during the workshop.**

integrate a modified LilyPad Arduino that simplifies electrical connections thus providing older adults the ability to quickly and safely craft innovative prototypes.

This paper makes three primary contributions: (1) we present Craftec, an electronic toolkit designed to support older adults in making and innovation using common crafting skills; (2) we describe findings from a pilot study of 8 younger adults and evaluation workshops with 17 older adults demonstrating the toolkit efficiency; and (3) we discuss implications for designing electronic toolkits for older adults to engage in maker activities.

## RELATED WORK

HCI researchers have created hybrid computational and crafting approaches by exploring crafting for tangible interaction and improved maker electronics toolkits. We focus on the relationship between crafting and electronic toolkits.

### Crafting and HCI

The HCI community has a growing interest in how crafting relates to people's tangible interactions with technology and the physical artifacts people create. Many researchers have focused on integrating digital technology into crafting [11, 18, 44, 22, 48, 58, 59]. Buechley et al.'s [8] creation of the LilyPad Arduino abstracted low-level electronics knowledge and integrated maker electronics into fabric projects via alternative, fabric-oriented conductive materials. Tsaknaki et al. [56] explored hybrid crafting – the integration of physical crafting and digital media [21] – with silversmiths to integrate small sensors into their crafted artifacts. Materiality – the feel for the materials and their inherent properties – is often discussed in conjunction with crafting in HCI [14, 18, 35, 41]. Giles and van der Linden [20] conducted e-textile workshops with blind and visually impaired, including several older adults. Similarly, we aim to use crafting as a bridge between older adults and maker electronics.

By integrating crafting and technology, researchers have reached more diverse populations than typical makers [18]. Hybrid crafting projects, such as LilyPad and Chibitronics, reach diverse audiences, particularly crafters, artists, and educators [10, 47]. Much of the craft-focused research has seen similar gender diversity in their participant pools [21, 41, 44]. Supporting diverse communities, especially older adults, creates opportunities for equitable technology literacy levels that can benefit broader communities, improve quality of life, and teach future generations [25]. Stewart et al. [54] actively sought out e-textiles as a way to support gender diversity in the design of engineered audio systems. Similarly, we see the integration of crafting practices into maker electronics as a way to create an inclusive atmosphere for older adults to build electronically enhanced artifacts, especially for a group that globally is largely women [45]. Lazar et al. [33, 35] engaged older adults with cognitive disabilities in creative practices as a part of art therapy which assisted participants in expressing themselves more clearly. We built upon this success with older adults by incorporating crafting.

### Maker Electronic Toolkits

Maker-oriented electronic toolkits have facilitated more accessible creating and building with electronics by lay people. Blikstein [6, 7] provides an overview of the development of electronic toolkits for children's education highlighting how toolkits have developed from programmable bricks [50, 49] to focusing on specific form factors [4, 8] and computers on chips [16, 17]. Blikstein [6] discusses the importance many toolkits have in abstracting technical knowledge so children can focus on more important ideas. Blikstein's framework, which informed Craftec, includes differentiating between toolkits based on level of selective exposure, detection of error correction, and ability to influence power [7].

Many maker electronic toolkits promote electronics concepts and encourage building electronically-enhanced artifacts. littleBits, which caters to STEM education programs [4], consist of pre-programmed electronic modules that snap together with magnets, allowing people to "*play with electronics without knowing electronics*" and explore computing logic while avoiding such issues as polarity reversals [4]. littleBits requires tape or Legos to create an artifact that integrates objects outside of its modules (e.g., wearable testing [32]). MakerWear expanded the concept of magnetic connections by providing children with pre-programmed hexagonal modules that snap into stiff boards sewn into objects to create different effects [31, 30, 32]. MakerWear demonstrated that they supported children's engagement in maker electronics by creating wearable artifacts while teaching them computing logic. mCookie [26] uses Lego-style stacking of components to create artifacts. Craftec builds upon these successes in easily building artifacts, but supports mediums such as wood and fabric to include broader groups of older adult crafters.

Some maker toolkit designers approached creativity by integrating crafts – such as sewing with fabric in the LilyPad Arduino toolkit [8] and exploring paper craft with Chibitronics [48]. Posch and Fitzpatrick [46] designed a series of prototype tools for e-textile makers and demonstrated the value of creating tools grounded in a particular craft.

People benefit in creating their own personally meaningful artifacts because it increases their satisfaction with the end result – a phenomenon known as the 'IKEA' effect [43]. Eduwear, a toolkit designed for the construction of wearable technology, capitalizes on this principle by enabling novices to create personally meaningful artifacts [29]. Building on this finding, Ananthanarayan et al. [2] found that those who spent over ninety minutes crafting their wearable device (electronics and design), used it more often. We extend these findings by emphasizing the hands-on crafting of electronically enhanced objects with Craftec.

## THE CRAFTEC SYSTEM

The Craftec system is composed of interchangeable toolkits that are extendable to incorporate commodity inputs and outputs within the LilyPad Arduino power and pin constraints. We started with three toolkits – Hard, Soft, and Stackable – before narrowing down to the Hard and Soft toolkits after the pilot study. We chose different crafting mediums and orientations to facilitate prototyping with hard and soft materials while being mindful of space constraints by increasing component placement degrees of freedom (i.e., the flexibility to orient and attach components in multiple dimensions).

### System Overview

The Craftec system is a medium-fidelity set of toolkits geared towards supporting older adults to prototype new technologies, such as IoT systems, where interchangeable components can be switched between toolkits. With Craftec, participants created examples using an LED and a light sensor.

One key benefit of integrating crafting into Craftec is that older adults participate in crafts already (some list it as their favorite activity [55]), making it ideal for expanding maker technology to them. Crafting can bridge between diverse groups and maker electronics as craft-focused toolkits have demonstrated [10, 39, 47]. Crafters can select the Hard toolkit for projects like woodworking, or the Soft toolkit for soft-mediums, such as fabric. We caution, however, that since Craftec integrates with combustible materials (e.g., fabric and wood), short circuits are of particular concern because they can cause fires, injure people, destroy crafts, and question one's confidence in creating with electronics.

The Craftec system builds on the rich design space of maker toolkits. The core of the design are modified LilyPad Arduino components [8]. Similar to other toolkits, we adopted snaps [1, 9], wires [23, 52], and magnets [53] to facilitate safe, secure connections. We iterated on snaps to form connections by leveraging conductive fabric for easier integration with sewing. We appreciated the quick prototyping of the 4 pin cables in Phidgets [23], so we integrated cables into the Hard toolkit. Based on the success of abstracting pins with colors [31] and differentiating inputs vs. output with shapes [48], we integrated both to accommodate varying visual acuity. In Craftec, we investigated how these affordances worked together in one system to empower older adults to build electronics using their crafting skills.

Craftec is the only system of toolkits designed for older adults to engage in maker activities by creating electronically enhanced artifacts using their crafting skills. Craftec's support for hard and soft craft mediums and the high component placement degrees of freedom is a unique combination.

### Hard Toolkit

The Hard toolkit is designed to connect components in a malleable orientation to allow for freedom of movement when placing components (Figures 1-a). Each component in the Hard toolkit was laser cut from balsa wood and engraved with the component name. We soldered a 5mm snap to each pin on the LilyPad Arduino sensors and outputs. We used the LilyPad Arduino SimpleSnap[1] and sewed the corresponding 8mm snaps into the laser cut base. Conductive thread established connections between the snaps on the bases and the magnets. Components snap into the base and each snap is conductively connected to a magnet. Insulated wires with jewelry clasps on the end connect magnets of different components to hold the connection in place. The Hard toolkit differentiates between outputs, which are rectangular, and inputs, which are circular. Colored puffy paint on the edges of the base guides users in creating correct electrical connections to other color-coded LilyPad components with yellow indicating analog, teal indicating digital, black indicating ground, and pink indicating power.

### Soft Toolkit

The Soft toolkit provides long conductive fabric strips that extend from the LilyPad Arduino, as shown in Figure 1-b, to provide room to machine or hand sew the circuit. The fabric strips were made from woven conductive fabric[2] that we laser cut. The conductive fabric strips were soldered to the LilyPad SimpleSnap Protoboard[3], so the LilyPad Arduino SimpleSnap could be securely snapped into place. Since the conductive fabric strips were smaller, we sewed the snaps directly into the strips using conductive thread.

The fabric strips eliminate difficulties involved with securing thread around the small pin holes of the LilyPad Arduino by allowing for machine sewing. Electronic components snap into the fabric circuit extensions, permitting their safe removal for washing and reuse in future projects with the interchangeable Craftec system. The fabric backing on the Soft toolkit's circuit extensions are differentiated by shape and color, with inputs being gray and circular and outputs being teal and rectangular. Pins were color coded the same as the Hard toolkit. The conventional power pin (+) was not used, and the conductive fabric strip was intentionally absent to decrease the likelihood of short circuits. Instead, the A5 pin was indicated as the power pin to reduce short circuits. Most sensors for the LilyPad

[1]https://www.sparkfun.com/products/10941
[2]https://www.adafruit.com/product/1168
[3]https://www.sparkfun.com/products/10940

Arduino require a connection to an analog pin, power, and ground, but the arrangement of the pins on the sensors make it difficult to use the conventional power pin (+) without crossing ground. We decided to simplify circuit creation by indicating A5 as the power pin, thus reducing the occurrence of short circuits.

### Stackable Toolkit

The other hard-medium circuit toolkit, Stackable, connected electrical components in a vertical orientation similar to the Lego stacking of mCookie [26] (Figure 1-c). The circuit extension bases were laser cut from balsa wood and marked with an image that represented the sensor or output to be used with the base. Electronics were secured to the Stackable toolkit bases by winding conductive thread through the circuit extensions' base and the pin holes of the electronics. Then, color-coded 3D printed magnet holders were glued onto the circular openings of the circuit extensions. The magnet holders contained 6mm x 2mm nickel-copper plated magnets onto the appropriate plastic magnet holders to facilitate electronic connections. The color of the magnet holders correlated to different pins, with red indicating power, green indicating digital pins, blue indicating analog pins, and black indicating ground. To reduce the occurrence of short-circuits, the red-colored power source on the base of the LilyPad Arduino was repositioned from its traditional location beside the ground pin to a location corresponding to the LilyPad Arduino's A2 analog pin. Because of the vertical nature of the circuit extensions, sensors must be placed on top of other electronic components to ensure full detection of environmental stimuli (e.g., Figure 1-c). As we discuss later, usability issues with the Stackable toolkit caused us to remove it from the Craftec system.

## PILOT STUDY WITH YOUNGER ADULTS

### Method

We conducted a two-hour ethics board approved pilot study with 8 younger adults to test the effectiveness of all three Craftec toolkits – Hard, Soft, and Stackable (Figure 1) – in comparison to an unmodified LilyPad Arduino. Six participants were men, and ages ranged from 20 to 31 years old (average = 26 years old) from Bloomington, Indiana using snowball sampling and personal contacts. They were Caucasian (5), Asian (2), and African American (1). We recruited computing-oriented college students who would give us unfiltered feedback about Craftec without thinking mistakes reflected on their own skills. Participants were matched with a researcher and completed four activities in separate rooms. The participants were compensated with $20 for their time.

#### *Procedure*

We administered a pre-survey first to gather basic demographic information and gauge participants' prior knowledge of maker electronics concepts. Participants tested the three Craftec toolkits and an unmodified LilyPad kit for comparison by creating two circuits. The first circuit consisted of an Arduino and an LED, and the second circuit added the light sensor to the first circuit. The four kits were purposefully randomized so that the participants did not interact with the kits in the same order.

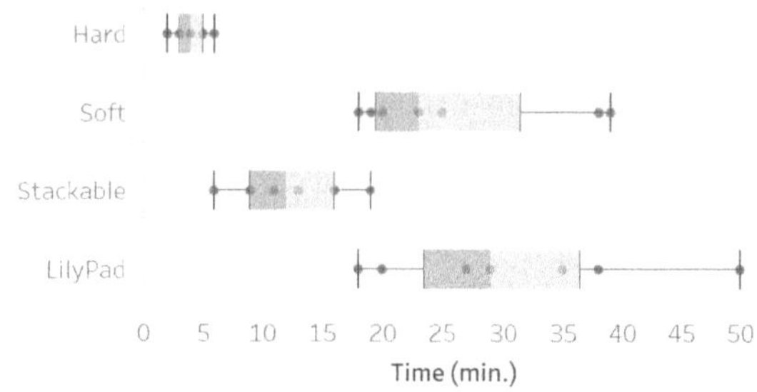


**Figure 2. Box and whisker plot of the total time to complete building both circuits during the pilot study.**

After working with each version of the toolkit, participants filled out a questionnaire about what they enjoyed and what they disliked about each version they used. When finished with each toolkit, participants completed a questionnaire gauging any change in circuitry or electronics knowledge and commenting on the toolkits.

#### *Analysis*

We recorded details on participants' interactions with the toolkits including the circuit completion times, number of short circuits, whether connections were secure, and challenges they faced. The surveys, researcher notes, video, and audio were analyzed using a mixed methods approach similar to other toolkit evaluation workshops [2, 31, 41].

### Results

#### *Participant Backgrounds*

The majority of participants considered their sewing skills as beginner-level, and most had programming experience. Two of the eight participants demonstrated a familiarity with electronic circuits, breadboards, and LEDs; and three of the eight participants demonstrated a familiarity with small electronics, sensors, and robots.

#### *Toolkit Efficiency*

We measured toolkit efficiency by evaluating circuit completion times (a common toolkit evaluation measure [36]), how frequently short circuits occurred, whether participants completed the circuits correctly, and difficulties encountered when working with each toolkit.

Circuits that required sewing took more **time to complete** than those that used magnets. Participants took about the same amount of time with the unmodified LilyPad Arduino (avg. 29.6 min) and Soft toolkit (avg. 25.1 min.), however, creating a circuit using the Stackable toolkit took less than half of the time (avg. 12.3 min.) as shown in Figure 2. Using the Hard toolkit was the fastest (avg. 4.5 min.).

Participants created significantly more **short circuits** when using the unmodified LilyPad Arduino as opposed to the Craftec system. No participants created a short circuit when working with the Soft or Stackable toolkits, but 1 of the 8 participants created a short circuit while using the Hard toolkit. In total, 7 participants created a short circuit while using the unmodified LilyPad Arduino. Most of the short circuits from the unmodified LilyPad were attributable to the conductive thread crossing.

**Circuit correctness** varied depending on the toolkit used, but people were largely successful. For the Hard toolkit, two participants had their LED circuits corrected by researchers, but all participants correctly completed the light sensor circuit. All participants completed the LED and light sensor circuits correctly with the Soft toolkit. Everyone completed the LED circuit correctly for the Stackable toolkit, but 1 participant did not correctly complete the light sensor circuit. One participant did not complete the LED circuit correctly with the unmodified LilyPad Arduino; similarly, another participant did not correctly complete the light sensor circuit.

Participants faced several **obstacles constructing functional, reliable circuits** while experimenting with the bases. Participants sometimes struggled with forming secure connections between the Hard toolkit's wires and magnets, and had issues working with inflexible wire connections. Soft toolkit problems included piercing the conductive fabric with a needle and overlapping strips of conductive fabric. Stackable toolkit difficulties included the magnetic strength and polarity, reliability of the magnets, and getting a good visual of the structure. With the LilyPad Arduino toolkits, participants experienced difficulties sewing, ensuring that the conductive thread formed a secure connection to the pins, avoiding loose or overlapping conductive thread, tracing electrical connections without the guidance of color, and creating tight stitches.

### *Design Considerations*

Participants noted that the Hard toolkit was quick to use, enabled intuitive prototyping, helped guard against short circuits due to insulated wires and color coding, was less of a hassle to use, and was more visually appealing. Participants praised the Soft toolkit for its reliable connections, color coding, and innovative combination of sewing and electronics. They noted that the conductive thread is a good visual representation of electrical connections and that the long fabric strips make short circuits less likely. Participants appreciated the novelty of the Stackable's structure, however they found manipulating the magnets in a vertical orientation challenging. They had difficult checking the magnetic connections unless the whole base was taken apart, keeping the bases level with each other, and the design's overall stability. Participants noted the versatility and design freedom that the LilyPad provided, but wanted more affordances in the design.

Based on these findings, we chose to narrow our evaluation of toolkits to the Hard and Soft toolkits by removing the Stackable toolkit from the system. The relative success of Hard and Soft compared to the difficulties people faced with the Stackable toolkit pushed us to narrow Craftec's focus. We made small changes to the Hard and Soft toolkits to resolve minor issues such as tighter connections between the Hard toolkit's wires and jewelry clasps to improve connections.

## EVALUATION WITH OLDER ADULTS

### Methods

We evaluated the Hard and Soft toolkits from the Craftec system in comparison to a LilyPad Arduino with 17 older adults in two 2-hour, ethics board approved, single session workshops. Ten participants (P1-P10) completed the first workshop, while the second workshop was run with 7 participants (P11-P17). Ten participants were women. All were white, and their ages ranged from 65-75 years old (average = 70.1). We collaborated with Parkview Research Center, a not-for-profit community health system in the US, who recruited participants on our behalf from a cardiology practice embedded in the health system's provider group - Parkview Physician's Group. Participants received $20 for their time and travel expenses.

### *Procedure*

Participants began with a pre-survey on demographics and their prior knowledge of maker electronics. Participants then read training materials discussing important electronics basics (e.g., input vs. output, circuit definition) and completed a second assessment of their circuits knowledge. Then, participants organized into self-selected groups of 2-4 people at each table to start individually working with a toolkit. One researcher was assigned to each table.

Participants tested as many toolkits as time allowed depending upon how quickly they were able to complete the activities. We did not set time constraints per toolkit because we were interested in correct completion and did not want to pressure participants. As in the pilot, they were asked to complete two circuits using an LED and light sensor for each toolkit. In addition to creating the circuits, in the workshop we asked participants to construct a craft-like artifact using their kits to envision how they could be incorporated into a craft project. Hard toolkits were adhered to a laser-cut balsa wood box, while Soft toolkits were sewn into a bag (Figure 3).

We altered the toolkit activity ordering procedure slightly between workshops to improve the participant experience and data collection. For the first workshop, participants determined their first toolkit by choosing a table to start at, but in the second workshop, everyone started with the Hard toolkit before continuing with the Soft or LilyPad Arduino toolkits. Starting participants with the quick success of the Hard toolkit was important to finishing all 3 toolkits in the 75 minutes allotted to working with the toolkits.

After completing each kit's circuits, we administered a brief survey to identify what participants enjoyed and struggled with. As the workshop concluded, participants completed a questionnaire reflecting on their overall use of the toolkits and an assessment of their circuit knowledge.

### *Analysis*

We collected researchers' notes of participants' interactions with each toolkit version to get a sense of how well they were able to complete the activities. Note that due to stricter data collection limitations of the medical center research environment, we collected audio and non-identifiable pictures of participants rather than video. The results were analyzed using a mixed methods approach similar to other toolkit workshops [2, 31, 41].

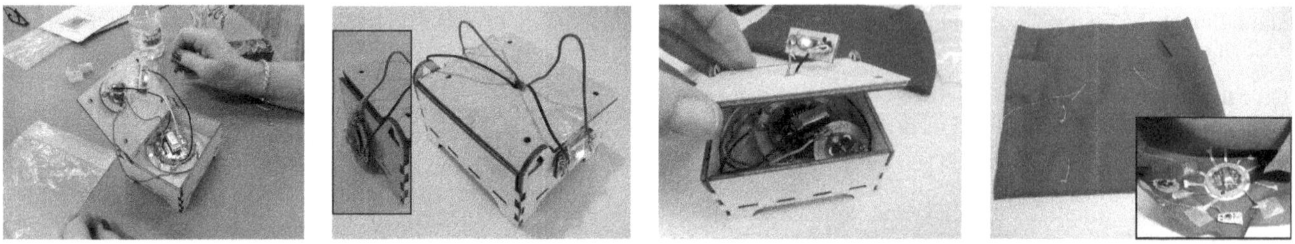

(a) Completed Box (b) Completed Box (c) Completed Box (d) Completed Bag

**Figure 3. These are examples of crafted boxes and bags. The boxes (a-c) use the Hard toolkit in feature different ways participants organized the components. The bag (d) uses the Soft toolkit.**

## Results

### *Participant Backgrounds*

Most workshop participants were unfamiliar with sewing or electronics. Most (12 of 17) rated their sewing skills as beginner. Only 2 participants said they were familiar with small electronics (e.g., LEDs, sensors) and programming, while 3 were familiar with circuits. For 4 participants, high school was their highest level of education, 2 had vocational school degrees, 8 had completed college, and 3 completed graduate or professional education.

### *Toolkit Efficiency*

Similar to the pilot study, we measured toolkit efficiency by evaluating the data collected during the workshop – circuit completion time, the number of short circuits, and the issues older adults faced with the toolkits. These included tearing conductive fabric, small port labels, and usability challenges for the LilyPad Arduino. Overall, 3 participants attempted only one toolkit with 1 completing their attempt, 11 attempted two toolkits with 10 completing both, and 3 attempted three toolkits with 2 completing all three. In total, 14 evaluated the Hard toolkit, 10 evaluated the Soft toolkit, and 10 evaluated the LilyPad Arduino toolkit.

Older adult participants took more **time to complete** the LED and light sensor circuits than the pilot participants. As displayed in Figure 4, workshop participants were the fastest with the Hard toolkit (avg. 9.6 min.). The Soft toolkit was the next fastest (avg. 31.3 min.), followed by the LilyPad Arduino (avg. 47.9 min.), which saw P3 and P6 struggle to complete in the 76 minutes allotted for circuit building.

Most participants were able to build circuits with more than one toolkit, especially in the second workshop where we started participants with the Hard toolkit. Some participants were able to build both circuits and the crafted box without any help from the research team. Several noted how the Hard toolkit was "Easier to understand" (P8) and "... easier to work with" (P7). By starting P11-P17 with the Hard toolkit, everyone in that workshop was able to complete more than one toolkit activity so they could compare between them, including P12 and P15 who completed all three. Several participants commented how much they enjoyed turning on the LEDs and learning new skills.

**Short circuits** were a common problem with the LilyPad Arduino toolkit, while the Craftec system saw few. Half of LilyPad Arduino participants (5/10) created a short circuit,

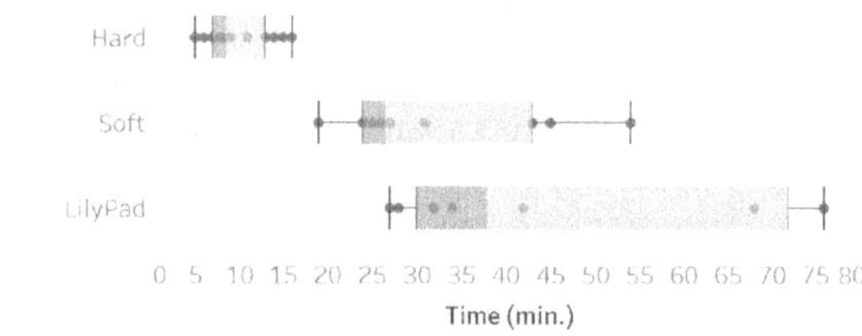


**Figure 4. Box and whisker plot of the total time to complete building both the LED and light sensor circuits during the workshop evaluation.**

especially as a result of loose and overlapping conductive thread. Two of 10 participants caused a short by crossing over threads they sewed into their fabric, while no one caused one with the Hard Toolkit.

### *Obstacles Creating Reliable Circuits*

A common issue for the Soft toolkit was the **torn conductive fabric extensions**, which slowed people down until the research team was able to fix them. The conductive fabric's soldered connection to the LilyPad SimpleSnap Protoboard would tear as participants operated the sewing machines or, in one case, when a participant shook their crafted bag. P14, who had experience with small electronics, was slowed by taking the time to fix his own connections.

With each kit, older adult participants disliked how difficult it was to read the **small port labels** on the Arduinos and components. We hoped that Craftec's reliance on coloring and shape would suffice, however our code was only set for specific ports.

There were a few **unique issues specific to the unmodified LilyPad Arduino toolkit** reflecting on the Craftec design decisions. Several participants disliked the difficulties they had with handling the tiny LED. They struggled to decide what length of thread to cut. If it was too short, then they were constantly rethreading the needle. If it was too long, then they were likely to tangle up the conductive thread. In addition, some participants struggled making tight connections with the ports, which requires looping the conductive thread through the pin holes several times, leading to finicky connections.

### *Crafted Boxes and Bags*

Craftec provided the older adults with the ability to quickly integrate maker electronics into a crafted balsa wood box and a fabric bag (Figure 3). Nearly everyone who worked on a box or a bag completed it shortly after completing both introductory circuits. For the Hard toolkit, participants often quickly reconfigured the LED and light sensor as they were constructing the box so it would function as they envisioned. They placed the Hard toolkit in several arrangements with some choosing to turn the light inside the box on when opened (Figure 3-a), while others lit up the box top when opened (Figure 3-c). Participants' most common concern was undoing their wired connections to place the LED and light sensor where they wanted.

The Soft toolkit bag offered fewer degrees of freedom for placing components since we gave participants a fabric template to machine sew their LED and light sensor circuits (Figure 3-d). Thus, the bags all lit up when opened.

When asked how they could use their crafted object or what project they could complete with one of the toolkits, participants highlighted several crafting projects. In the post-survey, most participants either agreed or strongly agreed that they could see opportunities for how electronics could be used. P12 suggested using the Soft toolkit to create a bag for their cell phones similar to the workshop. P10 said she would use the Hard toolkit for a kid's box or bag, or the LilyPad Arduino to modify her Christmas tree.

## DISCUSSION AND CONCLUSIONS

This paper contributes the Craftec system – an extendable maker electronics toolkit that supports older adults to incorporate electronics into their crafts. Craftec builds on Blikstein's educational children's toolkits framework [7] because it offers more selective exposure to concepts and power with embedded error correction (similar to PicoCricket [12] and Lego Mindstorms [24]). Craftec's support of multiple craft mediums and component placement degrees of freedom makes it a valuable addition to the toolkit community, who are often focused on STEM education. Our findings demonstrate that older adults – an overlooked group not often contributing to the DIY and Maker Movements – were able to efficiently build with the Hard and Soft toolkits. We discuss the implications of designing electronic toolkits for older adults to engage in maker activities through crafting.

Craftec compared favorably to the LilyPad Arduino [8] during the pilot study and workshop. Simplifying the connections between components with wires, magnets, conductive fabric, and conductive thread was key to Craftec's success. The Hard toolkit was much faster to complete than the unmodified LilyPad because it facilitated the ability to quickly prototype and modify the circuit configurations with magnets and wires. More work is needed to *investigate how to transition the Hard toolkit from prototyping to more permanent connections for an IoT object* in a living environment.

The Soft toolkit was faster on average for older adults using sewing machines than the LilyPad despite several participants having issues with torn conductive fabric. Similar results hold for the number of short circuits; the Craftec toolkits had very few (7.5% for both toolkits during the pilot and workshops), while many participants using LilyPad Arduino ran into issues (66.7%). Thus, we show the potential to *further abstract toolkit connections and increase degrees of freedom to facilitate safer making.*

Although machine sewing requires knowledge and resources, it *provides easier mechanisms to make secure, permanent connections that even novice participants can complete.* Hand sewing requires dexterity and visual acuity to thread the needle and stitch tight connections without bunching up thread. The Soft toolkit simplified this by allow participants to machine sew between conductive fabric strips – providing a large sewing area and tight pin connections.

### Implications for Designing Older Adult Toolkits

**Crafting** is a great way to engage older adults in maker electronics. Researchers found similar results with other demographics when bridging digital technology and crafting [11, 18, 44, 22, 48, 58, 59]. Allowing for varying crafting mediums opens up the possibilities of what older adults with diverse crafting skills can create. In the pilot, many younger adults viewed the Hard toolkit as an effective tool for teaching others about electronics, but the crafted boxes encouraged older adult participants to think of unique ideas for what projects to build. We encourage future toolkit creators to *take advantage of crafting to engage older adults in making with electronics* through a crafted object.

Several workshop participants who crafted their boxes used the Hard toolkit's extra **component placement degrees of freedom** to experiment with the physical design of the completed box. After seeing the initial interactions, participants reconfigured the sensors and LEDs to ensure the interaction worked as they envisioned. Older adults could have also tested their Soft toolkit bags by temporarily holding together the conductive fabric prior to sewing to envision how their toolkit interacted, allowing them to alter the layout of their components, however most did not because it would be awkward with the flexible bases. Currently, the design of Craftec connections imply permanence to participants – magnets could move, whereas sewing was a one time endeavor. *Toolkits should offer flexibility in how they are configured so participants can quickly see intended interactions and modify circuitry – providing participants with the ability to move from prototyping to permanent connections.*

Older adult participants struggled to read port numbers despite color and shape abstractions and expressed frustration if they accidentally connected to the incorrect port number. We *encourage toolkit researchers to integrate **flexible programming** with pins to increase degrees of freedom in creating circuits* and decrease programming pin constraints. We will improve the ease of use of Craftec's toolkits by leveraging recent toolkit advances such as Adafruit's Circuit Playground[4] to use on-board RGB LEDs for users to dynamically indicate ports with I/O based on the Craftec color abstractions.

### Limitations

We acknowledge both single session workshops should have been conducted identically using within-subjects study design. Since older adults needed more time to complete sewing kits,

[4] https://www.adafruit.com/product/3333

we altered the order in the second workshop to collect quality data. We were able to recruit a more gender diverse group in comparison to older adult HCI studies [13, 37, 38, 57] by working with a medical research center. However, we were restricted to collecting researcher notes, audio, and unidentifiable images. Since we did not have video in compliance with stricter medical research rules, some interaction data may have been lost.

## ACKNOWLEDGEMENTS

We thank participants and reviewers for providing valuable feedback. We also thank Parkview Research Center, Parkview Physician's Group, Haley MacLeod, Juan F. Maestre, and Evan Ahmed for their assistance. Funding for this research was provided in part by NSF Grants DGE-1342962, IIS-1439241, IIS-1814725, and CNS-1560276. Any opinions, findings, and conclusions or recommendations expressed in this material are those of the author(s) and do not necessarily reflect the views of the National Science Foundation.

## REFERENCES

[1] Swamy Ananthanarayan, Nathan Lapinski, Katie Siek, and Michael Eisenberg. 2014. Towards the crafting of personal health technologies. In *Proceedings of the 2014 conference on Designing interactive systems - DIS '14*. ACM Press, New York, New York, USA, 587–596. DOI: http://dx.doi.org/10.1145/2598510.2598581

[2] Swamy Ananthanarayan, Katie Siek, and Michael Eisenberg. 2016. A Craft Approach to Health Awareness in Children. In *Proceedings of the 2016 ACM Conference on Designing Interactive Systems*. ACM, Brisbane, QLD, Australia, 724–735. DOI: http://dx.doi.org/10.1145/2901790.2901888

[3] Ingrid Arreola, Zan Morris, Matthew Francisco, Kay Connelly, Kelly Caine, Ginger White, Ingrid Arreola, Zan Morris, Matthew Francisco, Kay Connelly, Kelly Caine, and Ginger White. 2014. From checking on to checking in: designing for low socio-economic status older adults. In *Proceedings of the 32nd annual ACM conference on Human factors in computing systems - CHI '14*. ACM Press, New York, New York, USA, 1933–1936. DOI: http://dx.doi.org/10.1145/2556288.2557084

[4] Ayah Bdeir and Ayah. 2009. Electronics as material: littleBits. In *Proceedings of the 3rd International Conference on Tangible and Embedded Interaction - TEI '09*. ACM Press, New York, New York, USA, 397. DOI: http://dx.doi.org/10.1145/1517664.1517743

[5] Susan M. Behuniak. 2011. The living dead? The construction of people with Alzheimer's disease as zombies. *Ageing and Society* 31, 1 (2011), 70–92. DOI: http://dx.doi.org/10.1017/S0144686X10000693

[6] Paulo Blikstein. 2013. Gears of our childhood: constructionist toolkits, robotics, and physical computing, past and future. In *Proceedings of the 12th International Conference on Interaction Design and Children - IDC '13*. ACM Press, New York, New York, USA, 173–182. DOI: http://dx.doi.org/10.1145/2485760.2485786

[7] Paulo Blikstein. 2015. Computationally Enhanced Toolkits for Children: Historical Review and a Framework for Future Design. *Foundations and Trends® in Human-Computer Interaction* 9, 1 (2015), 1–68. DOI: http://dx.doi.org/10.1561/1100000057

[8] Leah Buechley, Mike Eisenberg, Jaime Catchen, and Ali Crockett. 2008. The LilyPad Arduino: using computational textiles to investigate engagement, aesthetics, and diversity in computer science education. In *Proceeding of the twenty-sixth annual CHI conference on Human factors in computing systems - CHI '08*. 423. DOI: http://dx.doi.org/10.1145/1357054.1357123

[9] Leah Buechley, Nwanua Elumeze, Camille Dodson, and Michael Eisenberg. 2005. Quilt snaps: A fabric based computational construction kit. In *Proceedings - IEEE International Workshop on Wireless and Mobile Technologies in Education, WMTE 2005*, Vol. 2005. 219–221. DOI: http://dx.doi.org/10.1109/WMTE.2005.55

[10] Leah Buechley and Benjamin Mako Hill. 2010. LilyPad in the Wild: How Hardware's Long Tail is Supporting New Engineering and Design Communities. In *Proceedings of the 8th ACM Conference on Designing Interactive Systems (DIS '10)*. ACM, New York, NY, USA, 199–207. DOI: http://dx.doi.org/10.1145/1858171.1858206

[11] Leah Buechley and Hannah Perner-Wilson. 2012. Crafting technology: Reimagining the processes, materials, and cultures of electronics. *ACM Transactions on Computer-Human Interaction* 19, 3 (oct 2012), 1–21. DOI: http://dx.doi.org/10.1145/2362364.2362369

[12] The Playful Invention Company. 2010. PicoCricket - the invention that integrates art and technology. (2010). https://www.picocricket.com.

[13] Raymundo Cornejo, Robin Brewer, Caroline Edasis, and Anne Marie Piper. 2016. Vulnerability, Sharing, and Privacy: Analyzing Art Therapy for Older Adults with Dementia. In *Proceedings of the 19th ACM Conference on Computer-Supported Cooperative Work & Social Computing (CSCW '16)*. ACM, New York, NY, USA, 1572–1583. DOI: http://dx.doi.org/10.1145/2818048.2819960

[14] Kristin N. Dew and Daniela K. Rosner. 2018. Lessons from the Woodshop: Cultivating Design with Living Materials. In *Proceedings of the 2018 CHI Conference on Human Factors in Computing Systems (CHI '18)*. ACM, New York, NY, USA, Article 585, 12 pages. DOI: http://dx.doi.org/10.1145/3173574.3174159

[15] Dale Dougherty. 2012. Maker Market Study. (2012). https://cdn.makezine.com/make/bootstrap/img/etc/Maker-Market-Study.pdf.

[16] BeagleBoard.org Foundation. 2018a. Beagle Board. (2018). http://beagleboard.org/.

[17] RaspberryPi.org Foundation. 2018b. Raspberry Pi. (2018). http://raspberrypi.org/.

[18] Raune Frankjær and Peter Dalsgaard. 2018. Understanding Craft-Based Inquiry in HCI. In *Proceedings of the 2018 on Designing Interactive Systems Conference 2018 - DIS '18*. ACM Press, New York, New York, USA, 473–484. DOI: http://dx.doi.org/10.1145/3196709.3196750

[19] Tova Gamliel. 2017. Education in civic participation: Children, seniors and the challenges of an intergenerational information and communications technology program. *New Media & Society* 19, 9 (2017), 1388–1405. DOI: http://dx.doi.org/10.1177/1461444816639971

[20] Emilie Giles and Janet van der Linden. 2015. Imagining Future Technologies: ETextile Weaving Workshops with Blind and Visually Impaired People. In *Proceedings of the 2015 ACM SIGCHI Conference on Creativity and Cognition (C&C '15)*. ACM, New York, NY, USA, 3–12. DOI: http://dx.doi.org/10.1145/2757226.2757247

[21] Connie Golsteijn, Elise Van Den Hoven, David Frohlich, and Abigail Sellen. 2014. Hybrid crafting: Towards an integrated practice of crafting with physical and digital components. *Personal and Ubiquitous Computing* 18, 3 (2014), 593–611. DOI: http://dx.doi.org/10.1007/s00779-013-0684-9

[22] Elizabeth Goodman and Daniela Rosner. 2011. From garments to gardens: negotiating material relationships online and 'by hand'. In *Proceedings of the 2011 annual conference on Human factors in computing systems - CHI '11*. ACM Press, New York, New York, USA, 2257. DOI: http://dx.doi.org/10.1145/1978942.1979273

[23] Saul Greenberg and Chester Fitchett. 2001. Phidgets: Easy Development of Physical Interfaces Through Physical Widgets. In *Proceedings of the 14th Annual ACM Symposium on User Interface Software and Technology (UIST '01)*. ACM, New York, NY, USA, 209–218. DOI: http://dx.doi.org/10.1145/502348.502388

[24] The Lego Group. 2018. Lego Mindstorms. (2018). https://www.lego.com/en-us/mindstorms.

[25] Philip J. Guo. 2017. Older Adults Learning Computer Programming: Motivations, Frustrations, and Design Opportunities. In *Proceedings of the 2017 CHI Conference on Human Factors in Computing Systems (CHI '17)*. ACM, New York, NY, USA, 7070–7083. DOI: http://dx.doi.org/10.1145/3025453.3025945

[26] Microduino Inc. 2018. mCookie. (2018). http://microduinoinc.com/products/mcookie-parts/.

[27] Adafruit Industries. 2018. Adafruit Flora. (2018). https://www.adafruit.com/category/92.

[28] Kelly Joyce and Meika Loe. 2010. A sociological approach to ageing, technology and health. *Sociology of Health & Illness* 32, 2 (2010), 171–180. DOI: http://dx.doi.org/10.1111/j.1467-9566.2009.01219.x

[29] Eva-Sophie Katterfeldt, Nadine Dittert, and Heidi Schelhowe. 2009. EduWear: Smart Textiles as Ways of Relating Computing Technology to Everyday Life. In *Proceedings of the 8th International Conference on Interaction Design and Children*. ACM, Como, Italy, 9–17. DOI: http://dx.doi.org/10.1145/1551788.1551791

[30] Majeed Kazemitabaar, Liang He, Katie Wang, Chloe Aloimonos, Tony Cheng, and Jon E. Froehlich. 2016. ReWear: Early Explorations of a Modular Wearable Construction Kit for Young Children. In *Proceedings of the 2016 CHI Conference Extended Abstracts on Human Factors in Computing Systems - CHI EA '16*. ACM Press, New York, New York, USA, 2072–2080. DOI: http://dx.doi.org/10.1145/2851581.2892525

[31] Majeed Kazemitabaar, Jason McPeak, Alexander Jiao, Liang He, Thomas Outing, and Jon E. Froehlich. 2017. MakerWear: A Tangible Approach to Interactive Wearable Creation for Children. In *Proceedings of the 2017 CHI Conference on Human Factors in Computing Systems - CHI '17*. ACM Press, New York, New York, USA, 133–145. DOI: http://dx.doi.org/10.1145/3025453.3025887

[32] Majeed Kazemitabaar, Leyla Norooz, Mona Leigh Guha, and Jon E. Froehlich. 2015. MakerShoe: Towards a Wearable E-Textile Construction Kit to Support Creativity, Playful Making, and Self-Expression. In *Proceedings of the 14th International Conference on Interaction Design and Children - IDC '15*. ACM Press, New York, New York, USA, 449–452. DOI: http://dx.doi.org/10.1145/2771839.2771883

[33] Amanda Lazar, Raymundo Cornejo, Caroline Edasis, and Anne Marie Piper. 2016. Designing for the Third Hand: Empowering Older Adults with Cognitive Impairment through Creating and Sharing. In *Proceedings of the 2016 ACM Conference on Designing Interactive Systems - DIS '16*. ACM Press, New York, New York, USA, 1047–1058. DOI: http://dx.doi.org/10.1145/2901790.2901854

[34] Amanda Lazar, Caroline Edasis, and Anne Marie Piper. 2017. A Critical Lens on Dementia and Design in HCI. In *Proceedings of the 2017 CHI Conference on Human Factors in Computing Systems - CHI '17*. ACM Press, New York, New York, USA, 2175–2188. DOI: http://dx.doi.org/10.1145/3025453.3025522

[35] Amanda Lazar, Jessica L. Feuston, Caroline Edasis, and Anne Marie Piper. 2018. Making as Expression: Informing Design with People with Complex Communication Needs. In *Proceedings of the 2018 CHI Conference on Human Factors in Computing Systems - CHI '18*. ACM Press, New York, New York, USA, 1–16. DOI: http://dx.doi.org/10.1145/3173574.3173925

[36] David Ledo, Steven Houben, Jo Vermeulen, Nicolai Marquardt, Lora Oehlberg, and Saul Greenberg. 2018. Evaluation Strategies for HCI Toolkit Research. In *Proceedings of the 2018 CHI Conference on Human*

*Factors in Computing Systems (CHI '18)*. ACM, New York, NY, USA, Article 36, 17 pages. DOI: http://dx.doi.org/10.1145/3173574.3173610

[37] Matthew L. Lee and Anind K. Dey. 2014. Real-time Feedback for Improving Medication Taking. In *Proceedings of the 32Nd Annual ACM Conference on Human Factors in Computing Systems (CHI '14)*. ACM, New York, NY, USA, 2259–2268. DOI: http://dx.doi.org/10.1145/2556288.2557210

[38] Michael Massimi and Daniela Rosner. 2013. Crafting for Major Life Events: Implications for Technology Design and Use. In *Proceedings of the 27th International BCS Human Computer Interaction Conference (BCS-HCI '13)*. British Computer Society, Swinton, UK, UK, Article 34, 6 pages. http://dl.acm.org/citation.cfm?id=2578048.2578091

[39] Janis Lena Meissner, Angelika Strohmayer, Peter Wright, and Geraldine Fitzpatrick. 2018. A Schnittmuster for Crafting Context-Sensitive Toolkits. In *Proceedings of the 2018 CHI Conference on Human Factors in Computing Systems - CHI '18*. ACM Press, New York, New York, USA, 1–13. DOI: http://dx.doi.org/10.1145/3173574.3173725

[40] Janis Lena Meissner, John Vines, Janice McLaughlin, Thomas Nappey, Jekaterina Maksimova, and Peter Wright. 2017. Do-It-Yourself Empowerment As Experienced by Novice Makers with Disabilities. In *Proceedings of the 2017 Conference on Designing Interactive Systems (DIS '17)*. ACM, New York, NY, USA, 1053–1065. DOI: http://dx.doi.org/10.1145/3064663.3064674

[41] David A. Mellis, Sam Jacoby, Leah Buechley, Hannah Perner-Wilson, and Jie Qi. 2013. Microcontrollers as material: crafting circuits with paper, conductive ink, electronic components, and an "untoolkit". In *Proceedings of the 7th International Conference on Tangible, Embedded and Embodied Interaction - TEI '13*. ACM Press, New York, New York, USA, 83. DOI: http://dx.doi.org/10.1145/2460625.2460638

[42] Louis Neven. 2015. By any means? Questioning the link between gerontechnological innovation and older people's wish to live at home. *Technological Forecasting and Social Change* 93 (2015), 32 – 43. DOI: http://dx.doi.org/https://doi.org/10.1016/j.techfore.2014.04.016 Science, Technology and the "Grand Challenge" of Ageing.

[43] Michael I. Norton, Daniel Mochon, and Dan Ariely. 2011. The 'IKEA Effect': When Labor Leads to Love. *Harvard Business School Marketing Unit* 11, 091 (2011). DOI: http://dx.doi.org/10.2139/ssrn.1777100

[44] Hannah Perner-Wilson, Leah Buechley, and Mika Satomi. 2011. Handcrafting Textile Interfaces from a Kit-of-no-parts. In *Proceedings of the Fifth International Conference on Tangible, Embedded, and Embodied Interaction (TEI '11)*. ACM, New York, NY, USA, 61–68. DOI: http://dx.doi.org/10.1145/1935701.1935715

[45] Population Division, Department of Economic and Social Affairs. 2002. *World Population Aging: 1950-2050*. Technical Report ST/ESA/SER.A/207. United Nations.

[46] Irene Posch and Geraldine Fitzpatrick. 2018. Integrating Textile Materials with Electronic Making: Creating New Tools and Practices. In *Proceedings of the Twelfth International Conference on Tangible, Embedded, and Embodied Interaction - TEI '18*. ACM Press, New York, New York, USA, 158–165. DOI: http://dx.doi.org/10.1145/3173225.3173255

[47] Jie Qi, Leah Buechley, Andrew "bunnie" Huang, Patricia Ng, Sean Cross, and Joseph A. Paradiso. 2018. Chibitronics in the Wild: Engaging New Communities in Creating Technology with Paper Electronics. In *Proceedings of the 2018 CHI Conference on Human Factors in Computing Systems - CHI '18*. ACM Press, New York, New York, USA, 1–11. DOI: http://dx.doi.org/10.1145/3173574.3173826

[48] Jie Qi, Andrew "bunnie" Huang, and Joseph Paradiso. 2015. Crafting technology with circuit stickers. In *Proceedings of the 14th International Conference on Interaction Design and Children - IDC '15*. ACM Press, New York, New York, USA, 438–441. DOI: http://dx.doi.org/10.1145/2771839.2771873

[49] Mitchel Resnick, Fred Martin, Randy Sargent, and Brian Silverman. 1996. Programmable Bricks: Toys to think with. *IBM Systems Journal* 35, 3.4 (1996), 443–452. DOI: http://dx.doi.org/10.1147/sj.353.0443

[50] Mitchel Resnick and Stephen Ocko. 1991. *Constructionism* (1991), 141–150.

[51] Yvonne Rogers, Jeni Paay, Margot Brereton, Kate L. Vaisutis, Gary Marsden, and Frank Vetere. 2014. Never too old: engaging retired people inventing the future with MaKey MaKey. In *Proceedings of the 32nd annual ACM conference on Human factors in computing systems - CHI '14*. ACM Press, New York, New York, USA, 3913–3922. DOI: http://dx.doi.org/10.1145/2556288.2557184

[52] Eric Rosenbaum and Jay Silver. 2018. MaKey MaKey. (Aug. 2018). Retrieved August 1, 2018 from http://www.makeymakey.com/

[53] Arnan Sipitakiat and Nusarin Nusen. 2012. Robo-Blocks: designing debugging abilities in a tangible programming system for early primary school children. In *Proceedings of the 11th International Conference on Interaction Design and Children - IDC '12*. ACM Press, New York, New York, USA, 98. DOI: http://dx.doi.org/10.1145/2307096.2307108

[54] Rebecca Stewart, Sophie Skach, and Astrid Bin. 2018. Making Grooves with Needles: Using e-textiles to Encourage Gender Diversity in Embedded Audio Systems Design. In *Proceedings of the 2018 on*

*Designing Interactive Systems Conference 2018 - DIS '18*. ACM Press, New York, New York, USA, 163–172. DOI:http://dx.doi.org/10.1145/3196709.3196716

[55] Sarah L. Szanton, Rachel K. Walker, Laken Roberts, Roland J. Thorpe, Jennifer Wolff, Emily Agree, David L. Roth, Laura N. Gitlin, and Christopher Seplaki. 2015. Older adults' favorite activities are resoundingly active: Findings from the NHATS study. *Geriatric Nursing* 36, 2 (2015), 131 – 135. DOI:http://dx.doi.org/https://doi.org/10.1016/j.gerinurse.2014.12.008

[56] Vasiliki Tsaknaki, Ylva Fernaeus, Emma Rapp, and Jordi Solsona Solsona. 2017. Articulating challenges of hybrid crafting for the case of interactive silversmith practice. *DIS 2017 - Proceedings of the 2017 ACM Conference on Designing Interactive Systems* 2 (2017), 1187–1200. DOI: http://dx.doi.org/10.1145/3064663.3064718

[57] Stephen Uzor, Lynne Baillie, and Dawn Skelton. 2012. Senior Designers: Empowering Seniors to Design Enjoyable Falls Rehabilitation Tools. In *Proceedings of the SIGCHI Conference on Human Factors in Computing Systems (CHI '12)*. ACM, New York, NY, USA, 1179–1188. DOI: http://dx.doi.org/10.1145/2207676.2208568

[58] Maarten Versteeg, Elise van den Hoven, and Caroline Hummels. 2016. Interactive Jewellery: A Design Exploration. In *Proceedings of the TEI '16: Tenth International Conference on Tangible, Embedded, and Embodied Interaction (TEI '16)*. ACM, New York, NY, USA, 44–52. DOI: http://dx.doi.org/10.1145/2839462.2839504

[59] Clement Zheng and Michael Nitsche. 2017. Combining Practices in Craft and Design. In *Proceedings of the Tenth International Conference on Tangible, Embedded, and Embodied Interaction - TEI '17*. ACM Press, New York, New York, USA, 331–340. DOI: http://dx.doi.org/10.1145/3024969.3024973

# Upcycling Tree Branches as Architectural Elements through Collaborative Design and Fabrication

**Hironori Yoshida**
the University of Tokyo
Preferred Networks, Inc.
hironoriyh@gmail.com

**Maria Larsson**
the University of Tokyo
ma.ka.larrson@gmail.com

**Takeo Igarashi**
the University of Tokyo
takeo@acm.com

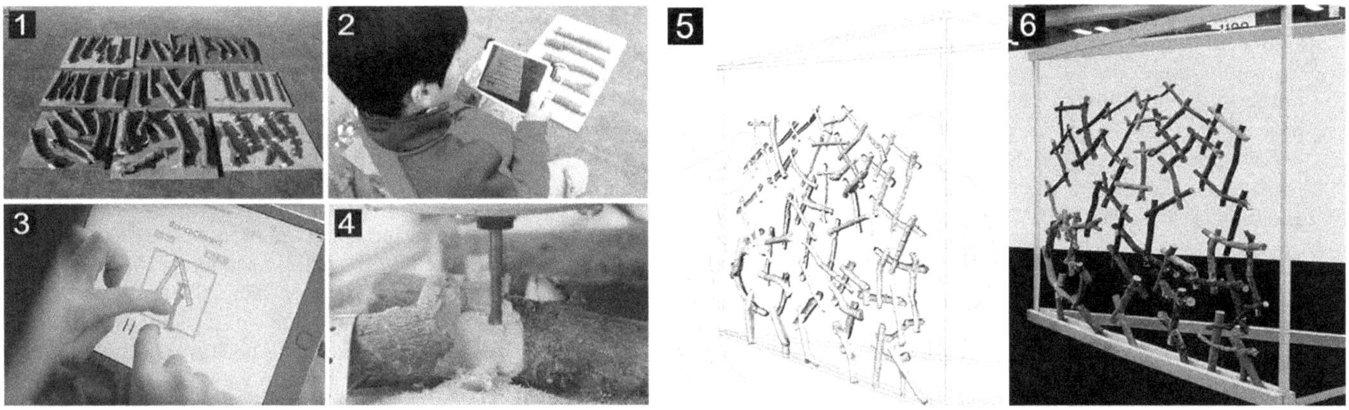

**Figure 1. Workflow overview: 1.fix branches on plates 2.scan the plates and upload the model 3. play the game with scanned branches 4.fabricate joineries by a CNC router 5. The layout of a screen wall designed for South by South West (SXSW). 6. An assembled screen wall.**

## ABSTRACT

While tree trunks are standardized as lumber, branches are typically chipped or burned. This paper proposes a workflow to upcycle such mundane and diverse natural material to architectural elements. Introducing an online design interface, we let users participate in the design and fabrication workflow from collecting branches to CNC milling. The branches are first scanned, and then key geometrical features are extracted and uploaded to the online game "BranchConnect". This application lets multiple non-expert users create 2D-layouts. At the point of intersection between two branches, the geometry of a lap joint and its cutting path are calculated on-the-fly. A CNC router mills out the joints accordingly, and the branches are assembled manually. Through this workflow, users go back-and-forth between physical and digital representations of tree branches. The process was validated with two case studies.

## Author Keywords

Design and Fabrication, Crowdsourcing, Upcycling


*TEI '19, March 17–20, 2019, Tempe, AZ, USA.*

ACM ISBN 978-1-4503-6196-5 /19/03 ...$15.00.
http://dx.doi.org/10.1145/3294109.3295639

## CCS Concepts

**•Applied computing → Computer-aided design; •Human-centered computing →** *Participatory design;* Please use the 2012 Classifiers and see this link to embed them in the Tex: `https://dl.acm.org/ccs/ccs_flat.cfm`

## INTRODUCTION

Effective use of natural resources is becoming an important theme in architectural design. Although wood has been used for building throughout history, it is nowadays particularly promoted as a sustainable construction material [16]. While tree trunks are processed and standardized into lumber, the rest of the tree, mostly branches and bark, are typically chipped or burned as fuel. In the DIY community we can observe some activity making objects out of naturally shaped branches, but these are often limited to handmade decorations. Since tree branches account for 25 % of a whole tree, there is a large potential contribution to the effective use of natural resources if we can use branches for building. [1].

More than being resourceful, the use of tree branches can provide a desired character for architectural design. Active use of local materials is a recognized design approach, called vernacular architecture [12]. Weston claims that a building made out of local materials represents the local community, which helps to foster a sense of belonging [15]. We put emphasis on this hub aspect of local materials. We take fabrication as an opportunity for non-experts to foster their knowledge, skills, and even the sense-of-belonging [5]. In terms of educating or supporting non-experts, various tools have been developed to assist non-experts to complete and realize their designs [6]. We also developed the design game which assists users to complete their designs, however, our motivation is to provide opportunities to connect others. In this sense, tree branches perform as tangible medium to participate in a community [4, 10].

This paper proposes a method to upcycle organically shaped materials to fabricate architectural elements leveraging computational fabrication techniques. For collecting and designing, we developed an online interface where users can freely post branches they have found. Further, users can create and post layout designs of branches through the online game BranchConnect. The submitted layout designs are directly translated to custom lap joints. As lap joints work as rigid joints and do not require additional systems such as screws, the assembly process of is simple and user-friendly (Figure 1.4). In this paper, we share the technical details of our workflow, and report from two case studies where we let non-expert users design and build a 2D screen wall. In summary, our contributions are

- A workflow enabling to use diverse and natural material as design components.
- An online game-based approach to collaborative architectural design.
- A method to design and fabricate customized non-orthogonal lap joints using high-resolution contours.

## RELATED WORK

Several design and fabrication projects focused on organic shape of trees. Monier and colleagues virtually explored architectural design with branch-like components, and Wood Barn project realized a structure from forked tree trunks built with custom joineries milled by a robot arm [11, 9]. While they used large tree trunks, our work uses tree branches, which are more obtainable and reasonable size for crowdsourcing without requiring special equipment. The challenge is the size and fragility of branches, thus it is more difficult to process. Schindler and colleagues used digitally scanned tree branches for furniture and interior design elements [13]. While they demonstrated the capability of digital fabrication processes to handle irregularly shaped branches, the design process was dependent on experts. Our work scaled their approach by gamified collaborative design interface and fabrication workflow for non-experts. Architectural design is inherently collaborative among users and architects. Computer mediated participatory design in architecture was further explored by Cimerman [2]. Talton and colleagues developed a collaborative design tool for users to design trees and plants [14]. FoldIt crowdsourced protein structure prediction to game players [3]. DrawAFriend is an app to collect stroke data for auto-stroke assistance [8]. Human-in-the-loop construction methods were proposed in architecture-scale [17, 7]. While these works take users either on design or fabrication, our work let users participate in the whole processes not only for problem solving but also for providing experience.

## WORKFLOW

The workflow is summarized as follows (also see the left of Figure 1). Branches are first collected and attached to plywood plates. Then they are scanned, processed and uploaded to the online game BranchConnect. Players create their layout design by moving branches around in the game. Once a design is finished, it is exported to another application that calculates the unique milling paths of each pair of joints. The CNC router mills out the joints accordingly, and users assemble the branches by hand.

### Collecting and Scanning Branches

The first step is to collect branches. Then they need to be trimmed down below a fixed length, determined by the reachable area of the CNC router used for fabricating. In our setup, the maximum length is about 50 *cm*. Branches are manually cut using a saw. Then they are attached to plywood plates, with about 5-8 branches per plate. They need to be firmly fixed to stay in place during the milling process. We use metal fixtures and screws to attach them.

To be able to import the collected branches to the game, their shapes are captured by digital 3D-scanning. After a textured mesh model is acquired, we extract skeleton, contour, and radius as a simplified representation of the branch. First the branches are segmented from the background by simply applying a height threshold. The top view 2D contours of each branch are obtained by contour detection. The skeleton is detected by applying Delaunay Triangulation to the contours and extracting the middle points from the triangles. After extracting the skeleton points, their order is analyzed, and a curve is drawn to connect them. In this process we need to consider the case of a grafting branch (Y-shaped) consisting of multiple segments. To avoid cutting metal fixtures during milling, their locations are identified by mouse-clicks and marked with a red dot. After all required data is extracted, it is uploaded to a cloud database, and the game is ready to run. The left of Figure 2 shows a textured mesh model on the left, and corresponding contours and skeletons on the right.

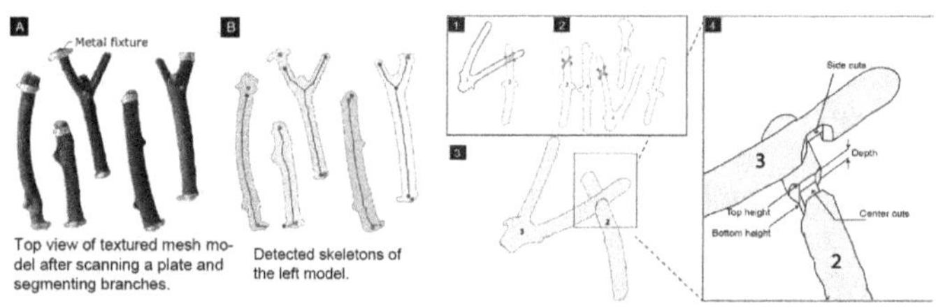


**Figure 2. Left: A and B show an interface of branch importer. Right: diagram of our joints. 1. A layout design 2. Branches on a plate with milling paths in red 3.An assembled pair of branches 4. A close-up joint geometry.**

### BranchConnect: The Game

The goal of the game is to connect predefined target points on a frame with a limited number of branches. Users can pick a branch from the available set displayed on the bottom and create layouts by moving, rotating, and mirroring branches. The user continuously receives visual feedback and a score, guiding the user to a feasible design. The game is completed when all the target points are connected. It is, however, still possible to keep modifying the layout to improve the design and to try to reach a higher score. Joint and group evaluation are the two key functions of the game, and the basis for the scoring system.

### *Joint Condition Score*

A joint is detected when two branch skeletons are intersecting. An important rule of the game is that every other branch needs to be flipped, i.e., mirrored, in order to make a valid joint. This is due to fabrication constraint of the CNC router which can approach a branch only from above. Mirrored branches are indicated by a thicker outline in the game. Figure 3 presents other joint conditions for calculating score.

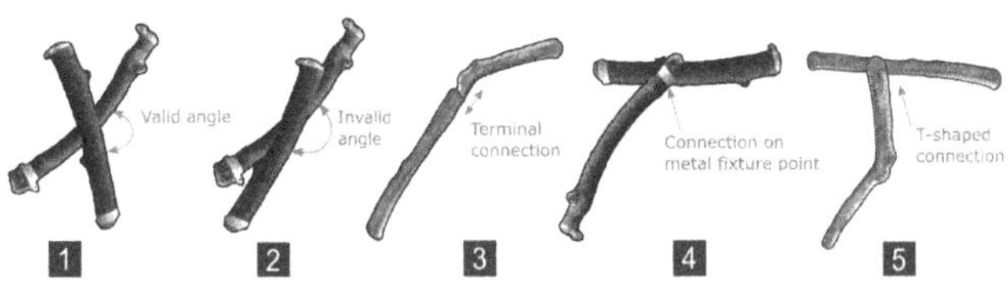


**Figure 3. Joint conditions. 1. Valid joint. 2. Invalid - angle out of range. 3. Invalid - terminal connection. 4. Invalid - metal fixture point. 5. Invalid - T-shaped connection.**

Iterating all branches in a frame $\mathscr{B}$, we get the number of all valid/invalid joints and connected target points, $N_{valid}$, $N_{invalid}$, $Ntarget$ respectively. When a branch $b_i \in \mathscr{B}$ is connected to one of target points, the number of the connected target points $N_{target}$ is appended and the branch is trimmed at the target point. We calculate the score of joint conditions $\mathscr{S}_{\text{joint}}$ as follows.

$$\begin{aligned} \mathscr{S}_{\text{joint}} &= w_1 N_{valid} + w_2 N_{invalid} + w_3 N_{target} \\ \text{s.t. } & w_j \in \mathbb{R} \wedge \forall j \in 1, \ldots, 3 \\ & N_{target} \leq T_{all} \in \mathbb{R} \end{aligned} \tag{1}$$

### *Group Condition Score*

Major group conditions are detected as in Figure 4. After updating the group, group condition and the connectivity of target points are evaluated. Denoting a group and a set of groups as $g_k$ and $\mathscr{G}$ respectively, we check each branch $b_i \in g_k \in \mathscr{G}$ whether it has a connection with a target point or not. If it has, the target point is stored in the group $g_k$. Denoting

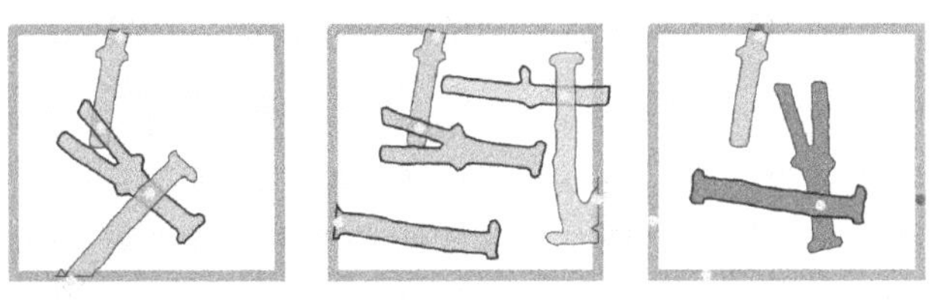

**Figure 4. Left: valid group with two target points connected. Middle: valid but non-optimal because there is more than one group. Right: invalid due to *Islanded* situation.**

the number of groups as $N_{group}$, the number of islanded groups as $N_{island}$, the number of bridged target points as $N_{bridged}$, the sum of distance of bridged target points as $Dist_{bridged}$ the score of group conditions $\mathscr{S}_{group}$ is calculated as

$$\begin{aligned} \mathscr{S}_{\text{group}} &= w_5 N_{island} + w_6 N_{bridged} + w_7 Dist_{bridged} + w_8 N_{cycle} \\ \text{s.t. } & w_j \in \mathbb{R} \wedge \forall j \in 1, \ldots, 4 \\ & N_{bridged} \leq T_{all} \\ & N_{island} \leq Br \end{aligned} \tag{2}$$

The game is completed when $N_{group}$ is one, and all the target points are connected to the group without invalid joints. The state of completion $\mathscr{C}_{\text{complete}}$ is binary and described as

$$\mathscr{C}_{\text{complete}} = \begin{cases} 1, & \text{if } N_{group} = 1 \wedge N_{bridged} = T_{all} \wedge N_{invalid} = 0 \\ 0, & \text{otherwise} \end{cases} \tag{3}$$

We calculate the score $S_{\text{all}}$ by adding the results from Eq 1, Eq 2, and Eq 3. Note that the weights $w_1 \ldots w_9$ are non-negative weight coefficients pre-adjusted in advance by the authors.

$$\begin{aligned} S_{\text{all}} &= \mathscr{S}_{\text{joint}} + \mathscr{S}_{\text{group}} + w_9 \mathscr{C}_{\text{complete}} \\ & \text{s.t. } w_9 \in \mathbb{R} \end{aligned} \tag{4}$$

## Fabrication and Assembly

After a design is selected for fabrication, fabricatability of the design is further analyzed in a high-resolution model. If an invalid joint is detected, the layout can be modified by adjusting the branch positions using the mouse. Users can also control fabrication parameters such as milling bit diameter, joint depth, cutting speed, moving height and so on. After confirming the fabrication settings and joint validity, G-Code is exported to the CNC by one click. The joint is a lap-joint with full side cuts and a half-way-down center cut. The resulting geometry creates rigid joints, adapted to the unique branch shapes and angles of intersection (the right of Figure 2).

## CASE STUDIES

### Workshop

We organized a design and fabrication workshop to examine the feasibility of our system. It was hosted in a public community house close to a forest. The participants were four children (aged 4, 7, 9, and 10) and two parents. We set the goal to create a screen wall (2000 $mm$ x 900 $mm$) divided into 8 sub-frames (500 $mm$ x 450 $mm$).

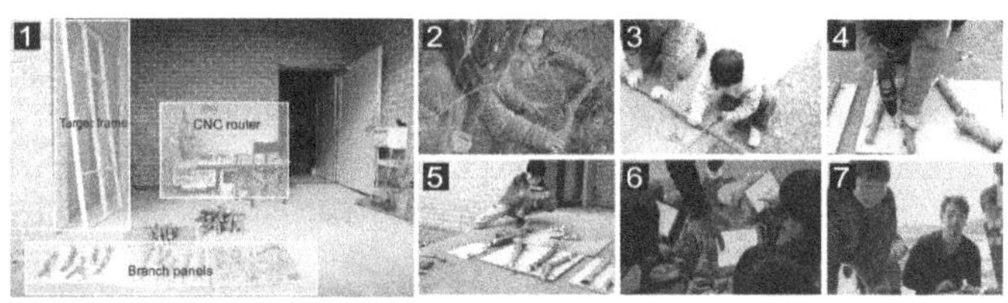


**Figure 5. An overview of the workshop. 1. The overview of the space. 2. Collect branches. 3. Cut in specified lengths 4. Attach on a plate 5. Scan the plate 6. Play the game 7. CNC milling.**

Firstly the participants were asked to collect branches with 2-10 $cm$ diameters. The collected branches were cut in appropriate lengths. They could construct two plates by themselves and the rest plates were built by authors. Each plate was scanned using iSence camera running on iPad minis. Figure 6 the left shows the scanned branches on plates. When the plates are scanned, simplified branches were uploaded online. We set 30 minutes for playing the game, including practice to get started. Figure 6 the right shows example layouts in score-descending order. Finally, participants were asked to assemble the branches by hand. The whole workshop took 4.6 hours to complete, including introduction, moving, and breaks.

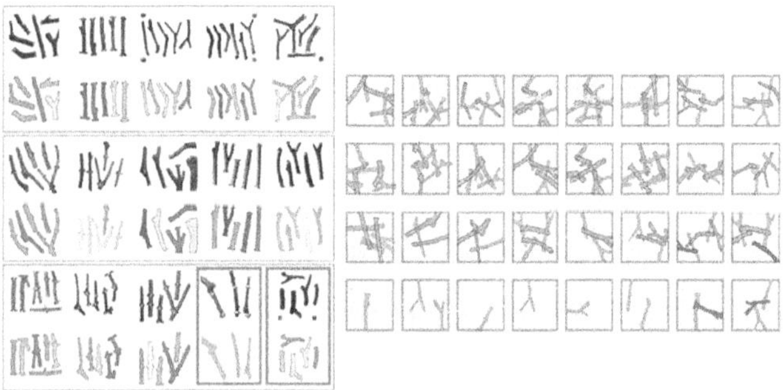

**Figure 6. Left: An overview of all the 15 scanned plates. Ortho-top views of scanned mesh models and segmented branches are shown for each raw, top and bottom respectively. The plates with red rectangles are built by participants in the workshop. Right: Example layouts created by the authors in score-descending order. The highest score is top-left and the lowest score is bottom-right.**

### SXSW Exhibition

What we learned from the workshop is that participants preferred to complete a large wall without subdividing frames. In this case study, a 2D screen wall with a single large frame was designed and built to exhibit at SXSW. The wall size is 2 by 2 *m* and we used 74 branches. Compared to the workshop, we used diverse types of trees and a wider range of shapes. The CNC milling took two weeks in total and the assembly took less than an hour with three people.

The main challenge of this study was to decide the best layout of over 70 branches all to be fitted in a frame. At the beginning, a designer focused on the layout task, but we soon realized that it was overwhelming for one person. Eventually we overcame the issue by virtually subdividing the frame into several work areas and restricting the number of branches per area. Each area became a micro-task, thus multiple designers could work collaboratively. For international shipping, branches went through fumigating process to eliminate insects in the branches. The final outcome is shown in Figure 1.6.

## CONCLUSION AND FUTURE WORK

We have presented a participatory workflow to upcycle tree branches as architectural elements. The participants collect, scan, mill, and assemble branches by themselves, guided by the system. The layout is also designed by the participants in an online game. We run two case studies where the participants successfully constructed wooden screen walls using our workflow. Our study only confirmed the feasibility of our approach. Further investigation is necessary to examine the effectiveness of the collaborative gamification approach in improving the layout quality and in nurturing the sense of belonging. The fabrication process is limited to 2D and inefficient. For future work, it is valuable to work on design and fabrication of 3D structures. The fabrication process has to accommodate higher degree of freedom either by robot arm or other approaches. Structural analysis is lacking in this study and can be integrated in the design process.

## ACKNOWLEDGEMENTS

This research was supported by JST Act-I Grant Number JPMJPR17UT, also partially supported by JSPS KAKENHI Grant Number 17H00752.

## REFERENCES

[1] Ahmed Abdel-Rahman. 2003. The Full paper making process. http://individual.utoronto.ca/abdel_rahman/paper/fpmp.html. (2003).

[2] Benjamin Cimerman. 2000. Participatory Design in Architecture: can computers help?. In *PDC*. 40–48.

[3] Seth Cooper, Firas Khatib, Adrien Treuille, Janos Barbero, Jeehyung Lee, Michael Beenen, Andrew Leaver-Fay, David Baker, Zoran Popović, and others. 2010. Predicting protein structures with a multiplayer online game. *Nature* 466, 7307 (2010), 756–760.

[4] Tanja Döring, Axel Sylvester, and Albrecht Schmidt. 2013. A Design Space for Ephemeral User Interfaces. In *Proceedings of the 7th International Conference on Tangible, Embedded and Embodied Interaction (TEI '13)*. ACM, New York, NY, USA, 75–82. DOI: http://dx.doi.org/10.1145/2460625.2460637

[5] Patrick Tobias Fischer, Eva Hornecker, and Christian Zoellner. 2013. SMSlingshot: An Expert Amateur DIY Case Study. In *Proceedings of the 7th International Conference on Tangible, Embedded and Embodied Interaction (TEI '13)*. ACM, New York, NY, USA, 9–16. DOI:http://dx.doi.org/10.1145/2460625.2460627

[6] Takeo Igarashi. 2016. Design Everything by yourself - User Interfaces for Graphics, CAD Modeling, and Robots. (2 2016). http://tei.acm.org/2016/keynote.html Keynote at the 10th TEI'16, Eindhoven, the Netherlands [Accessed: 2018 11 01].

[7] Benjamin Lafreniere, Tovi Grossman, Fraser Anderson, Justin Matejka, Heather Kerrick, Danil Nagy, Lauren Vasey, Evan Atherton, Nicholas Beirne, Marcelo H Coelho, and others. 2016. Crowdsourced Fabrication. In *Proceedings of the 29th Annual Symposium on User Interface Software and Technology*. ACM, 15–28.

[8] Alex Limpaecher, Nicolas Feltman, Adrien Treuille, and Michael Cohen. 2013. Real-time drawing assistance through crowdsourcing. *ACM Transactions on Graphics (TOG)* 32, 4 (2013), 54.

[9] Jessica Mairs. 2016. AA Design and Make students use a robotic arm to build a woodland barn. http://pr2016.aaschool.ac.uk/2014-15--Woodchip-Barn. (2016). Accessed: 2018-07-30.

[10] Marshall McLuhan and Quentin Fiore. 1967. The medium is the message. *New York* 123 (1967), 126–128.

[11] Vincent Monier, Jean Claude Bignon, and Gilles Duchanois. 2013. Use of irregular wood components to design non-standard structures. In *Advanced Materials Research*, Vol. 671. Trans Tech Publ, 2337–2343.

[12] Paul Oliver. 1997. *Encyclopedia of vernacular architecture of the world*. Cambridge University Press.

[13] Christoph Schindler, Martin Tamke, Ali Tabatabai, Martin Bereuter, and Hironori Yoshida. 2014. Processing Branches: Reactivating the performativity of natural wooden form with contemporary information technology. *International Journal of Architectural Computing* 12, 2 (2014), 101–115.

[14] Jerry O Talton, Daniel Gibson, Lingfeng Yang, Pat Hanrahan, and Vladlen Koltun. 2009. Exploratory modeling with collaborative design spaces. *ACM Transactions on Graphics-TOG* 28, 5 (2009), 167.

[15] Richard Weston. 2003. *Materials, form and architecture*. Yale University Press.

[16] Swedish Wood. 2018. Wood is a sustainable construction material. www.swedishwood.com. (2018). Accessed: 2018-07-26.

[17] Hironori Yoshida, Takeo Igarashi, Yusuke Obuchi, Yosuke Takami, Jun Sato, Mika Araki, Masaaki Miki, Kosuke Nagata, Kazuhide Sakai, and Syunsuke Igarashi. 2015. Architecture-scale Human-assisted Additive Manufacturing. *ACM Trans. Graph.* 34, 4, Article 88 (July 2015), 8 pages. DOI: http://dx.doi.org/10.1145/2766951

# A Pattern-Based, Design Framework for Designing Collaborative Environments

**Yixiao Wang**
Cornell University
Ithaca, NY, USA
yw697@cornell.edu

**Keith Evan Green**
Cornell University
Ithaca, NY, USA
keg95@cornell.edu

## ABSTRACT
Communication theory suggests that people tend to interact with interactive artifacts as if these were human. For decades, this understanding has been applied to designing singular, embedded artifacts at a small physical scale. In this paper, we extend the same theory and practice to the dimension of space—to designing interactive, physical environments and their components. A conceptual ground for this is found in a "pattern language" developed by Alexander et al. for designing static physical environments. Upon this ground, we construct a systematic framework for designing "collaborative environments" shaped, as well, by our own concepts, *Direct Mapping*, *Conveyed Mapping*, and *Space Agency*, to strive for more human-human-like interactions between human beings and their physical surroundings. Our lab-based study generates a hypothetical design as qualitative validation of the framework, which has significance for designing tangible, embedded, and embodied interaction as it extends, inevitably, to the dimension of space, entertaining, serving, and augmenting us.

### Author Keywords
Design patterns; transdisciplinary research methods; critical making; spatial interaction; spatial reconfiguration.

### CCS Concepts
• Human-centered computing → Human-Computer Interaction (HCI) → Interaction paradigms

## INTRODUCTION
*A Pattern Language* (1977) [4] by Alexander, Ishikawa, and Silverstein was highly influential in architecture but has since become more impactful on computer science and its allied disciplines (as reviewed by [12]). *A Pattern Language* is comprised of 253 patterns guiding environmental design, presented as drawn diagrams and written narratives which "represent our best guess as to what arrangement...will work to solve...a problem which occurs over and over again" [4]. For instance, pattern 185, "Sitting Circle" (figure 1), offers an arrangement of living room furniture, whereby the selection of furnishings and their placement, relative to the walls defining the room, allow for an intimate correspondence between those who are seated as well as a path for others to circumvent this intimate gathering with the least disruption and most efficient movement. Recognize that pattern 185, typical of *A Pattern Language*, was as much about how people interact with each other—how they collaborate—as how people interact with their physical surroundings. Patterns were meant to be assembled into familiar routines of people and places that define our everyday lives.

In computer science and its allied disciplines, a pattern-based framework has been applied to the design of software (e.g. "reusable object-oriented software" [11]); to computer games (e.g. [22]; and to the expanding realm of IoT [36], given that a networked suite of interactive devices is inherently spatial as compared to human-computer interaction with a singular device, which is 1:1. A pattern-based framework has also been impactful in social and assistive robot research (see [20] for an overview), where it informs robot-environment interaction (in navigation and perceptual tasks within a room) and also robot-human interaction (whereby the robot exhibits human-like "behavioral patterns" perceived by humans as approachable, familiar, or what we define here as "collaborative"). As will be explored later in this paper, a pattern-based framework may also prove productive to the emerging domain of interactive and intelligent environments first imagined, tellingly, by a circle of

Figure 1. Pattern number 185, "Sitting Circle" [2].


*TEI '19*, March 17–20, 2019, Tempe, AZ, USA

ACM ISBN 978-1-4503-6196-5/19/03...$15.00
https://doi.org/10.1145/3294109.3295652

| Sequence | Research Activity | Interactive System | The "Lens" Used |
|---|---|---|---|
| 1st | Ethnographic Study | Human-Human | Observation |
| 2nd | Coding of Interaction Patterns | Human-Human | *From the literature:*<br>• Grounded Theory Coding<br>• Design Partnerships<br>• Joint Action<br>• CSCW Creative Workplace |
| 3rd | Coding of Interaction Patterns | Human-Collaborative Environment | *Our own:*<br>• Direct Mapping<br>• Conveyed Mapping<br>• Space Agency |

**Table 1. The design-research framework based on studies, theories, and other literatures.**

researchers to which Alexander belonged that included Nicholas Negroponte (as elaborated in *Soft Architecture Machines*, [32]) and Gordan Pask (in "The Architectural Relevance of Cybernetics," [35]).

But the pattern language of Alexander et al., being based on professional "best guesses" [4] and conceived for designing static environments, is arguably an inadequate framework for designing computational systems that are spatial, collaborative, or both, given the complex interactions such systems afford. Consequently, this paper posits the question, *What is a pattern-based framework for designing computational artifacts that are integral to or constitute a collaborative environment*? In our effort to respond, we recognize such artifacts as "agents," defined as "any complex environment, including the built environment" [2], that is aware of, transmits, and receives information from the world, and also manipulates aspects of the world.

Rather than a framework drawn from "best guesses," our pattern-based framework overviewed in Table 1 is: (a) based in ethnography, (b) informed by a consideration of the literature (especially, communications theory), and (c) shaped by three of our own concepts—*Direct Mapping*, *Conveyed Mapping*, and *Space Agency*. Later in this paper, as a means to validate our framework, we report on a lab study that sought patterns in human-human interaction that we translated into patterns of interaction between humans and a collaborative environment of our own design. This singular case suggests an early, qualitative validation of the framework. We envision, in the future, our framework informing the design of wide-ranging tangible, embedded, and embodied artifacts as these become increasingly collaborative with us and extend, inevitably, to the dimension of space—supporting, entertaining, and augmenting us.

## THEORETICAL FOUNDATIONS

In developing our pattern-based framework, we drew inspiration from the literature of communication theory—particularly the two concepts, "Computer as Social Actor" (CASA) [30] and "The Media Equation" [37], both of which suggest that people tend to interact with interactive artifacts as if these were human. This intimate, "Pygmalion," human-artifact relationship in fact dates to antiquity [33, 46], was recuperated in the Renaissance [3]), and persists still today in embedded artifacts. CASA and the Media Equation are concepts that advance our understanding of the human-artifact rapport when the artifact is interactive or intelligent by way of digital means. Collaborative environments and their integral components heighten the complexity of this rapport still further. In this section, we consider CASA and the Media Equation, and their import to the framework.

### CASA and the Media Equation

With the rapid development of computational technologies, and as computer-embedded systems become more interactive and intelligent, researchers of the 1990s conceptualized the research paradigm, Computer as Social Actors (CASA) [30]. As part of this conceptualization, Reeve and Nass proposed "The Media Equation" (1996), a general communication theory that describes the tendency of people to interact and communicate with computer media as if this media were human [37]. Since then, many psychological experiments studying human communications have informed human-computer interaction design [31]. Initially, design researchers applied these psychological findings to virtual, avatar designs [45]. More recently, design researchers have been transferring "common, interpersonal communication phenomena" [31, 37] to tangible, embedded, and embodied systems such as social robots [14, 15], and robotic furniture [42] (the latter being pertinent to our case study, presented later in this paper). As will be elaborated here, our case study extends this conceptualization to a robotics-embedded collaborative environment supporting and potentially augmenting work activity. The case study aims to make evident that studying human-human collaboration reveals patterns of interactions that translate to patterns of how people and a collaborative environment might interact. Such patterns could then shape how collaborative environments and their components are designed, and the interactions such agents afford.

## ANALYTICAL FOUNDATIONS

In developing our pattern-based framework, we also drew inspiration from four analytical foundations from the literature: the grounded theory coding method, and the literatures of design partnerships, Joint Action, and Creative Workplaces drawn from the CSCW (Computer-Supported Cooperative Work) community. We briefly consider these foundations and their import to the framework.

### Grounded Theory Coding Method

"Grounded theory coding method" [8] is a well-accepted and commonly used coding technique for analyzing transcripts of ethnographic studies [24]. Charmaz identifies four steps [8] in the grounded theory coding process: "initial coding," "focused coding," "axle coding," and "theoretical coding." At a minimum, grounded theory coding should include "initial coding" and "focused coding" (as our research team accomplished in the case study, soon to be considered).

There are several reasons to use grounded theory coding method in a pattern-based design framework; the most important one is that grounded theory coding requires researchers to "stop and ask analytic questions" of the data collected [8]. Such questions not only "further our understandings to the studied life," but also "help us direct subsequent data-gathering toward the analytic issues we are defining." [8] In this way, design researchers are not only identifying interaction patterns, but also exploring deeper questions such as the *why* and *how* certain interactions occur. Asking these questions is vital for deeply understanding human-human interaction that lends well to coding robust, human-artifact interaction patterns.

### Design Partnerships, Joint Action, and CSCW

In developing our framework, we attended to a review of the literature pertaining to how design partners "design-think" [10, 23, 25] and both gesture and communicate through design, with special consideration of "face-to-face gestural interactions" occurring during the design process [6]. Insights from this literature inform the ethnographic study of human-human collaboration, offering sign-posts to the activity of observation.

From the psychology literature (e.g. [21]), interactions between human beings working closely together may be categorized as "joint actions," which describes both "emergent coordination" and "planned coordination." People perform "joint actions" when they "coordinate their actions in space and time to produce a joint outcome" [21]. When two people work together (as we observed in our case study of collaborating, human designers), the collaborating couple or group performs "joint actions" with clear goals and purposes, a "coordination" pattern of human-human actions characterized as "planned." Human-human coordination may also "emerge," unplanned [21].

Furthermore, our framework was informed by the literature from "design communication" (e.g. [43]) and CSCW. We found particular relevance in CSCW research focusing on Creative Workplaces [38, 47] with a focus on empirical studies recording sequences and frequencies of different design activities [43] and properties of "work space informal communications" such as "frequency, duration, and whether [such communications are] pre-arranged" [47]. These studies inspired us to further investigate how social cues "shape task coordination and communication" [38].

### Creative Workplaces

Towards conceptualizing our framework, we also found inspiration in empirical studies focused on physical settings salient to creativity in the workplace. Martens [26] outlined typically characteristics of the creative office: it is "informal," "family like," and provides a degree of user "control over the space." Furthermore, McCoy and Evans [27] identify five abstract dimensions of the creative workspace: "nature," "challenge," "freedom," "support," and "coherence." For each of these, McCoy and Evans elaborated its formal characteristics: "spatial form (size, dimension & shape)," "light," "internal organization of objects," "characteristics of bounding surface," "color," "texture," and so on. [27]. Stokols et al. [44] meanwhile argue that "levels of environmental distraction (noise, foot traffic, etc.)" are significantly related to "perceived support for creativity at work" [44]. Additionally, Martens [26] and McCoy [27, 28] performed literature reviews on "physical work spaces" and "creativity" that suggest that creative workplaces offer a variety of personalized spaces, secluded private spaces (offering "freedom, security and control") and "open offices" [26]. The Creative Workplaces findings and characterizations were helpful to us in forming an understanding of the physical context that shapes the collaboration of human partners.

What might seem a haphazard encounter with various literature has, taken together, significant implications for understanding human-human partnerships as afforded by the physical environment, and especially those environments which are interactive and moreover "collaborative."

## THREE NEW "TRANSLATIONAL" CONCEPTS

Designing an environment that is perceived as human-like, or what we call here "collaborative," brings new design challenges. In designing a collaborative environment, the designer transfers observable human-human interaction patterns as much as, and as precisely as possible, to human-environment interactions so that users interact with their physical surroundings as if the environment and its component parts were human-like in at least some respects. Towards this aspiration, we introduce three novel concepts to guide the design process of mapping human-human interaction patterns to human-environment interaction patterns.

### Direct Mapping

In the proposed design framework (as captured in Table 1), observations of human-human interaction are coded as patterns—a coding procedure that is not trivial but also not unfamiliar to many design researchers. Subsequently, such human-human interaction patterns are translated into human-environment interaction patterns. This translation is very much itself a design process—part-science, part-art. Some human-human interaction patterns can be "directly mapped" to human-environment interaction patterns. For instance, people actively engaged in collaboration with one another frequently use their arms to form gestures that communicate their ideas. In direct mapping, these physical gestures formed by human arms are recreated rather directly in the cyber-physical system.

We use the term "Direct Mapping," thus, to describe a design process in which human-human interaction patterns are directly copied, imitated, and applied to human-environment interaction designs. For instance, a robotic arm might closely replicate the gestures observed in the human-human work space. Presumably, the same gestures enacted by the robotic artifacts would convey the same messages to a collaborating human as did the human arm. This presumption has already been verified in human-robot interaction research [13, 14, 19], and [41] where Direct Mapping predominates. For example, Hoffman et al. designed a lamp robot called "Kip" [13] that directly maps various human expressions. Another example focused on the built environment, comes from Ju et al. [19], whereby an automatic door "gestures" those entering a building as if it were a doorman opening the door.

### Conveyed Mapping

There are many human-human interaction patterns that cannot be directly mapped to human-environment interactions. Obvious examples include eye contact, facial expressions, a sense of humor, and other subtle gestures. It is indeed difficult to imagine how an environment-as-agent, no matter how interactive or intelligent, could offer "eye contact" "smile," or "wink" to its human collaborators. Many of these subtle but significant social cues are used for reaching a common ground amongst human collaborators, during verbal communication, as defined and studied in the theory of "Grounding in Communication" [9]. Although these communications cannot be directly mapped to, say, a smart device, the meaning of these communications delivered by such a device—the messages it conveys—can be understood by human recipients. Consequently, we strive to design human-machine interactions in which the artifact conveys sufficient (i.e. discernable, perceivable) approximations of cues that humans naturally convey using subtle, social cues. For example, although a room cannot "nod its head" to encourage a conversation, maybe the room can "blink" green LED lights during a conversation to convey a semblance of encouragement to a human partner. We therefore use the term Conveyed Mapping to describe a design process in which human-human interaction patterns cannot be directly mapped to an artifact but nevertheless can be mapped in such a way as to convey the same core message as found in human-human interactions. The conveyance comes by way of a substituted gesture that the system is designed to deliver (e.g. approval by "green blinking lights" as a conveyance of "head nodding").

### Space Agency

In recent years, HCI research has, on one hand, focused on designing objects that might take a more figurative form (e.g. the aforementioned "Kip" [15]) or a more abstract form (e.g. a "mechanical ottoman" [41]) that is, in both cases, perceived by users as human-like. On the other hand, HCI research has increasingly focused on the dimension of space, extending "ubiquitous computing" to (for one) "smart cities" with special attention to "natural interfaces, context-aware applications, and automated capture and access" [1]. These two tendencies of HCI suggest the importance of human-like agency and "cyberspace" [17] that, taken together, suggest the need of HCI designers to focus attention increasingly on realizing an "information space" [7], one that seems familiar, or (at least) one that invites collaboration. However, HCI researchers entering this research domain have tended to focus more on embedding technologies into *existing infrastructure* rather than designing newly realized, cyber-human environments [1]. We call the latter a "Space Agent" (see figure 2) an interactive or intelligent artifact that is both environmental (i.e. space-making) and human-like in (at least some of) its behaviors. Situated in HCI's intellectual landscape

**Figure 2. Our vision of how Space Agents (here, robot surfaces) might be implemented in a fully-autonomous car.**

| Focused Coding | Initial Coding | Insights from Former Research & Theories |
|---|---|---|
| Non-verbal, bodily communication | arm gestures; shape, direction & feelings; mimicking characters, etc. | Four types of gestures for design tasks and meetings: kinetic, spatial, pointing & other [6]. |
| Inspiration cues | brain storming; abstract ideas; bold designs; share personal stories and experiences; ideas on drawing boards, etc. | Create idea maps and leverage ideas from others to generate more creative and diverse ideas [40]. |
| Facial expressions, eye contact, social cues. | eye contact with audience; showing interest and enthusiasm; positive confirmation; conversational encouragements, etc. | Four themes (with 13 models) for observed social cues and task outcomes; rapport in negotiation (laugh); establish procedural grounding (gaze); deictic in shared contexts gestures (points); non-verbal feedback to avoid interruptions (nod) [38]. |
| Cheerful & relaxed atmosphere | funny pictures or news; smiling face stickers on walls; cheerful talks; chatting and gossip; snacks, etc. | "SYMLOG three-dimensional-space"—a positive working atmosphere encouraging creative discussions and improving work efficiency [5]. |
| Place-based cues | Tell stories of a remote place: travelled there before; lived there before; having friends there; perception of the culture; local practices and policies, etc. | Using lights, sounds and movements to simulate environment, seasons, feelings of the places described in story books [39]. |

**Table 2. Study results of the initial design partnership study – five examples.**

somewhere in the space between smart objects, intelligent environments, and smart cities, Space Agents are capable of performing some manipulation tasks we might expect from a humanoid or industrial robot (e.g. grasping, reaching, supporting, pointing, twisting, carrying, pushing, lifting) while also capable of reconfiguring the spatial envelope of the room to shape, essentially, "different rooms" matched to the unfolding of human-artifact collaboration.

We use the term "Space Agency," thus, to describe that design attribute in which human-human interaction patterns are embodied in a collaborative environment or its constituent components to forge productive and satisfying human-environment interactions.

## CASE STUDY: COLLABORATIVE WORK ENVIRONMENT

We used our pattern-based framework, overviewed in Table 1 and elaborated in the previous sections, to design a collaborative work environment inspired by recent interactive and intelligent environments, including the *InteractiveWall* [16] by the Hyperbody Research Group (TU Delft), *Lift-Bit* [34] by Carlo Ratti (MIT), *AWE* [12] by co-author of this paper Keith Evan Green (Cornell), and the *ambientROOM* by Hiroshi Ishii (MIT) [18]. We envisioned our collaborative environment comprised, in part, by one or more Space Agents. For this collaborative environment (in more practical terms), we envisioned a Space Agent as a tendon-driven robot surface that is a cross between a human arm and a physically reconfigurable "ribbon" several feet in length (see figure 2). Performing manipulation tasks and defining the physical envelopes of rooms, Space Agents have potential, promising application to interiors of many kinds, including dwellings, hospitals, autonomous vehicles, spacecraft, and space habitation. Figure 2 shows our Space Agent robot surface implemented in a fully-autonomous ("level-5") vehicle. Our design objective is twofold: (a) to provide inhabitants many "rooms" configured by these robotic surfaces within a relatively compact habitable space; and (b) to envision such robotic surfaces not as components of a passive frame but as intelligent agents partnering with their inhabitants in human-collaborative environment activity—what we've called here "Space Agency."

We began the design cycle by observing human pairs partnering on a design task. From these observations, we generated patterns modeling human-human interactions which we then translated to patterns of interaction for a human designer collaborating with an intelligent, "human-like," physical space to accomplish the same design task. Interactions of human design partners were systematically coded as informed by Charmaz's "grounded theory coding technique" [8], design-partnership studies defined as "joint action" [21], and the CSCW literatures [47] (particularly that of the "Creative Workplace") [26]. Study results were mapped to human-environment interaction patterns guided by our three concepts introduced here for the first time: Direct Mapping, Conveyed Mapping, and Space Agency.

### Ethnographic Studies of Design Partnerships

Our ethnographic study focused on understanding face-to-face interactions between design partners collaborating on a design task. In our study, we observed four groups of designers (12 participants in total), each group comprised of two to four designers. The first three groups were formed by undergraduate design majors at Cornell University, while the fourth group had one professional architect and one design-focused doctoral student. Members of the three groups of undergraduate designers granted us permission to conduct observations of and interviews on their design processes, and to record field notes, pictures and videos. Members of the fourth group—the design professional and the Ph.D. student—only permitted us to conduct interviews with them. We did a forty-minute in-depth interview with this one group. For each of the three undergraduate student groups, we observed each group's design process in their studio workspaces for no less than 1.5 hours and as many as 3 hours, and recorded their interactions using video cameras, digital cameras, and hand-written field notes. At the end of each session, we did a 15-minute interview with one member of each team.

Following the observations, we coded our field notes and digital photos, and transcribed the video recordings [29], analyzing the transcribed materials using Charmaz's grounded theory coding techniques (i.e. "initial coding" and "focused coding") [8]. Given this paper's focus on a design-research framework, and given the paper's page-limit, we present here in Table 2 (found on the previous page) only the coding results and their associations with what we learned from the most relevant literatures.

### Mapping Human-Human Interactions to Human-Environment Interactions

From the coding results and insights, we identified four distinct human-human interaction patterns as a means to validate our design-research framework:

- *Arm Gestures* are a means of pointing and communicating shape, size, directionality, and other forms of communication produced by the upper limbs.
- *Positive Social Cues* express enthusiasm, encouragement, or agreement.
- *Inspirational Cues* include storytelling and sharing abstract ideas.
- *Place-based Cues* reference remote places, including their histories, cultures, local living styles, policies, etc.

*Arm Gestures* are interaction patterns involving physical movements of the arms. For Arm Gestures, we used Direct Mapping, given that these physical gestures can be transferred directly to the physical trajectories of the space agents.

*Positive Social Cues* such as those communicating enthusiasm are difficult to directly map to the Space Agent. Thus, we use Conveyed Mapping to convey the same messages by creating new forms of interaction that can be achieved via the Space Agents. For instance, a Space Agent might express enthusiasm through its animated movements and flashing rainbow colors produced by embedded LEDs.

*Inspirational Cues* are the stories and shared experiences people tell each other to get inspired. There are many ways a room might tell a story. Direct Mapping could, for instance, suggest having the room and human designer "exchange" stories with the use of a whiteboard: the human designer can use the whiteboard to post ideas, and the room's intelligent system then uses this input to search the internet for relevant stories (news reports, documentaries, fictional accounts etc.) based on the keywords of the post. This information can be presented on a display embedded in the Space Agent or on the wall or ceiling, and the Space Agent might move and emit color and audio to bring attention to the story and even capture the atmosphere of it (as our lab has done previously with the LIT ROOM [28]).

*Place-based Cues* might communicate information about a remote place that is relevant and informative to the work at hand. While the human designer may use only words and nonverbal communication such as hand gestures to describe a remote place, Indirect Mapping might make full use of the Space Agents with its embedded lighting and audio to evoke the site environment and its atmosphere, rendering the whole of the environment a "portal" to somewhere else [12]. This use of ambient media is partly inspired by Ishii's ambientROOM [18] cited earlier, which communicates information more in the background than the foreground of our attention. However, for our case-study design, we imagine ambient media also being, when appropriate, in the *foreground* of our attention, depending on the context.

For our case study (at least), a key contribution of the Space Agent robot surface is its capacity to bring an element of surprise to the creative process that, for Cross [10] and Maher [25], offers that "impetus for framing and reframing the problem, thereby avoiding routine," [10] rather unproductive behavior in the designer.

In the design activity, one should recognize that the application of either Direct Mapping, Conveyed Mapping, or Indirect Mapping is a design decision made by design researchers. Similarly, even with the same mapping method, different designers might arrive at different design outcomes because of the creative nature of implementing the pattern-based framework. The three mapping strategies of our pattern-based framework—Direct and Conveyed Mapping, and Space Agency—are intended to generate inspired design solutions rather than rigid or formulaic outcomes.

## FROM HUMAN-ENVIRONMENT INTERACTIONS TO DESIGN PATTERNS

In this section, we explore how the human-environment interaction patterns of our case study might generate "design patterns" for a collaborative environment supporting and even augmenting design activity. Helpful to us in this translation was the "Creative Workplace" literature, for instance, in suggesting the use of "fluid shapes" in space [27] for fostering creativity. As follows, the Space Agents (of continuum robot technology [12]) allow for fluid rather than rigid motion and shape-making. Additionally, following Martens' suggestion[26] that workspaces provide users with some measure of control over their physical environment, we designed an environment that may be physically shaped by direct control of its human collaborators.

Table 3 illustrates the human-environment interaction patterns and the corresponding design patterns generated. We recognize that these patterns are neither the only patterns nor the best design patterns. Nonetheless, these patterns are reasonable and logical ones based on our human-environment interaction patterns and what we drew from the Creative Workplace literature. In Table 3, we present these patterns in the manner of *A Pattern Language*—as both diagrams and brief narratives.

As Alexander et al. reminds us, "no pattern is an isolated entity"—a pattern can only exist "supported by other patterns: the larger patterns in which it is embedded, the patterns of the same size that surround it, and the smaller patterns which are embedded in it" [4]. For the few patterns presented in this paper, each of these patterns can follow another one in time; and at one time, one pattern can be

| **Human-Environment Interaction Pattern** | **Design Pattern Diagram** | **Design Pattern Narrative** |
|---|---|---|
| Arm Gestures<br>to<br>Space Agents | 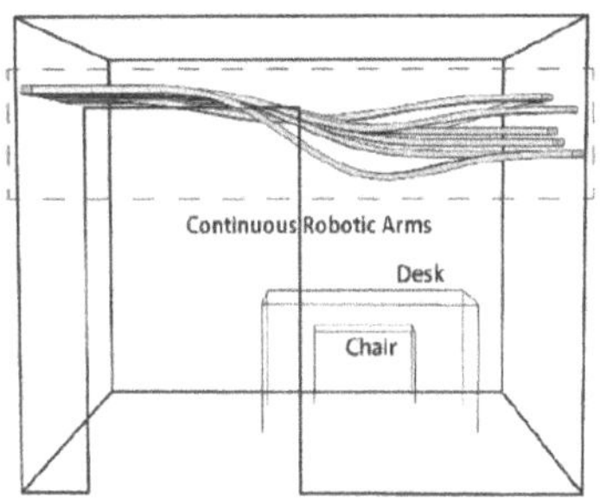 | Space agents (continuum robot surfaces) physically reconfigure to "point" and to convey shape, orientation, direction, and the like. These robot surfaces can be mounted on or embedded flush with ceiling and wall surfaces or, alternatively, be free-standing within the volume of the room. |
| Positive Social Cues<br>to<br>lighting effects | 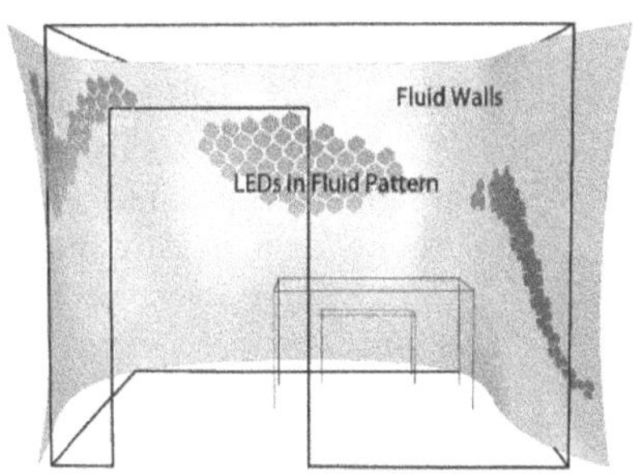 | Lighting is one means to convey "positive social cues." Changes in color, intensity, patterning, and periodicity/duration may be perceived by the human collaborator as a form of encouragement. Such lighting may be combined with the movement of the space agents to further the impact. |
| Inspiration Cues (story-telling)<br>to<br>white board input by human designer and responsive content content identified by AI, presented on displays | 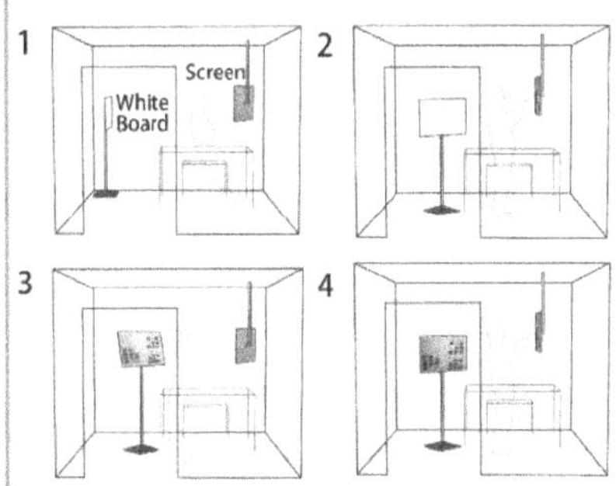 | The collaborative environment and human designer can "exchange" stories with use of a whiteboard: the human designer can use the whiteboard to post ideas, and the room's intelligent system then uses this input to search the internet for relevant stories based on the keywords on the posts. This information can then be presented on a display, embedded in the space agent, or projected on the wall or ceiling to capture the atmosphere of it. |
| Place-based Cues<br>to<br>multi-media display | 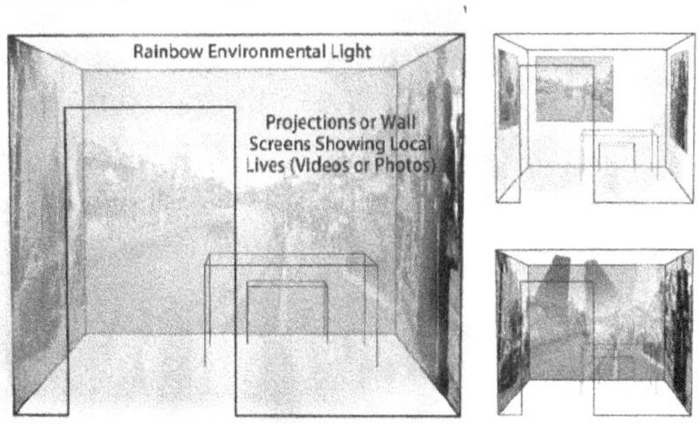 | Using images, video, audio, and lighting to evoke a remote place that might stimulate creative thinking. The space agents might work in concert with this audio-visual output, rendering the whole of the collaborative environment a "portal" to somewhere else. |

**Table 3. Five human-environment interaction patterns and their corresponding design patterns.**

layered upon another one, which collectively constitute larger patterns. In Table 3, for instance, we see the design patterns not operating in isolation (e.g. only the Space Agent's impact, as presented in the uppermost row) but combined with the effects found in rows beneath it, so that the shape-making Space Agents operate in concert with the lighting effects and audio of the room to offer Place-based Cues [6].

Admittedly, each of the patterns presented in Table 3 require further investigations to ensure that human users understand the conveyance of the human-like interactions offered by the collaborative environment. Such experiments would undoubtedly alter the patterns of Table 3 and may yet generate additional patterns which would, as Alexander et al. offer, represent "more true (sic), more profound patterns" that over time become "a common language, which all of us can share" [4].

## CONCLUSIONS AND FUTURE WORK

In this paper, we presented a pattern-based framework for designing interactive artifacts that are spatial and human-like, following (in part) from communication theory and related literature. In so doing, we have explored how human-human interaction can be studied, analyzed and translated to interactions of people and their cyber-physical surroundings—the latter we defined here as "collaborative environments." As part of our framework, we introduced three novel, translational strategies: *Direct Mapping*, *Conveyed Mapping*, and *Space Agency*. Our case study—the design of a collaborative environment for design activity—served as a means to elaborate and validate the framework. As prescribed by our pattern-based framework, the case study traced the following sequence of activities: ethnographic studies of human-human interactions, mapping human-human interactions to human-environment interactions, generating design patterns based on human-environment interaction patterns, and generating the collaborative environment design from these design patterns. Our future work involving human participants will (a) investigate if and how-well distinct patterns generated through the case study communicate (e.g. enthusiasm) to participants as we intended, and (b.) measure the impact of the Space Agents (i.e. robot surfaces) in their physical surroundings on a single human designer undertaking a design task, as comparted to a control in which two human designers partner on the same design task.

Increasingly, our physical surroundings are becoming interactive and intelligent by way of embedded system. The authors of this paper, by no means, contend that our pattern-based design framework is the only way to design interactive and intelligent artifacts. However, it is difficult to identify embedded artifacts that are without spatial implications, given their numbers, their networking, and their other, expanded behaviors. Furthermore, for such artifacts, we tend to expect from them behaviors that are natural and familiar to us—that are perceived by us as collaborative. And so, as design researchers strive for more human-human-like interactions between human beings and their cyber-physical surrounding, our framework holds particular promise.

## REFERENCES


[1] Gregory D. Abowd and Elizabeth D. Mynatt. 2000. Charting past, present, and future research in ubiquitous computing. *ACM Transactions on Computer-Human Interaction* 7, 1: 29-58.

[2] Henri Achten. 2014. One and Many: An Agent Perspective on Interactive Architecture. In *Proceedings of the 34th Annual Conference of the Association for Computer Aided Design in Architecture* (ACADIA 2014), 479-486.

[3] Leon Battista Alberti. 1988. *On the Art of Building in Ten Books*, trans. Joseph Rykwert, Neil Leach, and Robert Tavernor. The MIT Press.

[4] Christopher Alexander, Sara Ishikawa, Murray Silverstein, and Max Jacobson. 2013. *A Pattern Language: Towns, Buildings, Construction*. Oxford University Press.

[5] Robert Freed. Bales, Stephen A. Williamson, and Stephen P. Cohen. 1979. *Symlog: a system for the multiple level observation of groups*. Free Press.

[6] Mathilde M. Bekker, Judith S. Olson, and Gary M. Olson. 1995. Analysis of gestures in face-to-face design teams provides guidance for how to use groupware in design. In *Proceedings of the conference on Designing interactive systems processes, practices, methods, & techniques* (DIS '95). http://dx.doi.org/10.1145/225434.225452

[7] David Benyon. 2001. The new HCI navigation of information space. *Knowledge-Based Systems* 14, 8: 425-430.

[8] Kathy Charmaz. 2014. *Constructing grounded theory*. SAGE Press.

[9] Herbert H. Clark and Susan E. Brennan. 1991. Grounding in communication. *Perspectives on socially shared cognition* 13, 127–149.

[10] Kees Dorst and Nigel Cross. 2001. Creativity in the design process: co-evolution of problem–solution. *Design Studies* 22, 5: 425-437. https://doi.org/10.1016/S0142-694X(01)00009-6

[11] Erich Gamma, Richard Helm, Ralph Johnson, and John Vlissides. 1995 *Design Patterns: Elements of Reusable Object-Oriented Software*. Addison-Wesley Longman Press.

[12] Keith Evan Green. 2016. *Architectural Robotics: Ecosystems of Bits, Bytes, and Biology*. The MIT Press.

[13] Erel Hadas, Guy Hoffman, and Oren Zuckerman. 2018. Interpreting Non-Anthropomorphic Robots' Social Gestures. In *Proceedings of The HRI'2018 Workshop on Explainable Robotic Systems* (HRI '18). http://dx.doi.org/10.1145/258549.258715

[14] Guy Hoffman and Wendy Ju. 2014. Designing Robots with Movement in Mind. *Journal of Human-Robot Interaction* 3, 1: 89.

[15] Guy Hoffman, Oren Zuckerman, Gilad Hirschberger, Michal Luria, and Tal Shani Sherman. 2015. Design and Evaluation of a Peripheral Robotic Conversation Companion. In *Proceedings of the Tenth Annual ACM/IEEE International Conference on Human-Robot Interaction* (HRI '15). http://dx.doi.org/10.1145/2696454.2696495

[16] Hyperbody. InteractiveWall. Retrieved November 7, 2018 from http://www.hyperbody.nl/research/projects/interactive wall/

[17] Hiroshi Ishii and Brygg Ullmer. 1997. Tangible bits: towards seamless interfaces between people, bits and atoms. In *Proceedings of the ACM SIGCHI Conference on Human Factors in Computing Systems* (CHI '97), 234-241.

[18] Hiroshi Ishii, Craig Wisneski, Scott Brave, Andrew Dahley, Matt Gorbet, Brygg Ullmer, and Paul Yarin. 1998. ambientROOM: integrating ambient media with architectural space. In *CHI 98 Conference Summary on Human Factors in Computing Systems* (CHI '98). http://dx.doi.org/10.1145/286498.286652

[19] Wendy Ju and Takayama Leila. 2009. Approachability: How people interpret automatic door movement as gesture. *International Journal of Design* 3, 2: 1-10.

[20] Peter H. Kahn, Nathan G. Freier, Takayuki Kanda, Hiroshi Ishiguro, Jolina H. Ruckert, Rachel L. Severson, and Shaun K. Kane. 2008. Design patterns for sociality in human-robot interaction. In *Proceedings of the 3rd ACM/IEEE international conference on Human robot interaction* (HRI '08). https://doi.org/10.1145/1349822.1349836

[21] Günther Knoblich, Stephen Butterfill, and Natalie Sebanz. 2011. Psychological Research on Joint Action. *Advances in Research and Theory Psychology of Learning and Motivation*, 59-101.

[22] Bernd Kreimeier. 2002. "The Case for Game Design Patterns." Retrieved November 7 from http://echo.iat.sfu.ca/library/kreimeier_02_game_patterns.pdf

[23] Bryan Lawson. 2005. *How Designers Think.* Routledge Press.

[24] John Lofland. 2009. *Analyzing social settings: a guide to qualitative observation and analysis.* Wadsworth Press.

[25] Mary Lou Maher, Josiah Poon, and Sylvie Boulanger. 1996. Formalising design exploration as co-evolution: a combined gene approach. In *Advances in formal design methods for CAD*, J. S. Gero and F. Sudweeks (eds.). Chapman and Hall, London, UK.

[26] Yuri Martens. 2011. Creative workplace: instrumental and symbolic support for creativity. *Facilities* 29, 1/2: 63-79.

[27] Janetta Mitchell Mccoy and Gary W. Evans. 2002. The Potential Role of the Physical Environment in Fostering Creativity. *Creativity Research Journal* 14, 3-4: 409-426.

[28] Janetta Mitchell Mccoy. 2005. Linking the Physical Work Environment to Creative Context. *The Journal of Creative Behavior* 39, 3: 167-189.

[29] Matthew B. Miles and A. Michael. Huberman. *Qualitative data analysis: an expanded sourcebook.* Sage Press.

[30] Clifford Nass, Jonathan Steuer, and Ellen R. Tauber. 1994. Computers are social actors. In *Proceedings of the SIGCHI conference on Human factors in computing systems celebrating interdependence* (CHI '94). http://dx.doi.org/10.1145/191666.191703

[31] Clifford Nass and Corina Yen. 2010. *The man who lied to his laptop: what machines teach us about human relationships.* Current Press.

[32] Nicholas Negroponte. 1975. *Soft Architecture Machines*. The MIT Press.

[33] Ovid. 1 A.D. *Metamorphoses*, translated by Sir Samuel Garth, John Dryden, et al. Retrieved November 7, 2018 from http://classics.mit.edu/Ovid/metam.html

[34] Carlo Ratti. Lift Bit. In Matt Burgess. 2016. "There's a sofa you can control you're your phone." WIRED (April 8, 2016). Retrieved November 7, 2018 from https://www.wired.co.uk/article/lift-bit-internet-of-things-sofa

[35] Gordon Pask. 1969. The architectural relevance of cybernetics. *Architectural Design* 39, 9: 494-496.

[36] Pedro Martins Pontes, Bruno Lima, and João Pascoal Faria. 2018. Test patterns for IoT. In *Proceedings of the 9th ACM SIGSOFT International Workshop on Automating TEST Case Design, Selection, and Evaluation* (A-TEST 2018). https://doi.org/10.1145/3278186.3278196

[37] Byron Reeves and Clifford Nass. 1996. *The media equation: how people treat computers, television, and new media like real people and places*. Cambridge University Press.

[38] Allison Sauppé and Bilge Mutlu. 2014. How social cues shape task coordination and communication. In *Proceedings of the 17th ACM conference on Computer supported cooperative work & social computing* (CSCW '14). http://dx.doi.org/10.1145/2531602.2531610

[39] George Schafer, Keith Green, Ian Walker, Susan King Fullerton, and Elise Lewis. 2014. An interactive, cyber-physical read-aloud environment. *Proceedings of the 2014 Conference on Designing Interactive Systems* (DIS 14). http://dx.doi.org/10.1145/2598510.2598562

[40] Pao Siangliulue, Kenneth C. Arnold, Krzysztof Z. Gajos, and Steven P. Dow. 2015. Toward Collaborative Ideation at Scale. In *Proceedings of the 18th ACM Conference on Computer Supported Cooperative Work & Social Computing* (CSCW '15). http://dx.doi.org/10.1145/2675133.2675239

[41] David Sirkin, Brian Mok, Stephen Yang, and Wendy Ju. 2015. Mechanical Ottoman. In *Proceedings of the Tenth Annual ACM/IEEE International Conference on Human-Robot Interaction* (HRI '15). http://dx.doi.org/10.1145/2696454.2696461

[42] Marco Spadafora, Victor Chahuneau, Nikolas Martelaro, David Sirkin, and Wendy Ju. 2016. Designing the Behavior of Interactive Objects. In *Proceedings of the TEI 16: Tenth International Conference on Tangible, Embedded, and Embodied Interaction* (TEI'16). http://dx.doi.org/10.1145/2839462.2839502

[43] Joachim Stempfle and Petra Badke-Schaub. 2002. Thinking in design teams: an analysis of team communication. *Design Studies* 23, 5: 473–496.

[44] Daniel Stokols, Chip Clitheroe, and Mary Zmuidzinas. 2002. Qualities of Work Environments that Promote Perceived Support for Creativity. *Creativity Research Journal* 14, 2: 137–147.

[45] T. Franklin Waddell, Bo Zhang, and S. Shyam Sundar. 2015. Human–Computer Interaction. *Encyclopedia of Interpersonal Communication*, 1–9.

[46] Marcus Pollio Vitruvius. c. 80–70 BC (1931). *De Architectura (Ten Books)*, trans. F. Granger. Harvard University Press.

[47] Steve Whittaker, David Frohlich, and Owen Daly-Jones. 1994. What is it like and how might we support it? *Conference Companion on Human factors in Computing Systems* (CHI '94). http://dx.doi.org/10.1145/259963.260328

# Decomposition as Design: Co-Creating (with) Natureculture

**Szu-Yu (Cyn) Liu, Jeffrey Bardzell, Shaowen Bardzell**
School of Informatics, Computing, and Engineering, Indiana University, Bloomington, IN, USA
cynliu@iu.edu, jbardzel@indiana.edu, selu@indiana.edu

## ABSTRACT
HCI in recent years has shown an increasing interest in decentering humans in design. This decentering is a response to concerns about environmental sustainability, technology obsolescence, and consumerism. Scholars have introduced theoretical notions such as natureculture from feminist technoscience. Yet how such theories translate into material design practices remains an open question. This research seeks to broaden the repertoire of nonanthropocentric design practices in HCI. Specifically, it draws on the natural processes of decomposition as a creative approach to develop and test design tactics. To do so, we curate and critique hundreds of examples of decomposition in architecture, design, textile, crafting, and food making. We observe that decomposition often depends on what we call a "scaffold," and we further propose four variants of it as design tactics: fragmenting, aging, liberating, and tracing. We then tested the tactics over a period of four months in a ceramics studio using diverse materials, with a mixture of successes and failures. We conclude by reflecting on how the design tactics might be deployed in nonanthropocentric HCI/design.

### Author Keywords
Natureculture; decomposition; nonanthropocentric HCI; decentering humans; research through design; ceramics.

### CCS Concepts
• Human-centered computing → Interaction design • Social and professional topics → Sustainability

## INTRODUCTION
Humans are not the only but one of the entities on the planet, living alongside with other nonhumans actors such as plants, animals, and microorganisms. In the past decade, researchers in Human-Computer Interaction (HCI) have argued the need to move from a human-centric design agenda to one that encompasses a multispecies worldview [24,25,38]. This body of research not only provides insights to design for multispecies interaction and cohabitation [3,29,38], but also reflects on how interspecies collaboration opens new opportunities to environmental sustainability, collaborative survival, and aesthetic interaction [3,24,25,27]. This is an exciting step in HCI toward nurturing a mutualistic relationship between humans and other-than-human actors with and through technology.

However, the philosophy of de-centering humans in design remains quite abstract and theoretical to date. Except for a few examples [7,19,20,25,38], little research has been done to translate nonanthropocentric theories into actual design practices. With an interest in designing with nonhumans in mind, we ask, what exactly can designers do once we get out of the realm of high-flying theories and get our hands dirty? In this paper, we draw from the theory of natureculture—a concept that resists a human-centric perspective by "dis-objectify[ing] nonhuman worlds by exposing their liveliness and agency" [33:7]—and engage in design activities to explore concrete ways of co-creating with nature.

Under the theory of natureculture, we look into the process of winemaking. In turning grapes into wine, a series of collaborations between humans (e.g., grape farmers, wine producers) and nonhuman agencies (e.g., soil, grapevine, yeast) are involved. For example, wine makers provide yeast with sugary grape juice and an oxygen free environment, within which yeast drives the fermentation process and converts sugar into alcohol and carbon dioxide [1]. We are particularly inspired by the idea of human actors cultivating a space of co-creation that invites nonhumans to participate, sometimes even to take over the original composition. A similar concept, decomposition—breaking down organic matters to smaller particles—is yet another process of destruction and reconfiguration driven by nonhuman agencies such as earthworms and fungi. Although the term decomposition is often associated with negative connotations such as decay, rotting, aging, and death, it also opens new pathways to growth, renewal, transformation, and rebirth [6]. We consider decomposition as a creative process through which nonhuman others bring their own form of agency into the creative process and add value, character, function, aesthetics, and sustainability into design.

Within HCI, nonanthropocentric perspectives have become increasing popular in addressing and overcoming the present sociotechnical challenges. For example, sustainable HCI researchers have explored ways of urban farming and



*TEI '19, March 17-20, 2019, Tempe, AZ, USA*

ACM 978-1-4503-6196-5/19/03...$15.00.
https://doi.org/10.1145/3294109.3295653

foraging in response to issues over food safety, scarcity, and environmental sustainability. Scholars in urban informatics have suggested integrating ideas such as hybridity [9,43], coproduction [8], cohabitation [38], organic sensing [21], collaborative citymaking [10,12], and collaborative survival [25] to expand the current landscape of interactive technologies. We situate our work in nonanthropocentric HCI to contribute to the growing interest in building collaborative kinship with other species. In this paper, we build on the natural process of decomposition and explore through design curation, analysis, and making the concrete ways of designing with nature. We propose the notion of decomposition as a tangible and actionable design tactic in incorporating nature into design.

Our contribution to HCI is multi-fold. First, we present the natural process of decomposition as a way of natureculture co-creating with humans though actions of destruction. Such a provocation has the potential to spark the imagination of what designers can do to engage in creative activities with nonhuman actors. Second, we concretize the theoretical concept of natureculture and decomposition by curating and analyzing the physical representation of natureculture in design works, and experimenting with materials and objects to produce our own representations. And finally, we propose the concept of "scaffolding" and conclude by presenting fragmenting, aging, liberating, and tracing as actionable design tactics for those who are interested in experimenting with nonanthropocentric approaches to design.

## NATURECULTURE AND DECOMPOSITION

This work departs from the provocation of decentering the human in design. For [33], such an attempt requires a shift in perspectives that considers "the social as a tissue of associations between humans, nonhumans, and objects working in the realization of new relational formations." Central to our theoretical foundation is the concept of natureculture, which advocates for humans to (re-)connect with nonhumans and move away from the perspective of species isolation and superiority [14,23]. Anthropologist Anna Tsing describes this raise in awareness as the "arts of noticing" [41]; constituted in these arts is cultivating our ability to notice, appreciate, respond, and imagine outside of anthropocentric norms [25]. When applying the concept of natureculture into design, we are better positioned to understand design activities not as a pure cultural practice but as a creative space where humans "can be both actively involved and passively fascinated" [16:376]. Within the context of natureculture design, we are particularly inspired by Light et al.'s recent call to "embrace the rhythms of life and death around us" with and through design [24]. She writes, "the radical act of paying attention to things that we do not wish to see and that make us uncomfortable can be aided by design if it takes up the challenge of resisting smoothness and self-centeredness" [24]. We build upon this invitation to explore moments of vulnerability once we get out of the realm of human exceptionalism and come to interact with the nonhuman lifeworld.

In the context of this paper, we focus our inquiry of natureculture design on the notion of decomposition—a natural phenomenon that implies a constant process of "death and rebirth", "loss and renewal" [6]—as well as its analogous concepts such as decay, aging, corruption, destruction, decline, obsolescence, and death. As much as we try to avoid these unpleasant encounters, they are simply natural and inevitable during the course of life—for humans, animals, plants, artifacts, and technologies alike. In response to the call of "staying with the trouble" [15], HCI researchers have explored ways of adding value to design through deconstructive actions; they have also argued that designers might intervene into deconstructive processes, which often are beyond human capacity to control. For example, work on breakdown and repair investigates how forms of meaning, care, and creativity can be enacted through the limits of engineering-centered infrastructure design [17,19,28,36,39]. Rosner et al. [18,37] and Giaccardi et al. [13] experiment through material forms and reveal how traces of use present a quality that is aesthetically pleasing and emotionally meaningful in constructing relationships with technologies. Murer and colleagues [31] go further by suggesting "un-crafting" and other deconstructive practices as an initial and essential part of creating interactive artifacts. This body of work resonates with the theoretical foundation that we aim to emphasize in this work: the notion of decomposition and its synonyms provide an alternative trajectory of adding value (e.g., durability, sustainability, function, personality, aesthetics) to design through a course of destruction and reconfiguration unfolding across humans and nonhuman agencies.

## DESIGN PROCESS & METHODS

We consider decomposition not as a form of degradation but as a pathway towards transformation and as such, a potentially creative process. Such a process can be driven by a collaborative effort between humans and nonhuman agencies through and manifested in material forms. In this paper, we ask, how can designers draw from the process of decomposition to cultivate a space of natureculture co-creation? A primary goal of this paper is to concretize the notion of decomposition by moving it from an abstract theoretical argument towards actionable design tactics. To gain insights to this inquiry, our methods are twofold, involving design analysis and research through design.

### Curating and Analyzing Design: Design Tactics

In the first phase of the research, we aim to illustrate through actual design exemplars the physical manifestations of decomposition and explore tactics of designing with nature through destructive actions. We build a design inventory with more than 100 cases in analogous fields such as product design, architecture, textile, interaction design, and crafting. We searched popular design websites, blogs, competitions, and magazines to curate exemplars that suggested the involvement of natural forces, actors, and courses such as destruction and decay in the design-making process. To make sense of the emerging collection, help shape its growth, and discover patterns and clusters within it, we turned to interaction criticism. According to [4], interaction criticism entails "rigorous interpretive interrogations of the complex relationships between (a) the interface, including its material and perceptual qualities as well as its broader situatedness in visual languages and culture and (b) the user experience, including the meanings, behaviors, perceptions, affects, insights, and social sensibilities that arise in the context of interaction and its outcomes" [4:604].

In practice, this part of the research involved iteratively identifying design exemplars and producing critical discourse about them; two separate activities are involved: aesthetic description and aesthetic interpretation. *Aesthetic description* refers to an attempt to characterize the exemplars in question, to articulate their qualities, materials, and forms in a language both rich and relatively objective. It is rich in that it makes use of associations and metaphors to capture subtle nuances and qualities, and it is objective in that its purpose is to characterize the object in a way that most qualified viewers would agree to. Aesthetic description responds to questions such as the following: what is it? what is the broader context of creating? how is it made? And it results in a set of annotations that characterize the form, function, material, and medium of the design. *Aesthetic interpretation* refers to our take, that is, our own efforts after meaning. An interpretation is more subjective than the description, that is, dependent on the perception, imagination, literacy, and deepening understanding of an individual interpreter (or, in this case, small team of them). An interpretation also reflects an intellectual purpose; in our case, it was to perceive and appreciate diverse ways that processes of decomposition contribute to design by accounting for the nonhuman actors, what is there to be decomposed, what drives the process, and what forms of interaction it entails. We iteratively compared and contrasted the exemplars and their qualities to discover patterns and to identify possible categorizations, leading to a set of possible processes that designers might be able to emulate—what we would come to think of as design tactics.

As an outcome of this work, we identified four design tactics of decomposition: fragmenting, aging, liberating, and tracing. These four tactics diversely demonstrate how the notion of decomposition can (co-)create material forms. We also note that the tactics are not mutually exclusive but complement one another. We describe each tactic through actual design cases and reflect on how different modes of working with nature can be promoted and perceived through material forms. Our aim is not to develop an exhaustive list of design strategies; rather, it is intended to help us move from promising yet vague, toward something that is actionable enough to develop design experiments that could be tested.

### *Fragmenting*

Fragmenting is a tactic focusing on material fabrication. It breaks, combines, and repurposes the original materials to create a new composite that displays qualities of one-off products, manifested in patterns, textures, and aesthetics.

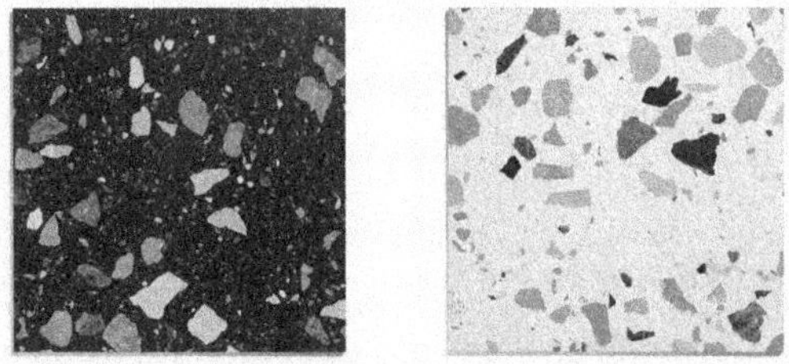

**Figure 1. Marmoreal (2014). ©Dzek and Max Lamb.**

Decomposition is a natural process when organic composites break down to simpler particles through physical, chemical, or organic means. We observed that this natural process has inspired designers to create new material composites by first fragmenting and then reassembling the original constituents through pressure, heat, and adhesives. The notion of decomposition in this case involves the physical breakdown of materials, the process then opens up a space for material re-composition and rearrangement, which often results in unique, unexpected, even enchanting and decorative patterns and embellishments.

For example, Marmoreal is an engineered marble designed by Max Lamb and produced by Dzek (figure 1) [45]. Composed of different types of classic Italian marbles from the Verona region, Marmoreal can be used for various interior applications ranging from tiles to furniture. The production process celebrates the sustainable root of terrazzo, sourcing waste stones from local Italian quarries. Combining together approximately 95% marble mix and 5% polyester resin, the material is casted in molds using a mixture of pressure, vibration, and vacuum. The new composite is stronger and more durable than natural marbles because the small batch of polyester resin fills the porous structure in the original stones. Max Lamb considers this material exploration as one that "celebrates the individual qualities of these stones while acknowledging that the sum of its parts makes for something far more compelling [22]."

Through the example of Marmoreal, we can see that fragmenting as a design tactic envisions a new form of natureculture co-creation, which is particularly useful in fabricating novel materials. Through a process of recycling, smashing, shuffling, and reassembling, the original ingredients remain visible while the new composite offers a wider possibility in aesthetics, function, and durability. The tactic of fragmenting can be easily integrated into the highly controlled mass production processes to add ambiguity and uniqueness to standardized products.

### *Aging*

Aging is a material exploration tactic, which incorporates materials that are sensitive to the passage of time, manifested in physical transformations such as form, texture, and color.

**Figure 2. The Rust Collection (2015). ©Ariane Prin.**

Aging is a natural phenomenon that amplifies the inevitable passage of life—carried through a course of "death and rebirth", "loss and renewal" [6]. The tactic of aging addresses the beauty of ephemeral presentation and continual evolution. Such appreciation of decay is coined in literature as "graceful aging" [35] and "aesthetic obsolescence" [5]. Aging as design tactic tends to emphasize the process of rotting and deteriorating by including materials that are sensitive and responsive to their surroundings. This tactic is closely related to the aesthetic of Wabi-Sabi, which aims to manifest the beauty that is imperfect, impermanent, and incomplete by capturing the inherently unstable, fleeting moments of deterioration [26,30]. A common design approach to aging is to mix metal powders (e.g., copper, brass, iron) with resin composites to create a marble-like finish. The color and texture of the object changes over time as the metal oxidizes to signify the process of aging.

For example, for Rust Collection (figure 2), designer Ariane Prin recycles leftover metal dusts and mixes them with plaster and Jesmonite to create containers that change the color and texture overtime as the metal oxidizes [32]. "Every time I go to my studio I'm excited to see the objects' changing textures. It's like each one of them was alive and mutating with time," she explains [32]. The corrosion of metal powders is then stopped with a layer of water-resistant coating, so one can safely use them as regular pots, trays, vases and jewelry boxes. In the process of creating, the designer lets the materials take their own life to develop patterns and colors that are unique and unpredictable.

Regardless of the form or material of an object, all surfaces inevitably display changes of their original qualities through time, reflecting the use context, the nature of material, and the environment. Though most products focus on enhancing the durability and stability while preventing deteriorating and ruining of artifacts, aging as a design tactic harnesses the passage of decay to develop a natural, un-replicable look and feel of objects. It refuses to treat objects as static substances but allows materials take on their own life. Means of human intervention include using heat, humidity, and chemical erosion to catalyze the transformation. Aging as a design tactic explores and utilizes the natural process of material degradation and deconstruction to entail the uniqueness of objects. In this making, human intervention presumably constructs the overall aesthetic qualities, but as nature takes part in the creative process, no finished products will be exactly the same.

*Liberating*

Liberating is a production tactic that resists posing physical controls and constraints during the course of forming. It encourages an honest presentation of materials and often results in objects of fluidity and randomness.

**Figure 3. Ripple (2013). ©Poetic Lab.**

Here, we focus on how the notion of decomposition arrests the temporality, sensitivity, and resiliency of materials during the formation of an object. Liberating as a design tactic rejects standardization. Specifically, thinking about mass-produced products, we are likely to picture artifacts that are precisely engineered, well-defined, and perfectly polished. To achieve this, molds are combined with matrixes of control to regulate the manufacturing process. The result is products of uniformity, where traces of manual labor are nowhere to be found [35]. On the contrary, the tactic of liberating strives to capture the material properties during the course of design production. When standardized molds and manufacturing formulas are removed, the tactic of liberating facilitates the creation of one-off products that display different qualities in forms, textures, and finishes.

The design tactic of liberating celebrates the beauty of craftsmanship through a poetic encounter between the craftsman, the environment, and the material. For example, Ripple (figure 3) purposefully incorporates a mouth-blowing technique to create an uneven glass dome that resembles the ever-changing ripple pattern. Molds and jigs were still used to assist forming and measuring, but they did not define the final look of the product. Designers Hanhsi Chen and Shikai Tseng state, "the process starts with this hot tube of [glass] material, and interacts with the air, gravity, and movements of the blower. [...] Time and memory is frozen [...] and with a small pinch of light, you can extract that moment" and "it's about the experience and the emotion that is created by this moving light" [44]. Indeed, designers or crafters do not have full control over the finishing look; it is the entangled correlation between material properties, human movements, and environmental conditions that co-create the product.

In industrial manufacturing, defects occur due to inaccurate control. The notion of decomposition pictures imperfections as aesthetic and desirable. Liberating as a design tactic deliberately seeks to release the subject from rigid human interventions and machine control during the phase of forming. It amplifies the properties of materials and conditions of environment by intentionally adding anomalies to create uniqueness—passages of making are inscribed in imperfections (e.g., bubbles, dimensional changes, uneven surfaces) to add value to the product.

*Tracing*

Tracing is the tactic of foregrounding traces of force, use, and repair. The history of an artifact is objectified and synthesized in terms of forms, textures, patterns, or breakages.

**Figure 4. Ripening Rugs (2015). ©Adrianus Kundert.**

The predominate production technology has been driven by the pursuit of perfection and endurance, aiming to produce objects in their pristine states. However, while scratches, breakages, and blemishes are often considered as defects, traces of use and repair inscribe the relations between an artifact and its user, adding a value that goes beyond the functional significance, and moves towards becoming an extension of the user [18,19,34]. Tracing as a design tactic not only calls attention to the entanglement between the object and its user, but also raises questions about durability, fragility, and resilience. Here, a common design tactic is to highlight the degradations with contrasting materials.

For instance, designer Adrianus Kundert believes that the durability of an object increases through use. The beauty of wear and tear is captured in his Ripening Rugs collection: the rugs gradually change their colors, patterns, and texture as the outer layer of the yarn is worn and the inner weave is revealed through use (figure 4). Kundert says, "the gradual erosion is what makes these floor coverings gain in attractiveness, each in its own way, instead of rendering them valueless and ending their lifetime." In this case, traces mark the identity of a product and signify its evolution. Another strategy of strengthening the emotional resonance to an artifact is through actions of repair. For example, Kintsugi—a Japanese crafting practice of restoring broken ceramic potteries mixing powers of gold, silver, or platinum with lacquer [11]—captures the notion of tracing through repairing. Kintsugi shows no attempt to hide the damages but to appreciate and illuminate the traces of use with contrasting color and material.

Tracing can be considered a creative practice emerging from the course of use and repair. Whether deliberate or accidental, every crack inscribes and manifests the story behind an artifact. As a design tactic, tracing appreciates and harnesses the use traces (e.g., breakage, wear, and tear) and material imperfections (e.g., impurity, asymmetry, and roughness) of an artifact; in other words, it shows no attempt to hide the damages or touches of repair, but to illuminate them as an aesthetic existence and the signature of an object. Here, decomposition is treated as both the process and result of justification and identification. At an objective level, designers can utilize the tactic of tracing to produce un-replicable objects and foreground signs of break and repair by presenting them as decorative arts. At a subjective level, end users are empowered to create unique products and express emotional resonance through marks of use and decay. Eventually, the tactic of tracing constructs personal memories and shared experiences over time, making an object one of a kind both on a physical and emotional level—a long-lasting relationship triggered and sustained by the imperfection of materiality.

*Section Conclusion: To Decompose Is to Scaffold*

From curating and analyzing design exemplars, we arrived at four decomposition-inspired design tactics—fragmenting, aging, liberating, and tracing—that all might be understood to fall under the broader umbrella of "scaffolding." In architectural practice, a scaffold is a temporary structure that supports construction efforts (e.g., holds materials or workers). In the context of this paper, we define a scaffold as a *soft structure*, a *transient composition* that is intentionally built to invite natural entities to build upon and eventually take over the original cultural construct. In a scaffold, both time and space are constructive media of the design.

The notion of scaffolding we propose here differs from anthropocentric design approaches: whereas in traditional design processes, phenomena outside of human control are avoided to reduce rates of product deficiency or slow down technology obsolescence, in scaffolding co-creation with nature, they are intentionally incorporated and celebrated as part of the design practice. In other words, we consider decomposition as a creative process through which nonhumans bring their own form of agency into design to add value, character, function, aesthetics, and sustainability. To further illustrate, let us compare a scaffold to the mold, a common manufacturing tool in mass production process that gives standardized shapes to materials. With precise environmental and material control, a mold can produce up to a million pieces of product with exact, pre-defined shapes within its life expectancy [42]. If we describe an industrial mold as a "hard structure" that foregrounds regulation, standardization, and efficiency, then a scaffold can be considered a "soft structure" that loosens human control, brings nonhuman agency into design, and celebrates the in-expectancy and un-replicability of the final outcome.

To further unpack the notion of scaffolding, we look into the concept of structure-preserving transformations, proposed by architect and design theorist Christopher Alexander as the way nature constructs and evolves the environment. He writes, "throughout nature, we see a continuous smooth unfolding of the wholeness, which preserves structure at every moment, even when it seems to be introducing new structure" [2:56]. We consider the natural process of decomposition as a structure-preserving transformation though which decaying organic matter is broken down to smaller particles, culturing new forms of lives. Through the course of decomposition, "nothing entirely new has been injected—the newness has been created by intensification of what exists" [2:53]. The design framing of scaffolding (as opposed to molding) we propose here, then, is a result of translating and leveraging the natural process of decomposition into actionable design tactics, further consolidated as design actions including fragmenting, aging, liberating, and tracing.

We are aware that the cases we select to present here are not interaction design exemplars but instances of product design; this reflects the training of the lead author. We have described earlier in the methods section that interpretation is an important means of knowledge production; as a result, we turn to our own expertise as a resource for translating nonanthropocentric theories into material design practices. In addition, every interaction design is also a product, with a specific form, function, aesthetic, material, character, and value orientation. We believe that the lessons learned from curating and analyzing product design examples are applicable to tangible and interactive interfaces. Finally, and perhaps most importantly, issues of consumerism, obsolescence, and sustainability, have long been explored and addressed in realm of product design; we believe it is important for HCI researchers and practitioners to learn and leverage what has been done in this analogous field.

### Research through Design: Creating "Scaffolds"

So far, we have concluded four design tactics and proposed scaffolding as an overarching strategy in co-creating with natureculture. Next, we experiment the tactics by embodying them through material forms. To do so, we first generated twelve design concepts, entailing a wide selection of materials in its execution: ceramics, glass, papers, silicone, metals (e.g., brass, copper, nickel, silver), fabrics (e.g., cotton, silk, denim, wool), foods (e.g., chocolate, tea, coffee, breakfast cereal), resins (e.g., epoxy, Jesmonite), and organic matters (e.g., mushroom, chia, moss, flower, sponge). All of our concepts were built directly from the tactics to reflect the different ways of engaging in the notion of decomposition through design. With the goal to actually engage in activities of making, we presented our conceptual sketches to three different studio coordinators to discuss the feasibility of execution, including ceramics and printing, metalsmithing, and digital fabrication. We considered factors such as material availability, facility accessibility, time flexibility, and financial feasibility. Since our goal was to experiment with the tactics through material forms, we were not very picky about what type of material or process we wanted to focus on; we decided to initiate our experiment in the ceramic studio, where we were generously granted a personal working space and the accessibility to all tool, facilities, and materials within the studio.

## DESIGN THROUGH DECOMPOSITION WITH CERAMICS

The design experiments presented in the following sections were led by Liu; the execution was supported by Wei Tseng, a senior undergraduate student, a novice in design and crafting. All authors had little experiences in ceramics making, so we turned to Chase Gamblin, the ceramics studio coordinator who has over 20 years of experiences. He showed us how to properly use the facilities and tools in the studio, but he encouraged us to engage in trial and error ourselves. Every little adjustment in the ceramics making process can lead to dramatic changes in the outcomes, "you might fail, you might succeed," he always said.

We started by getting our hands dirty, playing with clay and ceramic slip. Probably not surprising, many of our concepts failed—in a sense that the design outcomes did not follow our expectations. From an analytical perspective, the designs failed because we were not familiar with the material properties to the point that many of our designs cracked and fell apart during the course of drying. However, from a research through design perspective, the decomposed ceramics served quite well in manifesting and materializing the notion of decomposition. For instance, we were inspired by the tactic of tracing and had an idea of creating cracks on the surface of the clay body by leaving it outside in the snow during the course of drying. Our plan was to then use resins to fill the cracks to trace and foreground nature's force. Within this experiment, the scaffold is the clay bowl we made, which is considered as a soft structure because the material is still pliable with external forces. The nonhuman factor is the natural environment, filled with unpredictable weather conditions. Our hypothesis was that through fast freezing and drying, the surface of the clay might decompose and result in distinct patterns. However, the clay bowl become slushy and eventually fell apart as the snow melted.

We started to obtain some basic understanding of the clay's material properties after a few failures: it cracks during fast-drying, becomes sloppy when it meets water, and shrinks significantly while drying. In what follows, we present our design iteration on the tactic of liberating using slip. Slip is a liquid state of clay made by suspending clay particles in water. Slip is often used to create sophisticated shapes by casting it with molds or using it to paint the surface of wet clay bodies to make decorative patterns. In testing the tactic of liberating through slip, we resisted using molds but employed different types of scaffolds for slip to build upon. Here, the notion of decomposition takes place during two different stages of making: when the original scaffolds are covered and obscured with slip and when the scaffolds are eventually brunt away during the firing process.

### Experiment 1: Waxed Paper Cups + Slip

**Figure 5. Forces acting with the shrinking, drying slip left surprising polygonal patterns in the paper cups.**

In our first experiment, testing the tactic of liberating, we used waxed paper cups as the scaffold and slip as the natural entity whose performance is defined by multiple factors in the environment (e.g., gravity, temperature, humidity). By free dripping slip onto the paper cups we turned the cups into soft structures which allow slip to cover, alter, and take over the original surface with different shapes and patterns. In this process, we as designers still exerted a certain degree of control to reach our desired aesthetics. For example, we can choose, to a certain degree, where on the cups we want to pour the slip, how much slip we want to pour, how fast we want to pour, and even how fast we want the slip to dry (we used the heat gun to facilitate the drying process for some). However, the outcomes of the design remains ambiguous because there are many constraints to how much the we can actually control. For instance, a paper cup can only hold slip up to a certain amount; once it exceeds the capability of friction, the slip falls. However, we have also noticed that the slip poured onto the paper cups need to maintain a certain thickness or the design will soon crack and fall apart when it starts drying.

We envisioned applying the tactic of liberating to capture through slip an intricate interaction between slip, gravity, paper cups, and friction. However, the final result is again against our expectation. Specifically, slip shrinks when it dries but the wax layer on the paper cups prevents the slip from shrinking; the pressure got accumulated and eventually cracked the slip when it hardened. The ceramic master predicted the crack but he still encouraged us to try because "you might succeed, since the wax inside the cup is not too thick." The final result reveals the unruly and unpredictable quality of slip and the fact that if we want to "work with" (including understanding and experimenting in our case) this unruly material, we need to find alternative scaffold materials.

What is surprising and completely unexpected is that the pressure from the shrinking clay has imprinted polygonal patterns onto the waxed paper cups, leaving a unique trace of natureculture co-creation (figure 5). This experiment has challenged and pushed forward our previous analysis. Specifically, we pictured a scaffold as the foundation for natureculture co-creation to build upon and something to be discarded afterwards (e.g., burnt away during firing). We did not foresee the scaffold turning into a beautiful design object itself. Through this ceramic making activity, we discovered that a scaffold is not only "soft" in the way that it loosens factors of human control; it is also "soft" and malleable in itself, allowing force to leave unique marks and traces onto the scaffold. Such a process seems to resemble the tactic of *tracing* more than *liberating*, suggesting from this experiment that the tactics we concluded in the previous section are not mutually exclusive to one another. Indeed, natureculture co-creation is a space where designers "can [be] both actively involved and passively fascinated" [16:376].

**Experiment 2: Kitchen Towels + Slip**

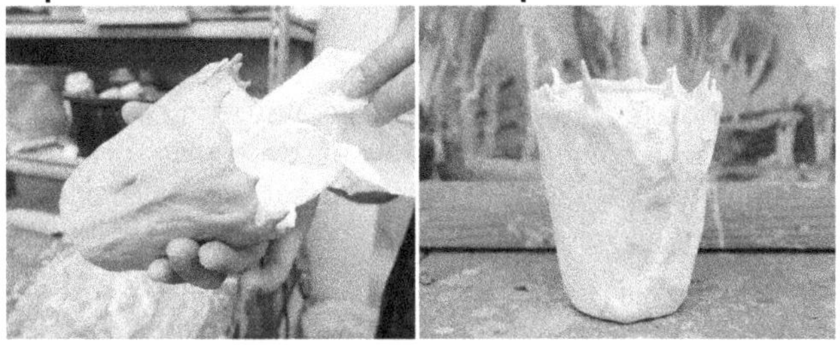

**Figure 6. (Left) removing paper cups to prevent the slip from cracking. (Right) the final result displays a hybrid materiality.**

With the goal of capturing and displaying through clay the negotiation between the cultured scaffold and the natural environment, we iterated on the material selection of the scaffold. We learned from experiences that the scaffold needed to be hard enough to maintain its shape while holding the weight of slip, and yet the scaffold also needed to be soft enough to allow the slip to shrink during the course of drying. We decided to use two different versions of scaffold in our next experiment. In execution, we first wrapped or taped kitchen towels onto the waxed paper cups and free dripped slip onto their surfaces. We then let the slip sit and dry for about 30 minutes when its surface became hard enough to sustain the shape without actually having a cup underneath it. Next, we carefully removed the waxed paper cups and set the slip covered kitchen towels on the drying rack for two days.

This time our ceramic work did not crack; instead, the final result displayed a hybrid materiality of all materials involved in the process of making (figure 6). Specifically, paper cups scaffolded the slip to display a certain unity and hardness of the pre-made containers, the texture and layers of the kitchen towels were inscribed onto the design as unique patterns, and the ceramic slip managed to visualize its own fluidity and stickiness when it came to interact with force (e.g., gravity and friction) in the environment. After firing, the kitchen towels dissolved while the clay body converted into bisque: a durable, much more permanent state of the clay. In this experiment, both the scaffolds and the nonhuman factors deformed to a degree by taking shape of one another. This hybridity almost obscures what is there to be changed and what is there to initiate the transformation. What can be observed through the material forms is that the process of decomposition transforms the soft, temporal, and invisible into something much harder, permanent, and physical.

**Experiment 3: Fabrics + Slip**

**Figure 7. (Left) slip dried on the fabric scaffold. (Right) the flaky edge on the bisque resembles the texture of the fabric.**

In the following experiment, we stitched and folded fabrics to create three-dimensional objects to replace the pre-made paper cups. We did so to gain more freedom in determining what our design may look like by not restricting it to ready-made industrial goods. In other words, we as designers tried to soften the scaffold even further so that nonhuman entities can have more voice in the co-creation process.

We used denim to make the scaffolds by cutting, layering, folding, and loosely stitching the fabrics together. We selected denim because it has enough firmness to hold the slip without collapsing; the fabric is also soft enough for the slip to shape and dry without cracking. In execution, we put our hands inside the fabrics and dipped them into a bucket of slip. The items were placed on the shelf to dry and then sent to the kiln for firing. In figure 7, we can see that the denim scaffold was brunt away during firing, leaving a thin layer of clay in the state of bisque. The final result displays a mixed property of fabric and clay. On the one hand, it has flaky edges that resemble the threads on the brink of the denim, with wrinkles and folds that capture the softness and thinness of fabrics. On the other hand, the wrinkles and folds are permanent: they no longer deform with gentle touches.

## CONCLUDING DISCSSION: DESIGNING [WITH/THROUGH] DECOMPOSITION

This research responds to a recent call in HCI that proposes shifting from a human-centric agenda towards one that integrates a multispecies worldview. This paper draws from the theoretical concept of natureculture to transgress the boundary between nature and culture and explore how this shift in perspective might reorient our design practices. In writing about natureculture, Anna Tsing describes her excitement about mushroom foraging, "these mushrooms are not the product of my labour, and because I have not toiled and worried over them, they jump into my hands with all the pleasures of the unasked for and the unexpected. For a moment, my tired load of guilt is absolved, and, like a lottery winner, I am alight with the sweetness of life itself [40:142]." Such a delight is experienced when she receives a gift from nature—intimate, unanticipated, and probably also quite tasty. In many cases, humans seem to live the best while cohabitating with nature: treating dogs, cats, and other living organisms as our "significant others" [14]; planting trees and flowers to decorate the dull concrete blocks in the cities; and traveling into the forest and natural parks to enjoy a tranquil moment with other lifeforms on Earth. It seems to be human nature having the desire to get close to nature. Such a desire goes beyond meeting the basic needs in order to survive but to also find joy and fulfillment in life. However, this is only one side of the story. In constructing the material world, through design and engineering, we assert and enforce boundaries between nature and culture. In cities, skyscrapers roar into the skyline, competing with trees for the sunlight which they depend on for their lives; lands are taken by roads and buildings, expelling wildlife from nesting and foraging; and soils are covered with all sorts of construction, leaving no room for plants and animals to thrive.

In this paper, we wish to rediscover the excitement of designing with intimate connections with nature, a joy we lost while drawing boundaries separating nature and culture. In exploring ways of reconnecting with nature through design, we observe the natural process of decomposition and use it as the guiding principle in collecting, thinking, writing, and making designs. With the interest in co-creating with natureculture, we propose to loosen factors of precision and control in design practices. We consider design as an activity of scaffolding, which is more about cultivating a space to facilitate nature's participation than trying to exclude it from design. From a design perspective, we have showed that a proper scaffold balances the constraint and freedom it offers for natureculture co-creation. From a theory-building perspective, we have made more tangible the theoretical concept of natureculture by focusing on the natural process of decomposition and materializing it through physical forms. We have learned through our various design research activities that the visual language of natureculture often exhibits mixed material properties of the cultural (e.g., the scaffold) and the natural (e.g., the nonhuman actors and the environment), and the product of natureculture co-creation can't ever be fully predicted or replicated—such a result is not so much about the designers' incapability, but more about their willingness to listen, observe, and respond to what nature has to say, as well as learning to be vulnerable and amazed in the design process.

Much of this paper has been about materials, forms, crafting, design processes, and the material involved in our making experiments—ceramics, papers, and fabrics. These may seem to be unfamiliar to interaction design researchers. Even so, the lessons learned in our research activities might offer some thoughts in designing interactive systems. For example, we might consider the design tactic behind artificial intelligence as a digital version of scaffolding, in so far that computer engineers lay out the basic logic of processing, but the machine evolves and develops its own way of thinking. In addition, designers can also draw from the hybrid materiality created by the scaffold to sketch new forms of tangible bits—such as fabricating a sensing outfit that turns hard and functions as a shield when there is an external strike towards the wearer. In extending the present work, we see an urgency to address directly ways of incorporating the notion of decomposition in developing interactive technologies. Moving on, we will experiment with the tactics by embodying them in tangible bits—this work is part of a larger project of connecting nature and culture through technology and design.

## ACKNOWLEDGMENTS

Heartfelt thanks to Chase Gamblin and Wei Tseng for their enormous support in our ceramics-making experiments. We gratefully acknowledge Patrycja Zdziarska and our anonymous reviewers for their thoughtful comments. This work is supported in part by the Ministry of Education, Taiwan, as well as the National Science Foundation under Grant No. #1513604.

## REFERENCES


[1] Luisa Alba-Lois and Claudia Segal-Kischinevzky. 2010. Yeast Fermentation and the Making of Beer and Wine. *Nature Education* 3, 9: 17. Retrieved from https://www.nature.com/scitable/topicpage/yeast-fermentation-and-the-making-of-beer-14372813

[2] Christopher Alexander. 2002. *The Nature of Order: An Essay on the Art of Building and the Nature of the Universe*. Center for Environmental Structure.

[3] Fredrik Aspling, Jinyi Wang, and Oskar Juhlin. 2016. Plant-computer interaction, beauty and dissemination. In *Proceedings of the Third International Conference on Animal-Computer Interaction - ACI '16*, 1–10.

[4] Jeffrey Bardzell. 2011. Interaction criticism: An introduction to the practice. *Interacting with Computers* 23, 6: 604–621.

[5] Brian Burns. 2010. Re-evaluating Obsolescence and Planning for It. In *Longer Lasting Products: Alternatives to the Throwaway Society*, Tim Cooper (ed.). Gower Publishing Limited, 39–60.

[6] Caitlin DeSilvey. 2006. Observed Decay: Telling Stories with Mutable Things. *Journal of Material Culture* 11, 3: 318–338.

[7] Laura Devendorf and Daniela K. Rosner. 2015. Reimagining Digital Fabrication as Performance Art. In *Proceedings of the 33rd Annual ACM Conference Extended Abstracts on Human Factors in Computing Systems - CHI EA '15*, 555–566.

[8] Laura Devendorf and Daniela K Rosner. 2017. Beyond Hybrids: Metaphors and Margins in Design. In *Proceedings of the 2017 ACM Conference on Designing Interactive Systems (DIS '17)*, 995–1000.

[9] Laura Devendorf and Kimiko Ryokai. 2015. Being the Machine: Reconfiguring Agency and Control in Hybrid Fabrication. In *Proceedings of the 2015 CHI Conference on Human Factors in Computing Systems - CHI '15*, 2477–2486.

[10] Carl DiSalvo and Jonathan Lukens. 2011. Nonanthropocentrism and the Nonhuman in Design: Possibilities for Designing New Forms of Engagement with and through Technology. In *From Social Butterfly to Engaged Citizen : Urban Informatics, Social Media, Ubiquitous Computing, and Mobile Technology to Support Citizen Engagement*, Marcus Foth, Judith Donath and Laura Forlano (eds.). MIT Press, 421–436.

[11] Val Jon Farris. 2014. From Broken to Beautiful: The Power of "Kintsugi." *The Huffington Post*. Retrieved April 11, 2017 from http://www.huffingtonpost.com/val-jon-farris/from-broken-to-beautiful-_b_5903994.html

[12] Laura Forlano. 2016. Decentering the Human in the Design of Collaborative Cities. *Design Issues* 32, 3: 42–54.

[13] Elisa Giaccardi, Elvin Karana, Holly Robbins, and Patrizia D'Olivo. 2014. Growing traces on objects of daily use. In *Proceedings of the 2014 conference on Designing interactive systems - DIS '14*, 473–482.

[14] Donna Haraway. 2016. *Staying with the Trouble: making Kin in the Chthulucene*. Duke University Press.

[15] Donna Haraway. 2003. *The Companion Species Manifesto: Dogs, People, And Signigicant Otherness*. Prickly Paradigm Press.

[16] Russell Hitchings. 2006. Expertise and Inability. *Journal of Material Culture* 11, 3: 364–381.

[17] Lara Houston, Steven J. Jackson, Daniela K. Rosner, Syed Ishtiaque Ahmed, Meg Young, and Laewoo Kang. 2016. Values in Repair. In *Proceedings of the 2016 CHI Conference on Human Factors in Computing Systems - CHI '16*, 1403–1414.

[18] Miwa Ikemiya and Daniela K. Rosner. 2014. Broken probes: Toward the design of worn media. *Personal and Ubiquitous Computing* 18, 3: 671–683.

[19] Steven J. Jackson and Laewoo Kang. 2014. Breakdown, Obsolescence and Reuse: HCI and the Art of Repair. In *Proceedings of the 2014 ACM annual conference on Human Factors in Computing Systems - CHI '14*, 449–458.

[20] Hiroki Kobayashi, Ryoko Ueoka, and Michitaka Hirose. 2009. Human Computer Biosphere Interaction: Towards Sustainable Society. In *Proceedings of the 29th Annual ACM Conference Extended Abstracts on Human Factors in Computing Systems - CHI EA '09*, 2509–2518.

[21] Stacey Kuznetsov, William Odom, James Pierce, and Eric Paulos. 2011. Nurturing natural sensors. In *UbiComp'11 - Proceedings of the 2011 ACM Conference on Ubiquitous Computing*, 227–236.

[22] Max Lamb. 2014. 157- Marmoreal. *Max Lamb*. Retrieved August 5, 2018 from http://maxlamb.org/157-marmoreal/

[23] Joanna Latimer. 2013. Being Alongside: Rethinking Relations amongst Different Kinds. *Theory, Culture & Society* 30, 8: 77–104.

[24] Ann Light, Irina Shklovski, and Alison Powell. 2017. Design for Existential Crisis. In *Conference on Human Factors in Computing Systems - Proceedings*, 722–734.

[25] Jen Liu, Daragh Byrne, and Laura Devendorf. 2018. Design for Collaborative Survival : An Inquiry into Human-Fungi Relationships. In *CHI'18: Proceedings of the SIGCHI Conference on Human Factors in Computing Systems*, 1–13.

[26] Leonard Loren. 1998. *Wabi-Sabi: for Artists, Designers, Poets, and Philosophers*. Stone Bridge Press, Berkeley.

[27] Peter Lyle, Jaz Hee-jeong Choi, and Marcus Foth. 2015. Growing Food in the City: Design Ideations for Urban

Residential Gardeners. In *Proceedings of the 7th International Conference on Communities and Technologies - C&T '15*, 89–97.

[28] Leah Maestri and Ron Wakkary. 2011. Understanding repair as a creative process of everyday design. In *ACM SIGCHI conference on Creativity & Cognition*, 81–90.

[29] Clara Mancini and Jussi Lehtonen. 2018. The Emerging Nature of Participation in Multispecies Interaction Design. In *DIS '18 Proceedings of the 2018 Designing Interactive Systems Conference*, 907–918.

[30] Richard Martin. 2007. Wabi-Sabi. *Photo Life*, 14–18. Retrieved from http://dt.pepperdine.edu/courses/greatbooks_v/gbv_101/Wabi- Sabi.PDF

[31] Martin Murer, Verena Fuchsberger, and Manfred Tscheligi. 2017. Un-Crafting : De-Constructive Engagements with Interactive Artifacts. In *TEI* '17 Proceedings of the Eleventh International Conference on Tangible, Embedded, and Embodied Interaction, 67–77.

[32] Ariane Prin. 2017. Prin London. Retrieved August 31, 2017 from http://www.prin.in/

[33] María Puig de la Bellacasa. 2010. Ethical doings in naturecultures. *Ethics, Place and Environment* 13, 2: 151–169.

[34] Holly Robbins, Elisa Giaccardi, Elvin Karana, and Patrizia D 'olivo. 2015. Understanding and Designing with (and for) Material Traces. *Studies in Material Thinking* 13.

[35] Valentina Rognoli and Elvin Karana. 2014. Toward a New Materials Aesthetic Based on Imperfection and Graceful Aging. In *Materials Experience: Fundamentals of Materials and Design*, Elvin Karana, Owain Pedgley and Valentina Rognoli (eds.). 145–154.

[36] Daniela K. Rosner and Morgan Ames. 2014. Designing for repair? Infrastructures and materialities of breakdown. In *Proceedings of the 17th ACM conference on Computer supported cooperative work & social computing - CSCW '14*, 319–331.

[37] Daniela K. Rosner, Miwa Ikemiya, Diana Kim, and Kristin Koch. 2013. Designing with Traces. *Proceedings of the SIGCHI Conference on Human Factors in Computing Systems - CHI '13*: 1649.

[38] Nancy Smith, Shaowen Bardzell, and Jeffrey Bardzell. 2017. Designing for Cohabitation: Naturecultures, Hybrids, and Decentering the Human in Design. In *CHI'17: Proceedings of the SIGCHI Conference on Human Factors in Computing Systems*, 1714–1725.

[39] Vanessa Thomas;, Christian Remy, and Oliver Bates. 2017. The Limits of HCD: Reimagining the Anthropocentricity of ISO 9241-210. In *LIMITS '17 Proceedings of the 2017 Workshop on Computing Within Limits*.

[40] Anna Tsing. 2012. Unruly Edges: Mushrooms as Companion Species. *Environmental Humanities* 1, 1: 141–154.

[41] Anna Tsing. 2015. *The Mushroom at the End of the World*. Princeton University Press.

[42] Hans Ullmer. Injection Mold Life Expectancy. *BASF Corporation*. Retrieved August 6, 2018 from http://www2.basf.us//PLASTICSWEB/displayanyfile?id=0901a5e180004878

[43] Amit Zoran, Roy Shilkrot, Suranga Nanyakkara, and Joseph Paradiso. 2014. The Hybrid Artisans: A Case Study in Smart Tools. *ACM Transactions on Computer-Human Interaction* 21, 3: 1–29.

[44] Ripple. *Poetic Lab*. 2013. Retrieved September 3, 2017 from http://www.poetic-lab.com/ripple-1/

[45] Marmoreal. *dzek*. 2018. Retrieved August 5, 2018 from http://dzekdzekdzek.com/products/white-marmoreal

# inFORCE: Bi-directional 'Force' Shape Display For Haptic Interaction

**Ken Nakagaki**[1] **Daniel Fitzgerald**[1] **Zhiyao (John) Ma**[2] **Luke Vink**[1] **Daniel Levine**[1] **Hiroshi Ishii**[1]
[1]MIT Media Lab
Cambridge, USA
{ken_n, djfitz, lajv, dvlevine, ishii}@media.mit.edu
[2]MIT EECS
Cambridge, USA
majohn@mit.edu

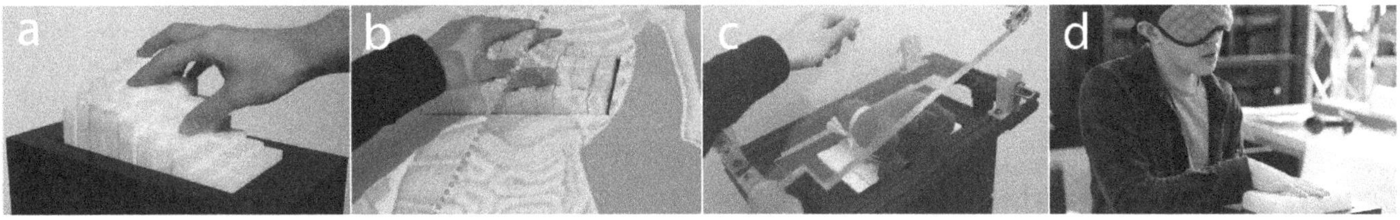


**Figure 1. a: *inFORCE* the bi-directional 'Force' Shape Display, b: Displaying Multi-layer Medical Data with Dynamic Shape and Haptic Properties c: Scanning Physical Material Compliances, d: User Study for Haptic Perception Evaluation**

## ABSTRACT

While previously proposed hardware on pin-based shape display has improved various technical aspects, there has been a clear limitation on the haptic quality of variable 'force' feedback. In this paper, we explore a novel haptic interaction design space with 'force' controlled shape display. Utilizing high performance linear actuators with current reading functionality, we built a 10 x 5 'force' shape display, named *inFORCE*, that can both detect and exert variable force on individual pins. By integrating closed-loop force control, our system can provide real-time variable haptic feedback in response to the way users press the pins. Our haptic interaction design space includes volumetric haptic feedback, material emulation, layer snapping, and friction. Our proposed interaction methods, for example, enables people to "press through" computationally rendered dynamic shapes to understand the internal structure of 3D volumetric information. We also demonstrate a material property capturing functionality. Our technical evaluation and user study assesses the hardware capability and haptic perception through interaction with *inFORCE*. We also discuss application spaces that 'force' shape display can be used for.

## CCS Concepts

**•Human-centered computing → Haptic devices;**

## Author Keywords

Shape Changing Interfaces; Shape Display; Force Feedback; Haptics



*TEI '19*, March 17–20, 2019, Tempe, AZ, USA



DOI: https://doi.org/10.1145/3294109.3295621

## INTRODUCTION

Shape Changing Interfaces has been one of the major realms in the field of HCI to physically embody shapes of digital data and dynamically adapt to users and contents [7, 16, 29]. However, various objects including the human body and layers of earth have volumetric structures and material properties cannot be represented only by shape rendering capabilities. While some research in actuated interfaces propose methods to render dynamic material stiffness and other material properties on-top of dynamic shapes, such replicated properties are either only on the surface layer or just homogeneous especially in volumetric layers.

We propose a novel pin-based shape display system which can detect and exert variable force for novel haptic interaction. Haptic interaction includes material property emulation and volumetric data representation. We propose a method to embed haptic effects to the volume of Shape Changing Interfaces as a novel way for users to understand volumetric structural data with multi-material properties mapped within a shape. Such interfaces could help medical students to understand biomedical structures and organ properties, or geo-scientists to understand the varying properties of different layers of the earth by touching and pressing through haptics-effects-encoded shape.

As a proof of concept prototype for the above interactions, we introduce *inFORCE*, a 'force' shape display which can detect variable force being applied to each pin and exert variable force on contact hands and objects. Technically, our hardware is composed with an array of linear motors that are faster and stronger than most of the previously proposed shape display hardware [18], which expands the design space of haptic interactions. Our approach takes advantage of Tangible and Shape Changing Interfaces, and extends them to give an extra dimension of haptic effects rendering capability beyond shape by integrating variable force control.

The contributions of this paper include;

- Presenting the haptic interaction design space with the bi-directional 'force' shape display.
- Development of *inFORCE* hardware and software to detect and represent variable force for creating interactive haptic effects.
- Evaluation of the force emulation capability and haptic perceptions of *inFORCE* through a technical evaluation and user study.
- Proposing an application space that benefits from the haptic interaction capability with *inFORCE.*

## RELATED WORK

### Haptic Interfaces

Various types of haptic feedback devices have been explored to present the sensation of virtual objects [15]. Object properties such as surface texture and heaviness have been reproduced through technical approaches including Vibro-Tactile Feedback [24, 26], or Electro-Stimulation [20, 37].

For kinetic compliance control, haptic devices have made use of various form factors, existing in the form of utensils (pens) styluses[21], grasping gloves[5], fingertip texture feedback[4]. Some of these works explore spatial volumetric data representation [3, 31]. In our work we use a shape-changing interface for its ability to create affordances dynamically and enable users' bare hands to interact with emulated data and material. Additionally, generating precise force control to emulate elastic properties in haptic research is also investigated widely using a closed-loop control system [6]. In part of our haptic effects, we also combine such control system to provide a perception of compliance stiffness, but with the shape display.

### Shape Changing Interfaces

While variety types of interfaces have been explored in the research realm of Shape Changing Interfaces [29, 16, 7], recent review paper pointed out that "future shape-changing interfaces should render haptic material properties, in addition to shape alone [1]." Some of previous research in HCI technically addressed this challenge by combining pneumatic actuation with jamming [34, 27, 11], and we apply this dual capability (shape + haptic property) to pin-based shape display systems to explore novel haptic interactions.

Pin-based shape displays have been recently explored widely as a general platform of Shape Changing Interfaces for prototyping a range of interactive applications (e.g. remote communication and dynamic affordances [12]) with a range of technical improvements (e.g. higher resolution with movable base [33] and modular design [14]). Volumetric data representation has been introduced with visually overlaying images on shape display system with AR, but without dynamic haptic or force feedback [19]. *Materiable* aimed to emulate material properties through illusionary haptic perception with an interaction framework of touch sensing and a physics simulation model [23]. While this method was a visually effective way to replicate illusionary material perception using actuators with weak force (<1N) and coarse touch detection (required to be pressed-in at least 5mm to detect touch), the integration of actual force control (<4N) with precise force sensitivity to a pin-based shape display directs to an open research space for exploring human perception through digitally rendered material and novel tangible interaction.

### Capturing Material Property

Finally, the scanning material properties itself is also widely explored in the engineering systems for material and body measurements [28, 25]. Our system, by taking the pin-based shape display approach, would be the first system that has capability of both capturing and replicating material property. We explore the new interaction design space enabled with this dual capabilities, through multiple applications including CAD (copy, paste and edit digital material) and body adaptation.

## INFORCE - BI-DIRECTIONAL 'FORCE' SHAPE DISPLAY

We aim to expand haptic interaction for pin-based shape display by means of variable force and shape control. Figure 2 shows the design space for haptic tangible interaction with pin-based force shape display, categorized into Haptic Feedback (displaying tactile feedback) and Sensing (capturing physical activity).

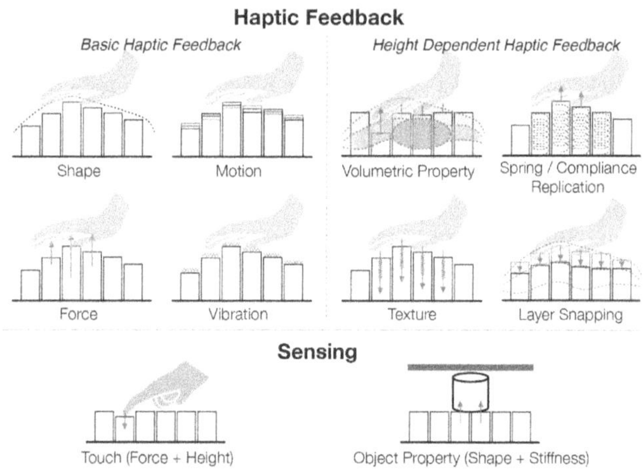


**Figure 2. Design Space of *inFORCE* for presenting variable haptic effects and touch / object sensing.**

### Haptic Feedback

Within Haptic Feedback, *Basic Haptic Feedback* presents a set of primitive haptic properties that 'force' shape displays can present, including not only static shape and motion (which are already common elements in previous shape display research), but also force and vibration. Force is a primitive effect that can be provided when each pin is in contact with user's body. Each pin can have a preset-force that can resist the pressed force until the pressed force becomes higher than the preset-force. Vibration effects simply provide vibration with a desired frequency to provide haptic effects similar to vibro-tactile feedback on each pin.

*Height Dependent Haptic Feedback* is a type of effect that can be presented based on how users touch or press the display surface. For example, *Volumetric Properties* can be provided, wherein volumetric haptic effects (e.g. stiffness, vibration etc) can be distributed depending on the pin heights when users press into the pins. To replicate the haptic effect of *a spring constant / compliance material*, the force can be gradually increased as users press downwards. *Texture effects* can be rendered by providing vibration + force effects according to the speed and height pins are pressed in [36]. Lastly, *Layer Snapping* is a haptic effect that the surface shape snaps to pre-defined heights when users apply force on the interactive layer. Each layer can have different force thresholds to convey properties (e.g. rigid vs soft) between each layer.

### Sensing

For the sensing capability of the 'force' shape display, it can detect human touch - how much force is applied as well as how far the pin is pressed in. It can also recognize object properties - it can measure the weight of objects placed on the pin array, and the shape and stiffness of the object when they are pressed by pins against a flat rigid overhead surface.

## DESIGN AND IMPLEMENTATION

The overall system of our prototype is composed of the *inFORCE* shape display itself and a computer that runs a software to control the hardware (Figure 3). The shape display consists of a 10 x 5 array of pins where each pin has a size of 19.2mm square with spacing of 0.8 mm. The overall display size (200x400mm) was chosen to fulfill the size of human hand for demonstrating haptic interaction, while we hope to create larger surfaces in the future.

To demonstrate some of the applications, we included peripheral devices such as projector for mapping images on three sides of the pins (Figure 11), and a USB camera for capturing the appearance of scanning objects (Figure 13). Also for scanning material, we fabricated a scanner attachment counter board for the *inFORCE* system that users can easily place overhead the pin display, so that pin displays can push material to be scanned towards the counter board to capture compliance data (Figure 1c).

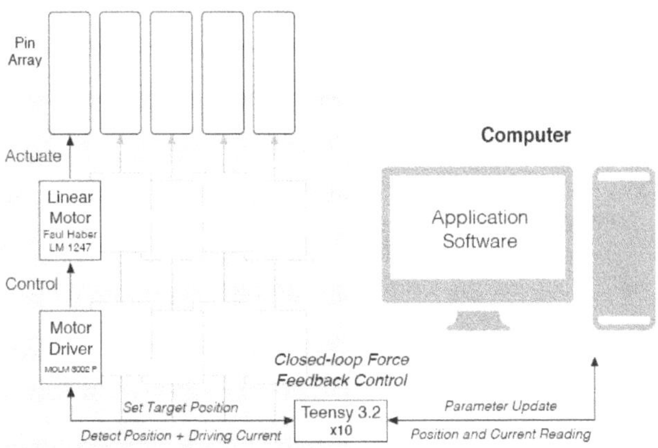


**Figure 3. System Overview.**

### Hardware Design

The hardware of the *inFORCE* shape display contains ten *Teensy 3.2* micro controllers and each micro controller controls five motor drivers through CAN. Each motor driver controls a single linear actuator. We used the "*QUICKSHAFT LM 1247 11 120*" linear actuator and "*MCLM 3002 P*" motor driver both produced by *Faulhaber*. As shown in the Figure 4, motors for one row of pins (10 total) were located on a single layer of a acrylic panel. To compensate for the space and resolution of the hardware, five of them were placed on the bottom of the panel and another five were placed on the top. Metal shafts were used to connect the motor shaft to the pins. Pins were made of white photo-polymer fabricated with a commercial SLA 3D printer. The total weight for the motor to lift was 70g for the top row motors and 95g for the bottom. Each *Teensy* operates at 60Hz to communicate with the motor driver, and the motor driver has the control frequency of $\leq$ 400kHz.

One of the core technologies incorporated into our implementation is the use of the high performance linear actuator *QUICKSHAFT*. This actuator is composed of a 3-phase self-supporting coil together with 3 hall sensors to offer micro-positioning applications [9]. The designated motor driver has its own PID control for position control when it receives command through CAN from *Teensy* and sends back sensor data including position and drawing current. We used this drawing current data to detect force. According to their datasheet, it is able to generate a continuous force of 3.6N and a peak Force 10.7N, with precision of 120μm and maximum speed of 3.2m/s. Each motor is running with 28V and the current it draws under force resistance is in maximum of 1.2A (the motor driver has the current limit function) resulting in up to 1680W in total.

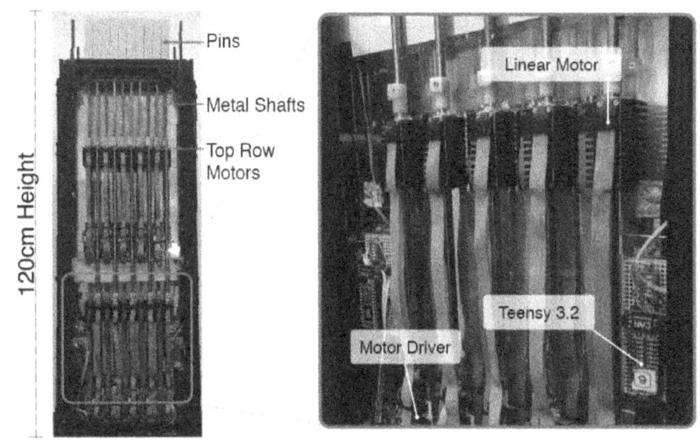


**Figure 4. Overall components on a single panel with 10 actuators and zoomed-in view of the top row of motors.**

### Software

Our software runs on a Windows computer with a frequency of 60Hz and is developed in a C++ environment.

#### *Force Detection*

While our motors did not have built-in force sensors, we were able to develop a custom control algorithm to emulate force feedback based on current sensing functionality within the motor driver and position output. Briefly, the current induced in the motor is roughly proportional to the force on the motor: the higher the load on the motor, the higher the induced current in general. However, there are confounding effects that we had to filter out, that we will describe below.

There are two effects that are necessary to be filtered out: additional current due to the movement of the pin, and additional current due to a magnetic pattern present within the motors. The following model suitably governs this relationship:

$$Current \propto (ExternalForce + Movement) \cdot Magnetic$$

Movement describes the additional current required to move the pin, if the pin is moving, and depends on the direction of movement and the location of the pin. If the pin is still, *Movement*=0. *Magnetic* describes the effect of the magnetic pattern encoded in the shaft of the motor, and is usually a value between 0.9 and 1.1 with no load, depending on the location of the pin. However, this value saturates when there is a load on the motor. Therefore, to form a good estimate of the latent variable Force from the observed variable Current, we must first have good estimates of the *Movement* and *Magnetic* variables. We do this during the calibration step, where for each pin, we run a data collection routine where we gather the values of *Movement* and *Magnetic*. We had to run the calibration several times, once with no weights and two with adding different weight to the pins to characterize the linear proportion of saturation for *Magnetic*. We later use these stored values, in addition to the observed current, to estimate the actual force.

### Compliance Material Representation

The algorithm that describes the movement of the pins in response to force is as follows. Each pin height is mapped to a "target force", which is the force that the finger should feel when pressing down on the pin at that height. For example, the target force could linearly map from 0N of force at maximum height to 3N at minimum height, simulating an object following Hooke's Law:

$$TargetForce = SpringConstant \cdot PinHeight \tag{1}$$

A PD control loop then tries to make the force on the pin equal to the target force. If the force on the pin is greater than the target force, the pin moves downwards with velocity proportional to the difference; vice versa, if the force on the pin is smaller than the target force, the pin moves upwards similarly. The kP proportionality constant (in addition to target force) helps control the perceived stiffness of the material. This closed control loop was implemented locally on each Teensy and the software on the computer temporally updates the parameters. Additionally, we developed a control system for an overall shape behavior in response to touch deformation similar to the one proposed in [23].

### Rendering Height Dependent Haptic Feedback

The method of creating the dynamic haptic effects is briefly covered below:

*Material Emulation*: the pins emulate the stiffness and feel of various materials, using the Material Representation algorithm described above.

*Volumetric Property*: Different target forces were mapped to pin heights. Users could feel the stiffness distribution by pressing-down on the pins.

*Layer Snapping*: When pressed at the specified force (sum of the force applied for multiple pins) for that layer, the pins snap down to the next layer. This method can be applied to replicating mechanical systems such as switches and toggles.

*Vibration Effects*: the pins are able to vibrate at a set frequency by oscillating the height up and down around a middle point. We observed that the oscillation is noticeable up to 30Hz. Additionally, by providing vibration as users press down the pins, we were able to generate a rough texture.

### Material Stiffness Scanning

Our method to scan the stiffness properties of a material are as follows. The object is first held in place above the pins by a user. Then, each pin moves upwards until it can detect the object. From then, it moves upwards in increments of predefined distance (we used 2.5mm for our prototype), and gathers the force detected from the material onto the pin. After hitting the limit of current (force load) or maximum height, the data of height-dependent force is stored. This data can directly be used as material emulation data to present the amount of force to provide depending on the distance each pin becomes pressed in. Figure 5 shows the material samples of foam and actual scanned data for each material as a reference. This data was used in a user study.

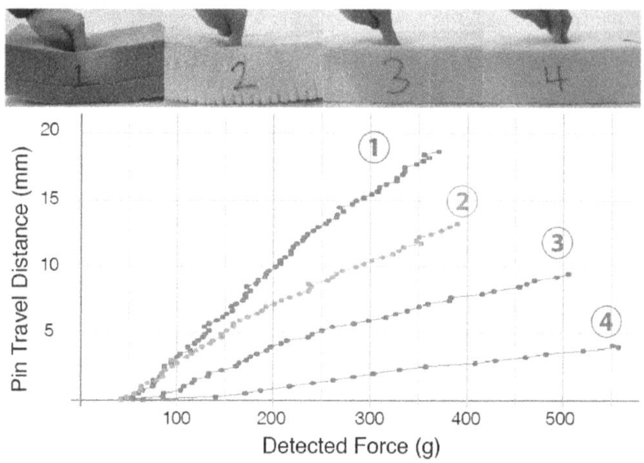


**Figure 5. Four scanned foams as material samples (above) and a graph of scanned data results based on a single pin travel distance vs detected force at the relative distance (below). Material 4 is stiffer than 1.**

## Technical Evaluation for Bi-directional Force Control

We validated bi-directional force control capability of *inFORCE* system. Regarding the force sensing aspect, we first measured the minimum weight the system can detect as external force. We placed weights on each pin (in increments of 10g) and observed the software to start detecting the weight. The average of all data was 57g with SD of 26.04. The resolution of measurement was approximately 0.4g. The maximum weight pins could detect depended on the motor torque as the motor driver had functionality to turn off the motor for a few seconds after drawing too much current. With this, the maximum weight pins could detect was 680g (70g STD) for peak force, and 380g (45g STD) for continuous force.

We also evaluated the force output control capability. As shown in the left of Figure 6, we fixed an analog force gauge above hardware and measured 8 different levels of target force output in a range of 100 - 300g for all 50 pins. Right of Figure 6 shows the results with a graph that shows relationship of target force determined in the system vs actual measured force (average of all 50 pins). The average error was 30.22g.

While the force-controlled shape display itself is novel, these technical evaluation results imply further challenges in accuracy improvements. It could be improved either by in-depth characterization of relationship between force and measured current to update our algorithm. Applying other state-of-the-art force sensing / control methods[6, 17] is another solution.

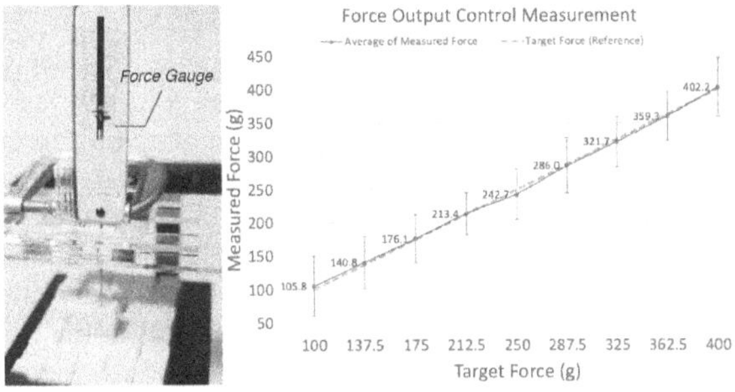


**Figure 6. Left: Force output evaluation setup with a force gauge, Right: Graph of the result - target force vs average of measured force.**

## USER STUDY

In order to evaluate the haptic representation capability of the *inFORCE* system, we conducted three preliminary studies.

*Compliance Stiffness* - Our first study was conducted to validate the stiffness perception rating based on the material replication algorithm described by Hooke's law in equation 1 where *SpringConstant* was set to 1 of 6 different parameters (0.01, 0.02, 0.04, 0.08, 0.1 and 0.64) that we chose through preliminary adjustments. Due to time constraints, each participant was tested twice for each emulated stiffness (12 trials in total) and we asked them to answer the perceived stiffness in their own scale [8, 35].

*Material Comparison* - The purpose of this study was to evaluate the haptic replication capability of scanned material compliance properties. We utilized both the captured data and the actual material samples presented in Figure 5. Participants were asked to compare the rendered material on *inFORCE* and actual material through haptic exploration and give a number on how close they are (100 being perfect). Since *inFORCE* is not capable of rendering the surface texture of materials, we prepared a pin display-based haptic filter with the same dimensions as *inFORCE* which can be placed on top of material samples (Figure 7). This filter replicates the compliance force while keeping the surface texture / structure functionally identical to *inFORCE*. Participants were asked to compare four sets of haptic explorations for four different materials (16 total) in random order, and for the closest score they gave in each digitally emulated material they were also asked why it was close and how it could be perfect.

*Multi-Layer* - Finally, *Multi-Layer* study was conducted to evaluate the volumetric haptic effects distributed in multi-layers as users pressed the pins down. The *Layer Snapping* haptic effect (Figure 2) with multi-layer of flat surface shapes was used in this evaluation. After applying force and snapping to next layer, participants were asked to answer the stiffness value and layer thickness (distance to snap to next layer) they just felt in their own scale. Participants rated a total of 20 layers of stiffness and thickness. The stiffness value and thickness values were generated randomly every time within a range of 130 - 2800g for stiffness, and 5 - 25mm for thickness.

Because the main purpose of all three studies was to evaluate the stiffness, volumetric and material property perception, we set the shape of the surface to be flat by default.

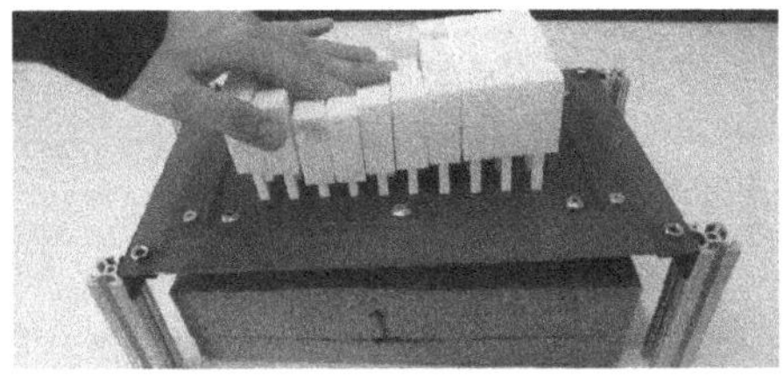

**Figure 7. Pin display based-haptic filter replicated with same dimension of *inFORCE* system to use in Material Comparison Study. Materials in Figure 5 are placed below the filter so users can feel the compliance stiffness through pressing the pins.**

### Procedure and Participants

For all three studies, users were asked to wear an eye mask to remove visual bias and communicate with the experimenters vocally. They were asked to use their dominant hand to press the pins throughout all studies. They were also advised to touch or press the pins in various ways (e.g. with finger tips and palms, or with different speeds and forces). Participants (N = 10, 5 female, 5 male), aged 18-32 (M = 23.78, SD = 5.87) were recruited for these studies and received 15 USD gift cards as compensation. Three studies were conducted in a row which lasted approximately 30 - 45 minutes total, including 3 minutes of break in-between. At the end of the study, they were asked to fill in a short questionnaire about their experiences.

### Results and Discussion

Figure 8, 9, and 10 show the results of all three studies respectively. The results of the *Compliance Stiffness* and *Multi-Layer* studies show overall proportional responses relative to the emulated stiffness properties, while the *Material Comparison* showed some unintended results. In the study, for material 4, which was the most rigid material among others, people tended to answer highest closeness score for the correct one. However, participants seemed to mix up three of the other softer material data; many identified replicated materials 1-3 as being closest to the haptic sensation of Material 3. While the material scanning results showed a relatively linear value in Figure 5 for stiffness reading, there can be a problem in the scanning quality to detect more complex material properties such as elasticity - how fast a material pushes back after compression. Some participants reported the big difference between the rendered material and actual material was the speed it comes back to its original shape. Some participants also reported that there was a small oscillation when pins were pressed down in depth, which implies several further improvements on control including calibration, update frequency, and algorithms. Because the softer emulated materials could more easily be pressed down, this can also be the reason Material 1-2 had low scores in closeness. Both these problems can be a challenge for future improvements both in material scanning and emulation. Furthermore, it also suggests that a comparative study would be needed to validate how well people can perceive the closeness between actual material samples with our filter on Figure 7.

In the post-study survey, we asked the question "How well were you able to feel the stiffness / emulated material for the following methods of touching? Pressing with finger tip(s) vs. pressing with a palm" that was to be answered in a 5-point likert scale (5 meaning very good and 1 meaning very poor). The average score for finger tip(s) was 3.5, and palm was 4.1. We assume this was because individual motor was not strong enough when they were strongly poked by finger tip(s) (over 6.8N based on our evaluation), while when using palms the load was distributed over multiple pins so it was harder to press beyond the intended position. We believe adding a mechanical clutch or brake mechanism to individual pins might be one of the solutions for future improvement.

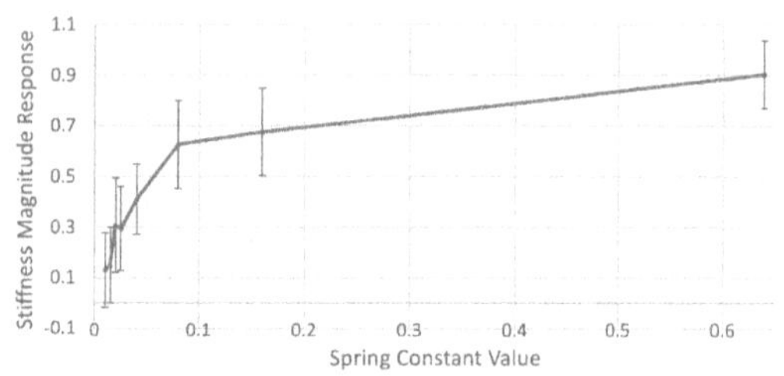


**Figure 8. Result of stiffness magnitude response for digitally rendered stiffness with 6 levels of *SpringConstant* values. The error bars represent the standard deviation values.**

| | | Actual Material Samples | | | |
|---|---|---|---|---|---|
| | | Material1 | Material2 | Material3 | Material4 |
| Replicated Materials | Material1 | 64.5 [19.7] | 54.1 [18.0] | 82.3 [6.5] | 46.4 [21.0] |
| | Material2 | 47.1 [15.5] | 54.1 [20.1] | 80.5 [13.0] | 50.5 [29.1] |
| | Material3 | 45.0 [19.4] | 52.5 [16.9] | 78.6 [10.7] | 61.2 [14.8] |
| | Material4 | 39.0 [17.4] | 36.8 [15.7] | 63.6 [14.5] | 85.0 [11.2] |

**Figure 9. Table of comparison with actual material samples and replicated material data on *inFORCE*. Values are the average scores of closeness ratings from all participants' responses (100 to be perfect closeness.). Values in [ ] represents the standard deviation for each data.**

## APPLICATION SPACE

We present potential applications that demonstrate the capability of bi-directional force and shape rendering, as well as haptic interaction techniques of the *inFORCE* shape display.

### Geological Data Representation

The expressivity of *inFORCE* display can present various kinds of data to present multi-dimensional data including shape and volumetric material data. Geo-science data is one

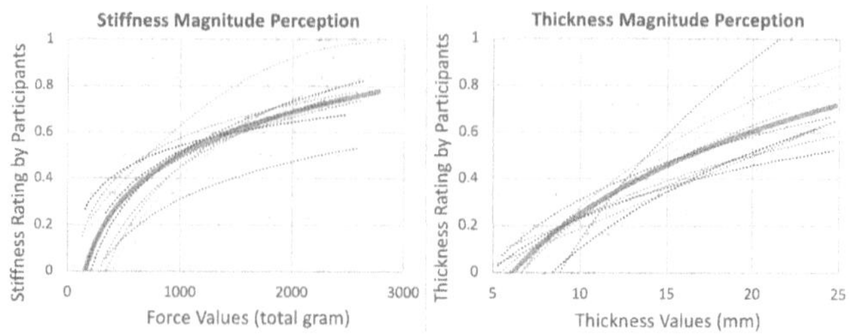


**Figure 10. Result of *Multi-Layer* study for stiffness and thickness perception. The thick red line represents the logarithmic trend line of collected responses from all participants, while each dotted-line represents the trend line from each participant's responses.**

of them. Seismic geo-science data contains multi-layered data with each layer having unique material properties. Geoscientists commonly view such complex data on screens as layers of section-cut visualized data. It is therefore difficult to comprehensively understand the 3D volumetric layered data and seismic properties. Getting an intuitive understanding for such a spatial and material property is a very important task for a range of fields including the oil and gas domains [13]. For example, as we discussed with oil companies, we learned that geo-scientists need to find a rigid layer of earth to estimate where the oil might be contained. Figure 11 shows an example of a user exploring through different layers of replicated earth seismic data. As a user press in the pins, the rendered shape snaps to different layers of seismic data according to the amount of force the user applies. This force can be variable depending on the geo-property data for each layer, so that the user can intuitively understand both the material property and shape of each layer.

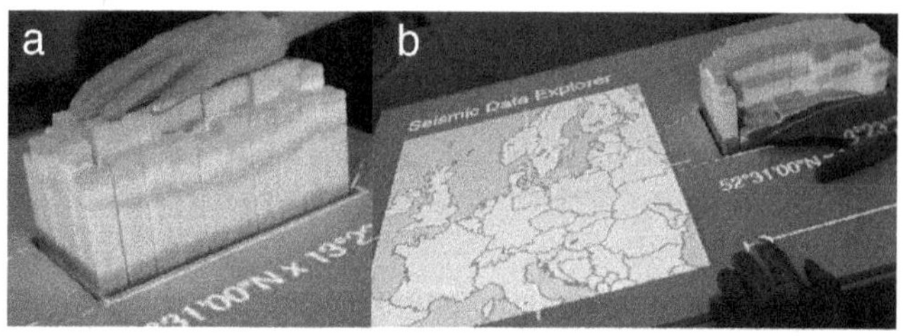


**Figure 11. Geoscience Data Exploration (a: Zoomed-in view of earth layers projected on the sides of pins, b: Zoomed-out view of the GeoScience UI for users to choose location to render layer data.)**

### Medical Data Replication

Another promising field for data representation using *inFORCE* is the medical field, wherein the haptic display can be used to train doctors in the palpation of different parts of the body [38]. Usually when medical students learns the body structure and surgery, they require a cadaver (which can be expensive), large 2D screens (which lacks the tactile sensation) [2], or a static anatomy model (which has limits to dynamically render different shapes and conditions). While similar applications have been presented in the field of haptics and shape changing interfaces [23], the *inFORCE* system allows rendering of depth and force feedback without wearing any device on our body. With the height dependent force feedback capability, a user can experience touching the volumetric body data that can only be perceived when pressing in by certain amount. Haptic perception of a tumor can be replicated when it is presented stiffer as a user pressed replicated body with specific depth, and heart pulse can be replicated by presenting a certain frequency of vibration with specific depth (Figure 12a). Figure 12b shows how *inFORCE* can be used for CRP training which requires specific force and timing. The training can be tracked and evaluated by the system for learning. The scanning functionality of *inFORCE* can be combined with this application scenario, where a female user can scan her own breast and use that data to replicate breast tumor information specific to her own body, to learn the proper way to find a breast tumor.

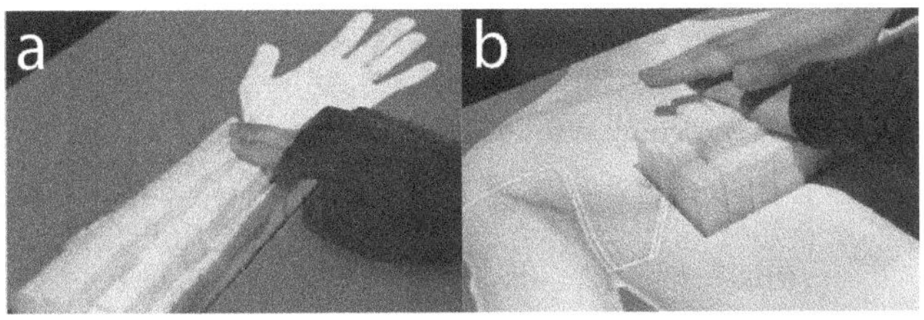


**Figure 12. Medical Application Prototype (a: Human arm model that people can feel pulse from only when pressed with appropriate force, b: Chest model for CRP training which requires appropriate force and timing that can be rated by the system.)**

### CAD Interface for Designing Multi-Material Model

As multi-material fabrication and 3D printing have been rising research topics in recent years, CAD interfaces also need to provide flexibility and intuitiveness for a range of users to easily design their desired shape and material property. Utilizing our system, users can tangibly shape forms, 'paint' material stiffness, and instantly check how the material property feels through their hands and bodies. The volumetric shape rendering capability allow users to modify volumetric material property as well. Additionally, with the material scanning capability, users can take real-world physical objects and materials to bring the physical stiffness in the digital CAD model, and apply the material property in their digital model. This is similar to the ideas of previous work where researchers explored capturing color or shape in the physical environments so that users can create their own digital painting or 3D model [30, 10]. Now, with our system, the material property can be incorporated in computational design for tangibly designing multi-material 3D model 13. Although there is still an interaction design challenge on how to create a UI for such a complex system, it is an exciting research space to tangibly design multi-material 3D models.

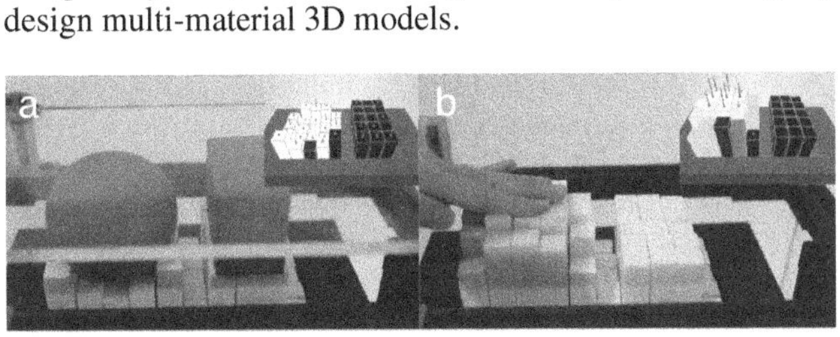


**Figure 13. Scanning and replicating Shape, stiffness and appearance of physical materials. Red ball is soft and blue block is rigid. The top right images show the software that represents black pins as detecting rigid material, and white pins as soft material. (a:Scanning material, b: Replicating the captured material.)**

### Body Adaptation

Based on the dual capability of scanning and rendering material stiffness, the *inFORCE* system has a potential to computationally capture our body data and provide appropriate comfort according to the captured data. This could be the future of furniture where beds, pillow, and chairs can understand our body states and dynamically adapt depending on personal body status and health issues (e.g. injury, pregnancy, etc). While the current system requires a counter plate for object property scanning, a seamless scanning method to capture body states is a primary research challenge for this application domain.

## LIMITATION AND FUTURE WORK

While our perception study was purely haptic, the novel interaction method in this paper such as snapping to layer or feeling stiffness through the layer would be interesting to combine with a visual system, just like the projection mapping methods we experimented within our application demonstration. Other types of visual augmentation, such as AR/VR may bring an interesting haptic perception study for multi-modal interaction (e.g. generate visuo-haptic illusion of users penetrating through a larger distance of layer in HMD, to compensate for the limited vertical movement range of the shape display.)

In our user study, we found several limitation of our system and technical challenges to provide intended haptic perception and discussed potential improvements. There are further challenges to enrich and expand other types of haptic properties such as surface texture, or adhesion. Another possible technical improvements include scaling up the size or increasing the resolution of the pin-display. Once it operates at the furniture scale, it may provide body scale interaction in the form of beds or floors, and multi-user interactions in social space [39]. While other researchers work on higher resolution pin display systems [33], it should not be difficult to apply our method to utilize the drawing current on the electrical actuator to generate a force feedback loop. We are excited to see how the interaction quality improves with higher resolution devices. Beyond haptic effects, actuating other materials with force-responsive shape displays is an exciting direction [22, 32]. The strong force may enable advanced object manipulation (e.g. throw, deform, etc), and also the force sensitivity of pins can be used to track the object location and weight.

## CONCLUSION

In this paper, we brought force detection and feedback control in pin-based shape displays to explore novel haptic interaction. We introduced the design and implementation of 'force' shape display with closed-loop control software to enable a range of haptic effects. We proposed application spaces to demonstrate how the haptic effects enabled by *inFORCE* could be utilized for volumetric data representation in geoscience and medical fields as well as material scanning and replication in multi-material CAD tools and body adaptation systems. We believe the force interactivity in Shape Changing Interfaces would expand the interaction beyond shape with volumetric materiality and haptic effects to convey rich information to users.

## ACKNOWLEDGMENTS

We thank all those who contributed to the hardware development of inFORCE, including: Clark Della Silva, Rebecca Li, Hanjun Li, Daniel Mendelsohn, Baian "Andrew" Chen, Luke Hyman, Yasmine Hassan, Sam Chin, Mary and the "Merry Band of Oliners" (Olin College) and The Norwell High School Robotics Team. We also thank Joanne Leong for reviewing the paper.

## REFERENCES

[1] Jason Alexander, Anne Roudaut, Jürgen Steimle, Kasper Hornbæk, Miguel Bruns Alonso, Sean Follmer, and Timothy Merritt. 2018. Grand Challenges in Shape-Changing Interface Research. In *Proceedings of the SIGCHI Conference on Human Factors in Computing Systems - CHI '18*. ACM Press, New York, New York, USA. DOI: http://dx.doi.org/10.1145/2470654.2466191

[2] Anatomage. Anatomage Table. https://www.anatomage.com/table/. https://www.anatomage.com/table/, Accessed: 2018-11-20.

[3] Ricardo S Avila and Lisa M Sobierajski. 1996. A haptic interaction method for volume visualization. In *Visualization'96. Proceedings*. IEEE, 197–204.

[4] Hrvoje Benko, Christian Holz, Mike Sinclair, and Eyal Ofek. 2016. Normaltouch and texturetouch: High-fidelity 3d haptic shape rendering on handheld virtual reality controllers. In *Proceedings of the 29th Annual Symposium on User Interface Software and Technology*. ACM, 717–728.

[5] Mourad Bouzit, Grigore Burdea, George Popescu, and Rares Boian. 2002. The Rutgers Master II-new design force-feedback glove. *IEEE/ASME Transactions on mechatronics* 7, 2 (2002), 256–263.

[6] Craig R Carignan and Kevin R Cleary. 2000. Closed-loop force control for haptic simulation of virtual environments. (2000).

[7] Marcelo Coelho and Jamie Zigelbaum. 2011. Shape-changing interfaces. *Personal and Ubiquitous Computing* 15, 2 (feb 2011), 161–173. DOI: http://dx.doi.org/10.1007/s00779-010-0311-y

[8] Alexandra Delazio, Ken Nakagaki, Roberta L Klatzky, Scott E Hudson, Jill Fain Lehman, and Alanson P Sample. 2018. Force Jacket: Pneumatically-Actuated Jacket for Embodied Haptic Experiences. In *Proceedings of the 2018 CHI Conference on Human Factors in Computing Systems*. ACM, 320.

[9] FAULHABER. Linear DC-Servomotors Series LM 1247...11. https://www.faulhaber.com/en/products/series/lm-124711/. https://www.faulhaber.com/en/products/series/lm-124711/, Accessed: 2018-11-20.

[10] Sean Follmer and Hiroshi Ishii. 2012. KidCAD. In *Proceedings of the 2012 ACM annual conference on Human Factors in Computing Systems - CHI '12*. ACM Press, New York, New York, USA, 2401. DOI: http://dx.doi.org/10.1145/2207676.2208403

[11] Sean Follmer, Daniel Leithinger, Alex Olwal, Nadia Cheng, and Hiroshi Ishii. 2012. Jamming user interfaces: programmable particle stiffness and sensing for malleable and shape-changing devices. In *Proceedings of the 25th annual ACM symposium on User interface software and technology*. ACM, 519–528.

[12] Sean Follmer, Daniel Leithinger, Alex Olwal, Akimitsu Hogge, and Hiroshi Ishii. 2013. inFORM. In *Proceedings of the 26th annual ACM symposium on User interface software and technology - UIST '13*. ACM Press, New York, New York, USA, 417–426. DOI: http://dx.doi.org/10.1145/2501988.2502032

[13] B Frohlich, Stephen Barrass, Björn Zehner, John Plate, and M Gobel. 1999. Exploring geo-scientific data in virtual environments. In *Visualization'99. Proceedings*. IEEE, 169–173.

[14] John Hardy, Christian Weichel, Faisal Taher, John Vidler, and Jason Alexander. 2015. Shapeclip: towards rapid prototyping with shape-changing displays for designers. In *Proceedings of the 33rd Annual ACM Conference on Human Factors in Computing Systems*. ACM, 19–28.

[15] Vincent Hayward, Oliver R Astley, Manuel Cruz-Hernandez, Danny Grant, and Gabriel Robles-De-La-Torre. 2004. Haptic interfaces and devices. *Sensor Review* 24, 1 (2004), 16–29.

[16] Hiroshi Ishii, Dávid Lakatos, Leonardo Bonanni, and Jean-Baptiste Labrune. 2012. Radical atoms. *interactions* 19, 1 (jan 2012), 38. DOI: http://dx.doi.org/10.1145/2065327.2065337

[17] Hyung-Kew Lee, Jaehoon Chung, Sun-Il Chang, and Euisik Yoon. 2008. Normal and shear force measurement using a flexible polymer tactile sensor with embedded multiple capacitors. *Journal of Microelectromechanical Systems* 17, 4 (2008), 934–942.

[18] Daniel Leithinger, Sean Follmer, Alex Olwal, and Hiroshi Ishii. 2015. Shape displays: Spatial interaction with dynamic physical form. *IEEE computer graphics and applications* 35, 5 (2015), 5–11.

[19] Daniel Leithinger, Sean Follmer, Alex Olwal, Samuel Luescher, Akimitsu Hogge, Jinha Lee, and Hiroshi Ishii. 2013. Sublimate: State-Changing Virtual and Physical Rendering to Augment Interaction with Shape Displays. In *Proceedings of the SIGCHI Conference on Human Factors in Computing Systems - CHI '13*. ACM Press, New York, New York, USA, 1441. DOI: http://dx.doi.org/10.1145/2470654.2466191

[20] Pedro Lopes, Sijing Young, Lung-pan Cheng, P Marwecki, and Patrick Baudisch. 2017. Providing Haptics to Walls and Other Heavy Objects in Virtual Reality by Means of Electrical Muscle Stimulation. In *Proc. Conf. Human Factors in Computing Systems (CHI)*.

[21] Thomas H Massie, J Kenneth Salisbury, and others. 1994. The phantom haptic interface: A device for probing virtual objects. In *Proceedings of the ASME winter annual meeting, symposium on haptic interfaces for virtual environment and teleoperator systems*, Vol. 55. Citeseer, 295–300.

[22] Ken Nakagaki, Udayan Umapathi, Daniel Leithinger, and Hiroshi Ishii. 2017. AnimaStage: Hands-on Animated Craft on Pin-based Shape Displays. In *Proceedings of the 2017 Conference on Designing Interactive Systems*. ACM, 1093–1097.

[23] Ken Nakagaki, Luke Vink, Jared Counts, Daniel Windham, Daniel Leithinger, Sean Follmer, and Hiroshi Ishii. 2016. Materiable. In *Proceedings of the 2016 CHI Conference on Human Factors in Computing Systems - CHI '16*. ACM Press, New York, New York, USA, 2764–2772. DOI: http://dx.doi.org/10.1145/2858036.2858104

[24] Yoichi Ochiai, Takayuki Hoshi, Jun Rekimoto, and Masaya Takasaki. 2014. Diminished haptics: Towards digital transformation of real world textures. In *International Conference on Human Haptic Sensing and Touch Enabled Computer Applications*. Springer, 409–417.

[25] Hakan Oflaz and ONDER Baran. 2014. A new medical device to measure a stiffness of soft materials. *Acta of bioengineering and biomechanics* 16, 1 (2014).

[26] Allison M Okamura, Jack T Dennerlein, and Robert D Howe. 1998. Vibration feedback models for virtual environments. In *Robotics and Automation, 1998. Proceedings. 1998 IEEE International Conference on*, Vol. 1. IEEE, 674–679.

[27] Jifei Ou, Lining Yao, Daniel Tauber, Jürgen Steimle, Ryuma Niiyama, and Hiroshi Ishii. 2014. jamSheets: thin interfaces with tunable stiffness enabled by layer jamming. In *Proceedings of the 8th International Conference on Tangible, Embedded and Embodied Interaction*. ACM, 65–72.

[28] Arthur Petron, Jean-Francois Duval, and Hugh Herr. 2017. Multi-Indenter Device for in Vivo Biomechanical Tissue Measurement. *IEEE Transactions on Neural Systems and Rehabilitation Engineering* 25, 5 (may 2017), 426–435. DOI: http://dx.doi.org/10.1109/TNSRE.2016.2572168

[29] Majken K. Rasmussen, Esben W. Pedersen, Marianne G. Petersen, and Kasper Hornbæk. 2012. Shape-changing interfaces. In *Proceedings of the 2012 ACM annual conference on Human Factors in Computing Systems - CHI '12*. ACM Press, New York, New York, USA, 735. DOI: http://dx.doi.org/10.1145/2207676.2207781

[30] Kimiko Ryokai, Stefan Marti, and Hiroshi Ishii. 2004. I/O brush. In *Proceedings of the 2004 conference on Human factors in computing systems - CHI '04*. ACM Press, New York, New York, USA, 303–310. DOI: http://dx.doi.org/10.1145/985692.985731

[31] J Kenneth Salisbury Jr. 1999. Making graphics physically tangible. *Commun. ACM* 42, 8 (1999), 74–81.

[32] Philipp Schoessler, Daniel Windham, Daniel Leithinger, Sean Follmer, and Hiroshi Ishii. 2015. Kinetic blocks: Actuated constructive assembly for interaction and display. In *Proceedings of the 28th Annual ACM Symposium on User Interface Software & Technology*. ACM, 341–349.

[33] Alexa F Siu, Eric J Gonzalez, Shenli Yuan, Jason B Ginsberg, and Sean Follmer. shapeShift: 2D Spatial Manipulation and Self-Actuation of Tabletop Shape Displays for Tangible and Haptic Interaction. (????). DOI: http://dx.doi.org/10.1145/3173574.3173865

[34] A. A. Stanley, J. C. Gwilliam, and A. M. Okamura. 2013. Haptic jamming: A deformable geometry, variable stiffness tactile display using pneumatics and particle jamming. In *2013 World Haptics Conference (WHC)*. IEEE, 25–30. DOI: http://dx.doi.org/10.1109/WHC.2013.6548379

[35] Stanley S Stevens. 1957. On the psychophysical law. *Psychological review* 64, 3 (1957), 153.

[36] Paul Strohmeier and Kasper Hornbæk. 2017. Generating Haptic Textures with a Vibrotactile Actuator. In *Proceedings of the 2017 CHI Conference on Human Factors in Computing Systems*. ACM, 4994–5005.

[37] Seiya Takei, Ryo Watanabe, Ryuta Okazaki, Taku Hachisu, and Hiroyuki Kajimoto. 2015. Presentation of Softness Using Film-Type Electro-Tactile Display and Pressure Distribution Measurement. In *Haptic Interaction*. Springer, 91–96.

[38] Sebastian Ullrich and Torsten Kuhlen. 2012. Haptic palpation for medical simulation in virtual environments. *IEEE Transactions on Visualization and Computer Graphics* 18, 4 (2012), 617–625.

[39] Luke Vink, Viirj Kan, Ken Nakagaki, Daniel Leithinger, Sean Follmer, Philipp Schoessler, Amit Zoran, and Hiroshi Ishii. 2015. Transform as adaptive and dynamic furniture. In *Proceedings of the 33rd Annual ACM Conference Extended Abstracts on Human Factors in Computing Systems*. ACM, 183–183.

# A Wearable Nebula
# Material Investigations of Implicit Interaction

**Vasiliki Tsaknaki**
KTH Royal Institute of Technology
Stockholm, Sweden
tsaknaki@kth.se

**Ludvig Elblaus**
KTH Royal Institute of Technology
Stockholm, Sweden
elblaus@kth.se

## ABSTRACT
In this paper we present the Nebula, a garment that translates intentional gestures and implicit interaction into sound. Nebula is a studded cloak made from a heavy fabric that envelopes the wearer with pendulous folds and has strong experiential qualities that were especially appreciated by performing artists. We describe the design process in detail, and highlight three material investigations that show material connections that were fundamental to the experience of the garment: How the draping and construction of the garment allowed for implicit interaction, how the studs were used both as a computational sensing material and a strong visual component, and how the sound design exploited tangible material qualities in the garment. We offer these three material investigations as contributions and discuss how material investigations more broadly can produce evocative connections in the materials available in design work, but also as a way to extract legible design intentions for other designers and researchers.

### Author Keywords
Implicit Interaction; Wearable technology; Crafting; Sound and Music Computing; Materials

### CCS Concepts
**•Human-centered computing → Interaction design; •Applied computing → Sound and music computing;**

## INTRODUCTION
A central challenge in the design of wearable technology is that it requires the fusion and interplay of a combination of knowledge from various domains of expertise, such as garment making, physical computing and electronics, and interaction design. For many decades research on wearable technology has been looking at how to develop solutions that are both meaningful in terms of interaction and well crafted [7, 35, 44, 42]. It is also a common topic in the TEI community.

In this paper, we present the process and main outcome of a collaborative project combining expertise from the fields of sound and music computing and interaction design. After two main design iterations accompanied by extensive material explorations, this process resulted in the Nebula interactive garment (Figure 1). The garment is a studded cloak that reacts to the movements of the wearer and responds with an ethereal soundscape. The design process was guided by the urge to explore implicit modes of interaction, including subtle movements, or shifting of body weight, in wearable contexts, from an open-ended material perspective. From reflecting on the design process in addition to the material and interactive qualities of the Nebula garment, we are extracting and presenting three main contributions, in the form of material investigations. These emerged throughout the design process in the work of combining the different areas of expertise that were present, and consequently the different types of material involved in this process.

The first material investigation concerns how the design process led to a garment with distinctly heavy and embracing qualities, which informed the design of the soundscape and consequently, the overall interactive experience that Nebula offers. The second material investigation summarizes how the active choice of studs as the main interactive and at the same time visual component of the garment, allowed for a seamless bridging of interaction and experiential qualities that can be sensed through wearables, what we called *functional aesthetics* [10]. The third material investigation concerns the designing of the sound in a wearable context, and in particular how we used the physical properties of the garment as a metaphor for crafting the audio modality.

The detailed articulation of the three material investigations consists the main contributions of this work. We propose that they can be viewed individually as specific examples of knowledge extracted from this particular project, and offer suggestions for exploring the space of implicit bodily interactions through physical and computational material qualities. They can also serve as a model for relating to and describing the work of integrating different materialities in the design of wearable technology or other fields with similar challenges.

## RELATED WORK
Wearable technology or *fashionable wearables*, has been defined by Seymour as "'designed' garments, accessories, or jewelry that combine aesthetics and style with functional technology" [36]. As a research area and application domain, wearable technology has recently seen resurgence in interaction design and in the TEI community, more specifically. This



*TEI '19*, March 17–20, 2019, Tempe, AZ, USA
© 2019 ACM. ISBN 978-1-4503-6196-5/19/03...15.00
DOI: 10.1145/3294109.3295623

**Figure 1. The second version of the Nebula garment.**

can be attributed, among other things, to recent technological developments that have broadened the space of possibilities for realizing more sophisticated interactive artefacts, including wearables. A number of toolkits and new types of materials have been gradually developed for wearable contexts, which utilize the particular properties of textiles, in an attempt to integrate technology seamlessly into garments. Early examples include the *Lilypad Arduino* prototyping board [5] designed specifically for wearable technology contexts, or the Kit-of-No-Parts approach by Perner-Wilson et al.[31] on handcrafting input and output sensors with soft and flexible materials, such as textiles or yarns that can be embedded into garments or accessories.

*Crafting interactive wearables* [41] is a rich material and crafts space, where computation meets textile design. This space can be also described as a *hybrid crafting practice* [15] since physical materials such as textiles and threads are combined with electronic components and computational materials, on the same artefact. This intersection entails many challenges that, apart from the quite divergent material space, include challenges on a level of bringing together and combining the diverse expertise involved in crafting wearables. As discussed by Gomez et al. [16] in a particular project they run that resulted in the development of a series of wearable technology concepts, this space can be seen as the intersection of art, (fashion) design and technology.

Interactive wearables developed for research purposes include mainly garments and accessories for sports, health applications, or assistive technology [6, 12, 20]. At the same time, many researchers have been exploring the expressive potential that different combinations of sensing and actuating modalities can offer, when worn on, or close to the body [45, 24]. These explorations often result in interactive wearables developed for performative or artistic contexts. Several research prototypes have been previously designed for music production. Some, like the influential *Musical Jacket* [32] or *Lizzy* [28], use intentional interaction with specific goals, such as triggering specific musical events by using explicit gestures. Another example that belongs to this category is the *hipDisk* [43], which is a self-contained wearable system for performance and play that augments the body with instrumental capabilities. These can be considered to be musical instruments that while worn, incorporate a controlled and intentional musical paradigm in their modes of interaction. Some other examples of research in this direction include *The Throat* [9], a singer-operated hand-worn artefact that embodies and extends particular notions of operatic singing techniques, the Future Grab [18], which maps hand gestures to human vowel pronunciation, and the *Rhythm'n'Shoes* [30], a wearable foot tapping interface with audio-tactile feedback. All of those examples seem to follow the tradition of the early groundbreaking work of Waisvisz [26] and Edwin van der Heide [4], who explored ways of using the hands and hand gestures for music making. While these projects and artefacts share many common characteristics with the Nebula garment, they explore a given musical paradigm with the explicit purpose of offering control over musical parameters to a dedicated performer, who in some cases can achieve virtuosity through enough practice over time.

The design and mapping of wearable musical instruments is of course more than the choice of explicit control or implicit interaction. One strategy, if the mode of performing is known, is to define a "movement vocabulary" that defines the repertoire of a professional performer and design the system to cater to that vocabulary, allowing the expertise in the original domain to be translated to the sonic output, such as the *kinesonic* approach of Hsu and Kemper [21]. If not only the tradition and mode of performance is known, but the wearable is designed for a particular theatrically staged piece, the design process can be integrated into the costume making for that piece and thereby exploit existing crafts knowledge [17]. However, such an approach is not without challenges, as the traditional organisational structures in theatres rely on division of labour with departments that rarely interact, e.g. costume designers and technical staff [19]. When collaboration between disciplines is needed, the use of *boundary objects* can help bridge divides and surface the materiality of designing wearable technology [47]. Cultural differences do not only exist between the ingoing disciplines involved in the creation of new artefacts, but also the performers' that will use the wearables on stage, and the technology created should be supportive of the different aesthetics and metaphysics of performance [3].

Another research approach in this domain is that of ambient data gathering through the use of wearable sensor systems, geared towards specific situations or actions being recorded through implicit interaction. One notable early example of this category of interactive garments is *The Conductors Jacket* [29]. Other, more contemporary examples include the work by Fujimoto et al. [13] or by Kapur et al. [25], who explored ways of creating music through body motions and performativity. This approach is also common in non-musical applications like the wearable American sign language recognizer [38], the *Flut-*

*ter* [33] or the *BodyScope* [46], as well as work on wearables that utilize music or sound as a mode of feedback through sonification of the sensed body [11]. This is a broad category of work that covers many different use cases, strategies, and intended design goals. Due to the open ended nature of the research process that resulted in the Nebula, and in particular the under-explored possibility of tuning the resulting sonification to convey information about gait or posture, the Nebula can be seen as related to, albeit not a continuation of this field of inquiry.

However, less work has been done on ambient data gathering for the production of artistic content using wearables, even though it is a common practice in the artistic forms of sonification and algorithmic data driven music composition, such as Sturm [39] and Collins [8]. While perhaps not wearable in the strictest sense, the mobile reactive music system *RjDj* [1] successfully explores ambient data gathering with artistic intent, playing with the ideas of implicit and explicit usage.

In this paper, we describe a material centered design process where implicit interaction was explored trough wearable artefacts that provided an open ended sensual and sonic experience. In contrast to the work described in this section, there was no performer, piece, or even performance tradition in mind. Instead, the goal was to create an evocative wearable that would meet a wide audience through exhibitions, to spark new ideas on how implicit interaction can be used in performance.

## THE NEBULA INTERACTIVE GARMENT

The conception and crafting of the Nebula took place as part of an interdisciplinary project called *Sound Clothes*, at the KTH Royal Institute of Technology university, in Stockholm, Sweden. It was an inter-department collaboration between the research groups of interaction design and sound and music computing that lasted for one year. The group also had expertise in craft-based research on electronic textiles, fashion design, musical composition and performing arts.

An exploratory and practice-based design research approach was followed [2, 27], starting from the available material space and project description. The design principles guiding the process were: To combine textiles, sound and interaction for exploring implicit modes of interaction, such as unintentional movements, slight changes in posture or subtle changes of the body weight, from an open-ended material perspective, building on what we referred to as functional aesthetics, a synergy between textiles, technology and sound.

The work was organized in bi-weekly meetings where initially each research group brought designed probes to be combined and tested together. As the design process evolved and the Nebula garment was conceived, those sessions took the form of collaborative crafting sessions, in which the researchers involved worked together on the actual garment. From then on, the goal was to find ways of developing an interpretation of body gestures in the auditory domain, with the aim to retain some of the particular characteristics and intentionality of the wearer in the final sonic outcome.

The design process resulted in an enveloping cloak designed for any gender and most body types, comprising of fabric, metal, and electronics, to create a nuanced interactive experience that enhances the sensation of one's bodily movements through sound. Visually as well as to the touch, the garment is defined by a contrast of soft fabric and a large number of sharp, metal studs. The opening and closing of the folds and the many studs that clash, apart from being the main visual element of the Nebula, are also the mechanic by which the garment is made interactive. The large folds of fabric that follow the movements of the wearer in a lagging, pendulum-like fashion are translated into sounds, in real time, through the studs, as it will be explained below. The garment has hidden buttons running along an opening in the front and it hangs from the shoulders and arms of the wearer. It is quite heavy and thick, and in motion, when the free-flowing fabric acts as a counterweight to the wearer's arms, it has a tactile and physical impact on the upper part of the wearer's body (Figure 1).

The garment is constructed in three layers. The first layer consists of four pieces of thick black cotton fabric stitched together in order to form the outer shell, comprised of two sleeves, the front and the back piece. The metal studs penetrate the first layer and create a physical conductive connection between the outside of the garment and the second layer. The second layer is a dense mesh of conductive thread that connects the metal studs to each other, in clusters, where groups of neighboring studs are interconnected. The clusters, in turn, are connected to an *X-OSC* circuit board [23], with some clusters connected to the analog inputs of the board, and some to the positive voltage output. The circuit board, together with a small battery that powers it, are placed inside a pocket stitched on the inside of the first layer, at the back of the garment. Finally, the third layer is a black polyester lining that protects the second layer with the mesh of conductive thread from the wearer.

Through this layered design, the studs form the end-points of a live electronic circuit that has the X-OSC board as its hub. If a cluster that is connected to a positive voltage source comes into contact with a cluster that is connected to an analog input, a detectable electrical connection is made. When the garment is worn, the input data are often composed of a stream of very brief connections. These are formed as two clusters are dragged through one another, and they come in contact. The X-OSC board has wireless capabilities, using Wi-Fi, and can transmit the detected connections to anything that can connect to a Wi-Fi network and receive OSC-messages.The transmitted OSC-messages from the X-OSC board are received on a laptop by custom software written in the *SuperCollider* [40] programming language. The software consists of two components, a data-processor and a sound generator. The data-processor takes the incoming streams of flickering connections from the studs and integrates those into a set of activity values, one for each cluster. These values are arranged in the order on which their corresponding clusters of studs are positioned on the garment, from top to bottom. In this way, the centroid of the resulting graph can be computed, adding an estimated measure of where on the body the current activity is positioned.

The garment has been exhibited extensively, always with at least one of the authors present, allowing for many discussions with a variety of people while they tried the garment. The public exhibitions were three open house events at the KTH Royal Institute of Technology, a demo session at the CHI'15 Conference in Seoul, South Korea [10], The Genoa Science Festival in Genoa, Italy, Ischia Musica in Ischia, and at the Sound and Music Computing Sweden Conference in Stockholm, Sweden. Furthermore, the garment has also been used with interaction design students at the KTH Royal Institute of Technology, as a starting point for discussions.

## MATERIAL INVESTIGATIONS

In this section, we present three material investigations that highlight three distinct but related themes that were extracted from the design process (shown in Figure 2) and from reflecting on the garment itself.

### Material Qualities Allowing for Implicit Interaction

Early on in the research process we decided to focus on the upper part of the body, mainly on the areas of the torso and the arms. This part of the body is very rich in terms of movements, ranging from subtle changes of posture such as shifting the weight on the one side, to bigger movements of turning or bending the torso. Consequently, we considered this to be a very rich design research space when it comes to combining wearables and interaction with sound. With a focus on this part of the body, we explored the broad material space that expands at the intersection of the different research domains involved. Our aim was firstly to build a shared material understanding in the research group, and then to find material combinations that would be relevant for the particular context.

Initially, an off-the-shelf garment was purchased and used as a platform for attaching the material probes that were gradually developed. This was for quick testing of the sensing capabilities on the body, rather than detached from it. The garment we chose was a long vest, open in the front, knitted out of thick wool. It had a lining, making it possible to slip electronics inside, allowing for relatively simple additions of material probes. The rationale was that in order to start testing the various materials closer to the body and start observing particular bodily movements that could be utilized for sound interaction, the material probes needed to be properly wearable without spending the time and resources to construct a finalized garment.

However, there was an increased concern with the somewhat rigid and stiff nature of the garment. Since it was knitted out of thick wool, the bodily movements and gestures of the wearer could not easily be translated into changes in the physical structure of the garment, such as folds that could trigger the sensors. After trying the garment with the embedded probes ourselves, we observed that sometimes the body moved but the garment remained still. This behavior was desirable from a perspective of explicit interaction, which was in line with some of the directions we explored, such as putting fabric-based buttons on the garment that needed to be actively interacted with, as a visible interface. But at the same time, it did not allow for implicit types of interaction, through sensing other aspects of the body such as implicit movements, slight changes in posture or subtle changes of the body weight, which was a main design goal for us. The combination of sensors, electronic components and computation were prototyped separately from the garment and then integrated on it, by stitching or pinning those on the garment's surface.

A new approach was deemed necessary and it was to become a big shift in the design process. Moving forward from focusing on the material samples and the sensing, the garment and the particular qualities of the garment when worn, were now put into focus. Using a very large piece of fabric, instead of the ready-made garment, many different ways of draping and pinning the fabric on the body were explored. The combined entity of wearer and wearable became the focal point, grounded on the physical characteristics of the garment that was being conceived- mainly on the flow, drapes and folds. Instead of trying to map behaviours to the prototyped sensors, the actual flow and liveliness of the folds and draping of the fabric informed and guided the subtleties of the interaction. We placed sensors on different areas of the garment, which were activated by bodily movements and gestures performed by the wearer, in areas where there was enough draping, folding, or extra fabric. At this stage, the approach was not a full integration of textile design and interaction design, since the technology was in a form of added-on components to the garment. But gradually the interactive garment was conceived as an entity, instead of creating individual components that were put together and tested. The use of the large piece of fabric turned out to be serendipitous, as it was very evocative and led to new design directions, where large amounts of free flowing fabric with many folds were found to be both visually pleasing as well as very easily activated by movement.

From the draping experiments, a concrete outcome was a garment designed in the form of a poncho, with free hanging fabric (Figure 3d). This was the first version of the garment, where metallic studs instead of e-textile materials were used as the sensing component. By reflecting on the properties of the fabric, together with the interactive qualities it allowed for and the sensing properties of the studs, we decided to use a much heavier fabric in order to create more of a swinging pendulum effect on the emerging folds. Furthermore, in the second version of the garment a more conscious way of creating folding patterns through pleating allowed for more nuanced implicit interaction. The long sleeves with the folding and hanging material were moving both when the wearer moved, but also while the wearer was largely still and only subtle bodily movements were performed.

We had two main insights from exhibiting the garment in regards to the draping and weight, and how those qualities influenced the interaction. When the wearer assumed a posture in which his/her arms were raised from the torso, either to the side or to the front, the draping and folding patterns of the Nebula were expanded as well. In this way a confined space like a womb or a shelter could be created around the wearer and within that space, the wearer, being enclosed, could explore a different set of soundscapes, as different clusters of studs were in contact with each other. The second insight

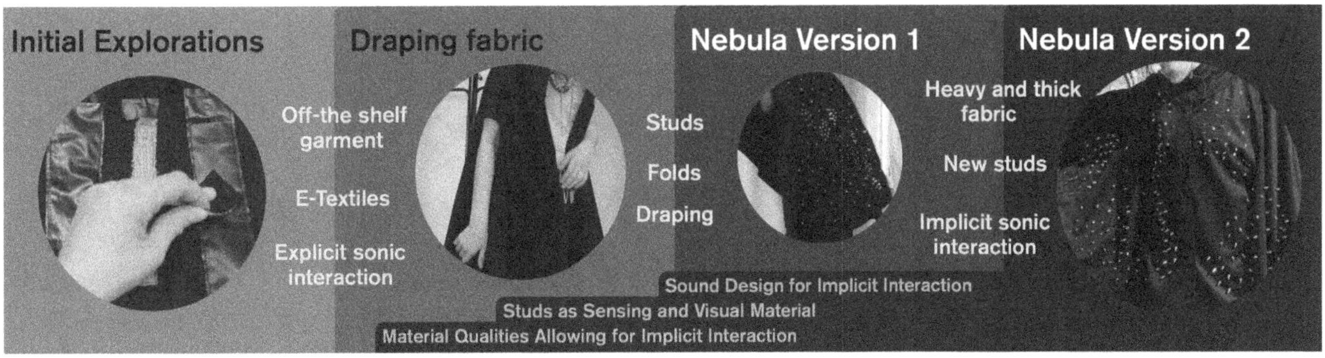


**Figure 2. A diagram showing the design iterations, versions of the garment, and material investigations.**

was when the person wearing the Nebula garment stood still with arms resting to the sides, and the folds and draping were resting on the wearer's body. In this resting posture, very subtle soundscapes could be explored, since the weight of the garment being felt on the body, and especially on the arms, created a slight pendulum-effect on the folds and draping hanging from the garment.

### Studs as Sensing and Visual Material

The materials involved in crafting the physical garment included fabric, thread and lining, and computational components, i.e. digital platforms and software for signal processing and communication. In order to become familiar with this diverse material space, we started by testing different types of e-textile materials in the form of soft and pliable electronics for wearable sensing. The e-textile materials used at this stage were: *EeonTex* conductive fabric [37], conductive fabric knitted with copper thread, velostat piezoresistive material, resistive yarn and silver plated nylon conductive thread. Additionally, we explored these different combinations of sensing and audio generation or audio modification, for example in the form of manipulation of recorded material.

Examples of material probes for sensing were soft and pliable patches functioning as buttons and sliders, constructed from fabric, resistive yarn and conductive textile. These were connected to the x-OSC circuit board in order to test data gathering and their potential for controlling sonic output. However, as we proceeded with exploring the material space of e-textiles for making soft input sensors integrated on the garment, we soon realized that we needed to find a different way of sensing the bodily movements of the wearer, translated from the folds and draping. Even though the flexible and soft sensors were functioning well as stand-alone components for explicit modes of interaction (i.e. actively pushing a textile button), when placed on the garment they did not provide the expected results in regard to more implicit modes of interaction.

To sense the folding and flowing of the fabric in motion, a different way of sensing was needed. During the material explorations we started to introduce metallic studs as a visual and tactile component and in realizing that some of the studs were conductive, we started to explore their potential as a sensing material. This led to us using a combination of metallic studs and copper thread as the central component of the activity sensing. In total, ten separate clusters of studs were wired with conductive thread, six on the chest area and two on the inside area of each arm. Each cluster is connected through a web of conductive thread with a wire connecting the web to the X-OSC microcontroller.

Investigating what types of materials could be used for sensing the movements of the wearer through their effects on the folds and draped fabric, was recognized as a significant feature of the design process. The decision to use metallic studs for both the computational sensing as well as a prominent visual component allowed the integration of the different material layers through a focus on interaction. Studs were seen as a new type of material in this context, merging exposed functionality and aesthetics into one element. Therefore, more broadly, this approach, can be also seen as eschewing common strategies of hiding or covering the materials that allow for computation in interactive wearables, and instead make those materials an active element of a garment's visual identity.

### Sound Design for Implicit Interaction

Initially, a direct intentionality was explored, where simple controls offered predictable results, such as a fabric-based button that played a sound, the same sound, every time it was pressed. However, such directness was not found to increase the engagement in the interaction with Nebula. It was not until we started to explore other ways of approaching intentionality, that the physical design of the garment and the sonic output fused into one coherent entity.

As the designs using studs and folds were articulated and explored through versions of the garment, a similar development was needed in the processing and sonification of the data received by the sensors. The direction that was chosen was based on using the evocative physical properties found. Instead of looking at discreet events with semantic meaning, similarly to the early stages of the design process, the guiding concepts became the clashing clusters of studs and the streams of events such clashes created. Similarly, instead of rewarding explicit intentionality with predictable results, a more ambient and soundscape-like approach was taken, where repeatability gave way to an engaging variety and unpredictability through implicit sensing that was translated to sound.

To realize these ideas the technique granular synthesis was chosen [34]. At its core, granular synthesis creates sound in

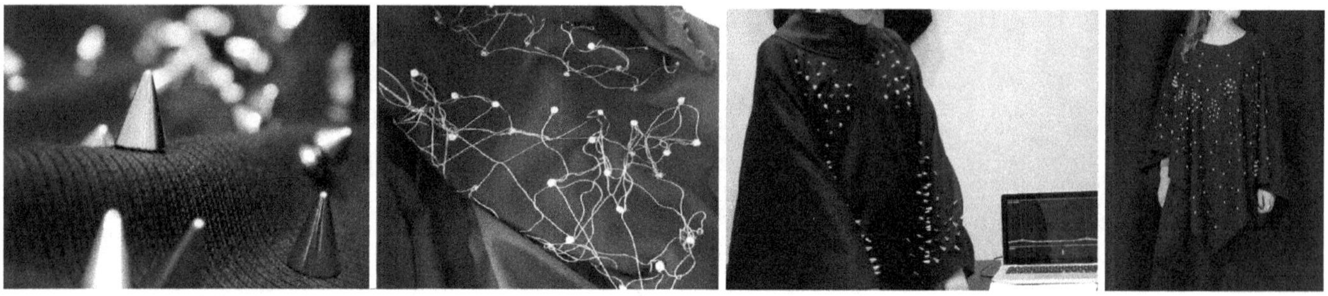

**Figure 3. From left to right: a) A closeup of the metallic studs that cover the garment, b) the webs of conductive thread that run between the outer fabric and the lining, c) the second version of Nebula in use during a demo session, d) the first version of Nebula.**

a bottom-up approach, where very short snippets of sound, often shorter than 0.1 seconds, are combined to create longer sounds. The short snippets are called grains and can be filled with synthesized sounds or short excerpts taken from an existing digital audio file. Often, these grains are not controlled individually, but rather shaped in groups, called clouds or streams. Using this type of audio synthesis exploited a very strong connection with the physical properties of the garment and the possibilities of interaction it finally allowed for. The clusters of studs colliding in places where there were folds or draping on the garment, could easily be thought of as clouds of grains, emanating from the movements of the wearer, that are lingering just as the pendulum-like swings of the folds take a while to settle. This quality of inertia was further exploited by the integration of the flickering activation signals, which were measured in the clusters into slower moving activity measures. Those signals had a variable speed in occasions of building-up and decay, making it possible to tune the connection between movement and sound.

The final material strategy explored was in the direction of letting the major characteristics of the physical design of the garment to serve as a model for the fundamental structure of the audio production. Specifically, the clashing clusters of studs were represented by clashing clusters of audio snippets, which were produced using sample-based granular synthesis. Our observations from exhibiting the garment can be summarized in two points, in regards to the sound design. On a micro scale, the richness and unpredictability in the resulting soundscape increased the engagement in the interaction with Nebula, as earlier, more direct and repeatable modes of sonification had done. On a macro scale, in which a gesture always creates a proportional sound, the responsiveness of the audio made it clear to the wearer that the sound was intrinsically linked to the particular physical experience of wearing the garment.

## DISCUSSION

The three material investigations presented above all point to a shift in how we approached the various materials involved, which allowed us to explore the design space of implicit interaction in relation to the body through the Nebula garment. The first material investigation concerned how the material qualities of the fabric and draping explorations led to the pendulous folds that allowed for rich implicit interaction. The second material investigation described the decision to use metallic studs as both the central sensing component, and a primary visual material. The studs acted as a conduit that also imparted a distinct new materiality to the interaction. The third material investigation focused on how the movements of the draped folds and the clashing clusters of studs resulted in streams of sensed events that informed the sound design.

In the beginning of the design process, the joint work was approached with the understanding of collaboration to be the combination of separately produced material probes, developed in separate contexts by researchers with skill sets that were particular to their domain. Moving from that, the later approach built on the notion of co-creation rather than combination. This allowed the members of the design team to shift their roles of domain experts and instead engage in a completely new and particular domain, or design space that emerged around the forming artefact. This shift can be described as a move towards a crafting approach where, instead of material qualities being treated as rigid, they were allowed to occur [22] throughout the making process. In doing so, the new material combinations that are described in the material investigations were found and explored.

Surfacing the major characteristics of the different materials involved in this design space and actively working with those, was central in order to create a rich interactive experience for the wearer. On the one hand, the physical design of the garment that informed and guided the fundamental structure of the audio production is somewhat perceivable, meaning that it can be felt by the wearer and it contributes to an engaging interaction with the Nebula. And this is because the audio production was built on the concept of clusters of studs, but also on the manifold juxtapositions of the enveloping folds and draping of the garment. On the other hand, the garment itself has several interesting experiential qualities. One thing of note is the way that it is interactive in all its material aspects, that is, it is not only the computational qualities that shape the interaction between the wearer and the garment. The heavy enveloping design with the pendulous counterweights immediately engages the wearer in a new physical experience by extending and interfering with the wearer's body. We embrace this quality and propose that it is by treating the design process as a crafting one, focusing on material investigations, that a close interrelation between material qualities, both computational and physical, can be achieved in a seamless and synergetic way.

Our intention with presenting this design process and its main outcome is not to suggest specific design guidelines that other researchers have to follow. Instead we hope that the three material investigations can offer useful guidance for how to approach the rich, and often complex, material space that unfolds when combining expertise from the domains of interaction design and sound and music computing, focusing on wearables. Reflecting on how they emerged throughout the process, they offered a way of surfacing not only evocative, but also exploitable combinations of materials. And more broadly, material investigations aim to strengthen the connection between disparate material categories, grounded on the interactive qualities of the intended designed artefact. Reflecting on the design process that resulted in the Nebula, we observed that a set of such strong links between material qualities has the potential to result in a new and engaging interactive experience. But at the same time, it can offer a fruitful way of extracting knowledge from a very unique and particular design process, as it is the case in every new design project, and make it legible through articulation, for other researchers and designers. This is because by extracting and isolating the specific qualities that support a particular intention in the design, a broader understanding of both the process and the resulting artefact can be made possible.

The garment was not originally designed for a particular setting or context. However, as is has been exhibited several times, a performance identity has evolved in conversation with the contemporary communities of music and dance. The average exhibition visitor enjoys the experience of wearing the garment, but many performers have also found the garment highly evocative of new artistic ideas, ultimately leading to the garment being used in a performance at the music festival *Ischia Musica* in Ischia, Italy. The qualities that seem to be most appreciated by performers can be summarized as an organic resistance, e.g. the garment allows the wearer to engage with it but not control it, giving the interaction a collaborative and exploratory feel. This could be reframed in the terms of our field as nuanced implicit interaction with feedback subtle enough for professional artistic performance. These are qualities that need further study, but the reactions indicate that wearable implicit interaction has great potential for artistic performance.

Therefore, one direction for future studies that we would like to pursue would be to further develop Nebula for a specific artistic work in collaboration with a performer, for example a dancer. In doing so, we could study and reflect on how the design principles followed in the design process presented here, being focused on a rather exploratory material perspective, can be re-addressed and re-adjusted based on the particular context of use, and consequently its limitations. In terms of future work, it would be also important to explore other types of wearables or even accessories designed similar to the Nebula and expand the understanding of implicit interaction arising through physical material qualities and their transformation into sound.

Through the particular design process that we present in this paper, we offer learnings in regard to the shaping of the intentionality of the wearer's actions, through implicit interaction with the Nebula. Moving from the direct, repeatable, and explicit to the ambient and implicit. More broadly, design processes are as valuable objects of study as designed artefacts. In interdisciplinary and evolving design domains in particular, as is the case with designing interactive wearables, there is a need for a strong corpus of practical investigations of design processes. The design process presented in this paper, but also the main outcome of it, the Nebula interactive garment, contributes to this research space. As previously stated, insights resulting from negotiations, mistakes or disruptions during a design process have as much great potential for knowledge production in the domain of interaction design, as presenting successful results [14]. This puts a further emphasis on the need for careful descriptions of design activities that contain valuable patterns or conceptualizations for future research in this domain to learn from.

## CONCLUSION

This paper has detailed the design work that produced the Nebula interactive garment. Three material investigations were presented that demonstrated how an integrated perspective that melds crafts knowledge and sensual qualities of all ingoing materials allow for functional aesthetics. Through these investigations, we found evocative connections between qualities in computational and non-computational materials, and exploited them to create a garment with strong experiential qualities that were especially appreciated by performing artists. In particular, designing for implicit interaction arising through the material qualities, was perhaps the defining quality in the second version of the garment. The use of material investigations is offered as a possible way to structure design work, but also as a way to extract legible design intentions for other designers and researchers.

## ACKNOWLEDGMENTS

The project *Sound Clothes*, in which Nebula has been developed, was funded by the *Small Visionary Projects* initiative at the KTH Royal Institute of Technology, in Stockholm, Sweden. We would like to thank our colleagues Vincent Lewandowski, Roberto Bresin and Ylva Fernaeus for their contribution to the project and the development of Nebula. Additionally, we are grateful to the people who tried Nebula and gave us feedback, in the different venues and occasions it has been exhibited.

## REFERENCES

[1] David Barnard, Joachim Bondo, Dan Burcaw, David Kaneda, Craig Kemper, Tim Novikoff, Chris Parris, Brad Ellis, Keith Peters, Jürgen Siebert, and others. 2009. Epilogue: Reactive Music and Invisible Interfaces. In *iPhone User Interface Design Projects*. Springer, 235–238.

[2] Thomas Binder and Johan Redström. 2006. Exemplary design research. (2006).

[3] Johannes Birringer and Michèle Danjoux. 2013. The sound of movement wearables: performing ukiyo. *Leonardo* 46, 3 (2013), 232–240.

[4] Bert Bongers. 1998. An interview with Sensorband. *Computer Music Journal* 22, 1 (1998), 13–24.

[5] Leah Buechley, Mike Eisenberg, Jaime Catchen, and Ali Crockett. 2008. The LilyPad Arduino: using computational textiles to investigate engagement, aesthetics, and diversity in computer science education. In *Proceedings of the SIGCHI conference on Human factors in computing systems*. ACM, 423–432.

[6] Daniel Cesarini, Thomas Hermann, and Bodo Ungerechts. 2014. A real-time auditory biofeedback system for sports swimming. In *Proceedings of the 20th International Conference on Auditory Display (ICAD 2014)*.

[7] Jessica Charlesworth. 2007. Wearables as "relationship tools". *Ai & Society* 22, 1 (2007), 63–84.

[8] Nick Collins. 2009. Musical form and algorithmic composition. *Contemporary Music Review* 28, 1 (2009), 103–114.

[9] Ludvig Elblaus, Kjetil Falkenberg Hansen, and Carl Unander-Scharin. 2012. Artistically directed prototyping in development and in practice. *Journal of New Music Research* 41, 4 (2012), 377–387.

[10] Ludvig Elblaus, Vasiliki Tsaknaki, Vincent Lewandowski, and Roberto Bresin. 2015. Nebula: An Interactive Garment Designed for Functional Aesthetics. In *Proceedings of the 33rd Annual ACM Conference Extended Abstracts on Human Factors in Computing Systems (CHI EA '15)*. ACM, New York, NY, USA, 275–278. DOI: http://dx.doi.org/10.1145/2702613.2725454

[11] Martin Eriksson and Roberto Bresin. 2010. Improving running mechanics by use of interactive sonification. *Proceedings of ISon* (2010), 95–98.

[12] Alexander Fiannaca, Ilias Apostolopoulous, and Eelke Folmer. 2014. Headlock: a wearable navigation aid that helps blind cane users traverse large open spaces. In *Proceedings of the 16th international ACM SIGACCESS conference on Computers & accessibility*. ACM, 19–26.

[13] Minoru Fujimoto, Naotaka Fujita, Yoshinari Takegawa, Tsutomu Terada, and Masahiko Tsukamoto. 2008. Musical B-boying: A Wearable Musical Instrument by Dancing. In *International Conference on Entertainment Computing*. Springer, 155–160.

[14] William Gaver, John Bowers, Tobie Kerridge, Andy Boucher, and Nadine Jarvis. 2009. Anatomy of a Failure: How We Knew when Our Design Went Wrong, and What We Learned from It. In *Proceedings of the SIGCHI Conference on Human Factors in Computing Systems (CHI '09)*. ACM, New York, NY, USA, 2213–2222. DOI:http://dx.doi.org/10.1145/1518701.1519040

[15] Connie Golsteijn, Elise Van Den Hoven, David Frohlich, and Abigail Sellen. 2014. Hybrid crafting: towards an integrated practice of crafting with physical and digital components. *Personal and ubiquitous computing* 18, 3 (2014), 593–611.

[16] Rafael E Gomez, Tricia Flanagan, and Rebekah M Davis. 2015. Designing experiences with wearables: A case study exploring the blurring boundaries of art, design, technology, culture and distance. In *Proceedings of the 6th IASDR (The International Association of Societies of Design Research Congress)*. IASDR (The International Association of Societies of Design Research), 805–820.

[17] Yu-I Ha and Yi-Kyung Kim. 2014. The design process of wearable computers for extending the performer?s expression. In *International Conference on Human-Computer Interaction*. Springer, 421–426.

[18] Yoonchang Han, Jinsoo Na, and Kyogu Lee. 2012. FutureGrab: A wearable synthesizer using vowel formants. *NIME'12* (2012).

[19] Michaela Honauer and Eva Hornecker. 2015. Challenges for creating and staging interactive costumes for the theatre stage. In *Proceedings of the 2015 ACM SIGCHI Conference on Creativity and Cognition*. ACM, 13–22.

[20] Brian Horsak, Michael Iber, Karin Bauer, Anita Kiselka, Anna-Maria Gorgas, Ronald Dlapka, and Jakob Doppler. 2015. A wireless instrumented insole device for real-time sonification of gait. Georgia Institute of Technology.

[21] Aurie Hsu and Steven Kemper. 2015. Kinesonic approaches to mapping movement and music with the remote electroacoustic kinesthetic sensing (RAKS) system. In *Proceedings of the 2nd International Workshop on Movement and Computing*. ACM, 45–47.

[22] Tim Ingold. 2010. The textility of making. *Cambridge Journal of Economics* 34, 1 (2010), 91–102. DOI: http://dx.doi.org/10.1093/cje/bep042

[23] X–io Technologies. 2018. X–OSC. (2018). http://x-io.co.uk/x-osc/

[24] Alexandra Ju. 2016. Functionality in Wearable Tech: Device, As Jewelry, As Body Mediator. In *Proceedings of the TEI '16: Tenth International Conference on Tangible, Embedded, and Embodied Interaction (TEI '16)*. ACM, New York, NY, USA, 641–646. DOI: http://dx.doi.org/10.1145/2839462.2856348

[25] Ajay Kapur, Eric L Yang, Adam R Tindale, and Peter F Driessen. 2005. Wearable sensors for real-time musical signal processing. In *Communications, Computers and signal Processing, 2005. PACRIM. 2005 IEEE Pacific Rim Conference on*. IEEE, 424–427.

[26] Volker Krefeld and Michel Waisvisz. 1990. The hand in the web: An interview with Michel Waisvisz. *Computer music journal* 14, 2 (1990), 28–33.

[27] Kari Kuutti and Liam J Bannon. 2014. The turn to practice in HCI: towards a research agenda. In *Proceedings of the 32nd annual ACM conference on Human factors in computing systems*. ACM, 3543–3552.

[28] Lizzy. 2018. (2018). http://lizzy.berlin

[29] Teresa Marrin and Rosalind W Picard. 1998. The" Conductor's Jacket": A Device for Recording Expressive Musical Gestures.. In *ICMC*.

[30] Stefano Papetti, Marco Civolani, and Federico Fontana. 2011. Rhythm'n'Shoes: a Wearable Foot Tapping Interface with Audio-Tactile Feedback.. In *NIME*. 473–476.

[31] Hannah Perner-Wilson, Leah Buechley, and Mika Satomi. 2011. Handcrafting textile interfaces from a kit-of-no-parts. In *Proceedings of the fifth international conference on Tangible, embedded, and embodied interaction*. ACM, 61–68.

[32] Ernest Rehmatulla Post, Maggie Orth, Peter R Russo, and Neil Gershenfeld. 2000. E-broidery: Design and fabrication of textile-based computing. *IBM Systems journal* 39, 3.4 (2000), 840–860.

[33] Halley Profita, Nicholas Farrow, and Nikolaus Correll. 2015. Flutter: An exploration of an assistive garment using distributed sensing, computation and actuation. In *Proceedings of the Ninth International Conference on Tangible, Embedded, and Embodied Interaction*. ACM, 359–362.

[34] Curtis Roads. 1988. Introduction to granular synthesis. *Computer Music Journal* 12, 2 (1988), 11–13.

[35] Thecla Schiphorst, Wynnie Wing Yi Chung, and Emily Ip. 2013. Wo. Defy: wearable interaction design inspired by a Chinese 19 th century suffragette movement. In *Proceedings of the 7th International Conference on Tangible, Embedded and Embodied Interaction*. ACM, 319–322.

[36] Sabine Seymour. 2008. *Fashionable technology: The intersection of design, fashion, science, and technology*. Springer Publishing Company, Incorporated.

[37] SparkFun. 2018. EeonTex. (2018). https://www.sparkfun.com/products/14110

[38] Thad Starner, Joshua Weaver, and Alex Pentland. 1998. Real-time american sign language recognition using desk and wearable computer based video. *IEEE Transactions on Pattern Analysis and Machine Intelligence* 20, 12 (1998), 1371–1375.

[39] Bob L Sturm. 2005. Pulse of an ocean: sonification of ocean buoy data. *Leonardo* 38, 2 (2005), 143–149.

[40] SuperCollider. 2018. (2018). https://supercollider.github.io/

[41] Oscar Tomico, Mascha van Zijverden, Tom Fejér, Yiyu Chen, Eef Lubbers, Meerthe Heuvelings, Sonia Aïssaoui, and Verena Schepperheyn. 2013. Crafting wearables: interaction design meets fashion design. In *CHI'13 Extended Abstracts on Human Factors in Computing Systems*. ACM, 2875–2876.

[42] Wouter Walmink, Danielle Wilde, and Florian'Floyd' Mueller. 2014. Displaying heart rate data on a bicycle helmet to support social exertion experiences. In *Proceedings of the 8th International Conference on Tangible, Embedded and Embodied Interaction*. ACM, 97–104.

[43] Danielle Wilde. 2012. hipDisk: experiencing the value of ungainly, embodied, performative, fun. In *CHI'12 Extended Abstracts on Human Factors in Computing Systems*. ACM, 979–982.

[44] Danielle Wilde and Sophie Birkmayer. 2004. Dress and Ange: coercing the address of highly personal body-centric issues. *Personal and Ubiquitous Computing* 8, 3-4 (2004), 264–273.

[45] Michele A. Williams, Asta Roseway, Chris O'Dowd, Mary Czerwinski, and Meredith Ringel Morris. 2015. SWARM: An Actuated Wearable for Mediating Affect. In *Proceedings of the Ninth International Conference on Tangible, Embedded, and Embodied Interaction (TEI '15)*. ACM, New York, NY, USA, 293–300. DOI: http://dx.doi.org/10.1145/2677199.2680565

[46] Koji Yatani and Khai N Truong. 2012. BodyScope: a wearable acoustic sensor for activity recognition. In *Proceedings of the 2012 ACM Conference on Ubiquitous Computing*. ACM, 341–350.

[47] Clint Zeagler, Maribeth Gandy, Scott M Gilliland, Delton Moore, Rocco Centrella, and Brandon Montgomery. 2017. In Harmony: Making a Wearable Musical Instrument as a Case Study of using Boundary Objects in an Interdisciplinary Collaborative Design Process.. In *Conference on Designing Interactive Systems*. 369–378.

# WindyWall: Exploring Creative Wind Simulations

David Tolley[1] Thi Ngoc Tram Nguyen[1] Anthony Tang[2]
Nimesha Ranasinghe[1,3] Kensaku Kawauchi[4] Ching-Chiuan Yen[1,5]
[1]Keio-NUS CUTE Centre
[4]Smart Systems Institute
[5]Division of Industrial Design
National University of Singapore
[2]Department of Computer Science
University of Calgary
[3]School of Computing and
Information Science
University of Maine

## ABSTRACT

Wind simulations are typically one-off implementations for specific applications. We introduce WindyWall, a platform for creative design and exploration of wind simulations. WindyWall is a three-panel 90-fan array that encapsulates users with 270° of wind coverage. We describe the design and implementation of the array panels, discussing how the panels can be re-arranged, where various wind simulations can be realized as simple effects. To understand how people perceive "wind" generated from WindyWall, we conducted a pilot study of wind magnitude perception using different wind activation patterns from WindyWall. Our findings suggest that: horizontal wind activations are perceived more readily than vertical ones, and that people's perceptions of wind are highly variable—most individuals will rate airflow differently in subsequent exposures. Based on our findings, we discuss the importance of developing a method for characterizing wind simulations, and provide design directions for others using fan arrays to simulate wind.

### Author Keywords

Multimodal Interaction; Novel Actuators / Displays; Tactile / Haptic Interaction

### CSS Concepts

• Human-centered computing~Haptic devices

## INTRODUCTION

Virtual Reality (VR), simulations have long focused on sight and sound as primary modalities for conveying immersion, or presence in a remote environment [38]. Recent work has begun to explore other sensory modalities, including haptics, temperature, olfactory, and taste (e.g. [32]). These modalities have been demonstrated to increase users' sense of presence in virtual spaces, with the impact of multiple combined modalities having a strong gestalt effect on immersion beyond each modality on its own. The present work lays down groundwork for VR simulations intended for relaxation, learning and therapy [10, 14, 30, 7], since effecting a strong sense of presence is crucial to the effectiveness of these simulations.



*TEI '19*, March 17–20, 2019, Tempe, AZ, USA

ACM 978-1-4503-6196-5/19/03…$15.00
https://doi.org/10.1145/3294109.3295624

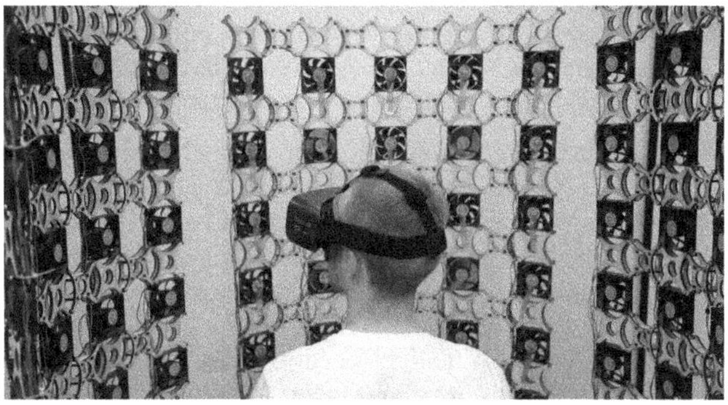

**Figure 1. WindyWall is a 3-panel array for simulating wind.**

Our focus is on designing wind simulations, where we are generating airflow on and across skin, and so we are interested in flexible ways to explore airflow simulations and understanding how people perceive these simulations. For instance, we are interested in being able to simulate scenarios such as a small puff of air, a gentle rolling breeze, a sweeping wind and an object rushing past the user. While knowing how to design wind simulations is useful for such VR experiences, this knowledge will also prove useful for a number of other applications, including ambient awareness [36, 13, 37], notifications [20, 17, 24, 27], and even subtle cuing of attention (e.g. [23]).

The problem is that we do not have a reproducible method for simulating wind, or a sufficiently nuanced understanding of the psychophysical experience of airflow for designing effective simulations. Wind as a modality is still largely understudied by the research community: most work has been limited to proof-of-concept systems for specific wind simulations and installations [1, 5, 8, 12, 18, 19, 21, 24, 25, 27, 35, 32], and as wind displays for feedback [17, 20, 29]. While these are fascinating, it is difficult for others to build on and creatively explore these ideas without the specific hardware in hand. Further, little work has explored how people experience airflow: for instance, how people experience the magnitude of airflow, whether the way airflow is directed at them affects this, or how people determine the source direction of airflow (and how accurate they are). Addressing these questions will help us in designing effective wind simulations that produce the sensation that designers are trying to achieve.

We take a three-pronged approach to address these problems: first, we introduce WindyWall, a general platform for exploring creative wind simulations; second, we develop an initial approach for characterizing specific elements of a wind simulation, giving others a way to parameterize and compare different wind simulations, and finally, we design and conduct a pilot experiment to understand how people perceive airflow as a function of how we manipulate parameters of WindyWall. WindyWall is a 90-fan array divided between three separate panels, where panels can be flexibly re-arranged, and individual fans can be actuated independently depending on the demands of a particular simulation. For instance, we can simulate a point-source gust of wind, or a column of wind, or modulate fan actuation timing to simulate more dynamic wind patterns.

Our pilot study informs future work with wind simulations by assessing users' perception of airflow magnitude. Our findings show that users are more sensitive to horizontal activation patterns of simulated wind (compared to vertical activation patterns), but that there are wide variations in how people perceive magnitude in airflow. These findings suggest that wind simulations need to be carefully designed and tested, and that our naïve expectations of how airflow is experienced may not be borne out in reality.

In this paper, we make the following contributions: first, we contribute the design of WindyWall, a fan array testbed to realize wind simulations; second, we outline requirements for characterizing wind simulations, and finally, through a pilot study, we provide new information to designers of wind simulations regarding how people perceive airflow as a function of different wind display parameters.

## RELATED WORK

### Simulating Wind for VR and Other Applications

Many researchers have used airflow as a modality to enhance the feeling of presence in virtual environments; however, the field has mainly produced a series of one-off system designs that are difficult to reproduce, each with its own idiosyncrasies. Some wind displays are embedded in environments [25, 36, 8], while others are embedded in everyday contexts, such as mounted to an existing display monitor [27, 24], or head-mounted [5, 17]. Collectively, these systems do not clearly build from one another, either in terms of design lessons, or technical approach; rather, each seems like a standalone, proof-of-concept design. While a comprehensive review is beyond the scope of this work, we outline exemplars of each of these approaches.

**Full Body Displays**. Some systems take a person-scale or room-scale approach to designing the airflow display. Moon & Kim [25] designed a 1m×1m×2m frame where 20 fans were affixed at three different heights. The authors found that fans blowing at the user's torso and head were most appropriate, whereas fans blowing at users' legs felt as though wind was blowing upward. In a study where participants viewed videos playing externally to the frame, the authors found that participants felt higher levels of immersion and presence in the VR simulation when the wind display was active. At an even larger scale, Verlinden et al. [36] report on a room-scale wind simulation, where fans are affixed to a frame hanging above a CAVE-like environment. The entire room was used for simulating sailing, where wind is an important decision-making modality for sailors. Participants in a study reported feeling more immersed in the simulation with the wind display. Such context-specific approaches have been demonstrated to improve performance. For instance, Deligiannidis & Jacob [8] show that wind and tactile feedback for a scooter simulation improve the speed through which participants complete a virtual obstacle course.

**Augmenting the Environment**. Some research augments conventional environments with fans to explore the design space of wind displays. For instance, Minakuchi & Nakamura [24] study mounting fans around a conventional computer monitor, and on the back of an office chair. Similarly, Mowafi et al. [27] assembled an array of six fans and nozzles along the top of a monitor to explore the extent to which people could differentiate between different patterns of activation. These kinds of approaches are more tractable explorations of wind displays, though not as common as head-mounted approaches.

**Head-Mounted Displays**. Head-mounted airflow displays align with the increasingly common approach to use head-mounted VR goggles. Ambiotherm, for instance, uses a pair of articulated fans mounted below the goggles to simulate wind [32]. In a study of the impact of multimodal stimulation (including temperature, sound, etc.), the authors demonstrated that using the fan to stimulate wind increased feelings of immersion. Other researchers use multiple actuators for more spatially localized airflow simulation. Cardin et al. [5] use multiple fans mounted on a specialized head-mounted frame, where eight different fans could be actuated at different times to simulate wind from different directions. Kojima et al. [17] take a similar, helmet-based approach, where the airflow is generated by using audio speakers to push air through small tubes at users' ears.

### Understanding Perception of Airflow to Design Effective Wind Displays

To effectively design with wind as a modality, we need to consider not only the technical aspects of building these airflow displays, but also gain a clear understanding of how airflow is perceived by people. Unfortunately, our current understanding of this is a patchwork of experimental results from one-off systems.

**Magnitude Estimation**. Agdas et al. [1] assessed peoples' ability to discern wind speed with a large turbine-style fan in a trailer, where airflow was simulated at rates of 10-70 mph. While the work was conducted in the context of public policy (i.e. are people effective in assessing the wind speed, and the risk of corporeal or property damage), the results are informative for design. Of particular interest, the authors observed a Weber-Fechner effect, where people's assessment of wind speed are non-linear to increases in actual wind speed. It would be interesting to understand how this relationship plays out at more appropriate wind speeds reasonable for VR simulations.

**Detection Thresholds**. Lee & Lee [20] report on a series of experiments to understand detection thresholds for airflow positioned and aimed at different parts of one's body. For instance, at what intensity does the airflow need to be detected (i.e. noticed) by a participant when the airflow is directed at different body parts (e.g. cheek, wrist, ankle, foot, etc.). Beyond intensity, the authors also explored duration threshold (i.e. how long does the user need to be exposed to airflow to detect airflow), and the distance threshold (i.e. how close does the device need to be for detection).

**Directionality**. Nakano et al. [29] present a study exploring how well people can differentiate between different fans, in angular terms, around their torso. Their study relied on a seven-fan array where fans were arranged 20 degrees apart from one another in a semi-circle with a radius of 80cm. This fan array was arranged around a participant's head (where the participant's head was fixed to a mount). The authors used a just-noticeable difference (JND) study design, where participants indicated whether two fans were the same or different fans. The authors report two JND values of 0° and 30°, depending on whether the airflow came from head-on, or the side. However, the authors also report on a small misalignment of one of the fans, which could have caused wide variation in their results. Notably, participants used different strategies to determine the source of the airflow; while some relied on sensations on their noses, others relied on sensations on their cheeks.

**Synthesis**. We have already seen a wide range of airflow displays designed for different scales; however, we do not yet have a good way of characterizing and parameterizing the wind displays (e.g. what are their characteristics of each simulation), nor do we yet have a coherent articulation of the psychophysical experience of airflow, particularly as it relates to design parameters that we can control. We do not know, for instance, how people perceive the magnitude of airflow when the contact surface area is varied. To address these issues and shortcomings, we designed WindyWall, a wind array that allows us to control various factors and understand how airflow is perceived by users.

## WINDYWALL PLATFORM

As illustrated in Figures 1 and 2, WindyWall is a hardware and software platform comprising of three independent panels of fans. Each panel comprises of 30 individual fans arranged in a 5×6 array (width × height), where each fan can be individually actuated. Each panel can be individually re-arranged or placed around a user in a 270° arrangement.

### Design Goals

We are motivated by an increasing interest in developing immersive VR simulations that incorporate wind. As such, we were initially interested in designing a platform that could simulate a range of wind scenarios, including a small puff of air, a gentle rolling breeze, a sweeping wind (e.g. a pedestal fan) or an object rushing past. Beyond this, our overriding goal in constructing the WindyWall platform was to design a platform to enable designers to creatively explore different possibilities within wind simulation. A reconfigurable platform would allow the designer to explore different types of setups, while the software interface would allow for semi high-level programming of the hardware platform.

Based on these ideas and our exploration of prior work, we developed four design goals for the WindyWall platform:

**DG1**: The platform needs to be designed for a single-person simulation for wind.

**DG2**: The platform must enable individually actuated sources of airflow, where each can be independently set to a specific power level.

**DG3**: The platform must be physically reconfigurable to allow for creative explorations of wind simulation.

**DG4**: Finally, the software platform ought to provide an easy mechanism to control groups of individually activated fans, where effects can be designed spatially and temporally.

### Design and Implementation

Our primary interest in this iteration is the design of a single-person simulation platform (DG1). While larger setups exist for different kinds of simulations (e.g. for groups, or for individuals), we were interested in designing for setups where an individual is immersed in a VR simulation, facilitated primarily through head-mounted stereo displays, rather than wall-projected CAVE systems. Such a setup is more portable, making it more suitable for traveling demonstrations as necessary. Furthermore, the reduced physical footprint would make it easier to replicate in multiple sites when designing multi-user experiences.

The central design tension we needed to resolve was how reconfigurable the platform ought to be (DG2, DG3, DG4) with regard to the ease of managing and designing a simulation. For instance, a fully-reconfigurable setup could involve individually positioned fans, each on a flexible arm clamp, but consistently recreating this setup would be time-consuming and onerous. In our process, we realized that if we were simply designing the platform to be experienced by a single individual at a time, we only needed to focus on the airflow experiences of the individual in that context—thus, it was only necessary to focus on fans whose airflow would touch the individual directly. To resolve the design tension, we settled on a partially reconfigurable set of panels (DG3), where each panel would contain a standard set of fans. These fans would all be pointed toward the user of the system, but individually not be reconfigurable within the panel itself. On the other hand, the software platform would enable the designer to access and control each of the individual fans (DG2), while a thin software layer could programmatically give the designer access to rows, columns, or arbitrarily assigned sets of fans as a group (DG4).

The final design has three panels providing 270° of coverage around a single user. Since the panels are easily reproducible and reconfigurable, they also allow other kinds of arrangements. Some possibilities include: (a) fully

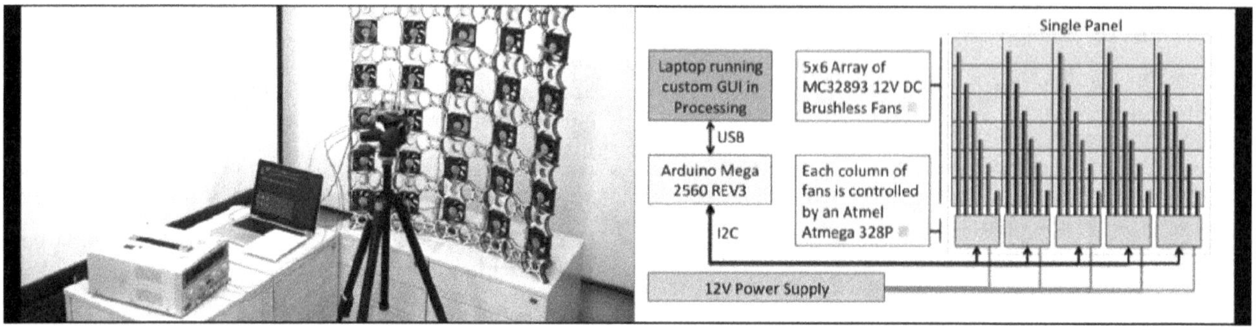


**Figure 2. The testing configuration for a single WindyWall panel (left). The schematic of the WindyWall (right).**

surrounding a user with panels; (b) a "hallway" of panels that allow a user to move through the space; (c) a "room" of panels, and (d) additional panels suspended from the ceiling to provide a "top down" sense of airflow as required.

Each panel comprises of 30 fans connected horizontally and vertically by wooden joints. Joints are 5mm thick pieces of laser-cut 5-ply plywood, connected to the corners of each fan. Angled at ~18° each, the horizontal joints connect each column of fans in an arc shape to form a curved wall, which covers an overall angle of 90°. Within the array, wooden joints create a horizontal spacing of 9.5cm and a vertical spacing of 8.5cm between each fan. When connected in this manner, each panel has a total height of 104.5cm and a curved width of 80cm. Each of the 90 fans is an MC32893 12V DC brushless fan, manufactured by Multicomp [28]. Individually, these fans are 80mm x 80mm x 25mm in size, have a rated power consumption of 1.7W and a rated airflow of 41CFM. Each column of 6 fans is connected to an Atmel ATmega328P [3] microprocessor and, in turn, each of these chips are connected to an Arduino Mega 2560 REV3 microcontroller [4], which acts as a "master" chip. Utilizing I2C protocol, both singular and multiple fans can be controlled through a custom GUI that has been created in Processing [31]. When a user wants to actuate specific fans, the Arduino Mega sends commands to the appropriate ATmega328P chips that are linked to the address of those target fans. Once each ATmega328P receives a command it will analyze it and execute any changes to fan-rotation speeds that are specified by the command.

### Designed Wind Effects

WindyWall is over-engineered to support our interest in designing wind effects. The platform was designed to give designers a wide range of capabilities for flexibly and creatively exploring the design of wind simulations. We expect, for instance, that the granularity of the individual fans to be far higher than what can be discerned by most human users; thus, a practical system for deployment might make use of far fewer actual fans. Furthermore, other kinds of wind simulations (i.e. for more than one person) would need different kinds of implementations. Nevertheless, to illustrate our approach, we designed several wind effects that could be conceived of as small scenario-based wind simulations:

- **Puff of Air**: A small number of closely located fans are simultaneously actuated at high fan speed for a short period of time. This can be used to simulate a short human breathe near a user's ear or an abrupt rush of air as a door is slammed shut near the user.
- **Rolling Breeze**: The fan speed of multiple fans is constantly modulated within a set range over time. This can be used to simulate continuous fluctuations of wind speed that are commonly experienced in outdoor environments. Here, this technique can be combined with broader or narrower configurations of fans to provide more or less ambient wind coverage as required (e.g. when simulating a user transitioning between two environments, such as walking in and out of a house).
- **Sweeping Wind Movement**: Adjacent fans are continuously actuated one after another to create a wind simulation that can sweep between any two points covered by the fans. This technique can be used to simulate the movement and orientation of the user or surrounding objects within a virtual environment. For example, a virtual rotating desk fan may be simulated by moderately-paced wind sweeps oscillating in the transverse plane. Alternatively, a sweeping motion may also be used to imply a user's movement past a virtual wind source (e.g. a user walking past an air vent).
- **Objects Rushing Past the User**: By combing the Sweeping Wind Movement and Puff of Air techniques, it is also possible to create more fast-paced sweeping wind simulations. These may be applied to scenarios where objects rush past a user in close proximity (e.g. a user dodging virtual projectiles that are being thrown at them).

## TOWARDS CHARACTERIZING A WIND SIMULATION

To compare various implementations of a wind simulations (e.g. each of our wind effects), we need a standard way of

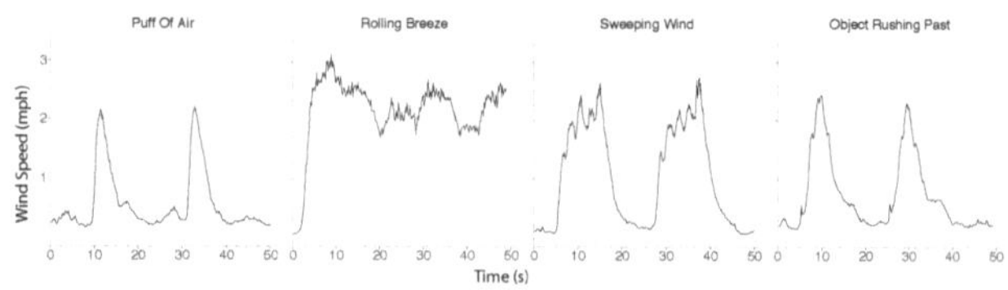


**Figure 3. Our characterization technique captures airflow magnitude over time, and visually allows us to distinguish between different airflow simulations. Left to right: Puff of Air, Rolling Breeze, Sweeping Wind and Object Rushing Past.**

characterizing how the airflow in the simulation is generated. Such a standardized method should allow researchers to describe and compare between setups and wind simulations (e.g. configurations, or effects) in an objective way. The method should emulate the experience of wind from the perspective of a human participant, measuring airflow, accounting for the ramp-up time of the airflow generator (e.g. fan, or other device), the sustained airflow rate (e.g. L/s), a way of describing the directionality of airflow (allowing for multiple directions of airflow), and how this airflow changes in relation to time (e.g. for an effect such as a gust of wind).

We developed a characterization strategy that satisfies the first two of these requirements.

**Measurement Device**: We use a thermal anemometer as our measurement device. The thermal anemometer (Rev P Wind Sensor [2]) relies on a hot-wire wind sensing mechanism, giving us appropriate resolution and consistency for the lower wind speeds generated by WindyWall (0-3 mph). We constructed a redundant measurement device using a pair of sensors, where each sensor samples wind speeds at 10Hz. In our setup (Figure 2, left), this device was affixed atop a tripod, and positioned to approximate the location of a seated user's nose (~60cm from the center fans).

**Collecting Data**: We collect wind speed data (mph) in an enclosed, temperature-controlled room (22°C) with minimal air circulation. In a typical situation, we will run the simulation multiple times (e.g. three times), collapsing the data across these multiple runs to get a more representative result, giving a clearer picture of the overall nature of a simulation apart from individual one-off sensor variations from a given measurement session.

**Visualizing Data**: Plotting the collapsed data as a time series plot shows the temporal windspeed variations, illustrating how each of the simulations are characteristically different.

To illustrate our approach, Figure 3 visualizes the characterization charts for the four wind effects described in the previous section. These show that Puff of Air is much briefer than Object Rushing Past, both of which are much shorter than Sweeping Wind and Rolling Breeze. Further, the peaks have a higher kurtosis than with the Rolling Breeze, which means the peak blowing-speed is briefer in Puff of Air than in Rolling Breeze. Finally, Sweeping Wind takes longer to reach its peak blowing-speed compared to Puff of Air. Thus, this simple visualization shows us ramp-up speeds, holds, sustained airflow rates, pauses, and ramp-downs in each airflow simulation. Even here, this technique provides designers a simple way to compare between different creative simulations with WindyWall.

While this strategy provides the first steps toward a wind characterization method, there is still considerable room for improvement. For instance, our technique does not yet account for airflow directionality, nor provide a broader "surface" for capturing airflow. Puff-of-air and object-rushing-past, for instance, look similar, even though an object rushing past sweeps by alongside one's body. This distinction is not captured in the visualization above, even though they are subjectively fairly different experiences. Currently, the measurement device only measures airflow from a single point, but we experience airflow along our entire bodies, thus a device that provides a larger surface area for air to impact it would be useful. Critically, future approaches need to emulate the experience of a human participant, which our strategy attempts to capture. This characterization technique should open the door to parameterizing wind simulations, allowing us to compare between different simulation platforms and effects.

## PILOT STUDY OF AIRFLOW MAGNITUDE PERCEPTION

Beyond objective characterizations of WindyWall airflow simulations, we are also interested in the subjective experience of airflow. To date, there is still very little work in this space, and since we are ultimately interested in designing wind simulations as part of immersive multisensory experiences, there were several questions that we wanted to address: for instance, is there a clear relationship between actual objective airflow rate and perceived airflow magnitude by users? Is this affected by how the airflow is directed at the user? To what extent, given repeated exposures, are individuals consistent in their assessments of the same airflow simulation? Across a group of users, are individuals consistent in their assessments of the same airflows? Answers to these basic questions are critical to designing simulations that can be dependably experienced as intended by the simulation's designer.

To address these questions, we designed a study where users' perceptions of airflow magnitude are compared to objective measures across several simple wind simulations. Our experiment asked participants to provide ratings of airflow— "How much wind do you feel?" (i.e. perceived magnitude of airflow) on a self-reported scale. We varied two parameters with WindyWall across airflow simulations:

- **Fan Rotation Speed**: High and Low (40% and 80% power, respectively, determined by early pilot studies for reliable and distinguishable fan speeds).
- **Size and Shape of Airflow Source**: Changing the number of fans, and the shape of the airflow simulation.

While studies have been conducted to explore this phenomenon given very high wind speeds (e.g. 10mph-60mph) [1], our focus was centered on investigating more tractable levels of airflow generation for the purpose of multisensory immersion (i.e. wind speeds of 0 – 3mph). For us, we wanted to compare wind blown at head level to match approaches from prior work (e.g. [29, 32, 24, 27]). Beyond this, we were also interested in exploring whether different spatial arrangements of active fans affected the perceived magnitude of the airflow to extend the arrangements explored from prior work (e.g. [25, 36]).

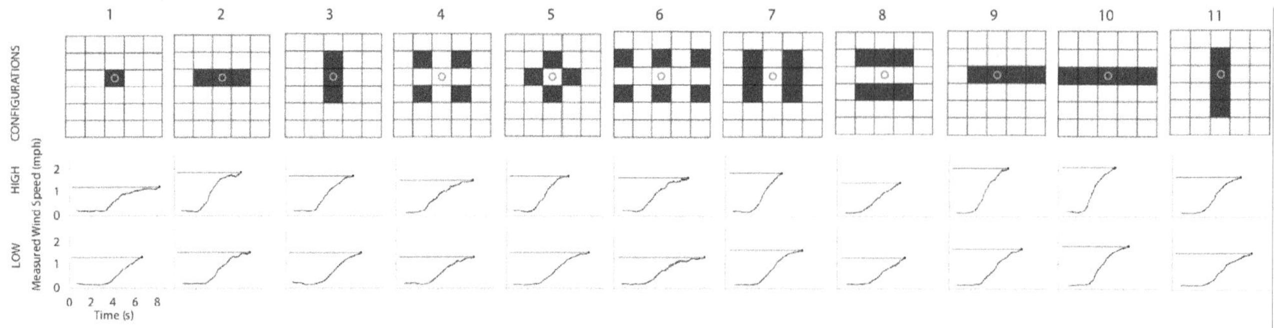


**Figure 4. Tested fan configurations at low and high power. The first row illustrates configuration on a single panel (dark = fan on; white = fan off; circle = central fan). Each chart illustrates the ramp up function for the fan array to reach the sustained wind speed (red line).**

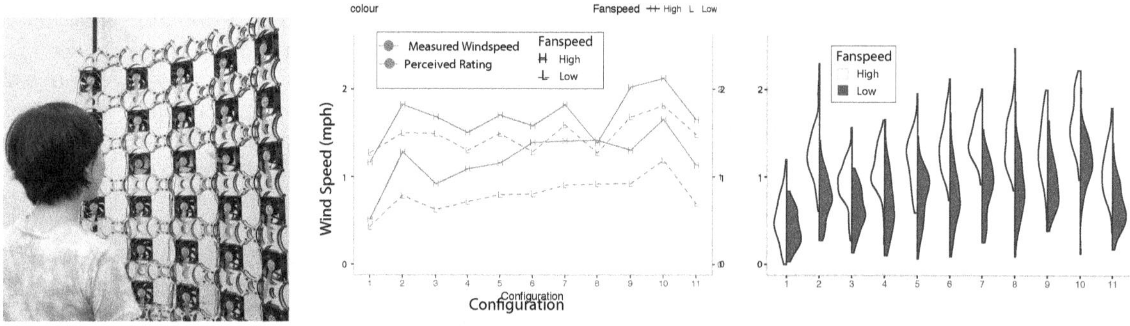


**Figure 5. The magnitude estimation experimental setup (left). Average perceived magnitude plotted against measured wind speed for each configuration and fan speed (center). Distribution of ratings for each configuration and fan speed (right).**

**Objective Data Collection.** To simplify the execution of our study, we used a single WindyWall panel, and very simple simulations (i.e. on/off). We explored eleven different fan configurations (illustrated in Figure 4), where the central fan was aimed directly at the sensor (or participant's head). Early pilots determined that the top and bottom two rows of fans could not be reliably felt if a participant was sitting. Thus, the fan configurations vary the number of fans (i.e. one fan to six fans), and also in different variations (i.e. horizontal, vertical, narrow, wide).

We collected wind speed data (mph) for the 11 fan configurations three times, each running at two different power levels (40% and 80%) that represented low and high fan speeds. This objective data is visualized in Figure 4.

**Pilot Study Design and Procedure.** Using a repeated-measures design, participants were asked to rate the same 11 configurations × 2 speeds a total of three times over the course of two weeks. The presentation order of the 22 simulations was randomized for each participant, with each configuration exposure time lasting for 20 seconds.

We recruited 16 participants (7 women) from our university, aged 19–33 (M=25, SD=3.39). Participants wore short-sleeve T-shirts to ensure consistent skin exposure. If participants normally wore glasses, they were asked to remove them for this study. As shown in Figure 5 (left), participants were seated facing the WindyWall panel at a distance of ~60cm. The height of the chair was adjusted so that the participant's nose was at the same height as the center fan of the third row. Participant were asked to close their eyes, and listened to white noise to cover fan noises.

Each round of exposure comprised of three events: (1) *Fans Activated*: Fans are actuated for the airflow simulation in this round, and given time to stabilize (5 seconds); (2) *Participant Provides Rating*: A bell sound plays, and participants provide a verbal rating of the perceived wind magnitude (10 seconds); (3) *Fans Deactivated*: Fans are allowed to come to rest (5 seconds). When providing ratings, participants were asked to rate the magnitude of the wind using the first wind simulation as a basis, subsequently providing ratings as ratios compared to their first exposure. In keeping with the *magnitude estimation procedure* outlined by [15], we did not limit the range that the participants could report, instead allowing participants to define their own ranges and to assign any number of their choice. To limit fatigue, we designed the study so that each rating exercise lasted no more than 15 minutes.

**Analysis.** As participants were free to give their ratings on any scale, we used a normalization technique to bring ratings into a consistent scale across the entire sample. Consistent with the process outlined in [15], raw ratings were normalized in two steps: first, we divided all ratings by their first one to give a consistent unit rating; second, we normalized all ratings such that an individual's mean ratings for 22 configurations are equal to 1.

### Pilot Study Results

We present preliminary findings from our pilot study, focusing on: the relationship between actual and perceived airflow intensity, the consistency of an individual's ratings and the consistency of ratings between individuals.

**Actual vs. Perceived Airflow Magnitude**. Figure 5 (center) shows a moderately positive correlation between participants' perceived airflow magnitude and objective measurements for each simulation (Pearson correlation coefficient=0.78). This suggests participants were able to perceive increases in airflow to some extent: wind magnitude ratings for airflows produced by high fan speeds were higher than those at the low fan speed. Participants' ratings of perceived airflow magnitude generally seemed to increase when exposed to a greater number of fans. As shown in Figure 5 (center), the simulations with the largest magnitude ratings all used either 5 or 6 fans.

Simulations with fans arranged on the transverse plane (horizontal around one's face, from one cheek to the other) were perceived to have a higher magnitude than those arranged in the sagittal plane (vertical from the top of the forehead to the chin). For instance, although configurations 2 and 3 both consisted of three fans, paired samples t-tests showed that configuration 2 (three horizontal fans) had significantly higher perceived ratings than configuration 3 (three vertical fans) at both high and low fan speeds, respectively: 2-high (M=1.28, SD=0.363) vs. 3-high (M=0.92, SD=0.252), $p < 0.005$; and 2-low (M=0.78, SD=0.254) vs. 3-low (M=0.62, SD=0.231), $p < 0.005$. Similarly, configurations 9 and 11 both consisted of four fans, and paired samples t-tests showed that configuration 9 (four horizontal fans) had significantly higher perceived ratings than configuration 11 (four vertical fans) at both high and low fan speeds, respectively: 9-high (M=1.298, SD=0.358) vs. 11-high (M=1.13, SD=0.349), $p = 0.014$; and 9-low (M=0.92, SD=0.309) vs. 11-low (M=0.69, SD=0.260), $p < 0.0005$.

**Reliability of an Individual's Ratings**. Individuals' ratings were either poorly or moderately reliable across their three sessions. Using Intraclass Correlation Coefficient (ICC), we measured each participant's reliability across multiple exposures for each configuration—i.e. intra-rater reliability [16]. Our analysis used 22 configurations, three measures (k=3), a two-way mixed model, absolute-agreement and single measurement as parameters. Across participants, ICC ranged from 0.37 to 0.76 (M=0.60, SD=0.097). Of our 16 participants, 3 participants' reliability would be considered poor (ICC < 0.50), 12 were considered moderate (0.50 < ICC < 0.75), while only one was considered good (0.75 < ICC < 0.90).

**Consistency Across Individuals' Ratings**. We found that participants did not agree on the perceived magnitude of each simulation. Figure 5 (right) illustrates the distribution of ratings across all participants for each simulation. The high amount of dispersion (i.e. lack of tightness around the central value) for each configuration indicates that agreement between participants is quite low: for any given simulation some participants rate the experience as being windy, while others might rate it as not being that windy. Many of the configurations seemed to provide a similar "magnitude" experience, even though naïvely, we would not expect this. As illustrated in Figure 5 (right), the distributions for many configurations share a lot of overlap, meaning that many different configurations essentially felt "the same" to participants. For instance, we might expect configurations 7 and 8 to feel similar given the similarity of the arrangement of the fans, and this is demonstrated in the distributions. On the other hand, configurations 2 and 6, which have different numbers and arrangement of fans, also appear to be experienced similarly by participants.

### Limitations

These findings should be considered only provisionary. First, we did not examine extended periods of repeated exposure (multiple repetitions per session). Second, the overall airflow volume produced by WindyWall may be too low for participants to distinguish various simulations. It may be the case that, for higher airflow volumes, participants may be more effective at distinguishing between different wind stimuli. This suggests that future iterations of WindyWall, or other wind interfaces, ought to be sufficiently higher powered to provide a greater range of airflow volumes that can be distinguished by users.

## DISCUSSION

### Characterizing Wind Simulations

We reiterate that it will be important to develop effective techniques to characterize wind simulations for reproducibility and comparison across different setups. Our efforts took initial steps toward developing this method, but we think there are still steps to be taken in experience capture, characterization, and visualization.

**Higher Fidelity Experience Capture**. Our major insight was that designers ought to try to characterize a wind simulation from the perspective of a typical human user. To this end, our capture device was a wind sensor made of two small anemometers placed where a user's face would be positioned when using WindyWall. Yet, a human's body is likely to have many places where it is sensitive to wind. If we assume that sensitivity is mainly in the face or ears [20, 29], then it may be more appropriate to outfit a mannequin bust with several such wind sensors (e.g. at the ears, at the nose, on the cheeks, on the forehead, neck, and so forth). Such an approach would allow us to capture not only a single point of data about airflow, but a mesh-style dataset accounting for airflow variation around a face.

Further, our lived experience suggests that bodies can differentiate between single and multiple sources of wind on the same patch of skin. For instance, if one was to have two separate fans blowing, this would feel different from a single fan blowing on the same patch of skin—not just in terms of airflow (i.e. volume), but also in that it actually feels like the wind is coming from two different sources. Currently, our anemometers only report a single airflow direction and airflow rate. While these are useful points of data, the sensor still remains a far cry from the sensitivity of our skin.

**Higher-Dimensional Characterization**. To effectively characterize wind simulations, we need to account for more than just airflow direction and volume: we also need to account for variations of the two parameters over time, and at a given moment, note that different places of our body may be experiencing different airflow direction and volume. For instance, consider the experience of a car that passes by quickly from one's left to right. Even if we do not touch this car, we do feel perturbations in the air due to fluid dynamics, and we feel this as a type of wind or airflow. Over time, this experience changes—we first feel it on the left side of our body, and as the car passes, we feel the wind on the right side of our body. The methods we use to characterize airflow need to be able to describe this change over time—not as theoretical constructs as in a fluid dynamics equation, but in terms of the experience as a human perceives it. Similarly, different points of our body experience different rates of airflow, and due to fluid dynamics, each part of the body may be experiencing the airflow from different directions.

**Distance from Fans.** Finally, how far people are from fans affects their experience of airflow. While in our work, we strictly control this factor (by placing people 1m away from fans), this will not be generally true in most real-life deployments. For instance, in the case of immersive VR experiences, people will be holding controllers such that their arms and hands will be closer than 0.6m from fans. This needs to be considered carefully in future work.

### Implications for Immersive Wind Simulations

Our explorations and findings suggest that people are far less capable of distinguishing and describing airflow than we had anticipated, that we need to think carefully about how people experience wind, and that our use of fans for simulation method may not be optimal.

**Variability in Sensitivity**. Our results suggest that people's sensitivity to airflow is highly variable—at least in terms of magnitude estimation: some are good at detecting subtle variations of airflow, while others are largely unable to detect meaningful variation. This presents challenges to designers of wind simulations, as it is difficult to know how to simulations are going to be experienced by a population of users. This suggests that we need to do more as a research community to explore the psychophysical experience of airflow, or how this modality acts in concert with others for virtual reality simulations.

**Passive vs. Active Exploration**. Most research in this area has assumed that people discover wind passively: they sit in a fixed location, and have wind blown at them. Yet, in a virtual simulation, a user will stand, move around, and try to explore the space (and thus experience wind) in an active manner. We still do not have enough understanding of how to account for and accommodate these kinds of situations, and thus do not know how to design effectively for it.

**Challenges with Fans**. Our experiences suggest that while fans are a cheap and easy method for simulating wind, this may not be the best approach. Fans have a "ramp-up" time (illustrated in Figure 4), adding to the latency in a simulation—for us, recorded latencies ranged between 2 and 4 seconds. Fans also produce vortices of wind, which may be undesirable in certain kinds of simulations. Recent efforts in developing haptic experiences (e.g. for feeling virtual objects, notifications, or force feedback) have explored the use of ultrasound and air pumps [22, 33, 34, 11]. It may be possible to use technologies in combination with fans to simulate foreground and background experiences of wind.

## CONCLUSIONS AND FUTURE WORK

WindyWall is a reconfigurable fan array that gives designers the power to creatively explore wind simulations. Our design allows the reconfiguration of the physical array, and allows each fan to be controlled individually, or in programmatic groups. We detail the issue of characterizing wind simulations, and its importance to the community as a whole. To understand the human experience of wind, we conducted an initial pilot study exploring the psychophysical experience of wind and airflow magnitude. Our results suggest that while overall trends exist, individual variation is extremely high. Our findings suggest that people may not be able to articulate their experience of wind effectively; instead, perhaps coarse-grained approaches may actually be sufficient for many applications. WindyWall opens up the possibility to explore these applications and ideas.

## ACKNOWLEDGEMENTS

This research is supported by the National Research Foundation, Prime Minister's Office, Singapore under its International Research Centres in Singapore Funding Initiative, and the National Science and Engineering Research Council of Canada. We thank Ivan Tan for supporting this work. We also thank participants of our study.

## REFERENCES

[1] Duzgun Agdas, Gregory D. Webster, and Forrest J. Masters. 2012. Wind speed perception and risk. *PloS one* 7. no. 11 (2012): e49944.

[2] AS220 Industries. https://moderndevice.com/product/wind-sensor-rev-p/.

[3] Atmel. https://en.wikipedia.org/wiki/ATmega328.

[4] Arduino. https://www.arduino.cc/en/uploads/Main/arduino-mega2560_R3-sch.pdf.

[5] Sylvain Cardin, Daniel Thalmann, and Frederic Vexo. 2007. Head mounted wind. In *Proceedings of the 20th annual conference on Computer Animation and Social Agents (CASA2007)*. no. VRLAB-CONF-2007-136, 101-108.

[6] Tom Carter, Sue Ann Seah, Benjamin Long, Bruce Drinkwater, and Sriram Subramanian. 2013. UltraHaptics: multi-point mid-air haptic feedback for touch surfaces. In *Proceedings of the 26th annual ACM symposium on User interface software and technology*. ACM, 505-514.

[7] Amber Choo, Xin Tong, Diane Gromala, and Ari Hollander. 2014. Virtual reality and mobius floe: cognitive distraction as non-pharmacological analgesic for pain management. In *Games for Health 2014*. Springer, 8-12.

[8] Leonidas Deligiannidis, and Robert JK Jacob. 2006. The vr scooter: Wind and tactile feedback improve user performance. In *IEEE Symposium on 3D User Interfaces (3DUI 2006)*. IEEE, 143-150.

[9] Mark H. Draper, Erik S. Viirre, Thomas A. Furness, and Valerie J. Gawron. 2001. Effects of image scale and system time delay on simulator sickness within head-coupled virtual environments. *Human factors* 43, no. 1 (2001): 129-146.

[10] Diane Gromala, Xin Tong, Amber Choo, Mehdi Karamnejad, and Chris D. Shaw. 2015. The virtual meditative walk: virtual reality therapy for chronic pain management. In *Proceedings of the 33rd Annual ACM Conference on Human Factors in Computing Systems*. ACM, 521-524.

[11] Sidhant Gupta, Dan Morris, Shwetak N. Patel, and Desney Tan. 2013. AirWave: non-contact haptic feedback using air vortex rings. In *Proceedings of the 2013 ACM international joint conference on Pervasive and ubiquitous computing*. ACM, 419-428.

[12] Felix Hülsmann, Julia Fröhlich, Nikita Mattar, and Ipke Wachsmuth. 2014. Wind and warmth in virtual reality: implementation and evaluation. In *Proceedings of the 2014 Virtual Reality International Conference*. ACM, 24.

[13] Hiroshi Ishii, Sandia Ren, and Phil Frei. 2001. Pinwheels: visualizing information flow in an architectural space. In *Ext. Abst. CHI 2001*: 111-112.

[14] Weina Jin, Amber Choo, Diane Gromala, Chris Shaw, and Pamela Squire. 2016. A virtual reality game for chronic pain management: a randomized, controlled clinical study. In *MMVR*. 154-160.

[15] Lynette A. Jones, and Hong Z. Tan. 2013. Application of psychophysical techniques to haptic research. *IEEE transactions on haptics* 6. IEEE, no. 3 (2013), 268-284.

[16] Terry K. Koo, and Mae Y. Li. 2016. A guideline of selecting and reporting intraclass correlation coefficients for reliability research. *Journal of Chiropractic Medicine* 15, no 2, PMC, 155-163.

[17] Yuichiro Kojima, Yuki Hashimoto, and Hiroyuki Kajimoto. 2009. A novel wearable device to present localized sensation of wind. In *Proceedings of the International Conference on Advances in Computer Enterntainment Technology*. ACM, 61-65.

[18] Sandip D. Kulkarni, Charles Fisher, Eric Pardyjak, Mark Minor, and John Hollerbach. 2009. Wind display device for locomotion interface in a virtual environment. In *EuroHaptics conference, 2009 and Symposium on Haptic Interfaces for Virtual Environment and Teleoperator Systems. World Haptics 2009. Third Joint*. IEEE, 184-189.

[19] Sandip D. Kulkarni, Mark A. Minor, Mark W. Deaver, and Eric R. Pardyjak. 2007. Output feedback control of wind display in a virtual environment. In *2007 IEEE International Conference on Robotics and Automation*. IEEE, 832-839.

[20] Jaeyeon Lee, and Geehyuk Lee. 2016. Designing a non-contact wearable tactile display using airflows. In *Proceedings of the 29th Annual Symposium on User Interface Software and Technology*. ACM, 183-194.

[21] Anke Lehmann, Christian Geiger, Bjorn Woldecke, and Jorg Stocklein. 2009. Poster: Design and evaluation of 3D content with wind output. In *IEEE Symposium on 3D User Interfaces (3DUI 2009)*. IEEE, 151-152.

[22] Benjamin Long, Sue Ann Seah, Tom Carter, and Sriram Subramanian. 2014. Rendering volumetric haptic shapes in mid-air using ultrasound. *ACM Transactions on Graphics (TOG)* 33, no. 6 (2014), 181.

[23] Weiquan Lu, Henry Been-Lirn Duh, Steven Feiner, and Qi Zhao. 2014. Attributes of subtle cues for facilitating visual search in augmented reality. *IEEE Trans. Vis. Comput. Graph. 20*, 3, 404-412.

[24] Mitsuru Minakuchi, and Satoshi Nakamura. 2007. Collaborative ambient systems by blow displays. In *Proceedings of the 1st international conference on Tangible and embedded interaction*. ACM, 105-108.

[25] Taeyong Moon, and Gerard J. Kim. 2004. Design and evaluation of a wind display for virtual reality. In *Proceedings of the ACM symposium on Virtual reality software and technology*. ACM, 122-128.

[26] Jason D. Moss, Jon Austin, James Salley, Julie Coats, Krysten Williams, and Eric R. Muth. 2011. The effects of display delay on simulator sickness. *Displays* 32, no. 4 (2011): 159-168.

[27] Omar Mowafi, Mohamed Khamis, and Wael Abouelsaadat. 2015. AirDisplay: Experimenting with air flow as a communication medium. In *Human-Computer Interaction*. Springer, 316-323.

[28] Multicomp. http://www.farnell.com/datasheets/1772996.pdf.

[29] Takuya Nakano, Shota Saji, and Yasuyuki Yanagida. 2012. Indicating wind direction using a fan-based wind display. In *International Conference on Human Haptic Sensing and Touch Enabled Computer Applications*. Springer, 97-102.

[30] Mark Nazemi, Diane Gromala, and Mehdi Karamnejad. 2014. Virtual reality as analgesia: an alternative approach for managing chronic pain. *International Journal of Creative Interfaces and Computer Graphics (IJCICG)* 5, no. 2 (2014): 75-86.

[31] Processing. https://processing.org/.

[32] Nimesha Ranasinghe, Pravar Jain, Shienny Karwita, David Tolley, and Ellen Yi-Luen Do. 2017. Ambiotherm: enhancing sense of presence in virtual reality by simulating real-world environmental conditions. In *Proceedings of the 2017 CHI Conference on Human Factors in Computing Systems*. ACM 1731-1742.

[33] Rajinder Sodhi, Ivan Poupyrev, Matthew Glisson, and Ali Israr. 2013. AIREAL: interactive tactile experiences in free air. *ACM Transactions on Graphics (TOG)* 32, no. 4 (2013): 134.

[34] Daniel Spelmezan, Rafael Morales González, and Sriram Subramanian. 2016. SkinHaptics: Ultrasound focused in the hand creates tactile sensations. In *2016 IEEE Haptics Symposium (HAPTICS)*. IEEE, 98-105.

[35] Yuriko Suzuki, and Minoru Kobayashi. 2005. Air jet driven force feedback in virtual reality. *IEEE computer graphics and applications* 25, no. 1 (2005): 44-47.

[36] Jouke C. Verlinden, Fabian A. Mulder, Joris S. Vergeest, Anna de Jonge, Darina Krutiy, Zsuzsa Nagy, Bob J. Logeman, and Paul Schouten. 2013. Enhancement of presence in a virtual sailing environment through localized wind simulation. *Procedia Engineering* 60 (2013): 435-441.

[37] Craig Wisneski, Hiroshi Ishii, Andrew Dahley, Matthew G. Gorbet, Scott Brave, Brygg Ullmer, and Paul Yarin. 1998. *CoBuild 1998*: 22-32.

[38] Bob G Witmer and Michael J Singer. 1998. Measuring presence in virtual environments: A presence questionnaire. *Presence: Teleoperators and virtual environments* 7, 3 (1998), 225–240.

# Designing Motion Matching for Real-World Applications: Lessons from Realistic Deployments

**David Verweij**
Northumbria
University Newcastle
Newcastle upon Tyne
david.verweij
@northumbria.ac.uk

**Augusto Esteves**
Edinburgh Napier
University
Edinburgh, UK
a.esteves@napier.ac.uk

**Saskia Bakker**
Eindhoven University
of Technology
Eindhoven, NL
s.bakker@tue.nl

**Vassilis-Javed Khan**
Eindhoven University
of Technology
Eindhoven, NL
v.j.khan@tue.nl

## ABSTRACT
Amongst the variety of (multi-modal) interaction techniques that are being developed and explored, the Motion Matching paradigm provides a novel approach to selection and control. In motion matching, users interact by rhythmically moving their bodies to track the continuous movements of different interface targets. This paper builds upon the current algorithmic and usability focused body of work by exploring the product possibilities and implications of motion matching. Through the development and qualitative study of four novel and different real-world motion matching applications — with 20 participants — we elaborate on the suitability of motion matching in different multi-user scenarios, the less pertinent use in home environments and the necessity for multi-modal interaction. Based on these learnings, we developed three novel motion matching based interactive lamps, which report on clear paths for further dissemination of the embodied interaction technique's experience. This paper hereby informs the design of future motion matching interfaces and products.

## CCS Concepts
**•Human-centered computing → Interaction techniques;** *Interactive systems and tools;*

## Author Keywords
Motion matching; motion correlation; smart watches; touchless interaction; gestural input.

## INTRODUCTION
The ability to remotely control the increasing number of smart devices is a recurrent challenge in HCI. This challenge has often been addressed by using tangible proxy devices, such as remote controllers [3, 15, 56]. Alternatively, researchers have explored input systems that leverage people's sensorimotor skills to provide intuitive, embodied and direct interaction, for example using body movement or gestures [5, 17, 28]. A recent class of such embodied interaction techniques, broadly described as *motion matching* [20, 46, 55] (synonyms include motion coincidence, motion pointing, rhythmic path mimicry), allows users to interact with digital systems by imitating a moving entity using bodily movements (e.g. moving one's hand to match a circular motion, see Fig. 1) [9, 11, 21, 48]. Compared to other touchless embodied systems, motion matching is seen as an interesting alternative for interaction with public displays and a growing number of smart appliances at home. For example, it works with unmodified off-the-shelf hardware such as web-cams [11] or smart watches [50]; does not require any gesture data training sets; and does not require gesture (or speech) discovery and memorization — making it an ideal candidate for spontaneous interaction [52]. On the other hand, previous work in this domain has focused primarily on seminal performance studies and technical developments. Our work contributes to these efforts by assessing a broad range of future user experiences with the technique.



*TEI '19*, March 17–20, 2019, Tempe, AZ, USA



ISBN 978-1-4503-6196-5/19/03...$15.00
DOI: https://doi.org/10.1145/3294109.3295628

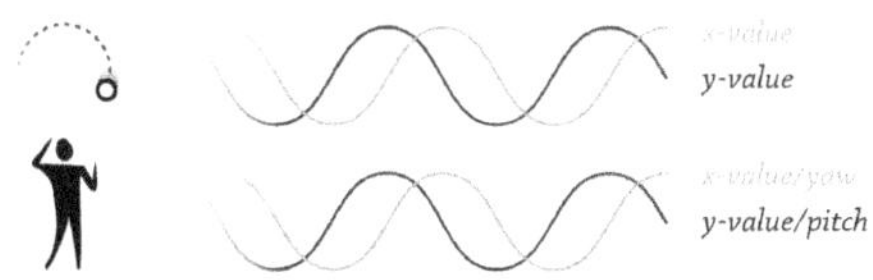


**Figure 1. Motion Matching is an embodied interaction technique that allows interaction based on mimicking (displayed) targets, resulting in matching movement characteristics (e.g. axes) between target and user.**

Related work has developed and studied a variety of technical implementations of motion matching interaction, using web-cams [11, 12], depth-sensors [9], eye-trackers [18, 25, 37, 48, 52], magnets [39], and inertial measurement units (IMUs) embedded in smart-watches [50], phones [4], and AR headsets [19]. These implementations are supplemented with work on further algorithmic developments and novel deployments [10, 16, 21, 27, 29, 47]. Taken together, these laboratory studies have shown that people are able to accurately interact with motion matching interfaces after a very short learning period. Given these promising developments, an important next step is to further explore how motion matching is experienced in broader real-world scenarios [13, 52], and in which settings it would be most valuable.

To support and promote the future design of motion matching products and interfaces — contrasting technical or algorithmic developments — we present the study of 20 participants who sequentially experienced four novel real-world motion matching implementations in a controlled environment. These four implementations explore existing anticipated uses for motion matching, as seen in prior work, for parameter control (e.g. [39, 18]), (multi-user) scenarios at home (e.g. [11, 51]) or in public spaces (e.g. [14, 52]) and explores (through the demos) social acceptance amongst these domains. This allows us to draw design relevant insights for the scenarios reflected in our implementations: smart home control, interactive television, smart classrooms, and public displays. Our findings demonstrate that motion matching seems more suitable for (semi) public spaces and focused interactions, and less pertinent for use in scenarios at home — particularly for simultaneous multi-user control. They furthermore indicate the necessity for multi-modal interaction for seamless integration of the technique in everyday life. We finalize this paper by exemplifying how these considerations could be put into practice. To this end, we present three novel interactive lamps which implement motion matching interaction and discuss practicalities for future integration of motion matching in consumer products.

## RELATED WORK

### Touchless Embodied Interaction

The advances in real-time body tracking have spurred the creation of a rich set of interaction techniques that rely on body movement and gestures as means of user input [30, 43, 44]. These techniques generally involve pointing-based approaches, where users control on-screen cursors through body or hand movements [31, 54]; gestural systems, where user input takes the form of discrete (semaphoric) mid-air gestures [2, 43, 54]; or an hybrid of the two [24, 28]. But while effective, pointing-based (ray casting) techniques tend to require rather larger body movements when dealing with larger interaction spaces (e.g., large displays or smart environments [23, 40]), and displaying cursors for multiple users has been found to lead to confusion in non-collaborative tasks [9]. Gestural systems, on the other hand, have users perform discrete, mid-air gestures with their arms, hands, or fingers [8]. These systems allow users to interact with smart spaces in a relatively scale- and orientation-free manner, but also requires them to learn and memorize the system's gestures and corresponding commands [1, 2], often leading to false activations [45]. Additionally, others have noted that several of these systems rely on gesture sets that are not entirely natural or intuitive [32, 33]. In sum, in domains where spontaneous interaction is necessary, such as in public spaces or in any unfamiliar smart environment, designing for motion-matching interaction might address many of these challenges.

### Motion Matching

The concept of motion matching was inspired by the early work of Williamson et al. [55], Fekete et al. [20], and more recently, Vidal et al. [52]. In motion matching, users interact not necessarily by pointing, nor by performing a discrete gesture, but by using their body to track the continuous and singular movements of different interface targets, see Fig. 1. User input and target movements are compared on their phase, speed, and direction — not on their position or scale. Because of this, interface targets can be positioned very close, or even superimposed onto each other [18]; and a small tracking motion is sufficient to interact with targets trajectory of any size or distance, leading to a less fatiguing experience when compared to interfaces that require pointing over large surfaces [11]. Furthermore, targets in motion matching interfaces encode the necessary input information in their singular movement. This makes for interfaces that are "self-revealing and highly discoverable" [11, 52], ideal for spontaneous interaction [14, 52]. This is particularly important in maintaining a consistent experience across various smart devices and smart environments, otherwise relying on a broad set of input gestures [48].

Current work on motion matching interfaces has explored a variety of ways to capture user input, with the majority relying on optical tracking. Examples include systems that track users' eyes as these follow a moving target [18, 25, 27, 48, 52]; depth-cameras that track users' hands [9, 21, 22]; and systems that rely on off-the-shelf web-cams to capture any input motion in their field-of-view (FOV), be it performed by the users' hands, feet, or even their heads [11]. But due to inherent limitations of computer vision, such as being restricted by their FOV (interaction space), being susceptible to changing-light conditions and occlusion, and introducing privacy concerns when used in the context of smart homes [7], recent work looks at other forms of input sensing for motion matching. Examples include passive magnets that capture the user's thumb movement [39], or inertial measurement units (IMUs) that capture users' head (AR headset [19]), arm (smartwatch [50]), or phone-based [4] rotations when following a moving target.

In addition to exploring different technical implementations of the technique, related works have also validated motion matching through a variety of lab studies. These have established the technique's accuracy [50], usability [18], and preference when compared to, e.g., pointing-based input [9]. But despite its promise and appeal, very little research has explored the use of motion matching in realistic, everyday scenarios. The few exceptions available describe how, when deployed in a real public display, motion matching facilitates discovery and rapid learning of interaction possibilities (Vidal et al. [52] describes 87.5% successful interactions with no guidance or instructions). With a high anticipated potential for this technique in a breadth of everyday scenarios — often envisioned in the related work — this leaves an important gap between research and product integration towards exemplifying motion matching product, and thus a crucial next step for this growing research area. This paper builds on the work described above and reports on the user experience across four realistic demos covering different use cases.

## FOUR MOTION MATCHING DEMOS

The complexity of integrating motion matching in everyday interactions at its current state is a delimiting factor for testing user experiences for motion matching. With the aim to inform the design and deployment of future motion matching systems, this study explores the user experience with the technique in different application scenarios, through four fully functional demos in a semi-controlled environment. These demos represent scenarios in personal and public spaces, single and multi-user control and individual and collaborative interactions, which allows us to draw design relevant insights for a broad spectrum of future potential implementations. We hypothesized the four demos (presented below) to elicit functional, attractive, and pleasurable experiences, whilst each scenario explores a different real-world setting. We varied the (graphical) implementation of the interaction technique amongst these demos to elicit different challenges that motion matching interfaces might encounter in future deployments. In this section, we introduce our technical implementation of motion matching, and present our four demos.

### Motion Matching Implementation

As addressed in the related work section, various technical implementations of motion matching interaction are possible, each with their own benefits and limitations. The aim of this work is to generalize insights that designers of future motion matching applications can build further upon. Therefore, we found it important that our implementation would rely on affordable, off-the-shelf hardware and could be used in a variety of real-life scenarios. To avoid the FOV limitations and privacy concerns of optical tracking, our implementation relies on the inertial measurement unit (IMU) in a smart-watch to track user's arm movements. For our studies we adopted the 'WaveTrace' implementation [50].

In line with the WaveTrace implementation, each of our four demos depicts rotating targets on a display. Each target is distinguishable by its own unique rotational phase and direction. To interact, users track the rotating movement of the target they wish to select with their arms, which is captured by a 9-DOF IMU (triple axis gyro, accelerometer, and magnetometer) embedded into an Android smart-watch (Sony Smartwatch 3) and represented as Euler angles (yaw, pitch, and roll). Using a 'rolling' window of 1500ms (~195Hz, ~292 data points for each axis), this data is then matched with all moving targets through a Pearson's correlation between the user's (the yaw/horizontal and pitch/vertical movements of the arm) and each target movement (respectively x- and y-axis). If the correlation coefficient, a value between -1 and 1, is above 0.8 in both axes, the target is selected. Continuous input is supported when users continue to track a target after the initial selection (to, e.g., increase playback volume). Whilst prior work has shown that variety of target trajectories are possible [9], we opted to constrain our implementation to circles, so as to remain comparable to the majority of related work on motion matching.

### Demonstrators

Based on ideation amongst the authors we developed four demos[1]: the 'Smart Home Control' aims to (seamlessly) blend a motion matching interface into users' smart homes (Fig. 2); an 'Interactive Television' demo aims to augment smart-TV interfaces with moving targets for co-located control (Fig. 3); a 'Smart Classroom' demo implements smart-watch use for classroom (Fig. 4); and, lastly, a 'Public Display' demo (Fig. 5)

[1] See youtu.be/Uyz0ubAhPy4 for a detailed video of each interface.

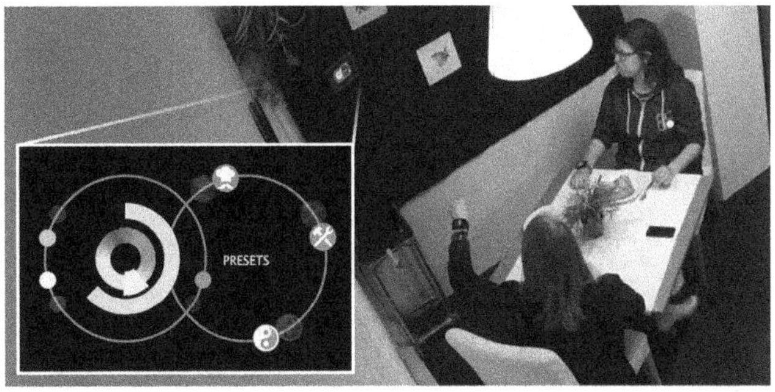


**Figure 2. Smart Home Control Demo. Left: clockwise tracking of the moving yellow target increases light intensity (counter clockwise decreases), whilst tracking the purple target navigates through the HUE color spectrum. Right: three room lighting presets.**

integrates motion matching with the aim to better facilitate the switch between implicit (e.g. user proximity) and explicit interaction (e.g. hand gestures) [53] in public and personal interaction spaces. Each demo consists of a custom Processing [38] application running on a laptop, which receives users' motion data over Wi-Fi. Each demo has a display appropriate for the context of use, which depicts the moving targets and provides feedback when a target is selected. To minimize false positives with everyday movements, an initial gesture needs to be performed to display (and activate) the targets. Kerber et al. [26] showed that a double flick of the wrist is a highly uncommon accidental movement. Applying such a delimiter also minimizes the amount of movement on the interface when no interaction is required. Unfortunately, using an Android-based smart-watch, a double flick requires the gesture recognition to be turned off due to conflicting with existing system gestures. Rather than building our own gesture recognition algorithm, we opted for using a single flick to represent the suggested double flick — which allowed us to use the built-in gesture recognition. All demos support up to two users interacting simultaneously (each wearing a smart-watch) and vary in their interface design.

#### *Demo 1 — Smart Home Control*

This smart home dashboard (Fig. 2) allows control over a Philips HUE smart lighting system [36]. A 5-inch display, embedded in a picture frame, displays a photo when the system is idle, attempting to hide the system in 'plain sight'. Upon activation, a motion matching menu is displayed. On the left, three (abstract) targets are displayed that manage the lights' brightness and color. The intensity of the lights increases or decreases upon continuous tracking of respectively clockwise or counterclockwise moving yellow targets. Continuous tracking of the purple target enables navigation through the HUE color spectrum. On the right, three (iconic) targets are displayed that once selected enable pre-defined light settings. Selection and the current light status is confirmed through brightness and color wheels displayed on the left.

#### *Demo 2 — Interactive Television*

A video on demand (VOD) interface (Fig. 3) focuses on multi-user interactions in a social setting — including a login, home and playback screen. Moving targets were implemented in several ways. For example, four out of six targets in the home screen (Fig. 3 - bottom) allowed for discrete navigation such

**Figure 3. Interactive TV Demo. Top: the menu during playback with five moving targets for basic video functionality. Bottom: the home screen menu with six moving targets. Both navigation menus contain two targets which allow for horizontal scrolling.**

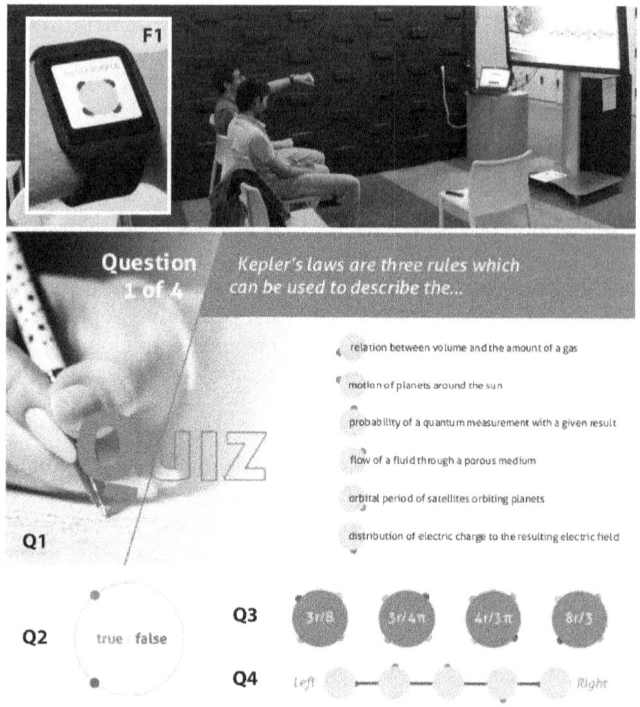


**Figure 4. Classroom Demo. Students choose an answer for in-class quiz questions. Each question differed in the implementation of moving targets (Q1-4) to explore their usability and experience.**

as up, down, play, and exit; whilst two other targets allowed horizontal navigation using continuous input. The volume targets in the playback menu (Fig. 3 — top) display a clock- and counterclockwise continuous target for respectively increasing or decreasing the volume, whilst the volume status is highlighted in their trajectory. Input from either user is received on a first-come-first-serve basis, where discrete input (e.g. 'play') disables input for 1.5 seconds to minimize accidental selection in the transition to a new view or state.

### *Demo 3 — Smart Classroom*

The classroom demo explores the use of motion matching in a public setting. Here, the benefits of our chosen wrist-worn motion sensor approach to motion matching become apparent, as capturing input on a classroom scale and complexity becomes feasible. The demo (Fig. 4) is an interactive quiz that provides additional haptic and graphical information and feedback that can be conveyed through the used smart-watch. Again, moving targets were implemented in several ways through the four types of questions: Q1 presented an individual target for each multiple-choice answer; Q2 displayed two targets moving in opposite direction on one trajectory; Q3 randomly assigned users a selection color to minimize shoulder surfing (Fig. 4 — F1), resulting in 16 displayed targets; lastly Q4 assigned an answer to each smart-watch screen, which was asked to 'position' on a 5-point presented scale using motion matching. Aggregate results are displayed on the large presentation screen, individual results on each user's smart-watch (if applicable).

### *Demo 4 — Public Display*

Finally, a train station departure board explores motion matching use around public displays in busy areas, and the benefit of cross-device interaction through users' own smart-watches (Fig. 5). Each platform icon in the departure board is a moving target which, upon selection, uploads additional information about the selected trip to the user's smart-watch — allowing for later retrieval of information.

## USER EXPERIENCE STUDY

We aim to evaluate current and potential future applications for motion matching interfaces. We are particularly interested in studying the suitability of the technique in the four application scenarios described above, and in generalizing our results to further practical application areas and to motion matching implementations other than WaveTrace [50].

### Setup and Procedure

We conducted a user evaluation with 20 participants (11F), aged between 19 and 30 (M = 23.7, SD = 2.83), to gather feedback and to invite participants to envision how these prototypes could be used in their everyday lives. Participants took part in pairs of two; paired with friends, family, acquaintances, or colleagues. This was done deliberately to promote open and frank discussions during the study, and to elicit honest opinions and experiences. Using a five-point Likert scale, participants rated their experience with computer technology and mobile devices as high (M = 3.95, SD = 0.89), and with wearable technology as average (M = 3.00, SD = 1.03). Most participants were students at a local institution (N=18), and none reported limited mobility. Each pair experienced each of the four demos consecutively. Demo 1 and 2 were set up in a room furnished as a living room. Demo 3 and 4 were set up in a hallway of a university building, to try and increase 'ecological validity'. Right before the study, all participants

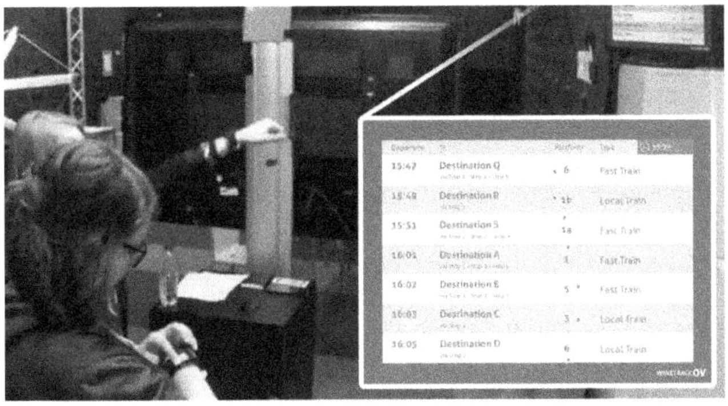

**Figure 5. Public Display Demo. By matching the motion of a certain train departure, users are provided with additional information about that trip on their smart-watches.**

took part in an individual training session to get accustomed to motion matching — similar to the performance study in [50].

We evaluated the demos using the Co-Constructing Stories method [34], a qualitative evaluation technique specifically geared towards evaluating the user experience of concepts or demos before they are turned into commercial products. The technique consists of a sensitization and elaboration phase, and is especially meant to help people imagine experiencing the demos in potential future use contexts. Before interacting with each demo, the researcher shared a simple fictional story that introduced the application scenario. To ensure *sensitization* with this scenario, participants were asked to recall their most recent (and where possible similar) experience related to that story. Participants were then invited to interact with the demo and all its functionalities. Afterward, participants engaged in a group (duo) discussion about their experience — the *elaboration* phase. In addition to any remarks or feedback on their experience with the demo, participants were asked to project it onto the experience they had described during the sensitization phase, and to reflect on this prospective experience. To provide a usability benchmark, we also asked each participant to individually fill in the System Usability Scale (SUS) [6] — a 10-item Likert scale questionnaire that assesses the perceived usability of an interface — after using each demo and before each discussion.

The order in which pairs used the four demos was balanced using a Latin Square. Each demo, including both phases and the SUS, took on average 30 minutes, resulting in a 2-hour session for each pair of participants. Upon request, participants were allowed to interact with any of the demos for a longer period of time. Finally, participants were compensated with a $30 gift voucher. We recorded audio and video of all sessions for further analysis.

## RESULTS

The SUS [6] is a 10-item Likert scale questionnaire that assesses the perceived usability of an interface. The participants' scores (see Table 1) can be compared with over 5000 SUS scores from previously assessed products and systems [41], see Table 1 bottom row. This positions the usability of the Smart Classroom and Public Display demos in the top 10%, and the other two demos substantially lower. These SUS re-

| | Home | TV | Classroom | Public |
|---|---|---|---|---|
| M (*SD*) | 64.0 (*18.3*) | 61.5 (*21.5*) | 83.6 (*12.1*) | 81.5 (*14.2*) |
| Percentile | 32 | 38 | 94 | 92 |

**Table 1. Perceived usability scores (using the SUS) for each demo, with their score translated into a percentile rank.**

sults reflect participants' shared view on these demos which we elaborate on below.

### Qualitative Findings

We extracted 547 quotes from the interviews' audio recordings, which address the overall user experience with the demos, motion matching, the context of the experience, envisioned user experiences, and suggested improvements. We analyzed the quotes using open coding [42]. One author and two independent researchers initial clustered part of their equal share of quotes independently, after which the emerged clusters were discussed and a intermediate set was agreed upon. The remaining quotes were collaboratively accommodated, whilst continuous discussion allowed for the clusters to evolve — resulting in eight clusters. Based on these clusters, we now present our findings (see Table 2) along three topics: *effort and social dynamics*, *application areas*, and *interface designs*.

#### *Effort and Social dynamics*

A recurring theme in the discussions revolved around the general use of motion matching, and often around the use of arm movements. Ten participants noted that tracking a moving target requires mental and visual effort. This was not deemed too problematic, especially in scenarios where the input and output share the same required focus space (**F1**)(e.g. the Smart Classroom or the Public Display demo). For other scenario's, seven participants emphasized that the moving target and interaction distracted from the task at hand (**F4**), for example, whilst scrolling through videos on the television. Overall, six participants expressed how they quickly got the hang of the interaction. They reasoned that using the technique has a (relatively) short learning curve. Only two participants expressed their concerns with physical fatigue, related to the stretched arm position.

Regarding moving targets as used in our interfaces, six participants envisioned that disambiguation through different trajectory shapes and speeds for different (type of) controls would assist in the technique's learnability and recognition of those controls (**F2**). Relatedly, eight participants reported that the current target speed (and thus the required arm movement speed) for particular continuous targets were uncharacteristic. This means that the input speed for, for example, changing a light's brightness felt too slow, and often did not match the output result (**F5**)(i.e. the speed of changing brightness). Ensuring a correct and characteristic translation between target movement and effect is also advocated by Esteves et al. [19] in their findings. Nine participants reported feeling unsure about whether the system was accurately capturing their input (**F6**). This is because most motion matching interfaces do not offer a hover state (doing so would increase acquisition times) — input feedback was provided purely upon selection as haptic feedback on participants' smart-watches. In cases of anonymous input (in the public domain demos), visual feedback was

| |
|---|
| **F1** - Tracking moving targets was not problematic |
| **F2** - Varying target trajectories could aid learnability |
| **F3** - Public input could motivate engagement/participation |
| **F4** - The moving targets could be distracting |
| **F5** - Target speeds could be too slow for their role |
| **F6** - User input feedback could be lacking and confusing |
| **F7** - Bodily moving input could be overtly public |
| **F8** - The interface design could be unnecessarily complex |
| **F9** - The interaction could be time consuming |
| **F10** - Pairing input techniques could help the experience |

**Table 2. Qualitative findings with their F# reference.**

intentionally left out. Five participants suggested adding additional output to confirm their bodily actions — P9: *'You want to know that the system knows you are aiming. That it understands that you are aiming but that you are not yet there'*. They believed this would increase their confidence in the selection mechanism. Relatedly, five participants explicitly reported that, because the technique does not include something akin to a cursor, they were not able to determine what the other participant was selecting, and as such, the transparency in the multi-user input control distribution was hampered (**F6**). This ability for multiple users to simultaneously interact caused ten participants to foresee issues if no priority system was implemented, particularly at home. In any case, these participants indicated that their selection concerns were mitigated over time, as they became more confident about how the demos responded to their input (and matching haptic feedback).

The visibility of the physical interaction to others (sometimes strangers) elicited discussions with thirteen participants on its social effect, especially on its potential awkwardness. Three participants expressed they felt awkward during the study when people actually passed by. When discussing whether the interaction would stay awkward in the future, 14 participants indicated it would depend on the location (e.g. at home or at the train station) or on how commonly known the interaction would be (**F7**). For example, P15 elaborates: *'[in a classroom] everyone needs to do the interaction and I think that that will slightly remove the awkwardness'*. Nine participants also mentioned that the visibility of interaction was a means to perceive other users' actions and decisions. As such, four participants anticipated that the technique could motivate engagement, especially in a classroom or presentation setting, as they could see if and when the other participant was engaging (**F3**). Alternatively, five participants commented on the negative effect of this visibility — for instance, the pressure when you are the last one to make a choice on a class quiz.

### *Application Areas*

Regarding the usefulness of the technique in the home domain, four participants discussed the need for simplicity (**F8**), and reported that there were too many targets, some of which redundant. They did, however, think it would be useful if they could use the technique to control multiple smart devices throughout the house, including an extractor hood (e.g. turn it off whilst eating dinner), lights, or the oven (e.g. to acquire a video feed from inside and check the state of the food).

Five participants expressed particular interest in extending the functionality to control their sound system through the dashboard interface as used in the Smart Home demo; they deemed it more useful than a lighting interface, which is not so commonly used. However, the physicality of the interaction was envisioned to become distracting for the casual environment of the home by six participants (**F4**). P13 states: *'... as we have used it now [in the study], it is totally distracting from the contact we have during dinner'*. Participants considered that this would not be an issue after the technique's adoption in the future, yet, it was deemed too distracting due to the visibility of the movement.

Participants moreover concurred on the usefulness of the motion matching interaction in the public domain, as reflected by the SUS scores. Seven participants envisioned that, in a classroom, the physicality and required focus aids in the engagement of the audience. This was emphasized by eleven participants who predicted that the physical movement would affect a lecture or presentation positively (**F3**). They envisioned the physical input to draw listeners out of their comfort zone and introduce interactive breaks, contrasting the envisioned distraction in the home domain. Seven participants reflected that regardless of functionality, the interaction would only prove its usefulness for public displays if passers-by have some time to spare (**F9**) — particularly in order to stand still. This reflects the limitation for interaction with public displays, regardless of the choice of (mid-air) input technique.

### *Interface Designs*

Whilst most participants were pleased with how the moving targets (seamlessly) augmented the interface in the Public Display demo, some commented on the lack of consistency between target movement, color, or size amongst the demos. Participants appreciated the haptic feedback as additional output in the public domain demos, with five participants indicating that this needs to be carefully considered to avoid unwanted distractions. The Perceived effort of the input technique, when compared to other input solutions, was also discussed. Eight participants considered the Public Display and Classroom demos to be more efficiently controlled using motion matching, while nine participants considered that existing input techniques were better suited for the Smart Home Control and Interactive Television demos (**F10**) — especially for menu navigation in the latter. Furthermore, the integration of the second screen (due to the use of a smart-watch) was considered useful and an advantage over current information sources by eight participants, especially for users in unknown places, such as whilst traveling. Finally, participants also expressed their interest in alternative input devices (e.g. fitness trackers), and in using traditional gestures in combination with the motion matching technique (**F10**).

## DISCUSSION

The purpose of this work is to support developments in motion matching through observations into its user experience, and its applicability in the four demos described. The discussion below offers insights that can drive motion matching development for broader systems and domains.

### Everyday Use

Overall, participants were positive about interacting in (semi) public spaces (**F1,F3,10**). Both the Smart Classroom and Public Display demos were rated high in the SUS which was qualitatively confirmed in the discussions with the participants. The two demos for the home elicited mixed responses (**F4,6,8,10**), highlighted by a low SUS. Participants reported they would not use the home demos due to their complexity (for their purpose), and because they were seen as too fatiguing or distracting. The TV demo also elicited a known limitation of motion matching interfaces: the lack of a cursor or hover state, making it challenging for users to know the system is aware of their input (**F6**). This was considered specifically challenging in multi-user scenarios with shared control (TV demo). These comments are common critiques of general gestural interfaces [32], and similar to what has been reported by other motion matching researchers [9]. Interestingly, the classroom demo, which allowed for multiple users to interact at once, did *not* allow for simultaneous control of shared parameters and thus did not elicit this critique. Instead, participants envisioned the embodied interaction in such a regulated context to be beneficial; to motivate participation and — even though individually tasked — collaboratively acted upon (**F7,3**). These findings suggest that the technique is particularly suitable in cases where it introduces new interaction possibilities (e.g. in the classroom or for public displays), or as an efficient interaction mechanism (e.g. turning up the volume whilst remain seated on the couch) — not as a replacement for (all) existing interaction modalities. This strengthens reflections from prior work on motion matching being predominantly useful in specific scenarios of use [14, 18, 19, 35, 39].

The aforementioned challenges become more apparent in the relaxed atmosphere of the home, in which participants preferred more straightforward interactions, even if this, for example, meant getting up and walking towards the light-switch (**F4,8,10**). Noticeably, participants' examples of other home control systems that could benefit from motion matching were based on these being out-of-reach, and enabling a smaller number of actions. This suggests that motion matching interfaces are most suitable for out-of-reach on-the-fly selection, as part of a multi-modal interaction flow. This contrasts prior implementations of motion matching input techniques that were designed to support precise parameter control [11, 19], or sustained interactions with public displays [9, 14].

### Interaction Model

The demos varied and iterated on prior implementations where targets travel the contour of a button. Participants commented that conveying input information through motion was useful, but could be enhanced by having trajectories that are (more) tightly coupled with their interaction metaphors (**F5**) — a round trajectory is suitable for knob-like actions such as increasing the volume, but not so much for perceived linear actions such as scrolling. The reported conflicts for continuous selection, such as potential physical fatigue or lack of input feedback, left us wondering whether continuous input is suitable for motion matching interfaces. Even though improvements in input feedback and algorithm optimization might improve the experience, these conflicts mirror findings by Esteves et al. [19] suggesting that IMU based motion matching is more suited for quick and discrete interaction. As several participants commented on a combination of motion matching and coarse gestures for continuous control, the multi-modal approach discussed earlier presents great potential for future implementations (**F10**).

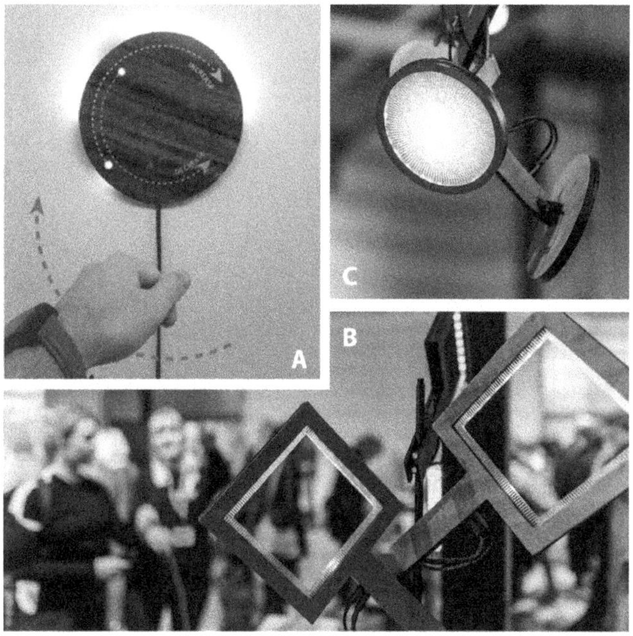


**Figure 6. The three proposed interactive lamps: the wall- (A), standing- (B) and ceiling-lamp (C). For the wall-lamp (A), tracking a blue or red LED traversing across the border of the lamp either increases or decreases the amount of light emitted. Photo B and C © Twycer and Mind the Step.**

## FROM RESEARCH TO DESIGN

To further study motion matching in real-life applications, we developed three interactive lamps - incorporating the aforementioned findings where possible. Whilst motion matching for at home seemed doubtful, connectivity in the smart-light consumer market is in full swing. We thereby further explore the (challenging) home domain by engaging researchers and consumers with product-finish motion matching lights — to be envisioned in their everyday lives. The three lamps[2] (a wall-, standing- and ceiling-lamp) have different output functionalities and form-factors (Fig. 6). The design choices and features partly respond to the earlier reported findings (see **F1-F10**). Their design is a concrete example of applying our research into practice, which can inform future developments. To emphasize the ease of implementation of motion matching using off-the-shelf hardware, and to further disseminate this body of work, we provide full supplementary materials (illustrator files, system design, source code and instructions) via the ACM Digital Library and GitHub (see [49]).

### Design Process and Implications

All three interactive lamp designs were built using RGBW LED strips that both emit light and any moving targets — using engraved Perspex for light refraction. We also opted

[2] See youtu.be/GawBbBrpR_A for a detailed video of each lamp.

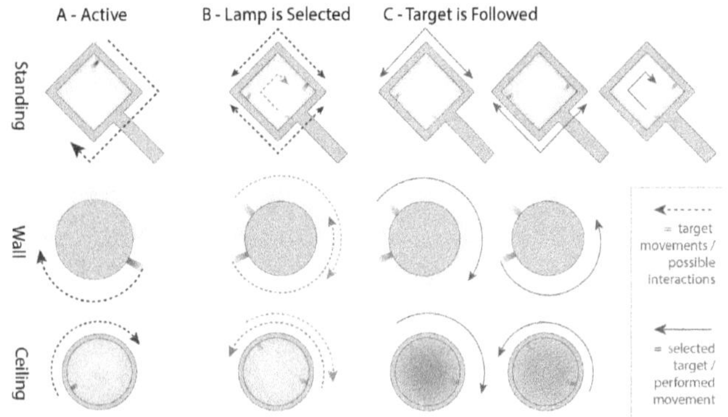


**Figure 7. All lights initially show their 'selection' target (A). Upon selection, a new set of targets is shown (B) — following one of these results (C) in a top, down or both light direction (Standing); different light beam angle (Wall); or a cold or warm color temperature (Ceiling). Note that a target might disappear when a maximum value or mode is reached.**

for using indirect light, as direct light sources would have been uncomfortable during prolonged use. These choices effectively enabled an in- and output space that was tightly coupled (**F1**) — something that was strongly suggested in the qualitative study. The interaction followed the same principle as before: after a flick of the wrist, the lamps display individual moving targets that enable their selection. Responding to participants' request for multi-modal input (**F10**), a tilt of the wrist (>23 degrees) in a clockwise or counterclockwise fashion would respectively increase or decrease the overall brightness of a selected lamp. After this, users simply need to lower their arms to deselect the lamp, and disable all moving targets (**F4**).

### *Trajectory and Product Shape*

To aid in target disambiguation (**F2**), the standing-lamp has rhomboidal shapes. This lamp can be set to direct light downwards (top LED's on), upwards (bottom LED's on) or both (all LED's on), see Fig. 7. To better support the interaction metaphor, the targets that trigger these behaviors respectively traverse back-and-forth on the top LEDs or bottom LEDs (blue targets), or circulate on all LEDs (green target). These implementations aim to adhere to how motion as input is reported to be more intuitive when the movements correspond to an expected functionality — i.e. it should use known interaction metaphors (**F5**). In addition, we envision the design of future systems to display moving targets on locations other than the 'main' display (if any) by using LEDs (e.g. around a button or perhaps embedded in the product logo). Therefore, future motion matching devices can be designed such that their shape is distinctive. This aids in their branding and in their input movement disambiguation from other (motion matching) devices. Alternatively, a transparent screen could be considered to allow more flexible placement in the intended environment. In such implementation, much like our see-through standing-lamp, the user potentially sees moving targets in a mirrored manner. The correlation algorithm must accommodate for such mirrored user input, and requires careful target disambiguation.

### *Omni-directional Field of View*

Whilst ensuring a high flexibility of use, embedding motion matching in consumer lighting products surfaced a few challenges. Firstly, all designs used in prior motion matching work, including our own demos, display moving targets in a 2D plane, often with an opaque background. As this limits placement due to the field of view and user's interaction space, the modules of the standing-lamp are see-through. Secondly, the standing- (and ceiling-) lamp consists of three modules, each spaced 120 degrees from each other to improve visibility from any angle. Lastly, in case of the ceiling-lamp, the modules are additionally angled down (roughly 45 degrees). Since the aforementioned 2D plane for a ceiling lamp would not contain a y-dimension (only x and z), a one-to-one correlation as used before would be impossible without additional sensing approaches. The angled modules reintroduce the y-dimension to maintain this accessible implementation. Future motion matching products that are not placed on or against a wall, should thereby carefully consider their potential placement in the design of their motion matching interface.

## LIMITATIONS AND FUTURE WORK

With our tracking approach [50], we acknowledge its need for an input device for each user, along with the potential ergonomic implications of using such arm movements longitudinally. Our studies showed the benefit of this implementation in the (semi) public domain, yet equally indicated improvements in other domains and applications. In addition, with the aim to present the building blocks for future researchers, we did not conduct a comparative study with alternative technical solutions. Such a comparative approach, alongside a field-based deployment, would contribute to this and equivalent motion matching interaction research. Our endeavor to develop motion matching based consumer products (the lights) allowed us to apply the insights gathered from the experience study. Although the reported practical challenges emerged due to our aim to explore physical designs (instead of screen-based solutions), they can nonetheless inform and inspire other researchers and practitioners to consider integrating the technique in their physical designs. We are particularly keen in further exploring the response to different combinations of user input (e.g. motion matching and discrete gestures or speech commands), colors and UI designs, and selection confirmation during discrete and continuous control. Our next steps will focus on studying the interactive lights in-situ, along with exploring the techniques potential in AR/VR environments.

## CONCLUSION

This paper contributes an in-depth, qualitative analysis of four motion matching implementations for a wide range of domains, reflecting upon these techniques as an appropriate input approach for spontaneous and touchless control of smart environments. The translation from theory to practice, through the screen-based demos and interactive lamps, elicits considerations for future motion matching products and services, including the design of targets and movements. The findings indicate motion matching as suitable in different multi-user scenarios, the less pertinent use in casual environments and the need for multi-modal interaction. This work nurtures future user experiences that draw on the strengths of different input techniques for interaction with a wide set of devices.

## ACKNOWLEDGEMENTS

We thank all participants for their time. This research was partly supported by the Design United foundation (C2E1707).

## REFERENCES

[1] Christopher Ackad, Andrew Clayphan, Martin Tomitsch, and Judy Kay. 2015. An In-the-wild Study of Learning Mid-air Gestures to Browse Hierarchical Information at a Large Interactive Public Display. In *Proceedings of the 2015 ACM International Joint Conference on Pervasive and Ubiquitous Computing (UbiComp '15)*. ACM, New York, NY, USA, 1227–1238. DOI: http://dx.doi.org/10.1145/2750858.2807532

[2] Thomas Baudel and Michel Beaudouin-Lafon. 1993. Charade: Remote Control of Objects Using Free-hand Gestures. *Commun. ACM* 36, 7 (July 1993), 28–35. DOI: http://dx.doi.org/10.1145/159544.159562

[3] Michael Beigl. 1999. Point & Click-Interaction in Smart Environments. In *Handheld and Ubiquitous Computing*, Hans-W. Gellersen (Ed.). Number 1707 in Lecture Notes in Computer Science. Springer Berlin Heidelberg, 311–313. DOI: http://dx.doi.org/10.1007/3-540-48157-5_31

[4] Peter Bennett, Stuart Nolan, Ved Uttamchandani, Michael Pages, Kirsten Cater, and Mike Fraser. 2015. Resonant Bits: Harmonic Interaction with Virtual Pendulums. In *Proceedings of the 9th International Conference on Tangible, Embedded, and Embodied Interaction (TEI '15)*. ACM, New York, USA, 49–52. DOI:http://dx.doi.org/10.1145/2677199.2680569

[5] Richard A. Bolt. 1980. 'Put-that-there': Voice and Gesture at the Graphics Interface. In *Proceedings of the 7th Annual Conference on Computer Graphics and Interactive Techniques (SIGGRAPH '80)*. ACM, New York, NY, USA, 262–270. DOI: http://dx.doi.org/10.1145/800250.807503

[6] John Brooke. 1996. SUS-A quick and dirty usability scale. In *Usability Evaluation in Industry*, Jordan Patrick W, Thomas B, McClelland Ian Lyall, and Weerdmeester Berarnd (Eds.). Taylor & Francis, London, 189–194.

[7] A.J. Bernheim Brush, Bongshin Lee, Ratul Mahajan, Sharad Agarwal, Stefan Saroiu, and Colin Dixon. 2011. Home Automation in the Wild: Challenges and Opportunities. In *Proceedings of the SIGCHI Conference on Human Factors in Computing Systems (CHI '11)*. ACM, New York, NY, USA, 2115–2124. DOI:http://dx.doi.org/10.1145/1978942.1979249

[8] Florian van de Camp, Alexander Schick, and Rainer Stiefelhagen. 2013. How to Click in Mid-Air. In *Distributed, Ambient, and Pervasive Interactions (Lecture Notes in Computer Science)*. Springer, Berlin, Heidelberg, 78–86. DOI: http://dx.doi.org/10.1007/978-3-642-39351-8_9

[9] Marcus Carter, Eduardo Velloso, John Downs, Abigail Sellen, Kenton O'Hara, and Frank Vetere. 2016. PathSync: Multi-User Gestural Interaction with Touchless Rhythmic Path Mimicry. In *Proceedings of the 2016 CHI Conference on Human Factors in Computing Systems (CHI '16)*. ACM, New York, NY, USA, 3415–3427. DOI: http://dx.doi.org/10.1145/2858036.2858284

[10] Christopher Clarke, Alessio Bellino, Augusto Esteves, and Hans Gellersen. 2017. Remote Control by Body Movement in Synchrony with Orbiting Widgets: An Evaluation of TraceMatch. *Proc. ACM Interact. Mob. Wearable Ubiquitous Technol.* 1, 3, Article 45 (Sept. 2017), 22 pages. DOI: http://dx.doi.org/10.1145/3130910

[11] Christopher Clarke, Alessio Bellino, Augusto Esteves>, Eduardo Velloso, and Hans Gellersen. 2016. TraceMatch: A Computer Vision Technique for User Input by Tracing of Animated Controls. In *Proceedings of the 2016 ACM International Joint Conference on Pervasive and Ubiquitous Computing (UbiComp '16)*. ACM, New York, NY, USA, 298–303. DOI: http://dx.doi.org/10.1145/2971648.2971714

[12] Christopher Clarke and Hans Gellersen. 2017. MatchPoint: Spontaneous Spatial Coupling of Body Movement for Touchless Pointing. In *Proceedings of the 30th Annual ACM Symposium on User Interface Software and Technology (UIST '17)*. ACM, New York, NY, USA, 179–192. DOI: http://dx.doi.org/10.1145/3126594.3126626

[13] Travis Cox, Marcus Carter, and Eduardo Velloso. 2016a. Public DisPLAY: Social Games on Interactive Public Screens. In *Proceedings of the 28th Australian Conference on Computer-Human Interaction (OzCHI '16)*. ACM, New York, NY, USA, 371–380. DOI: http://dx.doi.org/10.1145/3010915.3010917

[14] Travis Cox, Marcus Carter, and Eduardo Velloso. 2016b. Public DisPLAY: Social Games on Interactive Public Screens. In *Proceedings of the 28th Australian Conference on Computer-Human Interaction (OzCHI '16)*. ACM, New York, NY, USA, 371–380. DOI: http://dx.doi.org/10.1145/3010915.3010917

[15] Katie Derthick, James Scott, Nicolas Villar, and Christian Winkler. 2013. Exploring Smartphone-based Web User Interfaces for Appliances. In *Proceedings of the 15th International Conference on Human-computer Interaction with Mobile Devices and Services (MobileHCI '13)*. ACM, New York, NY, USA, 227–236. DOI:http://dx.doi.org/10.1145/2493190.2493239

[16] Murtaza Dhuliawala, Juyoung Lee, Junichi Shimizu, Andreas Bulling, Kai Kunze, Thad Starner, and Woontack Woo. 2016. Smooth Eye Movement Interaction Using EOG Glasses. In *Proceedings of the 18th ACM International Conference on Multimodal Interaction (ICMI 2016)*. ACM, New York, NY, USA, 307–311. DOI: http://dx.doi.org/10.1145/2993148.2993181

[17] Paul Dourish. 2001. *Where the Action is: The Foundations of Embodied Interaction*. MIT Press, Cambridge, MA, USA.

[18] Augusto Esteves, Eduardo Velloso, Andreas Bulling, and Hans Gellersen. 2015. Orbits: Gaze Interaction for Smart Watches Using Smooth Pursuit Eye Movements. In *Proceedings of the 28th Annual ACM Symposium on User Interface Software & Technology (UIST '15)*. ACM, New York, NY, USA, 457–466. DOI: http://dx.doi.org/10.1145/2807442.2807499

[19] Augusto Esteves, David Verweij, Liza Suraiya, Rasel Islam, Youryang Lee, and Ian Oakley. 2017. SmoothMoves: Smooth Pursuits Head Movements for Augmented Reality. In *Proceedings of the 30th Annual ACM Symposium on User Interface Software and Technology (UIST '17)*. ACM, New York, NY, USA, 167–178. DOI: http://dx.doi.org/10.1145/3126594.3126616

[20] Jean-Daniel Fekete, Niklas Elmqvist, and Yves Guiard. 2009. Motion-pointing: Target Selection Using Elliptical Motions. In *Proceedings of the SIGCHI Conference on Human Factors in Computing Systems (CHI '09)*. ACM, New York, NY, USA, 289–298. DOI: http://dx.doi.org/10.1145/1518701.1518748

[21] Euan Freeman, Stephen Brewster, and Vuokko Lantz. 2016. Do That, There: An Interaction Technique for Addressing In-Air Gesture Systems. In *Proceedings of the 2016 CHI Conference on Human Factors in Computing Systems (CHI '16)*. ACM, New York, NY, USA, 2319–2331. DOI: http://dx.doi.org/10.1145/2858036.2858308

[22] Euan Freeman, Gareth Griffiths, and Stephen A. Brewster. 2017. Rhythmic Micro-gestures: Discreet Interaction On-the-go. In *Proceedings of the 19th ACM International Conference on Multimodal Interaction (ICMI 2017)*. ACM, New York, NY, USA, 115–119. DOI:http://dx.doi.org/10.1145/3136755.3136815

[23] Franca Garzotto and Matteo Valoriani. 2013. Touchless Gestural Interaction with Small Displays: A Case Study. In *Proceedings of the Biannual Conference of the Italian Chapter of SIGCHI (CHItaly '13)*. ACM, New York, NY, USA, 26:1–26:10. DOI: http://dx.doi.org/10.1145/2499149.2499154

[24] Aakar Gupta, Thomas Pietrzak, Cleon Yau, Nicolas Roussel, and Ravin Balakrishnan. 2017. Summon and Select: Rapid Interaction with Interface Controls in Mid-air. In *Proceedings of the 2017 ACM International Conference on Interactive Surfaces and Spaces (ISS '17)*. ACM, New York, NY, USA, 52–61. DOI: http://dx.doi.org/10.1145/3132272.3134120

[25] Jari Kangas, Oleg Špakov, Poika Isokoski, Deepak Akkil, Jussi Rantala, and Roope Raisamo. 2016. Feedback for Smooth Pursuit Gaze Tracking Based Control. In *Proceedings of the 7th Augmented Human International Conference 2016 (AH '16)*. ACM, New York, NY, USA, Article 6, 8 pages. DOI: http://dx.doi.org/10.1145/2875194.2875209

[26] Frederic Kerber, Philipp Schardt, and Markus Löchtefeld. 2015. WristRotate: A Personalized Motion Gesture Delimiter for Wrist-worn Devices. In *Proceedings of the 14th International Conference on Mobile and Ubiquitous Multimedia (MUM '15)*. ACM, New York, NY, USA, 218–222. DOI: http://dx.doi.org/10.1145/2836041.2836063

[27] Mohamed Khamis, Carl Oechsner, Florian Alt, and Andreas Bulling. 2018. VRpursuits: Interaction in Virtual Reality Using Smooth Pursuit Eye Movements. In *Proceedings of the 2018 International Conference on Advanced Visual Interfaces (AVI '18)*. ACM, New York, NY, USA, 18:1–18:8. DOI: http://dx.doi.org/10.1145/3206505.3206522

[28] Mingyu Liu, Mathieu Nancel, and Daniel Vogel. 2015. Gunslinger: Subtle Arms-down Mid-air Interaction. In *Proceedings of the 28th Annual ACM Symposium on User Interface Software & Technology (UIST '15)*. ACM, New York, NY, USA, 63–71. DOI: http://dx.doi.org/10.1145/2807442.2807489

[29] Thomas Mattusch, Mahsa Mirzamohammad, Mohamed Khamis, Andreas Bulling, and Florian Alt. 2018. Hidden Pursuits: Evaluating Gaze-selection via Pursuits when the Stimuli's Trajectory is Partially Hidden. In *Proceedings of the 2018 ACM Symposium on Eye Tracking Research & Applications (ETRA '18)*. ACM, New York, NY, USA, 27:1–27:5. DOI: http://dx.doi.org/10.1145/3204493.3204569

[30] Tara Mullaney, Björn Yttergren, and Erik Stolterman. 2013. Positional Acts: Using a Kinect™ Sensor to Reconfigure Patient Roles Within Radiotherapy Treatment. In *Proceedings of the 8th International Conference on Tangible, Embedded and Embodied Interaction (TEI '14)*. ACM, New York, USA, 93–96. DOI:http://dx.doi.org/10.1145/2540930.2540943

[31] Ville Mäkelä, Tomi Heimonen, and Markku Turunen. 2014. Magnetic Cursor: Improving Target Selection in Freehand Pointing Interfaces. In *Proceedings of The International Symposium on Pervasive Displays (PerDis '14)*. ACM, New York, NY, USA, 112:112–112:117. DOI:http://dx.doi.org/10.1145/2611009.2611025

[32] Donald A. Norman and Jakob Nielsen. 2010. Gestural Interfaces: A Step Backward in Usability. *Interactions* 17, 5 (Sept. 2010), 46–49. DOI: http://dx.doi.org/10.1145/1836216.1836228

[33] Kenton O'hara, Richard Harper, Helena Mentis, Abigail Sellen, and Alex Taylor. 2013. On the Naturalness of Touchless: Putting the "Interaction" Back into NUI. *ACM Trans. Comput.-Hum. Interact.* 20, 1 (April 2013), 5:1–5:25. DOI: http://dx.doi.org/10.1145/2442106.2442111

[34] Derya Ozcelik Buskermolen and Jacques Terken. 2012. Co-constructing Stories: A Participatory Design Technique to Elicit In-depth User Feedback and Suggestions About Design Concepts. In *Proceedings of the 12th Participatory Design Conference: Exploratory Papers, Workshop Descriptions, Industry Cases - Volume 2 (PDC '12)*. ACM, New York, NY, USA, 33–36. DOI: http://dx.doi.org/10.1145/2348144.2348156

[35] Ken Pfeuffer, Melodie Vidal, Jayson Turner, Andreas Bulling, and Hans Gellersen. 2013. Pursuit Calibration: Making Gaze Calibration Less Tedious and More Flexible. In *Proceedings of the 26th Annual ACM Symposium on User Interface Software and Technology (UIST '13)*. ACM, New York, NY, USA, 261–270. DOI: http://dx.doi.org/10.1145/2501988.2501998

[36] Philips. 2017. Wireless and smart lighting. (2017). Retrieved 2017-09-13 from http://www2.meethue.com/en-us

[37] T. Piumsomboon, G. Lee, R. W. Lindeman, and M. Billinghurst. 2017. Exploring natural eye-gaze-based interaction for immersive virtual reality. In *2017 IEEE Symposium on 3D User Interfaces (3DUI)*. 36–39. DOI: http://dx.doi.org/10.1109/3DUI.2017.7893315

[38] Processing. 2017. Processing.org. (2017). Retrieved 2018-05-17 from https://www.processing.org/

[39] Gabriel Reyes, Jason Wu, Nikita Juneja, Maxim Goldshtein, W. Keith Edwards, Gregory D. Abowd, and Thad Starner. 2018. SynchroWatch: One-Handed Synchronous Smartwatch Gestures Using Correlation and Magnetic Sensing. *Proc. ACM Interact. Mob. Wearable Ubiquitous Technol.* 1, 4 (Jan. 2018), 158:1–158:26. DOI:http://dx.doi.org/10.1145/3161162

[40] Lawrence Sambrooks and Brett Wilkinson. 2013. Comparison of Gestural, Touch, and Mouse Interaction with Fitts' Law. In *Proceedings of the 25th Australian Computer-Human Interaction Conference: Augmentation, Application, Innovation, Collaboration (OzCHI '13)*. ACM, New York, NY, USA, 119–122. DOI:http://dx.doi.org/10.1145/2541016.2541066

[41] Jeff Sauro. 2011. *A Practical Guide to the System Usability Scale: Background, Benchmarks & Best Practices*. CreateSpace Independent Publishing Platform.

[42] John. V. Seidel. 1998. Qualitative Data Analysis. In *The Ethnograph v5.0: A Users Guide, Appendix E*. Colorado: Qualis Research, Colorado Springs. www.qualisresearch.com

[43] Toby Sharp, Cem Keskin, Duncan Robertson, Jonathan Taylor, Jamie Shotton, David Kim, Christoph Rhemann, Ido Leichter, Alon Vinnikov, Yichen Wei, Daniel Freedman, Pushmeet Kohli, Eyal Krupka, Andrew Fitzgibbon, and Shahram Izadi. 2015. Accurate, Robust, and Flexible Real-time Hand Tracking. In *Proceedings of the 33rd Annual ACM Conference on Human Factors in Computing Systems (CHI '15)*. ACM, New York, NY, USA, 3633–3642. DOI: http://dx.doi.org/10.1145/2702123.2702179

[44] Jamie Shotton, Toby Sharp, Alex Kipman, Andrew Fitzgibbon, Mark Finocchio, Andrew Blake, Mat Cook, and Richard Moore. 2013. Real-time Human Pose Recognition in Parts from Single Depth Images. *Commun. ACM* 56, 1 (Jan. 2013), 116–124. DOI: http://dx.doi.org/10.1145/2398356.2398381

[45] Radu-Daniel Vatavu and Ionut-Alexandru Zaiti. 2014. Leap Gestures for TV: Insights from an Elicitation Study. In *Proceedings of the 2014 ACM International Conference on Interactive Experiences for TV and Online Video (TVX '14)*. ACM, New York, NY, USA, 131–138. DOI: http://dx.doi.org/10.1145/2602299.2602316

[46] Eduardo Velloso, Marcus Carter, Joshua Newn, Augusto Esteves, Christopher Clarke, and Hans Gellersen. 2017. Motion Correlation: Selecting Objects by Matching Their Movement. *ACM Trans. Comput.-Hum. Interact.* 24, 3 (April 2017), 22:1–22:35. DOI: http://dx.doi.org/10.1145/3064937

[47] Eduardo Velloso, Flavio Luiz Coutinho, Andrew Kurauchi, and Carlos H Morimoto. 2018. Circular Orbits Detection for Gaze Interaction Using 2D Correlation and Profile Matching Algorithms. In *Proceedings of the 2018 ACM Symposium on Eye Tracking Research & Applications (ETRA '18)*. ACM, New York, NY, USA, 25:1–25:9. DOI: http://dx.doi.org/10.1145/3204493.3204524

[48] Eduardo Velloso, Markus Wirth, Christian Weichel, Augusto Esteves, and Hans Gellersen. 2016. AmbiGaze: Direct Control of Ambient Devices by Gaze. In *Proceedings of the 2016 ACM Conference on Designing Interactive Systems (DIS '16)*. ACM, New York, NY, USA, 812–817. DOI: http://dx.doi.org/10.1145/2901790.2901867

[49] David Verweij, Augusto Esteves, Saskia Bakker, and Khan Vassilis-Javed. 2018. davidverweij/motionmatching: TEI 2019 Release. (Nov. 2018). DOI:http://dx.doi.org/10.5281/zenodo.1490719

[50] David Verweij, Augusto Esteves, Vassilis Javed Khan, and Saskia Bakker. 2017a. WaveTrace: Motion Matching Input using Wrist-Worn Motion Sensors. In *CHI '17 Extended Abstracts on Human Factors in Computing Systems (CHI EA '17)*. ACM, Denver, CO, USA. DOI:http://dx.doi.org/10.1145/3027063.3053161

[51] David Verweij, Vassilis-Javed Khan, Augusto Esteves, and Saskia Bakker. 2017b. Multi-User Motion Matching Interaction for Interactive Television Using Smartwatches. In *Adjunct Publication of the 2017 ACM International Conference on Interactive Experiences for TV and Online Video (TVX '17 Adjunct)*. ACM, New York, NY, USA, 67–68. DOI: http://dx.doi.org/10.1145/3084289.3089906

[52] Mélodie Vidal, Andreas Bulling, and Hans Gellersen. 2013. Pursuits: Spontaneous Interaction with Displays Based on Smooth Pursuit Eye Movement and Moving Targets. In *Proceedings of the 2013 ACM International Joint Conference on Pervasive and Ubiquitous Computing (UbiComp '13)*. ACM, New York, NY, USA, 439–448. DOI: http://dx.doi.org/10.1145/2493432.2493477

[53] Daniel Vogel and Ravin Balakrishnan. 2004. Interactive Public Ambient Displays: Transitioning from Implicit to Explicit, Public to Personal, Interaction with Multiple Users. In *Proceedings of the 17th Annual ACM Symposium on User Interface Software and Technology (UIST '04)*. ACM, New York, NY, USA, 137–146. DOI: http://dx.doi.org/10.1145/1029632.1029656

[54] Daniel Vogel and Ravin Balakrishnan. 2005. Distant Freehand Pointing and Clicking on Very Large, High Resolution Displays. In *Proceedings of the 18th Annual ACM Symposium on User Interface Software and Technology (UIST '05)*. ACM, New York, NY, USA, 33–42. DOI:http://dx.doi.org/10.1145/1095034.1095041

[55] John Williamson and Roderick Murray-Smith. 2004. Pointing Without a Pointer. In *CHI '04 Extended Abstracts on Human Factors in Computing Systems (CHI EA '04)*. ACM, New York, NY, USA, 1407–1410. DOI:http://dx.doi.org/10.1145/985921.986076

[56] Gottfried Zimmermann, Gregg Vanderheiden, and Al Gilman. 2002. Prototype Implementations for a Universal Remote Console Specification. In *CHI '02 Extended Abstracts on Human Factors in Computing Systems (CHI EA '02)*. ACM, New York, NY, USA, 510–511. DOI: http://dx.doi.org/10.1145/506443.506454

# A Conversation with Actuators: An Exploratory Design Environment for Hybrid Materials

**Cesar Torres, Molly Jane Nicholas, Sangyeon Lee, Eric Paulos**
Electrical Engineering and Computer Sciences
University of California, Berkeley
[cearto, molecule, sangyeon, paulos]@berkeley.edu

## ABSTRACT
An exciting, expanding palette of hybrid materials is emerging that can be programmed to actuate by a range of external and internal stimuli. However, there exists a dichotomy between the physicality of the actuators and the intangible computational signal that is used to program them. For material practitioners, this lack of physical cues limits their ability to engage in a "conversation with materials" (CwM). This paper presents a creative workstation for supporting this epistemological style by bringing a stronger physicality to the computational signal and balance the conversation between physical and digital actors. The station utilizes a streaming architecture to distribute control across multiple devices and leverage the rich spatial cognition that a physical space affords. Through a formal user study, we characterize the actuation design practice supported by the CwM workstation and discuss opportunities for tangible interfaces to hybrid materials.

## CCS Concepts
•**Human-centered computing → Interactive systems and tools;** *Systems and tools for interaction design;*

## Author Keywords
Creativity support tools; Computational design; New Media

## INTRODUCTION
The studio, the atelier, the kitchen, the laboratory, and the makerspace are sites of creative expression. Their physical layout reflects the identity of their creators, bearing a mark of the process and creativity of the maker, of how they think, how they work, and how they move their body. In these spaces, the role of computational design is emerging as a prominent element, yet its ability to adapt to physical workflows is limited.

For many creative practitioners, a computer in the workspace acts as an anchor [26], confining the body and mind from leveraging the rich spatial cognition that a physical space affords. Systems that incorporate digital elements in a physical space are inherently brittle [9], affecting their reliability and


*TEI'19*, March 17–20, 2019, Tempe, AZ, USA

ACM ISBN 978-1-4503-6196-5/19/03.
https://doi.org/10.1145/3294109.3295643

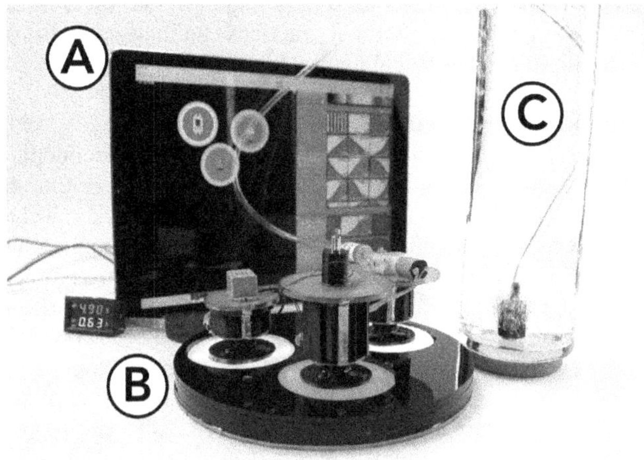


**Figure 1. Conversation with Actuators Workstation. a) A digital design tool is used to both simulate, track, and stream data signals to a physical workstation; b) a physical workstation provides high-current power and digital control to ready-made capacitive touch-enabled stages; c) each stage supports interfaces to external materials.**

ultimately their use. Particularly frustrating for practitioners is how little physical skills and material knowledge transfers compared to the computational know-how needed to navigate the computational design space.

*How might a creative environment allow practitioners to work with and experience computation in the same way they fluidly work with physical materials?* To explore this digital-physical boundary, we designed a hybrid workstation that facilitates working with actuators[1] controlled by a *digital* signal to produce *physical* changes in the environment via light, heat, motion, vibration, or pressure. The workstation is designed to support a thinking and working style common within physical practices known as a conversation with materials (CwM) [44]. The experience is characterized by materials taking on "a mind of their own," resisting or cooperating with the attempts of the practitioner to form them in a fashion that resembles understanding, persuading, and responding [11, 41]. However, for hybrid materials like actuators there exists a dichotomy between the physicality of the actuators and the intangible computational signal that is used to program them.

Our work aims to understand how design tools for hybrid materials can balance the conversation between physical and

[1] Actuation more precisely refers to physical motion; we use this term to refer to the range of possible physical outputs.

digital actors. In this paper, we first ground our discussion of a "conversation with materials" through an exemplar and motivate a set of design principles for facilitating a *conversation with actuators*. Through a formal analysis, we distill the conversational profile of actuators, identifying five material actors, both digital and physical. We then describe a workstation that foregrounds these actors and enables users to send digital signals to actuators through touch interactions. Lastly, we present the results of a formal user study and characterize the actuation design practice supported by the workstation.

## RELATED WORK

We review work in design theory and systems research that explores how computational practices can facilitate working with digital and physical materials.

### Supporting Material Practices

A large body of work derives from Schön's concept of reflection-in-action, an act of thinking and reflecting on action so as to influence future action [44]. This back and forth between designer and medium elicits a conversational relationship [53]. Many creativity support tools have been developed to foreground this conversation. To enable interactive device design development, d.tools [14] aligned its workflow with the design, test, and analysis of a reflective prototyping cycle. The conversation metaphor has also been explored explicitly as a dialog where an agent (a digital screen with a talking face) elicits reflection in the course of a design session [20]. More implicitly, artifacts that incorporate "slow technology"(e.g., [35, 34]) more naturally influence reflective behaviors.

Within HCI, discussions of materiality have grown from advances in physical computing and material science innovations [39]. Giaccardi and Karana [12] introduced a framework for articulating how materials participate in the making process, identifying four experiential levels: sensorial, interpretive, affective, and performative. Schilling et al. proposed discriminating the focus and attention of materials actors over time as a method of characterizing the "talk-back" that occurs during a creative session [42]. Our work builds on this discussion through the design of a physical system that gives a stronger physicality to digital actors.

### Supporting Working with Hybrid Materials

Smart and hybrid materials have expanded the landscape of creative artifacts and experiences, yet their co-existence with digital and physical ways of making produce several tensions. As new materials emerge within existing practices, Nitsche [33] observed the necessity of building on the material basis of the particular craft and rooting interaction in the complex interplay of materials. Vallgårda and Redström [51] advocated for the notion of computational elements as containing many of the same characteristics as physical materials such as substance, structure, and surface. Extending the concept of a computational composite, Liu et al. [28] describes smart materials having the ability to "[alter] a passive, static conversation into an active, sensorial interaction." Early work in hybrid craft introduced the idea of "conduits" or devices for transferring programs to physical media (such as a wand that transfers behaviors to objects) to facilitate interactions with hybrid media [4]. Such conduits are explored as a form of material programming with physical tools [50]. Digital materials complicate a conversation with materials, lacking a rich sensorial interaction that is central to a conversation with materials. Our work extends existing actuation design practices to interface with a wider range of materials, externalizing these 'conduits' as infrastructural, tangible elements in a creative space designed to facilitate the unique concerns of both physical and digital formal elements.

### Exploratory Environments and Actuation Design

Digital signal design has been a successful area supporting a variety of users and domains such as new media practitioners and flow-based programming (e.g. Max/MSP [38]), nonprogrammers and graphical simulations (e.g. LabVIEW [52]), or with children and tangible program-by-example (e.g. Topobo [40]). Other computational design practices leverage sketch-based interactions: Schneider et al. [43] demonstrate the additional flexibility of encoding actuation behaviors for vibration with spatially-aware vector representations. Sketch-based annotations have been further used to define how graphical elements move in virtual space, exposing time and space as formal variables within animation [22, 23], and encode optimized geometries for light displays [47] and mechanical linkage systems [24]. Similarly, firework [2] or Christmas light [1] displays encode the repertoire of the practice, incorporating mechanisms for choreographing control across multiple actors. Our work builds on these practices, introducing a decentralized streaming architecture that allows different devices to control and compose digital signals and make use of the spatial cognition afforded by physical, creative spaces.

## CWM DESIGN PRINCIPLES

To better ground our discussion of what facilitates a Conversation with Materials, we draw on the exemplar of clay situated within a ceramics studio and contrast it against actuators in an electronics design practice.

### 1. Expose a rich, responsive conversational profile

Clay exhibits multiple methods of conversing; as a physical material, clay can readily "talk back" through its sensorial profile. For example, to communicate its workability, clay redundantly communicates through a variety of sensory channels: visually, it displays its wetness and dryness; haptically, it responds to interactions with hands and tools; olfactorily, clay particles become suspended in the air. Even an awareness of the time spent in open air guides how ceramicist structure their creative process. As part of a long tradition, clay can converse symbolically through the cultural significance of its origin, or self-referentially through engagement with a set of methods, motifs, or artifacts within a particular practice. The sensorial interaction that clay exposes informs creative process.

Actuators have their own sensorial profile. While the rote capabilities of an actuator such as a motor are well-understood, working directly and actively with a motor exposes not only the motion it generates, but the sound and vibration it produces, the range of its speed, the extent of its torque on other objects, its presence in an environment, and the limits of its ability to transduce an electrical stimulus. However, the effort needed

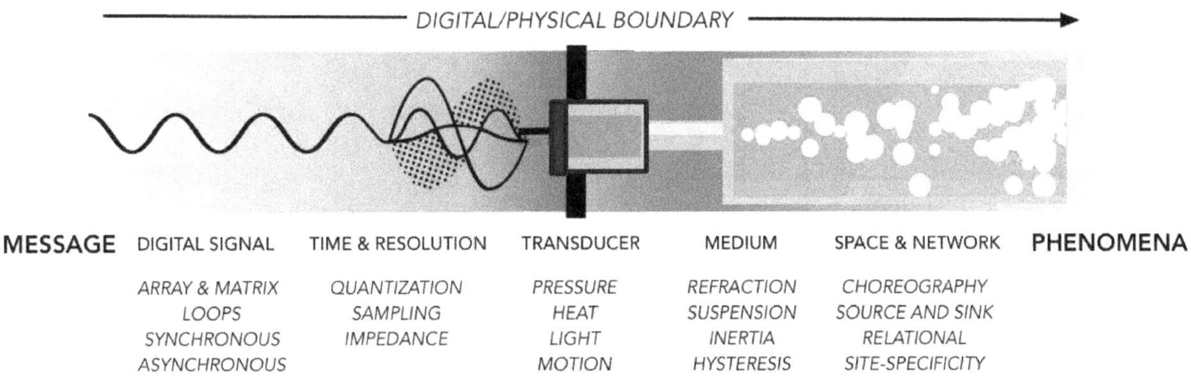


**Figure 2. Formal elements of a bubble display. Sampling a sine wave function forms a digital signal, which is stored as an integer and converted to an analog signal. The electrical signal is transported through a wire, distorting and acquiring noise. While the air pump is off, water fills the tube connecting it to a tank. This exerts an extra torque on the motor, increasing its internal resistance, and drawing more current. The signal is transduced, changing the internal air pressure and driving air through the water medium. The hysteresis of the medium causes the periodicity of the original sine wave to converge, forming groups of bubbles, propagating down the length of the tube, driven by buoyancy forces to escape towards its outlet, forming the final experienced phenomena.**

to appropriately house, power, and program actuators limits this type of conversational interaction [13].

*A CWM experience should communicate state and affordance, across both physical and digital materialities, through responsive multimodal interactions. Formal elements should be readily interpretable as creative agents.*

### 2. Support a constructionist learning experience

The ceramics studio facilitates a conversation through the versatility and ubiquity of the clay form — clay can exist in a variety of form factors (e.g., slips, slabs, coils), allowing for a body of techniques and methods to develop around a formfactor. Slip-casting, a technique where a liquid clay body is poured into a mold and allowed to set to and form a shell, is transferable across many material practices (e.g., chocolatiering, silicone molding). Instruction in such a space is fundamentally constructionist, where the ability to converse is developed through exploration, practice, and exposure to materials. The ceramics studio facilitates a conversation with clay wherein mistakes and accidents can be reconstituted and reclaimed using a pugmill and clay mixer, reducing the economic and emotional costs of engaging in a conversation [48].

In physical computing environments, the conversation is relatively expensive. Support for physical debugging is particularly limited [5], with more critical errors occurring across digital to physical translation. Programming is additionally complicated by the time-consuming need to flash code to microcontrollers, limiting exploratory behaviors in favor of attaining a minimal viable product.

*CWM environments should minimize the cost of exploration and allow the user to extract meaningful information or knowledge at any point during the workflow.*

### 3. Degrading gracefully

In concert with the vision of ubiquitous computing for computation to recede into the background, cyber-physical systems still require maintenance and repair. Relying too heavily on centralized systems introduces significant risk should they breakdown. A single loose wire should not break the entire interaction, nor should it disrupt a workflow. In a ceramics studio, a pottery wheel may break down, but it does not restrict the ability to continue using other clay-forming techniques.

*Systems in creative spaces need to communicate their seams [6] and be designed to degrade gracefully, maintaining some level of functionality at all times in the case that different components become unstable.*

## CONVERSATIONAL PROFILE OF ACTUATORS

To identify the conversational profile of actuators, we conducted a formal analysis [32, 3] to distill how form-giving elements are "arranged and function within a composition"(Figure 2). We specifically delineate the different established traditions and practices that influence each of these formal elements within New Media, art practice, interaction design, and HCI communities. We limit the analysis to actuation that is produced from a digital signal and reserve the much larger space of analog signal design and actuator-sensor design as an area of future exploration. Depicted in Figure 2, we present these formal elements in a linear order, beginning with the message, or concept, progressing through its evolution as a signal, and ending with the phenomena produced.

### SIGNAL

The digital signal is commonly expressed as a time-value pair, encoded as an array. The array as a digital material affords certain manipulations such as in-order atomic traversals, affine transformations, and interpolation. These manipulations produce unique artifacts to the signal constituting a characteristic digital aesthetic [15, 29, 51], namely: *atomicity*, that activations of the material occur with binary precision; *resolution*, or the error that arises from discretization and quantization during analog/digital signal conversion; *random-access*, also *indexability*, or the ability to access information without temporal or spatial restrictions; and *structural artifacts*, or the data structure present in the physical materialization of the digital material such as the pixel. Working with digital materials lowers risk, instead prioritizing interactions that reuse and repeat [29] as well as fragment and recombine [15].

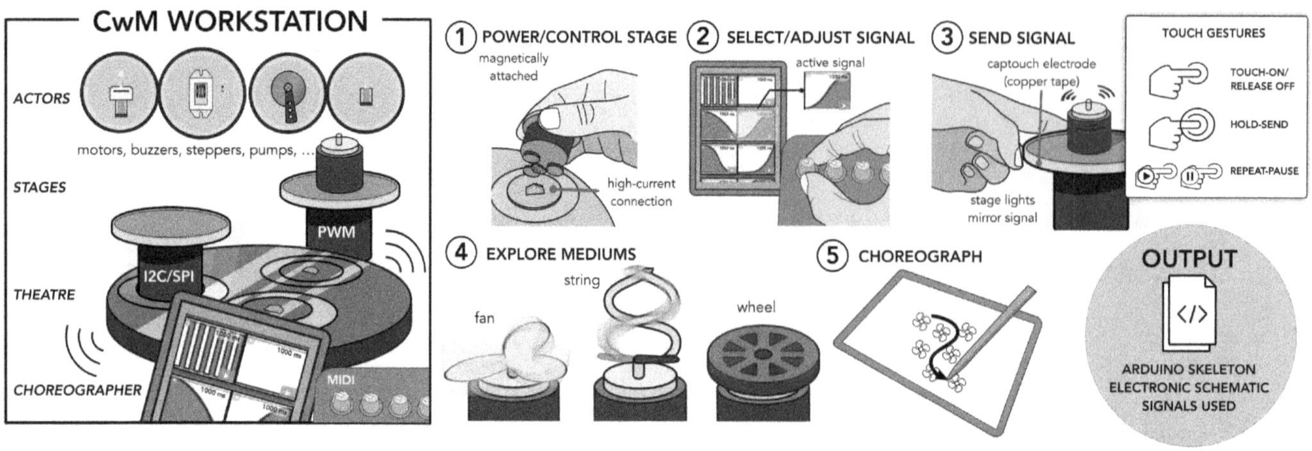


**Figure 3. A Conversation with Actuators. A physical workstations uses stages to interface with actuators. These stages dock to a central power station which exposes a websocket API for communicating with and controlling signals sent to actuators. 1) Embedded magnets allow for quick attachment to a high-current power source; 2) different devices can be used to select and adjust a signal; 3) a capacitive electrode is wrapped around the stage and senses touch events; these events trigger the active signal to be expressed by the stage. An LED ring under each stage mirrors the signal being sent to the actuator; 4) stages provide interfaces to external materials to gauge the characteristics of actuation; 5) a live representation of the scene is used to specify how a signal is sent to multiple actuators. Design files can be obtained at any point in the process.**

### TIME & RESOLUTION

As a signal travels through a transport layer (e.g., wire, open air), its resolution and period mediate how it arrives at the transducer. Time and resolution can affect the original signal through sampling error: signals may degrade and quantize from undersampling, fold from sampling at the Nyquist frequency, or exist in an anti-aliased form. While many systems remove noise and sampling artifacts, the incongruency between bandwidth and temporal resolution is a defining characteristic of early and current digital material practices that has given rise to several expressive and culturally significant media forms such as the pixel [16], the "8-bit aesthetic" [7] (e.g. chiptunes [21], bitmap art), and the glitch [31, 19].

### TRANSDUCER

A transducer sits on the digital/physical interface and can be used to refer to sensors or actuators. For actuators, a transducing element converts an electrical signal into light, heat, smell, sound, pressure, or motion. Each transducer has a unique conversational profile characterized by its physical and mechanical profile (e.g., response times). Within interaction design, these different profiles are leveraged to communicate information in the cognitive background (see ambientROOM [18]). Within each modality, a domain-specific vocabulary of behaviors exists, each with a narrow bandwidth of communication.

### PHYSICAL MEDIUM

The transduced physical stimulus is attenuated through an additional physical layer which we refer to as the medium. Various principles exist for expanding the legibility of the physical stimulus. Most prominent is the concept of "the medium is the message", a term popularized by McLuhan [30] used to describe how the content to be displayed (the message or signal) is inextricably tied, influenced, and altered by the medium that is used to transmit it. For heat, the thermal properties of materials define how heat is experienced over time. For light, reflectors and diffusers affect its presentation. For motion, linkages, gears, and other mechanical mechanisms can be used to amplify and redirect motion.

### SPACE & NETWORK

Actuators exist within a certain space and communication network. Spatial relationships can defined both physically and virtually (e.g. the range of a wireless network) causing actuators to form relationships and cliques. Work in HCI [23, 16] and New Media [46, 49, 25] has explored interactions that arise from these spatiotemporal relationships. Similarly, the context of the space can be leveraged to further alter the message, enabling distributed behaviors and control for constructing large collective displays [45, 10, 8, 27], or as site-specific constructions (e.g. urban street lighting [36]).

## SYSTEM DESIGN

In this section, we present a high-level overview of system components, annotate the design decisions that facilitate the conversational profile of actuators, and provide some implementation details. The workstation is designed as a piece of infrastructural equipment, similar to an oscilloscope, that is maintained and used within a communal space[2]. Figure 3 depicts the workstation and a typical interaction with the station, comprised of three elements:

- **THEATRE** - a central docking station exposes a common set of connections for ID, high-current power, a pair of GPIO pins, and a capacitive touch electrode. Each docking site is surrounded by a ring of smart LEDs, or *stage lights*, used to communicate system state. An application programming interface (API) exposes points to query or alter the theatre state via websockets.
- **STAGES** - modular, peripheral components magnetically attach to the theatre. The role of the stages is to house, showcase, and facilitate the exploration of the unique properties and design concerns of an actuator.
- **CHOREOGRAPHERS** - interfaces that facilitate communication between actuators connected to the theatre and the user. Choreographers were implemented as a web application and as a physical MIDI controller.

[2]The station design has been made available open source: `https://github.com/Hybrid-Ecologies/a-conversation-with-actuators`.

### Design Decisions

We examined how the workstation could increase the visibility and expose handles for creative control for each actor in an actuator's conversational profile (Fig 2).

Since the qualities of the **SIGNAL** are strongly tied to a synchronous programming workflow, we chose to allow users to issue actuation commands asynchronously through a streaming architecture. Asynchronous communication allows for multiple devices to act as signal generators; additionally, it prevents blocking code. For instance, commands for a stepper motor and an LED are interleaved, allowing both actuators to be controlled at the same time. We leverage the streaming architecture to generate and manipulate signal through different devices (Arduino, MIDI controllers, web applications). A MIDI knob, for example, could control the position of a stepper motor. With multiple devices capable of controlling actuation, communication is not delegated to a central point source but instead distributed throughout a space.

Once the signal is transmitted, it is susceptible to **TIME & RESOLUTION** and altered by the properties of the **TRANSDUCER**. For example, sending a sine wave to a motor produces an altered representation from both hysteresis and inertia. Since LEDs are the least susceptible to these actors, we use them to present a more faithful representation of an undistorted signal. Any signal sent to a stage is mirrored in the corresponding stage lights. A user can then compare the undistorted signal against the actuation expressed, exposing both noise and sampling artifacts as well as a transducer's profile.

The stages were designed to house actuators and facilitate interactions with different **MEDIUMS**. For example, a **LIGHT STAGE** would house LEDs in a recessed reflective cavity. A collection of interchangeable diffusing materials could then be used to explore different light textures. A **VIBRATION STAGE** would provide a collection of sound dampening or attenuating materials. A **PNEUMATICS STAGE** would provide connectors, valves, and air tubes to interface with balloons, water, and other mediums. The types of stages in the makerspace would reflect the unique repertoire of actuators that are available; the expertise of the community could additionally be reflected in the collection of exploratory mediums.

As opposed to designing actuation in isolation, the choreographer provides a user more nuanced control over how a group of actuators within a **SPACE & NETWORK** interact with each other. The choreographer allows users to specify a high-order behavior (e.g. turn on from left to right) by drawing a vector path. Actuators are then ordered based on their projection onto the vector and sent a signal in turn. For a circular LED ring, a zig-zagging path would cause a interlaced LED behavior to be expressed (Figure 4).

## SYSTEM ARCHITECTURE

**Theatre Dock.** Actuators require more current than most microcontrollers can supply; a transistor or relay connected to an external power supply is typically used to supply the requisite current. In this configuration, the microcontroller serves only to supply low-current logic to trigger transistors or relays to activate and drive high-current actuators.

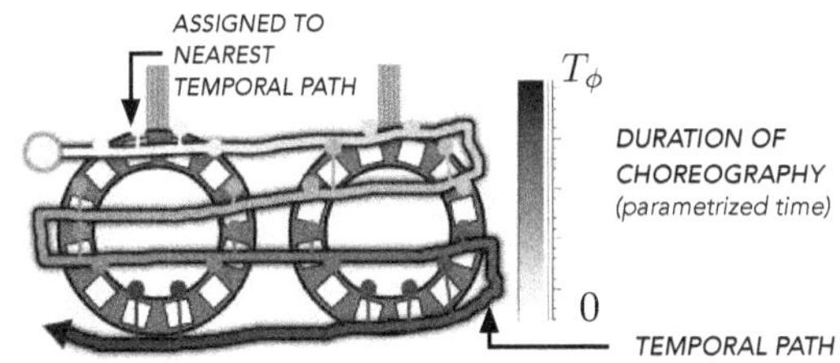


**Figure 4. Choreographed signals. Drawn arrows are used to specify when an actuator receives a signal over a period of time.**

The electrical design for the CWM workstation follows this pattern (Figure 5): an Arduino (atmega32) microcontroller is used to generate a logic-level signal which is amplified using n-channel "low-side" MOSFET transistors (P30N06LE) connected to an external high-current power source. Although an Arduino can produce PWM signal, we connect an external 12-bit PWM driver board (PCA9685) to the I2C bus, freeing up microcontroller timers and processing to instead be delegated to processing serial communication.

The theatre was constructed from a custom two-layer PCB designed to route control and power to all components. The theatre served as a breakout board to then be connected to a form factor for housing stages. Sets of six pins were exposed through the theatre: a high-current PWM signal, a common ground, two general purpose input/output (GPIO) pins, an ID pin specified through a unique voltage divider circuit, and an electrode routed from a capacitive touch controller (MPR121).

**Theatre API.** The theatre implemented an event listener for dock changes (when a stage is moved in or out of a docking site) and capacitive touch changes (touch and release); it additionally exposed API points for changing the PWM frequency being sent to each dock, and changing the color and intensity of the dock LEDs. Our system processed bi-directional `UART` serial information from peripherals coordinated through a middleware server (`Ruby EventMachine`) accessible via websockets. The input and output streams of devices were exposed to applications as subscribable services.

To introduce this functionality to off-the-shelf Arduino devices, we supply a library that provides streaming functionality without interfering with programming logic, minimizing the footprint of incorporating this architecture into current physical computing practices. With the addition of a Bluetooth Serial interface (e.g., HC-06, JY-MCU), the system additionally supports mobile interactions.

**Stages.** Stages are held to the theatre dock magnetically (Figure 5). A 3D printed enclosure holds a custom PCB, 6 pogo pins and 3 neodymium magnets that pair with a symmetric configuration on the theatre board. The PCB is configurable to match the needs of a specific actuator. In its simplest form, the PCB exposes only the load power and ground pins, allowing current-driven devices (e.g., piezos, motors, LEDs, buzzers) to be connected to the system. Alternatively, the two GPIO pins can be used to communicate via an I2C or SPI protocol. Each stage has a touch-enabled surface enabled by wrapping copper tape along the edge of the stage and connecting it to the capacitive touch electrode.

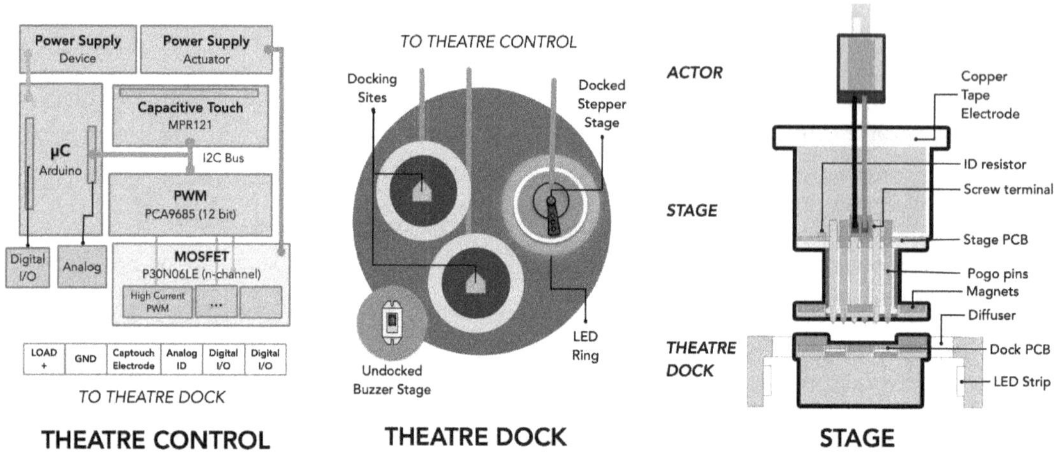


**Figure 5. System architecture. The theatre control board exposes a common set of electrical connections for digital control, high-current power, and capacitive touch. A PWM signal generator is used to trigger high-current gates. These connections are routed to a docking station where stages are magnetically held in place. Six pogo pins in the stage route electrical connections to the facilitate the unique needs of a target actuator.**

The stage can be configured in one of four touch interaction modes. A *tap-on* mode would send a high signal on touch and a low signal on release; should the system be reduced to only the theatre/stage, the CwM station would assume this mode allowing for its continued use degrading gracefully. A *hold-send* mode would send the active signal only when a stage was being pressed required users to actively touch and perceive the stimulus coming from the actuator.

**Choreographer Web App.** A web application running on an iPad was used to select, compose, and adjust data signals sent to a target actuator (Figure 3-2). The application subscribes to TheatreEvents via a websocket and keeps a live, updated representation of the elements connected to the theatre, presenting it visually through an SVG representation. Data signals are presented as manipulable visual blocks that are sortable and composable along a time track, following the visual metaphor and direct manipulation interactions common within video editing and sound composition design tools. The data signal is internally represented as a sequence of commands $\tau = \langle t, I \rangle$ where $t$ is the desired time (ms) of execution and $I$ is intensity. Externally, the blocks can be configured to display the signal as a line graph, as a hue, or as a position. These signal blocks could be composed through track operations (Figure 6) including concatenation and separation (**WELD**, **CUT**) or transformations (**REFLECT**). We include an initial sampling of common signals (on, off, pulse), and a series of common easing signals (e.g. linear, cubic) used in motion design.

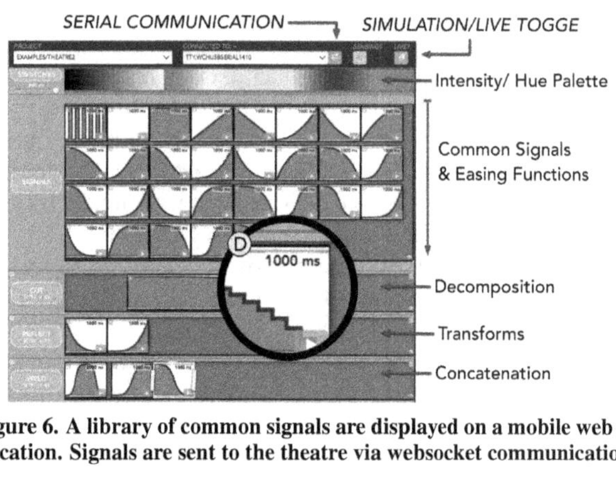


**Figure 6. A library of common signals are displayed on a mobile web application. Signals are sent to the theatre via websocket communication.**

**Choreographer-MIDI Controller.** A MIDI controller with 8 touchpads, each with 2 associated knob controllers, is connected to the theatre via a websocket. It coordinates with the web application to allow users to delegate a pad to store and playback a specific signal. Knobs were used to control playback position and signal duration.

## EVALUATION

The goal of our user study was to understand how foregrounding digital and physical actors alters the design decisions taken by practitioners. We survey the current repertoire of actuation design practices, evaluate the usability of the system, and describe the material conversations that occurred with the system.

*Participants.* The study was conducted with 18 novice interactive device designers (avg. 22 years, 8 female, 10 male, 0 nonbinary) with previous exposure to electronics recruited from university mailing lists in Art, Architecture, Design, and Computer Science. Proficiency was self-reported in a preliminary survey; all participants indicated experience working with actuators.

*Study design.* Participants were invited to meet with us in our studio space for an hour-long workshop and paid $20/hr. Each session surveyed participants on personal actuation design practices; a warm-up tutorial; a think-out-loud with a series of exploratory design tasks; and a post-study interview. Participants engage with the system in one of two configurations:

- *Multimodal.* Participants were exposed to three stages containing a buzzer, a vibrotactile motor, and an air pump connected to an airstone submerged in water; participants were tasked with brainstorming designs that incorporated any of these elements.
- *Multi-actor.* Participants were exposed to a non-matrix 25 RGB LED display and asked to design an ambient display for a high-energy location (e.g., parade, hospital ER, nightclub) or a low-energy location (e.g., park, beach).

## RESULTS

We report survey responses and qualitative results from participant interactions with the workstation and interview responses. We synthesize common themes and insights to support the design of future tangible interfaces for hybrid materials.

### Survey Results: Complexity drives opportunistic actions

In our initial survey, participants reported experience with a variety of interactive devices including RC cars, art installations, lighting displays, and robotics. Actuators were used for their rote purpose, as a spectacle element, or for communicating information. Software complexity was the chief deciding factor that influenced decisions on how actuation was used in personal projects. All participants reported major challenges with the Arduino programming experience. While it had helped them enter the physical computing space, the perceived time requirements to develop more complex actuator behaviors was prohibitive, and most users left even functional actuator design to the very end:

> **P5** With software, you have to put enough time to understand what you're doing, and I just don't have time. But I don't want to just take code from StackOverflow because it feels like cheating.

Actuators used as system state indicators were often directly mapped to sensor values to minimize complexity; legibility remained a common issue.

### Experiential encounters drive conversations

Each participant explored the station differently, guided by the most salient material actor. For the multimodal task, a majority of participants gravitated towards the unique sound that each actuator produced. Participants attributed proclivity to their perception of the capacitive touch interaction as that of a DJ, reinforced by the use of a MIDI controller commonly used in such performances. Other participants were drawn to the signal design interface, finding familiarity in the waveforms, specifically recalling and attempting to emulate the common yet evocative fade-and-pulse behavior.

Others were captured by the unfamiliarity of the air pump, attempting to decipher the blackbox around the transducer mechanism or the strangeness of an open bottle of water next to electronics. Few participants could interpret the nature of an actuator by sight, but all participants had encountered them before and could immediately recognize them through their expressions.

### Conversations elicit memory and evocation

Many participants were uncomfortable sending signals to the buzzer, initially avoiding it completely. However, its unique semiotic association to alarm clocks made it an evocative stimulus. As participants experimented with other actuators, it built familiarity and confidence to test the signals with the buzzer.

> **P12** Oh! [touching and startled by the buzzer] This... this is the sound of a toy train my grandpa used to have. And people would drop it because they were startled.

The responsive feedback from the system drove participants to create noises, searching for and responding to sounds that evoked laughter or a memory, speculating on which touch-triggered sound to incorporate in personal projects that would otherwise remain static.

### Immediacy of feedback builds reliability

Exposing the capabilities of the actuators drove exploration. Overall, participants considered the CwM station to be characterized most strongly by the immediacy of feedback from touch, by the lights, or through the SVG simulation. In particular, the visual-forward interface better represented the materials at hand.

Notably, one participant decided to explore the physical medium, cutting impromptu fan blades from styrofoam, modeling their design against a nearby fan. Placed on the shaft of the vibrotactile motor, the participant sent a high signal to the stage. The stage lights flashed, indicating that the signal had been sent, yet the fan had not moved. The participant repeated sending the signal without success. He removed the fan blades and transmitted the signal without it, surprised at the vibrotactile motor whirring to life. He realized that the fan, positioned too close to the end of the motor shaft, produces more friction than the motor can overcome.

Another participant contrasted their experience of encountering a similar difficulty: she was unclear whether the actuator was defective or misconfigured, abandoned the attempt and moved on to use a different component. For her, the workstation "removed the guesswork" and confirmed the validity of her design. The value of immediate feedback allowed both participants to recover and constructively build an understanding of the limits of the actuator.

### Streaming commands enables design complexity

While participants reported that the task was a comfortable fit with their current experience level of programming, they thought that creating a similar effect, especially with the number of actuators and other components in the system, would be incredibly tedious to accomplish without the tool (P9: "It would take me a month!"). In considering how they would create their finished designs in Arduino code, participants universally anticipated a dramatic increase in difficulty:

> **P3** [Programming that same interaction] in Arduino would be terrible. I'd have to manually put in all of the different values, and it would be really difficult to keep track of all of the values. For loops would also be annoying especially since there are so many different regions that you're controlling at the same time, so I think programming it would be a complete mess.

> **P1** It would be painstaking, and a real annoyance, but you could do it...That would be a whole bunch of loops, and yeah I wouldn't want to do that.

For the multi-actor condition, several users focused on the hue, saturation, and brightness of the LEDs, exploring the possibilities of working with these elements in ways that differed dramatically from the binary on-off typically used in their personal projects. Participants were surprised by how subtle timing differences dramatically altered choreographies.

By the end of the workshop, users found the choreography control to be appealing with more than half incorporating it into their final design. This evolving relationship to the formal elements of actuators demonstrates the importance of exposing the conversational profile as a means of enabling creativity.

We see the conversational model the workstation affords as clearly supporting a more exploratory process that enables complex designs and supported an exploratory design workflow, even with the additional complexity of driving many actuators.

### New vocabulary reflects deeper engagement

Participants with a stronger programming background initially found the tool challenging their existing mental model of design-programming (e.g., **P6:**I want to toggle each one individually.) In probing mental interaction models, we found consensus in how users approached manipulating LEDs (and other actuators) by using an array or matrix, going as far as having the virtual form dictate the design.

> **P3** My approach would probably be to figure out how to identify each individual LED, then run the cycle of light changes ... and just iterate through all the IDs in the right order.

We argue that the new mental models introduced by the tool caused users to shift from this thinking, focusing instead on the design rather than the underlying architecture. As they gained familiarity with the tool and began generating spatial designs, we noted a shift in think-out-loud language. In particular, participants described their workshop creations and practice in spatial and relational terms, using the choreography to program their desired spatially-meaningful messages, with their language mirroring the effect they wished to communicate.

> **P7** It looks scattered, or maybe the concentricity is a little too prominent, and I want it to be a little subtler. As far as getting someone to tap that, it's drawing me toward [the center]. Then for more visual effects there's really more emphasis on the pulsing.

Several engaged with the more conceptual thinking behind what the actuation was doing, and the context of the environment.

> **P5** It would make things a lot easier than just writing code, especially for people who are more visual design focused and less software focused like me. I know enough software technicalities to think of algorithms, but I don't necessarily have the skills to implement them as I want them to, so this provides a bridge between what I want to happen - the conceptualizing step - and the actual "making-this-happen" step.

Additionally, users continued to identify as authors despite the automatic code-generation of the workstation, and did not view this generation as taking away from the design process.

## DISCUSSION

As digital fabrication evolves, we aim to bring many of the same familiar fluid elements of creativity found within the established artistic practices to this domain in the hope that such efforts will broaden participation, improve inclusively, and enable new forms of creativity, innovations, products, and art. From our user study, we observed how defamiliarizing standing expectations of how artifacts should look and behave enhanced aesthetic literacy, or the "conceptual awareness which allows diverse persons to more actively become agents in their environment, combining knowledge, imagination, feeling, and skills" [17].

### Supporting sensors in a CWM workflow

Although the scope of the work is focused on actuation, the larger ecology of electronic and hybrid materials face similar challenges. Inverting the formal analysis (Figure 2) yields some starting points for supporting sensors in a conversation with materials workflow. For instance, how might creative environments expose the phenomenology of the sensed stimuli (e.g., from a heartbeat, from the environment), convey the limits of its observation (e.g., single point sample, distributed sensing), or communicate how it was processed and encoded (e.g., thresholding, machine learning). From an interaction design lens, there is additional opportunities for extending the formal properties of triggers to move beyond "if this then that" and occur probabilistically or evolve dynamically.

### Curating creative spaces

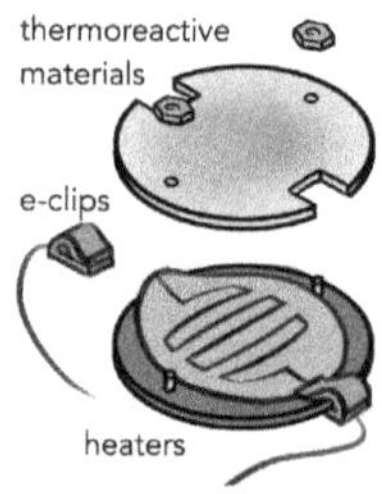


From this exploration, we see potential trajectories for tangible interfaces to emerging hybrid material practices such as e-textiles or paper electronics. Stages may offer an exploration, testing, and reflection environment custom to the unique challenges and concerns of a practice including organics, biologicals, chemicals. For instance, a paper electronics station for resistive heaters could offer specialized power and control terminals as well as curate and affix a host of different thermoreactive materials to explore heat as a material. For e-textiles, a stage could incorporate more of the physical practice, exposing power and control through a mannequin, in conjunction with electronic tools translated to the textiles domain [37].

## CONCLUSION

This work presented the design of a novel, creative workstation to support a "conversation with materials", aiming to expose the different physical and digital material actors present within actuation design. We treated the data signal as a computational material and exposed its distortions, capabilities, and its influence on actuators and space as a creative agent. Through a tangible, networked, and modular interface, we demonstrated the value of distributing creative agency across multiple form factors and of defamiliarizing computational design practices to expand on the aesthetic literacy of hybrid design elements.

## ACKNOWLEDGEMENTS

We thank Jasper O'Leary for his part in early explorations of this work, Tina Taleb for aiding with video documentation, and the anonymous reviewers for their valuable feedback. This research was supported by a Microsoft Research Dissertation Grant and NSF Graduate Research Fellowships.

## REFERENCES


[1] 2003. Light-O-Rama. (2003). http://www1.lightorama.com/

[2] 2010. Finale Fireworks. (2010). http://www.finalefireworks.com/

[3] Sylvan Barnet. 2011. *A short guide to writing about art.* Pearson/Prentice Hall.

[4] Glenn Blauvelt, Tom Wrensch, and Michael Eisenberg. 1999. Integrating Craft Materials and Computation. In *Proceedings of the 3rd Conference on Creativity & Cognition (C&C '99).* ACM, New York, NY, USA, 50–56. DOI:http://dx.doi.org/10.1145/317561.317572

[5] Tracey Booth, Simone Stumpf, Jon Bird, and Sara Jones. 2016. Crossed Wires: Investigating the Problems of End-User Developers in a Physical Computing Task. In *Proceedings of the 2016 CHI Conference on Human Factors in Computing Systems (CHI '16).* ACM, New York, NY, USA, 3485–3497. DOI: http://dx.doi.org/10.1145/2858036.2858533

[6] Matthew Chalmers, Ian MacColl, and Marek Bell. 2003. Seamful design: Showing the seams in wearable computing. (2003).

[7] Karen Collins. 2007. In the Loop: Creativity and Constraint in 8-bit Video Game Audio. *Twentieth-Century Music* 4, 2 (Sept. 2007), 209–227. DOI:http://dx.doi.org/10.1017/S1478572208000510

[8] Tejaswi Digumarti, Javier Alonso-Mora, Roland Siegwart, and Paul Beardsley. 2016. Pixelbots 2014. In *ACM SIGGRAPH 2016 Art Gallery (SIGGRAPH '16).* ACM, New York, NY, USA, 366–367. DOI: http://dx.doi.org/10.1145/2897843.2915197

[9] W Keith Edwards and Rebecca E Grinter. 2001. At home with ubiquitous computing: Seven challenges. In *International conference on ubiquitous computing.* Springer, 256–272.

[10] Sean Follmer, Daniel Leithinger, Alex Olwal, Akimitsu Hogge, and Hiroshi Ishii. 2013. inFORM: Dynamic Physical Affordances and Constraints Through Shape and Object Actuation. In *Proceedings of the 26th Annual ACM Symposium on User Interface Software and Technology (UIST '13).* ACM, New York, NY, USA, 417–426. DOI: http://dx.doi.org/10.1145/2501988.2502032

[11] Verena Fuchsberger, Martin Murer, and Manfred Tscheligi. 2013. Materials, Materiality, and Media. In *Proceedings of the SIGCHI Conference on Human Factors in Computing Systems (CHI '13).* ACM, New York, NY, USA, 2853–2862. DOI: http://dx.doi.org/10.1145/2470654.2481395

[12] Elisa Giaccardi and Elvin Karana. 2015. Foundations of materials experience: An approach for HCI. In *Proceedings of the 33rd Annual ACM Conference on Human Factors in Computing Systems.* ACM, 2447–2456.

[13] Björn Hartmann, Scott Doorley, and Scott R. Klemmer. 2008. Hacking, Mashing, Gluing: Understanding Opportunistic Design. *IEEE Pervasive Computing* 7, 3 (July 2008), 46–54. DOI: http://dx.doi.org/10.1109/MPRV.2008.54

[14] Björn Hartmann, Scott R. Klemmer, Michael Bernstein, Leith Abdulla, Brandon Burr, Avi Robinson-Mosher, and Jennifer Gee. 2006. Reflective Physical Prototyping Through Integrated Design, Test, and Analysis. In *Proceedings of the 19th Annual ACM Symposium on User Interface Software and Technology (UIST '06).* ACM, New York, NY, USA, 299–308. DOI: http://dx.doi.org/10.1145/1166253.1166300

[15] N. Katherine Hayles. 2004. Print Is Flat, Code Is Deep: The Importance of Media-Specific Analysis. *Poetics Today* 25, 1 (March 2004), 67–90. DOI: http://dx.doi.org/10.1215/03335372-25-1-67

[16] Kelly Bowman Heaton. 2000. *Physical pixels.* Ph.D. Dissertation. Massachusetts Institute of Technology. http: //xenia.media.mit.edu/~kelly/physPix/heatonThesis.pdf

[17] Pat Hutchings. 2005. Aesthetic Literacy Across The Curriculum: A Conversation. Published by The Carnegie Foundation for the Advancement of Teaching. https://www.researchgate.net/profile/Nader_Aghakhani/post/Is_there_any_study_on_aesthetic_literacy_in_Adult_Education/

[18] Hiroshi Ishii and Brygg Ullmer. 1997. Tangible bits: towards seamless interfaces between people, bits and atoms. In *Proceedings of the ACM SIGCHI Conference on Human factors in computing systems.* 234–241. http://dl.acm.org/citation.cfm?id=258715

[19] Yuichi Ito, Carl Stone, Masashi Yamada, and Shinya Miyazaki. 2014. Datamoshing Technique for Video Art Production. *The journal of the Society For Art and Science* 13, 3 (2014), 154–168. http://art-science.org/journal/v13n3/v13n3pp154/artsci-v13n3pp154.pdf

[20] Malte F. Jung, Nik Martelaro, Halsey Hoster, and Clifford Nass. 2014. Participatory Materials: Having a Reflective Conversation with an Artifact in the Making. In *Proceedings of the 2014 Conference on Designing Interactive Systems (DIS '14).* ACM, New York, NY, USA, 25–34. DOI: http://dx.doi.org/10.1145/2598510.2598591

[21] Maximos A. KaliakatsosâĂŞPapakostas, Michael G. Epitropakis, Andreas Floros, and Michael N. Vrahatis. 2012. Interactive Evolution of 8âĂŞbit melodies with Genetic Programming towards finding aesthetic measures for sound. In *Evolutionary and Biologically Inspired Music, Sound, Art and Design.* Springer, 141–152. http://link.springer.com/chapter/10.1007/978-3-642-29142-5_13

[22] Rubaiat Habib Kazi, Fanny Chevalier, Tovi Grossman, and George Fitzmaurice. 2014a. Kitty: Sketching Dynamic and Interactive Illustrations. In *Proceedings of the 27th Annual ACM Symposium on User Interface Software and Technology (UIST '14)*. ACM, New York, NY, USA, 395–405. DOI: http://dx.doi.org/10.1145/2642918.2647375

[23] Rubaiat Habib Kazi, Fanny Chevalier, Tovi Grossman, Shengdong Zhao, and George Fitzmaurice. 2014b. Draco: Bringing Life to Illustrations with Kinetic Textures. In *Proceedings of the SIGCHI Conference on Human Factors in Computing Systems (CHI '14)*. ACM, New York, NY, USA, 351–360. DOI: http://dx.doi.org/10.1145/2556288.2556987

[24] Han-Jong Kim, Yunwoo Jeong, Ju-Whan Kim, and Tek-Jin Nam. 2016. M.Sketch: Prototyping Tool for Linkage-Based Mechanism Design. In *Proceedings of the 29th Annual Symposium on User Interface Software and Technology (UIST '16 Adjunct)*. ACM, New York, NY, USA, 75–77. DOI: http://dx.doi.org/10.1145/2984751.2985709

[25] Brian Knep. 2017. Brian Knep :: Healing Pool. (2017). http://www.blep.com/works/healing-series/healing-pool/

[26] Jarrod Knibbe, Tovi Grossman, and George Fitzmaurice. 2015. Smart makerspace: An immersive instructional space for physical tasks. In *Proceedings of the 2015 International Conference on Interactive Tabletops & Surfaces*. ACM, 83–92.

[27] Mathieu Le Goc, Lawrence H. Kim, Ali Parsaei, Jean-Daniel Fekete, Pierre Dragicevic, and Sean Follmer. 2016. Zooids: Building Blocks for Swarm User Interfaces. In *Proceedings of the 29th Annual Symposium on User Interface Software and Technology (UIST '16)*. ACM, New York, NY, USA, 97–109. DOI: http://dx.doi.org/10.1145/2984511.2984547

[28] Szu-Yu Liu, Tung-Jen Tsai, and Daniel Alenquer. 2016. Exploring Computational Composite: An Approach To Sensorial Interaction. In *Proceedings of the 19th ACM Conference on Computer Supported Cooperative Work and Social Computing Companion (CSCW '16 Companion)*. ACM, New York, NY, USA, 337–340. DOI:http://dx.doi.org/10.1145/2818052.2869083

[29] Lev Manovich. 1999. Database as Symbolic Form. *Convergence* 5, 2 (June 1999), 80–99. DOI: http://dx.doi.org/10.1177/135485659900500206

[30] Marshall McLuhan. 1994. *Understanding media: The extensions of man*. MIT press.

[31] Rosa Menkman. 2011. Glitch studies manifesto. *Video vortex reader II: Moving images beyond YouTube* (2011), 336–347.

[32] Marjorie Munsterberg. 2009. *Writing about art*. http://writingaboutart.org/pages/formalanalysis.html

[33] Michael Nitsche, Andrew Quitmeyer, Kate Farina, Samuel Zwaan, and Hye Yeon Nam. 2014. Teaching Digital Craft. In *CHI '14 Extended Abstracts on Human Factors in Computing Systems (CHI EA '14)*. ACM, New York, NY, USA, 719–730. DOI: http://dx.doi.org/10.1145/2559206.2578872

[34] William Odom, Richard Banks, David Kirk, Richard Harper, Siân Lindley, and Abigail Sellen. 2012a. Technology Heirlooms?: Considerations for Passing Down and Inheriting Digital Materials. In *Proceedings of the SIGCHI Conference on Human Factors in Computing Systems (CHI '12)*. ACM, New York, NY, USA, 337–346. DOI: http://dx.doi.org/10.1145/2207676.2207723

[35] William Odom, Mark Selby, Abigail Sellen, David Kirk, Richard Banks, and Tim Regan. 2012b. Photobox: On the Design of a Slow Technology. In *Proceedings of the Designing Interactive Systems Conference (DIS '12)*. ACM, New York, NY, USA, 665–668. DOI: http://dx.doi.org/10.1145/2317956.2318055

[36] Pablo Paredes, Ryuka Ko, Eduardo Calle-Ortiz, John Canny, Björn Hartmann, and Greg Niemeyer. 2016. Fiat-Lux: Interactive Urban Lights for Combining Positive Emotion and Efficiency. In *Proceedings of the 2016 ACM Conference on Designing Interactive Systems (DIS '16)*. ACM, New York, NY, USA, 785–795. DOI: http://dx.doi.org/10.1145/2901790.2901832

[37] Irene Posch and Geraldine Fitzpatrick. 2018. Integrating Textile Materials with Electronic Making: Creating New Tools and Practices. In *Proceedings of the Twelfth International Conference on Tangible, Embedded, and Embodied Interaction (TEI '18)*. ACM, New York, NY, USA, 158–165. DOI: http://dx.doi.org/10.1145/3173225.3173255

[38] M Puckette and D Zicarelli. 1990. Max MSP software. (1990).

[39] Isabel P. S. Qamar, Rainer Groh, David Holman, and Anne Roudaut. 2018. HCI Meets Material Science: A Literature Review of Morphing Materials for the Design of Shape-Changing Interfaces. In *Proceedings of the 2018 CHI Conference on Human Factors in Computing Systems (CHI '18)*. ACM, New York, NY, USA, Article 374, 23 pages. DOI: http://dx.doi.org/10.1145/3173574.3173948

[40] Hayes Raffle. 2010. Topobo: Programming by Example to Create Complex Behaviors. In *Proceedings of the 9th International Conference of the Learning Sciences - Volume 2 (ICLS '10)*. International Society of the Learning Sciences, Chicago, Illinois, 126–127. http://dl.acm.org/citation.cfm?id=1854509.1854565

[41] Daniela K. Rosner. 2012. The Material Practices of Collaboration. In *Proceedings of the ACM 2012 Conference on Computer Supported Cooperative Work (CSCW '12)*. ACM, New York, NY, USA, 1155–1164. DOI:http://dx.doi.org/10.1145/2145204.2145375

[42] Markus Lorenz Schilling, Ron Wakkary, and William Odom. 2018. Focus Framework: Tracking Prototypes' Back-Talk. In *Proceedings of the Twelfth International Conference on Tangible, Embedded, and Embodied Interaction (TEI '18)*. ACM, New York, NY, USA, 684–693. DOI: http://dx.doi.org/10.1145/3173225.3173259

[43] Oliver S. Schneider, Ali Israr, and Karon E. MacLean. 2015. Tactile Animation by Direct Manipulation of Grid Displays. In *Proceedings of the 28th Annual ACM Symposium on User Interface Software & Technology (UIST '15)*. ACM, New York, NY, USA, 21–30. DOI: http://dx.doi.org/10.1145/2807442.2807470

[44] Donald Schon. 1983. The reflective practitioner. (1983).

[45] Julia Schwarz, David Klionsky, Chris Harrison, Paul Dietz, and Andrew Wilson. 2012. Phone as a pixel: enabling ad-hoc, large-scale displays using mobile devices. In *Proceedings of the 2012 ACM annual conference on Human Factors in Computing Systems*. ACM, 2235–2238. http://dl.acm.org/citation.cfm?id=2208378

[46] Scott Snibbe. 2005. Central Mosaic. (2005). https://www.snibbe.com/digital-art/

[47] Cesar Torres, Jasper O'Leary, Molly Nicholas, and Eric Paulos. 2017. Illumination Aesthetics: Light As a Creative Material Within Computational Design. In *Proceedings of the 2017 CHI Conference on Human Factors in Computing Systems (CHI '17)*. ACM, New York, NY, USA, 6111–6122. DOI: http://dx.doi.org/10.1145/3025453.3025466

[48] Cesar Torres, Sarah Sterman, Molly Nicholas, Richard Lin, Eric Pai, and Eric Paulos. 2018. Guardians of Practice: A Contextual Inquiry of Failure-Mitigation Strategies Within Creative Practices. In *Proceedings of the 2018 Designing Interactive Systems Conference (DIS '18)*. ACM, New York, NY, USA, 1259–1267. DOI: http://dx.doi.org/10.1145/3196709.3196795

[49] Camille Utterback. 2000. Liquid Time Series. (2000). http://camilleutterback.com/projects/liquid-time-series/

[50] Anna Vallgårda, Laurens Boer, Vasiliki Tsaknaki, and Dag Svanaes. 2016. Material Programming: A New Interaction Design Practice. In *Proceedings of the 2016 ACM Conference Companion Publication on Designing Interactive Systems (DIS '16 Companion)*. ACM, New York, NY, USA, 149–152. DOI: http://dx.doi.org/10.1145/2908805.2909411

[51] Anna Vallgårda and Johan Redström. 2007. Computational Composites. In *Proceedings of the SIGCHI Conference on Human Factors in Computing Systems (CHI '07)*. ACM, New York, NY, USA, 513–522. DOI: http://dx.doi.org/10.1145/1240624.1240706

[52] Lisa K Wells and Jeffrey Travis. 1996. *LabVIEW for everyone: graphical programming made even easier*. Prentice-Hall, Inc.

[53] Terry Winograd. 1996. Reflective conversation with materials an interview with Donald Schön by John Bennett. *Bringing Design to Software (1st ed.) Harlow: Addison Wesley* (1996), 171–189.

# Sequential Support: 3D Printing Dissolvable Support Material for Time-Dependent Mechanisms

**Martin Nisser, Junyi Zhu, Tianye Chen, Katarina Bulovic, Parinya Punpongsanon, Stefanie Mueller**
MIT CSAIL, Cambridge, MA, USA
{nisser, junyizhu, tianyec, kbulovic, parinya, stefanie.mueller}@mit.edu

## ABSTRACT

In this paper, we propose a different perspective on the use of support material: rather than printing support structures for overhangs, our idea is to make use of its transient nature, i.e. the fact that it can be dissolved when placed in a solvent, such as water. This enables a range of new use cases, such as quickly dissolving and replacing parts of a prototype during design iteration, printing temporary assembly labels directly on the object that leave no marks when dissolved, and creating time-dependent mechanisms, such as fading in parts of an image in a shadow art piece or releasing relaxing scents from a 3D printed structure sequentially overnight. Since we use regular support material (PVA), our approach works on consumer 3D printers without any modifications.

To facilitate the design of objects that leverage dissolvable support, we built a custom 3D editor plugin that includes a simulation showing how support material dissolves over time. In our evaluation, our simulation predicted geometries that are statistically similar to the example shapes within 10% error across all samples.

**Author Keywords:** 3D printing; support material.

## INTRODUCTION

Early on in the development of 3D printing, researchers realized that building objects bottom-up, layer-by-layer comes with an inherent issue: some geometries would have nothing underneath them to hold them up [1]. To solve this issue, researchers developed support structures to keep overhangs upright [9].

Early 3D printers that had only a single extruder used one material for both the model geometry and the support structures. Once the 3D print was finished, the support was broken off to reveal the object. However, this left visual artifacts and was not suitable for support material inside small holes as users were not able to reach in and remove it.

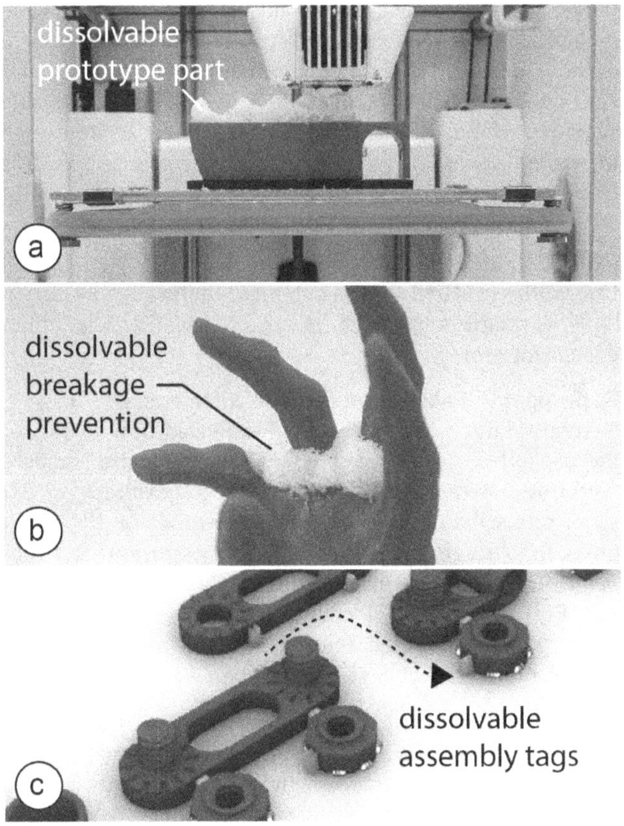


**Figure 1. We leverage the transient nature of support material to create new application scenarios: (a) a dissolvable prototype part for design iteration, (b) breakage prevention that can be dissolved after transport, (c) dissolvable assembly labels that leave no marks. In addition to these discrete use cases, we also developed mechanisms that continuously dissolve over time.**

Dissolvable support material [9] solved these problems: since it decomposes in a solvent, such as water, it creates smooth surfaces and leaves no visual marks. Because water can better access small holes, dissolvable structures can more easily be removed. Due to its many benefits, dissolvable support material (e.g., PVA) is now a widely used alternative to physically breaking off the support.


*TEI '19*, March 17–20, 2019, Tempe, AZ, USA

ACM ISBN 978-1-4503-6196-5/19/03...$15.00
https://doi.org/10.1145/3294109.3295630

Since printing support structures requires extra time and material, the use of support has so far been perceived as an inconvenient necessity to extend the range of printable geometries. In this paper, we take a different approach. Rather than using support material to print support structures, our idea is to make use of its transient nature, i.e. the fact that it can be dissolved when placed in a solvent, such as water, to enable a range of new use cases.

Our contributions include: (1) an exploration of alternative use cases of 3D printable support material in two categories: those that require controlled dissolving behavior for timing and sequencing events and those that do not need precise control and only require the support material to dissolve eventually; (2) a design interface in the form of a 3D editor plugin that facilitates designing with dissolvable support material; (3) a simulation integrated in the design interface that visualizes how the support material dissolves over time; and (4) a step-by-step procedure to characterize the simulation parameters for different environments.

## RELATED WORK

Our work is related to research that repurposes fabrication tools, optimizes support material, and models time-dependent geometries.

### Repurposing Fabrication Devices & Materials

Several research projects have investigated how to extend the capabilities of 3D printers by changing the standard workflow. *WirePrint* [11], for instance, extrudes in 3D space rather than layer-by-layer; *3D printed hair* [8] repurposes the stringing behavior of plastic extrusion; and *Embedded textiles* [18] embeds fabric layers during 3D printing. Finally, *Encore* [3] allows to print on top or around existing objects. These methods do not modify the 3D printer, rather they change how it is being operated.

Similar explorations exist for other fabrication processes. For stereolithography, *Cillia* [16] generates bitmaps rather than CAD models to enable high-resolution structures; and *FusePrint* [32] inserts existing objects directly into the resin to produce molds. For laser-cutting, *LaserOrigami* [12] makes 3D objects by using the laser for cutting and bending a single sheet, while *LaserStacker* [24] creates 3D objects by welding multiple sheets together. Other innovative fabrication techniques create multi-material bendable (*Foldem* [17]) and inflatable 3D objects (*BlowFab* [29]).

### Optimizing Support Structures

Several research projects have developed methods to print support structures in a way that minimizes the overall amount of support required. For instance, *Branching Support* [21] and *Clever Support* [25] optimize support structures by reducing the number of its connection points to the object. *Bridging Support* [4] uses the stringing behavior of plastic extrusion printers in order to build support structures that resemble horizontal bridges. Finally, *Perceptual Support* [31] lays out support structures to minimize visual artifacts. Support structures have also been used for innovative use cases: For instance, to prevent smearing from oozed-out material, a rampart structure made of support has been shown to work well [6]. Closest to our work is *Printable Hydraulics* [10], which uses the liquid support material in inkjet 3D printing as a means of fabricating hydraulic actuators with pre-filled fluidic channels.

### Modeling Time-Dependent Structures

Since we provide a simulation tool for how the support material dissolves over time, our work is also related to modeling tools for time-dependent geometries. *Transformative Appetite* [26], for instance, simulates the swelling and bending of edible 2D films that fold into 3D shapes during cooking. Similarly, *BioLogic* [30] comes with a simulation to preview how biofilms curve under humidity. Other predictive models have been developed for controlling bending angles in pneumatically actuated devices [13] and shape memory polymers that are activated by heat [14].

## SEQUENTIAL SUPPORT OVERVIEW

The main idea behind *Sequential Support* is to make use of the transient nature of support material, i.e. the fact that it can be dissolved when placed in a solvent, such as water, to enable a range of new application scenarios.

### Discrete vs. Continuous Dissolving

We classify our application scenarios into two categories: (1) *discrete* and (2) *continuous* dissolution.

In *discrete* dissolving, the timing and sequencing of how the support material dissolves plays no role, i.e. it is only of importance that the support material dissolves eventually. For instance, when iterating over a design, rather than reprinting the entire object, we use dissolvable support material for the part that requires iteration (Figure 1a). After dissolving the prototype part that required a change, we can print the new iteration directly on top of the object.

In *continuous* dissolving, in contrast, the timing and sequencing of how the support material dissolves does matter. For instance, we can use dissolvable support capsules to release relaxing scents on a night stand overnight in a particular *sequence* and at pre-defined *time steps* (see Figure 2). We release the scents in the order of red, blue, green and at 86 min, 115 min and 158 min respectively.

### Design Tool including Support Material Simulation

Our design tool, implemented as a plugin to the 3D editor Rhino3D, supports both types of use cases, discrete and continuous. Users start by creating a regular 3D model, then assign either regular plastic ('PLA') or dissolvable support material ('PVA') as a shader to the different object parts. Once users have assigned the material, our design tool enables a 'time-slider' that when dragged provides the user with a preview of how the support material will dissolve over time. The user can change the object geometry to explore different dissolving outcomes and then choose the design which produces the desired dissolved geometry to export for 3D printing. We provide a more detailed illustration of our design tool in the next section using a variety of use cases.

## APPLICATION USE CASES

In this section, we will illustrate five applications, including two continuous and three discrete examples. For each example, we will show the use of our design tool, and report on the fabrication and dissolving time as well as the simulation accuracy.

### #1 Overnight Scent Release (Continuous)

As mentioned above, we can use dissolvable support capsules to release relaxing scents overnight at pre-defined time steps. For this, we printed three support material spheres and filled them with essential oils (paused the print half way through, filled the capsule, continued the print as described in *Printed Optics* [28]). We then placed the capsules in a water container on the night stand in our bed room.

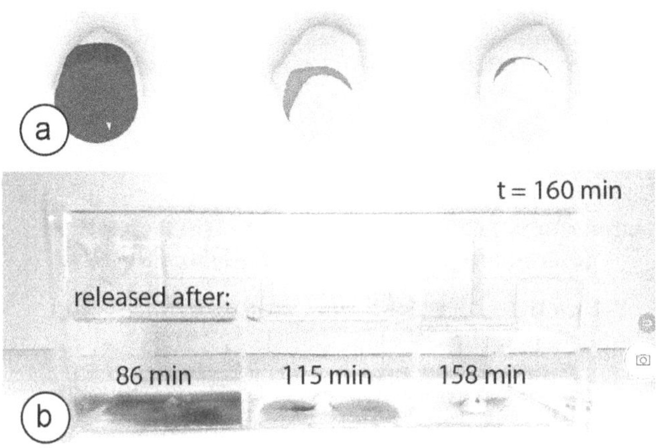


**Figure 2. This nightstand box releases relaxing scents in a pre-defined sequence: the red scent first, then blue, and finally green. (a) Simulation, and (b) actual release.**

Since each sphere had a different wall thickness (2.5mm, 3mm, 4mm), the scents were released one after another after 86 min, 115 min, and 158 min respectively. We had previously explored the timing using *Sequential Support's* simulation tool, which had predicted times of 86 min, 135 min, and 163 min for the red, blue, and green capsules.

### #2 Animating Shadow Art (Continuous)

By leveraging the timing and sequencing prediction of our support material simulation, we can use dissolving support to create shadow art. Figure 3 shows an example: Before the support material dissolves, the shadow art shows the initial image, i.e. a figure standing under a sunny sky. Once The shadow art starts dissolving, the sun turns into a cloud, the raindrops become visible, and finally an umbrella appears above the figure. The setup that we used to create this sequence consisted of the 3D printed object submersed in a water container and a light source mounted above it.

The dissolution time predicted by the simulation was 428 min vs. 380 min for the actual dissolving; the clouds, rain-drops, and umbrella were mostly dissolved at 1/2, 3/4T and at T, respectively, for both simulation and experiment.

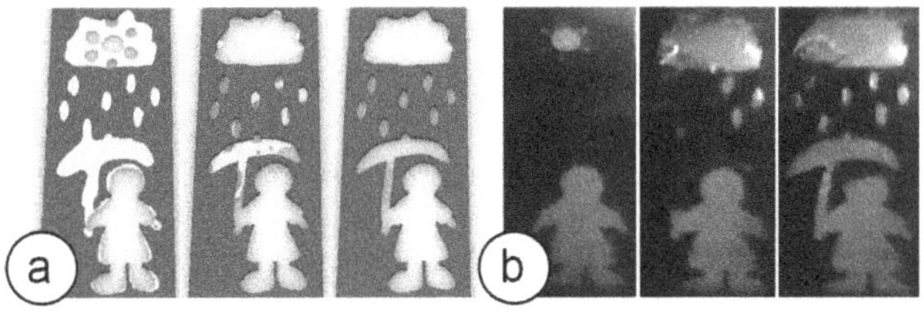


**Figure 3. (a) Simulation: We time the dissolving support to first convert the sun into a cloud, then show the raindrops, and finally an umbrella. (b) Physical result.**

### #3: Design Iteration Partially Replacing a Part (Discrete)

Rather than reprinting the entire object during prototyping, we can use dissolvable support material for the parts that require iteration. Figure 4 illustrates this using a Kinect handle that has been 3D printed to provide the user with a steadier grip while 3D scanning. We are unsure about the exact curvature and spacing for the grip and thus decide to print the grip part in dissolvable support.

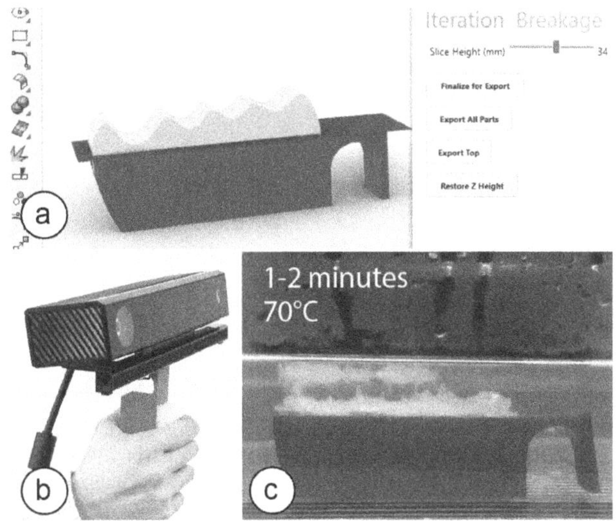


**Figure 4. (a) Splitting the model, (b) testing, (c) dissolving the top part before fabricating the next version.**

We use *Sequential Support's* user interface to split the model into two parts (bottom: red PLA, top: white dissolvable PVA) using the 'slicing height' slider. After printing and testing, we notice that the handle does not allow for a firm grip. We thus place it into hot water (70°C), which dissolves the top part within 1-2 minutes (note that discrete scenarios work with a higher water temperature (70°C vs. 45°C, thus dissolving faster). We return to the 3D editor, modify the 3D model, then export again. To reprint the top portion of the grip, we place the previously printed bottom part onto the build plate (using a custom mount and double sided tape) and print the new part directly on top.

Printing the new part took only 1h 41 min vs. 5h 16 min for printing the object from scratch (68% faster), and only took 16g material vs. 54g (71% less material). We test the handle again and now it feels right. We dissolve the top one more time and reprint it in red PLA to produce the final version of the design.

#### #4 Breakage Support: Dissolvable Packaging (Discrete)

To prevent fragile regions from breaking during transport, we use support material to reinforce them. Figure 5 shows an example: We print this phone stand in a FabLab but are afraid it might break as we transport it home. (a) After clicking *Sequential Support's* 'stress analysis' button, we see that the phone stand is likely going to break in the regions close to the fingers. (b) By dragging the 'support level' slider, the regions identified by the stress analysis (FEA) are covered in additional dissolvable material.

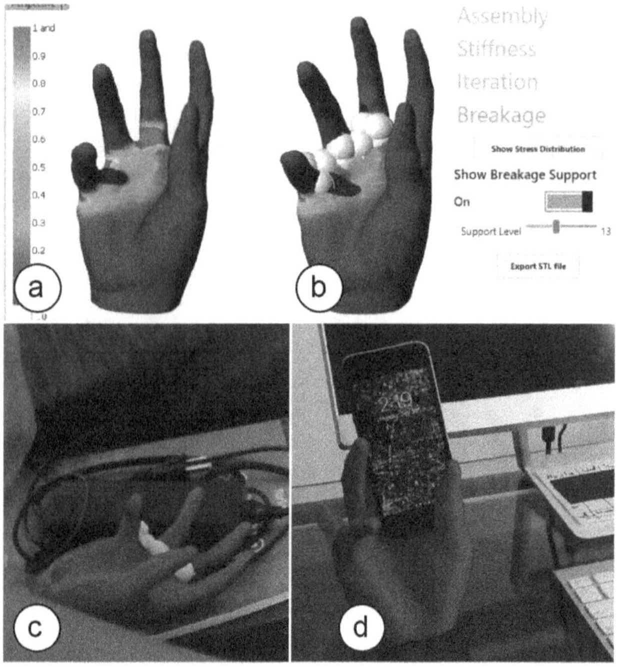


**Figure 5. (a) Stress map, (b) breakage support. (c) Transporting the object, and (d) after dissolving the support material on arrival use the phone stand.**

Adding the support increased printing time by only 19% (17h51 vs. 15h01) and required only 6g of support added to 107g PLA. After transporting the object, softening the support using hot water (70°C) took only 4 minutes; we then wiped off the rest by hand and were ready to use the object within 15 minutes.

#### #5 Assembly: Temporary Labels (Discrete)

In our final use case, we use support material to simplify assembly. Here, we design a lamp that consists of 10 different parts. First, we use *Sequential Support's* interface and attach matching labels to the parts of the object that belong together using the 'label' buttons (Figure 1c).

Next, we create 'stickers', i.e., small support structures that can be used to connect two parts together (Figure 6a). These structures work as temporary adhesives to put parts that belong together close to each other (e.g., a nut that belongs to a particular threaded protrusion). Users can break them off during assembly and dissolve the rest later together with the labels (ca. 2-3 min in 70°C).

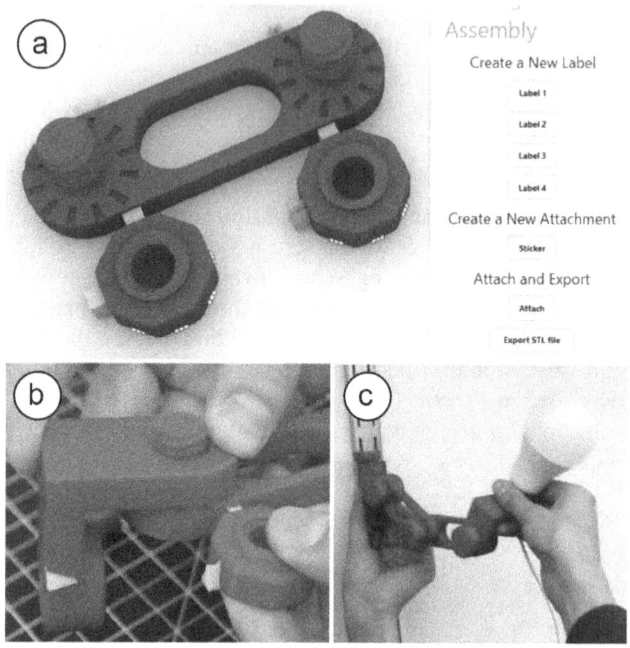


**Figure 6. (a) Small support structures can be used as connectors, to hold parts in place for (b) later assembly. (c) Mounting the assembled lamp onto the wall.**

## SIMULATION OF DISSOLVING SUPPORT MATERIAL

In the next section, we describe the algorithm used in our support material simulation that enables the continuous-time application scenarios. Our simulation takes into account different factors involved in dissolving support material, which we primarily base on related research on dissolving crystals in solvents [2], [5], [15].

#### Step #1: Voxelizing the Model

As soon as the user assigns support material ('PVA') as a shader to a part of a 3D model, we begin pre-processing the part to enable the simulation. We begin by voxelizing the part: We first compute the part's bounding box and then fill it with voxels of size N (we use: side length = 0.3mm; the higher the resolution the more accurate the simulation, however, this comes with the trade-off of increased computational complexity that limits interactive exploration in the design interface). We then keep all voxels that intersect with the part's surface and discard the rest.

#### Step #2: Dissolution Probability for Number of Faces

Each remaining voxel can have one of two states: dissolving in the current time step or not dissolving. To determine the probability that a voxel will dissolve, we use the following equation (initially proposed by Gilmer et al. [5] and extended by Briese et al. [2]):

$$P_d = v^{-\frac{f\phi}{kT}}$$

As can be seen in the formula, the probability that a voxel dissolves increases exponentially with the *number of faces f* exposed to the solvent. A voxel that is attached on only one side and thus has 5 faces exposed to the solvent, has a much higher chance of dissolving than a voxel with only one exposed face (Figure 7). This is why support structures on a model's surface dissolve faster than those in small inlets (e.g., screw holes), and why sparse structures dissolve faster than solids.

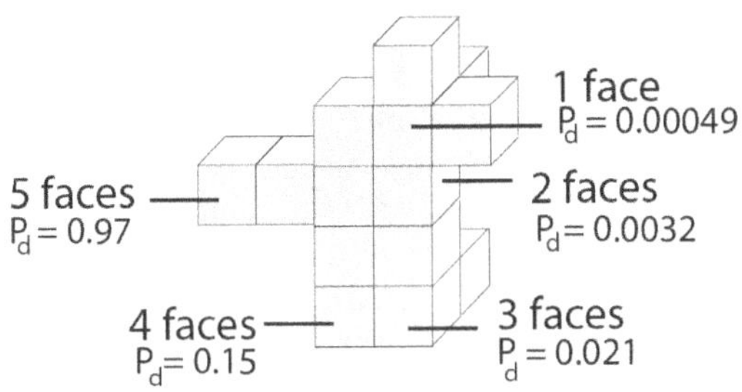


**Figure 7. The more faces of a voxel are exposed to the solvent, the higher the probability that it dissolves.**

In the formula, $T$ is the temperature of the water in Kelvin (constant at 318K or 45°C), $k$ is Boltzmann's constant ($1.38064852 \times 10^{-23}$ $m^2kg/s^2K$), and $v$ and $\varphi$ are constants that influence the speed of dissolution. We determined $v$ and $\varphi$ for our setup as described in section 'Characterizing simulation parameters' ($v = 6.5$, $\varphi = 1.9$).

Inserting all values into the formula, and varying the numbers of faces $f$ from 1-5 gives us the probability for a voxel to dissolve based on its number of faces: $f_1 = 0.00049$, $f_2 = 0.0032$, $f_3$=0.021, $f_4$=0.15, $f_5$=0.97 (Figure 7).

### Step #3: Drawing a Random Sample

We then use these probabilities as inputs to a kinetic Monte Carlo simulation as described in Briese et al. [2].

We start by drawing a random number n from a uniform distribution on the interval [0,1]. This number is then compared to the probability that each voxel will dissolve. If the random number is smaller than the dissolution probability of the voxel, the voxel is dissolved. If not, it stays put.

After removing all dissolved voxels in the current time step, new surface voxels are generated to ensure that the voxel layer remains 1 voxel thick. We then repeat step #2 and #3. Figure 9 shows some results from our simulation.

### Step #4: Rendering

We then convert the voxel model into a continuous surface using the Laplacian smoothing algorithm from the *Weaverbird* [27] Grasshopper add-on to render a more visually compelling result.

## CHARACTERIZING SIMULATION PARAMETERS

Next, we explain how we determine the two input parameters $v$ and $\varphi$ for the dissolution formula experimentally.

### Factors v (global dissolve speed) and ϕ (local speed)

The factor $v$ represents the *global* dissolve speed independent of the number of faces. The factor $\varphi$, in contrast, represents the *local* speed with which each voxel dissolves based on the number of its exposed faces $f$.

For instance, consider the effect of varying v and $\varphi$ on a 'star' shape. If $\varphi$ is small, the number of faces exposed to the solvent has less of an effect on the probability of dissolution of each voxel. As a result, voxels at the tips of the star (containing more exposed faces) will be dissolved at rates similar to those voxels composing the flat sides of the star (fewer exposed faces). Therefore, with small $\varphi$, the star will remain star-shaped. In contrast, if $\varphi$ is large, the number of faces exposed will play a greater role and the tips of the star will dissolve faster than the flat sides of the star, leading the star to become sphere-like.

### Collecting Test Data

To determine the parameters v and φ, we printed different shapes (sphere, star, cube). We dissolved them in water and captured images using a front view camera (Figure 8). The shapes measured: *cube* length: 15mm, *sphere* diameter: 15mm, and *star* outside diameter: 24mm.

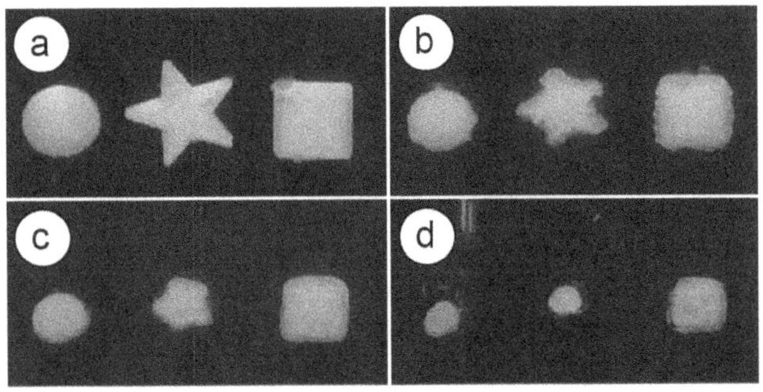


**Figure 8. Dissolving shapes over time.**

We used a 3-liter water tank and heated the water to a temperature of 45°C. This was the highest temperature chosen based on a trade-off between faster dissolution times and a tendency of the solvent to become cloudy at elevated temperatures, preventing us from recording the experiment.

We also created a mild current by using a 20mm magnetic stirrer at 600rpm. The reason we use stirring is that when support material dissolves, the resulting particles stay close to the location where they dissolved, i.e., close to the object's surface. The more particles are floating close to the surface, the slower the support material dissolves.

After immersing the objects in water, we took pictures every 8 minutes (Figure 8). We collected the same data from our simulation, i.e., we ran our simulation with an initial set of parameters for factor $v$ and $\varphi$ on the three test shapes and took screenshots from the same angle that the physical camera took photos of the real objects (Figure 9).

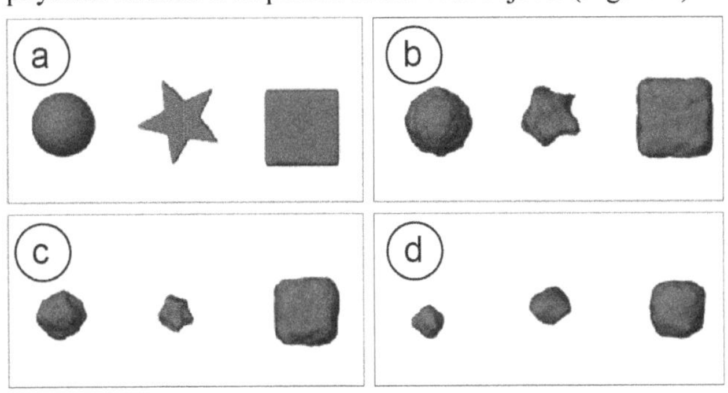


**Figure 9. Simulation pictures.**

### Extracting & Comparing Shape Contours

We used OpenCV to extract and then compare the shape contours. We first thresholded the images and then extracted huMoments to gain a feature vector describing the contours in a translation-, rotation-, and scale-invariant manner. We applied the same procedure to both the photos and the screenshots to gain a feature vector for each.

### Computing Error and Adjusting Simulation Parameters

We then used the two feature vectors to compute the error (Euclidean distance) between the actual physical behavior and our simulation. This error is thus based on the compared 2D images (photos and simulation screenshots), which we use as a proxy for the difference between the full 3D shapes.

We then chose another set of simulation parameters v and φ, re-ran our simulation with the new *v* and *φ* and compared the error to the error from the previous parameters (we always first picked *φ*, and then adjusted the corresponding *v* (global speed) until the probability for a voxel that has 5 faces ($f_5$) was 97%). The results for each set of *φ* and *v* can be seen in Figure 10.

We found that $\varphi = 1.9$ and $v = 6.5$ lead to the best results across the three different shapes (lowest average error between the feature vectors over all time steps). Figure 10 summarizes the result for dissolving the same objects (star, sphere, cube) twice. We found that the error between the two experiments differed by less than 10%.

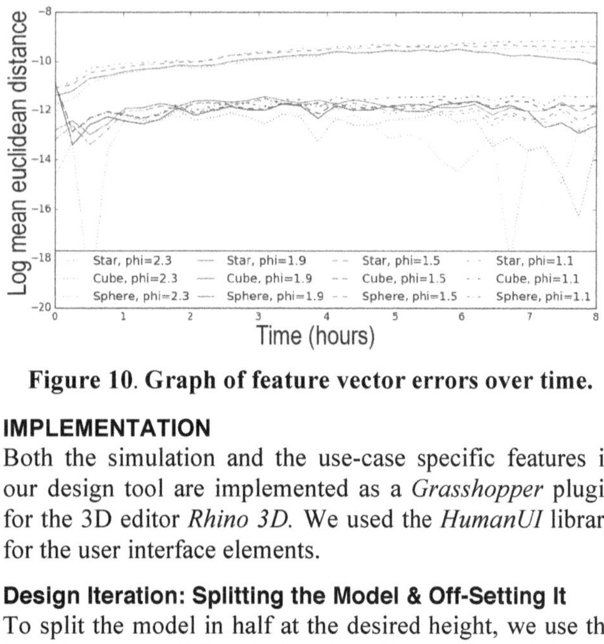


**Figure 10. Graph of feature vector errors over time.**

## IMPLEMENTATION

Both the simulation and the use-case specific features in our design tool are implemented as a *Grasshopper* plugin for the 3D editor *Rhino 3D*. We used the *HumanUI* library for the user interface elements.

### Design Iteration: Splitting the Model & Off-Setting It

To split the model in half at the desired height, we use the Grasshopper *SplitBrep()* function. On export of the .stl files, the two parts are merged into a closed solid using the Grasshopper *Cap* function. After splitting and capping, the two geometries are baked to a new layer in Rhino using the function *GH_Bake()*. We use a custom script to export each geometry on the *GH_Bake* layer as individual .stl files (both are regular closed meshes, i.e. the parts can have sparse infills but will be separated by a solid layer).

When printing a new iteration, the system only exports the top geometry as an .stl file. We then run a python script in the background that offsets the gcode commands in the Z direction by the height of the PLA part.

### Stress Analysis using Finite Element Analysis

To create the stress analysis for our model, we use Rhino's *Scan&Solve* plugin. The plugin comes with a function called *AddFaceVectorLoad()*, which we give a set of input forces with a uniform load of 100N pointing from the top to the bottom. To display the resulting stress distribution we use the function *SolutionDisplayEnable()*. We then get the points of the highest stress using the function *QuerySolutionValue()*, which returns a list of stress values at all points on the model. We sort this list using a custom python script and then create a number of spherical support structures to cover the stress points commensurate with a value chosen using the slider in the user interface.

### Assembly Instructions

To set up the snap locations on both the object and the instruction labels, we generate 'point' objects in Rhino. When the user connects two parts, we call Rhino's *orient()* function to snap the instruction label onto the reference point. We use the same approach for the *attach* option.

### Scent Release and Shadow Art

Both examples use the simulation described previously in section 'Simulation of Dissolving Support Material'.

## LIMITATIONS

While our approach enables new application scenarios, it is subject to the following limitations: *(1) single-use only:* once the support is dissolved, we cannot repeat the functionality. Thus, using support material works best for scenarios that require functionality only once, such as during assembly, product configuration, or transportation. *(2) Simulation Precision:* Since our set of sample shapes was small and the parameters were only optimized over a narrow range, the simulation should be fine-tuned in future work using additional shapes. *(3) Speed:* While the process of dissolving is fast at high water temperatures and for small amounts of support (only a few minutes for thicknesses in the vicinity of 1mm), it can take hours at low temperatures and when a lot of support material needs to dissolve. Thus, our work is limited to application scenarios with an extended time span, such as the overnight scent release or the slowly changing shadow art piece that could be displayed in a public plaza. (4) *Overhangs:* The support material cannot be used to print support structures for overhangs if those interfere with the main dissolving geometry. (5) *Adherence:* Current PVA support material is challenging to print since it does not adhere well to the regular PLA printing material. Printing on large flat surfaces (e.g. as in the design iteration case) facilitates adherence, while more complex geometries, such as the phone stand, are more difficult to print.

## DISCUSSION

In this paper, we provided a first exploration into how support material can be used for different application use cases. However, for each individual use case, a more extensive exploration is required to analyze the trade-offs of using support material vs. traditional approaches.

For instance, using support material in the design iteration use case can accomplish the same function (i.e. replacing a part of the object geometry) as by using a milling machine (see *Patching Physical Objects* [22]). Compared to using a mill, our approach has the benefit of not requiring additional hardware and being faster when a high temperature bath is used (minutes of dissolving vs. hours for milling). However, when using a mill, the user can decide which part to replace *after* printing, whereas in our approach the user needs to decide which part requires iteration *before* printing. In both processes, alignment and delamination are challenges that need further investigation. In contrast to approaches that use joints to connect parts [7], [20] or rafts / brims, our method does not require modifying the model.

Similar trade-offs need to be explored for the other use cases, such as the breakage support. For instance, the benefit of our approach compared to traditional packaging is that it reinforces the object locally at its most fragile locations; this is different from packaging foam, which provides aggregate protection across the entire object. In addition, our approach provides additional breakage support even after being removed from the main packaging and during handling, until dissolved by the end user. On the other hand, if the amount of protective support is large and requires a long time to print, the high speed of traditional wrapping techniques might outweigh the advantage of local support. Finally, depending on the circumstances, the soluble support packaging may need to be protected against humidity as this could weaken the structure over time.

## CONCLUSION

We presented *Sequential Support,* a system that enables users to use support material in 3D printing as a feature and not as a time- and material-consuming necessity. We showed how *Sequential Support* allows users to create a variety of objects for different application scenarios, such as dissolvable prototype parts, breakage support, assembly labels, and time- and sequence-dependent shadow art and scent release mechanisms. For future work, we plan to run a qualitative study in which we will investigate how our method changes participants' design practices. We will also use this study to explore additional application scenarios with participants. In particular, we are interested to further explore use cases in fabrication in which objects have a limited life-span such as those outlined in *Mobile Fabrication* [19], which include temporary tools and short-term fixes to everyday objects.

## ACKNOWLEDGMENTS

We thank Dishita G. Turakhia and Yini Qi for their help with video editing.

## REFERENCES

[1] Patrick Baudisch, and Stefanie Mueller, Personal Fabrication. *Foundations and Trends® in Human–Computer Interaction* 10, 3–4, 165-293, 2017.

[2] Laura Briese, Rolf S. Arvidson, Andreas Luttge. The effect of crystal size variation on the rate of dissolution – A kinetic Monte Carlo study. In *Geochimica et Cosmochimica Acta* 212, 167-175, 2017.

[3] Xiang 'Anthony' Chen, Stelian Coros, Jennifer Mankoff, and Scott E. Hudson. Encore: 3D Printed Augmentation of Everyday Objects with Printed-Over, Affixed and Interlocked Attachments. In *Proceedings of the 28th Annual ACM Symposium on User Interface Software & Technology* (UIST '15), 73-82.

[4] Jérémie Dumas, Jean Hergel, and Sylvain Lefebvre. Bridging the gap: automated steady scaffoldings for 3D printing. In *ACM Transactions on Graφcs* 33, 4, Article 98, 2014.

[5] G.H. Gilmer. Computer Models of Crystal Growth. In *Science* 208, 4442, 355-363, 1980.

[6] Jean Hergel and Sylvain Lefebvre. Clean color: Improving multi-filament 3D prints. In Computer Graφcs Forum 33, 2, 469-478, 2014.

[7] Jeeeun Kim, Anhong Guo, Tom Yeh, Scott E. Hudson, and Jennifer Mankoff. Understanding Uncertainty in Measurement and Accommodating its Impact in 3D Modeling and Printing. In *Proceedings of the 2017 Conference on Designing Interactive Systems* (DIS '17), 1067-1078.

[8] Gierad Laput, Xiang 'Anthony' Chen, and Chris Harrison. 3D Printed Hair: Fused Deposition Modeling of Soft Strands, Fibers, and Bristles. In *Proceedings of the 28th Annual ACM Symposium on User Interface Software & Technology* (UIST '15), 593-597.

[9] John Lang Lombardi, Dragan Popovich, Gregory John Artz. Water soluble rapid prototyping support and mold material. *US Patent US6070107 A,* filed May 20, 1998.

[10] Robert MacCurdy, Robert Katzschmann, Youbin Kim, Daniela Rus. Printable hydraulics: A method for fabricating robots by 3D co-printing solids and liquids. In *International Conference on Robotics and Automation* (ICRA), 3878-3885, 2016.

[11] Stefanie Mueller, Sangha Im, Serafima Gurevich, Alexander Teibrich, Lisa Pfisterer, François Guimbretière, and Patrick Baudisch. WirePrint: 3D printed previews for fast prototyping. In *Proceedings of the 27th annual ACM symposium on User interface software and technology* (UIST '14), 273-280.

[12] Stefanie Mueller, Bastian Kruck, and Patrick Baudisch. LaserOrigami: laser-cutting 3D objects. In *Proceedings of the SIGCHI Conference on Human Factors in Computing Systems* (CHI '13), 2585-2592.

[13] Ryuma Niiyama, Xu Sun, Cynthia Sung, Byoungkwon An, Daniela Rus, and Sangbae Kim. Pouch Motors: Printable Soft Actuators Integrated with Computational Design. In *Soft Robotics* 2, 2, 59–70, 2015.

[14] Martin E. W. Nisser, Samuel M. Felton, Michael T. Tolley, Michael Rubenstein, Robert J. Wood. Feedback-controlled self-folding of autonomous robot collectives. In *International Conference on Intelligent Robots and Systems* (IROS), 2016.

[15] Noyes-Whitney Equation: http://www.pharmpress.com/files/docs/remington-education-physical-pharmacy-sample-chapter-3.pdf

[16] Jifei Ou, Gershon Dublon, Chin-Yi Cheng, Felix Heibeck, Karl Willis, and Hiroshi Ishii. Cilllia: 3D Printed Micro-Pillar Structures for Surface Texture, Actuation and Sensing. In *Proceedings of the 2016 CHI Conference on Human Factors in Computing Systems* (CHI '16), 5753-5764.

[17] Varun Perumal C and Daniel Wigdor. Foldem: Heterogeneous Object Fabrication via Selective Ablation of Multi-Material Sheets. In *Proceedings of the 2016 CHI Conference on Human Factors in Computing Systems* (CHI '16), 5765-5775.

[18] Michael L. Rivera, Melissa Moukperian, Daniel Ashbrook, Jennifer Mankoff, and Scott E. Hudson. Stretching the Bounds of 3D Printing with Embedded Textiles. In *Proceedings of the 2017 CHI Conference on Human Factors in Computing Systems (CHI '17)*, 497-508.

[19] Thijs Roumen, Bastian Kruck, Tobias Dürschmid, Tobias Nack, and Patrick Baudisch. Mobile Fabrication. In *Proceedings of the 29th Annual Symposium on User Interface Software and Technology* (UIST '16), 3-14.

[20] Thijs Jan Roumen, Willi Müller, and Patrick Baudisch. Grafter: Remixing 3D-Printed Machines. In *Proceedings of the 2018 CHI Conference on Human Factors in Computing Systems* (CHI '18), Paper 63.

[21] Ryan Schmidt and Nobuyuki Umetani. Branching support structures for 3D printing. In *ACM SIGGRAPH 2014 Studio* (SIGGRAPH '14), Article 9.

[22] Alexander Teibrich, Stefanie Mueller, François Guimbretière, Robert Kovacs, Stefan Neubert, and Patrick Baudisch. Patching Physical Objects. In *Proceedings of the 28th Annual ACM Symposium on User Interface Software & Technology* (UIST '15), 83-91.

[23] Ultimaker PVA. https://ultimaker.com/en/products/materials/pva

[24] Udayan Umapathi, Hsiang-Ting Chen, Stefanie Mueller, Ludwig Wall, Anna Seufert, and Patrick Baudisch. LaserStacker: Fabricating 3D Objects by Laser Cutting and Welding. In *Proceedings of the 28th Annual ACM Symposium on User Interface Software & Technology* (UIST '15), 575-582.

[25] Juraj Vanek, J. A. Garcia Galicia, and Bedrich Benes. Clever Support: Efficient Support Structure Generation for Digital Fabrication. In *Computer Graφcs Forum* 33, 5, 117-125, 2014.

[26] Wen Wang, Lining Yao, Teng Zhang, Chin-Yi Cheng, Daniel Levine, and Hiroshi Ishii. Transformative Appetite: Shape-Changing Food Transforms from 2D to 3D by Water Interaction through Cooking. In *Proceedings of the 2017 CHI Conference on Human Factors in Computing Systems* (CHI '17), 6123-6132.

[27] Weaverbird Grasshopper Plugin. http://www.giuliopiacentino.com/weaverbird/

[28] Karl Willis, Eric Brockmeyer, Scott Hudson, and Ivan Poupyrev. Printed optics: 3D printing of embedded optical elements for interactive devices. In *Proceedings of the 25th annual ACM symposium on User interface software and technology* (UIST '12), 589-598.

[29] Junichi Yamaoka, Ryuma Niiyama, and Yasuaki Kakehi. BlowFab: Rapid Prototyping for Rigid and Reusable Objects using Inflation of Laser-cut Surfaces. In *Proceedings of the 30th Annual ACM Symposium on User Interface Software and Technology* (UIST '17), 461-469.

[30] Lining Yao, Jifei Ou, Chin-Yi Cheng, Helene Steiner, Wen Wang, Guanyun Wang, and Hiroshi Ishii. bioLogic: Natto Cells as Nanoactuators for Shape Changing Interfaces. In *Proceedings of the 33rd Annual ACM Conference on Human Factors in Computing Systems* (CHI '15), 1-10.

[31] Xiaoting Zhang, Xinyi Le, Athina Panotopoulou, Emily Whiting, and Charlie C. L. Wang. Perceptual models of preference in 3D printing direction. In *ACM Transactions on Graφcs* 34, 6, Article 215, 2015.

[32] Kening Zhu, Alexandru Dancu, and Shengdong (Shen) Zhao. FusePrint: A DIY 2.5D Printing Technique Embracing Everyday Artifacts. In *Proceedings of the 2016 ACM Conference on Designing Interactive Systems* (DIS '16), 146-157.

# Interactive Fabrication of CSG Models with Assisted Carving

**Ammar Hattab**
School of Engineering, Brown University
Providence, RI, USA
ammar_hattab@brown.edu

**Gabriel Taubin**
School of Engineering, Brown University
Providence, RI, USA
gabriel_taubin@brown.edu

**Figure 1. We assist users in carving a physical CAD model. Given a target CAD model (Left). We generate a series of cutting instructions (Middle) and use a projector to project them to a block of material to guide the user in carving them. Until the user reaches the target physical replica (Right).**

## ABSTRACT

We propose a method that helps an unskilled user to carve a physical replica of a 3D CAD model while only using manual cutting tools. The method starts by analyzing the input CAD model and generates a set of carving instructions. Then using a projector, we project the instructions sequentially one at a time to a block of material to guide the user in performing each of them. After each cutting step, we use the projector-camera setup to 3D scan the object after cutting. And automatically align the scanned point cloud to the CAD model, to prepare the position for the next instruction. We demonstrate a complete system to support this operation and show several examples manually carved while using the system.

### Author Keywords

Interactive Fabrication; Assisted Carving; Constructive Solid Modeling (CSG); Spatial Augmented Reality.

### CCS Concepts

**•Human-centered computing → Human computer interaction (HCI);**


*TEI '19, March 17–20, 2019, Tempe, AZ, USA.*

ACM ISBN 978-1-4503-6196-5 /19/03 ...$15.00.
http://dx.doi.org/10.1145/3294109.3295644

## INTRODUCTION

In the early stages of prototyping, users usually use digital and physical tools to create their design. They might start by creating a digital CAD model, then creating a physical mock-up prototype by hand using foams. This allows them to feel the shape of the model and to make adjustments, before going back to digital again. The process of transforming a digital CAD model into a physical mock-up is very important at this stage. Some users use 3D printers for that, but they cannot use a prototyping material like foam or wood. CNC milling machines, on the other hand, could work on foam or wood, but they are usually large and expensive or they require some process planning to produce the 3D model from all directions. For this reason, a large amount of fabrication at this stage is done using hand tools.

Manually carving a model is an important skill for new designers. While many prefer digital design, there's something important lost when you cannot touch the thing you are making. Fabricating something with your hands is a very different cognitive process than drawing something on a screen. When designing models on the screen, it is necessary to make assumptions about the form and the function since the model is more abstract.

But the process of manually carving a digital model out of a block of material is still hard for novice users. Precise cutting is a painstaking job and figuring out the cutting steps in 3D is not trivial especially for complex models. Motivated by this problem, we present a method that can automatically analyze a CAD model and generates a series of manual cutting instructions. Then using a projector to project these instructions to guide the user in performing the cut until he reaches the target shape. The system has two main components; a method to generate manual cutting instructions, and a projector-camera calibrated setup to project those instructions, and to perform 3D scanning.

There are many 3D CAD representations, the most popular are boundary representations (B-Rep) and constructive solid geometry (CSG). In CSG, the CAD model is built using a tree of Boolean operations (like union, intersection, and subtraction) applied on simpler objects (like a sphere, cylinder, box, etc). In this work, we want to generate a series of subtraction instructions that remove parts of a block of material. So, we decided to use CSG for its volumetric representation. Starting from a block of material, each cutting instruction removes some part of the material until we reach the target model.

## RELATED WORK

### Interactive Fabrication

Fabrication machines were not fully automated when they were invented but involved a lot of human interaction. Programmers were required to write low-level commands to drive the machines. Conversational (CNC) allowed a higher level of interaction with the machines. While the (CAM) controlled machines became fully automated with time.

Many previous papers tried to increase the involvement of humans in the fabrication process, leading to what's called "interactive fabrication". The term "interactive fabrication" was first coined by [17] where they developed several interactive prototyping devices, "Constructable" [9] is another early break-through for making functional physical prototype interactively where users interact with the fabrication machine by drafting directly on the work-piece using a hand-held laser pointer, "Drill Sergeant" [14] project developed smart tools by augmenting common workshop tools (drill/driver, saw, router) with measurement and interactive feedback devices, and used them to provide the user with interactive in-situ step instructions, "Shaper Origin" [12] project combined manual and automatic tool positioning to precisely move a hand-held milling tool along a 2D path, and more recently in "RoMA" project [10] they combined augmented guidance with head display for interactive fabrication.

Within the interactive fabrication research a few previous papers proposed techniques to help novice users in carving, the closest to our work are the "Sculpting by Numbers" [11], "ShapeShift" [16], and Marner's work [7] where they used a projector to help users in sculpting clay or carving foam. The main difference between these papers and our work is that they provide a general guidance for the user by projecting the depth or the goal object on the remaining material and let the user figure out how to reach that goal. Whereas our method leads the user one step at a time through their process. Being more prescriptive than the other approaches, our method might be more suitable for novice users with little experience in carving or 3D. While the other papers might work better for more experienced users. In fact, this approach was one of the recommendations of the expert review in [7]. We also allow the user to move the model freely by hand to perform the cut, and then we automatically align the model for the next cutting step.

Besides using a projector, in the "FreeD" project [18] they proposed a hybrid carving technique, where they developed a hand-held digital milling device that helps the user in carving the 3D model. Although the carving could be faster than our work, they normally produce rougher output, which is more suitable for free-form sculptures rather than CAD models.

### Automatic Process Planning

The method described in this paper starts by analyzing the CAD model and generates a list of cutting instructions, then it leads the user one step at a time to perform these cutting operations. While this might be suitable for beginner users, it's also very similar to the automated fabrication machines, where usually the CAD model is analyzed and a list of additive or subtractive instructions are generated and sent to the machine. In general, we call this process planning.

Additive machines like 3D printers, analyze the model by slicing it first and generate tool-paths from these slices. Milling machines, on the other hand, might require a more complex analysis, especially if the milling is to be performed from multiple directions, or in multiple stages using different machines. There has been a lot of work to automatically plan the fabrication process using different machines. Part of this work was focused on automatically discovering manufacturable features in the CAD model like holes, slots, and pockets, etc. See [5] for a survey of this work. The planning process might require segmenting the model into different surfaces, especially if a hybrid additive and subtractive fabrication is used as in [3].

### Spatially Augmented Reality

In this paper, we use a projector to project cutting instructions onto a block of material. This creates an augmented reality on top of a real physical object. An approach that is called spatially augmented reality. See for example [2]. In general, this approach uses the projector intrinsic and extrinsic parameters for the rendering cameras, such that the rendering is performed from the same position and orientation of the projector with respect to the environment. The projector itself is considered as an inverse camera. Many previous papers used this approach, especially for educational purposes. Some papers used this approach for guiding the user to perform certain tasks, such as sculpting [16, 11], or painting [4], or placing objects in a certain position. The benefit here is that the user does not need to wear any special devices to see the virtual reality.

## METHOD

### System Design

In terms of hardware, the system is composed of a camera and a projector calibrated and fixed with regard to each other. The projector is used to project the cutting instructions on a block of material where it will illuminate the regions that should be removed by the user. The camera is used to capture the 3D shape of the object -together with the projector, see Figure 2.

In terms of software, the system is composed mainly of five components:

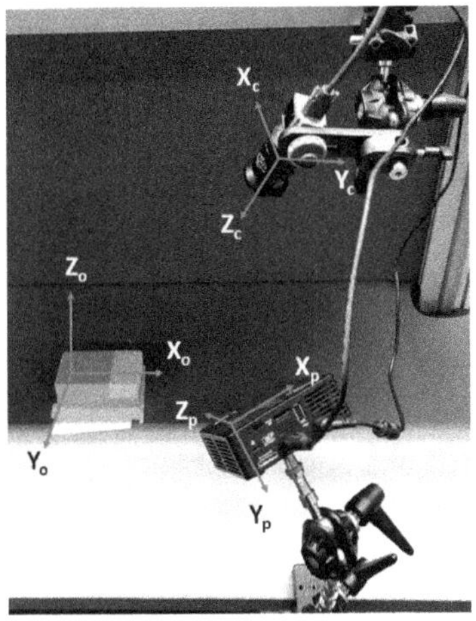


Figure 2. A projector-camera setup is used in this work

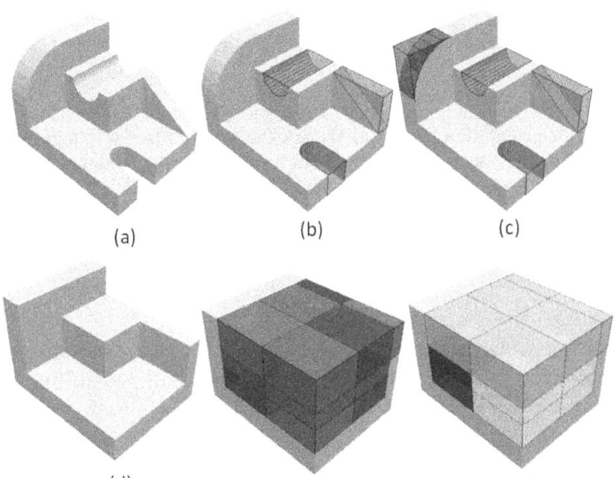


**Figure 3. Method steps. (a) Given a CAD model. (b) We add negative objects instructions. (c) And we add simple positive objects instructions. This finishes stage 1 which results in a (d) union of bounding boxes object. (e) We construct a voxel grid of the remaining space. (f) And we segment the voxel grid by merging voxels.**

### *Instructions Generator*

The input to this step is a CSG CAD model, and the goal is to generate a series of cutting instructions to cut that CAD model out of a block of material. Each cutting instruction should remove a part of that block. And each cutting instruction should be simple enough to be done using hand tools. The union of all removed parts is equal to subtracting the CAD model from its the bounding box. So basically, to generate these cutting instructions, we turn the problem into a 3D segmentation problem of the negative space (The space resulting from subtracting the model from its bounding box). The algorithm performs the segmentation in two stages. See Figure 3 for a general overview of the algorithm.

In the first stage, we generate a cutting instruction for each simple geometry shape in the CSG tree (cube, cylinder, cone, etc). At first, for the negative shapes (shapes that are subtracted in the CSG tree), they are added directly to the list of instructions

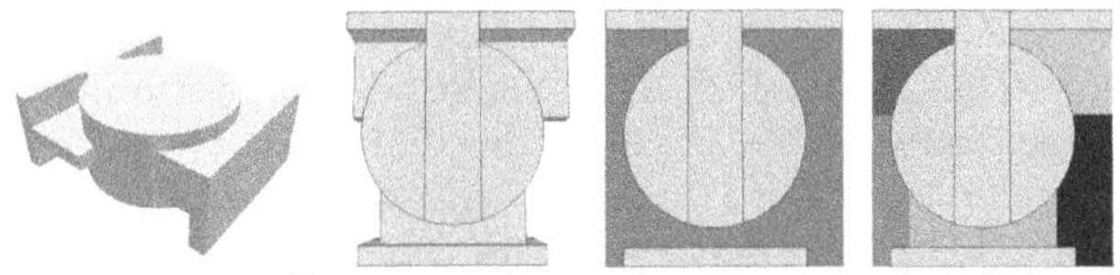


**Figure 4. Segmenting the remaining volume by depth. (a) Bounding boxes object the result of stage 1. (b) Remaining volume shown in red color. (c) Segmenting the remaining volume by depth.**

as the last cutting instructions. While for the positive shapes, if they are simple we add the negative space of the positive shape (its bounding box subtract the shape itself).

In the second stage, we start with the remaining volume to be cut, we define a voxel grid around it. Then we segment it by merging the small cells in the grid to get the remaining regions to be cut. We mark and exclude the filled voxels in this grid. Since the user usually starts cutting from the top, we need to look to the model from above. Starting from the top, for each remaining voxel, we compute the depth under this voxel (how many connected voxels under this voxel are marked as filled by the remaining volume). And, we run a region growing algorithm starting from that voxel (add the voxels that have the same depth to the same segment). After segmenting the voxels of certain z-level according to the depth, we start growing the segments down to the bottom levels. And we do so until no voxels are left. See Figure 4.

### *3D Scanning*

We need to capture the shape of the current object to find the correct alignment in order to project the next instruction. And to show the user how far he is from the target instruction. There are many 3D scanning techniques, but since we are using a projector to project the instructions, we can use it for 3D scanning as well. So, we used structured-light gray-code 3D scanning, and we used the method of [8] to calibrate the projector-camera setup.

Notice in Figure 2 that we have three coordinate systems, one for the camera, one for the projector and one for the 3D model. We choose to use the projector coordinate system as the main coordinate system and to convert all points and transformations to this coordinate system. Because the projector is the common thing between the two operations; 3D scanning with the camera, and 3D rendering with the 3D model. The point cloud resulting from scanning is converted to the projector coordinate system by a simple transformation using the rotation and translation matrices (we obtain them during the calibration process):

$$P_p = RP_c + T$$

While the 3D model is transformed into the projector coordinate system by the next 3D alignment step.

### *3D Alignment*

Fully carving a CAD model requires the ability to cut the model from several different orientations to cover the model details from all directions. Also, the user might want to hold the model in his hands or move it freely in any direction to use a specific tool. So, to allow a fluid process, we cannot restrict the model to a certain location or orientation. For this reason, after each cutting step, we must perform a 3D alignment step between the scanned 3D point-cloud and the current instruction 3D model. We used the iterative closest point (ICP) method to perform the automatic alignment [1].

The ICP method requires a good initial alignment to succeed. Otherwise, it could easily get stuck on some local minima. For this reason, after each cutting step, we ask the user to place the object roughly in the same position and orientation of the current instruction model. We do that by projecting a 2D guidance contour on the table and ask the user to place the object roughly on that contour. We generate that contour by slicing the bottom of the current instruction model. This usually provides a good initial alignment for the ICP to succeed. Otherwise, we allow the user to fix the initial alignment manually.

### *Detecting Changes*

We also allow the user to use the result of 3D scanning to verify the previous cut. We calculate the distance between each point of the 3D scanned point cloud and the current instruction model, and visualize these distances using colors as in [6]. This visualization helps the user in fixing any deviation introduced during the last cut operation, unless if the deviation is an over-cut (which cannot be fixed easily in the context of carving). In the case of over-cut, the user might choose to update the current CAD model with the actual cut operation as detected by 3D scanning. To do that, we first find the changed regions in the 3D scanned point cloud by using the method of [6] where the user specifies a threshold distance after which the point is considered among the changed points. The minimum change that can be detected by the system depends on the resolution of the used 3D scanner. After detecting the changed regions, we use RANSAC method [13] to detect planes, cylinders or other basic shapes in the changed regions. Then, we use the detected shapes to update the shape of the actual CAD model using CSG operations. Sometimes, the system fails to detect the correct changed regions or the correct shapes due to noise or gaps in the 3D scans. In these cases, we allow the user to manually correct the changed regions or to ignore falsely detected regions.

### *3D Rendering and Projection*

Now, after alignment of the scanned point cloud and the current instruction model. The model is ready for projecting the next instruction. So, we use WebGL to render the next instruction while using the projector intrinsic parameters for the rendering camera [15], and we show the rendering on the projector screen. At the same time, we show a rendering of the whole model with the current instruction highlighted on the computer screen to allow the user to visualize it.

## EXPERIMENTS AND DISCUSSION

### Carving Process

The carving process starts from a block of material with the same dimensions as the bounding box of the CAD model, then we project a sequence of cutting instructions and ask the user to perform them, for each cutting instruction we need to perform the steps shown in Figure 5.

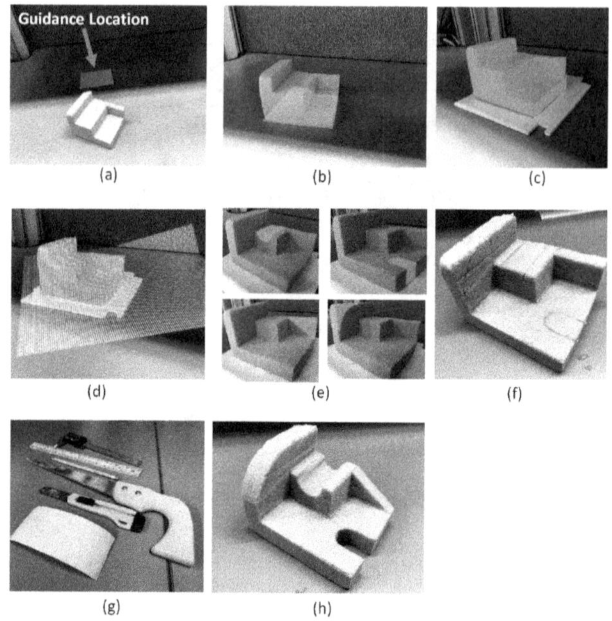


**Figure 5. General process step. For a specific instruction, first, we find the best orientation. Then (a) We ask the user to place it in a guidance location. (b) The user roughly places the object in the guidance location (c) We project the whole object again for a better rough alignment. (d) We perform 3D Scanning. (e) We project the instruction(s). (f) The user marks the places to be carved. (g) The user performs the carving using hand tools. (h) result ready for the next instruction.**

For each instruction, we need to find the best orientation to show it to the user that gives the best projector visibility. We simply want to choose from the six basic orientations; front, back, left, right, top and bottom. We do so by shooting rays starting from each polygon on the surface of the instruction in each of these directions. And choosing the direction that gives the best visibility (gives a larger visible area where these rays do not intersect the remaining volume). After choosing the best orientation we show it to the user and ask him to orient the part in the specified orientation.

### Carving Experiments

In Figure 6, we show some examples of CAD models and the manual carving process. To perform these experiments, we used a low-resolution Optoma projector (960 X 540 pixels) and a Basler camera (1928 X 1208). The projector and camera were fixed at a certain angle of the workspace table to allow projecting the instructions from several directions.

### Future Work

There are some constraints on the type of CAD models that the method can handle. At first, we expect each part of the model surface to be visible from some direction, otherwise, the algorithm will generate instructions that cannot be performed. One way to handle these cases is to split the CAD model to make its whole surface visible from some angle. Currently, we only compute the best orientation from the six basic orientations. But in the future, we want to develop a more complex algorithm that selects the best orientation in general.

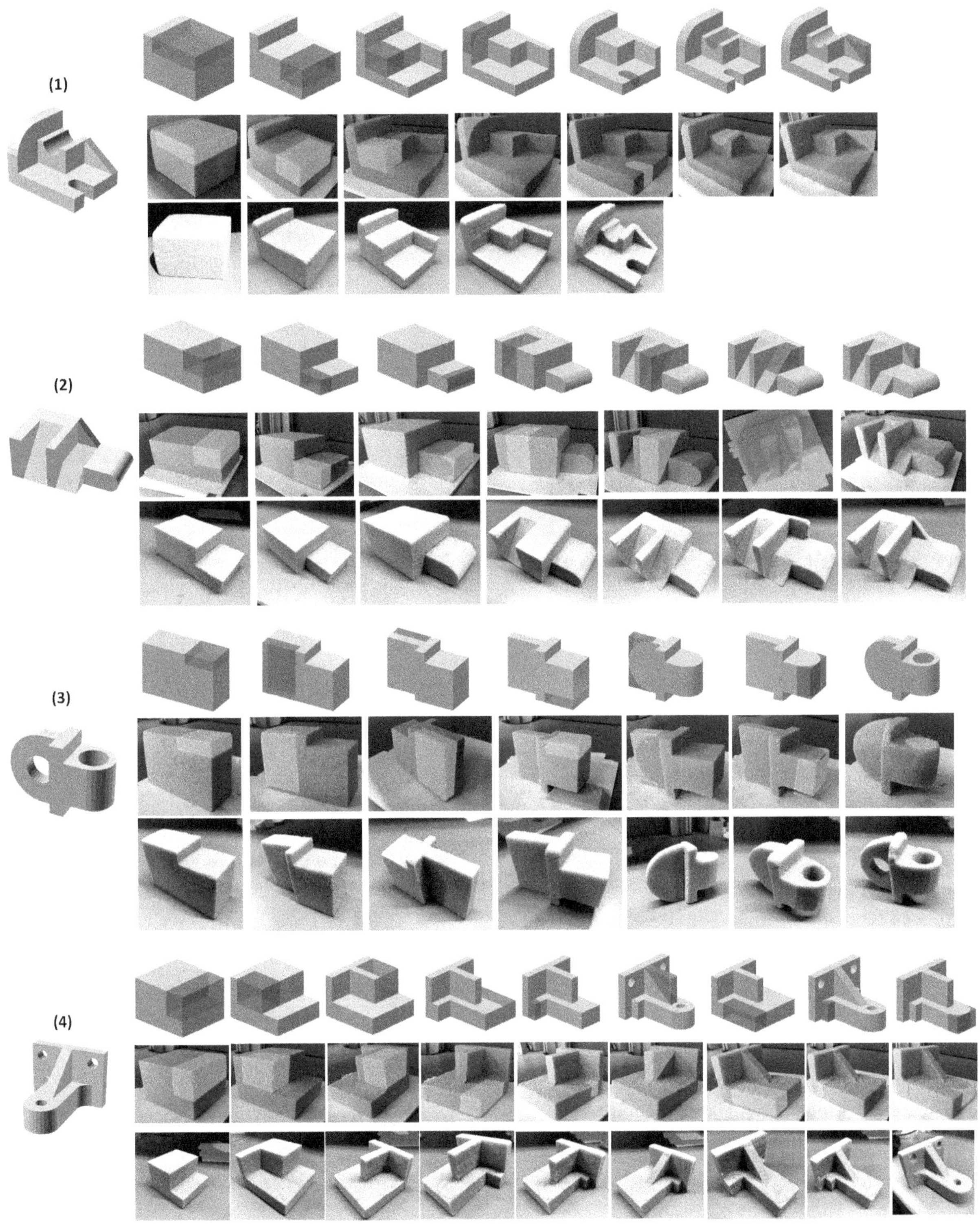


Figure 6. Some examples of CAD models and their manual carving process, with the rendered instructions on the top row, projected instructions on the middle row and the actual cutting result on the bottom row.

That algorithm should also take into account that we want the model to stand by itself while projecting this orientation.

Besides the visibility constraints, we should order the instructions such that we minimize the number of times where the user must move the object. This will help the user in performing multiple instructions at once. Another limitation of the method is that it does not always match the user preferences. Sometimes there are multiple possible good segmentations, and in general, the user might have his own preference, and he might not like the instructions given. Some other times the instructions given are too long for the user. To help with that, we give the user the option to combine multiple instructions, to skip instructions, or to change the order of instructions. In the future, we want to allow the user to do his own special cuts, and then rerun the algorithm starting from the user operation.

## CONCLUSION

In this preliminary work, we demonstrated a system that helps unskilled users in carving CAD models. We noticed that carving is a hard process for novice users, as they need help figuring out the steps to cut a specific 3D model and to measure and mark the locations to perform these cuts. We presented a method to generate carving instructions for an input CAD model and used a projector to project these instructions to a block of material. To generate the instructions, we need to solve a segmentation problem of the negative space of the CAD model. The method must take into account the visibility constraints and some other factors. 3D alignment is an important step in the system that prepares the system for projecting the next instruction. The system flexibility helps the user to match his preference in merging instructions, changing their order or defining custom instructions.

## ACKNOWLEDGMENTS

The work described herein was partially supported by a Brown Fellowship and by NSF grants IIS-1717355 and IIP-1500249.

## REFERENCES

[1] Paul J Besl and Neil D McKay. 1992. Method for registration of 3-D shapes. In *Sensor Fusion IV: Control Paradigms and Data Structures*, Vol. 1611. International Society for Optics and Photonics, 586–607.

[2] Oliver Bimber and Ramesh Raskar. 2005. *Spatial augmented reality: merging real and virtual worlds*. CRC press.

[3] YC Chang, JM Pinilla, JH Kao, J Dong, K Ramaswami, and FB Prinz. 1999. Automated layer decomposition for additive/subtractive solid freeform fabrication. In *Proceedings of the Solid Freeform Fabrication Symposium, The University of Texas at Austin*. 111–120.

[4] Matthew Flagg and James M Rehg. 2006. Projector-guided painting. In *Proceedings of the 19th annual ACM symposium on User interface software and technology*. ACM, 235–244.

[5] JungHyun Han, Mike Pratt, and William C Regli. 2000. Manufacturing feature recognition from solid models: a status report. *IEEE Transactions on Robotics and Automation* 16, 6 (2000), 782–796.

[6] Ammar Hattab, Ian Gonsher, Daniel Moreno, and Gabriel Taubin. 2017. Differential 3D Scanning. *IEEE computer graphics and applications* 38, 3 (2017), 43–51.

[7] Michael R Marner and Bruce H Thomas. 2010. Augmented foam sculpting for capturing 3D models. In *3D User Interfaces (3DUI), 2010 IEEE Symposium on*. IEEE, 63–70.

[8] Daniel Moreno and Gabriel Taubin. 2012. Simple, accurate, and robust projector-camera calibration. In *3D Imaging, Modeling, Processing, Visualization and Transmission (3DIMPVT), 2012 Second International Conference on*. IEEE, 464–471.

[9] Stefanie Mueller, Pedro Lopes, and Patrick Baudisch. 2012. Interactive construction: interactive fabrication of functional mechanical devices. In *Proceedings of the 25th annual ACM symposium on User interface software and technology*. ACM, 599–606.

[10] Huaishu Peng, Jimmy Briggs, Cheng-Yao Wang, Kevin Guo, Joseph Kider, Stefanie Mueller, Patrick Baudisch, and François Guimbretière. 2018. RoMA: Interactive Fabrication with Augmented Reality and a Robotic 3D Printer. (2018).

[11] Alec Rivers, Andrew Adams, and Frédo Durand. 2012a. Sculpting by numbers. *ACM Transactions on Graphics (TOG)* 31, 6 (2012), 157.

[12] Alec Rivers, Ilan E Moyer, and Frédo Durand. 2012b. Position-correcting tools for 2D digital fabrication. *ACM Transactions on Graphics (TOG)* 31, 4 (2012), 88.

[13] Ruwen Schnabel, Roland Wahl, and Reinhard Klein. 2007. Efficient RANSAC for point-cloud shape detection. In *Computer graphics forum*, Vol. 26. Wiley Online Library, 214–226.

[14] Eldon Schoop, Michelle Nguyen, Daniel Lim, Valkyrie Savage, Sean Follmer, and Björn Hartmann. 2016. Drill Sergeant: Supporting physical construction projects through an ecosystem of augmented tools. In *Proceedings of the 2016 CHI Conference Extended Abstracts on Human Factors in Computing Systems*. ACM, 1607–1614.

[15] Kyle Simek. 2013. Calibrated Cameras in OpenGL. `http://ksimek.github.io/2013/06/03/calibrated_cameras_in_opengl`. (2013). Accessed: 2018-04-12.

[16] Christopher Skeels and James M Rehg. 2007. ShapeShift: A projector-guided sculpture system. In *Proc. UIST*, Vol. 7.

[17] Karl DD Willis, Cheng Xu, Kuan-Ju Wu, Golan Levin, and Mark D Gross. 2011. Interactive fabrication: new interfaces for digital fabrication. In *Proceedings of the fifth international conference on Tangible, embedded, and embodied interaction*. ACM, 69–72.

[18] Amit Zoran, Roy Shilkrot, and Joseph Paradiso. 2013. Human-computer interaction for hybrid carving. In *Proceedings of the 26th annual ACM symposium on User interface software and technology*. ACM, 433–440.

# When is it not Craft? Materiality and Mediation when Craft and Computing Meet

**Michael Nitsche**
Georgia Institute of Technology
Atlanta, GA, USA
michael.nitsche@gatech.edu

**Anna Weisling**
Georgia Institute of Technology
Atlanta, GA, USA
aweisling@gatech.edu

## ABSTRACT
Craft has emerged as an important reference point for HCI. To avoid a misrepresenting, all-encompassing application of craft to interaction design, this position paper first discerns craft from HCI. It develops material engagement and mediation as differentiating factors to reposition craft in relation to tangible interaction design. The aim is to clarify craft's relation to interaction design and to open up new opportunities and questions that follow from this repositioning.

### Author Keywords
Craft; tangible interaction design; design research; physical computing.

### ACM Classification Keywords
• Human-centered computing~Interaction design theory, concepts and paradigms • Human-centered computing~Interaction devices • Human-centered computing~Interface design prototyping

## INTRODUCTION
Craft has become a major influence in Human-Computer Interaction (HCI) and related fields in computing. Among others, it has been integrated with a view to education in making [1] as well as Computer Science [2]; as material practice in relation to physical computing [3] and in the role of fabrication tools for production [4]; as reference for experience design [5] and collaborative practices [6]. Combinations of craft and HCI go hand in hand with a rise of maker-cultures and have shaped countless projects, often fueled by technologies that have become increasingly accessible. The meeting of craft and interaction design as originally separate disciplines has proven to be a fruitful intersection for debate and project development and has led to the notion of "hybrid crafting" [7] or "Neocraft" [8]. But the emerging field has also drawn criticism.


*TEI '19*, March 17–20, 2019, Tempe, AZ, USA

ACM ISBN 978-1-4503-6196-5/19/03...$15.00
https://doi.org/10.1145/3294109.3295651

Devendorf and Rosner question whether the limitations of a "hybrid" approach hinder the inclusion of additional references and thus build on a too restrictive perspective [9]. Frayling - an early proponent for the original method of research through design and inclusion of material practices - questions the direct projection of craft onto other fields [10]. Others draw attention to the possible incompatibilities or challenges of such a merger [11, 12]. The practical intersections between craft and interaction design are productive, but far from unproblematic.

Craft, defined by Sennet as work done "well for its own sake" [13] has encountered fundamental changes in the period of industrialization, which led Pye to separate between a workmanship of *risk* (which is largely tied to human performance and possibility of failure) and one of *certainty* (tied to mechanically optimized fabrication) [14]. The digital age continues to challenge craft. As digital technology enters craft processes, any skill- and knowledge-based craft concepts must embrace abstract tools, too. Dormer states that "[i]t is not craft as 'handcraft' that defines contemporary craftsmanship: it is craft as knowledge that empowers a maker to take charge of technology. " [15] In the continuation of these shifts we find a friction between craft and interaction design. The field of tangible interaction design is defined by its use of physical/ tangible components not only for *representation* but also for direct *manipulation* [16]. This focus on materials invites craft as a reference point, but it does not mean that tangible interfaces practice craft by definition.

The goal of this paper is a critical re-positioning of craft to interaction design. It aims to provide a theoretical discussion along three short example cases to sketch out a preliminary relation model.

## PROBLEMATIZING CRAFT
To provide an initial structure for this encounter of the domains, we first propose to talk about craft in a framing vs operational way. Any tangible design project can be approached and analyzed "*as* craft," meaning: we are free to deploy craft-related theories, practices, histories, and methods as critical means or as analytical perspectives to further tangible interaction design. In this case, the fields do not merge but open critical perspectives through their differences. In contrast, a tangible interaction design "*is* craft" when it includes actual craft practice in the direct encounter of the material and the computer as a tool in as

unmediated ways as possible, as we will discuss below. Following our own division, this paper focuses on examples where interaction and its design "*is* craft." As we shall see, even these cases are conflicted.

### Case: Hybrid Crafting

Zoran and Buechley speak of a "hybrid" approach in their combination of crafted and scanned/3D printed components into a mixed material piece "to merge digital fabrication with traditional craft, thereby combining two creative processes that rarely overlap" [17].

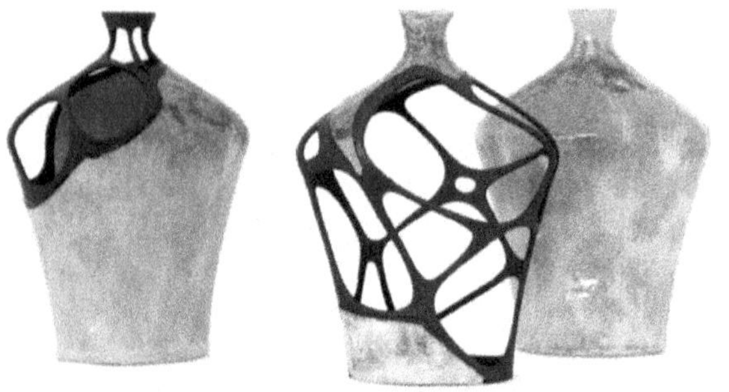

**Figure 1. Zoran's "hybrid" crafting combines and contrasts traditional ceramics with 3D printing [17].**

The merger is performed as a destruction of the initially traditionally crafted ceramics and a consciously non-functional filling of the resulting holes with 3D printed components (see fig. 1). The critical encounter emerges quite literally from the conflict between the two conditions: the crafted vs the 3D printed. The project is a successful example for a combined approach but not one of an uncomplicated merger. Instead, it operates through the differentiation between the two traditions of craft and personal fabrication/digital media.

Differences between the two disciplines, such as focus on distinct materials and divergent practices, histories, and communities, have fueled emerging interdisciplinary approaches, but also endanger the fields to diffuse into an unspecific amalgamation of neither. This smoldering is further driven by significant commercial forces, such as 3D printing and scanning industries, patents, and publishing interests. The related term of the "maker" is rightly being re-interrogated [18] and has spawned a critical rethinking of what is means to "make" [19]. Some of this critique tackles the making process itself in its formulation and publication (see the self-assembled booklets by Hertz [20]), not unlike Zoran's dysfunctional vases.

The goal, thus, is to avoid a simplistic blending that threatens to stifle the stimulating differences between craft and interaction design. We have to emphasize their differences and incompatibilities to ensure the identity of the partners involved in this obviously productive debate. To this end, we identify two differentiating factors as principles through which we can define whether HCI "*is* craft" or not: *Mediation*, and *Material Encounters*.

## MEDIATION

Looking at the improvements in user interface design and inspired by McLuhan, Alan Kay proclaimed in the early 90s "The computer is a medium! I had always thought of it as a tool, perhaps a vehicle-a much weaker conception." [21] The very same notion that computers mediate is reflected in the "multimedia" capabilities associated with computers, the interplay of hypermediacy and immediacy [22] and the idea of "transcoding" one media component into another [23]. Computers mediate by means of transcoding and simulation. By definition, these are processes that detach from the source, from whatever is remediated or transcoded. This inherited detachment prevents computer media such as video games or online worlds from qualifying as craft, instead we "invent the medium" [24] as designers and hand over the result to the user. Not every mediation has to go through a complete numerical abstraction, but digital mediation does. Based on this specificity, we suggest to differentiate between "mediated" (namely transcoded through digital technology) and "unmediated" (namely not transcoded). Mediation's abstraction, then, poses a separating factor from crafting.

Differentiating between "mediated" on one side, and "unmediated" on the other is to be understood as a preliminary tool. Media permeate lived environments and change them, blurring definitions and historic boundaries (see the changing notion of "liveness" [25]). This differentiation proposes not an absolute horizon but a departure from established divisions in HCI into material vs immaterial [26], or tangible/graspable vs intangible [16, 27].

## ENCOUNTERS WITH MATERIALS

Traditional crafting practices position the creator and the tool in a very specific relationship toward a physical material [28]. The material is the target of and partner in a process which is enabled by this crafter-tool dynamic, eventually resulting in an artifact which has been transformed, revealed, or made to emerge. During this process, tools are used not only to create, change, or give shape to a material, but also to relay information from the material itself to the crafter, which can in turn inform the crafting process. This is a reciprocal encounter with materials which are continuously revealing themselves and being revealed by us. Although tools have a defined practical function in this encounter, they are also part of the larger relational network at work (for a recent reading of this Heideggerian approach see [29]).

Because each material engages differently, traditional crafting practices vary. However, they all differ from the process of computational mediation/transcoding in several key ways, which can be thought of in terms of the difference between tool and machine. A transcoding media machine necessitates detachment, whereas the craft tool is a conduit for material "listening" as well as physical manipulation. When we put our hands to clay or a chisel to marble, we leave visible traces of our actions, connecting the body directly to the emerging object [30]. Reciprocally, our bodies are attuned to the reality of the artifact which is emerging through the state changes of the tool which connects us to it. As Merleau-Ponty describes in his example of a blind man's walking cane: the cane-tool extends the "area of sensitivity" [31]. Heidegger makes similar arguments, famously observing that the carpenter is not involved with the hammer, but rather with the nail *through* the hammer, the wood through the nail and so on. The hammer, the nail, and the crafter realize connection and potential within that context [32]. Feedback from the changing materials, felt through the tool, is imperative to the process of crafting. The human control of the tool, and the varying nuances associated with it, such as skill and dexterity, determine that material change as well as the emerging skill and role of the crafter.

In contrast, the computer, operating as a media machine and as a transcoder, will execute a procedure successfully or unsuccessfully, and relay that outcome to the user. The result might be the anticipated realization of the objective, or a crash, freeze, or other instantiation of failure. As we will argue below, computers and hardware can operate on the level of tools, but if we type on the keyboard or operate the mouse, the embodied action does not tell us anything about the process which is making something appear on the screen. Bridging this disconnect between input and output has been a motivating factor in tangible interaction design since its beginnings [16]. One might consider touch-screens on which you can draw with varying levels of pressure, vibrotactile communication devices [33], or haptic software interfaces [34], as a "craft-like." But the operations which facilitate this feedback to us remain ambivalent to our actions as the one interacting with these devices. We might be experts in their use but remain largely ignorant of their workings. Though we are trained in efficient use as we type on our keyboard, we do not receive information back through that same channel. The keys do not shock us. The material properties of the tool—electricity traveling through circuits—are invisible and not incorporated into the experiential participation. The operation – a finger pressing, swipe, pinch, grasp – is mediated to the user. McCullough sees in such expert handling a notion of crafting even if it is interacting with a computer. His skill-based definition of craft argues that the computer as medium "or communications device is inherently a tool for the *mind*-not the hands" [35], but it is a tool in the crafting sense, a "software tool" working via "analogy" and "metaphor" in its interaction design [35]. This might apply to handling interfaces, such as operating the mouse or shortcuts in an application, but is less clear when it comes to the material qualities we highlight here. For McCullough, "[c]oncepts become things" through computers but the role of those things' materials and their changes are less clear.

That is why we turn to Shiner, who presents a strong delineation between hand-tool craft and hand-computer making. Both are separated by the engagement with tacit knowledge on the part of the crafter. For Shiner, the enactment of tacit knowledge reflects a way of making which is characterized by the embodiment of the crafter herself: "Mastery in the crafts is a matter of mind and hand working instinctively together, a kind of practical know-how or tacit knowledge." [36] Shiner is able to distinguish this kind of making from digital design practices, in which, "the designer or craftsperson combines digital design with digital fabrication, the body's contact with 'materials' is so radically diminished that the flow of tacit knowledge normally gained through physical contact and feedback from alterations in the material becomes primarily visual and intellectual" [37]. In that way, digital design tools and related interfaces such as the *Reactable* are still remediators with the additional quality of tangible design integrated into the process of that mediation. Oreggia and White engage this philosophy in their discussion of art and musical practices in particular, stating that, "as with brushstrokes in painting, the materiality of [a] musical instrument leaves traces on the performance, and thus the materiality of the instrument is essential to the semantics of the performance in a way in which the materiality of a computer is not essential to the semantics of programs that are executed on it." [38] We encounter the *Reactable* as physical device but its materiality does not relate to its underlying transcoding operations. The material encounter traced here, as well as by Shiner, presents a second defining moment to differentiate the abstraction of digital production from material crafting.

So far, the argument has introduced *mediation* and *material encounters* as possible differentiating factors between craft and computing. These are based on different forms of engagement with materials: transcoded/mediated vs non-mediated/ tool-driven.

## VISUALIZING INTERACTION DYNAMICS

Using the differentiation laid out above, a model can be sketched out that first puts particular modes of production in relation to these two means of the computer as either tool or media machine. Based on such a mapping of modes of engagement, we will later propose a basic mapping of the roles within such a system.

First, the two defining means of computers' role, as media machine or as tool, can help to map out different modes of computer's use. The two key modes here are those of creation (in a direct encounter with the material, e.g. through tacit knowledge) and consumption (in a condition of abstracted mediation of processes, e.g. when using opaque applications).

Second, the combined position of such modes and means on our spectrum of mediated-to-material-encounter can help illuminate the role of the maker, particularly within hybrid practices which draw from both craft and HCI practices.

The model isolates the differences between craft and HCI practices, but it also emphasizes the hybridity of many emergent practices and the flexibility of varying roles of practitioners who move in-between them. In this schema, a computer may be used as a tool when it primarily accommodates material encounters, or as a media machine when it operates as an opaque abstracting machine of transcoded signs. Likewise, the role of a practitioner may align with various disciplines suggested by the mode of engagement, from designer to producer, crafter to consumer.

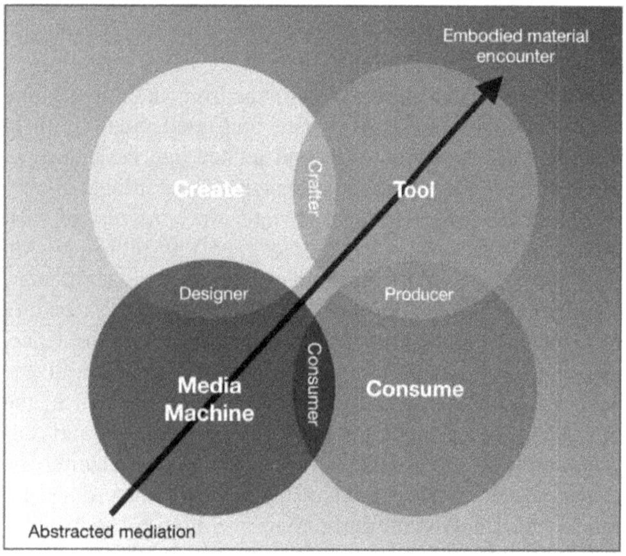


**Figure 2. Mapping the different positions of interactors in relation to possible functions of the computer as device.**

When a tool is used to create something in the embodied way outlined above, there is an associated direct material encounter which places the creator in a crafting role. In contrast, a media machine being used for the consumption of transcoded media positions the individual in the role of a consumer. Subsequently, the areas in which a media machine is being used to create, or the tool is used for consumer purposes, are where you find hybrid practices such as design and production. The chart presents a broad model, but it helps to position different practices "as craft" versus "is craft" by offering an entry point into interrogating the maker's relationship to their means and mode of production.

## ENCOUNTERS WITH TECHNOLOGY

Two short reference cases in tangible interaction design are presented as examples for possible material encounters that support the proposed turn to mediated vs unmediated practice.

### Case: Soft Circuits

The field of soft circuits inherently utilizes craft practices and materials: it applies craft-like assemblies and hybrid materials that might be conductive as well as protective, worn as well as sensing, functioning and fashionable. Yet, even the most craft-centric approaches remain obscure to most users as long as the operations remain opaque-as-mediated to them. The end user who purchases a prepared wearable remains oblivious about the way conductivity changes in a soft circuit button or a stretching potentiometer. In that regard, the tangible component represents a physical mediation, much like that envisioned by Ullmer and Ishii [16]. It may be a tangible input-output link, as craft materials are directly experienced in the use of the object. Users get the physical and tactile sensation of a carefully constructed material encounter, but this remains a transcoded encounter. If one wants to integrate craft as an active quality and practice in its own right, then this represents a missed opportunity.

Within soft circuitry, various scholars have addressed this. We argue that the reason why Perner-Wilson's work is valuable in the context of craft in tangible interaction design is not only the resulting object and how it integrates textiles and electronics but also because of the documentation leading up to it.

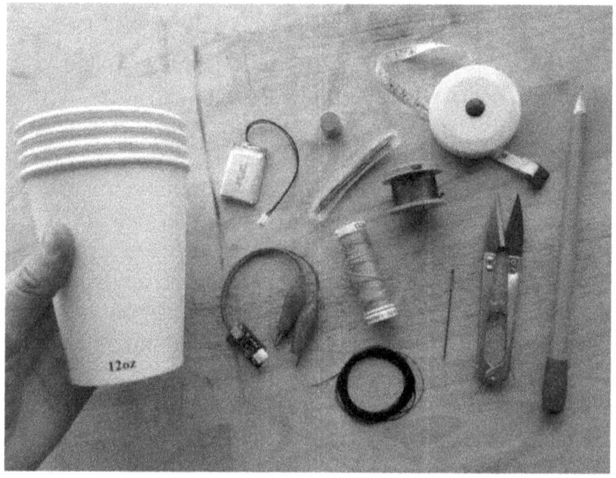

**Figure 3. Perner-Wilson's "Woven Paper Cup Speaker" from the online Instructable [39].**

In her online Instructable *Woven Paper Cup Speaker*, Perner-Wilson explains step-by-step the crafting of the simple speaker object and explains the underlying logic. A classic mediating device, a speaker, turns into a material encounter.

If only the final product is concerned, then craft practices, such as sewing, crocheting, or stitching remain obscured as they are not handled by the user but performed by an external maker. Because Perner-Wilson provides extensive documentation on how to create her pieces, these practices become accessible (see also [1, 40]). Craft, as a productive action, is integrated into the design of workshops and educational conditions. Such a productive stance includes designing for a creative encounter of the underlying materials. In such a craft-inspired interaction design approach, the user is not encountering a crafted artifact but engages in crafting as process to deal with the artifact. Digital component involved in this process turn from a mediating device into a tool.

Within the proposed model, Perner-Wilson's artifact construction is a creative act in which material encounters and computation are closely connected – it draws mainly from traditional crafting tools. In the creation of the work itself, the role of the maker is defined by the use of physical tools and the emergence of a material artifact through that relationship. Here the dynamic between the creator and what is created involves reciprocal engagement of raw materials and that which emerges from a crafting process. This portion of the work, then, sees the role of the maker in a crafting role. However, we must also recognize the shifting role of the maker in later portions of the work, which incorporate computational elements as media: a major function of the piece relies on recording and deployment of documentation via the internet, and so we can see the maker's role shift from that of crafter to a more mediated activity. The role of the maker is fluid, shifting between roles based on the levels of material encounter and mediation in the means and mode of production.

### Case: Circuit Bending & No-input Mixing

Musicians who engage in no-input mixing (also known as inputless mixing or zero input mixing) and circuit bending deliberately dismantle the protective shell designed to keep consumers from the inner workings of mechanical systems in order to exploit the electrical activity within the devices. Often, the individuals engaged in this type of destruction-as-construction are non-experts more concerned with "[traversing] through the hidden content inside of a technological system for the joy of entertaining its concealed underlayer" than with complying with the usages imposed by manufacturers and designers of the objects [41]. As Hertz and Parikka explain, this "depunctualization" of black-box technology makes that which is purposefully designed to be invisible to the user, in a technological object which is constructed for a singular use, into an instrument which is technically "broken" yet functional for new, creative purposes.

Similarly, no-input mixing exploits the traditionally undesirable "noise" which is inherent to any electrical system (in this case a sound mixer) and redirects that noise as an input back into the system itself. By amplifying the system noise and passing that signal through the mixer in different ways, a chaotic (unpredictable) feedback loop is created within the circuit, producing pitched loops and beats entirely dependent on the constraints of the largely unknown system. The results are somewhat the opposite of the carefully crafted soft circuits, most often unpredictable, non-linear, and potentially destructive.

"Blackboxing," as a design philosophy, is a method of separating the individual from the material conditions of a system, rendering us users rather than crafters. By re-exposing, repurposing, and redirecting the raw materials of an object, we engage in a craft-like relationship with those objects, even as we potentially destroy them in the process. When engaging in no-input mixing or live circuit bending, the musician not only changes the flow of electricity within the system itself, but imparts their own noise into the process. One of the most prolific no-input mixer musicians, Toshimaru Nakamura, describes the relationship between himself and his instrument: "I often lose my awareness of who does what. One 'who' is the no-input mixing board (my set up for acquiring feedbacks), and the other 'who' is me. Am I playing the machines? Or, are these machines playing me? ... It seems like there is quite an equal relationship." [42]

The ongoing encounter with the materials of the object, which are unique to each mixer and instrument, define and shape the creative direction taken by the musician, and the musicians themselves change how the fundamental materials of the object operate—often to detrimental effect. Because the musician is engaging with a mixer on a material level and adapting to the physical properties which emerge as the material is manipulated, they are in a crafting role when performing. There is an ongoing process of creative adaptation to the new and emerging physical and material states of the instrument, and meaning emerges through the in-situ decision-making on the part of the performer.

At the same time, the musician is also playing the role of producer of a mediated experience, as they are likely creating music for an audience who are consuming a product as they attend a performance, and possibly also later through distributed recordings. The extreme end of this production cycle is the consumer who streams a recording of the performance at home, or buys the CD recording for later listening. In this activity, both the means (media machine) and mode (consumption) are highly mediated, placing the performer in a role of producer, and recipients in the role of consumer.

Both sample cases show how material encounter with the immediate operational components of a hybrid piece "is craft." They also show how these pieces shift to mediation and engagement becomes more detached. Roles can shift quickly even within a single performance or maker project.

## LOOKING FORWARD

Ultimately, these examples highlight the difficult task we face within the discussion of craft in tangible interaction design. They complicate issues of identity and purpose across disciplines and practices which evolve and change. Today, practitioners have both tools and media machines at their disposal, and depending on their use, one can quickly turn into the other. Increasingly we must account for what Simondon called "technological objects," which can exist "not only by virtue of [their] functioning...but by virtue of phenomena of which [they are], [themselves], the center." [43] This dynamic is reflected in our model, at the poles of the computer as tool vs mediating machine. It is not resolved but mapped in correlation, and through this context we can position any interactor's role as well as the standing of craft in interaction design.

This has the potential to open up a new problem space and opportunity for tangible interaction design.

### Moving Craft to Interaction

We differentiate between the computer as a media machine that allows users to produce content through its functionality and the computer as a tool that allows participants to shape and master its functionality in an as immediate as possible encounter with the technology and material at hand. We used this dualism to map creative and consumer activities in relation to these modes and are able to identify different productive roles for the human participant. Computers as tools allow the interactor to work with the computer as crafter. Here, the tangible interaction design "is craft" in an immediate encounter with the technology on a material level that allows for creation of new practices, objects, even tools themselves. But the two case studies also show that this is not a stable role. In practice, makers shift between different modes of engagement, at times even fulfilling two in parallel. Thus, we can illustrate the dynamic relationship between media machine vs tool and connect it to the role of the interactor in a basic schema, divided into the two positions the technological objects can take and the differing roles for the participator who engages with them. This shifting use of the role of the computer as differentiator mirrors Simondon's approach to technological objects:

"Now, in order that the human function be meaningful, it is absolutely necessary that each man employed at a technical task should acquaint himself with every conceivable aspect of the machine, should arrive at some sort of understanding of it, and should pay attention as much to its elements as to its integration into the functional ensemble." [43]

This necessity refers not only to the human to improve the encounter with the technological object, it ultimately refers to the construction of a "functional ensemble." Much like Simondon's call for a balanced ensemble, we call for a balanced combination of craft and interaction design that is constantly in a state of growing "acquaintance," but based on a differentiation between the two. We suggest *mediation* and *material encounter* as measures of any such growing acquaintance and propose an initial model to map the resulting opportunities. Those opportunities are in the dynamics as much as in the differentiation. We hope to support discussion on two tiers. First, the separation model should help other scholars to position their own projects and/ or discuss craft-related interaction design of others in a new way. Second, we call for more coverage of the transitional states that thrive in workshop settings and educational framings. It is not enough to optimize a project or technology for a single use--in order to feed the necessary growing "acquaintance" we need to support transitional engagements between modes.

## ACKNOWLEDGMENTS

Michael Nitsche's contribution is partially based upon work supported by the National Science Foundation under Grant No. #1612686 (NSF AISL program).

## REFERENCES


[1] Kylie Peppler, Katie Salen Tekinbas, Melissa Gresalfi, and Rafi Santo. 2014. *Short Circuits. Crafting e-Puppets with DIY Electronics*. MIT Press, London, Cambridge, MA.

[2] Michael Eisenberg. 2003. Mindstuff: Educational Technology Beyond the Computer. *Convergence*, 9, 2, 29-53.

[3] Jenny Bergström, Brendon Clark, Alberto Frigo, Ramia Mazé, Johan Redström, and Anna Vallgårda. 2010. Becoming materials: material forms and forms of practice. *Digital Creativity*, 21, 3, 155-172.

[4] Jennifer Jacobs, David Mellis, Amit Zoran, Cesar Torres, Joel Brandt, and Joshua Tanenbaum. 2016. Digital Craftsmanship: HCI Takes on Technology as an Expressive Medium. In *Proceedings of the 2016 ACM Conference Designing Interactive Systems DIS '16*, 57-60.

[5] Nithikul Nimkulrat. 2012. Hands-On Intellect: Integrating Craft Practice into Design Research. *International Journal of Design*, 6, 3, 1-14.

[6] Clement Zheng, and Michael Nitsche. 2017. Combining Practices in Craft and Design. In *Proceedings of the 11th International Conference on Tangible, Embedded and Embodied Interactions TEI ' 17*, 331-340.

[7] Connie Golsteijn, Elise Hoven, David Frohlich, and Abigail Sellen. 2014. Hybrid crafting: towards an integrated practice of crafting with physical and digital components. *Personal Ubiquitous Comput.*, 18, 3, 593-611.

[8] Sandra Alfoldy. 2010. *NeoCraft: Modernity and the Crafts*. The Press of the Nova Scotia College of Art and Design, Halifax.

[9] Laura Devendorf, and Daniela K. Rosner. 2017. Beyond Hybrids: Metaphors and Margins in Design. In *Proceedings of the 2017 ACM Conference Designing Interactive Systems DIS 2017*, 995-1000.

[10] Christopher Frayling. 2011. *On Craftsmanship. Towards a new Bauhaus*. Oberon Books, London.

[11] Eric Paulos. 2007. HCI Cannot be used to Evaluate Art. In *Proceedings of the Workshop position paper for HCI and New Media Arts: Methodology and Evaluation* at ACM SIGCHI,

[12] Phoebe Sengers, and Chris Csikszentmihalyi. 2003. HCI and the arts: a conflicted convergence? In *Proceedings of the CHI '03 Extended Abstracts on Human Factors in Computing Systems*, 876-877.

[13] Richard Sennet. 2008. *The Craftsman*. Yale University Press, New Haven; London.

[14] David Pye. 1968. *The Nature and Art of Workmanship*. Cambium Press, Bethel.

[15] Peter Dormer. 1997. *Craft and the Turing Test for practical Thinking*. Manchester University Press, Manchester, 1997.

[16] Brygg Ullmer, and Hiroshi Ishii. 2001. Emerging frameworks for tangible user interfaces. *IBM Syst. J.*, 39, 3-4, 915-931.

[17] Amit Zoran, and Leah Buechley. 2010. Hybrid Reassemblage: An Exploration of Craft, Digital

Fabrication and Artifact Uniqueness. *Leonardo*, 46, 1, 4-10.

[18] Jonathan Bean, and Daniela Rosner. 2014. Making: Movement or Brand? *ACM Interactions*, 21, 1, 26-27.

[19] Matt Ratto. 2011. Critical Making: conceptual and material studies in technology and social life. *The Information Society: An International Journal*, 27, 4, 252-260.

[20] Garnett Hertz. 2012. *Critical Making*. Telharmonium Press, Hollywood.

[21] Alan Kay. 1990. User Interface: A Personal View. In *The Art of Human-Computer Interface Design*, ed. by B. Laurel, Addison-Wesley Publ. Co., Reading, 191-209.

[22] Jay D. Bolter, and Richard Grusin. 1999. *Remediation: Understanding New Media*. MIT Press, Cambridge; London.

[23] Lev Manovich. 2001. *The Language of New Media*. MIT Press, Cambridge; London.

[24] Janet Murray. 2012. Inventing the Medium. Principles of Interaction Design as Cultural Practice. MIT Press, Cambridge; London.

[25] Phil Auslander. 2008. *Liveness. Performance in a Mediatized Culture*. Routledge, London, New York.

[26] Paul Milgram, and Fumio Kishino. 1994. A Taxonomy of Mixed Reality Visual Displays. *IEICE Transactions on Information Systems*, E77-D, 12 (December 1994), 1321-1329.

[27] George W. Fitzmaurice, and William Buxton. 1997. An empirical evaluation of graspable user interfaces: towards specialized, space-multiplexed input. In *Proceedings of the 1997 ACM SIGCHI Conference on Human factors in computing systems*, 43-50.

[28] Howard Risatti. 2007. *A Theory of Craft. Function and Aesthetic Expression*. University of North Carolina, Chapel Hill.

[29] Graham Harman. 2009. Technology, Objects and Things in Heidegger. *Cambridge Journal of Economics*, 34, 1, 17-25.

[30] Richard Sennett. 2008. *The Craftsman*. Yale University Press, New Haven; London.

[31] Maurice Merleau-Ponty. 1962. *The Phenomenology of Perception*. Routledge, London.

[32] Martin Heidegger. 1962. *Being and Time*. SCM Press, London.

[33] Angela Chang, Sile O'Modhrain, Rob Jacob, Eric Gunther, and Hiroshi Ishii. 2002. ComTouch: design of a vibrotactile communication device. In *Proceedings of the 4th conference on Designing interactive systems: processes, practices, methods, and techniques (DIS '02)*, ACM, New York, 312-320.

[34] Lonny L. Chu. 2002. User performance and haptic design issues for a force-feedback sound editing interface. In *CHI '02 Extended Abstracts on Human Factors in Computing Systems (CHI EA '02)*, ACM, New York, 544-545.

[35] Malcolm McCullough. 1998. *Abstracting Craft: The Practiced Digital Hand*. MIT Press, Cambridge.

[36] Larry Shiner. 2010. *The Fate of Craft*. The Press of the Nova Scotia College of Art and Design, Halifax.

[37] Larry Shiner. 2012. "Blurred Boundaries"? Rethinking the concept of craft and its relation to art and design. *Philosophy Compass*, 7, 4 (2012), 230-244.

[38] Eleonora Oreggia, and Graham White. 2016. Because there was no user in art: Imagining a technological sublime. In *xCoAx 2016: Proceedings of the Fourth Conference on Computation, Communication, Aesthetics and X*, Bergamo, 187-200

[39] Plusea. 2016. Woven Paper Cup Speaker. *Instructables.com*, https://www.instructables.com/id/Woven-Paper-Cup-Speaker/. (accessed: 18 Nov 2018).

[40] Leah Buechley, and Kanjun Qiu. 2014. *Sew Electric*. HTL Press, Cambridge.

[41] Garnet Hertz, and Jussi Parikka. 2012. Zombie Media: Circuit Bending Media Archaeology into an Art Method. *Leonardo*, 45, 5, 424-430

[42] Toshimaru Nakamura. 2002. A few of my waking times. *Resonance*, 9, 2.

[43] Gilbert Simondon. 1980 (1958). *On the Mode of Existence of Technical Objects*. University of Paris, Paris.

# Critical Materiality: Creating Toolkits and Methods for Engaging Materiality in HCI

**Joanna Berzowska**
Concordia University
Montreal, QC H3G 1M8, Canada
joanna.berzowska@concordia.ca

**Aisling Kelliher**
Virginia Tech
Blacksburg, VA 24061, USA
aislingk@vt.edu

**Daniela K. Rosner**
University of Washington
Seattle, WA 98195, USA
dkrosner@uw.edu

**Matt Ratto**
University of Toronto
Toronto, ON M5S 3H7, Canada
matt.ratto@utoronto.ca

**Suzanne Kite**
Concordia University
Montreal, QC H3G 1M8, Canada
suzannekite@alum.calarts.edu



*TEI '19*, March 17–20, 2019, Tempe, AZ, USA

ACM ISBN 978-1-4503-6196-5/19/03.
https://doi.org/10.1145/3294109.3295656

## Abstract

The miniaturization of electronic technologies, as well as advances in organic and material science, have contributed to the development of composite, smart, and computational materials that create promising narratives for the future of ubiquitous computing. The goal of this one-day studio is to develop tools to acquire a deeper conceptual and critical understanding of materiality in HCI. The studio will draw on strategies from a broad range of sources including critical making, speculative design, experiential prototyping, and indigenous ontologies, in order to map out key questions and concerns. The studio will give the participants the opportunity to discuss the concept of Critical Materiality as a framework for developing tangible, embedded, and embodied interfaces, by brainstorming narratives around the past lives, current uses, and the future imaginaries of materials. Participants will co-develop a shared vocabulary and theoretical framework for Critical Materiality as a strategy to be deployed in conceiving and implementing HCI artifacts and experiences. The studio will culminate in the design and production of a deck of cards that propose keywords, questions, concerns, and opportunities for Hybrid Materials within this Critical Materiality framework. The deck of cards will be made available during the conference and distributed online.

## Author Keywords
Hybrid Materials; Materiality; Critical Frameworks; Design Toolkits; Design Methods

## CCS Concepts
• Human-centered computing~Interaction design theory, concepts and paradigms • Human-centered computing~Systems and tools for interaction design

## Introduction
The past decade has generated a broad range of research that considers the materials of interaction as increasingly important to the field of HCI [14]. The miniaturization of electronic technologies, as well as advances in organic and material science, have contributed to the development of composite, smart, and computational materials that create promising narratives for the future of ubiquitous computing. The future vision of Hybrid Materials allows for truly seamless flow between physical and digital. Earlier work in transitive materials [7], programming materiality [6], organic user interfaces [7], and Radical Atoms [9] can benefit from approaches emanating from the fields of Critical Making [11], Material Studies [12], Critical Craft, and Art and Design, to allow space for critical thinking.

Building on previous work that considered "material studies in theorizing digital culture, in developing digital media and information technologies" [12], we propose the concept of Critical Materiality as a useful framework for mapping out this theoretical space. The goal of this one-day studio is to develop tools and strategies to acquire a deeper conceptual and critical understanding of materiality in HCI.

## Studio Proposal
The Hybrid Material vision imagines that the very materials of our physical world can increasingly be augmented, mechanized, actuated, deformed, and animated, so as to fulfill the vision of a truly programmable material world. Our future materials and our material futures will be smart, active, responsive, and perhaps even disobedient [1]. The studio will give the participants the opportunity to discuss the concept of Critical Materiality as a framework for developing tangible, embedded, and embodied interfaces, by brainstorming narratives around the past lives, current uses, and the future imaginaries of materials.

Participants will co-develop a shared vocabulary and theoretical framework for "Critical Materiality" as a strategy to be deployed in conceiving and implementing HCI artifacts and experiences. The participants will begin by using some popular design method toolkits and card-decks as "objects to think with" [13] in exploring their own perceptions about the design process and the act of making. Toolkit examples include IDEO Method Cards, The Thing from the Future from Situationlab, Design with Intent by Dan Lockton, and Nesta's Designing for Public Service.

The participants will be provided with a number of suggested interrogative lenses to critique the toolkits with respect to themes and concepts such as material expressivity, ecological footprints, or indigenous ontologies. The goal of this inductive exercise is to identify opportunity spaces for expanding the perceived affordances of the toolkits and the activities and behaviors they support with respect to materials and materiality. The outcomes of this exercise will help direct the generative components of the studio, where the convenors and participants will work on making their own individual and collective toolkits to fill the gaps identified earlier.

The studio structure involves brainstorming, sketching, hands-on experimentation, drawing, and collage as a means for the development of a deck of method cards. The studio participants will decide on 3 or 4 categories or themes and split into groups to develop them. The process will give the participants the opportunity to discuss the role of Critical Materiality as a framework for developing tangible embedded and embodied interfaces.

## Theoretical Influences

Our workshop activities begin with a shared commitment to interrogate our materials as part of wider historical, political, and industrial forces—foregrounding legacies of practice and oppression that live in the shadows of industrial capitalism. These theoretical commitments take the form of analytic frameworks and methodological reworkings at the interface of HCI and critical technoscience [2, 3, 5]. Whether through disability activism [8, 10] or feminist theorizing [4], these literatures interrogate the micro interactions implicated in the macro worlds of financial capital, transactional politics, and care regimes. We explore the forms and interactions our materials produce as sites to not resolve or solve technological problems, but rather to complicate and extend our understanding of design's possibilities, foreclosures and consequences beyond the individual user or device-level engagement.

## Studio Topics to be Covered

The studio will give the participants the opportunity to discuss the concept of Critical Materiality as a framework for developing tangible, embedded, and embodied interfaces, by brainstorming narratives around the past lives, current uses, and the future imaginaries of materials. Questions and topics to be covered include:

- Provenance of materials (ecological footprints, ethical considerations, cultural appropriation, decolonizing materials, etc...)
- Ways of describing materiality.
- The expressive qualities of materials.
- Indigenous Ontologies and how do materials become "animated"?
- Composite/Hybrid materials and Future Imaginaries.
- How do our ways of performing HCI perpetuate erasure?
- Materiality and embodiment.
- Sustainability and material practices.
- Political, historical, and social contexts of material practice.
- How do we animate materials as we use them, shape them, misuse them, and transform them?
- How can we embed critical thinking in working with the materials of interaction?

## Studio Learning Goals/Discussion Objectives

Participants will co-develop a shared vocabulary and theoretical framework for "Critical Materiality" as a strategy to be deployed in conceiving and implementing HCI artifacts and experiences. The studio will culminate in the design and production of a deck of cards that propose keywords, questions, issues, and opportunities for Hybrid Materials within this Critical Materiality framework. The deck of cards will be made available during the conference and distributed online on the studio website. Studio submissions will remain on the workshop site and shared with TEI attendees. The studio website will be maintained, allowing for participants to continue discussions and collaborations and support future research.

## References


[1] Morehshin Allahyari and Daniel Rourke. 2015. *The 3D Additivist Manifesto*.

[2] Sareeta Amrute. 2016. *Encoding race, encoding class: Indian IT workers in Berlin*. Duke University Press.

[3] Anne Balsamo. 2011. *Designing culture: The technological imagination at work*. Duke University Press.

[4] Shaowen Bardzell. 2010. Feminist HCI: taking stock and outlining an agenda for design. In *Proceedings of the SIGCHI Conference on Human Factors in Computing Systems* (CHI '10). 1301-1310. https://doi.org/10.1145/1753326.1753521

[5] Shaowen Bardzell. 2014. Utopias of participation: design, criticality, and emancipation. In *Proceedings of the 13th Participatory Design Conference: Short Papers, Industry Cases, Workshop Descriptions, Doctoral Consortium papers, and Keynote abstracts - Volume 2* (PDC '14), 189-190. http://dx.doi.org/10.1145/2662155.2662213

[6] Joanna Berzowska. 2012. Programming materiality. In *Proceedings of the Sixth International Conference on Tangible, Embedded and Embodied Interaction* (TEI '12), Stephen N. Spencer (Ed.). https://doi.org/10.1145/2148131.2148136

[7] Marcelo Coelho, Ivan Poupyrev, Sajid Sadi, Roel Vertegaal, Joanna Berzowska, Leah Buechley, Pattie Maes, and Neri Oxman. 2009. Programming reality: from transitive materials to organic user interfaces. In *CHI '09 Extended Abstracts on Human Factors in Computing Systems* (CHI EA '09). 4759-4762. https://doi.org/10.1145/1520340.1520734

[8] Katie Ellis, Gerard Goggin, and Mike Kent. "Disability's digital frictions: Activism, technology, and politics." *The Fibreculture Journal* 26 (2015): 7-31.

[9] Hiroshi Ishii. 2015. TRANSFORM: Beyond Tangible Bits, Towards Radical Atoms. In *Proceedings of the 3rd ACM Symposium on Spatial User Interaction* (SUI '15). 1-1. https://doi.org/10.1145/2788940.2788958

[10] Alison Kafer. 2013. *Feminist, queer, crip*. Indiana University Press.

[11] Matt Ratto. 2011. Critical Making: Conceptual and Material Studies in Technology and Social Life. *The Information Society* 27, 4 (July 2011), 252-260. http://dx.doi.org/10.1080/01972243.2011.583819

[12] Daniela Rosner, Jean-François Blanchette, Leah Buechley, Paul Dourish, and Melissa Mazmanian. 2012. From materials to materiality: connecting practice and theory in HCI. CHI EA '12. 2787-2790. https://doi.org/10.1145/2212776.2212721

[13] Sherry Turkle. 2007. *Evocative Objects Things We Think With*. MIT Press, Cambridge, MA.

[14] Mikael Wiberg, Hiroshi Ishii, Paul Dourish, Anna Vallgårda, Tobie Kerridge, Petra Sundström, Daniela Rosner, and Mark Rolston. 2013. Materiality matters---experience materials. *Interactions 20*, 2 (March 2013), 54-57. https://doi.org/10.1145/2427076.2427087

# Be the Meeple: New Perspectives on Traditional Board Games

**Dorothé Smit**
University of Salzburg
Salzburg, Austria
dorothe.smit@sbg.ac.at

**Jens Reinhardt**
Hamburg University of Applied Sciences
Hamburg, Germany
jens.reinhardt@haw-hamburg.de

**Bernhard Maurer**
University of Salzburg
Salzburg, Austria
bernhard.maurer@sbg.ac.at

**Katrin Wolf**
Hamburg University of Applied Sciences
Hamburg, Germany
katrin.wolf@haw-hamburg.de

**Martin Murer**
University of Salzburg
Salzburg, Austria
martin.murer@sbg.ac.at


*TEI '19*, March 17–20, 2019, Tempe, AZ, USA
ACM 978-1-4503-6196-5/19/03.
https://doi.org/10.1145/3294109.3295657

## Abstract
Games are a great objective for research on tangible and embodied interaction as they not only have a long tradition in both the analogue and the digital game domain; they also perfectly represent the tangible and the embodiment through the nature of game play. In this Studio, we will go beyond the analogue characteristics of board games, not just by adding a visual digital layer, but by examining new game play mechanics for board games through digital technology. We will do this by introducing a new role in board games as an immersed 'character' in the game. For this, we use a very specific technology (virtual reality live streaming from a miniature perspective) as a new lens on (existing) board games. Through experimentation with and exploration of existing board games through this new lens, we will conceptualize and prototype game play mechanics for this new notion of game participation.

## Author Keywords
mixed reality; board games; perspectives; game mechanics.

## Introduction
Analogue table-top games are hugely popular, both among the general public, as well as niche groups. Play contexts range from low-commitment social settings among friends, to board game enthusiasts attending specified game fairs and playing games in competitive settings. Traditionally,

board games are a social, collective activity, played with two or more people. On the other side, video games – and other electronic games – are more focused on interaction with the system [6]. Cue hybrid games: a research area that explores traditional board games and digital games, and aims to find out how digital environments can add value to tactile, physical, or material experiences [10].

Previous research has specifically looked into materiality aspects of board game play. In that regard, Rogerson et al. [7] in detail investigated the user experience of analogue board game play. They illustrate where the enjoyment of board gaming stems from and highlight aspects of sociality, intellectual challenge, variety and materiality.More specifically, cooperation, competition and social interaction are main drivers of user experience in board game play and the general hobby involved [8]. Additionally, "Board game play is a form of cooperative work that is situated, embodied, distributed and articulated" [8]. Although recent attempts have been made to add the digital into board games through those hybrid games, those concepts are often limited to adding visual, graphic layers onto (existing) board games, rather than introducing technology as a design 'game-changer' for physical board games.

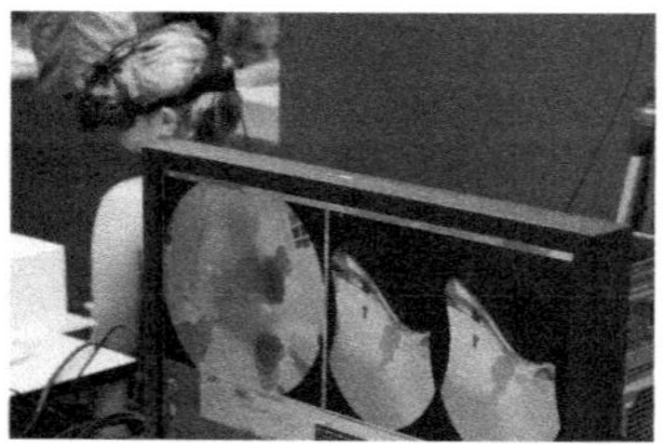

**Figure 1:** The live 360°-video feed provides the perspective of a Meeple in a board game.

## Studio Proposal

In this Studio, we will examine new game play mechanics for board games by initially introducing a new role in board games as an immersed 'character' (or 'meeple': a small figure with a stylized human form, used as a playing piece in certain board games [4]) in the game. For this, we use a very specific technology (virtual reality live streaming from a miniature perspective) as a new lens on (existing) board games. The aim is to foster research on hybrid gaming [6, 10], which combines the tangible, virtual, digital, tactile and social aspects of gameplay. The organizers will pre-select different games to be played and explored throughout the studio. This selection will be based on different cooperative or competitive game mechanics, different approaches to components and materiality, various turn structures and timings, as well as diverse player roles. Participants are also invited to bring their own (selection of) board games. This will stimulate participants to think about the Studio ahead of time, and bring inspiration in the form of board games and ideas.

The organizers will provide 360°-cameras with the ability to live stream, and head-mounted devices through which these streams can be watched. Starting out from 'general' game play, we will challenge the participants to introduce the camera to their game and assess the way the game play mechanics are – or could be – altered by introducing this new perspective. Participants will be encouraged to explore different roles in board games, ranging from passive bystander (e.g., the dealer in poker), to constructive game component (e.g., dice, blocks from Jenga) to active participation (e.g., the 'meeple' in Carcasonne).

Throughout the first part of the Studio, participants will explore games in two rounds. The organizers will make sure that the participants play a range of different game styles and mechanics. Following these explorations, the Studio participants are encouraged to create new board game concepts and game play mechanics, starting from the perspective of a character in a board game. The participants will then prototype their game, incorporating the knowledge they have gathered earlier about different game types and mechanics. Throughout the ideation and prototyping stages, the organizers will reflect with the participants on the game mechanics that work (and do not work) from a meeple's point of view. By starting with an immersed perspective, the participants will be challenged to use the VR

**Figure 2:** A board game player immersed in Meeple Perspective Virtual Reality.

technology as a design material, rather than a visual layer, added on top of the existing game play in later stages of the design of a board game.

## Studio Topics

**Game Play Mechanics.** The organizers will give an introduction to 'modern' board games and highlights of different genres. Thereby, participants will learn about, games that follow innovative perspectives on materiality and physical game components, unusual social interactions as well as general design considerations when it comes to game mechanics.

**Hybrid Games.** We will further discuss existing products and concepts of board games that incorporate technology, therefore being considered hybrid. Approaches such as externalizing computation from players to a smart phone (as in Alchemists [1]), assistance for randomized board setups, narration and rules introduction (as seen in Decent [3] and XCom [2]), will be discussed. In doing so, we also highlight technical aspects and related design consideration.

**Introduction to VR live streaming and VVVV.** We will provide participants with the hardware and software necessities to explore VR live streaming on the spot. Additionally, participants will be introduced to VVVV[1], a visual programming environment. Getting started with VVVV is low-threshold, and we are confident that participants from any programming skill-level will be able to apply the software in their projects.

**Constructive Design Strategies for VR.** In the Studio, we will take a bottom-up approach to design strategies for VR. We will start from the introduction of a new technology, and move quickly into paper prototyping, so that participants – regardless of prototyping skill level or knowledge about VR – can benefit from the new perspectives introduced to them in this Studio.

## Learning Goals & Outcomes

We seek tinkerers, programmers, makers, gamers, and anyone interested in tangible interaction and the opportunities of virtual reality (live streaming) to come join this Studio. At the end of this one-day Studio, participants – from all skill levels – will be (introduced to and) more familiar with the medium of Virtual Reality, and have new tools at their disposal to incorporate this technology in their work. Participants will further have experienced hybrid game play and deeper explored VR live stream games. They will have explored novel game design ideas and will present concepts (and prototypes) of new, hybrid board games that incorporate the virtual perspective from the get-go. We will reflect on the possibilities and limitations that this specific technology introduces into the design and game play mechanics of board games, as well as on the opportunities and obstacles that come with the development of hybrid board games in general.

This Studio aims at providing new insights about game play mechanics, tangible interactions and the power of perspectives that can be integrated, not just in the conceptualization of new (hybrid) games, but also in other fields, such as computer-supported collaborative work, tangible interaction, interactive architecture, and of course the growing area of virtual and augmented reality. Currently, this area and tangible interaction seem to be at odds with each other. The total obfuscation of the real world often leads to high immersion in the virtual world [9], giving the users a sense of presence: the experience of being located in a space other than where the body is located [5]. At the same time, tangible interactions should be observable not just visually, but also

[1] https://vvvv.org/

haptically, so that they can be understood by anyone with knowledge about the basic behaviours of the physical world [11]. In this Studio, we explore how returning the physical body to the plane of interactions in Virtual Reality affects immersion and sense of presence.

## Acknowledgements

This work is supported by the Austrian Science Fund (FWF): I 3580-N33 and the Research Foundation Flanders (FWO) and the German Ministry of Education and Research (BMBF) within the GEVAKUB project (01JKD1701B)

## References

[1] 2014. Czech Games Edition, Alchemists. `https://boardgamegeek.com/boardgame/161970/alchemists`. (2014). Accessed: 2018-08-27.

[2] 2015. XCOM: The Boardgame, Fantasy Flight Games. `https://boardgamegeek.com/boardgame/163602/xcom-board-game`. (2015). Accessed: 2018-04-11.

[3] 2016. Decent Road to Legend App, Fantasy Flight Games. `https://www.fantasyflightgames.com/en/news/2016/3/15/road-to-legend/`. (2016). Accessed: 2018-08-27.

[4] 2018. ‘Meeple’. Oxford Online Dictionary. (2018). Retrieved August 27, 2018 from `https://en.oxforddictionaries.com/definition/meeple`.

[5] Frank Biocca. 1997. The Cyborg's Dilemma: Progressive Embodiment in Virtual Environments. *Journal of Computer-Mediated Communication* 3, 2 (Sept. 1997), 0–0. DOI:`http://dx.doi.org/10.1111/j.1083-6101.1997.tb00070.x`

[6] Regan L. Mandryk and Diego S. Maranan. 2002. False Prophets: Exploring Hybrid Board/Video Games. In *CHI '02 Extended Abstracts on Human Factors in Computing Systems (CHI EA '02)*. ACM, New York, NY, USA, 640–641. DOI: `http://dx.doi.org/10.1145/506443.506523`

[7] Melissa J Rogerson, Martin Gibbs, and Wally Smith. 2016. I Love All the Bits: The Materiality of Boardgames. In *Proceedings of the 2016 CHI Conference on Human Factors in Computing Systems*. ACM, 3956–3969.

[8] Melissa J. Rogerson, Martin R. Gibbs, and Wally Smith. 2018. Cooperating to Compete: The Mutuality of Cooperation and Competition in Boardgame Play. In *Proceedings of the 2018 CHI Conference on Human Factors in Computing Systems (CHI '18)*. ACM, New York, NY, USA, Article 193, 13 pages. DOI: `http://dx.doi.org/10.1145/3173574.3173767`

[9] Thomas Schubert, Frank Friedmann, and Holger Regenbrecht. 1999. Embodied Presence in Virtual Environments. In *In Ray Paton & Irene Neilson (Eds.), Visual Representations and Interpretations.* Springer-Verlag, 269–278.

[10] Heikki Tyni, Annakaisa Kultima, and Frans Mäyrä. 2013. Dimensions of Hybrid in Playful Products. In *Proceedings of International Conference on Making Sense of Converging Media (AcademicMindTrek '13)*. ACM, New York, NY, USA, Article 237, 8 pages. DOI: `http://dx.doi.org/10.1145/2523429.2523489`

[11] Brygg Ullmer, Hiroshi Ishii, and Robert J. K. Jacob. 2005. Token+constraint systems for tangible interaction with digital information. *ACM Transactions on Computer-Human Interaction* 12, 1 (March 2005), 81–118. DOI: `http://dx.doi.org/10.1145/1057237.1057242`

# Hybrid Ways of Disseminating Interaction Design Research

**Jeroen Peeters**
RISE Interactive
Umeå, Sweden
jeroen.peeters@ri.se

**Rosa van der Veen**
RISE Interactive
Umeå, Sweden
rosa.v.d.veen@ri.se



*TEI '19*, March 17–20, 2019, Tempe, AZ, USA

ACM ISBN 978-1-4503-6196-5/19/03.
https://doi.org/10.1145/3294109.3295658

## Abstract
This studio will constructively explore hybrid publication formats for the dissemination of interaction design research in an academic context. We start from the premise that there is a gap between the richness of the artefacts created in interaction design research and the formal publication formats that exist today. Interactive artefacts and the experiences they elicit in use, possess a richness that is difficult to communicate in text and images alone. Through prototyping, we will explore this gap: what are key elements of artefact based research, that might benefit from alternative media, and how might we design such media to become useful supplements to existing dissemination formats? By bringing together a diverse group of participants from the TEI community to explore this topic, we aim at bringing forth a discussion on how we might stretch the boundaries of academic publication of interaction design research.

**Author Keywords** Design Research; Dissemination; Embodiment; Active Perception ACM

**Classification Keywords**
Human-centered computing~Interaction design theory, concepts and paradigms

## Introduction

This studio focuses on exploring hybrid ways of communicating research outcomes in an academic context. Within the TEI community, many research efforts involve the creation of interactive artefacts, and it is often is the design process, or a form of reporting on the final result, that forms the basis for the process of generating new knowledge about interaction design.These artefacts, as research vehicles, possess a richness that is fundamental to design research [3]. We might describe this richness as the potential of artefacts to become more than their strictly functional characteristics, possessing the ability to resonate with an individuals' intentionality and sensitivity, embedded within a socio-cultural context [11]. The richness of interacting with a design is essential to its meaning, yet this meaning is easily lost in the descriptive nature of publications. The TEI community is diverse and builds on different theoretical foundations. However, one could consider ecological psychology [4], phenomenology [5], and embodied cognition [1] among common foundations employed to some of the work to understand human experience in interaction. Such foundations share a notion of embodiment: we perceive the world by acting in it [2].

This starts to sketch a fundamental incongruence between the knowledge that interaction design research aims at communicating, and the largely passive experience a reader has with the publications intended to communicate this knowledge to peers. We therefore find it important to question and critically examine how existing rmal dissemination formats might better accommodate the richness found in the artefacts created in this research, as well as the theoretical underpinnings that inform it.

The wider, overlapping fields of design research and HCI have started to explore ways to accommodate such richness in formal publications and dissemination formats. One example is the Arts Track at the TEI Conference, that allows researchers to exhibit technical or experience prototypes and have a dialogue about their work directly with others in the community. Other examples include the Pictorial track at the ACM DIS Conference since 2014, that allow for richer visual material, the Video track at the ACM CHI Conference that allow for dynamics of interaction to become more visible, or the Research Through Design Conference that places artefacts at the centre attention through "Rooms of Interest". Dissertations are another example of formal dissemination formats that have started to be explored. For example Ambra Trotto's Ph.D dissertation [10], published as an iPad application to allow the key element of her work, active perception, to be experienced. A different example is Nick Sousanis Ed.D. dissertation. In his work, "Unflattening" [9], he communicates the consequences of the primacy of words over images in Western culture in the form of a graphic novel. Although, strictly speaking, this last example does not belong to the field of design research itself, it illustrates how within the academic world new ways of disseminating research are explored.

## Studio Proposal

In this studio, we aim to examine this emergent area from the perspective of constructive design research: by prototyping hybrid ways of disseminating interaction design research we aim at probing tacit practices around communication of research outcomes.

In earlier design research projects, we have explored the boundaries of publications by designing ways in which we might leverage active engagement for the reader to assist in communicating about research. For example, in the *Interactive Dissertation* project [7], we explored how the printed version of a PhD thesis [6] in interaction design may embody experiential qualities of the interactive systems presented in the thesis' textual content. In this project, we created several booklets in which interactive elements were combined with the textual and graphical content of a publication, to actively engage readers and highlight key aspects of an original design's interactivity. In another case, we explored how we might elicit active bodily engagement from the reader through exercises presented on the pages of a pictorial publication [8]. These exercises ask the reader to actively contribute graphical content herself, within the constraints offered by the exercise presented on the pages of the publication. Through this process, we aimed at eliciting a better understanding for the reader of what we as researchers aimed communicate about this design process.

Our previous work in this area, the process of engaging with the content of a traditional publication through the medium of (interactive) print design, has informed the proposal for this studio. On a practical level, we have learned that it is important for the researcher to have a thorough understanding of the research content one attempts to transpose into a new medium. Moreover, it is difficult to give experiential form to an entire publication, it has proven to be more constructive to focus on a key element: for example a detail of a research finding, design process or interactive artefact crucial to the research. On a broader level, we have found that prototyping is a useful way to trigger discussion about tacit practices of dissemination: physical prototypes make concrete what key elements of a research contribution are. This studio will build on the previous work by constructively exploring hybrid publication formats. The final prototypes created by participants will be experiential publications, which will be achieved through the following steps. The organisers will guide participants through the process and offer support where necessary. The workshop will provide the necessary tools for participants to explore and prototype their experiential publications.

*Phase 0: Preparation*
Participants are asked to contribute an existing publication, preferably their own, as the starting point or case for the workshop. In the *Call for Position Statements*, we ask participants to discuss in a short video why they perceive this particular paper as a valuable candidate to be prototyped as a in experiential publication.

*Phase 1: Understanding what to communicate*
To stimulate dialogue, the day will continue in pairs. In the first phase, pairs will be asked to explain to each other what key elements in their respective publications may be of relevance to transpose into a new medium. The aim of this phase is to find a joint starting point for exploratory prototyping.

*Phase 2: Explorative prototyping of how to communicate*
In pairs, participants will prototype three ways to explore how the key element(s) that emerged in Phase 1 could be communicated interactively. The aim of this phase is to develop a deeper understanding of what more or less practical ways exist and how effective they may be to communicate research content to future reader of the experiential publication.

*Phase 3: Developing a final prototype*
In pairs, participants will develop their explorations into a final prototype of an experiential publication as a probe to discuss the boundaries of dissemination formats. The aim of this phase is to understand the relationship between the interactive element developed in the previous phases and the traditional media used in publication formats, such as text and images.

*Phase 4: Presentation, discussion, and reflection*
The final phase concludes the workshop with a presentation of the prototypes created during the day, and a shared discussion on what opportunities and caveats have emerged with regards to the dissemination of interaction design research through hybrid publication formats.

## Studio Learning Goals/Discussion Objectives

On a practical level, this studio aims to inspire participants by eliciting a fresh perspective on their own work, and to develop skills that may lead to creative and fitting ways to use publication formats in future research projects. On a broader level, the studio aims at the development of a library of examples that support a curated discussions around:

- What do we risk losing when we communicate interactive artefacts and the experiences they elicit in existing publication formats?
- What could be ways in which we might mitigate this risk, e.g. through supplemental material or the "hacking" of formal formats, etc.

Through this discussion, we aim to contribute to the field's understanding of the effects that dissemination formats have in both opening up or constraining the transferring of knowledge within an academic community.

## References

[1] Clark, Andy. 1997. Being There: Putting Brain, Body and World Together Again. Cambridge: MIT Press.

[2] Dourish, Paul. 2001. Where the Action is: The Foundations of Embodied Interaction. Cambridge: MIT Press.

[3] Gaver, William. 2012. "What Should We Expect from Research Through Design?" Proc. CHI '12.

[4] Merleau-Ponty, Maurice. 1962. Phenomenology of Perception. Trans. Colin Smith, New York: Humanities Press.

[5] Merleau-Ponty, Maurice. 1962. Phenomenology of Perception. Trans. Colin Smith, New York: Humanities Press.

[6] Peeters, Jeroen. 2017 Perpetual Perspectives - On Designing for Aesthetic Engagement. Ph.D. Diss., Umeå University.

[7] Peeters, Jeroen., Peeters Marlies, and Trotto, Ambra. 2017. Exploring Active Perception in Disseminating Design Research. In Proceedings of the 2017 Conference on Designing Interactive Systems (DIS '17). ACM, New York, NY, USA.

[8] Jeroen Peeters and Ambra Trotto. 2018. Designing Expressions of Movement Qualities. In Proceedings of the 2018 Designing Interactive Systems Conference (DIS '18). ACM, New York, NY, USA.

[9] Sousanis, Nick. (2015). Unflattening. Ed.d. Diss., Harvard University Press.

[10] Trotto, Ambra. 2011. Rights through Making. Ph.D. Diss., Eindhoven University of Technology.

[11] Trotto, Ambra and Hummels, Caroline. 2013. "Designing in Skills, Nurturing Personal Engagement in Design". Proceedings of IASDR '13.

# Designing Interactive Olfactory Experience in Real Context and Applications

**Mei-Kei Lai**
Design Programme, School of Arts, Macao Polytechnic Institute, Macao

mklai@ipm.edu.mo

**Yan Yan Cao**
Graduate School of Media Design, Keio University, Japan

yanyan.cao@gmail.com


ACM ISBN 978-1-4503-6196-5/19/03.
https://doi.org/10.1145/3294109.3295659

## Abstract

Olfactory experience has become a popular topic in TEI community as its novelty in inviting new type of storytelling and new dimension of medium in embodied interaction. This studio focuses on the experiential approach of designing interactive olfactory experience in real world contexts. We will show two case studies on how to adapt contextual inquiry into designing olfactory interactions. We will also demo prototypes and introduce a set of basic digital tools for creating olfactory interactions. Based on the tools and demo, the participants will work in groups to design olfactory experience for their proposed contexts and applications. The aim of the studio is to establish a community in discussion of a new perspective in designing and evaluating interactive olfactory experience in real contexts and applications.

## Author Keywords

Olfactory experience, interaction design; smell; odor.

## ACM Classification Keywords

• Human-centered computing~Human computer interaction (HCI)

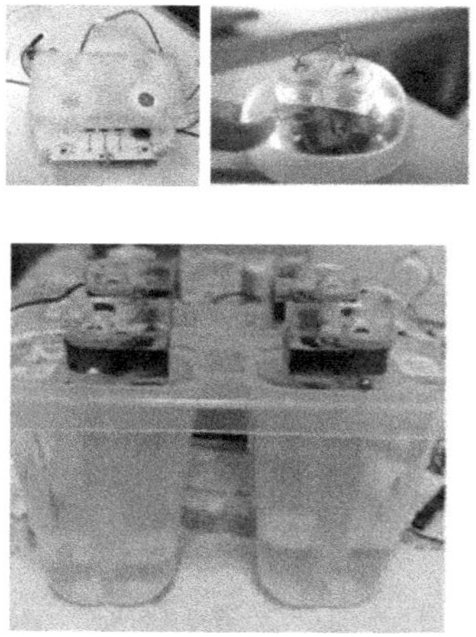

Figure 1. Digital diffusers integrated in different contexts and applications, to be shown at the TEI studio. Top left: Diffuser control module with digital control unit driving digital piezo diffuser and liquid container. Top right: Digital diffuser control module used in a prototype. Bottom: multiple digital diffuser sets.

## Introduction

Interactive olfactory experience has drawn considerable attention in TEI community in recent years, especially its potential in embodied interaction and multisensory engagement. Many studies address olfactory technologies and its new form of interactions. For example, retrieving scent combination through manipulating malleable clay [1], using olfaction with other modalities to evoke mental imageries [2], engaging users with an artifact's historical contexts through scents [3]. These researches showed the proof-of-concepts to explore the boundaries between bodies and environments through the sense of smell. Among wider HCI communities, researchers have also shown interests in multisensory interactions and held a series of workshops [4][5] to address how to integrate multisensory design experience with smell.

In addition to experiments and mechanism of new forms of interactions, the focus of olfactory experience design also expands from supporting conventional audiovisual entertainment [6] to real world experience, such as reading [7], car driving [8], cocktail drinking [9] and funeral rituals [10]. Obrist et al [11] are calling for new ways to design meaningful interactive olfactory experience instead of enhancing task performance only.

Based on our recent research in olfactory interactions, we believe the next step is to integrate interactive olfactory in real contexts and applications. In our approach, we have used ethnographic research method i.e.: fieldwork or customer journey mapping to analyze the experience. We have also brought proof-of concepts to real contexts and gained insights from users' experience directly. As shown by earlier research, olfaction is a subjective experience based on early encountered experience [12] compared to other modalities. The role of odours in daily life mainly is to link the people to the affective appreciation of surrounding and the episodic memories [13]. Each scent has its own meaning toward different people under different culture contexts. Therefore, we think we can discover more opportunities and values of interactive olfactory experience by applying them in real contexts.

In this studio, we would like to present preliminary findings from our case studies, in which we create specific contexts and potential value for interactive olfactory experience. We provide two case studies where the design process is ethnographic and experience-based. In the first case study, interaction with smells is used explicitly to enhance family bonding through smells that are related to family events and memories. In the second case study, it attempts to opens up opportunities of building interactive ambience of smell as part of service design.

We aim to open discussion on new contexts and scenarios where interactive olfactory experiences can be applied. We will provide hands-on design session to stimulate their thinking on how to design for specific contexts and applications.

## Detailed Proposal Discussions

In this studio, we will recruit 12-18 participants from academic or industry background. Our studio will include four sessions: introduction with case studies, brainstorming on contexts and applications, sketching interactions, final group presentation and discussions.

Figure 2: Examples of integrating interactive olfactory experience into real contexts and applications. Top: Creating interaction scenario in hotel lounge by using digital diffusers, sensors, props and everyday items. Bottom: Early sketching of integrating interactive olfactory experience into everyday bathing environment.

The case studies and introduction will give participants an overview of how we have used experiential approach in our own work. What kind of considerations we have given and challenges we have met while designing for specific contexts. In the brainstorming session, participants will work in groups of 3-4 people. They are encouraged to bring in contexts related to the fields they are familiar with, or from their own background and studies.

Organizers will introduce a set of digital tools for quick prototyping of olfactory interaction. Based on proposed context in the brainstorming session, participants will sketch interactions using combination of digital tools and general prototyping materials. The main purpose is for them to think through the realistic scenarios and think about the challenges of integrating the experience and actual interactions. In the final presentation, participants are encouraged to use a combination of image collages, videos and skits to present the holistic experience they will bring about, and discuss the value and opportunities it brings for the interactive olfactory experience design.

## Topics to be Covered

- Challenges and Opportunities of Interactive Olfactory Experience
- Experience-based Approach for Olfactory Interactions
- Role of Interaction Designer in Interactive Olfactory Design
- Evaluation Framework for Interactive Olfactory Design

The studio will provide a platform to show participants the unique challenges and characteristics of olfactory interactions. We will explore its future contexts and applications. We will present our contextual inquiry approach used in two case studies and discuss on how it can be applied in other contexts and applications.

By sharing of how we practice the research and conduct field tests in real contexts, we hope to highlight the role of interaction designer in discovering value of interactive olfactory experience. We are calling on interaction designers to create future scenarios, to build into real contexts, to bring the interactive olfactory experience closer to reality. We would like to see if forming a structured experiential method for olfactory interactions is possible and will create a structured evaluation framework for future research.

## Learning Goals & Discussion Objectives

- Learning about the interactive olfactory technologies and how to integrate them into applications
- Designing the potential new contexts and application areas through toolkit and interaction methods
- Learning how to use experiential approach in interactive olfactory design: mainly two case studies as well as hands-on group work
- Discuss the evaluation of value in interactive olfactory experience

Participants will learn both through case studies and hands-on group work how to integrate interactive olfactory experience design into real contexts and applications. Through this studio, we would also like to engage with the wider community of interaction designers and researchers and enable further exploration and integrations.

## References


[1] Hsin-Liu Kao, Ermal Dreshaj, Judith Amores, Sang-won Leigh, Xavier Benavides, Pattie Maes, Ken Perlin, and Hiroshi Ishii. 2015. clayodor: Retrieving scents through the manipulation of malleable material. In Proceedings of the Ninth International Conference on Tangible, Embedded, and Embodied Interaction, pp. 697-702. ACM.

[2] Yan Yan Cao, and Naohito Okude. 2015. Scented pebbles: interactive ambient experience with smell and lighting. In *Proceedings of the Ninth International Conference on Tangible, Embedded, and Embodied Interaction*, pp. 409-410. ACM.

[3] Jamie Kwan, Jean Ho Chu, Daniel Harley, Melanie McBride, and Ali Mazalek. 2016. Grasping Cultural Context through Multisensory Interactions. In *Proceedings of the TEI'16: Tenth International Conference on Tangible, Embedded, and Embodied Interaction*, pp. 482-487. ACM.

[4] Adrian D. Cheok, Jordan Tewell, Gilang A. Pradana, and Koki Tsubouchi. 2013. Touch, Taste, and Smell: Multi-sensory Entertainment. In *Advances in Computer Entertainment*, pp. 516-518. Springer, Cham.

[5] Assunta Matassa, Luca Console, Leonardo Angelini, Maurizio Caon, and Omar Abou Khaled. 2015. Workshop on full-body and multisensory experience in ubiquitous interaction. In *Adjunct Proceedings of the 2015 ACM International Joint Conference on Pervasive and Ubiquitous Computing and Proceedings of the 2015 ACM International Symposium on Wearable Computers*, pp. 923-926. ACM.

[6] Niall Murray, Oluwakemi A. Ademoye, Gheorghita Ghinea, and Gabriel-Miro Muntean. 2017. A tutorial for olfaction-based multisensorial media application design and evaluation. *ACM Computing Surveys (CSUR)* 50, no. 5: 67.

[7] Monica Bordegoni, Marina Carulli, Yuan Shi, and Daniele Ruscio. 2017. Investigating the effects of odour integration in reading and learning experiences. *INTERACTION DESIGN AND ARCHITECTURES*(32), 104–125.

[8] Dmitrijs Dmitrenko, Emanuela Maggioni, Chi Thanh Vi, and Marianna Obrist. 2017. What Did I Sniff?: Mapping Scents Onto Driving-Related Messages." In *Proceedings of the 9th International Conference on Automotive User Interfaces and Interactive Vehicular Applications*, pp. 154-163. ACM.

[9] Nimesha Ranasinghe, Thi Ngoc Tram Nguyen, Yan Liangkun, Lien-Ya Lin, David Tolley, and Ellen Yi-Luen Do. 2017. Vocktail: A virtual cocktail for pairing digital taste, smell, and color sensations. In *Proceedings of the 2017 ACM on Multimedia Conference*, pp. 1139-1147. ACM.

[10] Daisuke Uriu, William Odom, Mei-Kei Lai, Sai Taoka, and Masahiko Inami. 2018. SenseCenser: an Interactive Device for Sensing Incense Smoke & Supporting Memorialization Rituals in Japan." In *Proceedings of the 19th International ACM SIGACCESS Conference on Computers and Accessibility*, pp. 315-318. ACM.

[11] Marianna Obrist, Carlos Velasco, Chi Thanh Vi, Nimesha Ranasinghe, Ali Israr, Adrian D. Cheok, Charles Spence, and Ponnampalam Gopalakrishnakone. 2016. Touch, taste, & smell user interfaces: The future of multisensory HCI. In *Proceedings of the 2016 CHI Conference Extended Abstracts on Human Factors in Computing Systems*, pp. 3285-3292. ACM.

[12] Trygg Engen. 1991. *Odor sensation and memory*. Greenwood Publishing Group.

[13] Egon P. Köster, Per Møller, and Jos Mojet. 2014. A "Misfit" Theory of Spontaneous Conscious Odor Perception (MITSCOP): reflections on the role and function of odor memory in everyday life." *Frontiers in psychology* 5: 64.

# Composing Ecosystemically in Responsive Environments with Gestural Media, Objects and Textures

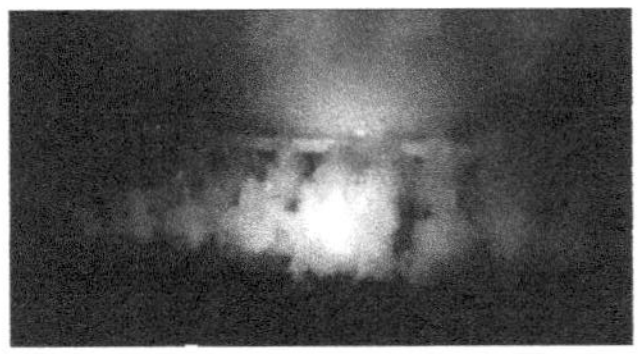

**Figure 1:** Atmospheres: dense arrays of ultrasonic atomizers are used to create clouds as displays, which can be modulated from other instruments or the global state of the responsive environment.

**Figure 2:** Experiential Model of the Atmosphere: continuous state changes and parameterization of a steerable model of cloud physics provides immersive atmospheres and rich dynamics.

**Brandon Mechtley**
**Todd Ingalls**
**Lauren Hayes**
**Byron Lahey**
**Jessica Rajko**
**Seth Thorn**
**Robert LiKamWa**
Arizona State University
Tempe, AZ 85287, USA
bmechtley@asu.edu

**Julian Stein**
**Garrett Johnson**
**Emiddio Vasquez**
**Connor Rawls**
**Peter Weisman**
**Assegid Kidane**
**Sha Xin Wei**


ACM ISBN 978-1-4503-6196-5/19/03.
https://doi.org/10.1145/3294109.3295660

## Abstract
In this workshop, participants will try their hand at a variety of tangible, embodied, and embedded sensing and feedback technologies including vibrotactile instruments, expressive mechatronics, gesturally modulated fields of light, sound, mist, and realtime steerable immersive atmospheres. Working through hands-on experience by theme, participants will be introduced to compositional and experimental methodologies. In the second half of the workshop, participants will compose together some simple "ecosystems" using the Synthesis Center's hardware-software media choreography architecture (sc), in the iStage experimental theater-scale blackbox space.

## Author Keywords
Responsive environment; ensemble; ecosystemic design; new materialism; touch; haptics; gesture; ethico-aesthetic; play; realtime media; responsive media; gestural media; mixed reality; immersive environment; sensors; movement and computing; electronic music; performance.

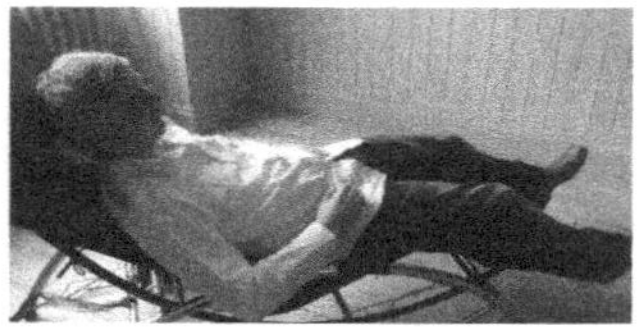

**Figure 3:** Skin Music (Hayes): Audio-haptic actuators and transducers provide vibrotactile feedback for a physical perception of music.

**Figure 4:** Rhythm: Coordinating multiple instruments produces complex rhythmic structures throughout an environment.

**Figure 5:** "Windowless" (Thorn) is a computational system for violin and alto.glove, a physical-digital interface for augmented violin performance.

## Introduction

This studio introduces the extensive set of research-creation expertise related to tangible, embodied, and, extended experience, at the School of Arts, Media + Engineering (AME) at Arizona State University, and is hosted at the Synthesis Center's iStage, an experimental "blackbox" space. The iStage has hosted large scale experiments in movement-based arts, sensing, machine-perception, realtime media, gesture, rhythm, critical and speculative studies. In this workshop, participants will explore composing for whole environments with multiple instruments created by AME researchers.

## Studio Proposal

We introduce people to a suite of techniques for creating and exploring tangible, embodied, and extended experience in the iStage environment, a theater-scale blackbox at ASU. Studio leads will work with participants to try techniques at different scales: (0) objects: enchanted objects, puppetry (Lahey); (1) body: audio-haptics (Hayes, [1, 2]), virtual haptics (LiKamWa/Sagheb), "sense-organs" crossing vision and pressure (Rawls); augmented multichannel violin (Thorn, [6, 7]); (2) ensemble: thermal economies (Johnson, [4]); (3) texture: gesturally modulated mist and theatrical lightfields / soundfields; (4) ecosystem: steerable immersive atmosphere simulations (Mechtley, [5]).

## Studio Topics to Be Covered

This studio will cover performance, composition, and design practice considerations for vibrotactile feedback, mechatronic puppetry, enchanted objects and computational materials, virtual haptics, performer-centric augmented instruments, gesturally modulated mist and theatrical light- and soundfields, and steerable immersive complex system simulations.

In addition, the studio will cover how these techniques can be combined in ecosystemic and holistic ways to create coherent responsive environments.

## Studio Learning Goals / Discussion Objectives

1. Familiarization with techniques for body-, ensemble-, environment-scale technologies for experience modulated by realtime, responsive (not "interactive") tangible media, materials, objects [8, 9].
2. Distinguishing body- or ego-centric, anthropocentric, vs. ecosytemic design approaches.
3. Thinking through material / analog vs. digital computation.
4. Introducing methodologies for research oriented by whole experience, embodied experience, felt meaning [3], and pre-individual subjectivity.

## Studio Supporting Web Documents

Please check the studio website for the latest information: improvisationalenvironments.weebly.com

- Steerable Weather: vimeo.com/synthesiscenter/ema
- Audio-Haptic Composition: https://vimeo.com/77170690
- Synthesis Atelier-based Research: http://synthesiscenter.net/research
- iStage timelapse: http://vimeo.com/synthesiscenter/slsa2
- Augmented violin: https://vimeo.com/251840089

## Acknowledgements

We thank affiliates of Synthesis and staff, faculty, and students from the School of Arts, Media + Engineering / ASU, including: Luke Kautz, Shahab Sagheb, Chris Ziegler, Megan Patzem, Ben Nandin, Leslie Smith, Alexia Lopez Klein, Lisette Borja.

## References

[1] Lauren Hayes. 2014. *Audio-Haptic Relationships as Compositional and Performance Strategies*. Ph.D. Dissertation.

[2] Lauren Hayes. 2015. Skin Music (2012): an Audio-Haptic Composition for Ears and Body. In *Proceedings of 2015 ACM SIGCHI Conference on Creativity and Cognition*. ACM, 359–360.

[3] Lauren Hayes and Jessica Rajko. 2017. Towards an Aesthetics of Touch. In *Proceedings of the 4th International Conference on Movement Computing (MOCO '17)*. ACM, New York, NY, USA, Article 22, 8 pages. DOI: http://dx.doi.org/10.1145/3077981.3078028

[4] Garrett Laroy Johnson, Britta Joy Peterson, Todd Ingalls, and Sha Xin Wei. 2018. Lanterns: An Enacted and Material Approach to Ensemble Group Activity with Responsive Media. In *Proceedings of the 5th International Conference on Movement and Computing (MOCO '18)*. ACM, New York, NY, USA, Article 37, 4 pages. DOI: http://dx.doi.org/10.1145/3212721.3212848

[5] Brandon Mechtley, Christopher Roberts, Julian Stein, Ben Nandin, and Xin Wei Sha. 2018. Enactive Steering of an Experiential Model of the Atmosphere. In *Proceedings of the International Conference on Virtual and Mixed Reality (VAMR)*. Springer, Cham.

[6] Seth Thorn. 2018. Alto.Glove: New Techniques for Augmented Violin. In *Proceedings of the International Conference on New Interfaces for Musical Expression*. Blacksburg.

[7] Seth Thorn. 2019. A Computational System for Violin: Synthesis and Dissolution in Windowless. *Leonardo Music Journal* (2019).

[8] Sha Xin Wei. 2013. *Poeisis and Enchantment in Topological Matter*. MIT Press.

[9] Sha Xin Wei. 2016. Theater Without Organs: Co-Articulating Gesture and Substrate in Responsive Environments. In *Living Architecture Systems Group White Papers*.

# Breaking the fourth wall: Embodied Interfaces for a Better Algorithmic Experience with Recommender Algorithms

**Oscar Alvarado**
Department of Computer Sciences,
KU Leuven
Leuven, Belgium
oscar.alvarado@cs.kuleuven.be

## ABSTRACT
Recommender algorithms deal with most of our contemporary culture consumption. Algorithmic Experience (AX) emerges in HCI to guide users' experience with algorithms. To the best of our knowledge, previous work on recommender systems does not consider tangible interfaces to support positive AX and better algorithmic awareness. The ongoing research proposes to expand the design space for the current AX debate by designing an embodied interface suited for movie recommender algorithms.

## CONTEXT AND MOTIVATION
Culture has been transformed by algorithms. They enact a function of cultural gatekeeping, sorting, ranking, managing, distributing and even producing existing music, movies or tv shows, video streaming and other kinds of cultural expressions, becoming relevant cultural objects [9].

Unfortunately, there is a general low algorithmic awareness among users [8]. Furthermore, algorithms produce negative user experiences such as threats of invisibility, anxiety and inequalities [4], bias in personalization processes [5], and user categorizations based on mere profit [20].

Different academic researchers have tried to solve these issues. Examples include invitations for human-centered algorithmic systems [3,18] or paradigm proposals towards algorithmic experience (AX) [1,19]. Similarly, recommender systems efforts address transparency, trust, and interaction issues [12,16]. Interestingly, no "embodied or tangible" design addresses yet the black-box nature of algorithms, promotes users' awareness or improves the experience with algorithmic systems [12,16].

Therefore, this research examines the design, interaction, pros and cons of embodied interfaces to improve AX. To delimit the scope, movie recommender algorithms have been chosen due to four main reasons strictly related with qualities that only tangible interfaces could provide. First, the "abstract" and complex notion of "algorithm" for most users could be overcome by tangible interfaces that could represent a more concrete idea of what the algorithm does, how to control it and increase its awareness among users. Second, the existent varied and broadly accepted tangible opportunities to represent the algorithmic outcomes in this application domain such as archetypes for movie categories, figures or toys related with commonly known shows, and common interaction signs such as "thumbs up/down" to interact with the recommender system. Third, the opportunities that tangible interfaces offer could open collective and shareable experiences in such a social cultural practice. Fourth, the everyday use of movie recommender algorithms rises sensible social issues and design opportunities, such as more control and transparency over recommendations and promotion of small or not mainstream content creators. TEI possesses here an unexplored and novel occasion to expand the design space in the current academic algorithms debate and bring new embodied interactions.


*TEI '19, March 17–20, 2019, Tempe, AZ, USA*

ACM ISBN 978-1-4503-6196-5/19/03...$15.00
https://doi.org/10.1145/3294109.3302931

## OBJECTIVES AND RESEARCH QUESTIONS
To guide this research, a main research question and three research sub-questions were proposed: How can tangible interaction improve the algorithmic experience of movie recommender algorithms?

**RSQ1**: Which tangible interface is more suitable to address the interaction with movie recommender algorithms?

**RSQ2:** How can we design the interaction of an embodied interface to improve AX in movie recommender algorithms?

**RSQ3:** To what extent can embodied interactions improve the AX of movie recommender algorithms?

## BACKGROUND
Different academic efforts have described the relevance of algorithms in the cultural context and in audience definition. For instance, Striphas proposes *algorithmic culture* as "the enfolding of human thought, conduct, organization and expression into the logic of big data and large-scale computation" [21:396]. Additionally, Gomez-Uribe and Hunt describes Netflix's intentions to promote audiences that are too small to exist [10:6] and increase the overall engagement with the platform [10:7]. Similarly, Hallinan and Striphas

explore how Netflix's recommender was improved during a contest called the Netflix Prize [11].

Unfortunately, there are also negative experiences with algorithms. Eslami et al. have studied users low awareness of algorithm curation existence [8], which translates into surprise and anger. Additionally, discriminatory practices, anxiety and panic had been reported by Bishop [4] in YouTube. Also, Bozdag described the layers in which algorithmic personalization could be human biased [5].

Therefore, the interaction with algorithms has been also explored. For example, Diakopolous presents a transparency standard for algorithms [7]. Oh et al. picture a novel chapter in HCI based on *algorithmic experience* "as a new stream of research on user experience" [19:2531] to consider long term relationships with algorithms. Similarly, Alvarado and Waern propose Algorithmic Experience (AX) as "...the ways in which users experience systems and interfaces that are heavily influenced by algorithmic behavior." [1:7] and suggest design areas for social media [1:6].

Other works center in the interaction with recommender systems. Jugovac and Jannach survey research about interaction with recommender systems [16], while their "black boxed" nature is analyzed by He, Parra and Verbert in their survey about interactive recommender systems [12]. Regarding recommender systems evaluation, Knijnenburg et al. present a user-centered framework to test recommender systems interaction [17], while Tintarev and Masthoff evaluate seven different aims for recommender explanations [24]. Similarly, Bakalov et al. evaluate user models and personalization effects for recommender algorithms [2], while Cramer et al evaluate an art recommender system [6].

In this context, tangible interface design has elaborated various examples towards a materialization of interaction with digital information such as algorithms. For example, Sundström et al proposed *inspirational bits* to represent digital design materials [22], while Vallgårda and Redström suggested *computational composites*: mixtures between digital computations and other materials to give diverse properties to digital tools [25]. Ishii's *tangible bits* couple digital information with everyday physical objects and surfaces [19], providing a physical form to digital information. Similarly, *radical atoms* [15] propose "...interactions with dynamic physical materials that are computationally transformable and reconfigurable" [15:45].

## PRELIMINARY RESULTS

A first study has been published as a full paper at CHI [1] and used a semiotic inspection and sensitizing workshops to analyze the user experience with Facebook's newsfeed [1:3–5]. Both methods collected different negative experiences expressed by the users in relation with the curating algorithms in their newsfeed and produced different design solutions to improve the experience with the system. The results proposed the concept of *algorithmic experience* (AX) as a way to define explicitly the interaction with and experience of algorithms [1:1] and suggested a framework for AX pictured in Figure 1. It is composed of five different design areas to improve AX in social media: profiling transparency and management, algorithmic awareness and control, and selective algorithmic memory [1:6].

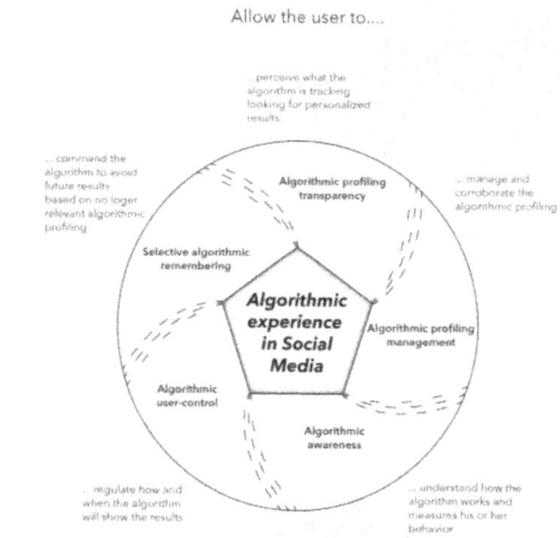


**Figure 1 Design areas for AX in social media** [1:6]

A second study took the AX framework and applied five sensitizing design workshops to explore the AX of Netflix's recommender algorithm. Additionally, the method opened the opportunity for the users to propose their "algorithm material representation" answering the question: "How does Netflix see you?" with different materials and creative tools such as LEGOS™, Play-Doh™, pilots, pens, markers, construction paper, and others. Figure 2 shows the exercise results validating that users possess different tangible and material ways to represent their algorithmic profiling and recommendations. As can be seen in the figure, these forms could be grouped in two main categories: abstract and archetypical representations. Abstract representations are defined by graphs and structured forms, while archetypes are reflected in clowns, castle-like TVs, characterized people sitting in front of the system and using props, and others.

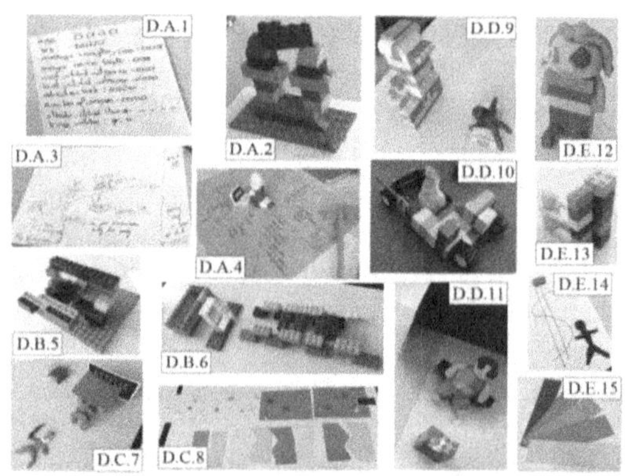


**Figure 2 Users' material representations**

Furthermore, the study provided other results related with AX for recommender algorithms, extending the original framework with two new design areas: algorithmic social practices and algorithmic usefulness. It also produced suggestions for possible tangible representations for algorithms for AX improvement. A paper describing these results has been written and will be submitted to DIS 2019.

## RESEARCH DESIGN AND METHODOLOGY

PhD research will follow a research through design methodology and a mixed approach as shown in Table 1.

| Research sub-question | Data collection | RtD action/ result | Analysis methods |
|---|---|---|---|
| RSQ1 | Literature review about embodied and tangible interfaces | Select a group of tangible interfaces (TI) for the selected domain | Guided by Radical Atoms [15], similar theories and properties for abstract and archetypical possibilities |
| | Think aloud and observation | Design a final TI based on the previous group to address the next RSQs | |
| RSQ2 | Co design explorations | Design an appropriate TI interaction language for the selected domain | Guided by AX framework for recommender algorithms [1] |
| RSQ3 | Sensitized workshops and interviews | Provide an analysis of TI's potential and limitations to improve AX for the selected domain | |
| | Surveys and questionnaires | | |

**Table 1 Data collection and analysis methods**

## TIMELINE

Since the ongoing research is just starting its second year, it still possesses 3 years left according to the initial founding agreement. January 2021 is the date in which all the research questions should be addressed, and the final thesis defended.

1. From January 2019 to July 2019: It is intended to implement a movie recommender prototype based on academically proven movie recommendation algorithms and datasets. Possibly, a paper will be elaborated to evaluate AX improvement in recommender algorithms.
2. From July 2019 to January 2020: RSQ1, a literature review about tangible/embodied interfaces will be done to determine the most suitable implementation for the intended research. Additionally, a think-aloud/observational study will be performed to discover user's behaviors towards movie recommender algorithms during movie watching in their use context.
3. From January 2020 to July 2020: RSQ2, co-design exploration, and an iterative prototype development method together with users will be done for the tangible interface interaction and operational design.
4. From July 2020 to January 2021: RSQ3, sensitized workshop together with interviews, surveys and questionnaires will be done to evaluate the effects on AX.

## CONTRIBUTIONS

This research could provide many outcomes for the TEI community. For instance, it could offer a first proposal for positive Algorithmic Experience (AX) using Tangible Interfaces (TI). Similarly, it will provide an approximation to address the black-box nature of algorithms using TI with movie recommender algorithms as an application domain. Finally, it could open a novel design space to develop a "killer app" for TI in different algorithm-related contexts.

## ACKNOWLEDGEMENTS

The author is indebted with prof. dr. Katrien Verbert for her support and supervision. Research is possible thanks to University of Costa Rica (Universidad de Costa Rica) and the KU Leuven Research Council (grant C24/16/017).

## REFERENCES

[1] Oscar Alvarado and Annika Waern. 2018. Towards Algorithmic Experience. In Proceedings of the 2018 CHI Conference on Human Factors in Computing Systems - CHI '18, 1–9. https://doi.org/10.1145/3173574.3173860

[2] Fedor Bakalov, Marie-Jean Meurs, Birgitta König-Ries, Bahar Sateli, René Witte, Greg Butler, and Adrian Tsang. 2013. An approach to controlling user models and personalization effects in recommender systems. Proceedings of the 2013 international conference on Intelligent user interfaces - IUI '13: 49–56. https://doi.org/10.1145/2449396.2449405

[3] Eric PS Baumer. 2017. Toward human-centered algorithm design. Big Data & Society: 1–12. https://doi.org/10.1177/2053951717718854

[4] Sophie Bishop. 2018. Anxiety, panic and self-optimization. Convergence: The International Journal of Research into New Media Technologies 24, 1: 69–84. https://doi.org/10.1177/1354856517736978

[5] Engin Bozdag. 2013. Bias in algorithmic filtering and personalization. Ethics and Information Technology 15, 3: 209–227. https://doi.org/10.1007/s10676-013-9321-6

[6] Henriette Cramer, Vanessa Evers, Satyan Ramlal, Maarten Van Someren, Lloyd Rutledge, Natalia Stash,

Lora Aroyo, and Bob Wielinga. 2008. The effects of transparency on trust in and acceptance of a content-based art recommender. User Modeling and User-Adapted Interaction 18, 5: 455–496. https://doi.org/10.1007/s11257-008-9051-3

[7] Nicholas Diakopoulos. 2016. Accountability in algorithmic decision making. Communications of the ACM 59, 2: 56–62. https://doi.org/10.1145/2844110

[8] Motahhare Eslami, Aimee Rickman, Kristen Vaccaro, Amirhossein Aleyasen, Andy Vuong, Karrie Karahalios, Kevin Hamilton, and Christian Sandvig. 2015. "I always assumed that I wasn't really that close to [her]." In Proceedings of the 2015 CHI Conference on Human Factors in Computing Systems - CHI '15, 153–162. https://doi.org/10.1145/2702123.2702556

[9] Tarleton Gillespie. 2016. #trendingistrending: When algorithms become culture. Algorithmic Cultures: Essays on Meaning, Performance and New Technologies 189: 52–75. https://doi.org/10.4324/9781315658698

[10] Carlos A. Gomez-Uribe and Neil Hunt. 2015. The Netflix Recommender System. ACM Transactions on Management Information Systems 6, 4: 1–19. https://doi.org/10.1145/2843948

[11] B. Hallinan and T. Striphas. 2016. Recommended for you: The Netflix Prize and the production of algorithmic culture. New Media & Society 18, 1: 117–137. https://doi.org/10.1177/1461444814538646

[12] Chen He, Denis Parra, and Katrien Verbert. 2016. Interactive recommender systems: A survey of the state of the art and future research challenges and opportunities. Expert Systems with Applications: An International Journal 56, C: 9–27. https://doi.org/10.1016/j.eswa.2016.02.013

[13] H. Ishii and B. Ullmer. 1997. Tangible bits: towards seamless interfaces between people, bits, and atoms. In Proceedings of the ACM SIGCHI Conference on Human factors in computing systems CHI '97, 234–241. https://doi.org/10.1145/604045.604048

[14] Hiroshi Ishii. 2008. Tangible bits: beyond pixels. In Proceedings of the 2nd international conference on Tangible and embedded interaction TEI 08, xv–xxv. https://doi.org/10.1145/1347390.1347392

[15] Hiroshi Ishii, Dávid Lakatos, Leonardo Bonanni, and Jean-Baptiste Labrune. 2012. Radical Atoms : Beyond Tangible Bits , Toward Transformable Materials. Interactions, 38–51. https://doi.org/10.1145/2065327.2065337

[16] Michael Jugovac and Dietmar Jannach. 2017. Interacting with Recommenders – Overview and Research Directions. ACM Transactions on Interactive Intelligent Systems (TiiS) 7, 3: 1–46. https://doi.org/10.1145/3001837

[17] Bart P. Knijnenburg, Martijn C. Willemsen, Zeno Gantner, Hakan Soncu, and Chris Newell. 2012. Explaining the user experience of recommender systems. User Modeling and User-Adapted Interaction 22, 4–5: 441–504. https://doi.org/10.1007/s11257-011-9118-4

[18] Min Kyung Lee, Ji Tae Kim, and Leah Lizarondo. 2017. A Human-Centered Approach to Algorithmic Services: Considerations for Fair and Motivating Smart Community Service Management that Allocates Donations to Non- Profit Organizations. In Proceedings of the 2017 CHI Conference on Human Factors in Computing Systems - CHI '17, 3365–3376. https://doi.org/10.1145/3025453.3025884

[19] Changhoon Oh, Taeyoung Lee, Yoojung Kim, SoHyun Park, Sae bom Kwon, and Bongwon Suh. 2017. Us vs. Them: Understanding Artificial Intelligence Technophobia over the Google DeepMind Challenge Match. In Conference on Human Factors in Computing Systems - CHI '17, 2523–2534. https://doi.org/10.1145/3025453.3025539

[20] Robert Prey. 2017. Nothing personal: algorithmic individuation on music streaming platforms. Media, Culture & Society: 016344371774514. https://doi.org/10.1177/0163443717745147

[21] Ted Striphas. 2015. Algorithmic culture. European Journal of Cultural Studies 18, 4–5: 395–412. https://doi.org/10.1177/1367549415577392

[22] Petra Sundström, Alex S Taylor, Katja Grufberg, Niklas Wirstrom, and Jordi S Belenguer. 2011. Inspirational bits: towards a shared understanding of the digital material. In Proceedings of the 2011 CHI Conference on Human Factors in Computing Systems - CHI '11, 1561–1570. https://doi.org/10.1145/1978942.1979170

[23] Nava Tintarev and Judith Masthoff. 2007. A survey of explanations in recommender systems. Proceedings - International Conference on Data Engineering: 801–810. https://doi.org/10.1109/ICDEW.2007.4401070

[24] Nava Tintarev and Judith Masthoff. 2012. Evaluating the effectiveness of explanations for recommender systems: Methodological issues and empirical studies on the impact of personalization. User Modeling and User-Adapted Interaction 22, 4–5: 399–439. https://doi.org/10.1007/s11257-011-9117-5

[25] Anna Vallgårda and Johan Redström. 2007. Computational composites. In Proceedings of the SIGCHI conference on Human factors in computing systems - CHI '07, 513–522. https://doi.org/10.1145/1240624.1240706

# TetRotation: Utilising Multimodal Analytics and Gestural Interaction to Nurture Mental Rotation Skills

**Serena Lee-Cultura**
Norwegian University of Science and Technology
Trondheim, Norway
serena.leecultura@ntnu.no

## ABSTRACT

Embodied Interaction (EI) offers unique opportunities to uncover novel ways to achieve experiential learning whilst keeping students stimulated and engaged. Spatial abilities have been repeatedly demonstrated as a success predictor for educations and professions in Science, Technology, Engineering and Mathematics. However, many researchers argue that training and assessment of this pertinent reasoning skill is vastly under-represented in the school curriculum. This paper presents TetRotation, a PhD centred on how affordances coming from Multimodal Analytics can be coupled with EI to nurture Mental Rotation (MR) skills. The overarching objectives of the project are two fold. First, the TetRotation Interaction Design study will highlight best practices identified through the assessment of efficiency, level of engagement and learning gains achieved when using gesture based EI to solve MR tasks. Next, in the TetRotation Game study, these design practices will guide the implementation of an interactive serious game purposed to support the development of MR skills. This research relies on mixed method techniques, including data collections from users' actions, like motion sensing, EEG, gaze tracking, video-recordings, click streams, interviews and surveys.

### Author Keywords

Embodied interaction; gesture; multimodal analytics; rotation; spatial cognition; spatial skills; serious game.

### CCS Concepts

**•Human-centered computing → Gestural input; •Applied computing → Interactive learning environments;**

## INTRODUCTION & MOTIVATION

Research in learning technology and interaction design is in constant pursuit of innovative ways to enhance students' learning experience [6, 11]. Advancements in sensing technologies (eg. Kinect, Leap Motion) enable smooth collection of large scale data sets from multimodal inputs [1, 2]. The richness offered by these Multimodal Analytics (MMA) affords researchers opportunities to deepen their understanding of the complex nature of multidimensional learning environments.



*TEI '19*, March 17–20, 2019, Tempe, AZ, USA



ISBN 978-1-4503-6196-5/19/03...$15.00
DOI: https://doi.org/10.1145/3294109.3302932

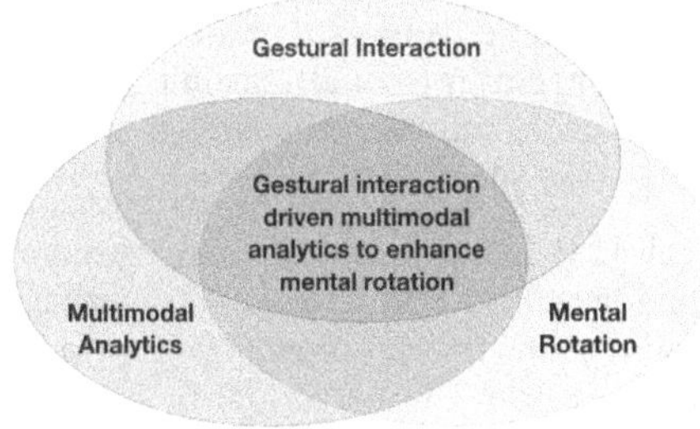


**Figure 1. PhD research domain.**

The intersect of EI and MMA boasts significant impact on helping researchers understand the effectiveness of embodied learning environments [1, 2, 19]. Notable studies have harnessed the power of MMA, such as fine-grained logs of hand movement and gaze data, to identify the significance of temporality in data modelling [2], as well as understand the correlation between student movement and learning gains [1]. These findings endorse embodied MMA as a persuasive instrument for advancing user-experience during learning (i.e., learner experience).

Clifton et al. [7] claim that Tangible, Embedded and Embodied Interaction Interfaces (TEI) systems are especially well suited to exploit the natural relationship between the body and spatial cognition in pursuit of developing spatial skills. Additionally, spatial abilities have been repeatedly demonstrated as a success predictor for educations and professions in Science, Technology, Engineering and Mathematics (STEM) [7, 12, 17]. However, many researchers argue that training and assessment of this pertinent reasoning skill is vastly under-represented in the school curriculum [7, 17]. From this, emanates a powerful motivator for pursuing the intersect of embodied interaction, MMA and spatial skills.

Mental Rotation (MR) is the spatial sub-domain that deals with visualizing the rotation of an object around an axis in 2 or 3 dimensional space [9]. Studies show that from a young age, males significantly outperform females in MR [4, 9, 15]. The contribution of this PhD centres on developing a collective understanding of users' MR skills through the lens of MMA and EI, see Figure 1. Specifically, the proposed research attempts to answer the following questions.

- RQ1: How can MMA be used to properly assess MR skills?
- RQ2: What are the most efficient and engaging gesture based EI to employ in order to understand/solve MR tasks?
- RQ3: How can the integration of MMA influence the creation of more efficient and engaging design practices for using gesture based EI to develop MR skills?

## RELATED WORK

Here we highlight some noteworthy contributions that demonstrate the importance of EI and MMA into providing new ways to understand and actively participate in scientific learning, particularly concerning spatial reasoning. We also discuss limitations of each study to acknowledge areas where future research may take shape.

Zander et al. [18] demonstrated that touch gesture interactions, in conjunction with dynamic on-screen virtual objects, elevated learning gains for participants with prior acquired MR skills. Findings from Chiu et al. [5, 6] suggest that gesture based EI applied to MR and projection problems, promote deeper engagement in the cognitive process resulting in slower but more deliberate manipulations. It should be mentioned that each of these papers cited a small number of participants, which can cause "lack of explanatory power" [18]. As well, Zander et al. did not administer pre/post test of spatial skills, while Chiu et al. stated that their assessment was not robust enough due to an observed ceiling effect. Regardless, these studies support the claim that spatial abilities are malleable [7, 16], while also demonstrating that EI serves as an appropriate method for supporting and enhancing spatial skills.

Andrade et al. [2] used log data to illustrate the importance of temporality during gesture analysis of elicited bimanual hand movements. Their findings revealed that temporal analytics played a vital role in determining an appropriate data model for sequential gestures. In a similar study [1], fine-grained logs of hand movement and gaze data informed the correlation of student performed actions to learning gains. However, the lack of control group in these studies removed the possibility of determining if the student learning experience decreased in response to the induced cognitive load imposed by performing gestures and also by requiring that participants pay attention to dynamic on-screen population graphs. Furthermore, the elicited gestures were restricted to simple up/down hand movements, leaving much room for future analysis involving a more complex gesture set. Notwithstanding, in these inspiring works EI driven MMA amplified researchers understanding of the interplay between EI and learning, by enabling researchers to accurately infer students' theoretical proficiency.

There is limited empirical research combining EI with both MMA and spatial cognition. However, it is worth highlighting the works of Zhang et al. [19], which employed MMA to develop Bayesian Attentional Networks (BANs); a new structure to model the relationship between level of attention, EI input modality and feedback mechanism, while reasoning time sensitive visual-spatial navigation problems. Although an interesting method for determining user attention, BANs are not without limitation. They are computationally expensive and not yet capable of determining levels of attention in real time. Furthermore, researchers utilised a minimal number of input datastreams during observations; though they plan to extend their approach to include Electroencephalography (EEG) and other wearable technologies in future experiments.

Collectively, these contributions demonstrate that EI supported by MMA demonstrate potential for nurturing spatial skills more effectively than traditional methods, while also increasing learner enjoyment. As well, they comprise a starting space for further development in EI based interventions by suggesting an initial set of design principles.

To account for the limitation discussed in the aforementioned studies, the TetRotation Project (TetRotation) will employ a between group study with relatively high number of participants to ensure reliability and in various contexts/settings to ensure validity of data. In addition, we will use a diversified influx of MMA derived from: motion sensing technology, EEG, video-recordings, real time eye tracking, click streams, interviews and surveys. This will foster opportunities for a more holistic analysis of the students' multidimensional learning experience. Lastly, the assessed gesture set will represent greater range motion than simple up/down hand movement.

## RESEARCH APPROACH & METHODS

TetRotation aims to address the aforementioned research questions. Design and development of TetRotation will be achieved by two case studies; TetRotation Interaction Design (TetRoID) and TetRotation Game (TetRoG), which investigate gesture based EI principles and their interplay with game design, respectively.

### Literature Review & Pilot Study

In order to develop a comprehensive understanding of previous empirical and theoretical knowledge, we have conducted a Systematic Literature Review (SLR) in the domain of EI and spatial abilities. We identified a collection of successes, failures, and pertinent design guidelines from relevant works centred on gesture based systems and MR tasks [5, 6, 14]. In addition, we aim to conduct an exploratory pilot study to examine users' natural gestural tendencies when manipulating virtual objects around the x, y and z axes, as defined by the right hand rule. Findings from the pilot study and SLR will guide the initial design decisions for TetRoID. Specifically, we are motivated by the success of the rotation and translation gestures described by Radkowski et al. [14], and look to this gesture set, with possible adaptation from pilot study results as our starting point.

### TetRotation: Interaction Design

TetRoID will use MMA to assess the learning gains, efficiency and engagement of the gestures proposed for reasoning about MR. Additionally, it serves as research into the interaction space that drives the input modalities utilised in TetRoG. High levels of engagement are associated with a wider breadth of knowledge, a deeper understanding of learned material, and

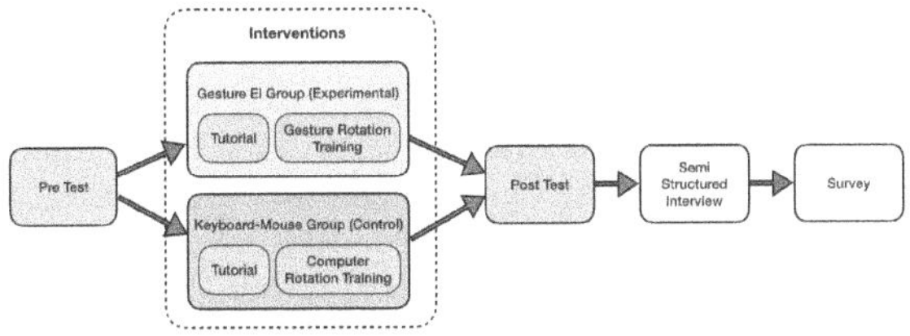


**Figure 2. The 5 phases of the TetRotation Interaction Design Study.**

increased achievement [10]. Moreover, our desire to realise a MR training system with potential to integrate into a formal learning scenario motivates the need for efficiency.

TetRoID will adhere to a mixed methods between groups embedded design. Embedded design is implemented when a traditionally quantitative (or qualitative) research design integrates the collection and analysis of both qualitative and quantitative data types [8]. TetRoID is predominantly quantitative and will consist of five distinct phases; illustrated in Figure 2. The experimental group will be familiarised with a set of motion tracked hand gestures. Participants will be asked to solve a collection of exercises concerned with rotating virtual 2D and 3D objects that appear on screen. A control group will solve the same exercises using traditional keyboard and mouse interactions.

An influx of different multimodal data streams will be collected during the intervention phase of TetRoID. EEG and eye tracking technology will be utilised to capture brain wave patterns and gaze data, respectively. Motivated by the frequency of its use in pre-exsting studies [3, 6], Leap Motion has been selected for gesture tracking and collection of related data. Click stream data from the control group will be captured using custom written event tracking software. In addition, participants' MR skills will undergo pre and post assessment. A video/audio-recorded semi-structured interview will be administered, whereby participants will be asked to solve an object rotation task without the use of pen or paper. Participants will also complete an attitudinal survey.

The quantitative data will be used to evaluate the MR learning gains achieved by a participant, inform on the efficiency of the proposed gesture set, as well as provide insights into participant engagement. Collection of the qualitative data will supplement and refine the quantitative results through explanation of participants interaction preferences and levels of engagement. In addition, qualitative data will offer opportunities to observe participants while working through MR tasks, and solicit additional feedback to be used during extraction of hypothesised design principles informing best practices for gesture based EI and MR. Collectively, this data will address the concerns of RQ1 and RQ2, as well as provide insights into RQ3.

### TetRotation: Game Design

TetRoG aims to develop an interactive serious video game purposed to support and enhance MR skills through the support of MMA and gesture based EI. Conceptually, it extends the classic video game Tetris, with an embodied twist. That is, a player controls virtual game pieces through motion tracked body movement. Unlike the original Tetris, TetRoG will offer interactive play in both 2 and 3 dimensions. Design principles resulting from the aforementioned TetRoID will provide a framework for the initial incarnation of TetRoG. Implementation will follow the design based research methodology, and will involve iterations whereby participants interact with the game based training environment, are assessed for learning gains and provide feedback to be considered during theoretical design principle refinement. We will investigate if the harmony between efficiency and engagement to optimise learning, persists through the game play experience. As well, we will solicit suggested changes to foster an improved user experience. Figure 3 illustrates this life cycle. Findings from this study will further address RQ3 by exploring the integration of MMA verified gestures into a serious game.

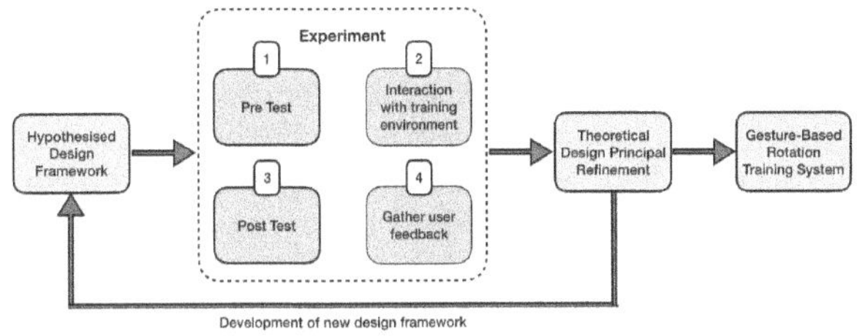


**Figure 3. Life cycle of the TetRotation Game Study.**

### Data Analysis

This section discusses the data to be measured and analysed to address metrics raised in the proposed research questions.

*Learning Gains:* are defined as the improvements of a target ability in response to a stimulus over a given period of time [2]. In TetRotation, learning gains are the change in MR skills attained by a participant's engagement with TetRoG, as measured by the difference in performance between the pre and post assessment conducted in each study.

*Efficiency:* describes the ratio of useful work to actual work performed [13] and will be determined through comparison between a participant's input and the optimal input utilised when solving a problem. The number of gestures and number of clicks performed in relation to each other and the minimum number required to solve the given problem [6], as well as the speed of transitions between gestures and clicks [2], will be considered when analyzing mental and temporal efficiency. Data offered by EEG will determine if use of gestures reduces efficiency by imposing excess cognitive load.

*Engagement:* refers to the level of involvement demonstrated by a participant throughout their interactions. To determine this metric, eye tracking data, EEG, and survey response will be collectively analysed.

## CONCLUSION

Further research efforts possess the potential to unlock valuable information capable of transcending how researchers and students interact with learning materials while developing and amplifying spatial abilities. In this paper, we present relevant literature that motivates our research questions. We also discuss the successes and limitations of notable related studies.

We present TetRotation; a project that builds upon elements of the aforementioned research by examining the capacity of MMA to nurture pedagogical opportunities involving spatial abilities by exploring new ways to incorporate gesture based EI into the training and evaluation of MR. The findings we gather during TetRotation will address the overarching research objectives to (1) incorporate MMA across heterogeneous data sets to identify efficient and engaging design principles that achieve optimal learning gains, and (2) deliver an interactive serious video game purposed to amplify MR skills through EI. This research broadens the domain for development of gesture driven technologies that require a solid understanding and execution of mental rotation. Some examples include interactive geometry applications (i.e., rotating a 2D shape in a 3D environment to explore the relationship between it's area and volume), as well as gesture controlled robotics as tools to perform in hazardous or unpredictable conditions (i.e., spacecraft mechanics).

## ACKNOWLEDGEMENTS

I would like to thank my supervisor Prof. Michail Giannakos. This work is supported by the Research Council of Norway under the project FUTURE LEARNING (255129/H20).

## REFERENCES

[1] Alejandro Andrade. 2017. Understanding Student Learning Trajectories Using Multimodal Learning Analytics within an Embodied-Interaction Learning Environment. In *Proceedings of the Seventh International Learning Analytics & Knowledge Conference*. ACM, 70–79.

[2] Alejandro Andrade, Joshua A Danish, and Adam V Maltese. 2017. A Measurement Model of Gestures in an Embodied Learning Environment: Accounting for Temporal Dependencies. *Journal of Learning Analytics* 4, 3 (2017), 18–46.

[3] Jack Shen-Kuen Chang, Georgina Yeboah, Alison Doucette, Paul Clifton, Michael Nitsche, Timothy Welsh, and Ali Mazalek. 2017. TASC: Combining Virtual Reality with Tangible and Embodied Interactions to Support Spatial Cognition. In *Proceedings of the 2017 Conference on Designing Interactive Systems*. ACM, 1239–1251.

[4] Isabelle D Cherney. 2008. Mom, let me play more computer games: They improve my mental rotation skills. *Sex Roles* 59, 11-12 (2008), 776–786.

[5] Po-Tsung Chiu. 2017. *Supporting spatial skill learning with gesture-based embodied interaction*. Master's thesis. University of Illinois at Urbana-Champaign.

[6] Po-Tsung Chiu, Helen Wauck, Ziang Xiao, Yuqi Yao, and Wai-Tat Fu. 2018. Supporting Spatial Skill Learning with Gesture-Based Embodied Design. In *23rd International Conference on Intelligent User Interfaces*. ACM, 67–71.

[7] Paul G Clifton, Jack Shen-Kuen Chang, Georgina Yeboah, Alison Doucette, Sanjay Chandrasekharan, Michael Nitsche, Timothy Welsh, and Ali Mazalek. 2016. Design of Embodied Interfaces for Engaging Spatial Cognition. *Cognitive Research: Principles and Implications* 1, 1 (2016), 24.

[8] John W Creswell and VL Plano Clark. 2011. Choosing a mixed methods design. *Designing and conducting mixed methods research* (2011), 53–106.

[9] Richard De Lisi and Jennifer L Wolford. 2002. Improving children's mental rotation accuracy with computer game playing. *The Journal of genetic psychology* 163, 3 (2002), 272–282.

[10] Elizabeth A Linnenbrink and Paul R Pintrich. 2003. The role of self-efficacy beliefs in student engagement and learning in the classroom. *Reading &Writing Quarterly* 19, 2 (2003), 119–137.

[11] Laura Malinverni and Narcis Pares. 2014. Learning of Abstract Concepts Through Full-Body Interaction: A Systematic Review. *Journal of Educational Technology & Society* 17, 4 (2014), 100.

[12] Nora S Newcombe. 2010. Picture This: Increasing Math and Science Learning by Improving Spatial Thinking. *American Educator* 34, 2 (2010), 29.

[13] Henri Palleis and Heinrich Hussmann. 2016. Indirect 2D Touch Panning: How Does It Affect Spatial Memory and Navigation Performance?. In *Proceedings of the 2016 CHI Conference on Human Factors in Computing Systems*. ACM, 1947–1951.

[14] Rafael Radkowski and Christian Stritzke. 2012. Interactive hand gesture-based assembly for augmented reality applications. In *Proceedings of the 2012 International Conference on Advances in Computer-Human Interactions*. Citeseer, 303–308.

[15] Melissa S Terlecki, Nora S Newcombe, and Michelle Little. 2008. Durable and generalized effects of spatial experience on mental rotation: Gender differences in growth patterns. *Applied Cognitive Psychology: The Official Journal of the Society for Applied Research in Memory and Cognition* 22, 7 (2008), 996–1013.

[16] David H Uttal, Nathaniel G Meadow, Elizabeth Tipton, Linda L Hand, Alison R Alden, Christopher Warren, and Nora S Newcombe. 2013. The Malleability of Spatial Skills: A meta-analysis of training studies. *Psychological bulletin* 139, 2 (2013), 352.

[17] Jonathan Wai, David Lubinski, and Camilla P Benbow. 2009. Spatial Ability for STEM Domains: Aligning Over 50 Years of Cumulative Psychological Knowledge Solidifies its Importance. *Journal of Educational Psychology* 101, 4 (2009), 817.

[18] Steffi Zander, Stefanie Wetzel, and Sven Bertel. 2016. Rotate it!–Effects of touch-based gestures on elementary school students' solving of mental rotation tasks. *Computers & Education* 103 (2016), 158–169.

[19] Ting Zhang, Yu-Ting Li, and Juan P Wachs. 2017. The Effect of Embodied Interaction in Visual-Spatial Navigation. *ACM Transactions on Interactive Intelligent Systems (TiiS)* 7, 1 (2017), 3.

# Multi-Party Mixed Reality Interaction for Earth Sciences Education

**Yan-Ming Chiou**
Computer and Information Sciences
University of Delaware
Newark, Delaware
steveice@udel.edu

## ABSTRACT
Collaborative learning has been shown to be beneficial for children's learning performance, increasing the curiosity and intensity of the ability of cooperation. Mixed-Reality with collaborative learning is the trending research topic in the Human-Computer Interaction (HCI) area. Additionally, with the rise of attention to global warming which brings in more extreme weather and climate conditions, the earth science education would be one of the crucial topics for the next generation. Moreover, there are few augmented reality and mixed reality applications on earth science subject. In this paper, we propose a Mixed Reality Tornado Simulator which offers an earth science education in a collaborative setting. Students and the instructor can cooperate on learning the knowledge of the formation and its damage cause on human-built structures, farming, and vegetation by using our mixed reality application with the Microsoft HoloLens. Also, for evaluating the learning performance in this mixed reality setting, we propose to study the cognitive load while the student is learning the abstract knowledge in Earth Science. We will separate the student into a control group and experimental groups and use different teaching instruments to test the difference of cognitive load.

## CCS Concepts
**•Human-centered computing → Mixed / augmented reality; •Applied computing → Computer-assisted instruction; Interactive learning environments; Collaborative learning;**

## Author Keywords
Mixed Reality, Interactive Earth Sciences Education, Microsoft HoloLens, Collaborative Learning

## INTRODUCTION
From the climate data in National Aeronautics and Space Administration (NASA) [10], global temperatures have risen about 1.62 degrees Fahrenheit since the late 19th century, sea level increases 3.2 millimeters per year, Arctic ice decrease by 12.8 percent per decade and the extreme weather events happen more often since the 19th century. NASA also predicted that the hurricanes, also known as typhoons, will become frequent and stronger, sea level will rise 1-4 feet by 2020 and the Arctic likely to become ice-free before mid-21st-century [10].

With these concerns in mind, it is crucial for the human being to work together to make the global climate change speed become slower. One immediate step is to raise the awareness about climate change with the education of our students in K12 earth science classes. In the United States, middle and high school teachers teach earth and space science (ESS) which is included in the new Next Generation Science Standards (NGSS) for K-12 science education [5]. In ESS [1] disciplinary core ideas including earth's place in the universe, earth's system and earth and human activity. Students will learn the knowledge of earth science from primary school (K-2) to high school (9 - 12 grades) which is sufficient enough to cultivate the earth science knowledge. With the development of advanced immersive technologies, the class material could go beyond the textbook and the videos. Research shows that students learn more efficiently when the instructor uses technology instruments in class and deploys interactive learning activity along with the class materials [12, 14]. For example, the instructor can introduce some recent significant or severe weather events that have occurred on the earth, such as hurricanes, tornadoes, and tsunami and use some interaction e-learning websites [7, 13] to show how these events happen and what is the damage would cause by these natural events.

Moreover, by leveraging mixed-reality (MR), bringing digital learning into another stage offers active learning methods by introducing embodied interventions. In the MR world, we can utilize all the real world elements as an object to interact with the virtual object. Furthermore, MR can bridge the communication gap between teacher and students. For instance, we can place a virtual Newton avatar on the table to teach Newton's three laws of motion, and also reproduce Trojan Horse story from the Trojan War on the table; within these two different areas of learning to arrange, we can add more interactive activities inside the MR application to provide an engagement and collaborative learning environment. Also,



*TEI '19*, March 17–20, 2019, Tempe, AZ, USA



DOI: https://doi.org/10.1145/3294109.3302933

when students get lost in the MR environment, the teacher can join the session remotely to guide the student.

Nevertheless, most of the MR applications on the education area are provided visualization information from the textbook as the supplement content instead of facilitating learning through different kinds of collaborative and constructionist activities to interact in the real world [9]. Collaborative learning is a setting in which two or more people are learning or solving a problem together. During the problem-solving process in collaborative learning, students can share their ideas while others can evaluate and discuss the approach to find the solution.

## RELATED WORK

In this section, the literature review of the mixed/augmented reality applications in education, with special focus on earth science subject, and some works about collaborative learning will be discussed.

### Mixed Reality and Augmented Reality on Education

Carlos Delgado-Kloos et al. [8] summarized twenty-eight augmented reality projects on the educational area, and most of them used location-based and image-based approaches to guide student to explore physics, life sciences, mathematics, and earth sciences topics. However, most of these work only provides exploration or simulation activities for single student and only a few of the works includes the cooperative and collaborative concept. Shodhan et al. [12] designed Voyage which is a multiuser mobile virtual reality (VR) experience application to promote collaboration among students and teachers. The students were separated into groups, and they wore Google Daydream[1] devices to have a forest field trip in the virtual world, and the teacher used the Apple iPad[2] to guide and monitor the exploration status for all the groups. Zeynep et al. [14] studied the cognitive loads of students to learn abstract concepts in a geology course between using mobile augmented reality and traditional textbook. They used image-based augmented reality application which student can use their smartphone to scan the image on the textbook and then the virtual objects including 2D, 3D and video would be shown on the smartphone. Khan et al [9] developed a mixed reality collaborative educational application called Mathland. In Mathland, students can explore and experiment the mathematics and physics concept by using virtual items that created by the author and use the customized tangible object to interact with these virtual objects in mixed reality.

### Collaborative Earth Science Education

Natalie et al. [3] built an augmented reality grand canyon field trips game, and used the location-based approach to allow students to explore the virtual grand canyon around the school campus. During the progress of the virtual field trip, students learned geologic time, geologic structure and horologic processes from the mobile devices. Chen et al. [4] used screen-based augmented reality with tangible objects to teach the earth science phenomena of day, night, and seasons for middle school students. They used three-stage instruction process to integrate with digital instruments into the education progress; 1) knowledge presentation stage, 2) exploration of the augmented reality world and 3) reinforcement stage to discover how many concepts were acquired by study.

[1]https://vr.google.com/daydream/
[2]https://www.apple.com/ipad/

## APPROACH

### Overview

Mixed Reality Tornado Simulator is a multi-party interaction application to teach the formation of tornado, and destructive power of tornado. Students will have the capability to work with their peers simultaneously to build the tornado by choosing different ground environment, airflow, and physical parameters.

To enhance learning performance and to reduce the cognitive load of the students, we propose a mixed reality intervention with collaborative learning in the context of tornado formation and its damage to the living place. With this research goal, it points out our research goal as following 1) How to design a collaborative learning environment (setting) in mixed reality for earth science education? 2) How to reduce students' cognitive load and increase students' motivation?

### Collaborative Learning with Mixed Reality

In the classroom setting, collaborative learning not only involves jointly intellectual effort in students but students and teachers by working on interdependent learning activities [6]. With the integration of Mixed Reality, the teacher can design some experiment and activities on the virtual environment without any physical boundaries and limitation while students can explore the knowledge together by manipulating the virtual objects via a tangible or embodied controller.

### Apparatus

The hardware consists of three Microsoft HoloLens, a Dell Alienware 17 (8th Generation Intel Core i7-8750H, Nvidia GeForce GTX 1080 OC with 6GB GDDR5 and 32GB DDR4 of RAM) and a wireless network router with IEEE 802.11 ac supported. The laptop is using as the server for coordinating the virtual environment and collecting the experimental data. A pair of the Microsoft HoloLens headsets is used by students to build a tornado and design the virtual city on the ground collaboratively, and another HoloLens is used by the instructor to observe and guide students during the experiment. Also, we plan to integrate HoloLens with Leap Motion sensor to detect the hand gesture for offering embodied interaction feature.

### Prototype

For prototyping Multi-Party Mixed Reality Tornado Simulator, we will make terrain and environment similar to Figure 2. In our setting, the 3D topographic map will be presented on the table, and the extreme weather condition would be zoomed in between the two participants. Moreover, we will provide a toolset in the right-hand side of each participant, so they can discuss together about the environment and manipulate the weather control panel together to control the form of the simulated tornado.

In the Mixed Reality Tornado Simulator menu shown in Figure 1. The video feature plays the online education video

**Figure 1. Mixed Reality Tornado Simulator - Menu & Tornado Builder**

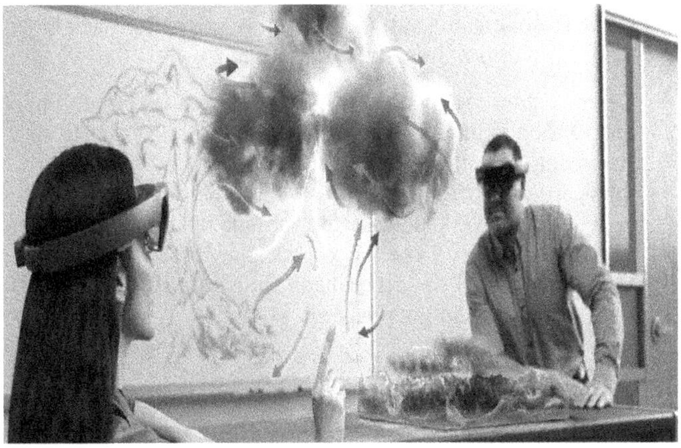

**Figure 2. Microsoft HoloLens concept Idea for lighting. Adapted from "Microsoft Mixed Realtiy, https://www.microsoft.com/en-us/mixed"**

about Tornado 101 [3] provided by National Geography Website which explains the formation of the tornado in details. The document feature provides the digital textbook content for students to reference the material. The setting feature enables the students to choose terrain or 3D topographic map. Ask the teacher feature enables students to invite the instructor to join the experiment session remotely to monitor and answer students' questions. Tornado builder feature, it will pop-up a button menu with three different parameter sliders; students can use the slider to change the funnel width, pressure difference and rotation speed. The test run feature, based on the intensity of the pre-built tornado and other setting such as ground temperature, students can hit the play button to see how tornado might destroy the city where that create by manipulating and placing objects into 3D scenes on Figure 1.

For offering a tangible interaction feature, students can use *Bloom* gesture, which is holding out the hand with all fingers then open the hand, to open the control menu. With *Air Tap* gesture, students can choose the feature on the menu to ask teacher, create tornado, read document, test the destructive power of tornado and modified the setting. Also, with HoloLens, students can walk around freely without the limitation of the wired-cable connected. Students can observe the tornado in different angles and discuss how to create the virtual city with the collaborators and teacher.

### Experiment Design

**Research hypothesis H1**: Using mixed reality with multi-party collaborate learning method for learning the tornado formation and destruction would reduce the students' cognitive load compared to the web-based education application.

**Research hypothesis H2**: Using mixed reality with multi-party collaborate learning method for learning the tornado formation and destruction would provide profoundly immersive experience compared to the tablet/digital 2D visualization.

For H1, We will consider two different approaches to monitor cognitive load from the students. First, using the electroencephalography (EEG) device, such as InteraXon Muse[4], to monitor the brain wave activity through the study. We will analyze the brain wave difference during the learning stages of both the control group and experiment group. Secondly, we will do the qualitative analysis by studying the video and finding the nonverbal behavior of the students; such as body language and facial expression. For example, when people feel confused, they will bite their lips, crossed arms, brow furled and blinked the eye more often[2].

For H2, we want to identify the level of immersive experience in mixed reality tornado experiment by measuring the presence from the student. In order to measure the presence of the mixed reality, we plan to use Igroup Presence Questionnaire (IPQ) [11]. The questions Items (e.g." In the computer-generated world, I had a sense of "being there," Somehow I felt that the virtual world surrounded me.", "I was not aware of my real environment.", "I was completely captivated by the virtual world.") are measured in a 5-point Likert scale from 1 = strongly disagree to 5 = strongly agree.

### Participants

Approximately sixty individuals, including teachers and students, from a research-partner high school in Newark, Delaware, United States will be recruited. We expect to have 50 (age 12-14) students and 10 teachers in the study. We will follow the ethics research guidelines including the IRB procedure from the University of Delaware, parental consents, children consents, and parental approval for pictures and videos.

### Overview of the Pilot Study

For the pilot study, we will recruit two teachers and eight students from the nearby middle school and separated them into two groups. Each group consists of one teacher and four students.

The sessions are conducting in a classroom in the nearby high school. There are two settings for each group; the control group has four students using the tablet or digital 2D visualization while the experiment group also have four students

[3]https://video.nationalgeographic.com/video/news/101-videos/00000144-0a31-d3cb-a96c-7b3d903d0000

[4]https://choosemuse.com/

using HoloLens to learn the concept the tornado. Each session would last approximately for an hour.

Before each session starts, students are required to do the pre-test, which is based on K-12 Tornado practice questions [7]. After that, the teacher starts to teach about the formation and the destruction of the tornado for 15 minutes. Afterwards, students would be asked to create a tornado by digital instruments. Then, students will use the tornado they create to destroy the virtual city. After the experiment, students will fill out the IPQ questionnaire, and the post-test.

### Case Study

For the case study, we will recruit six teachers and forty students from the nearby high school. Similar to the pilot, we will separate them into two groups so each group consists of three teachers and twenty students. We will repeat the same research and experiment procedure as mentioned in the pilot study.

### Expected Findings

We expect to observe a meaningful difference on cognitive load between control and experiment groups during the session. We aim that our collected data will provide evidence to support hypothesis H1. Also, we expect to find a considerable difference between two groups on the IPQ questionnaire responses as stated in hypothesis H2.

## FUTURE WORK

In this paper, we propose the research plan and the prototype of the multi-party mixed reality interaction for earth sciences education. Also, I list the related previous work, inspiring designs, educational theory, projects and mixed reality user-interface (UI) and user experience (UX) design, along with the research hypothesis and experiment design. The timeline of this work will last for a year which includes, finalizing the prototype, developing the mixed reality intervention software, preparing the institutional review board (IRB) document and send to the IRB office for approving experiment, pilot study, modify the software based on the feedback from pilot study, case study and data analysis. I expect to finish this project in the middle of my fourth year of the Ph.D. program. In the following years, I plan to increase the number of participants and build a large-scale mixed reality application and expand the collaborative learning with multi-modal deep learning method for enhancing the learning performance by providing the a personalized learning environment.

## REFERENCES


[1] National Science Teachers Association. 2018. Disciplinary Core Ideas. (2018). `https://ngss.nsta.org/DisciplinaryCoreIdeasMid.aspx?id=3`, Accessed:11/09/2018.

[2] Judee K Burgoon, Laura K Guerrero, and Kory Floyd. 2016. *Nonverbal communication*. Routledge.

[3] Natalie Bursztyn, A Walker, B Shelton, and Joel Pederson. 2017. Increasing undergraduate interest to learn geoscience with GPS-based augmented reality field trips on students' own smartphones. *GSA Today* 27, 5 (2017), 4–11.

[4] Cheng-ping Chen and Chang-Hwa Wang. 2015. Employing augmented-reality-embedded instruction to disperse the imparities of individual differences in earth science learning. *Journal of Science Education and Technology* 24, 6 (2015), 835–847.

[5] National Research Council and others. 2013. *Next generation science standards: For states, by states.*

[6] Pierre Dillenbourg. 1999. *Collaborative learning: Cognitive and computational approaches. advances in learning and instruction series.* ERIC.

[7] CK-12 Foundation. 2018. CK-12 Foundation:Tornado. (2018). `https://www.ck12.org/Earth-Science/Tornadoes/?referrer=concept_details`, Accessed:11/09/2018.

[8] María-Blanca Ibáñez and Carlos Delgado-Kloos. 2018. Augmented reality for STEM learning: A systematic review. *Computers & Education* (2018).

[9] Mina Khan, Fernando Trujano, and Pattie Maes. 2018. Mathland: Constructionist Mathematical Learning in the Real World Using Immersive Mixed Reality. In *Immersive Learning Research Network*, Dennis Beck, Colin Allison, Leonel Morgado, Johanna Pirker, Anasol Peña-Rios, Todd Ogle, Jonathon Richter, and Christian Gütl (Eds.). Springer International Publishing, Cham, 133–147.

[10] NASA. 2018. Climate change: How do we know? (2018). `https://climate.nasa.gov/evidence/`, Accessed:11/09/2018.

[11] Thomas Schubert, Frank Friedmann, and Holger Regenbrecht. 2001. The experience of presence: Factor analytic insights. *Presence: Teleoperators & Virtual Environments* 10, 3 (2001), 266–281.

[12] Shodhan Sharan, Korzeniowsky Julian, Mukundan Rajeev, Kim Na-yeon, He Sijia, John Balash, and Mark J. W. Lee. 2018. Fostering Collaborative Interactions in the Classroom Using Mobile VR. ACM.

[13] NASA Space Place team. 2018. SciKinks:Tornado Simulator. (2018). `https://scijinks.gov/tornado-simulation/`, Accessed:11/09/2018.

[14] Zeynep Turan, Elif Meral, and Ibrahim Fevzi Sahin. 2018. The impact of mobile augmented reality in geography education: achievements, cognitive loads and views of university students. *Journal of Geography in Higher Education* (2018), 1–15.

# Tangible Interactions for Privacy Management

**Vikram Mehta**
The Open University,
Milton Keynes, UK
vikram.mehta@open.ac.uk

## ABSTRACT
Due to the ubiquity of IoT devices, privacy violations can now occur across our cyber-physical-social lives. An individual is often not aware of the possible privacy implications of their actions and commonly lacks the ability to dynamically control the undesired access to themselves or their information. Present approaches to privacy management lack an immediacy of feedback and action, tend to be complex and non-engaging, are intrusive and socially inappropriate, and are inconsistent with users' natural interactions with the physical and social environment. This results in ineffective end-user privacy management. To address these challenges, I focus on designing tangible systems, which promise to provide high levels of stimulation, rich feedback, direct, and engaging interaction experiences. This is achieved through intuitive awareness mechanisms and control interactions, conceptualizing interaction metaphors, implementing tangible interfaces for privacy management and demonstrating their utility within various real life scenarios.

### Author Keywords
Tangibles for privacy management; End-user privacy; Cyber-physical-social environments; Interaction design.

## CONTEXT AND MOTIVATION FOR DISSERTATION
The ever-increasing proliferation of ubicomp systems in our everyday spaces has nurtured the growth of cyber-physical-social environments (CPSE). The private territory of an individual now expands beyond their physical boundaries to include virtual (cyber) territory [7]. Personal information can be sensed (or observed) from users' physical actions by observers (human and technological), and uploaded invisibly to the Internet without warning. The constant interaction with, and interruptions (or disturbances) from disturbers (human and technological) around a user can have a detrimental effect on their social relationships and mental wellbeing. Such observations and disturbances can be termed as privacy threats, which originate from the cyber, physical and social worlds that individuals inhabit. Many people are unable to perceive or control who is observing or disturbing them in their extended private territory, leading to a lack of awareness of possible privacy implications, resulting in inadequate protection practices.

## RESEARCH OBJECTIVES AND CHALLENGES
My research objective is to build solutions to enable end-users to effectively (in a proactive and reactive manner) manage privacy in CPSE. I identify the following challenges: **RC1:** To engage inexperienced users in privacy management. **RC2:** To actively (without overloading) raise awareness of potential violations without disrupting user's social and functional lives in runtime. **RC3:** To enable direct and intuitive controls without requiring them to go through high and technical learning curves.

## BACKGROUND/LITERATURE REVIEW
Privacy is about managing the disclosure of ones' physical space and personal information to others. In the context of CPSE, it is an individual's right to be aware of potential observations and disturbances, and their right to control undesired ones [7]. Due to bi-directional nature of privacy [1], an individual may sometimes also experience too much privacy (social isolation).

Existing interfaces that support privacy awareness and control can be categorized into three non-exclusive sets: (1) UIs for online privacy [3], (2) UIs for mobile privacy [2], and (3) UIs for UbiComp privacy [7]. Through a wide survey of the end-user privacy management literature, I have determined that for a contextual task of privacy management, present approaches can lack immediacy of feedback and action, tend to be complex and non-engaging, and are inconsistent to users' natural interactions with the physical and social environment. The intrusive nature of many existing privacy alert mechanisms, and the cumbersome and non-discreet nature of existing privacy controls results in ineffective solutions.

Literature shows that Tangible User Interfaces (TUIs) hold the potential to provide high levels of realism and stimulation, rich feedback and intuitiveness of interaction to users. In the context of privacy, this is also supported by my early research on on-body privacy warnings and controls [8]. Tangible forms of interaction cover a range of computational systems and interfaces that share "tangibility and materiality, physical embodiment of data, embodied interaction and bodily movement as an essential part of interaction, and embeddedness in real space " [5]. I propose


*TEI '19*, March 17–20, 2019, Tempe, AZ, USA

ACM 978-1-4503-6196-5/19/03…$15.00
https://doi.org/10.1145/3294109.3302934

to design such tangible interactions to enable end-users manage their privacy in complex scenarios of CPSE.

## PROBLEM STATEMENT/RESEARCH QUESTION

Main research question is: **How can tangible interactions engage and enable end-users to continuously, intuitively and efficiently manage their territorial privacy in cyber-physical-social environments?**

**"Manage"** here refers to enhancing awareness and enabling control. I split the usability aspects into four features: engaging, continuous, intuitive and efficient. **"Engage"** means being able to involve users in managing their privacy in a delightful and pleasing manner. **"Continuous"** means the proposed solution must be able to actively raise user's awareness and enable control at all times whenever the user desires or is urgently required to manage their privacy. It should not annoy users through constant notifications. Information should be presented at different levels from coarse-grained to fine-tuned depending on how much the user wants to know and control. **"Intuitive"** means the ease of use in different contexts. It aims to make the interactions natural and direct to the user, without high (or technical) learning curves and cognitive load. **"Efficient"** means increasing the speed of use and reducing the number of steps required to manage privacy in a given context.

These features should be implemented and evaluated in cohesion to assess overall effectiveness of the proposed solution. Social appropriateness of the interaction should be considered, ensuring that awareness is raised through discreet methods, and to provide non-intrusive controls. I further divide the main research question into 2 sub-questions: (a) how can we exploit culturally specific or biologically grounded metaphors in the design of tangible interactions that raise awareness and enable control of privacy in daily settings? (b) How can we use alternative tangible modalities to raise awareness and enable control of privacy in daily settings?

## SAMPLE PROBLEM SCENARIOS

**Figure 1: (a) fraud calls to gain access to remote desktop, (b) access to personal device by someone in a party**

In figure 1, I illustrate two real-life scenarios where privacy management is practically challenging.

## RESEARCH APPROACH AND METHODS

Privacy is highly personal and contextual in nature. To design effective methods and tools I keep end-users at the center of my research approach. My research includes three basic activities of interaction design: (1) Identifying needs and establishing requirements, (2) Designing and building prototypes, and (3) Evaluation. To **identify user needs**, I am utilizing exploratory methods and findings from literature. In the **design & build** step, I am conceptualizing and designing cultural or biologically grounded metaphors and models that underpin the established socio-centric privacy theories into tangible approaches for interaction. I also plan to instantiate conceptual designs by building low and medium fidelity prototypes using off the shelf microelectronics, digital fabrication, software and other prototyping tools. I plan to **evaluate** user engagement, continuous nature, intuitiveness, efficiency and appropriateness of our proposed solutions through empirical methods involving lab and field-testing.

I follow an iterative and incremental approach and hence execute these activities in 3 phases (see figure 2). Findings from each phase inform future phases. Across all of these phases, I use a combination of common data collection techniques including questionnaires, structured and semi-structured interviews (one-to-one, focus group), participatory design (co-design workshops) and direct observations. Qualitative (e.g. thematic analysis) and quantitative methods (statistical analysis) are used for data analysis and to explore and identify significant patterns.

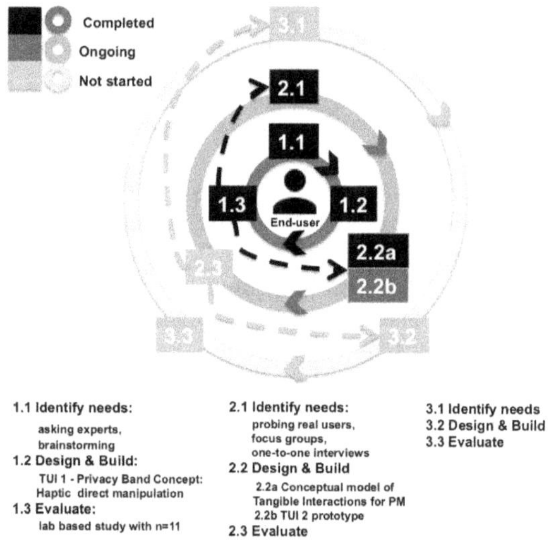


**Figure 2: Iterative User-Centered Research Methodology**

## RESULTS TO DATE

Figure 2 also illustrates the status of my three-phased research. I have finished phase 1. Initial enquiry into the problem space was done through the exploratory literature review and brainstorming with experts. One key requirement was to provide users with subtle, real-time privacy warnings and non-obtrusive control capabilities. This is particularly important in social situations such as when in meetings. To fulfill this, I designed and prototyped Privacy Band (see figure 3): a forearm wearable that provides users with interactive capabilities to manage their cyber-physical privacy reactively in an ad-hoc, continuous and eyes free manner [8]. Initial work (lab user study with 11 participants) has shown that it can help raise the privacy awareness of its' user through discreet haptic vibrations (metaphorical 'privacy itch') at distinct locations and prompt them to react (or control) their privacy in an intuitive and immediate manner through direct manipulation (metaphorical 'privacy scratch').

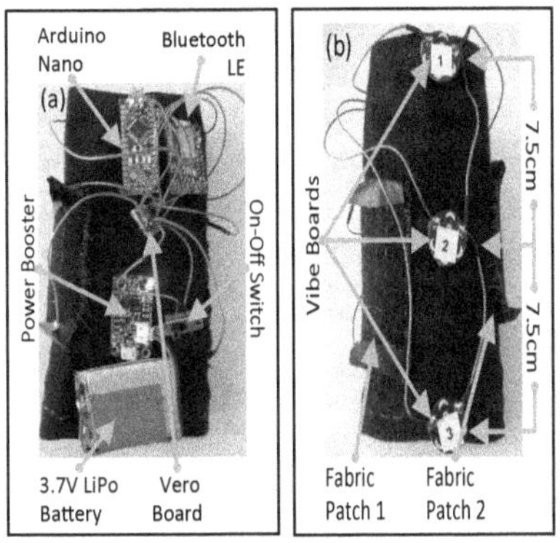


**Figure 3: Privacy Band (a) "Front" view, (b) Back view**

A sample scenario for Privacy Band: Adam has a wide network of friends and enables the Buddy Tracker app on his smartphone, which allows selected friends to locate him for serendipitous meetings. He wants to have some control over his privacy so he connects the Buddy Tracker app to the Privacy Band. While in a café with Bob he feels a slight itch on his forearm indicating that an observer has checked his location. He does not want his chat with Bob to be disturbed so he subtly scratches (haptic direct manipulation) the inner side of his forearm indicating that he wants to keep this information private and the Buddy Tracker app stops revealing his location. If instead he wanted to meet the observer at the café he could have scratched his outer forearm to indicate that he is happy for his location to be shared.

In the 2nd phase, I have explored the needs of end-users. Focusing on older adults (aged 60+), I have completed 5 focus groups (n=15) to explore the privacy concerns, mitigation approaches and challenges faced by them in CPSE. I found that older adults are highly prone to undesired observations and disturbances in their day-to-day living and these occur across cyber, physical and social spaces. They try to block and avoid, log, confront or even allow the access but face various challenges in doing so. There is a clear lack of technological solutions that are appropriate and sufficient for multiple contexts in CPSE. In addition, many are either not aware of the presence of existing tools for privacy management or are unable to interact with them. They desire regulated awareness and intuitive controls to manage their privacy. Based on the findings and literature, I have constructed a conceptual model (see figure 4) that can be used to design interfaces to help end-users manage privacy reactively and proactively.

The model consists of two integral components: Awareness and Control (see Table 1 and 2), which are inherent to any tangible interface [6], and are equally essential for the user's sense of personal privacy.

| **Awareness Component** | |
|---|---|
| **Mechanisms** | 1. Feed-back: report<br>2. Feed-forward: prompt |
| **Medium (Modalities)** | 1. Tangible: Haptics (e.g. vibration, temperature)<br>2. Intangible: Peripheral vision, sound, smell |
| **Features** | 1. Characteristics of access:<br>a. People (who), b. Purpose (why), c. Method (what, when)<br>2. Time of awareness input: a. real-time, b. end-of-the-day<br>3. Position of awareness input: a. on-body, b. ambient |

**Table 1. Awareness Characteristics**

| **Control Component** | |
|---|---|
| **Mechanisms (Actions)** | 1. Pro-act, 2. React |
| **Medium (Modalities)** | 1. Direct manipulation, 2. Body postures, 3. Full body movements |
| **Features** | Forms of control:<br>a. Allow, b. Block, c. Confront (fight back), d. Log |

**Table 2. Control Characteristics**

Depending on the users' context (age, time, location, activity), capabilities (physical, cognitive, social and technical abilities), and privacy needs [4] (intimate, personal, social, public), when an external application senses potential privacy violation, it informs **(A.2, figure 4)** the digital element of the awareness (representation) component with characteristics of the violation or risk. Violations could span across cyber, physical and social spaces of the user. Some of the user's context, capabilities, privacy needs and preferences for notification and control, are manually fed into system at the time of setup **(A.1, figure 4)**. Those that change often can be sensed through TUI sensors or user's existing devices like smartphones.

Not all elements of potential access need to be informed to the user. Depending upon user's preference and context, the digital element also decides on the time and position to deliver the awareness notification (for e.g. discreet on-body notification when in meeting or ambient notification when sitting in a private cabin). This information can then, tangibly or intangibly, be communicated (feed-forward) to the user to warn of a future threat or potential access as part of the physical element of the awareness system. The affordance of the tangible interface at that point prompts and guides **(A.3, figure 4)** the user to react (or control) **(A.4, figure 4)** their privacy in an intuitive and immediate manner through direct manipulation, body postures or full body movements. These interactions depend on users' preference, context and capabilities. I plan to investigate the suitable awareness and control modalities empirically.

The user could allow, block, confront or log the violations as per their context, capabilities and privacy needs. These user actions occur in the physical element of the control component. The system gives inherent feedback [9] to the user in scenarios that involve haptic direct manipulation. This restores (or helps collect evidence) **(A.5, figure 4)** of users' privacy and updates the digital and physical state of the tangible interface **(A.6, figure 4)**. In the end, the user receives functional feedback [9] **(A.7, figure 4)** of her actions (whether privacy has been restored as desired or not) through the awareness component.

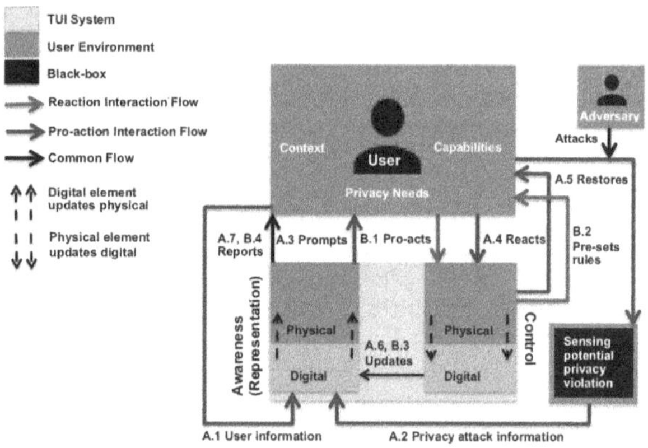


**Figure 4. Conceptual Model for Designing Tools for End-User Privacy Management in CPSE.**

Another possible flow is when user follows a proactive approach. In this case, the user may sense the need to control their privacy and pro-acts **(B.1, figure 4)** in a manner similar to the workflow described above. This may pre-set **(B.2, figure 4)** privacy rules/needs of the user and update **(B.3, figure 4)** the digital and physical state of the tangible interface. The system reports acknowledgment to the user through functional feedback **(B.4, figure 4)**.

## DISSERTATION STATUS AND NEXT STEPS

I plan to continue with phase 2 activity of building an improved TUI prototype for privacy management. This will be followed by a simulated lab-based evaluation. 3rd phase will involve co-designing with end-users and developing the final prototype. Time permitting; I intend to conduct a field study involving carefully planned targeted privacy violations in the physical and digital environments of the participants. I plan to finish fieldwork by the beginning of 2020 and complete thesis writing by mid-2020.

## CURRENT AND EXPECTED CONTRIBUTIONS

I have proposed the concept of tangible interactions for end-user privacy management. I have demonstrated the concept through implementing on-body interfaces for alerting users about personal privacy breaches, and providing them the ability to directly control the access to their information in a discreet and non-obtrusive manner. I plan to contribute an empirically grounded and validated model (substantiated with prototypes) to help designers build interfaces and interactions for effective end-user privacy management in CPSE. I also plan to use this model for generating relevant metaphors.

The concepts of Privacy as well as methods for violation and protection have evolved over time and need greater attention than ever before. With this research, I aim to empower end-users by providing them with intuitive, engaging, continuous and effective interaction methods and tools for managing privacy as and when desired.

## ACKNOWLEDGEMENTS

My work is supported by ERC Advanced Grant 291652, EPSRC Grants EP/K033522/1 and EP/P01013X/1.

## REFERENCES

[1] Irwin Altman. 1976. Privacy: A conceptual analysis. *Environment and behavior* 8, 1: 7–29.

[2] Rebecca Balebako, Jaeyeon Jung, Wei Lu, Lorrie Faith Cranor, and Carolyn Nguyen. 2013. Little brothers watching you: Raising awareness of data leaks on smartphones. In *Proc of 9th SOUPS'13*, 12.

[3] Lorrie Faith Cranor, Praveen Guduru, and Manjula Arjula. 2006. User interfaces for privacy agents. *ACM TOCHI'06* 13, 2: 135–178.

[4] Edward T. Hall, Ray L. Birdwhistell, Bernhard Bock, Paul Bohannan, A. Richard Diebold Jr, Marshall Durbin, Munro S. Edmonson, J. L. Fischer, Dell Hymes, Solon T. Kimball, and others. 1968. Proxemics. *Current anthropology* 9, 2/3: 83–108.

[5] Eva Hornecker and Jacob Buur. 2006. Getting a grip on tangible interaction: a framework on physical space and social interaction. In *Proc of SIGCHI CHI'06*, 437–446.

[6] Hiroshi Ishii. 2008. Tangible bits: beyond pixels. In *Proc of the 2nd TEI*, xv–xxv.

[7] Bastian Könings. 2015. User-centered awareness and control of privacy in Ubiquitous Computing. PhD diss., Universität Ulm.

[8] Vikram Mehta, Arosha K. Bandara, Blaine A. Price, and Bashar Nuseibeh. 2016. Privacy Itch and Scratch: On Body Privacy Warnings and Controls. In EA CHI'16, 2417–2424.

[9] Stephan AG Wensveen, Johan Partomo Djajadiningrat, and C. J. Overbeeke. 2004. Interaction frogger: a design framework to couple action and function through feedback and feedforward. In *Proc of 5th DIS*, 177–184.

# Virtual Adornments: Haute Couture Practices for IoT Connecting Apparel

**Caroline McMillan**
RMIT University
Melbourne, Australia
cazmcmillan@hotmail.com

## ABSTRACT

The Internet of Things (IoT) [3, 16, 35] is a physical-digital ecosystem of compliant technologies and heterogeneous parts, enabling vast transmissions of data and candid, pervasive presence of things [40]. Fashion, on the other hand, is an embodied practice, an information medium of material, social, cultural, economic and political forces. Many wearables are outfitted to actuate data input sources as a visualised display. However, the impact and rich possibilities of fashion adornment practices for embodied data engagement in IoT wearables design have been overlooked. Introducing computational materials of the IoT to physical properties pushes this virtual system into the physical realm. In this research, an aesthetic criterion of haute couture practices considers the material turn [34, 39]. Design cases of fashion-led adornment style are a promising path to follow in the context of designing wearables for an *Internet of Worn Things*.

### Author Keywords

Wearables; Internet of Things; fashion; haute couture; research through design; material cultures.

### CSS Concepts

• **Human-centered computing~Interface design prototyping** • *Applied computing~Performing arts* • Computer systems organization~Robotic components

## LITERATURE REVIEW

The IoT's ubiquitous [41], enmeshed ecology enables autonomous processing and aggregation of big data transactions amongst the digital-physical world. Data security vulnerabilities are addressed as a key issue [42, 14], as is locating dynamic topologies [31] of IoT connected *worn things*. Moreover, our shifting engagement with computational material, wireless technologies and data, provokes diverse aesthetic and material dialogue; the material turn, notions of screen essentialism [4, 13, 25], computational medial affordances such as glitches, pattern recognition, autonomous behaviours [6, 36] and disembodied aesthetics [12, 32]. As wearables, IoT systems, have notably advanced tracking practices, such as the Quantified self [23, 37] and remote social interactions [9]. Given the susceptibility of networked denizens in a pervasive socio-technical system, it is timely to question the habitual IoT paradigm [2, 26], framing the networked *body-worn things* in this ecology. Accordingly, worn quantified data visualisation is critiqued [18], as are aesthetic data input sources [7, 25] and bodily-sensory outputs [1, 38, 44]. While ornamental textile approaches have been explored for textile computation (5, 11, 15, 25, 33], my research draws from rich fashion traditions of haute couture [8, 10, 28], whose embellishment practices offer a tactile, aesthetic refinement for wearables.


*TEI '19, March 17–20, 2019, Tempe, AZ, USA*

ACM 978-1-4503-6196-5/19/03…$15.00
https://doi.org/10.1145/3294109.3302935

## RESEARCH QUESTIONS

By foregrounding a fashion perspective, networked *worn things* are viewed through a computational material lens.

- In what ways can fashion-led, embodied material practices craft computational material into meaningful data visualisation, for networked wearables in an *Internet of Worn Things* ecology?
- How can computational material and its medial affordances interrogate aesthetic expression for haute couture adornment practices, to broaden bodily-sensory modes of output?

## APPROACH

In my research inquiry, I adapt Research through Design (RtD) [14], to the specific context of crafting IoT connected fashion wearables and extend it by integrating antidisciplinary [20] and performative [17, 19, 27] tactics. RtD supports my investigation of embodied engagement with computational materials through fashion design processes as a mode of inquiry. In this research, a collection of IoT connected garments - *Virtual Adornments* are devised to customise wireless technologies and data-sets for use in haute couture adornment style, to probe networks of *worn things*. Using the design mechanisms and conditions relevant for garments, future outcomes are imagined, emergent material prototypes constructed and artefacts devised to engage with broader ethics of dynamic, networked, worn data transactions. Making negotiates antidisciplinary interventions and performative observations, using material investigation, prototyping material artefacts to incite feedback, see emergent patterns and to articulate unfamiliar conditions. Methods employed in this approach are drawn from RtD design processes: *contextual review of practice and literature, material and aesthetic investigation and ideation, material probes[21] and embodied ideation[43], action research diaries, prototypes, testing, performative artefacts, wearer interventions.*

## WORK IN PROGRESS

### Prototypes

The *Virtual Adornments* collection explores visual and tactile bodily-sensory aesthetic expressions for empowered data input and refined output systems, through consistent haute couture adornment style. This approach is unique, in the sense that hardware components are replaced before tailored on garments. This creates significant differences in the aesthetic expression since the reworked materials correspond to tactile textures, reminiscent of fashion haute couture collections. Two exploratory works in this series are; *Live:scape BLOOM* [29, 30], an IoT dress with robotic embellishment that kinetically responds to quantified weather phenomena, and *Aura:maton*, IoT connected corsetry that electronically releases scent based on quantified physiological data. Both garments explore embodied, autonomous behaviour of data expression in the IoT.

**Figure 1. Video still of *Live:scape BLOOM*. Haute couture robotic embellishment detail.**

### Embodied Design Workshops

Further, an initial phase of embodied design workshops with new media, theatre, fashion and interaction design students, faculty, and dancers has been conducted. Additional requirements were necessary to deepen ideation for what future networked data expressions may fit, move, perform, look and feel. The aim was to probe tactile, bodily experience through materials and movement gestures, and program IoT wearables into the act of wearing. Early analysis unearths that the resulting wearables conceptualisations are specific to individual material, sensory, bodily, style and cultural orientation.

### Performative artefacts

Exhibiting *Live:scapeBLOOM* as a performative artefact revealed a range of individual responses — many described desires for broader sensory-aesthetic expression, such as added LED's for greater effect, scent producing flower embellishment, or more reciprocative interaction behaviour than autonomous live streams of quantified wind data. A hardware 'glitch' in *Live:scape BLOOM* created coquettish movement and provoked intrigue from one viewer. Rather than debug the glitch, it is a compelling shaping material to reconceptualise autonomous computational pattern recognition and medial affordances into the wearables design process: *embellishment repeat patterns, materials, garment patternmaking, silhouettes, data input sources and output hardware, performative interaction design, embodied, dynamic prototyping, testing interventions, film presentation.*

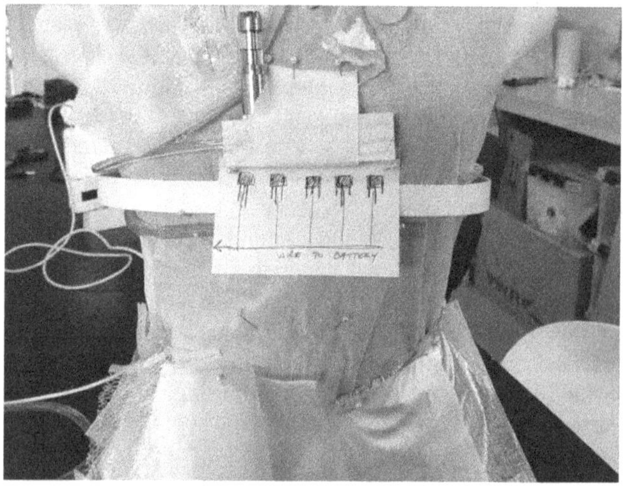

**Figure 2. Detail of an emergent material prototype in the design process of making an olfactory output for data expression.**

## DISCUSSION AND FUTURE WORK

Performative analysis of *Livescape:BLOOM* has informed aesthetic direction for *Aura:maton.* In consideration of data-triggered scent embellishment, material investigations for ambient scent as opposed to skin worn, and required hardware options, the overall expression was drastically modified to accommodate the volatile, temporal behaviour of scent material. Instead, immaterial forms such as fog, temporal traces, and fabric transparency were used to capture aesthetic properties metaphorically. My objective is to value the practice and material improvisation of fashion haute couture for IoT wearables, so they can be worn as everyday garments and appreciated for augmented wireless data visualisation. The approach of aligning established fashion and textile embellishment with computational material practices for the field of IoT, while drawing on familiar routines in the design process, proves suitable for this research. Wearables can be more than computational display. Rather, artefacts of identification within dynamic, physical-digital systems, contributing to the grounding of the fashion wearables design as a bodily-sensory practice. Ongoing work explores wearer probes, that scaffold interactions of IoT mediated garments to leverage broader public responses and experiential accounts of the *Virtual Adornments* collection.

**Figure 3. Video still of *AURA:maton*. Performative analysis of haute couture robotic corsetry.**

## CONCLUSION

My research reveals what can be considered failures of autonomous technological processing, as crucial to material and design innovation. This view advances practice in fashion-led IoT connected wearables, critiquing inclinatiotoward designing for seamless technological functionality. By looking outside the boundaries of IoT usage, and introducing a fashion perspective for an *Internet of Worn Things*, my work resists ubiquitous technological scenarios of automated network assembly and function, to propose more nuanced responses of fashion wearables as a complex, layered, embodied practice.

## ACKNOWLEDGMENTS

I would like to thank my supervisors Danielle Wilde and Lijing Wang for their ongoing encouragement and support. Funding from the Australian Research Training Program Scholarship is gratefully acknowledged. I would also like to thank the reviewers for their helpful comments. *Live:scape BLOOM* was developed during the Deutsche Telekom Fashion Fusion Award Berlin Germany 2016. 

## REFERENCES

[1] Judith Amores and Patti Maes. 2017, May. Essence: Olfactory interfaces for unconscious influence of mood and cognitive performance. In *Proceedings of the 2017 CHI Conference on Human Factors in Computing Systems* (pp. 28-34). ACM.

[2] Luigi Atzori, Antonio Iera and Giacomo Morabito. 2010. The internet of things: A survey. *Computer networks*, *54*(15), 2787-2805.

[3] Kevin Ashton. 2009. That 'internet of things' thing. *RFID journal*, *22*(7), 97-114.

[4] David M. Berry and Michael Dieter. 2015. Thinking postdigital aesthetics: Art, computation and design. In *Postdigital Aesthetics: Art, Computation and Design* (pp. 1-11). Palgrave Macmillan.

[5] Joanna Berzowska and Marcelo Coelho. 2005, October. Kukkia and vilkas: Kinetic electronic garments. In *Wearable Computers, 2005. Proceedings. Ninth IEEE International Symposium on* (pp. 82-85). IEEE.

[6] James Bridle. 2019. New Aesthetic. Retrieved January 6, 2019 from http://new-aesthetic.tumblr.com/

[7] Sophia Brueckner and Rachel Freire. 2018. (October). Embodisuit: a wearable platform for embodied knowledge. In *Proceedings of the 2018 ACM International Symposium on Wearable Computers* (pp. 242-247). ACM.

[8] Chanel. 2015. Making-of the CHANEL Spring-Summer 2015 Haute Couture Collection, Retrieved April 20, 2018 from https://www.youtube.com/watch?v=3cDhTzoMj_s

[9] Cute Circuit. The Hug Shirt; The Twitter Dress. Retrieved January 6, 2018 from http://cutecircuit.com/

[10] Delpozo. 2018. Embroidery. Retrieved November 7, 2018 from https://www.delpozo.com/en/atelier-delpozo-2/embroidery/

[11] Laura Devendorf, Joanne Lo, Noura Howell, Jung Lin Lee, Nan-Wei Gong, M. Emre Karagozler, Shiho Fukuhara, Ivan Poupyrev, Eric Paulos and Kimiko Ryokai. 2016. May. I don't Want to Wear a Screen: Probing Perceptions of and Possibilities for Dynamic Displays on Clothing. In *Proceedings of the 2016 CHI Conference on Human Factors in Computing Systems* (pp. 6028-6039). ACM.

[12] Dezeen. 2012. Li Edelkoort at Dezeen Live. Video. (21 December 2012.) Retrieved January 9, 2019 from https://vimeo.com/56121730

[13] Virginia Eubanks. 2018. Automating inequality: How high-tech tools profile, police, and punish the poor. St. Martin's Press.

[14] Christopher Frayling. 1993. Research in Art and Design.Royal College of Art Research Papers series 1.1, 1-5.

[15] Ying Gao. 2017. Possible Tomorrows. Retrieved 4 May, 2018 from http://yinggao.ca/possible-tomorrows/

[16] Neil Gershenfeld, Raffi Krikorian and Danny Cohen. 2004. The internet of things. *Scientific American, 291*(4), 76-81.

[17] Brad Haseman. 2006. A manifesto for performative research. *Media International Australia incorporating Culture and Policy*, *118*,1, 98-106.

[18] James N. Gilmore. 2016. Everywear: The quantified self and wearable fitness technologies. *New Media & Society*, *18*(11), 2524-2539.

[19] Giulio Jacucci and Ina Wagner. 2007. Performative roles of materiality for collective creativity. In *Proceedings of the 6th ACM SIGCHI conference on Creativity & cognition* (pp. 73-82). ACM.

[20] Joi Ito. 2014. Antidisciplinary. *MIT Media Lab Blog October*, *2*, 2014.

[21] Heekyoung Jung and Erik Stolterman. 2011. Material probe: exploring materiality of digital artifacts. In *Proceedings of the fifth international conference on Tangible, embedded, and embodied interaction* (pp. 153-156). ACM.

[22] Heekyoung Jung, Erik Stolterman, Will Ryan, Tonya Thompson and Marty Siegel. 2008. Toward a framework for ecologies of artifacts: how are digital artifacts interconnected within a personal life?. In *Proceedings of the 5th Nordic conference on Human-computer interaction: building bridges* (pp. 201-210). ACM.

[23] Kevin Kelly. 2007. What is the quantified self. *The Quantified Self*, *5*, 2007.

[24] Rebecca Kleinberger, Alisha Panjwani. 2018, March. Digitally Enchanted Wear: a Novel Approach in the Field of Dresses as Dynamic Digital Displays. In *Proceedings of the Twelfth International Conference on Tangible, Embedded, and Embodied Interaction* (pp. 27-34). ACM.

[25] Kobakant. Smart Rituals; The Crying Dress. Retrieved March 11, 2018 from: http://www.kobakant.at/DIY/?p=6204

[26] Treffyn Lynch Koreshoff, Tuck Was Long, Tony Robertson. 2013. Approaching a human-centred Internet of Things.

[27] Valerie Lamontagne. 2017. *Performative Wearables: Bodies, Fashion and Technology*. Ph.D Dissertation. Concordia University, Montréal, Canada.

[28] @marchesafashion. 2016. Marchesa x IBM. Instagram post. (May 2, 2016). Retrieved August 6, 2018 from https://www.instagram.com/p/BE42oJbhStN/?hl=en

[29] Caroline McMillan. 2018, June. Live:Scape BLOOM: Connecting Smart Fashion to the IoT Ecology. In *International Conference on Artificial Intelligence*

[30] Caroline McMillan. 2018. Live:scape BLOOM. Video. (6 November 2018) Retrieved 9 January 2019 from https://vimeo.com/299296620

[31] Friedemann Mattern, Christian Floerkemeier. 2010. From the Internet of Computers to the Internet of Things. In *From active data management to event-based systems and more* (pp. 242-259). Springer, Berlin, Heidelberg.

[32] Bruna Petreca. 2017. Giving Body to Digital Fashion Tools. In *Digital Bodies* (pp. 191-204). Palgrave Macmillan, London.

[33] Irene Posch. 2017. The Embroidered Computer. Retrieved January 6, 2018 fromhttp://www.ireneposch.net/the-embroidered-computer/

[34] Erica Robles and Mikael Wiberg. 2010. Texturing the material turn in interaction design. In *Proceedings of the fourth international conference on Tangible, embedded, and embodied interaction* (pp. 137-144). ACM.

[35] Bruce Sterling. 2014. The epic struggle of the Internet of Things. Moscow: Strelka Press.

[36] Bruce Sterling, 2012. An essay on the new aesthetic. *Group*, *1*, 1-4.

[37] Melanie Swan. 2013. The quantified self: Fundamental disruption in big data science and biological discovery. *Big Data*, *1*,2, 85-99.

[38] Jenny Tillotson. 2015. eScent. Retrieved November 9, 2018 from https://www.escent.ai/fashion-tech

[39] Anna Vallgårda, & Johan Redström. 2007. Computational composites. In *Proceedings of the SIGCHI conference on Human factors in computing systems* (pp. 513-522). ACM.

[40] Ron Wakkary Doenja Oogjes, Sabrina Hauser, Henry Lin, Cheng Cao, Leo Ma, Tijs Duel. 2017, June. Morse Things: A Design Inquiry into the Gap Between Things and Us. In *Conference on Designing Interactive Systems* (pp. 503-514).

[41] Mark Weiser. 1991. The Computer for the 21st Century. *Scientific american*, 265,3: 94-105.

[42] Matthew Wynn, Sandra Rueda, Kyle Tillotson, Ryan Kao, Andrea Calderon, Andreas Murillo, Javier Camargo, Rafael Mantilla, Brahian Rangel, Alvaro A. Cardenas. 2017. Sexual Intimacy in the Age of Smart Devices: Are We Practicing Safe IoT?. In *Proceedings of the 2017 Workshop on Internet of Things Security and Privacy* (pp. 25-30). ACM.

[43] Danielle Wilde, Anna Vallgårda and Oscar Tomico. 2017. Embodied design ideation methods: analysing the Power of estrangement. In *Proceedings of the 2017 CHI Conference on Human Factors in Computing Systems* (pp. 5158-5170). ACM.

[44] Danielle Wilde and Patricia Marti. 2018, June. Exploring Aesthetic Enhancement of Wearable Technologies for Deaf Women. In *Proceedings of the 2018 on Designing Interactive Systems Conference 2018* (pp. 201-213). ACM.

# Exploring the Potential for Tangible Social Technologies for Childhood Cancer Patients within the Hospital

**Jillian L. Warren**
School of Interactive Arts & Technology (SIAT)
Simon Fraser University
Surrey, Canada
Jlw29@sfu.ca

**ABSTRACT**

Through a multi-phased mixed method study with childhood cancer patients (8-12 years old) and their team of caregivers within US and Canadian hospitals we will explore (1) the ways the cancer experience impacts patient's social/emotional well-being, (2) how existing technologies fail to provide feelings of connectedness to friends/peers, and (3) how novel tangible technology could improve connectedness. We aim to (1) empower children with cancer by allowing them to voice their own experiences with isolation, loneliness, and loss of a normal childhood, as well as how technology may better support their needs, (2) contribute design knowledge about how to support meaningful social interaction and play that is age and 'ability' appropriate, and (3) provide insight for future design and evaluation studies by better understanding constraints/opportunities for social tangible technologies intended for use in a real world pediatric hospitals.

**Author Keywords**

child-computer interaction; design research; childhood cancer; social health; in-situ hospital studies; children.

## THE IMPACT OF CHILDHOOD CANCER & NEED FOR DESIGN-RESEARCH IN CHILDHOOD CANCER CARE

While leaps have been made to increase childhood cancer survivorship, the reality is that childhood cancer patients face many challenges on their way to recovery – outside of the obvious impacts on their physical bodies. During cancer treatment children's lives and the lives of their family members are upended. Treatment often leaves children isolated from friends and peers within a hospital environment and lacking the physical capabilities or energy to play 'normally'. From decades of child development and psychology research we understand that play is an essential part of how children come to understand their own bodies, sense of self, and the 'workings' of the world around them (e.g. social/cultural norms, physics and dynamics between different physical properties, emotion recognition and regulation, etc.). Research positioned within the tangible and embodied computing paradigm has focused on the embodied and social nature of play and opportunities to support or augment such play. Child-computer interaction research under this umbrella relies on assumptions about how physical interaction in and with the world underlies both internal and external ways of 'knowing'. Research focused on promoting normal and healthy child development point to the need for play, in particular for children with illness that are confined to hospital environments (e.g. [1, 5, 9, 13, 15]). For example, play is now widely recognized in the medical field as a way to reduce fear and anxiety (among other things) produced by medical procedures and the hospital itself [16, 20]. Many hospitals have explicitly created play environments for children that range from purely physical spaces (e.g. Vancouver Canucks-themed playroom at B.C. Children's Hospital [8]) to immersive environments (e.g. Infusionarium at Children's Hospital of Orange County [17]), and have also employed staff – play specialists, play therapists, etc. – who specialize in using play to meet the myriad needs of hospitalized children (e.g. [1, 9, 15, 16]). Yet there is little research that focuses on how social tangible technologies might support playful social interactions for children who are hospitalized and are isolated from friends.

Designing 'play' artifacts and spaces that promote social interaction and/or aid physical development can be extremely challenging as children enter *middle childhood* – a period of key developmental, social and contextual changes between the ages of 6-12 years old [28]. At this stage of life children seek increased autonomy and independence as they transition into adolescence by spending a large portion of time outside of the home by attending school, engaging in extracurricular activities, and playing/socializing with friends more independently, etc. [28]. However, children in middle childhood with cancer are robbed of time they would normally dedicate to these everyday activities – activities that provide opportunities for personal interest development, increased autonomy and independent decision-making, deep friendship building, exploration of peer connectedness, and maintaining physical health and a positive body image [28]. Despite efforts to provide opportunities to play and socialize – both in-person as well as through digital or virtual channels – children with cancer still report "feelings of loneliness and


*TEI '19, March 17–20, 2019, Tempe, AZ, USA*

ACM ISBN 978-1-4503-6196-5/19/03…$15.00
https://doi.org/10.1145/3294109.3302958

isolation" and "loss of a normal childhood" [26]. These reports are especially interesting in a world where so many 'socially-focused' technologies exist (e.g. mobile social games, social media, video enabled call services, internet enabled gaming platforms, etc.) that can connect people regardless of time and location. While I do not believe there will be a way to fully alleviate feelings of isolation, this leaves me with many questions about the efficacy of play spaces and readily available technologies intended to support meaningful play and social interaction for children within a hospital environment. Thus far efforts to explore existing and novel technologies that can help reduce these feelings by improving social connectedness and enhanced opportunities for play have been limited.

Few design research studies explore how technology can support childhood cancer patients, especially in dealing with feelings of loneliness, isolation and loss of normal childhood. For example, searching "cancer" within Association for Computing Machinery (ACM) Conference Proceedings reveals only 6 articles discussing childhood cancer patients. In the proceedings, the *Interaction Design and Children* (IDC) conference had 4 articles, the *Conference on Human Factors in Computing Systems* (CHI) had 2, and the *Tangible and Embedded Interaction* (TEI) conference had 0. Only two are for social support ([22, 30]). The ACM Journals database had 0 articles. Despite the gap in literature, there is a recent call to action within the field of human-computer interaction to explore the "potential and value of technologies to augment our everyday social interactions" [18], including play (e.g. [2, 7, 25]), and to design meaningful technology for health/well-being [27]. Furthermore, Freed argued that play in middle childhood is essential to normal emotional and social development and exploring novel ways that "tangible" technologies can be created to produce meaningful play experiences is important especially for children who cannot play face-to-face [12]. It is within this context that I hope to explore the potential for socially-focused tangible technologies that can help children feel more like children despite the constraints imposed by childhood cancer, their treatment and their environment. My overarching research questions are as follows:

1. *In what ways do children (aged 8-12) experience feelings of social isolation, loneliness and/or loss of a normal childhood due to hospitalization and cancer treatment? In what ways do existing technologies help support/constrain social interaction?*
2. *In what ways does the hospital environment and/or treatment impact the use of interactive socially-focused technology within the hospital for children with cancer who report these feelings?*
3. *What types of concerns/rules do parents have in regard to their child with cancer's use of socially-focused technologies? Why? How does this compare to studies of parents of healthy children?*
4. *What design considerations are necessary for social tangible technology aimed at alleviating these issues for child patients in the hospital environment?*

## DESIGN SPACE: EXPANDING TANGIBLE SOCIAL PLAY INTO THE HOSPITAL

Decades of research across many fields has explored play as an integral part of not only normal child development, but also as a means to help children 'heal' within a hospital environment. As we've come to conceptualize play as the 'work of children', child research has expanded to examine the role play objects and environments have on children's development, relationships and health/well-being. This includes inquiries into computational, interactive technology that harness both the physical and digital world to promote play. Many researchers trace the origins of pervasive, augmented, and mixed reality games back to Ubicomp. Many of these explored ways to support play (e.g. [3, 4, 6, 7, 14, 19, 23]) and the authors in [23] pointed out that pervasive gaming encompasses many different areas that show potential for providing play opportunities for social interaction and improving feelings of connectedness to others: (1) smart toys, (2) affective gaming, (3) augmented tabletop games, (4) location-aware games, and (5) augmented reality games. This large landscape also overlaps with tangible computing and embodied interaction, where researchers work from "an understanding that you cannot separate the individual from the world in which that individual lives and acts" [11] because of the innate inseparability between the mind, body and environment. Research positioned within the tangible and embodied umbrella have focused heavily on children since there are assumptions about the 'naturalness' of physical interaction that capitalizes on children's intertwined motor and cognitive capacities. Dourish [11] pointed out that the field of tangible computing encompasses many different activities, which include: (1) creating smart environments that may include proximity based computational qualities, (2) augmenting everyday objects with computational faculties, and (3) capitalizing on physical manipulation of representational objects to directly interact with an interface. Shaer and Hornecker [29] discussed the breadth of tangible user interfaces, which can include: *tangible augmented reality* (combine tangible input with AR output), *tangible tabletop interaction* (includes tangible objects and interactive multi-touch surfaces), *ambient displays* (inspired by Ishii's Tangible Bits, now focuses on monitors and wall display), and *embodied user interfaces* (considers how technology can take advantage of or enhance bodily knowing). They pointed out that understanding the perspectives associated with tangible interaction requires that we unify or at least acknowledge different conceptualizations of computing, which include *tangible computing*, *tangible interaction*, and *reality-based interaction* (a broad area that includes studies involving VR, AR, UbiComp/Pervasive computing, handheld interaction, and tangible interaction).

Given existing inquiries in human and child-computer interaction using these computing/design paradigms one can envision ways to augment physical spaces and artifacts to encourage both active and passive social interaction for children (with cancer) isolated within a hospital. It seems that many existing technologies implemented in hospitals that fall under this computing paradigm, like CHOC's Infusionarium and Immersive Healing Experiences ([31]), take users 'elsewhere' as opposed to providing ways to re-imagine or re-purpose the physical spaces children already occupy through 'layers' of computation. One can imagine that changing the narrative experience around the space one occupies by embedding within it meaningful ways to maintain and build relationships through play can have positive impacts on children required to be in the space for long periods at a time – especially if these spaces are normally associated with fear, anxiety and/or pain. While the 'distraction' method is an effective best practice for children actively undergoing treatment that require them to remain stationary (e.g. chemotherapy), it seems that there are many opportunities to integrate novel technologies to increase feelings of *connectedness* as well as promote feelings of *autonomy* and *active participation* in their journey to healing. Technology has the potential to capitalize on these needs sought out by children during middle childhood – needs normally satisfied by spending increased time away from their direct family and home life via school and other activities. In order to ethically design technology to meet these needs first requires that we understand more about children's preferences for and access to interactive technologies within the hospital environment, particularly as it has to do with promoting and maintaining meaningful social interaction and connectedness to friends and peers. Furthermore, while we assume children in developed countries now have a fluency and an overall positive outlook on everyday technology use as 'digital natives', we also understand there may be many barriers in this design space, including issues like parental concerns/rules regarding 'social' technology use, hospital spaces, and hospital rules.

## METHODOLOGY

Using a mixed methods in-situ design research approach with a vulnerable population we plan to triangulate data from observation of pediatric hospital spaces and conduct in-depth semi-structured interviews with multiple stakeholders (child patients, caregivers, parents) in both Vancouver, Canada and the US to answer our exploratory research questions. Overall, the exploratory study will be made up of several phases (See Figure 1). All interviews will be audio recorded and be administered with an interview guide. Phase 1 includes a pilot study to assess the understandability of child interview questions. Phase 2 includes conducting interviews with children and then using the interview data to help inform interviews in Phase 3 with caregivers (e.g. doctors and nurses) and parents. In Phase 4 a follow up with each child about data from parent and caregiver interviews will be done to better understand differences in point of view between participant groups. Throughout Phases 2-4 we will collect observational data in the form of notes and photos that help document spaces, contexts and/or technologies discussed throughout the interviewing process. These may be used as independent data but may also act as a means to better communicate questions or issues during the interviewing process. All participants will be recruited in person from B.C. Children's Hospital and from the Children's Hospital of Orange County in the United States. Data analysis will be as follows: (1) Transcribe interviews; (2) Open coding of transcribed interviews to produce primary themes [24], rigor ensured through statistical methods for intercoder reliability [10]; (3) Comparison of themes across ages of children; (4) Axial coding and comparison of themes between children and parents and caregivers to produce design considerations.

Child participants are included for the following reasons, which also motivate my first goal/contribution below: (1) there is a gap in the literature providing child accounts of the cancer experience and studies point to discrepancies in how parents and their children with cancer report the child's 'quality' of life (e.g. [21]), and (2) adults and children have different points of view on the necessity, expectations and relevance of technology intended for social purposes.

## GOALS & CONTRIBUTION

We aim to (1) empower children with cancer by allowing them to voice their own experiences with isolation, loneliness, and loss of a normal childhood, as well as how technology may better support their needs, by integrating them as a primary data source for our study, (2) contribute design knowledge about how to support meaningful social interaction and play that is age and 'ability' appropriate, and (3) provide insight for future design and evaluation studies by better understanding constraints/opportunities for social tangible technologies intended for use in a real world pediatric hospital environment.

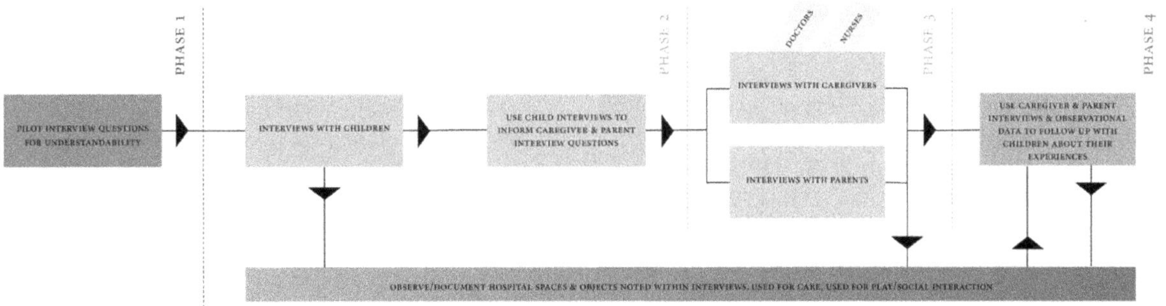


**Figure 1. Proposed Study Process for Data Collection**

## REFERENCES


[1] Adams, M.A. 1976. A hospital play program: Helping children with serious illness. *American Journal of Orthopsychiatry*. 46, 3 (1976), 416.

[2] Al Mahmud, A. et al. 2007. aMAZEd: Designing an Affective Social Game for Children. *Proceedings of the 6th International Conference on Interaction Design and Children* (New York, NY, USA, 2007), 53–56.

[3] Avontuur, T. et al. 2014. Play It Our Way: Customization of Game Rules in Children's Interactive Outdoor Games. *Proceedings of the 2014 Conference on Interaction Design and Children* (New York, NY, USA, 2014), 95–104.

[4] Bekker, T. et al. 2010. Designing playful interactions for social interaction and physical play. *Personal and Ubiquitous Computing*. 14, 5 (Jul. 2010), 385–396.

[5] Bohg, R. et al. 1986. Unstructured play in hospital settings: An internal locus of control rationale. *Children's Health Care*. 15, 2 (1986), 101–107.

[6] Boon, B. et al. 2016. Playscapes: a Design Perspective on Young Children's Physical Play. *Proceedings of the The 15th International Conference on Interaction Design and Children* (2016), 181–189.

[7] Brederode, B. et al. 2005. pOwerball: The Design of a Novel Mixed-reality Game for Children with Mixed Abilities. *Proceedings of the 2005 Conference on Interaction Design and Children* (New York, NY, USA, 2005), 32–39.

[8] Canucks Playroom offers fun space for sick kids at BC Children's Hospital – The Columbia Valley Pioneer: *www.columbiavalleypioneer.com/trending-now/canucks-playroom-offers-fun-space-for-sick-kids-at-bc-childrens-hospital/*. Accessed: 2018-11-17.

[9] Constantinou, M. 2007. *The effect of Gestalt play therapy on feelings of anxiety experienced by the hospitalized oncology child*. Univ. of South Africa.

[10] Creswell, J.W. 2013. *Qualitative Inquiry and Research Design: Choosing Among Five Approaches*. SAGE Publications, Incorporated.

[11] Dourish, P. 2001. *Where the action is: the foundations of embodied interaction*. MIT Press.

[12] Freed, N. 2010. Toys Keeping in Touch: Technologies for Distance Play. *Proceedings of the Fourth International Conference on Tangible, Embedded, and Embodied Interaction* (NY, NY, USA, 2010), 315–316.

[13] Gariépy, N. and Howe, N. 2003. The therapeutic power of play: examining the play of young children with leukaemia. *Child: care, health and development*. 29, 6 (2003), 523–537.

[14] Guo, B. et al. 2012. Design-in-play: improving the variability of indoor pervasive games. *Multimedia Tools and Applications*. 59, 1 (Jul. 2012), 259–277.

[15] Haiat, H. et al. 2003. The world of the child: a world of play even in the hospital. *Journal of Pediatric Nursing*. 18, 3 (2003), 209–214.

[16] Hubbuck, C. 2009. *Play for Sick Children : Play Specialists in Hospitals and Beyond*. Jessica Kingsley Publishers.

[17] Infusionarium comes to CHOC Children's: 2014. *https://blog.chocchildrens.org/worlds-first-infusionarium-comes-choc-childrens/*. Accessed: 2018-11-17.

[18] Isbister, K. 2016. Connecting through play. *ACM Interactions*.

[19] Jegers, K. and Wiberg, M. 2006. Pervasive gaming in the everyday world. *IEEE Pervasive Computing*. 5, 1 (Jan. 2006), 78–85.

[20] Jun-Tai, N. 2008. Play in hospital. *Paediatrics and Child Health*. 18, 5 (May 2008), 233–237.

[21] Klassen, A.F. et al. 2009. Quality of life questionnaires for children with cancer and childhood cancer survivors: a review of the development of available measures. *Supportive Care in Cancer*. 18, 9 (Oct. 2009), 1207–1217.

[22] Lindberg, S. et al. 2014. Designing Digital Peer Support for Children: Design Patterns for Social Interaction. *Proceedings of the 2014 Conference on Interaction Design and Children* (New York, NY, USA, 2014), 47–56.

[23] Magerkurth, C. et al. 2005. Pervasive Games: Bringing Computer Entertainment Back to the Real World. *Comput. Entertain.* 3, 3 (Jul. 2005), 4–4.

[24] Maxwell, J.A. 2012. *Qualitative Research Design: An Interactive Approach*. SAGE Publications, Inc.

[25] Miura, A. et al. 2013. Social Playware with an Enhanced Reach for Facilitating Group Interaction. *CHI '13 Extended Abstracts on Human Factors in Computing Systems* (New York, NY, USA, 2013), 1155–1160.

[26] Moody, K. et al. 2006. Exploring concerns of children with cancer. *Supportive Care in Cancer*. 14, 9 (2006), 960–966.

[27] Schneiderman, B. et al. 2016. Grand challenges for HCI researchers | ACM Interactions. *ACM Interactions*.

[28] Schonert-Reichl, K.A. and Rowcliffe, P. 2011. *Middle Childhood Inside and Out: The Psychological and Social Worlds of Canadian Children Ages 9-12: Full Report*. The United Way of the Lower Mainland.

[29] Shaer, O. and Hornecker, E. 2010. Tangible user interfaces: past, present, and future directions. *Foundations and Trends in Human-Computer Interaction*. 3, 1–2 (2010), 1–137.

[30] Wärnestå, P. and Nygren, J. 2013. Building an Experience Framework for a Digital Peer Support Service for Children Surviving from Cancer. *Proceedings of the 12th International Conference on Interaction Design and Children* (New York, NY, USA, 2013), 269–272.

[31] products | Reimagine Well.

# Designing a System to Facilitate Intergenerational Story Sharing and Preservation for Older Adults

**Cun Li**
Eindhoven University of Technology
Eindhoven, the Netherlands
Cun.li@tue.nl

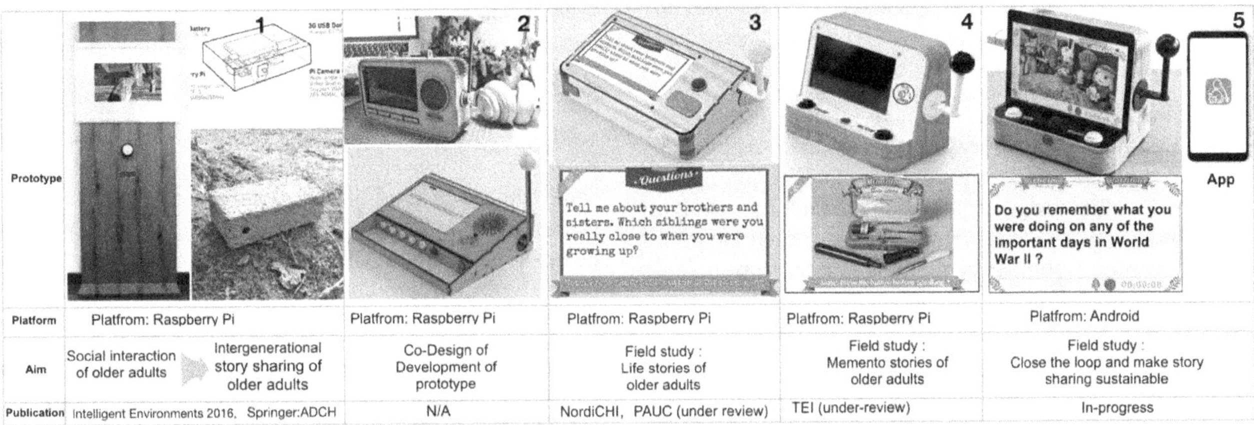


**Figure 1. Iterations Overview**

## ABSTRACT

My PhD research focuses on intergenerational story sharing for older adults, which is conducted in a Research-through-Design manner. It includes five iterations: It started from an exploration prototype Interactive Gallery (1st iteration), and its findings helped to narrow down my research area and define my research question. To answer it, the 2nd iteration was continued, which was a co-design process of developing prototypes. 3rd and 4th iteration focused on older adults' life stories and memento stories respectively. While the 5th iteration is in the process, which aims to facilitate intergenerational story sharing and preservation in a sustainable manner.

### Author Keywords

Research-through-design; elderly; storytelling; tangible interface; social interaction

### ACM Classification Keywords

• Human-centered computing~Interaction devices
• Human-centered computing~Collaborative and social computing • Social and professional topics~Seniors
• Hardware~Haptic devices


*TEI '19, March 17–20, 2019, Tempe, AZ, USA*

ACM ISBN 978-1-4503-6196-5/19/03…$15.00
https://doi.org/10.1145/3294109.3302957

## CONTEXT AND MOTIVATION

Aging society is coming. Social interaction is a critical factor affecting the quality of life of older adults. The quality and quantity of individuals' social relationships have been linked not only to mental health but also to both morbidity and mortality[6]. People lacking social contacts are more susceptible to diseases, infarction, stroke, and the onset of Alzheimer's disease[15]. However, social isolation is widespread among older adults[16], they have limited involvement in social connections[11].

Social interaction of old adults is a broad research area, and my research focuses on its subset: intergenerational storytelling of older adults. Storytelling of older adults serves multiple functions: Social function, maintaining social relationships[7], creating meaning beyond the individual and providing a sense of and in relation to family members [4]. Physiological function, improving self-esteem, mood, and well-being, and reducing loneliness as one ages [3]. Cultural function, their stories are treasured intangible source of cultural heritage [17].

However, storytelling and preservation are still problematic for older adults: First, while social media like Facebook helps to share and preserve the stories to some extent, these platforms are more about the "now" moments and less about the past[10]. Second, digital online applications and websites for story sharing are normally inaccessible for most older adults (especially for those live in nursing home), who are disconnected from the mainstream online social circles due to lack of technology that resonate with them [18]. Third, despite that sitting together to communicate face-to-face is obviously the most common and enjoyable way to share stories[9], whereas they don't have many such opportunities because most of them live separately with their children.

## RESEARCH QUESTION AND APPROACH

Research question of my PhD research is: *How can we use technology to facilitate intergenerational story sharing and preservation of older adults?* To answer this research question, three sub-research questions are formulated: *(1) What are their stories about? (2) How to facilitate them to tell and preserve their stories? (3) How to involve the young generation to make the story sharing sustainable?*

The research approach we adopt is Research-through-Design. It is conceptualizing research done using the practice of design activity, revealing research insights [20]. It features that knowledge is gained by conducting a design exercise based on prototype [5]. In our case, each iteration broadly consists of contextual inquiry, research prototype, field study, and reflection.

## RELATED WORK

Regarding social technology for older adults, existing research indicates that their social interaction could be promoted either by strengthening connections between older adults and their existing social circles (friends, family, etc.)[13], or expanding their social circle by knowing more friends[18]. In our study, we found as personal stories were private and personal, older adults preferred to share them with their existing social circle, especially their children.

Regarding applications of intergenerational storytelling, there are smartphone applications or webs for creating multimedia stories [1], software of managing family stories[10], software for videos to be saved in real-world locations, shared with family[2], and software support digital reminiscing of the family[14]. Current applications are mostly smartphone apps or website, which are normally inaccessible for the elderly users.

Regarding research on mementos and related stories include lifelogging technologies which capture mementos memories[19]; Organizing and archiving digital mementos [8];making connections between objects and stories[12]. However, current research give more attention to personal digital content, while mementos of older adults are mostly in physical format.

## ITERATIVE DESIGN APPROACH

### 1st iteration: Interactive Gallery

**Aim**: Our first prototype-Interactive Gallery was an explorative prototype, designed to uncover the related potential factors, narrow down research goal and define PhD research question. (Figure1-(1))

**Contextual inquiry**: To understand the basic social pattern of older adults in nursing home, we conducted semi-structured interviews with older adults and caregivers. The following are a brief overview of the findings: Older adults encountered difficulties in connecting with their fellow residents. The nursing home was not a fully open community, which made it a relatively isolated and independent. Their daily routines remained the same, and most of them couldn't operate digital devices.

**Prototype and field study**: Interactive Gallery system consists of a set of scenery-collectors and a gallery-like interactive installation. The formers are distributed to volunteers from local communities to share real-time scenery photos with older adults, and the latter is placed in the nursing home which enables older adults to watch and start conversations. Communication between sharers and receivers will also be connected through a "postcard-sending" metaphor: The older adults could print scenery photos as postcards by simply pressing the button. They could choose to send back to sharers, or keep them. It was implemented in a local nursing home for five weeks. Direct observation method (including baseline observation and intervention observation) and semi-structured interviews were adopted successively.

**Reflection**: The field study proved tangible interface employing metaphor reduces using barriers for them. Their memories were evoked by the familiar scenery photos. They'd like to share memories with their children, as memories were personal and private. Also, memory triggers need to be highlighted.

## IDENTIFICATION OF RESEARCH QUESTION

Results of 1st iteration indicated that older adults could be deemed as story content producers, and their children were their listeners. This drove us to narrow down our research goal and further identify the research question, which guided our planning and execution of the following project.

### 2nd iteration: Co-design process of prototype

**Contextual inquiry**: To understand the status quo of intergenerational storytelling of older adults, and define design requirement. Semi-structured interviews were conducted with both the older adults and their children.

**Design requirements**: Memory trigger. Tangible interface employing metaphor. Using audio as the storage medium of stories. Could be used either face-to-face or separately by older adults and their children.

**Mock-ups and user consultation**: Three concepts were built based on the design requirements and were developed to be mock-ups. Older adults were consulted to evaluate them. Slots-story employing metaphor of slots-machine was chosen and further detailed. (Figure1-(2))

**Final prototype**: Slots-story, a slots machine-like device, aims to facilitate inter-generational life story sharing and preservation. It utilizes with the metaphor of slots machine, and integrates functions of memory cue generator, story recording, and preservation. By default, there are 40 trigger questions covering most aspects of an entire life. It could either be used face-to-face or separately by older adults and their children. (Figure1-(3))

### 3rd iteration: life stories of old adults

**Field study**: eight pairs of participants (each pair consisted of an old adult and his/her child) from nursing home were recruited to use the prototype for around five days. Totally 359 stories were collected. Semi-structured interviews were conducted with both older adults and the young. Stories were transcribed and analyzed.

**Reflection**: As some stories were related to their mementos, such as album, souvenir, etc., which were also ideal memory triggers as they provided visual clues. This inspired us to explore their mementos and related stories in the next iteration. Additionally, the appearance of porotype should be refined according to older adults' feedback.

### 4th iteration: memento stories of adults

**Contextual inquiry**: It aimed to gain a better understanding of the status quo of their memento storytelling, and defined design requirements. We interviewed with older adults and young adults separately. We first asked them to arrange a brief guided tour of their homes, aiming to examine their mementos for displaying and stored in hidden places. We then conducted semi-structured interviews with them.

**Design requirements**: Integrating mementos into older adults' daily environments. Cross-generational cooperation. Tangible interface employing metaphor and intuitive interaction. Using audio as the storage medium of stories. Could be used either face-to-face or separately by older adults and their children.

**Description**: We focused on memento stories of older adults in this iteration. The prototype was refined based on the feedback of the 3rd iteration: Prototype's decorative effects needed to be highlighted to make it unobtrusive when putting it at older adults' home. (Figure1-(4)). It was used in a cross-generational operation manner: the young took photos of older adults' mementos and copied them to the prototype, while older adults used the prototype to tell stories related to the mementos.

**Field study**: Ten pairs of participants (each pair consisted of an old adult and child) were recruited to use the prototype for around seven days. 283 mementos were collected. Semi-structured interviews were conducted with older adults and their children. Mementos were categorized and analyzed. Stories were firstly transcribed, then were analyzed.

**Reflection**: Sustainability of the intergenerational sharing was necessary. Next, a cellphone application will be designed for the young side.

### 5th iteration: make intergenerational story sharing sustainable (in process)

**Aim**: In this iteration, we will close the intergenerational storytelling loop by designing an App for the young generation: aiming to facilitate intergenerational story sharing and preservation in a sustainable manner.

**System**: A system consisting of a slot machine-like device used by older adults, a cellphone application used by the young. It focuses on two kinds of stories of older adults: life stories and family memento stories (Figure 2).

## CONCLUSION AND FUTURE WORK

Table 1 shows the overview progress of the five iterations. The knowledge generated in our study are threefold: First, design and implementation of a tangible system for facilitating intergenerational sharing for the elderly. Second, insights on our research question regarding intergenerational storytelling for older adults. Third, lessons learnt in our iterative research have a universal significance for RTD application study, especially for older adults. During the last 3 years, I have finished 4 iterations, and the making of the 5th iteration's prototype is in process. Before its formal implementation, an initial evaluation will be first conducted. In formal field study, it will be used by the participants in a relatively long-term manner (for 2-3 weeks). Lastly, data analyzing and interviews will be conducted.

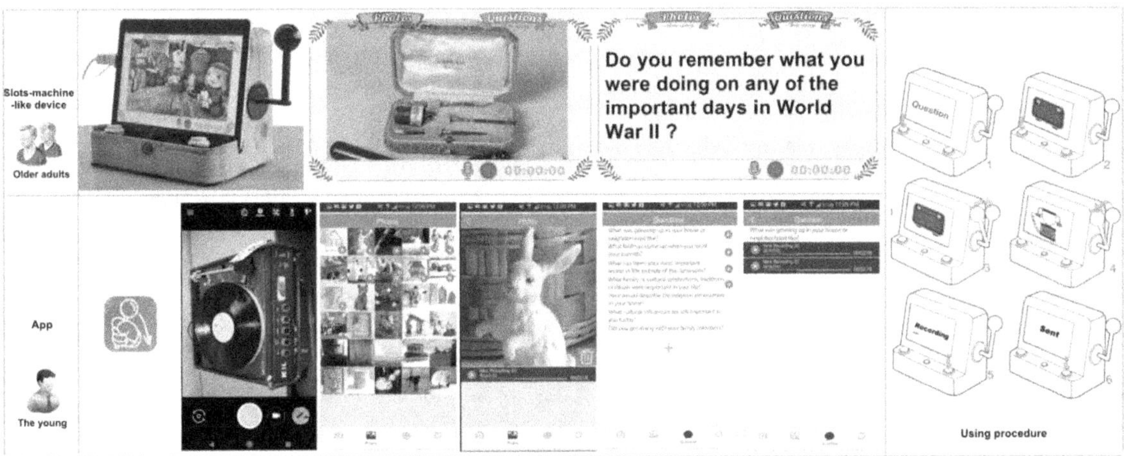


**Figure 2. Prototype of 5th iteration**

## REFERENCES

[1] Frank R. Bentley, Santosh Basapur, and Sujoy Kumar Chowdhury. 2011. The use of StoryKit: design implications for intergenerational mobile storytelling. *Proceedings of the 13th international conference on Ubiquitous computing*, ACM, 31–40.

[2] Frank R Bentley, Santosh Basapur, and Sujoy Kumar Chowdhury. 2011. Promoting intergenerational communication through location-based asynchronous video communication. Proceedings of the 13th international conference on Ubiquitous computing, ACM, 31–40.

[3] Kai-Jo Chiang, Hsin Chu, Hsiu-Ju Chang, et al. 2010. The effects of reminiscence therapy on psychological well-being, depression, and loneliness among the institutionalized aged. International Journal of Geriatric Psychiatry 25, 4: 380–388.

[4] Robyn Fivush. 2011. Intergenerational narratives: How collective family stories Relate to adolescents' emotional well-being. Aurora. Revista de Arte, Mídia e Política. ISSN 1982-6672 10: 51.

[5] Danny Godin and Mithra Zahedi. 2014. Aspects of research through design: a literature review. Proceedings of DRS: 1667–1680.

[6] Julianne Holt-Lunstad, Timothy B. Smith, and J. Bradley Layton. 2010. Social relationships and mortality risk: a meta-analytic review. PLoS medicine 7, 7: e1000316.

[7] Ira E Hyman. 1994. Conversational remembering: Story recall with a peer versus for an experimenter. Applied Cognitive Psychology 8, 1: 49–66.

[8] Sarah de Leeuw. 2009. Evocative Objects: Things We Think With. Emotion, Space and Society 2, 2: 131–132.

[9] Siân E. Lindley and Andrew F. Monk. 2008. Social enjoyment with electronic photograph displays: Awareness and control. International Journal of Human-Computer Studies 66, 8: 587–604.

[10] Aaron Marcus. 2015. The Story Machine: Combining Information Design/Visualization with Persuasion Design to Change Family-Story Sharing Behavior. In Mobile Persuasion Design. Springer London, London, 163–260.

[11] V. Mor, K. Branco, J. Fleishman, et al. 1995. The Structure of Social Engagement among Nursing Home Residents. The Journals of Gerontology Series B: Psychological Sciences and Social Sciences 50B, 1: P1–P8.

[12] Daniela Petrelli, Steve Whittaker, and Jens Brockmeier. 2008. AutoTopography: what can physical mementos tell us about digital memories? Proceedings of the SIGCHI conference on Human Factors in computing systems, ACM, 53–62.

[13] Pedro C. Santana, Marcela D. Rodríguez, Víctor M. González, Luís A. Castro, and Ángel G. Andrade. 2005. Supporting emotional ties among mexican elders and their families living abroad. CHI'05 Extended Abstracts on Human Factors in Computing Systems, ACM, 2099–2103.

[14] Elizabeth Thiry and Mary Beth Rosson. 2012. Unearthing the family gems: design requirements for a digital reminiscing system for older adults. CHI'12 Extended Abstracts on Human Factors in Computing Systems, ACM, 1715–1720.

[15] J. Tomaka. 2006. The Relation of Social Isolation, Loneliness, and Social Support to Disease Outcomes Among the Elderly. Journal of Aging and Health 18, 3: 359–384.

[16] Mary Jane Tremethick. 2001. Alone in a crowd: A study of social networks in home health and assisted living. Journal of Gerontological Nursing 27, 5: 42–47.

[17] David R. Unruh. 1983. Death and Personal History: Strategies of Identity Preservation. Social Problems 30, 3: 340–351.

[18] Jenny Waycott, Frank Vetere, Sonja Pedell, et al. 2013. Older adults as digital content producers. Proceedings of the SIGCHI Conference on Human Factors in Computing Systems, ACM, 39–48.

[19] Steve Whittaker, Ofer Bergman, and Paul Clough. 2010. Easy on that trigger dad: a study of long term family photo retrieval. Personal and Ubiquitous Computing 14, 1: 31–43.

[20] John Zimmerman, Erik Stolterman, and Jodi Forlizzi. 2010. An analysis and critique of Research through Design: towards a formalization of a research approach. Proceedings of the 8th ACM Conference on Designing Interactive Systems, ACM, 310–319.

# Tangible Signals - Physical Representation of Sound and Haptic Control Feedback

**Jens Vetter**
University of Art and Design
Linz, Austria
jensvetter@ymail.com

## ABSTRACT

This paper describes the Ph.D. research project *Tangible Signals* which is currently in its initial phase. This project investigates the dynamic physical representation and haptic feedback control of computer music and sound data using motorized and augmented objects. The research focuses on artistic and performative contributions that this approach offers. Special attention is given to the collaboration with visually impaired people, as they are very limited in the use of exclusively GUI-based interaction. On the following pages the background of the project will be described and methods, research questions and work progress will be presented.

### Author Keywords

Tangible Interaction, Haptic Control Feedback, Dynamic Data Physicalization, Physical Sound Representation

### CCS Concepts

**•Human-centered computing → Natural language interfaces; Haptic devices; User centered design;** *User interface toolkits;* **•Hardware → Haptic devices;**

## INTRODUCTION

The creation and manipulation of sounds is fascinating and challenging. The availability and ease of use of microcontrollers, sensors and easily accessible programming environments supported the transition from Graphical User Interfaces (GUI) to Tangible User Interfaces (TUI) [4]. In interfaces like e.g. the *reacTable* [5], techniques were developed to control digital sound generation with the help of physical tokens. With the re-entering into the physical material, tangible interaction and haptic feedback is also embedded in numerous New Interfaces for Musical Expression (NIME). Some of them, like *Beatbearing* [1] or the *Tquencer* [6] even allow the creation of sounds and the operation of music interfaces through purely tangible interaction, without being dependent on visual feedback (e.g. no visual menus).



*TEI '19*, March 17–20, 2019, Tempe, AZ, USA
© 2019 ACM. ISBN 978-1-4503-6196-5/19/03...$15.00
DOI: https://doi.org/10.1145/3294109.3302958

But while many NIMEs and TUIs concentrate on enabling the creation and control of digital data, especially the control of musical parameters through the availability of tangible interaction, yet there are only a few interfaces and devices which are able to dynamically represent data in a physical way and at the same time offer the possibility to control or change this data representation and thus the data itself. This intermediate step between on the one hand the digital sound generation on the computer and on the other hand the playback or listening to the musical contents could be a useful and inspiring tool, especially for musical purposes. Especially when the physical representation of the data would be controllable and modifiable, enhanced by haptic feedback.

The physical representation and modification of digital sound data including haptic feedback is the core of this research work *Tangible Signals*. The audience is at first visually impaired musicians who are limited in their work with GUIs, but also sighted musicians who want to integrate a physical level into their creative process. In addition, this research may also be of interest to other disciplines that benefit from physical representation and modification of data.

## BACKGROUND

Music-making on the computer is a combination between the creation and input of musical information, the processing of musical events and the output of the musical content. For the creation of sound, there exists now a large number of new musical interfaces, some of them that also provide physical interaction which is tangible or contains haptic feedback, like the SeaBoard [1]. More and more studies on physical and haptic feedback processes show the potential of the implementation of haptic feedback in the musical context. For example Sile O'Modhrain and R. Brent Gillespie argue for a dynamic coupling of musical input and physical output in the book *Musical Haptics* [8]. However, the further processing of the sound, e.g. in digital audio workstations (Logic Pro, Reaper, etc.) is still mostly GUI based, supported by midi controllers, which have at most motorized sliders or knobs. In these systems there is no physical representation happening. Considering the manipulation of sound in digital audio workstations as part of the creative process, the absence of physical representation and tangible interaction is a limitation and may prevent new

[1] Seabord: https://roli.com/products/seaboard/

**Figure 1. SoundFORM - © A. Colter, P. Davivongsa et al.**

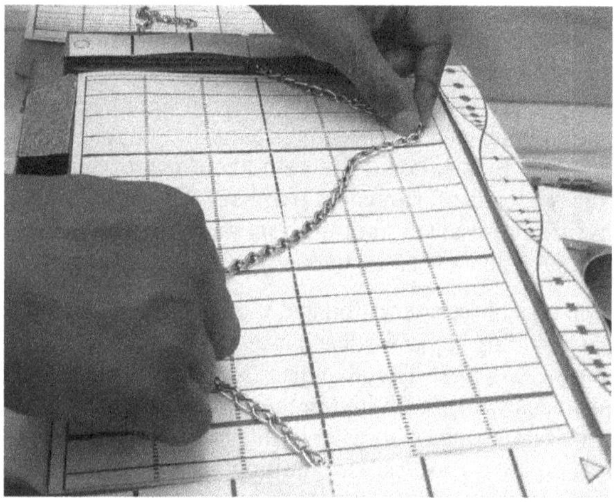

**Figure 2. HaptEQ - © Aaron Karp**

approaches and concepts to the treatment and understanding of sound.

### Physical Manipulation

There are only few interfaces that try to implement the representational manipulation of sound at this level. For example the *SoundFORM* [2] (see Fig.1), a pin-based display that follows a physical approach. It displays digital data using a grid of 24 x 24 motorized pins, a dynamic display of sound information, e.g. simple waveforms or the physical display of sound events in a sequence. There have been several previous attempts to physically represent data based on pin displays, such as Ivan Poupyrev's *LUMEN* [9], a prototype of a refreshable pin display. Another example is the *HaptEQ* [7] (see Fig.2), which allows the configuration of a digital equalizer by means of an understandable physical form. This allows to adjust the equalizer without having to use the graphical interface from the corresponding software by camera tracking of a chain-like physical object on a prepared surface. However, the object is a passive input and is not able to react to changes in the digital configuration.

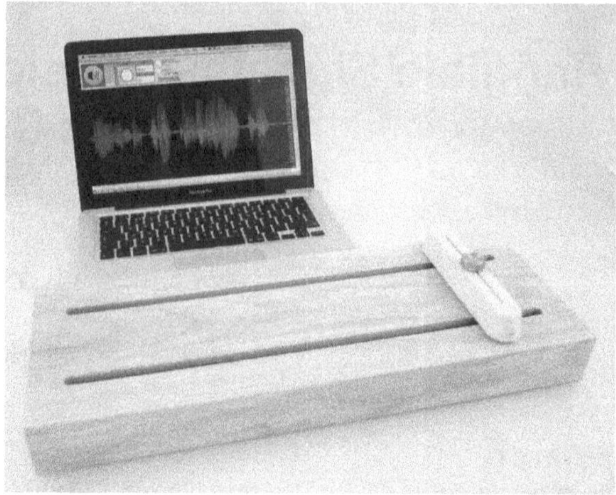

**Figure 3. Haptic Wave - © A. Tanaka and A. Parkinson**

An unfinished project, still, is the *Holy Braille* [3] by Sile O'Modhrain and her team, a refreshable pin display, which many blind and visually impaired people are longing for. Here already the naming shows how essential and important interfaces for the physical representation of data are especially for blind people. Which is why one of the few interfaces which is actually able to display digital sound information haptically has been developed for visually impaired people and is called the *Haptic Wave* [10] (see Fig. 3). It aims to make digital sound information, in this case the waveform, tangible. For this purpose, the interface provides a handle that can be moved on a rail, which makes it possible to scan a waveform with the help of haptic feedback and thus, for instance, find particularly loud or particularly quiet spots in the waveform. Also the development of the *Haptic Wave* has been initiated for visually impaired sound engineers and was appreciated as a valuable tool in sound production.

So far, only two of these interfaces, the *Haptic Wave* and the *SoundFORM* are able to display sound information in a dynamic-physical way. Both interfaces have their limitations, one is the focus on the waveform, the other on the low resolution. But what becomes visible in both examples is the focused interest in interactive physical representation of data, which currently still has to build up its own vocabulary and experience.

### Haptic Control Feedback

While many NIMEs and TUIs concentrate on enabling the creation and control of digital data, especially the control of musical parameters through the availability of tangible input devices, there are, like mentioned above, not many examples of interfaces that are able both to physically represent sound information and to control or change the displayed sound. This union or cycle of digital representation and physical representation of sound and haptic control feedback is an obvious and promising field of research. It could extend the existing chain of transformation of digital sound , i.e. digital-to-analog conversion (D/A converter) and playback of music through loudspeaker systems.

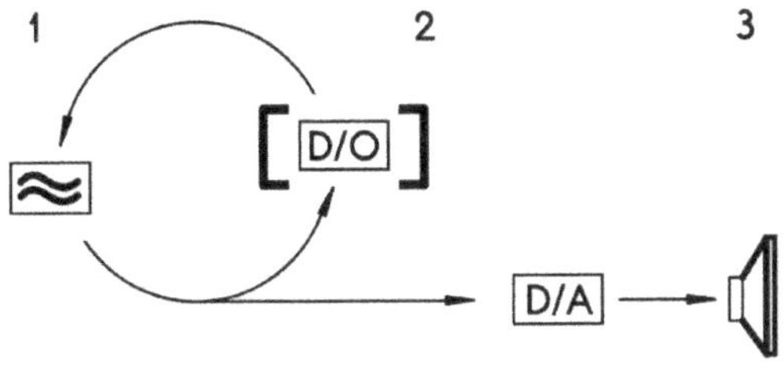


**Figure 4. Digital-to-Object Conversion - 1 digital musical data processing in the computer - 2 converting to both D/A and D/O (allows for manipulation) - 3 finally playback via loudspeaker**

But it is not only technical solutions (actuators, materials, digital protocols, etc.) that need to be reconsidered; new vocabulary and new approaches also have to be found on a conceptual level. In order to already make a proposal here that is metaphorically based on the D/A converter, I would like to suggest the introduction of another type of conversion: the *Digital-to-Object Conversion* (D/O converter) (see Fig.4). Here, digital characteristics of sound would not only be reproduced as sound, but as physical object-like representation, which in turn could be controlled and manipulated.

The outcomes could not only lead to a new understanding of tangible interfaces and their use in the musical context, but also to new ways of experiencing sound and sound information, also - but not only - for visually impaired musicians. The findings could even be of significance in other non-musical fields of application, for example in mathematics, physics or architecture, i.e. wherever 2D functions are to be displayed. It might also be possible to integrate resulting methods or devices into digital workflows in terms of accessibility. Another field of application could be stage-based musical live performances, in which non-visual tangible information and manipulations could also enable particularly interesting interactions.

## SPECIFIC AIMS

The specific aims of this research is to theoretically, practically and artistically expand the current state of knowledge regarding the physical representation of sound and its haptic feedback control. Based on approaches from artistic research, prototypes are to be developed that embody the hitherto little-explored digital-to-object conversion. The cycle of digital sound representation, physical representation and haptic control feedback described above will be investigated in more detail and explored in practice. Apart from technical considerations, musical representation of sound will be analyzed in relation to its output as physical representation. This includes the analysis of suitable properties and images of sounds (waveform, volume, frequency spectrum, bundling of properties), possible merging of sound areas, and other states of sound that are suitable for physical representation. Thus, an essential aspect is the necessary relationship of the resolution of sound aspects in relation to the resolution of physical representation. The development of individual control software will be necessary for the practical implementation of prototypes and experimental approaches. This software will be implemented based on the programming languages SuperCollider and Javascript. The use of other programming languages is conceivable, as required.

## RESEARCH QUESTION

- How can the physical representation of sound and haptic feedback control contribute to the process of sound generation, sound processing and artistic performance?
- How does the physical representation of sound and its haptic control feedback open up new inspiration and creativity in artistic-musical expression?
- How does the interaction with the physical representation of sound and its haptic control feedback compare to GUI-based workflows?

## RESEARCH METHODS

This research takes place in an artistic-musical context in the department *Tangible Music Lab* (TamLab), which is part of the Institute for Media Studies at the University of Art and Design Linz. A special focus therefore is on musical interaction, tangible interfaces and the experimental-artistic extension of existing knowledge and practical experiences. The openness and impulses that arise from an artistic research approach can also be applied to this research topic, since it will be an exploration between design, research and art that builds on one another. The work steps will take place partly simultaneously, partly one after the other.

- Iterative design process - Iterative design of multifunctional prototypes (see below)
- Qualitative analysis - Based on observation of musicians (sighted, visually impaired) using the means of physical representation and haptic feedback control, embodied in prototypes that are being developed.
- Cooperation with the Institute for the Blind in Vienna - Lectures, Workshops, Development of Braille-based music-systems
- Artistic works - Development of musical-artistic works in relation to the topic (stage-based, art installation, etc.)
- Prepared Discussions - Organized discussion (e.g. a symposium) with artists, musicians, scientists from neighbouring fields.
- Publication of research results - scientific publications at conferences (NIME, TEI, etc.) and journals

## GOALS & OUTCOMES

The goal of this research project is to answer the questions raised, to extend the existing concepts and approaches concerning the physical representation of sound and haptic feedback control, to create new vocabulary, interface approaches and experiences. The technical solutions, artistic processes and side developments will be documented and will contribute to a more comprehensive view of this area. On a social and educational level, the cooperation with the School for the Blind in Vienna will open new doors for visually impaired students to engage with computer sound production.

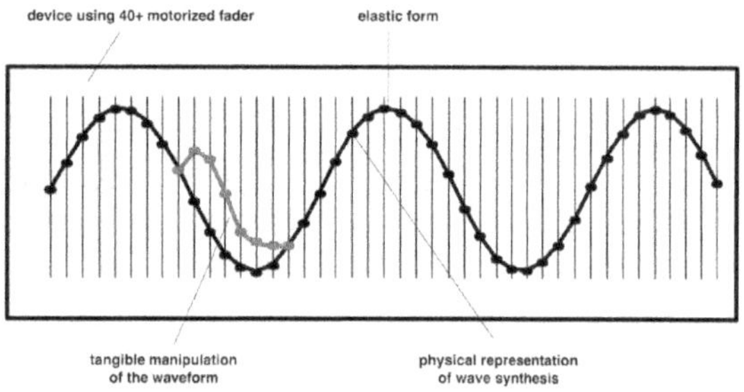


**Figure 5. Tangible Wavetable Synthesis**

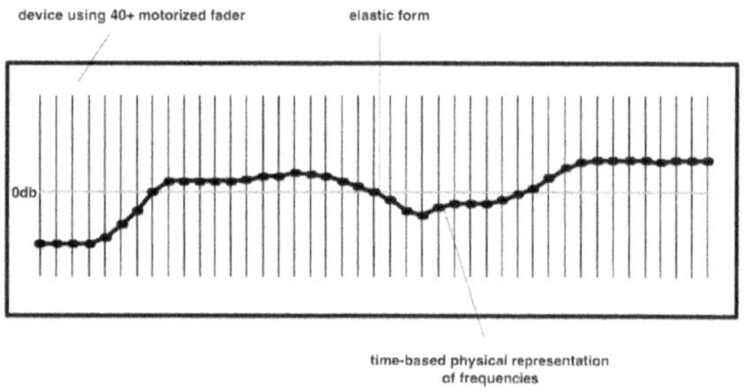


**Figure 6. Tangible EQ**

## WORK PROGRESS

This research project started in October 2018 and thereby it is still at its very beginning. On the one hand I focus on the realization of prototypes that deal with the physical representation of sound and haptic feedback control (see below). On the other hand, a collaboration with the Institute for the Blind in Vienna started in order to slowly come into contact with visually impaired teenagers and to sensitize them to the topic of physical representation of sound and haptic feedback control. For this purpose I will develop a small mobile music system based on a Raspberry Pi (including loudspeakers), which makes it possible to use the Braille keyboard as a musical instrument and later acts as a starting point to form a Braille orchestra. Here the finished modules can also be used for the physical representation of sound and haptic feedback control in the musical performance.

### Prototypes

The *Tangible EQ* (see Fig.6) is a prototype designed to explore and embody the above principles of digital-to-object conversion. It expands the ideas and concepts of the *HaptEQ*.The digital sound and its frequency characteristics are represented in a time-based manner over approx. 40 motorized faders. One of the special features of the *Tangible EQ* is the continuous elastic connection of the individual faders. The frequency curve is displayed but can be controlled to manipulate the original sound. Haptic force feedback is implemented to display the activities of the sounds in the different frequencies.

Similarly the *Tangible Wavetable Synthesizer* (see Fig.5) is a representation of a generated sine wave. It allows the representation of a sine wave (or sawtooth wave, etc.) and can not only visualize the sound physically, but allows a manipulation that corresponds to the wavetable synthesis. The waveform can be changed manually as desired, which in turn changes the basic sound. Seth Kranzler took a similar approach in his interface Wavetable Synthesizer [18], except that he concentrated more on controlling digital synthesis and less on physical representation.

## ACKNOWLEDGEMENTS

I would like to thank my Ph.D. supervisor, Prof. Dr. Martin Kaltenbrunner, Head of the Tangible Music Lab Department, for his inspiring and constructive feedback and suggestions on my research work.

## REFERENCES

[1] Peter Bennett and Sile O'Modhrain. 2008. The BeatBearing: a tangible rhythm sequencer. In *Proceedings of NordiCHI 2008: 5th Nordic Conference on Computer-Human Interaction*, Vol. 2008. 1–12.

[2] Aubrey Colter, Patlapa Davivongsa, Donald Derek Haddad, Halla Moore, Brian Tice, and Hiroshi Ishii. 2016. SoundFORMS : Manipulating Sound Through Touch. *CHI Extended Abstracts on Human Factors in Computing Systems* (2016), 2425–2430.

[3] Brent Gillespie, Alex Russomanno, Mark Burns, and Sile O'Modhrain. 2016. The Holy Braille: A Tablet For The Visually Impaired. *Popular Science* May/June issue (2016).

[4] Hiroshi Ishii and Brygg Ullmer. 1997. Tangible bits. In *Proceedings of the SIGCHI conference on Human factors in computing systems - CHI '97*. 234–241.

[5] Sergi Jordà, Günter Geiger, Marcos Alonso, and Martin Kaltenbrunner. 2007. The reacTable : Exploring the Synergy between Live Music Performance and Tabletop Tangible Interfaces. In *Proceedings of Conference on Tangible and Embedded Interaction TEI '07*. 139–146.

[6] Martin Kaltenbrunner and Jens Vetter. 2018. Tquencer : A Tangible Musical Sequencer Using Overlays. In *TEI 2018*. 429–434.

[7] Aaron Karp. 2017. HaptEQ : A Collaborative Tool For Visually Impaired Audio Producers. In *the 12th International Audio Mostly Conference*. ACM Press, New York, USA, 1–4.

[8] Sile O'Modhrain and R. Brent Gillespie. 2018. Once More, with Feeling: Revisiting the Role of Touch in Performer-Instrument Interaction. In *Musical Haptics*. Chapter 2, 11–27.

[9] Ivan Poupyrev, Tatsushi Nashida, Shigeaki Maruyama, Jun Rekimoto, and Yasufumi Yamaji. 2004. Lumen: interactive visual and shape display for calm computing. *SIGGRAPH '04: SIGGRAPH 2004 Emerging technologies* (2004), 17.

[10] Atau Tanaka and Adam Parkinson. 2016. Haptic Wave. In *Proceedings of the 2016 CHI Conference on Human Factors in Computing Systems - CHI '16*. 2150–2161.

# transFORM - A Cyber-Physical Artefact Augmenting Social Interaction in Residual Public Spaces

**Carlos Henrique Araujo de Aguiar**
Architectural Robotic Lab Cornell University
Ithaca, USA
ca449@cornell.edu

## ABSTRACT
The emergence of social networks and apps has reduced the importance of physical space as a locus for social interaction. In response, we introduce transFORM, a cyber-physical environment installed in under-used, outdoor, public spaces. transFORM embodies our understanding of how a responsive, cyber-physical architecture can augment social relationship and increase place attachment. In this paper we critically examine the social interaction problem in the context of our increasingly digital society, present our ambition, and introduce our prototype, which we will iteratively design, and test. Cyber-physical interventions at large scale in public spaces are an inevitable future, and this paper serves to establish the fundamental terms of this frontier.

### Author Keywords
HCI; co-design at scale; cyber-physical artefact; place attachment; social interaction.

### ACM Classification Keywords
• Human-centered computing~Interactive systems and tools • Human-centered computing~Interaction design process and methods • Human-centered computing~User centered design

## INTRODUCTION
The subject of place attachment in public and semi-public urban spaces is an important contemporary issue that calls for careful examination and further comprehension in a technologically changing world. "Place attachment" is the cognitive and emotional bond that individuals develop towards a place [[13]]. Place attachment helps to explain and predict other outcomes, such as behaviors, perceptions and emotions [[15], [12]]. As a setting for all sorts of social engagement, public outdoor places like plazas have been a remarkable example of beloved and attached places [[24]].


*TEI '19, March 17–20, 2019, Tempe, AZ, USA*

ACM ISBN 978-1-4503-6196-5/19/03...$15.00
https://doi.org/10.1145/3294109.3302959

Traditionally, these positively-viewed outdoor spaces have been the capacious settings for people's interaction in many cultures and societies, such as the Agora (Figure 1) in ancient Greece. However, digital and networked technologies have drastically changed the way people interact with each other, and the way people interact with the built environment [[11], [21], [9], [16], [20], [14]]. Such change has shown significant impact on the levels of place attachment to such spaces.

In response to public outdoor spaces being supplanted by social networks and apps, our team from design, computing, digital humanities, and library science, partnering with a library and local government, proposes *transFORM*, a cyber-physical environment at room scale, installed in underused outdoor, public squares. Our objective: to enhance information access, use, and archivlng outside the walls of public libraries and to foster social interaction and place attachment in public, urban spaces. Our main goal is to rethink the relationship between people, space and technology, and ultimately, to redesign urban, outdoor spaces as a vehicle for human interaction embedded with today's digital technologies. The key is not to negate technology, but to reintegrate it into the built environment [[8]] in order to, in William J. Mitchell words, "create fresh urban relationships, processes, and patterns that have the social and cultural qualities we seek for the twenty-first century." [[23]]

**Figure 1. Agora, by Edward Dodwell. Photo on Wikipedia.**

## RESEARCH QUESTIONS
Based on these concerns, this research posits two major research questions:

1. What are the key design features that lead to enhanced social interaction?

2. How does a responsive cyber-physical environment affect social interaction and place attachment in a public outdoor space?

**Figures 2, 3 and 4. Three different configurations – two "open" and one "closed".**

## transFORM: GOAL AND DESIGN PROCESS

transFORM will serve as the physical manifestation of our understanding of how an intelligent, cyber-physical environment can augment social interaction and place attachment in urban, outdoor space. transFORM is an architectural-robotic origami that creates various meaningful scenarios, setting premises for people's appropriation in urban space.

Practically, transFORM is a collection of folding, hinged origami that aims to support several activities for urban dwellers. By physically changing its shape, color and sound, transFORM offers different activities, varying from one to another according to user's needs (Figures 2-4).

Origami is mostly recognized as a three-dimensional sculpture formed by folding a sheet of paper. A variation of origami called kirigrami, also known as "pop-up" origami, introduces a single, internal cut into the folded sheet of paper to expand the formal possibilities of the resulting form. Using numerical computing program (MATLAB), we analyzed the gravitational forces actuating in the geometry of our first prototype in order to find the reaction force necessary to accomplish static equilibrium (Figure 5).

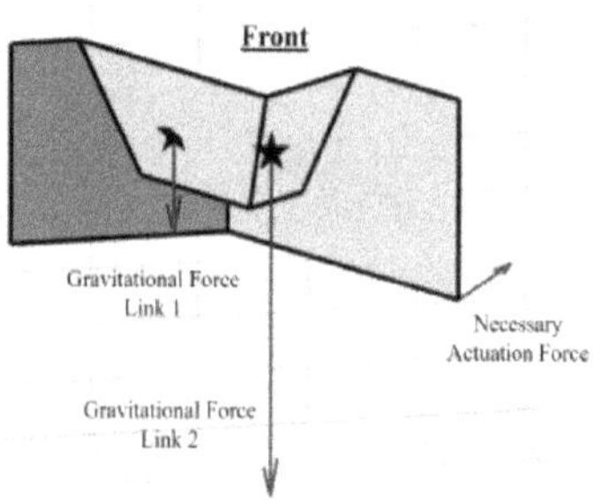


**Figure 5. Geometrical Analysis of transFORM using MATLAB**

## CO-DESIGN AT SCALE: INITIAL STUDY TO GENERATE DESIGN REQUIREMENTS

Our main goal is to design for an under-used public space a responsive environment with imbedded information technologies matched to what people do with them. Therefore, the objective of this first (out of two) co-design study is to understand "*Who* does *what* with *whom* using *what* physical and digital resources?" To seek responses, we conducted a survey asking 41 participants (ages 16-68) to select three activities they would like to do in the under-used place under three different conditions: (a) being alone, (b) being with family/friends, and (c) being with strangers.

Following from the results of the survey, we invited participants to engage in a co-design activity (Figure 6) where they designed a space that supported the top selected activities correspondent to each of the three conditions (i.e. treatments (a)-(c)). Participants were be given six fundamental components to design such a space – screen, light, bench, floor, canopy and table (Figure 6).

It'd be extensive to report the complete analysis in this paper given its level of complexity. As an example, however, in Figure 7 shows the most used components for each of the top 4 activities engaged by people when they are with family/friends. These matrixes enable us to create a collection of human behavior-environmental patterns and their associated fundamental components.

In addition to the co-design activity, we also asked participants to 'think out loud' as they imagined and described their behavior in the space.

**Figure 6. Coding of a Co-Design Activity**

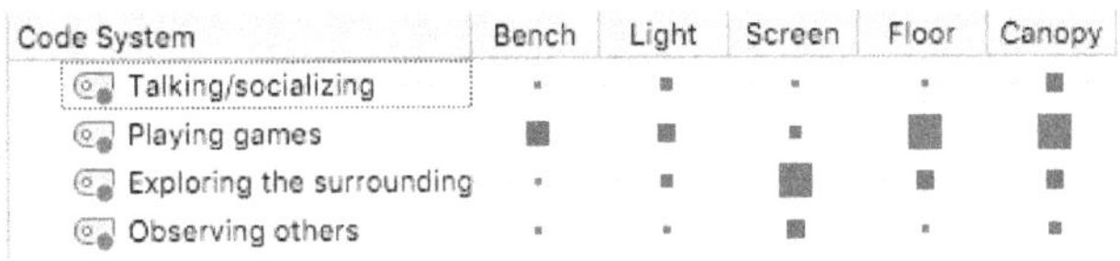


**Figure 7. Actor-Activity-Component matrix**

An interesting pattern we identified refers to the participants' behavior when they approach the space populated with strangers. Some of the participants said they would first observe from afar what others are doing, a behavior that we call "Observing Others"; then, if they became interested, they would approach the screen, canopy or lights to "*...see what others are doing*." In instances when they became interested, they reported that they would engage in a deeper interaction with the installation. We call this behavior "Exploring Surrounding" characterized by participants' exploration in terms of learning and discovering the spatial attributes and affordances. Finally, some participants said they would engage in either "Talking/Socializing" or "Playing Games" with strangers. This behavior suggests that the installation facilitate the interaction among strangers. Figure 8 shows the taxonomy of interaction just described.

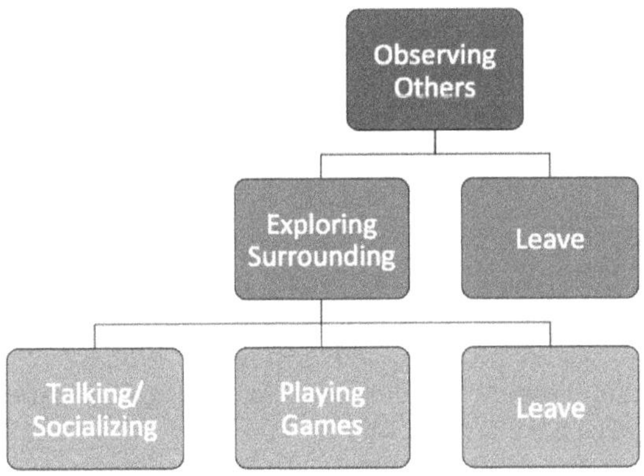


**Figure 8. Taxonomy of Interaction when Interacting with Strangers**

## CURRENT AND FUTURE WORK

In current work, we are constructing a full-scale prototype of transFORM in our lab. We will then invite participants to engage in a second co-design activity, this time using a full-scale prototype. The aim of this second co-design study is to gain more detailed input regarding the attributes and affordances of transFORM artefact. Following this, we will iterate the design and test the full-scale prototype in-situ where we'll measure the effect of transFORM in social interaction and place attachment. For this quasi-experiment, we'll do five observations: two before the installation of *transFORM*; two after its installation; and one after its removal (Figure 9). We expect to see no major change in the levels of place attachment in the first two observations (O1 and O2) (see figures 9 and 10). However, we do expect to see a significant increase in place attachment levels after the installation of transFORM (O3 and O4). Lastly, we expect lower levels of place attachment after the removal of transFORM.

$$O_1O_2\,X\,O_3O_4\,\underline{X}\,O_5$$

**Figure 9. Quasi-Experiment, Remove Treatment with Pre- and Post Test. The letters 'O' means observations. Letter 'X' means add intervention, in this case transFORM. Letter 'X' means remove intervention.**

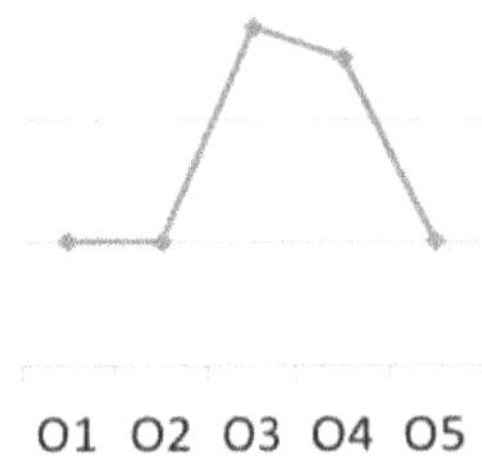


**Figure 10. Expected levels of place attachment for each observation.**

## IMPLICATIONS FOR TEI COMMUNITY

transFORM will probe unexplored opportunities in public, outdoor places for Tangible, Embedded and Embodied Interaction (TEI) at large physical scale, and will provide a deeper understanding of how people perceive and interact with each other in such new places. Others have created larger-scale interactive installations [[17], [5], [3], [6], [18], [1], [2], [7], [10], [19], [4], [22]], but transFORM is distinct from these in its objective to foster place attachment and offer information services beyond the walls of the library. Servings as a design exemplar of large-scale outdoor HCI, transFORM offers a replicable installation and resources to underserved communities

## REFERENCES

[1] A. Morrison, C. Maresa-Yee, W. Jensen, N. Eshraghi. 2016. The Humming Wall: Vibrotactile and Vibroacustic Interactions in an Urben Environment. In *Proceedings of the Designing Interactive Systems Conference,* Brisbane, Australia, 818-822.

[2] C. Ardito, P. Buono, M. Costabile, G. Desolda. 2015. Interaction with Large Displays: A Survey. In *ACM Comput. Surv.* 47, 3: 46:1–46:38. http://doi.org/10.1145/2682623

[3] C. Fortin, K. Hennessy, H. Sweeney. 2014. Roles of an Interactive Media Façade in a Digital Agora. In *Proceedings of The International Symposium on Pervasive Displays,* (June 2014), 7-12.

[4] D. Vogel, R. Balakrishnan. 2004. Interactive public ambient displays: Transitioning from implicit to

explicit, public to personal, interaction with multiple users. In *Proceedings of the 17th annual ACM symposium on User interface software and technology* (Santa Fe, New Mexico, USA, October 24 - 27, 2004.). UIST '04. ACM, New York, NY, 137-146. DOI= http://doi.acm.org/10.1145/1029632.1029656

[5] D. Williams, J. Roggenbuck. 1989. Measuring Place Attachment: Some Preliminary Results. In *Abstracts of the 1989 Leisure Research Symposium.* 20–24.

[6] E. Grönvall, S. Kinch, M. G. Petersen, M. K. Rasmussen. 2014. Causing commotion with a shape-changing bench: experiencing shape-changing interfaces in use. In *Proceedings of SIGCHI Conference on Human Factors in Computing Systems*, (May, 2014), 2559-2568.

[7] G. Dublon, E. Portocarrero. 2014. Listentree: Audio-Haptic Display in the Natural Environment. In *Proceedings 20th International Conference on Auditory Display* (ICAD–2014)

[8] G. Pask. 1969. The Architectural Relevance Of Cybernetics. Architectural Design 39.9: 494-496. Trivedi, Deepak, et al. "Soft robotics: Biological inspiration, state of the art, and future research." Applied Bionics and Biomechanics 5.3 (2008): 99-117.

[9] K. Easterling. 2011. The Action Is The Form. In *Sentient City: Ubiquitous computing, architecture, and the future of urban space.* Edited by Mark Shepard. The Architect League of New York, The MIT Press, 154-158.

[10] K. Grønbæk, K. Kortbek, C. Møller, J. Nielsen, L. Stenfeldt. 2012. Designing Playful Interactive Installations for Urban Environments – The SwingScape Experience. In *Advances in Computer Entertainment SE* - 16 , Anton Nijholt, Teresa Romão and Dennis Reidsma (eds.). Springer Berlin Heidelberg, 230–245. http://doi.org/10.1007/978-3-642-34292-9_16

[11] K. Oungrinis. 2006. Transformations: Paradigms for Designing Transformable Spaces. Harvard Design School, Cambridge, MA, 7-16.

[12] L. Cuba, M. D. Hummon. 1993. A Place to Call Home: Identification with Dwellings, Community, and Region. In *Sociological Quartely*, 34, 111-131.

[13] L. Scannel, R. Gifford. 2010. Defining Place Attachment: A Tripartite Organizing Framework. In *Journal of Environmental Psychology*, 30, 1-10.

[14] L. Winner. 1999. Do artifacts have politics? In *The Social Shaping of Technology* (2nd. ed.), Donald MacKenzie and Judy Wajcman (Eds.). Open University Press, Buckingham, UK, 28-40.

[15] M. Fullilove. 1996. Psychiatric Implications of Displacement: Contributions from the Psychology of Place. In *American Journal of Psychiatry*, 153, 1516-1523.

[16] M. McLuhan.1994. Understanding Media. The MIT press, Cambridge, MA.

[17] N. Memarovic, M. Langheinrich, F. Alt, I. Eihart, S. Hosio and E. Rubegni. 2012. Using public displays to stimulate passive engagement, active engagement, and discovery in public spaces. In *Proceedings of the 4thMedia Architecture Biennale Conference,* (November, 2012), 55-64.

[18] P. Fisher, F. Gerlach, J. Acuna, D. Pollack, I. Schäfer, J. Trautmann, E. Hornecker. 2014. Movable, Kick-/Flickable Light Fragments Eliciting Ad-hoc Interaction in Public Space. In *Proceedings of The International Symposium on Pervasive Displays,* (June, 2014), 50-55.

[19] P. Peltonen, E. Kurvinen, A. Salovaara, et al. 2008. It's Mine, Don'T Touch!: Interactions at a Large Multi-touch Display in a City Centre. In *Proceedings of the SIGCHI Conference on Human Factors in Computing Systems*, ACM, 1285–1294. http://doi.org/10.1145/1357054.1357255

[20] R. Anderson. 1992. Social impacts of computing: Codes of professional ethics. *Soc Sci Comput Rev* 10, 2: 453-469.

[21] S. Sassen. 2011. Unsettling Topographic Representation. In *Sentient City: Ubiquitous computing, architecture, and the future of urban space.* Edited by Mark Shepard. The Architect League of New York, The MIT Press, 192-198.

[22] S. Schroeter, M. Foth, S. Satchell. 2012. People, content, location: sweet spotting urban screens for situated engagement. In *Proceedings of the Designing Interactive Systems Conference* (Newcastle, England, June 11 - 15, 2012). DIS '12. ACM, New York, NY, 146-155. DOI= http://doi.acm.org/10.1145/2317956.2317980

[23] W. Mitchell. 1999. E-topia: 'Urban life, Jim – but not as we know it'. The MIT Press, Cambridge, MA, 2-8.

[24] W. Whyte. 1980. The Social Life of Small Urban Spaces. Project for Public Spaces. New York, New York.

# Toward New Ecologies of Cyberphysical Representational Forms, Scales, and Interaction Modalities

**Alexandre G. de Siqueira**
Clemson, SC, United States
gomesde@clemson.edu


### ABSTRACT
Research on tangible user interfaces commonly focuses on tangible interfaces acting alone or in comparison with multi-touch or graphical interfaces. In contrast, hybrid approaches can be seen as the norm for established "mainstream" interaction paradigms. In my work, I propose interfaces that support complementary interaction modalities, representational forms and scales, toward hybrid systems which are more legible and actionable than any strategy considered separately. I describe systems involving dial-like tangibles, which are passive and active, and systems combining interaction modalities such as tangible and multi-touch, and tangible and VR interaction. I briefly describe some of the planned and performed evaluations, and draw lessons from an already completed study involving a computationally-mediated scientific poster platform with content developed by undergraduate students.



### CCS Concepts
•**Human-centered computing** → **Haptic devices;** *Mixed / augmented reality; Virtual reality;* •**Hardware** → **Haptic devices;**

### Author Keywords
Hybrid Interaction; tangible user interfaces; tangible interaction; multi-touch interaction; Virtual Reality Interaction; cyberphysical interfaces;


### INTRODUCTION
Screen-based graphics and text still remain the primary means for representing digital information. Screens, both big and small, in our desks, pockets, head-mounted, or embedded in the environment that surrounds us, usually in combination with general-purpose input devices, are still the predominant paradigm in human-computer interaction.

While successful, one recognized limitation of graphical user interfaces (GUI) in general, and the "WIMP" (windows-icon-menu-pointer) in particular is the "input" and "output" asymmetry. About this issue, Ullmer [13] asserts:


*TEI '19*, May 17–20, 2019, Tempe, AZ, USA
ACM 978-1-4503-6196-5/19/03. . . $15.00
DOI: https://doi.org/10.1145/3294109.3302960

**Figure 1. Tangibles created toward hybrid forms, interaction, and mediation modalities** *(top row) Capacitive sensed dials were part of poster sessions at several venues in a system combining tangibles and multi-touch interaction. (top right) Active challenge coin combines LED and electronic paper mediation to provide legibility and user feedback. (bottom) VintagePong controllers and VRFishing Rod were part of a conference workshop and a demo session, toward interfaces which combine tangibles and Virtual Reality simulations.*

> *"While often employing millions of pixels of graphical output, WIMP interfaces generally rely upon a single locus of pointer-driven input, in a style largely devoid of physical and kinesthetic affordances, or other handles for engaging with a world of multiple users, each with two hands and a lifetime of physical skills ."*

The last decades have seen a number of research efforts, and commercially available systems, exploring ways to overcome these limitations, and better link the physical and digital worlds. These efforts have inspired several research areas, such as virtual and augmented reality, ubiquitous computing, wearable computing, research on tangible user interfaces (TUI), and driven the popularization of diverse interaction paradigms such as gestural interaction, and voice activated systems.

While tangible interfaces offer interaction beyond the trio screen-mouse-keyboard, within the tangible interaction field, research often focuses on tangible interfaces acting by themselves, or tangible interfaces in comparison with "competing" interaction techniques (e.g. graphical and multi-touch interfaces [17, 1]). In contrast, when considering established "mainstream" interaction paradigms, hybrid approaches can be seen as more the norm than the exception.

Reflecting upon the Xerox Star system, its creators warned not to be dogmatic about the direct manipulation on Desktop metaphors [6]. Contemporary operating systems and desktop computer applications tend to combine both graphical user interfaces and textual/command-line interfaces. Operating systems, in particular smart-phone platforms, typically blend multi-touch with more "traditional" applications (e.g., web browsers), or even voice commands [2]. Voice activated devices, such as Amazon Echo [10], often come in a number of sizes, and do not rely solely on audio input/output, instead they combine a primary voice-activated interaction with buttons for input, and sound and (LED) illumination for output.

These combinations of forms, fabrication approaches, materials, scales, input and output modalities may be key to circumventing issues and limitations of interfaces embodying single-approach prospects. In my research, I investigate ecologies of systems combining a number of cyberphysical representational forms, scales, and interaction modalities. I anticipate that hybrids of multiple complimentary scales, forms, and mediation modalities – including passive and dynamic, physical and virtual, or combinations thereof – can be more legible and actionable than any of them considered alone. Figure 1 shows some artifacts created for interfaces that combine hybrid forms, mediation and interaction modalities.

### Design Heuristics and Approach

The systems I research engage multiple computationally-mediated forms, scales, and interaction modalities, including touching something, moving something, rotating something, and beyond. Typical challenges of computationally-mediated systems relate to how one can tell what, how, and when to *do* something, especially at a first exposure to a system. One common term associated with these challenges is Donald Norman's "affordance" [5]: perceived properties (that may not actually exist), which may provide suggestions or clues as to how, or when to use such properties. As illustrated by Donald Norman's work, even a single affordance may pose a design challenge (e.g. exploring the rotational affordance of a door knob is a typical example [5]). These become even more complex as a number of forms, scale and modalities are combined.

Partly in response to such design challenges, I co-authored with Ullmer and others the LAVA heuristics [12]. The LAVA heuristics – **L**egible, **A**ctionable, **V**eritable, and **A**spirational – provide a conceptual tool for regarding different aspects of representational forms, scales and modalities within interaction design. Here, I will focus on the first two concepts:

- **legible:** *are artifacts expressed in physical and visual representational forms that allow users and systems to "read" them?* For *human legibility*, functions may be labeled with words or icons. However, form, choice of materials, spatial distribution, etc. may overcome this need, possibly leading to more elegant designs. In either case, human and system legibility is important [12]. If a user cannot distinguish (e.g.) a functional from a non-functional element (e.g., a button, RFID/NFC sensing zone, etc.), it is difficult for her to engage. *System legibility* relates to the sensing and communication strategies employed by the system to perceive its elements. These may be active (e.g. Bluetooth communication), or passive (e.g. constellations of conductive touch points on a multi-touch screen), and may be legible only by the systems, or by both humans and systems. A tracking label that communicates information to a system (e.g. via a computer vision) and, at the same time, is legible by humans is an example of an artifact which is legible by both humans and systems.
- **actionable:** *do the physical artifacts provide paths to access and/or manipulate aspects of their cyberphysical associations?* Interaction with physical objects should be reflected both in the physical and virtual spaces, and users should be able to perceive such actions as expressed by one or more forms of feedback.

In my work, I analyze and discuss the design and interaction of computationally-mediated systems consisting of a number of scales, forms and mediation modalities in light of the LAVA heuristics. In particular, how these hybrid systems can be more legible and actionable than when those mediation modalities are considered separately.

## THESIS STATEMENT

My dissertation works to support the following thesis:

> *Computationally-mediated systems consisting of hybrids of complimentary cyberphysical representational forms, scales, and mediation modalities can be more legible and actionable than non-hybrid ones.*

The systems proposed by my dissertation often offer functionality *with* and *without* tangibles, and *with* and *without* virtual/"soft" interactors, including combinations of both. I regard (e.g.) "pure-multitouch" and "pure-tangible" variants, big or small, with active and passive artifacts, as well as hybrids thereof, all as "first class citizens". In this sense, the proposed systems are often not strictly a "tangible interface" system alone, but rather (inspired by [8, 9, 7]) what I and others have begun to consider as *cyberphysical interfaces* – systems designed to integrate support for multiple physical and virtual interaction.

## RESEARCH APPROACH AND EVALUATION

Mark Weiser, when discussing ubiquitous computing for the twenty-first century [14] envisioned devices of three scales: tabs, pads and boards. Inch-scale devices, which he envisioned as active Post-it notes; foot-scale devices, like a sheet of paper, a book, or magazine, and yard-scale devices, equivalent to blackboards. Each with particular roles, and affordances. In this work, I explore inch-scale devices such as passive and active dials, and active challenge coins (Fig. 2); foot scale devices such as computationally mediated books, clocks, and table-sized tangible work-spaces, as well as room-sized interfaces which may combine all of the above into a single system.

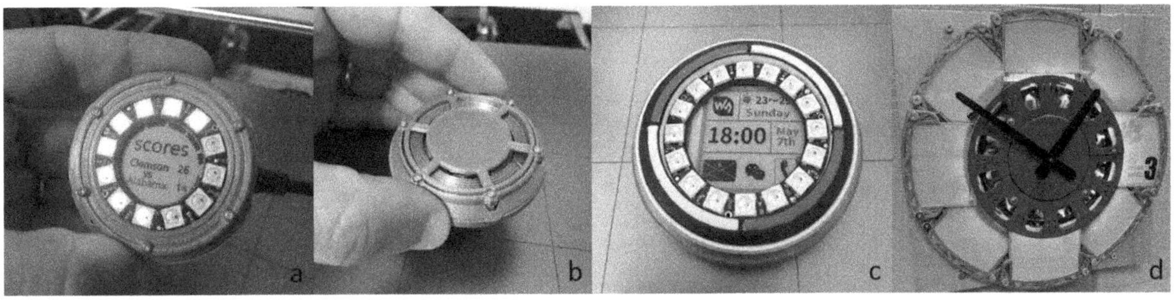


**Figure 2. Active Challenge Coins and Clock mediating information through combinations of electronic paper and LED rings.** *a) 12-LED tethered challenge coin. b) Active challenge coin equipped with wireless-charging. c) 16-LED active challenge coin equipped with wireless data communication via wifi showing iconic and textual information. d) Detail of a Challenge Clock.*

In my preliminary work, I investigate the class of tangibles that involves passive and active cylinders, wheels, dials, pucks, and knobs. I explore combining diverse shapes, materials, fabrication approaches (e.g. 3D printing and laser cutting), and sensing strategies toward dials which are reproducible, and interact with multiple systems. I am currently evaluating active challenge coins (evaluation planned to be completed by February 2019), which provide legibility to users both with e-ink displays and and LED rings (Fig. 2a). Toward characterizing how their unique combination of electronic-paper and LEDs can lead to more legible artifacts, I plan to measure an index of conspicuity, considering a single active challenge coin. As defined by Wertheim [15, 16], conspicuity is the extent to which an object, when viewed peripherally, is visually masked by its embedding surroundings. I will also measure glance legibility of an interface composed of groups of active challenge coins. Glance legibility measures the time a user takes looking at an interface before being able to answer a question about said interface. I expect that combinations of LED and electronic-paper mediation will provide higher levels conspicuity and glance legibility when compared to tokens employing any of the mediation strategies separately.

In another study, (mostly qualitative – completed) I have explored combining diverse interaction modalities, such as tangible and multi-touch interaction into a single experience, with neither being considered intrinsically superior to the other [4]. Here, a computationally-mediated scientific poster platform was created, combining both tangible and multi-touch interaction. Six undergraduate students participated in a number of workshops offered by us, created several posters with their own content, and presented as part of a summer undergraduate research program. Some of the observed results were that in general, poster creators tended to use buttons and gui interactors while developing the posters. "Hard" tangibles were mainly used for testing purposes during short periods of time, independently of the activity performed (e.g. selecting content or zooming an image). When presenting the posters in a public setting, most poster creators tended to use all three modes of interaction (hard, soft tangibles and multi-touch interaction,) with choice depending on the activity being performed. The apparent contrasting behavior toward tangibles we observed between poster creators while developing posters in the lab, and while presenting the posters seems to be in agreement with observations by others. Tangibles tend to be chosen more often when multiple users are collaborating, and not as often when working individually [3, 11]. This supports our hybrid interaction approach, optimizing the system for single and multiple-user modalities, instead of favoring one or the other.

Following that work, I have explored other combinations of interaction modalities, such as tangible and virtual reality (VR), including immersive, non-immersive VR simulations, and combinations of both. Evaluation of this work will be done by analyzing qualitative and quantitative (task performance) of pure tangible interaction, pure VR, and utilization of tangibles while immersed in the VR environment to accomplish a number of tasks. This final evaluation step is planned to be completed by July 2019.

Lastly, a number of artifacts have been completed (e.g. a number of passive and active tokens, active challenge coins, active challenge clocks, and active challenge books). Currently, beyond the envisionments, which have already been realized, a table-sized interface is being prototyped, in the context of a larger room-sized "inteface", also under development. However, given the current state of development, evaluations of systems at these (larger) scales are beyond the scope of my dissertation, and I plan to pursue them as future work.

## THESIS CONTRIBUTION

In supporting the thesis statement, this research makes a number of specific contributions.

1. *Identification and characterization of hybrid representational forms, scales, and modalities as an approach toward more legible and actionable cyberphysical systems.*

   The thesis is broadly concerned with the design and characterization of systems embodying hybrids of "cyberphysical representational forms, scales, and modalities." This approach is supported both by systems designed toward the thesis, as well as other previous work. However, the identification, expression, and characterization of these hybrids as promoting more legible and actionable cyberphysical systems is original to the work of this thesis.

2. *Realization and demonstration of a number of prototyped cyberphysical systems, which embody multiple complimentary representational forms, scales, and mediation modalities.*

   The thesis develops the use of cyberphysical systems, which embody a number of representational forms, scales and mediation modalities. I argue and empirically demonstrate that such systems may be more legible and actionable than non-hybrid ones.

3. *Entrada Poster Platform* The Entrada Poster Platform proposes a platform for scientific poster presentation combining tangible and multi-touch interaction, with large (approx. 55-inch) displays, and small-scale (tablet sized) variants, with and without physical interactors. This work is followed by a number of others, such as combining tangibles and virtual reality.
4. *Experimental comparison of tangible tokens combining electronic paper and LED mediation modalities, toward more legible artifacts.* Conspicuity legibility and glance legibility will be evaluated with a single active challenge coin, and a group of active challenge coins, informing the design of more legible interfaces with token-like elements.
5. *Experimental comparison of hybrids of tangible and VR interaction.* Hybrids of tangible and VR interaction systems will be experimentally compared with pure tangible and pure VR interfaces. These user studies will seek to empirically establish quantitative and qualitative benefits of hybrid cyberphysical systems embodying combinations of those interaction modalities.

## STATEMENT OF MOTIVATION

The Graduate Student Consortium represents an opportunity to share current and planned directions of my research, as well as, receive valuable insights toward evolving and enhancing the work. Beyond the scope of one's thesis, this event also gives graduate students the opportunity to have one-to-one discussions with senior researchers and investigators in the field, which is invaluable for the current and future prospects as graduate students assume faculty, or post-doc positions. With this opportunity, I look forward to receive feedback from fellow students, and senior investigators, and hopefully contribute with my own constructive feedback toward the work of other graduate students. I find that in many occasions, by looking critically at the work of others, I can identify strengths and weaknesses of my own work. In particular, I hope that this experience can help me identify intersections and future collaboration opportunities that I hope can last for years beyond this much appreciated event.

## ACKNOWLEDGEMENTS

This research was partially supported by NSF MRI CNS-1828611, and the Coordination for the Improvement of Higher Education Personnel (CAPES). I thank Dr. Brygg Ullmer who provided insight and opportunities that supported this research. I thank the undergraduate students Wajdi Halabi, and Carson Wood, and graduate students Moloud Nasiri, and Jing Lyu for their work and dedication supporting the development of the prototypes discussed in this paper.

## REFERENCES

[1] Alissa N Antle and Sijie Wang. 2013. Comparing motor-cognitive strategies for spatial problem solving with tangible and multi-touch interfaces. In *Proc. of TEI'13*. ACM, 65–72.

[2] Jacob Aron. 2011. How innovative is Apple's new voice assistant, Siri? (2011).

[3] Jonathan Cohen, Meg Withgott, and Philippe Piernot. 1999. Logjam: a tangible multi-person interface for video logging. In *Proc. of the SIGCHI conference on Human Factors in Computing Systems*. ACM, 128–135.

[4] Alexandre G de Siqueira, Brygg Ullmer, Mark Delarosa, Chris Branton, and Miriam K Konkel. 2018. Hard and Soft Tangibles: Mixing Multi-touch and Tangible Interaction in Scientific Poster Scenarios. In *Proc. of the Twelfth International Conference on Tangible, Embedded, and Embodied Interaction*. ACM, 476–486.

[5] Norman Donald. 1988. The design of everyday things. *Doubled Currency* (1988).

[6] J. Johnson, T.L. Roberts, W. Verplank, D.C. Smith, C.H. Irby, M. Beard, and K. Mackey. 1989. The Xerox Star: a retrospective. *Computer* 22, 9 (Sep. 1989), 11 –26. DOI: http://dx.doi.org/10.1109/2.35211

[7] P Venkata Krishna. 2014. *Challenges, Opportunities, and Dimensions of Cyber-Physical Systems*. IGI Global.

[8] E. Lee. 2008. Cyber Physical Systems: Design Challenges. In *Proc. of ISORC'08*. 363–369.

[9] Jay Lee, Behrad Bagheri, and Hung-An Kao. 2015. A cyber-physical systems architecture for industry 4.0-based manufacturing systems. *Manufacturing Letters* 3 (2015), 18–23.

[10] Amanda Purington, Jessie G Taft, Shruti Sannon, Natalya N Bazarova, and Samuel Hardman Taylor. 2017. Alexa is my new BFF: social roles, user satisfaction, and personification of the amazon echo. In *Proc. of the 2017 CHI Conference Extended Abstracts on Human Factors in Computing Systems*. ACM, 2853–2859.

[11] Bertrand Schneider, Patrick Jermann, Guillaume Zufferey, and Pierre Dillenbourg. 2011. Benefits of a tangible interface for collaborative learning and interaction. *IEEE Transactions on Learning Technologies* 4, 3 (2011), 222–232.

[12] Brygg Ullmer, Alexandre Siqueira, Chris Branton, and Miriam K Konkel. 2016. Weaving peripheral interaction within habitable architectures. In *Peripheral Interaction*. Springer, 253–272.

[13] Brygg Anders Ullmer and Hiroshi Ishii. 2002. *Tangible interfaces for manipulating aggregates of digital information*. Ph.D. Dissertation. Citeseer.

[14] Mark Weiser. 1995. The computer for the 21st century: specialized elements of hardware and software, connected by wires, radio waves and infrared, will be so ubiquitous that no one will notice their presence. In *Readings in Human–Computer Interaction*. Elsevier, 933–940.

[15] AH Wertheim. 1989. A quantitative conspicuity index: theoretical foundation and experimental validation of a measurement procedure. *Report C-20 (in Dutch). TNO Human Factors Research Institute, Soesterberg, The Netherlands* (1989).

[16] Alexander H Wertheim. 2010. Visual conspicuity: a new simple standard, its reliability, validity and applicability. *Ergonomics* 53, 3 (2010), 421–442.

[17] Lesley Xie, Alissa N Antle, and Nima Motamedi. 2008. Are tangibles more fun?: comparing children's enjoyment and engagement using physical, graphical and tangible user interfaces. In *Proc. of TEI'08*. ACM, 191–198.

# Using Biometrics as a Social Intervention in Gaming

**Raquel Robinson**
University of Saskatchewan
Saskatoon, SK Canada
raquel.robinson@usask.ca

### ABSTRACT
My doctoral research examines the use of biometrics as a design intervention in games to increase social closeness. I have built an overlay for Twitch that reveals streamer biometrics to spectators (All the Feels [16]). Using this tool, along with additional design interventions, I plan to explore and expand communication possibilities between players, streamers and spectators in order to facilitate social connection. In this abstract I briefly describe the three projects I am currently working on through my doctoral work: In the Same Boat, Twitch Plays 'All the Feels', and Turnin' the Beat Around.

### Author Keywords
Digital games; Haptics; Live streaming; Biometrics; Emotions.

### CCS Concepts
•**Human-centered computing** → **Human computer interaction (HCI); Collaborative interaction;** *Haptic devices;*

### INTRODUCTION
People who care about each other, work together, or know one another don't always live in the same geographical location. As social closeness—i.e., feeling connected to others—is vital for our well-being [17], building and evaluating tools that help connect people over a distance has been a priority for designers and researchers in human-computer interaction (HCI). For example, technology-enabled communication, such as always-on video chat [9], mobile streaming of experiences on-the-go [7], and connected tangibles [10], have helped people feel closer and more connected to one another over a distance.

Games and playful activities have been long used to support co-located social interactions: pick-up sports leagues or board game nights can help us satisfy our need to feel related to others [18] and create shared experiences that draw us together. With recent technological advances, these shared game experiences can now connect people over a distance as well. Gamers spend an average of 6 hours/week playing with others online and 5 hours/week playing with others in person [3]. More than half of frequent gamers report that video games help them connect with their friends and family [3].

From another angle, we consider the game live streaming experience, which adds another level to distributed social gaming. Since the advent of televised digital gaming in the 1990s, sharing gameplay video footage has been a fundamental part of gaming culture and activity. In the last decade, video sharing services such as YouTube have become more prominent. Additionally, esports (playing computer games in tournaments with spectators) have become an emerging phenomenon, driving interest in sharing both live and recorded gameplay. The intense popularity of the streaming phenomenon in recent years is largely due to the creation of Twitch. Twitch was founded in 2011 and has since become the leading service for gameplay streaming. The popularity of gameplay streaming continues to rise, with 100+ million unique viewers per month and 1.7+ million broadcasters per month [1]. The videogame live streaming market continues to grow with sites (such as YouTube) creating communities of their own. Spectators using Twitch do not simply view a player's stream passively; they can interact with the streamer during play. The Twitch platform allows spectators to chat using both typed text and emotes engaging in lively side conversation in real time. Twitch also provides a fertile environment for experiments in sociability due to the customizability and robust chat features it offers. For example, Twitch Plays Pokémon turned the chat room into a game controller, allowing users around the world to collaborate and directly interface with the game [2]. Both streamers and spectators regularly customize their Twitch experience in order to interact more effectively. In recent years there has been a rise in the desire to increase interactivity between the audience and online performers [19]. This is partially because websites like YouTube and Twitch make it more accessible for people around the world to become performers [21]. The role of an audience ranges from observing the performance passively to the audience becoming the performers.

I consider both social games and live streaming in my research goal to use biometrics as the main mechanic for designing emotional experiences that will support people to form or maintain intimacy and trust over a distance. I will explore this through three projects: 1. In the Same Boat: an embodied physiological mirroring game designed to explore social closeness between players over a distance; 2. Twitch Plays 'All the Feels': exploring audience interactivity in a horror game in which spectators have access to the streamers' vitals,



*TEI '19,* March 17–20, 2019, Tempe, AZ, USA



DOI: https://doi.org/10.1145/3294109.3302961

looking at spectator/streamer interactions and how visualizing biometrics can change the experience; and 3. Turnin' the Beat Around: considering which contexts to use haptic communication of performers' heart rate data in live-performance experiences (type of performance e.g. sports, gaming, music events or type of emotional experience)? Although each project was designed to facilitate different experiences, all of these projects hope to increase trust, intimacy, and social closeness among spectators and players.

## RELATED WORK

### Biometrics and Game Live Streaming

Over the last decade, biometric sensors have been explored in the context of game design and research. Sensors have primarily been used as novel (interaction) inputs to games (e.g. [13]), and as tools to evaluate games and their effect in players [11, 12]. Visualizing sensor data is rarely used as a design tool, and instead primarily for information tracking and quantified self reports. My doctoral work takes a different direction, examining how such sensors can enhance social closeness for both players and live streaming spectators.

In this regard, research and design in the domain of interactive performances can be illuminating, for example Reeves et al.'s investigation of spectator experience of interactive installations [15], and Wang et al.'s work assessing audience engagement with a theater performance [24]. Tennent et al. [23] engaged in a similar project during a prototype TV show, displaying physiological data from actors. The goals of these authors – to allow the audience to engage in "sense-making practices when watching actors" and "potentially enhance the vicarious nature of viewing another's experience – resonate with our goal of providing a rich spectator experience. The same research team has also implemented a tool for capturing video, audio, heartrate, and acceleration data of those riding a roller coaster, streaming this live to spectators, thus transforming riders into performers [22].

In the realm of game design, biometrics to enrich the spectator experience were used during Dreamhack, a biannual European eSports event where key players around the world gather to play competitive games that are broadcasted on a large scale. In 2011, Dreamhack equipped players with heart rate monitors while streaming games, which was commented and celebrated by the audience: "I think it's a great addition and I'm really getting more into the player's minds by knowing how stressed they are in the particular moment." [14] Unfortunately, subsequent Dreamhack events discontinued the display of this biometric feature, which some fans attributed to distraction for the players [14]. This intervention shows the potential of displaying the players' biometrics for the sake of a rich spectator experience. Yet, this is an underexplored topic that needs to be further examined.

Physiological input has been used as a novel input approach, designed to enhance engagement through intimate interaction with the system. For example, Nacke et. al [13] built a system in which a game played using a traditional controller is augmented using both direct (e.g., facial expressions) and indirect (e.g., galvanic skin response) physiological sensor input.

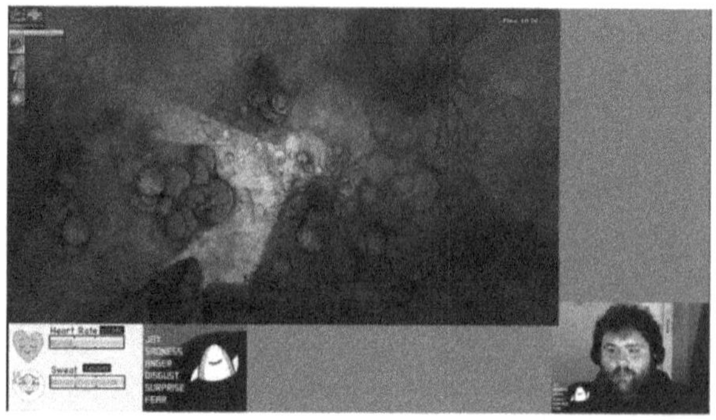

**Figure 1. Current version of All the Feels. Lower left portion of the screen shows the heart rate, GSR, and facial expression data of streamer.**

Combining both physiological signals and bodily movement as input to the game, Zangouei et. al [25] created an emotional game experience for co-located players in which they solve riddles to progress.

### All the Feels

All the Feels is a tool I created in my master's work that provides an overlay of biometric and webcam-derived data onto the interface of the popular video game streaming service, Twitch [16]. This overlay provides visualization of heart rate, skin conductance, and facial emotion recognition. The tool consists of the Empatica E4 wristband capturing the heart rate and skin conductance (sweat), and a tailored version of the Affdex software capturing levels of the emotions: joy, sadness, anger, disgust, surprise, and fear (see Figure 1). These levels are displayed as a side bar graph, filling up when one of the emotion levels is at maximum. To the right of this, an emoji displays the prominent emotion of the player at the time. For example, the player smiles, the "joy" bar fills up, and a happy face emoji displays to the right. The addition is intended to enhance the spectator experience and improve streamer-spectator connection. I conducted a preliminary live test with the tool involving a female streamer and 25 spectators. I found that All the Feels seemed to increase perceived connection between the spectator and the streamer, while offering an engaging and enjoyable experience for spectators. These preliminary results of the study align with prior work done, showing increased enjoyment, engagement, and viewership among live stream spectators [16]. The player did not find the software obtrusive and appreciated the supportive dialog that ensued from spectators who saw her emotion data. I believe this research shows that All the Feels is a promising addition to gameplay streams, to be proven out in more in-depth, extended field testing which I will describe in a later section. The results of this research support that biometric data could be used as an additional layer of information to spark conversation and enhance streamer and spectator experience.

## CURRENT WORK AND TIMELINE

For my Ph.D. I will focus on three projects that expand on All the Feels: In the Same Boat, Twitch Plays 'All the Feels', and Turnin' the Beat Around. For all projects, players/spectators will fill out a mixture of validated scales asking about trust formation and social connection. With these projects, I plan

**Figure 2. Example of game In the Same Boat. Here one player is syncing a smile with their partner (pictured off screen) and together they are jumping over a whirlpool.**

**Figure 3. Game setup: Webcam, circuit playground with pulse sensor attached to finger, and game on screen.**

to explore several research questions, including: I) As social closeness is important for an individual's health and well-being, how can we best design games to support and foster social closeness? II) In what ways do streamers communicate with their audience and what ways can we augment this experience in terms of emote usage, extensions, and Twitch chat in general add to the social experience? III) In which live-performance contexts does haptic heart rate feedback provide the most value?

### Project 1: In the Same Boat

Building off work by Isbister [8], Mandryk [4, 13], and Robinson [16], we created an embodied mirroring game—In the Same Boat—to explore social closeness between players over a distance. We leverage the synchronization of both players' physiological data (heart rate, breathing, facial expressions) mapped to an input scheme to control the movement of a canoe down a river. The game is a two-player infinite runner, played over a network, in which players use their physiological input to control a canoe riding down a river, while dodging obstacles along the way (see Figure 2).

This work aims to validate the following hypothesis:

- *H1: Using biometrics as a control schema in an interdependent and cooperative game will further increase social closeness amongst distributed players.*

The two players must sync their facial expressions to dodge obstacles that occur in the middle lane of the river, and they must sync their heart rate (or breathing rate in an alternate version) to stay in the middle of the river. If they fail to synchronize in time, the canoe will move to either the left or right portion of the river, which has more obstacles and therefore increases the game difficulty. The synchrony of physiological input acts as the mechanic that realized cooperation and interdependence (both dynamics which support trust formation and social closeness in games [4]) in the game. In the Same Boat was designed to promote an intimate interaction, by focusing on embodied interaction using physiological input, mirroring emotions through synching, and networked play. The game was coded in Unity, and the Circuit Playground Express by Adafruit (biometric controller), Affdex (facial recognition technology), the Pulse Sensor Amped (heart rate sensor) are the hardware used in the game (see Figure 3). The heart rate is calibrated for each player to their baseline beats per minute (BPM). For each player, if they are within 20BPM of their baseline heart rate, they are considered synchronized with the other player by the system. The Circuit Playground has a built-in microphone which picks up peaks when blown into and calculates a breath rate value based on that.

Currently, preliminary studies have been conducted with 6 groups (12 participants). This game version (using emotions as a controller) is compared against one using the keyboard as a controller. We use Likert scale ratings to measure participants' perceived feelings of trust before and after the game, relatedness, and enjoyment. These studies have shown that trust formation increases from before to after playing in both versions of the game, participants enjoy the emotion controls version more than the keyboard controls, and overall people communicated with each other well to maneuver the canoe. This shows that using biometrics in this social context *can* further enhance the social closeness between players over a distance. To the best of our knowledge, this game is the first to leverage physiological syncing over a distance and has the potential to help geographically-distributed friends, family, and partners to feel closer through playful interaction. Further iteration and testing will allow us to explore different physiological input methods and gain more insight into designing for intimate distributed play experiences. This project is in progress and will complete by April 2019.

### Project 2: Twitch Plays 'All the Feels'

The second project will test All the Feels within the horror genre, which was the genre spectators indicated as most interesting in our prior work. This project is in collaboration with Jessica Hammer at Carnegie Mellon University, using inspiration from a game their lab created called 'What Lurks in the Dark' [5], which is a Twitch-based horror game that allows for audience participation.

Using their game as a design inspiration, we explore the following hypotheses:

- *H1: Visualizing streamers biometric data will enhance the spectators' emotional experience, making them feel closer and more connected to the experience and the live streamer.*

**Figure 4. Example of the game map, audience voting system, and All the Feels. Orange circle shows the game plus 'All the Feels', the green circle shows the game-map, and the red circle shows the Twitch chat feed.**

- *H2: Seeing the affect their decisions have on the player's biometric data will give the spectators clear feedback about how their actions affect not only the gameplay, but also the player.*

We are creating a horror game called, 'What Lurks in the Deep', which is a top down puzzle horror game where the streamer-player is trapped in a boat with monsters lurking in the depths outside. There are five different monsters in the game, each with a different set of strengths and weaknesses. The player is unaware of which monster is lurking outside the boat, so must understand and prepare for monsters based on sound alone. They will be able to use lights on the boat to hide from or attack the monster. The audience has a larger overview of the map, and has access to information the player-streamer does not, including which monster is approaching the boat.

The audience determines if they want to help or hurt the streamer and plan their actions accordingly. This game explores themes such as viewer sympathy, the challenges of teamwork in online spaces, and the balance of power between streamer and audience. Combining What Lurks in the Deep with All the Feels, I will be able to determine what dynamics change when viewers are able to see the streamers' vitals. I am interested in how seeing this internal information change interactions, decisions to help/hurt the streamer, and the overall communication in chat. The study will consist of the streamer playing the game while using All the Feels (see setup in Figure 4). This project is in the early stages, as we are currently re-designing portions of the game and changing elements of the audience interactions. This project is in progress and the user testing will be done by the end of the summer in 2019.

### Turnin' the Beat Around

The third project iterates on prior work differently – testing the best ways of communicating the biometric information to the spectators in terms of modality. My preliminary work [16] focuses on visualization of the biometric information. However, other studies in this same area consider the relative effectiveness of modality – haptic vs. visuals on audience's experience. Other work has shown that haptic feedback providing additional information to users interacting with technology can provide a more enriching experience [6].

This project is in collaboration with a colleague Alina Striner, who has researched the audience experience in different contexts [21, 20]. Prior unpublished work in this area (conducted by Striner et. al) suggests that haptic heart rate information is more effective at engaging audiences over visual or visual plus haptic data. In their study, they showed participants three different videos of different sports activities: figure skating, poker, and gymnastics. Analyses suggest that the figure skating video was the only video in which seeing the performer's heart rate information *did not* enhance the spectator experience. They found a strong haptic main effect in the poker video and gymnastics video over the skating video in several metrics: Feelings, engagement-absorption, and connectedness.

Based on these findings, our work explores the following hypotheses:

- *H1: More context surrounding the drama of the experience creates more empathy with performer which may increase value of heart rate data.*
- *H2: Increased feedback about performer state (or feelings toward this state) increases value of heart rate feedback, because it provides an interpretive context.*
- *H3: Points feedback allows the viewer to better understand the stakes, which provides an interpretive context for the heart rate data.*

As a followup to this study by Striner et al, our research explores haptic heart rate in particular (as opposed to visual) to find out why heart rate information was not valuable in the context of figure skating. To study this, we will have participants watch 2 videos. One video will consist of a pre- and post-interviews with the figure skater added before and after showing the nervousness and suspense building up to the routine, as well as the feelings and reactions of the skater after the routine. This allows the audience to not only have more context behind the video, but also have increased feedback about the ice skater's emotional well-being. Having access to someone's emotional state is important for emotion interpretation, and this is not easy to detect in an ice-skating performance. Ice skaters are often hiding their internal state during the routine by smiling throughout the performance. Additionally, we will overlay a points feedback system at the upper right corner of the screen. As for heart rate data, we will communicate the skater's heart rate information to the spectators through vibrations from a haptic motor encased in fabric, vibrating in time with the skater's heart beat. Heart rate data will be faked, and peaks will be synchronized with peak moments of the performance (jumps, tricks, etc.). Preliminary studies will be run in the Winter of 2019, and the project will primarily take place in the summer of 2019.

### REFERENCES

[1] 2011. Twitch. (2011). http://www.twitch.tv

[2] 2014. Twitch Plays Pokemon. (2014). https://www.twitch.tv/twitchplayspokemon

[3] 2018. 2018 Essential Facts About The Computer And Video Game Industry. (2018). http://www.theesa.com/wp-content/uploads/2018/05/EF2018_FINAL.pdf

[4] Ansgar E Depping and Regan L Mandryk. 2017. Cooperation and Interdependence: How Multiplayer Games Increase Social Closeness. *CHI PLAY 2017 - Proceedings of the 2017 Annual Symposium on Computer-Human Interaction in Play* (2017). DOI: http://dx.doi.org/10.1145/3116595.3116639

[5] Justin Fanzo, Rachel Gu, Jinchao Han, Ketul Majmudar, Tony Deng, Flora Cheng, Chaoya Li, and Jessica Hammer. 2017. What Lurks in the Dark: An Audience Participation Horror Game. *Extended Abstracts Publication of the Annual Symposium on Computer-Human Interaction in Play* (2017), 621–624. DOI:http://dx.doi.org/10.1145/3130859.3130865

[6] David Hannah, Martin Halvey, Graham Wilson, and Stephen A Brewster. 2011. Using Multimodal Interactions for 3D Television and Multimedia Browsing. In *Proceedings of the 9th European Conference on Interactive TV and Video (EuroITV '11)*. ACM, New York, NY, USA, 181–184. DOI: http://dx.doi.org/10.1145/2000119.2000156

[7] Kori Inkpen, Brett Taylor, Sasa Junuzovic, John Tang, and Gina Venolia. 2013. Experiences2Go: Sharing Kids' Activities Outside the Home with Remote Family Members. In *Proceedings of the 2013 Conference on Computer Supported Cooperative Work (CSCW '13)*. ACM, New York, NY, USA, 1329–1340. DOI: http://dx.doi.org/10.1145/2441776.2441926

[8] Katherine Isbister. 2012. How to stop being a buzzkill. *Proceedings of the 14th international conference on Human-computer interaction with mobile devices and services companion - MobileHCI '12* (2012), 1. DOI: http://dx.doi.org/10.1145/2371664.2371666

[9] Tejinder K Judge, Carman Neustaedter, and Andrew F Kurtz. 2010. The Family Window: The Design and Evaluation of a Domestic Media Space. In *Proceedings of the SIGCHI Conference on Human Factors in Computing Systems (CHI '10)*. ACM, New York, NY, USA, 2361–2370. DOI: http://dx.doi.org/10.1145/1753326.1753682

[10] Joseph 'Jofish' Kaye and Liz Goulding. 2004. Intimate Objects. In *Proceedings of the 5th Conference on Designing Interactive Systems: Processes, Practices, Methods, and Techniques (DIS '04)*. ACM, New York, NY, USA, 341–344. DOI: http://dx.doi.org/10.1145/1013115.1013175

[11] Regan L. Mandryk. 2008. A physiological approach for continuously modeling user emotion in interactive play environments. *Measuring Behavior 2008* 2008 (2008), 93–94. DOI: http://dx.doi.org/10.1016/j.ijhcs.2006.11.011

[12] Regan L. Mandryk and Kori M. Inkpen. 2004. Physiological Indicators for the Evaluation of Co-located Collaborative Play. In *Proceedings of the 2004 ACM Conference on Computer Supported Cooperative Work (CSCW '04)*. ACM, New York, NY, USA, 102–111. DOI: http://dx.doi.org/10.1145/1031607.1031625

[13] Lennart E. Nacke, Michael Kalyn, C Lough, and Regan L. Mandryk. 2011. Biofeedback game design: using direct and indirect physiological control to enhance game interaction. *Proceedings of the SIGCHI ...* (2011), 103–112. DOI: http://dx.doi.org/10.1145/1978942.1978958

[14] Reddit. 2012. what happened to the heart monitors in tournaments? (2012). https://www.reddit.com/r/starcraft/comments/qncru/what_happened_to_the_heart_monitors_in_tournaments/

[15] Stuart Reeves, Sarah Martindale, Paul Tennent, Steve Benford, Joe Marshall, and Brendan Walker. 2015. The Challenges of Using Biodata in Promotional Filmmaking. *ACM Transactions on Computer-Human Interaction (TOCHI)* 22, 3 (2015), 11. DOI: http://dx.doi.org/10.1145/2699758

[16] Raquel Robinson, Zachary Rubin, Elena Márquez Segura, and Katherine Isbister. 2017. All the Feels: Designing a Tool That Reveals Streamers' Biometrics to Spectators. In *Proceedings of the 12th International Conference on the Foundations of Digital Games (FDG '17)*. ACM, New York, NY, USA, 36:1–36:6. DOI: http://dx.doi.org/10.1145/3102071.3102103

[17] R. Ryan and E. Deci. 2000. Self-determination theory and the facilitation of intrinsic motivation. *American Psychologist* 55, 1 (2000), 68–78. DOI: http://dx.doi.org/10.1037/0003-066X.55.1.68

[18] Richard M. Ryan, C. Scott Rigby, and Andrew Przybylski. 2006. The motivational pull of video games: A self-determination theory approach. *Motivation and Emotion* 30, 4 (2006), 347–363. DOI: http://dx.doi.org/10.1007/s11031-006-9051-8

[19] Joseph Seering, Saiph Savage, Michael Eagle, Joshua Churchin, Rachel Moeller, Jeffrey P Bigham, and Jessica Hammer. 2017. Audience Participation Games: Blurring the Line Between Player and Spectator. In *Proceedings of the 2017 Conference on Designing Interactive Systems (DIS '17)*. ACM, New York, NY, USA, 429–440. DOI: http://dx.doi.org/10.1145/3064663.3064732

[20] Alina Striner, Sasha Azad, and Chris Martens. 2017. A Common Framework for Audience Interactivity. *CoRR* abs/1710.0 (2017). http://arxiv.org/abs/1710.03320

[21] Alina Striner and Brenna McNally. 2017. Transitioning Between Audience and Performer: Co-Designing Interactive Music Performances with Children. In *Proceedings of the 2017 CHI Conference Extended Abstracts on Human Factors in Computing Systems (CHI EA '17)*. ACM, New York, NY, USA, 2115–2122. DOI:http://dx.doi.org/10.1145/3027063.3053171

[22] Burak S Tekin and Stuart Reeves. 2017. Ways of spectating : Unravelling spectator participation in Kinect play. In *Forthcoming CHI '17*. Denver, CO.

[23] Paul Tennent, Stuart Reeves, Steve Benford, Brendan Walker, Joe Marshall, Patrick Brundell, Rupert Meese, and Paul Harter. 2012. The machine in the ghost. In *Proceedings of the 2012 ACM annual conference extended abstracts on Human Factors in Computing Systems Extended Abstracts - CHI EA '12*. 91. DOI: http://dx.doi.org/10.1145/2212776.2212787

[24] Chen Wang, Erik N. Geelhoed, Phil P. Stenton, and Pablo Cesar. 2014. Sensing a live audience. In *Chi '14*. 1909–1912. DOI: http://dx.doi.org/10.1145/2556288.2557154

[25] Farnaz Zangouei, Mohammad Ali Babazadeh Gashti, Kristina Höök, Tim Tijs, Gert-Jan de Vries, and Joyce Westerink. 2010. How to stay in the emotional rollercoaster. *Proceedings of the 6th Nordic Conference on Human-Computer Interaction Extending Boundaries - NordiCHI '10* (2010), 571. DOI: http://dx.doi.org/10.1145/1868914.1868978

# Design Interactions between Robot Surfaces and Human Designers

**Yixiao Wang**
Cornell University
Ithaca, NY
Yw697@cornell.edu

## ABSTRACT
This paper presents the rationale and current progress of my Ph.D. dissertation: "design interactions between robot surfaces and human designers." This specific topic serves as a case study trying to explore the question of how to design an interactive and partially intelligent space. We proposed the concept of "space agent" defined as "interactive and intelligent environments perceived by users as human agents" based on communication theories. Built upon this concept, we proposed a design framework for interactive environments. Then we further explored literatures about what space agent could contribute to human users specifically for the case of interior designers' work space. Research questions and research designs are introduced in this paper, followed by the discussions of experiments design.

### Author Keywords
Space agent; interaction design; work space design; continuous robot surfaces; reconfigurable space.

### ACM Classification Keywords
• Human-centered computing~Collaborative interaction
• Human-centered computing~User interface design
• Human-centered computing~User centered design
• Human-centered computing~Interaction design theory, concepts and paradigms

## INTRODUCTION
In an increasingly digital society, we have witnessed many environments or installations which are intelligent and interactive. Famous examples include "HypoSurface" by MIT Media Lab [[1]] and "MuscleBody" by TU Delft Hyperbody Research Group [[2]]. Most of these interactive architectural installations focus on providing new and interesting interactions to the users without further discussing the essential questions such as why we would like to enable such interactions (theoretical foundations); what influences such an interactive environment would have on human users; how we should design such interactive environment effectively; and how to evaluate the interactive environment. The answers to these questions are important not only as the justifications of the project, but also the rationales through which new designs could be better informed and consequently, improved. Inspired by these questions, the authors decide to explore interactive environment design through the research and design of an "intelligent and interactive work environment for interior designers," which serves as the specific case to narrow down the scope of our research topic.


*TEI '19, March 17–20, 2019, Tempe, AZ, USA*

ACM ISBN 978-1-4503-6196-5/19/03...$15.00
https://doi.org/10.1145/3294109.3302962

## SPACE AGENT
As computer-embedded systems become more interactive and more intelligent due to rapid development of computational technologies. Researchers of the 1990s conceptualized the research paradigm, CASA (Computer as Social Actors) [[3]]. As part of this conceptualization, Reeve and Nass proposed "The Media Equation" as a general communication theory that describes the tendency of people to interact and communicate with computer media as if this media is a human being [[4]]. Since then, many psychological experiments studying human communications have been conducted to inform human-computer interaction design [[5]]. Design researchers initially applied these psychological findings to virtual, avatar designs. More recently, design researchers have been transferring "common interpersonal communication phenomena" [[5],[4]] to computer-embedded systems such as robotic furniture [[6]] and social robots [[7]].

Herein, the authors suggest that a computer-embedded intelligent space, such as an intelligent work space, may also be perceived by users as a human being—partner, friend, collaborator, which is the definition of "space agent." Consequently, studying human-human interaction may predict how people would like to communicate and interact with an intelligent space. This concept could greatly influence and richly inform how interactive and intelligent spaces are designed, and the interactions these spatial artifacts afford. We will further discuss the "space agent" concept and corresponding design pattern framework in the TEI 2019 conference presentation for our paper "Designing Interactive Spaces as if They Were Human: A Design Pattern Framework for the 3rd Dimension."

## INTELLIGENT WORK SPACE AS A SPACE AGENT

What should an intelligent work space look like? In Figure 1, below, we list four different spaces with different intelligence levels and interaction patterns.

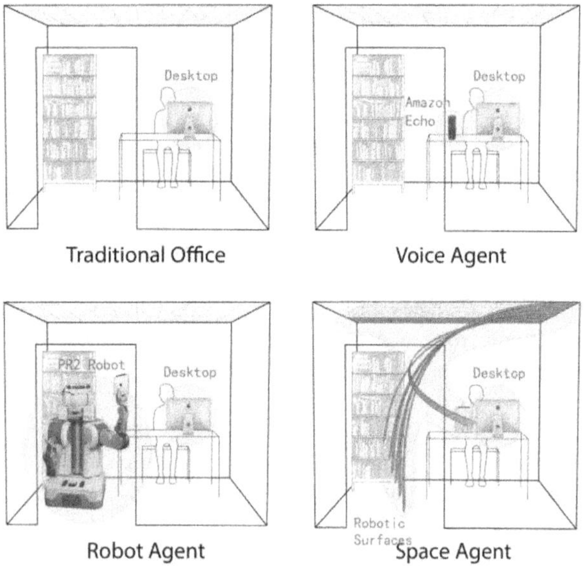


**Figure 1. Diagram of four different work spaces: traditional office, voice agent, robot agent, and space agent.**

The first one is our everyday office with a chair, a desk, a desktop computer, and hopefully a bookshelf. There is no intelligence or interactions in the space. Recently, people start to have an "Amazon Echo" or "Google Home" on their desks. These "Voice Agents" could perform some simple tasks with users such as turning on the light or TV, which gives certain level of intelligence and verbal interactions to the work space. Or, we could have a "Robot Agent" in the room. A well programmed PR2 robot, as shown in Figure 1, could do some simple tasks with certain level of intelligence and support some verbal and non-verbal interactions. Finally, we have the option of designing the work space as a "space agent," which could proactively reconfigure the physical work space to support different activities as if a partner to the users. It gives user the ability to control physical space configurations, while at the same time manifests intelligent partnership by perceiving what users are doing and being supportive. In Figure 1, the "Space Agents" are designed as robot surfaces peeling off the ceiling, which divides the work space into two parts.

## A STORY OF JOANNE

Now let's look at how "Space Agent" could partner with our persona "Joanne," an interior designer, in her various design activities in the following scenario. The sentences in *italic font* below are descriptions of sub-tasks performed by the "space agent."

**Figure 2. Robotic surfaces as a space agent applied in autonomous car interior: meeting clients.**

**Figure 3. Robotic surfaces as a space agent applied in autonomous car interior: private working.**

Joanne is an interior designer. Her office is an intelligent work space with robotic surfaces attached to the ceiling, capable of reconfiguring and redefining the interior space. Today, Joanne needs to design a chair for her clients. She steps into the office in the morning and sits beside her desk. *One of the robotic surfaces embedded in the ceiling gently bent down to provide her a tablet in a comfortable position (see Figure 2).* After checking her email on the tablet, Joanne keeps staring at computer screens and still doesn't feel in the mood of creating new chair designs for her clients from Switzerland. *The robotic surface with the tablet tentatively moves into Joanne's eye sight with two words on the screen: "need inspirations?"* Joanne nods her head slowly. *The screen then suggests: "site environment simulation" and the robotic surfaces start to create the feeling of "cold winter in Switzerland" using lights, movements, and sounds.* Joanne feels the atmosphere and starts to sketch on the paper. Suddenly, her calendar reminds her that an online conference with her clients is happening in 10 minutes. *Joanne quickly picks up her old and new sketches while some robotic surfaces start to bend down together forming a pin-up wall surface beside Joanne*, so that she could pin her drawings in an organized way for her clients. Meanwhile, her colleagues are coming into the office. *Some other robotic surfaces gently bent down to separate Joanne and her colleagues spatially and block the noise (Figure 3).* After some time, Joanne feels tired and wants to have a rest. She stands up and leans towards a soft robotic surface on the wall. *The soft robotic surface changes its surface curvature in a way providing both ergonomic and comfortable body support for her leaning gesture.*

## SPACE AGENT AS A DESIGN PARTNER

In the scenario above, we see how the space agent (robotic surfaces) could detect user activities and proactively reconfigure the interior space to support design activities. We believe that the more "Joanne" working with the space agent, the more space agent could understand her behavior patterns and become her design partners. Why do we believe "space agent" could become a design partner? What does this partnership mean to the designers? What influences could "space agent" environment have to the users? And finally, what are the previous examples I could build upon? In this section, we reviewed some literatures to give meaningful answers to these questions.

### Three Key Characteristics of a Good Partner

Bratman (1992) proposed the "Trio of features characteristic of SCA" which are "mutual responsiveness," "commitment to joint activity," and "commitment to mutual support" [[8]]. Based on the current AI technology, space agent could perceive what users are doing well enough to infer the goal of the current task. Meanwhile, "space agent" is trying to be supportive to the users by being responsive to user's non-verbal behaviors. These characteristics qualifies a "partner" in a "Share Cooperative Activity." However, because of the time limit of my dissertation, I would only expect a "temporary partnership" between "space agent" and participants in the performance experiment.

### Space Agent – Spatial Support – Creativity

Space Agent is a reconfigurable space that is not only proactive to user behaviors, but also under control of users. For instance, if certain reconfiguration is not favored by the users, the users could gesture the room to return to the previous configuration. The proactive part of space agent is conveying the idea of being supportive. McCoy and Evans suggest that environmental supports (both social and physical) are salient to creativity [[9]]. Amabile and his colleagues have studied how social environment could influence creativity [[10]]. As McCoy and Evans suggest that "just as the social environment provides support, the physical environment may reflect and reinforce that support." [[9]] In summary, the literatures support the following rationale: Space Agent may proactively provide spatial supports which could be salient to creativity.

### Space Agent – Control over Space – Work Environment Satisfaction

Previous studies suggest that staying in control over the space could allow workers to better focus on their jobs [[11]]. For instance, the space agent could provide privacy and block noises. The control over space, together with the active spatial support provided by the space agent, could potentially improve the work environment satisfaction of the users, which could further contribute to many other things such as working efficiency and creativity [[11]]. Luck in his Ph.D. dissertation also suggests that "locus of control" and "perceived control" could positively influence "workplace preferences" and "job satisfaction" [[12]].

### Space Agent – Partnership (Friendship) – Creativity

James Somers, in his recent New Yorker magazine article, specifically described how partnership and friendship become a power horse of creativity at Google [[13]]. Good partners complement each other in a dynamic way, cultivating a good relationship (friendship) which in return positively influence the complementary partnership. Michael in her book argues that creativity is born from collaborations and the friendship among the collaborators [[14]]. She used examples and related studies to support this argument in her book.

### Previous Example

I would like to position my dissertation topic in the domain of "architectural robotics", which is a sub-field of interactive architecture. "Architectural robotics" is described as an "interactive, partly intelligent, and meticulously designed physical environment." [[15]] One "architectural robotics" example closely related to my dissertation project is "Animated Work Environment" (AWE), which is a reconfigurable work station consist of a one-dimensional bending structure [[16]]. Compared to "AWE," "space agent" expand the reconfigurable space scale to the whole office and emphasis specifically on the interactions and relationships between the space and users.

## TECHNICAL BOUNDARIES

Specifically, we need supervised learning and classification algorithms operating with large enough database and fast enough computational speed. We have already developed the prototype of this technology using MATLAB for model training and grasshopper for implementation [[17]]. However, to achieve a proper space agent behavior, we should integrate cost-based prediction functions [[18]] or HMM smoothing, filtering, and prediction [[19]]. Further explorations in AI algorithms are still needed to achieve proper partnership interactions between "space agent" and designers.

## RESEARCH QUESTIONS AND RESEARCH DESIGN

Based on the concept of "Space Agent" and literature reviews above, we have the following research questions:

- How to design the interactions between "Space Agent" and human user, so that it can develop a temporary partnership with human designer?
- Could the "space agent environment" and the "temporary partnership" together, increase designers' "work environment satisfaction" and "creative work performance?"

For the first research questions, we propose three different interaction patterns to be explored in the pilot study, which will be further explained in the "experiment design" section:

- *Interaction pattern 1*: users need to push a button to enable certain space reconfiguration;
- *Interaction pattern 2*: space agent always asks for permissions before it actively reconfigures the space;
- *Interaction pattern 3*: space agent proactively reconfigures the space without asking for permissions but will return to its former configuration when users gesture it to stop.

For the second research question, we plan to explore it in the "performance experiment." The research design for this research question is illustrated in Figure 4.

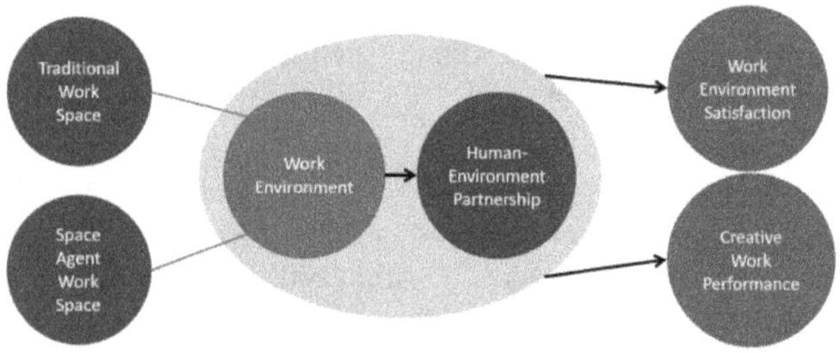


**Figure 4. Research design diagram**

As shown in Figure 4, the independent variable is work environment, which is a categorical variable with two levels: "Traditional Work Space" and "Space Agent Work Space." We believe the "space agent work space" could develop a temporary partnership with its users by providing proactive spatial support based on its understanding to the human activities. Meanwhile, the human users will experience his control over the work space in this partnership. The dependent variables are "work environment satisfaction" and "creative work performance." These two variables are based upon previous literature reviews and can be measured by existed scales.

## EXPERIMENT DESIGN

### Experiment-1: Pilot Study of Interaction Patterns and Spatial Configurations for Each Sub-task

In this pilot study, we'll invite 12 interior designers to go through the exact scenario we described in the "story of Joanne," by performing the same design task (design a chair) inside a space agent environment. we're going to ask participants to co-design with us the spatial configuration for each sub-task (the sub-tasks are specified in the scenario using italic font). Then We'll use VOZ technique to simulate three different interaction patterns (specified in "research question and research design" section) for each sub-task and ask participants which one they prefer and why. Table 1 shows five sub-tasks and corresponding interaction patterns we will explore in this pilot study.

### Experiment-2: Performance Studies

In our performance studies, 22 participants will be asked to perform tasks based on the scenarios. We will: (a) measure how robot surfaces facilitate a human participant performing specific tasks; and (b) observe, measure, and characterize human-robot activity patterns and processes. Quantitative methods will be used to measure proposed variables. For "creative work performance," we will organize a design expert panel to evaluate the outcome of performed tasks such as the quality and quantity of design works or ideas generated by the participants. For "work environment satisfaction," we will give participants a validated scale after they performed the required tasks in the "space agent" work space. Qualitative methods used in the performance studies are the same as those used for the usability and user experience studies: a mix of observations, interviews, think alouds, surveys, and coded video-recording of sessions. Analysis of these data will be a key factor in informing the team members of the absolute and relative merits of the surface robot designs.

| Sub-tasks | Interaction pattern 1 | Interaction pattern 2 | Interaction pattern 3 |
|---|---|---|---|
| Providing tablet for email checking | Push a button, then tablet is provided by a robotic surface | SA asks for permission first, then provides the tablet | SA provides the tablet without asking for permission |
| Simulating site environment | Push a button, then SA starts to simulate site environment | SA asks for permission first, then simulates site environment | SA simulates site environment without asking for permission |
| Forming a pin-up wall | Push a button, then pin-up wall is provided in the right position | SA asks for permission first, then starts to form pin-up wall | SA forms the pin-up wall without asking for permission |
| Spatially separating users into different groups | Push a button, then robotic surfaces come down to separate different user groups | SA asks for permission first, then form the partitions | SA forms separating partitions without asking for permission |
| Providing comfortable surfaces for leaning gestures | Push a button, then robotic surfaces change curvatures to support leaning gesture | SA asks for permission first, then provides the leaning surface | SA provides leaning surfaces without asking for permission |

**Table 1. Three interaction patterns for five sub-tasks ("SA" represents "Space Agent")**

## REFERENCES


[1] deCOI and MIT. "Hyposurface." Available at http://www.decoi-architects.org/2011/10/hyposurface/

[2] Hyperbody Research Group, TU Delft. "Muscle Body." Available at http://www.bk.tudelft.nl/en/about-faculty/departments/architectural-engineering-and-technology/organisation/hyperbody/research/applied-research-projects/muscle-body/.http://www.acm.org/class/how_to_use.html

[3] Clifford Nass, Jonathan Steuer, and Ellen R. Tauber. 1994. Computers are social actors. In *Conference Companion on Human Factors in Computing Systems* (CHI '94), Catherine Plaisant (Ed.). ACM, New York, NY, USA, 204-. DOI:https://doi.org/10.1145/259963.260288

[4] Byron Reeves and Clifford Nass. 1996. *The media equation: how people treat computers, television, and new media like real people and places*. Cambridge University Press.

[5] Clifford Nass and Corina Yen. 2010. *The man who lied to his laptop: what machines teach us about human relationships*. New York: Current.

[6] David Sirkin, Brian Mok, Stephen Yang, and Wendy Ju. 2015. Mechanical Ottoman: How Robotic Furniture Offers and Withdraws Support. In *Proceedings of the Tenth Annual ACM/IEEE International Conference on Human-Robot Interaction* (HRI '15). ACM, New York, NY, USA, 11-18. DOI: https://doi.org/10.1145/2696454.2696461

[7] G. Hoffman, O. Zuckerman, G. Hirschberger, M. Luria, and T. S. Sherman. 2015. Design and Evaluation of a Peripheral Robotic Conversation Companion. In *Proceedings of the Tenth Annual ACM/IEEE International Conference on Human-Robot Interaction* (HRI 15).

[8] Michael E. Bratman. 1992. Shared Cooperative Activity. *The Philosophical Review* 101, 2 (1992), 327. DOI:http://dx.doi.org/10.2307/2185537

[9] McCoy, Janetta Mitchell, and Gary W. Evans. 2002. The Potential Role of the Physical Environment in Fostering Creativity, *Creat. Res. J.,* 14, 3-4: 409-426.

[10] Amabile, Teresa M., and Nur D. Gryskiewicz. 1989. The creative environment scales: Work environment inventory. *Creativity research journal*, 2, 4: 231-253.

[11] Samani, Sanaz Ahmadpoor, Siti Zaleha Binti Abdul Rasid, and Saudah bt Sofian. 2015. Individual Control over the Physical Work Environment to Affect Creativity. *Ind. Eng. Manag. Syst.,* 14, 1: 94-103.

[12] Luck Gypsi. 2003. *The Relationship of an Innovative Thinking Style, Locus of Control and Perceived Control on Job Satisfaction and Workspace Preferences Among Knowledge Workers*. California School of Professional Psychology.

[13] James Somers. 2018. The Friendship That Made Google Huge. (December 2018). Retrieved December 21, 2018 from https://www.newyorker.com/magazine/2018/12/10/the-friendship-that-made-google-huge

[14] Michael P. Farrell. 2003. *Collaborative circles: friendship dynamics & creative work*, Chicago, IL: University of Chicago Press.

[15] Keith Evan Green. 2016. *Architectural robotics: ecosystems of bits, bytes, and biology*, Cambridge, MA: The MIT Press.

[16] K. E. Green, I. D. Walker, L. J. Gugerty, and J. C. Witte. 2006. Three robot-rooms: the AWE project. In *CHI '06 Extended Abstracts on Human Factors in Computing Systems* (CHI EA '06). ACM, New York, NY, USA, 809-814. DOI=http://dx.doi.org/10.1145/1125451.1125611

[17] Dongheng Jing and Yixiao Wang. 2018. MAE 6710 final video. (December 2018). Retrieved December 21, 2018 from https://youtu.be/Y1vD4bpKFSg

[18] G. Hoffman and C. Breazeal. 2007. Cost-Based Anticipatory Action Selection for Human–Robot Fluency. *IEEE Transactions on Robotics.,* 23, 5: 952-961. DOI:http://dx.doi.org/10.1109/tro.2007.907483

[19] Stuart J. Russell and Peter Norvig. 2018. *Artificial intelligence: a modern approach*, Upper Saddle River: Pearson.

# Author Index

www.ingramcontent.com/pod-product-compliance
Lightning Source LLC
LaVergne TN
LVHW080105011026
849160LV00013B/1037

*9781450370684*